Collins

ARABIC POCKET DICTIONARY

HarperCollins Publishers
HarperCollins Publishers, 195 Broadway,
New York, NY 10007

COLLINS POCKET ARABIC DICTIONARY

First Edition 2017

10 9 8 7 6 5 4 3

ISBN 978-0-06-219181-6

www.harpercollins.com

HarperCollins books may be purchased for educational, business, or sales promotional use. For information, please write to: Special Markets Department, HarperCollins Publishers, 10 East 53rd Street, New York, NY 10022

A catalogue record for this book is available from the British Library

Typesetting by Lingea s.r.o.

Printed and bound in China

Acknowledgements
We would like to thank those authors and publishers who kindly gave permission for copyright material to be used in the Collins Corpus. We would also like to thank Times Newspapers Ltd for providing valuable data.

Series Editor
Rob Scriven

Managing Editor
Gaëlle Amiot-Cadey

Editor
Susanne Reichert

CONTENTS
المحتويات

INTRODUCTION

We are delighted that you have decided to buy this Arabic-English, English-Arabic dictionary and hope that you will enjoy and benefit from using it at home, on holiday or at work.

مقدمة

يسرنا أنك قررت شراء هذا القاموس عربي – إنجليزي، إنجليزي عربي ونأمل أن تستمتع وتستفيد من إستعماله في المنزل، أو أثناء الإجازات أو في العمل.

ABBREVIATIONS — الاختصارات

adjective	*adj*	صفة
adverb	*adv*	ظرف
exclamation	*excl*	تعجب
preposition	*prep*	حرف ج
pronoun	*pron*	ضمير
noun	*n*	اسم
plural	*pl*	جمع
verb	*v*	فعل
intransitive verb	*vi*	فعل لازم
transitive verb	*vt*	فعل متعدٍّ

النطق باللغة الإنجليزية/ENGLISH PRONUNCIATION

الأصوات اللينة

	English example	*Explanation*
[ɑ:]	f**a**ther	ألف فتح مثل: ب**ا**ت /م**ا**ت
[ʌ]	b**u**t, c**o**me	فتح خفيف قصر مثل: **مَ**ن /**عَ**ن
[æ]	m**a**n, c**a**t	فتح طويل يشبه الألف اللينة مثل: مش**ى**
[ə]	fath**er**, **a**go	فتحة قصيرة مثل: **أَ**ب
[ə:]	b**ir**d, h**ear**d	كسر طويل
[ɛ]	g**e**t, b**e**d	كسر طويل وخفيف
[ɪ]	**i**t, b**i**g	كسر قصير قوي
[i:]	t**ea**, s**ee**	[ياء مد] مثل: يأت**ي** / صائم**ي**ن
[ɔ]	h**o**t, w**a**sh	ضم منتهي بسكون
[ɔ:]	s**aw**, **a**ll	ضم ممدود
[u]	p**u**t, b**oo**k	[ضم] مثل: **مُ**ستعد /**قُ**م
[ʊ]	t**oo**, y**ou**	[واو مد] مثل: ي**و**لد/ ي**و**جد

الأصوات المدغمة

	English example	*Explanation*
[ai]	fl**y**, h**i**gh	ألف فتح منتهي بياء ساكنة محي**ايْ**
[au]	h**ow**, h**ou**se	ألف فتح منتهي بضم مثل: **واو**
[ɛə]	th**ere**, b**ear**	كسر طويل خفيف منتهي بياء مفتوحة مثل: بِ**يَ**دي
[ei]	d**ay**, ob**ey**	فتح منهي بياء مثل: **أَيْ**ن
[iə]	h**ere**, h**ear**	كسر قوي قصير منهي بفتح
[əu]	g**o**, n**o**te	ضم منتهي بسكون مثل: **مُ**نتهي
[əi]	b**oy**, **oi**l	ضم منتهي بياء ساكنة
[uə]	p**oo**r, s**ure**	ضم منتهي بفتح مثل **و**اسع

الأصوات الساكنة

	English example	*Explanation*
[b]	**b**ig, lo**bb**y	[**ب**] مثل: **ب**ا**ب** /م**ب**لغ /لع**ب**
[d]	mende**d**	[**د**] مثل: **د**خل /م**د**ح /أبا**د**
[g]	**g**o, **g**et, bi**g**	[**ج**] بدون تعطيش كما تنطق في العامية المصرية
[ʤ]	**g**in, ju**dg**e	[**ج**] مع المبالغة في التعطيش لتنطق وكأنها / **د+ج**/
[ŋ]	si**ng**	تشبه حكم **إخفاء النون** في قراءة القرآن الكريمكما في قوله تعالى "ناصيةٍ كاذبة
[h]	**h**ouse, **h**e	[**هـ**] مثل: **ه**و /مل**ه**ى /أخرج**ه**
[j]	**y**oung, **y**es	[**ى**] /**الألف اللينة**/ مثل **ي**جري /هذ**ي**ان/ جر**ى**
[k]	**c**ome, mo**ck**	[**ك**] مثل: **ك**امل /ت**ك**لم / مل**ك**
[r]	**r**ed, t**r**ead	[**ر**] مثل: **ر**مى /م**ر**مى /م**ر**
[s]	**s**and, ye**s**	[**س**] مثل: **س**مير/م**س**مار/رأ**س**
[z]	ro**s**e, **z**ebra	[**ز**] مثل: **ز**عم/م**ز**روع /فا**ز**
[ʃ]	**sh**e, ma**ch**ine	[**ش**] مثل: **ش**ارع /م**ش**روع /معا**ش**
[tʃ]	**ch**in, ri**ch**	[**تش**] مثل:
[v]	**v**alley	[**ڤ**]مثل [ف] ولكن تنطق بوضع الأسنان العلوية على الجزء الخارجي من الشفاه السفلية: مثل الري**ف**يرا
[w]	**w**ater, **wh**ich	[**و**] مثل: **و**جد /م**و**جود
[ʒ]	vi**s**ion	تنطق ما بين [**ش**] و [**ج**] بحيث يكون الفك العلوي ملامسا للشفاه السفلى واللسانقريب من اللثة العليا بحيث يخرج الهواء محدثا صوتا إحتكاكيا
[θ]	**th**ink, my**th**	[**ث**] مثل: **ث**رى /م**ث**ل**ث**
[ð]	**th**is, **th**e	[**ذ**] مثل **ذ**ئب /م**ذ**يب /ملا**ذ**

ARABIC ALPHABET

Isolated Letter	Name	End	Mid.	Beg.	Explanation	IPA
ا	alif	ـا	ـا	ا	m**a**n	ʔ
ب	baa	ـب	ـبـ	بـ	**b**oy	b
ت	taa	ـت	ـتـ	تـ	**t**oy	t
ث	thaa	ـث	ـثـ	ثـ	**th**ree	θ
ج	jeem	ـج	ـجـ	جـ	gara**ge** - vi**si**on	ʒ
ح	ħaa	ـح	ـحـ	حـ	pronounced from the middle of the throat with back tongue a little higher	ħ
خ	kha	ـخ	ـخـ	خـ	pronounced with back tongue in a position between the position for /h/ and that for /k/ like (lo**ch**) in Scots	x
د	dal	ـد	ـدـ	دـ	**d**ay	d
ذ	dhal	ـذ	ـذـ	ذـ	**th**e	ð
ر	raa	ـر	ـرـ	رـ	**r**un	r
ز	zay	ـز	ـزـ	زـ	**z**oo	z
س	seen	ـس	ـسـ	سـ	**s**orry	s
ش	sheen	ـش	ـشـ	شـ	**sh**ow	ʃ
ص	ṣaad	ـص	ـصـ	صـ	heavy /s/	$s^{ʕ}$

ض	ḍaaḍ	ـض	ـضـ	ضـ	strong /d/	$d^{ʕ}$
ط	ṭaa	ـط	ـطـ	طـ	heavy /t/	$t^{ʕ}$
ظ	ḍhaa	ـظ	ـظـ	ظـ	heavy /Dh/	$z^{ʕ}$
ع	,aeen	ـع	ـعـ	عـ	**a**rm but pronounced with back tongue a little lower	ʕ
غ	gheen	ـغ	ـغـ	غـ	**g**irl but pronounced with back tongue a little lower	ɣ
ف	faa	ـف	ـفـ	فـ	**f**ree	f
ق	,qaaf	ـق	ـقـ	قـ	**q**uarter but with back tongue a little higher	q
ك	kaaf	ـك	ـكـ	كـ	**c**amp	k
ل	lam	ـل	ـلـ	لـ	**l**eg	l
م	meem	ـم	ـمـ	مـ	**m**oon	m
ن	noon	ـن	ـنـ	نـ	**n**ight	n
هـ	haa	ـه	ـهـ	هـ	**h**igh	h
و	wow	ـو	ـو-	و-	**w**ow	w
ي	yaa	ـي	ـيـ	يـ	**y**ear	j

NUMBERS — الأعداد

zero	0	صفر	٠
one	1	واحد	١
two	2	اثنان	٢
three	3	ثلاث	٣
four	4	أربع	٤
five	5	خمس	٥
six	6	ست	٦
seven	7	سبع	٧
eight	8	ثمان	٨
nine	9	تسع	٩
ten	10	عشر	١٠
eleven	11	أحد عشر	١١
twelve	12	اثنا عشر	١٢
thirteen	13	ثلاث عشر	١٣
fourteen	14	أربع عش	١٤
fifteen	15	خمس عشر	١٥
sixteen	16	ست عشر	١٦
seventeen	17	سبع عشر	١٧
eighteen	18	ثمان عشر	١٨
nineteen	19	تسع عشر	١٩
twenty	20	عشرون	٢٠
twenty-one	21	واحد وعشرون	٢١

twenty-two	22	اثنان وعشرون	٢٢
twenty-three	23	ثلاث وعشرون	٢٣
thirty	30	ثلاثون	٣٠
thirty-one	31	واحد وثلاثون	٣١
fourty	40	أربعون	٤٠
fifty	50	خمسون	٥٠
sixty	60	ستون	٦٠
seventy	70	سبعون	٧٠
eighty	80	ثمانون	٨٠
ninety	90	تسعون	٩٠
one hundred	100	مائة	١٠٠
one hundered and ten	110	مائة وعشر	١١٠
two hundred	200	مائتان	٢٠٠
two hundred and fifty	250	مائتان وخمسون	٢٥٠
three hundred	300	ثلاثمائه	٣٠٠
one thousand	1,000	ألف	١٠٠٠
one million	1,000,000	مليون	١٠٠٠٠٠٠

DAYS OF THE WEEK | أيام الأسبوع

Monday	الاثنين
Tuesday	الثلاثاء
Wednesday	الأربعاء
Thursday	الخميس
Friday	الجمعة
Saturday	السبت
Sunday	الأحد

MONTHS | الشهور

January	كانون الثاني
February	شباط
March	آذار
April	نيسان
May	أيّار
June	حزيران
July	تمّوز
August	آب
September	أيلول
October	تشرين أوّل
November	تشرين ثاني
December	كانون أوّل

ENGLISH-ARABIC
إنجليزي – عربي

a [eɪ] *art*; **Is there a cash machine here?** هل توجد ماكينة صرف آلي هنا؟ [hal tojad makenat ṣarf aaly huna?]; **This is a gift for you** إنها هدية لك [inaha hadyia laka]
abandon [əˈbændən] *v* يَهْجر [jahʒaru]
abbey [ˈæbɪ] *n* دَيْر الرهبان [Deer al-rohban]
abbreviation [əˌbriːvɪˈeɪʃən] *n* اختصار [ixtisˤaːr]
abdomen [ˈæbdəmən; æbˈdəʊ-] *n* بَطْن [batˤn]
abduct [æbˈdʌkt] *v* يَخطَف [jaxtˤafu]
ability [əˈbɪlɪtɪ] *n* قدرة [qudra]
able [ˈeɪbəl] *adj* قادِر [qaːdir]
abnormal [æbˈnɔːməl] *adj* غير طبيعي [Ghayer ṭabeʼaey]
abolish [əˈbɒlɪʃ] *v* يلغي [julɣiː]
abolition [ˌæbəˈlɪʃən] *n* إلغاء [ʔilɣaːʔ]
abortion [əˈbɔːʃən] *n* إجهاض [ʔiʒhaːdˤ]
about [əˈbaʊt] *adv* حوالي [ħawaːlaj] ▷ *prep* عن [ʕan]; **Do you have any leaflets about...?** هل يوجد لديكم أي مطبوعات عن... [hal yujad laday-kum ay maṭ-boʼaat ʻaan...?]
above [əˈbʌv] *prep* فوق [fawqa]
abroad [əˈbrɔːd] *adv* بالخارج [Bel-kharej]
abrupt [əˈbrʌpt] *adj* مفاجئ (خطير) [mufaːʒiʔ]
abruptly [əˈbrʌptlɪ] *adv* بشكل مفاجئ [Be-sakl mofajeya]
abscess [ˈæbsɛs; -sɪs] *n* خُرَّاج [xurraːʒ]
absence [ˈæbsəns] *n* غياب [ɣijaːb]
absent [ˈæbsənt] *adj* غائب [ɣaːʔibb]
absent-minded [ˌæbsənˈtˈmaɪndɪd] *adj* شارِد الذهن [Shared al-dhehn]
absolutely [ˌæbsəˈluːtlɪ] *adv* بكل تأكيد [Bekol taakeed]
abstract [ˈæbstrækt] *adj* نظري [nazˤarij]
absurd [əbˈsɜːd] *adj* سَخيف [saxiːf]
Abu Dhabi [ˈæbuː ˈdɑːbɪ] *n* أبو ظبي [ʔabu zˤabj]
abuse *n* [əˈbjuːs] سوء استعمال [Sooa esteʼamal] ▷ *v* [əˈbjuːz] يُسيء استخدام [Yosea estekhdam]; **child abuse** *n* سوء معاملة الأطفال [Soo moʼaamalat al-aṭfaal]
abusive [əˈbjuːsɪv] *adj* مؤذي [muʔðiː]
academic [ˌækəˈdɛmɪk] *adj* أكاديمي [ʔakaːdiːmij]; **academic year** *n* عام دراسي [ʻaam derasey]
academy [əˈkædəmɪ] *n* أكاديمية [ʔakaːdiːmijja]
accelerate [ækˈsɛləˌreɪt] *v* يُسْرِع [jusriʕu]
acceleration [ækˌsɛləˈreɪʃən] *n* تسريع [tasriːʕ]
accelerator [ækˈsɛləˌreɪtə] *n* معجل [muʕaʒʒil]
accept [əkˈsɛpt] *v* يَقْبَل [jaqbalu]
acceptable [əkˈsɛptəbəl] *adj* مقبول [maqbuːl]
access [ˈæksɛs] *n* وصول [wusˤuːl] ▷ *v* يَدخُل [jadxulu]
accessible [əkˈsɛsəbəl] *adj* سهل الوصول [Sahl al-woṣool]
accessory [əkˈsɛsərɪ] *n* كماليات [kamaːlijjaːt]
accident [ˈæksɪdənt] *n* حادث [ħaːdiθ]; **accident & emergency department** *n* إدارة الحوادث والطوارئ [Edarat al-hawadeth wa-al-tawarea]; **accident insurance** *n* تأمين ضد الحوادث

[Taameen ḍed al-hawaadeth]; **by accident** *adv* بالصُدْفَة [Bel-ṣodfah]; **I've had an accident** تعرضت لحادث [ta'aar-ḍto le-ḥadith]; **There's been an accident!** كانت هناك حادثة [kanat hunaka ḥadetha]; **What do I do if I have an accident?** ماذا أفعل عند وقوع حادث؟ [madha af'aal 'aenda wi-'qoo'a ḥadeth?]

accidental [ˌæksɪ'dɛntᵊl] *adj* عرضي [ʕaradʕij]

accidentally [ˌæksɪ'dɛntəlɪ] *adv* بالصُدْفَة [Bel-ṣodfah]

accommodate [ə'kɒməˌdeɪt] *v* يُجهِز (يوفر) [juʒahhizu]

accommodation [əˌkɒmə'deɪʃən] *n* مسكن [maskan]

accompany [ə'kʌmpənɪ; ə'kʌmpnɪ] *v* يُرافق [juraːfiqu]

accomplice [ə'kɒmplɪs; ə'kʌm-] *n* شريك في جريمة [Shareek fee jareemah]

according [ə'kɔːdɪŋ] *prep*; **according to** *prep* وفقاً لـ [wifqan-li]

accordingly [ə'kɔːdɪŋlɪ] *adv* بناء على [Benaa ala]

accordion [ə'kɔːdɪən] *n* أكورديون [ʔakuːrdjuːn]

account [ə'kaʊnt] *n* *(in bank)* حساب [ħisaːb], *(report)* بيان (بالأسباب) [bajaːn]; **account number** *n* رقم الحساب [Ra'qm al-hesab]; **bank account** *n* حساب بنكي [Hesab bankey]; **current account** *n* حساب جارى [Hesab tejarey]; **joint account** *n* حساب مشترك [Hesab moshtarak]

accountable [ə'kaʊntəbᵊl] *adj* مسؤول [masʔuːl]

accountancy [ə'kaʊntənsɪ] *n* مُحَاسَبَة [muħaːsaba]

accountant [ə'kaʊntənt] *n* محاسب [muħaːsib]

account for [ə'kaʊnt fɔː] *v* يُبَرر [jubariru]

accuracy ['ækjʊrəsɪ] *n* دِقّة [diqqa]

accurate ['ækjərɪt] *adj* دقيق [daqiːq]

accurately ['ækjərɪtlɪ] *adv* بِدِقّة [Bedae'qah]

accusation [ˌækjʊ'zeɪʃən] *n* اتهام [ittihaːm]

accuse [ə'kjuːz] *v* يَتّهم [jattahimu]

accused [ə'kjuːzd] *n* متهم [muttaham]

ace [eɪs] *n* واحد [waːħid]

ache [eɪk] *n* ألَمْ [ʔalam] ▷ *v* يؤلم [juʔlimu]

achieve [ə'tʃiːv] *v* يُحقِق [juħaqqiqu]

achievement [ə'tʃiːvmənt] *n* إنجاز [ʔinʒaːz]

acid ['æsɪd] *n* حمض [ħimdʕ]; **acid rain** *n* أمطار حمضية [Amṭar ḥemdeyah]

acknowledgement [ək'nɒlɪdʒmənt] *n* اعتراف [iʕtiraːf]

acne ['æknɪ] *n* حب الشباب [Hob al-shabab]

acorn ['eɪkɔːn] *n* ثمرة البلوط [Thamarat al-balooṭ]

acoustic [ə'kuːstɪk] *adj* سَمعي [samʕij]

acre ['eɪkə] *n* أكْر [ʔakr]

acrobat ['ækrəˌbæt] *n* أكروبات [ʔakruːbaːt]

acronym ['ækrənɪm] *n* اسم مُختَصَر [Esm mokhtaṣar]

across [ə'krɒs] *prep* عبر [ʕabra]

act [ækt] *n* فِعل [fiʕl] ▷ *v* يَقُوم بعمل [Ya'qoom be]

acting ['æktɪŋ] *adj* نائب [naːʔibb] ▷ *n* تمثيل [tamθiːll]

action ['ækʃən] *n* فِعْلٌ [fiʕl]

active ['æktɪv] *adj* نشيط [naʃiːtʕ]

activity [æk'tɪvɪtɪ] *n* نشاط [naʃaːtʕ]; **activity holiday** *n* أجازة لممارسة الأنشطة [ajaaza lemomarsat al 'anshe ṭah]

actor ['æktə] *n* ممثل (عامل) [mumaθθil]

actress ['æktrɪs] *n* ممثلة [mumaθθila]

actual ['æktʃʊəl] *adj* فعلي [fiʕlij]

actually ['æktʃʊəlɪ] *adv* في الواقع [Fee al-wa'qe'a]

acupuncture ['ækjʊˌpʌŋktʃə] *n* وخز بالإبر [Wakhz bel-ebar]

ad [æd] *abbr* إعلان [ʔiʕlaːnun]; **small ads** *npl* إعلانات صغيرة [E'alanat ṣaghera]

AD [eɪ diː] *abbr* بعد الميلاد [Ba'ad al-meelad]

adapt [ə'dæpt] *v* يَتَكَيف [jatakajjafu]
adaptor [ə'dæptə] *n* مُحَوِّل كهربي [Moḥawel kahrabey]
add [æd] *v* يُضيف [judˤi:fu]
addict ['ædɪkt] *n* مدمن [mudmin]; **drug addict** *n* مدمن مخدرات [Modmen mokhadarat]
addicted [ə'dɪktɪd] *adj* مُدمن [mudmin]
additional [ə'dɪʃənᵊl] *adj* إضافي [ʔidˤa:fij]
additive ['ædɪtɪv] *n* إضَافة [ʔidˤa:fa]
address [ə'drɛs] *n (location)* عنوان [ʕunwa:n], *(speech)* خِطَاب [xitˤa:b]; **address book** *n* دفتر العناوين [Daftar al-'aanaaween]; **home address** *n* عنوان المنزل ['aonwan al-manzel]; **web address** *n* عنوان الويب ['aonwan al-web]; **My email address is...** عنوان بريدي الالكتروني هو... ['ainwan ba-reedy al-ali-kitrony howa...]; **Please send my mail on to this address** من فضلك قم بتحويل رسائلي إلى هذا العنوان [min faḍlak 'qum be-taḥweel rasa-ely ela hadha al-'ainwan]; **The website address is...** عنوان موقع الويب هو... ['ainwan maw-'q i'a al-web howa...]; **What is your email address?** ما هو عنوان بريدك الالكتروني؟ [ma howa 'ain-wan bareed-ak al-alikit-rony?]; **Will you write down the address, please?** هل يمكن لك أن تدون العنوان، إذا تفضلت؟ [hal yamken laka an tudaw-win al-'aenwaan, edha tafaḍalt?]
add up [æd ʌp] *v* يُجَمِع [juʒammiʕu]
adjacent [ə'dʒeɪsᵊnt] *adj* مجاور [muʒa:wir]
adjective ['ædʒɪktɪv] *n* صفة [sˤifa]
adjust [ə'dʒʌst] *v* يَضْبِط [jadˤbitˤu]
adjustable [ə'dʒʌstəbᵊl] *adj* يُمْكِن ضبطه [Yomken ḍabṭoh]
adjustment [ə'dʒʌstmənt] *n* ضَبْط [dˤabtˤ]
administration [əd,mɪnɪ'streɪʃən] *n* إدارة [ʔida:ra]
administrative [əd'mɪnɪ,strətɪv] *adj* إداري [ʔida:rij]
admiration [,ædmə'reɪʃən] *n* إعجاب [ʔiʕʒa:b]
admire [əd'maɪə] *v* يُعجب بـ [Yo'ajab be]
admission [əd'mɪʃən] *n* اعتراف [iʕtira:f]; **admission charge** *n* رَسْم الالتحاق [Rasm al-elteha'q]
admit [əd'mɪt] *v (allow in)* يَسمَح بالدخول [Yasmaḥ bel-dokhool], *(confess)* يُقِر [juqiru]
admittance [əd'mɪtᵊns] *n* اذن بالدخول [Edhn bel-dekhool]
adolescence [,ædə'lɛsəns] *n* سِن المراهقة [Sen al-moraha'qah]
adolescent [,ædə'lɛsᵊnt] *n* مراهق [mura:hiq]
adopt [ə'dɒpt] *v* يَتَبَنى (يُقر) [jatabanna:]
adopted [ə'dɒptɪd] *adj* مُتَبَنًّى [mutabanna:]
adoption [ə'dɒpʃən] *n* تَبَنّي [tabanni:]
adore [ə'dɔ:] *v* يَعْشق [jaʕʃaqu]
Adriatic [,eɪdrɪ'ætɪk] *adj* أدرياتيكي [ʔadrija:ti:ki:]
Adriatic Sea [,eɪdrɪ'ætɪk si:] *n* البحر الأدرياتيكي [Albahr al adriạteky]
adult ['ædʌlt; ə'dʌlt] *n* بَالِغْ [ba:liɣ]; **adult education** *n* تعليم الكبار [Ta'aleem al-kebar]
advance [əd'vɑ:ns] *n* تَحسُن [taħass] ▷ *v* يَتقَدم [jataqadamu]; **advance booking** *n* حجز مقدم [Hajz mo'qadam]
advanced [əd'vɑ:nst] *adj* متقدم [mutaqaddim]
advantage [əd'vɑ:ntɪdʒ] *n* ميزة [mi:za]
advent ['ædvɛnt; -vənt] *n* نزول المسيح [Nezool al-maseeḥ]
adventure [əd'vɛntʃə] *n* مغامرة [muɣa:mara]
adventurous [əd'vɛntʃərəs] *adj* مُغامر [muɣa:mir]
adverb ['æd,vɜ:b] *n* ظرف [zˤarf]
adversary ['ædvəsərɪ] *n* خَصْم [xasˤm]
advert ['ædvɜ:t] *n* إعلان [ʔiʕla:n]
advertise ['ædvə,taɪz] *v* أذاع [ʔaða:ʕa]
advertisement [əd'vɜ:tɪsmənt; -tɪz-] *n* إعلان [ʔiʕla:n]
advertising ['ædvə,taɪzɪŋ] *n* صناعة الإعلان [Ṣena'aat al e'alan]

advice [ədˈvaɪs] *n* نصيحة [nasˤi:ħa]
advisable [ədˈvaɪzəbᵊl] *adj* من مستحسن [Men al-mostahsan]
advise [ədˈvaɪz] *v* ينصح [jansˤaħu]
aerial [ˈɛərɪəl] *n* هوائي [hawa:ʔij]
aerobics [ɛəˈrəʊbɪks] *npl* أيروبكس [ʔajru:bi:k]
aerosol [ˈɛərəˌsɒl] *n* هباء جوي [Habaa jawey]
affair [əˈfɛə] *n* شأن [ʃaʔn]
affect [əˈfɛkt] *v* يُؤثِر [juaθθiru]
affectionate [əˈfɛkʃənɪt] *adj* حنون [ħanu:n]
afford [əˈfɔːd] *v* يقدر [jaqdiru]
affordable [əˈfɔːdəbᵊl] *adj* يُمْكِن شراؤه [jumkinu ʃira:ʔuhu]
Afghan [ˈæfgæn; -gən] *adj* أفغاني [ʔafɣa:nij] ▷ *n* أفغاني [ʔafɣa:nij]
Afghanistan [æfˈgænɪˌstɑːn; -ˌstæn] *n* افغانستان [ʔafɣa:nista:n]
afraid [əˈfreɪd] *adj* خائف [xa:ʔif]
Africa [ˈæfrɪkə] *n* إفريقيا [ʔifri:qja:]; **North Africa** *n* شمال أفريقيا [Shamal afreekya]; **South Africa** *n* جنوب أفريقيا [Janoob afree'qya]
African [ˈæfrɪkən] *adj* أفريقي [ʔifri:qij] ▷ *n* إفريقي [ʔifri:qij]; **Central African Republic** *n* جمهورية أفريقيا الوسطى [Jomhoreyat afre'qya al-wosṭa]; **North African** *n* شخص من شمال إفريقيا [Shakhs men shamal afree'qya]من , شمال إفريقيا [Men shamal afree'qya]; **South African** *n* جنوب أفريقي [Janoob afree'qy]شخص من جنوب أفريقيا , [Shkhṣ men janoob afree'qya]
Afrikaans [ˌæfrɪˈkɑːns; -ˈkɑːnz] *n* اللغة الأفريكانية [Al-loghah al-afreekaneyah]
Afrikaner [afriˈkɑːnə; ˌæfrɪˈkɑːnə] *n* جنوب أفريقي من أصل أوربي وخاصة من المستوطنين الهولنديين [ʒanu:bu ʔifri:qijjin min ʔasˤlin ʔu:rubbi: waxa:sˤsˤatan mina al-mustawtˤini:na al-hu:landijji:na]
after [ˈɑːftə] *conj* بَعْد [baʕda] ▷ *prep* بَعْدَما [Ba'dama]
afternoon [ˌɑːftəˈnuːn] *n* بَعْد الظهر [Ba'ada al-ḍhohr]
afters [ˈɑːftəz] *npl* أوقات الظهيرة [Aw'qat aldhaherah]
aftershave [ˈɑːftəˌʃeɪv] *n* عِطْر الكولونيا ['aeṭr alkoloneya]
afterwards [ˈɑːftəwədz] *adv* بَعْد ذلك [Ba'ad dhalek]
again [əˈgɛn; əˈgeɪn] *adv* مرة ثانية [Marrah thaneyah]
against [əˈgɛnst; əˈgeɪnst] *prep* ضد [dˤiddun]
age [eɪdʒ] *n* سِن المرء [Sen al-mara]; **age limit** *n* حد السّن [Had alssan]; **Middle Ages** *npl* العصور الوسطى [Al-'aoṣoor al-wosṭa]
aged [ˈeɪdʒɪd] *adj* مُسِن [musinn]
agency [ˈeɪdʒənsɪ] *n* وكالة [wika:la]; **travel agency** *n* وكالة سفريات [Wakalat safareyat]
agenda [əˈdʒɛndə] *n* جدول أعمال [Jadwal a'amal]
agent [ˈeɪdʒənt] *n* وكيل [waki:l]; **estate agent** *n* سِمسار عقارات [Semsaar a'qarat]; **travel agent** *n* وكيل سفريات [Wakeel safareyat]
aggressive [əˈgrɛsɪv] *adj* عدواني [ʕudwa:nij]
AGM [eɪ dʒiː ɛm] *abbr* الاجتماع السنوي للجمعية العمومية [Al-jtema'a alsanawey leljam'ayah al'aomomeyah]
ago [əˈgəʊ] *adv*; **a month ago** منذ شهر [mundho shahr]; **a week ago** منذ أسبوع [mundho isboo'a]
agony [ˈægənɪ] *n* (سكرة الموت) أَلَمْ [ʔalam]
agree [əˈgriː] *v* يَقْبَل [jaqbalu]
agreed [əˈgriːd] *adj* مُتفق عليه [Moṭafa'q 'alayeh]
agreement [əˈgriːmənt] *n* اتفاق [ʔittifa:q]
agricultural [ˈægrɪˌkʌltʃərəl] *adj* زراعي [zira:ʕij]
agriculture [ˈægrɪˌkʌltʃə] *n* زِرَاعة [zira:ʕa]
ahead [əˈhɛd] *adv* قُدُماً [qudumaan]
aid [eɪd] *n* عون [ʕawn]; **first aid** *n* إسعافات أولية [Es'aafat awaleyah];

first-aid kit *n* أدوات الإسعافات الأولية [Adawat al-es'aafaat al-awaleyah]; **hearing aid** *n* وسائل المساعدة السمعية [Wasael al-mosa'adah al-sam'aeyah]
AIDS [eɪdz] *n* الإيدز [alʔi:dz]
aim [eɪm] *n* هدف [hadaf] ▷ *v* يَسعَى إلى [Yas'aaa ela]
air [ɛə] *n* هواء [hawa:ʔ]; **air hostess** *n* مضيفة جوية [Moḍeefah jaweyah]; **air-traffic controller** *n* مراقبة جوية [Mora'qabah jaweyah]; **Air Force** *n* سلاح الطيران [Selaḥ al-ṭayaran]; **Can you check the air, please?** هل يمكن مراجعة ضغط الهواء في الإطارات من فضلك؟ [hal yamken mura-ja'aat ḍaghṭ al-hawaa fee al-eṭaraat min faḍlak?]
airbag [ɛəbæg] *n* وِسَادة هوائية [Wesadah hwaaeyah]
air-conditioned [ɛəkən'dɪʃənd] *adj* مُكيف الهواء [Mokaeyaf al-hawaa]
air conditioning [ɛə kən'dɪʃənɪŋ] *n* تكييف الهواء [Takyeef al-hawaa]
aircraft ['ɛəˌkrɑ:ft] *n* طائرة [tˤa:ʔira]
airline ['ɛəˌlaɪn] *n* شركة طيران [Sharekat ṭayaraan]
airmail ['ɛəˌmeɪl] *n* بريد جوي [Bareed jawey]
airport ['ɛəˌpɔ:t] *n* مطار [matˤa:r]; **airport bus** *n* أتوبيس المطار [Otobees al-maṭar]; **How do I get to the airport?** كيف يمكن أن أذهب إلى المطار [Kayf yomken an adhhab ela al-maṭar]; **How much is the taxi to the airport?** ما هي أجرة التاكسي للذهاب إلى المطار؟ [ma heya ejrat al-taxi lel-thehaab ela al-maṭaar?]; **Is there a bus to the airport?** هل يوجد أتوبيس يتجه إلى المطار؟ [Hal yojad otobees yatjeh ela al-maṭaar?]
airsick ['ɛəˌsɪk] *adj* دوار الجو [Dawar al-jaw]
airspace ['ɛəˌspeɪs] *n* مجال جوي [Majal jawey]
airtight ['ɛəˌtaɪt] *adj* مُحكم الغلق [Moḥkam al-ghal'q]
aisle [aɪl] *n* ممشى [mamʃa:]
alarm [ə'lɑ:m] *n* إنذار [ʔinða:r]; **alarm call** *n* نداء استغاثة [Nedaa esteghathah]; **alarm clock** *n* منبه [munabbihun]; **false alarm** *n* إنذار كاذب [endhar kadheb]; **fire alarm** *n* إنذار حريق [endhar Haree'q]; **smoke alarm** *n* كاشف الدُخان [Kashef al-dokhan]
alarming [ə'lɑ:mɪŋ] *adj* مُرْعِبٌ [murʕib]
Albania [æl'beɪnɪə] *n* ألبانيا [ʔalba:nja:]
Albanian [æl'beɪnɪən] *adj* ألباني [ʔalba:nij] ▷ *n (language)* اللغة الألبانية [Al-loghah al-albaneyah], *(person)* ألباني [ʔalba:nij]
album ['ælbəm] *n* ألبوم [ʔalbu:m]; **photo album** *n* ألبوم الصور [Albom al sewar]
alcohol ['ælkəˌhɒl] *n* كحول [kuħu:l]; **Does that contain alcohol?** هل يحتوى هذا على الكحول؟ [hal yaḥ-tawy hadha 'aala al-kiḥool?]; **I don't drink alcohol** أنا لا أشرب الكحول [ana la ashrab al-koḥool] لا أتناول المشروبات الكحولية , [la ata-nawal al-mashro-baat al-kiḥol-iyah]
alcohol-free ['ælkəˌhɒlfri:] *adj* خالي من الكحول [Khaley men al-koḥool]
alcoholic [ˌælkə'hɒlɪk] *adj* كحولي [kuħu:lij] ▷ *n* سكير [sikki:r]
alert [ə'lɜ:t] *adj* منتبه [muntabih] ▷ *v* يُنَبِه [junabbihu]
Algeria [æl'dʒɪərɪə] *n* الجزائر [ʔal-ʒaza:ʔiru]
Algerian [æl'dʒɪərɪən] *adj* جزائري [ʒaza:ʔirij] ▷ *n* شخص جزائري [Shakhṣ jazayry]
alias ['eɪlɪəs] *adv* اسم مستعار [Esm mostaar] ▷ *prep* الشهير بـ [Al-shaheer be-]
alibi ['ælɪˌbaɪ] *n* دفع بالغيبة [Dafa'a bel-ghaybah]
alien ['eɪljən; 'eɪlɪən] *n* أجنبي [ʔaʒnabij]
alive [ə'laɪv] *adj* على قيد الحياة [Ala 'qayd al-hayah]
all [ɔ:l] *adj* جميع [ʒami:ʕ] ▷ *pron* كُلّ [kulla]
Allah ['ælə] *n* الله [allahu]
allegation [ˌælɪ'geɪʃən] *n* إدّعَاء [ʔiddiʕa:ʔ]

alleged [əˈlɛdʒd] *adj* مَزْعوم [mazʕu:m]
allergic [əˈlɜːdʒɪk] *adj* مثير للحساسية [Mother lel-hasaseyah]
allergy [ˈælədʒɪ] *n* حساسية [ħasa:sijja]; **peanut allergy** *n* حساسية تجاه الفول السوداني [Hasaseyah tejah al-fool alsodaney]
alley [ˈælɪ] *n* زُقَاق [zuqa:q]
alliance [əˈlaɪəns] *n* تَحَالُف [taħa:luf]
alligator [ˈælɪˌgeɪtə] *n* تمساح أمريكي [Temsaah amreekey]
allow [əˈlaʊ] *v* يَسمَح [jasmaħu]
all right [ɔːl raɪt] *adv* على ما يُرام [ˈaala ma yoram]
ally [ˈælaɪ; əˈlaɪ] *n* حليف [ħali:f]
almond [ˈɑːmənd] *n* لوز [lawz]
almost [ˈɔːlməʊst] *adv* تقريباً [taqri:ban]
alone [əˈləʊn] *adj* وحيد [waħi:d]
along [əˈlɒŋ] *prep* على طول [Ala ṭool]
aloud [əˈlaʊd] *adv* بصوت مرتفع [Beṣot mortafe'a]
alphabet [ˈælfəˌbɛt] *n* أبجدية [ʔabaʒadijja]
Alps [ælps] *npl* جبال الألب [ʒiba:lu al-ʔalbi]
already [ɔːlˈrɛdɪ] *adv* بالفعل [bi-al-fiʕli]
alright [ɔːlˈraɪt] *adv*; **Are you alright?** هل أنت على ما يرام [hal anta 'aala ma yoraam?]
also [ˈɔːlsəʊ] *adv* أيضا [ʔajdˤan]
altar [ˈɔːltə] *n* مذبح الكنيسة [madhbaḥ al-kaneesah]
alter [ˈɔːltə] *v* يُبَدل [jubaddilu]
alternate [ɔːlˈtɜːnɪt] *adj* مُتَناوب [mutana:wibb]
alternative [ɔːlˈtɜːnətɪv] *adj* بَدِيل [badi:l] ▷ *n* بديل [badi:l]
alternatively [ɔːlˈtɜːnətɪvlɪ] *adv* بالتبادل [bittaba:dali]
although [ɔːlˈðəʊ] *conj* بالرغم من [Bel-raghm men]
altitude [ˈæltɪˌtjuːd] *n* عُلُوْ [ʕuluww]
altogether [ˌɔːltəˈgɛðə; ˈɔːltəˌgɛðə] *adv* تماما [tama:man]
aluminium [ˌæljʊˈmɪnɪəm] *n* ألومونيوم [ʔalu:minju:m]
always [ˈɔːlweɪz; -wɪz] *adv* دائما [da:ʔiman]
a.m. [eɪɛm] *abbr* صباحا [sˤaba:ħan]; **I will be leaving tomorrow morning at ten a.m.** سوف أغادر غدا في الساعة العاشرة صباحا [sawfa oghader ghadan fee al-sa'aa al-'aashera ṣaba-han]
amateur [ˈæmətə; -tʃə; -ˌtjʊə; ˌæməˈtɜː] *n* هاوٍ [ha:win]
amaze [əˈmeɪz] *v* يُذهِل [juðhilu]
amazed [əˈmeɪzd] *adj* مندهش [mundahiʃ]
amazing [əˈmeɪzɪŋ] *adj* رائع [ra:ʔiʕ]
ambassador [æmˈbæsədə] *n* سَفير [safi:r]
amber [ˈæmbə] *n* كهرمان [kahrama:n]
ambition [æmˈbɪʃən] *n* طُموح [tˤamu:ħ]
ambitious [æmˈbɪʃəs] *adj* طَموح [tˤumu:ħ]
ambulance [ˈæmbjʊləns] *n* سيارة إسعاف [Sayarat es'aaf]
ambush [ˈæmbʊʃ] *n* كمين [kami:n]
amenities [əˈmiːnɪtɪz] *npl* أسباب الراحة [Asbab al-rahah]
America [əˈmɛrɪkə] *n* أمريكا [ʔamri:ka:]; **Central America** *n* أمريكا الوسطى [Amrika al wostaa]; **North America** *n* أمريكا الشمالية [Amreeka al- Shamaleyah]; **South America** *n* أمريكا الجنوبية [Amrika al janobeyiah]
American [əˈmɛrɪkən] *adj* أمريكي [ʔamri:kij] ▷ *n* أمريكي [ʔamri:kij]; **American football** *n* كرة القدم الأمريكية [Korat al-'qadam al-amreekeyah]; **North American** *n* شخص من أمريكا الشمالية [Shkhṣ men Amrika al shamalyiah]من أمريكا الشمالية , [men Amrika al shamalyiah]; **South American** *n* جنوب أمريكي [Janoob amriky]شخص من أمريكا الجنوبية , [Shakhṣ men amreeka al-janoobeyah]
ammunition [ˌæmjʊˈnɪʃən] *n* ذَخِيرة [ðaxi:ra]
among [əˈmʌŋ] *prep* وسطَ [wasatˤa]
amount [əˈmaʊnt] *n* مبلغ [mablaɣ]
amp [æmp] *n* أمبير [ʔambi:r]

amplifier ['æmplɪˌfaɪə] *n* مكبر [mukabbir]
amuse [ə'mjuːz] *v* يُسَلي [jusalliː]; **amusement arcade** *n* لعبة ترفيهية [Lo'abah trafeheyah]
an [ɑːn] *art* أداة تنكير [ʔadaːtu tankiːr]
anaemic [ə'niːmɪk] *adj* مُصاب بالأنيميا [Moṣaab bel-aneemeya]
anaesthetic [ˌænɪs'θɛtɪk] *n* مُخَدِّرٌ [muxaddir]; **general anaesthetic** *n* مٌخَدِر كلي [Mo-khader koley]; **local anaesthetic** *n* عقار مخدر موضعي ['aa'qar mokhader mawde'aey]
analyse ['ænəˌlaɪz] *v* يُحلِل [juħallilu]
analysis [ə'nælɪsɪs] *n* تحليل [taħliːl]
ancestor ['ænsɛstə] *n* سَلف [salaf]
anchor ['æŋkə] *n* مرساة [mirsaːt]
anchovy ['æntʃəvɪ] *n* أنشوجة [ʔunʃuːda]
ancient ['eɪnʃənt] *adj* قديم [qadiːm]
and [ænd; ənd; ən] *conj* و [wa]; **a whisky and soda** ويسكي بالصودا [wesky bil-ṣoda]; **in black and white** باللون الأسود والأبيض [bil-lawn al-aswad wa al-abyaḍ]
Andes ['ændiːz] *npl* جبال الأنديز [ʒibaːlu al-ʔandiːzi]
Andorra [æn'dɔːrə] *n* إمارة أندورة [ʔimaːratu ʔanduːrata]
angel ['eɪndʒəl] *n* ملاك [malaːk]
anger ['æŋgə] *n* غضب [ɣadˤab]
angina [æn'dʒaɪnə] *n* ذبحة صدرية [dhabhah ṣadreyah]
angle ['æŋgəl] *n* زاوية [zaːwija]; **right angle** *n* زاوية يُمنى [Zaweyah yomna]
angler ['æŋglə] *n* سمك الشص [Samak al-shaṣ]
angling ['æŋglɪŋ] *n* صيد بالسِنَّارة [Ṣayd bel-sayarah]
Angola [æŋ'gəʊlə] *n* أنجولا [ʔanʒuːlaː]
Angolan [æŋ'gəʊlən] *adj* أنجولي [ʔanʒuːlij] ▷ *n* أنجولي [ʔanʒuːlij]
angry ['æŋgrɪ] *adj* غاضب [ɣaːdˤib]
animal ['ænɪməl] *n* حيوان [ħajawaːn]
aniseed ['ænɪˌsiːd] *n* يانسون [jaːnsuːn]
ankle ['æŋkəl] *n* رُسغ القدم [rosgh al-'qadam]

anniversary [ˌænɪ'vɜːsərɪ] *n* ذِكْرى سنوية [dhekra sanaweyah]; **wedding anniversary** *n* عيد الزواج ['aeed al-zawaj]
announce [ə'naʊns] *v* يُعلن [juʕlinu]
announcement [ə'naʊnsmənt] *n* إعلان [ʔiʕlaːn]
annoy [ə'nɔɪ] *v* يُضايق [judˤaːjiqu]
annoying [ə'nɔɪɪŋ; an'noying] *adj* مضايق [mudˤaːjiq]
annual ['ænjʊəl] *adj* سنوي [sanawij]
annually ['ænjʊəlɪ] *adv* كل عام [Kol-'aaam]
anonymous [ə'nɒnɪməs] *adj* غير مسمى [ghayr mosama]
anorak ['ænəˌræk] *n* جاكيت ثقيل [Jaket tha'qeel]
anorexia [ˌænɒ'rɛksɪə] *n* فقدان الشهية [Fo'qdaan al-shaheyah]
anorexic [ˌænɒ'rɛksɪk] *adj* مُفقِد للشهية [Mof'qed lel-shaheyah]
another [ə'nʌðə] *adj* آخَر [ʔaːxaru]
answer ['ɑːnsə] *n* إجابة [ʔiʒaːba] ▷ *v* يُجيب [juʒiːbu]
answerphone ['ɑːnsəfəʊn] *n* تليفون مزود بوظيفة الرد الآلي [Telephone mozawad be-waḍheefat al-rad al-aaley]
ant [ænt] *n* نملة [namla]
antagonize [æn'tægəˌnaɪz] *v* يُعادي [juʕaːdiː]
Antarctic [ænt'ɑːktɪk] *adj* القارة القطبية الجنوبية [Al-'qarah al-'qoṭbeyah al-janoobeyah]; **the Antarctic** *n* قطبي جنوبي ['qoṭbey janoobey]
Antarctica [ænt'ɑːktɪkə] *n* قطبي جنوبي ['qoṭbey janoobey]
antelope ['æntɪˌləʊp] *n* ظبي [zˤabjj]
antenatal [ˌæntɪ'neɪtəl] *adj* جنيني [ʒaniːnij]
anthem ['ænθəm] *n* نشيد [naʃiːd]
anthropology [ˌænθrə'pɒlədʒɪ] *n* الأنثروبولوجيا [ʔal-ʔanθiruːbuːluːʒjaː]
antibiotic [ˌæntɪbaɪ'ɒtɪk] *n* مضاد حيوي [Moḍad ḥayawey]
antibody ['æntɪˌbɒdɪ] *n* جسم مضاد [Jesm moḍad]

anticlockwise [ˌæntɪˈklɒkˌwaɪz] *adv* عكس عقارب الساعة [ʻaaks ʻaaʼqareb al-saaʼah]
antidepressant [ˌæntɪdɪˈprɛsᵊnt] *n* مضاد للاكتئاب [Moḍad lel-ekteaab]
antidote [ˈæntɪˌdəʊt] *n* ترياق [tirja:q]
antifreeze [ˈæntɪˌfriːz] *n* مانع للتجمد [Maneʼa lel-tajamod]
antihistamine [ˌæntɪˈhɪstəˌmiːn; -mɪn] *n* مضاد للهستامين [Moḍad lel-hestameen]
antiperspirant [ˌæntɪˈpɜːspərənt] *n* مضاد لإفراز العرق [Moḍad le-efraz al-ʼaarʼq]
antique [ænˈtiːk] *n* عتيق [ʕati:q]; **antique shop** *n* متجر المقتنيات القديمة [Matjar al-moʼqtanayat al-ʼqadeemah]
antiseptic [ˌæntɪˈsɛptɪk] *n* مُطهر [mutˁahhir]
antivirus [ˈæntɪˌvaɪrəs] *n* مضاد للفيروسات [Moḍad lel-fayrosat]
anxiety [æŋˈzaɪɪtɪ] *n* توق شديد [Tooʼq shaded]
any [ˈɛnɪ] *pron* أي [ʔajju]أي من , [Ay men]; **Do you have any vegan dishes?** هل يوجد أي أطباق نباتية؟ [hal yujad ay aṭbaaʼq nabat-iya?]; **I don't have any cash** ليس معي أية أموال نقدية [laysa maʼay ayat amwaal naʼq-diya]
anybody [ˈɛnɪˌbɒdɪ; -bədɪ] *pron* أي شخص [Ay shakhṣ]
anyhow [ˈɛnɪˌhaʊ] *adv* بأي طريقة [Be-ay ṭareeʼqah]
anyone [ˈɛnɪˌwʌn; -wən] *pron* أحد [ʔaħadun]
anything [ˈɛnɪˌθɪŋ] *pron* أي شيء [Ay shaya]; **Do you need anything?** هل تحتاج إلى أي شيء؟ [hal taḥtaaj ela ay shay?]
anyway [ˈɛnɪˌweɪ] *adv* على أي حال [Ala ay ḥal]
anywhere [ˈɛnɪˌwɛə] *adv* في أي مكان [Fee ay makan]
apart [əˈpɑːt] *adv* بشكل مُنفَصِل [Beshakl monfaṣel]
apart from [əˈpɑːt frɒm] *prep* بخلاف [Be-khelaf]
apartment [əˈpɑːtmənt] *n* شَقّة [ʃuqqa]
aperitif [ɑːˌpɛrɪˈtiːf] *n* مشروب فاتح للشهية [Mashroob fateḥ lel shaheyah]
aperture [ˈæpətʃə] *n* ثقب [θuqb]
apologize [əˈpɒləˌdʒaɪz] *v* يعتذر [jaʕtaðiru]
apology [əˈpɒlədʒɪ] *n* اعتذار [ʔiʕtiða:r]
apostrophe [əˈpɒstrəfɪ] *n* فاصلة علوية [Faṣela aʼolweyah]
appalling [əˈpɔːlɪŋ] *adj* مروع [murawwiʕ]
apparatus [ˌæpəˈreɪtəs; -ˈrɑːtəs; ˈæpəˌreɪtəs] *n* جهاز [ʒiha:z]
apparent [əˈpærənt; əˈpɛər-] *adj* ظاهر [zˁa:hir]
apparently [əˈpærəntlɪ; əˈpɛər-] *adv* من الواضح [Men al-waḍeḥ]
appeal [əˈpiːl] *n* استئناف [ʔistiʔna:f] ▷ *v* يَستأنِف حكما [Yastaanef al-hokm]
appear [əˈpɪə] *v* يَظْهَر [jazˁharu]
appearance [əˈpɪərəns] *n* مظهر [mazˁhar]
appendicitis [əˌpɛndɪˈsaɪtɪs] *n* التهاب الزائدة [Eltehab al-zaedah]
appetite [ˈæpɪˌtaɪt] *n* شهية [ʃahijja]
applaud [əˈplɔːd] *v* يُطْرِي [jutˁri:]
applause [əˈplɔːz] *n* تصفيق [tasˁfi:q]
apple [ˈæpᵊl] *n* تفاحة [tuffa:ħa]; **apple pie** *n* فطيرة التفاح [Faṭeerat al-tofaaḥ]
appliance [əˈplaɪəns] *n* جهاز [ʒiha:z]
applicant [ˈæplɪkənt] *n* مُقدم الطلَب [Moʼqadem al-ṭalab]
application [ˌæplɪˈkeɪʃən] *n* طلب [tˁalab]; **application form** *n* نموذج الطلب [Namozaj al-ṭalab]
apply [əˈplaɪ] *v* يَتقَدم بطلب [Yataʼqadam be-ṭalab]
appoint [əˈpɔɪnt] *v* يُعين [juʕajjinu]
appointment [əˈpɔɪntmənt] *n* موعد [mawʕid]; **Can I have an appointment with the doctor?** هل يمكنني تحديد موعد مع الطبيب؟ [hal yamken -any taḥdeed mawʼaid maʼaa al-ṭabeeb?]; **Do you have an**

appointment? هل تحدد لك موعدًا؟ [hal taḥa-dada laka maw'aid?]; **I have an appointment with...** لدي موعد مع.....؟ [la-daya maw-'aid m'aa...]; **I'd like to make an appointment** أود في تحديد موعد [awid fee taḥdeed maw'aid]
appreciate [ə'priːʃɪˌeɪt; -sɪ-] *v* يُقَدِر [jaqdiru]
apprehensive [ˌæprɪ'hɛnsɪv] *adj* خائف [xaːʔif]
apprentice [ə'prɛntɪs] *n* مهني مبتدئ [Mehaney mobtadea]
approach [ə'prəʊtʃ] *v* يَقْتَرِب [jaqtaribu]
appropriate [ə'prəʊprɪɪt] *adj* ملائم [mulaːʔim]
approval [ə'pruːvᵊl] *n* موافقة [muwaːfaqa]
approve [ə'pruːv] *v* يوافق [juwaːfiqu]
approximate [ə'prɒksɪmɪt] *adj* تقريبي [taqriːbij]
approximately [ə'prɒksɪmɪtlɪ] *adv* تقريبا [taqriːban]
apricot ['eɪprɪˌkɒt] *n* مشمش [miʃmiʃ]
April ['eɪprəl] *n* أبريل [ʔabriːl]; **April Fools' Day** *n* يوم كذبة أبريل [yawm kedhbat abreel]
apron ['eɪprən] *n* مريلة مطبخ [Maryalat maṭbakh]
aquarium [ə'kwɛərɪəm] *n* حوض سمك [Hawḍ al-samak]
Aquarius [ə'kwɛərɪəs] *n* الدلو [addaluː]
Arab ['ærəb] *adj* عربي الجنسية ['arabey al-jenseyah] ▷ *n* *(person)* شخص عربي [Shakhṣ 'arabey]; **United Arab Emirates** *npl* الإمارات العربية المتحدة [Al-emaraat al'arabeyah al-motaḥedah]
Arabic ['ærəbɪk] *adj* عربي [ʕarabij] ▷ *n* *(language)* اللغة العربية [Al-loghah al-arabeyah]
arbitration [ˌɑːbɪ'treɪʃən] *n* تحكيم [taħkiːm]
arch [ɑːtʃ] *n* قنطرة [qantˤara]
archaeologist [ˌɑːkɪ'ɒlədʒɪst] *n* عالم آثار ['aalem aathar]
archaeology [ˌɑːkɪ'ɒlədʒɪ] *n* عِلم الآثار ['Aelm al-aathar]
archbishop ['ɑːtʃ'bɪʃəp] *n* رئيس أساقفة [Raees asa'qefah]
architect ['ɑːkɪˌtɛkt] *n* معماري [miʕmairjj]
architecture ['ɑːkɪˌtɛktʃə] *n* فن العمارة [Fan el-'aemarah]
archive ['ɑːkaɪv] *n* أرشيف [ʔarʃiːf]
Arctic ['ɑːktɪk] *adj* قطبي شمالي ['qoṭbey shamaley]; **Arctic Circle** *n* الدائرة القطبية الشمالية [Al-daerah al'qoṭbeyah al-Shamaleyah]; **Arctic Ocean** *n* المحيط القطبي الشمالي [Al-moḥeeṭ al-'qoṭbey al-shamaley]; **the Arctic** *n* قطبي شمالي ['qoṭbey shamaley]
area ['ɛərɪə] *n* مجال [maʒaːl]; **service area** *n* منطقة تقديم الخدمات [Menta'qat ta'qdeem al- khadamat]
Argentina [ˌɑːdʒən'tiːnə] *n* الأرجنتين [ʔal-ʔarʒuntiːn]
Argentinian [ˌɑːdʒən'tɪnɪən] *adj* أرجنتيني [ʔarʒuntiːnij] ▷ *n* *(person)* أرجنتيني [ʔarʒuntiːnij]
argue ['ɑːgjuː] *v* يُجادل [juʒaːdilu]
argument ['ɑːgjʊmənt] *n* مشادة كلامية [Moshadah kalameyah]
Aries ['ɛəriːz] *n* الحَمَل [alħamal]
arm [ɑːm] *n* ذِرَاع [ðiraːʕ]
armchair ['ɑːmˌtʃɛə] *n* كرسي مزود بذراعين [Korsey mozawad be-dhera'aayn]
armed [ɑːmd] *adj* مُسلح [musallaħ]
Armenia [ɑː'miːnɪə] *n* أرمنيا [ʔarminjaː]
Armenian [ɑː'miːnɪən] *adj* أرمني [ʔarminij] ▷ *n* *(language)* اللغة الأرمنية [Al-loghah al-armeeneyah], *(person)* أرمني [ʔarminij]
armour ['ɑːmə] *n* دِرْع [dirʕ]
armpit ['ɑːmˌpɪt] *n* إبط [ʔibitˤ]
army ['ɑːmɪ] *n* جيش [ʒajʃ]
aroma [ə'rəʊmə] *n* عبير [ʕabiːr]
aromatherapy [əˌrəʊmə'θɛrəpɪ] *n* علاج بالعطور ['aelaj bel-oṭoor]
around [ə'raʊnd] *adv* حول [ħawla] ▷ *prep* في مكان قريب [fiː makaːnin qariːbin]
arrange [ə'reɪndʒ] *v* يُرتب [jurattibu]
arrangement [ə'reɪndʒmənt] *n* ترتيب

[tarti:b]
arrears [əˈrɪəz] *npl* متأخرات [mutaʔaxxira:tun]
arrest [əˈrɛst] *n* اعتقال [ʔiʕtiqa:l] ▷ *v* يَقْبض على [jaqbudˤu ʕala:]
arrival [əˈraɪvᵊl] *n* وصول [wusˤu:l]
arrive [əˈraɪv] *v* يَصل [jasˤilu]
arrogant [ˈærəgənt] *adj* متعجرف [mutaʕaʒrif]
arrow [ˈærəʊ] *n* سهم [sahm]
arson [ˈɑːsᵊn] *n* إشعال الحرائق [Esha'aal alḥarae'q]
art [ɑːt] *n* (مهارة) فن [fann]; **art gallery** *n* جاليري فني [Jalery faney]; **art school** *n* كلية الفنون [Koleyat al-fonoon]; **work of art** *n* عمل فني ['amal faney]
artery [ˈɑːtərɪ] *n* شُريان [ʃurja:n]
arthritis [ɑːˈθraɪtɪs] *n* التهاب المفاصل [Eltehab al-mafaṣel]
artichoke [ˈɑːtɪˌtʃəʊk] *n* خرشوف [xarʃu:f]
article [ˈɑːtɪkᵊl] *n* مقالة [maqa:la]
artificial [ˌɑːtɪˈfɪʃəl] *adj* اصطناعي [ʔisˤtˤina:ʕij]
artist [ˈɑːtɪst] *n* فنان [fanna:n]
artistic [ɑːˈtɪstɪk; arˈtistic] *adj* فني [fanij]
as [əz] *adv* حيث أن [Hayth ann] ▷ *conj* بينما [bajnama:] ▷ *prep* كما [kama:]
asap [eɪsæp] *abbr* بأسرع ما يُمكن [Beasraa'a ma yomken]
ascent [əˈsɛnt] *n*; **When is the last ascent?** ما هو موعد آخر هبوط للتزلج؟ [ma howa maw-'aid aakhir hibooṭ lel-tazaluj?]
ashamed [əˈʃeɪmd] *adj* خجلان [xaʒla:n]
ashore [əˈʃɔː] *adv*; **Can we go ashore now?** أيمكننا العودة إلى الشاطئ الآن؟ [a-yamkun-ana al-'awdah ela al-shaṭee al-aan?]
ashtray [ˈæʃˌtreɪ] *n* طفاية السجائر [Ṭafayat al-sajayer]
Asia [ˈeɪʃə; ˈeɪʒə] *n* آسيا [ʔa:sja:]
Asian [ˈeɪʃən; ˈeɪʒən] *adj* أسيوي [ʔa:sjawij] ▷ *n* أسيوي [ʔa:sjawij]
Asiatic [ˌeɪʃɪˈætɪk; -zɪ-] *adj* أسيوي [ʔa:sjawij]
ask [ɑːsk] *v* يَسْأل [jasʔalu]
ask for [ɑːsk fɔː] *v* يَطلُب [jatˤlubu]
asleep [əˈsliːp] *adj* نائم [na:ʔim]
asparagus [əˈspærəgəs] *n* نبات الاسبراجوس [naba:tu ala:sbara:ʒu:s]
aspect [ˈæspɛkt] *n* ناحية [na:ħija]
aspirin [ˈæsprɪn] *n* أسبرين [ʔasbiri:n]; **I can't take aspirin** لا يمكنني تناول الأسبرين [la yam-kinuni tanawil al-asbireen]; **I'd like some aspirin** أريد بعض الأسبرين [areed ba'aḍ al-asbereen]
assembly [əˈsɛmblɪ] *n* اجتماع [ʔiʒtima:ʕ]
asset [ˈæsɛt] *n* شيء ثمين [ʃajʔun θami:n]; **assets** *(property)* أصل [ʔasˤlun]
assignment [əˈsaɪnmənt] *n* مهمة [mahamma]
assistance [əˈsɪstəns] *n* مساعدة [musa:ʕada]; **I need assistance** أحتاج إلى مساعدة [aḥtaaj ela musa-'aada]
assistant [əˈsɪstənt] *n* مساعد [musa:ʕid]; **personal assistant** *n* مساعد شخصي [Mosa'aed shakhṣey]; **sales assistant** *n* مساعد المبيعات [Mosa'aed al-mobee'aat]; **shop assistant** *n* مساعد في متجر [Mosa'aed fee matjar]
associate *adj* [əˈsəʊʃɪɪt]مساعد [musa:ʕid] ▷ *n* [əˈsəʊʃɪɪt]مرافق [mura:fiq]
association [əˌsəʊsɪˈeɪʃən; -ʃɪ-] *n* جمعية [ʒamʕijja]
assortment [əˈsɔːtmənt] *n* تصنيف [tasˤni:f]
assume [əˈsjuːm] *v* يَفْتَرِض [jaftaridˤu]
assure [əˈʃʊə] *v* يُطَمئن [jatˤmaʔinnu]
asthma [ˈæsmə] *n* الربو [Al-rabw]
astonish [əˈstɒnɪʃ] *v* يُدهِش [judhiʃu]
astonished [əˈstɒnɪʃt] *adj* مذهول [maðhu:l]
astonishing [əˈstɒnɪʃɪŋ] *adj* مذهل [muðhil]
astrology [əˈstrɒlədʒɪ] *n* علم التنجيم [A'elm al-tanjeem]
astronaut [ˈæstrəˌnɔːt] *n* رائد فضاء [Raeed faḍaa]
astronomy [əˈstrɒnəmɪ] *n* علم الفلك ['aelm al-falak]

asylum [ə'saɪləm] *n* ملتجأ آمن [Moltajaa aamen]; **asylum seeker** *n* طالب لجوء سياسي [ṭ aleb lejoa seyasy]
at [æt] *prep* عند [ʕinda]; **at least** *adv* على الأقل ['ala ala'qal]
atheist ['eɪθɪˌɪst] *n* مُلحِد [mulħid]
athlete ['æθliːt] *n* لاعب رياضي [La'aeb reyaḍey]
athletic [æθ'lɛtɪk] *adj* (رياضي) متعلق بالرياضة البدنية [(Reyaḍy) mota'ale'q bel- Reyaḍah al-badabeyah]
athletics [æθ'lɛtɪks] *npl* ألعاب القوى [ʔalʕaːbun ʔalqiwaː]
Atlantic [ət'læntɪk] *n* أطلنطي [ʔatˤlantˤij]
atlas ['ætləs] *n* الأطلس [ʔal-ʔatˤlasu]
atmosphere ['ætməsˌfɪə] *n* جَوّ [ʒaww]
atom ['ætəm] *n* ذَرَّة [ðarra]; **atom bomb** *n* قنبلة ذرية ['qobelah dhareyah]
atomic [ə'tɒmɪk] *adj* ذَري [ðarij]
attach [ə'tætʃ] *v* يُرْفِق [jurfiqu]
attached [ə'tætʃt] *adj* ملحق [mulħaq]
attachment [ə'tætʃmənt] *n* رَبْط [rabtˤ]
attack [ə'tæk] *n* هجوم [huʒuːm] ▷ *v* يهاجم [juhaːʒimu]; **heart attack** *n* أزمة قلبية [Azmah 'qalbeyah]; **terrorist attack** *n* هجوم إرهابي [Hojoom 'erhaby]; **I've been attacked** لقد تعرضت لهجوم [la'qad ta-'aaraḍto lel-hijoom]
attempt [ə'tɛmpt] *n* محاولة [muħaːwala] ▷ *v* يُحاوِل [juħaːwilu]
attend [ə'tɛnd] *v* يَحضِر [juħadˤdˤiru]
attendance [ə'tɛndəns] *n* الحاضرين [ʔal-ħaːdˤiriːna]
attendant [ə'tɛndənt] *n*; **flight attendant** *n* مضيف الطائرة [moḍeef al-ṭaaerah]
attention [ə'tɛnʃən] *n* انتباه [ʔintibaːh]
attic ['ætɪk] *n* طابق علوي [Ṭabe'q 'aolwei]
attitude ['ætɪˌtjuːd] *n* مَوْقِف [mawqif]
attorney [ə'tɜːnɪ] *n* وكيل [wakiːl]
attract [ə'trækt] *v* يَجذِب [jaʒðibu]
attraction [ə'trækʃən] *n* جاذبية [ʒaːðibijja]
attractive [ə'træktɪv] *adj* جذاب [ʒaððaːb]
aubergine ['əʊbəˌʒiːn] *n* باذنجان [baːðinʒaːn]
auburn ['ɔːbᵊn] *adj* أسمر محمر [Asmar mehmer]
auction ['ɔːkʃən] *n* مزاد [mazaːd]
audience ['ɔːdɪəns] *n* جمهور [ʒumhuːr]
audit ['ɔːdɪt] *n* مراجعة حسابية [Moraj'ah ḥesabeyah] ▷ *v* يدقق الحسابات [Yoda'qe'q al-ḥesabat]
audition [ɔː'dɪʃən] *n* حاسة السمع [Hasat al-sama'a]
auditor ['ɔːdɪtə] *n* مراجع حسابات [Moraaje'a ḥesabat]
August ['ɔːgəst] *n* أغسطس [ʔuɣustˤus]
aunt [ɑːnt] *n* (خالة) عمة [ʕamma]
auntie ['ɑːntɪ] *n* زنجية عجوز [Enjeyah 'aajooz]
au pair [əʊ 'pɛə; o pɛr] *n* أجنبي مقيم [Ajnabey mo'qeem]
austerity [ɒ'stɛrɪtɪ] *n* تقشُف [taqʃifu]
Australasia [ˌɒstrə'leɪzɪə] *n* أوسترالاسيا [ʔuːstraːlaːsjaː]
Australia [ɒ'streɪlɪə] *n* أستراليا [ʔustraːlijaː]
Australian [ɒ'streɪlɪən] *adj* أسترالي [ʔustraːlij] ▷ *n* أسترالي [ʔustraːlij]
Austria ['ɒstrɪə] *n* النمسا [ʔa-nnamsaː]
Austrian ['ɒstrɪən] *adj* نمساوي [namsaːwij] ▷ *n* نمساوي [namsaːwij]
authentic [ɔː'θɛntɪk] *adj* مُوثق [muwaθθiq]
author, authoress ['ɔːθə, 'ɔːθəˌrɛs] *n* المؤلف [ʔal-muallifu]
authorize ['ɔːθəˌraɪz] *v* يُفَوض [jufawwidˤu]
autobiography [ˌɔːtəʊbaɪ'ɒgrəfɪ; ˌɔːtəbaɪ-] *n* سيرة ذاتية [Seerah dhateyah]
autograph ['ɔːtəˌgrɑːf; -ˌgræf] *n* أوتوجراف [ʔuːtuːʒraːf]
automatic [ˌɔːtə'mætɪk] *adj* آلي [ajj]; **An automatic, please** سيارة تعمل بنظام نقل السرعات الآلي من فضلك [sayara ta'amal be-neḍham na'qil al-sur'aat al-aaly, min faḍlak]; **Is it an automatic**

car? هل هذه السيارة تعمل بنظام نقل السرعات الآلي؟ [hal hadhy al-sayarah ta'amal be-neḍham na'qil al-sur'aaat al-aaly?]
automatically [ˌɔːtəˈmætɪklɪ] *adv* آلياً [ajjan]
autonomous [ɔːˈtɒnəməs] *adj* متمتّع بحُكْم ذاتي [Motamet'a be-ḥokm dhatey]
autonomy [ɔːˈtɒnəmɪ] *n* حُكْم ذاتي [ḥokm ḍhatey]
autumn [ˈɔːtəm] *n* الخريف [Al-khareef]
availability [əˈveɪləbɪlɪtɪ] *n* تَوَفُّرٌ [tawaffur]
available [əˈveɪləbᵊl] *adj* متوفر [mutawaffir]
avalanche [ˈævəˌlɑːntʃ] *n* انهيار [ʔinhijaːr]
avenue [ˈævɪˌnjuː] *n* طريق مشجر [ṭaree'q moshajar]
average [ˈævərɪdʒ; ˈævrɪdʒ] *adj* متوسط [mutawassitˤ] ▷ *n* معدل [muʕaddal]
avocado, avocados [ˌævəˈkɑːdəʊ, ˌævəˈkɑːdəʊs] *n* ثمرة الأفوكاتو [Thamarat al-afokatoo]
avoid [əˈvɔɪd] *v* يَتَجنب [jataʒanabbu]
awake [əˈweɪk] *adj* مُستيقظ [mustajqizˤ] ▷ *v* يفَيق [jafiːqu]
award [əˈwɔːd] *n* جائزة [ʒaːʔiza]
aware [əˈwɛə] *adj* مدرك [mudrik]
away [əˈweɪ] *adv* بعيداً [baʕiːdan]; **away match** *n* مباراة الذهاب [Mobarat al-dhehab]
awful [ˈɔːfʊl] *adj* شنيع [ʃaniːʕ]
awfully [ˈɔːfəlɪ; ˈɔːflɪ] *adv* بفظاعة [befaḍha'aah]
awkward [ˈɔːkwəd] *adj* أخْرَق [ʔaxraq]
axe [æks] *n* بَلْطَة [baltˤa]
axle [ˈæksəl] *n* محور الدوران [Meḥwar al-dawaraan]
Azerbaijan [ˌæzəbaɪˈdʒɑːn] *n* أذربيجان [ʔaðarbajʒaːn]
Azerbaijani [ˌæzəbaɪˈdʒɑːnɪ] *adj* أذربيجاني [ʔaðarbiːʒaːnij] ▷ *n* أذربيجاني [ʔaðarbiːʒaːnij]

B&B [biː ænd biː] *n* مبيت وإفطار [Mabeet wa efṭaar]
BA [bɑː] *abbr* ليسانس [lajsaːns]
baby [ˈbeɪbɪ] *n* طفل رضيع [Ṭefl readea'a]; **baby milk** *n* لبن أطفال [Laban aṭfaal]; **baby wipe** *n* منديل أطفال [Mandeel aṭfaal]; **baby's bottle** *n* زجاجة رضاعة الطفل [Zojajat reḍa'aat al-ṭefl]
babysit [ˈbeɪbɪsɪt] *v* يُجالس الأطفال [Yojales al-aṭfaal]
babysitter [ˈbeɪbɪsɪtə] *n* جليس أطفال [Jalees aṭfaal]
babysitting [ˈbeɪbɪsɪtɪŋ] *n* مجالسة الأطفال [Mojalasat al-atfaal]
bachelor [ˈbætʃələ; ˈbætʃlə] *n* أعزب [ʔaʕzab]
back [bæk] *adj* متجه خلفاً [Motajeh khalfan] ▷ *adv* إلى الوراء [Ela al-waraa] ▷ *n* ظَهر [zˤahr] ▷ *v* يُرجع [jurʒiʕu]; **back pain** *n* أَلَمْ الظهر [Alam al-ḍhahr]
backache [ˈbækˌeɪk] *n* أَلَمْ الظهر [Alam al-ḍhahr]
backbone [ˈbækˌbəʊn] *n* عمود فقري ['amood fa'qarey]
backfire [ˌbækˈfaɪə] *v* يُخّلِف نتائج عكسية [Yokhalef nataaej 'aakseyah]
background [ˈbækˌgraʊnd] *n* خلفية

[xalfijja]
backing [ˈbækɪŋ] *n* دَعْم [daʕm]
back out [bæk aʊt] *v* يتراجع عن [jatara:ʒaʕu ʕan]
backpack [ˈbækˌpæk] *n* حقيبة الظهر [Ha'qeebat al-ḍhahr]
backpacker [ˈbækˌpækə] *n* حامل حقيبة الظهر [Hamel ha'qeebat al-ḍhahr]
backpacking [ˈbækˌpækɪŋ] *n* حمل حقيبة الظهر [Hamal ha'qeebat al-ḍhahr]
backside [ˌbækˈsaɪd] *n* مُؤَخِرَّةٌ [muʔaxirra]
backslash [ˈbækˌslæʃ] *n* شرطة مائلة للخلف [Sharṭah maelah lel-khalf]
backstroke [ˈbækˌstrəʊk] *n* ضربة خلفية [Ḍarba khalfeyah]
back up [bæk ʌp] *v* يدعم [jadʕamu]
backup [bækˌʌp] *n* نسخة احتياطية [Noskhah eḥteyaṭeyah]
backwards [ˈbækwədz] *adv* للخلف [Lel-khalf]
bacon [ˈbeɪkən] *n* لحم خنزير مقدد [Laḥm khanzeer me'qaded]
bacteria [bækˈtɪərɪə] *npl* بكتريا [baktirja:]
bad [bæd] *adj* سيء [sajjiʔ]
badge [bædʒ] *n* شارَة [ʃa:ra]
badger [ˈbædʒə] *n* حيوان الغُرَير [Ḥayawaan al-ghoreer]
badly [ˈbædlɪ] *adv* على نحو سيء [Ala nahw saye]
badminton [ˈbædmɪntən] *n* تنس الريشة [Tenes al-reshah]
bad-tempered [bædˈtɛmpəd] *adj* شَرِسٌ [ʃaris]
baffled [ˈbæfəld] *adj* متحير [mutaħajjir]
bag [bæg] *n* حقيبة [ħaqi:ba]; **bum bag** *n* حقيبة صغيرة [Ha'qeebah ṣagheerah]; **carrier bag** *n* كيس مشتريات [Kees moshtarayat]; **overnight bag** *n* حقيبة للرحلات القصيرة [Ha'qeebah lel-rahalat al-'qaṣeerah]; **plastic bag** *n* كيس بلاستيكي [Kees belasteekey]; **polythene bag** *n* حقيبة من البوليثين [Ha'qeebah men al-bolytheleyn]; **shopping bag** *n* كيس التسوق [Kees al-tasawo'q]; **sleeping bag** *n* كيس النوم [Kees al-nawm]; **tea bag** *n* كيس شاي [Kees shaay]; **toilet bag** *n* حقيبة أدوات الاستحمام [Ha'qeebat adwat al-estehmam]; **I don't need a bag, thanks** شكرًا لا أحتاج إلى حقيبة [shukran la aḥtaj ela ḥa'qeba]
baggage [ˈbægɪdʒ] *n* أمتِعَة [ʔamtiʕa]; **baggage allowance** *n* وَزْن الأمتعة المسموح به [Wazn al-amte'aah al-masmooh beh]; **baggage reclaim** *n* استلام الأمتعة [Estelam al-amte'aah]; **excess baggage** *n* وزن زائد للأمتعة [Wazn zaed lel-amte'aah]
baggy [ˈbægɪ] *adj* مرهوظ [marhu:zˤ]
bagpipes [ˈbægˌpaɪps] *npl* مزامير القربة [Mazameer al-'qarbah]
Bahamas [bəˈhɑːməz] *npl* جزر الباهاما [ʒuzuru ʔal-ba:ha:ma:]
Bahrain [bɑːˈreɪn] *n* البحرين [al-baħrajni]
bail [beɪl] *n* كفالة [kafa:la]
bake [beɪk] *v* يَخبز [jaxbizu]
baked [beɪkt] *adj* مخبوز [maxbu:z]; **baked potato** *n* بطاطس بالفرن [Baṭaṭes bel-forn]
baker [ˈbeɪkə] *n* خباز [xabba:z]
bakery [ˈbeɪkərɪ] *n* مخبز [maxbaz]
baking [ˈbeɪkɪŋ] *n* خَبْز [xubz]; **baking powder** *n* مسحوق خبز [Masḥoo'q khobz]
balance [ˈbæləns] *n* توازن [tawa:z]; **balance sheet** *n* ميزانية [mi:za:nijjatun]; **bank balance** *n* حساب بنكي [Hesab bankey]
balanced [ˈbælənst] *adj* متوازن [mutawa:zinn]
balcony [ˈbælkənɪ] *n* شُرْفَة [ʃurfa]
bald [bɔːld] *adj* أصلع [ʔasˤlaʕ]
Balkan [ˈbɔːlkən] *adj* بلقاني [balqa:nij]
ball [bɔːl] *n (dance)* حفل راقص [Half ra'qeṣ], *(toy)* كرة [kura]
ballerina [ˌbæləˈriːnə] *n* راقصة باليه [Ra'ṣat baleeh]
ballet [ˈbæleɪ; bæˈleɪ] *n* باليه [ba:li:h]; **ballet dancer** *n* راقص باليه [Ra'qeṣ baleeh]; **ballet shoes** *npl* حذاء الباليه

[hedhaa al-baleeh]; **Where can I buy tickets for the ballet?** أين يمكنني أن أشتري تذاكر لعرض الباليه؟ [ayna yamken-any an ashtray tadhaker le-'aarḍ al-baleh?]
balloon [bə'lu:n] *n* بالون [ba:lu:n]
bamboo [bæm'bu:] *n* خَيْزُرَان [xajzura:n]
ban [bæn] *n* حظر [ħazˁr] ▷ *v* يَمنَع [jamnaʕu]
banana [bə'nɑ:nə] *n* موز [mawz]
band [bænd] *n (musical group)* فرقة موسيقية [Fer'qah mose'qeyah], *(strip)* رباط [riba:tˁ]; **brass band** *n* فرقة الآلات النحاسية [Fer'qat al-aalat al-naḥaseqeyah]; **elastic band** *n* رباط مطاطى [rebaṭ maṭaṭey]; **rubber band** *n* شريط مطاطي [shareeṭ maṭaṭey]
bandage ['bændɪdʒ] *n* ضمادة [dˁamma:da] ▷ *v* يُضَمد [judˁammidu]; **I'd like a bandage** أريد ضمادة جروح [areed ḍimadat jirooḥ]; **I'd like a fresh bandage** أريد ضمادة جديدة [areed ḍimada jadeeda]
Band-Aid [bændeɪd] *n* لصقة طبية [Laṣ'qah ṭebeyah]
bang [bæŋ] *n* ضَجّة [dˁaʒʒa] ▷ *v* يُحْدِث ضجة
Bangladesh [ˌbɑ:ŋglə'dɛʃ; ˌbæŋ-] *n* بنجلاديش [banʒla:di:ʃ]
Bangladeshi [ˌbɑ:ŋglə'dɛʃɪ; ˌbæŋ-] *adj* بنجلاديشي [banʒla:di:ʃij] ▷ *n* بنجلاديشي [banʒla:di:ʃij]
banister ['bænɪstə] *n* دَرابِزين [dara:bizi:n]
banjo ['bændʒəʊ] *n* آلة البانجو الموسيقية [Aalat al-banjoo al-mose'qeyah]
bank [bæŋk] *n (finance)* بنك [bank], *(ridge)* ضفة [dˁiffa]; **bank account** *n* حساب بنكي [Hesab bankey]; **bank balance** *n* حساب بنكي [Hesab bankey]; **bank charges** *npl* مصاريف بنكية [Maṣareef Bankeyah]; **bank holiday** *n* عطلة شعبية [A'otalh sha'abeyah]; **bank statement** *n* كشف بنكي [Kashf bankey]; **bottle bank** *n* مستودع الزجاجات [Mostawda'a al-zojajat]; **merchant bank** *n* بنك تجاري [Bank Tejarey]; **How far is the bank?** ما هي المسافة بينا وبين البنك؟ [Ma heya al-masafa bayna wa been al-bank?]; **I would like to transfer some money from my bank in...** أرغب في تحويل بعض الأموال من حسابي البنكي في... [arghab fee taḥweel ba'aḍ al-amwal min ḥisaaby al-banki fee...]; **Is the bank open today?** هل البنك مفتوح اليوم؟ [hal al-bank maf-tooḥ al-yawm?]; **Is there a bank here?** هل يوجد بنك هنا؟ [hal yujad bank huna?]; **When does the bank close?** متى ينتهي عمل البنك؟ [mata yan-tahy 'aamal al-bank?]
banker ['bæŋkə] *n* موظف بنك [mowaḍhaf bank]
banknote ['bæŋkˌnəʊt] *n* ورقة مالية [Wara'qah maleyah]
bankrupt ['bæŋkrʌpt; -rəpt] *adj* مُفلس [muflis]
banned [bænd] *adj* مُحَرّم [muħarram]
Baptist ['bæptɪst] *n* كنيسة معمدانية [Kaneesah me'amedaneyah]
bar [bɑ:] *n (alcohol)* بار [ba:r], *(strip)* قالب مستطيل ['qaleb mostaṭeel]; **snack bar** *n* متجر الوجبات السريعة [Matjar al-wajabat al-sarey'aa]; **Where is the bar?** أين يوجد بار المشروبات؟ [ayna yujad bar al-mash-roobat?]
Barbados [bɑ:'beɪdəʊs; -dəʊz; -dɒs] *n* البربادوس [ʔalbarba:du:s]
barbaric [bɑ:'bærɪk] *adj* همجي [hamaʒij]
barbecue ['bɑ:bɪˌkju:] *n* شواء اللحم [Shewaa al-lahm]
barber ['bɑ:bə] *n* حَلاق [ħalla:q]
bare [bɛə] *adj* مُجرد [muʒarrad] ▷ *v* يَكْشِف عن [Yakshef 'an]
barefoot ['bɛəˌfʊt] *adj* حافي القدمين [Ḥafey al-'qadameyn] ▷ *adv* حافي القدمين [Ḥafey al-'qadameyn]
barely ['bɛəlɪ] *adv* بجهد شديد [Bejahd shaded]
bargain ['bɑ:gɪn] *n* صفقة [sˁafqa]
barge [bɑ:dʒ] *n* زورق بخاري مخصص لقائد الأسطول [Zawra'q bokharee mokhaṣaṣ

le-'qaaed al-osṭool]
bark [bɑːk] *v* ينبح [janbaħu]
barley ['bɑːlɪ] *n* شَعِير [ʃaʕiːrr]
barmaid ['bɑːˌmeɪd] *n* مضيفة بار [Moḍeefat bar]
barman, barmen ['bɑːmən, 'bɑːmɛn] *n* مضيف بار [Moḍeef bar]
barn [bɑːn] *n* مخزن حبوب [Makhzan ḥoboob]
barrel ['bærəl] *n* برميل [birmiːl]
barrier ['bærɪə] *n* حاجز [ħaːʒiz]; **ticket barrier** *n* حاجز وضع التذاكر [Hajez wad'a al-tadhaker]
bartender ['bɑːˌtɛndə] *n* ساقي البار [Sa'qey al-bar]
base [beɪs] *n* قاعدة [qaːʕida]
baseball ['beɪsˌbɔːl] *n* بيسبول [biːsbuːl]; **baseball cap** *n* قُبَعة البيسبول ['qoba'at al-beesbool]
based [beɪst] *adj* مؤسس على [Moasas ala]
basement ['beɪsmənt] *n* بدروم [bidruːm]
bash [bæʃ] *n* ضربة [dˤarba] ▷ *v* يَضرِب بعنف [Yaḍreb be'aonf]
basic ['beɪsɪk] *adj* أساسي [ʔasaːsij]
basically ['beɪsɪklɪ] *adv* بشكل أساسي [Beshkl asasy]
basics ['beɪsɪks] *npl* أساسيات [ʔasaːsijjaːtun]
basil ['bæzᵊl] *n* رَيحان [rajħaːnn]
basin ['beɪsᵊn] *n* حوض [ħawdˤdˤ]
basis ['beɪsɪs] *n* أساس [ʔasaːs]
basket ['bɑːskɪt] *n* سلة [salla]; **wastepaper basket** *n* سلة الأوراق المهملة [Salat al-awra'q al-mohmalah]
basketball ['bɑːskɪtˌbɔːl] *n* كرة السلة [Korat al-salah]
Basque [bæsk; bɑːsk] *adj* باسكي [baːskiː] ▷ *n (language)* اللغة الباسكية [Al-loghah al-bakestaneyah], *(person)* باسكي [baːskiː]
bass [beɪs] *n* سمك القاروس [Samak al-faros]; **bass drum** *n* طبلة كبيرة رنانة غليظة الصوت [Ṭablah kabeerah rannanah ghaleeḍhat al-ṣawt]; **double bass** *n* الدُبَلْبَس وهي أكبر آله في الأسرة الكمانية [addubalbas wa hija ʔakbaru aːlatu fiː alʔusrati alkamaːnijjati]
bassoon [bəˈsuːn] *n* مزمار [mizmaːr]
bat [bæt] *n (mammal)* خُفَّاش [xuffaːʃ], *(with ball)* مضرب [midˤrab]
bath [bɑːθ] *n*; **bubble bath** *n* سائل استحمام [Saael estehmam]
bathe [beɪð] *v* يَستحِم [jastaħimmu]
bathrobe ['bɑːθˌrəʊb] *n* بُرْنس حمام [Bornos hammam]
bathroom ['bɑːθˌruːm; -ˌrʊm] *n* حمام [ħammaːm]; **Does the room have a private bathroom?** هل يوجد حمام خاص داخل الحجرة [hal yujad ḥamam khaṣ dakhil al-ḥujra?]; **The bathroom is flooded** الحمام تغمره المياه [al-ḥamaam taghmurho al-me-aa]
baths [bɑːθz] *npl* حمامات [ħammaːmaːtun]
bathtub ['bɑːθˌtʌb] *n* حوض استحمام [Hawḍ estehmam]
batter ['bætə] *n* عجينة الكريب ['aajenat al-kreeb]
battery ['bætərɪ] *n* بطارية [batˤtˤaːrijja]; **I need a new battery** أريد بطارية جديدة [areed baṭaariya jadeeda]; **The battery is flat** البطارية فارغة [al-baṭareya faregha]
battle ['bætᵊl] *n* معركة [maʕraka]
battleship ['bætᵊlˌʃɪp] *n* سَفينة حربية [Safeenah ḥarbeyah]
bay [beɪ] *n* خليج [xaliːʒ]; **bay leaf** *n* ورق الغار [Wara'q alghaar]
BC [biː siː] *abbr* قبل الميلاد ['qabl al-meelad]
be [biː; bɪ] *v* يَكون [jakuːnu]
beach [biːtʃ] *n* شاطئ [ʃaːtˤiʔ]; **How far is the beach?** ما هي المسافة بيننا وبين الشاطئ؟ [ma heya al-masafa bay-nana wa bayn al-shaṭee?]; **I'm going to the beach** سوف أذهب إلى الشاطئ [sawfa adhab ela al-shaṭee]; **Is there a bus to the beach?** هل يوجد أتوبيس إلى الشاطئ؟ [Hal yojad otobees elaa al-shaṭea?]
bead [biːd] *n* خرزة [xurza]

beak [biːk] *n* منقار [minqaːr]
beam [biːm] *n* عَارِضَةٌ خَشَبِيَّةٌ [ʻaareḍeh khashabeyah]
bean [biːn] *n* فُولٌ [fuːl]; **broad bean** *n* فول [fuːlun]; **coffee bean** *n* حبوب البن [Ḥobob al-bon]; **French beans** *npl* فاصوليا خضراء [Faṣoleya khaḍraa]; **runner bean** *n* فاصوليا خضراء متعرشة [faṣoleya khadraa mota'aresha]
beansprout ['biːnspraʊt] *n*; **beansprouts** *npl* براعم الفول [Braa'em al-fool]
bear [bɛə] *n* دُبّ [dubb] ▷ *v* يَحتمِل [juħtamalu]; **polar bear** *n* الدب القطبي [Al-dob al-shamaley]; **teddy bear** *n* دُب تيدي بير [Dob tedey beer]
beard [bɪəd] *n* لحية [liħja]
bearded [bɪədɪd] *adj* مُلتح [multaħin]
bear up [bɛə ʌp] *v* يَصْمُد [jasˤmudu]
beat [biːt] *n* نبضة [nabdˤa] ▷ *v* *(outdo)* يَهْزِم [jahzimu], *(strike)* يَضرب [jadˤribu]
beautiful ['bjuːtɪfʊl] *adj* جَميل [ʒamiːl]
beautifully ['bjuːtɪflɪ; 'beautifully] *adv* بشكل جميل [Beshakl jameel]
beauty ['bjuːtɪ] *n* جمال [ʒamaːl]; **beauty salon** *n* صالون تجميل [Ṣalon ḥela'qa]; **beauty spot** *n* شامة [ʃaːmatun]
beaver ['biːvə] *n* قندس [qundus]
because [bɪ'kɒz; -'kəz] *conj* لأن [liʔanna]
become [bɪ'kʌm] *v* يُصبِح [jusˤbiħu]
bed [bɛd] *n* سَرير [sariːrr]; **bed and breakfast** *n* مبيت وإفطار [Mabeet wa efṭaar]; **bunk beds** *npl* سَرير بدورين [Sareer bedoreen]; **camp bed** *n* سَرير رحلات [Sareer raḥalat]; **double bed** *n* سَرير مُزدوج [Sareer mozdawaj]; **king-size bed** *n* فراش كبير الحجم [Ferash kabeer al-ḥajm]; **single bed** *n* سَرير فردي [Sareer fardey]; **sofa bed** *n* كنبة سرير [Kanabat sereer]; **twin beds** *npl* سريرين منفصلين [Sareerayn monfaṣelayen]
bedclothes ['bɛd,kləʊðz] *npl* بياضات [bajjaːdˤaːtun]
bedding ['bɛdɪŋ] *n* شراشف [ʃaraːʃif]
bedroom ['bɛd,ruːm; -,rʊm] *n* غرفة النوم [Ghorfat al-noom]
bedsit ['bɛd,sɪt] *n* شقة بغرفة واحدة [Sh'qah be-ghorfah waḥedah]
bedspread ['bɛd,sprɛd] *n* غطاء سرير [Gheṭa'a sareer]
bedtime ['bɛd,taɪm] *n* وَقْت النوم [Wa'qt al-nawm]
bee [biː] *n* نحلة [naħla]
beech [biːtʃ] *n*; **beech (tree)** *n* شجرة الزان [Shajarat al-zaan]
beef [biːf] *n* لحم بقري [Laḥm ba'qarey]
beefburger ['biːf,bɜːgə] *n* شرائح اللحم البقري المشوي [Shraeḥ al-laḥm al-ba'qarey al-mashwey]
beer [bɪə] *n* بيرة [biːra]; **another beer** كأس آخر من البيرة [kaas aakhar min al-beera]; **A draught beer, please** كأس من البيرة من فضلك [kaas min al-beera min faḍlak]
beetle ['biːtᵊl] *n* خُنْفِسَاء [xunfusaːʔ]
beetroot ['biːt,ruːt] *n* بنجر [banʒar]
before [bɪ'fɔː] *adv* أمام [ʔamaːma] ▷ *conj* قبل أن ['qabl an] ▷ *prep* أمام [ʔamaːma]
beforehand [bɪ'fɔː,hænd] *adv* مقدماً [muqaddaman]
beg [bɛg] *v* يَستجدي [jastaʒdiː]
beggar ['bɛgə] *n* المتسول [Almotasawel]
begin [bɪ'gɪn] *v* يبدأ [jabdaʔu]; **When does it begin?** متى يبدأ العمل هنا؟ [mata yabda al-'aamal huna?]
beginner [bɪ'gɪnə] *n* المبتدئ [Almobtadea]
beginning [bɪ'gɪnɪŋ] *n* بداية [bidaːja]; **at the beginning of June** في بداية شهر يونيو [fee bedayat shaher yon-yo]
behave [bɪ'heɪv] *v* يَتَصَرف [jatasˤarrafu]
behaviour [bɪ'heɪvjə] *n* سلوك [suluːk]
behind [bɪ'haɪnd] *adv* خلف [xalfa] ▷ *n* مُؤَخَّرَه [muʔaxxirra] ▷ *prep* خلف [xalfa]; **lag behind** *v* يَتخلف [jataxallafu]; **I've been left behind** لقد تخلفت عنه [la'qad takha-lafto 'aanho]
beige [beɪʒ] *adj* بيجْ [biːʒ]
Beijing ['beɪ'dʒɪŋ] *n* بكين [bikiːn]
Belarus ['bɛlə,rʌs; -,rʊs] *n* روسيا البيضاء [ruːsjaː ʔal-bajdˤaːʔu]

Belarussian [ˌbɛləʊˈrʌʃən; ˌbjɛl-] *adj* بيلاروسي [biːlaːruːsij] ▷ *n (language)* اللغة البيلاروسية [Al-loghah al-belaroseyah], *(person)* بيلاروسي [biːlaːruːsij]
Belgian [ˈbɛldʒən] *adj* بلجيكي [bilʒiːkij] ▷ *n* بلجيكي [bilʒiːkij]
Belgium [ˈbɛldʒəm] *n* بلجيكا [bilʒiːkaː]
belief [bɪˈliːf] *n* اعتقاد [ʕtiqaːd]
believe [bɪˈliːv] *vi* يُؤْمِن [juminu] ▷ *vt* يُصدِّق [jusˤaddiqu]
bell [bɛl] *n* جرس [ʒaras]
belly [ˈbɛlɪ] *n* بَطْن [batˤn]; **belly button** *n* سُرَّة البطن [Sorrat al-baṭn]
belong [bɪˈlɒŋ] *v* يخُص [jaxusˤsˤu]; **belong to** *v* ينتمي إلى [Yantamey ela]
belongings [bɪˈlɒŋɪŋz] *npl* متعلقات [mutaʕalliqaːtun]
below [bɪˈləʊ] *adv* تحت [taħta] ▷ *prep* تحت [taħta]
belt [bɛlt] *n* حزام [ħizaːm]; **conveyor belt** *n* سير متحرك [Sayer motaḥrrek]; **money belt** *n* حزام لحفظ المال [Hezam lehefḍh almal]; **safety belt** *n* حزام الأمان [Hezam al-aman]
bench [bɛntʃ] *n* نضد [nadˤad]
bend [bɛnd] *n* التواء [ʔiltiwaːʔ] ▷ *v* يَثْني [jaθniː]; **bend down** *v* يَمْيل [jamiːlu]; **bend over** *v* ينحني [janħaniː]
beneath [bɪˈniːθ] *prep* أسفلُ [ʔasfalu]
benefit [ˈbɛnɪfɪt] *n* فائدة [faːʔida] ▷ *v* يَستفْيد [jastifiːdu]
bent [bɛnt] *adj (dishonest)* منحني [munħanij], *(not straight)* منثني [munθanij]
beret [ˈbɛreɪ] *n* بيريه [biːriːh]
berry [ˈbɛrɪ] *n* تَوت [tuːtt]
berth [bɜːθ] *n* مرسى [marsaː]
beside [bɪˈsaɪd] *prep* بجانب [Bejaneb]
besides [bɪˈsaɪdz] *adv* بالإضافة إلى [Bel-edafah ela]
best [bɛst] *adj* أَفْضَل [ʔafdˤalu] ▷ *adv* أكثر [ʔakθaru]; **best man** *n* إشبين العريس [Eshbeen al-aroos]
bestseller [ˌbɛstˈsɛlə] *n* الأكثر مبيعا [Al-akthar mabe'aan]
bet [bɛt] *n* رهان [rihaːn] ▷ *v* يُراهن [juraːhinu]
betray [bɪˈtreɪ] *v* يَخون [jaxuːnu]
better [ˈbɛtə] *adj* أفْضَل [ʔafdˤalu] ▷ *adv* أكثر [ʔakθaru]
betting [bɛtɪŋ] *n* مراهنة [muraːhana]; **betting shop** *n* مكتب المراهنة [Maktab al-morahanah]
between [bɪˈtwiːn] *prep* بين [bajna]
bewildered [bɪˈwɪldəd] *adj* مُتحير [mutaħajjir]
beyond [bɪˈjɒnd] *prep* وراء [waraːʔa]
biased [ˈbaɪəst] *adj* متحيز [mutaħajjiz]
bib [bɪb] *n* صدرية طفل [Ṣadreyat ṭefl]
Bible [ˈbaɪbᵊl] *n* الإنجيل [al-ʔinʒiːlu]
bicarbonate [baɪˈkɑːbənɪt; -ˌneɪt] *n*; **bicarbonate of soda** *n* ثاني كربونات الصوديوم [Thaney okseed al-karboon]
bicycle [ˈbaɪsɪkᵊl] *n* دراجة [darraːʒa]; **bicycle pump** *n* منفاخ دراجة [Monfakh draajah]
bid [bɪd] *n* مناقصة [munaːqasˤa] ▷ *v (at auction)* يُزايد [juzaːjidu]
bifocals [baɪˈfəʊkᵊlz] *npl* ثنائي البؤرة [Thonaey al-booarah]
big [bɪg] *adj* كبير [kabiːr]; **It's too big** إنه كبير جدا [inaho kabeer jedan]; **The house is quite big** المنزل كبير بالفعل [al-manzil kabeer bil-fi'ail]
bigger [bɪgə] *adj* أكبر [ʔakbaru]; **Do you have a bigger one?** هل لديك غرف أكبر من ذلك؟ [hal ladyka ghuraf akbar min dhalik?]
bigheaded [ˈbɪgˌhɛdɪd] *adj* متورم [mutawarrim]
bike [baɪk] *n* دراجة هوائية [Darrajah hawaeyah]; **mountain bike** *n* دراجة الجبال [Darrajah al-jebal]
bikini [bɪˈkiːnɪ] *n* بيكيني [biːkiːniː]
bilingual [baɪˈlɪŋgwəl] *adj* ناطق بلغتين [Naṭe'q be-loghatayn]
bill [bɪl] *n (account)* فاتورة رسمية [Fatoorah rasmeyah], *(legislation)* مشروع قانون [Mashroo'a 'qanooney]; **phone bill** *n* فاتورة تليفون [Fatoorat telefon]
billiards [ˈbɪljədz] *npl* لعبة البلياردو [Lo'abat al-belyardo]
billion [ˈbɪljən] *n* مِلْيَار [miljaːr]

bin [bɪn] *n* صندوق [sˤundu:q]; **litter bin** *n* سلة المهملات [Salat al-mohmalat]
binding ['baɪndɪŋ] *n*; **Can you adjust my bindings, please?** هل يمكنك ضبط الأربطة لي من فضلك؟ [hal yamken -aka ḍabṭ al-arbe-ṭa lee min faḍlak?]; **Can you tighten my bindings, please?** هل يمكنك إحكام الأربطة لي من فضلك؟ [hal yamken -aka eḥkaam al-arbe-ṭa lee min faḍlak?]
bingo ['bɪŋɡəʊ] *n* لعبة البنجو [Lo'abat al-benjo]
binoculars [bɪ'nɒkjʊləz; baɪ-] *npl* منظار [minzˤa:run]
biochemistry [ˌbaɪəʊ'kɛmɪstrɪ] *n* كيمياء حيوية [Kemyaa ḥayaweyah]
biodegradable [ˌbaɪəʊdɪ'ɡreɪdəbᵊl] *adj* قابل للتحلل بالبكتريا ['qabel lel-tahalol bel-bekteriya]
biography [baɪ'ɒɡrəfɪ] *n* سيرة [si:ra]
biological [ˌbaɪə'lɒdʒɪkᵊl] *adj* بيولوجي [bju:lu:ʒij]
biology [baɪ'ɒlədʒɪ] *n* بيولوجيا [bju:lu:ʒja:]
biometric [ˌbaɪəʊ'mɛtrɪk] *adj* بيولوجي إحصائي [Bayology ehṢaey]
birch [bɜ:tʃ] *n* شجر البتولا [Ahjar al-betola]
bird [bɜ:d] *n* طائر [tˤa:ʔir]; **bird flu** *n* إنفلوانزا الطيور [Enfelwanza al-ṭeyor]; **bird of prey** *n* طيور جارحة [Ṭeyoor jareḥah]
birdwatching [bɜ:dwɒtʃɪŋ] *n* ملاحظة الطيور [molaḥaḍhat al-ṭeyoor]
Biro® ['baɪrəʊ] *n* ®بيرو [bi:ru:]
birth [bɜ:θ] *n* ميلاد [mi:la:d]; **birth certificate** *n* شهادة ميلاد [Shahadat meelad]; **birth control** *n* تنظيم النسل [tanḍheem al-nasl]; **place of birth** *n* مكان الميلاد [Makan al-meelad]
birthday ['bɜ:θˌdeɪ] *n* عيد ميلاد ['aeed al-meelad]; **Happy birthday!** عيد ميلاد سعيد ['aeed meelad sa'aeed]
birthplace ['bɜ:θˌpleɪs] *n* محل الميلاد [Mahal al-meelad]
biscuit ['bɪskɪt] *n* بسكويت [baskawi:t]
bishop ['bɪʃəp] *n* أسْقُف [asquf]
bit [bɪt] *n* جزء صغير [Joza ṣagheer]
bitch [bɪtʃ] *n* كلبة [kalb]
bite [baɪt] *n* قضمة [qadˤma] ▷ *v* يلسع [jalsaʕu]
bitter ['bɪtə] *adj* مر [murr]
black [blæk] *adj* أسود [ʔaswad]; **black ice** *n* ثلج أسود [thalj aswad]; **in black and white** باللون الأسود والأبيض [bil-lawn al-aswad wa al-abyaḍ]
blackberry ['blækbərɪ] *n* ثمرة العُليق [Thamrat al-'alay'q]
blackbird ['blækˌbɜ:d] *n* شحرور [ʃaħru:r]
blackboard ['blækˌbɔ:d] *n* سبورة [sabu:ra]
blackcurrant [ˌblæk'kʌrənt] *n* كِشمِش أسود [Keshmesh aswad]
blackmail ['blækˌmeɪl] *n* ابتزاز [ʔibtiza:z] ▷ *v* يبتز [jabtazzu]
blackout ['blækaʊt] *n* تعتيم [taʕti:m]
bladder ['blædə] *n* مثانة [maθa:na]; **gall bladder** *n* مَرَارَة [marra:ratun]
blade [bleɪd] *n* نصل [nasˤl]; **razor blade** *n* شفرة حلاقة [Shafrat hela'qah]; **shoulder blade** *n* لَوْح الكَتِف [Looh al-katef]
blame [bleɪm] *n* لوم [lawm] ▷ *v* يَلوم [jalu:mu]
blank [blæŋk] *adj* فارغ [fa:riɣ] ▷ *n* أبيض [ʔabjadˤ]; **blank cheque** *n* شيك على بياض [Sheek ala bayad]
blanket ['blæŋkɪt] *n* بطانية [batˤa:nijja]; **electric blanket** *n* بطانية كهربائية [Baṭaneyah kahrobaeyah]; **Please bring me an extra blanket** من فضلك أريد بطانية إضافية [min faḍlak areed baṭa-nya eḍa-fiya]
blast [blɑ:st] *n* لفحة [lafħa]
blatant ['bleɪtᵊnt] *adj* صَارِخ [sˤa:rix]
blaze [bleɪz] *n* وهج [wahaʒ]
blazer ['bleɪzə] *n* بليزر [blajzir]
bleach [bli:tʃ] *n* يُبيِّض [jubajjidˤu]
bleached [bli:tʃt] *adj* مُبَيَّض [mubajjidˤ]
bleak [bli:k] *adj* منعزل [munʕazil]
bleed [bli:d] *v* ينزف [janzifu]
bleeper ['bli:pə] *n* جهاز النداء الآلي [Jehaz

al-nedaa al-aaley]
blender ['blɛndə] *n* خلاط كهربائي [Khalaṭ kahrabaey]
bless [blɛs] *v* يبارك [juba:riku]
blind [blaɪnd] *adj* ضرير [dˤari:r] ▷ *n* ستارة النافذة [Setarat al-nafedhah]; **Venetian blind** *n* ستارة مُعتِمة [Setarah mo'atemah]
blindfold ['blaɪnd,fəʊld] *n* معصوب العينين [Ma'aṣoob al-'aainayn] ▷ *v* يَعْصِبُ العينين [Ya'aṣeb al-ozonayn]
blink [blɪŋk] *v* يُومِض [ju:midˤu]
bliss [blɪs] *n* نعيم [naʕi:m]
blister ['blɪstə] *n* بَثْرَة [baθra]
blizzard ['blɪzəd] *n* عاصفة ثلجية عنيفة ['aasefah thaljeyah 'aneefah]
block [blɒk] *n (buildings)* بِنَايَة [bina:ja], *(obstruction)* كُتلة خشبية أو حجرية [Kotlah khashebeyah aw hajareyah], *(solid piece)* كُتلة [kutla] ▷ *v* يقولب [jaqu:labu]
blockage ['blɒkɪdʒ] *n* انسداد [insida:d]
blocked [blɒkt] *adj* مسدود [masdu:d]
blog [blɒg] *n* مُدَوَّنة [mudawwana] ▷ *v* يُدَون [judawwinu]
bloke [bləʊk] *n* فَتى [fata:]
blonde [blɒnd] *adj* أشقر [ʔaʃqar]
blood [blʌd] *n* دم [dam]; **blood group** *n* فصيلة دم [faṣeelat dam]; **blood poisoning** *n* تسمم الدم [Tasamom al-dam]; **blood pressure** *n* ضغط الدم [ḍaghṭ al-dam]; **blood sports** *n* رياضة دموية [Reyaḍah damaweyah]; **blood test** *n* اختبار الدم [Ekhtebar al-dam]; **blood transfusion** *n* نقل الدم [Na'ql al-dam]; **My blood group is O positive** فصيلة دمي O موجب [faṣeelat damey O mojab]; **This stain is blood** هذه البقعة بقعة دم [hathy al-bu'q-'aa bu'q-'aat dum]
bloody ['blʌdɪ] *adj* دموي [damawij]
blossom ['blɒsəm] *n* زهرة الشجرة المثمرة [Zahrat al-shajarah al-mothmerah] ▷ *v* يُزهر [juzhiru]
blouse [blaʊz] *n* بلَوزة [blu:za]
blow [bləʊ] *n* لطمة [latˤma] ▷ *v* يَهُبّ [jahubbu]
blow-dry [bləʊdraɪ] *n* تجفيف الشعر [Tajfeef al-saha'ar]
blow up [bləʊ ʌp] *v* ينفجر [janfaʒiru]
blue [blu:] *adj* أزرق [ʔazraq]
blueberry ['blu:bərɪ; -brɪ] *n* تُوتْ أزرق [Toot azra'q]
blues [blu:z] *npl* كآبة [kaʔa:batun]
bluff [blʌf] *n* خديعة [xadi:ʕa] ▷ *v* يَخدَع [jaxdaʕu]
blunder ['blʌndə] *n* خطأ فادح [Khata fadeh]
blunt [blʌnt] *adj* متبلد [mutaballid]
blush [blʌʃ] *v* يَستحِي [jastaħi:]
blusher ['blʌʃə] *n* أحمر خدود [Ahmar khodod]
board [bɔ:d] *n (meeting)* هيئة [hajʔa], *(wood)* لوح [lawħ] ▷ *v (go aboard)* لوح [lawħun]; **board game** *n* لعبة طاولة [Lo'abat ṭawlah]; **boarding card** *n* كارت ركوب [Kart rekoob]; **boarding pass** *n* تصريح الركوب [Taṣreeh al-rokob]; **boarding school** *n* مدرسة داخلية [Madrasah dakheleyah]; **bulletin board** *n* لوحة النشرات [Looḥat al-nasharaat]; **diving board** *n* لوح غطس [Looḥ ghaṭs]; **draining board** *n* لوحة تجفيف [Lawhat tajfeef]; **half board** *n* نصف إقامة [Neṣf e'qamah]; **ironing board** *n* لوح الكي [Looḥ alkay]; **notice board** *n* لوحة الملاحظات [Looḥat al-molahḍhat]; **skirting board** *n* وَزَرة [wizratun]
boarder ['bɔ:də] *n* تلميذ داخلي [telmeedh dakhely]
boast [bəʊst] *v* يَتَبَاهى [jataba:ha:]
boat [bəʊt] *n* مَركب [markab]; **fishing boat** *n* قارب صيد ['qareb ṣayd]; **rowing boat** *n* قارب تجديف ['qareb tajdeef]; **sailing boat** *n* قارب ابحار ['qareb ebḥar]
body ['bɒdɪ] *n* جسم [ʒism]
bodybuilding ['bɒdɪ,bɪldɪŋ] *n* كمال الأجسام [Kamal al-ajsaam]
bodyguard ['bɒdɪ,gɑ:d] *n* حارس شخصي [ḥares shakhṣ]
bog [bɒg] *n* مستنقع [mustanqaʕ]
boil [bɔɪl] *vi* يَغْلي [jaɣli:] ▷ *vt* يَسلُق

[jasluqu]
boiled [bɔɪld] *adj* مغلي [maɣlij]; **boiled egg** *n* بيضة مسلوقة [Bayḍah maslo'qah]
boiler ['bɔɪlə] *n* مرجل [mirʒal]
boiling ['bɔɪlɪŋ] *adj* غليان [ɣalaja:n]
boil over [bɔɪl 'əʊvə] *v* يَخرُج عن شعوره [jaxruʒu ʕan ʃuʕu:rihi]
Bolivia [bə'lɪvɪə] *n* بوليفيا [bu:lijfja:]
Bolivian [bə'lɪvɪən] *adj* بوليفي [bu:li:fij] ▷ *n* بوليفي [bu:li:fij]
bolt [bəʊlt] *n* صامولة [sˤa:mu:la]
bomb [bɒm] *n* قنبلة [qunbula] ▷ *v* يَقصف [jaqsˤifu]; **atom bomb** *n* قنبلة ذرية ['qobelah dhareyah]
bombing [bɒmɪŋ] *n* تفجير [tafʒi:r]
bond [bɒnd] *n* سَند [sanad]
bone [bəʊn] *n* عظمة [ʕazˤama]; **bone dry** *adj* جاف تماماً [Jaf tamaman]
bonfire ['bɒn,faɪə] *n* إشعال النار [Esh'aal al-naar]
bonnet ['bɒnɪt] *n* *(car)* قلنسوة [qulunsuwa]
bonus ['bəʊnəs] *n* علاوة [ʕala:wa]
book [bʊk] *n* كتاب [kita:b] ▷ *v* يَحجز [jaħʒizu]; **address book** *n* دفتر العناوين [Daftar al-'aanaaween]
bookcase ['bʊk,keɪs] *n* خزانة كتب [Khezanat kotob]
booking ['bʊkɪŋ] *n* حجز [ħaʒz]; **advance booking** *n* حجز مقدم [Hajz mo'qadam]; **booking office** *n* مكتب الحجز [Maktab al-ḥjz]; **Can I change my booking?** هل يمكن أن أغير الحجز الذي قمت به؟ [hal yamken an aghyir al-ḥajiz al-ladhy 'qumt behe?]; **I want to cancel my booking** أريد إلغاء الحجز الذي قمت به؟ [areed el-ghaa al-ḥajiz al-ladhy 'qumto behe]; **Is there a booking fee?** هل يوجد مصاريف للحجز؟ [hal yujad maṣareef lel-ḥajz?]
booklet ['bʊklɪt] *n* كُتَيِّب [kutajjib]
bookmark ['bʊk,mɑːk] *n* علامة مميزة ['alamah momayazah]
bookshelf ['bʊk,ʃɛlf] *n* رَف الكُتُب [Raf al-kotob]
bookshop ['bʊk,ʃɒp] *n* مكتبة لبيع الكتب [Maktabah le-bay'a al-kotob]
boost [bu:st] *v* يُعزز [juʕazzizu]
boot [bu:t] *n* حذاء عالي السَاق [hedhaa 'aaley al-sa'q]
booze [bu:z] *n* إسراف في الشراب [Esraf fee alsharab]
border ['bɔ:də] *n* حاشية [ħa:ʃijja]
bore [bɔ:] *v* *(be dull)* يَثْقب [jaθqubu], *(drill)* يَثْقب [jaθqubu]
bored [bɔ:d] *adj* يُسبِب الملل [Yosabeb al-malal]
boredom ['bɔ:dəm] *n* سَأم [saʔam]
boring ['bɔ:rɪŋ] *adj* ممل [mumill]
born [bɔ:n] *adj* مولود [mawlu:d]
borrow ['bɒrəʊ] *v* يَستدين [jastadijinu]
Bosnia ['bɒznɪə] *n* البوسنَة [ʔal-bu:snatu]; **Bosnia and Herzegovina** *n* البوسنة والهرسك [ʔal-bu:snatu wa ʔal-hirsik]
Bosnian ['bɒznɪən] *adj* بوسنيّ [bu:snij] ▷ *n* *(person)* بوسني [bu:snij]
boss [bɒs] *n* زعيم [zaʕi:m]
boss around [bɒs ə'raʊnd] *v* يُمْلي عليه [Yomely 'aleyh]
bossy ['bɒsɪ] *adj* دكتاتوري [dikta:tu:rij]
both [bəʊθ] *adj* كلًا من [Kolan men] ▷ *pron* كلاهما [kila:huma:]
bother ['bɒðə] *v* يُقْلَقْ [jaqlaqu]
Botswana [bʊ'tʃwɑːnə; bʊt'swɑːnə; bɒt-] *n* بتسوانا [butswa:na:]
bottle ['bɒtᵊl] *n* زجاجة [zuʒa:ʒa]; **baby's bottle** *n* زجاجة رضاعة الطفل [Zojajat reḍa'aat al-ṭefl]; **bottle bank** *n* مستودع الزجاجات [Mostawda'a al-zojajat]; **hot-water bottle** *n* زجاجة مياه ساخنة [Zojajat meyah sakhenah]; **a bottle of mineral water** زجاجة مياه معدنية [zujaja meaa ma'adan-iya]; **a bottle of red wine** زجاجة من النبيذ الأحمر [zujaja min al-nabeedh al-aḥmar]; **Please bring another bottle** من فضلك أحضر لي زجاجة أخرى [min faḍlak iḥḍir lee zujaja okhra]
bottle-opener ['bɒtᵊl'əʊpənə] *n* فتاحة الزجاجات [Fatahat al-zojajat]
bottom ['bɒtəm] *adj* أسفلُ [ʔasfalu] ▷ *n*

قاع [qa:ʕ]
bought [bɔːt] *adj* جاهز [ʒa:hiz]
bounce [baʊns] *v* يَرتدّ [jartaddu]
bouncer ['baʊnsə] *n* المتبجح [al-mutabaʒʒiħ]
boundary ['baʊndərɪ; -drɪ] *n* حد [ħadd]
bouquet ['buːkeɪ] *n* بَاقَة [ba:qa]
bow *n* [bəʊ](*weapon*) قوس [qaws] ▷ *v* [baʊ]انحناء [inħina:ʔun]
bowels ['baʊəlz] *npl* سُلطانية [sultˤa:nijjatun]
bowl [bəʊl] *n* وعاء [wiʕa:ʔ]
bowling ['bəʊlɪŋ] *n* لعبة البولينج [Lo'aba al-boolenj]; **bowling alley** *n* مسار كرة البولينج [Maser korat al-boolenj]; **tenpin bowling** *n* لعبة البولنغ العشرية [Lo'aba al-boolenj al-'ashreyah]
bow tie [bəʊ] *n* رباط عنق على شكل فراشة [Rebaṭ 'ala shakl frashah]
box [bɒks] *n* صندوق [sˤundu:q]; **box office** *n* شباك التذاكر [Shobak al-taḍhaker]; **call box** *n* كابينة تليفون [Kabeenat telefoon]; **fuse box** *n* علبة الفيوز ['aolbat al-feyoz]; **gear box** *n* علبة التروس ['aolbat al-teroos]
boxer ['bɒksə] *n* ملاكم [mula:kim]; **boxer shorts** *npl* شورت بوكسر [Short boksar]
boxing ['bɒksɪŋ] *n* ملاكمة [mula:kama]
boy [bɔɪ] *n* ولد [walad]
boyfriend ['bɔɪˌfrɛnd] *n* رفيق [rafi:q]
bra [brɑː] *n* حَمَّالة صَدْر [Hammalat ṣadr]
brace [breɪs] *n* (*fastening*) سناد [sana:d]
bracelet ['breɪslɪt] *n* سُوَار [suwa:r]
braces ['breɪsɪz] *npl* حمالة [ħamma:latun]
brackets ['brækɪts] *npl* أقواس [ʔaqwa:sun]
brain [breɪn] *n* دِمَاغ [dima:ɣ]
brainy ['breɪnɪ] *adj* ذكي [ðakij]
brake [breɪk] *n* فرامل [fara:mil] ▷ *v* يُفَرْمِل [jufarmilu]; **brake light** *n* مصباح الفرامل [Mesbaḥ al-faramel]; **The brakes don't work** الفرامل لا تعمل [Al-faramel la ta'amal]
bran [bræn] *n* نُخالة [nuxa:la]
branch [brɑːntʃ] *n* فرع [farʕ]
brand [brænd] *n* ماركة [ma:rka]; **brand name** *n* العلامة التجارية [Al-'alamah al-tejareyah]
brand-new [brænd'njuː] *adj* ماركة جديدة [Markah jadeedah]
brandy ['brændɪ] *n* براندي [bra:ndi:]; **I'll have a brandy** سأتناول براندي [sa-ata-nawal brandy]
brass [brɑːs] *n* نحاس أصفر [Nahas aṣfar]; **brass band** *n* فرقة الآلات النحاسية [Fer'qat al-aalat al-naḥaseqeyah]
brat [bræt] *n* طفل مزعج [Ṭefl moz'aej]
brave [breɪv] *adj* شجاع [ʃuʒa:ʕ]
bravery ['breɪvərɪ] *n* شجاعة [ʃaʒa:ʕa]
Brazil [brə'zɪl] *n* البرازيل [ʔal-bara:zi:lu]
Brazilian [brə'zɪljən] *adj* برازيلي [bara:zi:lij] ▷ *n* برازيلي [bara:zi:lij]
bread [brɛd] *n* خُبز [xubz]; **bread roll** *n* خبز ملفوف [Khobz malfoof]; **brown bread** *n* خبز أسمر [Khobz asmar]
bread bin [brɛdbɪn] *n* نشّابة [naʃʃa:ba]
breadcrumbs ['brɛdˌkrʌmz] *npl* بُقسماط مطحون [Bo'qsomat maṭhoon]
break [breɪk] *n* فترة راحة [Fatrat raaḥ a] ▷ *v* يكسر [jaksiru]; **lunch break** *n* استراحة غداء [Estrahet ghadaa]
break down [breɪk daʊn] *v* يَتعطل [jataʕatˤtˤalu]
breakdown ['breɪkdaʊn] *n* تَعَطّل [taʕatˤul]; **breakdown truck** *n* شاحنة قَطْر [Shaḥenat 'qaṭr]; **breakdown van** *n* عربة الأعطال ['arabat al-a'ataal]; **nervous breakdown** *n* إنهيار عصبي [Enheyar aṣabey]
breakfast ['brɛkfəst] *n* إفطار [ʔiftˤa:r]; **bed and breakfast** *n* مبيت وإفطار [Mabeet wa efṭaar]; **continental breakfast** *n* إفطار كونتيننتال [Efṭaar kontenental]; **Can I have breakfast in my room?** هل يمكن أن أتناول الإفطار داخل غرفتي؟ [hal yamken an ata-nawal al-efṭaar dakhil ghurfaty?]; **Is breakfast included?** هل يشمل ذلك الإفطار؟ [hal yash-mil dhalik al-ifṭaar?]; **with**

breakfast شاملة الإفطار [shamelat al-eftaar]; **without breakfast** غير شاملة للإفطار [gheyr shamela lel-eftaar]; **What time is breakfast?** ما هو موعد الإفطار [ma howa maw-'aid al-eftaar?]; **What would you like for breakfast?** ماذا تريد تناوله في الإفطار [madha tureed tana-wilho fee al-eftaar?]

break in [breɪk ɪn] *v* يسطو على [Yasṭo 'ala]; **break in (on)** *v* يقتحم

break-in [breɪkɪn] *n* اقتحام [iqtiħa:m]

break up [breɪk ʌp] *v* يُجَزِأ [juʒazziʔu]

breast [brɛst] *n* ثَدْي [θadjj]

breast-feed ['brɛst,fiːd] *v* يَرضع [jardˤiʕu]

breaststroke ['brɛst,strəʊk] *n* سباحة الصدر [Sebaḥat al-ṣadr]

breath [brɛθ] *n* نَفَس [nafs]

Breathalyser® ['brɛθə,laɪzə] *n* بريثاليزر® [bri:θa:lajzr]

breathe [briːð] *v* يَتنفَس [jatanafasu]

breathe in [briːð ɪn] *v* يَستنشق [jastanʃiqu]

breathe out [briːð aʊt] *v* يَزْفِر [jazfiru]

breathing ['briːðɪŋ] *n* تنفس [tanaffus]

breed [briːd] *n* نسل [nasl] ▷ *v* يَتناسَل [jatana:salu]

breeze [briːz] *n* نسيم [nasi:m]

brewery ['brʊərɪ] *n* مصنع البيرة [maṣna'a al-beerah]

bribe [braɪb] *v* يَرشو [jarʃu:]

bribery ['braɪbərɪ; 'bribery] *n* رشوة [raʃwa]

brick [brɪk] *n* طوبة [tˤu:ba]

bricklayer ['brɪk,leɪə] *n* بنّاء [banna:ʔ]

bride [braɪd] *n* عروس [ʕaru:s]

bridegroom ['braɪd,gruːm; -,grʊm] *n* عريس [ʕari:s]

bridesmaid ['braɪdz,meɪd] *n* وصيفة العروس [Waṣeefat al-'aroos]

bridge [brɪdʒ] *n* جسر [ʒisr]; **suspension bridge** *n* جسر معلق [Jesr mo'aala'q]

brief [briːf] *adj* ملخص [mulaxxasˤ]

briefcase ['briːf,keɪs] *n* حقيبة أوراق جلدية [Ha'qeebat awra'q jeldeyah]

briefing ['briːfɪŋ] *n* إصدار التعليمات [Eṣdar al ta'alemat]

briefly ['briːflɪ] *adv* باختصار [bekhteṣaar]

briefs [briːfs] *npl* سروال تحتي قصير [Serwal taḥtey 'qaṣeer]

bright [braɪt] *adj* ساطع [sa:tˤiʕ]

brilliant ['brɪljənt] *adj* شخص متقد الذكاء [shakhṣ mota'qed al-dhakaa]

bring [brɪŋ] *v* يُحضِر [juħadˤdˤiru]

bring back [brɪŋ bæk] *v* يُعْيد [juʕi:du]

bring forward [brɪŋ 'fɔːwəd] *v* يُقدم [juqaddimu]

bring up [brɪŋ ʌp] *v* يُربي [jurabbi:]

Britain ['brɪtᵊn] *n* بريطانيا [bri:tˤa:nja:]

British ['brɪtɪʃ] *adj* بريطاني [bri:tˤa:nij] ▷ *n* بريطاني [bri:tˤa:nij]

broad [brɔːd] *adj* واسع [wa:siʕ]

broadband ['brɔːd,bænd] *n* نطاق واسع [Neṭ'q wase'a]

broadcast ['brɔːd,kɑːst] *n* إذاعة [ʔiða:ʕa] ▷ *v* يُذيع [juði:ʕu]

broad-minded [brɔːd'maɪndɪd] *adj* واسع الأفق [Wase'a al-ofo'q]

broccoli ['brɒkəlɪ] *n* قرنبيط [qarnabi:tˤ]

brochure ['brəʊʃjʊə; -ʃə] *n* كتيب إعلاني [Kotayeb e'alaaney]

broke [brəʊk] *adj* مفلس [muflis]

broken ['brəʊkən] *adj* مكسور [maksu:r]; **broken down** *adj* مُعَطّل [muʕatˤtˤalun]; **The lock is broken** القفل مكسور [al-'qiful maksoor]; **This is broken** إنها مكسورة [inaha maksoora]

broker ['brəʊkə] *n* سِمسار [samsa:r]

bronchitis [brɒŋ'kaɪtɪs] *n* التهاب شُعَبي [Eltehab sho'aaby]

bronze [brɒnz] *n* برونز [bru:nz]

brooch [brəʊtʃ] *n* بروش [bru:ʃ]

broom [bruːm; brʊm] *n* مكنسة [miknasatu]

broth [brɒθ] *n* مرق [maraq]

brother ['brʌðə] *n* أخ [ʔax]

brother-in-law ['brʌðə ɪn lɔː] *n* زوج الأخت [zawj alokht]

brown [braʊn] *adj* بُنيٌّ [bunnij]; **brown bread** *n* خبز أسمر [Khobz asmar]; **brown rice** *n* أرز أسمر [Orz asmar]

browse [braʊz] *v* يتصفح [jatasˤaffaħu]
browser ['braʊzə] *n* مُتَصفِّح [mutasˤaffiħ]
bruise [bru:z] *n* كدمة [kadama]
brush [brʌʃ] *n* فرشاة [furʃa:t] ▷ *v* يُنَظِف بالفرشاة [yonaḍhef bel-forshah]
brutal ['bru:tᵊl] *adj* وحشي [waħʃij]
bubble ['bʌbᵊl] *n* فُقَّاعة [fuqa:ʕa]; **bubble bath** *n* سائل استحمام [Saael estehmam]; **bubble gum** *n* لبان بالون [Leban balloon]
bucket ['bʌkɪt] *n* دَلْو [dalw]
buckle ['bʌkᵊl] *n* إبزيم [ʔibzi:m]
Buddha ['bʊdə] *n* بوذا [bu:ða:]
Buddhism ['bʊdɪzəm] *n* البوذية [al-bu:ðijjatu]
Buddhist ['bʊdɪst] *adj* بوذي [bu:ðij] ▷ *n* بوذي [bu:ðij]
budgerigar ['bʌdʒərɪˌgɑ:] *n* بغبغاء [babbaɣa:ʔ]
budget ['bʌdʒɪt] *n* ميزانية [mi:za:nijja]
budgie ['bʌdʒɪ] *n* بغبغاء [babbaɣa:ʔ]
buffalo ['bʌfəˌləʊ] *n* جاموسة [ʒa:mu:sa]
buffet ['bʊfeɪ] *n* سُفرة [sufra]; **buffet car** *n* عربة البوفيه ['arabat al-boofeeh]
bug [bʌg] *n* بقة [baqqa]
bugged ['bʌgd] *adj* مُراقب [mura:qib]
buggy ['bʌgɪ] *n* عربة صغيرة خفيفة ['arabah ṣagheerah khafeefah]
build [bɪld] *v* يَبْني [jabni:]
builder ['bɪldə] *n* بنَّاء [banna:ʔ]
building ['bɪldɪŋ] *n* بِنَاء [bina:ʔ]; **building site** *n* موقع البناء [Maw'qe'a al-benaa]
bulb [bʌlb] *n* *(electricity)* بصلة النبات [baṣalat al-nabat], *(plant)* لَحاء [liħa:ʔ]
Bulgaria [bʌl'gɛərɪə; bʊl-] *n* بلغاريا [bulɣa:rja:]
Bulgarian [bʌl'gɛərɪən; bʊl-] *adj* بلغاري [balɣa:ri:] ▷ *n* *(language)* اللغة البلغارية [Al-loghah al-balghareyah], *(person)* بلغاري [balɣa:ri:]
bulimia [bju:'lɪmɪə] *n* شراهة الأكل [Sharahat alakal]
bull [bʊl] *n* ثور [θawr]
bulldozer ['bʊlˌdəʊzə] *n* جرافة [ʒarra:fa]
bullet ['bʊlɪt] *n* رصاصة [rasˤa:sˤa]
bully ['bʊlɪ] *n* بلطجي [baltˤaʒij] ▷ *v* يستأسد على [jastaʔsidu ʕala:]
bum [bʌm] *n* عَجِيزَةٌ [ʕaʒi:za]; **bum bag** *n* حقيبة صغيرة [Ha'qeebah ṣagheerah]
bumblebee ['bʌmbᵊlˌbi:] *n* نحلة ضخمة [Naḥlah ḍakhmah]
bump [bʌmp] *n* ضَربة [dˤarba]; **bump into** *v* يتصادف مع [Yataṣaadaf ma'a]
bumper ['bʌmpə] *n* مصد [musˤidd]
bumpy ['bʌmpɪ] *adj* وَعِر [waʕir]
bun [bʌn] *n* كعكة [kaʕka]
bunch [bʌntʃ] *n* حزمة [ħuzma]
bungalow ['bʌŋgəˌləʊ] *n* بيت من طابق واحد [Bayt men ṭabe'q wahed]
bungee jumping ['bʌndʒɪ] *n* قفز بالحبال ['qafz bel-ḥebal]; **Where can I go bungee jumping?** أين يمكن أن أذهب للقفز بالحبال المطاطية؟ [ayna yamken an adhhab lil-'qafiz bel-ḥebal al-maṯaṯiya?]
bunion ['bʌnjən] *n* التفاف إبهام القدم [Eltefaf ebham al-'qadam]
bunk [bʌŋk] *n* سَرير مبيت [Sareer mabeet]; **bunk beds** *npl* سَرير بدورين [Sareer bedoreen]
buoy [bɔɪ; 'bu:ɪ] *n* عَوَّامَةٌ [ʕawa:ma]
burden ['bɜ:dᵊn] *n* عبء [ʕibʔ]
bureaucracy [bjʊə'rɒkrəsɪ] *n* بيروقراطية [bi:ru:qra:tˤijjati]
bureau de change ['bjʊərəʊ də 'ʃɒnʒ] *n* مكتب صرافة [Maktab ṣerafah]; **I need to find a bureau de change** أريد الذهاب إلى مكتب صرافة [areed al-dhehaab ela maktab ṣerafa]; **Is there a bureau de change here?** هل يوجد مكتب صرافة هنا؟ [hal yujad maktab ṣerafa huna?]; **When is the bureau de change open?** متى يبدأ مكتب الصرافة عمله؟ [mata yabda maktab al-ṣirafa 'aamalaho?]
burger ['bɜ:gə] *n* هامبُرجَر [ha:mbarʒar]
burglar ['bɜ:glə] *n* لص المنازل [Leṣ al-manazel]; **burglar alarm** *n* إنذار سرقة [endhar sare'qa]
burglary ['bɜ:glərɪ] *n* سَطو [satˤw]
burgle ['bɜ:gᵊl] *v* يَسطو [jastˤu:]
Burma ['bɜ:mə] *n* بورما [bu:rma:]

Burmese [bɜːˈmiːz] *adj* بورمي [buːrmij] ▷ *n (language)* اللغة البورمية [Al-loghah al-bormeyah], *(person)* بورمي [buːrmij]
burn [bɜːn] *n* حرق [ħuriqa] ▷ *v* يَحرق [jaħriqu]
burn down [bɜːn daʊn] *v* يَحترق عن آخره [Yaḥtare'q 'an aakherh]
burp [bɜːp] *n* تَجَشُّؤ [taʒaʃʃuʔ] ▷ *v* يَتجشأ [jataʒaʃʃaʔu]
burst [bɜːst] *v* ينفجر [janfaʒiru]
bury [ˈbɛrɪ] *v* يَدفِن [jadfinu]
bus [bʌs] *n* أوتوبيس [ʔuːtuːbiːs]; **airport bus** *n* أتوبيس المطار [Otobees al-maṭar]; **bus station** *n* محطة أوتوبيس [Mahaṭat otobees]; **bus stop** *n* موقف أوتوبيس [Maw'qaf otobees]; **bus ticket** *n* تذكرة أوتوبيس [tadhkarat otobees]
bush [bʊʃ] *n (shrub)* شُجَيْرَة [ʃuʒajra], *(thicket)* دَغَل [duɣl]
business [ˈbɪznɪs] *n* أعمال تجارية [A'amaal tejareyah]; **business class** *n* درجة رجال الأعمال [Darajat rejal ala'amal]; **business trip** *n* رحلة عمل [Reḥlat 'aamal]; **show business** *n* مجال الاستعراض [Majal al-este'araḍ]
businessman, businessmen [ˈbɪznɪsˌmæn; -mən, ˈbɪznɪsˌmɛn] *n* رَجُل أعمال [Rajol a'amal]
businesswoman, businesswomen [ˈbɪznɪsˌwʊmən, ˈbɪznɪsˌwɪmɪn] *n* سيدة أعمال [Sayedat a'amaal]; **I'm a businesswoman** أنا سيدة أعمال [ana sayidat a'amaal]
busker [ˈbʌskə] *n* فنان متسول [Fanan motasawol]
bust [bʌst] *n* صَدْر [sˤadr]
busy [ˈbɪzɪ] *adj* مشغول [maʃɣuːl]; **busy signal** *n* إشارة إنشغال الخط [Esharat ensheghal al-khat]
but [bʌt] *conj* لكن
butcher [ˈbʊtʃə] *n* جزار [ʒazzaːr]
butcher's [ˈbʊtʃəz] *n* محل الجزار [Maḥal al-jazar]
butter [ˈbʌtə] *n* زُبْدَة [zubda]; **peanut butter** *n* زُبْدَة الفستق [Zobdat al-fosto'q]
buttercup [ˈbʌtəˌkʌp] *n* عُشْب الحَوْذان ['aoshb al-hawdhan]
butterfly [ˈbʌtəˌflaɪ] *n* فراشة [faraːʃa]
buttocks [ˈbʌtəkz] *npl* أَرْدَافٌ [ʔardaːfun]
button [ˈbʌtᵊn] *n* زِرٌّ [zirr]; **belly button** *n* سُرَّة البطن [Sorrat al-baṭn]
buy [baɪ] *v* يَشتَري [jaʃtariː]
buyer [ˈbaɪə] *n* مشتري [muʃtariː]
buyout [ˈbaɪˌaʊt] *n* شراء كامل [Sheraa kaamel]
by [baɪ] *prep* بواسطة [biwaːsitˤati]
bye-bye [baɪbaɪ] *excl* إلى اللقاء [ela al-le'qaa]
bypass [ˈbaɪˌpɑːs] *n* ممر جانبي [Mamar janebey]

C

cab [kæb] *n* سيارة أجرة [Sayarah ojarah]
cabbage ['kæbɪdʒ] *n* كُرُنبٌ [kurnub]
cabin ['kæbɪn] *n* كابينة [ka:bi:na]كوخ , [ku:x]; **cabin crew** *n* كابينة الطاقم [Kabbenat al-ṭa'qam]; **a first-class cabin** كابينة من الدرجة الأولى [kabeena min al-daraja al-o-la]; **a standard class cabin** كابينة من الدرجة العادية [kabeena min al-daraja al-'aadiyah]; **Where is cabin number five?** أين توجد الكابينة رقم خمسة؟ [Ayn tojad al-kabeenah ra'qm khamsah?]
cabinet ['kæbɪnɪt] *n* خِزانة [xiza:na]
cable ['keɪbᵊl] *n* كابل [ka:bil]; **cable car** *n* تَرام [tra:mun]; **cable television** *n* وَصْلَة تلفزيونية [Wṣlah telefezyoneyah]
cactus ['kæktəs] *n* صبار [sˁabba:r]
cadet [kə'dɛt] *n* طالب عسكري [Ṭaleb 'askarey]
café ['kæfeɪ; 'kæfɪ] *n* مقهى [maqha:]; **Internet café** *n* مقهى الانترنت [Ma'qha al-enternet]; **Are there any Internet cafés here?** هل يوجد أي مقهى للإنترنت هنا؟ [hal yujad ay ma'qha lel-internet huna?]
cafeteria [ˌkæfɪ'tɪərɪə] *n* كافيتريا [kafijtirja:]
caffeine ['kæfiːn; 'kæfɪˌiːn] *n* كافين [ka:fi:n]
cage [keɪdʒ] *n* قفص [qafasˁ]
cagoule [kə'guːl] *n* معطف المطر [Me'ataf lel-maṭar]
cake [keɪk] *n* كعك [kaʕk]
calcium ['kælsɪəm] *n* كالسيوم [ka:lsju:m]
calculate ['kælkjʊˌleɪt] *v* يَعُد [jaʕuddu]
calculation [ˌkælkjʊ'leɪʃən] *n* حُسبان [ħusba:n]
calculator ['kælkjʊˌleɪtə] *n* آلة حاسبة [Aalah ḥasbah]; **pocket calculator** *n* آلة حاسبة للجيب [Alah haseba lel-jeeb]
calendar ['kælɪndə] *n* تقويم [taqwi:m]
calf, calves [kɑːf, kɑːvz] *n* عجل [ʕiʒl]
call [kɔːl] *n* مكالمة [muka:lama] ▷ *v* يَستدعِي [jastadʕi:]; **alarm call** *n* نداء استغاثة [Nedaa esteghathah]; **call box** *n* كابينة تليفون [Kabeenat telefoon]; **call centre** *n* مركز الاتصال [Markaz al-eteṣal]; **roll call** *n* تَفَقُّد الحضور [Tafa'qod al-ḥoḍor]; **I must make a phonecall** يجب أن أقوم بإجراء مكالمة تليفونية [yajib an a'qoom be-ijraa mukalama talefonia]; **I'd like to make a reverse charge call** أريد إجراء مكالمة تليفونية مدفوعة من الطرف الآخر [areed ejraa mukalama talefonia mad-fo'aa min al-ṭaraf al-aakhar]
call back [kɔːl bæk] *v* يُعاوِد الاتصال [Yo'aaawed al-eteṣaal]
call for [kɔːl fɔː] *v* يَدْعو إلى [Yad'aoo ela]
call off [kɔːl ɒf] *v* يَزْجُر [jazʒuru]
calm [kɑːm] *adj* ساكن [sa:kin]
calm down [kɑːm daʊn] *v* يَهْدَأ [juhaddiʔu]
calorie ['kælərɪ] *n* سُعْر حراري [So'ar hararey]
Cambodia [kæm'bəʊdɪə] *n* كامبوديا [ka:mbu:dja:]
Cambodian [kæm'bəʊdɪən] *adj* كمبودي [kambu:dij] ▷ *n (person)* شخص كمبودي[Shakhṣ kamboodey]
camcorder ['kæmˌkɔːdə] *n* كاميرا فيديو نقّال [Kamera fedyo na'q'qaal]
camel ['kæməl] *n* جمل [ʒamal]

camera ['kæmərə; 'kæmrə] *n* كاميرا [ka:mi:ra:]; **camera phone** *n* تليفون بكاميرا [Telefoon bekamerah]; **digital camera** *n* كاميرا رقمية [Kameera ra'qmeyah]; **video camera** *n* كاميرا فيديو [Kamera fedyo]
cameraman, cameramen ['kæmərə,mæn; 'kæmrə-, 'kæmərə,mɛn] *n* مُصَوِّر [musˤawwir]
Cameroon [,kæmə'ru:n; 'kæmə,ru:n] *n* الكاميرون [al-ka:mi:ru:n]
camp [kæmp] *n* معسكر [muʕaskar] ▷ *v* يُخيم [juxajjimu]; **camp bed** *n* سَرير رحلات [Sareer raḥalat]
campaign [kæm'peɪn] *n* حملة [ħamla]
camper ['kæmpə] *n* مُعَسكِر [muʕaskar]
camping ['kæmpɪŋ] *n* تنظيم المعسكرات [Tanṭeem al-mo'askarat]; **camping gas** *n* موقد يعمل بالغاز للمعسكرات [Maw'qed ya'amal bel-ghaz lel-mo'askarat]
campsite ['kæmp,saɪt] *n* موقع المعسكر [Maw'qe'a al-mo'askar]
campus ['kæmpəs] *n* الحرم الجامعي [Al-ḥaram al-jame'aey]
can [kæn] *n* علبة [ʕulba] ▷ *v* يستطيع [jastatˤi:ʕu]; **watering can** *n* رشاش مياه [Rashah meyah]
Canada ['kænədə] *n* كندا [kanada:]
Canadian [kə'neɪdɪən] *adj* كندي [kanadijj] ▷ *n* شخص كندي [Shakhṣ kanadey]
canal [kə'næl] *n* قناة [qana:t]
Canaries [kə'nɛəri:z] *npl* طيور الكناري [tˤuju:ru al-kana:rijji]
canary [kə'nɛərɪ] *n* طائر الكناري [Ṭaaer al-kanarey]
cancel ['kænsᵊl] *v* يُبْطِل [jubtˤil]
cancellation [,kænsɪ'leɪʃən] *n* إلغاء [ʔilɣa:ʔ]; **Are there any cancellations?** هل تم إلغاء أي حجز؟ [hal tam-a el-gha ay ḥajiz?]
cancer ['kænsə] *n (illness)* مرض السرطان [Maraḍ al-saraṭan]
Cancer ['kænsə] *n (horoscope)* برج السرطان [Borj alsaraṭan]
candidate ['kændɪ,deɪt; -dɪt] *n* مُرَشَح [muraʃʃaħ]
candle ['kændᵊl] *n* شمعة [ʃamʕa]
candlestick ['kændᵊl,stɪk] *n* شمعدان [ʃamʕada:n]
candyfloss ['kændɪ,flɒs] *n* غزل البنات [Ghazl al-banat]
canister ['kænɪstə] *n* علبة صغيرة ['aolbah ṣagherah]
cannabis ['kænəbɪs] *n* حشيش [ħaʃi:ʃ]
canned [kænd] *adj* مُعَلَّبَةٌ [muʕallabat]
canoe [kə'nu:] *n* صندل [sˤandal]
canoeing [kə'nu:ɪŋ] *n* تجديف [taʒdi:f]; **Where can we go canoeing?** أين يمكن أن أمارس رياضة التجديف بالقوارب الصغيرة؟ [ayna yamken an omares riyaḍat al-tajdeef bil- 'qawareb al-ṣaghera?]
can-opener ['kæn'əʊpənə] *n* فتاحة علب التصبير [Fatahat 'aolab al-taṣdeer]
canteen [kæn'ti:n] *n* مطعم [matˤʕam]
canter ['kæntə] *v* يُخِب الفرس [Yokheb al-faras]
canvas ['kænvəs] *n* قماش الرسم ['qomash al-rasm]
canvass ['kænvəs] *v* يَستطلع الرأي [Yastaṭle'a al-ray]
cap [kæp] *n* غطاء قنينة [Gheṭa'a 'qeneenah]; **baseball cap** *n* قُبَعة البيسبول ['qoba'at al-beesbool]
capable ['keɪpəbᵊl] *adj* مؤهل [moahhal]
capacity [kə'pæsɪtɪ] *n* سعة [siʕa]
capital ['kæpɪtᵊl] *n* عاصمة [ʕa:sˤima]
capitalism ['kæpɪtə,lɪzəm] *n* رأسمالية [raʔsuma:lijja]
Capricorn ['kæprɪ,kɔ:n] *n* الجَدْي [alʒadjju]
capsize [kæp'saɪz] *v* يَنقلب [janqalibu]
capsule ['kæpsju:l] *n* كبسولة [kabsu:la]
captain ['kæptɪn] *n* رئيس [raʔijs]
caption ['kæpʃən] *n* تعليق [taʕli:q]
capture ['kæptʃə] *v* يْأسِر [jaʔsiru]
car [kɑ:] *n* سَيارة [sajja:ra]; **cable car** *n* ترام [tra:mun]; **car hire** *n* إيجار سيارة [Ejar sayarah]; **car park** *n* موقف انتظار [Maw'qaf enteḍhar]; **car rental** *n* تأجير سيارة [Taajeer sayarah]; **car wash** *n*

غسيل سيارة [ghaseel sayaarah]; **company car** *n* سيارة الشركة [Sayarat al-sharekah]; **dining car** *n* عربة تناول الطعام في القطار ['arabat tanawool al-ṭa'aaam fee al-'qeṭar]; **estate car** *n* سيارة بصالون متحرك المقاعد [Sayarah be-ṣalon motaḥarek al-ma'qaed]; **hired car** *n* سيارة مستأجرة [Sayarah mostaajarah]; **patrol car** *n* سيارة الدورية [Sayarah al-dawreyah]; **racing car** *n* سيارة السباق [Sayarah al-seba'q]; **rental car** *n* سيارة إيجار [Sayarah eejar]; **saloon car** *n* سيارة صالون [Sayarah ṣalon]; **sleeping car** *n* عربة النوم ['arabat al-nawm]

carafe [kə'ræf; -'rɑːf] *n* غرّافة [ɣarra:fa]

caramel ['kærəməl; -ˌmɛl] *n* كرميل [karami:l]

carat ['kærət] *n* قيراط [qi:ra:tˤ]

caravan ['kærəˌvæn] *n* مَقْطُورَةٌ [maqtˤu:ra]; **caravan site** *n* موقع المَقْطُورَة [Maw'qe'a al-ma'qṭorah]

carbohydrate [ˌkɑːbəʊ'haɪdreɪt] *n* كَارْبُوهَيْدْرَات [ka:rbu:hajdra:t]

carbon ['kɑːbᵊn] *n* كربون [karbu:n]; **carbon footprint** *n* بصمة كربونية [Baṣma karbonyah]

carburettor [ˌkɑːbjʊ'rɛtə; 'kɑːbjʊˌrɛtə; -bə-] *n* المكربن [Al-makreen]

card [kɑːd] *n* بطاقة [bitˤa:qa]; **boarding card** *n* كارت ركوب [Kart rekoob]; **credit card** *n* كارت ائتمان [Kart eateman]; **debit card** *n* كارت سحب [Kart sahb]; **greetings card** *n* بطاقة تهنئة [Beṭaqat tahneaa]; **ID card** *abbr* بطاقة شخصية [beṭ a'qah shakhṣeyah]; **membership card** *n* بطاقة عضوية [Beṭaqat 'aodweiah]; **playing card** *n* بطاقة لعب [Beṭaqat la'aeb]; **report card** *n* تقرير مدرسي [Ta'qreer madrasey]; **top-up card** *n* كارت إعادة الشحن [Kart e'aadat shaḥn]

cardboard ['kɑːdˌbɔːd] *n* ورق مقوى [Wara'q mo'qawa]

cardigan ['kɑːdɪgən] *n* سترة صوفية [Sotrah ṣofeyah]

cardphone ['kɑːdfəʊn] *n* كارت تليفون [Kart telefone]

care [kɛə] *n* عناية [ʕina:ja] ▷ *v* يعتني [jaʕtani:]; **intensive care unit** *n* وحدة العناية المركزة [Weḥdat al-'aenayah al-morkazah]

career [kə'rɪə] *n* حقل النشاط [Ha'ql al-nashaṭ]

careful ['kɛəfʊl] *adj* حَذِرٌ [ħaðir]

carefully ['kɛəfʊlɪ] *adv* بِعناية [Be-'aenayah]

careless ['kɛəlɪs] *adj* مهمل [muhmil]

caretaker ['kɛəˌteɪkə] *n* مشرف على بيت [Moshref ala bayt]

car-ferry ['kɑːfɛrɪ] *n* معدية سيارات [Me'adeyat sayarat]

cargo ['kɑːgəʊ] *n* حُمولة [ħumu:la]

Caribbean [ˌkærɪ'biːən; kə'rɪbɪən] *adj* كاريبي [ka:rajbi:] ▷ *n* البحر الكاريبي [Al-baḥr al-kareebey]

caring ['kɛərɪŋ] *adj* مهتم بالآخرين [Mohtam bel-aakhareen]

carnation [kɑː'neɪʃən] *n* قرنفل [qaranful]

carnival ['kɑːnɪvᵊl] *n* كرنفال [karnafa:l]

carol ['kærəl] *n* أغنية مرحة [oghneyah mareha]

carpenter ['kɑːpɪntə] *n* نجار [naʒʒa:r]

carpentry ['kɑːpɪntrɪ] *n* نجارة [niʒʒa:ra]

carpet ['kɑːpɪt] *n* سجادة [saʒa:dda]; **fitted carpet** *n* سجاد مثبت [Sejad mothabat]

carriage ['kærɪdʒ] *n* حافلة [ħa:fila]

carriageway ['kærɪdʒˌweɪ] *n*; **dual carriageway** *n* طريق مزدوج الاتجاه للسيارات [Taree'q mozdawaj al-etejah lel-sayarat]

carrot ['kærət] *n* جزر [ʒazar]

carry ['kærɪ] *v* يَحمِل [juħmalu]

carrycot ['kærɪˌkɒt] *n* سرير محمول للطفل [Sareer maḥmool lel-ṭefl]

carry on ['kærɪ ɒn] *v* يَستمِر [jastamirru]

carry out ['kærɪ aʊt] *v* يُنَفِذ [junaffiðu]

cart [kɑːt] *n* عربة [ʕaraba]

carton ['kɑːtᵊn] *n* علبة كارتون ['aolbat kartoon]

cartoon [kɑːˈtuːn] *n* رسوم متحركة [Rosoom motaharekah]
cartridge [ˈkɑːtrɪdʒ] *n* خرطوشة [xartˤuːʃa]
carve [kɑːv] *v* يَنْحِت [janħutu]
case [keɪs] *n* قضية [qadˤijja]; **pencil case** *n* مقلمة [miqlamatun]
cash [kæʃ] *n* نَقْد [naqd]; **cash dispenser** *n* ماكينة صرافة [Makenat ṣerafah]; **cash register** *n* ماكينة تسجيل الكاش [Makenat tasjeel al-kaash]
cashew [ˈkæʃuː; kæˈʃuː] *n* ثمرة الكاجو [Thamarat al-kajoo]
cashier [kæˈʃɪə] *n* صَرَّافٌ [sˤarraːf]
cashmere [ˈkæʃmɪə] *n* شال من الصوف الناعم [Shal men al-Ṣoof al-na'aem]
casino [kəˈsiːnəʊ] *n* كازينو [kaːziːnuː]
casserole [ˈkæsəˌrəʊl] *n* كسرولة [kasruːlatu]
cassette [kæˈsɛt] *n* كاسيت [kaːsiːt]
cast [kɑːst] *n* يَصُبّ [jasˤubu]
castle [ˈkɑːsəl] *n* قلعة [qalʕa]
casual [ˈkæʒjʊəl] *adj* طارئ [tˤaːriʔ]
casually [ˈkæʒjʊəlɪ] *adv* بشكل عَارِض [Beshakl 'aareḍ]
casualty [ˈkæʒjʊəltɪ] *n* مُصَاب [musˤaːb]
cat [kæt] *n* قطة [qitˤa]
catalogue [ˈkætəˌlɒg] *n* كتالوج [kataːluːʒ]; **I'd like a catalogue** أريد مشاهدة الكتالوج [areed mu-shahadat al-kataloj]
cataract [ˈkætəˌrækt] *n (eye)* مياه بيضاء [Meyah bayḍaa], *(waterfall)* شَلّال كبير [Shallal kabeer]
catarrh [kəˈtɑː] *n* نَزْلَة [nazla]
catastrophe [kəˈtæstrəfɪ] *n* نكبة [nakba]
catch [kætʃ] *v* يمسك [jumsiku]
catching [ˈkætʃɪŋ] *adj* فاتن [faːtin]
catch up [kætʃ ʌp] *v* لحق ب [laħiqa bi]
category [ˈkætɪgərɪ] *n* فئة [fiʔa]
catering [ˈkeɪtərɪŋ] *n* توريد الطعام [Tarweed al-ṭa'aam]
caterpillar [ˈkætəˌpɪlə] *n* يَرَقَانَةٌ [jaraqaːna]
cathedral [kəˈθiːdrəl] *n* كاتدرائية [kaːtidraːʔijja]; **When is the cathedral open?** متى تُفتح الكاتدرائية؟ [mata tuftaḥ al-katid-ra-eya?]
Catholic [ˈkæθəlɪk; ˈkæθlɪk] *adj* كاثوليكي [kaːθuːliːkij] ▷ *n* شخص كاثوليكي [Shakhṣ katholeykey]; **Roman Catholic** *n* روماني كاثوليكي [Romaney katholeykey]شخص روماني كاثوليكي , [shakhṣ romaney katholeekey]
cattle [ˈkætəl] *npl* ماشية [maːʃijjatun]
Caucasus [ˈkɔːkəsəs] *n* قُوقَاز [quːqaːz]
cauliflower [ˈkɒlɪˌflaʊə] *n* قنبيط [qanbiːtˤ]
cause [kɔːz] *n (ideals)* سبب [sabab], *(reason)* سبب [sabab] ▷ *v* يُسبب [jusabbibu]
caution [ˈkɔːʃən] *n* حَذَر [ħaðar]
cautious [ˈkɔːʃəs] *adj* حذِر [ħaðir]
cautiously [ˈkɔːʃəslɪ] *adv* بحذر [beḥadhar]
cave [keɪv] *n* كهف [kahf]
CCTV [siː siː tiː viː] *abbr* دائرة تلفزيونية مغلقة [Daerah telefezyoneyah moghla'qa]
CD [siː diː] *n* اسطوانة [ustˤuwaːna]; **CD burner** *n* ناسخ الاسطوانة [Nasekh al-esṭewanah]; **CD player** *n* مشغل الاسطوانات [Moshaghel al-esṭewanat]; **When will the CD be ready?** متى ستكون الاسطوانة جاهزة؟ [mata sata-koon al-esṭ-ewana jaheza?]
CD-ROM [-ˈrɒm] *n* دُرج الأسطوانات المدمجة [Dorj al-esṭewanaat al-modmajah]
ceasefire [ˈsiːsˈfaɪə] *n* وَقْف إطلاق النار [Wa'qf eṭlaa'q al-naar]
ceiling [ˈsiːlɪŋ] *n* سَقف [saqf]
celebrate [ˈsɛlɪˌbreɪt] *v* يَحْتفل [jaħtafilu]
celebration [ˈsɛlɪˌbreɪʃən] *n* احتفال [iħtifaːl]
celebrity [sɪˈlɛbrɪtɪ] *n* شُهْرَة [ʃuhra]
celery [ˈsɛlərɪ] *n* كرفس [kurfus]
cell [sɛl] *n* خلية [xalijja]
cellar [ˈsɛlə] *n* قبو [qabw]
cello [ˈtʃɛləʊ] *n* كمنجة كبيرة [Kamanjah kabeerah]

cement [sɪ'mɛnt] *n* أسمنت [ʔasmant]
cemetery ['sɛmɪtrɪ] *n* مقبرة [maqbara]
census ['sɛnsəs] *n* إحصاء رسمي [Ehṣaa rasmey]
cent [sɛnt] *n* سِنت [sint]
centenary [sɛn'ti:nərɪ] *n* قَرْن [qarn]
centimetre ['sɛntɪ,mi:tə] *n* سنتيمتر [santi:mitar]
central ['sɛntrəl] *adj* مركزي [markazijjat]; **central heating** *n* تدفئة مركزية [Tadfeah markazeyah]; **Central America** *n* أمريكا الوسطى [Amrika al wostaa]
centre ['sɛntə] *n* وسطٌ [wasatˤ]; **call centre** *n* مركز الاتصال [Markaz al-eteṣal]; **city centre** *n* وسط المدينة [Wasaṭ al-madeenah]; **job centre** *n* مركز العمل [markaz al-'aamal]; **leisure centre** *n* مركز ترفيهي [Markaz tarfehy]; **shopping centre** *n* مركز تسوق [Markaz tasawe'q]; **town centre** *n* وَسَطْ المدينة [Wasaṭ al-madeenah]; **visitor centre** *n* مركز زائري [Markaz zaerey]
century ['sɛntʃərɪ] *n* قرن [qarn]
CEO [si: i: əʊ] *abbr* مدير الإدارة التنفيذية [Modeer el-edarah al-tanfeedheyah]
ceramic [sɪ'ræmɪk] *adj* خزفي [xazafij]
cereal ['sɪərɪəl] *n* حبوب [ħubu:b]
ceremony ['sɛrɪmənɪ] *n* مراسم [mara:sim]
certain ['sɜ:tᵊn] *adj* محدد [muħadadd]
certainly ['sɜ:tᵊnlɪ] *adv* بلا شَكْ [Bela shak]
certainty ['sɜ:tᵊntɪ] *n* يقين [jaqi:n]
certificate [sə'tɪfɪkɪt] *n* شهادة [ʃaha:da]; **birth certificate** *n* شهادة ميلاد [Shahadat meelad]; **marriage certificate** *n* عقد زواج ['aa'qd zawaj]; **medical certificate** *n* شهادة طبية [Shehadah ṭebeyah]; **I need a 'fit to fly' certificate** أحتاج إلى شهادة تفيد أنني مؤهلة للسفر بالطائرة [aḥtaaj ela shahada tufeed inna-ni mo-ah-ala lel-safar bil-ṭaa-era]
Chad [tʃæd] *n* تشاد [tʃa:d]
chain [tʃeɪn] *n* سِلسة [silsila]
chair [tʃɛə] *n (furniture)* كرسي [kursij]; **easy chair** *n* كرسي مريح [Korsey moreeḥ]; **rocking chair** *n* كرسي هَزَّاز [Korsey hazzaz]
chairlift ['tʃɛə,lɪft] *n* تليفريك [tili:fri:k]
chairman, chairmen ['tʃɛəmən, 'tʃɛəmɛn] *n* رئيس المجلس [Raees al-majlas]
chalk [tʃɔ:k] *n* طباشير [tˤaba:ʃi:r]
challenge ['tʃælɪndʒ] *n* تحدّ [taħaddin] ▷ *v* يتحدى [jataħadda:]
challenging ['tʃælɪndʒɪŋ; 'challenging] *adj* صعب [sˤaʕb]
chambermaid ['tʃeɪmbə,meɪd] *n* خادمة فى فندق [Khademah fee fodo'q]
champagne [ʃæm'peɪn] *n* شامبانيا [ʃa:mba:nja:]
champion ['tʃæmpɪən] *n* بطل *(competition)* [batˤal]
championship ['tʃæmpɪən,ʃɪp] *n* بطولة [butˤu:la]
chance [tʃɑ:ns] *n* مصادفة [musˤa:dafa]; **by chance** *adv* بالصُدْفَة [Bel-ṣodfah]
change [tʃeɪndʒ] *n* تغيير [taɣji:r] ▷ *vi* يَتغَير [jataɣajjaru] ▷ *vt* يُغّير [juɣajjiru]; **changing room** *n* غرفة تبديل الملابس [Ghorfat tabdeel al-malabes]; **I want to change my ticket** أريد تغيير تذكرتي [areed taghyeer tadhkeraty]; **I want to change some... into...** أرغب في تغيير بعض... إلى... [arghab fee taghyeer ba'aḍ... ela...]; **I'd like to change my flight** أريد تغيير رحلتي الجوية [areed taghyeer reḥlaty al-jaw-wya]; **I'd like to change one hundred... into...** أرغب في تغيير مائة... إلى... [arghab fee taghyeer ma-a... ela...]; **Where are the changing rooms?** أين توجد غرفة تغيير الملابس؟ [ayna tojad ghurfat taghyeer al-malabis?]; **Where can I change some money?** أين يمكنني تغيير بعض النقود؟ [ayna yamken-any taghyeer ba'aḍ al-ni'qood?]; **Where can I change the baby?** أين يمكنني تغيير ملابس الرضيع؟ [ayna yamken-any taghyeer ma-labis al-raḍee'a?]

changeable ['tʃeɪndʒəbᵊl] *adj* قابل للتغيير ['qabel lel-tagheyer]
channel ['tʃænᵊl] *n* مجرى نهر [Majra nahr]
chaos ['keɪɒs] *n* فوضى [fawdˤa:]
chaotic [keɪ'ɒtɪk] *adj* مشوش [muʃawwaʃ]
chap [tʃæp] *n* فَتى [fata:]
chapel ['tʃæpᵊl] *n* كنيسة صغيرة [Kanesah ṣagherah]
chapter ['tʃæptə] *n* فصل [fasˤl]
character ['kærɪktə] *n* شخصية [ʃaxsˤijja]
characteristic [ˌkærɪktə'rɪstɪk] *n* سمة [sima]
charcoal ['tʃɑːˌkəʊl] *n* فَحْم نباتي [Faḥm nabatey]
charge [tʃɑːdʒ] *n (accusation)* تُهمة [tuhma], *(electricity)* شحن [ʃaħn], *(price)* رسم [rasm] ▷ *v (accuse)* يَتّهِم [jattahimu], *(electricity)* يَحشو [jaħʃu:], *(price)* يَطْلُبُ سِعْرا [jatˤlubu siʕran]; **admission charge** *n* رَسْم الالتحاق [Rasm al-elteha'q]; **cover charge** *n* المصاريف المدفوعة مقدما [Al-maṣaareef al-madfoo'ah mo'qadaman]; **service charge** *n* رَسْم الخدمة [Rasm al-khedmah]; **It's not charging** إنها لا تقبل الشحن [inaha la ta'qbal al-shaḥin]; **It's not holding its charge** لا تحتفظ بشحنها [la taḥtafiḍh be-shaḥ-neha]; **Where can I charge my mobile phone?** أين يمكن أن أشحن تليفوني المحمول؟ [ayna yamken an ash-ḥan talefony al-maḥmool?]
charger ['tʃɑːdʒə] *n* شاحِن [ʃa:ħin]
charity ['tʃærɪtɪ] *n* إحسان [ʔiħsa:n]; **charity shop** *n* محل لبضائع متبرع بها لجهة خيرية [Maḥal lebaḍae'a motabar'a beha lejahah khayryah]
charm [tʃɑːm] *n* فتنة [fitna]
charming ['tʃɑːmɪŋ] *adj* ساحر [sa:ħir]
chart [tʃɑːt] *n* رسم بياني [Rasm bayany]; **pie chart** *n* رسم بياني دائري [Rasm bayany daery]
chase [tʃeɪs] *n* مطاردة [mutˤa:rada] ▷ *v* يُطارِد [jutˤa:ridu]
chat [tʃæt] *n* دردشة [dardaʃa] ▷ *v* يدردش [judardiʃu]; **chat show** *n* برنامج حواري [Barnamaj hewary]
chatroom ['tʃætˌruːm; -ˌrʊm] *n* غرفة محادثة [ghorfat mohadathah]
chauffeur ['ʃəʊfə; ʃəʊ'fɜː] *n* سائق سيارة [Saae'q sayarah]
chauvinist ['ʃəʊvɪˌnɪst] *n* شوفيني [ʃu:fi:ni:]
cheap [tʃiːp] *adj* رخيص [raxi:sˤ]
cheat [tʃiːt] *n* غش [ɣaʃʃa] ▷ *v* يَغُش [jaɣiʃʃu]
Chechnya ['tʃɛtʃnjə] *n* الشيشان [aʃ-ʃi:ʃa:n]
check [tʃɛk] *n* فحص [faħsˤ] ▷ *v* يفحص [jafħasˤu]; **Can you check the water, please?** أتسمح بفحص الماء بالسيارة؟ [a-tas-maḥ be-faḥiṣ al-maa-i bil-sayara?]
checked [tʃɛkt] *adj* ذو مربعات [dho moraba'aat]
check in [tʃɛk ɪn] *v* يتسجل فى فندق [Yatasajal fee fondo'q]
check-in [tʃɛkɪn] *n* التسجيل فى فندق [Al-tasjeel fee fondo'q]
check out [tʃɛk aʊt] *v* يغادر الفندق [Yoghader al-fodo'q]
checkout ['tʃɛkaʊt] *n* مغادرة الفندق [Moghadarat al-fondo'q]
check-up [tʃɛkʌp] *n* فحص طبى عام [Faḥṣ ṭebey 'aam]
cheek [tʃiːk] *n* خد [xadd]
cheekbone ['tʃiːkˌbəʊn] *n* عظم الوجنة [aḍhm al-wajnah]
cheeky ['tʃiːkɪ] *adj* وَقِح [waqiħ]
cheer [tʃɪə] *n* ابتهاج [ibtiha:ʒ] ▷ *v* يبتهج [jabtahiʒu]
cheerful ['tʃɪəfʊl] *adj* مبهج [mubhaʒ]
cheese [tʃiːz] *n* جُبن [ʒubn]; **cottage cheese** *n* جبن قريش [Jobn 'qareesh]
chef [ʃɛf] *n* رئيس الطهاة [Raees al-ṭohah]
chemical ['kɛmɪkᵊl] *n* مادة كيميائية [Madah kemyaeyah]
chemist ['kɛmɪst] *n* كِيمِيَائِيٌّ [ki:mija:ʔij]; **chemist('s)** *n* معمل كيميائي [M'amal

kemyaeay]
chemistry ['kɛmɪstrɪ] *n* كيمياء [ki:mija:ʔ]
cheque [tʃɛk] *n* شِيك بنكي [Sheek bankey]; **blank cheque** *n* شيك على بياض [Sheek ala bayad]; **traveller's cheque** *n* شِيك سياحي [Sheek seyahey]
chequebook ['tʃɛk,bʊk] *n* دفتر شيكات [Daftar sheekaat]
cherry ['tʃɛrɪ] *n* كرز [karaz]
chess [tʃɛs] *n* شطرنج [ʃatˤranʒ]
chest [tʃɛst] *n (body part)* صَدْر [sˤadr], *(storage)* صندوق [sˤundu:q]; **chest of drawers** *n* خزانة ملابس بأدراج [Khezanat malabes be-adraj]
chestnut ['tʃɛs,nʌt] *n* كَسْتِناء [kastana:ʔ]
chew [tʃu:] *v* يَمضُغ [jamdˤuɣu]; **chewing gum** *n* علكة [ʕilkatun]
chick [tʃɪk] *n* كتكوت [kutku:t]
chicken ['tʃɪkɪn] *n* دَجَاجَةٌ [daʒa:ʒa]
chickenpox ['tʃɪkɪn,pɒks] *n* حُماق [ħumq]
chickpea ['tʃɪk,pi:] *n* حبة الحمص [Habat al-hommoṣ]
chief [tʃi:f] *adj* رئيسي [raʔi:sij] ▷ *n* سيد [sajjid]
child, children [tʃaɪld, 'tʃɪldrən] *n* غِر [ɣirr]; **child abuse** *n* سوء معاملة الأطفال [Soo mo'aamalat al-aṭfaal]
childcare ['tʃaɪld,kɛə] *n* رعاية الأطفال [Re'aayat al-aṭfal]
childhood ['tʃaɪldhʊd] *n* طفولة [tˤufu:la]
childish ['tʃaɪldɪʃ] *adj* طُفُولِيٌّ [tˤufu:lij]
childminder ['tʃaɪld,maɪndə] *n* جليسة أطفال [Jaleesat aṭfaal]
Chile ['tʃɪlɪ] *n* دولة تشيلي [Dawlat tesheeley]
Chilean ['tʃɪlɪən] *adj* تشيلي [tʃi:lij] ▷ *n* مواطن تشيلي [Mowaṭen tsheeley]
chill [tʃɪl] *v* يبرِّد [jubarridu]
chilli ['tʃɪlɪ] *n* فلفل أحمر حار [Felfel aḥmar ḥar]
chilly ['tʃɪlɪ] *adj* مُثْلِج [muθallaʒ]
chimney ['tʃɪmnɪ] *n* مَدخَنة [midxana]
chimpanzee [,tʃɪmpæn'zi:] *n* شمبانزي [ʃamba:nzij]
chin [tʃɪn] *n* ذَقْن [ðaqn]
china ['tʃaɪnə] *n* آنية من الصيني [Aaneyah men al-ṣeeney]
China ['tʃaɪnə] *n* الصين [asˤ-sˤi:nu]
Chinese [tʃaɪ'ni:z] *adj* صيني [sˤi:nij] ▷ *n (language)* اللغة الصينية [Al-loghah al-ṣeeneyah], *(person)* صيني [sˤi:nij]
chip [tʃɪp] *n (electronic)* شريحة [ʃari:ħatt], *(small piece)* رقاقة [ruqa:qa]; **silicon chip** *n* شريحة السليكون [Shreeḥah men al-selekoon]
chips [tʃɪps] *npl* شرائح [ʃara:ʔiħun]
chiropodist [kɪ'rɒpədɪst] *n* مُعَالِج القدم [Mo'aaleg al-'qadam]
chisel ['tʃɪzᵊl] *n* إزميل خشبي [Ezmeel khashabey]
chives [tʃaɪvz] *npl* ثوم معمر [Thoom mo'aamer]
chlorine ['klɔ:ri:n] *n* كلور [klu:r]
chocolate ['tʃɒkəlɪt; 'tʃɒklɪt; -lət] *n* شوكولاتة [ʃu:ku:la:ta]; **milk chocolate** *n* شيكولاتة باللبن [Shekolata bel-laban]; **plain chocolate** *n* شيكولاتة سادة [Shekolatah sada]
choice [tʃɔɪs] *n* اختيار [ixtija:r]
choir [kwaɪə] *n* جَوْقَةٌ [ʒawqa]
choke [tʃəʊk] *v* يَختنق [jaxtaniqu]
cholesterol [kə'lɛstə,rɒl] *n* كولِسْتِرُول [ku:listiru:l]
choose [tʃu:z] *v* يختار [jaxta:ru]
chop [tʃɒp] *n* فرم [faram] ▷ *v* يَفْرُم [jafrumu]; **pork chop** *n* شَريحة لحم خنزير [Shareehat laḥm khenzeer]
chopsticks ['tʃɒpstɪks] *npl* عيدان الأكل فى الصين [ʕi:da:ni alʔakla fi: assˤi:ni]
chosen ['tʃəʊzᵊn] *adj* مختار [muxta:r]
Christ [kraɪst] *n* المَسِيح [al-masi:ħu]
christening ['krɪsᵊnɪŋ; 'christening] *n* حفلة التعميد [Ḥaflat alt'ameed]
Christian ['krɪstʃən] *adj* مَسيحي [masi:ħij] ▷ *n* مَسيحي [masi:ħij]; **Christian name** *n* اسم مَسيحي [Esm maseeḥey]
Christianity [,krɪstɪ'ænɪtɪ] *n* المَسيحية

[al-masi:ħijjatu]
Christmas ['krɪsməs] *n* عيد الميلاد المجيد ['aeed al-meelad al-majeed]; **Christmas card** *n* كارت الكريسماس [Kart al-kresmas]; **Christmas Eve** *n* عشية عيد الميلاد ['aasheyat 'aeed al-meelad]; **Christmas tree** *n* شجرة عيد الميلاد [Shajarat 'aeed al-meelad]
chrome [krəʊm] *n* كُروم [ku:ru:mu]
chronic ['krɒnɪk] *adj* مزمن [muzmin]
chrysanthemum [krɪ'sænθəməm] *n* الاقحوان [al-uqħuwa:nu]
chubby ['tʃʌbɪ] *adj* مُمْتَلِئ [mumtaliʔ]
chunk [tʃʌŋk] *n* قطعة غليظة قصيرة ['qet'aah ghaleḍhah]
church [tʃɜːtʃ] *n* كنيسة [kani:sa]; **Can we visit the church?** أيمكننا زيارة الكنيسة؟ [a-yamkun-ana zeyarat al-kaneesa]
cider ['saɪdə] *n* عصير تفاح ['aaṣeer tofaḥ]
cigar [sɪ'gɑː] *n* سيجار [si:ʒa:r]
cigarette [ˌsɪgə'rɛt] *n* سيجارة [si:ʒa:ra]; **cigarette lighter** *n* قداحة [qadda:ħatun]
cinema ['sɪnɪmə] *n* سينما [si:nima:]; **What's on at the cinema?** ماذا يعرض الآن على شاشات السينما؟ [madha yu'a-raḍ al-aan 'aala sha-shaat al-senama?]
cinnamon ['sɪnəmən] *n* قرفة [qirfa]
circle ['sɜːkᵊl] *n* دائرة [da:ʔira]; **Arctic Circle** *n* الدائرة القطبية الشمالية [Al-daerah al'qoṭbeyah al-Shamaleyah]
circuit ['sɜːkɪt] *n* دارة [da:ra]
circular ['sɜːkjʊlə] *adj* دائري [da:ʔirij]
circulation [ˌsɜːkjʊ'leɪʃən] *n* دَوَران [dawara:n]
circumstances ['sɜːkəmstənsɪz] *npl* ظروف [zˤuru:fun]
circus ['sɜːkəs] *n* سيرك [si:rk]
citizen ['sɪtɪzᵊn] *n* مواطن [muwa:tˤin]; **senior citizen** *n* شخص متقدم العمر [Shakhṣ mota'qadem al-'aomr]
citizenship ['sɪtɪzənˌʃɪp] *n* الانتماء الوطني [Al-entemaa alwaṭaney]
city ['sɪtɪ] *n* مدينة [madi:na]; **city centre** *n* وسط المدينة [Wasaṭ al-madeenah]; **Is there a bus to the city?** هل يوجد أتوبيس إلى المدينة؟ [Hal yojad otobees ela al-madeenah?]; **Please take me to the city centre** من فضلك أريد الذهاب إلى وسط المدينة [min faḍlak areed al-dhehaab ela waṣaṭ al-madena]; **Where can I buy a map of the city?** أين يمكن أن أشتري خريطة للمدينة؟ [ayna yamken an ash-tary khareeṭa lil-madena?]
civilian [sɪ'vɪljən] *adj* مدني [madanijjat] ▷ *n* مدني [madanijja]
civilization [ˌsɪvɪlaɪ'zeɪʃən] *n* حضارة [ħadˤa:ra]
claim [kleɪm] *n* مطالبة [mutˤa:laba] ▷ *v* يُطالِب [jutˤa:libu]; **claim form** *n* استمارة مطالبة [Estemarat moṭalabah]
clap [klæp] *v* يُصَفِق [jusˤaffiqu]
clarify ['klærɪˌfaɪ] *v* يُوضِح [juwadˤdˤiħu]
clarinet [ˌklærɪ'nɛt] *n* كلارينت [kla:ri:nit]
clash [klæʃ] *v* يَصْطَدِم [jasˤtˤadimu]
clasp [klɑːsp] *n* يُصافح [jusˤa:fiħu]
class [klɑːs] *n* طَبَقَة إجْتِماعِيَّة [tˤabaqatun iʒtima:ʕijja]; **business class** *n* درجة رجال الأعمال [Darajat rejal ala'amal]; **economy class** *n* درجة سياحية [Darjah seyaḥeyah]; **second class** *n* درجة ثانية [Darajah thaneyah]
classic ['klæsɪk] *adj* كلاسيكي [kla:si:kij] ▷ *n* كلاسيكي [kla:si:kij]
classical ['klæsɪkᵊl] *adj* كلاسيكي [kla:si:kij]
classmate ['klɑːsˌmeɪt] *n* زميل الفصل [Zameel al-faṣl]
classroom ['klɑːsˌruːm; -ˌrʊm] *n* حجرة دراسية [Ḥojrat derasah]; **classroom assistant** *n* مساعد المدرس [Mosa'aed al-modares]
clause [klɔːz] *n* مادة [ma:dda]
claustrophobic [ˌklɔːstrə'fəʊbɪk; ˌklɒs-] *adj* خائف من الأماكن المغلقة [Khaef men al-amaken al-moghla'ah]
claw [klɔː] *n* ظُفْرٌ [zˤufr]
clay [kleɪ] *n* صلصال [sˤalsˤa:l]
clean [kliːn] *adj* نظيف [nazˤi:f] ▷ *v* يُنَظِف [junazˤzˤifu]; **Can you clean the room,**

please? هل يمكن من فضلك تنظيف الغرفة؟ [hal yamken min faḍlak tanḍheef al-ghurfa?]; **I need this dry-cleaned** احتاج أن أنظف هذا تنظيفا جافًا [aḥtaaj an ana-ḍhif hadha tan-ḍheefan jaafan]; **I'd like to get these things cleaned** أود تنظيف هذه الأشياء [awid tanḍheef hadhy al-ashyaa]; **The room isn't clean** الغرفة ليست نظيفة [al-ghurfa laysat naḍhefa]; **Where can I get this cleaned?** أين يمكنني تنظيف هذا؟ [ayna yamken-any tanḍheef hadha?]

cleaner ['kliːnə] *n* خادم للتنظيف [Khadem lel-tanḍheef]

cleaning ['kliːnɪŋ] *n* تنظيف [tanzˤiːf]; **cleaning lady** *n* عاملة النظافة ['aamelat al-nadhafah]

cleanser ['klɛnzə] *n* غَسُولٌ [ɣasuːl]

clear [klɪə] *adj* واضح [waːdˤiħ]

clearly ['klɪəlɪ] *adv* بوضوح [biwudˤuːħin]

clear off [klɪə ɒf] *v* يَذهَب بسرعة [yaḍhab besor'aa]

clear up [klɪə ʌp] *v* يُزيل الغموض [Yozeel al-ghmooḍ]

clementine ['klɛmənˌtiːn; -ˌtaɪn] *n* نوع من البرتقال الناعم [nawʕun min alburtuqaːli alnaːʕimi]

clever ['klɛvə] *adj* شاطر [ʃaːtˤir]

click [klɪk] *n* نقرة [naqra] ▷ *v* ينقر [janquru]

client ['klaɪənt] *n* زبون [zabuːn]

cliff [klɪf] *n* جُرف [ʒarf]

climate ['klaɪmɪt] *n* مناخ [munaːx]; **climate change** *n* تغير المناخ [Taghyeer almonakh]

climb [klaɪm] *v* يَتسلق [jatasallaqu]

climber ['klaɪmə] *n* متسلق الجبال [Motasale'q al-jebaal]

climbing ['klaɪmɪŋ] *n* تسلق [tasalluq]

clinic ['klɪnɪk] *n* عيادة [ʕijaːda]

clip [klɪp] *n* مشبك [maʃbak]

clippers ['klɪpəz] *npl* ماكينة حلاقة [Makeenat ḥelaqah]

cloakroom ['kləʊkˌruːm; -ˌrʊm] *n* حجرة لحفظ المعاطف [Hojarah le-hefḍh al-ma'atef]

clock [klɒk] *n* ساعة حائط [Saa'ah ḥaaeṭ]; **alarm clock** *n* منبه [munabbihun]

clockwise ['klɒkˌwaɪz] *adv* باتجاه عقارب الساعة [Betejah a'qareb al-saa'ah]

clog [klɒg] *n* قبقاب [qubqaːb]

clone [kləʊn] *n* استنساخ [istinsaːx] ▷ *v* يَسْتَنْسِخ [jastansix]

close *adj* [kləʊs] حميم [ħamiːm] ▷ *adv* [kləʊs] بإحكام [biʔiħkaːmin] ▷ *v* [kləʊz] يُغْلِق [juɣliqu]; **close by** *adj* قريب من ['qareeb men]; **closing time** *n* وَقْت الإغلاق [Wa'qt al-eghlaa'q]

closed [kləʊzd] *adj* مغلق [muɣlaq]

closely [kləʊslɪ] *adv* مغلقاً [muɣlaqan]

closure ['kləʊʒə] *n* إغلاق [ʔiɣlaːq]

cloth [klɒθ] *n* قماش [qumaːʃ]

clothes [kləʊðz] *npl* ملابس [malaːbisun]; **clothes line** *n* حبل الغسيل [ḥ abl al-ghaseel]; **clothes peg** *n* مشبك الغسيل [Mashbak al-ghaseel]; **Is there somewhere to dry clothes?** هل يوجد مكان ما لتجفيف الملابس؟ [hal yujad makan ma le-tajfeef al-malabis?]; **My clothes are damp** ملابسي بها بلل [mala-bisy beha balal]

clothing ['kləʊðɪŋ] *n* ألبسة [ʔalbisa]

cloud [klaʊd] *n* سحابة [saħaːba]

cloudy ['klaʊdɪ] *adj* غائم [ɣaːʔim]

clove [kləʊv] *n* فص ثوم [Faṣ thawm]

clown [klaʊn] *n* مهرج [muharriʒ]

club [klʌb] *n (group)* نادي [naːdiː], *(weapon)* هراوة [haraːwa]; **golf club** *n* نادي الجولف [Nady al-jolf]; **Where is there a good club?** هل يوجد نادي جيدة؟ [Hal yojad nady jayedah]

club together [klʌb tə'gɛðə] *v* تشاركوا معاً [Tasharakoo ma'aan]

clue [kluː] *n* مفتاح لغز [Meftaḥ loghz]

clumsy ['klʌmzɪ] *adj* أخرق [ʔaxraq]

clutch [klʌtʃ] *n* قَابَض [qaːbidˤ]

clutter ['klʌtə] *n* ضوضاء [dˤawdˤaːʔ]

coach [kəʊtʃ] *n (trainer)* مدرب [mudarrib], *(vehicle)* مَركَبَة [markaba]

coal [kəʊl] *n* فحم [faħm]

coarse [kɔːs] *adj* فظ [fazˤzˤ]

coast [kəʊst] *n* ساحل [saːħil]

coastguard ['kəʊst,gɑːd] *n* خفر السواحل [Khafar al-ṣawaḥel]
coat [kəʊt] *n* سترة [sutra]; **fur coat** *n* معطف فرو [Me'ataf farw]
coathanger ['kəʊt,hæŋə] *n* شماعة المعاطف [Shama'aat al-ma'aatef]
cobweb ['kɒb,wɛb] *n* بيت العنكبوت [Bayt al-'ankaboot]
cocaine [kə'keɪn] *n* كوكايين [ku:ka:ji:n]
cock [kɒk] *n* دِّيك [di:k]
cockerel ['kɒkərəl; 'kɒkrəl] *n* ديِّك صغير [Deek ṣagheer]
cockpit ['kɒk,pɪt] *n* حُجَيْرَةُ الطَّيّار [Ḥojayrat al-ṭayar]
cockroach ['kɒk,rəʊtʃ] *n* صرصور [sˤarsˤu:r]
cocktail ['kɒk,teɪl] *n* كوكتيل [ku:kti:l]; **Do you sell cocktails?** أتقدمون الكوكتيلات؟ [a-tu'qade-moon al-koktailaat?]
cocoa ['kəʊkəʊ] *n* كاكاو [ka:ka:w]
coconut ['kəʊkə,nʌt] *n* جوزة الهند [Jawzat al-hend]
cod [kɒd] *n* سمك القد [Samak al'qad]
code [kəʊd] *n* شفرة [ʃafra]; **dialling code** *n* كود الاتصال بمنطقة أو بلد [Kod al-eteṣal bemanṭe'qah aw balad]; **Highway Code** *n* مجموعة قوانين السير في الطرق السريعة [Majmo'aat 'qwaneen al-sayer fee al-ṭoro'q al-ṣaree'aah]
coeliac ['siːlɪ,æk] *adj* بَطْنِيّ [batˤnij]
coffee ['kɒfɪ] *n* قهوة [qahwa]; **black coffee** *n* قهوة سادة ['qahwa sadah]; **coffee bean** *n* حبوب البن [Ḥobob al-bon]; **decaffeinated coffee** *n* قهوة منزوعة الكافيين ['qahwa manzo'aat al-kafayen]; **A white coffee, please** قهوة باللبن من فضلك ['qahwa bil-laban min faḍlak]; **Could we have another cup of coffee, please?** هل يمكن الحصول على فنجان آخر من القهوة من فضلك؟ [hal yamken al-ḥuṣool 'aala fin-jaan aakhar min al-'qahwa min faḍlak?]
coffeepot ['kɒfɪ,pɒt] *n* أبريق القهوة [Abreeq al-'qahwah]
coffin ['kɒfɪn] *n* تابوت [ta:bu:t]
coin [kɔɪn] *n* عملة معدنية [Omlah ma'adaneyah]
coincide [,kəʊɪn'saɪd] *v* يَتَزامن [jataza:manu]
coincidence [kəʊ'ɪnsɪdəns] *n* تزامن [taza:mana]
Coke® [kəʊk] *n* كوك® [ku:k]
colander ['kɒləndə; 'kʌl-] *n* مصفاة [misˤfa:t]
cold [kəʊld] *adj* بارِد [ba:rid] ▷ *n* زكام [zuka:m]; **cold sore** *n* قرحة البرد حول الشفاة ['qorḥat al-bard ḥawl al-shefah]
coleslaw ['kəʊl,slɔː] *n* سَلاطة الكرنب والجزر [Salaṭ at al-koronb wal-jazar]
collaborate [kə'læbə,reɪt] *v* يتعاون [jataʕa:wanu]
collapse [kə'læps] *v* ينهار [janha:ru]
collar ['kɒlə] *n* قلادة قصيرة ['qeladah 'qaṣeerah]
collarbone ['kɒlə,bəʊn] *n* تُرْقُوة [turquwa]
colleague ['kɒliːg] *n* زميل [zami:l]
collect [kə'lɛkt] *v* يجمع [juʒammiʕu]
collection [kə'lɛkʃən] *n* مجموعة [maʒmu:ʕa]
collective [kə'lɛktɪv] *adj* جماعي [ʒama:ʕij] ▷ *n* منظمة تعاونية [monaḍhamah ta'aaaweneyah]
collector [kə'lɛktə] *n* مُحصِّل [muħasˤsˤil]; **ticket collector** *n* جامع التذاكر [Jame'a al-tadhaker]
college ['kɒlɪdʒ] *n* كُلِية [kulijja]
collide [kə'laɪd] *v* يتصادم [jatasˤa:damu]
collie ['kɒlɪ] *n* كلب اسكتلندى ضخم [Kalb eskotalandey dakhm]
colliery ['kɒljərɪ] *n* منجم فحم [Majam fahm]
collision [kə'lɪʒən] *n* تصادم [tasˤa:dum]; **I'd like to arrange a collision damage waiver** أريد عمل الترتيبات الخاصة بالتنازل عن تعويض التصادم [areed 'aamal al-tar-tebaat al-khaṣa bil-tanazul 'aan ta'aweeḍ al-ta-ṣadum]
Colombia [kə'lɒmbɪə] *n* كولومبيا [ku:lu:mbija:]

Colombian [kə'lɒmbɪən] *adj* كولومبي [ku:lu:mbi:] ▷ *n* شخص كولومبي [Shakhṣ kolombey]
colon ['kəʊlən] *n* قولون [qu:lu:n]
colonel ['kɜ:nᵊl] *n* كولونيل [ku:lu:ni:l]
colour ['kʌlə] *n* لون [lawn]; **A colour film, please** فيلم ملون من فضلك [filim mola-wan min faḍlak]; **Do you have this in another colour?** هل يوجد لون آخر غير ذلك اللون؟ [hal yujad lawn aakhar ghayr dhalika al-lawn?]; **I don't like the colour** أنا لا أحب هذا اللون [ana la oḥibo hadha al-lawn]; **I'd like a colour photocopy of this, please** أرجو الحصول على نسخة ضوئية ملونة من هذا المستند [arjo al-ḥuṣool 'aala nuskha mu-lawana min hadha al-mustanad min faḍlak]
colour-blind ['kʌlə'blaɪnd] *adj* مصاب بعمى الألوان [Moṣaab be-'ama al-alwaan]
colourful ['kʌləfʊl] *adj* غني بالألوان [Ghaney bel-alwaan]
colouring ['kʌlərɪŋ] *n* تلوين [talwi:n]
column ['kɒləm] *n* عمود [ʕamu:d]
coma ['kəʊmə] *n* غيبوبة عميقة [Ghaybobah 'amee'qah]
comb [kəʊm] *n* مشط [muʃtˤ] ▷ *v* يَمْشّط [jamʃutˤu]
combination [ˌkɒmbɪ'neɪʃən] *n* مجموعة مؤتلفة [Majmo'aah moatalefa]
combine [kəm'baɪn] *v* يُوحد [juwaħħidu]
come [kʌm] *v* يأتي [jaʔti:]
come back [kʌm bæk] *v* يعود [jaʕu:du]
comedian [kə'mi:dɪən] *n* ممثل هزلي [Momthel hazaley]
come down [kʌm daʊn] *v* يَنْخَفِض [janxafidˤu]
comedy ['kɒmɪdɪ] *n* كوميديا [ku:mi:dja:]
come from [kʌm frəm] *v* يَأتي من [Yaatey men]
come in [kʌm ɪn] *v* يَدخُل [jadxulu]
come off [kʌm ɒf] *v*; **The handle has come off** لقد سقط مقبض الباب [la'qad sa'qaṭa me-'qbaḍ al-baab]
come out [kʌm aʊt] *v* يبْرُز من [Yabroz men]
come round [kʌm raʊnd] *v* يَستفيق [jastafi:qu]
comet ['kɒmɪt] *n* نجم ذو ذنب [Najm dho dhanab]
come up [kʌm ʌp] *v* يطلع [jutˤliʕu]
comfortable ['kʌmftəbᵊl; 'kʌmfətəbᵊl] *adj* مريح [muri:ħ]
comic ['kɒmɪk] *n* هزلي [hazlijja]; **comic book** *n* كتاب هزلي [Ketab hazaley]; **comic strip** *n* سلسلة رسوم هزلية [Selselat resoom hazaleyah]
coming ['kʌmɪŋ] *adj* مقبل [muqbil]
comma ['kɒmə] *n* فاصلة [fa:sˤila]; **inverted commas** *npl* فواصل معقوفة [Fawaṣel ma'a'qoofah]
command [kə'mɑ:nd] *n* سلطة [sultˤa]
comment ['kɒmɛnt] *n* ملاحظة [mula:ħazˤa] ▷ *v* يُعَلِق على [Yo'alle'q ala]
commentary ['kɒməntərɪ; -trɪ] *n* تعليق [taʕli:q]
commentator ['kɒmənˌteɪtə] *n* مُعلِق [muʕalliq]
commercial [kə'mɜ:ʃəl] *n* إعلان تجارى [E'alaan tejarey]; **commercial break** *n* فاصل إعلاني [Faṣel e'alaany]
commission [kə'mɪʃən] *n* عمولة [ʕumu:la]; **Do you charge commission?** هل تطلب عمولة؟ [hal taṭlub 'aumoola?]; **What's the commission?** ما هي العمولة؟ [ma heya al-'aumola?]
commit [kə'mɪt] *v* يَرتكِب [jartakibu]
committee [kə'mɪtɪ] *n* لجنة [laʒna]
common ['kɒmən] *adj* شائع [ʃa:ʔiʕ]; **common sense** *n* الحِس العام [Al-ḥes al-'aaam]
communicate [kə'mju:nɪˌkeɪt] *v* يَتَصِل بـ [Yataṣel be]
communication [kəˌmju:nɪ'keɪʃən] *n* اتصال [ittisˤa:l]
communion [kə'mju:njən] *n* مُشارَكة [muʃa:raka]
communism ['kɒmjʊˌnɪzəm] *n* شيوعية [ʃuju:ʕijja]
communist ['kɒmjʊnɪst] *adj* شيوعي [ʃuju:ʕij] ▷ *n* شيوعي [ʃuju:ʕij]

community [kə'mju:nɪtɪ] *n* مُجتَمع [muʒtamaʕ]
commute [kə'mju:t] *v* يُسافر يومياً من وإلى مكان عمله [Yosafer yawmeyan men wa ela makan 'amaleh]
commuter [kə'mju:tə] *n* القائم برحلات يومية من وإلى عمله [Al-'qaem beraḥlaat yawmeyah men wa ela 'amaleh]
compact ['kəm'pækt] *adj* مضغوط [madˤɣu:tˤ]; **compact disc** *n* قرص مضغوط ['qorṣ maḍghooṭ]
companion [kəm'pænjən] *n* صاحب [sˤa:ħib]
company ['kʌmpənɪ] *n* شركة [ʃarika]; **company car** *n* سيارة الشركة [Sayarat al-sharekah]; **I would like some information about the company** أريد الحصول على بعض المعلومات عن الشركة [areed al-ḥuṣool 'aala ba'aḍ al-ma'aloomat 'an al-shareka]
comparable ['kɒmpərəbᵊl] *adj* قابل للمقارنة ['qabel lel-mo'qaranah]
comparatively [kəm'pærətɪvlɪ] *adv* نسبياً [nisbijjan]
compare [kəm'pɛə] *v* يُقارن [juqa:rinu]
comparison [kəm'pærɪsᵊn] *n* مقارنة [muqa:rana]
compartment [kəm'pɑ:tmənt] *n* مقصورة [maqsˤu:ra]
compass ['kʌmpəs] *n* بوصلة [bawsˤala]
compatible [kəm'pætəbᵊl] *adj* متوافق [mutawa:fiq]
compensate ['kɒmpɛn,seɪt] *v* يُعَوض [juʕawwidˤu]
compensation [,kɒmpɛn'seɪʃən] *n* تعويض [taʕwi:dˤ]
compere ['kɒmpɛə] *n* مقدم برامج [Mo'qadem bramej]
compete [kəm'pi:t] *v* يَتنافَس [jatana:fasu]
competent ['kɒmpɪtənt] *adj* مختص [muxtasˤsˤ]
competition [,kɒmpɪ'tɪʃən] *n* منافسة [muna:fasa]
competitive [kəm'pɛtɪtɪv] *adj* تنافسي [tana:fusij]
competitor [kəm'pɛtɪtə] *n* مُنافِس [muna:fis]
complain [kəm'pleɪn] *v* يَشكو [jaʃku:]
complaint [kəm'pleɪnt] *n* شكوى [ʃakwa:]; **I'd like to make a complaint** إني أرغب في تقديم شكوى [inny arghab fee ta'qdeem shakwa]
complementary [,kɒmplɪ'mɛntərɪ; -trɪ] *adj* متمم [mutammim]
complete [kəm'pli:t] *adj* كامل [ka:mil]
completely [kəm'pli:tlɪ] *adv* بالكامل [bialka:mili]
complex ['kɒmplɛks] *adj* مُرَكَب [markab] ▷ *n* مادة مركبة [Madah morakabah]
complexion [kəm'plɛkʃən] *n* بَشْرَة [baʃra]
complicated ['kɒmplɪ,keɪtɪd] *adj* معقد [muʕaqqad]
complication [,kɒmplɪ'keɪʃən] *n* تعقيد [taʕqi:d]
compliment *n* ['kɒmplɪmənt] مجاملة [muʒa:mala] ▷ *v* ['kɒmplɪ,mɛnt] يُجامل [juʒa:milu]
complimentary [,kɒmplɪ'mɛntərɪ; -trɪ] *adj* مُجامِل [muʒa:mil]
component [kəm'pəʊnənt] *adj* مكون [mukawwin] ▷ *n* مكون [mukawwin]
composer [kəm'pəʊzə] *n* مؤلف موسيقى [Moaalef mosee'qy]
composition [,kɒmpə'zɪʃən] *n* تركيب [tarki:b]
comprehension [,kɒmprɪ'hɛnʃən] *n* إدراك [ʔidra:k]
comprehensive [,kɒmprɪ'hɛnsɪv] *adj* شامل [ʃa:mil]
compromise ['kɒmprə,maɪz] *n* تسوية [taswija] ▷ *v* يُسوى بحل وَسَط [juswa: biħalli wasatˤin]
compulsory [kəm'pʌlsərɪ] *adj* إلزامي [ʔilza:mij]
computer [kəm'pju:tə] *n* كمبيوتر [kumbiju:tar]; **computer game** *n* لعبة الكترونية [Lo'abah elektroneyah]; **computer science** *n* علوم الحاسب الآلى ['aoloom al-ḥaseb al-aaly]; **May I use**

your computer? هل لي أن استخدم الكمبيوتر الخاص بك؟ [hal lee an astakhdim al-computer al-khaaṣ bik?]; **My computer has frozen** لقد تعطل جهاز الكمبيوتر [la'qad ta-'aaṭal jehaaz al-computer]; **Where is the computer room?** أين توجد غرفة الكمبيوتر؟ [ayna tojad ghurfat al-computer]

computing [kəm'pju:tɪŋ] *n* استخدام الحاسب الآلي [Estekhdam al-haseb al-aaly]

concentrate ['kɒnsən,treɪt] *v* يُركز [jurakkizu]

concentration [,kɒnsən'treɪʃən] *n* تركيز [tarki:z]

concern [kən'sɜ:n] *n* اهتمام [ihtima:m]

concerned [kən'sɜ:nd] *adj* مَعنيّ [maʕnij]

concerning [kən'sɜ:nɪŋ] *prep* فى ما يتعلق بـ [Fee maa yata'ala'q]

concert ['kɒnsɜ:t; -sət] *n* حفلة موسيقية [Haflah mose'qeyah]

concerto, concerti [kən'tʃɛətəʊ, kən'tʃɛətɪ] *n* لحن منفرد [Laḥn monfared]

concession [kən'sɛʃən] *n* امتياز [imtija:z]

concise [kən'saɪs] *adj* موجز [mu:ʒaz]

conclude [kən'klu:d] *v* يَختَتِم [jaxtatimu]

conclusion [kən'klu:ʒən] *n* خاتمة [xa:tima]

concrete ['kɒnkri:t] *n* خرصانة [xarasˤa:na]

concussion [kən'kʌʃən] *n* ارتجاج في المخ [Ertejaj fee al-mokh]

condemn [kən'dɛm] *v* يُدين [judi:nu]

condensation [,kɒndɛn'seɪʃən] *n* تكثيف [takθi:f]

condition [kən'dɪʃən] *n* شَرط [ʃartˤ]

conditional [kən'dɪʃənᵊl] *adj* مشروط [maʃru:tˤ]

conditioner [kən'dɪʃənə; con'ditioner] *n* ملطف [mulatˤtˤif]

condom ['kɒndɒm; 'kɒndəm] *n* عازل طبى لمنع الحمل ['aazel ṭebey le-man'a al-haml]

conduct [kən'dʌkt] *v* يُوصِل [ju:sˤilu]

conductor [kən'dʌktə] *n* قائد فرقة موسيقية ['qaaed fer'qah mose'qeyah]; **bus conductor** *n* موصل [mu:sˤilun]

cone [kəʊn] *n* مخروط [maxru:tˤ]

conference ['kɒnfərəns; -frəns] *n* مؤتمر [muʔtamar]; **press conference** *n* مؤتمر صحفي [Moatamar ṣaḥafey]; **Please take me to the conference centre** من فضلك أريد الذهاب إلى مركز المؤتمرات [min faḍlak areed al-dhehaab ela markaz al-muta-marat]

confess [kən'fɛs] *v* يعترف [jaʕtarifu]

confession [kən'fɛʃən] *n* إقرار [ʔiqrar]

confetti [kən'fɛtɪ] *npl* قُصَاصَات ورقية [qusˤaːsˤaːtu waraqijjatu]

confidence ['kɒnfɪdəns] *n (secret)* ثقة [θiqa], *(self-assurance)* ثقة بالنفس [The'qah bel-nafs], *(trust)* ثقة [θiqa]

confident ['kɒnfɪdənt] *adj* واثق [wa:θiq]

confidential [,kɒnfɪ'dɛnʃəl] *adj* سِريّ [sirij]

confirm [kən'fɜ:m] *v* يُؤَكِد على [Yoaked ala]

confirmation [,kɒnfə'meɪʃən] *n* تأكيد [taʔki:d]

confiscate ['kɒnfɪ,skeɪt] *v* يُصَادِر [jusˤa:diru]

conflict ['kɒnflɪkt] *n* صراع [sˤira:ʕ]

confuse [kən'fju:z] *v* يُربِك [jurbiku]

confused [kən'fju:zd; con'fused] *adj* مُرتبك [murtabik]

confusing [kən'fju:zɪŋ; con'fusing] *adj* مُربِك [murbik]

confusion [kən'fju:ʒən] *n* ارتباك [irtiba:k]

congestion [kən'dʒɛstʃən] *n* احتقان [iħtiqa:n]

Congo ['kɒŋgəʊ] *n* الكونغو [al-ku:nɣu:]

congratulate [kən'grætjʊ,leɪt] *v* يُهنئ [juhanniʔ]

congratulations [kən,grætjʊ'leɪʃənz] *npl* تهنئة [tahniʔat]

conifer ['kəʊnɪfə; 'kɒn-] *n* شجرة الصنوبر المخروطية [Shajarat al-ṣonobar

al-makhrooṭeyah]
conjugation [ˌkɒndʒʊˈgeɪʃən] *n* تصريف الأفعال [Taṣreef al-afaal]
conjunction [kənˈdʒʌŋkʃən] *n* حرف عطف [Harf 'aaṭf]
conjurer [ˈkʌndʒərə] *n* دَجَّال [daʒʒa:l]
connect [kəˈnɛkt] *v* يَفْصِل [jafsˁilu]
connection [kəˈnɛkʃən] *n* رَابِطة [ra:bitˁa]
conquer [ˈkɒŋkə] *v* يَغْزو [jaɣzu:]
conscience [ˈkɒnʃəns] *n* ضمير إنساني [Ḍameer ensaney]
conscientious [ˌkɒnʃɪˈɛnʃəs] *adj* حي الضمير [Hay al-Ḍameer]
conscious [ˈkɒnʃəs] *adj* واعٍ [wa:ʕin]
consciousness [ˈkɒnʃəsnɪs] *n* وَعى [waʕa:]
consecutive [kənˈsɛkjʊtɪv] *adj* متعاقب [mutaʕa:qib]
consensus [kənˈsɛnsəs] *n* إجماع [ʔiʒma:ʕ]
consequence [ˈkɒnsɪkwəns] *n* عاقبة [ʕa:qiba]
consequently [ˈkɒnsɪkwəntlɪ] *adv* بالتالى
conservation [ˌkɒnsəˈveɪʃən] *n* المُحافظة على الموارد الطبيعية [Al-moḥafadhah ala al-mawared al-ṭabe'aeyah]
conservative [kənˈsɜːvətɪv] *adj* شخص محافظ [Shakhṣ moḥafeḍh]
conservatory [kənˈsɜːvətrɪ] *n* مستنبت زجاجي [mustanbatun zuʒa:ʒij]
consider [kənˈsɪdə] *v* يُفَكِر في [Yofaker fee]
considerate [kənˈsɪdərɪt] *adj* مُراعٍ لمشاعر الآخرين [Moraa'a le-masha'aer al-aakhareen]
considering [kənˈsɪdərɪŋ] *prep* بالنظر إلى [Bel-naḍhar elaa]
consist [kənˈsɪst] *v*; **consist of** *v* يَتَأَلف من [Yataalaf men]
consistent [kənˈsɪstənt] *adj* متماسك [mutama:sik]
consonant [ˈkɒnsənənt] *n* حرف ساكن [ḥarf saken]
conspiracy [kənˈspɪrəsɪ] *n* مؤامرة [muʔa:mara]
constant [ˈkɒnstənt] *adj* مستمر [mustamirr]
constantly [ˈkɒnstəntlɪ] *adv* بِثَبَات [biθaba:tin]
constipated [ˈkɒnstɪˌpeɪtɪd] *adj* مصاب بالامساك [Moṣab bel-emsak]
constituency [kənˈstɪtjʊənsɪ] *n* دائرة انتخابية [Daaera entekhabeyah]
constitution [ˌkɒnstɪˈtjuːʃən] *n* دستور [dustu:r]
construct [kənˈstrʌkt] *v* يُنْشِئ [junʃiʔ]
construction [kənˈstrʌkʃən] *n* إنشاء [ʔinʃa:ʔ]
constructive [kənˈstrʌktɪv] *adj* بَنَّاء [banna:ʔ]
consul [ˈkɒnsᵊl] *n* قنصل [qunsˁul]
consulate [ˈkɒnsjʊlɪt] *n* قنصلية [qunsˁulijja]
consult [kənˈsʌlt] *v* يَستشير [jastaʃi:ru]
consultant [kənˈsʌltᵊnt] *n (adviser)* مستشار [mustaʃa:r]
consumer [kənˈsjuːmə] *n* مُسْتَهلِك [mustahlik]
contact *n* [ˈkɒntækt] اتصال [ittisˁa:l] ▷ *v* [kənˈtækt] يَتَصِل [jattasˁilu]; **contact lenses** *npl* عدسات لاصقة ['adasaat laṣe'qah]; **Where can I contact you?** أين يمكنني الاتصال بك؟ [ayna yamken-any al-etiṣal beka?]; **Who do we contact if there are problems?** من الذي يمكن الاتصال به في حالة حدوث أي مشكلات؟ [man allaði: jumkinu alittisˁa:lu bihi fi: ħa:latin ħudu:θin ʔajji muʃkila:tin]
contagious [kənˈteɪdʒəs] *adj* ناقل للعدوى [Na'qel lel-'aadwa]
contain [kənˈteɪn] *v* يَحتوي [jaħtawi:]
container [kənˈteɪnə] *n* حاوية [ħa:wija]
contemporary [kənˈtɛmprərɪ] *adj* معاصر [muʕa:sˁiru]
contempt [kənˈtɛmpt] *n* احتقار [iħtiqa:r]
content [ˈkɒntɛnt] *n* رضا [ridˁa:]; **contents** *npl (list)* محتويات [muħtawaja:tun]
contest [ˈkɒntɛst] *n* مسابقة

[musa:baqa]
contestant [kən'tɛstənt] *n* مُنازِع [muna:ziʕ]
context ['kɒntɛkst] *n* سياق [sija:q]
continent ['kɒntɪnənt] *n* قارة [qa:rra]
continual [kən'tɪnjʊəl] *adj* متواصل [mutawasˤil]
continually [kən'tɪnjʊəlɪ] *adv* باستمرار [bistimrarin]
continue [kən'tɪnju:] *vi* يَستأنِف [jasta?nifu] ▷ *vt* يستمر [jastamirru]
continuous [kən'tɪnjʊəs] *adj* مستمر [mustamirr]
contraception [ˌkɒntrə'sɛpʃən] *n* منع الحمل [Man'a al-ḥml]; **I need contraception** أحتاج إلى منع الحمل [aḥtaaj ela mani'a al-ḥamil]
contraceptive [ˌkɒntrə'sɛptɪv] *n* مواد مانعة للحمل [Mawad mane'aah lel-haml]
contract ['kɒntrækt] *n* عقد [ʕaqd]
contractor ['kɒntræktə; kən'træk-] *n* مقاول [muqa:wil]
contradict [ˌkɒntrə'dɪkt] *v* يناقض [juna:qidˤu]
contradiction [ˌkɒntrə'dɪkʃən] *n* تناقض [tana:qudˤ]
contrary ['kɒntrərɪ] *n* مُعَاكِس [muʕa:kis]
contrast ['kɒntrɑ:st] *n* تباين [taba:j]
contribute [kən'trɪbju:t] *v* يسهم [jushimu]
contribution [ˌkɒntrɪ'bju:ʃən] *n* إسهام [?isha:m]
control [kən'trəʊl] *n* تَحَكُم [taħakkum] ▷ *v* يضبط [jadˤbitˤu]; **birth control** *n* تنظيم النسل [tanḍheem al-nasl]; **passport control** *n* الرقابة على جوازات السفر [Al-re'qabah ala jawazat al-safar]; **remote control** *n* التحكم عن بعد [Al-taḥakom an bo'ad]
controller [kən'trəʊlə] *n*; **air-traffic controller** *n* مراقبة جوية [Mora'qabah jaweyah]
controversial ['kɒntrə'vɜ:ʃəl] *adj* جَدَلي [ʒadalij]
convenient [kən'vi:nɪənt] *adj* مناسب [muna:sib]
convent ['kɒnvənt] *n* دَيْر الراهبات [Deer al-rahebat]
conventional [kən'vɛnʃənᵊl] *adj* تقليدي [taqli:dij]
conversation [ˌkɒnvə'seɪʃən] *n* محادثة [muħa:daθa]
convert [kən'vɜ:t] *v* يتحّول [jataħawwalu]; **catalytic converter** *n* منظم الضارة [monaḍhem al-ḍarah]
convertible [kən'vɜ:təbᵊl] *adj* قابل للتحويل ['qabel lel-taḥweel] ▷ *n* سيارة كوبيه [Sayarah kobeeh]
convict [kən'vɪkt] *v* يُجَرِّم [juʒarrimu]
convince [kən'vɪns] *v* يُقْنِع بـ [Yo'qn'a be]
convincing [kən'vɪnsɪŋ; con'vincing] *adj* مقنع [muqniʕ]
convoy ['kɒnvɔɪ] *n* موكب [mawkib]
cook [kʊk] *n* طَبَّاخ [tˤabba:x] ▷ *v* يَطْهو [jatˤhu:]
cookbook ['kʊkˌbʊk] *n* كتاب طهى [Ketab ṭahey]
cooker ['kʊkə] *n* مَوْقِد [mu:qid]; **gas cooker** *n* موقد يعمل بالغاز [Maw'qed ya'amal bel-ghaz]
cookery ['kʊkərɪ] *n* فن الطبخ [Fan al-ṭabkh]; **cookery book** *n* كتاب فن الطهي [Ketab fan alṭahey]
cooking ['kʊkɪŋ] *n* طَهْيٌ [tˤahj]
cool [ku:l] *adj (cold)* مائِل للبرودة [Mael lel-brodah], *(stylish)* متبلد الحس [Motabled al-ḥes]
cooperation [kəʊˌɒpə'reɪʃən] *n* تعاون [taʕa:w]
cop [kɒp] *n* شرطي [ʃartˤij]
cope [kəʊp] *v*; **cope (with)** *v* يَتَغْلَب على [Yatghalab 'ala]
copper ['kɒpə] *n* نحاس [nuħa:s]
copy ['kɒpɪ] *n (reproduction)* نَسْخ [nasx], *(written text)* نسخة [nusxa] ▷ *v* ينسخ [jansixu]
copyright ['kɒpɪˌraɪt] *n* حقوق الطبع والنشر [Ho'qoo'q al-ṭab'a wal-nashr]
coral ['kɒrəl] *n* مُرجان [marʒa:n]
cord [kɔ:d] *n*; **spinal cord** *n* الحبل الشوكي

[Al-ḥabl alshawkey]
cordless ['kɔːdlɪs] *adj* لا سلكى [La-selkey]
corduroy ['kɔːdəˌrɔɪ; ˌkɔːdə'rɔɪ] *n* قماش قطنى متين ['qomash 'qoṭ ney mateen]
core [kɔː] *n* لُبّ [lubb]
coriander [ˌkɒrɪ'ændə] *n* كزبرة [kuzbara]
cork [kɔːk] *n* فلين [filli:n]
corkscrew ['kɔːkˌskruː] *n* نازعة السدادات [na:ziʕatu assada:da:ti]
corn [kɔːn] *n* ذُرَة [ðura]
corner ['kɔːnə] *n* زاوية [za:wija]
cornet ['kɔːnɪt] *n* بوق [bu:q]
cornflakes ['kɔːnˌfleɪks] *npl* رقائق الذُرَة [Ra'qae'a al-dorrah]
cornflour ['kɔːnˌflaʊə] *n* نشا الذرة [Nesha al-zorah]
corporal ['kɔːpərəl; -prəl] *n* عرّيف [ʕari:f]
corpse [kɔːps] *n* جثة [ʒuθθa]
correct [kə'rɛkt] *adj* صحيح [sˤaħi:ħ] ▷ *v* يُصحِح [jusˤaħħiħu]
correction [kə'rɛkʃən] *n* تصحيح [tasˤħi:ħ]
correctly [kə'rɛktlɪ] *adv* بشكل صحيح [Beshakl ṣaheeḥ]
correspondence [ˌkɒrɪ'spɒndəns] *n* مراسلة [mura:salatu]
correspondent [ˌkɒrɪ'spɒndənt] *n* مُرَاسِل [mura:sil]
corridor ['kɒrɪˌdɔː] *n* رِوَاق [riwa:q]
corrupt [kə'rʌpt] *adj* فاسد [fa:sid]
corruption [kə'rʌpʃən] *n* فساد [fasa:d]
cosmetics [kɒz'mɛtɪks] *npl* مستحضرات تزيين [Mostaḥdarat tazyeen]
cost [kɒst] *n* تكلفة [taklufa] ▷ *v* يُكَلِف [jukallifu]; **cost of living** *n* تكلفة المَعيشة [Taklefat al-ma'aeeshah]; **How much does it cost?** كم تبلغ تكلفة هذا؟ [kam tablugh taklifat hadha?]; **How much will the repairs cost?** كم تكلفة التصليح؟ [kam taklifat al-taṣleeḥ?]
Costa Rica ['kɒstə 'riːkə] *n* كوستاريكا [ku:sta:ri:ka:]
costume ['kɒstjuːm] *n* زِي [zajj]; **swimming costume** *n* زي السباحَة [Zey sebaḥah]
cosy ['kəʊzɪ] *adj* دافئ ومريح [Dafea wa moreeḥ]
cot [kɒt] *n* مهد [mahd]
cottage ['kɒtɪdʒ] *n* كوخ لقضاء العطلة [Kookh le-'qadaa al-'aotlah]; **cottage cheese** *n* جبن قريش [Jobn 'qareesh]
cotton ['kɒtᵊn] *n* قطن [qutˤn]; **cotton bud** *n* رأس البرعم القطني [Raas al-bor'aom al-'qaṭaney]; **cotton wool** *n* قطن طبي ['qoṭn ṭebey]
couch [kaʊtʃ] *n* مَضْجَع [madˤʒaʕ]
couchette [kuː'ʃɛt] *n* مضجع صغير [Maḍja'a ṣagheer]
cough [kɒf] *n* سُعال [suʕa:l] ▷ *v* يَسْعُل [jasʕulu]; **cough mixture** *n* مُركّب لعلاج السعال [Morakab le'alaaj also'aal]
council ['kaʊnsəl] *n* مجلس [maʒlis]; **council house** *n* دار المجلس التشريعى [Dar al-majles al-tashre'aey]
councillor ['kaʊnsələ] *n* عضو مجلس ['aodw majles]
count [kaʊnt] *v* يَحسَب [jaħsibu]
counter ['kaʊntə] *n* طاولة بيع [Ṭawelat bey'a]
count on [kaʊnt ɒn] *v* يعتمد على [jaʕtamidu ʕala:]
country ['kʌntrɪ] *n* بَلَد [balad]; **developing country** *n* بَلَد نامٍ [Baladen namen]
countryside ['kʌntrɪˌsaɪd] *n* رِيفْ [ri:f]
couple ['kʌpᵊl] *n* زوجان [zawʒa:ni]
courage ['kʌrɪdʒ] *n* إقدام [ʔiqda:m]
courageous [kə'reɪdʒəs] *adj* مِقدام [miqda:m]
courgette [kʊə'ʒɛt] *n* كوسة [ku:sa]
courier ['kʊərɪə] *n* ساعي [sa:ʕi:]; **I want to send this by courier** أريد إرسال ساعي لتوصيل ذلك [areed ersaal sa'ay le-tawṣeel hadha]
course [kɔːs] *n* دَوْرَة تعليمية [Dawrah ta'aleemeyah]; **golf course** *n* ملعب الجولف [Mal'aab al-jolf]; **main course** *n* طبق رئيسي [Ṭaba'q raeesey]; **refresher**

course *n* دورة تنشيطية [Dawrah ṭansheeṭeyah]; **training course** *n* دروة تدريبية [Dawrah tadreebeyah]
court [kɔːt] *n* بلاط القصر [Balaṭ al-'qaṣr]; **tennis court** *n* ملعب تنس [Mal'aab tenes]
courtyard ['kɔːt,jɑːd] *n* ساحة الدار [Sahat al-dar]
cousin ['kʌzᵊn] *n* ابن العم [Ebn al-'aam]
cover ['kʌvə] *n* غطاء [ɣitˤaːʔ] ▷ *v* يُغَطّي [juɣatˤtˤiː]; **cover charge** *n* المصاريف المدفوعة مقدما [Al-maṣaareef al-madfoo'ah mo'qadaman]
cow [kaʊ] *n* بقرة [baqara]
coward ['kaʊəd] *n* جبان [ʒabaːn]
cowardly ['kaʊədlɪ] *adj* جبان [ʒabaɪn]
cowboy ['kaʊ,bɔɪ] *n* راعى البقر [Ra'aey al-ba'qar]
crab [kræb] *n* حيوان السرطان [Ḥayawan al-saraṭan]
crack [kræk] *n (cocaine)* مُخَدِر [muxaddir], *(fracture)* صَدْع [sˤadʕ] ▷ *v* يَصْدع [jasˤdaʕu]; **crack down on** *v* يَتخذ اجراءات صارمة ضد [yatakhedh ejraat ṣaremah ḍed]
cracked [krækt] *adj* متصدع [mutasˤaddiʕ]
cracker ['krækə] *n* كسارة الجوز [Kasarat al-jooz]
cradle ['kreɪdᵊl] *n* مَهْد [mahd]
craft [krɑːft] *n* حرفة [ħirfa]
craftsman ['krɑːftsmən] *n* حِرَفي [ħirafij]
cram [kræm] *v* يحشو [jaħʃuː]
crammed [kræmd] *adj* محشو [maħʃuww]
cranberry ['krænbərɪ; -brɪ] *n* توت برى [Toot barrey]
crane [kreɪn] *n (bird)* رافعة [raːfiʕa], *(for lifting)* ونْش [winʃ]
crash [kræʃ] *n* تَحَطّم [taħatˤum] ▷ *vi* يَتْحَطم [jataħatˤtˤamu] ▷ *vt* يتَحطَم [jataħatˤtˤamu]
crawl [krɔːl] *v* يَزْحف [jazħafu]
crayfish ['kreɪ,fɪʃ] *n* جراد البحر [Jarad al-bahr]
crayon ['kreɪən; -ɒn] *n* أقلام ملونة [A'qlaam molawanah]
crazy ['kreɪzɪ] *adj* ضعيف [dˤaʕiːf]
cream [kriːm] *adj* كريمي [kriːmiː] ▷ *n* قشدة [qiʃda]; **ice cream** *n* آيس كريم [aayes kreem]; **shaving cream** *n* كريم الحلاقة [Kereem al-helaka]; **whipped cream** *n* كريمة مخفوقة [Keremah makhfoo'qah]
crease [kriːs] *n* ثنية [θanja]
creased [kriːst] *adj* متغضن [mutaɣadˤdˤin]
create [kriː'eɪt] *v* يُبْدِع [jubdiʕu]
creation [kriː'eɪʃən] *n* إبداع [ʔibdaːʕ]
creative [kriː'eɪtɪv] *adj* خلاق [xallaːq]
creature ['kriːtʃə] *n* مخلوق [maxluːq]
crêche [krɛʃ] *n* حضانة أطفال [Haḍanat aṭfal]
credentials [krɪ'dɛnʃəlz] *npl* أوراق اعتماد [Awra'q e'atemaad]
credible ['krɛdɪbᵊl] *adj* موثوق فيه [Mawthoo'q beh]
credit ['krɛdɪt] *n* ائتمان [iʔtimaːn]; **credit card** *n* كارت ائتمان [Kart eateman]; **Can I pay by credit card?** هل يمكنني الدفع ببطاقة الائتمان؟ [hal yamken -any al-daf'a be- beṭa-'qat al-etemaan?]; **Do you take credit cards?** هل يتم قبول بطاقات الائتمان؟ [hal yatum 'qubool be-ṭa'qaat al-eeteman?]
crematorium, crematoria [,krɛmə'tɔːrɪəm, ,krɛmə'tɔːrɪə] *n* مَحْرَقة [maħraqa]
cress [krɛs] *n* نبات رشاد [Nabat rashad]
crew [kruː] *n* طاقم [tˤaːqam]; **crew cut** *n* قصة شعر قصيرة ['qaṣat sha'ar]
cricket ['krɪkɪt] *n (game)* لعبة الكريكيت [Lo'abat al-kreeket], *(insect)* حشرة صرار الليل [Hashrat ṣarar al-layl]
crime [kraɪm] *n* جريمة [ʒariːma]
criminal ['krɪmɪnᵊl] *adj* جنائي [ʒinaːʔij] ▷ *n* مجرم [muʒrim]
crisis ['kraɪsɪs] *n* أزمة [ʔazma]
crisp [krɪsp] *adj* هش [haʃʃ]
crisps [krɪsps] *npl* شرائح البطاطس [Sharaeh al- baṭaṭes]

crispy ['krɪspɪ] *adj* هش [haʃʃ]
criterion, criteria [kraɪ'tɪərɪən, kraɪ'tɪərɪə] *n* معيار [miʕjir]
critic ['krɪtɪk] *n* نَاقِد [na:qid]
critical ['krɪtɪkᵊl] *adj* انتقادي [intiqa:dij]
criticism ['krɪtɪˌsɪzəm] *n* نَقْد [naqd]
criticize ['krɪtɪˌsaɪz] *v* ينتقد [jantaqidu]
Croatia [krəʊ'eɪʃə] *n* كرواتيا [karwa:tja:]
Croatian [krəʊ'eɪʃən] *adj* كرواتي [kruwa:tijjat] ▷ *n (language)* اللغة الكرواتية [Al-loghah al-korwateyah], *(person)* كرواتي [kruwa:tijja]
crochet ['krəʊʃeɪ; -ʃɪ] *v* يُحْبِك [juħbiku]
crockery ['krɒkərɪ] *n*; **We need more crockery** نحن في حاجة إلى المزيد من أواني الطهي [naḥno fee ḥaja ela al-mazeed min awany al-ṭahy]
crocodile ['krɒkəˌdaɪl] *n* تمساح [timsa:ħ]
crocus ['krəʊkəs] *n* زعفران [zaʕfara:n]
crook [krʊk] *n* خُطاف [xutˤa:f], *(swindler)* خُطاف [xutˤa:f]
crop [krɒp] *n* محصول [maħsˤu:l]
cross [krɒs] *adj* مُتَقَاطِع [mutaqa:tˤiʕ] ▷ *n* صليب [sˤali:b] ▷ *v* يَعَبُر [juʕabbiru]; **Red Cross** *n* الصليب الأحمر [Al-Ṣaleeb al-aḥmar]
cross-country ['krɒs'kʌntrɪ] *n* سباق الضاحية [Seba'q al-ḍaheyah]
crossing ['krɒsɪŋ] *n* عبور [ʕubu:r]; **level crossing** *n* مزلقان [mizlaqa:nun]; **pedestrian crossing** *n* ممر خاص لعبور المشاه [Mamar khaṣ leaboor al-moshah]; **pelican crossing** *n* عبور المشاه سيراً على الأقدام ['aobor al-moshah sayran ala al-a'qdam]; **zebra crossing** *n* ممر للمشاة ملون بالأبيض والأسود [Mamar lel-moshah molawan bel-abyaḍ wal-aswad]; **How long does the crossing take?** ما هي المدة التي يستغرقها العبور؟ [ma heya al-mudda al-laty yasta-ghri'q-uha al-'auboor?]; **How much is the crossing for a car and four people?** ما هي تكلفة عبور سيارة وأربعة أشخاص؟ [ma heya taklifat 'auboor sayara wa arba'aat ash-khaṣ?]; **The crossing was rough** كان العبور صعبا [kan il-'aobor ṣa'aban]
cross out [krɒs aʊt] *v* يَشطُب [jaʃtˤubu]
crossroads ['krɒsˌrəʊdz] *n* طرق متقاطعة [Ṭaree'q mot'qat'ah]
crossword ['krɒsˌwɜːd] *n* كلمات متقاطعة [Kalemat mota'qat'aa]
crouch down [kraʊtʃ daʊn] *v* يَرْبِض [jarbidˤu]
crow [krəʊ] *n* غراب [ɣura:b]
crowd [kraʊd] *n* حشد [ħaʃd]
crowded [kraʊdɪd] *adj* مزدحم [muzdaħim]
crown [kraʊn] *n* تاج [ta:ʒ]
crucial ['kruːʃəl] *adj* عصيب [ʕasˤi:b]
crucifix ['kruːsɪfɪks] *n* صَليب [sˤali:b]
crude [kruːd] *adj* فَج [faʒʒ]
cruel ['kruːəl] *adj* قاسي [qa:si:]
cruelty ['kruːəltɪ] *n* قسوة [qaswa]
cruise [kruːz] *n* رحلة بحرية [Rehalh bahreyah]
crumb [krʌm] *n* كِسْرة خبز [Kesrat khobz]
crush [krʌʃ] *v* يَسحق [jasħaqu]
crutch [krʌtʃ] *n* عكاز [ʕukka:z]
cry [kraɪ] *n* بُكَاء [buka:ʔ] ▷ *v* يَصرخ [jasˤruxu]
crystal ['krɪstᵊl] *n* بُلّور [billawr]
cub [kʌb] *n* شِبْل [ʃibl]
Cuba ['kjuːbə] *n* كوبا [ku:ba:]
Cuban ['kjuːbən] *adj* كوبي [ku:bij] ▷ *n* كوبي [ku:bij]
cube [kjuːb] *n* مكعب [mukaʕʕab]; **ice cube** *n* مكعب ثلج [Moka'aab thalj]; **stock cube** *n* مكعب حساء [Moka'aab ḥasaa]
cubic ['kjuːbɪk] *adj* مكعب [mukaʕʕab]
cuckoo ['kʊkuː] *n* طائر الوقواق [Ṭaaer al-wa'qwa'q]
cucumber ['kjuːˌkʌmbə] *n* خِيَار [xija:r]
cuddle ['kʌdᵊl] *n* عناق [ʕina:q] ▷ *v* يُعانِق [juʕa:niqu]
cue [kjuː] *n (billiards)* إلماع [ʔilma:ʕ]
cufflinks ['kʌflɪŋks] *npl* أزرار كم القميص [Azrar kom al'qameeṣ]
culprit ['kʌlprɪt] *n* مُذنِب [muðnib]

cultural ['kʌltʃərəl] *adj* ثقافي [θaqa:fij]
culture ['kʌltʃə] *n* ثقافة [θaqa:fa]
cumin ['kʌmɪn] *n* كَمّون [kammu:n]
cunning ['kʌnɪŋ] *adj* ماكر [ma:kir]
cup [kʌp] *n* فنجان [finʒa:n]; **World Cup** *n* كأس العالم [Kaas al-'aalam]
cupboard ['kʌbəd] *n* خزانة للأطباق والكؤوس [Khezanah lel aṭba'q wal-koos]
curb [kɜːb] *n* شكيمة [ʃaki:ma]
cure [kjʊə] *n* شفاء [ʃifa:ʔ] ▷ *v* يُعالِج [juʕa:liʒu]
curfew ['kɜːfjuː] *n* حضر التجول [haḍr al-tajawol]
curious ['kjʊərɪəs] *adj* محب للاستطلاع [Moḥeb lel-esteṭlaa'a]
curl [kɜːl] *n* يَعْقِص الشعر [Ya'aqeṣ al-sha'ar]
curler ['kɜːlə] *n* ماكينة تجعيد الشعر [Makeenat taj'aeed sha'ar]
curly ['kɜːlɪ] *adj* معقوص [maʕqu:sˤ]
currant ['kʌrənt] *n* زبيب [zabi:b]
currency ['kʌrənsɪ] *n* عملة متداولة [A'omlah motadawlah]
current ['kʌrənt] *adj* حالي [ħa:lij] ▷ *n* *(electricity)* تيار [tajja:r], *(flow)* تدفق [tadaffuq]; **current account** *n* حساب جارى [Hesab tejarey]; **current affairs** *npl* شؤون الساعة [Sheoon al-saa'ah]; **Are there currents?** هل يوجد تيارات مائية في هذه الشواطئ؟ [hal yujad taya-raat maiya fee hadhy al-shawaṭy]
currently ['kʌrəntlɪ] *adv* حالياً [ħa:lijjan]
curriculum [kə'rɪkjʊləm] *n* منهج دراسى [Manhaj derasey]; **curriculum vitae** *n* سيرة ذاتية [Seerah dhateyah]
curry ['kʌrɪ] *n* كاري [ka:ri:]; **curry powder** *n* مسحوق الكاري [Mashoo'q alkaarey]
curse [kɜːs] *n* لعنة [laʕna]
cursor ['kɜːsə] *n* مُؤَشّر [muʔaʃʃir]
curtain ['kɜːtᵊn] *n* ستارة [sita:ra]
cushion ['kʊʃən] *n* مخفف الصدمات [Mokhafef al-ṣadamat]
custard ['kʌstəd] *n* كسترد [kustard]
custody ['kʌstədɪ] *n* وصاية [wisˤa:ja]
custom ['kʌstəm] *n* عرف [ʕurf]
customer ['kʌstəmə] *n* عميل [ʕami:l]
customized ['kʌstə,maɪzd] *adj* مَصْنُوع وفقاً لطلب الزبون [masˤnu:ʕun wafqan litˤalabi azzabu:ni]
customs ['kʌstəmz] *npl* رسوم جمركية [Rosoom jomrekeyah]; **customs officer** *n* مسئول الجمرك [Masool al-jomrok]
cut [kʌt] *n* جرح [ʒurħ] ▷ *v* يَقطّع [jaqtˤaʕu]; **crew cut** *n* قصة شعر قصيرة ['qaṣat sha'ar]; **power cut** *n* انقطاع التيار الكهربي [En'qetaa'a al-tayar alkahrabey]; **He has cut himself** لقد جرح نفسه [la'qad jara-ḥa naf-sehe]
cutback ['kʌt,bæk] *n* تخفيض الانتاج [Takhfeeḍ al-entaj]
cut down [kʌt daʊn] *v* يَقطّع شجرة [juqatˤtˤaʕu ʃaʒaratan]
cute [kjuːt] *adj* حَذِق [ħaðiq]
cutlery ['kʌtlərɪ] *n* سَكاكين المائدة [Skakeen al-maeadah]
cutlet ['kʌtlɪt] *n* شَريحة لحم مشوية [Shareehat laḥm mashweyah]
cut off [kʌt ɒf] *v* يَتوَقف عن العمل [jatawaqqafu ʕan alʕamali]
cutting ['kʌtɪŋ] *n* قطع [qitˤaʕ]
cut up [kʌt ʌp] *v* يَقطّع بالسكين [Ya'qta'a bel-sekeen]
CV [siː viː] *abbr* سيرة ذاتية [Seerah dhateyah]
cybercafé ['saɪbə,kæfeɪ; -,kæfɪ] *n* مقهى الانترنت [Ma'qha al-enternet]
cybercrime ['saɪbə,kraɪm] *n* جرائم الكمبيوتر والانترنت [Jraem al-kmobyoter wal-enternet]
cycle ['saɪkᵊl] *n* *(bike)* دراجة بخارية [Darrajah bokhareyah], *(recurring period)* دورة [dawra] ▷ *v* يُدَوِّر [jadu:ru]; **cycle lane** *n* زُقاق دائري [Zo'qa'q daerey]; **cycle path** *n* ممر الدراجات [Mamar al-darajat]
cycling ['saɪklɪŋ] *n* تدوير [tadwi:ru]
cyclist ['saɪklɪst] *n* راكب الدراجة [Rakeb al-darrajah]
cyclone ['saɪkləʊn] *n* زَوْبَعة [zawbaʕa]
cylinder ['sɪlɪndə] *n* اسطوانة

[ustˤuwa:na]
cymbals ['sɪmbᵊlz] *npl* آلة الصنج الموسيقية [Alat al-ṣanj al-mose'qeyah]
Cypriot ['sɪprɪət] *adj* قبرصي [qubrusˤij] ▷ *n (person)* قبرصي [qubrusˤij]
Cyprus ['saɪprəs] *n* قبرص [qubrusˤ]
cyst [sɪst] *n* مَثانة [maθa:na]
cystitis [sɪ'staɪtɪs] *n* التهاب المثانة [El-tehab al-mathanah]
Czech [tʃɛk] *adj* تشيكي [tʃi:kij] ▷ *n (language)* اللغة التشيكية [Al-loghah al-teshekeyah], *(person)* شخص تشيكي [Shakhṣ tesheekey]; **Czech Republic** *n* جمهورية التشيك [Jomhoreyat al-tesheek]

d

dad [dæd] *n* أب [ʔab]
daddy ['dædɪ] *n* بابا [ba:ba:]
daffodil ['dæfədɪl] *n* نرجس [narʒis]
daft [dɑ:ft] *adj* أحمَق [ʔaħmaq]
daily ['deɪlɪ] *adj* يَوْمي [jawmij] ▷ *adv* يومياً [jawmijjaan]
dairy ['dɛərɪ] *n* مصنع منتجات الألبان [maṣna'a montajat al-alban]; **dairy produce** *n* منتج ألبان [Montej albaan]; **dairy products** *npl* منتجات الألبان [Montajat al-baan]
daisy ['deɪzɪ] *n* زهرة الأقحُوان [Thamrat al-o'qḥowan]
dam [dæm] *n* سد [sadd]
damage ['dæmɪdʒ] *n* ضرر [dˤarar] ▷ *v* يَضُر [jadˤurru]
damaged ['dæmɪdʒd] *adj*; **My luggage has been damaged** لقد تعرضت حقائبي للضرر [la'qad ta-'aaraḍat ḥa'qa-eby lel-ḍarar]; **My suitcase has arrived damaged** لقد تعرضت حقيبة السفر الخاصة بي للضرر [la'qad ta-'aaraḍat ḥa'q-ebat al-safar al-khaṣa bee lel-ḍarar]
damn [dæm] *adj* لعين [laʕi:nu]
damp [dæmp] *adj* نَدِي [nadij]
dance [dɑ:ns] *n* رَقصَة [raqsˤa] ▷ *v* يَرقص

[jarqusˁu]
dancer ['dɑːnsə] *n* راقص [raːqisˁu]
dancing ['dɑːnsɪŋ] *n* رَقْص [raqsˁ]; **ballroom dancing** *n* رقص ثنائي [Ra'qṣ thonaaey]
dandelion ['dændɪˌlaɪən] *n* نبات الهندباء البرية [Nabat al-hendbaa al-bareyah]
dandruff ['dændrəf] *n* قشرة الرأس ['qeshart al-raas]
Dane [deɪn] *n* دانماركي [daːnmaːrkij]
danger ['deɪndʒə] *n* خطر [xatˁar]; **Is there a danger of avalanches?** هل يوجد خطر من وجود الكتلة الجليدية المنحدرة؟ [hal yujad khatar min wijood al-kutla al-jalee-diya al-muḥadera?]
dangerous ['deɪndʒərəs] *adj* خطير [xatˁiːr]
Danish ['deɪnɪʃ] *adj* دانماركي [daːnmaːrkij] ▷ *n (language)* اللغة الدانمركية [Al-loghah al-danmarkeyah]
dare [dɛə] *v* يَجرُؤ [jaʒruʔu]
daring ['dɛərɪŋ] *adj* جرئ [ʒariʔ]
dark [dɑːk] *adj* مظلم [muzˁlim] ▷ *n* ظلام [zˁalaːm]
darkness ['dɑːknɪs] *n* ظُلْمَة [zˁulma]
darling ['dɑːlɪŋ] *n* حبيب [ħabiːb]
dart [dɑːt] *n* سَهْم [sahm]
darts [dɑːts] *npl* لعبة رمي السهام [Lo'abat ramey al-seham]
dash [dæʃ] *v* يندفع [jandafiʕu]
dashboard ['dæʃˌbɔːd] *n* حجاب واقى [Ḥejab wara'qey]
data ['deɪtə; 'dɑːtə] *npl* بيانات [bajaːnaːtun]
database ['deɪtəˌbeɪs] *n* قاعدة بيانات ['qaedat bayanat]
date [deɪt] *n* تاريخ [taːriːx]; **best-before date** *n* يُفضل استخدامه قبل التاريخ المُحدد [Yofaḍḍal estekhdamoh 'qabl al-tareekh al-mohaddad]; **expiry date** *n* تاريخ الانتهاء [Tareekh al-entehaa]; **sell-by date** *n* تاريخ انتهاء الصلاحية [Tareekh enthaa al-ṣalaḥeyah]; **What is the date?** ما هو التاريخ؟ [ma howa al-tareekh?]; **What is today's date?** ما هو تاريخ اليوم؟ [ma howa tareekh al-yawm?]
daughter ['dɔːtə] *n* ابنة [ibna]
daughter-in-law ['dɔːtə ɪn lɔː] (*pl* **daughters-in-law**) *n* زوجة الابن [Zawj al-ebn]
dawn [dɔːn] *n* فَجْر [faʒr]
day [deɪ] *n* يوم [jawm]; **day return** *n* تذكرة ذهاب وعودة في نفس اليوم [tadhkarat dhehab we-'awdah fee nafs al-yawm]; **Valentine's Day** *n* عيد الحب ['aeed al-ḥob]; **Do you run day trips to...?** هل تنظمون رحلات يومية إلى...؟ [hal tunaḍh-emoon reḥlaat yaw-mlya ela...?]; **What a lovely day!** يا له من يوم جميل! [ya laho min yawm jameel]; **What are your rates per day?** ما هو الإيجار اليومي؟ [ma howa al-ejaar al-yawmi?]; **What day is it today?** أي الأيام تكون اليوم؟ [ay al-ayaam howa al- yawm?]; **What is the dish of the day?** ما هو طبق اليوم [ma howa ṯaba'q al-yawm?]
daytime ['deɪˌtaɪm] *n* فترة النهار [Fatrat al-nehaar]
dead [dɛd] *adj* متوفى [mutawaffin] ▷ *adv* تماماً [tamaːman]; **dead end** *n* طريق مسدود [Taree'q masdood]
deadline ['dɛdˌlaɪn] *n* موعد الانتهاء [Maw'aed al-entehaa]
deaf [dɛf] *adj* أصم [ʔasˁamm]
deafening ['dɛfᵊnɪŋ] *adj* مسبب الصمم [Mosabeb lel-ṣamam]
deal [diːl] *n* صفقة [sˁafqa]
dealer ['diːlə] *n* تاجر [taːʒir]; **drug dealer** *n* تاجر مخدرات [Tajer mokhaddrat]
deal with [diːl wɪð] *v* يُعالِج [juʕaːliʒu]
dear [dɪə] *adj (expensive)* عزيزي [ʕaziːziː], *(loved)* عزيز [ʕaziːz]
death [dɛθ] *n* مَوْت [mawt]
debate [dɪ'beɪt] *n* مناقشة [munaːqaʃa] ▷ *v* يناقش [junaːqiʃu]
debit ['dɛbɪt] *n* مَدين [madiːn] ▷ *v* يُسجِل على حساب [jusʒilu ʕalaː ħisaːbin]; **debit card** *n* كارت سحب [Kart sahb]; **direct debit** *n* يخصم مباشرةً من حساب العميل [Yokhṣam mobasharatan men hesab al'ameel]

debt [dɛt] *n* دَيْن [dajn]
decade ['dɛkeɪd; dɪ'keɪd] *n* عقد من الزمن ['aa'qd men al-zaman]
decaffeinated [dɪ'kæfɪˌneɪtɪd] *adj* منزوع منه الكافيين [Manzoo'a menh al-kafayeen]; **decaffeinated coffee** *n* قهوة منزوعة الكافيين ['qahwa manzo'aat al-kafayen]
decay [dɪ'keɪ] *v* يَتعفن [jataʕaffanu]
deceive [dɪ'siːv] *v* يَغش [jaɣiʃʃu]
December [dɪ'sɛmbə] *n* ديسمبر [diːsambar]; **on Friday the thirty first of December** يوم الجمعة الموافق الحادي والثلاثين من ديسمبر [yawm al-jum'aa al- muwa-fi'q al-ḥady waal-thalatheen min desambar]
decent ['diːsᵊnt] *adj* مهذب [muhaððab]
decide [dɪ'saɪd] *v* يُقَرر [juqarriru]
decimal ['dɛsɪməl] *adj* عشري
decision [dɪ'sɪʒən] *n* قرار [qaraːr]
decisive [dɪ'saɪsɪv] *adj* حاسم [ħaːsim]
deck [dɛk] *n* ظهر المركب [ḍhahr al-mrkeb]; **How do I get to the car deck?** كيف يمكن الوصول إلى السيارة على ظهر المركب؟ [kayfa yamkin al-wiṣool ela al-sayarah 'ala ḍhahr al-markab?]
deckchair ['dɛkˌtʃɛə] *n* كرسي طويل قابل لظهر المركب [kursijjun tˤawiːlun qaːbilun lizˤahri almarkabi]
declare [dɪ'klɛə] *v* يُعْلِن [juʕlinu]
decorate ['dɛkəˌreɪt] *v* يُزَخرف [juzaxrifu]
decorator ['dɛkəˌreɪtə] *n* مُزَخْرَف [muza-xraf]
decrease *n* ['diːkriːs] النقص [an-naqsˤu] ▷ *v* [dɪ'kriːs] ينقص [janqusˤu]
dedicated ['dɛdɪˌkeɪtɪd] *adj* متفرغ [mutafarriɣ]
dedication [ˌdɛdɪ'keɪʃən] *n* تكريس [takriːs]
deduct [dɪ'dʌkt] *v* يَقْتَطِع [jaqtatˤiʕu]
deep [diːp] *adj* عميق [ʕamiːq]
deep-fry [diːpfraɪ] *v* يَقلي [jaqliː]
deeply ['diːplɪ] *adv* بعمق [biʕumqin]
deer [dɪə] **(***pl* **deer)** *n* أيْل [ʔajl]
defeat [dɪ'fiːt] *n* هزيمة [haziːmunt] ▷ *v* يهزم [jahzimu]
defect [dɪ'fɛkt] *n* عيب [ʕajb]
defence [dɪ'fɛns] *n* دفاع [difaːʕ]
defend [dɪ'fɛnd] *v* يُدافع [judaːfiʕu]
defendant [dɪ'fɛndənt] *n* مُدَعى عليه [Moda'aa 'aalayh]
defender [dɪ'fɛndə] *n* مُدَافِع [mudaːfiʕ]
deficit ['dɛfɪsɪt; dɪ'fɪsɪt] *n* عجز في الميزانية ['ajz fee- almezaneyah]
define [dɪ'faɪn] *v* يُعَرف [jaʕrifu]
definite ['dɛfɪnɪt] *adj* واضح [waːdˤiħ]
definitely ['dɛfɪnɪtlɪ] *adv* بكل تأكيد [Bekol taakeed]
definition [ˌdɛfɪ'nɪʃən] *n* تعريف [taʕriːf]
degree [dɪ'griː] *n* درجة [daraʒa]; **degree centigrade** *n* درجة حرارة مئوية [Draajat ḥaraarah meaweyah]; **degree Celsius** *n* درجة حرارة سلزيوس [Darajat ḥararah selezyos]; **degree Fahrenheit** *n* درجة حرارة فهرنهايتي [Darjat hararh ferhrenhaytey]
dehydrated [diː'haɪdreɪtɪd] *adj* مُجَفَف [muʒaffif]
de-icer [diː'aɪsə] *n* ماكينة إزالة الثلوج [Makenat ezalat al-tholo'j]
delay [dɪ'leɪ] *n* تأخير [taʔxiːr] ▷ *v* يتأَخر [jataʔaxxaru]
delayed [dɪ'leɪd] *adj* متأخر [mutaʔaxxir]
delegate *n* ['dɛlɪˌgeɪt] انتداب [intidaːb] ▷ *v* ['dɛlɪˌgeɪt] ينتدب [jantadibu]
delete [dɪ'liːt] *v* يَحذِف [jaħðifu]
deliberate [dɪ'lɪbərɪt] *adj* مُتَعَمد [mutaʕammad]
deliberately [dɪ'lɪbərətlɪ] *adv* بشكل متعمد [Be-shakl mota'amad]
delicate ['dɛlɪkɪt] *adj* رقيق [raqiːq]
delicatessen [ˌdɛlɪkə'tɛsᵊn] *n* أطعمة معلبة [a ṭ'aemah mo'aalabah]
delicious [dɪ'lɪʃəs] *adj* شهي [ʃahij]; **The meal was delicious** كانت الوجبة شهية [kanat il-wajba sha-heyah]
delight [dɪ'laɪt] *n* بهجة [bahʒa]
delighted [dɪ'laɪtɪd] *adj* مسرور جداً [Masroor jedan]
delightful [dɪ'laɪtfʊl] *adj* سار جداً [Sar jedan]
deliver [dɪ'lɪvə] *v* يُسَلِم [jusallimu]

delivery [dɪˈlɪvərɪ] *n* تسليم [tasli:m]; **recorded delivery** *n* بعلم الوصول [Be-'aelm al-woṣool]
demand [dɪˈmɑːnd] *n* حاجة ملحة [Hajah molehah] ▷ *v* يُطَالِب ب [Yoṭaleb be]
demanding [dɪˈmɑːndɪŋ] *adj* كثير المطالب [Katheer almaṭaleb]
demo, demos [ˈdɛməʊ, ˈdiːmɒs] *n* تجربة إيضاحية [Tajrebah eeḍaheyah]
democracy [dɪˈmɒkrəsɪ] *n* ديمقراطية [di:muqra:tˤijja]
democratic [ˌdɛməˈkrætɪk] *adj* ديمقراطي [di:muqra:tˤij]
demolish [dɪˈmɒlɪʃ] *v* يَهْدِم [jahdimu]
demonstrate [ˈdɛmənˌstreɪt] *v* يُبَرْهِن [jubarhinu]
demonstration [ˌdɛmənˈstreɪʃən] *n* مُظَاهَرة [muzˤa:hara]
demonstrator [ˈdɛmənˌstreɪtə] *n* معيد [muʕi:d]
denim [ˈdɛnɪm] *n* قماش الدنيم القطنى ['qomash al-deneem al-'qotney]
denims [ˈdɛnɪmz] *npl* سروال من قماش الدِنيم القطنى [Serwal men 'qomash al-deneem al-'qotney]
Denmark [ˈdɛnmɑːk] *n* الدانمارك [ad-da:nma:rk]
dense [dɛns] *adj* كثيف [kaθi:f]
density [ˈdɛnsɪtɪ] *n* كثافة [kaθa:fa]
dent [dɛnt] *n* أسنان [ʔasna:nu] ▷ *v* يَنْبَعِج [janbaʕiʒu]
dental [ˈdɛntᵊl] *adj* متعلق بطب الأسنان [Mota'ale'q be-ṭeb al-asnan]; **dental floss** *n* خَيْط تنظيف الأسنان [Khayṭ tandheef al-asnan]
dentist [ˈdɛntɪst] *n* طبيب أسنان [Ṭabeeb asnan]; **I need a dentist** أحتاج إلى الذهاب إلى طبيب أسنان [aḥtaaj ela al-dhehaab ela ṭabeeb asnaan]
dentures [ˈdɛntʃəz] *npl* أطقم أسنان صناعية [Aṭ'qom asnan ṣena'aeyah]
deny [dɪˈnaɪ] *v* ينُكر [junkiru]
deodorant [diːˈəʊdərənt] *n* مزيل رائحة العرق [Mozeel raaehat al-'aara'q]
depart [dɪˈpɑːt] *v* يَرحل [jarħalu]
department [dɪˈpɑːtmənt] *n* قِسم [qism]; **accident & emergency department** *n* إدارة الحوادث والطوارئ [Edarat al-hawadeth wa-al-tawarea]; **department store** *n* محل مكون من أقسام [Maḥal mokawan men a'qsaam]
departure [dɪˈpɑːtʃə] *n* مغادرة [muɣa:dara]; **departure lounge** *n* صالة المغادرة [Ṣalat al-moghadarah]
depend [dɪˈpɛnd] *v* يعتمد على [jaʕtamidu ʕala:]
deport [dɪˈpɔːt] *v* ينفي [janfi:]
deposit [dɪˈpɒzɪt] *n* يُوْدِع [judiʕu]
depressed [dɪˈprɛst] *adj* محبط [muħbatˤ]
depressing [dɪˈprɛsɪŋ] *adj* محزن [muħzin]
depression [dɪˈprɛʃən] *n* إحباط [ʔiħba:tˤ]
depth [dɛpθ] *n* عمق [ʕumq]
descend [dɪˈsɛnd] *v* ينحدر [janħadiru]
describe [dɪˈskraɪb] *v* يَصِف [jasˤifu]
description [dɪˈskrɪpʃən] *n* وَصف [wasˤf]
desert [ˈdɛzət] *n* صحراء [sˤaħra:ʔu]; **desert island** *n* جزيرة استوائية غير مأهولة [Jozor ghayr maahoolah]
deserve [dɪˈzɜːv] *v* يَستحق [jastaħiqqu]
design [dɪˈzaɪn] *n* تصميم [tasˤmi:m] ▷ *v* يُصمم [jusˤammimu]
designer [dɪˈzaɪnə] *n* مُصَمِم [musˤammim]; **interior designer** *n* مُصَمِم داخلي [Moṣamem dakheley]
desire [dɪˈzaɪə] *n* رغبة [raɣba] ▷ *v* يَرغب [jarɣabu]
desk [dɛsk] *n* مكتب [maktab]; **enquiry desk** *n* مكتب الاستعلامات [Maktab al-este'alamaat]; **May I use your desk?** هل لي أن أستخدم المكتب الخاص بك؟ [hal lee an astakhdim al-maktab al-khaaṣ bik?]
despair [dɪˈspɛə] *n* يأس [jaʔs]
desperate [ˈdɛspərɪt; -prɪt] *adj* يئوس [jaʔu:s]
desperately [ˈdɛspərɪtlɪ] *adv* بيأس [bijaʔsin]
despise [dɪˈspaɪz] *v* يَحتقر [jaħtaqiru]

despite [dɪ'spaɪt] *prep* بالرغم [Bel-raghm]
dessert [dɪ'zɜːt] *n* تحلية [taħlija]; **dessert spoon** *n* ملعقة الحلويات [Mel'a'qat al-ḥalaweyat]
destination [ˌdɛstɪ'neɪʃən] *n* مَقصَد [maqsˤid]
destiny ['dɛstɪnɪ] *n* قَدَر [qadar]
destroy [dɪ'strɔɪ] *v* يُدمِر [judammiru]
destruction [dɪ'strʌkʃən] *n* تدمير [tadmiːr]
detail ['diːteɪl] *n* تفصيل [tafsˤiːl]
detailed ['diːteɪld] *adj* مُفَصّل [mufasˤsˤal]
detective [dɪ'tɛktɪv] *n* شرطة سرية [Shorṭah serryah]
detention [dɪ'tɛnʃən] *n* احتجاز [iħtiʒaːz]
detergent [dɪ'tɜːdʒənt] *n* مادة منظفة [Madah monaḍhefah]
deteriorate [dɪ'tɪərɪəˌreɪt] *v* يَفْسَد [jafsadu]
determined [dɪ'tɜːmɪnd] *adj* عاقد العزم ['aaa'qed al-'aazm]
detour ['diːtʊə] *n* تَحَوُّل [taħawwul]
devaluation [diːˌvæljuː'eɪʃən; deˌvalu'ation] *n* تخفيض قيمة العملة [Takhfeeḍ 'qeemat al'aomlah]
devastated ['dɛvəˌsteɪtɪd] *adj* مدمر [mudammar]
devastating ['dɛvəˌsteɪtɪŋ] *adj* مسبب لدمار هائل [Mosabeb ledamar haael]
develop [dɪ'vɛləp] *vi* يتطور [jatatˤawwaru] ▷ *vt* يُطَور [jutˤawwiru]; **developing country** *n* بَلَد نام [Baladen namen]
development [dɪ'vɛləpmənt] *n* تطور [tatˤawwur]
device [dɪ'vaɪs] *n* مُعَدَّة [muʕadda]
devil ['dɛvᵊl] *n* شيطان [ʃajtˤaːn]
devise [dɪ'vaɪz] *v* يَبتكِر [jabtakiru]
devoted [dɪ'vəʊtɪd] *adj* مكرس [mukarras]
diabetes [ˌdaɪə'biːtɪs; -tiːz] *n* مرض السكر [Maraḍ al-sokar]
diabetic [ˌdaɪə'bɛtɪk] *adj* مصاب بالسكري [Moṣab bel sokkarey] ▷ *n* شخص مصاب بالبول السكرى [Shakhṣ moṣaab bel-bol al-sokarey]
diagnosis [ˌdaɪəg'nəʊsɪs] *n* تشخيص [taʃxiːsˤ]
diagonal [daɪ'ægənᵊl] *adj* قطري [qutˤrij]
diagram ['daɪəˌgræm] *n* رسم بياني [Rasm bayany]
dial ['daɪəl; daɪl] *v* يَتَصِل [jattasˤilu]; **dialling code** *n* كود الاتصال بمنطقة أو بلد [Kod al-eteṣal bemanṭe'qah aw balad]; **dialling tone** *n* نغمة الاتصال [Naghamat al-eteṣal]
dialect ['daɪəˌlɛkt] *n* لهجة [lahʒa]
dialogue ['daɪəˌlɒg] *n* حوار [ħiwaːru]
diameter [daɪ'æmɪtə] *n* قُطْر [qutˤr]
diamond ['daɪəmənd] *n* ماس [maːs]
diarrhoea [ˌdaɪə'rɪə] *n* إسهال [ʔishaːl]; **I have diarrhoea** أعاني من الإصابة بالإسهال [o-'aany min al-eṣaaba bel-es-haal]
diary ['daɪərɪ] *n* يوميات [jawmijjaːt]
dice, die [daɪs, daɪ] *npl* نَرْد [nardun]
dictation [dɪk'teɪʃən] *n* إملاء [ʔimlaːʔ]
dictator [dɪk'teɪtə] *n* ديكتاتور [diːktaːtuːr]
dictionary ['dɪkʃənərɪ; -ʃənrɪ] *n* قاموس [qaːmuːs]
die [daɪ] *v* يموت [jamuːtu]
diesel ['diːzᵊl] *n* وقود الديزيل [Wa'qood al-deezel]
diet ['daɪət] *n* نظام غذائي [Neḍhaam ghedhey] ▷ *v* يلتزم بحمية غذائية معينة [Yalazem beḥemyah ghedhaeyah mo'ayanah]; **I'm on a diet** أتبع نظام غذائي خاص [atba'a neḍham ghedha-ee khaaṣ]أنا أتبع نظام غذائي خاص , [ana atb'a neḍham ghedhaey khaaṣ]
difference ['dɪfərəns; 'dɪfrəns] *n* اختلاف [ixtilaːf]
different ['dɪfərənt; 'dɪfrənt] *adj* مختلف [muxtalif]; **I would like something different** أريد شيئا مختلفا [areed shyan mukh-talefan]
difficult ['dɪfɪkᵊlt] *adj* صَعْب [sˤaʕb]
difficulty ['dɪfɪkᵊltɪ] *n* صعوبة [sˤuʕuːba]
dig [dɪg] *v* يَحفُر [jaħfuru]
digest [dɪ'dʒɛst; daɪ-] *v* يَهضِم [jahdˤimu]
digestion [dɪ'dʒɛstʃən; daɪ-] *n* هضم

[hadˁm]
digger ['dɪgə] *n* حفار [ħaffa:r]
digital ['dɪdʒɪtᵊl] *adj* رقمي [raqmij]; **digital camera** *n* كاميرا رقمية [Kameera ra'qmeyah]; **digital radio** *n* راديو رقمي [Radyo ra'qamey]; **digital television** *n* تليفزيون رقمي [telefezyoon ra'qamey]; **digital watch** *n* ساعة رقمية [Sa'aah ra'qameyah]
dignity ['dɪgnɪtɪ] *n* كرامة [kara:ma]
dilemma [dɪ'lɛmə; daɪ-] *n* معضلة [muʕdˁila]
dilute [daɪ'lu:t] *v* يُخفِف [juxafiffu]
diluted [daɪ'lu:tɪd] *adj* مخفف [muxaffaf]
dim [dɪm] *adj* باهت [ba:hit]
dimension [dɪ'mɛnʃən] *n* بُعْد [buʕd]
diminish [dɪ'mɪnɪʃ] *v* يُقَلِل [juqallilu]
din [dɪn] *n* ضجيج [dˁaʒi:ʒ]
diner ['daɪnə] *n* متناول العشاء [Motanawal al-'aashaa]
dinghy ['dɪŋɪ] *n* زورق تجديف [Zawra'q]
dinner ['dɪnə] *n* وَجْبَة الطعام [Wajbat al-ṭa'aam]; **dinner jacket** *n* جاكت العشاء [Jaket al-'aashaa]; **dinner party** *n* حفلة عشاء [Ḥaflat 'aashaa]; **dinner time** *n* وَقْت العشاء [Wa'qt al-'aashaa]
dinosaur ['daɪnə,sɔ:] *n* ديناصور [di:na:sˁu:r]
dip [dɪp] *n (food/sauce)* غَمْس [ɣams] ▷ *v* يَغْمِس [jaɣmisu]
diploma [dɪ'pləʊmə] *n* دبلوما [diblu:ma:]
diplomat ['dɪplə,mæt] *n* دبلوماسي [diblu:ma:sij]
diplomatic [,dɪplə'mætɪk] *adj* دبلوماسي [diblu:ma:sij]
dipstick ['dɪp,stɪk] *n* قضيب قياس العمق ['qaḍeeb 'qeyas al-'aom'q]
direct [dɪ'rɛkt; daɪ-] *adj* مباشر [muba:ʃir] ▷ *v* يُوجه [juwaʒʒihu]; **direct debit** *n* يخصم مباشرةً من حساب العميل [Yokhṣam mobasharatan men hesab al'ameel]; **I'd prefer to go direct** أفضل الذهاب مباشرة [ofaḍel al-dhehaab muba-sharatan]; **Is it a direct train?** هل يتجه هذا القطار مباشرة إلى...؟ [hal yata-jih hadha al-'qeṭaar muba-sha-ratan ela...?]
direction [dɪ'rɛkʃən; daɪ-] *n* توجيه [tawʒi:h]
directions [dɪ'rɛkʃənz; daɪ-] *npl* توجيهات [tawʒi:ha:tun]
directly [dɪ'rɛktlɪ; daɪ-] *adv* مباشرةً [muba:ʃaratan]
director [dɪ'rɛktə; daɪ-] *n* مُدِير [mudi:r]; **managing director** *n* عضو مُنتَدب ['aḍow montadab]
directory [dɪ'rɛktərɪ; -trɪ; daɪ-] *n* دليل [dali:l]; **directory enquiries** *npl* استعلامات دليل الهاتف [Este'alamat daleel al-hatef]; **telephone directory** *n* دليل الهاتف [Daleel al-hatef]
dirt [dɜ:t] *n* قذارة [qaða:ra]
dirty ['dɜ:tɪ] *adj* ملوث [mulawwaθ]
disability [,dɪsə'bɪlɪtɪ] *n* عجز [ʕaʒz]
disabled [dɪ'seɪbᵊld] *adj* عاجز [ʕa:ʒiz]
disadvantage [,dɪsəd'vɑ:ntɪdʒ] *n* عَيْب [ʕajb]
disagree [,dɪsə'gri:] *v* يتعارَض [jataʕa:radˁu]
disagreement [,dɪsə'gri:mənt] *n* اختلاف الرأى [Ekhtelaf al-raaey]
disappear [,dɪsə'pɪə] *v* يَخْتفي [jaxtafi:]
disappearance [,dɪsə'pɪərəns] *n* اختفاء [ixtifa:ʔ]
disappoint [,dɪsə'pɔɪnt] *v* يُخِيب [juxajjibu]
disappointed [,dɪsə'pɔɪntɪd] *adj* مُحبَط [muħbatˁ]
disappointing [,dɪsə'pɔɪntɪŋ] *adj* مُحبِط [muħbitˁ]
disappointment [,dɪsə'pɔɪntmənt] *n* خيبة الأمل [Khaybat al-amal]
disaster [dɪ'zɑ:stə] *n* كارثه [ka:riθa]
disastrous [dɪ'zɑ:strəs] *adj* كارثي [ka:riθij]
disc [dɪsk] *n* قرص [qursˁ]; **compact disc** *n* قرص مضغوط ['qorṣ maḍghooṭ]; **disc jockey** *n* مشغل الأغنيات المسجلة [Moshaghel al-oghneyat al-mosajalah]; **slipped disc** *n* إنزلاق غضروفي [Enzela'q

ghodrofey]
discharge [dɪs'tʃɑːdʒ] *v*; **When will I be discharged?** متى سأخرج من المستشفى؟ [mata sa-akhruj min al-mus-tashfa?]
discipline ['dɪsɪplɪn] *n* تأديب [taʔdiːb]
disclose [dɪs'kləʊz] *v* يُفْشي [juffiː]
disco ['dɪskəʊ] *n* ديسكو [diːskuː]
disconnect [ˌdɪskə'nɛkt] *v* يَفْصِل [jafsˤilu]
discount ['dɪskaʊnt] *n* خَصم [xasˤm]; **student discount** *n* خصم للطلاب [Khaṣm lel-ṭolab]
discourage [dɪs'kʌrɪdʒ] *v* يُثبَط من الهمة [yothabeṭ men al-hemah]
discover [dɪ'skʌvə] *v* يَكْتَشِف [jaktaʃifu]
discretion [dɪ'skrɛʃən] *n* تعقل [taʕaqqul]
discrimination [dɪˌskrɪmɪ'neɪʃən] *n* تمييز [tamjiːz]
discuss [dɪ'skʌs] *v* يُناقِش [junaːqiʃu]
discussion [dɪ'skʌʃən] *n* مناقشة [munaːqaʃa]
disease [dɪ'ziːz] *n* مرض [maradˤ]; **Alzheimer's disease** *n* مرض الزهايمر [Maraḍ al-zehaymar]
disgraceful [dɪs'greɪsfʊl] *adj* شَائِن [ʃaːʔin]
disguise [dɪs'gaɪz] *v* يَتنكَر [jatanakkaru]
disgusted [dɪs'gʌstɪd] *adj* مشمئز [muʃmaʔizz]
disgusting [dɪs'gʌstɪŋ] *adj* مثير للاشمئزاز [Mother leḻ-sheazaz]
dish [dɪʃ] *n (food)* أَكْلٌ, *(plate)* طبق [tˤabaq]; **dish towel** *n* فوطة تجفيف الأطباق [Foṭah tajfeef al-aṭbaa'q]; **satellite dish** *n* طبق قمر صناعي [Ṭaba'q ṣena'aey]; **soap dish** *n* طبق صابون [Ṭaba'q ṣaboon]; **How do you cook this dish?** كيف يطهي هذا الطبق؟ [Kayfa yoṭhaa hadha alṭaba'q]; **How is this dish served?** كيف يقدم هذا الطبق؟ [kayfa yu'qadam hatha al-ṭaba'q?]; **What is in this dish?** ما الذي في هذا الطبق؟ [ma al-lathy fee hatha al-ṭaba'q?]; **What is the dish of the day?** ما هو طبق اليوم [ma howa ṭaba'q al-yawm?]
dishcloth ['dɪʃˌklɒθ] *n* قماشة لغسل الأطباق ['qomash le-ghseel al-aṭbaa'q]
dishonest [dɪs'ɒnɪst] *adj* غير أمين [Gheyr amen]
dishwasher ['dɪʃˌwɒʃə] *n* غسالة أطباق [ghasalat aṭba'q]
disinfectant [ˌdɪsɪn'fɛktənt] *n* مبيد الجراثيم [Mobeed al-jaratheem]
disk [dɪsk] *n* مكتب [maktab]; **disk drive** *n* سواقة أقراص [Sowa'qat a'qraṣ]
diskette [dɪs'kɛt] *n* قرص صغير ['qorṣ ṣagheyr]
dislike [dɪs'laɪk] *v* يكره [jakrahu]
dismal ['dɪzməl] *adj* موحش [muːħiʃ]
dismiss [dɪs'mɪs] *v* يَصْرِفْ [jasˤrifu]
disobedient [ˌdɪsə'biːdɪənt] *adj* عاصي [ʕaːsˤiː]
disobey [ˌdɪsə'beɪ] *v* يَعْصي [jaʕsˤiː]
dispenser [dɪ'spɛnsə] *n* صُنبور توزيع [Ṣonboor twazea'a]; **cash dispenser** *n* ماكينة صرافة [Makenat ṣerafah]
display [dɪ'spleɪ] *n* ابداء [ibdaːʔ] ▷ *v* يَعْرِض [jaʕridˤu]
disposable [dɪ'spəʊzəbᵊl] *adj* ممكن التخلص منه [Momken al-takhalos menh]
disqualify [dɪs'kwɒlɪˌfaɪ] *v* يٌجَرِده من الأهلية [juʒarriduhu min alʔahlijjati]
disrupt [dɪs'rʌpt] *v* يُمَزِق [jumazziqu]
dissatisfied [dɪs'sætɪsˌfaɪd] *adj* غير راض [Ghayr raḍ]
dissolve [dɪ'zɒlv] *v* يُذيب [juðiːbu]
distance ['dɪstəns] *n* مسافة [masaːfa]
distant ['dɪstənt] *adj* بعيد [baʕiːd]
distillery [dɪ'stɪlərɪ] *n* معمل التقطير [Ma'amal alta'qteer]
distinction [dɪ'stɪŋkʃən] *n* فارق [faːriq]
distinctive [dɪ'stɪŋktɪv] *adj* مميز [mumajjaz]
distinguish [dɪ'stɪŋgwɪʃ] *v* يُمَيز [jumajjizu]
distract [dɪ'strækt] *v* يَصْرِف الانتباه [jusˤrifu aliːntibaːhu]
distribute [dɪ'strɪbjuːt] *v* يوزع [juwazziʕu]
distributor [dɪ'strɪbjʊtə] *n* موزع

[muwazziʕ]
district [ˈdɪstrɪkt] *n* منطقة [mintˤaqa]
disturb [dɪˈstɜːb] *v* يُزعِج [juzʕiʒu]
ditch [dɪtʃ] *n* مَصْرَف [masˤrif] ▷ *v* يَحفُر خندقاً [Yaḥfor khanda'qan]
dive [daɪv] *n* غطس [ɣatˤasa] ▷ *v* يغطس [jaɣtˤisu]
diver [ˈdaɪvə] *n* غطاس [ɣatˤtˤaːs]
diversion [daɪˈvɜːʃən] *n* انحراف [inħiraːf]
divide [dɪˈvaɪd] *v* يُقَسِم [juqassimu]
diving [ˈdaɪvɪŋ] *n* الغوص [al-ɣawsˤu]; **diving board** *n* لوح غطس [Looḥ ghaṭs]; **scuba diving** *n* غوص بأجهزة التنفس [ghawṣ beajhezat altanafos]
division [dɪˈvɪʒən] *n* تقسيم [taqsiːm]
divorce [dɪˈvɔːs] *n* طلاق [tˤalaːq] ▷ *v* طلاق [tˤalaːqun]
divorced [dɪˈvɔːst] *adj* مُطَلَق [mutˤallaq]
DIY [diː aɪ waɪ] *abbr* افعلها بنفسك [Ef'alhaa be-nafsek]
dizzy [ˈdɪzɪ] *adj* دُوار [duwaːr]
DJ [diː dʒeɪ] *abbr* دي جيه [D J]
DNA [diː ɛn eɪ] *n* الحمض النووي [alħamdˤu annawawijju]
do [dʊ] *v* يَفْعل [jafʕalu]
dock [dɒk] *n* حوض السفن [Hawḍ al-sofon]
doctor [ˈdɒktə] *n* طبيب [tˤabiːb]; **Call a doctor!** اتصل بالطبيب [itaṣel bil-ṭabeeb]; **I need a doctor** أحتاج إلى طبيب [aḥtaaj ela ṭabeeb]; **Is there a doctor who speaks English?** هل يوجد طبيب هنا يتحدث الإنجليزية؟ [hal yujad ṭabeeb huna yata-ḥadath al-injile-ziya?]; **Please call the emergency doctor** من فضلك اتصل بطبيب الطوارئ [min faḍlak itaṣil beṭa-beeb al-ṭawaree]
document [ˈdɒkjʊmənt] *n* مستند [mustanad]; **I want to copy this document** أريد نسخ هذا المستند [areed naskh hadha al-mustanad]
documentary [ˌdɒkjʊˈmɛntərɪ; -trɪ] *n* فيلم وثائقي [Feel wathaae'qey]
documentation [ˌdɒkjʊmɛnˈteɪʃən] *n* توثيق [tawθiːq]
documents [ˌdɒkjʊmɛnts] *npl* مستندات [mustanadaːtun]
dodge [dɒdʒ] *v* يراوغ [juraːwiɣu]
dog [dɒg] *n* كلب [kalb]; **guide dog** *n* كلب هادي مدرب للمكفوفين [Kalb hadey modarab lel-makfoofeen]; **hot dog** *n* نقانق ساخنة [Na'qane'q sakhenah]
dole [dəʊl] *n* إعانة بَطالة [E'anat baṭalah]
doll [dɒl] *n* دُمْيَة [dumja]
dollar [ˈdɒlə] *n* دُولَار [duːlaːr]
dolphin [ˈdɒlfɪn] *n* دُولفين [duːlfiːn]
domestic [dəˈmɛstɪk] *adj* داخلي [daːxilij]
Dominican Republic [dəˈmɪnɪkən rɪˈpʌblɪk] *n* جمهورية الدومنيكان [Jomhoreyat al-domenekan]
domino [ˈdɒmɪˌnəʊ] *n* لعبة الدومينو [Loabat al-domeno]
dominoes [ˈdɒmɪˌnəʊz] *npl* أحجار الدومينو [Ahjar al-domino]
donate [dəʊˈneɪt] *v* يَتَبْرع [jatabarraʕu]
done [dʌn] *adj* مُستَكمَل [mustakmal]
donkey [ˈdɒŋkɪ] *n* حمار [ħimaːr]
donor [ˈdəʊnə] *n* مَانِح [maːniħ]
door [dɔː] *n* بَابْ [baːb]; **door handle** *n* مقبض الباب [Me'qbaḍ al-bab]
doorbell [ˈdɔːˌbɛl] *n* جرس الباب [Jaras al-bab]
doorman, doormen [ˈdɔːˌmæn; -mən, ˈdɔːˌmɛn] *n* بواب [bawwaːb]
doorstep [ˈdɔːˌstɛp] *n* درجة الباب [Darajat al-bab]
dorm [dɔːm] *n*; **Do you have any single sex dorms?** هل يوجد لديكم أسرة فردية بدورين؟ [Hal yoojad ladaykom aserah fardeyah bedoorayen?]
dormitory [ˈdɔːmɪtərɪ; -trɪ] *n* دَار إيوَاء [Dar eewaa]
dose [dəʊs] *n* جرعة [ʒurʕa]
dot [dɒt] *n* نقطة [nuqtˤa]
double [ˈdʌbᵊl] *adj* مضاعف [mudˤaːʕaf] ▷ *v* يُضاعف [judˤaːʕifu]; **double bass** *n* الدُبَلْبَس وهي أكبر آله في الأسرة الكمانية [addubalbas wa hija ʔakbaru aːlatu fiː alʔusrati alkamaːnijjati]; **double bed** *n* سَرير مُزدوج [Sareer mozdawaj]; **double glazing** *n* طبقتين من الزجاج

[Ṭaba'qatayen men al-zojaj]; **double room** *n* غرفة مزدوجة [Ghorfah mozdawajah]
doubt [daʊt] *n* شَكٌّ [ʃak] ▷ *v* يَرتَاب [jarta:bu]
doubtful ['daʊtfʊl] *adj* مشكوك فيه [Mashkook feeh]
dough [dəʊ] *n* عجينه [ʕaʒi:na]
doughnut ['dəʊnʌt] *n* كعكات محلاة مقلية [Ka'akat moḥallah ma'qleyah]
do up [dʊ ʌp] *v* يثبّت [juθabbitu]
dove [dʌv] *n* يمامة [jama:ma]
do without [dʊ wɪ'ðaʊt] *v* يَستغْني عن [Yastaghney 'aan]
down [daʊn] *adv* نحو الأرض [naħwa alʔardˤi]
download ['daʊn,ləʊd] *n* تحميل [taħmi:l] ▷ *v* يحمل [juħammalu]
downpour ['daʊn,pɔː] *n* سَيْل [sajl]
downstairs ['daʊn'stɛəz] *adj* سُفلى [sufla:] ▷ *adv* سفلياً [suflijjan]
downtown ['daʊn'taʊn] *adv* واقع في قلب المدينة [Wa'qe'a fee 'qalb al-madeenah]
doze [dəʊz] *v* ينعس [janʕasu]
dozen ['dʌzᵊn] *n* دستة [dasta]
doze off [dəʊz ɒf] *v* يَبْدأ بالنوم الخفيف [jabdaʔu binnawmi alxafi:fi]
drab [dræb] *adj* رَتيب [rati:b]
draft [drɑːft] *n* مسودة [muswadda]
drag [dræg] *v* يَنسحِب [jansaħibu]
dragon ['drægən] *n* تنين [tinni:n]
dragonfly ['drægən,flaɪ] *n* يَعْسُوب [jaʕsu:b]
drain [dreɪn] *n* مصرف للمياه [Maṣraf lel-meyah] ▷ *v* يُصَرّف ماءً [Yoṣṣaref maae]; **draining board** *n* لوحة تجفيف [Lawhat tajfeef]
drainpipe ['dreɪn,paɪp] *n* أنبوب التصريف [Anboob altaṣreef]
drama ['drɑːmə] *n* دراما [dra:ma:]
dramatic [drə'mætɪk] *adj* درامي [dra:mij]
drastic ['dræstɪk] *adj* عنيف [ʕani:f]
draught [drɑːft] *n* مسودة [muswadda]
draughts [drɑːfts] *npl* شطرنج [ʃatˤranʒun]
draw [drɔː] *n (lottery)* سَحْب [saħb], *(tie)* تَعَادُل الفَرِيقَين ▷ *v (equal with)* يتعادل مع [Yata'aaadal ma'a], *(sketch)* يَرسِم [jarsumu]
drawback ['drɔː,bæk] *n* مال يرد بعد دفعه [Maal yorad daf'ah]
drawer ['drɔːə] *n* دُرْج [durʒ]
drawers [drɔːz] *n*; **chest of drawers** *n* خزانة ملابس بأدراج [Khezanat malabes be-adraj]
drawing ['drɔːɪŋ] *n* رسم [rasm]
drawing pin ['drɔːɪŋ pɪn] *n* دبوس تثبيت اللوائح [Daboos tathbeet al-lawaeh]
dreadful ['drɛdfʊl] *adj* مفزع [mufziʕ]
dream [driːm] *n* حلم [ħulm] ▷ *v* يَحلُم [jaħlumu]
drench [drɛntʃ] *v* يُبَلِل [jubalilu]
dress [drɛs] *n* فستان [fusta:n] ▷ *v* يلبس [jalbasu]; **evening dress** *n* ملابس السهرة [Malabes al-sahrah]; **wedding dress** *n* فستان الزفاف [Fostaan al-zefaf]; **Can I try on this dress?** هل يمكن أن أجرب هذا الفستان؟ [hal yamken an ajar-reb hadha al-fustaan?]
dressed [drɛst] *adj* متأنق [mutaʔanniq]
dresser ['drɛsə] *n* مساعد اللبس [Mosa'aed al-lebs]
dressing ['drɛsɪŋ] *n*; **salad dressing** *n* صلصة السلطة [Ṣalṣat al-salata]
dressing gown ['drɛsɪŋ gaʊn] *n* رُوب الحَمَّام [Roob al-ḥamam]
dressing table ['drɛsɪŋ 'teɪbᵊl] *n* طَاوِلَة زينة [Ṭawlat zeenah]
dress up [drɛs ʌp] *v* يتَأَنق [jataʔannaqu]
dried [draɪd] *adj* مجفف [muʒaffif]
drift [drɪft] *n* جرف [ʒurf] ▷ *v* يَنْجَرِف [janʒarifu]
drill [drɪl] *n* مِثْقَاب [miθqa:b] ▷ *v* يَثْقب بمثقاب [Yath'qob bemeth'qaab]; **pneumatic drill** *n* مثقاب هوائي [Meth'qaab hawaey]
drink [drɪŋk] *n* مَشروب [maʃru:b] ▷ *v* يَشرب [jaʃrabu]; **binge drinking** *n* الإفراط في تناول الشراب [Al-efraaṭ fee tanawol alsharab]; **drinking water** *n* مياه الشرب

[Meyah al-shorb]; **soft drink** *n* مشروب غازي [Mashroob ghazey]
drink-driving ['drɪŋk'draɪvɪŋ] *n* القيادة تحت تأثير الكحول [Al-'qeyadh taḥt taatheer al-koḥool]
drip [drɪp] *n* سائل متقطّر [Sael mota'qaṭer] ▷ *v* يَقْطِر [jaqtˤiru]
drive [draɪv] *n* نزهة في سيارة [Nozhah fee sayarah] ▷ *v* يقود [jaqu:du]; **driving instructor** *n* معلم القيادة [Mo'alem al-'qeyadh]; **four-wheel drive** *n* الدَفْع الرباعي [Al-daf'a al-roba'aey]; **left-hand drive** *n* سيارة مقودها على الجانب الأيسر [Sayarh me'qwadoha ala al-janeb al-aysar]; **right-hand drive** *n* عجلة القيادة اليمنى ['aajalat al-'qeyadah al-yomna]
driver ['draɪvə] *n* سائق [sa:ʔiq]; **learner driver** *n* سائق مبتدئ [Sae'q mobtadea]; **lorry driver** *n* سائق لوري [Sae'q lorey]; **racing driver** *n* سائق سيارة سباق [Sae'q sayarah seba'q]; **truck driver** *n* سائق شاحنة [Sae'q shahenah]
driveway ['draɪv,weɪ] *n* درب [darb]
driving lesson ['draɪvɪŋ 'lɛsᵊn] *n* دَرْس القيادة [Dars al-'qeyadah]
driving licence ['draɪvɪŋ 'laɪsəns] *n* رُخْصَة القيادة [Rokhṣat al-'qeyadah]; **Here is my driving licence** ها هي رخصة القيادة الخاصة بي [ha heya rikhṣat al-'qiyada al-khaṣa bee]; **I don't have my driving licence on me** أحمل رخصة قيادة، لكنها ليست معي الآن [Aḥmel rokhṣat 'qeyadah, lakenaha laysat ma'aey al-aan]; **My driving licence number is...** رقم رخصة قيادتي هو... [ra'qim rikhṣat 'qeyad-aty howa...]
driving test ['draɪvɪŋ 'tɛst] *n* اختبار القيادة [Ekhtebar al-'qeyadah]
drizzle ['drɪzᵊl] *n* رذاذ [raða:ð]
drop [drɒp] *n* قطرة [qatˤra] ▷ *v* يَسقُط [jasqutˤu]; **eye drops** *npl* قطرة للعين ['qaṭrah lel-'ayn]
drought [draʊt] *n* جفاف [ʒafa:f]
drown [draʊn] *v* يَغْرَق [jaɣraqu]
drowsy ['draʊzɪ] *adj* نعسان [naʕsa:n]
drug [drʌg] *n* مخدرات [muxaddira:t]; **drug addict** *n* مدمن مخدرات [Modmen mokhadarat]; **drug dealer** *n* تاجر مخدرات [Tajer mokhaddrat]
drum [drʌm] *n* طبلة [tˤabla]
drummer ['drʌmə] *n* طبال [tˤabba:l]
drunk [drʌŋk] *adj* ثَمِل [θamil] ▷ *n* سكران [sakra:n]
dry [draɪ] *adj* جاف [ʒa:ff] ▷ *v* يُجَفِف [juʒaffifu]; **bone dry** *adj* جاف تماماً [Jaf tamaman]; **A dry sherry, please** كأس من مشروب الشيري الجاف من فضلك [Kaas mashroob al-sheery al-jaf men faḍlek]; **I have dry hair** أنا شعري جاف [ana sha'ary jaaf]
dry-cleaner's ['draɪ'kli:nəz] *n* محل التنظيف الجاف [Mahal al- tanḍheef al-jaf]
dry-cleaning ['draɪ'kli:nɪŋ] *n* تنظيف جاف [tanḍheef jaf]
dryer ['draɪə] *n* مُجَفّف [muʒaffif]; **spin dryer** *n* مُجَفِف دوار [Mojafef dwar]; **tumble dryer** *n* مجفف ملابس [Mojafef malabes]
dual ['dju:əl] *adj*; **dual carriageway** *n* طريق مزدوج الاتجاه للسيارات [Taree'q mozdawaj al-etejah lel-sayarat]
dubbed [dʌbt] *adj* يسمى بعضهم بالكنية [jusma: baʕdˤuhum bilkanijjati]
dubious ['dju:bɪəs] *adj* مريب [muri:b]
duck [dʌk] *n* بطة [batˤtˤa]
due [dju:] *adj* مستحق الدفع [Mostaḥa'q al-daf'a]
due to [dju: tʊ] *prep* نتيجة لـ [Nateejah le]
dull [dʌl] *adj* فاتر [fa:tir]
dumb [dʌm] *adj* أبكم [ʔabkam]
dummy ['dʌmɪ] *n* أبكم [ʔabkam]
dump [dʌmp] *n* نفاية [nufa:ja] ▷ *v* يُلْقي النفايات [Yol'qy al-nefayat]; **rubbish dump** *n* مقلب النفايات [Ma'qlab al-nefayat]
dumpling ['dʌmplɪŋ] *n* زلابية [zala:bijja]
dune [dju:n] *n*; **sand dune** *n* كثبان رملية [Kothban ramleyah]
dungarees [,dʌŋgə'ri:z] *npl* ملابس قطنية خشنة [Malabes 'qotneyah

khashenah]
dungeon ['dʌndʒən] *n* برج محصن [Borj moḥaṣṣan]
duration [djʊ'reɪʃən] *n* مُدَّة [mudda]
during ['djʊərɪŋ] *prep* أثناء
dusk [dʌsk] *n* غَسَقْ [ɣasaq]
dust [dʌst] *n* غبار [ɣuba:r] ▷ *v* ينفض [janfudˤu]
dustbin ['dʌst,bɪn] *n* صندوق القمامة [Ṣondok al-'qemamah]
dustman, dustmen ['dʌstmən, 'dʌstmɛn] *n* الزَبّال [az-zabba:lu]
dustpan ['dʌst,pæn] *n* جاروف الكناسة [Jaroof al-kannasah]
dusty ['dʌstɪ] *adj* مغبر [muɣbarr]
Dutch [dʌtʃ] *adj* هولندي [hu:landij] ▷ *n* هولندي [hu:landij]
Dutchman, Dutchmen ['dʌtʃmən, 'dʌtʃmɛn] *n* رَجُل هولندي [Rajol holandey]
Dutchwoman, Dutchwomen [,dʌtʃwʊmən, 'dʌtʃ,wɪmɪn] *n* هولندية [hu:landijja]
duty ['dju:tɪ] *n* واجب [wa:ʒib]; **(customs) duty** *n* رسوم جمركية [Rosoom jomrekeyah]
duty-free ['dju:tɪ'fri:] *adj* معفى من الرسوم الضريبية [Ma'afee men al-rosoom al-ḍareebeyah] ▷ *n* مَعْفِي من الضرائب [Ma'afey men al-ḍaraaeb]
duvet ['du:veɪ] *n* غطاء مخملى [Gheṭa'a makhmaley]
DVD [di: vi: di:] *n* اسطوانة دى في دي [Esṭwanah DVD]; **DVD burner** *n* ناسخ لاسطوانات دى في دي [Nasekh le-sṭewanat D V D]; **DVD player** *n* مشغل اسطوانات دى في دي [Moshaghel esṭwanat D V D]
dye [daɪ] *n* صبغة [sˤibɣa] ▷ *v* يَصبِغ [jasˤbiɣu]
dynamic [daɪ'næmɪk] *adj* ديناميكي [di:na:mi:kajj]
dyslexia [dɪs'lɛksɪə] *n* عسر التكلم ['aosr al-takalom]
dyslexic [dɪs'lɛksɪk] *adj* متعسر النطق [Mota'aer alnoṭ'q] ▷ *n* شخص متعسر النطق [Shakhṣ mota'aser al-noṭ'q]

e

each [iːtʃ] *adj* كل [kulla] ▷ *pron* كل امرئ [Kol emrea]
eagle [ˈiːɡəl] *n* عُقاب [ʕuqaːb]
ear [ɪə] *n* أذن [ʔuð]
earache [ˈɪərˌeɪk] *n* ألم الأذُن [Alam al odhon]
eardrum [ˈɪəˌdrʌm] *n* طبلة الأذن [Ṭablat alozon]
earlier [ˈɜːlɪə] *adv* أقدم [aqdam]
early [ˈɜːlɪ] *adj* مبكر [mubakkir] ▷ *adv* باكراً [baːkiran]; **We arrived early/late** لقد وصلنا مبكرًا [la'qad waṣalna mu-bakiran]
earn [ɜːn] *v* يَكْتَسِب [jaktasibu]
earnings [ˈɜːnɪŋz] *npl* مكاسب [makaːsibun]
earphones [ˈɪəˌfəʊnz] *npl* سماعات الأذن [Sama'at al-odhon]
earplugs [ˈɪəˌplʌgz] *npl* سِدادات الأذن [Sedadat alodhon]
earring [ˈɪəˌrɪŋ] *n* قرط [qirtˤ]
earth [ɜːθ] *n* الأرض [al-ʔardˤi]
earthquake [ˈɜːθˌkweɪk] *n* زلزال [zilzaːl]
easily [ˈiːzɪlɪ] *adv* بسهولة [bisuhuːlatin]
east [iːst] *adj* شرقي [ʃarqij] ▷ *adv* شرقاً [ʃarqan] ▷ *n* شرق [ʃarq]; **Far East** *n* الشرق الأقصى [Al-shar'q al-a'qsa]; **Middle East** *n* الشرق الأوسط [Al-shar'q al-awṣaṭ]
eastbound [ˈiːstˌbaʊnd] *adj* متجه شرقاً [Motajeh sharqan]
Easter [ˈiːstə] *n* عيد الفصح ['aeed al-feṣḥ]; **Easter egg** *n* بيض عيد الفصح [Bayḍ 'aeed al-feṣḥ]
eastern [ˈiːstən] *adj* شرقي [ʃarqij]
easy [ˈiːzɪ] *adj* سهل [sahl]; **easy chair** *n* كرسي مريح [Korsey moreeḥ]
easy-going [ˈiːzɪˈɡəʊɪŋ] *adj* سهل الانقياد [Sahl al-en'qyad]
eat [iːt] *v* يأكل [jaʔkulu]
e-book [ˈiːˈbʊk] *n* كتاب الكتروني [Ketab elektrooney]
eccentric [ɪkˈsɛntrɪk] *adj* لا متراكز [La motrakez]
echo [ˈɛkəʊ] *n* صَدَى [sˤadaː]
ecofriendly [ˈiːkəʊˌfrɛndlɪ] *adj* صديق للبيئة [Ṣadeek al-beeaah]
ecological [ˌiːkəˈlɒdʒɪkəl] *adj* بيئي [biːʔij]
ecology [ɪˈkɒlədʒɪ] *n* علم البيئة ['aelm al-beeah]
e-commerce [ˈiːkɒmɜːs] *n* تجارة الكترونية [Tejarah elektroneyah]
economic [ˌiːkəˈnɒmɪk; ˌɛkə-] *adj* اقتصادي [iqtisˤaːdij]
economical [ˌiːkəˈnɒmɪkəl; ˌɛkə-] *adj* مُقتصِد [muqtasˤid]
economics [ˌiːkəˈnɒmɪks; ˌɛkə-] *npl* علم الاقتصاد ['aelm al-e'qtesad]
economist [ɪˈkɒnəmɪst] *n* عالم اقتصادي ['aaalem e'qteṣaadey]
economize [ɪˈkɒnəˌmaɪz] *v* يَقْتَصِد [jaqtasˤidu]
economy [ɪˈkɒnəmɪ] *n* اقتصاد [iqtisˤaːd]; **economy class** *n* درجة سياحية [Darjah seyaḥeyah]
ecstasy [ˈɛkstəsɪ] *n* نشوي [naʃawij]
Ecuador [ˈɛkwəˌdɔː] *n* الاكوادور [al-ikwaːduːr]
eczema [ˈɛksɪmə; ɪɡˈziːmə] *n* اكزيما [ikziːmaː]
edge [ɛdʒ] *n* حافة [ħaːffa]
edgy [ˈɛdʒɪ] *adj* قاطع [qaːtˤiʕ]

edible ['ɛdɪbᵊl] *adj* صالح للأكل [Ṣaleḥ lel-aakl]
edition [ɪ'dɪʃən] *n* طبعة [tˤabʕa]
editor ['ɛdɪtə] *n* مُحَرر [muħarrir]
educated ['ɛdjʊˌkeɪtɪd] *adj* متعلم [mutaʕallim]
education [ˌɛdjʊ'keɪʃən] *n* تعليم [taʕli:m]; **adult education** *n* تعليم الكبار [Ta'aleem al-kebar]; **higher education** *n* تعليم عالي [Ta'aleem 'aaaly]
educational [ˌɛdjʊ'keɪʃənᵊl] *adj* تربوي [tarbawij]
eel [i:l] *n* سَمكة الأنقليس [Samakat al-anfalees]
effect [ɪ'fɛkt] *n* أثر [ʔaθar]; **side effect** *n* آثار جانبية [Aathar janeebyah]
effective [ɪ'fɛktɪv] *adj* فعال [faʕʕa:l]
effectively [ɪ'fɛktɪvlɪ] *adv* بفعالية [bifaʕa:lijjatin]
efficient [ɪ'fɪʃənt] *adj* كاف [ka:fin]
efficiently [ɪ'fɪʃəntlɪ] *adv* بكفاءة [bikafa:ʔatin]
effort ['ɛfət] *n* جهد [ʒuhd]
e.g. [i: dʒi:] *abbr* على سبيل المثال ['ala sabeel al-methal]
egg [ɛg] *n* بيضة [bajdˤa]; **boiled egg** *n* بيضة مسلوقة [Bayḍah maslo'qah]; **egg white** *n* بياض البيض [Bayaḍ al-bayḍ]; **egg yolk** *n* صفار البيض [Ṣafar al-bayḍ]; **Easter egg** *n* بيض عيد الفصح [Bayḍ 'aeed al-feṣh]; **scrambled eggs** *npl* بيض مخفوق [Bayḍ makhfou'q]
eggcup ['ɛgˌkʌp] *n* كأس البيضة [Kaas al-bayḍah]
Egypt ['i:dʒɪpt] *n* مصر [misˤru]
Egyptian [ɪ'dʒɪpʃən] *adj* مصري [misˤrij] ▷ *n* مِصْري [misˤrij]
eight [eɪt] *number* ثمانية [θama:nijatun]
eighteen ['eɪ'ti:n] *number* ثمانية عشر [θama:nijata ʕaʃara]
eighteenth ['eɪ'ti:nθ; 'eigh'teenth] *adj* الثامن عشر [aθ-θa:min ʕaʃar]
eighth [eɪtθ] *adj* الثامن [aθθa:min] ▷ *n* ثُمن [θum]
eighty ['eɪtɪ] *number* ثمانون [θama:nu:na]
Eire ['ɛərə] *n* أيرلندا [ʔajrlanda:]
either ['aɪðə; 'i:ðə] *adv (with negative)* فوق ذلك [Faw'q dhalek] ▷ *conj* إما (ro ..) ▷ *pron* أي من [Ay men]; **either... or** *conj* إما... أو [Emma...aw]
elastic [ɪ'læstɪk] *n* مطاط [matˤtˤa:tˤ]; **elastic band** *n* رباط مطاطى [rebaṭ maṭaṭey]
Elastoplast® [ɪ'læstəˌplɑ:st] *n* لاصق من نوع إلاستوبلاست ® [la:sˤiq min nawʕi ʔila:stu:bla:st]
elbow ['ɛlbəʊ] *n* مِرفق [mirfaq]
elder ['ɛldə] *adj* أكبر سِنّاً [Akbar senan]
elderly ['ɛldəlɪ] *adj* كهولي [kuhu:lij]
eldest ['ɛldɪst] *adj* الأكبر سناً [Al-akbar senan]
elect [ɪ'lɛkt] *v* يَنتخِب [jantaxibu]
election [ɪ'lɛkʃən] *n* انتخاب [intixa:b]; **general election** *n* انتخابات عامة [Entekhabat 'aamah]
electorate [ɪ'lɛktərɪt] *n* جمهور الناخبين [Jomhoor al-nakhebeen]
electric [ɪ'lɛktrɪk] *adj* مكهرب [mukahrab]; **electric blanket** *n* بطانية كهربائية [Baṭaneyah kahrobaeyah]; **electric shock** *n* صَدْمَة كهربائية [Ṣadmah kahrbaeyah]
electrical [ɪ'lɛktrɪkᵊl] *adj* كهربائي [kahraba:ʔij]
electrician [ɪlɛk'trɪʃən; ˌi:lɛk-] *n* مشتغل بالكهرباء [Moshtaghel bel-kahrabaa]
electricity [ɪlɛk'trɪsɪtɪ; ˌi:lɛk-] *n* كهرباء [kahraba:ʔ]; **Do we have to pay extra for electricity?** هل يحب علينا دفع مصاريف إضافية للكهرباء؟ [hal yajib 'aala-yna daf'a maṣa-reef eḍafiya lel-kah-rabaa?]; **Is the cost of electricity included?** هل يشمل ذلك تكلفة الكهرباء؟ [hal yash-mil dhalik tak-lifat al-kah-rabaa?]; **There is no electricity** لا توجد كهرباء [la tojad kah-rabaa]; **Where is the electricity meter?** أين يوجد عداد الكهرباء؟ [ayna yujad 'aadad al-kah-raba?]
electronic [ɪlɛk'trɒnɪk; ˌi:lɛk-] *adj*

الكتروني [iliktru:nijjat]
electronics [ɪlɛk'trɒnɪks; ˌi:lɛk-] *npl* الكترونيات [ilikturu:nijja:tun]
elegant ['ɛlɪgənt] *adj* أنيق [ʔani:q]
element ['ɛlɪmənt] *n* عنصر [ʕunsˤur]
elephant ['ɛlɪfənt] *n* فيل [fi:l]
eleven [ɪ'lɛvᵊn] *number* أحد عشر [ʔaħada ʕaʃar]
eleventh [ɪ'lɛvᵊnθ; e'leventh] *adj* الحادي عشر [al-ħa:di: ʕaʃar]
eliminate [ɪ'lɪmɪˌneɪt] *v* يحذف [juħðafu]
elm [ɛlm] *n* شجر الدردار [Shajar al-dardaar]
else [ɛls] *adj* أيضا [ʔajdˤan]
elsewhere [ˌɛls'wɛə] *adv* فى مكان آخر [Fee makaan aakhar]
email ['i:meɪl] *n* بريد الكتروني [Bareed elektrooney] ▷ *vt (a person)* يُرْسِل بريدا إلكترونيا [Yorsel bareedan electroneyan]; **email address** *n* عنوان البريد الإلكتروني ['aonwan al-bareed al-electrooney]
embankment [ɪm'bæŋkmənt] *n* جِسر [ʒisr]
embarrassed [ˌɪm'bærəst] *adj* مُحرَج [muħraʒ]
embarrassing [ɪm'bærəsɪŋ; em'barrassing] *adj* مُحرِج [muħriʒ]
embassy ['ɛmbəsɪ] *n* سِفارة [sifa:ra]
embroider [ɪm'brɔɪdə] *v* يُزَين [juzajjinu]
embroidery [ɪm'brɔɪdərɪ] *n* تطريز [tatˤri:z]
emergency [ɪ'mɜ:dʒənsɪ] *n* حالة طارئة [Ḥalah ṭareaa]; **accident & emergency department** *n* إدارة الحوادث والطوارئ [Edarat al-hawadeth wa-al-tawarea]; **emergency exit** *n* مخرج طوارئ [Makhraj ṭawarea]; **emergency landing** *n* هبوط اضطراري [Hoboot edterary]; **It's an emergency!** إنها حالة طارئة [inaha ḥala ṭareaa]
emigrate ['ɛmɪˌgreɪt] *v* يهاجر [juha:ʒiru]
emotion [ɪ'məʊʃən] *n* عاطفة [ʕa:tˤifa]
emotional [ɪ'məʊʃənᵊl] *adj* عاطفي [ʕa:tˤifij]
emperor, empress ['ɛmpərə, 'ɛmprɪs] *n* إمبراطور [ʔimbara:tˤu:r]
emphasize ['ɛmfəˌsaɪz] *v* يُؤَكِد [juakiddu]
empire ['ɛmpaɪə] *n* إمبراطورية [ʔimbara:tˤu:rijja]
employ [ɪm'plɔɪ] *v* يوظف [juwazˤzˤifu]
employee [ɛm'plɔɪi:; ˌɛmplɔɪ'i:] *n* موظف [muwazˤzˤaf]
employer [ɪm'plɔɪə] *n* صاحب العمل [Ṣaheb 'aamal]
employment [ɪm'plɔɪmənt] *n* وظيفة [wazˤi:fa]
empty ['ɛmptɪ] *adj* خال [xa:lin] ▷ *v* يُفْرِغ [jufriɣu]
enamel [ɪ'næməl] *n* طلاء المينا [Ṭelaa al-meena]
encourage [ɪn'kʌrɪdʒ] *v* يُشجع [juʃaʒʒiʕu]
encouragement [ɪn'kʌrɪdʒmənt] *n* تشجيع [taʃʒi:ʕ]
encouraging [ɪn'kʌrɪdʒɪŋ] *adj* مشجع [muʃaʒʒiʕ]
encyclopaedia [ɛnˌsaɪkləʊ'pi:dɪə] *n* موسوعة [mawsu:ʕa]
end [ɛnd] *n* نهاية [niha:ja] ▷ *v* يَنْتَهي [jantahi:]; **dead end** *n* طريق مسدود [Taree'q masdood]; **at the end of June** في نهاية شهر يونيو [fee nehayat shahr yon-yo]
endanger [ɪn'deɪndʒə] *v* يُعَرِض للخطر [Yo'areḍ lel-khaṭar]
ending ['ɛndɪŋ] *n* انتهاء [intiha:ʔ]
endless ['ɛndlɪs] *adj* لا نهائي [La nehaaey]
enemy ['ɛnəmɪ] *n* عدو [ʕaduww]
energetic [ˌɛnə'dʒɛtɪk] *adj* ملئ بالطاقة [Maleea bel-ṭa'qah]
energy ['ɛnədʒɪ] *n* طاقة [tˤa:qa]
engaged [ɪn'geɪdʒd] *adj* مشغول [maʃɣu:l]; **engaged tone** *n* رنين انشغال الخط [Raneen ensheghal al-khaṭ]; **It's engaged** إنه مشغول [inaho mash-ghool]
engagement [ɪn'geɪdʒmənt] *n* ارتباط [irtiba:tˤ]; **engagement ring** *n* خاتم الخطوبة [Khatem al-khotobah]
engine ['ɛndʒɪn] *n* محرك [muħarrik]; **search engine** *n* محرك البحث [moḥarek

al-baḥth]; **The engine is overheating** المحرك حرارته مرتفعه [al-muḥar-ik ḥarara-tuho murtafe'aa]

engineer [ˌɛndʒɪˈnɪə] *n* مهندس [muhandis]

engineering [ˌɛndʒɪˈnɪərɪŋ] *n* هندسة [handasa]

England [ˈɪŋɡlənd] *n* إنجلترا [ʔinʒiltira:]

English [ˈɪŋɡlɪʃ] *adj* إنجليزي [ʔinʒili:zij] ▷ *n* إنجليزي [ʔinʒili:zij]; **Do you speak English?** هل تتحدث الإنجليزية [hal tata- ḥadath al-injileez-iya?]; **Does anyone speak English?** أيوجد هنا من يتحدث الإنجليزية؟ [ayujad huna min yata-ḥadath al-injile-ziya?]; **I don't speak English** أنا لا أتحدث الإنجليزية [ana la ata-ḥadath al-injile-ziya]; **I speak very little English** أنا أتحدث الإنجليزية قليلا جدا [ana ata-ḥadath al-injile-ziya 'qaleelan jedan]

Englishman, Englishmen [ˈɪŋɡlɪʃmən, ˈɪŋɡlɪʃmɛn] *n* مواطن انجليزي [mowaṭen enjeleezey]

Englishwoman, Englishwomen [ˈɪŋɡlɪʃˌwʊmən, ˈɪŋɡlɪʃˌwɪmɪn] *n* مواطنة إنجليزية [Mowaṭenah enjlezeyah]

engrave [ɪnˈɡreɪv] *v* يَنقُش [janquʃu]

enjoy [ɪnˈdʒɔɪ] *v* يَستمتِع ب [jastamtiʕu bi]

enjoyable [ɪnˈdʒɔɪəbᵊl] *adj* ممتع [mumtiʕ]

enlargement [ɪnˈlɑːdʒmənt; enˈlargement] *n* تكبير [takbi:r]

enormous [ɪˈnɔːməs] *adj* ضخم [dˤaxm]

enough [ɪˈnʌf] *adj* كاف [ka:fin] ▷ *pron* مقدار كاف [Me'qdaar kaaf]

enquire [ɪnˈkwaɪə] *v* يَستعَلِم عن [jastaʕlimu ʕan]

enquiry [ɪnˈkwaɪərɪ] *n* استعلام [istiʕla:m]; **enquiry desk** *n* مكتب الاستعلامات [Maktab al-este'alamaat]; **What is the number for directory enquiries?** ما هو رقم استعلامات دليل التليفون؟ [ma howa ra'qim esti'a-lamaat daleel al-talefon?]

ensure [ɛnˈʃʊə; -ˈʃɔː] *v* يَكْفُل [jakfulu]

enter [ˈɛntə] *v* يُدخِل [judxilu]

entertain [ˌɛntəˈteɪn] *v* يَستضيف (يسلي) [jastadˤi:fu]

entertainer [ˌɛntəˈteɪnə] *n* فنان مشترك في حفلة عامة (فنان) [Fanan moshtarek fe ḥaflah 'aama]

entertaining [ˌɛntəˈteɪnɪŋ] *adj* مسل [musallin]

entertainment [ˌɛntəˈteɪnmənt] *n*; **What entertainment is there?** ما وسائل التسلية المتاحة؟ [ma wasa-el al-tas-leya al-mutaa-ḥa?]

enthusiasm [ɪnˈθjuːzɪˌæzəm] *n* حماسة [ħama:sa]

enthusiastic [ɪnˌθjuːzɪˈæstɪk; enˌthusiˈastic] *adj* متحمس [mutaħammis]

entire [ɪnˈtaɪə] *adj* صحيح [sˤaħi:ħ]

entirely [ɪnˈtaɪəlɪ] *adv* بشكل كامل [Beshakl kaamel]

entrance [ˈɛntrəns] *n* مدخل [madxal]; **entrance fee** *n* رَسْم الدخول [Rasm al-dokhool]; **Where is the wheelchair-accessible entrance?** أين يوجد المدخل المخصص للكراسي المتحركة؟ [ayna yujad al-madkhal al-mukhaṣaṣ lel-karasy al-muta-ḥareka?]

entry [ˈɛntrɪ] *n* دخول (مادة) [duxu:l]; **entry phone** *n* تليفون المدخل [Telefoon al-madkhal]

envelope [ˈɛnvəˌləʊp; ˈɒn-] *n* مغلف [muɣallaf]

envious [ˈɛnvɪəs] *adj* حسود [ħasu:d]

environment [ɪnˈvaɪrənmənt] *n* بيئة [bi:ʔit]

environmental [ɪnˌvaɪrənˈmɛntəˌl] *adj* بيئي [bi:ʔij]; **environmentally friendly** *adj* صديق للبيئة [Ṣadeek al-beeaah]

envy [ˈɛnvɪ] *n* حسد [ħasad] ▷ *v* يَحسُد [jaħsudu]

epidemic [ˌɛpɪˈdɛmɪk] *n* وباء [waba:ʔ]

epileptic [ˌɛpɪˈlɛptɪk] *n* مريض بالصَرَعْ [Mareeḍ bel-ṣara'a]; **epileptic fit** *n* نوبة صرع [Nawbat ṣar'a]

episode [ˈɛpɪˌsəʊd] *n* سلسلة متتابعة

[Selselah motatabe'ah]
equal ['iːkwəl] *adj* مساو [musa:win] ▷ *v* يُساوي [jusa:wi:]
equality [ɪ'kwɒlɪtɪ] *n* مساواة [musa:wa:t]
equalize ['iːkwəˌlaɪz] *v* يُساوي بين [Yosawey bayn]
equation [ɪ'kweɪʒən; -ʃən] *n* مُعادلة [muʕa:dala]
equator [ɪ'kweɪtə] *n* خط الاستواء [Khaṭ al-estwaa]
Equatorial Guinea [ˌɛkwə'tɔːrɪəl 'ɡɪnɪ] *n* غينيا الاستوائية [ɣi:nja: al-istiwa:ʔijjatu]
equipment [ɪ'kwɪpmənt] *n* مُعدات [muʕadda:t]
equipped [ɪ'kwɪpt] *adj* مجهز [muʒahhaz]
equivalent [ɪ'kwɪvələnt] *n* مُساوي [musa:wi:]
erase [ɪ'reɪz] *v* يمحو [jamħu:]
Eritrea [ˌɛrɪ'treɪə] *n* إريتريا [ʔiri:tirja:]
erotic [ɪ'rɒtɪk] *adj* مُثير للشهوة الجنسية [Motheer lel shahwah al-jenseyah]
error ['ɛrə] *n* غلطة [ɣaltˤa]
escalator ['ɛskəˌleɪtə] *n* سلم متحرك [Solam motaḥarek]
escape [ɪ'skeɪp] *n* هروب [huru:b] ▷ *v* يَفِرْ [jafirru]; **fire escape** *n* سُلَم النجاة من الحريق [Solam al-najah men al-ḥaree'q]
escort [ɪs'kɔːt] *v* يُصَاحِب [jusˤa:ħibu], يرافق [jura:fiqu]
especially [ɪ'spɛʃəlɪ] *adv* خصوصاً [xusˤwusˤan]
espionage ['ɛspɪəˌnɑːʒ; ˌɛspɪə'nɑːʒ; 'ɛspɪənɪdʒ] *n* جاسوسية [ʒa:su:sijja]
essay ['ɛseɪ] *n* مقال [maqa:l]
essential [ɪ'sɛnʃəl] *adj* جَوهَري [ʒawharij]
estate [ɪ'steɪt] *n* عِزبة [ʕizba]; **estate agent** *n* سِمسار عقارات [Semsaar a'qarat]; **estate car** *n* سيارة بصالون متحرك المقاعد [Sayarah be-ṣalon motaḥarek al-ma'qaed]
estimate *n* ['ɛstɪmɪt] تقدير [taqdi:r] ▷ *v* ['ɛstɪˌmeɪt] يُقيِّم [juqajjimu]
Estonia [ɛ'stəʊnɪə] *n* إستونيا [ʔistu:nja:]
Estonian [ɛ'stəʊnɪən] *adj* إستوني [ʔistu:nij] ▷ *n* *(language)* اللغة الإستونية [Al-loghah al-estwaneyah], *(person)* إستوني [ʔistu:nij]
etc [ɪt 'sɛtrə] *abbr* إلخ [ʔilax]
eternal [ɪ'tɜːnᵊl] *adj* خالد [xa:lid]
eternity [ɪ'tɜːnɪtɪ] *n* خُلود [xulu:d]
ethical ['ɛθɪkᵊl] *adj* أخلاقي مِهَنِي [Akhla'qy mehany]
Ethiopia [ˌiːθɪ'əʊpɪə] *n* إثيوبيا [ʔiθju:bja:]
Ethiopian [ˌiːθɪ'əʊpɪən] *adj* إثيوبي [ʔiθju:bij] ▷ *n* مواطن إثيوبي [Mowaṭen ethyobey]
ethnic ['ɛθnɪk] *adj* عرقي [ʕirqij]
e-ticket ['iː'tɪkɪt] *n* تذكرة إلكترونية [Tadhkarah elektroneyah]
EU [iː juː] *abbr* الاتحاد الأوروبي [Al-tehad al-orobey]
euro ['jʊərəʊ] *n* يورو [ju:ru:]
Europe ['jʊərəp] *n* أوروبا [ʔu:ru:bba:]
European [ˌjʊərə'pɪən] *adj* أوروبي [ʔu:ru:bij] ▷ *n* شخص أوروبي [Shakhs orobby]; **European Union** *n* الاتحاد الأوروبي [Al-tehad al-orobey]
evacuate [ɪ'vækjʊˌeɪt] *v* يُخلِي [juxli:]
eve [iːv] *n* عشية [ʕaʃijja]
even ['iːvᵊn] *adj* مستو [mustawin] ▷ *adv* حتى [ħatta:]
evening ['iːvnɪŋ] *n* مساء [masa:ʔ]; **evening class** *n* صف مسائي [Ṣaf masaaey]; **evening dress** *n* ملابس السهرة [Malabes al-sahrah]; **Good evening** مساء الخير [masaa al-khayer]; **in the evening** في المساء [fee al-masaa]; **The table is booked for nine o'clock this evening** هذه المائدة محجوزة للساعة التاسعة من هذا المساء [hathy al-ma-eda maḥjoza lel-sa'aa al-tase'aa min hatha al-masaa]; **What are you doing this evening?** ما الذي ستفعله هذا المساء [ma al-lathy sataf-'aalaho hatha al-masaa?]; **What is there to do in the evenings?** ماذا يمكن أن نفعله في المساء؟ [madha yamken an naf-'aalaho fee al-masaa?]

event [ɪ'vɛnt] *n* حدث [ħadaθ]
eventful [ɪ'vɛntfʊl] *adj* زاخر بالأحداث (خطير) [Zakher bel-aḥdath]
eventually [ɪ'vɛntʃʊəlɪ] *adv* لاحقاً [la:ħiqan]
ever ['ɛvə] *adv* في أي وقت [Fee ay wa'qt]
every ['ɛvrɪ] *adj* تام [ta:mm]
everybody ['ɛvrɪˌbɒdɪ] *pron* الجميع [Aljamee'a]
everyone ['ɛvrɪˌwʌn; -wən] *pron* كل شخص [Kol shakhṣ]
everything ['ɛvrɪθɪŋ] *pron* كل شيء [Kol shayea]
everywhere ['ɛvrɪˌwɛə] *adv* حيثما [ħajθuma:]
evidence ['ɛvɪdəns] *n* دليل [dali:l]
evil ['i:vᵊl] *adj* شرير [ʃirri:r]
evolution [ˌi:və'lu:ʃən] *n* نشوء [nuʃwuʔ]
ewe [ju:] *n* شاة [ʃa:t]
exact [ɪg'zækt] *adj* مضبوط [madˤbu:tˤ]
exactly [ɪg'zæktlɪ] *adv* تماماً [tama:man]
exaggerate [ɪg'zædʒəˌreɪt] *v* يُبالِغ [juba:liɣu]
exaggeration [ɪg'zædʒəˌreɪʃən] *n* مبالغة [muba:laɣa]
exam [ɪg'zæm] *n* امتحان [imtiħa:n]
examination [ɪgˌzæmɪ'neɪʃən] *n* *(medical)* فحص [faħsˤ], *(school)* فحص (فحص) [faħsˤ]
examine [ɪg'zæmɪn] *v* يَتَفْحَص (يستجوب) [jatafaħħasˤu]
examiner [ɪg'zæmɪnə] *n* الفاحص [al-fa:ħisˤu]
example [ɪg'zɑ:mpᵊl] *n* مثال [miθa:l]
excellent ['ɛksələnt] *adj* ممتاز [mumta:z]
except [ɪk'sɛpt] *prep* ما عدا [Ma 'aada]
exception [ɪk'sɛpʃən] *n* استثناء [istiθna:ʔ]
exceptional [ɪk'sɛpʃənᵊl] *adj* استثنائي [istiθna:ʔij]
excessive [ɪk'sɛsɪv] *adj* مفرط [mufritˤ]
exchange [ɪks'tʃeɪndʒ] *v* يَتَبَادل [jataba:dalu]; **exchange rate** *n* سِعر الصرف [Se'ar al-ṣ arf]; **rate of exchange** *n* سِعر الصرف [Se'ar al-ṣ arf]; **stock exchange** *n* سُوق الأوراق المالية [Soo'q al-awra'q al-maleyah]
excited [ɪk'saɪtɪd] *adj* مُثار [muθa:r]
exciting [ɪk'saɪtɪŋ] *adj* مثير [muθi:r]
exclude [ɪk'sklu:d] *v* يَستبعد [justabʕadu]
excluding [ɪk'sklu:dɪŋ] *prep* باستثناء
exclusively [ɪk'sklu:sɪvlɪ] *adv* على وجه الحصر ['ala wajh al-ḥaṣr]
excuse *n* [ɪk'skju:s] عذر [ʕuðran] ▷ *v* [ɪk'skju:z] يَعْذُر [jaʕðuru]; **Excuse me** معذرة [maʕðiratun]; **Excuse me, that's my seat** معذرة، هذا هو مقعدي؟ [ma'a-dhera, hadha howa ma'q'aady]
execute ['ɛksɪˌkju:t] *v* يعدم [juʕdimu]
execution [ˌɛksɪ'kju:ʃən] *n* تنفيذ [tanfi:ð]
executive [ɪg'zɛkjʊtɪv] *n* سُلطة تنفيذية (مدير) [Soltah tanfeedheyah]
exercise ['ɛksəˌsaɪz] *n* تمرين [tamri:n]
exhaust [ɪg'zɔ:st] *n*; **The exhaust is broken** لقد انكسرت ماسورة العادم [Le'aad enkasarat masoorat al-'adem]
exhausted [ɪg'zɔ:stɪd] *adj* مرهق [murhiq]
exhibition [ˌɛksɪ'bɪʃən] *n* معرض [maʕridˤ]
ex-husband [ɛks'hʌzbənd] *n* زوج سابق [Zawj sabe'q]
exile ['ɛgzaɪl; 'ɛksaɪl] *n* منفى [manfa:]
exist [ɪg'zɪst] *v* يوجد [ju:ʒadu]
exit ['ɛgzɪt; 'ɛksɪt] *n* مخرج [maxraʒ]; **emergency exit** *n* مخرج طوارئ [Makhraj ṭawarea]
exotic [ɪg'zɒtɪk] *adj* دخيل [daxi:l]
expect [ɪk'spɛkt] *v* يَتَوَقع [jatawaqqaʕu]
expedition [ˌɛkspɪ'dɪʃən] *n* بِعْثَة [biʕθa]
expel [ɪk'spɛl] *v* يَطْرُد [jatˤrudu]
expenditure [ɪk'spɛndɪtʃə] *n* نَفَقة [nafaqa]
expenses [ɪk'spɛnsɪz] *npl* نفقات [nafaqa:tun]
expensive [ɪk'spɛnsɪv] *adj* مرتفع الثمن [mortafe'a al-thaman]
experience [ɪk'spɪərɪəns] *n* خبرة [xibra]; **work experience** *n* خبرة العمل

[Khebrat al'aamal]
experienced [ɪk'spɪərɪənst] *adj* مُجَرَب [muʒarrib]
experiment [ɪk'spɛrɪmənt] *n* تجربة [taʒriba]
expert ['ɛkspɜːt] *n* خبير [xabiːr]
expire [ɪk'spaɪə] *v* ينتهي [janqadˤiː]
explain [ɪk'spleɪn] *v* يَشرح [jaʃraħu]
explanation [ˌɛksplə'neɪʃən] *n* شَرح [ʃarħ]
explode [ɪk'spləʊd] *v* يُفجِر [jufaʒʒiru]
exploit [ɪk'splɔɪt] *v* يَستغِل [jastaɣillu]
exploitation [ˌɛksplɔɪ'teɪʃən] *n* استغلال [istiɣlaːl]
explore [ɪk'splɔː] *v* يَستكشف [jastakʃifu]
explorer [ɪk'splərə] *n* مستكشف (مسبار) [mustakʃif]
explosion [ɪk'spləʊʒən] *n* انفجار [infiʒaːr]
explosive [ɪk'spləʊsɪv] *n* مادة متفجرة [Madah motafajerah]
export *n* ['ɛkspɔːt](تصدير) صادِر [sˤaːdir] ▷ *v* [ɪk'spɔːt] يٌصَدِر [jusˤaddiru]
express [ɪk'sprɛs] *v* يُعَبِر عن [Yo'aber 'an]
expression [ɪk'sprɛʃən] *n* تعبير [taʕbiːr]
extension [ɪk'stɛnʃən] *n* امتداد (توسع) [imtidaːd]; **extension cable** *n* وَصْلَة تمديد [Waṣlat tamdeed]
extensive [ɪk'stɛnsɪv] *adj* ممتد [mumtadd]
extensively [ɪk'stɛnsɪvlɪ] *adv* بشكل مُوَسَّع [Beshakl mowasa'a]
extent [ɪk'stɛnt] *n* مدى [madaː]
exterior [ɪk'stɪərɪə] *adj* خارجي [xaːriʒij]
external [ɪk'stɜːnᵊl] *adj* سطحي [satˤħij]
extinct [ɪk'stɪŋkt] *adj* منقرض [munqaridˤ]
extinguisher [ɪk'stɪŋgwɪʃə] *n* طفاية الحريق [Ṭafayat ḥaree'q]
extortionate [ɪk'stɔːʃənɪt] *adj* مُستَغِل [mustaɣill]
extra ['ɛkstrə] *adj* زَائِد [zaːʔid] ▷ *adv* إلى درجة فائقة [Ela darajah fae'qah]
extraordinary [ɪk'strɔːdᵊnrɪ; -dᵊnərɪ] *adj* استثنائي [istiθnaːʔij]
extravagant [ɪk'strævɪgənt] *adj* مسرف [musrif]
extreme [ɪk'striːm] *adj* شديد [ʃadiːd]
extremely [ɪk'striːmlɪ] *adv* بدرجة شديدة [Bedarajah shadeedah]
extremism [ɪk'striːmɪzəm] *n* تطرف [tatˤarruf]
extremist [ɪk'striːmɪst] *n* متطرف [mutatˤarrif]
ex-wife [ɛks'waɪf] *n* زوجة سابقة [Zawjah sabe'qah]
eye [aɪ] *n* عين [ʕajn]; **eye drops** *npl* قطرة للعين ['qaṭrah lel-'ayn]; **eye shadow** *n* ظل العيون [ḍhel al-'aoyoon]; **I have something in my eye** يوجد شيء ما في عيني [yujad shay-un ma fee 'aynee]; **My eyes are sore** إن عيناي ملتهبتان [enna 'aynaya multa-hebatan]
eyebrow ['aɪˌbraʊ] *n* حاجب [ħaːʒib]
eyelash ['aɪˌlæʃ] *n* رِمش العين [Remsh al'ayn]
eyelid ['aɪˌlɪd] *n* جفن [ʒafn]
eyeliner ['aɪˌlaɪnə] *n* قلم تحديد العينين ['qalam taḥdeed al-'ayn]
eyesight ['aɪˌsaɪt] *n* مجال البصر [Majal al-baṣar]

f

fabric ['fæbrɪk] *n* قماش [quma:ʃ]
fabulous ['fæbjʊləs] *adj* غير قابل للتصديق [Ghayr 'qabel leltaṣdee'q]
face [feɪs] *n* وجه [waʒh] ▷ *v* يواجه [juwa:ʒihu]; **face cloth** *n* مِنشَفة الوجه [Menshafat al-wajh]
facial ['feɪʃəl] *adj* وجهي [waʒhij] ▷ *n* تدليك الوجه [Tadleek al-wajh]
facilities [fə'sɪlɪtɪz] *npl* منشآت (تسهيلات) [munʃaʔa:tun]
fact [fækt] *n* حقيقة [ħaqi:qa]
factory ['fæktərɪ] *n* مصنع [masˤnaʕ]
fade [feɪd] *v* يَذوي [jaðawwi:]
fag [fæg] *n* كدح [kadaħ]
fail [feɪl] *v* يَفْشَل [jafʃalu]
failure ['feɪljə] *n* فشل [faʃal]
faint [feɪnt] *adj* خائر القوى [Khaaer al-'qowa] ▷ *v* يُصَاب بإغماء [yoṣab be-eghmaa]
fair [fɛə] *adj (light colour)* فَاتِح [fa:tiħ], *(reasonable)* عادل [ʕa:dil] ▷ *n* سوق خيرية [Soo'q khayreyah]
fairground ['fɛəˌgraʊnd] *n* أرض المعارض [Arḍ al ma'ariḍ]
fairly ['fɛəlɪ] *adv* بإنْصَاف [bi-ʔinsˤa:fin]
fairness ['fɛənɪs] *n* عدَل [ʕadl]
fairy ['fɛərɪ] *n* جنية [ʒinnija]
fairytale ['fɛərɪˌteɪl] *n* أحد حكايات الجان [Aḥad ḥekayat al-jan]
faith [feɪθ] *n* إيمان (إخلاص) [ʔi:ma:n]
faithful ['feɪθfʊl] *adj* مخلص [muxlisˤ]
faithfully ['feɪθfʊlɪ] *adv* بصِدْق [bisˤidqin]
fake [feɪk] *adj* مُزَيَّف [muzajjaf] ▷ *n* زائف (مدع) [za:ʔif]
fall [fɔːl] *n* سُقوط [suqu:tˤ] ▷ *v* يَقَع [jaqaʕu]
fall down [fɔːl daʊn] *v* يَسْقُط (يخر ساجدا) [jasqutˤu]
fall for [fɔːl fɔː] *v* يقع في غرامها [Ya'qah fee ghrameha]
fall out [fɔːl aʊt] *v* يَتَشاجر (يتفرق) [jataʃa:ʒaru]
false [fɔːls] *adj* زائف [za:ʔif]; **false alarm** *n* إنذار كاذب [endhar kadheb]
fame [feɪm] *n* سُمْعَة [sumʕa]
familiar [fə'mɪlɪə] *adj* مألوف [maʔlu:f]
family ['fæmɪlɪ; 'fæmlɪ] *n* عائلة [ʕa:ʔila]
famine ['fæmɪn] *n* مجاعة [maʒa:ʕa]
famous ['feɪməs] *adj* مَشهور [maʃhu:r]
fan [fæn] *n* مروحة [mirwaħa]; **fan belt** *n* سير المروحة [Seer almarwaha]; **Does the room have a fan?** هل يوجد مروحة بالغرفة [hal yujad mirwa-ḥa bil-ghurfa?]
fanatic [fə'nætɪk] *n* شخص متعصب [Shakhṣ motaṣeb]
fancy ['fænsɪ] *v* يَتخيل [jataxajjalu]; **fancy dress** *n* زي تَنكري [Zey tanakorey]
fantastic [fæn'tæstɪk] *adj* خَيَالِي [xaja:lij]
FAQ [ɛf eɪ kjuː] *abbr* سُؤال مُتكرر [Soaal motakarer]
far [fɑː] *adj* بعيد [baʕi:d] ▷ *adv* على مسافة بعيدة [Ala masafah ba'aedah]; **Far East** *n* الشرق الأقصى [Al-shar'q al-a'qsa]; **Is it far?** هل المسافة بعيدة؟ [hal al-masafa ba'aeda?]; **It's not far** المسافة ليست بعيدة [al-masaafa laysat ba'aeeda]; **It's quite far** المسافة ليست بعيدة جدا [al-masaafa laysat ba'aeedah jedan]
fare [fɛə] *n* أجرة السفر [Ojrat al-safar]
farm [fɑːm] *n* مزرعة [mazraʕa]
farmer ['fɑːmə] *n* مزارع [maza:riʕ]

farmhouse ['fɑːmˌhaʊs] *n* منزل ريفي [Mazel reefey]
farming ['fɑːmɪŋ] *n* زراعة [ziraːʕa]
Faroe Islands ['fɛərəʊ 'aɪləndz] *npl* جزر فارو [Jozor faaw]
fascinating ['fæsɪˌneɪtɪŋ] *adj* فاتِن [faːtin]
fashion ['fæʃən] *n* موضة (نمط) [muːdˤa]
fashionable ['fæʃənəbᵊl] *adj* مواكب للموضة [Mowakeb lel-moḍah]
fast [fɑːst] *adj* سريع [sariːʕ] ▷ *adv* بسرعة [Besor'aah]; **He was driving too fast** كان يقود السيارة بسرعة كبيرة [kaːna jaquːdu assajjaːrata bisurʕatin kabiːratin]
fat [fæt] *adj* سَمين [samiːn] ▷ *n* بَدِين [badiːn]
fatal ['feɪtᵊl] *adj* مميت (مقدر) [mumiːt]
fate [feɪt] *n* قَدَر [qadar]
father ['fɑːðə] *n* والِد [waːlid]
father-in-law ['fɑːðə ɪn lɔː] **(***pl* **fathers-in-law)** *n* الحمو [alħamuː]
fault [fɔːlt] *n (defect)* عيب [ʕajb], *(mistake)* عيب [ʕajb]
faulty ['fɔːltɪ] *adj* معيوب [maʕjuːb]
fauna ['fɔːnə] *npl* حيوانات [ħajwaːnaːt]
favour ['feɪvə] *n* معروف [maʕruːf]
favourite ['feɪvərɪt; 'feɪvrɪt] *adj* مفضل [mufadˤdˤal] ▷ *n* شخص مُقَرّب [Shakhṣ mo'qarab]
fax [fæks] *n* فاكس [faːks] ▷ *v* يُرسِل رسالةً بالفاكس [Yorsel resalah bel-fax]; **Do you have a fax?** هل يوجد فاكس؟ [hal yujad fax?]; **How much is it to send a fax?** كم تبلغ تكلفة إرسال رسالة بالفاكس؟ [Kam tablogh taklefat ersal resalah bel-faks?]; **I want to send a fax** أريد إرسال فاكس [areed ersaal fax]; **Is there a fax machine I can use?** هل توجد ماكينة فاكس يمكن استخدامها؟ [hal tojad makenat fax yamken istekh-damuha?]; **Please resend your fax** رجاء إعادة إرسال الفاكس [rejaa e-'aadat ersaal al-fax]; **There is a problem with your fax** هناك مشكلة ما في الفاكس [Honak moshkelah ma fel-faks]; **What is the fax number?** ما هو رقم الفاكس؟ [ma howa ra'qim al-fax?]
fear [fɪə] *n* خَوف [xawf] ▷ *v* يخاف [jaxaːfu]
feasible ['fiːzəbᵊl] *adj* عملي [ʕamalij]
feather ['fɛðə] *n* رِيشَة [riːʃa]
feature ['fiːtʃə] *n* سِمة [sima]
February ['fɛbrʊərɪ] *n* فبراير [fabraːjir]
fed up [fɛd ʌp] *adj* سَئِمَ [saʔima]
fee [fiː] *n* أجر (رسم) [ʔaʒr]; **entrance fee** *n* رَسْم الدخول [Rasm al-dokhool]; **tuition fees** *npl* رسوم التعليم [Rasm al-ta'aleem]
feed [fiːd] *v* يُطْعِم [jutˤʕimu]
feedback ['fiːdˌbæk] *n* الإفادة بالرأي [Al-efadah bel-raay]
feel [fiːl] *v* يَشعُر [jaʃʕuru]
feeling ['fiːlɪŋ] *n* شُعُور [ʃuʕuːr]
feet [fiːt] *npl* أقدام [ʔaqdaːmun]
felt [fɛlt] *n* لباد [libaːd]
female ['fiːmeɪl] *adj* مُؤنث [muʔannaθ] ▷ *n* أنثى [ʔunθaː]
feminine ['fɛmɪnɪn] *adj* مؤنث [muʔannaθ]
feminist ['fɛmɪnɪst; 'feminist] *n* شخص موال لمساواة المرأة بالرجل [Shakhṣ mowal le-mosawat al-maraah bel-rajol]
fence [fɛns] *n* سِياج [sijaːʒ]
fennel ['fɛnᵊl] *n* نبات الشمر [Nabat al-shamar]
fern [fɜːn] *n* نبات السراخس [Nabat al-sarakhes]
ferret ['fɛrɪt] *n* النِمْس [an-nimsu]
ferry ['fɛrɪ] *n* معدية [muʕdija]
fertile ['fɜːtaɪl] *adj* خِصب [xisˤb]
fertilizer ['fɜːtɪˌlaɪzə] *n* سِماد [samaːd]
festival ['fɛstɪvᵊl] *n* مهرجان [mihraʒaːn]
fetch [fɛtʃ] *v* يجلب [jaʒlibu]
fever ['fiːvə] *n* حمى [ħummaː]; **hay fever** *n* مرض حمى القش [Maraḍ ḥomma al-'qash]; **He has a fever** أنه يعاني من الحمى [inaho yo-'aany min al- ḥomma]
few [fjuː] *adj* بعض [baʕdˤu] ▷ *pron* قليل [qaliːlun]
fewer [fjuːə] *adj* أقل [ʔaqallu]
fiancé [fɪ'ɒnseɪ] *n* خطيب [xatˤiːb]
fiancée [fɪ'ɒnseɪ] *n* خطيبة [xatˤiːba]
fibre ['faɪbə] *n* ألياف [ʔaljaːf]

fibreglass [ˈfaɪbəˌɡlɑːs] *n* مادة ألياف الزجاج [Madat alyaf alzojaj]
fiction [ˈfɪkʃən] *n* قصة خيالية [ˈqeṣah khayaleyah]; **science fiction** *n* خيال علمي [Khayal ˈaelmey]
field [fiːld] *n* حقل [ħaql]; **playing field** *n* ملعب رياضي [Mal'aab reyady]
fierce [fɪəs] *adj* مفترس [muftaris]
fifteen [ˈfɪfˈtiːn] *number* خَمْسة عشر [xamsata ʕaʃar]
fifteenth [ˈfɪfˈtiːnθ; ˈfifteenth] *adj* الخامس عشر [al-xaːmis ʕaʃar]
fifth [fɪfθ] *adj* خامس [xaːmis]
fifty [ˈfɪftɪ] *number* خَمْسُون [xamsuːna]
fifty-fifty [ˈfɪftɪˈfɪftɪ] *adj* مقسم مناصفة [Mo'qassam monaṣafah] ▷ *adv* مناصفة [munaːsˤafatan]
fig [fɪɡ] *n* تين [tiːn]
fight [faɪt] *n* قتال [qitaːl] ▷ *v* يُحارِب [juħaːribu]
fighting [faɪtɪŋ] *n* قتال [qitaːl]
figure [ˈfɪɡə; ˈfɪɡjər] *n* رقم [raqm]
figure out [ˈfɪɡə aʊt] *v* يَتبين [jatabajjanu]
Fiji [ˈfiːdʒiː; fiːˈdʒiː] *n* فيجي [fiːʒiː]
file [faɪl] *n (folder)* ملف [milaff], *(tool)* ملف [milaff] ▷ *v (folder)* يَحفَظ في ملف [yahfaḍh fee malaf], *(smoothing)* يبرد بمبرد [Yobared bemobared]
Filipino, Filipina [ˌfɪlɪˈpiːnəʊ, ˌfɪlɪˈpiːna] *adj* فلبيني [filibbiːnij] ▷ *n* مواطن فلبيني [Mowaṭen felebeeney]
fill [fɪl] *v* يَمْلأ [jamlʔu]
fillet [ˈfɪlɪt] *n* شريحة لحم مخلية من العظام (عصابة رأس) [Shreeḥat laḥm makhleyah men al-eḍham] ▷ *v* يُقَطِّع إلى شرائح [Yo'qaṭe'a ela shraeḥ]
fill in [fɪl ɪn] *v* يَمْلأ الفراغ [Yamlaa al-faragh]
filling [ˈfɪlɪŋ] *n*; **A filling has fallen out** لقد تآكل الحشو [la'qad ta-aa-kala al-ḥasho]; **Can you do a temporary filling?** هل يمكنك عمل حشو مؤقت؟ [hal yamken -aka ˈaamal ḥasho mo-a'qat?]
fill up [fɪl ʌp] *v* يَملأ ب [Yamlaa be]
film [fɪlm] *n* فيلم [fiːlm]; **film star** *n* نجم سينمائي [Najm senemaaey]; **horror film** *n* فيلم رعب [Feelm ro'ab]; **A colour film, please** فيلم ملون من فضلك [filim mola-wan min faḍlak]; **Can you develop this film, please?** هل يمكنك تحميض هذا الفيلم من فضلك؟ [hal yamken -aka taḥmeeḍ hadha al-filim min faḍlak?]; **The film has jammed** لقد توقف الفيلم بداخل الكاميرا [la'qad tiwa-'qaf al-filim bedakhil al-kamera]; **When does the film start?** متى يبدأ عرض الفيلم؟ [mata yabda ˈaarḍ al-filim?]; **Where can we go to see a film?** متى يمكننا أن نذهب لمشاهدة فيلمًا سينمائيا؟ [Mata yomkenona an nadhab le-moshahadat feelman senemaeyan]; **Which film is on at the cinema?** أي فيلم يعرض الآن على شاشة السينما؟ [ay filim ya'aruḍ al-aan ˈala sha-shat al-senama?]
filter [ˈfɪltə] *n* جهاز ترشيح [Jehaz tarsheeh] ▷ *v* يُصَفِي [jusˤaffiː]
filthy [ˈfɪlθɪ] *adj* قذر [qaðir]
final [ˈfaɪnᵊl] *adj* نهائي [nihaːʔij] ▷ *n* نهائي [nihaːʔij]
finalize [ˈfaɪnəˌlaɪz] *v* يُنْهي [junhiː]
finally [ˈfaɪnəlɪ] *adv* أخيرا [ʔaxiːran]
finance [fɪˈnæns; ˈfaɪnæns] *n* تمويل [tamwiːl] ▷ *v* يُمَول [jumawwilu]
financial [fɪˈnænʃəl; faɪ-] *adj* مالي [maːlij]; **financial year** *n* سَنة مالية [Sanah maleyah]
find [faɪnd] *v* يَجِد [jaʒidu]
find out [faɪnd aʊt] *v* يَكْتَشِف [jaktaʃifu]
fine [faɪn] *adj* (رقيق) رائع [raːʔiʕ] ▷ *adv* على نحو رائع [Ala nahw rae'a] ▷ *n* غرامة [ɣaraːma]; **How much is the fine?** كم تبلغ الغرامة؟ [kam tablugh al-gharama?]; **Where do I pay the fine?** أين تدفع الغرامة؟ [ayna tudfa'a al-gharama?]
finger [ˈfɪŋɡə] *n* إصبع [ʔisˤbaʕ]; **index finger** *n* اصبع السبابة [Eṣbe'a al-sababah]
fingernail [ˈfɪŋɡəˌneɪl] *n* ظُفر [zˤufr]
fingerprint [ˈfɪŋɡəˌprɪnt] *n* بصمة الإصبع [Baṣmat al-eṣba'a]

finish ['fɪnɪʃ] *n* نهاية [niha:ja] ▷ *v* يَخْتَتِم [jaxtatimu]
finished ['fɪnɪʃt] *adj* مُنجَزْ [munʒaz]
Finland ['fɪnlənd] *n* فنلندا [finlanda:]
Finn ['fɪn] *n* مواطن فنلندي [Mowaṭen fenlandey]
Finnish ['fɪnɪʃ] *adj* فنلندي [fanlandij] ▷ *n* اللغة الفنلندية [Al-loghah al-fenlandeyah]
fir [fɜː] *n*; **fir (tree)** *n* شجر التنوب [Shajar al-tanob]
fire [faɪə] *n* نار [na:ru]; **fire alarm** *n* إنذار حريق [endhar Haree'q]; **fire brigade** *n* فرقة مطافيء [Fer'qat maṭafeya]; **fire escape** *n* سُلَم النجاة من الحريق [Solam al-najah men al-ḥaree'q]; **fire extinguisher** *n* طفاية الحريق [Ṭafayat ḥaree'q]
fireman, firemen ['faɪəmən, 'faɪəmɛn] *n* رَجُل المطافئ [Rajol al-maṭafeya]
fireplace ['faɪəˌpleɪs] *n* مستوقد [mustawqid]
firewall ['faɪəˌwɔːl] *n* الجدار الواقي [Al-jedar al-wa'qey]
fireworks ['faɪəˌwɜːks] *npl* ألعاب نارية [Al-'aab nareyah]
firm [fɜːm] *adj* راسخ [ra:six] ▷ *n* مؤسسة [muʔassasa]
first [fɜːst] *adj* أول [ʔawwal] ▷ *adv* أولًا [ʔawwala:] ▷ *n* أول [ʔawwal]; **first aid** *n* إسعافات أولية [Es'aafat awaleyah]; **first name** *n* الاسم الأول [Al-esm al-awal]; **This is my first trip to...** هذه هي أول رحلة لي إلى... [Hadheh hey awal reḥla lee ela]; **When does the first chair-lift go?** متى يتحرك أول ناقل للمتزلجين؟ [mata yata-ḥarak awal na'qil lel-muta-zall-jeen?]; **When is the first bus to...?** ما هو موعد أول أتوبيس متجه إلى... [ma howa maw-'aid awal baaṣ mutajih ela...?]
first-class ['fɜːst'klɑːs] *adj* درجة أولى [Darajah aula]
firstly ['fɜːstlɪ] *adv* أولًا [ʔawwala:]
fiscal ['fɪskᵊl] *adj* أميري [ʔami:rij]; **fiscal year** *n* سنة ضريبية [Sanah ḍareebeyah]
fish [fɪʃ] *n* سَمكة [samaka] ▷ *v* يَصطاد [jasˤatˤdu]; **freshwater fish** *n* سَمكة مياه عذبة [Samakat meyah adhbah]
fisherman, fishermen ['fɪʃəmən, 'fɪʃəmɛn] *n* صياد السمك [Sayad al-samak]
fishing ['fɪʃɪŋ] *n* صيد السمك [Ṣayd al-samak]; **fishing boat** *n* قارب صيد ['qareb ṣayd]; **fishing rod** *n* سِنارة [sˤanna:ratun]; **fishing tackle** *n* معدات صيد السمك [Mo'aedat ṣayed al-samak]
fishmonger ['fɪʃˌmʌŋgə] *n* تاجر الأسماك [Tajer al-asmak]
fist [fɪst] *n* قبضة [qabdˤa]
fit [fɪt] *adj* جيد [ʒabad] ▷ *n* نوبة [nawba] ▷ *v* يُناسِب [junasibu]; **epileptic fit** *n* نوبة صرع [Nawbat ṣar'a]; **fitted kitchen** *n* مطبخ مجهز [Maṭbakh mojahaz]; **fitted sheet** *n* ملاءة مثبتة [Melaah mothabatah]; **fitting room** *n* غرفة القياس [ghorfat al-'qeyas]
fit in [fɪt ɪn] *v* يَتلائَم مع [Yatalaam ma'a]
five [faɪv] *number* خَمْسة [xamsatun]
fix [fɪks] *v* يُثَبِت [juθabbitu]
fixed [fɪkst] *adj* ثابت [θa:bit]
fizzy ['fɪzɪ] *adj* فوار [fuwa:r]
flabby ['flæbɪ] *adj* رَخْو [raxw]
flag [flæg] *n* عَلَم [ʕalam]
flame [fleɪm] *n* لهب [lahab]
flamingo [flə'mɪŋgəʊ] *n* طائر الفلامنجو [Ṭaaer al-flamenjo]
flammable ['flæməbᵊl] *adj* قابل للاشتعال ['qabel lel-eshte'aal]
flan [flæn] *n* فطيرة فْلَان [Faṭerat folan]
flannel ['flænᵊl] *n* صوف فانيلة [Ṣoof faneelah]
flap [flæp] *v* يُرفرِف [jurafrifu]
flash [flæʃ] *n* وميض [wami:dˤ] ▷ *v* يوُمض [ju:midˤu]
flashlight ['flæʃˌlaɪt] *n* وميض [wami:dˤ]
flask [flɑːsk] *n* دَورَق [dawraq]
flat [flæt] *adj* منبسط [munbasitˤ] ▷ *n* مُسَطّح [musatˤtˤah]; **studio flat** *n* شقة ستديو [Sha'qah stedeyo]
flat-screen ['flæt͵skriːn] *adj* شاشة مسطحة [Shasha mosṭahah]
flatter ['flætə] *v* يُطري [jutˤri:]

flattered ['flætəd] *adj* شاعر بالإطراء [Shaa'aer bel-eṭraa]
flavour ['fleɪvə] *n* نكهة [nakha]
flavouring ['fleɪvərɪŋ] *n* مادة منكهة [Madah monakahah]
flaw [flɔː] *n* نقص [naqsʕ]
flea [fliː] *n* برغوث [barɣuːθ]; **flea market** *n* سُوق للسلع الرخيصة [Soo'q lel-sealaa al-ṣgheerah]
flee [fliː] *v* يَتفَادى [jatafaːdaː]
fleece [fliːs] *n* صوف الخروف [Ṣoof al-kharoof]
fleet [fliːt] *n* قافلة [qaːfila]
flex [flɛks] *n* سِلك كهربائي (لي) [Selk kahrabaey]
flexible ['flɛksɪbəl] *adj* مرن [marin]
flexitime ['flɛksɪˌtaɪm] *n* ساعات عمل مرنة [Sa'aat 'aamal marenah]
flight [flaɪt] *n* رحلة جوية [Rehalah jaweyah]; **charter flight** *n* رحلة جوية مُؤجَرة [Rehalh jaweyah moajarah]; **flight attendant** *n* مضيف الطائرة [moḍeef al-ṭaaerah]; **scheduled flight** *n* رحلة منتظمة [Reḥlah montaḍhemah]
fling [flɪŋ] *v* يَطْرَح جانبا [Yaṭraḥ janeban]
flip-flops ['flɪp'flɒpz] *npl* شِبشِب [ʃubʃubun]
flippers ['flɪpəz] *npl* زعانف الغطس [Za'aanef al-ghaṭs]
flirt [flɜːt] *n* غزل (حركة خاطفة) [ɣazl] ▷ *v* يُغَازِل [juɣaːzilu]
float [fləʊt] *n* عوامة [ʕawaːma] ▷ *v* يطفو [jatʕfuː]
flock [flɒk] *n* سِرب [sirb]
flood [flʌd] *n* طوفان [tʕuːfaːn] ▷ *vi* يفيض [jafiːdʕu] ▷ *vt* يَغْمُر [jaɣmuru]
flooding ['flʌdɪŋ] *n* فيضان [fajadʕaːn]
floodlight ['flʌdˌlaɪt] *n* وحدة إضاءة كشافة [Weḥdah eḍafeyah kashafah]
floor [flɔː] *n* أرضية [ʔardʕijja]; **ground floor** *n* الدور الأرضي [Aldoor al-arḍey]
flop [flɒp] *n* فَشَل [faʃal]
floppy ['flɒpɪ] *adj*; **floppy disk** *n* قرص مرن ['qorṣ maren]
flora ['flɔːrə] *npl* نباتات [nabaːtaːt]
florist ['flɒrɪst] *n* بائع زهور [Bae'a zohor]
flour ['flaʊə] *n* دقيق طحين [Da'qee'q ṭaheen]
flow [fləʊ] *v* يَتدفق [jatadaffaqu]
flower ['flaʊə] *n* زهرة [zahra] ▷ *v* يُزهر [juzhiru]
flu [fluː] *n* الإنفلوانزا [Alenfolwanza]; **bird flu** *n* إنفلوانزا الطيور [Enfelwanza al-ṭeyor]
fluent ['fluːənt] *adj* سَلس (فصيح) [salis]
fluorescent [ˌflʊəˈrɛsənt; ˌfluoˈrescent] *adj* فلوري [fluːrij]
flush [flʌʃ] *n* نضارة [nadʕdʕaːra] ▷ *v* يَتورد (يتدفق) [jatawarradu]
flute [fluːt] *n* آلة الفلوت [Aalat al-felot]
fly [flaɪ] *n* ذُبَابَة [ðubaːba] ▷ *v* يَطير [jatʕiːru]
fly away [flaɪ əˈweɪ] *v* يَهْرُب مسرعا [Yahrab mosre'aan]
foal [fəʊl] *n* مهر [mahr]
foam [fəʊm] *n*; **shaving foam** *n* رغوة الحلاقة [Raghwat ḥela'qah]
focus ['fəʊkəs] *n* بُؤْرة [buʔra] ▷ *v* يَتركَز [jatarakkazu]
foetus ['fiːtəs] *n* جنين [ʒaniːn]
fog [fɒg] *n* ضباب [dʕabaːb]; **fog light** *n* مصباح الضباب [Mesbaḥ al-ḍabab]
foggy ['fɒgɪ] *adj* غائم [ɣaːʔim]
foil [fɔɪl] *n* رقاقة معدنية [Re'qaeq ma'adaneyah]
fold [fəʊld] *n* طي (حظيرة خراف) [tʕajj] ▷ *v* يَطْوي [jatʕwiː]
folder ['fəʊldə] *n* حافظة [ħaːfizʕa]
folding [fəʊldɪŋ] *adj* قابل للطي ['qabel lel-ṭay]
folklore ['fəʊkˌlɔː] *n* فولكلور [fuːlkluːr]
follow ['fɒləʊ] *v* يَتبِع [jatbaʕu]
following ['fɒləʊɪŋ] *adj* لاحِق [laːħiq]
food [fuːd] *n* طعام [tʕaʕaːm]; **food poisoning** *n* التسمم الغذائي [Al-tasmom al-ghedhaaey]; **food processor** *n* محضر الطعام [Moḥder al-ṭa'aam]; **Do you have food?** هل يوجد لديكم طعام؟ [hal yujad laday-kum ṭa'aam?]; **The food is too hot** إن الطعام ساخن أكثر من اللازم [enna al-ṭa'aam sakhen akthar min al-laazim]; **The food is very greasy** الطعام كثير الدسم [al-ṭa'aam katheer

al-dasim]
fool [fuːl] *n* مُغَفّل [muɣaffl] ▷ *v* يُضَلِل [jundˤallilu]
foot, feet [fʊt, fiːt] *n* قدم [qadam]; **My feet are a size six** مقاس قدمي ستة [ma'qas 'qadamy sit-a]
football ['fʊt,bɔːl] *n* كرة القدم [Korat al-'qadam]; **American football** *n* كرة القدم الأمريكية [Korat al-'qadam al-amreekeyah]; **football match** *n* مباراة كرة قدم [Mobarat korat al-'qadam]; **football player** *n* لاعب كرة القدم [La'aeb korat al-'qadam]; **Let's play football** هلم نلعب كرة القدم؟ [haloma nal'aab kurat al-'qadam]
footballer ['fʊt,bɔːlə] *n* لاعب كرة قدم [La'eb korat 'qadam]
footpath ['fʊt,pɑːθ] *n* ممر المشاة [mamar al-moshah]
footprint ['fʊt,prɪnt] *n* أَثَر القدم [Athar al'qadam]
footstep ['fʊt,stɛp] *n* أثر القدم [Athar al-'qadam]
for [fɔː; fə] *prep* لأجل [liʔaʒli]
forbid [fə'bɪd] *v* يُحَرم [juħarrimu]
forbidden [fə'bɪdᵊn] *adj* ممنوع [mamnuːʕ]
force [fɔːs] *n* قوة عسكرية ['qowah askareyah] ▷ *v* يُجْبِر [juʒbiru]; **Air Force** *n* سلاح الطيران [Selaḥ al-ṭayaran]
forecast ['fɔː,kɑːst] *n* تنبؤ [tanabuʔ]
foreground ['fɔː,graʊnd] *n* أمامي [ʔamaːmij]
forehead ['fɒrɪd; 'fɔː,hɛd] *n* جبهة [ʒabha]
foreign ['fɒrɪn] *adj* أجنبي [ʔaʒnabij]
foreigner ['fɒrɪnə] *n* أجنبي [ʔaʒnabij]
foresee [fɔː'siː] *v* يتنَبأ ب [Yatanabaa be]
forest ['fɒrɪst] *n* غابة [ɣaːba]
forever [fɔː'rɛvə; fə-] *adv* إلى الأبد [Ela alabad]
forge [fɔːdʒ] *v* يُزَور [juzawwiru]
forgery ['fɔːdʒərɪ] *n* تزوير [tazwiːr]
forget [fə'gɛt] *v* ينسى [jansaː]
forgive [fə'gɪv] *v* يَغْفِر [jaɣfiru]
forgotten [fə'gɒtᵊn] *adj* منسي [mansijju]
fork [fɔːk] *n* شوكة طعام [Shawkat ṭa'aaam]
form [fɔːm] *n* شَكْل [ʃakl]; **application form** *n* نموذج الطلب [Namozaj al-ṭalab]; **order form** *n* نموذج طلبية [Namodhaj ṭalabeyah]
formal ['fɔːməl] *adj* عُرفي [ʕurafij]
formality [fɔː'mælɪtɪ] *n* شكل رسمي [Shakl rasmey]
format ['fɔːmæt] *n* تنسيق [tansiːq] ▷ *v* يُعْيد تهيئة [Yo'aeed taheyaah]
former ['fɔːmə] *adj* سابق [saːbiq]
formerly ['fɔːməlɪ] *adv* سابقاً
formula ['fɔːmjʊlə] *n* صيغة [sˤiːɣa]
fort [fɔːt] *n* حصن [ħisˤn]
fortnight ['fɔːt,naɪt] *n* يومان [jawmaːni]
fortunate ['fɔːtʃənɪt] *adj* سعيد [saʕiːd]
fortunately ['fɔːtʃənɪtlɪ] *adv* لحسن الحظ [Le-hosn al-haḍh]
fortune ['fɔːtʃən] *n* حظ سعيد [haḍh sa'aeed]
forty ['fɔːtɪ] *number* أربعون [ʔarbaʕuːna]
forward ['fɔːwəd] *adv* إلى الأمام [Ela al amam] ▷ *v* يرسل [jursilu]; **forward slash** *n* شرطة مائلة للأمام [Sharṭah maelah lel-amam]; **lean forward** *v* يَتَكئ للأمام [Yatakea lel-amam]
foster ['fɒstə] *v* يُعزز (يتبنى) [juʕazzizu]; **foster child** *n* طفل متبنى [Ṭefl matabanna]
foul [faʊl] *adj* غادِر [ɣaːdir] ▷ *n* مخالفة [muxaːlafa]
foundations [faʊn'deɪʃənz] *npl* أساسات [ʔasaːsaːtun]
fountain ['faʊntɪn] *n* نافورة [naːfuːra]; **fountain pen** *n* قلم حبر ['qalam ḥebr]
four [fɔː] *number* أربعة [ʔarbaʕatun]
fourteen ['fɔː'tiːn] *number* أربعة عشر [ʔarbaʕata ʕaʃr]
fourteenth ['fɔː'tiːnθ] *adj* الرابع عشر [ar-raːbiʕu ʕaʃari]
fourth [fɔːθ] *adj* رابع [raːbiʕu]
fox [fɒks] *n* ثعلب [θaʕlab]
fracture ['fræktʃə] *n* كَسْر [kasr]
fragile ['frædʒaɪl] *adj* قابل للكسر ['qabel

lel-kassr]
frail [freɪl] *adj* واهن [wa:hin]
frame [freɪm] *n* إطار [ʔitˁa:r]; **picture frame** *n* إطار الصورة [Eṭar al ṣorah]; **Zimmer® frame** *n* هيكل زيمر المساعد على المشي [hajkalun zajmiri almusa:ʕidi ʕala: almaʃʃi]
France [frɑːns] *n* فرنسا [faransa:]
frankly ['fræŋklɪ] *adv* بصراحة [Beṣaraḥah]
frantic ['fræntɪk] *adj* شديد الاهتياج [Shdeed al-ehteyaj]
fraud [frɔːd] *n* احتيال [iħtija:l]
freckles ['frɛkᵊlz] *npl* نمش [namʃun]
free [friː] *adj (no cost)* مجاني [maʒʒa:nij], *(no restraint)* حر [ħurr] ▷ *v* يُحَرر [juħarriru]; **free kick** *n* ضربة حرة [Ḍarba ḥorra]
freedom ['friːdəm] *n* حرية [ħurrijja]
freelance ['friːˌlɑːns] *adj* يعمل بشكل حر [Ya'amal beshakl ḥor] ▷ *adv* بشكل مُستَقل [Beshakl mosta'qel]
freeze [friːz] *v* يَتَجمد [jataʒammadu]
freezer ['friːzə] *n* فريزر [fri:zar]
freezing ['friːzɪŋ] *adj* شديد البرودة [Shadeedat al-broodah]; **It's freezing cold** الجو شديد البرودة [al-jaw shaded al-boroda]
freight [freɪt] *n* شُحنة [ʃuħna]
French [frɛntʃ] *adj* فرنسي [faransij] ▷ *n* اللغة الفرنسية [All-loghah al-franseyah]; **French beans** *npl* فاصوليا خضراء [Faṣoleya khaḍraa]; **French horn** *n* بوق فرنسي [Boo'q faransey]
Frenchman, Frenchmen ['frɛntʃmən, 'frɛntʃmɛn] *n* مواطن فرنسي [Mowaṭen faransey]
Frenchwoman, Frenchwomen ['frɛntʃwʊmən, 'frɛntʃˌwɪmɪn] *n* مواطنة فرنسية [Mowaṭenah faranseyah]
frequency ['friːkwənsɪ] *n* تردد [taraddud]
frequent ['friːkwənt] *adj* متكرر [mutakarrir]
fresh [frɛʃ] *adj* طازج [tˁa:zaʒ]
freshen up ['frɛʃən ʌp] *v* يُنْعِش [junʕiʃu]
fret [frɛt] *v* يَغْيظ [jaɣi:zˁu]
Friday ['fraɪdɪ] *n* الجمعة [al-ʒumuʕatu]; **Good Friday** *n* الجمعة العظيمة [Al-jom'ah al-'aaḍheemah]; **on Friday the thirty first of December** يوم الجمعة الموافق الحادي والثلاثين من ديسمبر [yawm al-jum'aa al- muwa-fi'q al-ḥady waal-thalatheen min desambar]; **on Friday** في يوم الجمعة [fee yawm al-jum'aa]
fridge [frɪdʒ] *n* ثلاجة [θalla:ʒa]
fried [fraɪd] *adj* مقلي [maqlij]
friend [frɛnd] *n* صديق [sˁadi:q]
friendly ['frɛndlɪ] *adj* ودود [wadu:d]
friendship ['frɛndʃɪp] *n* صداقة [sˁada:qa]
fright [fraɪt] *n* رُعْب [ruʕb]
frighten ['fraɪtᵊn] *v* يُرْعِب [jurʕibu]
frightened ['fraɪtənd] *adj* مرعوب [marʕu:b]
frightening ['fraɪtᵊnɪŋ] *adj* مرعب [murʕib]
fringe [frɪndʒ] *n* هُداب [huda:b]
frog [frɒg] *n* ضفدع [dˁifdaʕ]
from [frɒm; frəm] *prep* مِنْ [min]
front [frʌnt] *adj* أمامي [ʔama:mij] ▷ *n* واجهة [wa:ʒiha]
frontier ['frʌntɪə; frʌn'tɪə] *n* تخم [tuxm]
frost [frɒst] *n* صقيع [sˁaqi:ʕ]
frosting ['frɒstɪŋ] *n* تغطية الكيك [taghṭeyat al-keek]
frosty ['frɒstɪ] *adj* تَكَوَّنْ الصقِيع [Takawon al-sa'qee'a]
frown [fraʊn] *v* يَعْبَس [jaʕbasu]
frozen ['frəʊzᵊn] *adj* متجمد [mutaʒammid]
fruit [fruːt] *n (botany)* فاكهة [fa:kiha], *(collectively)* فاكهة [fa:kiha]; **fruit juice** *n* عصير الفاكهة ['aṣeer fakehah]; **fruit machine** *n* آلة كشف الشذوذ الجنسي [aalat kashf al sheḍhoḍh al jensy]; **fruit salad** *n* سَلاطة فواكه [Salaṭat fawakeh]; **passion fruit** *n* فاكهة العشق [Fakehat al-'aesh'q]
frustrated [frʌ'streɪtɪd] *adj* مخيب [muxajjib]
fry [fraɪ] *v* يَقلي [jaqli:]; **frying pan** *n* قلاية

[qala:jjatun]
fuel [fjʊəl] *n* وقود [waqunwdu]
fulfil [fʊl'fɪl] *v* يُنْجِز [junʒizu]
full [fʊl] *adj* ممتليء [mumtali:ʔʔ]; **full moon** *n* بَدْر [badrun]; **full stop** *n* نُقْطَة [nuqtˤatun]
full-time ['fʊl,taɪm] *adj* دوام كامل [Dawam kamel] ▷ *adv* بدوام كامل [Bedawam kaamel]
fully ['fʊlɪ] *adv* تماما [tama:man]
fumes [fju:mz] *npl* أبخِرَة [ʔabxiratun]; **exhaust fumes** *npl* أدخنة العادم [Adghenat al-'aadem]
fun [fʌn] *adj* مزحي [mazħij] ▷ *n* لهو [lahw]
funds [fʌndz] *npl* موارد مالية [Mawared maleyah]
funeral ['fju:nərəl] *n* جنازة [ʒana:za]; **funeral parlour** *n* قاعة إعداد الموتى ['qaat e'adad al-mawta]
funfair ['fʌn,fɛə] *n* ملاهي [mala:hijju]
funnel ['fʌnᵊl] *n* قمع [qamʕ]
funny ['fʌnɪ] *adj* مضحك [mudˤħik]
fur [fɜ:] *n* فرو [farw]; **fur coat** *n* معطف فرو [Me'ataf farw]
furious ['fjʊərɪəs] *adj* مهتاج [muhta:ʒ]
furnished ['fɜ:nɪʃt] *adj* مفروش [mafru:ʃ]
furniture ['fɜ:nɪtʃə] *n* أثاث [ʔaθa:θ]
further ['fɜ:ðə] *adj* تالي [ta:li:] ▷ *adv* علاوة على ذلك ['aelawah ala ḍalek]; **further education** *n* نظام التعليم الإضافي [neḍham al-ta'aleem al-eḍafey]
fuse [fju:z] *n* صمام كهربائي [Ṣamam kahrabaey]; **fuse box** *n* علبة الفيوز ['aolbat al-feyoz]
fusebox ['fju:z,bɒks] *n*; **Where is the fusebox?** أين توجد علبة المفاتيح الكهربية [ayna tojad 'ailbat al-mafateeḥ al-kahraba-eya?]
fuss [fʌs] *n* جَلَبة [ʒalaba]
fussy ['fʌsɪ] *adj* صَعْب الإرضاء (منمق) [Ṣa'ab al-erḍaa]
future ['fju:tʃə] *adj* مستقبلي [mustaqbalij] ▷ *n* مستقبل [mustaqbal]

g

Gabon [gə'bɒn] *n* الجابون [al-ʒa:bu:n]
gain [geɪn] *n* مَكْسَب [maksab] ▷ *v* يَربَح [jarbaħu]
gale [geɪl] *n* ريح هوجاء [Reyḥ ḥawjaa]
gallery ['gælərɪ] *n* جاليري [ʒa:li:ri:]; **art gallery** *n* جاليري فني [Jalery faney]
gallop ['gæləp] *n* عدو الفرس (جري) [adow al-faras] ▷ *v* يَجْري بالفرس [Yajree bel-faras]
gallstone ['gɔ:l,stəʊn] *n* حصاة المرارة [Haṣat al-mararah]
Gambia ['gæmbɪə] *n* جامبيا [ʒa:mbija:]
gamble ['gæmbᵊl] *v* يقُامِر [juqa:miru]
gambler ['gæmblə] *n* مقامر [muqa:mir]
gambling ['gæmblɪŋ] *n* مقامرة [muqa:mara]
game [geɪm] *n* مباراة [muba:ra:t]; **board game** *n* لعبة طاولة [Lo'abat ṭawlah]; **games console** *n* وحدة التحكم في ألعاب الفيديو [Wehdat al-tahakom fee al'aab al-vedyoo]
gang [gæŋ] *n* عصابة [ʕisˤa:ba]
gangster ['gæŋstə] *n* عضو في عصابة ['aoḍw fee eṣabah]
gap [gæp] *n* فجوة [faʒwa]
garage ['gærɑ:ʒ; -rɪdʒ] *n* جراج [ʒara:ʒ]; **Which is the key for the garage?** أين

يوجد مفتاح الجراج؟ [ayna yujad muftaaḥ al-jaraj?]
garbage [ˈɡɑːbɪdʒ] *n* نفاية [nufaːja]
garden [ˈɡɑːdᵊn] *n* حديقة [ħadiːqa]; **garden centre** *n* مشتل [maʃtalun]
gardener [ˈɡɑːdnə; ˈgardener] *n* بُستاني [bustaːnij]
gardening [ˈɡɑːdᵊnɪŋ; ˈgardening] *n* بَسْتَنة [bastana]
garlic [ˈɡɑːlɪk] *n* ثوم [θuːm]; **Is there any garlic in it?** هل به ثوم؟ [hal behe thoom?]
garment [ˈɡɑːmənt] *n* ثوب [θawb]
gas [ɡæs] *n* غاز [ɣaːz]; **gas cooker** *n* موقد يعمل بالغاز [Maw'qed ya'amal bel-ghaz]; **natural gas** *n* غاز طبيعي [ghaz ṭabeeaey]; **I can smell gas** أنني أشم رائحة غاز [ina-ny ashum ra-e-hat ghaaz]; **Where is the gas meter?** أين يوجد عداد الغاز؟ [ayna yujad 'aadad al-ghaz?]
gasket [ˈɡæskɪt] *n* سِدادة (مرسة شراع) [saddaːda]
gate [ɡeɪt] *n* بوابة [bawwaːba]; **Please go to gate...** توجه من فضلك إلى البوابة رقم... [tawa-jah min faḍlak ela al-bawa-ba ra'qum...]; **Which gate for the flight to...?** ما هي البوابة الخاصة بالرحلة المتجهة إلى... [ma heya al-baw-aba al-khaṣa bel-reḥla al-mutajiha ela...?]
gateau, gateaux [ˈɡætəʊ, ˈɡætəʊz] *n* جاتوه [ʒaːtuː]
gather [ˈɡæðə] *v* يَجتمِع [jaʒtamiʕu]
gauge [ɡeɪdʒ] *n* مقياس [miqjaːs] ▷ *v* يُعايِر [juʕaːjiru]
gaze [ɡeɪz] *v* يُحدِق [juħaddiqu]
gear [ɡɪə] *n* *(equipment)* جهاز [ʒihaːz], *(mechanism)* تعشيقة [taʕʃiːqa]; **gear box** *n* علبة التروس ['aolbat al-teroos]; **gear lever** *n* ذِراع الفتيس [dhera'a al-fetees]; **gear stick** *n* ذراع نقل السرعة [Dhera'a na'ql al-sor'aah]
gearbox [ˈɡɪəˌbɒks] *n*; **The gearbox is broken** لقد انكسرت علبة التروس [la'qad inkasarat 'ailbat al-tiroos]
gearshift [ˈɡɪəˌʃɪft] *n* مُغَيِّر السرعة [Moghaey al-sor'aah]
gel [dʒɛl] *n* جل [ʒil]; **hair gel** *n* جل الشعر [Jel al-sha'ar]
gem [dʒɛm] *n* حجر كريم [Ajar kareem]
Gemini [ˈdʒɛmɪˌnaɪ; -ˌniː] *n* الجوزاء [al-ʒawzaːʔu]
gender [ˈdʒɛndə] *n* النَوْع [an-nawʕu]
gene [dʒiːn] *n* جين وراثي [Jeen werathey]
general [ˈdʒɛnərəl; ˈdʒɛnrəl] *adj* عام [ʕaːm] ▷ *n* فكرة عامة [Fekrah 'aamah]; **general anaesthetic** *n* مٌخَدِر كلي [Mo-khader koley]; **general election** *n* انتخابات عامة [Entekhabat 'aamah]; **general knowledge** *n* معلومات عامة [Ma'aloomaat 'aamah]
generalize [ˈdʒɛnrəˌlaɪz] *v* يُعَمِم [juʕammimu]
generally [ˈdʒɛnrəlɪ] *adv* عادةً [ʕaːdatun]
generation [ˌdʒɛnəˈreɪʃən] *n* جيل [ʒiːl]
generator [ˈdʒɛnəˌreɪtə] *n* مولد [muwalid]
generosity [ˌdʒɛnəˈrɒsɪtɪ] *n* كَرَم [karam]
generous [ˈdʒɛnərəs; ˈdʒɛnrəs] *adj* سخي [saxij]
genetic [dʒɪˈnɛtɪk] *adj* جيني [ʒiːnnij]
genetically-modified [dʒɪˈnɛtɪklɪˈmɒdɪˌfaɪd] *adj* معدل وراثيا [Mo'aaddal weratheyan]
genetics [dʒɪˈnɛtɪks] *n* علم الوراثة [A'elm al-weratha]
genius [ˈdʒiːnɪəs; -njəs] *n* شخص عبقري [Shakhṣ'ab'qarey]
gentle [ˈdʒɛntᵊl] *adj* نبيل المحتد [Nabeel al-moḥtad]
gentleman, gentlemen [ˈdʒɛntᵊlmən, ˈdʒɛntᵊlmɛn] *n* رَجُل نبيل [Rajol nabeel]
gently [dʒɛntlɪ] *adv* بلطف [bilutˤfin]
gents' [dʒɛnts] *n* دَوْرة مياه للرجال [Dawrat meyah lel-rejal]
genuine [ˈdʒɛnjʊɪn] *adj* أصلي [ʔasˤlij]
geography [dʒɪˈɒɡrəfɪ] *n* جغرافيا [ʒuɣraːfjaː]
geology [dʒɪˈɒlədʒɪ] *n* جيولوجيا

[ʒjuːluːʒjaː]
Georgia [ˈdʒɔːdʒjə] *n (country)* جورجيا [ʒuːrʒjaː], *(US state)* ولاية جورجيا [Welayat jorjeya]
Georgian [ˈdʒɔːdʒjən] *adj* جورجي [ʒuːrʒij] ▷ *n (person)* مواطن جورجي [Mowaṭen jorjey]
geranium [dʒɪˈreɪnɪəm] *n* نبات الجيرانيوم [Nabat al-jeranyom]
gerbil [ˈdʒɜːbɪl] *n* يَربوع [jarbuːʕ]
geriatric [ˌdʒɛrɪˈætrɪk] *adj* شيخوخي [ʃajxuːxij] ▷ *n* طب الشيخوخة [Ṭeb al-shaykhokhah]
germ [dʒɜːm] *n* جرثومة [ʒurθuːma]
German [ˈdʒɜːmən] *adj* ألماني [ʔalmaːnij] ▷ *n (language)* اللغة الألمانية [Al loghah al almaniyah], *(person)* ألماني [ʔalmaːnij]; **German measles** *n* حصبة ألمانية [Haṣbah al-maneyah]
Germany [ˈdʒɜːmənɪ] *n* ألمانيا [ʔalmaːnijjaː]
gesture [ˈdʒɛstʃə] *n* إيماءة [ʔiːmaːʔa]
get [gɛt] *v* يَحصُل على [Taḥṣol ʻala], *(to a place)* يَحصُل على [Taḥṣol ʻala]
get away [gɛt əˈweɪ] *v* يَنْصَرف [jansˤarifu]
get back [gɛt bæk] *v* يَستَرِد [jastariddu]
get in [gɛt ɪn] *v* يركب [jarrkabu]
get into [gɛt ˈɪntə] *v* يَتوَرط في [Yatawaraṭ fee]
get off [gɛt ɒf] *v* ينزل [janzilu]
get on [gɛt ɒn] *v* يركب [jarrkabu]
get out [gɛt aʊt] *v* يَخرُج [jaxruʒu]
get over [gɛt ˈəʊvə] *v* يَتَغلب على [Yatghalab ʻala]
get through [gɛt θruː] *v*; **I can't get through** لا يمكنني الوصول إليه [la yam-kinuni al-wiṣool e-lay-he]
get together [gɛt təˈgɛðə] *v* يجتمع [jaʒtamiʕu]
get up [gɛt ʌp] *v* ينهض [janhadˤu]
Ghana [ˈgɑːnə] *n* غانا [ɣaːnaː]
Ghanaian [gɑːˈneɪən] *adj* غاني [ɣaːnij] ▷ *n* مواطن غاني [Mowaṭen ghaney]
ghost [gəʊst] *n* شبح [ʃabaħ]
giant [ˈdʒaɪənt] *adj* عملاق [ʕimlaːq] ▷ *n* مارد [maːrid]
gift [gɪft] *n* هبة [hiba]; **gift shop** *n* متجر هدايا [Matjar hadaya]; **gift voucher** *n* قسيمة هدية [ʻqaseemat hadeyah]
gifted [ˈgɪftɪd] *adj* موهوب [mawhuːb]
gigantic [dʒaɪˈgæntɪk] *adj* عملاق [ʕimlaːq]
giggle [ˈgɪgᵊl] *v* يُقَهْقِه [juqahqihu]
gin [dʒɪn] *n* شراب الجين المُسكِر (محلج القطن) [Sharaab al-jobn al-mosaker]
ginger [ˈdʒɪndʒə] *adj* بني مائل إلى الحُمرة [banniː maːʔilun ʔila alħumrati] ▷ *n* زَنْجَبيل [zanʒabiːl]
giraffe [dʒɪˈrɑːf; -ˈræf] *n* زرافة [zaraːfa]
girl [gɜːl] *n* بِنْت [bint]
girlfriend [ˈgɜːlˌfrɛnd] *n* صديقة [sˤadiːqa]
give [gɪv] *v* يُعْطِي [juʕtˤiː]
give back [gɪv bæk] *v* يَرُد [jaruddu]
give in [gɪv ɪn] *v* يَستسلم [jastaslimu]
give out [gɪv aʊt] *v* يُوَزِّع [juwazziʕu]
give up [gɪv ʌp] *v* يُقْلِع عن [Yoʼqleʼa an]
glacier [ˈglæsɪə; ˈgleɪs-] *n* نهر جليدي [Nahr jaleedey]
glad [glæd] *adj* سعيد [saʕiːd]
glamorous [ˈglæmərəs] *adj* فاتن [faːtin]
glance [glɑːns] *n* لمحة [lamħa] ▷ *v* يلمح [jalmaħu]
gland [glænd] *n* غدة [ɣuda]
glare [glɛə] *v* (يسطع) يُحملِق [juħamliqu]
glaring [ˈglɛərɪŋ] *adj* ساطع [saːtˤiʕ]
glass [glɑːs] *n* زُجَاج [zuʒaːʒ], *(vessel)* زُجَاج [zuʒaːʒ]; **magnifying glass** *n* عدسة مكبرة [ʻadasat takbeer]; **stained glass** *n* زجاج مُعَشَّق [Zojaj moashaʼq]
glasses [ˈglɑːsɪz] *npl* نظارة [nazˤzˤaːratun]
glazing [ˈgleɪzɪŋ] *n*; **double glazing** *n* طبقتين من الزجاج [Ṭabaʼqatayen men al-zojaj]
glider [ˈglaɪdə] *n* طائرة شراعية [Ṭaayearah ehraeyah]
gliding [ˈglaɪdɪŋ] *n* التحليق في الجو [Al-taḥleeʼq fee al-jaw]
global [ˈgləʊbᵊl] *adj* عالمي [ʕaːlamij]; **global warming** *n* ظاهرة الاحتباس

الحراري [dhaherat al-eḥtebas al-ḥararey]
globalization [ˌɡləʊbəlaɪˈzeɪʃən] *n* عَوْلَمَة [ʕawlama]
globe [ɡləʊb] *n* الكرة الأرضية [Al-korah al-ardheyah]
gloomy [ˈɡluːmɪ] *adj* كئيب [kaʔijb]
glorious [ˈɡlɔːrɪəs] *adj* جليل [ʒaliːl]
glory [ˈɡlɔːrɪ] *n* مجد [maʒd]
glove [ɡlʌv] *n* قفاز [quffaːz]; **glove compartment** *n* دُرج العربة [Dorj al-'aarabah]; **oven glove** *n* قفاز فرن ['qoffaz forn]; **rubber gloves** *npl* قفازات مطاطية ['qoffazat maṭaṭeyah]
glucose [ˈɡluːkəʊz; -kəʊs] *n* جلوكوز [ʒlukuːz]
glue [ɡluː] *n* غراء [ɣiraːʔ] ▷ *v* يُغَرِّي [juɣarriː]
gluten [ˈɡluːtən] *n* جلوتين [ʒluːtiːn]; **Could you prepare a meal without gluten?** هل يمكن إعداد وجبة خالية من الجلوتين؟ [hal yamken e'adad wajba khaliya min al-jilo-teen?]; **Do you have gluten-free dishes?** هل توجد أطباق خالية من الجلوتين؟ [hal tojad aṭba'q khaleya min al-jiloteen?]
go [ɡəʊ] *v* يَذهَب [jaðhabu]
go after [ɡəʊ ˈɑːftə] *v* يَسعَى وراء [Yas'aa waraa]
go ahead [ɡəʊ əˈhɛd] *v* ينطلق [jantˤaliqu]
goal [ɡəʊl] *n* هدف [hadaf]
goalkeeper [ˈɡəʊlˌkiːpə] *n* حارس المرمى [Hares al-marma]
goat [ɡəʊt] *n* ماعز [maːʕiz]
go away [ɡəʊ əˈweɪ] *v* يُغَادر مكانا [Yoghader makanan]
go back [ɡəʊ bæk] *v* يَرْجِع [jarʒiʕu]
go by [ɡəʊ baɪ] *v* يَمُرّ [jamurru]
god [ɡɒd] *n* إله [ʔilah]
godchild, godchildren [ˈɡɒdˌtʃaɪld, ˈɡɒdˌtʃɪldrən] *n* ربيب [rabiːb]
goddaughter [ˈɡɒdˌdɔːtə] *n* ربيبة [rabiːba]
godfather [ˈɡɒdˌfɑːðə] *n* *(baptism)* أب روحي [Af rooḥey], *(criminal leader)* رئيس عصابة [Raees eṣabah]
godmother [ˈɡɒdˌmʌðə] *n* الأم المُربية [al om almorabeyah]
go down [ɡəʊ daʊn] *v* ينزل [janzilu]
godson [ˈɡɒdˌsʌn] *n* ربيب [rabiːb]
goggles [ˈɡɒɡəlz] *npl* نظارة واقية [naḍharah wa'qeyah]
go in [ɡəʊ ɪn] *v* يَتدخل [jatadaxxalu]
gold [ɡəʊld] *n* ذَهَبْ [ðahab]
golden [ˈɡəʊldən] *adj* ذَهَبِي [ðahabij]
goldfish [ˈɡəʊldˌfɪʃ] *n* سمك ذهبي [Samak dhahabey]
gold-plated [ˈɡəʊldˈpleɪtɪd] *adj* مطلي بالذهب [Maṭley beldhahab]
golf [ɡɒlf] *n* رياضة الجولف [Reyadat al-jolf]; **golf club** *n* نادي الجولف [Nady al-jolf]; **golf course** *n* ملعب الجولف [Mal'aab al-jolf]
gone [ɡɒn] *adj* راحل [raːħil]
good [ɡʊd] *adj* جَيِد [ʒajjid]
goodbye [ˌɡʊdˈbaɪ] *excl* وداعا! [wadaːʕan]
good-looking [ˈɡʊdˈlʊkɪŋ] *adj* حسن المظهر [Hosn al-maḍhar]
good-natured [ˈɡʊdˈneɪtʃəd] *adj* دَمِث الأخلاق [Dameth al-akhla'q]
goods [ɡʊdz] *npl* بضائع [badˤaːʔiʕun]
go off [ɡəʊ ɒf] *v* ينقطع [janqatˤiʕu]
Google® [ˈɡuːɡəl] *v* يبحث على موقع جوجل® [jabħaθu ʕalaː mawqiʕi ʒuːʒl]
go on [ɡəʊ ɒn] *v* يستمر [jastamirru]
goose, geese [ɡuːs, ɡiːs] *n* إوزة [ʔiwazza]; **goose pimples** *npl* قشعريرة الجلد ['qash'aarerat al-jeld]
gooseberry [ˈɡʊzbərɪ; -brɪ] *n* كشمش [kuʃmuʃ]
go out [ɡəʊ aʊt] *v* يُغادِر المكان [Yoghader al-makanan]
go past [ɡəʊ pɑːst] *v* يَتَجاوز [jatazaːwazu]
gorgeous [ˈɡɔːdʒəs] *adj* فائق الجمال [Faae'q al-jamal]
gorilla [ɡəˈrɪlə] *n* غوريلا [ɣuːriːlaː]
go round [ɡəʊ raʊnd] *v* يَلِفْ [jalifu]
gospel [ˈɡɒspəl] *n* إنجيل [ʔinʒiːl]
gossip [ˈɡɒsɪp] *n* نَميمة [namiːma] ▷ *v*

يَنْهَمِك في القيل والقال [Yanhamek fee al-'qeel wa al-'qaal]
go through [gəʊ θruː] *v* يَجْتَاز [jaʒtaːzu]
go up [gəʊ ʌp] *v* يَرتفِع [jartafiʕu]
government ['gʌvənmənt; 'gʌvəmənt] *n* حكومة [ħukuwamt]
gown [gaʊn] *n*; **dressing gown** *n* رُوب الحَمَّام [Roob al-ḥamam]
GP [dʒiː piː] *abbr* طبيب باطني [Ṭabeeb baṭney]
GPS [dʒiː piː ɛs] *abbr* نظام تحديد المواقع العالمي [nizˤaːmun taħdiːdu almuwaːqiʕi alʕaːlamijji]
grab [græb] *v* يَتَلَقف [jatalaqqafu]
graceful ['greɪsfʊl] *adj* لَبِق [labiq]
grade [greɪd] *n* مَنْزِلة [manzila]
gradual ['grædjʊəl] *adj* تدريجي [tadriːʒij]
gradually ['grædjʊəlɪ] *adv* بالتدريج [bi-at-tadriːʒi]
graduate ['grædjʊɪt] *n* خريج [xirriːʒ]
graduation [ˌgrædjʊ'eɪʃən] *n* تخرج [taxarruʒ]
graffiti, graffito [græ'fiːtiː, græ'fiːtəʊ] *npl* نقوش أثرية [No'qoosh athareyah]
grain [greɪn] *n* حبة [ħabba]
grammar ['græmə] *n* علم النحو والصرف ['aelm al-naḥw wal-ṣarf]
grammatical [grə'mætɪkᵊl] *adj* نحوي [naħwij]
gramme [græm] *n* جرام [ʒraːm]
grand [grænd] *adj* عظيم [ʕazˤiːm]
grandchild ['grænˌtʃaɪld] *n* حفيد [ħafiːd]; **grandchildren** *npl* أحفاد [ʔaħfaːdun]
granddad ['grænˌdæd] *n* جد [ʒadd]
granddaughter ['grænˌdɔːtə] *n* حفيدة [ħafiːda]
grandfather ['grænˌfɑːðə] *n* جد [ʒadd]
grandma ['grænˌmɑː] *n* جدة [ʒadda]
grandmother ['grænˌmʌðə] *n* أم الأب أو الأم [Om al-ab aw al-om]
grandpa ['grænˌpɑː] *n* جد [ʒadd]
grandparents ['grænˌpɛərəntz] *npl* الجدين [al-ʒaddajni]
grandson ['grænsʌn; 'grænd-] *n* ابن الإبن [Ebn el-ebn]
granite ['grænɪt] *n* حجر الجرانيت [Ḥajar al-jraneet]
granny ['grænɪ] *n* جدة [ʒadda]
grant [grɑːnt] *n* منحة [minħa]
grape [greɪp] *n* عنب [ʕinab]
grapefruit ['greɪpˌfruːt] *n* جريب فروت [ʒriːb fruːt]
graph [grɑːf; græf] *n* تخطيط بياني [Takhṭeeṭ bayany]
graphics ['græfɪks] *npl* رسوم جرافيك [Rasm jrafek]
grasp [grɑːsp] *v* يَقْبِض على [jaqbudˤu ʕalaː]
grass [grɑːs] *n (informer)* واشي [waːʃiː], *(marijuana)* حشيش مخدر [Hashesh mokhader], *(plant)* عشب [ʕuʃb]
grasshopper ['grɑːsˌhɒpə] *n* جراد الجندب [Jarad al-jandab]
grate [greɪt] *v* (يحك بسطح خشن) يَبْشُر [jabʃuru]
grateful ['greɪtfʊl] *adj* ممتن [mumtann]
grave [greɪv] *n* قبر [qabr]
gravel ['grævᵊl] *n* حصى [ħasˤaː]
gravestone ['greɪvˌstəʊn] *n* شاهد القبر [Shahed al-'qabr]
graveyard ['greɪvˌjɑːd] *n* مدفن [madfan]
gravy ['greɪvɪ] *n* مرقة اللحم [Mara'qat al-laḥm]
grease [griːs] *n* شحم [ʃaħm]
greasy ['griːzɪ; -sɪ] *adj* دُهْني [duhnij]
great [greɪt] *adj* عظيم [ʕazˤiːm]
Great Britain ['greɪt 'brɪtᵊn] *n* بريطانيا العظمى [Beretanyah al-'aoḍhma]
great-grandfather ['greɪt'grænˌfɑːðə] *n* الجَدّ الأكبر [Al-jad al-akbar]
great-grandmother ['greɪt'grænˌmʌðə] *n* الجدة الأكبر [Al-jaddah al-akbar]
Greece [griːs] *n* اليونان [al-juːnaːni]
greedy ['griːdɪ] *adj* جشع [ʒaʃiʕ]
Greek [griːk] *adj* يوناني [juːnaːnij] ▷ *n* *(language)* اللغة اليونانية [Al-loghah al-yonaneyah], *(person)* يوناني [juːnaːnij]

green [gri:n] *adj (colour)* أخضر [ʔaxdˤar], *(inexperienced)* مغفّل [muɣaffal] ▷ *n* أخضر [ʔaxdˤar]; **green salad** *n* سَلاطة خضراء [Salaṭat khadraa]
greengrocer's ['gri:nˌgrəʊsəz] *n* متجر الخضر والفاكهة [Matjar al-khoḍar wal-fakehah]
greenhouse ['gri:nˌhaʊs] *n* صوبة زراعية [Ṣobah zera'aeyah]
Greenland ['gri:nlənd] *n* جرينلاند [ʒri:nala:ndi]
greet [gri:t] *v* يُرحِب ب [Yoraḥeb bee]
greeting ['gri:tɪŋ] *n* تحية [taħijja]; **greetings card** *n* بطاقة تهنئة [Beṭaqat tahneaa]
grey [greɪ] *adj* رمادي [rama:dij]
grey-haired [ˌgreɪ'hɛəd] *adj* رمادي الشعر [Ramadey al-sha'ar]
grid [grɪd] *n* شبكة قضبان مُتصالِبة [Shabakat 'qodban motaṣalebah]
grief [gri:f] *n* أسى [ʔasa:]
grill [grɪl] *n* شواية [ʃawwa:ja] ▷ *v* يَشوي [jaʃwi:]
grilled [grɪld; grilled] *adj* مشوي [maʃwij]
grim [grɪm] *adj* مروع [murawwiʕ]
grin [grɪn] *n* ابتسامة عريضة [Ebtesamah areeḍah] ▷ *v* يكشّر [jukaʃʃiru]
grind [graɪnd] *v* يَطْحَن [jatˤħanu]
grip [grɪp] *v* يمسك بإحكام [Yamsek be-ehkam]
gripping [grɪpɪŋ] *adj* مُثير [muθi:r]
grit [grɪt] *n* حبيبات خشنة [Ḥobaybat khashabeyah]
groan [grəʊn] *v* يئِنّ [jaʔinnu]
grocer ['grəʊsə] *n* بَقّال [baqqa:l]
groceries ['grəʊsərɪz] *npl* بِقَالة [baqa:latun]
grocer's ['grəʊsəz] *n* متجر البقالة [Matjar al-be'qalah]
groom [gru:m; grʊm] *n* سائس خيل [Saaes kheel], *(bridegroom)* عريس [ʕari:s]
grope [grəʊp] *v* يَتلَمس طريقه في الظلام [Yatalamas ṭaree'qah fee al-ḍhalam]
gross [grəʊs] *adj (fat)* هائل [ha:ʔil], *(income etc.)* هائل [ha:ʔil]
grossly [grəʊslɪ] *adv* بفظاظة [bifazˤa:zˤatin]
ground [graʊnd] *n* سَطح الأرض [Saṭh alarḍ] ▷ *v* يَضع على الأرض [Yaḍa'a ala al-arḍ]; **ground floor** *n* الدور الأرضي [Aldoor al-arḍey]
group [gru:p] *n* جماعة [ʒama:ʕa]
grouse [graʊs] *n (complaint)* شكوى [ʃakwa:], *(game bird)* طائر الطيهوج [Ṭaaer al-ṭayhooj]
grow [grəʊ] *vi* ينمو [janmu:] ▷ *vt* يَنمو [janmu:]
growl [graʊl] *v* يُهْدِر [juhdiru]
grown-up [grəʊnʌp] *n* بالغ [ba:liɣ]
growth [grəʊθ] *n* نمو [numuww]
grow up [grəʊ ʌp] *v* ينضج [jandˤuʒu]
grub [grʌb] *n* يَرَقْة دودية [Yara'qah doodeyah]
grudge [grʌdʒ] *n* ضغينة [dˤaɣi:na]
gruesome ['gru:səm] *adj* رَهيب [rahi:b]
grumpy ['grʌmpɪ] *adj* سَئ الطبع [Sayea al-ṭabe'a]
guarantee [ˌgærən'ti:] *n* ضمان [dˤama:n] ▷ *v* يَضمن [jadˤmanu]; **It's still under guarantee** إنها لا تزال داخل فترة الضمان [inaha la tazaal dakhel fatrat al-ḍaman]
guard [gɑ:d] *n* حارس [ħa:ris] ▷ *v* يَحْرُس [jaħrusu]; **security guard** *n* حارس الأمن [Ḥares al-amn]
Guatemala [ˌgwɑ:tə'mɑ:lə] *n* جواتيمالا [ʒwa:ti:ma:la:]
guess [gɛs] *n* تخمين [taxmi:n] ▷ *v* يُخمِن [juxamminu]
guest [gɛst] *n* ضيف [dˤajf]
guesthouse ['gɛstˌhaʊs] *n* دار ضيافة [Dar eḍafeyah]
guide [gaɪd] *n* مرشد [murʃid] ▷ *v* مرشد [murʃidun]; **guide dog** *n* كلب هادي مدرب للمكفوفين [Kalb hadey modarab lel-makfoofeen]; **guided tour** *n* جولة إرشادية [Jawlah ershadeyah]; **tour guide** *n* مرشد سياحي [Morshed seyaḥey]; **Do you have a guide to local walks?** هل يوجد لديكم مرشد لجولات السير المحلية؟ [hal yujad

laday-kum murshid le-jaw-laat al-sayr al-mahal-iya?]; **Is there a guide who speaks English?** هل يوجد مرشد سياحي يتحدث باللغة الإنجليزية؟ [hal yujad murshid seyahy yata-hadath bil-lugha al-injile-ziya]

guidebook ['gaɪd,bʊk] *n* كُتَيِّب الإرشادات [Kotayeb al-ershadat]

guilt [gɪlt] *n* ذَنْب [ðanab]

guilty ['gɪltɪ] *adj* مذنب [muðnib]

Guinea ['gɪnɪ] *n* غينيا [ɣi:nja:]; **guinea pig** *n (for experiment)* حقل للتجارب [Ha'ql lel-tajareb], *(rodent)* خنزير غينيا [Khnzeer ghemyah]

guitar [gɪ'tɑː] *n* جيتار [ʒi:ta:r]

gum [gʌm] *n* لثة [laθatt]; **chewing gum** *n* علكة [ʕilkatun]

gun [gʌn] *n* بندقية [bunduqijja]; **machine gun** *n* رشاش [raʃʃa:ʃun]

gust [gʌst] *n* انفجار عاطفي [Enfejar 'aatefy]

gut [gʌt] *n* معي [maʕjj]

guy [gaɪ] *n* فَتى [fata:]

Guyana [gaɪ'ænə] *n* جيانا [ʒuja:na:]

gym [dʒɪm] *n* جمانزيوم [ʒimna:zju:mi]

gymnast ['dʒɪmnæst] *n* أخصائي الجمنازيوم [akheșaaey al-jemnazyom]

gymnastics [dʒɪm'næstɪks] *npl* تدريبات الجمنازيوم [Tadreebat al-jemnazyoom]

gynaecologist [,gaɪnɪ'kɒlədʒɪst] *n* طبيب أمراض نساء [Ṭabeeb amraḍ nesaa]

gypsy ['dʒɪpsɪ] *n* غَجَرِيّ [ɣaʒarij]

h

habit ['hæbɪt] *n* عادة سلوكية ['aadah selokeyah]

hack [hæk] *v* يَتَسلل (كمبيوتر) [jatasallalu]

hacker ['hækə] *n* قراصنة الكمبيوتر (كمبيوتر) ['qarașenat al-kombyotar]

haddock ['hædək] *n* سمك الحدوق [Samak al-ḥadoo'q]

haemorrhoids ['hɛmə,rɔɪdz] *npl* داء البواسير [Daa al-bawaseer]

haggle ['hægᵊl] *v* يُساوم [jusa:wimu]

hail [heɪl] *n* بَرَد (مطر) [bard] ▷ *v* يَنْزِلُ البَرَد [Yanzel al-barad]

hair [hɛə] *n* شَعْر [ʃaʕr]; **hair gel** *n* جل الشعر [Jel al-sha'ar]; **hair spray** *n* سْبراي الشعر [Sbray al-sha'ar]

hairband ['hɛə,bænd] *n* عصابة الرأس ['eșabat al-raas]

hairbrush ['hɛə,brʌʃ] *n* فرشاة الشعر [Forshat al-sha'ar]

haircut ['hɛə,kʌt] *n* قصة الشعر ['qașat al-sha'ar]

hairdo ['hɛə,duː] *n* تسريحة الشعر [Tasreehat al-sha'ar]

hairdresser ['hɛə,drɛsə] *n* مُصفف الشعر [Moșafef al-sha'ar]

hairdresser's ['hɛə,drɛsəz] *n* صالون

حلاقة [Ṣalon ḥelaqah]
hairdryer ['hɛəˌdraɪə] *n* مُجَفِف الشعر [Mojafef al-sha'ar]
hairgrip ['hɛəˌɡrɪp] *n* دبوس شعر [Daboos sha'ar]
hairstyle ['hɛəˌstaɪl] *n* تصفيف الشعر [taṣfeef al-sha'ar]
hairy ['hɛərɪ] *adj* كثير الشعر [Katheer sha'ar]
Haiti ['heɪtɪ; hɑː'iːtɪ] *n* هايتي [ha:jti:]
half [hɑːf] *adj* نصفي [nisˁfaj] ▷ *adv* نصفيا [nisˁfijja:] ▷ *n* نصف [nisˁf]; **half board** *n* نصف إقامة [Neṣf e'qamah]; **It's half past two** الساعة الثانية والنصف [al-sa'aa al-thaneya wal-nuṣf]
half-hour ['hɑːfˌaʊə] *n* نصف ساعة [Neṣf saa'aah]
half-price ['hɑːfˌpraɪs] *adj* نصف السعر [Neṣf al-se'ar] ▷ *adv* بنصف السعر [Be-nesf al-se'ar]
half-term ['hɑːfˌtɜːm] *n* عطلة نصف الفصل الدراسي ['aoṭlah neṣf al-faṣl al-derasey]
half-time ['hɑːfˌtaɪm] *n* نِصْف الوقت [Nesf al-wa'qt]
halfway [ˌhɑːf'weɪ] *adv* إلى منتصف المسافة [Ela montaṣaf al-masafah]
hall [hɔːl] *n* قاعة [qa:ʕa]; **town hall** *n* دار البلدية [Dar al-baladeyah]
hallway ['hɔːlˌweɪ] *n* رُدهَة [radha]
halt [hɔːlt] *n* وقوف [wuqu:f]
ham [hæm] *n* فخذ الخنزير المدخن [Fakhdh al-khenzeer al-modakhan]
hamburger ['hæmˌbɜːɡə] *n* هامبرجر [ha:mbarʒar]
hammer ['hæmə] *n* شَاكوش [ʃa:ku:ʃ]
hammock ['hæmək] *n* الأرجوحة الشبكية [Al orjoha al shabakiya]
hamster ['hæmstə] *n* حيوان الهمستر [Heyawaan al-hemester]
hand [hænd] *n* يد [jadd] ▷ *v* يُسَلِم [jusallimu]; **hand luggage** *n* أمتعة محمولة في اليد [Amte'aah maḥmoolah fee al-yad]; **Where can I wash my hands?** أين يمكن أن أغسل يدي؟ [ayna yamken an aghsil yady?]
handbag ['hændˌbæɡ] *n* حقيبة يد [Ha'qeebat yad]
handball ['hændˌbɔːl] *n* كرة اليد [Korat al-yad]
handbook ['hændˌbʊk] *n* دليل [dali:l]
handbrake ['hændˌbreɪk] *n* فرملة يَدّ [Farmalat yad]
handcuffs ['hændˌkʌfs] *npl* القيود [al-quju:du]
handicap ['hændɪˌkæp] *n*; **My handicap is...** ...إعاقتي هي [...e'aa'qaty heya]; **What's your handicap?** ما إعاقتك؟ [ma e-'aa'qa-taka?]
handkerchief ['hæŋkətʃɪf; -tʃiːf] *n* منديل قماش [Mandeel 'qomash]
handle ['hændᵊl] *n* مقبض [miqbadˁ] ▷ *v* يُعَامل [juʕa:malu]; **The door handle has come off** لقد سقط مقبض الباب [la'qad sa'qaṭa me-'qbaḍ al-baab]
handlebars ['hændᵊlˌbɑːz] *npl* مقود [miqwadun]
handmade [ˌhænd'meɪd] *adj* يَدوي [jadawij]
hands-free ['hændzˌfriː] *adj* غير يدوي [Ghayr yadawey]; **hands-free kit** *n* سماعات [samma:ʕa:tun]
handsome ['hændsəm] *adj* وسيم [wasi:m]
handwriting ['hændˌraɪtɪŋ] *n* خط اليد [Khaṭ al-yad]
handy ['hændɪ] *adj* في المتناول [Fee almotanawal]
hang [hæŋ] *vi* يَشنِق [jaʃniqu] ▷ *vt* يُعَلِق [juʕalliqu]
hanger ['hæŋə] *n* حمالة ثياب [Hammalt theyab]
hang-gliding ['hæŋ'ɡlaɪdɪŋ] *n* رياضة الطائرة الشراعية الصغيرة [Reyadar al-Ṭaayearah al-ehraeyah al-ṣagherah]
hang on [hæŋ ɒn] *v* ينتظر [jantazˁiru]
hangover ['hæŋˌəʊvə] *n* عادة من الماضى ['aadah men al-maḍey]
hang up [hæŋ ʌp] *v* يَضَع سَمّاعَة التلفون [jadˁaʕu samma:ʕata attilfu:n]

hankie ['hæŋkɪ] *n* منديل [mindi:l]
happen ['hæpᵊn] *v* يَحْدُث [jaħduθu]
happily ['hæpɪlɪ] *adv* بسعادة [Besa'aaadah]
happiness ['hæpɪnɪs] *n* سَعادة [saʕa:da]
happy ['hæpɪ] *adj* سعيد [saʕi:d]; **Happy birthday!** عيد ميلاد سعيد ['aeed meelad sa'aeed]
harassment ['hærəsmənt] *n* مُضايقة [mudˤa:jaqa]
harbour ['hɑːbə] *n* ميناء [mi:na:ʔ]
hard [hɑːd] *adj (difficult)* صَعْب [sˤaʕb], *(firm, rigid)* صَلْب [sˤalb] ▷ *adv* بقوة [Be-'qowah]; **hard disk** *n* قرص صلب ['qorṣ ṣalb]; **hard shoulder** *n* كتف طريق صلب [Katef ṭaree'q ṣalb]
hardboard ['hɑːdˌbɔːd] *n* لوح صلب [Looḥ ṣolb]
hardly ['hɑːdlɪ] *adv* بالكَاد [bil-ka:di]
hard up [hɑːd ʌp] *adj* معسر [muʕassir]
hardware ['hɑːdˌwɛə] *n* مكونات مادية [Mokawenat madeyah]
hare [hɛə] *n* أرنب [ʔarnab]
harm [hɑːm] *v* يَضُر [jadˤurru]
harmful ['hɑːmfʊl] *adj* مؤذي [muʔði:]
harmless ['hɑːmlɪs] *adj* غير مؤذ [Ghayer modh]
harp [hɑːp] *n* قيثار [qi:θa:ra]
harsh [hɑːʃ] *adj* خشن [xaʃin]
harvest ['hɑːvɪst] *n* حصاد [ħasˤa:d] ▷ *v* يحصد [jaħsˤudu]
hastily [heɪstɪlɪ] *adv* في عُجالة [Fee 'aojalah]
hat [hæt] *n* قبعة [qubaʕa]
hatchback ['hætʃˌbæk] *n* سيارة بباب خلفى [Sayarah be-bab khalfey]
hate [heɪt] *v* يَبْغَض [jabɣadˤu]
hatred ['heɪtrɪd] *n* بغض [buɣdˤ]
haunted ['hɔːntɪd] *adj* مُطَارَد [mutˤa:rad]
have [hæv] *v* يَمْلِك [jamliku]
have to [hæv tʊ] *v* يَجِب عليه [Yajeb alayh]
hawthorn ['hɔːˌθɔːn] *n* زعرور بلدي [Za'aroor baladey]
hay [heɪ] *n* تبن [tibn]; **hay fever** *n* مرض حمى القش [Maraḍ ḥomma al-'qash]
haystack ['heɪˌstæk] *n* كومة مضغوطة من القش [Kawmah maḍghoṭah men al-'qash]
hazelnut ['heɪzᵊlˌnʌt] *n* البندق [al-bunduqi]
he [hiː] *pron* هو
head [hɛd] *n (body part)* رَأْس [raʔs], *(principal)* قائد [qa:ʔid] ▷ *v* يَرْأَس [jarʔasu]; **deputy head** *n* نائب الرئيس [Naeb al-raaes]; **head office** *n* مكتب رئيسي [Maktab a'ala]
headache ['hɛdˌeɪk] *n* صُدَاع [sˤuda:ʕ]
headlamp ['hɛdˌlæmp] *n* مصباح علوي [Mesbaḥ 'aolwey]
headlight ['hɛdˌlaɪt] *n* مصباح أمامى [Mesbaḥ amamey]
headline ['hɛdˌlaɪn] *n* عُنوان رئيسي ['aonwan raaesey]
headphones ['hɛdˌfəʊnz] *npl* سماعات الرأس [Samaat al-raas]
headquarters [ˌhɛd'kwɔːtəz] *npl* مراكز رئيسية [Marakez raeaseyah]
headroom ['hɛdˌrʊm; -ˌruːm] *n* فتحة سقف السيارة [fatḥ at saa'qf al-sayaarah]
headscarf, headscarves ['hɛdˌskɑːf, 'hɛdˌskɑːvz] *n* وِشاح غطاء الرأس [Weshaḥ gheṭaa al-raas]
headteacher ['hɛdˌtiːtʃə] *n* مدرس أول [Modares awal]
heal [hiːl] *v* يشفى [juʃfa:]
health [hɛlθ] *n* صحة [sˤiħħa]
healthy ['hɛlθɪ] *adj* صحي [sˤiħij]
heap [hiːp] *n* كومة [ku:ma]
hear [hɪə] *v* يَسمَع [jasmaʕu]
hearing ['hɪərɪŋ] *n* سَمْع [samʕ]; **hearing aid** *n* وسائل المساعدة السمعية [Wasael al-mosa'adah al-sam'aeyah]
heart [hɑːt] *n* قلب [qalb]; **heart attack** *n* أزمة قلبية [Azmah 'qalbeyah]; **I have a heart condition** أعاني من حالة مرضية في القلب [o-'aany min ḥala maraḍiya fee al-'qalb]
heartbroken ['hɑːtˌbrəʊkən] *adj* مكسور القلب من شدة الحزن [Maksoor

al-'qalb men shedat al-ḥozn]
heartburn ['hɑːtˌbɜːn] *n* حرقة في فم المعدة [Ḥor'qah fee fom al-ma'adah]
heat [hiːt] *n* حرارة [ħaraːra] ▷ *v* يُسَخِن [jusaxxinu]; **I can't sleep for the heat** لا يمكنني النوم بسبب حرارة الغرفة [la yam-kinuni al-nawm be-sabab ḥararat al-ghurfa]
heater ['hiːtə] *n* سخان [saxxaːn]; **How does the water heater work?** كيف يعمل سخان المياه؟ [kayfa ya'amal sikhaan al-meaah?]
heather ['hɛðə] *n* نبات الخَلَنج [Nabat al-khalnaj]
heating ['hiːtɪŋ] *n* تسخين [tasxiːn]; **central heating** *n* تدفئة مركزية [Tadfeah markazeyah]
heat up [hiːt ʌp] *v* يُسَخِن [junsaxxinu]
heaven ['hɛvᵊn] *n* جَنّة [ʒanna]
heavily ['hɛvɪlɪ] *adv* بصورة مُكَثّفة [Beṣorah mokathafah]
heavy ['hɛvɪ] *adj* ثقيل [θaqiːl]; **This is too heavy** إنه ثقيل جدا [inaho tha'qeel jedan]
hedge [hɛdʒ] *n* سِياج من الشجيرات [Seyaj men al-shojayrat]
hedgehog ['hɛdʒˌhɒg] *n* قنفذ [qunfuð]
heel [hiːl] *n* كعب [kaʕb]; **high heels** *npl* كعوب عالية [Ko'aoob 'aleyah]
height [haɪt] *n* ارتفاع [irtifaːʕ]
heir [ɛə] *n* وريث [wariːθ]
heiress ['ɛərɪs] *n* وريثة [wariːθa]
helicopter ['hɛlɪˌkɒptə] *n* هيلكوبتر [hiːlikuːbtir]
hell [hɛl] *n* جحيم [ʒaħiːm]
hello [hɛ'ləʊ] *excl* أهلا! [ʔahlan]
helmet ['hɛlmɪt] *n* خوذة [xuwða]; **Can I have a helmet?** هل يمكن أن أحصل على خوذة؟ [hal yamken an aḥṣal 'aala khoo-dha?]
help [hɛlp] *n* مساعدة [musaːʕada] ▷ *v* يُساعد [jusaːʕidu]; **Fetch help quickly!** سرعة طلب المساعدة [isri'a be-ṭalab al-musa-'aada]; **Help!** مساعدة [musaːʕadatun]
helpful ['hɛlpfʊl] *adj* مفيد [mufiːd]
helpline ['hɛlpˌlaɪn] *n* حبل الإنقاذ [Habl elen'qadh]
hen [hɛn] *n* دجاجة [daʒaːʒa]; **hen night** *n* ليلة خروج الزوجات فقط [Laylat khorooj alzawjaat fa'qaṭ]
hepatitis [ˌhɛpə'taɪtɪs] *n* التهاب الكبد [El-tehab al-kabed]
her [hɜː; hə; ə] *pron* ضمير الغائبة المتصل, خاص بالمفردة الغائبة
herbs [hɜːbz] *npl* أعشاب [ʔaʕʃaːbun]
herd [hɜːd] *n* سِرب [sirb]
here [hɪə] *adv* هنا [hunaː]; **I'm here for work** أنا هنا للعمل [ana huna lel-'aamal]; **I'm here on my own** أنا هنا بمفردي [ana huna be-mufrady]
hereditary [hɪ'rɛdɪtərɪ; -trɪ] *adj* وراثي [wiraːθij]
heritage ['hɛrɪtɪdʒ] *n* موروث [mawruːθ]
hernia ['hɜːnɪə] *n* فتق [fatq]
hero ['hɪərəʊ] *n* بطل *(novel)* [batˤal]
heroin ['hɛrəʊɪn] *n* هيروين [hiːrwiːn]
heroine ['hɛrəʊɪn] *n* بَطَلة [batˤala]
heron ['hɛrən] *n* مالك الحزين [Malek al ḥazeen]
herring ['hɛrɪŋ] *n* سمك الرِنجَة [Samakat al-renjah]
hers [hɜːz] *pron* خاصتها
herself [hə'sɛlf] *pron* نفسها; **She has hurt herself** لقد جرحت نفسها [la'qad jara-ḥat naf-saha]
hesitate ['hɛzɪˌteɪt] *v* يَتَردد [jataraddadu]
heterosexual [ˌhɛtərəʊ'sɛksjʊəl] *adj* مشتهِ للجنس الآخر [Mashtah lel-jens al-aakahar]
HGV [eɪtʃ dʒiː viː] *abbr* مركبات البضائع الثقيلَة [Markabat albaḍaaea altha'qeelah]
hi [haɪ] *excl* مرحبا! [marħaban]
hiccups ['hɪkʌps] *npl* زُغُطَّة [zuɣtˤatun]
hidden ['hɪdᵊn] *adj* خفي [xafij]
hide [haɪd] *vi* يَختَبئ [jaxtabiʔ] ▷ *vt* يُخفِي [juxfiː]
hide-and-seek [ˌhaɪdænd'siːk] *n* لعبة الاستغماية [Lo'abat al-estoghomayah]
hideous ['hɪdɪəs] *adj* بَشِعْ [baʃiʕ]

hifi [ˈhaɪˈfaɪ] *n* هاي فاي [Hay fay]
high [haɪ] *adj* عالي [ʕa:lijju] ▷ *adv* مرتفع [murtafiʕun]; **high heels** *npl* كعوب عالية [Ko'aoob 'aleyah]; **high jump** *n* قفزة عالية ['qafzah 'aaleyah]; **high season** *n* موسم ازدهار [Mawsem ezdehar]
highchair [ˈhaɪˌtʃɛə] *n* كُرْسي مُرتَفِع [Korsey mortafe'a]
high-heeled [ˈhaɪˌhiːld] *adj* كعب عالى [Ka'ab 'aaaley]
highlight [ˈhaɪˌlaɪt] *n* جزء ذو أهمية خاصة [Joza dho ahammeyah khaṣah] ▷ *v* يُلْقي الضوء على [Yol'qy al-ḍawa 'aala]
highlighter [ˈhaɪˌlaɪtə] *n* مادة تجميلية تبرز الملامح [Madah tajmeeleyah tobrez al-malameḥ]
high-rise [ˈhaɪˌraɪz] *n* بِنَايَة عالية [Benayah 'aaleyah]
hijack [ˈhaɪˌdʒæk] *v* يَختطِف [jaxtatˤifu]
hijacker [ˈhaɪˌdʒækə] *n* مُختَطِف [muxtatˤif]
hike [haɪk] *n* نزهة طويلة سيراً على الأقدام [nazhatun tˤawi:latun sajran ʕala: alʔaqda:mi]
hiking [haɪkɪŋ] *n* تنزه [tanazzuh]
hilarious [hɪˈlɛərɪəs] *adj* مرح [maraħ]
hill [hɪl] *n* تل [tall]; **I'd like to go hill walking** أريد صعود التل سيرا على الأقدام [areed ṣi'aood al-tal sayran 'aala al-a'qdaam]
hill-walking [ˈhɪlˌwɔːkɪŋ] *n* التنزه بين المرتفعات [Altanazoh bayn al-mortaf'aat]
him [hɪm; ɪm] *pron* ضمير المفرد الغائب
himself [hɪmˈsɛlf; ɪmˈsɛlf] *pron* نفسه; **He has cut himself** لقد جرح نفسه [la'qad jara-ḥa naf-sehe]
Hindu [ˈhɪnduː; hɪnˈduː] *adj* هندوسي [hindu:sij] ▷ *n* هندوسي [hindu:sij]
Hinduism [ˈhɪndʊˌɪzəm] *n* هندوسية [hindu:sijja]
hinge [hɪndʒ] *n* مِفصلة [mifsˤala]
hint [hɪnt] *n* تلميح [talmi:ħ] ▷ *v* يَرْمُز إلى [Yarmoz ela]
hip [hɪp] *n* رَدف الجسم [Radf al-jesm]
hippie [ˈhɪpɪ] *n* هِيبِزْ [hi:biz]
hippo [ˈhɪpəʊ] *n* فرس النهر [Faras al-nahr]
hippopotamus, hippopotami [ˌhɪpəˈpɒtəməs, ˌhɪpəˈpɒtəmaɪ] *n* فرس النهر [Faras al-nahr]
hire [ˈhaɪə] *n* أجَّرَ [ʔaʒʒara] ▷ *v* يستأجر [jastaʔʒiru]; **car hire** *n* إيجار سيارة [Ejar sayarah]; **hire car** *n* استئجار سيارة [isti-jar sayara]
his [hɪz; ɪz] *adj* خاصته ▷ *pron* ضمير الغائب المتصل
historian [hɪˈstɔːrɪən] *n* مُؤَرِّخ [muʔarrix]
historical [hɪˈstɒrɪkᵊl] *adj* تاريخي [ta:ri:xij]
history [ˈhɪstərɪ; ˈhɪstrɪ] *n* تاريخ [ta:ri:x]
hit [hɪt] *n* ضربة [dˤarba] ▷ *v* يُصْيب [jusˤi:bu]
hitch [hɪtʃ] *n* حركة مفاجئة [Ḥarakah mofajeah]
hitchhike [ˈhɪtʃˌhaɪk] *v* يُسافر متطفلًا [Yosaafer motaṭafelan]
hitchhiker [ˈhɪtʃˌhaɪkə] *n* مسافر يوقف السيارات ليركبها مجانا [Mosafer yo'qef al-sayarat le-yarkabha majanan]
hitchhiking [ˈhɪtʃˌhaɪkɪŋ] *n* طلب التوصيل [Ṭalab al-tawseel]
HIV *abbr* إصابة بالإيدز- إيجابية! [Eṣabah bel-eedz – ejabeyah!]
HIV-negative [eɪtʃ aɪ viː ˈnɛgətɪv] *adj* إصابة بالإيدز- سلبية [Eṣaba bel edz – sal-beyah]
HIV-positive [eɪtʃ aɪ viː ˈpɒzɪtɪv] *adj* إصابة بالإيدز- إيجابية [Eṣaba bel edz – eja-beyah]
hobby [ˈhɒbɪ] *n* هواية [hiwa:ja]
hockey [ˈhɒkɪ] *n* لعبة الهوكي [Lo'abat alhookey]; **ice hockey** *n* لعبة الهوكي على الجليد [Lo'abat alhookey 'ala aljaleed]
hold [həʊld] *v* يَحتَفظ ب [taḥtafeḍh be]
holdall [ˈhəʊldˌɔːl] *n* جراب [ʒira:b]
hold on [həʊld ɒn] *v* ينتظر قليلا [yantḍher 'qaleelan]
hold up [həʊld ʌp] *v* يٌعَطِل [junʕatˤtˤilu]
hold-up [həʊldʌp] *n* سطو مُسلح [Saṭw mosalaḥ]
hole [həʊl] *n* حفرة [ħufra]

holiday ['hɒlɪˌdeɪ; -dɪ] *n* أجازة [ʔaʒa:za]; **activity holiday** *n* أجازة لممارسة الأنشطة [ajaaza lemomarsat al 'anshe ṭah]; **bank holiday** *n* عطلة شعبية [A'otalh sha'abeyah]; **holiday home** *n* منزل صيفى [Manzel ṣayfey]; **holiday job** *n* وَظيفة فى فترة الأجازة [waḍheefah fee fatrat al-ajaazah]; **package holiday** *n* خطة عطلة شاملة الإقامة والانتقال [Khoṭ at 'aoṭlah shamelat al-e'qamah wal-ente'qal]; **public holiday** *n* أجازة عامة [ajaaza a'mah]; **Enjoy your holiday!** أجازة سعيدة [ejaaza sa'aeeda]; **I'm here on holiday** أنا هنا في أجازة [ana huna fee ejasa]

Holland ['hɒlənd] *n* هولندا [hu:landa:]

hollow ['hɒləʊ] *adj* أجوف [ʔaʒwaf]

holly ['hɒlɪ] *n* نبات شائك الأطراف [Nabat shaek al-aṭraf]

holy ['həʊlɪ] *adj* مقدس [muqadas]

home [həʊm] *adv* بالبَيْت [bi-al-bajti] ▷ *n* منزل [manzil]; **home address** *n* عنوان المنزل ['aonwan al-manzel]; **home match** *n* مباراة الإياب فى ملعب المضيف [Mobarat al-eyab fee mal'aab al-moḍeef]; **home page** *n* صفحة رئيسية [Ṣafḥah raeseyah]; **mobile home** *n* منزل متحرك [Mazel motaḥarek]; **nursing home** *n* دار التمريض [Dar al-tamreeḍ]; **stately home** *n* منزل فخم [Mazel fakhm]; **Would you like to phone home?** هل لديك رغبة في الاتصال بالمنزل؟ [hal ladyka raghba fee al-itiṣal bil-manzil?]

homeland ['həʊmˌlænd] *n* موطن أصلي [Mawṭen aṣley]

homeless ['həʊmlɪs] *adj* شريد [ʃari:d]

home-made ['həʊm'meɪd] *adj* مصنع منزلياً [Maṣna'a manzeleyan]

homeopathic [ˌhəʊmɪ'ɒpæθɪk] *adj* معالج مثلي [Moalej methley]

homeopathy [ˌhəʊmɪ'ɒpəθɪ] *n* العلاج المِثْلي [Al-a'elaj al-methley]

homesick ['həʊmˌsɪk] *adj* حنين إلى الوطن [Ḥaneem ela al-waṭan]

homework ['həʊmˌwɜ:k] *n* واجب منزلى [Wajeb manzeley]

Honduras [hɒn'djʊərəs] *n* الهندوراس [al-handu:ra:si]

honest ['ɒnɪst] *adj* أمين [ʔami:n]

honestly ['ɒnɪstlɪ] *adv* بأمانة [biʔama:nati]

honesty ['ɒnɪstɪ] *n* أمانة [ʔama:na]

honey ['hʌnɪ] *n* عسل [ʕasal]

honeymoon ['hʌnɪˌmu:n] *n* شَهْر العسل [Shahr al-'asal]

honeysuckle ['hʌnɪˌsʌkᵊl] *n* شُجيرة غنية بالرحيق [Shojayrah ghaneyah bel-raḥee'q]

honour ['ɒnə] *n* شَرف [ʃaraf]

hood [hʊd] *n* غطاء للرأس والعنق [Gheṭa'a lel-raas wal-a'ono'q]

hook [hʊk] *n* عقيفة [ʕaqi:fa]

Hoover® ['hu:və] *n* مكنسة كهربائية [Meknasah kahrobaeyah]; **hoover** *v* يَكْنِس بالمكنسة الكهربائية [Yaknes bel-maknasah al-kahrabaeyah]

hope [həʊp] *n* أمَلْ [ʔamal] ▷ *v* يأمل [jaʔmalu]

hopeful ['həʊpfʊl] *adj* واعِد [wa:ʕid]

hopefully ['həʊpfʊlɪ] *adv* مفعم بالأمل [Mof-'am bel-amal]

hopeless ['həʊplɪs] *adj* يائس [ja:ʔis]

horizon [hə'raɪzᵊn] *n* الأفق [al-ʔufuqi]

horizontal [ˌhɒrɪ'zɒntᵊl] *adj* أُفُقِي [ʔufuqij]

hormone ['hɔ:məʊn] *n* هرمون [hurmu:n]

horn [hɔ:n] *n* بوق [bu:q]; **French horn** *n* بوق فرنسي [Boo'q faransey]

horoscope ['hɒrəˌskəʊp] *n* خريطة البروج [khareeṭat al-brooj]

horrendous [hɒ'rɛndəs] *adj* رهيب [rahi:b]

horrible ['hɒrəbᵊl] *adj* رهيب [rahi:b]

horrifying ['hɒrɪˌfaɪɪŋ] *adj* مرعب [murʕib]

horror ['hɒrə] *n* فَزَع [fazaʕ]; **horror film** *n* فيلم رعب [Feelm ro'ab]

horse [hɔ:s] *n* حصان [ħisˁa:n]; **horse racing** *n* سباق الخيول [Seba'q al-kheyol]; **horse riding** *n* ركوب الخيل [Rekoob

al-khayl]; **rocking horse** *n* حصان خشبي هزاز [Heṣan khashabey hazaz]
horseradish ['hɔːsˌrædɪʃ] *n* فجل حار [Fejl ḥar]
horseshoe ['hɔːsˌʃuː] *n* حدوة الحصان [Hedawat heṣan]
hose [həʊz] *n* خُرطوم [xurtˤawm]
hosepipe ['həʊzˌpaɪp] *n* خرطوم المياه [Kharṭoom al-meyah]
hospital ['hɒspɪtᵊl] *n* مستشفى [mustaʃfaː]; **maternity hospital** *n* مستشفى توليد [Mostashfa tawleed]; **psychiatric hospital** *n* مستشفى أمراض عقلية [Mostashfa amraḍ 'aa'qleyah]; **How do I get to the hospital?** كيف يمكن أن أذهب إلى المستشفى؟ [kayfa yamkin an athhab ela al-mustashfa?]; **We must get him to hospital** علينا أن ننقله إلى المستشفى ['alayna an nan-'quloho ela al-mustashfa]; **Where is the hospital?** أين توجد المستشفى؟ [ayna tojad al-mustashfa?]; **Will he have to go to hospital?** هل سيجب عليه الذهاب إلى المستشفى؟ [hal sayajib 'aalyhe al-dhehaab ela al-mustashfa?]
hospitality [ˌhɒspɪ'tælɪtɪ] *n* حُسن الضيافة [Ḥosn al-ḍeyafah]
host [həʊst] *n (entertains)* مُضِيف [mudˤiːf], *(multitude)* حَشْد [ħaʃd]
hostage ['hɒstɪdʒ] *n* رهينة [rahiːna]
hostel ['hɒstᵊl] *n* بيت الشباب [Bayt al-shabab]
hostess ['həʊstɪs] *n*; **air hostess** *n* مضيفة جوية [Moḍeefah jaweyah]
hostile ['hɒstaɪl] *adj* عدائي [ʕidaːʔij]
hot [hɒt] *adj* حار [ħaːrr]; **hot dog** *n* نقانق ساخنة [Na'qane'q sakhenah]; **The room is too hot** هذه الغرفة حارة أكثر من اللازم [hathy al-ghurfa ḥara ak-thar min al-laazim]
hotel [həʊ'tɛl] *n* فندق [funduq]; **Can you book me into a hotel?** أيمكنك أن تحجز لي بالفندق؟ [a-yamkun-ika an taḥjuz lee bil-finda'q?]; **He runs the hotel** إنه يدير الفندق [inaho yodeer al-finda'q]; **I'm staying at a hotel** أنا مقيم في فندق [ana mu'qeem fee finda'q]; **Is your hotel accessible to wheelchairs?** هل يمكن الوصول إلى الفندق بكراسي المقعدين المتحركة؟ [hal yamken al-wiṣool ela al-finda'q be-karasi al-mu'q'aadeen al-mutaḥarika?]; **What's the best way to get to this hotel?** ما هو أفضل طريق للذهاب إلى هذا الفندق [Ma howa afḍal taree'q lel-dhehab ela al-fondo'q]
hour [aʊə] *n* ساعة [saːʕa]; **office hours** *npl* ساعات العمل [Sa'aat al-'amal]; **opening hours** *npl* ساعات العمل [Sa'aat al-'amal]; **peak hours** *npl* ساعات الذروة [Sa'aat al-dhorwah]; **rush hour** *n* وَقْت الذروة [Wa'qt al-dhorwah]; **visiting hours** *npl* ساعات الزيارة [Sa'at al-zeyadah]; **How much is it per hour?** كم يبلغ الثمن لكل ساعة؟ [kam yablugh al-thaman le-kul sa'a a?]
hourly ['aʊəlɪ] *adj* محسوب بالساعة [Mahsoob bel-saa'ah] ▷ *adv* كل ساعة [Kol al-saa'ah]
house [haʊs] *n* بيت [bajt]; **council house** *n* دار المجلس التشريعى [Dar al-majles al-tashre'aey]; **detached house** *n* منزل منفصل [Manzel monfaṣelah]; **semi-detached house** *n* منزل نصف متصل [Mazel neṣf motaṣel]
household ['haʊsˌhəʊld] *n* أهل البيت [Ahl al-bayt]
housewife, housewives ['haʊsˌwaɪf, 'haʊsˌwaɪvz] *n* رَبّة المنزل [Rabat al-manzel]
housework ['haʊsˌwɜːk] *n* أعمال منزلية [A'amaal manzelyah]
hovercraft ['hɒvəˌkrɑːft] *n* حَوّامَة [ħawwaːma]
how [haʊ] *adv* كيف [kajfa]; **How are you?** كيف حالك؟ [kayfa ḥaluka?]; **How do I get to...?** كيف يمكن أن أصل إلى...؟ [kayfa yamkin an aṣal ela...?]; **How does this work?** كيف يعمل هذا؟ [Kayfa ya'amal hatha?]
however [haʊ'ɛvə] *adv* ومع ذلك
howl [haʊl] *v* يعوي [jaʕwiː]
HQ [eɪtʃ kjuː] *abbr* مركز رئيسي [markazun

ra?i:sijjun]
hubcap ['hʌbˌkæp] *n* غطاء للوقاية أو الزينة [Gheṭa'a lel-we'qayah aw lel-zeenah]
hug [hʌg] *n* تشبث [taʃabbuθ] ▷ *v* يُعَانِقُ [juʕa:niqu]
huge [hju:dʒ] *adj* هائل [ha:?il]
hull [hʌl] *n* جسم السفينة [Jesm al-safeenah]
hum [hʌm] *v* يَتَرنم [jatarannamu]
human ['hju:mən] *adj* بَشَري [baʃarij]; **human being** *n* إنسان [?insa:nun]; **human rights** *npl* حقوق الإنسان [Ho'qoo'q al-ensan]
humanitarian [hju:ˌmænɪ'tɛərɪən] *adj* مُحسِن [muħsin]
humble ['hʌmbᵊl] *adj* متواضع [mutawa:dˤiʕ]
humid ['hju:mɪd] *adj* رَطِب [ratˤb]
humidity [hju:'mɪdɪtɪ] *n* رطوبة [rutˤu:ba]
humorous ['hju:mərəs] *adj* فكاهي [fuka:hij]
humour ['hju:mə] *n* دُعَابة [duʕa:ba]; **sense of humour** *n* حس الفكاهة [Ḥes al-fokahah]
hundred ['hʌndrəd] *number* مائة [ma:?itun]; **I'd like five hundred...** أرغب في الحصول على خمسمائة... [Arghab fee al-ḥoṣol alaa khomsamah...]
Hungarian [hʌŋ'gɛərɪən] *adj* مجري [maʒrij] ▷ *n (person)* مَجَري الجنسية [Majra al-jenseyah]
Hungary ['hʌŋgərɪ] *n* المجر [al-maʒari]
hunger ['hʌŋgə] *n* جوع [ʒu:ʕ]
hungry ['hʌŋgrɪ] *adj* جوعان [ʒawʕa:n]
hunt [hʌnt] *n* يَصيد [jasˤi:du] ▷ *v* يَصيد [jasˤi:du]
hunter ['hʌntə] *n* صياد [sˤajja:d]
hunting ['hʌntɪŋ] *n* صيد [sˤajd]
hurdle ['hɜ:dᵊl] *n* سياج نقال [Seyaj na'qal]
hurricane ['hʌrɪkᵊn; -keɪn] *n* إعصار [?iʕsˤa:r]
hurry ['hʌrɪ] *n* استعجال [istiʕʒa:l] ▷ *v* يُسْرِع [jusriʕu]
hurry up ['hʌrɪ ʌp] *v* يَستعجِل [jastaʕʒilu]
hurt [hɜ:t] *adj* مستاء [musta:?] ▷ *v* يؤذي [juðiː]
husband ['hʌzbənd] *n* زَوْج [zawʒ]
hut [hʌt] *n* كوخ [ku:x]; **Where is the nearest mountain hut?** أين يوجد أقرب كوخ بالجبل؟ [ayna yujad a'qrab kookh bil-jabal?]
hyacinth ['haɪəsɪnθ] *n* هياسنت [haja:sint]
hydrogen ['haɪdrɪdʒən] *n* هيدروجين [hi:dru:ʒi:n]
hygiene ['haɪdʒi:n] *n* نظافة [nazˤa:fa]
hymn [hɪm] *n* ترنيمة [tarni:ma]
hypermarket ['haɪpəˌmɑ:kɪt] *n* متجر كبير جدا [Matjar kabeer jedan]
hyphen ['haɪfᵊn] *n* شرطة قصيرة [Sharṭah 'qaṣeerah]

i

I [aɪ] *pron* أنا [ʔana]; **I don't like...** أنا لا أحب... [ana la oḥibo...]; **I like...** أنا أفضل... [ana ofaḍel...]; **I love...** أنا أحب... [ana aḥib]
ice [aɪs] *n* جليد [ʒali:d]; **black ice** *n* ثلج أسود [thalj aswad]; **ice cube** *n* مكعب ثلج [Moka'aab thalj]; **ice hockey** *n* لعبة الهوكي على الجليد [Lo'abat alhookey 'ala aljaleed]; **ice lolly** *n* ستيك الآيس كريم [Steek al-aayes kreem]; **ice rink** *n* حلبة من الجليد الصناعي [Ḥalabah men aljaleed alṣena'aey]
iceberg ['aɪsbɜːg] *n* جبل جليدي [Jabal jaleedey]
icebox ['aɪs,bɒks] *n* صندوق الثلج [Ṣondoo'q al-thalj]
ice cream ['aɪs 'kriːm] *n* آيس كريم [aayes kreem]; **I'd like an ice cream** أريد تناول آيس كريم [areed tanawil ice kreem]
Iceland ['aɪslənd] *n* أيسلندا [ʔajslanda:]
Icelandic [aɪs'lændɪk] *adj* أيسلاندي [ʔajsla:ndi:] ▷ *n* الأيسلندي [Alayeslandey]
ice-skating ['aɪs,skeɪtɪŋ] *n* تَزَلُج على الجليد [Tazaloj 'ala al-jaleed]
icing ['aɪsɪŋ] *n* تَزْيين الحلوى [Tazyeen al-ḥalwa]; **icing sugar** *n* سكر ناعِم [Sokar na'aem]
icon ['aɪkɒn] *n* أيقونة [ʔajqu:na]
icy ['aɪsɪ] *adj* جليدي [ʒali:dij]
idea [aɪ'dɪə] *n* فكرة [fikra]
ideal [aɪ'dɪəl] *adj* مثالي [miθa:lij]
ideally [aɪ'dɪəlɪ] *adv* بشكل مثالي [Be-shakl methaley]
identical [aɪ'dɛntɪkᵊl] *adj* متطابق [mutatˤa:biq]
identification [aɪ,dɛntɪfɪ'keɪʃən] *n* تعريف الهوية [Ta'areef al-haweyah]
identify [aɪ'dɛntɪ,faɪ] *v* يُعَيِّنُ الهوِيَّة [Yo'aeyen al-haweyah]
identity [aɪ'dɛntɪtɪ] *n* هَوِيّة [huwijja]; **identity card** *n* بطاقة شخصية [beṭa'qah shakhṣeyah]; **identity theft** *n* سرقة الهوية [Sare'qat al-hawyiah]
ideology [,aɪdɪ'ɒlədʒɪ] *n* أيدولوجية [ʔajdu:lu:ʒijja]
idiot ['ɪdɪət] *n* أبْلَه [ʔablah]
idiotic [,ɪdɪ'ɒtɪk] *adj* أحمق [ʔaħmaq]
idle ['aɪdᵊl] *adj* عَاطِل [ʕa:tˤil]
i.e. [aɪ iː] *abbr* أيَ أن [Ay an]
if [ɪf] *conj* إذا [ʔiða:]
ignition [ɪg'nɪʃən] *n* اشتعال [iʃtiʕa:l]
ignorance ['ɪgnərəns] *n* جهل [ʒahl]
ignorant ['ɪgnərənt] *adj* جاهل [ʒa:hil]
ignore [ɪg'nɔː] *v* يَتَجاهل [jataʒa:halu]
ill [ɪl] *adj* سقيم [saqi:m]
illegal [ɪ'liːgᵊl] *adj* غير قانوني [Ghayer 'qanooney]
illegible [ɪ'lɛdʒɪbᵊl] *adj* غير مقروء [Ghayr ma'qrooa]
illiterate [ɪ'lɪtərɪt] *adj* أمي [ʔumijju]
illness ['ɪlnɪs] *n* داء [da:ʔ]
ill-treat [ɪl'triːt] *v* يُعامِل معاملة سيئة [Yo'aamal mo'aamalh sayeah]
illusion [ɪ'luːʒən] *n* وهم [wahm]
illustration [,ɪlə'streɪʃən] *n* توضيح [tawdˤi:ħ]
image ['ɪmɪdʒ] *n* صورة [sˤu:ra]
imaginary [ɪ'mædʒɪnərɪ; -dʒɪnrɪ] *adj* تَخَيُلي [taxajjulij]
imagination [ɪ,mædʒɪ'neɪʃən] *n* خيال [xaja:l]
imagine [ɪ'mædʒɪn] *v* يتَخَيَل [jataxajjalu]

imitate [ˈɪmɪˌteɪt] *v* يُقَلِد [juqallidu]
imitation [ˌɪmɪˈteɪʃən] *n* محاكاة [muħa:ka:t]
immature [ˌɪməˈtjʊə; -ˈtʃʊə] *adj* غير ناضج [Ghayr naḍej]
immediate [ɪˈmi:dɪət] *adj* فوري [fawrij]
immediately [ɪˈmi:dɪətlɪ] *adv* فى الحال [Fee al-hal]
immigrant [ˈɪmɪgrənt] *n* وَافِد [wa:fid]
immigration [ˌɪmɪˈgreɪʃən] *n* هِجْرَة [hiʒra]
immoral [ɪˈmɒrəl] *adj* لا أخلاقي [La Akhla'qy]
impact [ˈɪmpækt] *n* تأثير [taʔθi:r]
impaired [ɪmˈpɛəd] *adj*; **I'm visually impaired** أعاني من ضعف البصر [o-'aany min ḍu'auf al-baṣar]
impartial [ɪmˈpɑ:ʃəl] *adj* غير متحيز [Ghayer motaḥeyz]
impatience [ɪmˈpeɪʃəns] *n* نفاذ الصبر [nafadh al-ṣabr]
impatient [ɪmˈpeɪʃənt] *adj* غير صبور [Ghaeyr ṣaboor]
impatiently [ɪmˈpeɪʃəntlɪ] *adv* بدون صبر [Bedon ṣabr]
impersonal [ɪmˈpɜ:sənᵊl] *adj* موضوعي [mawdˤu:ʕij]
import *n* [ˈɪmpɔ:t] استيراد [istijra:d] ▷ *v* [ɪmˈpɔ:t] يَستورد [jastawridu]
importance [ɪmˈpɔ:tᵊns] *n* أهمية [ʔahamijja]
important [ɪmˈpɔ:tᵊnt] *adj* هام [ha:mm]
impossible [ɪmˈpɒsəbᵊl] *adj* مستحيل [mustaħi:l]
impractical [ɪmˈpræktɪkᵊl] *adj* غير عملي [Ghayer 'aamaley]
impress [ɪmˈprɛs] *v* يُؤثِر فى [Yoather fee]
impressed [ɪmˈprɛst] *adj* متأثر [mutaʔaθirr]
impression [ɪmˈprɛʃən] *n* انطباع [intˤibba:ʕ]
impressive [ɪmˈprɛsɪv] *adj* مؤثر [muʔaθir]
improve [ɪmˈpru:v] *v* يُحْسِن [juħsinu]
improvement [ɪmˈpru:vmənt] *n* تحسين [taħsi:n]
in [ɪn] *prep* في [fi:]; **in a month's time** في غضون شهر [fee ghoḍon shahr]; **in summer** في الصيف [fee al-ṣayf]; **in the evening** في المساء [fee al-masaa]; **I live in...** ...أسكن في [askun fee..]; **Is the museum open in the morning?** هل المتحف مفتوح في الصباح؟ [hal al-mat-ḥaf maf-tooḥ fee al-ṣabaḥ]; **We'll be in bed when you get back** عند العودة سوف نكون في الفراش ['aenda al-'aoda sawfa nakoon fee al-feraash]
inaccurate [ɪnˈækjʊrɪt; inˈaccurate] *adj* غير دقيق [Ghayer da'qee'q]
inadequate [ɪnˈædɪkwɪt] *adj* غير ملائم [Ghayr molaem]
inadvertently [ˌɪnədˈvɜ:tᵊntlɪ] *adv* بدون قَصْد [Bedoon 'qaṣd]
inbox [ˈɪnbɒks] *n* صندوق الوارد [Ṣondok alwared]
incentive [ɪnˈsɛntɪv] *n* باعث [ba:ʕiθ]
inch [ɪntʃ] *n* بوصة [bawsˤa]
incident [ˈɪnsɪdənt] *n* حدث عرضي [Hadth 'aradey]
include [ɪnˈklu:d] *v* يَتَضمن [jatadˤammanu]
included [ɪnˈklu:dɪd] *adj* مُرفق [murfiq]
including [ɪnˈklu:dɪŋ] *prep* بما فى ذلك [Bema fee ḍhalek]
inclusive [ɪnˈklu:sɪv] *adj* جامع [ʒa:miʕ]
income [ˈɪnkʌm; ˈɪnkəm] *n* دَخْل [daxala]; **income tax** *n* ضريبة دخل [Ḍareebat dakhl]
incompetent [ɪnˈkɒmpɪtənt] *adj* غير كفؤ [Ghayr kofa]
incomplete [ˌɪnkəmˈpli:t] *adj* ناقص [na:qisˤ]
inconsistent [ˌɪnkənˈsɪstənt] *adj* متضارب [mutadˤa:rib]
inconvenience [ˌɪnkənˈvi:njəns; -ˈvi:nɪəns] *n* عدم المُلاءمة ['adam al-molaamah]
inconvenient [ˌɪnkənˈvi:njənt; -ˈvi:nɪənt] *adj* غير ملائم [Ghayr molaem]
incorrect [ˌɪnkəˈrɛkt] *adj* خاطئ [xa:tˤiʔ]
increase *n* [ˈɪnkri:s] زيادة [zija:da] ▷ *v*

[ɪnˈkriːs] يَزيد [jaziːdu]
increasingly [ɪnˈkriːsɪŋlɪ] *adv* بشكل متزايد [Beshakl motazayed]
incredible [ɪnˈkrɛdəbᵊl] *adj* لا يصدق [La yoṣda'q]
indecisive [ˌɪndɪˈsaɪsɪv] *adj* غير حاسم [Ɵahyr hasem]
indeed [ɪnˈdiːd] *adv* حقاً [ħaqqan]
independence [ˌɪndɪˈpɛndəns] *n* استقلال [istiqlaːlu]
independent [ˌɪndɪˈpɛndənt] *adj* مستقل [mustaqil]
index [ˈɪndɛks] *n (list)* فهرس [fahras], *(numerical scale)* فهرس [fahras]; **index finger** *n* اصبع السبابة [Eṣbe'a al-sababah]
India [ˈɪndɪə] *n* الهند [al-hindi]
Indian [ˈɪndɪən] *adj* هندي [hindij] ▷ *n* هندي [hindij]; **Indian Ocean** *n* المحيط الهندي [Almoḥeeṭ alhendey]
indicate [ˈɪndɪˌkeɪt] *v* يشير إلى [Yosheer ela]
indicator [ˈɪndɪˌkeɪtə] *n* مُؤَشِّر [muʔaʃʃir]
indigestion [ˌɪndɪˈdʒɛstʃən] *n* عسر الهضم ['aosr al-haḍm]
indirect [ˌɪndɪˈrɛkt] *adj* غير مباشر [Ghayer mobasher]
indispensable [ˌɪndɪˈspɛnsəbᵊl] *adj* لا مفر منه [La mafar menh]
individual [ˌɪndɪˈvɪdjʊəl] *adj* فردي [fardijjat]
Indonesia [ˌɪndəʊˈniːzɪə] *n* أندونيسيا [ʔanduːniːsjjaː]
Indonesian [ˌɪndəʊˈniːzɪən] *adj* أندونيسى [ʔanduːniːsij] ▷ *n (person)* أندونيسي [ʔanduːniːsij]
indoor [ˈɪnˌdɔː] *adj* داخلي [daːxilij]; **What indoor activities are there?** ما الأنشطة الرياضية الداخلية المتاحة؟ [ma al-anshiṭa al-reyaḍya al-dakhiliya al-mutaḥa?]
indoors [ˌɪnˈdɔːz] *adv* داخلياً [daːxilijjan]
industrial [ɪnˈdʌstrɪəl] *adj* صناعي [sˤinaːʕij]; **industrial estate** *n* عقارات صناعية ['aa'qarat ṣenaeyah]
industry [ˈɪndəstrɪ] *n* صناعة [sˤinaːʕa]
inefficient [ˌɪnɪˈfɪʃənt] *adj* غير فعال [Ghayer fa'aal]
inevitable [ɪnˈɛvɪtəbᵊl] *adj* محتوم [maħtuːm]
inexpensive [ˌɪnɪkˈspɛnsɪv] *adj* بَخْس [baxs]
inexperienced [ˌɪnɪkˈspɪərɪənst] *adj* قليل الخبرة ['qaleel al-khebrah]
infantry [ˈɪnfəntrɪ] *n* سلاح المُشَاة [Selaḥ al-moshah]
infection [ɪnˈfɛkʃən] *n* عدوى [ʕadwaː]
infectious [ɪnˈfɛkʃəs] *adj* مُعْد [muʕdin]
inferior [ɪnˈfɪərɪə] *adj* أدنى درجة [Adna darajah] ▷ *n* مرؤوس [marʔuws]
infertile [ɪnˈfɜːtaɪl] *adj* قاحل [qaːħil]
infinitive [ɪnˈfɪnɪtɪv] *n* مَصْدَر [masˤdar]
infirmary [ɪnˈfɜːmərɪ] *n* مَشْفَى [maʃfaː]
inflamed [ɪnˈfleɪmd] *adj* مشتعل [muʃtaʕil]
inflammation [ˌɪnfləˈmeɪʃən] *n* التهاب [ʔiltihaːb]
inflatable [ɪnˈfleɪtəbᵊl] *adj* قابل للنفخ ['qabel lel-nafkh]
inflation [ɪnˈfleɪʃən] *n* تَضَخُّم [tadˤaxxum]
inflexible [ɪnˈflɛksəbᵊl] *adj* غير مَرِن [Ghayer maren]
influence [ˈɪnflʊəns] *n* أَثَرْ [ʔaθar] ▷ *v* يُؤثِر فى [Yoather fee]
influenza [ˌɪnflʊˈɛnzə] *n* أنفلونزا [ʔanfulwanzaː]
inform [ɪnˈfɔːm] *v* يُبْلغ عن [Yoballegh an]
informal [ɪnˈfɔːməl] *adj* غير رسمي [Ghayer rasmey]
information [ˌɪnfəˈmeɪʃən] *n* معلومات [amaʕluːmaːt]; **information office** *n* مكتب الاستعلامات [Maktab al-este'alamaat]; **Here's some information about my company** تفضل بعض المعلومات المتعلقة بشركتي [tafaḍal ba'aḍ al-ma'a-lomaat al-muta'a-le'qa be-share-katy]; **I'd like some information about...** أريد الحصول على بعض المعلومات عن... [areed al-ḥuṣool 'aala ba'aḍ al-ma'aloomat

'an...]
informative [ɪn'fɔːmətɪv] *adj* تثقيفي [taθqiːfij]
infrastructure ['ɪnfrəˌstrʌktʃə] *n* بِنْيَة أساسية [Benyah asaseyah]
infuriating [ɪn'fjʊərɪeɪtɪŋ] *adj* مثير للغضب [Mother lel-ghaḍab]
ingenious [ɪn'dʒiːnjəs; -nɪəs] *adj* مبدع [mubdiʕ]
ingredient [ɪn'griːdɪənt] *n* مُكَوِّن [mukawwan]
inhabitant [ɪn'hæbɪtənt] *n* ساكن [saːkin]
inhaler [ɪn'heɪlə] *n* بَخَّاخ [baxxaːx]
inherit [ɪn'hɛrɪt] *v* يَرِث [jariθu]
inheritance [ɪn'hɛrɪtəns] *n* ميراث [miːjraːθ]
inhibition [ˌɪnɪ'bɪʃən; ˌɪnhɪ-] *n* كَبْح [kabħ]
initial [ɪ'nɪʃəl] *adj* ابتدائي [ibtidaːʔij] ▷ *v* يُوقِع بالحرف الأول من اسمه [Yowa'qe'a bel-harf alawal men esmeh]
initially [ɪ'nɪʃəlɪ] *adv* مبدئياً [mabdaʔijjan]
initials [ɪ'nɪʃəlz] *npl* الأحرف الأولى [Al-aḥrof al-ola]
initiative [ɪ'nɪʃɪətɪv; -'nɪʃətɪv] *n* مبادرة [mubaːdara]
inject [ɪn'dʒɛkt] *v* يَحقِن [jaħqinu]
injection [ɪn'dʒɛkʃən] *n* حقن [ħaqn]; **I want an injection for the pain** أريد أخذ حقنة لتخفيف الألم [areed akhdh ḥu'qna le-takhfeef al-alam]; **Please give me an injection** من فضلك أعطني حقنة [min faḍlak i'a-ṯiny ḥi'qna]
injure ['ɪndʒə] *v* يجرح [jaʒraħu]
injured ['ɪndʒəd] *adj* مجروح [maʒruːħ]
injury ['ɪndʒərɪ] *n* إصابة [ʔisˤaːba]; **injury time** *n* وَقْت بدل الضائع [Wa'qt badal ḍaye'a]
injustice [ɪn'dʒʌstɪs] *n* ظلم [zˤulm]
ink [ɪŋk] *n* حِبر [ħibr]
in-laws [ɪnlɔːz] *npl* أصهار [ʔasˤhaːrun]
inmate ['ɪnˌmeɪt] *n* شريك السكن [Shareek al-sakan]
inn [ɪn] *n* خان [xaːna]
inner ['ɪnə] *adj* باطني [baːtˤinij]; **inner tube** *n* أنبوب داخلي [Anboob dakheley]
innocent ['ɪnəsənt] *adj* برئ [bariːʔ]
innovation [ˌɪnə'veɪʃən] *n* ابتكار [ibtikaːr]
innovative ['ɪnəˌveɪtɪv] *adj* ابتكاري [ibtikaːrij]
inquest ['ɪnˌkwɛst] *n* استجواب [istiʒwaːb]
inquire [ɪn'kwaɪə] *v* يَسأَل عن [Yasaal 'an]
inquiry [ɪn'kwaɪərɪ] *n* استعلام [istiʕlaːm]; **inquiries office** *n* مكتب الاستعلامات [Maktab al-este'alamaat]
inquisitive [ɪn'kwɪzɪtɪv] *adj* محب للبحث والتحقيق [moḥeb lel-baḥth wal-taḥ'qeeq]
insane [ɪn'seɪn] *adj* مجنون [maʒnuːn]
inscription [ɪn'skrɪpʃən] *n* نقش [naqʃ]
insect ['ɪnsɛkt] *n* حشرة [ħaʃara]; **insect repellent** *n* طارد للحشرات [Ṭared lel-ḥasharat]; **stick insect** *n* الحشرة العصوية [Al-hasherah al-'aodweia]
insecure [ˌɪnsɪ'kjʊə] *adj* غير آمن [Ghayr aamen]
insensitive [ɪn'sɛnsɪtɪv] *adj* غير حساس [Ghayr hasaṣ]
inside *adv* [ˌɪn'saɪd] داخلًا [daːxilaː] ▷ *n* ['ɪn'saɪd] دَاخِل [daːxila] ▷ *prep* ضمن [Ḍemn]
insincere [ˌɪnsɪn'sɪə] *adj* منافق [munaːfiq]
insist [ɪn'sɪst] *v* يُصِر على [Yoṣer 'aala]
insomnia [ɪn'sɒmnɪə] *n* أرق [ʔaraq]
inspect [ɪn'spɛkt] *v* يَفْحَص [jafħasˤu]
inspector [ɪn'spɛktə] *n* مفتش [mufattiʃ]; **ticket inspector** *n* مفتش التذاكر [Mofatesh taḍhaker]
instability [ˌɪnstə'bɪlɪtɪ] *n* عدم الثبات ['adam al-thabat]
instalment [ɪn'stɔːlmənt] *n* تركيب [tarkiːb]
instance ['ɪnstəns] *n* مرحلة [marħala]
instant ['ɪnstənt] *adj* ملح [milħ]
instantly ['ɪnstəntlɪ] *adv* بالحاح [bi-ilħaːħin]

instead [ɪn'stɛd] *adv* بدلًا من ذلك [Badalan men ḍhalek]; **instead of** *prep* بدلًا من [badalan men]
instinct ['ɪnstɪŋkt] *n* غريزة [ɣari:za]
institute ['ɪnstɪˌtju:t] *n* معهد [maʕhad]
institution [ˌɪnstɪ'tju:ʃən] *n* مؤسسة [muʔassasa]
instruct [ɪn'strʌkt] *v* يُعلِم [juʕallimu]
instructions [ɪn'strʌkʃənz] *npl* تعليمات [taʕli:ma:tun]
instructor [ɪn'strʌktə] *n* مُعَلِم [muʕallim]; **driving instructor** *n* معلم القيادة [Mo'alem al-'qeyadh]
instrument ['ɪnstrəmənt] *n* أداة [ʔada:t]; **musical instrument** *n* آلة موسيقية [Aala mose'qeyah]
insufficient [ˌɪnsə'fɪʃənt] *adj* غير كافي [Ghayr kafey]
insulation [ˌɪnsjʊ'leɪʃən] *n* عَازَل [ʕa:zil]
insulin ['ɪnsjʊlɪn] *n* أنسولين [ʔansu:li:n]
insult *n* ['ɪnsʌlt]إهانة [ʔiha:na] ▷ *v* [ɪn'sʌlt]يُهْين [juhi:nu]
insurance [ɪn'ʃʊərəns; -'ʃɔ:-] *n* تأمين [taʔmi:n]; **accident insurance** *n* تأمين ضد الحوادث [Taameen ḍed al-hawaadeth]; **car insurance** *n* تأمين سيارة [Taameen sayarah]; **insurance policy** *n* بوليصة تأمين [Booleeṣat taameen]; **life insurance** *n* تأمين على الحياة [Taameen 'ala al-hayah]; **third-party insurance** *n* تتأمين عن الطرف الثالث[Tameen lada algheer]; **travel insurance** *n* تأمين السفر [Taameen al-safar]; **Do you have insurance?** هل لديك تأمين؟ [hal ladyka ta-meen?]; **Give me your insurance details, please** من فضلك أعطني بيانات التأمين الخاصة بك [min faḍlak i'a-ṭiny baya-naat al-ta-meen al-khaṣa bik]; **Here are my insurance details** تفضل هذه هي بيانات التأمين الخاص بي [Tafaḍal hadheh heya beyanaat altaameen alkhaṣ bee]; **How much extra is comprehensive insurance cover?** ما هو المبلغ الإضافي لتغطية التأمينية الشاملة؟ [ma: huwa almablaɣu alʔidˤa:fijju litaɣtˤijjati attaʔmi:nijjati aʃʃa:milati]; **I don't have dental insurance** ليس لدي تأمين صحي لأسناني [laysa la-daya ta-meen ṣiḥee le-asnany]; **I'd like to arrange personal accident insurance** أريد عمل الترتيبات الخاصة بالتأمين ضد الحوادث الشخصية [areed 'aamal al-tar-tebaat al-khaṣa bil-taameen ḍid al-ḥawadith al-shakhṣiya]; **Is fully comprehensive insurance included in the price?** هل يشمل السعر التأمين الشامل والكامل؟ [hal yash-mil al-si'ar al-taameen al-shamil wal-kamil?]; **Will the insurance pay for it?** هل ستدفع لك شركة التأمين مقابل ذلك [hal sa-tadfaa laka share-kat al-tameen ma'qabil dhalik?]
insure [ɪn'ʃʊə; -'ʃɔ:] *v* يُؤَمن [juamminu]
insured [ɪn'ʃʊəd; -'ʃɔ:d] *adj* مؤمن عليه [Moaman 'aalayh]
intact [ɪn'tækt] *adj* سليم [sali:m]
intellectual [ˌɪntɪ'lɛktʃʊəl] *adj* فِكْري [fikrij] ▷ *n* فِكْري [fikrij]
intelligence [ɪn'tɛlɪdʒəns] *n* ذكاء [ðaka:ʔ]
intelligent [ɪn'tɛlɪdʒənt] *adj* ذَكِي [ðakij]
intend [ɪn'tɛnd] *v*; **intend to** *v* يَعْتَزِم [jaʕtazimu]
intense [ɪn'tɛns] *adj* مجهد [muʒhid]
intensive [ɪn'tɛnsɪv] *adj* شديد [ʃadi:d]; **intensive care unit** *n* وحدة العناية المركزة [Weḥdat al-'aenayah al-morkazah]
intention [ɪn'tɛnʃən] *n* نية [nijja]
intentional [ɪn'tɛnʃənᵊl] *adj* مقصود [maqsˤu:d]
intercom ['ɪntəˌkɒm] *n* نظام الاتصال الداخلي [nedhaam aleteṣaal aldakheley]
interest ['ɪntrɪst; -tərɪst] *n (curiosity)* اهتمام [ihtima:m], *(income)* مصلحة [masˤlaħa] ▷ *v* يُثير اهتمام [yotheer ehtemam]; **interest rate** *n* معدل الفائدة [Moaadal al-faaedah]
interested ['ɪntrɪstɪd; -tərɪs-] *adj* مهتم [muhttam]; **Sorry, I'm not interested**

معذرة، أنا غير مهتم بهذا الأمر [maʕðaratun ʔana: ɣajru muhtammin biha:ða: alʔamri]
interesting ['ɪntrɪstɪŋ; -tərɪs-] *adj* مُشَوق [muʃawwiq]
interior [ɪn'tɪərɪə] *n* دَاخِلٌ [da:xil]; **interior designer** *n* مُصَمِم داخلي [Moșamem dakheley]
intermediate [ˌɪntə'mi:dɪɪt] *adj* أوسط [ʔawsatˤ]
internal [ɪn'tɜ:nᵊl] *adj* داخلي [da:xilij]
international [ˌɪntə'næʃənᵊl] *adj* دَولِي [dawlij]
Internet ['ɪntəˌnɛt] *n* الانترنت [al-intirnit]; **Internet café** *n* مقهى الانترنت [Ma'qha al-enternet]; **Internet user** *n* مُستَخدِم الانترنت [Mostakhdem al-enternet]
interpret [ɪn'tɜ:prɪt] *v* يُفَسِر [jufassiru]
interpreter [ɪn'tɜ:prɪtə] *n* مُفَسِّر [mufassir]
interrogate [ɪn'tɛrəˌgeɪt] *v* يَستجوب [jastaʒwibu]
interrupt [ˌɪntə'rʌpt] *v* يُقَاطِعُ [juqa:tˤiʕu]
interruption [ˌɪntə'rʌpʃən] *n* مقاطعة [muqa:tˤaʕa]
interval ['ɪntəvəl] *n* فاصل [fa:sˤil]
interview ['ɪntəˌvju:] *n* مقابلة [muqa:bala] ▷ *v* يُقابِل [juqa:bilu]
interviewer ['ɪntəˌvju:ə] *n* محاور [muħa:wir]
intimate ['ɪntɪmɪt] *adj* حميم [ħami:m]
intimidate [ɪn'tɪmɪˌdeɪt] *v* يُخوِّف [juxawwifu]
into ['ɪntu:; 'ɪntə] *prep* بداخل [bida:xili]; **bump into** *v* يتصادف مع [Yatașaadaf ma'a]
intolerant [ɪn'tɒlərənt] *adj* مُتَعصِب [mutaʕasˤibb]
intranet ['ɪntrəˌnɛt] *n* شبكة داخلية [Shabakah dakheleyah]
introduce [ˌɪntrə'dju:s] *v* يُقَدِم [juqaddimu]
introduction [ˌɪntrə'dʌkʃən] *n* مقدمة [muqadima]
intruder [ɪn'tru:də; in'truder] *n* متطفل [mutatˤafil]
intuition [ˌɪntjʊ'ɪʃən] *n* حَدَسْ [ħads]
invade [ɪn'veɪd] *v* يغزو [jaɣzu:]
invalid ['ɪnvəˌli:d] *n* مريض [mari:dˤ]
invent [ɪn'vɛnt] *v* يَخترِع [jaxtariʕu]
invention [ɪn'vɛnʃən] *n* اختراع [ixtira:ʕ]
inventor [ɪn'vɛntə] *n* مُختَرِع [muxtaraʕ]
inventory ['ɪnvəntərɪ; -trɪ] *n* مخزون [maxzu:n]
invest [ɪn'vɛst] *v* يَستثمر [jastaθmiru]
investigation [ɪnˌvɛstɪ'geɪʃən] *n* تحقيق [taħqi:qu]
investment [ɪn'vɛstmənt] *n* استثمار [istiθma:r]
investor [ɪn'vɛstə] *n* مُسْتَثمر [mustaθmir]
invigilator [ɪn'vɪdʒɪˌleɪtə] *n* مُرَاقِب [mura:qib]
invisible [ɪn'vɪzəbᵊl] *adj* غير منظور [Ghayr monaḍhoor]
invitation [ˌɪnvɪ'teɪʃən] *n* دعوة [daʕwa]
invite [ɪn'vaɪt] *v* يَدْعو [jadʕu:]
invoice ['ɪnvɔɪs] *n* فاتورة تجارية [Fatoorah tejareyah] ▷ *v* يُعِد فاتورة [Yo'aed al-fatoorah]
involve [ɪn'vɒlv] *v* يَشمَل [jaʃmalu]
iPod® ['aɪˌpɒd] *n* الآي بود® [alʔa:j bu:d]
IQ [aɪ kju:] *abbr* معامل الذكاء [Mo'aamel aldhakaa]
Iran [ɪ'rɑ:n] *n* إيران [ʔi:ra:n]
Iranian [ɪ'reɪnɪən] *adj* إيراني [ʔi:ra:nij] ▷ *n* *(person)* إيراني [ʔi:ra:nij]
Iraq [ɪ'rɑ:k] *n* العراق [al-ʕira:qi]
Iraqi [ɪ'rɑ:kɪ] *adj* عراقي [ʕira:qij] ▷ *n* عراقي [ʕira:qij]
Ireland ['aɪələnd] *n* أيرلندا [ʔajrlanda:]; **Northern Ireland** *n* أيرلندة الشمالية [Ayarlanda al-shamaleyah]
iris ['aɪrɪs] *n* قزحية العين ['qazeḥeyat al-'ayn]
Irish ['aɪrɪʃ] *adj* أيرلندي [jralandij] ▷ *n* الأيرلندي [Alayarlandey]
Irishman, Irishmen ['aɪrɪʃmən, 'aɪrɪʃmɛn] *n* رَجُل إيرلندي [Rajol ayarlandey]
Irishwoman, Irishwomen

['aɪrɪʃwʊmən, 'aɪrɪʃwɪmɪn] *n* ايرلندية [ijrlandijja]
iron ['aɪən] *n* حديد [ħadi:d] ▷ *v* يَكْوي [jakwi:]
ironic [aɪ'rɒnɪk] *adj* تهكمي [tahakumij]
ironing ['aɪənɪŋ] *n* كيّ الملابس [Kay almalabes]; **ironing board** *n* لوح الكي [Looḥ alkay]
ironmonger's ['aɪən,mʌŋgəz] *n* محل تاجر الحديد والأدوات المعدنية [Mahal tajer alḥadeed wal-adwat al-ma'adaneyah]
irony ['aɪrənɪ] *n* سُخرية [suxrijja]
irregular [ɪ'rɛgjʊlə] *adj* غير منتظم [Ghayr montaḍhem]
irrelevant [ɪ'rɛləvənt] *adj* غير متصل بالموضوع [Ghayr motaṣel bel-maeḍo'a]
irresponsible [,ɪrɪ'spɒnsəbᵊl] *adj* غير مسئول [Ghayr maswool]
irritable ['ɪrɪtəbᵊl] *adj* سريع الغضب [Saree'a al-ghaḍab]
irritating ['ɪrɪ,teɪtɪŋ] *adj* مثير للغضب [Mother lel-ghaḍab]
Islam ['ɪzlɑ:m] *n* الإسلام [al-ʔisla:mu]
Islamic ['ɪzləmɪk] *adj* إسلامي [ʔisla:mij]
island ['aɪlənd] *n* جزيرة [ʒazi:ra]; **desert island** *n* جزيرة استوائية غير مأهولة [Jozor ghayr maahoolah]
isolated ['aɪsə,leɪtɪd] *adj* معزول [maʕzu:l]
ISP [aɪ ɛs pi:] *abbr* مزود بخدمة الإنترنت [Mozawadah be-khedmat al-enternet]
Israel ['ɪzreɪəl; -rɪəl] *n* إسرائيل [ʔisra:ʔijl]
Israeli [ɪz'reɪlɪ] *adj* إسرائيلي [ʔisra:ʔi:lij] ▷ *n* إسرائيلي [ʔisra:ʔi:lij]
issue ['ɪʃju:] *n* إصدار [ʔisˁda:r] ▷ *v* يَصْدُر [jasˁduru]
it [ɪt] *pron* ضمير غائب مفرد لغير العاقل [dˁami:ru ɣa:ʔibun mufrad liɣajri alʕa:quli]
IT [aɪ ti:] *abbr* تكنولوجيا المعلومات [tiknu:lu:ʒija: almaʕlu:ma:t]
Italian [ɪ'tæljən] *adj* إيطالي [ʔi:tˁa:lij] ▷ *n* *(language)* اللغة الإيطالية [alloghah al etaleyah], *(person)* إيطالي [ʔi:tˁa:lij]
Italy ['ɪtəlɪ] *n* إيطاليا [ʔi:tˁa:ljja:]
itch [ɪtʃ] *v* يستحكه جلده [yastaḥekah jaldah]
itchy [ɪtʃɪ] *adj* يَتَطلب الحك [yataṭalab al-hak]
item ['aɪtəm] *n* بَنْد [bund]
itinerary [aɪ'tɪnərərɪ; ɪ-] *n* دليل السائح [Daleel al-saaeh]
its [ɪts] *adj* مِلْك
itself [ɪt'sɛlf] *pron* نفسه
ivory ['aɪvərɪ; -vrɪ] *n* عاج [ʕa:ʒ]
ivy ['aɪvɪ] *n* لِبْلاب [labla:b]

jab [dʒæb] *n* وخز [waxz]
jack [dʒæk] *n* رافعة [raːfiʕa]
jacket [ˈdʒækɪt] *n* سُترة [sutra]; **dinner jacket** *n* جاكت العشاء [Jaket al-'aashaa]; **jacket potato** *n* بطاطس مشوية بقشرها [Baṭaṭes mashweiah be'qshreha]; **life jacket** *n* سُترة النجاة [Sotrat al-najah]
jackpot [ˈdʒækˌpɒt] *n* مجموع مراهنات [Majmoo'a morahnaat]
jail [dʒeɪl] *n* سجن [siʒn] ▷ *v* يَسجِن [jasʒinu]
jam [dʒæm] *n* مربّى [murabbaː]; **jam jar** *n* وعاء المربّى [We'aaa almorabey]; **traffic jam** *n* ازدحام المرور [Ezdeḥam al-moror]
Jamaican [dʒəˈmeɪkən] *adj* جامايكي [ʒaːmaːjkij] ▷ *n* جامايكي [ʒaːmaːjkij]
jammed [dʒæmd] *adj* مضغوط [madˤɣuːtˤ]
janitor [ˈdʒænɪtə] *n* حاجب [ħaːʒib]
January [ˈdʒænjʊərɪ] *n* يناير [janaːjiru]
Japan [dʒəˈpæn] *n* اليابان [al-jaːbaːnu]
Japanese [ˌdʒæpəˈniːz] *adj* ياباني [jaːbaːniː] ▷ *n (language)* اللغة اليابانية [Al-lghah al-yabaneyah], *(person)* ياباني [jaːbaːniː]
jar [dʒɑː] *n* برطمان [bartˤamaːn]; **jam jar** *n* وعاء المربّى [We'aaa almorabey]
jaundice [ˈdʒɔːndɪs] *n* يرقان [jaraqaːn]
javelin [ˈdʒævlɪn] *n* رُمْح [rumħ]
jaw [dʒɔː] *n* فك [fakk]
jazz [dʒæz] *n* موسيقى الجاز [Mosey'qa al-jaz]
jealous [ˈdʒɛləs] *adj* غيور [ɣajuːr]
jeans [dʒiːnz] *npl* ملابس الجينز [Malabes al-jeenz]
jelly [ˈdʒɛlɪ] *n* جيلي [ʒiːliː]
jellyfish [ˈdʒɛlɪˌfɪʃ] *n* قنديل البحر ['qandeel al-baḥr]
jersey [ˈdʒɜːzɪ] *n* قميص من الصوف ['qameeṣ men al-ṣoof]
Jesus [ˈdʒiːzəs] *n* يسوع [jasuːʕ]
jet [dʒɛt] *n* أنبوب [ʔunbuːb]; **jet lag** *n* تعب بعد السفر بالطائرة [Ta'aeb ba'ad al-safar bel-ṭaerah]; **jumbo jet** *n* طائرة نفاثة [Ṭaayeara nafathah]
jetty [ˈdʒɛtɪ] *n* حاجز الماء [Hajez al-maa]
Jew [dʒuː] *n* يهودي [jahuːdiː]
jewel [ˈdʒuːəl] *n* جوهرة [ʒawhara]
jeweller [ˈdʒuːələ] *n* جواهرجي [ʒawaːhirʒiː]
jeweller's [ˈdʒuːələz] *n* محل جواهرجي [Maḥal jawaherjey]
jewellery [ˈdʒuːəlrɪ] *n* مجوهرات [muʒawharaːt]; **I would like to put my jewellery in the safe** أريد أن أضع مجوهراتي في الخزينة [areed an aḍa'a mujaw-haraty fee al-khazeena]
Jewish [ˈdʒuːɪʃ] *adj* عِبري [ʕibriː]
jigsaw [ˈdʒɪɡˌsɔː] *n* منشار المنحنيات [Menshar al-monḥanayat]
job [dʒɒb] *n* وَظيفة [wazˤiːfa]; **job centre** *n* مركز العمل [markaz al-'aamal]
jobless [ˈdʒɒblɪs; 'jobless] *adj* عاطل [ʕaːtˤil]
jog [dʒɒɡ] *v* يُمارِس رياضة العدو [Yomares reyaḍat al-'adw]
jogging [ˈdʒɒɡɪŋ] *n* هَرْوَلة [harwala]
join [dʒɔɪn] *v* يَربِط [jarbitˤu]
joiner [ˈdʒɔɪnə] *n* شخص اجتماعي [Shakhṣ ejtema'ay]
joint [dʒɔɪnt] *adj* مشترك [muʃtarak] ▷ *n*

(junction) وَصْلَة [wasˤla], *(meat)* مُفصَل [mafsˤal]; **joint account** *n* حساب مشترك [Hesab moshtarak]
joke [dʒəʊk] *n* نكتة [nukta] ▷ *v* يمزح [jamzaħu]
jolly [ˈdʒɒlɪ] *adj* بهيج [bahi:ʒ]
Jordan [ˈdʒɔːdᵊn] *n* الأردن [al-ʔurd]
Jordanian [dʒɔːˈdeɪnɪən] *adj* أردني [unrdunij] ▷ *n* أردني [unrdunij]
jot down [dʒɒt daʊn] *v* كتب بسرعة [Katab besor'aah]
jotter [ˈdʒɒtə] *n* دفتر صغير [Daftar ṣagheer]
journalism [ˈdʒɜːnᵊˌlɪzəm] *n* صحافة [sˤaħa:fa]
journalist [ˈdʒɜːnᵊlɪst] *n* صحفي [sˤaħafij]
journey [ˈdʒɜːnɪ] *n* رحلة [riħla]; **How long is the journey?** ما الفترة التي ستستغرقها الرحلة؟ [ma al-fatra al-laty sa-tasta-ghru'qiha al-reḥla?]; **The journey takes two hours** الرحلة تستغرق ساعتين [al-reḥla tasta-ghri'q sa'aatyin]
joy [dʒɔɪ] *n* بهجة [bahʒa]
joystick [ˈdʒɔɪˌstɪk] *n* عصا القيادة ['aaṣa al-'qeyadh]
judge [dʒʌdʒ] *n* قاضي [qa:dˤi:] ▷ *v* يُحاكِم [juħa:kamu]
judo [ˈdʒuːdəʊ] *n* جودو [ʒu:du:]
jug [dʒʌg] *n* إبريق [ibri:q]; **a jug of water** إبريق من الماء [ebree'q min al-maa-i]
juggler [ˈdʒʌglə; ˈjuggler] *n* مُشَعْوِذ [muʃaʕwið]
juice [dʒuːs] *n* عصير [ʕasˤi:ru]; **orange juice** *n* عصير برتقال [Aṣeer borto'qaal]
July [dʒuːˈlaɪ; dʒə-; dʒʊ-] *n* يوليو [ju:lju:]
jump [dʒʌmp] *n* قفزة طويلة ['qafzah ṭaweelah] ▷ *v* يَقْفِز [jaqfizu]; **high jump** *n* قفزة عالية ['qafzah 'aaleyah]; **jump leads** *npl* وصلة بطارية السيارة [Waṣlat baṭareyah al-sayarah]; **long jump** *n* قفزة طويلة ['qafzah ṭaweelah]
jumper [ˈdʒʌmpə] *n* مُوصِل (مِعْطف) [mu:sˤil]
jumping [dʒʌmpɪŋ] *n*; **show-jumping** *n* استعراضات القفز [Este'araḍat al-'qafz]
junction [ˈdʒʌŋkʃən] *n* وصلة [wasˤla]
June [dʒuːn] *n* يونيو [ju:nju:]; **at the beginning of June** في بداية شهر يونيو [fee bedayat shaher yon-yo]; **at the end of June** في نهاية شهر يونيو [fee nehayat shahr yon-yo]; **for the whole of June** طوال شهر يونيو [ṭewal shahr yon-yo]; **It's Monday fifteenth June** يوم الاثنين الموافق 51 يونيو [yawm al-Ithnain al-muwa-fi'q 15 yon-yo]
jungle [ˈdʒʌŋgᵊl] *n* دغل [daɣl]
junior [ˈdʒuːnjə] *adj* أصغر [ʔasˤɣaru]
junk [dʒʌŋk] *n* خُرْدة [xurda]; **junk mail** *n* بريد غير مرغوب [Bareed gheer marghoob]
jury [ˈdʒʊərɪ] *n* هيئة المحلفون [Hayaat moḥalefeen]
just [dʒəst] *adv* على وجه الضبط [Ala wajh al-ḍabṭ]
justice [ˈdʒʌstɪs] *n* عَدَالة [ʕada:la]
justify [ˈdʒʌstɪˌfaɪ] *v* يُعَلِل [juʕallilu]

k

kangaroo [ˌkæŋɡəˈruː] *n* كُنْغُر [kanɣur]
karaoke [ˌkɑːrəˈəʊkɪ] *n* غِنَاء مع الموسيقى [Ghenaa ma'a al-mose'qa]
karate [kəˈrɑːtɪ] *n* كراتيه [kara:ti:h]
Kazakhstan [ˌkɑːzɑːkˈstæn; -ˈstɑːn] *n* كازاخستان [ka:za:xista:n]
kebab [kəˈbæb] *n* كباب [kaba:b]
keen [kiːn] *adj* قاطع [qa:tˤiʕ]
keep [kiːp] *v* يَحفَظ [jaħfazˤu]
keep-fit [ˈkiːpˌfɪt] *n* المُحافظة على الرشاقة [Al-mohafaḍh ala al-rasha'qa]
keep out [kiːp aʊt] *v* يبتعِد عن [Yabta'aed 'an]
keep up [kiːp ʌp] *v* يلاحق خطوة بخطوة [Yolaḥek khoṭwa bekhoṭwah]; **keep up with** *v* يَبقى في حالة جيدة [Yab'qaa fee ḥalah jayedah]
kennel [ˈkɛnᵊl] *n* وجار الكلب [Wejaar alkalb]
Kenya [ˈkɛnjə; ˈkiːnjə] *n* كينيا [ki:nja:]
Kenyan [ˈkɛnjən; ˈkiːnjən] *adj* كيني [ki:nij] ▷ *n* شخص كيني [Shakhs keeny]
kerb [kɜːb] *n* حاجز حجرى [Hajez hajarey]
kerosene [ˈkɛrəˌsiːn] *n* كيروسين [ki:runwsi:n]
ketchup [ˈkɛtʃəp] *n* كاتشب [ka:tʃub]
kettle [ˈkɛtᵊl] *n* غلاية [ɣalla:ja]
key [kiː] *n (for lock)* مفتاح [mifta:ħ], *(music/computer)* نغمة مميزة [Naghamaah momayazah]; **car keys** *npl* مفاتيح السيارة [Meftaḥ al-sayarah]; **Can I have a key?** هل يمكنني الاحتفاظ بمفتاح؟ [hal yamken -any al-eḥtefaaḍh be-muftaaḥ?]; **I've forgotten the key** لقد نسيت المفتاح [la'qad nasyto al-muftaaḥ]; **the key for room number two hundred and two** مفتاح الغرفة رقم مائتين واثنين [muftaaḥ al-ghurfa ra'qim ma-atyn wa ithnayn]; **The key doesn't work** المفتاح لا يعمل [al-muftaaḥ la ya'amal]; **We need a second key** إننا في حاجة إلى مفتاح آخر [ena-na fee ḥaja ela muftaaḥ aakhar]; **What's this key for?** أين يوجد مفتاح... [le-ay ghurfa hadha al-muftaaḥ?]; **Where do we get the key...?** أين يمكن أن أحصل على المفتاح...؟ [ayna yamken an naḥṣal 'ala al-muftaaḥ...?]; **Where do we hand in the key when we're leaving?** أين نترك المفتاح عندما نغادر؟ [ayna natruk al-muftaaḥ 'aendama nughader?]; **Which is the key for this door?** أين يوجد مفتاح هذا الباب؟ [ayna yujad muftaaḥ hadha al-baab?]
keyboard [ˈkiːˌbɔːd] *n* لوحة مفاتيح [Looḥat mafateeḥ]
keyring [ˈkiːˌrɪŋ] *n* عَلَاقَة مفاتيح ['aalaqat mafateeḥ]
kick [kɪk] *n* رَكلة [rakla] ▷ *v* يَركُل [jarkulu]
kick off [kɪk ɒf] *v* يَستأنِف لعب كرة القدم [Yastaanef lo'ab korat al'qadam]
kick-off [kɪkɒf] *n* الركلة الأولى [Al-raklah al-ola]
kid [kɪd] *n* غلام [ɣula:m] ▷ *v* يَخدَع [jaxdaʕu]
kidnap [ˈkɪdnæp] *v* يَختطِف [jaxtatˤifu]
kidney [ˈkɪdnɪ] *n* كُلْيَة [kilja]
kill [kɪl] *v* يقتل [jaqtulu]
killer [ˈkɪlə] *n* سفاح [saffa:ħ]
kilo [ˈkiːləʊ] *n* كيلو [ki:lu:]
kilometre [kɪˈlɒmɪtə; ˈkɪləˌmiːtə] *n* كيلومتر [ki:lu:mitr]
kilt [kɪlt] *n* تنورة قصيرة بها ثنيات واسعة [Tannorah 'qaṣeerah beha thanayat wase'aah]

kind [kaɪnd] *adj* حنون [ħanu:n] ▷ *n* نوع [nawʕ]; **What kind of sandwiches do you have?** ما نوع الساندويتشات الموجودة؟ [ma naw'a al-sandweshaat al-maw-jooda?]
kindly ['kaɪndlɪ] *adv* لطفاً [lutˤfan]
kindness ['kaɪndnɪs] *n* لطف [lutˤf]
king [kɪŋ] *n* ملك [milk]
kingdom ['kɪŋdəm] *n* مملكة [mamlaka]
kingfisher ['kɪŋˌfɪʃə] *n* طائر الرفراف [Ṭaayer alrafraf]
kiosk ['ki:ɒsk] *n* كشك [kiʃk]
kipper ['kɪpə] *n* ذَكَر سمك السلمون [Dhakar samak al-salamon]
kiss [kɪs] *n* قبلة [qibla] ▷ *v* يُقَبِل [juqabbilu]
kit [kɪt] *n* صندوق العدة [Ṣondok al-'aedah]; **hands-free kit** *n* سماعات [samma:ʕa:tun]; **repair kit** *n* عدة التصليح ['aodat altaṣleeh]
kitchen ['kɪtʃɪn] *n* مطبخ [matˤbax]; **fitted kitchen** *n* مطبخ مجهز [Maṭbakh mojahaz]
kite [kaɪt] *n* طائرة ورقية [Ṭaayeara wara'qyah]
kitten ['kɪtᵊn] *n* هرة صغيرة [Herah ṣagheerah]
kiwi ['ki:wi:] *n* طائر الكيوي [Ṭaarr alkewey]
knee [ni:] *n* رُكبَة [rukba]
kneecap ['ni:ˌkæp] *n* الرضفة [aradˤfatu]
kneel [ni:l] *v* يَركَع [jarkaʕu]
kneel down [ni:l daʊn] *v* يَسجُد [jasʒudu]
knickers ['nɪkəz] *npl* سروال قصير [Serwal 'qaṣeer]
knife [naɪf] *n* سكينة [saki:na]
knit [nɪt] *v* يَعْقِد [jaʕqidu]
knitting ['nɪtɪŋ] *n* حَبك [ħibk]; **knitting needle** *n* إبرة خياطة [Ebrat khayṭ]
knob [nɒb] *n* مقبض [miqbadˤ]
knock [nɒk] *n* ضربة عنيفة [Darba 'aneefa] ▷ *v* يَقْرَع [jaqraʕu], *(on the door etc.)* يَقْرَع [jaqraʕu]
knock down [nɒk daʊn] *v* يَصْرَع [jasˤraʕu]
knock out [nɒk aʊt] *v* يَعمَل بعجلة من غير اتقان [jaʕmalu biʕaʒlatin min ɣajrin ʔitqa:ni]
knot [nɒt] *n* عقدة [ʕuqda]
know [nəʊ] *v* يعرف [jaʕrifu]
know-all ['nəʊɔ:l] *n* مدعي العلم بكل شيء [Moda'aey al'aelm bel-shaya]
know-how ['nəʊˌhaʊ] *n* القدرة الفنية [Al'qodarh al-faneyah]
knowledge ['nɒlɪdʒ] *n* معرفة [maʕrifa]
knowledgeable ['nɒlɪdʒəbᵊl] *adj* حسن الاطلاع [Hosn al-etela'a]
known [nəʊn] *adj* مشهور [maʃhu:r]
Koran [kɔ:'rɑ:n] *n* القُرآن [al-qurʔa:nu]
Korea [kə'ri:ə] *n* كوريا [ku:rja:]; **North Korea** *n* كوريا الشمالية [Koreya al-shamaleyah]; **South Korea** *n* كوريا الجنوبية [Korya al-janoobeyah]
Korean [kə'ri:ən] *adj* كوري [ku:rijjat] ▷ *n* *(language)* اللغة الكورية [Al-loghah al-koreyah], *(person)* كوري [ku:rijja]
kosher ['kəʊʃə] *adj* شَرْعِيّ [ʃarʕij]
Kosovo ['kɔsɔvɔ; 'kɒsəvəʊ] *n* كوسوفو [ku:su:fu:]
Kuwait [kʊ'weɪt] *n* الكويت [al-kuwi:tu]
Kuwaiti [kʊ'weɪtɪ] *adj* كويتي [kuwajtij] ▷ *n* كويتي [kuwajtij]
Kyrgyzstan ['kɪəgɪzˌstɑ:n; -ˌstæn] *n* كيرجستان [ki:raʒista:n]

lab [læb] *n* معمل [maʕmal]
label ['leɪbᵊl] *n* ملصق بيانات [Molsa'q bayanat]
laboratory [lə'bɒrətərɪ; -trɪ; 'læbrə,tɔːrɪ] *n* مُختَبَر [muxtabar]; **language laboratory** *n* مُختَبَر اللغة [Mokhtabar al-loghah]
labour ['leɪbə] *n* عمال [ʕummaːl]
labourer ['leɪbərə] *n* عَامِل [ʕaːmil]
lace [leɪs] *n* شريط الحذاء [Shreeṭ al-ḥedhaa]
lack [læk] *n* نقص [naqsˤ]
lacquer ['lækə] *n* ورنيش اللَك [Warneesh al-llak]
lad [læd] *n* صبي [sˤabij]
ladder ['lædə] *n* سُلَم [sullam]
ladies ['leɪdɪz] *n*; **ladies'** *n* سيدات [sajjidaːtun]; **Where is the ladies?** أين يوجد حمام السيدات؟ [Ayn yojad ḥamam al-saydat]
ladle ['leɪdᵊl] *n* مغرفة [miɣrafa]
lady ['leɪdɪ] *n* سيدة [sajjida]
ladybird ['leɪdɪ,bɜːd] *n* خُنْفِسَاء الدَعْسُوقَة [Khonfesaa al-da'aso'qah]
lag [læg] *n*; **jet lag** *n* تعب بعد السفر بالطائرة [Ta'aeb ba'ad al-safar bel-ṭaerah]; **I'm suffering from jet lag** أنا أعاني من الدوار عند ركوب الطائرة [ana o-'aany min al-dawaar 'aenda rukoob al-ṭa-era]
lager ['lɑːgə] *n* جعة معتقة [Jo'aah mo'ata'qah]
lagoon [lə'guːn] *n* بُحَيْرَة [buħajra]
laid-back ['leɪdbæk] *adj* مسترخي [mustarxiː]
lake [leɪk] *n* بُحَيْرة [buħajra]
lamb [læm] *n* حَمَل [ħiml]
lame [leɪm] *adj* كسيح [kasiːħ]
lamp [læmp] *n* مصباح [misˤbaːħ]; **bedside lamp** *n* مِصْبَاح بِسَرِيرِ [Meṣbaaḥ besareer]
lamppost ['læmp,pəʊst] *n* عمود النور ['amood al-noor]
lampshade ['læmp,ʃeɪd] *n* غطاء المصباح [Gheṭaa almeṣbaḥ]
land [lænd] *n* أرض [ʔardˤ] ▷ *v* يَهْبِط [jahbitˤu]
landing ['lændɪŋ] *n* هبوط [hubuːtˤ]
landlady ['lænd,leɪdɪ] *n* مالكة الأرض [Malekat al-arḍ]
landlord ['lænd,lɔːd] *n* صاحب الأرض [Ṣaheb ardh]
landmark ['lænd,mɑːk] *n* مَعلَم [maʕlam]
landowner ['lænd,əʊnə] *n* مالك الأرض [Malek al-arḍ]
landscape ['lænd,skeɪp] *n* منظر طبيعى [manḍhar ṭabe'aey]
landslide ['lænd,slaɪd] *n* انهيار أرضي [Enheyar ardey]
lane [leɪn] *n* زُقَاق [zuqaːq], *(driving)* زُقَاق [zuqaːq]; **cycle lane** *n* زُقَاق دائري [Zo'qa'q daerey]
language ['læŋgwɪdʒ] *n* لغة [luɣa]; **language laboratory** *n* مُختَبَر اللغة [Mokhtabar al-loghah]; **language school** *n* مدرسة لغات [Madrasah lo-ghaat]; **sign language** *n* لغة الإشارة [Loghat al-esharah]
lanky ['læŋkɪ] *adj* طويل مع هزال [Ṭaweel ma'aa hozal]
Laos [laʊz; laʊs] *n* جمهورية لاووس [Jomhoreyat lawoos]

lap [læp] *n* حضن [ħudˤn]
laptop ['læp,tɒp] *n* كمبيوتر محمول [Kombeyotar maḥmool]
larder ['lɑːdə] *n* موضع لحفظ الأطعمة [Mawḍe'a lehafḍh al-aṭ'aemah]
large [lɑːdʒ] *adj* عريض [ʕariːdˤ]
largely ['lɑːdʒlɪ] *adv* بدرجة كبيرة [Be-darajah kabeerah]
laryngitis [,lærɪn'dʒaɪtɪs] *n* التهاب الحنجرة [Eltehab al-hanjara]
laser ['leɪzə] *n* ليزر [lajzar]
lass [læs] *n* فتاة [fataːt]
last [lɑːst] *adj* أخير [ʔaxiːr] ▷ *adv* آخراً [ʔaːxiran] ▷ *v* يَستمِر [jastamirru]; **I'm delighted to meet you at last** يسعدني أن التقي بك أخيرًا [yas-'aedny an al-ta'qy beka akheran]
lastly ['lɑːstlɪ] *adv* أخيراً [ʔaxiːran]
late [leɪt] *adj (dead)* فقيد [faqiːd], *(delayed)* مُبطئ [mubtˤiʔ] ▷ *adv* متأخراً [mutaʔaxiran]
lately ['leɪtlɪ] *adv* منذ عهد قريب [monḍh 'aahd 'qareeb]
later ['leɪtə] *adv* فيما بعد [Feema baad]
Latin ['lætɪn] *n* لاتيني [laːtiːniː]
Latin America ['lætɪn ə'mɛrɪkə] *n* أمريكا اللاتينية [Amreeka al-lateeneyah]
Latin American ['lætɪn ə'mɛrɪkən] *adj* من أمريكا اللاتينية [men Amrika al lateniyah]
latitude ['lætɪ,tjuːd] *n* خط العرض [Khaṭ al-'arḍ]
Latvia ['lætvɪə] *n* لاتيفيا [laːtiːfjaː]
Latvian ['lætvɪən] *adj* لاتيفي [laːtiːfiː] ▷ *n (language)* اللغة الاتيفية [Al-loghah al-atefeyah], *(person)* شخص لاتيفي [Shakhs lateefey]
laugh [lɑːf] *n* ضحكة [dˤaħka] ▷ *v* يَضحَك [jadˤħaku]
laughter ['lɑːftə] *n* ضَحِك [dˤaħik]
launch [lɔːntʃ] *v* يُطلق [jutˤliqu]
Launderette® [,lɔːndə'rɛt; lɔːn'drɛt] *n* ®لاندريت [Landreet®]
laundry ['lɔːndrɪ] *n* مغسلة [miɣsala]
lava ['lɑːvə] *n* الحمم البركانية [Al-ḥemam al-borkaneyah]
lavatory ['lævətərɪ; -trɪ] *n* مرحاض [mirħaːdˤ]
lavender ['lævəndə] *n* لافندر [laːfandar]
law [lɔː] *n* قانون [qaːnuːn]; **law school** *n* كلية الحقوق [Kolayt al-ho'qooq]
lawn [lɔːn] *n* مرج [marʒ]
lawnmower ['lɔːn,maʊə] *n* جزازة العشب [Jazazt al-'aoshb]
lawyer ['lɔːjə; 'lɔɪə] *n* محامي [muħaːmij]
laxative ['læksətɪv] *n* ملين الأمعاء [Molayen al-am'aa]
lay [leɪ] *v* يَطْرَح [jatˤraħu]
layby ['leɪ,baɪ] *n* مكان انتظار [Makan enteḍhar]
layer ['leɪə] *n* طَبَقة [tˤabaqa]; **ozone layer** *n* طبقة الأوزون [Taba'qat al-odhoon]
lay off [leɪ ɒf] *v* يُسَرح [jusarriħu]
layout ['leɪ,aʊt] *n* مُخطط [muxatˤatˤ]
lazy ['leɪzɪ] *adj* كسول [kasuːl]
lead[1] [liːd] *n (in play/film)* دَور رئيسي [Dawr raaesey], *(position)* مقال رئيسي فى صحيفة [Ma'qal raaeaey fee ṣaheefah] ▷ *v* يَتْزَعَم [jatzaʕʕamu]; **jump leads** *npl* وصلة بطارية السيارة [Waṣlat baṭareyah al-sayarah]; **lead singer** *n* مُغَنّي حفلات [Moghaney ḥafalat]
lead[2] [lɛd] *n (metal)* قيادة [qijaːda]
leader ['liːdə] *n* قائد [qaːʔid]
lead-free [,lɛd'friː] *adj* خالى من الرصاص [Khaley men al-raṣaṣ]
leaf [liːf] *n* ورقة نبات [Wara'qat nabat]; **bay leaf** *n* ورق الغار [Wara'q alghaar]
leaflet ['liːflɪt] *n* نشرة [naʃra]
league [liːg] *n* جَمَاعَة [ʒamaːʕa]
leak [liːk] *n* تَسَرُب [tasarrub] ▷ *v* يسرب [jusarribu]
lean [liːn] *v* يَتَكئ [jattakiʔ]; **lean forward** *v* يَتَكئ للأمام [Yatakea lel-amam]
lean on [liːn ɒn] *v* يَستنِد على [Yastaned 'ala]
lean out [liːn aʊt] *v* يَتَكئ على [Yatakea ala]
leap [liːp] *v* يَثِب [jaθibu]; **leap year** *n* سَنة كبيسة [Sanah kabeesah]
learn [lɜːn] *v* يَتعلم [jataʕallamu]

learner ['lɜːnə; 'learner] *n* مُتَعَلِّم [mutaʕallinm]; **learner driver** *n* سائق مبتدئ [Sae'q mobtadea]
lease [liːs] *n* عقد إيجار ['aa'qd eejar] ▷ *v* يُؤَجِر منقولات [Yoajer man'qolat]
least [liːst] *adj* الأقل [Al'aqal]; **at least** *adv* على الأقل ['ala ala'qal]
leather ['lɛðə] *n* جلد مدبوغ [Jeld madboogh]
leave [liːv] *n* إجازة [ʔiʒaːza] ▷ *v* يَتْرك [jatruku]; **maternity leave** *n* أجازة وضع [Ajazat wad'a]; **paternity leave** *n* أجازة رعاية طفل [ajaazat re'aayat al ṭefl]; **sick leave** *n* أجازة مَرضِيَّة [Ajaza maraḍeyah]
leave out [liːv aʊt] *v* يَستبعِد [justabʕadu]
leaves [liːvz] *npl* أوراق الشجر [Awra'q al-shajar]
Lebanese [ˌlɛbə'niːz] *adj* لبناني [lubnaːnij] ▷ *n* لبناني [lubnaːnij]
Lebanon ['lɛbənən] *n* لبنان [lubnaːn]
lecture ['lɛktʃə] *n* محاضرة [muħaːdˤara] ▷ *v* يُحاضِر [juħaːdˤiru]
lecturer ['lɛktʃərə; 'lecturer] *n* محاضر [muħaːdˤir]
leek [liːk] *n* بَصَلْ أخضر [Baṣal akhḍar]
left [lɛft] *adj* يساري [jasaːrij] ▷ *adv* يساراً [jasaːran] ▷ *n* يسار [jasaːr]; **Go left at the next junction** اتجه نحو اليسار عند التقاطع الثاني [Etajh naḥw al-yasar 'aend al-ta'qato'a al-thaney]; **Turn left** اتجه نحو اليسار [Etajeh naḥw al-yasaar]
left-hand [ˌleft'hænd] *adj* أعسر [ʔaʕsar]; **left-hand drive** *n* سيارة مقودها على الجانب الأيسر [Sayarh me'qwadoha ala al-janeb al-aysar]
left-handed [ˌleft'hændɪd] *adj* أعسر [ʔaʕsar]
left-luggage [ˌleft'lʌgɪdʒ] *n* أمتعة مُخزَّنة [Amte'aah mokhazzanah]; **left-luggage locker** *n* خزانة الأمتعة المتروكة [Khezanat al-amte'ah al-matrookah]; **left-luggage office** *n* مكتب الأمتعة [Makatb al amte'aah]
leftovers ['lɛftˌəʊvəz] *npl* بقايا الطعام [Ba'qaya ṭ a'aam]
left-wing [ˌleftˌwɪŋ] *adj* جناح أيسر [Janah aysar]
leg [lɛg] *n* رِجل [riʒl]
legal ['liːgᵊl] *adj* قانوني [qaːnuːnij]
legend ['lɛdʒənd] *n* اسطورة [ʔustˤuːra]
leggings ['lɛgɪŋz] *npl* بنطلون صيق [Banṭaloon ṣaye'q]
legible ['lɛdʒəbᵊl] *adj* مقروء [maqruːʔ]
legislation [ˌlɛdʒɪs'leɪʃən] *n* تشريع [taʃriːʕ]
leisure ['lɛʒə; 'liːʒər] *n* راحة [raːħa]; **leisure centre** *n* مركز ترفيهي [Markaz tarfehy]
lemon ['lɛmən] *n* ليمون [lajmuːn]; **with lemon** بالليمون [bil-laymoon]
lemonade [ˌlɛmə'neɪd] *n* عصير الليمون المحلى ['aaṣeer al-laymoon al-moḥala]
lend [lɛnd] *v* يُقرِض مالا [Yo'qred malan]
length [lɛŋkθ; lɛŋθ] *n* طول [tˤuːl]
lens [lɛnz] *n* عدسة [ʕadasa]; **contact lenses** *npl* عدسات لاصقة ['adasaat laṣe'qah]; **zoom lens** *n* عدسة تكبير ['adasah mokaberah]
Lent [lɛnt] *n* الصَوْم الكبير [Al-ṣawm al-kabeer]
lentils ['lɛntɪlz] *npl* نبات العدس [Nabat al-'aads]
Leo ['liːəʊ] *n* ليو [lijuː]
leopard ['lɛpəd] *n* نمر منقط [Nemr men'qaṭ]
leotard ['lɪəˌtɑːd] *n* ثوب الراقص أو البهلوان [Thawb al-ra'qes aw al-bahlawan]
less [lɛs] *adv* بدرجة أقل [Be-darajah a'qal] ▷ *pron* أقل [ʔaqallu]
lesson ['lɛsᵊn] *n* دَرْس [dars]; **driving lesson** *n* دَرْس القيادة [Dars al-'qeyadah]
let [lɛt] *v* يَدَع [jadaʕu]
let down [lɛt daʊn] *v* يَتخلى عن [Yatkhala an]
let in [lɛt ɪn] *v* يَسْمَح بالدُّخول [Yasmah bel-dokhool]
letter ['lɛtə] *n (a, b, c)* حرف [ħarf], *(message)* خطاب [xitˤaːb]; **I'd like to send this letter** أريد أن أرسل هذا الخطاب [areed an arsil hadha al-kheṭab]

letterbox ['lɛtəˌbɒks] *n* صندوق الخطابات [Ṣondok al-kheṭabat]
lettuce ['lɛtɪs] *n* خَسّ [xussu]
leukaemia [luːˈkiːmɪə] *n* لوكيميا [luːkiːmjaː]
level ['lɛvᵊl] *adj* منبسط [munbasitˤ] ▷ *n* منبسط [munbasitˤ]; **level crossing** *n* مزلقان [mizlaqaːnun]; **sea level** *n* مستوى سطح البحر [Mostawa saṭh al-bahr]
lever ['liːvə] *n* عتلة [ʕatla]
liar ['laɪə] *n* كذاب [kaðaːb]
liberal ['lɪbərəl; 'lɪbrəl] *adj* تحرري [taħarurij]
liberation [ˌlɪbəˈreɪʃən] *n* تحرير [taħriːr]
Liberia [laɪˈbɪərɪə] *n* ليبيريا [liːbiːrjaː]
Liberian [laɪˈbɪərɪən] *adj* ليبيري [liːbiːrij] ▷ *n* ليبيري [liːbiːrij]
Libra ['liːbrə] *n* الميزان [al-miːzaːnu]
librarian [laɪˈbrɛərɪən] *n* أمين المكتبة [Ameen al maktabah]
library ['laɪbrərɪ] *n* مكتبة [maktaba]
Libya ['lɪbɪə] *n* ليبيا [liːbjaː]
Libyan ['lɪbɪən] *adj* ليبي [liːbij] ▷ *n* ليبي [liːbij]
lice [laɪs] *npl* قمل [qamlun]
licence ['laɪsəns] *n* رُخْصَة [ruxsˤa]; **driving licence** *n* رُخْصَة القيادة [Rokhṣat al-'qeyadah]
lick [lɪk] *v* يَلْعَق [jalʕaqu]
lid [lɪd] *n* غِطاء [ɣitˤaːʔ]
lie [laɪ] *n* كذبة [kiðba] ▷ *v* يَكْذِب [jakððibu]
Liechtenstein ['lɪktənˌstaɪn; 'lɪçtənʃtain] *n* لختنشتاين [lixtunʃtaːjan]
lie down [laɪ daʊn] *v* يَكْذِب [jakððibu]
lie in [laɪ ɪn] *v* الرقود في السرير [Alro'qood fel-sareer]
lie-in [laɪɪn] *n*; **have a lie-in** *v* الرقود في السرير [Alro'qood fel-sareer]
lieutenant [lɛfˈtɛnənt; luːˈtɛnənt] *n* ملازم أول [Molazem awal]
life [laɪf] *n* حياة [ħajaːt]; **life insurance** *n* تأمين على الحياة [Taameen 'ala al-hayah]; **life jacket** *n* سُترة النجاة [Sotrat al-najah]
lifebelt ['laɪfˌbɛlt] *n* حزام النجاة من الغرق [Hezam al-najah men al-ghar'q]
lifeboat ['laɪfˌbəʊt] *n* قارب نجاة ['qareb najah]
lifeguard ['laɪfˌgɑːd] *n* عامل الإنقاذ ['aamel alen'qaḍh]; **Get the lifeguard!** اتصل بعامل الإنقاذ [itaṣel be-'aamil al-en'qaadh]
life-saving ['life-ˌsaving] *adj* مُنقذ للحياة [Mon'qedh lel-ḥayah]
lifestyle ['laɪfˌstaɪl] *n* نمط حياة [Namaṭ hayah]
lift [lɪft] *n (free ride)* توصيلة مجانية [tawṣeelah majaneyah], *(up/down)* مصعد [misˤʕad] ▷ *v* يَرفَع [jarfaʕu]; **ski lift** *n* مِصْعَد التّزَلّج [Meṣ'aad al-tazalog]; **Do you have a lift for wheelchairs?** هل لديك مصعد لكراسي المقعدين المتحركة؟ [hal ladyka maṣ'aad le-karasi al-mu'q'aadeen al-mutaḥarika?]; **Is there a lift in the building?** هل يوجد مصعد في المبنى؟ [hal yujad maṣ'aad fee al-mabna?]; **Where is the lift?** أين يوجد المصعد؟ [ayna yujad al-maṣ'aad?]
light [laɪt] *adj (not dark)* خفيف [xafiːf], *(not heavy)* خفيف [xafiːf] ▷ *n* ضوء [dˤawʔ] ▷ *v* يُضِئ [judˤiʔ]; **brake light** *n* مصباح الفرامل [Mesbaḥ al-faramel]; **hazard warning lights** *npl* أضواء التحذير من الخطر [Aḍwaa al-tahdheer men al-khaṭar]; **light bulb** *n* مصباح اضاءة [Mesbaḥ eḍaah]; **pilot light** *n* شُعلة الاحتراق [Sho'alat al-eḥtera'q]; **traffic lights** *npl* إشارات المرور [Esharaat al-moroor]; **May I take it over to the light?** هل يمكن أن أشاهدها في الضوء؟ [hal yamken an osha-heduha fee al-ḍoe?]
lighter ['laɪtə] *n* قداحة [qaddaːħa]
lighthouse ['laɪtˌhaʊs] *n* منارة [manaːra]
lighting ['laɪtɪŋ] *n* اضاءة [idˤaːʔa]
lightning ['laɪtnɪŋ] *n* بَرْق [barq]
like [laɪk] *prep* مِثل ▷ *v* يُحِب [juħibbu]
likely ['laɪklɪ] *adj* محتمل [muħtamal]
lilac ['laɪlək] *adj* الليلك [allajlak] ▷ *n* لائِلاكْ [laːjlaːk]
Lilo® ['laɪləʊ] *n* ليلو® [Leelo®]
lily ['lɪlɪ] *n* زنبقة [zanbaqa]; **lily of the valley** *n* زَنْبَق الوادي [Zanba'q al-wadey]
lime [laɪm] *n (compound)* جير [ʒiːr], *(fruit)*

ليمون [lajmu:n]
limestone [ˈlaɪmˌstəʊn] *n* حجر الجير [Hajar al-jeer]
limit [ˈlɪmɪt] *n* قيد [qajd]; **age limit** *n* حد السّن [Had alssan]; **speed limit** *n* حد السرعة [Ḥad alsor'aah]
limousine [ˈlɪməˌziːn; ˌlɪməˈziːn] *n* ليموزين [li:mu:zi:n]
limp [lɪmp] *v* يعرُج [jaʕruʒu]
line [laɪn] *n* خط [xatˤtˤu]; **washing line** *n* خط الغسيل [Khat al-ghaseel]; **I want to make an outside call, can I have a line?** أريد إجراء مكالمة خارجية، هل يمكن أن تحول لي أحد الخطوط؟ [areed ejraa mukalama kharij-iya, hal yamkin an it-ḥawil le aḥad al-khiṭooṭ?]; **It's a bad line** هذا الخط مشوش [hatha al-khaṭ musha-wash]; **Which line should I take for...?** ما هو الخط الذي يجب أن أستقله؟ [ma howa al-khaṭ al-lathy yajeb an asta'qil-uho?]
linen [ˈlɪnɪn] *n* كتان [katta:n]; **bed linen** *n* بياضات الأسرّة [Bayaḍat al-aserah]
liner [ˈlaɪnə] *n* باخِرَة رُكّاب [Bakherat rokkab]
lingerie [ˈlænʒərɪ] *n* ملابس داخلية [Malabes dakheleyah]
linguist [ˈlɪŋɡwɪst] *n* عالم لغويات ['aalem laghaweyat]
linguistic [lɪŋˈɡwɪstɪk] *adj* لغوي [luɣawij]
lining [ˈlaɪnɪŋ] *n* بطَانَة [batˤa:na]
link [lɪŋk] *n* رابط [ra:bitˤ]; **link (up)** *v* يَصل بين [yaṣel bayn]
lino [ˈlaɪnəʊ] *n* مشمع الأرضية [Meshama'a al-arḍeyah]
lion [ˈlaɪən] *n* أسد [ʔasad]
lioness [ˈlaɪənɪs] *n* لبؤة [labuʔa]
lip [lɪp] *n* شفاه [ʃifa:h]; **lip salve** *n* كريم للشفاه [Kereem lel shefah]
lip-read [ˈlɪpˌriːd] *v* يَقْرَأ الشفاه [Ya'qraa al-shefaa]
lipstick [ˈlɪpˌstɪk] *n* أحمر شفاه [Ahmar shefah]
liqueur [lɪˈkjʊə; likœr] *n* مُسكِر [muskir]
liquid [ˈlɪkwɪd] *n* مادة سائلة [madah saaelah]; **washing-up liquid** *n* سائل غسيل الأطباق [Saael ghaseel al-aṭba'q]
liquidizer [ˈlɪkwɪˌdaɪzə] *n* مادة مسيلة [Madah moseelah]
list [lɪst] *n* قائمة [qa:ʔima] ▷ *v* يُعِد قائمة [Yo'aed 'qaemah]; **mailing list** *n* قائمة بريد ['qaemat bareed]; **price list** *n* قائمة أسعار ['qaemat as'aar]; **waiting list** *n* قائمة انتظار ['qaemat enteḍhar]; **wine list** *n* قائمة خمور ['qaemat khomor]; **The wine list, please** قائمة النبيذ من فضلك ['qaemat al-nabeedh min faḍlak]
listen [ˈlɪsᵊn] *v* يَستمِع [jastamiʕu]; **listen to** *v* يَستمِع إلى [Yastame'a ela]
listener [ˈlɪsnə] *n* مستمع [mustamiʕ]
literally [ˈlɪtərəlɪ] *adv* حرفياً [ħarfijjan]
literature [ˈlɪtərɪtʃə; ˈlɪtrɪ-] *n* أدب [dab]
Lithuania [ˌlɪθjʊˈeɪnɪə] *n* ليتوانيا [li:twa:nja:]
Lithuanian [ˌlɪθjʊˈeɪnɪən] *adj* ليتواني [li:twa:nij] ▷ *n (language)* اللغة الليتوانية [Al-loghah al-letwaneyah], *(person)* شخص ليتواني [shakhṣ letwaneyah]
litre [ˈliːtə] *n* لتر [litr]
litter [ˈlɪtə] *n* رُكَام مُبَعثَر [Rokaam moba'athar], *(offspring)* ولادة الحيوان [Weladat al-ḥayawaan]; **litter bin** *n* سلة المهملات [Salat al-mohmalat]
little [ˈlɪtᵊl] *adj* صغير [sˤaɣi:r]
live¹ [lɪv] *v* يعيش [jaʕi:ʃu]
live² [laɪv] *adj* حي [ħajj]; **Where can we hear live music?** أين يمكننا الاستماع إلى موسيقى حية؟ [ayna yamken-ana al-istima'a ela mose'qa ḥay-a?]
lively [ˈlaɪvlɪ] *adj* بحيوية [biħajawijjatin]
live on [lɪv ɒn] *v* يعيش على [Ya'aeesh ala]
liver [ˈlɪvə] *n* كَبِدْ [kabid]
live together [lɪv] *v* يعيش سوياً [Ya'aeesh saweyan]
living [ˈlɪvɪŋ] *n* رزق [rizq]; **cost of living** *n* تكلفة المعيشة [Taklefat al-ma'aeeshah]; **living room** *n* حجرة المعيشة [Ḥojrat al-ma'aeshah]; **standard of living** *n* مستوى المعيشة [Mostawa al-ma'aeeshah]
lizard [ˈlɪzəd] *n* السِحلية [as-siħlijjatu]

load [ləʊd] *n* حِمل [ħiml] ▷ *v* يتلقى حملا [Yatala'qa ḥemlan]
loaf, loaves [ləʊf, ləʊvz] *n* رغيف [raɣi:f]
loan [ləʊn] *n* قرض [qardˤ] ▷ *v* يُقْرض [juqridˤu]
loathe [ləʊð] *v* يَشمئِز من [Yashmaaez 'an]
lobby ['lɒbɪ] *n*; **I'll meet you in the lobby** سوف أقابلك في الردهة الرئيسية للفندق [sawfa o'qabe-loka fee al-radha al-raee-sya lel-finda'q]
lobster ['lɒbstə] *n* جَرَاد البحر [Garad al-baḥr]
local ['ləʊkᵊl] *adj* محلي [maħalij]; **local anaesthetic** *n* عقار مخدر موضعي ['aa'qar mokhader mawde'aey]; **I'd like to try something local, please** أريد أن أجرب أحد الأشياء المحلية من فضلك [areed an ajar-rub aḥad al-ashyaa al-maḥal-lya min faḍlak]; **We'd like to see local plants and trees** نريد أن نرى النباتات والأشجار المحلية [nureed an nara al-naba-taat wa al-ash-jaar al-maḥali-ya]; **What's the local speciality?** ما هو الطبق المحلي المميز؟ [ma howa al-ṭaba'q al-maḥa-ly al-muma-yaz?]
location [ləʊ'keɪʃən] *n* مكان [maka:n]; **My location is...** أنا في المكان... [ana fee al-makaan...]
lock [lɒk] *n* *(door)* هويس [huwajs], *(hair)* خُصلة شعر [Khoṣlat sha'ar] ▷ *v* يَقْفِل [jaqfilu]
locker ['lɒkə] *n* خزانة بقفل [Khezanah be-'qefl]; **left-luggage locker** *n* خزانة الأمتعة المتروكة [Khezanat al-amte'ah al-matrookah]
locket ['lɒkɪt] *n* دَلاَيَة [dala:ja]
lock out [lɒk aʊt] *v* يُحرِم شخصاً من الدخول [Yoḥrem shakhṣan men al-dokhool]
locksmith ['lɒkˌsmɪθ] *n* صانع المفاتيح [Ṣaane'a al-mafateeḥ]
lodger ['lɒdʒə] *n* نزيل [nazi:l]
loft [lɒft] *n* عِلية [ʕilja]
log [lɒg] *n* كُتْلَه خَشَبِيّه [kutlatun xaʃabijja]
logical ['lɒdʒɪkᵊl] *adj* منطقي [mantˤiqij]
log in [lɒg ɪn] *v* يُسجِل الدخول [Yosajel al-dokhool]
logo ['ləʊgəʊ; 'lɒg-] *n* شِعَار [ʃiʕa:r]
log off [lɒg ɒf] *v* يُسجِل الخروج [Yosajel al-khoroj]
log on [lɒg ɒn] *v* يَدخُل على شبكة المعلومات [Yadkhol 'ala shabakat alma'aloomat]
log out [lɒg aʊt] *v* يَخرُج من برنامج الكمبيوتر [Yakhroj men bernamej kombyotar]
lollipop ['lɒlɪˌpɒp] *n* مَصّاصَه [masˤsˤasˤa]
lolly ['lɒlɪ] *n* مَصّاصَة [masˤsa:ˤsˤa]
London ['lʌndən] *n* لندن [lund]
loneliness ['ləʊnlɪnɪs] *n* وِحْدَة [waħda]
lonely ['ləʊnlɪ] *adj* متوحد [mutawaħħid]
lonesome ['ləʊnsəm] *adj* مهجور [mahʒu:r]
long [lɒŋ] *adj* طويل [tˤawi:l] ▷ *adv* طويلًا [tˤawi:la:an] ▷ *v* يَتْوق إلى [Yatoo'q ela]; **long jump** *n* قفزة طويلة ['qafzah ṭaweelah]
longer [lɒŋə] *adv* أطول [ʔatˤwalu]
longitude ['lɒndʒɪˌtju:d; 'lɒŋg-] *n* خط طول [Khaṭ ṭool]
loo [lu:] *n* مِرْحَاض [mirħa:dˤ]
look [lʊk] *n* نظرة [nazˤra] ▷ *v* ينظر [janzˤuru]; **look at** *v* ينظر إلى [yanḍhor ela]
look after [lʊk ɑ:ftə] *v* يعتني بـ [Ya'ataney be]
look for [lʊk fɔ:] *v* يَبْحَث عن [Yabḥath an]
look round [lʊk raʊnd] *v* يَدْرِس الاحتمالات قبل وضع خطة [Yadros aleḥtemalaat 'qabl waḍ'a alkhoṭah]
look up [lʊk ʌp] *v* يَرفَع بصره [Yarfa'a baṣarah]
loose [lu:s] *adj* فضفاض [fadˤfa:dˤ]
lorry ['lɒrɪ] *n* شاحِنة لوري [Shaḥenah loorey]; **lorry driver** *n* سائق لوري [Sae'q lorey]
lose [lu:z] *vi* يَضْيع [judˤajjiʕu] ▷ *vt* يَخسر [jaxsaru]

loser ['luːzə] *n* الخاسر [al-xa:siru]
loss [lɒs] *n* خسارة [xasa:ra]
lost [lɒst] *adj* تائه [ta:ʔih]; **lost-property office** *n* مكتب المفقودات [Maktab al-maf'qodat]
lost-and-found ['lɒstænd'faʊnd] *n* مفقودات وموجودات [maf'qodat wa- maw-joodat]
lot [lɒt] *n*; **a lot** *n* نصيب [nasˤi:bun]
lotion ['ləʊʃən] *n* مُستحضر سائل [Mosthdar saael]; **after sun lotion** *n* لوشن بعد التعرض للشمس [Loshan b'ad al-t'arod lel shams]; **cleansing lotion** *n* سائل تنظيف [Sael tandheef]; **suntan lotion** *n* غسول سمرة الشمس [ghasool somrat al-shams]
lottery ['lɒtərɪ] *n* يانصيب [ja:nasˤi:b]
loud [laʊd] *adj* مدو [mudawwin]
loudly [laʊdlɪ] *adv* بصوت عال [Besot 'aaley]
loudspeaker [ˌlaʊd'spiːkə] *n* مكبر صوت [makbar sˤawt]
lounge [laʊndʒ] *n* حجرة الجلوس [Hojrat al-joloos]; **departure lounge** *n* صالة المغادرة [Ṣalat al-moghadarah]; **transit lounge** *n* صالة العبور [Ṣalat al'aoboor]
lousy ['laʊzɪ] *adj* خسيس [xasi:s]
love [lʌv] *n* حب [ħubb] ▷ *v* يُتَيِمّ ب [Yotayam be]; **I love...** ...أنا أحب [ana ahib]; **I love you** أحبك [ahibak]; **Yes, I'd love to** نعم، أحب القيام بذلك [na'aam, ahib al-'qiyam be-dhalik]
lovely ['lʌvlɪ] *adj* مُحبب [muħabbab]
lover ['lʌvə] *n* مُحِب [muħib]
low [ləʊ] *adj* منخفض [munxafidˤ] ▷ *adv* منخفضاً [munxafadˤan]; **low season** *n* فترة ركود [Fatrat rekood]
low-alcohol ['ləʊˌælkəˌhɒl] *adj* قليلة الكحول ['qaleelat al-kohool]
lower ['ləʊə] *adj* أدنى [ʔadna:] ▷ *v* ينخفض [janxafidˤu]
low-fat ['ləʊˌfæt] *adj* قليل الدسم ['qaleel al-dasam]
loyalty ['lɔɪəltɪ] *n* إخلاص [ʔixla:sˤ]
luck [lʌk] *n* حظ [ħazˤzˤ]
luckily ['lʌkɪlɪ] *adv* لحسن الطالع [Le-hosn altale'a]
lucky ['lʌkɪ] *adj* محظوظ [maħzˤu:zˤ]
lucrative ['luːkrətɪv] *adj* مربح [murbiħ]
luggage ['lʌgɪdʒ] *n* حقائب السفر [ha'qaeb al-safar]; **hand luggage** *n* أمتعة محمولة في اليد [Amte'aah mahmoolah fee al-yad]; **luggage rack** *n* حامل حقائب السفر [Hamel ha'qaeb al-safar]; **luggage trolley** *n* عربة حقائب السفر ['arabat ha'qaaeb al-safar]; **Can I insure my luggage?** هل يمكنني التأمين على حقائب السفر الخاصة بي؟ [hal yamken -any al-tameen 'aala ha'qa-eb al-safar al-khasa bee?]; **My luggage hasn't arrived** لم تصل حقائب السفر الخاصة بي بعد [Lam tasel ha'qaeb al-safar al-khasah bee ba'ad]; **Where is the luggage for the flight from...?** أين حقائب السفر للرحلة القادمة من...؟ [ayna ha'qaeb al-safar lel-rehla al-'qadema min...?]
lukewarm [ˌluːk'wɔːm] *adj* فاتر [fa:tir]
lullaby ['lʌləˌbaɪ] *n* تهويدة [tahwi:da]
lump [lʌmp] *n* ورم [waram]
lunch [lʌntʃ] *n* غداء [ɣada:ʔ]; **lunch break** *n* استراحة غداء [Estrahet ghadaa]; **packed lunch** *n* وجبة الغذاء المعبأة [Wajbat al-ghezaa al-mo'abaah]; **Can we meet for lunch?** هل يمكننا الاجتماع على الغداء؟ [hal yamken -ana al-ejte-maa'a 'aala al-ghadaa?]
lunchtime ['lʌntʃˌtaɪm] *n* وَقْت الغداء [Wa'qt al-ghadhaa]
lung [lʌŋ] *n* رئة [riʔit]
lush [lʌʃ] *adj* مزدهر [muzdahir]
lust [lʌst] *n* شهوة [ʃahwa]
Luxembourg ['lʌksəmˌbɜːg] *n* لكسمبورغ [luksambu:rɣ]
luxurious [lʌg'zjʊərɪəs] *adj* مترف [mutraf]
luxury ['lʌkʃərɪ] *n* رفاهية [rafa:hijja]
lyrics ['lɪrɪks] *npl* قصائد غنائية ['qasaaed ghenaaeah]

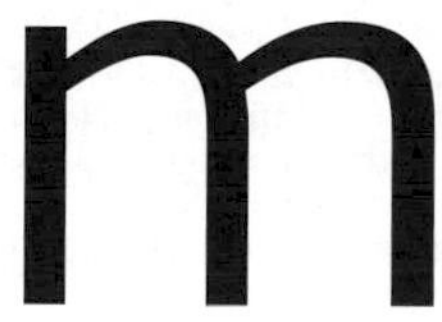

mac [mæk] *abbr* معطف واق من المطر [Me'ataf wa'qen men al-maarṭar]
macaroni [ˌmækəˈrəʊnɪ] *npl* مكرونة [makaru:natun]
machine [məˈʃiːn] *n* ماكينة [ma:ki:na]; **answering machine** *n* جهاز الرد الآلي [Jehaz al-rad al-aaly]; **machine gun** *n* رشاش [raʃʃa:ʃun]; **machine washable** *adj* قابل للغسل في الغسالة ['qabel lel-ghaseel fee al-ghassaalah]; **sewing machine** *n* ماكينة خياطة [Makenat kheyaṭah]; **slot machine** *n* ماكينة الشقبية [Makenat al-sha'qabeyah]; **ticket machine** *n* ماكينة التذاكر [Makenat al-taḍhaker]; **vending machine** *n* ماكينة بيع [Makenat bay'a]; **washing machine** *n* غسّالَة [ɣassa:latun]; **Can I use my card with this cash machine?** هل يمكنني استخدام بطاقتي في ماكينة الصرف الآلي هذه؟ [hal yamken -any esti-khdaam beṭa-'qatee fee makenat al-ṣarf al-aaly hadhy?]; **Is there a cash machine here?** هل توجد ماكينة صرف آلي هنا؟ [hal tojad makenat ṣarf aaly huna?]; **Is there a fax machine I can use?** هل توجد ماكينة فاكس يمكن استخدامها؟ [hal tojad makenat fax yamken istekh-damuha?]; **The cash machine swallowed my card** لقد ابتلعت ماكينة الصرف الآلي بطاقتي [la'qad ibtal-'aat makenat al-ṣarf al-aaly be-ṭa'qaty]; **Where is the nearest cash machine?** أين توجد أقرب ماكينة لصرف النقود؟ [ayna tojad a'qrab makena le-ṣarf al-no'qood?]
machinery [məˈʃiːnərɪ] *n* الآلية [al-ajjatu]
mackerel [ˈmækrəl] *n* سمك الماكريل [Samak al-makreel]
mad [mæd] *adj (angry)* مجنون [maʒnu:n], *(insane)* خبل [xabil]
Madagascar [ˌmædəˈgæskə] *n* مدغشقر [madaɣaʃqar]
madam [ˈmædəm] *n* زوجة [zawʒa]
madly [ˈmædlɪ] *adv* بجنون [biʒunu:nin]
madman [ˈmædmən] *n* مجنون [maʒnu:n]
madness [ˈmædnɪs] *n* جنون [ʒunu:n]
magazine [ˌmægəˈziːn] *n (ammunition)* ذخيرة حربية [dhakheerah ḥarbeyah], *(periodical)* مجلة [maʒalla]
maggot [ˈmægət] *n* يَرَقْة [jaraqa]
magic [ˈmædʒɪk] *adj* سَاحِر [sa:ħir] ▷ *n* سِحْر [siħr]
magical [ˈmædʒɪkəl] *adj* سِحري [siħrij]
magician [məˈdʒɪʃən] *n* ساحر [sa:ħir]
magistrate [ˈmædʒɪˌstreɪt; -strɪt] *n* قاضي [qa:dˤi:]
magnet [ˈmægnɪt] *n* مغناطيس [miɣna:tˤi:s]
magnetic [mægˈnɛtɪk] *adj* مغناطيسي [miɣna:tˤi:sij]
magnificent [mægˈnɪfɪsᵊnt] *adj* بديع [badi:ʕ]
magpie [ˈmægˌpaɪ] *n* طائر العَقْعَق [Ṭaaer al'a'qa'q]
mahogany [məˈhɒgənɪ] *n* خشب الماهوجني [Khashab al-mahojney]
maid [meɪd] *n* خادمة [xa:dima]
maiden [ˈmeɪdᵊn] *n*; **maiden name** *n* اسم المرأة قبل الزواج [Esm al-marah 'qabl alzawaj]
mail [meɪl] *n* بريد [bari:d] ▷ *v* يُرسِل بالبريد

[Yorsel bel-bareed]; **junk mail** *n* بريد غير مرغوب [Bareed gheer marghoob]; **Is there any mail for me?** هل تلقيت أي رسائل بالبريد الإلكتروني؟ [hal tala-'qyto ay rasa-el bil-bareed al-alekitrony?]
mailbox ['meɪl,bɒks] *n* صندوق البريد [Ṣondo'q bareed]
mailing list ['meɪlɪŋ 'lɪst] *n* قائمة بريد ['qaemat bareed]
main [meɪn] *adj* أساسي [ʔasa:sij]; **main course** *n* طبق رئيسي [Ṭaba'q raeesey]; **main road** *n* طريق رئيسي [ṭaree'q raeysey]
mainland ['meɪnlənd] *n* اليابسة [al-ja:bisatu]
mainly ['meɪnlɪ] *adv* في الدرجة الأولى [Fee al darajah al ola]
maintain [meɪn'teɪn] *v* يصون [jasˤu:nu]
maintenance ['meɪntɪnəns] *n* صيانة [sˤija:na]
maize [meɪz] *n* ذُرَة [ðura]
majesty ['mædʒɪstɪ] *n* جلالة [ʒala:la]
major ['meɪdʒə] *adj* أساسي [ʔasa:sij]
majority [mə'dʒɒrɪtɪ] *n* الأغلبية [al-ʔaɣlabijjatu]
make [meɪk] *v* يَصْنَع [jasˤnaʕu]
makeover ['meɪk,əʊvə] *n* تحول في المظهر [taḥawol fee almaḍhhar]
maker ['meɪkə] *n* صانع [sˤa:niʕ]
make up [meɪk ʌp] *v* يَخْتَلِق [jaxtaliqu]
make-up [meɪkʌp] *n* مستحضرات التجميل [Mostahdraat al-tajmeel]
malaria [mə'lɛərɪə] *n* ملاريا [mala:rja:]
Malawi [mə'lɑːwɪ] *n* ملاوي [mala:wi:]
Malaysia [mə'leɪzɪə] *n* ماليزيا [ma:li:zja:]
Malaysian [mə'leɪzɪən] *adj* ماليزي [ma:li:zij] ▷ *n* شخص ماليزي [shakhṣ maleezey]
male [meɪl] *adj* ذَكَرِي [ðakarij] ▷ *n* ذَكَر [ðakar]
malicious [mə'lɪʃəs] *adj* خبيث [xabi:θ]
malignant [mə'lɪgnənt] *adj* خَبِيث [xabi:θ]
malnutrition [,mælnjuː'trɪʃən] *n* سوء التغذية [Sooa al taghdheyah]
Malta ['mɔːltə] *n* مالطة [ma:ltˤa]
Maltese [mɔːl'tiːz] *adj* مالطي [ma:ltˤij] ▷ *n (language)* اللغة المالطية [Al-loghah al-malṭeyah], *(person)* مالطي [ma:ltˤij]
mammal ['mæməl] *n* لبون [labu:n]
mammoth ['mæməθ] *adj* ضخم [dˤaxm] ▷ *n* ماموث [ma:mu:θ]
man, men [mæn, mɛn] *n* رَجُل [raʒul]; **best man** *n* إشبين العريس [Eshbeen al-aroos]
manage ['mænɪdʒ] *v* يُدير [judi:ru]
manageable ['mænɪdʒəbᵊl] *adj* سهل القيادة [Sahl al-'qeyadah]
management ['mænɪdʒmənt] *n* إدارة [ʔida:ra]
manager ['mænɪdʒə] *n* مدير [mudi:r]; **I'd like to speak to the manager, please** من فضلك أرغب في التحدث إلى المدير [min faḍlak arghab fee al-taḥaduth ela al-mudeer]
manageress [,mænɪdʒə'rɛs; 'mænɪdʒə,rɛs] *n* مديرة [mudi:ra]
mandarin ['mændərɪn] *n (fruit)* يوسفي [ju:sufij], *(official)* اللغة الصينية الرئيسية [Al-loghah al-Ṣeneyah alraeseyah]
mangetout ['mɑ̃ʒ'tuː] *n* بِسِلَّة [bisallatin]
mango ['mæŋgəʊ] *n* مَنجا [manʒa:]
mania ['meɪnɪə] *n* هَوَس [hawas]
maniac ['meɪnɪ,æk] *n* مَجذوب [maʒðu:b]
manicure ['mænɪ,kjʊə] *n* تدريم الأظافر [Tadreem al-aḍhaafe] ▷ *v* يدرِّم [judarrimu]
manipulate [mə'nɪpjʊ,leɪt] *v* يُعالِج باليد [Yo'aalej bel-yad]
mankind [,mæn'kaɪnd] *n* بشرية [baʃarijja]
man-made ['mæn,meɪd] *adj* من صنع الإنسان [Men ṣon'a al-ensan]
manner ['mænə] *n* سلوك [sulu:k]
manners ['mænəz] *npl* سلوكيات [sulu:kijja:tun]
manpower ['mæn,paʊə] *n* قوة بشرية ['qowah bashareyah]
mansion ['mænʃən] *n* قصر ريفي ['qaṣr

reefey]
mantelpiece ['mæntᵊl,pi:s] *n* رف المستوقد [Raf al-mostaw'qed]
manual ['mænjʊəl] *n* دليل التشغيل [Daleel al-tashgheel]
manufacture [,mænjʊ'fæktʃə] *v* يُصَّنِع [jusˤsˤaniʕu]
manufacturer [,mænjʊ'fæktʃərə] *n* صاحب المصنع [Ṣaheb al-maṣna'a]
manure [mə'njʊə] *n* سماد عضوي [Semad 'aodwey]
manuscript ['mænjʊ,skrɪpt] *n* مخطوطة [maxtˤu:tˤa]
many ['mɛnɪ] *adj* كثير [kaθi:r] ▷ *pron* عديد [ʕadi:dun]
Maori ['maʊrɪ] *adj* ماوري [ma:wrij] ▷ *n (language)* اللغة الماورية [Al-loghah al-mawreyah], *(person)* شخص ماوري [Shakhṣ mawrey]
map [mæp] *n* خريطة [xari:tˤa]; **road map** *n* خريطة الطريق [Khareeṭat al-ṭaree'q]; **street map** *n* خارطة الشارع [khareṭat al-share'a]; **Can I have a map?** هل يمكن أن أحصل على خريطة؟ [hal yamken an aḥṣal 'aala khareeṭa?]; **Can you draw me a map with directions?** هل يمكن أن ترسم لي خريطة للاتجاهات؟ [Hal yomken an tarsem le khareeṭah lel-etejahaat?]; **Can you show me where it is on the map?** هل يمكن أن أري مكانه على الخريطة؟ [Hal yomken an ara makanah ala al-khareeṭah]; **Do you have a map of the tube?** هل لديكم خريطة لمحطات المترو؟ [hal ladykum khareeṭa le-muḥaṭ-aat al-metro?]; **I need a road map of...** أريد خريطة الطريق لـ... [areed khareeṭat al-ṭaree'q le...]; **Is there a cycle map of this area?** هل يوجد خريطة لهذه المنطقة؟ [hal yujad khareeṭa le-hadhy al-manṭa'qa?]; **Where can I buy a map of the area?** أي يمكن أن أشتري خريطة للمكان؟ [ayna yamkun an ash-tary khareeṭa lel-man-ṭa'qa?]
maple ['meɪpᵊl] *n* أشجار القيقب [Ashjaar al-'qay'qab]
marathon ['mærəθən] *n* سباق المارثون [Seba'q al-marathon]
marble ['mɑ:bᵊl] *n* رُخَام [ruxa:m]
march [mɑ:tʃ] *n* سَيْر [sajr] ▷ *v* يَسِير [jasi:ru]
March [mɑ:tʃ] *n* مارس [ma:ris]
mare [mɛə] *n* فرس [faras]
margarine [,mɑ:dʒə'ri:n; ,mɑ:gə-] *n* سَمْن نباتي [Samn nabatey]
margin ['mɑ:dʒɪn] *n* هامش [ha:miʃ]
marigold ['mærɪ,gəʊld] *n* الأقحوان [al-ʔuqħuwa:nu]
marijuana [,mærɪ'hwɑ:nə] *n* ماريجوانا [ma:ri:ʒwa:na:]
marina [mə'ri:nə] *n* حوض مرسى السفن [Hawḍ marsa al-sofon]
marinade *n* [,mærɪ'neɪd] ماء مالح [Maa maleḥ] ▷ *v* ['mærɪ,neɪd] يُخلل [juxallilu]
marital ['mærɪtᵊl] *adj*; **marital status** *n* الحالة الاجتماعية [Al-halah al-ejtemaayah]
maritime ['mærɪ,taɪm] *adj* بحري [baħrij]
marjoram ['mɑ:dʒərəm] *n* عُشب البَرْدَقُوش ['aoshb al-barda'qoosh]
mark [mɑ:k] *n* علامة [ʕala:ma] ▷ *v (grade)* يُعْطِي علامة مدرسية [Yo'aṭey a'alaamah madraseyah], *(make sign)* يُوَسِم [ju:simu]; **exclamation mark** *n* علامة تعجب ['alamah ta'ajob]; **question mark** *n* علامة استفهام ['alamat estefham]; **quotation marks** *npl* علامات الاقتباس ['aalamat al-e'qtebas]
market ['mɑ:kɪt] *n* سُوق [su:q]; **market research** *n* دراسة السوق [Derasat al-soo'q]; **stock market** *n* البورصة [al-bu:rsˤatu]
marketing ['mɑ:kɪtɪŋ] *n* تسويق [taswi:qu]
marketplace ['mɑ:kɪt,pleɪs] *n* السوق [as-su:qi]
marmalade ['mɑ:mə,leɪd] *n* هلام الفاكهة [Holam al-fakehah]
maroon [mə'ru:n] *adj* منبوذ [manbu:ð]
marriage ['mærɪdʒ] *n* زواج [zawa:ʒ]; **marriage certificate** *n* عقد زواج

['aa'qd zawaj]
married ['mærɪd] *adj* متزوج [mutazawwiʒ]
marrow ['mærəʊ] *n* نخاع العظم [Nokhaa'a al-'aḍhm]
marry ['mærɪ] *v* يَتَزوج [jatazawwaʒu]
marsh [mɑːʃ] *n* سبخة [sabxa]
martyr ['mɑːtə] *n* شهيد [ʃahiːd]
marvellous ['mɑːvᵊləs] *adj* مدهش [mudhiʃ]
Marxism ['mɑːksɪzəm] *n* الماركسية [al-maːrkisijjatu]
marzipan ['mɑːzɪˌpæn] *n* مَرْزيبان [marziːbaːn]
mascara [mæ'skɑːrə] *n* ماسكارا [maːskaːraː]
masculine ['mæskjʊlɪn] *adj* مذكر [muðakkar]
mask [mɑːsk] *n* قناع [qinaːʕ]
masked [mɑːskt; masked] *adj* متنكر [mutanakkir]
mass [mæs] *n (amount)* مقدار كبير [Me'qdaar kabeer], *(church)* قُدّاس [quddaːs]
massacre ['mæsəkə] *n* مذبحة [maðbaħa]
massage ['mæsɑːʒ; -sɑːdʒ] *n* تدليك [tadliːk]
massive ['mæsɪv] *adj* ضَخْم [dˤaxm]
mast [mɑːst] *n* صاري [sˤaːriː]
master ['mɑːstə] *n* مدرس [mudarris] ▷ *v* يُتْقِن [jutqinu]
masterpiece ['mɑːstəˌpiːs] *n* رائعة [raːʔiʕa]
mat [mæt] *n* ممسحة أرجل [Memsahat arjol]; **mouse mat** *n* لوحة الفأرة [Looḥat al-faarah]
match [mætʃ] *n (partnership)* شريك حياة [Shareek al-ḥayah], *(sport)* مباراة [mubaːraːt] ▷ *v* يُضاهي [judˤaːhiː]; **away match** *n* مباراة الذهاب [Mobarat al-dhehab]; **home match** *n* مباراة الإياب فى ملعب المضيف [Mobarat al-eyab fee mal'aab al-moḍeef]; **I'd like to see a football match** أود أن أشاهد مباراة كرة قدم؟ [awid an oshahed mubaraat korat 'qadam]
matching [mætʃɪŋ] *adj* مكافئ [mukaːfiʔ]
mate [meɪt] *n* رفيق [rafiːq]
material [mə'tɪərɪəl] *n* مادة [maːdda]
maternal [mə'tɜːnᵊl] *adj* متعلق بالأم [Mota'ale'q bel om]
mathematical [ˌmæθə'mætɪkᵊl; ˌmæθ'mæt-] *adj* (رياضي(متعلق بالرياضيات
mathematics [ˌmæθə'mætɪks; ˌmæθ'mæt-] *npl* رياضيات [rijaːdˤijjaːtun]
maths [mæθs] *npl* علم الرياضيات ['aelm al-reyaḍeyat]
matter ['mætə] *n* مسألة [masʔala] ▷ *v* يَهُم [jahummu]
mattress ['mætrɪs] *n* حشية [ħiʃʃa]
mature [mə'tjʊə; -'tʃʊə] *adj* ناضج [naːdˤiʒ]; **mature student** *n* طالب راشد [Ṭaleb rashed]
Mauritania [ˌmɒrɪ'teɪnɪə] *n* موريتانيا [muːriːtaːnjaː]
Mauritius [mə'rɪʃəs] *n* موريتاني [muːriːtaːnij]
mauve [məʊv] *adj* بنفسجي [banafsaʒij]
maximum ['mæksɪməm] *adj* أقصى [ʔaqsˤaː] ▷ *n* حد أقصى [Had a'qsa]
may [meɪ] *v*; **May I call you tomorrow?** هل يمكن أن أتصل بك غدا؟ [hal yamken an ataṣel beka ghadan?]; **May I open the window?** هل يمكن أن أفتح النافذة؟ [hal yamken an aftaḥ al-nafidha?]
May [meɪ] *n* مايو [maːjuː]
maybe ['meɪˌbiː] *adv* رُبما [rubbamaː]
mayonnaise [ˌmeɪə'neɪz] *n* ميونيز [majuːniːz]
mayor, mayoress [mɛə, 'mɛərɪs] *n* مُحَافِظ [muħaːfizˤ]
maze [meɪz] *n* متاهة [mataːha]
me [miː] *pron* إليَّ [ʔilajja]
meadow ['mɛdəʊ] *n* أرض خضراء [Arḍ khaḍraa]
meal [miːl] *n* وجبة [waʒba]; **Could you prepare a meal without eggs?** هل يمكن إعداد وجبة خالية من البيض؟ [hal yamken e'adad wajba khaliya min al-bayḍ?]; **Could you prepare a meal**

without gluten? هل يمكن إعداد وجبة خالية من الجلوتين؟ [hal yamken e'adad wajba khaliya min al-jilo-teen?]; **The meal was delicious** كانت الوجبة شهية [kanat il-wajba sha-heyah]
mealtime ['miːlˌtaɪm] *n* وَقْت الطعام [Wa'qt al-ṭa'aaam]
mean [miːn] *adj* حقير [ħaqiːr] ▷ *v* يَقْصِد [jaqsˤidu]
meaning ['miːnɪŋ] *n* معنى [maʕnaː]
means [miːnz] *npl* وَسائِل [wasaːʔilun]
meantime ['miːnˌtaɪm] *adv* في غضون ذلك [Fee ghodoon ḍhalek]
meanwhile ['miːnˌwaɪl] *adv* خلال ذلك [Khelal dhalek]
measles ['miːzəlz] *npl* حصبة [ħasˤabatun]; **German measles** *n* حصبة ألمانية [Haṣbah al-maneyah]; **I had measles recently** أصبت مؤخرًا بمرض الحصبة [oṣebtu mu-akharan be-maraḍ al- ḥaṣba]
measure ['mɛʒə] *v* يَقْيس [jaqisu]; **tape measure** *n* شريط قياس [Shreeṭ 'qeyas]
measurements ['mɛʒəmənts] *npl* قياسات [qijaːsaːtun]
meat [miːt] *n* لحم [laħm]; **red meat** *n* لحم أحمر [Laḥm aḥmar]; **I don't eat red meat** لا أتناول اللحوم الحمراء [la ata- nawal al-liḥoom al-ḥamraa]; **The meat is cold** إن اللحم باردة [En al-laḥm baredah]; **This meat is off** هذه اللحم ليست طازجة [Hadheh al-lahm laysat ṭazejah]
meatball ['miːtˌbɔːl] *n* كرة لحم [Korat laḥm]
Mecca ['mɛkə] *n* مكة [makkatu]
mechanic [mɪ'kænɪk] *n* ميكانيكي [miːkaːniːkij]; **Can you send a mechanic?** هل يمكن أن ترسل لي ميكانيكي؟ [hal yamken an tarsil lee meka-neeky?]
mechanical [mɪ'kænɪkᵊl] *adj* ميكانيكي [miːkaːniːkij]
mechanism ['mɛkəˌnɪzəm] *n* تقنية [tiqnija]
medal ['mɛdᵊl] *n* ميدالية [miːdaːlijja]
medallion [mɪ'dæljən] *n* مدالية كبيرة [Medaleyah kabeerah]
media ['miːdɪə] *npl* وَسائِل الإعلام [Wasaael al-e'alaam]
mediaeval [ˌmɛdɪ'iːvᵊl] *adj* متعلق بالقرون الوسطى [Mot'aale'q bel-'qroon al-wosṭa]
medical ['mɛdɪkᵊl] *adj* طبي [tˤibbij] ▷ *n* فحص طبي شامل [Fahṣ ṭebey shamel]; **medical certificate** *n* شهادة طبية [Shehadah ṭebeyah]
medication [ˌmɛdɪ'keɪʃən] *n*; **I'm on this medication** أنني أتبع هذا العلاج [ina-ny atba'a hadha al-'aelaaj]
medicine ['mɛdɪsɪn; 'mɛdsɪn] *n* دَوَاء [dawaːʔ]
meditation [ˌmɛdɪ'teɪʃən] *n* تَأَمُّل [taʔammul]
Mediterranean [ˌmɛdɪtə'reɪnɪən] *adj* متوسطي [mutawassitˤij] ▷ *n* البحر المتوسط [Al-bahr al-motawaseṭ]
medium ['miːdɪəm] *adj (between extremes)* معتدل [muʕtadil]
medium-sized ['miːdɪəmˌsaɪzd] *adj* متوسط الحجم [Motawaseṭ al-hajm]
meet [miːt] *vi* يَجتَمِع [jaʒtamiʕu] ▷ *vt* يُقَابِل [juqaːbilu]
meeting ['miːtɪŋ] *n* اجتماع [ʔiʒtimaːʕ]; **I'd like to arrange a meeting with...** أرغب في ترتيب إجراء اجتماع مع.....؟ [arghab fee tar-teeb ejraa ejtemaa ma'aa...]
meet up [miːt ʌp] *v* يَلْتَقي ب [Yalta'qey be]
mega ['mɛgə] *adj* كبير [kabiːr]
melody ['mɛlədɪ] *n* لحن [laħn]
melon ['mɛlən] *n* شَمَّام [ʃammaːm]
melt [mɛlt] *vi* يَذوب [jaðuːbu] ▷ *vt* يُذِيب [juðiːbu]
member ['mɛmbə] *n* عضو [ʕudˤw]; **Do I have to be a member?** هل يجب علي أن أكون عضوا؟ [hal yajib 'aala-ya an akoon 'auḍwan?]
membership ['mɛmbəˌʃɪp] *n* عضوية [ʕudˤwijja]; **membership card** *n* بطاقة عضوية [Beṭaqat 'aodweiah]

memento [mɪˈmɛntəʊ] *n* التذكِرة [at-taðkiratu]
memo [ˈmɛməʊ; ˈmiːməʊ] *n* مذكرة [muðakkira]
memorial [mɪˈmɔːrɪəl] *n* نُصُب تذكاري [Noṣob tedhkarey]
memorize [ˈmɛməˌraɪz] *v* يَحفَظ [jaħfazˤu]
memory [ˈmɛmərɪ] *n* ذَاكِرة [ðaːkira]; **memory card** *n* كارت ذاكرة [Kart dhakerah]
mend [mɛnd] *v* يُصْلِح [jusˤliħu]
meningitis [ˌmɛnɪnˈdʒaɪtɪs] *n* التهاب السحايا [Eltehab al-sahaya]
menopause [ˈmɛnəʊˌpɔːz] *n* سِن اليأس [Sen al-yaas]
menstruation [ˌmɛnstrʊˈeɪʃən] *n* طَمْث [tˤamθ]
mental [ˈmɛntᵊl] *adj* عقلي [ʕaqlij]
mentality [mɛnˈtælɪtɪ] *n* عقلية [ʕaqlijja]
mention [ˈmɛnʃən] *v* يَذْكُر [jaðkuru]
menu [ˈmɛnjuː] *n* قائمة طعام [ʻqaemat ṭa'aam]; **set menu** *n* قائمة مجموعات الأغذية [ʻqaemat majmo'aat al-oghneyah]
mercury [ˈmɜːkjʊrɪ] *n* زئبق [ziʔbaq]
mercy [ˈmɜːsɪ] *n* رحمة [raħma]
mere [mɪə] *adj* مجرد [muʒarrad]
merge [mɜːdʒ] *v* يَدمِج [judmiʒu]
merger [ˈmɜːdʒə] *n* دَمْج [damʒ]
meringue [məˈræŋ] *n* ميرنجو [miːrinʒuː]
mermaid [ˈmɜːˌmeɪd] *n* حورية الماء [Ḥooreyat al-maa]
merry [ˈmɛrɪ] *adj* بهيج [bahiːʒ]
merry-go-round [ˈmɛrɪgəʊˈraʊnd] *n* دوامة الخيل [Dawamat al-kheel]
mess [mɛs] *n* فوضى [fawdˤaː]
mess about [mɛs əˈbaʊt] *v* يَتلخبط [jatalaxbatˤu]
message [ˈmɛsɪdʒ] *n* رسالة [risaːla]; **text message** *n* رسالة نصية [Resalah naṣeyah]; **Can I leave a message with his secretary?** هل يمكنني ترك رسالة مع السكرتير الخاص به؟ [hal yamken -any tark resala ma'aa al-sikertair al-khaṣ behe?]; **Can I leave a message?** هل يمكن أن أترك رسالة؟ [hal yamken an atruk resala?]
messenger [ˈmɛsɪndʒə] *n* رسول [rasuːl]
mess up [mɛs ʌp] *v* يُخطِئ [juxtˤiʔ]
messy [ˈmɛsɪ] *adj* فوضوي [fawdˤawij]
metabolism [mɪˈtæbəˌlɪzəm] *n* عملية الأيض [ʻamaleyah al-abyaḍ]
metal [ˈmɛtᵊl] *n* معدن [maʕdin]
meteorite [ˈmiːtɪəˌraɪt] *n* حُطام النيزك [Ḥoṭaam al-nayzak]
meter [ˈmiːtə] *n* عداد [ʕaddaːd]; **parking meter** *n* عداد وقوف السيارة [ʻadaad wo'qoof al-sayarah]; **Do you have change for the parking meter?** هل معك نقود فكه لعداد موقف الانتظار؟ [Hal ma'ak ne'qood fakah le'adad maw'qaf al-ente ḍhar?]; **Where is the electricity meter?** أين يوجد عداد الكهرباء؟ [ayna yujad ʻaadad al-kah-raba?]; **Where is the gas meter?** أين يوجد عداد الغاز؟ [ayna yujad ʻaadad al-ghaz?]
method [ˈmɛθəd] *n* طريقة [tˤariːqa]
Methodist [ˈmɛθədɪst] *adj* منهجي [manhaʒij]
metre [ˈmiːtə] *n* متر [mitr]
metric [ˈmɛtrɪk] *adj* متري [mitrij]
Mexican [ˈmɛksɪkən] *adj* مكسيكي [miksiːkij] ▷ *n* مكسيكي [miksiːkij]
Mexico [ˈmɛksɪˌkəʊ] *n* المكسيك [al-miksiːku]
microchip [ˈmaɪkrəʊˌtʃɪp] *n* شريحة صغيرة [Shareehat ṣagheerah]
microphone [ˈmaɪkrəˌfəʊn] *n* ميكروفون [miːkuruːfuːn]; **Does it have a microphone?** هل يوجد ميكروفون؟ [hal yujad mekro-fon?]
microscope [ˈmaɪkrəˌskəʊp] *n* ميكروسكوب [miːkuruːskuːb]
mid [mɪd] *adj* أوسط [ʔawsatˤ]
midday [ˈmɪdˈdeɪ] *n* منتصف اليوم [Montaṣaf al-yawm]; **at midday** عند منتصف اليوم [ʻaenda muntaṣaf al-yawm]

middle [ˈmɪdᵊl] *n* وَسَطْ [wasatˤ]; **Middle Ages** *npl* العصور الوسطى [Al-'aoṣoor al-woṣṭa]; **Middle East** *n* الشرق الأوسط [Al-shar'q al-awṣaṭ]
middle-aged [ˈmɪdᵊlˌeɪdʒɪd] *adj* كهل [kahl]
middle-class [ˈmɪdᵊlˌklɑːs] *adj* من الطبقة الوسطى [men al-Ṭaba'qah al-wosṭa]
midge [mɪdʒ] *n* ذُبَابَة صغيرة [Dhobabah ṣagheerah]
midnight [ˈmɪdˌnaɪt] *n* منتصف الليل [montaṣaf al-layl]; **at midnight** عند منتصف الليل ['aenda muntaṣaf al-layl]
midwife, midwives [ˈmɪdˌwaɪf, ˈmɪdˌwaɪvz] *n* قَابِلة [qa:bila]
migraine [ˈmiːɡreɪn; ˈmaɪ-] *n* صداع النصفي [Ṣoda'a al-naṣføy]
migrant [ˈmaɪɡrənt] *adj* مهاجر [muha:ʒir] ▷ *n* مُهاجِر [muha:ʒir]
migration [maɪˈɡreɪʃən] *n* هجرة [hiʒra]
mike [maɪk] *n* ميكروفون [mi:kuru:fu:n]
mild [maɪld] *adj* لطيف [latˤi:f]
mile [maɪl] *n* مِيل [mi:l]
mileage [ˈmaɪlɪdʒ] *n* مسافة بالميل [Masafah bel-meel]
mileometer [maɪˈlɒmɪtə] *n* عداد الأميال المقطوعة ['adaad al-amyal al-ma'qto'aah]
military [ˈmɪlɪtərɪ; -trɪ] *adj* عسكري [ʕaskarij]
milk [mɪlk] *n* حليب [ħali:b] ▷ *v* يَحلِب [jaħlibu]; **baby milk** *n* لبن أطفال [Laban aṭfaal]; **milk chocolate** *n* شيكولاتة باللبن [Shekolata bel-laban]; **semi-skimmed milk** *n* حليب نصف دسم [Haleeb nesf dasam]; **skimmed milk** *n* حليب منزوع الدسم [Haleeb manzoo'a al-dasam]; **UHT milk** *n* لبن مبستر [Laban mobaster]; **with the milk separate** بالحليب دون خلطه [bil ḥaleeb doon khal-ṭuho]
milkshake [ˈmɪlkˌʃeɪk] *n* مخفوق الحليب [Makhfoo'q al-ḥaleeb]
mill [mɪl] *n* طاحونة [tˤa:ħu:na]
millennium [mɪˈlɛnɪəm] *n* الألفية [al-ʔalfijjatu]
millimetre [ˈmɪlɪˌmiːtə] *n* مليمتر [mili:mitr]
million [ˈmɪljən] *n* مليون [milju:n]
millionaire [ˌmɪljəˈnɛə] *n* مليونير [milju:ni:ru]
mimic [ˈmɪmɪk] *v* يّحاكِي [juħa:ki:]
mince [mɪns] *v* لحم مفروم [Laḥm mafroom]
mind [maɪnd] *n* عقل [ʕaqil] ▷ *v* يهتم [jahtammu]
mine [maɪn] *n* منجم [manʒam] ▷ *pron* ملكي
miner [ˈmaɪnə] *n* عامل مناجم ['aamel manajem]
mineral [ˈmɪnərəl; ˈmɪnrəl] *adj* غير عضوي [Ghayer 'aoḍwey] ▷ *n* مادة غير عضوية [Madah ghayer 'aodweyah]; **mineral water** *n* مياه معدنية [Meyah ma'adaneyah]
miniature [ˈmɪnɪtʃə] *adj* مُصَغَر [musˤaɣɣar] ▷ *n* شَكْل مُصَغّر [Shakl moṣaghar]
minibar [ˈmɪnɪˌbɑː] *n* ثلاجة صغيرة [Thallaja ṣagheerah]
minibus [ˈmɪnɪˌbʌs] *n* ميني باص [Meny baas]
minicab [ˈmɪnɪˌkæb] *n* سيارة أجرة صغيرة [Sayarah ojrah ṣagherah]
minimal [ˈmɪnɪməl; ˈminimal] *adj* أدنى [ʔadna:]
minimize [ˈmɪnɪˌmaɪz] *v* يُخفِض إلى الحد الأدنى [juxfidˤu ʔila: alħaddi alʔadna:]
minimum [ˈmɪnɪməm] *adj* أدنى [ʔadna:] ▷ *n* حد أدنى [Had adna]
mining [ˈmaɪnɪŋ] *n* تعدين [taʕdi:n]
miniskirt [ˈmɪnɪˌskɜːt] *n* جونلة قصيرة [Jonelah 'qaṣeerah]
minister [ˈmɪnɪstə] *n* *(clergy)* كاهن [ka:hin], *(government)* وزير [wazi:r]; **prime minister** *n* رئيس الوزراء [Raees al-wezaraa]
ministry [ˈmɪnɪstrɪ] *n* *(government)* وزارة [wiza:ra], *(religion)* كهنوت [kahnu:t]
mink [mɪŋk] *n* حيوان المِنْكْ [Ḥayawaan almenk]

minor ['maɪnə] *adj* ثانوي [θa:nawij] ▷ *n* شخص قاصر [Shakhṣ 'qaṣer]
minority [maɪ'nɒrɪtɪ; mɪ-] *n* أقلية [ʔaqallija]
mint [mɪnt] *n (coins)* دار سك العملة [Daar ṣaak al'aomlah], *(herb/sweet)* نعناع [naʕnaːʕ]
minus ['maɪnəs] *prep* طَرْح
minute *adj* [maɪ'nju:t] دقيق الحجم [Da'qee'q al-hajm] ▷ *n* ['mɪnɪt] دقيقة [daqi:qa]; **Could you watch my bag for a minute, please?** من فضلك، هل يمكن أن أترك حقيبتي معك لدقيقة واحدة؟ [min faḍlak, hal yamkin an atrik ḥa'qebaty ma'aak le-da'qe'qa waḥeda?]
miracle ['mɪrəkᵊl] *n* معجزة [muʕʒiza]
mirror ['mɪrə] *n* مرآة [mirʔa:t]; **rear-view mirror** *n* مرآة الرؤية الخلفية [Meraah al-roayah al-khalfeyah]; **wing mirror** *n* مرآة جانبية [Meraah janebeyah]
misbehave [ˌmɪsbɪ'heɪv] *v* يُسيء التصرف [Yoseea altaṣarof]
miscarriage [mɪs'kærɪdʒ] *n* إجهاض تلقائي [Ejhaḍ tel'qaaey]
miscellaneous [ˌmɪsə'leɪnɪəs] *adj* متنوع [mutanawwiʕ]
mischief ['mɪstʃɪf] *n* إزعاج [ʔizʕa:ʒ]
mischievous ['mɪstʃɪvəs] *adj* مؤذ [muʔðin]
miser ['maɪzə] *n* بَخيل [baxi:l]
miserable ['mɪzərəbᵊl; 'mɪzrə-] *adj* تعيس [taʕi:s]
misery ['mɪzərɪ] *n* بؤس [buʔs]
misfortune [mɪs'fɔ:tʃən] *n* سوء الحظ [Soa al-ḥaḍh]
mishap ['mɪshæp] *n* حظ عاثر [Ḥadh 'aaer]
misjudge [ˌmɪs'dʒʌdʒ] *v* يُخطئ في الحكم على [yokhṭea fee al-ḥokm ala]
mislay [mɪs'leɪ] *v* يضيّع [judʕajjiʕu]
misleading [mɪs'li:dɪŋ; mis'leading] *adj* مُضَلِل [mudʕallil]
misprint ['mɪsˌprɪnt] *n* خطأ مطبعي [Khata matba'aey]
miss [mɪs] *v* يفتقد [jaftaqidu]
Miss [mɪs] *n* آنسة [ʔa:nisa]
missile ['mɪsaɪl] *n* قذيفة صاروخية ['qadheefah ṣarookheyah]
missing ['mɪsɪŋ] *adj* مفقود [mafqu:d]
missionary ['mɪʃənərɪ] *n* مُبَشِر [mubaʃʃir]
mist [mɪst] *n* شَبّورة [ʃabuwra]
mistake [mɪ'steɪk] *n* غلط [ɣalatʕ] ▷ *v* يُخطئ [juxtʕiju]
mistaken [mɪ'steɪkən] *adj* مخطئ [muxtʕiʔ]
mistakenly [mɪ'steɪkənlɪ] *adv* عن طريق الخطأ [Aan ṭaree'q al-khataa]
mistletoe ['mɪsᵊlˌtəʊ] *n* نبات الهُدَال [Nabat al-hoddal]
mistress ['mɪstrɪs] *n* خليلة [xali:la]
misty ['mɪstɪ] *adj* ضبابي [dʕaba:bij]
misunderstand [ˌmɪsʌndə'stænd] *v* يُسِئ فهم [Yoseea fahm]
misunderstanding [ˌmɪsʌndə'stændɪŋ] *n* سوء فهم [Soa fahm]
mitten ['mɪtᵊn] *n* قفاز يغطي الرسغ ['qoffaz yoghaṭey al-rasgh]
mix [mɪks] *n* مزيج [mazi:ʒ] ▷ *v* يمزج [jamziʒu]
mixed [mɪkst] *adj* مخلوط [maxlu:tʕ]; **mixed salad** *n* سلاطة مخلوطة [Salata makhloṭa]
mixer ['mɪksə] *n* خلاط [xala:atʕ]
mixture ['mɪkstʃə] *n* خليط [xali:tʕ]
mix up [mɪks ʌp] *v* يَخلِط [jaxlitʕu]
mix-up [mɪksʌp] *n* تشوش [taʃawwuʃ]
MMS [ɛm ɛm ɛs] *abbr* خدمة رسائل الوسائط المتعددة [Khedmat rasael al-wasaaeṭ almota'aadedah]
moan [məʊn] *v* يَنْدُب [jandubu]
moat [məʊt] *n* خَنْدَق مائي [Khanda'q maaey]
mobile ['məʊbaɪl] *adj* مُتَحَرِّكٌ [mutaħarrik]; **mobile home** *n* منزل متحرك [Mazel motaḥarek]; **mobile number** *n* رقم المحمول [Ra'qm almahmool]; **mobile phone** *n* هاتف جوال [Hatef jawal]
mock [mɒk] *adj* مُزَوَر [muzawwir] ▷ *v* يَهزأ ب [Yah-zaa be]

mod cons ['mɒd kɒnz] *npl* وسائل الراحة الحديثة [Wasael al-rahah al-hadethah]
model ['mɒdᵊl] *adj* مثالي [miθa:lij] ▷ *n* طراز [tˤira:z] ▷ *v* يُشَكِل [juʃakkilu]
modem ['məʊdɛm] *n* مودم [mu:dim]
moderate ['mɒdərɪt] *adj* متوسط [mutawassitˤ]
moderation [ˌmɒdə'reɪʃən] *n* اعتدال [iʕtida:l]
modern ['mɒdən] *adj* عصري [ʕasˤrij]; **modern languages** *npl* لغات حديثة [Loghat hadethah]
modernize ['mɒdəˌnaɪz] *v* يُحَدِث [juħaddiθu]
modest ['mɒdɪst] *adj* معتدل [muʕtadil]
modification [ˌmɒdɪfɪ'keɪʃən] *n* تعديل [taʕdi:l]
modify ['mɒdɪˌfaɪ] *v* يُعَدِل [juʕadilu]
module ['mɒdju:l] *n* وحدة قياس [Weḥdat 'qeyas]
moist [mɔɪst] *adj* مُبْتَل [mubtall]
moisture ['mɔɪstʃə] *n* نداوة [nada:wa]
moisturizer ['mɔɪstʃəˌraɪzə; 'moistuˌrizer; 'moistuˌriser] *n* مرطب [muratˤtˤib]
Moldova [mɒl'dəʊvə] *n* مولدافيا [mu:lda:fja:]
Moldovan [mɒl'dəʊvən] *adj* مولدافي [mu:lda:fij] ▷ *n* مولدافي [mu:lda:fij]
mole [məʊl] *n (infiltrator)* حاجز الأمواج [Hajez al-amwaj], *(mammal)* الخُلْد [al-xuldu], *(skin)* خال [xa:l]
molecule ['mɒlɪˌkju:l] *n* جزيء [ʒuzajʔ]
moment ['məʊmənt] *n* لحظة [laħzˤa]; **Just a moment, please** لحظة واحدة من فضلك [laḥḍha waheda min faḍlak]
momentarily ['məʊməntərəlɪ; -trɪlɪ] *adv* كل لحظة [Kol laḥḍhah]
momentary ['məʊməntərɪ; -trɪ] *adj* خاطف [xa:tˤif]
momentous [məʊ'mɛntəs] *adj* هام جداً [Ham jedan]
Monaco ['mɒnəˌkəʊ; mə'nɑ:kəʊ; mɔnako] *n* موناكو [mu:na:ku:]
monarch ['mɒnək] *n* ملك [milk]
monarchy ['mɒnəkɪ] *n* أسرة حَاكمة [Osrah ḥakemah]
monastery ['mɒnəstərɪ; -strɪ] *n* دَيْر [dajr]
Monday ['mʌndɪ] *n* الإثنين [al-ʔiθnajni]
monetary ['mʌnɪtərɪ; -trɪ] *adj* متعلق بالعملة [Mota'ale'q bel-'omlah]
money ['mʌnɪ] *n* مال [ma:l]; **money belt** *n* حزام لحفظ المال [Hezam lehefḍh almal]; **pocket money** *n* مصروف الجيب [Maṣroof al-jeeb]; **Could you lend me some money?** هل يمكن تسليفي بعض المال؟ [hal yamken tas-leefy ba'aḍ al-maal?]; **I have no money** ليس معي مال [laysa ma'ay maal]; **I have run out of money** لقد نفذ مالي [la'qad nafatha malee]
Mongolia [mɒŋ'gəʊlɪə] *n* منغوليا [manɣu:lja:]
Mongolian [mɒŋ'gəʊlɪən] *adj* منغولي [manɣu:lij] ▷ *n (language)* اللغة المنغولية [Al-koghah al-manghooleyah], *(person)* منغولي [manɣu:lij]
mongrel ['mʌŋgrəl] *n* هجين [haʒi:n]
monitor ['mɒnɪtə] *n* شاشة [ʃa:ʃa]
monk [mʌŋk] *n* راهب [ra:hib]
monkey ['mʌŋkɪ] *n* قرد [qird]
monopoly [mə'nɒpəlɪ] *n* احتكار [iħtika:r]
monotonous [mə'nɒtənəs] *adj* مُمِل [mumill]
monsoon [mɒn'su:n] *n* ريح موسمية [Reeḥ mawsemeyah]
monster ['mɒnstə] *n* مسخ [masx]
month [mʌnθ] *n* شَهْر [ʃahr]
monthly ['mʌnθlɪ] *adj* شهري [ʃahrij]
monument ['mɒnjʊmənt] *n* مبنى نُصُب تذكاري [Mabna noṣob tedhkarey]
mood [mu:d] *n* حالة مزاجية [Halah mazajeyah]
moody ['mu:dɪ] *adj* متقلب المزاج [Mota'qaleb al-mazaj]
moon [mu:n] *n* قمر [qamar]; **full moon** *n* بَدْر [badrun]
moor [mʊə; mɔ:] *n* أرض سبخة [Arḍ sabkha] ▷ *v* يُوثِق [ju:θiqu]
mop [mɒp] *n* ممسحة تنظيف [Mamsaḥat

tandheef]
moped ['məʊpɛd] *n* دراجة آلية [darrajah aaleyah]
mop up [mɒp ʌp] *v* يمسح [jamsaħu]
moral ['mɒrəl] *adj* أخلاقي (معنوي) [ʔaxla:qij] ▷ *n* مغزى [maɣzan]
morale [mɒ'rɑ:l] *n* معنويات [maʕnawijja:t]
morals ['mɒrəlz] *npl* أخلاقيات [ʔaxla:qijja:tun]
more [mɔ:] *adj* أكثر [ʔakθaru] ▷ *adv* بدرجة أكبر [Be-darajah akbar] ▷ *pron* أكثر [ʔakθaru]; **Could you speak more slowly, please?** هل يمكن أن تتحدث ببطء أكثر إذا سمحت؟ [hal yamken an tata-ḥadath be-buṭi akthar edha samaḥt?]
morgue [mɔ:g] *n* مشرحة [maʃraħa]
morning ['mɔ:nɪŋ] *n* صباح [sˤaba:ħ]; **morning sickness** *n* غثيان الصباح [Ghathayan al-ṣabaḥ]; **Good morning** صباح الخير [ṣabaḥ al-khyer]; **in the morning** في الصباح [fee al-ṣabaḥ]; **I will be leaving tomorrow morning at ten a.m.** سوف أغادر غدا في الساعة العاشرة صباحا [sawfa oghader ghadan fee al-sa'aa al-'aashera ṣaba-han]; **I've been sick since this morning** منذ الصباح وأنا أعاني من المرض [mundho al-ṣabaah wa ana o'aany min al-maraḍ]; **Is the museum open in the morning?** هل المتحف مفتوح في الصباح؟ [hal al-mat-ḥaf maf-tooḥ fee al-ṣabaḥ]; **this morning** هذا الصباح [hatha al-ṣabaḥ]; **tomorrow morning** غدًا في الصباح [ghadan fee al-ṣabaḥ]
Moroccan [mə'rɒkən] *adj* مغربي [maɣribij] ▷ *n* مغربي [maɣribij]
Morocco [mə'rɒkəʊ] *n* المغرب [almaɣribu]
morphine ['mɔ:fi:n] *n* مورفين [mu:rfi:n]
Morse [mɔ:s] *n* مورس [mu:ris]
mortar ['mɔ:tə] *n* *(military)* مدفع الهاون [Madafa'a al-hawon], *(plaster)* ملاط [mala:tˤ]
mortgage ['mɔ:gɪdʒ] *n* رَهْن [rahn] ▷ *v* يَرْهن [jarhanu]
mosaic [mə'zeɪɪk] *n* فسيفساء [fusajfisa:ʔ]
Moslem ['mɒzləm] *adj* مُسلِم [muslim] ▷ *n* مُسْلِم [muslim]
mosque [mɒsk] *n* جامع [ʒa:miʕ]
mosquito [mə'ski:təʊ] *n* بعوضة [baʕu:dˤa]
moss [mɒs] *n* طُحْلُب [tˤuħlub]
most [məʊst] *adj* أقصى [ʔaqsˤa:] ▷ *adv* *(superlative)* إلى جد بعيد [Ela jad ba'aeed] ▷ *n* *(majority)* مُعظَم
mostly ['məʊstlɪ] *adv* في الأغلب [Fee al-aghlab]
MOT [ɛm əʊ ti:] *abbr* وزارة النقل [wiza:ratu annaqli]
motel [məʊ'tɛl] *n* استراحة [istira:ħa]
moth [mɒθ] *n* عثة [ʕaθθa]
mother ['mʌðə] *n* أُم [ʔumm]; **mother tongue** *n* اللغة الأم [Al loghah al om]; **surrogate mother** *n* الأم البديلة [al om al badeelah]
mother-in-law ['mʌðə ɪn lɔ:] **(***pl* **mothers-in-law)** *n* الحماة [al-ħama:tu]
motionless ['məʊʃənlɪs] *adj* ساكن [sa:kin]
motivated ['məʊtɪˌveɪtɪd] *adj* محفز [muħaffiz]
motivation [ˌməʊtɪ'veɪʃən; ˌmoti'vation] *n* تحفيز [taħfi:z]
motive ['məʊtɪv] *n* حافز [ħa:fiz]
motor ['məʊtə] *n* موتور [mawtu:r]; **motor mechanic** *n* ميكانيكي السيارات [Mekaneekey al-sayarat]; **motor racing** *n* سباق سيارات [Seba'q sayarat]
motorbike ['məʊtəˌbaɪk] *n* دراجة بمحرك [Darrajah be-moharrek]
motorboat ['məʊtəˌbəʊt] *n* زورق بمحرك [Zawra'q be-moḥ arek]
motorcycle ['məʊtəˌsaɪkᵊl] *n* دراجة نارية [Darrajah narreyah]
motorcyclist ['məʊtəˌsaɪklɪst] *n* سائق دراجة بخارية [Sae'q drajah bokhareyah]
motorist ['məʊtərɪst] *n* سائق سيارة [Saae'q sayarah]

motorway [ˈməʊtəˌweɪ] *n* طريق السيارات [ṭaree'q alsayaraat]
mould [məʊld] *n (fungus)* عفن [ʕafan], *(shape)* قالب [qa:lab]
mouldy [ˈməʊldɪ] *adj* متعفن [mutaʕaffin]
mount [maʊnt] *v* يَرتفع [jartafiʕu]
mountain [ˈmaʊntɪn] *n* جبل [ʒabal]; **mountain bike** *n* دراجة الجبال [Darrajah al-jebal]; **Where is the nearest mountain rescue service post?** أين يوجد أقرب مركز لخدمة الإنقاذ بالجبل؟ [ayna yujad a'qrab markaz le-khedmat al-en-'qaadh bil-jabal?]
mountaineer [ˌmaʊntɪˈnɪə] *n* متسلق الجبال [Motasale'q al-jebaal]
mountaineering [ˌmaʊntɪˈnɪərɪŋ] *n* تسلق الجبال [Tasalo'q al-jebal]
mountainous [ˈmaʊntɪnəs] *adj* جبلي [ʒabalij]
mount up [maʊnt ʌp] *v* يزيد من [Yazeed men]
mourning [ˈmɔːnɪŋ] *n* حداد [ħida:d]
mouse, mice [maʊs, maɪs] *n* فأر [faʔr]; **mouse mat** *n* لوحة الفأرة [Looḥat al-faarah]
mousse [muːs] *n* كريمة شيكولاتة [Kareemat shekolatah]
moustache [məˈstɑːʃ] *n* شارِب [ʃa:rib]
mouth [maʊθ] *n* فم [fam]; **mouth organ** *n* آلة الهرمونيكا الموسيقية [Alat al-harmoneeka al-mose'qeyah]
mouthwash [ˈmaʊθˌwɒʃ] *n* غسول الفم [Ghasool al-fam]
move [muːv] *n* انتقال [intiqa:l] ▷ *vi* يَتَحرك [jataħarraku] ▷ *vt* يُحَرِك [jaħarrik]
move back [muːv bæk] *v* يَتَحرك للخلف [Yatḥarak lel-khalf]
move forward [muːv fɔːwəd] *v* يَتَحرك إلى الأمام [Yatḥarak lel-amam]
move in [muːv ɪn] *v* ينتقل [jantaqilu]
movement [ˈmuːvmənt] *n* حركة [ħaraka]
movie [ˈmuːvɪ] *n* فيلم [fi:lm]
moving [ˈmuːvɪŋ] *adj* متحرك [mutaħarriki]
mow [məʊ] *v* يُجزُّ [jaʒuzzu]
mower [ˈmaʊə] *n* جَزَّازَة [ʒazza:za]
Mozambique [ˌməʊzəmˈbiːk] *n* موزمبيق [mu:zambi:q]
mph [maɪlz pə aʊə] *abbr* مِيل لكل ساعة [Meel lekol sa'aah]
Mr [ˈmɪstə] *n* السيد [asajjidu]
Mrs [ˈmɪsɪz] *n* السيدة [asajjidatu]
Ms [mɪz; məs] *n* لَقَب للسَّيِّدَه أو الآنِسَه [laqaba lissajjidati ʔaw alʔa:nisati]
MS [mɪz; məs] *abbr* مرض تصلب الأنسجة المتعددة [Maraḍ taṣalob al-ansejah al-mota'adedah]
much [mʌtʃ] *adj* كثير [kaθi:r] ▷ *adv* كثير [kaθi:run]|كثيرا , [kaθi:ran]; **There's too much... in it** يوجد به الكثير من... [yujad behe al-kather min...]
mud [mʌd] *n* طين [tˤi:n]
muddle [ˈmʌdᵊl] *n* تشوش [taʃawwuʃ]
muddy [ˈmʌdɪ] *adj* موحل [mu:ħil]
mudguard [ˈmʌdˌɡɑːd] *n* رفرف العجلة [Rafraf al-'ajalah]
muesli [ˈmjuːzlɪ] *n* حبوب الميوسلي [Ḥoboob al-meyosley]
muffler [ˈmʌflə] *n* لفاع [lifa:ʕ]
mug [mʌɡ] *n* مَجّ [maʒʒ] ▷ *v* يهاجم بقصد السرقة [Yohajem be'qaṣd al-sare'qah]
mugger [ˈmʌɡə] *n* تمساح نهري أسيوي [Temsaah nahrey asyawey]
mugging [mʌɡɪŋ] *n* هجوم للسرقة [Hojoom lel-sare'qah]
muggy [ˈmʌɡɪ] *adj*; **It's muggy** الجو رطب [al-jaw raṭb]
mule [mjuːl] *n* بَغْل [baɣl]
multinational [ˌmʌltɪˈnæʃənᵊl] *adj* متعدد الجنسيات [Mota'aded al-jenseyat] ▷ *n* شركة متعددة الجنسيات [Shreakah mota'adedat al-jenseyat]
multiple [ˈmʌltɪpᵊl] *adj*; **multiple sclerosis** *n* تَلَيُّف عصبي متعدد [Talayof 'aaṣabey mota'aded]
multiplication [ˌmʌltɪplɪˈkeɪʃən] *n* مضاعفة [mudˤa:ʕafa]
multiply [ˈmʌltɪˌplaɪ] *v* يُكْثِر [jukθiru]
mum [mʌm] *n* ماما [ma:ma:]
mummy [ˈmʌmɪ] *n (body)* مومياء

[mu:mja:ʔ], *(mother)* ماما [ma:ma:]
mumps [mʌmps] *n* التهاب الغدة النكفية [Eltehab alghda alnokafeyah]
murder [ˈmɜːdə] *n* جريمة قتل [Jareemat ʻqatl] ▷ *v* يقتل عمداً [Ya'qtol ʻaamdan]
murderer [ˈmɜːdərə] *n* قاتل [qa:til]
muscle [ˈmʌsᵊl] *n* عضلة [ʕadˤala]
muscular [ˈmʌskjʊlə] *adj* عضلي [ʕadˤalij]
museum [mjuːˈziːəm] *n* متحف [matħaf]; **Is the museum open every day?** هل المتحف مفتوح طوال الأسبوع؟ [hal al-mat-ḥaf maf-tooḥ ṭiwaal al-isboo'a?]; **When is the museum open?** متى يُفتح المتحف؟ [mata yoftaḥ al-matḥaf?]
mushroom [ˈmʌʃruːm; -rʊm] *n* عيش الغراب [ʻaaysh al-ghorab]
music [ˈmjuːzɪk] *n* موسيقى [mu:si:qa:]; **folk music** *n* موسيقى شعبية [Mose'qa sha'abeyah]; **music centre** *n* مركز موسيقى [Markaz mose'qa]; **Where can we hear live music?** أين يمكننا الاستماع إلى موسيقى حية؟ [ayna yamken-ana al-istima'a ela mose'qa ḥay-a?]
musical [ˈmjuːzɪkᵊl] *adj* موسيقي [mu:si:qij] ▷ *n* مسرحية موسيقية [Masraḥeyah mose'qeya]; **musical instrument** *n* آلة موسيقية [Aala mose'qeyah]
musician [mjuːˈzɪʃən] *n* عازف موسيقى [ʻaazef mose'qaa]
Muslim [ˈmʊzlɪm; ˈmʌz-] *adj* مُسلِم [muslim] ▷ *n* مُسْلِم [muslim]
mussel [ˈmʌsᵊl] *n* أم الخُلُول [Om al-kholool]
must [mʌst] *v* يَجِب [jaʒibu]
mustard [ˈmʌstəd] *n* خردل [xardal]
mutter [ˈmʌtə] *v* يُغَمْغِم [juɣamɣimu]
mutton [ˈmʌtᵊn] *n* لحم ضأن [Lahm ḍaan]
mutual [ˈmjuːtʃʊəl] *adj* متبادل [mutaba:dal]
my [maɪ] *pron* ي: ضمير المتكلم المضاف إليه
Myanmar [ˈmaɪænmɑː; ˈmjænmɑː] *n* ميانمار [mija:nma:r]
myself [maɪˈsɛlf] *pron* نفسي [nafsijjun]
mysterious [mɪˈstɪərɪəs] *adj* غامض [ɣa:midˤ]
mystery [ˈmɪstərɪ] *n* غموض [ɣumu:dˤ]
myth [mɪθ] *n* أسطورة [ʔustˤu:ra]
mythology [mɪˈθɒlədʒɪ] *n* علم الأساطير [ʻaelm al asateer]

naff [næf] *adj* قديم الطراز [‘qadeem al-ṭeraz]
nag [næg] *v* ينق [janiqqu]
nail [neɪl] *n* مسمار [misma:r]; **nail polish** *n* طلاء أظافر [Ṭelaa aḍhafer]; **nail scissors** *npl* مقص أظافر [Ma’qaṣ aḍhafer]; **nail varnish** *n* طلاء أظافر [Ṭelaa aḍhafer]; **nail-polish remover** *n* مزيل طلاء الأظافر [Mozeel ṭalaa al-aḍhafer]
nailbrush ['neɪl,brʌʃ] *n* فرشاة أظافر [Forshat aḍhafer]
nailfile ['neɪl,faɪl] *n* مبرد أظافر [Mabrad aḍhafer]
naive [nɑː'iːv; naɪ'iːv] *adj* ساذَج [sa:ðaʒ]
naked ['neɪkɪd] *adj* عار [ʕa:r]
name [neɪm] *n* اسم [ism]; **brand name** *n* العلامة التجارية [Al-’alamah al-tejareyah]; **first name** *n* الاسم الأول [Al-esm al-awal]; **maiden name** *n* اسم المرأة قبل الزواج [Esm al-marah ‘qabl alzawaj]; **I booked a room in the name of...** لقد قمت بحجز غرفة باسم... [La’qad ‘qomt behajz ghorfah besm...]; **My name is...** اسمي... [ismee..]; **What’s your name?** ما اسمك؟ [ma ismak?]
nanny ['nænɪ] *n* مربية [murabbija]
nap [næp] *n* غفوة [ɣafwa]
napkin ['næpkɪn] *n* منديل المائدة [Mandeel al-maaedah]
nappy ['næpɪ] *n* شراب مُسكِر [Sharaab mosker]
narrow ['nærəʊ] *adj* ضيق [dˤajjiq]
narrow-minded ['nærəʊ'maɪndɪd] *adj* ضَيّق الأُفُق [Ḍaye’q al-ofo’q]
nasty ['nɑːstɪ] *adj* كريه [kari:h]
nation ['neɪʃən] *n* أمة [ʔumma]; **United Nations** *n* الأمم المتحدة [Al-omam al-motahedah]
national ['næʃənᵊl] *adj* قومي [qawmijju]; **national anthem** *n* نشيد وطني [Nasheed waṭney]; **national park** *n* حديقة وطنية [Hadee’qah waṭaneyah]
nationalism ['næʃənə,lɪzəm; 'næʃnə-] *n* قَوْمِيّة [qawmijja]
nationalist ['næʃənəlɪst] *n* مُنَاصر للقومية [Monaṣer lel-’qawmeyah]
nationality [,næʃə'nælɪtɪ] *n* جنسية [ʒinsijja]
nationalize ['næʃənə,laɪz; 'næʃnə-] *v* يؤمِّم [juʔammimu]
native ['neɪtɪv] *adj* بلدي [baladij]; **native speaker** *n* متحدث باللغة الأم [motaḥdeth bel-loghah al-om]
NATO ['neɪtəʊ] *abbr* منظمة حلف الشمال الأطلنطي [munazˤzˤamatun ħalfa aʃʃima:li alʔatˤlantˤijji]
natural ['nætʃrəl; -tʃərəl] *adj* طبيعي [tˤabi:ʕij]; **natural gas** *n* غاز طبيعي [ghaz ṭabeeaey]; **natural resources** *npl* موارد طبيعية [Mawared ṭabe’aey]
naturalist ['nætʃrəlɪst; -tʃərəl-] *n* مُناصر للطبيعة [monaṢer lel-ṭabe’aah]
naturally ['nætʃrəlɪ; -tʃərə-] *adv* طبيعي [tˤabi:ʕijjun]
nature ['neɪtʃə] *n* طبيعة [tˤabi:ʕa]
naughty ['nɔːtɪ] *adj* شقي [ʃaqij]
nausea ['nɔːzɪə; -sɪə] *n* غثيان [ɣaθaja:n]
naval ['neɪvᵊl] *adj* بحري [baħrij]
navel ['neɪvᵊl] *n* سُرَّة [surra]
navy ['neɪvɪ] *n* أسطول [ʔustˤu:l]
navy-blue ['neɪvɪ'bluː] *adj* أزرق داكن

[Azra'q daken]
NB [ɛn biː] *abbr (notabene)* ملاحظة هامة [mulaːħazˁatun haːmatun]
near [nɪə] *adj* قريب [qariːb] ▷ *adv* قُرب [qurba] ▷ *prep* بالقُرب من [Bel-'qorb men]; **Are there any good beaches near here?** هل يوجد شواطئ جيدة قريبة من هنا؟ [hal yujad shawaṭee jayida 'qareeba min huna?]; **It's very near** هل المسافة قريبة جدا؟ [al-masafa 'qareeba jedan]
nearby *adj* ['nɪəˌbaɪ] مجاور [muʒaːwir] ▷ *adv* [ˌnɪə'baɪ] على نحو قريب [Ala naḥw 'qareeb]
nearly ['nɪəlɪ] *adv* على نحو وثيق ['aala naḥwen wathee'q]
near-sighted [ˌnɪə'saɪtɪd] *adj* قريب النظر ['qareeb al- naḍhar]
neat [niːt] *adj* نظيف [nazˁiːf]
neatly [niːtlɪ] *adv* بإتقان [biʔitqaːnin]
necessarily ['nɛsɪsərɪlɪ; ˌnɛsɪ'sɛrɪlɪ] *adv* بالضرورة [bi-adˁ-dˁaruːrati]
necessary ['nɛsɪsərɪ] *adj* ضروري [dˁaruːrij]
necessity [nɪ'sɛsɪtɪ] *n* ضرورة [dˁaruːra]
neck [nɛk] *n* رَقَبَة [raqaba]
necklace ['nɛklɪs] *n* قلادة [qilaːda]
nectarine ['nɛktərɪn] *n* خُوخ [xuːx]
need [niːd] *n* حاجة [ħaːʒa] ▷ *v* يَحتاج إلى [Taḥtaaj ela]
needle ['niːdᵊl] *n* إبرة [ʔibra]; **knitting needle** *n* إبرة خياطة [Ebrat khayṭ]; **Do you have a needle and thread?** هل يوجد لديك إبرة وخيط؟ [hal yujad ladyka ebra wa khyṭ?]
negative ['nɛgətɪv] *adj* سلبي [silbij] ▷ *n* إحجام [ʔiħʒaːmu]
neglect [nɪ'glɛkt] *n* إهمال [ʔihmaːl] ▷ *v* يُهْمِل [juhmilu]
neglected [nɪ'glɛktɪd] *adj* مهمل [muhmil]
negligee ['nɛglɪˌʒeɪ] *n* ثوب فضفاض [Thawb feḍeaḍ]
negotiate [nɪ'gəʊʃɪˌeɪt] *v* يَتفاوَض [jatafaːwadˁu]
negotiations [nɪˌgəʊʃɪ'eɪʃənz] *npl* مفاوضات [mufaːwadˁaːtun]
negotiator [nɪ'gəʊʃɪˌeɪtə] *n* مفاوض [mufaːwidˁ]
neighbour ['neɪbə] *n* جار [ʒaːr]
neighbourhood ['neɪbəˌhʊd] *n* مُجَاوِرة [muʒaːwira]
neither ['naɪðə; 'niːðə] *adv* فوق ذلك [Faw'q dhalek] ▷ *conj* لا هذا ولا ذاك [La hadha wala dhaak]
neon ['niːɒn] *n* غاز النيون [Ghaz al-neywon]
Nepal [nɪ'pɔːl] *n* نيبال [niːbaːl]
nephew ['nɛvjuː; 'nɛf-] *n* ابن الأخ [Ebn al-akh]
nerve [nɜːv] *n (boldness)* وقاحة [waqaːħa], *(to/from brain)* عصب [ʕasˁab]
nerve-racking ['nɜːv'rækɪŋ] *adj* مرهق الأعصاب [Morha'q al-a'aṣaab]
nervous ['nɜːvəs] *adj* عصبي المزاج ['aṣabey]; **nervous breakdown** *n* إنهيار عصبي [Enheyar aṣabey]
nest [nɛst] *n* عش [ʕuʃ]
net [nɛt] *n* شبكة [ʃabaka]
Net [nɛt] *n* صافي [sˁaːfiː]
netball ['nɛtˌbɔːl] *n* كرة الشبكة [Korat al-shabakah]
Netherlands ['nɛðələndz] *npl* هولندا [huːlandaː]
nettle ['nɛtᵊl] *n* نبات ذو وبر شائك [Nabat dho wabar shaek]
network ['nɛtˌwɜːk] *n* شبكة [ʃabaka]; **I can't get a network** لا أستطيع الوصول إلى الشبكة [la asta-ṭee'a al-wiṣool ela al-shabaka]
neurotic [njʊ'rɒtɪk] *adj* عصابي [ʕisˁaːbij]
neutral ['njuːtrəl] *adj* حيادي [ħijaːdij] ▷ *n* شخص محايد [Moḥareb moḥayed]
never ['nɛvə] *adv* أبداً [ʔabadan]
nevertheless [ˌnɛvəðə'lɛs] *adv* وبرغم ذلك [Wa-be-raghm dhalek]
new [njuː] *adj* جديد [ʒadiːd]; **New Year** *n* رَأس السَنَة [Raas alsanah]; **New Zealand** *n* نيوزلندا [njuːzilandaː]; **New Zealander** *n* نيوزلندي [njuːzilandiː]
newborn ['njuːˌbɔːn] *adj* طفل حديث الولادة [Ṭefl ḥadeeth alweladah]
newcomer ['njuːˌkʌmə] *n* وَافِد [waːfid]

news [nju:z] *npl* أخبار [ʔaxba:run]; **When is the news?** تى تعرض الأخبار؟ [Tee ta'areḍ alakhbaar]
newsagent ['nju:z,eɪdʒənt] *n* وكيل أخبار [Wakeel akhbaar]
newspaper ['nju:z,peɪpə] *n* صحيفة [sˤaħi:fa]
newsreader ['nju:z,ri:də] *n* قارئ الأخبار ['qarey al-akhbar]
newt [nju:t] *n* سَمندل الماء [Samandal al-maa]
next [nɛkst] *adj* تالي [ta:li:] ▷ *adv* تال [ta:lin]; **next to** *prep* بجوار; **When do we stop next?** متى سنتوقف في المرة التالية؟ [mata sa-nata-wa'qaf fee al-murra al-taleya?]; **When is the next bus to...?** ما هو الموعد التالي للأتوبيس المتجه إلى...؟ [ma howa al-maw'aid al-taaly lel-baaṣ al-mutajeh ela...?]
next-of-kin ['nɛkstɒv'kɪn] *n* أقرب أفراد العائلة [A'qrab afrad al-'aaleah]
Nicaragua [,nɪkə'rægjʊə; nika'raɣwa] *n* نيكاراجوا [ni:ka:ra:ʒwa:]
Nicaraguan [,nɪkə'rægjʊən; -gwən] *adj* من نيكاراجاو [Men nekarajwa] ▷ *n* نيكاراجاوي [ni:ka:ra:ʒa:wi:]
nice [naɪs] *adj* لطيف [latˤi:f]
nickname ['nɪk,neɪm] *n* كنية [kinja]
nicotine ['nɪkə,ti:n] *n* نيكوتين [ni:ku:ti:n]
niece [ni:s] *n* بَنْت الأخت [Bent al-okht]
Niger ['naɪ'dʒɪər] *n* النيجر [an-ni:ʒar]
Nigeria [naɪ'dʒɪərɪə] *n* نيجيريا [ni:ʒi:rja:]
Nigerian [naɪ'dʒɪərɪən] *adj* نيجيري [ni:ʒi:rij] ▷ *n* نيجيري [ni:ʒi:rij]
night [naɪt] *n* ليل [lajl]; **hen night** *n* ليلة خروج الزوجات فقط [Laylat khorooj alzawjaat fa'qaṭ]; **night school** *n* مدرسة ليلية [Madrasah layleyah]; **stag night** *n* (حفل توديع العزوبية) للرجال [(ḥafl tawdee'a al'aozobayah) lel-rejaal]; **at night** ليلًا [lajla:]; **Good night** ليلة سعيدة [layla sa'aeeda]; **How much is it per night?** كم تبلغ تكلفة الإقامة في الليلة الواحدة؟ [kam tablugh taklifat al-e'qama fee al-layla al-waḥida?]; **I want to stay an extra night** أريد البقاء لليلة أخرى [areed al-ba'qaa le-layla ukhra]; **I'd like to stay for two nights** أريد الإقامة لليلتين [areed al-e'qama le lay-la-tain]; **last night** الليلة الماضية [al-laylah al-maaḍiya]; **tomorrow night** غدًا في الليل [ghadan fee al-layl]
nightclub ['naɪt,klʌb] *n* نادي ليلي [Nadey layley]
nightdress ['naɪt,drɛs] *n* ثياب النوم [Theyab al-noom]
nightie ['naɪtɪ] *n* قميص نوم نسائي ['qamees noom nesaaey]
nightlife ['naɪt,laɪf] *n* الخدمات الترفيهية الليلية [Alkhadmat al-tarfeeheyah al-layleyah]
nightmare ['naɪt,mɛə] *n* كابوس [ka:bu:s]
nightshift ['naɪt,ʃɪft] *n* نوبة ليلية [Noba layleyah]
nil [nɪl] *n* لا شيء [La shaya]
nine [naɪn] *number* تسعة [tisʕatun]
nineteen [,naɪn'ti:n] *number* تسعة عشر [tisʕata ʕaʃara]
nineteenth [,naɪn'ti:nθ] *adj* التاسع عشر [atta:siʕa ʕaʃara]
ninety ['naɪntɪ] *number* تسعين [tisʕi:nun]
ninth [naɪnθ] *adj* تاسع [ta:siʕ] ▷ *n* تاسع [ta:siʕ]
nitrogen ['naɪtrədʒən] *n* نيتروجين [ni:tru:ʒi:n]
no [nəʊ] *pron* ليس كذا [Lays kadha]; **no one** *pron* لا أحد [la ahad]
nobody ['nəʊbədɪ] *pron* لا أحد [la ahad]
nod [nɒd] *v* يُومئ برأسه [Yomea beraaseh]
noise [nɔɪz] *n* ضوضاء [dˤawdˤa:ʔ]; **I can't sleep for the noise** لا استطيع النوم بسبب الضوضاء [la asta-ṭee'a al-nawm besa-bab al-ḍawḍaa]
noisy ['nɔɪzɪ] *adj* ضوضاء [dˤawdˤa:ʔ]; **It's noisy** إنها غرفة بها ضوضاء [inaha ghurfa beha ḍawḍaa]; **The room is too noisy** هناك ضوضاء كثيرة جدا بالغرفة [hunaka ḍaw-ḍaa kathera jedan bil-ghurfa]
nominate ['nɒmɪ,neɪt] *v* يُرَشِح

[juraʃʃiħu]
nomination [ˌnɒmɪˈneɪʃən; ˌnomiˈnation] *n* ترشيح [tarʃiːħ]
none [nʌn] *pron* لا شيء [La shaya]
nonsense [ˈnɒnsəns] *n* هراء [huraːʔ]
non-smoker [nɒnˈsməʊkə] *n* شخص غير مُدَخِن [Shakhṣ Ghayr modakhen]
non-smoking [nɒnˈsməʊkɪŋ] *adj* غير مُدَخِن [Ghayr modakhen]
non-stop [ˈnɒnˈstɒp] *adv* بدون توقف [Bedon tawa'qof]
noodles [ˈnuːdəlz] *npl* مكرونة اسباجتي [Makaronah spajety]
noon [nuːn] *n* ظُهْر [zˤuhr]
nor [nɔː; nə] *conj* ولا
normal [ˈnɔːməl] *adj* طبيعي [tˤabiːʕij]
normally [ˈnɔːməlɪ] *adv* بصورة طبيعية [beṣoraten ṭabe'aey]
north [nɔːθ] *adj* شمالي [ʃamaːlij] ▷ *adv* شمالا [ʃamaːlan] ▷ *n* شمال [ʃamaːl]; **North Africa** *n* شمال أفريقيا [Shamal afreekya]; **North African** *n* شخص من شمال إفريقيا [Shakhs men shamal afree'qya]من شمال إفريقيا , [Men shamal afree'qya]; **North America** *n* أمريكا الشمالية [Amreeka al- Shamaleyah]; **North American** *n* شخص من أمريكا الشمالية [Shkhṣ men Amrika al shamalyiah]من أمريكا الشمالية , [men Amrika al shamalyiah]; **North Korea** *n* كوريا الشمالية [Koreya al-shamaleyah]; **North Pole** *n* القطب الشمالي [A'qoṭb al-shamaley]; **North Sea** *n* البحر الشمالي [Al-baḥr al-Shamaley]
northbound [ˈnɔːθˌbaʊnd] *adj* متجه شمالًا [Motajeh shamalan]
northeast [ˌnɔːθˈiːst; ˌnɔːrˈiːst] *n* شمال شرقي [Shamal shar'qey]
northern [ˈnɔːðən] *adj* شمالي [ʃamaːlij]; **Northern Ireland** *n* أيرلندة الشمالية [Ayarlanda al-shamaleyah]
northwest [ˌnɔːθˈwɛst; ˌnɔːˈwɛst] *n* شمال غربي [Shamal gharbey]
Norway [ˈnɔːˌweɪ] *n* النرويج [ʔan-narwiːʒ]
Norwegian [nɔːˈwiːdʒən] *adj* نرويجي [narwiːʒij] ▷ *n (language)* اللغة النرويجية [Al-loghah al-narwejeyah], *(person)* نرويجي [narwiːʒij]
nose [nəʊz] *n* أنْف [ʔanf]
nosebleed [ˈnəʊzˌbliːd] *n* نزيف الأنف [Nazeef al-anf]
nostril [ˈnɒstrɪl] *n* فتحة الأنف [Fathat al-anf]
nosy [ˈnəʊzɪ] *adj* فضولي [fudˤuːlij]
not [nɒt] *adv* لا [laː]; **I'm not drinking** أنا لا أشرب. [ana la ashrab]
note [nəʊt] *n (banknote)* عملة وَرَقية [ʕumlatun waraqiːja], *(message)* ملاحظة [mulaːħazˤa], *(music)* نغمة [naɣama]; **sick note** *n* إذْن غياب مرضي [edhn gheyab maraḍey]
notebook [ˈnəʊtˌbʊk] *n* مفكرة [mufakkira]
note down [nəʊt daʊn] *v* يُدون [judawwinu]
notepad [ˈnəʊtˌpæd] *n* كتيب ملاحظات [Kotayeb molaḥaḍhat]
notepaper [ˈnəʊtˌpeɪpə] *n* ورقة ملاحظات [Wara'qat molaḥadhaat]
nothing [ˈnʌθɪŋ] *pron* شيء غير موجود [Shaya ghayr mawjood]
notice [ˈnəʊtɪs] *n (note)* إشعار [ʔiʃʕaːr], *(termination)* إنذار [ʔinðaːr] ▷ *v* يُنْذِر [junðiru]; **notice board** *n* لوحة الملاحظات [Looḥat al-molahḍhat]
noticeable [ˈnəʊtɪsəbəl] *adj* ملحوظ [malħuːzˤ]
notify [ˈnəʊtɪˌfaɪ] *v* يُعلِم [juʕallimu]
nought [nɔːt] *n* لا شيء [La shaya]
noun [naʊn] *n* اسم [ism]
novel [ˈnɒvəl] *n* رواية [riwaːja]
novelist [ˈnɒvəlɪst] *n* رُوَائي [riwaːʔij]
November [nəʊˈvɛmbə] *n* نوفمبر [nuːfumbar]
now [naʊ] *adv* الآن [ʔal-ʔaːn]; **Do I pay now or later?** هل يجب أن أدفع الآن أم لاحقا؟ [hal yajib an adfa'a al-aan am la-ḥe'qan?]; **I need to pack now** أنا في حاجة لحزم أمتعتي الآن [ana fee ḥaja le-ḥazem am-te-'aaty al-aan]
nowadays [ˈnaʊəˌdeɪz] *adv* في هذه الأيام [Fee hadheh alayaam]

nowhere ['nəʊˌwɛə] *adv* ليس في أي مكان [Lays fee ay makan]
nuclear ['nju:klɪə] *adj* نووي [nawawij]
nude [nju:d] *adj* ناقص [na:qisˤ] ▷ *n* صورة عارية [Ṣoorah 'aareyah]
nudist ['nju:dɪst] *n* مُناصر للعُرْي [Monaṣer lel'aory]
nuisance ['nju:səns] *n* إزعاج [ʔizʕa:ʒ]
numb [nʌm] *adj* خَدِر [xadir]
number ['nʌmbə] *n* رقم [raqm]; **account number** *n* رقم الحساب [Ra'qm al-hesab]; **mobile number** *n* رقم المحمول [Ra'qm almahmool]; **number plate** *n* لوحة الأرقام [Looḥ al-ar'qaam]; **phone number** *n* رقم التليفون [Ra'qm al-telefone]; **reference number** *n* رقم مرجعي [Ra'qm marje'ay]; **room number** *n* رقم الغرفة [Ra'qam al-ghorfah]; **wrong number** *n* رقم خطأ [Ra'qam khaṭaa]; **Can I have your phone number?** هل يمكن أن أحصل على رقم تليفونك؟ [hal yamken an aḥṣal 'aala ra'qm talefonak?]; **My mobile number is...** رقم تليفوني المحمول هو... [ra'qim talefony al-maḥmool howa...]; **What is the fax number?** ما هو رقم الفاكس؟ [ma howa ra'qim al-fax?]; **What is the number of your mobile?** ما هو رقم تليفونك المحمول؟ [ma howa ra'qim talefonak al-maḥmool?]; **What's the telephone number?** ما هو رقم التليفون؟ [ma howa ra'qim al-talefon?]; **You have the wrong number** هذا الرقم غير صحيح [hatha al-ra'qum ghayr ṣaḥeeḥ]
numerous ['nju:mərəs] *adj* متعدد [mutaʕaddid]
nun [nʌn] *n* راهبة [ra:hiba]
nurse [nɜ:s] *n* ممرضة [mumarridˤa]; **I'd like to speak to a nurse** أرغب في استشارة ممرضة [arghab fee es-ti-sharat mu-mareḍa]
nursery ['nɜ:srɪ] *n* حضانة [ħadˤa:na]; **nursery rhyme** *n* أغنية أطفال [Aghzeyat aṭfaal]; **nursery school** *n* مدرسة الحضانة [Madrasah al-ḥaḍanah]
nursing home ['nɜ:sɪŋ həʊm] *n* دار التمريض [Dar al-tamreeḍ]
nut [nʌt] *n (device)* صمولة [sˤamu:la], *(food)* جوزة [ʒawza]; **nut allergy** *n* حساسية الجوز [Hasaseyat al-joz]
nutmeg ['nʌtmɛg] *n* جوزة الطيب [Jozat al-ṭeeb]
nutrient ['nju:trɪənt] *n* مادة مغذية [Madah moghadheyah]
nutrition [nju:'trɪʃən] *n* تغذية [taɣðija]
nutritious [nju:'trɪʃəs] *adj* مغذي [muɣaððij]
nutter ['nʌtə] *n* جامع الجوز [Jame'a al-jooz]
nylon ['naɪlɒn] *n* نايلون [na:jlu:n]

oak [əʊk] *n* بَلُّوط [ballu:tˤ]
oar [ɔː] *n* مجداف [miʒda:f]
oasis, oases [əʊ'eɪsɪs, əʊ'eɪsiːz] *n* واحة [wa:ħa]
oath [əʊθ] *n* قَسَم [qism]
oatmeal ['əʊt,miːl] *n* دقيق الشوفان [Da'qee'q al-shofaan]
oats [əʊts] *npl* شوفان [ʃu:fa:nun]
obedient [ə'biːdɪənt] *adj* مطيع [mutˤi:ʕ]
obese [əʊ'biːs] *adj* بَدِين [badi:n]
obey [ə'beɪ] *v* يُطْيع [jutˤi:ʕu]
obituary [ə'bɪtjʊərɪ] *n* نَعْي [naʕj]
object ['ɒbdʒɪkt] *n* شيء [ʃajʔ]
objection [əb'dʒɛkʃən] *n* اعتراض [iʕtira:dˤ]
objective [əb'dʒɛktɪv] *n* موضوعي [mawdˤu:ʕij]
oblong ['ɒb,lɒŋ] *adj* مستطيل الشكل [Mostaṭeel al-shakl]
obnoxious [əb'nɒkʃəs] *adj* بغيض [baɣi:dˤ]
oboe ['əʊbəʊ] *n* أوبوا [ʔu:bwa:]
obscene [əb'siːn] *adj* فاحش [fa:ħiʃ]
observant [əb'zɜːvənt] *adj* شديد الانتباه [shaded al-entebah]
observatory [əb'zɜːvətərɪ; -trɪ] *n* نقطة مراقبة [No'qtat mora'qabah]
observe [əb'zɜːv] *v* يُلاحِظ [jula:ħizˤu]
observer [əb'zɜːvə; ob'server] *n* مراقب [mura:qib]
obsessed [əb'sɛst] *adj* مهووس [mahwu:s]
obsession [əb'sɛʃən] *n* حِيَازة [ħija:za]
obsolete ['ɒbsə,liːt; ,ɒbsə'liːt] *adj* مهجور [mahʒu:r]
obstacle ['ɒbstəkᵊl] *n* عقبة [ʕaqaba]
obstinate ['ɒbstɪnɪt] *adj* مستعص [mustaʕsˤin]
obstruct [əb'strʌkt] *v* يعوق [jaʕu:qu]
obtain [əb'teɪn] *v* يَكتسِب [jaktasibu]
obvious ['ɒbvɪəs] *adj* جَلّي [ʒalij]
obviously ['ɒbvɪəslɪ] *adv* بشكل واضح [Beshakl waḍeḥ]
occasion [ə'keɪʒən] *n* مُنَاسَبَة [muna:saba]
occasional [ə'keɪʒənᵊl] *adj* مناسبي [muna:sabij]
occasionally [ə'keɪʒənəlɪ] *adv* من وقت لآخر [Men wa'qt le-aakhar]
occupation [,ɒkjʊ'peɪʃən] *n (invasion)* احتلال [iħtila:l], *(work)* مهنة [mihna]
occupy ['ɒkjʊ,paɪ] *v* يَحتل [jaħtallu]
occur [ə'kɜː] *v* يقَع [jaqaʕu]
occurrence [ə'kʌrəns] *n* حدوث [ħudu:θ]
ocean ['əʊʃən] *n* مُحِيط [muħi:tˤ]; **Arctic Ocean** *n* المحيط القطبي الشمالي [Al-moḥeeṭ al-'qoṭbey al-shamaley]; **Indian Ocean** *n* المحيط الهندي [Almoḥeeṭ alhendey]
Oceania [,əʊʃɪ'ɑːnɪə] *n* أوسيانيا [ʔu:sja:nja:]
o'clock [ə'klɒk] *adv*; **after eight o'clock** بعد الساعة الثامنة [ba'ad al-sa'aa al-thamena]; **at three o'clock** في تمام الساعة الثالثة [fee tamam al-sa'aa al- thaletha]; **I'd like to book a table for four people for tonight at eight o'clock** أريد حجز مائدة لأربعة أشخاص الليلة في تمام الساعة الثامنة [areed ḥajiz ma-e-da le-arba'at ashkhaaṣ al-layla fee ta-mam al-sa'aa al-thamena]; **It's one o'clock** الساعة واحدة [al-sa'aa al-waḥeda]

October [ɒkˈtəʊbə] *n* أكتوبر [ʔuktu:bar]; **It's Sunday third October** يوم الأحد الموافق الثالث من أكتوبر [yawm al-aḥad al- muwa-fi'q al-thalith min iktobar]
octopus [ˈɒktəpəs] *n* أخطبوط [ʔuxtˤubu:tˤ]
odd [ɒd] *adj* شاذ [ʃa:ðð]
odour [ˈəʊdə] *n* شَذا [ʃaða:]
of [ɒv; əv] *prep* حرف وصل [ħarfu wasˤli]
off [ɒf] *adv* بعيداً [baʕi:dan] ▷ *prep* بعيد [baʕi:dun]; **time off** *n* أجازة [ʔaʒa:zatun]
offence [əˈfɛns] *n* إساءة [ʔisa:ʔa]
offend [əˈfɛnd] *v* يُسيء إلى [Yoseea ela]
offensive [əˈfɛnsɪv] *adj* مسيء [musi:ʔ]
offer [ˈɒfə] *n* اقتراح [iqtira:ħ] ▷ *v* يّقَدِم [juqaddimu]; **special offer** *n* عرض خاص [ʻaarḍ khaṣ]
office [ˈɒfɪs] *n* مكتب [maktab]; **booking office** *n* مكتب الحجز [Maktab al-ḥjz]; **box office** *n* شباك التذاكر [Shobak al-taḏhaker]; **head office** *n* مكتب رئيسي [Maktab a'ala]; **information office** *n* مكتب الاستعلامات [Maktab al-este'alamaat]; **left-luggage office** *n* مكتب الأمتعة [Makatb al amte'aah]; **lost-property office** *n* مكتب المفقودات [Maktab al-maf'qodat]; **office hours** *npl* ساعات العمل [Sa'aat al-'amal]; **post office** *n* مكتب البريد [maktab al-bareed]; **registry office** *n* مكتب التسجيل [Maktab al-tasjeel]; **ticket office** *n* مكتب التذاكر [Maktab al-taḏhaker]; **tourist office** *n* مكتب سياحي [Maktab seayaḥey]; **Do you have a press office?** هل لديك مكتب إعلامي؟ [hal ladyka maktab e'a-laamy?]; **How do I get to your office?** كيف يمكن الوصول إلى مكتبك؟ [kayfa yamkin al-wiṣool ela mak-tabak?]; **When does the post office open?** متى يفتح مكتب البريد؟ [mata yaftaḥ maktab al-bareed?]
officer [ˈɒfɪsə] *n* ضابط [dˤa:bitˤ]; **customs officer** *n* مسئول الجمرك [Masool al-jomrok]; **police officer** *n* ضابط شرطة [Ḍabeṭ shorṭah]; **prison officer** *n* ضابط سجن [Ḍabeṭ sejn]
official [əˈfɪʃəl] *adj* رسمي [rasmij]
off-licence [ˈɒfˌlaɪsəns] *n* رُخصَة بيع الخمور لتناولها خارج المحل [Rokhṣat baye'a al-khomor letnawolha kharej al-maḥal]
off-peak [ˈɒfˌpiːk] *adv* في غير وقت الذروة [Fee ghaeyr wa'qt al-dhorwah]
off-season [ˈɒfˌsiːzᵊn] *adj* موسم راكد [Mawsem raked] ▷ *adv* ركود [Rokood]
offside [ˈɒfˈsaɪd] *adj* خارج النطاق المُحَدد [Kharej al-neta'q al-mohadad]
often [ˈɒfᵊn; ˈɒftᵊn] *adv* غالباً [ɣa:liban]
oil [ɔɪl] *n* نفط (زيت) [naftˤ] ▷ *v* يُزيت [juzajjitu]; **olive oil** *n* زيت الزيتون [Zayt al-zaytoon]
oil refinery [ɔɪl rɪˈfaɪnərɪ] *n* معمل تكرير الزيت [Ma'amal takreer al-zayt]
oil rig [ɔɪl rɪg] *n* جهاز حفر آبار النفط [Gehaz ḥafr abar al-naft]
oil slick [ɔɪl slɪk] *n* طبقة زيت طافية على الماء [Ṭaba'qat zayt ṭafeyah alaa alma]
oil well [ɔɪl wɛl] *n* بئر بترول [Beear betrol]
ointment [ˈɔɪntmənt] *n* مرهم [marhamunS]
OK [ˌəʊˈkeɪ] *excl* حسناً [ħasanan]
okay [ˌəʊˈkeɪ] *adj* مقبول [maqbu:l]; **okay!** *excl* حسناً [ħasanan]
old [əʊld] *adj* عجوز [ʕaʒu:z]; **old-age pensioner** *n* صاحب معاش كبير السن [Ṣaheb ma'aash kabeer al-sen]
old-fashioned [ˈəʊldˈfæʃənd] *adj* دقة قديمة [Da'qah 'qadeemah]
olive [ˈɒlɪv] *n* زيتون [zajtu:n]; **olive oil** *n* زيت الزيتون [Zayt al-zaytoon]; **olive tree** *n* شجرة الزيتون [Shajarat al-zaytoon]
Oman [əʊˈmɑːn] *n* عمان [ʕuma:n]
omelette [ˈɒmlɪt] *n* الأومليت [ʔal-ʔu:mli:ti]
on [ɒn] *adv* على [ʕala:] ▷ *prep* على [ʕala:]; **on behalf of** *n* نيابة عن [Neyabatan 'an]; **on time** *adj* في الموعد المحدد [Fee al-maw'aed al-moḥadad]; **It's on the corner** على هذا الجانب ['ala hadha aljaneb]; **Take the first turning on your right** أتجه نحو أول منعطف على

اليمين [ʔattaʒihu naħwa ʔawwali munʕatʕafi ʕala: aljami:ni]; **The drinks are on me** المشروبات على حسابي [al-mashro-baat 'ala ḥesaby]; **What's on tonight at the cinema?** ماذا يعرض الليلة على شاشة السينما؟ [madha yu'a-raḍ al-layla 'aala sha-shat al-senama?]; **Which film is on at the cinema?** أي فيلم يعرض الآن على شاشة السينما؟ [ay filim ya'aruḍ al-aan 'ala sha-shat al-senama?]

once [wʌns] *adv* مرّةً [marratan]

one [wʌn] *number* واحد [wa:ħidun] ▷ *pron* شخص [ʃaxsʕun]; **no one** *pron* لا أحد [la ahad]

one-off [wʌnɒf] *n* مرة واحدة [Marah waḥedah]

onion ['ʌnjən] *n* بصل [basʕal]; **spring onion** *n* بصل أخضر [Baṣal akhdar]

online ['ɒn,laɪn] *adj* متصل بالإنترنت [motaṣel bel-enternet] ▷ *adv* متصلا بالإنترنت [Motaṣelan bel-enternet]

onlooker ['ɒn,lʊkə] *n* مُشاهِد [muʃa:hid]

only ['əʊnlɪ] *adj* الأفضل [Álafḍal] ▷ *adv* فقط [faqatʕ]

open ['əʊpᵊn] *adj* مفتوح [maftu:ħ] ▷ *v* يفتح [jaftaħu]; **opening hours** *npl* ساعات العمل [Sa'aat al-'amal]; **Is it open today?** هل هو مفتوح اليوم؟ [hal how maftooḥ al-yawm?]; **Is the castle open to the public?** هل القلعة مفتوحة للجمهور؟ [hal al-'qal'aa maf-tooḥa lel-jamhoor?]; **Is the museum open in the afternoon?** هل المتحف مفتوح بعد الظهر؟ [hal al-mat-ḥaf maf-tooḥ ba'ad al-ḍhihir?]

opera ['ɒpərə] *n* الأوبرا [ʔal-ʔu:bira:]; **soap opera** *n* مسلسل درامي [Mosalsal deramey]; **What's on tonight at the opera?** ماذا يعرض الآن في دار الأوبرا؟ [madha yu'a-raḍ al-aan fee daar al-obera?]

operate ['ɒpə,reɪt] *v* *(to function)* يُشَغِّلُ [juʃaɣɣilu], *(to perform surgery)* يُجرَي عملية جراحية [Yojrey 'amaleyah jeraḥeyah]

operating theatre ['ɒpə,reɪtɪŋ 'θɪətə] *n* غرفة عمليات [ghorfat 'amaleyat]

operation [,ɒpə'reɪʃən] *n* *(surgery)* عملية جراحية ['amaleyah jeraheyah], *(undertaking)* عملية [ʕamalijja]

operator ['ɒpə,reɪtə] *n* مُشغل [muʃaɣɣil]

opinion [ə'pɪnjən] *n* رَأي [raʔjj]; **opinion poll** *n* استطلاع الرأي [Eateṭla'a al-ray]; **public opinion** *n* الرأي العام [Al-raaey al-'aam]

opponent [ə'pəʊnənt] *n* خِصم [xasʕm]

opportunity [,ɒpə'tju:nɪtɪ] *n* فرصة [fursʕa]

oppose [ə'pəʊz] *v* يُعارِض [juʕa:ridʕu]

opposed [ə'pəʊzd] *adj* مقابل [muqa:bil]

opposing [ə'pəʊzɪŋ] *adj* معارض [muʕa:ridʕ]

opposite ['ɒpəzɪt; -sɪt] *adj* مضاد [mudʕa:d] ▷ *adv* تِجَاه [tiʒa:ha] ▷ *prep* مواجه [Mowajeh]

opposition [,ɒpə'zɪʃən] *n* مُعارضَة [muʕa:radʕa]

optician [ɒp'tɪʃən] *n* نظاراتي [nazʕzʕa:ra:ti:]

optimism ['ɒptɪ,mɪzəm] *n* تفاؤل [tafa:ʔul]

optimist ['ɒptɪ,mɪst] *n* مُتَفَائِل [mutafa:ʔil]

optimistic [ɒptɪ'mɪstɪk] *adj* متفائل [mutafa:ʔil]

option ['ɒpʃən] *n* خِيَار [xija:r]

optional ['ɒpʃənᵊl] *adj* اختياري [ixtija:rij]

opt out [ɒpt aʊt] *v* يقرر [juqarriru]

or [ɔ:] *conj* أو; **either... or** *conj* إما... أو [Emma…aw]

oral ['ɔ:rəl; 'ɒrəl] *adj* شفهي [ʃafahij] ▷ *n* فحص شفهي [Faḥṣ shafahey]

orange ['ɒrɪndʒ] *adj* برتقالي [burtuqa:lij] ▷ *n* برتقالة [burtuqa:la]; **orange juice** *n* عصير برتقال [Aṣeer borto'qaal]

orchard ['ɔ:tʃəd] *n* بستان [busta:n]

orchestra ['ɔ:kɪstrə] *n* الأوركسترا [ʔal-ʔu:rkistra:]

orchid ['ɔ:kɪd] *n* زهرة الأوركيد [Zahrat al-orkeed]

ordeal [ɔ:'di:l] *n* مأزق [maʔziq]

order ['ɔ:də] *n* طَلَبٌ [tʕalab] ▷ *v* *(command)*

يأمر [jaʔmuru], *(request)* يطلب [jatˤlubu]; **order form** *n* نموذج طلبية [Namodhaj ṭalabeyah]; **postal order** *n* حوالة مالية [Ḥewala maleyah]; **standing order** *n* أمر دفع شهري [Amr daf'a shahrey]
ordinary ['ɔːdᵊnrɪ] *adj* عادي [ʕaːdij]
oregano [ˌɒrɪ'gɑːnəʊ] *n* زَعْتَر بَري [Za'atar barey]
organ ['ɔːgən] *n (body part)* عضو في الجسد ['aoḍw fee al-jasad], *(music)* آلة الأرْغُن الموسيقية [Aalat al-arghan al-moseeqeyah]; **mouth organ** *n* آلة الهرمونيكا الموسيقية [Alat al-harmoneeka al-mose'qeyah]
organic [ɔː'gænɪk] *adj* عضوي [ʕudˤwij]
organism ['ɔːgəˌnɪzəm] *n* كائن حي [Kaaen ḥay]
organization [ˌɔːgənaɪ'zeɪʃən] *n* منظمة [munazˤzˤama]
organize ['ɔːgəˌnaɪz] *v* يُنَظِم [junazˤzˤimu]
organizer ['ɔːgəˌnaɪzə; 'orgaˌnizer; 'orgaˌniser] *n*; **personal organizer** *n* منظم شخصي [monaḍhem shakhṣey]
orgasm ['ɔːgæzəm] *n* هزة الجماع [Hezat al-jemaa'a]
Orient ['ɔːrɪənt] *n* المَشْرِق [ʔalmaʃriqi]
oriental [ˌɔːrɪ'ɛntᵊl] *adj* مَشرِقي [maʃriqij]
origin ['ɒrɪdʒɪn] *n* أصل *(source)* [ʔasˤl]
original [ə'rɪdʒɪnᵊl] *adj* أصيل [ʔasˤiːl]
originally [ə'rɪdʒɪnəlɪ] *adv* في الأصل [Fee al aṣl]
ornament ['ɔːnəmənt] *n* حلية [ħilijja]
orphan ['ɔːfən] *n* يَتْيم [jatiːm]
ostrich ['ɒstrɪtʃ] *n* نعامة [naʕaːma]
other ['ʌðə] *adj* أخر [ʔaxar]
otherwise ['ʌðəˌwaɪz] *adv* بطريقة أخرى [ṭaree'qah okhra] ▷ *conj* وإلا [Waelaa]
otter ['ɒtə] *n* ثعلب الماء [Tha'alab al-maaa]
ounce [aʊns] *n* الأونس [ʔal-ʔuːnsu]
our [aʊə] *adj* مِلكَنا
ours [aʊəz] *pron* مِلكَنا
ourselves [aʊə'sɛlvz] *pron* أنفسنا
out [aʊt] *adj* بعيد [baʕiːd] ▷ *adv* خارجاً [xaːriʒan]
outbreak ['aʊtˌbreɪk] *n* نشوب [nuʃuːb]
outcome ['aʊtˌkʌm] *n* ناتج [naːtiʒ]
outdoor ['aʊt'dɔː] *adj* خلوي [xalawij]
outdoors [ˌaʊt'dɔːz] *adv* في العراء [Fee al-'aaraa]
outfit ['aʊtˌfɪt] *n* مُعدات [muʕaddaːt]
outgoing ['aʊtˌgəʊɪŋ] *adj* منصرف [munsˤarif]
outing ['aʊtɪŋ] *n* نزهة [nuzha]
outline ['aʊtˌlaɪn] *n* مخطط تمهيدي [Mokhaṭaṭ tamheedey]
outlook ['aʊtˌlʊk] *n* مطل [matall]
out-of-date ['aʊtɒv'deɪt] *adj* متخلف [mutaxaliff]
out-of-doors ['aʊtɒv'dɔːz] *adv* في الهواء الطلق [Fe al-hawaa al-ṭal'q]
outrageous [aʊt'reɪdʒəs] *adj* شَنيع [ʃaniːʕ]
outset ['aʊtˌsɛt] *n* مُستَهل [mustahall]
outside *adj* ['aʊtˌsaɪd] خارجي [xaːriʒij] ▷ *adv* [ˌaʊt'saɪd] خارجاً [xaːriʒan] ▷ *n* ['aʊt'saɪd] خارج [xaːriʒ] ▷ *prep* إلى خارج [Ela al-kharej]; **I want to make an outside call, can I have a line?** أريد إجراء مكالمة خارجية، هل يمكن أن تحول لي أحد الخطوط؟ [areed ejraa mukalama kharij-iya, hal yamkin an it-ḥawil le aḥad al-khiṭooṭ?]
outsize ['aʊtˌsaɪz] *adj* مقاس كبير [Ma'qaas kabeer]
outskirts ['aʊtˌskɜːts] *npl* ضواح [dˤawaːħin]
outspoken [ˌaʊt'spəʊkən] *adj* صريح [sˤariːħ]
outstanding [ˌaʊt'stændɪŋ] *adj* معلق [muʕallaq]
oval ['əʊvᵊl] *adj* بيضوي [bajdˤawij]
ovary ['əʊvərɪ] *n* مِبْيَض [mabiːdˤ]
oven ['ʌvᵊn] *n* فرن [furn]; **microwave oven** *n* فرن الميكروويف [Forn al-maykroweef]; **oven glove** *n* قفاز فرن ['qoffaz forn]
ovenproof ['ʌvᵊnˌpruːf] *adj* مقاوم لحرارة الفرن [Mo'qawem le-ḥarart al-forn]
over ['əʊvə] *adj* منتهي [muntahij] ▷ *prep* فوق [fawqa]

overall [ˌəʊvər'ɔːl] *adv* عموما [ʕumuːman]
overalls [ˌəʊvə'ɔːlz] *npl* بدلة العمل [Badlat al-'aamal]
overcast ['əʊvəˌkɑːst] *adj* معتم [muʕtim]
overcharge [ˌəʊvə'tʃɑːdʒ] *v* يغالي في الثمن [Yoghaley fee al-thaman]
overcoat ['əʊvəˌkəʊt] *n* معطف [miʕtˤaf]
overcome [ˌəʊvə'kʌm] *v* يَتَغْلَب على [Yatghalab 'ala]
overdone [ˌəʊvə'dʌn] *adj* زائد الطهو [Zaed al-ṭahw]
overdose ['əʊvəˌdəʊs] *n* جرعة زائدة [Jor'aah zaedah]
overdraft ['əʊvəˌdrɑːft] *n* افراط السحب على البنك [Efraṭ al-saḥb ala al-bank]
overdrawn [ˌəʊvə'drɔːn] *adj* مبالغ فيه [mobalagh feeh]
overdue [ˌəʊvə'djuː] *adj* فات موعد استحقاقه [Fat maw'aed esteḥ'qa'qh]
overestimate [ˌəʊvər'ɛstɪˌmeɪt] *v* يُغَالي في التقدير [Yoghaley fee al-ta'qdeer]
overheads ['əʊvəˌhɛdz] *npl* مصاريف عامة [Maṣareef 'aamah]
overlook [ˌəʊvə'lʊk] *v* يَطُلْ على [Ya'aṣeb al-'aynayn]
overnight ['əʊvəˌnaɪt] *adv*; **Can I park here overnight?** هل يمكن أن أترك السيارة هنا إلى الصباح؟ [hal yamken an atruk al-sayara huna ela al-ṣabaḥ?]; **Can we camp here overnight?** هل يمكن أن نقوم بعمل مخيم للمبيت هنا؟ [hal yamken an na'qoom be-'aamal mukhyam lel-mabeet huna?]
overrule [ˌəʊvə'ruːl] *v* يَتحكم ب [Yataḥkam be]
overseas [ˌəʊvə'siːz] *adv* عبر البحار ['abr al-behar]
oversight ['əʊvəˌsaɪt] *n (mistake)* سهو [sahw], *(supervision)* إشراف [ʔiʃraːf]
oversleep [ˌəʊvə'sliːp] *v* يَستغَرق في النوم [yastagh'q fel nawm]
overtake [ˌəʊvə'teɪk] *v* يتجاوز [jataʒaːwazu]
overtime ['əʊvəˌtaɪm] *n* وَقْت إضافي [Wa'qt eḍafey]
overweight [ˌəʊvə'weɪt] *adj* زائد الوزن [Zaed alwazn]
owe [əʊ] *v* يدين [judiːnu]
owing to ['əʊɪŋ tuː] *prep* بسبب
owl [aʊl] *n* بومة [buːma]
own [əʊn] *adj* ملكه [mulkahu] ▷ *v* يَمْتَلِك [jamtaliku]
owner ['əʊnə] *n* مالك [maːlik]; **Could I speak to the owner, please?** من فضلك هل يمكنني التحدث إلى المالك؟ [min faḍlak hal yamkin-ani al-taḥaduth ela al-maalik?]
own up [əʊn ʌp] *v* يُقِر ب [Yo'qarreb]
oxygen ['ɒksɪdʒən] *n* أكسجين [ʔuksiʒiːn]
oyster ['ɔɪstə] *n* صَدَفَة [sˤadafa]
ozone ['əʊzəʊn; əʊ'zəʊn] *n* الأوزون [ʔal-ʔuːzuːni]; **ozone layer** *n* طبقة الأوزون [Taba'qat al-odhoon]

p

PA [piː eɪ] *abbr* م.ش. [miːm. ʃiːn.]
pace [peɪs] *n* سرعة السير [Sor'aat al-seer]
pacemaker ['peɪsˌmeɪkə] *n* منظم الخطوات [monaḍhem al-khaṭawat]
Pacific [pə'sɪfɪk] *n* المحيط الهادي [Al-moḥeeṭ al-haadey]
pack [pæk] *n* رزمة [ruzma] ▷ *v* يُحَزِم [jaħzimu]
package ['pækɪdʒ] *n* حُزمَة [ħuzma]; **package holiday** *n* خطة عطلة شاملة الإقامة والانتقال [Khoṭ at 'aoṭlah shamelat al-e'qamah wal-ente'qal]; **package tour** *n* خطة رحلة شاملة الإقامة والانتقالات [Khotah rehalah shamelah al-e'qamah wal-ente'qalat]
packaging ['pækɪdʒɪŋ] *n* تعبئة [taʕbiʔit]
packed [pækt] *adj* مغلف [muɣallaf]; **packed lunch** *n* وجبة الغذاء المعبأة [Wajbat al-ghezaa al-mo'abaah]
packet ['pækɪt] *n* رُزْمَة [ruzma]
pad [pæd] *n* وسادة رقيقة [Wesadah ra'qee'qah]
paddle ['pædᵊl] *n* محراك [miħraːk] ▷ *v* يُجَذِّف [juʒaðːifu]
padlock ['pædˌlɒk] *n* قفل [qufl]
paedophile ['piːdəʊˌfaɪl] *n* حب الأطفال [Hob al-atfaal]
page [peɪdʒ] *n* صفحة [sˤafħa] ▷ *v* يستدعي [jastadʕiː]; **home page** *n* صفحة رئيسية [Ṣafḥah raeseyah]; **Yellow Pages®** *npl* يلوبيدجز® [bloobeedjez®]
pager ['peɪdʒə] *n* جهاز النداء [Jehaaz al-nedaa]
paid [peɪd] *adj* مسدد [musaddad]
pail [peɪl] *n* دلو [dalw]
pain [peɪn] *n* أَلَمٌ [ʔalam]; **back pain** *n* أَلَمْ الظهر [Alam al-ḍhahr]
painful ['peɪnfʊl] *adj* مؤلم [mulim]
painkiller ['peɪnˌkɪlə] *n* مسكن آلام [Mosaken lel-alam]
paint [peɪnt] *n* دِهَان [dihaːn] ▷ *v* يَطْلِي [jatˤliː]
paintbrush ['peɪntˌbrʌʃ] *n* فرشاة الدهان [Forshat al-dahaan]
painter ['peɪntə] *n* رسام [rassaːm]
painting ['peɪntɪŋ] *n* لَوْحَة [lawħa]
pair [pɛə] *n* زوجان [zawʒaːni]
Pakistan [ˌpɑːkɪ'stɑːn] *n* باكستان [baːkistaːn]
Pakistani [ˌpɑːkɪ'stɑːnɪ] *adj* باكستاني [baːkistaːnij] ▷ *n* باكستاني [baːkistaːnij]
pal [pæl] *n* صديق [sˤadiːq]
palace ['pælɪs] *n* قصر [qasˤr]; **Is the palace open to the public?** هل القصر مفتوح للجمهور؟ [hal al-'qaṣir maf-tooḥ lel-jamhoor?]; **When is the palace open?** متى يُفتح القصر؟ [mata yoftaḥ al-'qaṣir?]
pale [peɪl] *adj* شاحب [ʃaːħib]
Palestine ['pælɪˌstaɪn] *n* فلسطين [filastˤiːnu]
Palestinian [ˌpælɪ'stɪnɪən] *adj* فلسطيني [filastˤiːnij] ▷ *n* فلسطيني [filastˤiːnij]
palm [pɑːm] *n (part of hand)* راحة اليد [Rahat al-yad], *(tree)* نخلة [naxla]
pamphlet ['pæmflɪt] *n* كتيب [kutajjib]
pan [pæn] *n* مقلاة [miqlaːt]; **frying pan** *n* قلاية [qalaːjjatun]
Panama [ˌpænə'mɑː; 'pænəˌmɑː] *n* بنما [banamaː]
pancake ['pænˌkeɪk] *n* فطيرة محلاة

[Faṭerah moḥalah]
panda ['pændə] *n* بَندَا [banda:]
panic ['pænɪk] *n* ذُعْر [ðuʕr] ▷ *v* يُذْعَر [juðʕaru]
panther ['pænθə] *n* نِمْر [namir]
panties ['pæntɪz] *npl* لباس داخلي [Lebas dakhely]
pantomime ['pæntəˌmaɪm] *n* التمثيل الصامت [altamtheel al-ṣamet]
pants [pænts] *npl* بَنطلون [bantˤalu:nun]
paper ['peɪpə] *n* ورقة [waraqa]; **paper round** *n* طريق توزيع الصحف [ṭaree'q tawze'a al-ṣohof]; **scrap paper** *n* ورق مسودة [Wara'q mosawadah]; **toilet paper** *n* ورق المرحاض [Wara'q al-merḥaḍ]; **tracing paper** *n* ورق شفاف [Wara'q shafaf]; **wrapping paper** *n* ورق التغليف [Wara'q al-taghleef]; **writing paper** *n* ورقة كتابة [Wara'qat ketabah]
paperback ['peɪpəˌbæk] *n* كتاب ورقي الغلاف [Ketab wara'qey al-gholaf]
paperclip ['peɪpəˌklɪp] *n* مشبك ورق [Mashbak wara'q]
paperweight ['peɪpəˌweɪt] *n* ثقالة الورق [Na'qalat al-wara'q]
paperwork ['peɪpəˌwɜːk] *n* أعمال مكتبية [A'amaal maktabeyah]
paprika ['pæprɪkə; pæ'priː-] *n* فُلْفُل مطحون [Felfel maṭhoon]
paracetamol [ˌpærə'siːtəˌmɒl; -'sɛtə-] *n*; **I'd like some paracetamol** أريد باراسيتامول [areed barasetamol]
parachute ['pærəˌʃuːt] *n* مِظَلة [mizˤalla]
parade [pə'reɪd] *n* استعراض [istiʕra:dˤ]
paradise ['pærəˌdaɪs] *n* جنة [ʒanna]
paraffin ['pærəfɪn] *n* بارافين [ba:ra:fi:n]
paragraph ['pærəˌɡrɑːf; -ˌɡræf] *n* فقرة [faqra]
Paraguay ['pærəˌɡwaɪ] *n* باراجواي [ba:ra:ʒwa:j]
Paraguayan [ˌpærə'ɡwaɪən] *adj* من باراجواي [Men barajway] ▷ *n* شخص من باراجواي [Shakhṣ men barajway]
parallel ['pærəˌlɛl] *adj* متوازي [mutawa:zi:]
paralysed ['pærəˌlaɪzd] *adj* مشلول [maʃlu:l]
paramedic [ˌpærə'mɛdɪk] *n* طبيب مساعد [Ṭabeeb mosaa'aed]
parcel ['pɑːsᵊl] *n* علبة [ʕulba]
pardon ['pɑːdᵊn] *n* عذر [ʕuðran]
parent ['pɛərənt] *n* والِد أو والدة [Waled aw waledah]; **parents** *npl* والدين [wa:lidajni]; **single parent** *n* أحد الوالدين [Aḥad al-waledayn]
parish ['pærɪʃ] *n* أبرشية [ʔabraʃijja]
park [pɑːk] *n* متنزه [mutanazzah] ▷ *v* يَركِن سيارة [jarkinu sajja:ratan]; **car park** *n* موقف انتظار [Maw'qaf enteḍhar]; **national park** *n* حديقة وطنية [Hadee'qah waṭaneyah]; **theme park** *n* حديقة ألعاب [Hadee'qat al'aab]
parking [pɑːkɪŋ] *n* موقف سيارات [Maw'qaf sayarat]; **parking meter** *n* عداد وقوف السيارة ['adaad wo'qoof al-sayarah]; **parking ticket** *n* تذكرة الركن [tadhkarat al-rokn]
parliament ['pɑːləmənt] *n* برلمان [barlama:n]
parole [pə'rəʊl] *n* إطلاق سراح مشروط [Eṭla'q ṣarah mashrooṭ]
parrot ['pærət] *n* ببغاء [babbaɣa:ʔ]
parsley ['pɑːslɪ] *n* بَقدُونِس [baqdu:nis]
parsnip ['pɑːsnɪp] *n* جزر أبيض [Jazar abyad]
part [pɑːt] *n* جزء [ʒuzʔ]; **spare part** *n* قطع غيار ['qaṭa'a gheyar]
partial ['pɑːʃəl] *adj* جزئي [ʒuzʔij]
participate [pɑː'tɪsɪˌpeɪt] *v* يَشتَرِك في [Yashtarek fee]
particular [pə'tɪkjʊlə] *adj* جدير بالذكر [Jadeer bel-dhekr]
particularly [pə'tɪkjʊləlɪ] *adv* على وجه الخصوص [Ala wajh al-khoṣoṣ]
parting ['pɑːtɪŋ] *n* رحيل [raħi:l]
partly ['pɑːtlɪ] *adv* جزئياً [ʒuzʔijan]
partner ['pɑːtnə] *n* شريك [ʃari:k]; **I have a partner** أنا مرتبط بشريك [Ana mortabeṭ beshareek]
partridge ['pɑːtrɪdʒ] *n* طائر الحَجل [Ṭaayer al-hajal]

part-time ['pɑːtˌtaɪm] *adj* غير مُتَفَرغ [Ghayr motafaregh] ▷ *adv* بدوام جزئي [Bedwam jozay]
part with [pɑːt wɪð] *v* يَتَخَلّى عن [Yatkhala 'an]
party ['pɑːtɪ] *n (group)* حزب [ħizb], *(social gathering)* حفلة [ħafla] ▷ *v* يَحضر حفل [Taḥdar ḥafl]; **dinner party** *n* حفلة عشاء [Ḥaflat 'aashaa]; **search party** *n* فريق البحث [Faree'q al-bahth]
pass [pɑːs] *n (in mountains)* مجاز [maʒaːz], *(meets standard)* متوافِق مع المعايير [Motawaf'q fee al-m'aayeer], *(permit)* جواز مرور [Jawaz moror] ▷ *v (an exam)* يجتاز [jaʒtaːzu] ▷ *vi* يَمُرّ [jamurru] ▷ *vt* يَجْتاز [jaʒtaːzu]; **boarding pass** *n* تصريح الركوب [Taṣreeh al-rokob]; **ski pass** *n* ممر التزحلق [Mamar al-tazahlo'q]
passage ['pæsɪdʒ] *n (musical)* رحلة [riħla], *(route)* ممر [mamarr]
passenger ['pæsɪndʒə] *n* راكب [raːkib]
passion ['pæʃən] *n* وَلَع [walaʕ]; **passion fruit** *n* فاكهة العشق [Fakehat al-'aesh'q]
passive ['pæsɪv] *adj* سلبي [silbij]
pass out [pɑːs aʊt] *v* يُغْمَى عليه [Yoghma alayh]
Passover ['pɑːsˌəʊvə] *n* تصريح خروج [Taṣreeh khoroj]
passport ['pɑːspɔːt] *n* جواز سفر [Jawaz al-safar]; **passport control** *n* الرقابة على جوازات السفر [Al-re'qabah ala jawazat al-safar]; **I've forgotten my passport** لقد نسيت جواز سفري [la'qad nasyto jawaz safary]; **I've lost my passport** لقد ضاع جواز سفري [la'qad ḍa'aa jawaz safary]; **My passport has been stolen** لقد سرق جواز سفري [la'qad sure'qa jawaz safary]; **Please give me my passport back** من فضلك، أريد أن أسترد جواز سفري [min faḍlak, areed an asta-rid jawaz safary]
password ['pɑːsˌwɜːd] *n* كلمة السر [Kelmat al-ser]
past [pɑːst] *adj* منصرم [munsˤarim] ▷ *n* ماضي [maːdˤiː] ▷ *prep* بَعْد [baʕda]
pasta ['pæstə] *n* باستا [baːstaː]
paste [peɪst] *n* معجون [maʕʒuːn]
pasteurized ['pæstəˌraɪzd] *adj* مبستر [mubastar]
pastime ['pɑːsˌtaɪm] *n* تسلية [taslija]
pastry ['peɪstrɪ] *n* معجنات [muʕaʒʒanaːt]; **puff pastry** *n* عجينة الباف باستري ['ajeenah aleyaf bastrey]; **shortcrust pastry** *n* فطيرة هَشْة [Faṭerah hashah]
patch [pætʃ] *n* رقعة [ruqʕa]
patched [pætʃt] *adj* مرقع [muraqqaʕ]
path [pɑːθ] *n* سبيل [sabiːl]; **cycle path** *n* ممر الدراجات [Mamar al-darajat]
pathetic [pə'θɛtɪk] *adj* مثير للحزن [Mother lel-ḥozn]
patience ['peɪʃəns] *n* صبر [sˤabr]
patient ['peɪʃənt] *adj* صبور [sˤabuːr] ▷ *n* مريض [mariːdˤ]
patio ['pætɪˌəʊ] *n* فناء مرصوف [Fenaa marṣoof]
patriotic ['pætrɪəˌtɪk] *adj* وطني [watˤanij]
patrol [pə'trəʊl] *n* دَورية [dawrijja]; **patrol car** *n* سيارة الدورية [Sayarah al-dawreyah]
pattern ['pætᵊn] *n* نمط [namatˤ]
pause [pɔːz] *n* وَقْفَةٌ [waqfa]
pavement ['peɪvmənt] *n* رصيف [rasˤiːfu]
pavilion [pə'vɪljən] *n* سُرادق [saraːdiq]
paw [pɔː] *n* كف الحيوان [Kaf al-ḥayawaan]
pawnbroker ['pɔːnˌbrəʊkə] *n* مُرهِن [murhin]
pay [peɪ] *n* دفع [dafʕ] ▷ *v* يَدفَع [jadfaʕu]; **sick pay** *n* الأجر المدفوع خلال الأجازة المرضية [Al-'ajr al-madfoo'a khelal al-'ajaza al-maraḍeyah]; **Can I pay by cheque?** هل يمكنني الدفع بشيك؟ [hal yamken -any al-daf'a be- shaik?]; **Do I have to pay duty on this?** هل يجب على دفع رسوم على هذا الشيء؟ [hal jaʒibu ʕala: dafʕin rusuːmin ʕala: haːðaː aʃʃajʔi]; **Do I pay in advance?** هل يجب الدفع مقدما؟ [hal yajib al-dafi'a mu'qad-aman?]; **Do I pay now or later?** هل يجب أن أدفع الآن أم لاحقا؟ [hal

yajib an adfa'a al-aan am la-ḥe'qan?]; **Do we have to pay extra for electricity?** هل يحب علينا دفع مصاريف إضافية للكهرباء؟ [hal yajib 'aala-yna daf'a maṣa-reef eḍafiya lel-kah-rabaa?]; **When do I pay?** متى أدفع؟ [mata adfa'a?]; **Where do I pay?** أين يتم الدفع؟ [ayna yatim al-daf'a?]; **Will I have to pay?** هل سيكون الدفع واجبًا علي؟ [hal sayakon al-dafi'a wajeban 'aalya?]; **Will the insurance pay for it?** هل ستدفع لك شركة التأمين مقابل ذلك [hal sa-tadfaa laka share-kat al-tameen ma'qabil dhalik?]

payable ['peɪəbᵊl] *adj* واجب دفعه [Wajeb daf'aaho]

pay back [peɪ bæk] *v* يُسدِد [jusaddidu]

payment ['peɪmənt] *n* دَفْع [dafʕ]

payphone ['peɪˌfəʊn] *n* هاتف عمومي [Hatef 'aomoomy]

PC [piː siː] *n* جهاز الكمبيوتر الشخصي [ʒihaːzu alkumbjuːtr aʃʃaxsˤijji]

PDF [piː diː ɛf] *n* ملف FDP [Malaf PDF]

peace [piːs] *n* سلام [salaːm]

peaceful ['piːsfʊl] *adj* مسالم [musaːlim]

peach [piːtʃ] *n* خُوخ [xuːx]

peacock ['piːˌkɒk] *n* طاووس [tˤaːwuːs]

peak [piːk] *n* قمة [qima]; **peak hours** *npl* ساعات الذروة [Sa'aat al-dhorwah]

peanut ['piːˌnʌt] *n* حبة فول سوداني [Ḥabat fool sodaney]; **peanut allergy** *n* حساسية تجاه الفول السوداني [Hasaseyah tejah al-fool alsodaney]; **peanut butter** *n* زُبْدَة الفستق [Zobdat al-fosto'q]

pear [pɛə] *n* كُمَّثرى [kummiθraː]

pearl [pɜːl] *n* لؤلؤة [luʔluʔa]

peas [piːs] *npl* بِسِلّة [bisalati]

peat [piːt] *n* سِمَاد طبيعي [Semad ṭabe'ay]

pebble ['pɛbᵊl] *n* حصاة [ħasˤaːt]

peculiar [pɪ'kjuːlɪə] *adj* فريد [fariːd]

pedal ['pɛdᵊl] *n* دَوَّاسة [dawwaːsa]

pedestrian [pɪ'dɛstrɪən] *n* مُرْتَجِل [murtaʒil]; **pedestrian crossing** *n* ممر خاص لعبور المشاه [Mamar khaṣ leaboor al-moshah]; **pedestrian precinct** *n* منطقة مشاه [Menta'qat moshah]

pedestrianized [pɪ'dɛstrɪəˌnaɪzd] *adj* محول إلى منطقة مشاه [Meḥawel ela manṭe'qat moshah]

pedigree ['pɛdɪˌgriː] *adj* أصل [ʔasˤl]

peel [piːl] *v* يُقَشِر [juqaʃʃiru]

peg [pɛg] *n* وتد [watad]

Pekinese [ˌpiːkɪŋ'iːz] *n* كلب بِكِيني [Kalb bekkeeney]

pelican ['pɛlɪkən] *n* بَجَعَة [baʒaʕa]; **pelican crossing** *n* عبور المشاه سيراً على الأقدام ['aobor al-moshah sayran ala al-a'qdam]

pellet ['pɛlɪt] *n* كرة صغيرة [Korat ṣagheerah]

pelvis ['pɛlvɪs] *n* الحوض [alħawdˤi]

pen [pɛn] *n* قلم [qalam]; **ballpoint pen** *n* قلم حبر جاف ['qalam ḥebr jaf]; **felt-tip pen** *n* قلم ذو سن من اللباد ['qalam dho sen men al-lebad]; **fountain pen** *n* قلم حبر ['qalam ḥebr]

penalize ['piːnəˌlaɪz] *v* يُجَرِم [juʒarrimu]

penalty ['pɛnᵊltɪ] *n* جزاء [ʒazaːʔ]

pencil ['pɛnsᵊl] *n* قلم رصاص ['qalam raṣaṣ]; **pencil case** *n* مقلمة [miqlamatun]; **pencil sharpener** *n* مبراة [mibraːtun]

pendant ['pɛndənt] *n* حلية متدلية [Halabh motadaleyah]

penfriend ['pɛnˌfrɛnd] *n* صديق بالمراسلة [Ṣadeek belmoraslah]

penguin ['pɛŋgwɪn] *n* بطريق [bitˤriːq]

penicillin [ˌpɛnɪ'sɪlɪn] *n* بنسلين [binisiliːn]

peninsula [pɪ'nɪnsjʊlə] *n* شبه الجزيرة [Shebh al-jazeerah]

penknife ['pɛnˌnaɪf] *n* سكين القلم [Sekeen al-'qalam]

penny ['pɛnɪ] *n* سِنْت [sint]

pension ['pɛnʃən] *n* معاش [maʕaːʃ]

pensioner ['pɛnʃənə; 'pensioner] *n* صاحب المعاش [Ṣaheb al-ma'aash]; **old-age pensioner** *n* صاحب معاش كبير السن [Ṣaheb ma'aash kabeer al-sen]

pentathlon [pɛn'tæθlən] *n* مباراة خماسية [Mobarah khomaseyah]

penultimate [pɪˈnʌltɪmɪt] *adj* قبل الأخير [ˈqabl al akheer]
people [ˈpiːpᵊl] *npl* ناس [naːs]
pepper [ˈpɛpə] *n* فُلْفُل [fulful]
peppermill [ˈpɛpəˌmɪl] *n* مطحنة الفلفل [maṭḥanat al-felfel]
peppermint [ˈpɛpəˌmɪnt] *n* نِعْنَاع [naʕnaːʕ]
per [pɜː; pə] *prep* لكل [likulli]; **per cent** *adv* بالمائة [biʕalmiʕati]; **How much is it per hour?** كم يبلغ الثمن لكل ساعة؟ [kam yablugh al-thaman le-kul sa'a a?]; **How much is it per night?** كم يبلغ الثمن لكل ساعة [kam yablugh al-thaman le-kul layla?]
percentage [pəˈsɛntɪdʒ] *n* نسبة مئوية [Nesbah meaweyah]
percussion [pəˈkʌʃən] *n* نَقْر [naqr]
perfect [ˈpɜːfɪkt] *adj* تام [taːmm]
perfection [pəˈfɛkʃən] *n* مِثاليّة [miθaːlijja]
perfectly [ˈpɜːfɪktlɪ] *adv* على نحو كامل [Ala naḥw kaamel]
perform [pəˈfɔːm] *v* يؤدي [juʔaddiː]
performance [pəˈfɔːməns] *n (artistic)* تمثيل [tamθiːll], *(functioning)* أداء [ʔadaːʔ]
perfume [ˈpɜːfjuːm] *n* عطر [ʕitˤr]
perhaps [pəˈhæps; præps] *adv* لَعَّل [laʕalla]
period [ˈpɪərɪəd] *n* مدة [mudda]; **trial period** *n* فترة المحاكمة [Fatrat al-moḥkamah]
perjury [ˈpɜːdʒərɪ] *n* الحنث باليمين [Al-ḥanth bel-yameen]
perm [pɜːm] *n* تمويج الشعر [Tamweej al-sha'ar]
permanent [ˈpɜːmənənt] *adj* دائم [daːʔim]
permanently [ˈpɜːmənəntlɪ] *adv* بشكل دائم [Beshakl daaem]
permission [pəˈmɪʃən] *n* إِذْن [ʔiðn]
permit *n* [ˈpɜːmɪt] تصريح [tasˤriːħ] ▷ *v* [pəˈmɪt] يسمح ب [jasmaħu bi]; **work permit** *n* تصريح عمل [Taṣreeh 'amal]; **Do you need a fishing permit?** هل أنت في احتياج إلى تصريح بالصيد؟ [hal anta fee iḥti-yaj ela taṣreeḥ bil-ṣayd?]
persecute [ˈpɜːsɪˌkjuːt] *v* يَضطهِد [jadˤtˤahidu]
persevere [ˌpɜːsɪˈvɪə] *v* يُثَابِر [juθaːbiru]
Persian [ˈpɜːʃən] *adj* فارسي [faːrisij]
persistent [pəˈsɪstənt] *adj* مُصِر [musˤirru]
person [ˈpɜːsᵊn] *n* فَرد [fard]
personal [ˈpɜːsənᵊl] *adj* شخصي [ʃaxsˤij]; **personal assistant** *n* مساعد شخصي [Mosa'aed shakhṣey]; **personal organizer** *n* منظم شخصي [monaḍhem shakhṣey]; **personal stereo** *n* جهاز الصوت المجسم الشخصي [Jehaz al-ṣawt al-mojasam al-shakhṣey]
personality [ˌpɜːsəˈnælɪtɪ] *n* هَوية [hawijja]
personally [ˈpɜːsənəlɪ] *adv* شخصياً [ʃaxsˤiːan]
personnel [ˌpɜːsəˈnɛl] *n* الموظفين [almuwazˤzˤafiːna]
perspective [pəˈspɛktɪv] *n* منظور [manzˤuːr]
perspiration [ˌpɜːspəˈreɪʃən] *n* تَعَرُّق [taʕarruq]
persuade [pəˈsweɪd] *v* يَحُثْ [jaħuθθu]
persuasive [pəˈsweɪsɪv] *adj* مقنع [muqniʕ]
Peru [pəˈruː] *n* بيرو [biːruː]
Peruvian [pəˈruːvɪən] *adj* بيروفي [biːruːfij] ▷ *n* بيروفي [biːruːfij]
pessimist [ˈpɛsɪˌmɪst] *n* مُتَشائِم [mutaʃaːʔim]
pessimistic [ˈpɛsɪˌmɪstɪk] *adj* متشائم [mutaʃaːʔim]
pest [pɛst] *n* وباء [wabaːʔ]
pester [ˈpɛstə] *v* يُضايق [judˤaːjiqu]
pesticide [ˈpɛstɪˌsaɪd] *n* مبيد حشرات [Mobeed hasharat]
pet [pɛt] *n* حيوان أليف [Ḥayawaan aleef]
petition [pɪˈtɪʃən] *n* التماس [iltimaːs]
petrified [ˈpɛtrɪˌfaɪd] *adj* متحجر [mutaħaʒʒir]
petrol [ˈpɛtrəl] *n* بنزين [binziːn]; **petrol station** *n* محطة بنزين [Mahaṭat benzene]; **petrol tank** *n* خزان بنزين

[Khazan benzeen]; **unleaded petrol** *n* بنزين خالي من الرصاص [Benzene khaly men al- raṣaṣ]; **I've run out of petrol** لقد نفذ البنزين من السيارة [la'qad nafatha al-banzeen min al-sayara]; **Is there a petrol station near here?** هل يوجد محطة بنزين قريبة من هنا؟ [hal yujad muḥaṯat banzeen 'qareeba min huna?]; **The petrol has run out** نفذ البنزين من السيارة [nafadh al-banzeen min al-sayara]

pewter ['pju:tə] *n* سبيكة البيوتر [Sabeekat al-beyooter]

pharmacist ['fɑ:məsɪst] *n* صيدلي [sˤajdalij]

pharmacy ['fɑ:məsɪ] *n* صيدلية [sˤajdalijja]

PhD [pi: eɪtʃ di:] *n* درجة الدكتوراه في الفلسفة [daraʒatu adduktu:ra:ti fi: alfalsafati]

pheasant ['fɛzᵊnt] *n* طائر التدرج [Ṭaear al-tadraj]

philosophy [fɪ'lɒsəfɪ] *n* فلسفة [falsafa]

phobia ['fəʊbɪə] *n* خوف مرضي [Khawf maraḍey]

phone [fəʊn] *n* هاتف [ha:tif] ▷ *v* يَتَصِل تليفونيا [jattasˤilu tili:fu:nijjan]; **camera phone** *n* تليفون بكاميرا [Telefoon bekamerah]; **entry phone** *n* تليفون المدخل [Telefoon al-madkhal]; **mobile phone** *n* هاتف جوال [Hatef jawal]; **phone bill** *n* فاتورة تليفون [Fatoorat telefon]; **phone number** *n* رقم التليفون [Ra'qm al-telefone]; **smart phone** *n* هاتف ذكي [Hatef zaky]; **I'd like some coins for the phone, please** أريد بعض العملات المعدنية من أجل الهاتف من فضلك [areed ba'aḍ al-'aimlaat al-ma'a-danya min ajil al-haatif min faḍlak]; **I'm having trouble with the phone** هناك مشكلة في الهاتف [hunaka mushkila fee al-haatif]; **May I use your phone?** هل يمكن أن أستخدم هاتفك؟ [hal yamken an asta-khdim ha-tifak?]

phonebook ['fəʊn,bʊk] *n* دفتر الهاتف [Daftar al-hatef]

phonebox ['fəʊn,bɒks] *n* كابينة تليفون [Kabeenat telefoon]

phonecall ['fəʊn,kɔ:l] *n* اتصال هاتفي [Eteṣal hatefey]

phonecard ['fəʊn,kɑ:d] *n* كارت تليفون [Kart telefone]; **A phonecard, please** أريد كارت تليفون من فضلك [areed kart talefon min faḍlak]

photo ['fəʊtəʊ] *n* صورة فوتوغرافية [Ṣorah fotoghrafeyah]; **photo album** *n* ألبوم الصور [Albom al ṣewar]

photocopier ['fəʊtəʊ,kɒpɪə] *n* ماكينة تصوير [Makenat taṣweer]

photocopy ['fəʊtəʊ,kɒpɪ] *n* نسخة ضوئية [niskha ḍaw-iyaa] ▷ *v* يستخرج نسخة [Yastakhrej noskhah]; **I'd like a photocopy of this, please** أرجو عمل نسخة ضوئية من هذا المستند [arjo al-ḥuṣool 'aala nuskha min hadha al-mustanad min faḍlak]

photograph ['fəʊtə,grɑ:f; -,græf] *n* صورة فوتوغرافية [Ṣorah fotoghrafeyah] ▷ *v* يُصور فوتوغرافيا [Yoṣawer fotoghrafeyah]

photographer [fə'tɒgrəfə; pho'tographer] *n* مصور فوتوغرافي [moṣawer fotoghrafey]

photography [fə'tɒgrəfɪ] *n* التصوير الفوتوغرافي [Al-taṣweer al-fotoghrafey]

phrase [freɪz] *n* عبارة [ʕiba:ra]

phrasebook ['freɪz,bʊk] *n* كتاب العبارات [Ketab al-'aebarat]

physical ['fɪzɪkᵊl] *adj* بدني [badanij] ▷ *n* متعلق بالبدن [Mota'ale'q bel-badan]

physicist ['fɪzɪsɪst] *n* فيزيائي [fi:zja:ʔij]

physics ['fɪzɪks] *npl* فيزياء [fi:zja:ʔun]

physiotherapist [,fɪzɪəʊ'θɛrəpɪst] *n* أخصائي العلاج الطبيعي [Akeṣaaey al-elaj al-ṭabeaey]

physiotherapy [,fɪzɪəʊ'θɛrəpɪ] *n* علاج طبيعي ['aelaj ṭabeye]

pianist ['pɪənɪst] *n* لاعب البيانو [La'aeb al-beyano]

piano [pɪ'ænəʊ] *n* بيانو [bija:nu:]

pick [pɪk] *n* انتقاء [intiqa:ʔ] ▷ *v* يختار [jaxta:ru]

pick on [pɪk ɒn] *v* يُسئ معاملة شخص [Yosee mo'amalat shakhṣ]
pick out [pɪk aʊt] *v* يَنتقِي [jantaqi:]
pickpocket ['pɪk,pɒkɪt] *n* نَشَّال [naʃʃa:l]
pick up [pɪk ʌp] *v* يَجْلِب [jaʒlibu]
picnic ['pɪknɪk] *n* نزهة في الهواء الطلق [Nozhah fee al-hawaa al-ṭal'q]
picture ['pɪktʃə] *n* صورة [sˤu:ra]; **picture frame** *n* إطار الصورة [Eṭar al ṣorah]; **Would you take a picture of us, please?** هل يمكن أن تلتقط لنا صورة هنا من فضلك؟ [hal yamken an talta-'qiṭ lana ṣoora min faḍlak?]
picturesque [,pɪktʃə'rɛsk] *adj* رائع [ra:ʔiʕ]
pie [paɪ] *n* فطيرة [fatˤi:ra]; **apple pie** *n* فطيرة التفاح [Faṭeerat al-tofaaḥ]; **pie chart** *n* رسم بياني دائري [Rasm bayany daery]
piece [pi:s] *n* قطعة [qitˤʕa]
pier [pɪə] *n* دعامة [daʕa:ma]
pierce [pɪəs] *v* يَخْرِق [jaxriqu]
pierced [pɪəst] *adj* مثقوب [maθqu:b]
piercing ['pɪəsɪŋ] *n* ثَقْب [θuqb]
pig [pɪg] *n* خنزير [xinzi:r]; **guinea pig** *n* *(for experiment)* حقل للتجارب [Ha'ql lel-tajareb], *(rodent)* خنزير غينيا [Khnzeer ghemyah]
pigeon ['pɪdʒɪn] *n* حمامة [ħama:ma]
piggybank ['pɪgɪ,bæŋk] *n* حصالة على شكل خنزير [Ḥaṣalah ala shakl khenzeer]
pigtail ['pɪg,teɪl] *n* ضفيرة [dˤafi:ra]
pile [paɪl] *n* خازوق [xa:zu:q]
piles [paɪlz] *npl* دعائم [daʕa:ʔimun]
pile-up [paɪlʌp] *n* تكدس [takaddus]
pilgrim ['pɪlgrɪm] *n* حَاجّ [ħa:ʒʒ]
pilgrimage ['pɪlgrɪmɪdʒ] *n* الحج [al-ħaʒʒu]
pill [pɪl] *n* حبة دواء [Habbat dawaa]; **sleeping pill** *n* حبة نوم [Habit nawm]
pillar ['pɪlə] *n* دعامة [daʕa:ma]
pillow ['pɪləʊ] *n* وِسَادة [wisa:da]
pillowcase ['pɪləʊ,keɪs] *n* غطاء الوسادة [gheṭaa al-wesadah]
pilot ['paɪlət] *n* ربان الطائرة [Roban al-ṭaaerah]; **pilot light** *n* شُعلة الاحتراق [Sho'alat al-eḥtera'q]
pimple ['pɪmpᵊl] *n* دُمّل [dumul]
pin [pɪn] *n* دبوس [dabbu:s]; **drawing pin** *n* دبوس تثبيت اللوائح [Daboos tathbeet al-lawaeh]; **rolling pin** *n* نَشّابة [naʃʃa:batun]; **safety pin** *n* دبوس أمان [Daboos aman]; **I need a safety pin** أحتاج إلى دبوس آمن [aḥtaaj ela dub-boos aamin]
PIN [pɪn] *npl* رقم التعريف الشخصي [Ra'qam alta'areef alshakhṣey]
pinafore ['pɪnə,fɔ:] *n* مئزر [miʔzar]
pinch [pɪntʃ] *v* يَقْرِصّ [jaqrusˤu]
pine [paɪn] *n* شجرة الصنوبر [Shajarat al-ṣonobar]
pineapple ['paɪn,æpᵊl] *n* أناناس [ʔana:na:s]
pink [pɪŋk] *adj* وردي [wardij]
pint [paɪnt] *n* باينت [ba:jant]
pip [pɪp] *n* حَبَّة [ħabba]
pipe [paɪp] *n* ماسورة [ma:su:ra]; **exhaust pipe** *n* ماسورة العادم [Masorat al-'aadem]
pipeline ['paɪp,laɪn] *n* خط أنابيب [Khaṭ anabeeb]
pirate ['paɪrɪt] *n* قُرْصان [qursˤa:n]
Pisces ['paɪsi:z; 'pɪ-] *n* الحوت [al-ħu:tu]
pistol ['pɪstᵊl] *n* مسدس [musaddas]
piston ['pɪstən] *n* مِكْبَس [mikbas]
pitch [pɪtʃ] *n* *(sound)* طبقة صوت [Ṭabaqat ṣawt], *(sport)* رَمْيَة [ramja] ▷ *v* يَرْمي [jarmi:]
pity ['pɪtɪ] *n* شفقة [ʃafaqa] ▷ *v* يُشفق على [Yoshfe'q 'aala]
pixel ['pɪksᵊl] *n* بِكْسِل [biksil]
pizza ['pi:tsə] *n* بيتزا [bi:tza:]
place [pleɪs] *n* مكان [maka:n] ▷ *v* يَضع في [Yaḍa'a fee]; **place of birth** *n* مكان الميلاد [Makan al-meelad]; **Do you know a good place to go?** أتعرف مكانا جيدا يمكن أن أذهب إليه؟ [a-ta'aruf makanan jayidan yamkin an adhhab e-lay-he?]
placement ['pleɪsmənt] *n* وَضْع [wadˤʕ]
plain [pleɪn] *adj* بسيط [basi:tˤ] ▷ *n* ارض منبسطة [ardˤu munbasatˤatin]; **plain chocolate** *n* شيكولاتة سادة [Shekolatah

sada]
plait [plæt] *n* طية [tˤajja]
plan [plæn] *n* خطة [xutˤtˤa] ▷ *v* يُخطِط [juxatˤtˤitˤu]; **street plan** *n* خريطة الشارع [Khareeṭat al-share'a]
plane [pleɪn] *n (aeroplane)* طائرة [tˤa:ʔira], *(surface)* سَطح مستوي [Saṭ mostawey], *(tool)* طائرة [tˤa:ʔira]
planet ['plænɪt] *n* كوكب [kawkab]
planning [plænɪŋ] *n* تخطيط [taxtˤi:tˤ]
plant [plɑ:nt] *n* نبات [naba:t], *(site/ equipment)* مباني وتجهيزات [Mabaney watajheezaat] ▷ *v* يزرع [jazraʕu]; **plant pot** *n* حوض نباتات [Hawḍ nabatat]; **pot plant** *n* نبات يزرع في حاوية [Nabat yozra'a fee ḥaweyah]; **We'd like to see local plants and trees** نريد أن نرى النباتات والأشجار المحلية [nureed an nara al-naba-taat wa al-ash-jaar al-maḥali-ya]
plaque [plæk; plɑ:k] *n* قِلادة [qila:da]
plaster ['plɑ:stə] *n (for wall)* جص [ʒibsˤ], *(for wound)* مادة لاصقة [Madah laṣe'qah]
plastic ['plæstɪk; 'plɑ:s-] *adj* بلاستيكي [bla:sti:kij] ▷ *n* بلاستيك [bla:sti:k]; **plastic bag** *n* كيس بلاستيكي [Kees belasteekey]; **plastic surgery** *n* جراحة تجميلية [Jerahah tajmeeleyah]
plate [pleɪt] *n* صحيفة [sˤaħi:fa]; **number plate** *n* لوحة الأرقام [Looḥ al-ar'qaam]
platform ['plætfɔ:m] *n* منصة [minasˤsˤa]
platinum ['plætɪnəm] *n* بلاتين [bla:ti:n]
play [pleɪ] *n* لعب [laʕib] ▷ *v (in sport)* يلعب [jalʕabu], *(music)* يَعْزِف [jaʕzifu]; **play truant** *v* يتغَيب [jataɣajjabu]; **playing card** *n* بطَاقة لعب [Beṭaqat la'aeb]; **playing field** *n* ملعب رياضي [Mal'aab reyady]; **We'd like to play tennis** نود أن نلعب التنس؟ [nawid an nal'aab al-tanis]; **Where can I play golf?** أين يمكنني أن ألعب الجولف؟ [ayna yamken-any an al-'aab al-jolf?]
player ['pleɪə] *n (instrumentalist)* آلة عَزْف [Aalat 'aazf], *(of sport)* لاعب [la:ʕib]; **CD player** *n* مشغل الاسطوانات [Moshaghel al-esṭewanat]; **MP3 player** *n* مشغل 3PM ملفات [Moshaghel malafat MP3]; **MP4 player** *n* 4PM مشغل ملفات [Moshaghel malafat MP4]
playful ['pleɪfʊl] *adj* لعوب [laʕu:b]
playground ['pleɪˌgraʊnd] *n* ملعب [malʕab]
playgroup ['pleɪˌgru:p] *n* مجموعة لعب [Majmo'aat le'aab]
PlayStation® ['pleɪˌsteɪʃən] *n* ®بلايستيشن [bla:jsiti:ʃn]
playtime ['pleɪˌtaɪm] *n* وَقْت اللعب [Wa'qt al-la'aeb]
playwright ['pleɪˌraɪt] *n* كاتب مسرحي [Kateb masrḥey]
pleasant ['plɛzᵊnt] *adj* سار [sa:rr]
please [pli:z] *excl* ot ekil d'I ?# أرجوك = esaelp ,ni kcehc أريد التسجيل في الرحلة من فضلك
pleased [pli:zd] *adj* مسرور [masru:r]
pleasure ['plɛʒə] *n* سرور [suru:r]; **It was a pleasure to meet you** من دواعي سروري أن التقي بك [min dawa-'ay siro-ry an al-ta'qy bik]; **It's been a pleasure working with you** من دواعي سروري العمل معك [min dawa-'ay siro-ry al-'aamal ma'aak]; **With pleasure!** بكل سرور [bekul siroor]
plenty ['plɛntɪ] *n* وَفْرة [wafra]
pliers ['plaɪəz] *npl* كمَّاشة [kamma:ʃatun]
plot [plɒt] *n (piece of land)* قطعة أرض ['qeṭ'aat arḍ], *(secret plan)* حبكة ▷ *v (conspire)* يتآمر [jataʔa:maru]
plough [plaʊ] *n* محراث [miħra:θ] ▷ *v* يَحْرُث [jaħruθu]
plug [plʌg] *n* قابس [qa:bis]; **spark plug** *n* شمعة إشعال [Sham'aat esh'aal]
plughole ['plʌgˌhəʊl] *n* فتحة التوصيل [Fathat al-tawṣeel]
plug in [plʌg ɪn] *v* يُوصِل بالقابس الكهربائي [ju:sˤilu bilqa:busi alkahraba:ʔijji]
plum [plʌm] *n* برقوق [barqu:q]
plumber ['plʌmə] *n* سباك [sabba:k]
plumbing ['plʌmɪŋ] *n* سِبَاكة [siba:ka]
plump [plʌmp] *adj* ممتلئ الجسم [Momtaleya al-jesm]
plunge [plʌndʒ] *v* يَغْطَس [jaɣtˤusu]

plural ['plʊərəl] *n* جمع [ʒamʕ]
plus [plʌs] *prep* زائد [za:ʔidun]
plywood ['plaɪˌwʊd] *n* خشب أبلكاج [Khashab ablakaj]
p.m. [pi: ɛm] *abbr* مساءً [masa:ʔun]; **Please come home by 11p.m.** رجاء العودة بحلول الساعة الحادية عشر مساءً [rejaa al-'aawda beḥilool al-sa'aa al-ḥade-a 'aashar masa-an]
pneumonia [nju:'məʊnɪə] *n* مرض ذات الرئة [Maraḍ dhat al-re'aa]
poached [pəʊtʃt] *adj* *(caught illegally)* مُتَلَبِّس بالجَريمَه [Motalabes bel-jareemah], *(simmered gently)* مسلوق [maslu:q]
pocket ['pɒkɪt] *n* جيب [ʒajb]; **pocket calculator** *n* آلة حاسبة للجيب [Alah haseba lel-jeeb]; **pocket money** *n* مصروف الجيب [Maṣroof al-jeeb]
podcast ['pɒdˌkɑ:st] *n* بودكاست [bu:dka:st]
poem ['pəʊɪm] *n* قصيدة [qasˤi:da]
poet ['pəʊɪt] *n* شاعر [ʃa:ʕir]
poetry ['pəʊɪtrɪ] *n* شِعْر [ʃiʕr]
point [pɔɪnt] *n* نقطة [nuqtˤa] ▷ *v* يُشير [juʃi:ru]
pointless ['pɔɪntlɪs] *adj* بلا مغزى [Bela maghdha]
point out [pɔɪnt aʊt] *v* يُوضح [ju:dˤiħu]
poison ['pɔɪzᵊn] *n* سُمّ [summ] ▷ *v* يُسَمِّم [jusammimu]
poisonous ['pɔɪzənəs] *adj* سام [sa:mm]
poke [pəʊk] *v* يَلْكُم [jalkumu]
poker ['pəʊkə] *n* لُعبَة البوكَر [Lo'abat al-bookar]
Poland ['pəʊlənd] *n* بولندة [bu:landat]
polar ['pəʊlə] *adj* قطبي [qutˤbij]; **polar bear** *n* الدب القطبي [Al-dob al-shamaley]
pole [pəʊl] *n* قطب [qutˤb]; **North Pole** *n* القطب الشمالي [A'qoṭb al-shamaley]; **pole vault** *n* قفز بالزانة ['qafz bel-zanah]; **South Pole** *n* القطب الجنوبي [Al-k'qotb al-janoobey]; **tent pole** *n* عمود الخيمة ['amood al-kheemah]
Pole [pəʊl] *n* بولندي [bu:landij]
police [pə'li:s] *n* شُرْطَة [ʃurtˤa]; **police officer** *n* ضابط شرطة [Ḍabeṭ shorṭah]; **police station** *n* قسم شرطة ['qesm shorṭah]
policeman, policemen [pə'li:smən, pə'li:smɛn] *n* ضابط شرطة [Ḍabeṭ shorṭah]
policewoman, policewomen [pə'li:swʊmən, pə'li:swɪmɪn] *n* ضابطة شرطة [Ḍaabeṭ shorṭah]
policy ['pɒlɪsɪ] *n*; **insurance policy** *n* بوليصة تأمين [Booleeṣat taameen]
polio ['pəʊlɪəʊ] *n* شلل أطفال [Shalal aṭfaal]
polish ['pɒlɪʃ] *n* مادة تلميع [Madah talmee'a] ▷ *v* يَجلو [jaʒlu:]; **nail polish** *n* طلاء أظافر [Telaa aḍhafer]; **shoe polish** *n* ورنيش الأحذية [Warneesh al-aḥḍheyah]
Polish ['pəʊlɪʃ] *adj* بولندي [bu:landij] ▷ *n* بولندي [bu:landij]
polite [pə'laɪt] *adj* مؤدب [muʔaddab]
politely [pə'laɪtlɪ] *adv* بأَدَب [Beadab]
politeness [pə'laɪtnɪs] *n* الكياسة [al-kija:satu]
political [pə'lɪtɪkᵊl] *adj* سياسي [sija:sij]
politician [ˌpɒlɪ'tɪʃən] *n* رجل سياسة [Rajol seyasah]
politics ['pɒlɪtɪks] *npl* سياسة [sija:sa]
poll [pəʊl] *n* اقتراع [iqtira:ʕ]; **opinion poll** *n* استطلاع الرأي [Eateṭla'a al-ray]
pollen ['pɒlən] *n* لقاح [liqa:ħ]
pollute [pə'lu:t] *v* يُلَوث [julawwiθu]
polluted [pə'lu:tɪd] *adj* مُلَوَث [mulawwaθ]
pollution [pə'lu:ʃən] *n* تلوث [talawwuθ]
Polynesia [ˌpɒlɪ'ni:ʒə; -ʒɪə] *n* بولينسيا [bu:li:nisja:]
Polynesian [ˌpɒlɪ'ni:ʒən; -ʒɪən] *adj* بولنسي [bu:linisij] ▷ *n* *(language)* اللغة البولينيسية [Al- loghah al-bolenseyah], *(person)* بولينيسي [bu:li:ni:sij]
pomegranate ['pɒmɪˌgrænɪt; 'pɒmˌgrænɪt] *n* رُمَّان [rumma:n]
pond [pɒnd] *n* بِرْكَة [birka]
pony ['pəʊnɪ] *n* فَرَس قَزم [Faras 'qezm]; **pony trekking** *n* رحلة على الجياد [Rehalah ala al-jeyad]

ponytail ['pəʊnɪˌteɪl] *n* ضفيرة [dˤafiːra]
poodle ['puːdᵊl] *n* كلب البودل [Kalb al-boodel]
pool [puːl] *n (resources)* حوض منتج للنفط [Hawḍ montej lel-nafṭ], *(water)* حَوْض [ħawdˤ]; **paddling pool** *n* حَوض سباحة للأطفال [Ḥaeḍ sebaha lel-aṭfaal]; **swimming pool** *n* حمام سباحة [Hammam sebaḥah]
poor [pʊə; pɔː] *adj* فقير [faqiːr]
poorly ['pʊəlɪ; 'pɔː-] *adj* بشكل سيء [Be-shakl sayea]
popcorn ['pɒpˌkɔːn] *n* فشار [fuʃaːr]
pope [pəʊp] *n* البابا [al-baːbaː]
poplar ['pɒplə] *n* خشب الحور [Khashab al-ḥoor]
poppy ['pɒpɪ] *n* خشخاش [xaʃxaːʃ]
popular ['pɒpjʊlə] *adj* شعبي [ʃaʕbij]
popularity ['pɒpjʊlærɪtɪ] *n* شعبية [ʃaʕbijjit]
population [ˌpɒpjʊ'leɪʃən] *n* سكان [sukkaːn]
pop-up [pɒpʌp] *n* قفز [qafaza]
porch [pɔːtʃ] *n* رواق [riwaːq]
pork [pɔːk] *n* لحم خنزير [Lahm al-khenzeer]; **pork chop** *n* شَريحة لحم خنزير [Shareehat laḥm khenzeer]
porn [pɔːn] *n (informal)* الإباحية [al-ʔibaːħijatu]
pornographic [pɔː'nɒgræfɪk] *adj* إباحي [ʔibaːħij]
pornography [pɔː'nɒgrəfɪ] *n* فن إباحي [Fan ebaḥey]
porridge ['pɒrɪdʒ] *n* عصيدة [ʕasˤiːda]
port [pɔːt] *n (ships)* منفذ جوي أو بحري [manfaḍh jawey aw baḥrey], *(wine)* نبيذ برتغالي [nabiːðun burtuɣaːlij]
portable ['pɔːtəbᵊl] *adj* محمول [maħmuːl]
porter ['pɔːtə] *n* شَيَّال [ʃajjaːl]
portfolio [pɔːt'fəʊlɪəʊ] *n* حقيبة أوراق [Ha'qeebat awra'q]
portion ['pɔːʃən] *n* حصة [ħisˤsˤa]
portrait ['pɔːtrɪt; -treɪt] *n* صورة للوجه [Ṣorah lel-wajh]
Portugal ['pɔːtjʊgᵊl] *n* البرتغال [al-burtuɣaːl]
Portuguese [ˌpɔːtjʊ'giːz] *adj* برتغالي [burtuɣaːlij] ▷ *n (language)* اللغة البرتغالية [Al-loghah al-bortoghaleyah], *(person)* برتغالي [burtuɣaːlij]
position [pə'zɪʃən] *n* مكانة [makaːna]
positive ['pɒzɪtɪv] *adj* إيجابي [ʔiːʒaːbij]
possess [pə'zɛs] *v* يمتلك [jamtaliku]
possession [pə'zɛʃən] *n* حيازة [ħijaːza]
possibility [ˌpɒsɪ'bɪlɪtɪ] *n* إمكانية [ʔimkaːnijja]
possible ['pɒsɪbᵊl] *adj* ممكن [mumkin]; **as soon as possible** في أقرب وقت ممكن [fee a'qrab wa'qt mumkin]
possibly ['pɒsɪblɪ] *adv* من الممكن [Men al-momken]
post [pəʊst] *n (mail)* نظام بريدي [neḍham bareedey], *(position)* موضع [mawdˤiʕ], *(stake)* عمود [ʕamuːd] ▷ *v* يُرسِل بالبريد [Yorsel bel-bareed]; **post office** *n* مكتب البريد [maktab al-bareed]
postage ['pəʊstɪdʒ] *n* أجرة البريد [ojrat al bareed]
postbox ['pəʊstˌbɒks] *n* صندوق البريد [Ṣondo'q bareed]
postcard ['pəʊstˌkɑːd] *n* بطاقة بريدية [Beṭaqah bareedyah]
postcode ['pəʊstˌkəʊd] *n* رمز بريدي [Ramz bareedey]
poster ['pəʊstə] *n* إعلان ملصق [E'alan Molṣa'q]
postgraduate [pəʊst'grædjʊɪt] *n* دراسات عليا [diraːsaːt ʕaljan]
postman, postmen ['pəʊstmən, 'pəʊstmɛn] *n* ساعي البريد [Sa'aey al-bareed]
postmark ['pəʊstˌmɑːk] *n* خاتم البريد [Khatem al-bareed]
postpone [pəʊst'pəʊn; pə'spəʊn] *v* يؤجل [juaʒʒilu]
postwoman, postwomen ['pəʊstwʊmən, 'pəʊstwɪmɪn] *n* ساعية البريد [Sa'aeyat al-bareed]
pot [pɒt] *n* إناء [ʔinaːʔ]; **plant pot** *n* حوض نباتات [Hawḍ nabatat]; **pot plant** *n* نبات يزرع في حاوية [Nabat yozra'a fee

ḥaweyah]
potato, potatoes [pəˈteɪtəʊ, pəˈteɪtəʊz] *n* بطاطس [batˤaːtˤis]; **baked potato** *n* بطاطس بالفرن [Baṭaṭes bel-forn]; **jacket potato** *n* بطاطس مشوية بقشرها [Baṭaṭes mashweiah be'qshreha]; **mashed potatoes** *npl* بطاطس مهروسة [Baṭaṭes mahrosah]; **potato peeler** *n* جهاز تقشير البطاطس [Jehaz ta'qsheer al-baṭaṭes]
potential [pəˈtɛnʃəl] *adj* ممكن [mumkin] ▷ *n* إمكانية [ʔimkaːnijja]
pothole [ˈpɒtˌhəʊl] *n* أُخْدُود [ʔuxduːd]
pottery [ˈpɒtərɪ] *n* مصنع الفخار [Maṣna'a al-fakhaar]
potty [ˈpɒtɪ] *n* نونية للأطفال [Noneyah lel-aṭfaal]; **Do you have a potty?** هل توجد نونية للأطفال؟ [hal tojad non-iya lil-aṭfaal?]
pound [paʊnd] *n* رطل [ratˤl]; **pound sterling** *n* جنيه استرليني [Jeneh esterleeney]
pour [pɔː] *v* يَسْكُب [jaskubu]
poverty [ˈpɒvətɪ] *n* فَقْر [faqr]
powder [ˈpaʊdə] *n* بودرة [buːdra]; **baking powder** *n* مسحوق خبز [Masḥoo'q khobz]; **soap powder** *n* مسحوق الصابون [Mashoo'q ṣaboon]; **talcum powder** *n* مَسْحوقُ الطَّلْق [Mashoo'q al-ṭal'q]; **washing powder** *n* مسحوق الغسيل [Mashoo'q alghaseel]
power [ˈpaʊə] *n* قوة [quwwa]; **power cut** *n* انقطاع التيار الكهربي [En'qetaa'a al-tayar alkahrabey]; **solar power** *n* طاقة شمسية [Ṭa'qah shamseyah]
powerful [ˈpaʊəfʊl] *adj* قوي [qawij]
practical [ˈpræktɪkᵊl] *adj* عملي [ʕamalij]
practically [ˈpræktɪkəlɪ; -klɪ] *adv* عمليا [ʕamalijan]
practice [ˈpræktɪs] *n* ممارسة [mumaːrasa]
practise [ˈpræktɪs] *v* يُمارس [jumaːrisu]
praise [preɪz] *v* يُثني على [Yothney 'aala]
pram [præm] *n* زورق صغير [Zawra'q ṣagheer]
prank [præŋk] *n* مزحة [mazħa]
prawn [prɔːn] *n* رُوبيَان [ruːbjaːn]
pray [preɪ] *v* يُصَلي [jusˤaliː]
prayer [prɛə] *n* صلاة [sˤalaːt]
precaution [prɪˈkɔːʃən] *n* حيطة [ħiːtˤa]
preceding [prɪˈsiːdɪŋ] *adj* سالِف [saːlif]
precinct [ˈpriːsɪŋkt] *n* دائرة انتخابية [Daaera entekhabeyah]; **pedestrian precinct** *n* منطقة مشاه [Menta'qat moshah]
precious [ˈprɛʃəs] *adj* نفيس [nafiːs]
precise [prɪˈsaɪs] *adj* مُحْكَم [muħkam]
precisely [prɪˈsaɪslɪ] *adv* بالتحديد [bi-at-taħdiːdi]
predecessor [ˈpriːdɪˌsɛsə] *n* سلف [salaf]
predict [prɪˈdɪkt] *v* يتنبأ [jatanabbaʔu]
predictable [prɪˈdɪktəbᵊl] *adj* مُتوَقع [mutawaqqaʕ]
prefect [ˈpriːfɛkt] *n* تلميذ مُفَوّض [telmeedh mofawaḍ]
prefer [prɪˈfɜː] *v* يُفَضِل [jufadˤdˤilu]
preferably [ˈprɛfərəblɪ; ˈprɛfrəblɪ] *adv* من الأفضل [Men al-'afḍal]
preference [ˈprɛfərəns; ˈprɛfrəns] *n* تفضيل [tafdˤiːl]
pregnancy [ˈprɛgnənsɪ] *n* حَمْل [ħaml]
pregnant [ˈprɛgnənt] *adj* حَبلى [ħublaː]
prehistoric [ˌpriːhɪˈstɒrɪk] *adj* متعلق بما قبل التاريخ [Mota'ale'q bema 'qabl al-tareekh]
prejudice [ˈprɛdʒʊdɪs] *n* إجْحَاف [ʔiʒħaːf]
prejudiced [ˈprɛdʒʊdɪst] *adj* متحامل [mutaħaːmil]
premature [ˌprɛməˈtjʊə; ˈprɛməˌtjʊə] *adj* مبتسر [mubatasir]
premiere [ˈprɛmɪˌɛə; ˈprɛmɪə] *n* بارز [baːriz]
premises [ˈprɛmɪsɪz] *npl* المبنى والأراضي التابعه له [Al-mabna wal-aradey al-taabe'ah laho]
premonition [ˌprɛməˈnɪʃən] *n* هاجس داخلي [Hajes dakheley]
preoccupied [priːˈɒkjʊˌpaɪd] *adj* مشغول البال [Mashghool al-bal]
prepaid [priːˈpeɪd] *adj* مدفوع مسبقا [Madfo'a mosba'qan]

preparation [ˌprɛpəˈreɪʃən] *n* إعداد [ʔiʕda:d]
prepare [prɪˈpɛə] *v* يُعِد [juʕidu]
prepared [prɪˈpɛəd] *adj* مُعَد [muʕadd]
Presbyterian [ˌprɛzbɪˈtɪərɪən] *adj* مشيخي [maʃjaxij] ▷ *n* كَنِيسة مَشْيَخِيَّة [Kaneesah mashyakheyah]
prescribe [prɪˈskraɪb] *v* يصف علاجا [Yaṣef ʻaelagan]
prescription [prɪˈskrɪpʃən] *n* وصفة طبية [Waṣfah ṭebeyah]
presence [ˈprɛzəns] *n* حضور [ħudˤu:r]
present *adj* [ˈprɛz] حاضر [ħa:dˤir] ▷ *n* [ˈprɛz] *(gift)* هدية [hadijja], *(time being)* حاضر [ħa:dˤir] ▷ *v* [prɪˈzɛnt] يُبْدي [jubdi:]; **I'm looking for a present for my husband** أنا أبحث عن هدية لزوجي [ana abḥath ʻaan hadiya le-zawjee]
presentation [ˌprɛzənˈteɪʃən] *n* تقديم [taqdi:m]
presenter [prɪˈzɛntə] *n* مقدم [muqaddim]
presently [ˈprɛzəntlɪ] *adv* تواً [tawwan]
preservative [prɪˈzɜːvətɪv] *n* مادة حافظة [Madah ḥafeḍhah]
president [ˈprɛzɪdənt] *n* رئيس [raʔijs]
press [prɛs] *n* نَشْر [naʃr] ▷ *v* يَضغط [jadˤɣatˤu]; **press conference** *n* مؤتمر صحفي [Moatamar ṣaḥafey]
press-up [prɛsʌp] *n* تمرين الضغط [Tamreen al- Ḍaghṭ]
pressure [ˈprɛʃə] *n* ضَغْط [dˤaɣtˤ] ▷ *v* يُلقي بضغط [Yol'qy be-ḍaghṭ]; **blood pressure** *n* ضغط الدم [ḍaghṭ al-dam]
prestige [prɛˈstiːʒ] *n* هيبة [hajba]
prestigious [prɛˈstɪdʒəs] *adj* مَهيب [mahi:b]
presumably [prɪˈzjuːməblɪ] *adv* بصورة محتملة [be ṣorah moḥtamalah]
presume [prɪˈzjuːm] *v* يُسَلِم ب [Yosalem be]
pretend [prɪˈtɛnd] *v* يَتظاهر [jatazˤa:haru]
pretext [ˈpriːtɛkst] *n* حجة [ħuʒʒa]
prettily [ˈprɪtɪlɪ] *adv* على نحو جميل [Ala nahw jameel]
pretty [ˈprɪtɪ] *adj* وَسيم [wasi:m] ▷ *adv* إلى حد معقول [Ela ḥad ma'a'qool]
prevent [prɪˈvɛnt] *v* يمنع [jumnaʕu]
prevention [prɪˈvɛnʃən] *n* وقاية [wiqa:ja]
previous [ˈpriːvɪəs] *adj* مُنصَرِم [munsˤarim]
previously [ˈpriːvɪəslɪ] *adv* من قبل [Men ʻqabl]
prey [preɪ] *n* فريسة [fari:sa]
price [praɪs] *n* سِعر [siʕr]; **price list** *n* قائمة أسعار [ʻqaemat as'aar]; **retail price** *n* سعر التجزئة [Se'ar al-tajzeah]; **selling price** *n* سعر البيع [Se'ar al-bay'a]
prick [prɪk] *v* يَثْقُب [jaθqubu]
pride [praɪd] *n* فخر [faxr]
priest [priːst] *n* قسيس [qasi:s]
primarily [ˈpraɪmərəlɪ] *adv* بصورة أساسية [Beṣorah asasiyah]
primary [ˈpraɪmərɪ] *adj* أولي [ʔawwalij]; **primary school** *n* مدرسة إبتدائية [Madrasah ebtedaeyah]
primitive [ˈprɪmɪtɪv] *adj* بدائي [bida:ʔij]
primrose [ˈprɪmˌrəʊz] *n* زهرة الربيع [Zahrat al-rabee'a]
prince [prɪns] *n* أمير [ʔami:r]
princess [prɪnˈsɛs] *n* أميرة [ʔami:ra]
principal [ˈprɪnsɪpᵊl] *adj* أصلي [ʔasˤlij] ▷ *n* مدير مدرسة [Madeer madrasah]
principle [ˈprɪnsɪpᵊl] *n* مبدأ [mabdau]
print [prɪnt] *n* نشرة مطبوعة [Nashrah maṭbo'aah] ▷ *v* يَطبَع [jatˤbaʕu]
printer [ˈprɪntə] *n (machine)* طابِعة [tˤa:biʕa], *(person)* طابعة [tˤa:biʕa]; **Is there a colour printer?** هل توجد طابعة ملونة؟ [hal tojad ṭabe-'aa mulawa-na?]
printing [ˈprɪntɪŋ] *n*; **How much is printing?** كم تكلفة الطباعة؟ [kam taklafati atˤtˤiba:ʕati]
printout [ˈprɪntaʊt] *n* مطبوعات [matˤbu:ʕa:t]
priority [praɪˈɒrɪtɪ] *n* أولوية [ʔawlawijja]
prison [ˈprɪzᵊn] *n* حَبْس [ħabs]; **prison officer** *n* ضابط سجن [Ḍabeṭ sejn]
prisoner [ˈprɪzənə] *n* سجين [saʒi:n]

privacy ['praɪvəsɪ; 'prɪvəsɪ] *n* سرية [sirrija]
private ['praɪvɪt] *adj* خصوصي [xusˤu:sˤij]; **private property** *n* مِلكِية خاصة [Melkeyah khaṣah]
privatize ['praɪvɪˌtaɪz] *v* يُخصِص [juxasˤsˤisˤu]
privilege ['prɪvɪlɪdʒ] *n* امتياز [imtija:z]
prize [praɪz] *n* جائزة [ʒa:ʔiza]
prize-giving ['praɪzˌɡɪvɪŋ] *n* تقديم الهدايا [Ta'qdeem al-hadayah]
prizewinner ['praɪzˌwɪnə] *n* الفائز بالجائزة [Al-faez bel-jaaezah]
probability [ˌprɒbə'bɪlɪtɪ] *n* احتمالية [iħtima:lijja]
probable ['prɒbəbᵊl] *adj* محتمل [muħtamal]
probably ['prɒbəblɪ] *adv* على الأرجح [Ala al-arjah]
problem ['prɒbləm] *n* مشكلة [muʃkila]; **There's a problem with the room** هناك مشكلة ما في الغرفة [Honak moshkelatan ma fel-ghorfah]
proceedings [prə'si:dɪŋz] *npl* دعوى قضائية [Da'awa 'qaḍaeyah]
proceeds ['prəʊsi:dz] *npl* عائدات [ʕa:ʔida:tun]
process ['prəʊsɛs] *n* عملية [ʕamalijja]
procession [prə'sɛʃən] *n* موكب [mawkib]
produce [prə'dju:s] *v* ينتج [juntiʒu]
producer [prə'dju:sə] *n* مُنتِج [muntiʒ]
product ['prɒdʌkt] *n* منتَج [mantu:ʒ]
production [prə'dʌkʃən] *n* إنتاج [ʔinta:ʒ]
productivity [ˌprɒdʌk'tɪvɪtɪ] *n* إنتاجية [ʔinta:ʒijja]
profession [prə'fɛʃən] *n* وظيفة [wazˤi:fa]
professional [prə'fɛʃənᵊl] *adj* مُحترِف [muħtarif] ▷ *n* محترف [muħtarif]
professionally [prə'fɛʃənəlɪ] *adv* باحتراف [Beḥteraaf]
professor [prə'fɛsə] *n* أستاذ جامعي [Ostaz jame'aey]
profit ['prɒfɪt] *n* رِبْح [ribħ]
profitable ['prɒfɪtəbᵊl] *adj* مربح [murbiħ]
program ['prəʊɡræm] *n* برنامج [barna:maʒ] ▷ *v* يُبَرمج [jubarmiʒu]
programme ['prəʊɡræm] *n* برنامج *(computer)* [barna:maʒ]
programmer ['prəʊɡræmə; 'programmer] *n* مُبَرْمِج [mubarmiʒ]
programming ['prəʊɡræmɪŋ] *n* برمجة [barmaʒa]
progress ['prəʊɡrɛs] *n* تقدُم [taqaddum]
prohibit [prə'hɪbɪt] *v* يَحظُر [jaħzˤuru]
prohibited [prə'hɪbɪtɪd] *adj* محظور [maħzˤu:r]
project ['prɒdʒɛkt] *n* مشروع [maʃru:ʕ]
projector [prə'dʒɛktə] *n* جهاز عرض [Jehaz 'ard]; **overhead projector** *n* جهاز العرض العلوي [Jehaz al-'ard al-'aolwey]
promenade [ˌprɒmə'nɑ:d] *n* نزهة [nuzha]
promise ['prɒmɪs] *n* عهد [ʕahd] ▷ *v* يُواعد [juwa:ʕidu]
promising ['prɒmɪsɪŋ] *adj* واعَد [wa:ʕada]
promote [prə'məʊt] *v* يُروج [jurawwiʒu]
promotion [prə'məʊʃən] *n* ترويج [tarwi:ʒ]
prompt [prɒmpt] *adj* يُحَفِز [juħaffizu]
promptly [prɒmptlɪ] *adv* فورا [fawran]
pronoun ['prəʊˌnaʊn] *n* ضمير [dˤami:r]
pronounce [prə'naʊns] *v* ينطق [jantˤiqu]
pronunciation [prəˌnʌnsɪ'eɪʃən] *n* نُطق [nutˤq]
proof [pru:f] *n (evidence)* دليل [dali:l], *(for checking)* إثبات [ʔiθba:t]
propaganda [ˌprɒpə'ɡændə] *n* دِعَايَة [diʕa:jat]
proper ['prɒpə] *adj* مناسب [muna:sib]
properly ['prɒpəlɪ] *adv* بشكل مناسب [Be-shakl monaseb]
property ['prɒpətɪ] *n* مِلكِية [milkijja]; **private property** *n* مِلكِية خاصة [Melkeyah khaṣah]
proportion [prə'pɔ:ʃən] *n* نسبة [nisba]

proportional [prəˈpɔːʃənᵊl] *adj* نسبي [nisbij]
proposal [prəˈpəʊzᵊl] *n* عرض [ʕardˤ]
propose [prəˈpəʊz] *v* يقترح [jaqtariħu]
prosecute [ˈprɒsɪˌkjuːt] *v* يضطهد [jadˤtˤahidu]
prospect [ˈprɒspɛkt] *n* تَوَقَعَ [tawaqqaʕa]
prospectus [prəˈspɛktəs] *n* نشرة دعائية [Nashrah de'aeyah]
prosperity [prɒˈspɛrɪtɪ] *n* إزدهار [ʔizdihaːr]
prostitute [ˈprɒstɪˌtjuːt] *n* عاهرة [ʕaːhira]
protect [prəˈtɛkt] *v* يَحمي [jaħmiː]
protection [prəˈtɛkʃən] *n* حماية [ħimaːja]
protein [ˈprəʊtiːn] *n* بروتين [bruːtiːn]
protest *n* [ˈprəʊtɛst]احتجاج [iħtiʒaːʒ] ▷ *v* [prəˈtɛst]يَعترض [jaʕtaridˤu]
Protestant [ˈprɒtɪstənt] *adj* بروتستانتي [bruːtistaːntij] ▷ *n* بروتستانتي [bruːtistaːntij]
proud [praʊd] *adj* فخور [faxuːr]
prove [pruːv] *v* يُثبت [juθbitu]
proverb [ˈprɒvɜːb] *n* مَثَل [maθal]
provide [prəˈvaɪd] *v* يزود [juzawwidu]; **provide for** *v* يُعْيل [juʕiːlu]
provided [prəˈvaɪdɪd] *conj* شَريطة أن [Shareeṭat an]
providing [prəˈvaɪdɪŋ] *conj* شَريطة أن [Shareeṭat an]
provisional [prəˈvɪʒənᵊl] *adj* شَرطي [ʃartˤij]
proximity [prɒkˈsɪmɪtɪ] *n* قرابة [quraːba]
prune [pruːn] *n* برقوق [barquːq]
pry [praɪ] *v* يُحَدِق بإمعان [Yoḥade'q be-em'aaan]
pseudonym [ˈsjuːdəˌnɪm] *n* اسم مُستعار [Esm most'aar]
psychiatric [ˌsaɪkɪˈætrɪk; ˌpsychiˈatric] *adj* نفسي [nafsij]
psychiatrist [saɪˈkaɪətrɪst] *n* طبيب نفساني [Ṭabeeb nafsaaney]
psychological [ˌsaɪkəˈlɒdʒɪkᵊl] *adj* سيكولوجي [sajkuːluːʒij]
psychologist [saɪˈkɒlədʒɪst] *n* عالم نفسي ['aalem nafsey]
psychology [saɪˈkɒlədʒɪ] *n* علم النفس ['aelm al-nafs]
psychotherapy [ˌsaɪkəʊˈθɛrəpɪ] *n* علاج نفسي ['aelaj nafsey]
PTO [piː tiː əʊ] *abbr* اقلب الصفحة من فضلك [E'qleb alṣafḥah men faḍlek]
pub [pʌb] *n* حانة [ħaːna]
public [ˈpʌblɪk] *adj* شعبي [ʃaʕbij] ▷ *n* شعب [ʃaʕb]; **public holiday** *n* أجازة عامة [ajaaza a'mah]; **public opinion** *n* الرأي العام [Al-raaey al-'aam]; **public relations** *npl* علاقات عامة ['ala'qat 'aamah]; **public school** *n* مدرسة عامة [Madrasah 'aamah]; **public transport** *n* نقل عام [Na'ql 'aam]
publican [ˈpʌblɪkən] *n* صاحب حانة [Ṣaheb hanah]
publication [ˌpʌblɪˈkeɪʃən] *n* منشور [manʃuːr]
publish [ˈpʌblɪʃ] *v* ينشر [janʃuru]
publisher [ˈpʌblɪʃə] *n* ناشر [naːʃir]
pudding [ˈpʊdɪŋ] *n* حلوى البودينج [Ḥalwa al-boodenj]
puddle [ˈpʌdᵊl] *n* بِرْكَة [birka]
Puerto Rico [ˈpwɜːtəʊ ˈriːkəʊ; ˈpwɛə-] *n* برتو ريكو [burtuː riːkuː]
pull [pʊl] *v* يَجذِب [jaʒðibu]
pull down [pʊl daʊn] *v* يَهْدِم [jahdimu]
pull out [pʊl aʊt] *vi* يَتَحرك بالسيارة ▷ *vt* يَقْتَلِع [jaqtaliʕu]
pullover [ˈpʊlˌəʊvə] *n* يُوْقِف السيارة [Yo'qef sayarah]
pull up [pʊl ʌp] *v* يَسْحَب [jasħabu]
pulse [pʌls] *n* نبضة [nabdˤa]
pulses [pʌlsɪz] *npl* نبضات [nabadˤaːtun]
pump [pʌmp] *n* مضخة [midˤaxxa] ▷ *v* يَضُخ [jadˤuxxu]; **bicycle pump** *n* منفاخ دراجة [Monfakh draajah]; **Pump number three, please** المضخة رقم ثلاثة من فضلك [al-maḍakha ra'qum thalath min faḍlak]
pumpkin [ˈpʌmpkɪn] *n* قَرْع [qarʕ]
pump up [pʌmp ʌp] *v* ينفخ [junfaxu]
punch [pʌntʃ] *n* *(blow)* مثقب [miθqab],

(hot drink) شراب البَنْش المُسكِر [Sharaab al-bensh al-mosker] ▷ *v* يخرّم [juxarrimu]
punctual [ˈpʌŋktjʊəl] *adj* مُنْضَبِط [mundˤabitˤ]
punctuation [ˌpʌŋktjʊˈeɪʃən] *n* وضع علامات الترقيم [Wad'a 'alamaat al-tar'qeem]
puncture [ˈpʌŋktʃə] *n* ثقب [θuqb]
punish [ˈpʌnɪʃ] *v* يُعَاقِب [juʕa:qibu]
punishment [ˈpʌnɪʃmənt] *n* عقاب [ʕiqa:b]; **capital punishment** *n* أقصى عقوبة [A'qsa 'aoqobah]; **corporal punishment** *n* عقوبة بدنية ['ao'qoba badaneyah]
punk [pʌŋk] *n* غلام الصوفان [ɣula:mu asˤsˤu:fa:ni]
pupil [ˈpjuːpᵊl] *n (eye)* بُؤبُؤ العَيْن [Boaboa al-'ayn], *(learner)* تلميذ [tllml:ð]
puppet [ˈpʌpɪt] *n* دمية متحركة [Domeyah motaḥarekah]
puppy [ˈpʌpɪ] *n* جرو [ʒarw]
purchase [ˈpɜːtʃɪs] *v* يَبتاَع [jabta:ʕu]
pure [pjʊə] *adj* نقي [naqij]
purple [ˈpɜːpᵊl] *adj* أرجواني [urʒuwa:nij]
purpose [ˈpɜːpəs] *n* غرض [ɣaradˤ]
purr [pɜː] *v* يخرخر [juxarxiru]
purse [pɜːs] *n* حافظة نقود [ḥafedhat ne'qood]
pursue [pəˈsjuː] *v* يُلاحِق [jula:ħiqu]
pursuit [pəˈsjuːt] *n* ملاحقة [mula:ħaqa]
pus [pʌs] *n* قيح [qajħ]
push [pʊʃ] *v* يَدفَع [jadfaʕu]
pushchair [ˈpʊʃˌtʃɛə] *n* عربة طفل ['arabat ṭefl]
push-up [pʊʃʌp] *n* تمرين الضغط [Tamreen al- Daghṭ]
put [pʊt] *v* يَضع [jadˤaʕu]
put aside [pʊt əˈsaɪd] *v* يَدخِر [jaddaxiru]
put away [pʊt əˈweɪ] *v* يَدخِر مالا [juddaxiru ma:la:]
put back [pʊt bæk] *v* يُرْجِع [jurʒiʕu]
put forward [pʊt fɔːwəd] *v* يُقَدِم [juqaddimu]
put in [pʊt ɪn] *v* يركب [jarrkabu]
put off [pʊt ɒf] *v* يؤخر [juʔaxiru]
put up [pʊt ʌp] *v* يَنْزِل في مكان [Yanzel fee makaan]
puzzle [ˈpʌzᵊl] *n* لغز [luɣz]
puzzled [ˈpʌzᵊld] *adj* مرتبك [murtabik]
puzzling [ˈpʌzlɪŋ] *adj* مُحير [muħajjir]
pyjamas [pəˈdʒɑːməz] *npl* بيجامة [bi:ʒa:matun]
pylon [ˈpaɪlən] *n* بُرج كهرباء [Borj kahrbaa]
pyramid [ˈpɪrəmɪd] *n* هرم [haram]

q

Qatar [kæ'tɑː] *n* قطر [qatˤar]
quail [kweɪl] *n* طائر السِمَّان [Ṭaaer al-saman]
quaint [kweɪnt] *adj* طريف [tˤari:f]
Quaker ['kweɪkə] *n* منتسب لجماعة الأصحاب [Montaseb le-jama'at al-aṣḥaab]
qualification [ˌkwɒlɪfɪ'keɪʃən] *n* مُؤهِل [muahhil]
qualified ['kwɒlɪˌfaɪd] *adj* مُؤهَل [muahhal]
qualify ['kwɒlɪˌfaɪ] *v* يؤهل [juʔahilu]
quality ['kwɒlɪtɪ] *n* جودة [ʒawda]
quantify ['kwɒntɪˌfaɪ] *v* يَقْيس مقدار [Ya'qees me'qdaar]
quantity ['kwɒntɪtɪ] *n* كمية [kammija]
quarantine ['kwɒrənˌtiːn] *n* حَجْر صحي [Ḥajar ṣeḥey]
quarrel ['kwɒrəl] *n* شجار [ʃiʒa:r] ▷ *v* يتشاجر مع [Yatashajar ma'a]
quarry ['kwɒrɪ] *n* طريدة [tˤari:da]
quarter ['kwɔːtə] *n* رُبْع [rubʕ]; **quarter final** *n* سباق الدور رُبع النهائي [Seba'q al-door roba'a al-nehaaey]
quartet [kwɔː'tɛt] *n* رباعية [ruba:ʕijjatu]
quay [kiː] *n* رصيف الميناء [Raṣeef al-meenaa]
queen [kwiːn] *n* ملكة [malika]
query ['kwɪərɪ] *n* تساؤل [tasa:ʔul] ▷ *v* يَسْتفهم [jastafhimu]
question ['kwɛstʃən] *n* سُؤال [sua:l] ▷ *v* يَستَجوب [jastaʒwibu]; **question mark** *n* علامة استفهام ['alamat estefham]
questionnaire [ˌkwɛstʃə'nɛə; ˌkɛs-] *n* استبيان [istibja:n]
queue [kjuː] *n* صَفْ [sˤaf] ▷ *v* يَصْطَف [jasˤtˤaffu]
quick [kwɪk] *adj* سريع [sari:ʕ]
quickly [kwɪklɪ] *adv* سريعاً [sari:ʕan]
quiet ['kwaɪət] *adj* هادئ [ha:diʔ]; **I'd like a quiet room** أفضل أن تكون الغرفة هادئة [ofaḍel an takoon al-ghurfa hade-a]; **Is there a quiet beach near here?** هل يوجد شواطئ هادئ قريب من هنا؟ [hal ju:ʒadu ʃawa:tˤiʔa ha:diʔi qari:bun min huna:]
quietly ['kwaɪətlɪ] *adv* بهدوء [bihudu:ʔin]
quilt [kwɪlt] *n* لحاف [liħa:f]
quit [kwɪt] *v* يُقَلِع عن [Yo'qle'a 'aan]
quite [kwaɪt] *adv* فعلا [fiʕlan]
quiz, quizzes [kwɪz, 'kwɪzɪz] *n* اختبار موجز [ekhtebar mojaz]
quota ['kwəʊtə] *n* نصيب [nasˤi:b]
quotation [kwəʊ'teɪʃən] *n* عرض أسعار ['aarḍ as'aar]; **quotation marks** *npl* علامات الاقتباس ['aalamat al-e'qtebas]
quote [kwəʊt] *n* اقتباس [iqtiba:s] ▷ *v* يَقْتِبس [jaqtabisu]

r

rabbi ['ræbaɪ] *n* حاخام [ħa:xa:m]
rabbit ['ræbɪt] *n* أرنب [ʔarnab]
rabies ['reɪbi:z] *n* داء الكلب [Daa al-kalb]
race [reɪs] *n (contest)* سباق [siba:q], *(origin)* سلالة [sula:la] ▷ *v* يَتَسابق [jatasa:baqu]; **I'd like to see a horse race** أود أن أشاهد سباقًا للخيول؟ [awid an oshahed seba'qan lil-khiyool]
racecourse ['reɪsˌkɔ:s] *n* حلبة السباق [ḥalabat seba'q]
racehorse ['reɪsˌhɔ:s] *n* جواد السباق [Jawad al-seba'q]
racer ['reɪsə] *n* مُسَابِق [musa:biq]
racetrack ['reɪsˌtræk] *n* حلبة السباق [ḥalabat seba'q]
racial ['reɪʃəl] *adj* عنصري [ʕunsʕurij]
racing ['reɪsɪŋ] *n*; **horse racing** *n* سباق الخيول [Seba'q al-kheyol]; **motor racing** *n* سباق سيارات [Seba'q sayarat]; **racing car** *n* سيارة السباق [Sayarah al-seba'q]; **racing driver** *n* سائق سيارة سباق [Sae'q sayarah seba'q]
racism ['reɪsɪzəm] *n* تمييز عنصري [Tamyeez 'aonory]
racist ['reɪsɪst] *adj* متحيز عنصريا [Motaḥeyz 'aonṣoreyan] ▷ *n* عنصري [ʕunsʕurij]
rack [ræk] *n* حامل [ħa:mil]; **luggage rack** *n* حامل حقائب السفر [Hamel ha'qaeb al-safar]
racket ['rækɪt] *n (racquet)* مضرب الراكيت [Maḍrab alrakeet]; **tennis racket** *n* مضرب تنس [Maḍrab tenes]
racoon [rə'ku:n] *n* حيوان الراكون [Ḥayawaan al-rakoon]
racquet ['rækɪt] *n* مضرب كرة الطاولة [Maḍrab korat al-ṭawlah]
radar ['reɪdɑ:] *n* رادار [ra:da:r]
radiation [ˌreɪdɪ'eɪʃən] *n* إشعاع [ʔiʃʕa:ʕ]
radiator ['reɪdɪˌeɪtə] *n* جهاز إرسال الإشعاع [Jehaz esrsaal al-esh'aaa'a]
radio ['reɪdɪəʊ] *n* راديو [ra:dju:]; **digital radio** *n* راديو رقمي [Radyo ra'qamey]; **radio station** *n* محطة راديو [Mahaṭat radyo]; **Can I switch the radio off?** هل يمكن أن أطفئ الراديو؟ [hal yamken an aṭfee al-radio?]; **Can I switch the radio on?** هل يمكن أن أشغل الراديو؟ [hal yamken an osha-ghel al-radio?]
radioactive [ˌreɪdɪəʊ'æktɪv] *adj* مشع [muʃiʕʕ]
radio-controlled ['reɪdɪəʊ'kən'trəʊld] *adj* متحكم به عن بعد [Motaḥkam beh an bo'ad]
radish ['rædɪʃ] *n* فجل [fiʒl]
raffle ['ræfᵊl] *n* بيع باليانصيب [Bay'a bel-yanaṣeeb]
raft [rɑ:ft] *n* طَوْف [tʕawf]
rag [ræg] *n* خرقة [xirqa]
rage [reɪdʒ] *n* غضب شديد [ghaḍab shaded]; **road rage** *n* مشاحنات على الطريق [Moshahanaat ala al-ṭaree'q]
raid [reɪd] *n* غارة [ɣa:ra] ▷ *v* يَشُن غارة [Yashen gharah]
rail [reɪl] *n* قضبان السكة الحديدية ['qoḍban al-sekah al-ḥadeedeyah]
railcard ['reɪlˌkɑ:d] *n* بطاقة للسفر بالقطار [Beṭa'qah lel-safar bel-kharej]
railings ['reɪlɪŋz] *npl* درابزينات [dara:bzi:na:tun]
railway ['reɪlˌweɪ] *n* سكة حديدية [Sekah haedeedyah]; **railway station** *n* محطة سكك حديدية [Mahaṭat sekak

ḥadeedeyah]
rain [reɪn] *n* مطر [matˤar] ▷ *v* يُمْطِر [jumtˤiru]; **acid rain** *n* أمطار حمضية [Amṭar ḥemdeyah]; **Do you think it's going to rain?** هل تظن أن المطر سوف يسقط؟ [hal taḍhun ana al-maṭar sawfa yas'qiṭ?]; **It's raining** إنها تمطر [Enha tomṭer]
rainbow ['reɪnˌbəʊ] *n* قوس قزح ['qaws 'qazh]
raincoat ['reɪnˌkəʊt] *n* معطف واق من المطر [Me'ataf wa'qen men al-maarṭar]
rainforest ['reɪnˌfɒrɪst] *n* غابات المطر بخط الاستواء [Ghabat al-maṭar be-khaṭ al-estwaa]
rainy ['reɪnɪ] *adj* مُمطر [mumtˤir]
raise [reɪz] *v* يُعْلي [juʕli:]
raisin ['reɪzᵊn] *n* زَبيب [zabi:b]
rake [reɪk] *n* آلة جمع الأعشاب [a:latun ʒamʕu alʔaʕʃa:bi]
rally ['rælɪ] *n* سباق الراليات [Seba'q al-raleyat]
ram [ræm] *n* كبش [kabʃ] ▷ *v* يَصْدِم بقوة [Yaṣdem be'qowah]
Ramadan [ˌræmə'dɑːn] *n* رَمَضان [ramadˤa:n]
rambler ['ræmblə] *n* مُتَجوِّل [mutaʒawwil]
ramp [ræmp] *n* طريق منحدر [Ṭaree'q monḥadar]
random ['rændəm] *adj* عشوائي [ʕaʃwa:ʔij]
range [reɪndʒ] *n (limits)* مَدَى [mada:], *(mountains)* سلسلة جبال [Selselat jebal] ▷ *v* يَتَراوح [jatara:waħu]
rank [ræŋk] *n (line)* صف [sˤaff], *(status)* مكانة [maka:na] ▷ *v* يُرَتب [jurattibu]
ransom ['rænsəm] *n* فدية [fidja]
rape [reɪp] *n (plant)* نبات اللفت [Nabat al-left], *(sexual attack)* اغتصاب [iɣtisˤa:b] ▷ *v* (يسلب) يغتصب [jaɣtasˤibu]; **I've been raped** لقد تعرضت للاغتصاب [la'qad ta-'aaraḍto lel-ighti-ṣaab]
rapids ['ræpɪdz] *npl* منحدر النهر [Monḥadar al-nahr]
rapist ['reɪpɪst; 'rapist] *n* مُغتَصِب [muɣtasˤib]
rare [rɛə] *adj (uncommon)* نادر [na:dir], *(undercooked)* نادر [na:dir]
rarely ['rɛəlɪ] *adv* نادرا [na:diran]
rash [ræʃ] *n* طفح جلدي [Ṭafh jeldey]; **I have a rash** أعاني من طفح جلدي [O'aaney men ṭafḥ jeldey]
raspberry ['rɑːzbərɪ; -brɪ] *n* توت [tu:tt]
rat [ræt] *n* جرذ [ʒurð]
rate [reɪt] *n* معدل [muʕaddal] ▷ *v* يُثَمِن [juθamminu]; **interest rate** *n* معدل الفائدة [Moaadal al-faaedah]; **rate of exchange** *n* سِعر الصرف [Se'ar al-ṣ arf]
rather ['rɑːðə] *adv* إلى حد ما [ʔila ħaddin ma:]
ratio ['reɪʃɪˌəʊ] *n* نسبة [nisba]
rational ['ræʃənᵊl] *adj* عقلاني [ʕaqla:nij]
rattle ['rætᵊl] *n* خشخيشة الأطفال [Khashkheeshat al-aṭfaal]
rattlesnake ['rætᵊlˌsneɪk] *n* الأفعى ذات الأجراس [Al-af'aa dhat al-ajraas]
rave [reɪv] *n* هذيان [haðaja:n] ▷ *v* يُربِك [jurbiku]
raven ['reɪvᵊn] *n* غراب أسود [Ghorab aswad]
ravenous ['rævənəs] *adj* مفترس [muftaris]
ravine [rə'viːn] *n* واد عميق وضيق [Wad 'amee'q wa-ḍaye'q]
raw [rɔː] *adj* خام [xa:m]
razor ['reɪzə] *n* موسى الحلاقة [Mosa alḥela'qah]; **razor blade** *n* شفرة حلاقة [Shafrat hela'qah]
reach [riːtʃ] *v* يَبْلُغ [jabluɣu]
react [rɪ'ækt] *v* يَتفاعل [jatafaaʕalu]
reaction [rɪ'ækʃən] *n* تَفَاعٌل [tafa:ʕul]
reactor [rɪ'æktə] *n* مُفَاعِل [mufa:ʕil]
read [riːd] *v* يَقْرَأ [jaqraʔu]
reader ['riːdə] *n* قارئ [qa:riʔ]
readily ['rɛdɪlɪ; 'readily] *adv* حالًا [ħa:la:]
reading ['riːdɪŋ] *n* قراءة [qira:ʔa]
read out [riːd] *v* يَقْرَأ بصوت مرتفع [Ya'qraa beṣawt mortafe'a]
ready ['rɛdɪ] *adj* متأهب [mutaʔahib]
ready-cooked ['rɛdɪ'kʊkt] *adj* مطهو

[matˁhuww]
real ['rɪəl] *adj* واقعي [wa:qiˁij]
realistic [ˌrɪə'lɪstɪk] *adj* واقعي [wa:qiˁij]
reality [rɪ'ælɪtɪ] *n* واقع [wa:qiˁ]; **reality TV** *n* تلفزيون الواقع [Telefezyon al-wa'qe'a]; **virtual reality** *n* واقع افتراضي [Wa'qe'a eftradey]
realize ['rɪəˌlaɪz] *v* يُدْرِك [judriku]
really ['rɪəlɪ] *adv* أحقاً [ħaqqan]
rear [rɪə] *adj* خلفي [xalfij] ▷ *n* مؤخرة الجيش [Mowakherat al-jaysh]; **rear-view mirror** *n* مرآة الرؤية الخلفية [Meraah al-roayah al-khalfeyah]
reason ['riːzᵊn] *n* مُبّرر [mubbarir]
reasonable ['riːzənəbᵊl] *adj* معقول [maʕquːlin]
reasonably ['riːzənəblɪ] *adv* على نحو معقول [Ala naḥw ma'a'qool]
reassure [ˌriːə'ʃʊə] *v* يُعْيد طَمْأنَتُه [Yo'aeed ṭomaanath]
reassuring [ˌriːə'ʃʊəɪŋ] *adj* مُطمئِن [mutˁmaʔin]
rebate ['riːbeɪt] *n* خَسْم [ħasm]
rebellious [rɪ'bɛljəs] *adj* متمرد [mutamarrid]
rebuild [riː'bɪld] *v* يُعْيد بناء [Yo'aeed benaa]
receipt [rɪ'siːt] *n* وَصْل [wasˁl]
receive [rɪ'siːv] *v* يَستلِم [jastalimu]
receiver [rɪ'siːvə] *n (electronic)* جهاز الاستقبال [Jehaz alest'qbal], *(person)* مُستَلِم [mustalim]
recent ['riːsᵊnt] *adj* حديث [ħadiːθ]
recently ['riːsəntlɪ] *adv* حديثاً [ħadiːθan]
reception [rɪ'sɛpʃən] *n* استقبال [istiqbaːl]
receptionist [rɪ'sɛpʃənɪst] *n* موظف الاستقبال [mowadhaf al-este'qbal]
recession [rɪ'sɛʃən] *n* انسحاب [insiħaːb]
recharge [riː'tʃɑːdʒ] *v* يُعْيد شحن بطارية [Yo'aeed shaḥn baṭareyah]
recipe ['rɛsɪpɪ] *n* وصفة طهي [Waṣfat ṭahey]
recipient [rɪ'sɪpɪənt] *n* مُتَلق [mutalaqi]
reckon ['rɛkən] *v* يحسب [jaħsubu]
reclining [rɪ'klaɪnɪŋ] *adj* منحني [munħanij]
recognizable ['rɛkəgˌnaɪzəbᵊl] *adj* ممكن تمييزه [Momken tamyezoh]
recognize ['rɛkəgˌnaɪz] *v* يَتْعَرف على [Yata'araf 'ala]
recommend [ˌrɛkə'mɛnd] *v* يُوصي [juːsˁiː]
recommendation [ˌrɛkəmɛn'deɪʃən] *n* توصية [tawsˁijja]
reconsider [ˌriːkən'sɪdə] *v* يُعْيد النظر في [Yo'aeed al-naḍhar fee]
record *n* ['rɛkɔːd] مَحضَر [maħdˁar] ▷ *v* [rɪ'kɔːd] يُسجِل [jusaʒʒilu]
recorded delivery [rɪ'kɔːdɪd dɪ'lɪvərɪ] *n* بعلم الوصول [Be-'aelm al-woṣool]
recorder [rɪ'kɔːdə] *n (music)* جهاز التسجيل [Jehaz al-tasjeel], *(scribe)* مُسَجِّل [musaʒʒal]
recording [rɪ'kɔːdɪŋ] *n* عملية التسجيل ['amalyat al-tasjeel]
recover [rɪ'kʌvə] *v* يَشفى [juʃfaː]
recovery [rɪ'kʌvərɪ] *n* شِفَاء [ʃifaːʔ]
recruitment [rɪ'kruːtmənt] *n* توظيف [tawzˁiːf]
rectangle ['rɛkˌtæŋgᵊl] *n* مستطيل [mustatˁiːl]
rectangular [rɛk'tæŋgjʊlə] *adj* مستطيل الشكل [Mostaṭeel al-shakl]
rectify ['rɛktɪˌfaɪ] *v* يُعدل [juʕaddilu]
recurring [rɪ'kʌrɪŋ] *adj* متكرر [mutakarrir]
recycle [riː'saɪkᵊl] *v* يُعْيد استخدام [Yo'aeed estekhdam]
recycling [riː'saɪklɪŋ] *n* إعادة تصنيع [E'aadat taṣnee'a]
red [rɛd] *adj* أحمر [ʔaħmar]; **red meat** *n* لحم أحمر [Laḥm aḥmar]; **red wine** *n* نبيذ أحمر [nabeedh aḥmar]; **Red Cross** *n* الصليب الأحمر [Al-Ṣaleeb al-aḥmar]; **Red Sea** *n* البحر الأحمر [Al-bahr al-ahmar]; **a bottle of red wine** زجاجة من النبيذ الأحمر [zujaja min al-nabeedh al-aḥmar]
redcurrant ['rɛd'kʌrənt] *n* عنب أحمر ['aenab aḥmar]

redecorate [riːˈdɛkəˌreɪt] *v* يُعْيد تزيين [Yo'aeed tazyeen]
red-haired [ˈrɛdˌhɛəd] *adj* أحمر الشعر [Aḥmar al-sha'ar]
redhead [ˈrɛdˌhɛd] *n* شَعْر أحمر [Sha'ar ahmar]
redo [riːˈduː] *v* يُعْيد عمل الشيء [Yo'aeed 'aamal al-shaya]
reduce [rɪˈdjuːs] *v* يُخَفِض [juxaffidˤu]
reduction [rɪˈdʌkʃən] *n* تقليل [taqliːl]
redundancy [rɪˈdʌndənsɪ] *n* إسهاب (حشو) [ʔishaːb]
redundant [rɪˈdʌndənt] *adj* مطنب [mutˤanabb]
reed [riːd] *n* قصبة [qasˤaba]
reel [riːl; rɪəl] *n* بَكَرَة [bakara]
refer [rɪˈfɜː] *v* يُشير إلى [Yosheer ela]
referee [ˌrɛfəˈriː] *n* حَكَم مباريات رياضية [Hosn almaḍhar]
reference [ˈrɛfərəns; ˈrɛfrəns] *n* مرجع [marʒaʕin]; **reference number** *n* رقم مرجعي [Ra'qm marje'ay]
refill [riːˈfɪl] *v* يُعْيد ملء [Yo'aeed mela]
refinery [rɪˈfaɪnərɪ] *n* مصفاة معمل التكرير [Meṣfaah ma'amal al-takreer]; **oil refinery** *n* معمل تكرير الزيت [Ma'amal takreer al-zayt]
reflect [rɪˈflɛkt] *v* يَعْكِس [jaʕkisu]
reflection [rɪˈflɛkʃən] *n* انعكاس [inʕikaːs]
reflex [ˈriːflɛks] *n* رد انعكاسي [Rad en'aekasey]
refreshing [rɪˈfrɛʃɪŋ; reˈfreshing] *adj* مُجدد للنشاط [Mojaded lel-nashaṭ]
refreshments [rɪˈfrɛʃmənts] *npl* وجبة طعام خفيفة [Wajbat ṭ a'aam khafeefah]
refrigerator [rɪˈfrɪdʒəˌreɪtə] *n* ثلاجة [θallaːʒa]
refuel [riːˈfjuːəl] *v* يُزود بوقود إضافي [juzawwadu biwuquːdin ʔidˤaːfijjin]
refuge [ˈrɛfjuːdʒ] *n* ملجأ [malʒa]
refugee [ˌrɛfjʊˈdʒiː] *n* لاجئ [laːʒiʔ]
refund *n* [ˈriːˌfʌnd] إعادة دفع [E'aadat daf'a] ▷ *v* [rɪˈfʌnd] يُعْيد مبلغ [juʕjidu mablaɣan]
refusal [rɪˈfjuːzəl] *n* رَفْض [rafdˤ]
refuse[1] [rɪˈfjuːz] *v* يَرفُض [jarfudˤu]
refuse[2] [ˈrɛfjuːs] *n* حثالة [ħuθaːla]
regain [rɪˈgeɪn] *v* يَستعيد [jastaʕiːdu]
regard [rɪˈgɑːd] *n* اهتمام [ihtimaːm] ▷ *v* يَعتبر [jaʕtabiru]
regarding [rɪˈgɑːdɪŋ] *prep* فيما يتعلق بـ (بشأن) [Feema yat'ala'q be]
regiment [ˈrɛdʒɪmənt] *n* فوج [fawʒu]
region [ˈriːdʒən] *n* إقليم [iqliːm]
regional [ˈriːdʒənəl] *adj* إقليمي [iqliːmij]
register [ˈrɛdʒɪstə] *n* سِجل [siʒʒil] ▷ *v* يُسجِل [jusaʒʒilu]; **cash register** *n* ماكينة تسجيل الكاش [Makenat tasjeel al-kaash]
registered [ˈrɛdʒɪstəd] *adj* مُسَجَل [mussaʒal]
registration [ˌrɛdʒɪˈstreɪʃən] *n* تسجيل [tasʒiːlu]; **Registration number...** رقم التسجيل هو... [ra'qim al-tasjeel howa...]
regret [rɪˈgrɛt] *n* نَدَم [nadima] ▷ *v* يأسف [jaʔsafu]
regular [ˈrɛgjʊlə] *adj* مُعتاد [muʕtaːd]
regularly [ˈrɛgjʊləlɪ] *adv* بانتظام [bentedham]
regulation [ˌrɛgjʊˈleɪʃən] *n* تنظيم [tanzˤiːm]لائِحَة ,
rehearsal [rɪˈhɜːsəl] *n* بروفة [bruːfa]
rehearse [rɪˈhɜːs] *v* يُكَرر [jukariru]
reimburse [ˌriːɪmˈbɜːs] *v* يُعوِّض عن [Yo'aweḍ 'an]
reindeer [ˈreɪnˌdɪə] *n* حيوان الرنة [ħajawaːnu arrannati]
reins [reɪnz] *npl* لِجَام [liʒaːmun]
reject [rɪˈdʒɛkt] *v* يَأبَى [jaʔbaː]
relapse [ˈriːˌlæps] *n* انتكاسة [intikaːsa]
related [rɪˈleɪtɪd] *adj* مرتبط [murtabitˤ]
relation [rɪˈleɪʃən] *n* علاقة [ʕalaːqa]; **public relations** *npl* علاقات عامة ['ala'qat 'aamah]
relationship [rɪˈleɪʃənʃɪp] *n* علاقة [ʕalaːqa]; **Sorry, I'm in a relationship** آسف، أنا على علاقة بأحد الأشخاص [ʔaːsifun ʔanaː ʕalaː ʕilaːqatin biʔaħadin alʔaʃxaːsˤi]
relative [ˈrɛlətɪv] *n* قريب [qariːb]
relatively [ˈrɛlətɪvlɪ] *adv* نسبيًا [nisbijan]

relax [rɪ'læks] *v* يَسترخِي [jastarxi:]
relaxation [ˌriːlæk'seɪʃən] *n* استرخاء [istirxa:ʔ]
relaxed [rɪ'lækst] *adj* مستريح [mustri:ħ]
relaxing [rɪ'læksɪŋ] *adj* يساعد على الراحة [Yosaed ala al-rahah]
relay ['riːleɪ] *n* تناوب [tana:wub]
release [rɪ'liːs] *n* إطلاق [ʔitˤla:q] ▷ *v* يُطلق سراح [Yoṭle'q sarah]
relegate ['rɛlɪˌgeɪt] *v* يُبْعِد [jubʕidu]
relevant ['rɛlɪvənt] *adj* وثيق الصلة [Wathee'q al-ṣelah]
reliable [rɪ'laɪəbᵊl] *adj* موثوق به [Mawthoo'q beh]
relief [rɪ'liːf] *n* راحة [ra:ħa]
relieve [rɪ'liːv] *v* يُخفِف [juxafiffu]
relieved [rɪ'liːvd] *adj* مرتاح [murta:ħ]
religion [rɪ'lɪdʒən] *n* دِينْ [dajn]
religious [rɪ'lɪdʒəs] *adj* ديني [di:nij]
reluctant [rɪ'lʌktənt] *adj* ممانع [muma:niʕ]
reluctantly [rɪ'lʌktəntlɪ] *adv* على مضض ['Ala maḍaḍ]
rely [rɪ'laɪ] *v*; **rely on** *v* يُعَوِل على [yo'awel 'ala]
remain [rɪ'meɪn] *v* يَبقى [jabqa:]
remaining [rɪ'meɪnɪŋ] *adj* متبقي [muta-baqij]
remains [rɪ'meɪnz] *npl* بقايا [baqa:ja:]
remake ['riːˌmeɪk] *n* إعادة صُنْع [E'aadat taṣnea'a]
remark [rɪ'mɑːk] *n* ملاحظة [mula:ħazˤa]
remarkable [rɪ'mɑːkəbᵊl] *adj* جدير بالملاحظة [Jadeer bel-molahaḍhah]
remarkably [rɪ'mɑːkəblɪ] *adv* رائعاً [ra:ʔiʕan]
remarry [riː'mærɪ] *v* يَتَزوج ثانية [Yatazawaj thaneyah]
remedy ['rɛmɪdɪ] *n* دواء [dawa:ʔ]
remember [rɪ'mɛmbə] *v* يَتَذكر [jataðakkaru]
remind [rɪ'maɪnd] *v* يُذكّر [juðakkiru]
reminder [rɪ'maɪndə; re'minder] *n* رسالة تذكير [Resalat tadhkeer]
remorse [rɪ'mɔːs] *n* ندم [nadam]
remote [rɪ'məʊt] *adj* ضئيل [dˤaʔijl]; **remote control** *n* التحكم عن بعد [Al-taḥakom an bo'ad]
remotely [rɪ'məʊtlɪ] *adv* عن بُعْد ['an bo'ad]
removable [rɪ'muːvəbᵊl] *adj* قابل للنقل ['qabel lel-na'ql]
removal [rɪ'muːvᵊl] *n* إزالة [ʔiza:la]; **removal van** *n* شاحِنة نقل [Shahenat na'ql]
remove [rɪ'muːv] *v* يُزيل [juzi:lu]
remover [rɪ'muːvə] *n*; **nail-polish remover** *n* مزيل طلاء الأظافر [Mozeel ṭalaa al-aḍhafer]
rendezvous ['rɒndɪˌvuː] *n* مَوْعِد [mawʕid]
renew [rɪ'njuː] *v* يُجَدِد [juʒaddidu]
renewable [rɪ'njuːəbᵊl] *adj* ممكن تجديده [Momken tajdedoh]
renovate ['rɛnəˌveɪt] *v* يُرمِم [jurammimu]
renowned [rɪ'naʊnd] *adj* شهير [ʃahi:r]
rent [rɛnt] *n* إيجار [ʔiʒa:r] ▷ *v* يُؤَجِر [juʔaʒʒiru]; **I'd like to rent a room** أريد غرفة للإيجار [areed ghurfa lil-eejar]
rental ['rɛntᵊl] *n* الأجرة [alʔuʒrati]; **car rental** *n* تأجير سيارة [Taajeer sayarah]; **rental car** *n* سيارة إيجار [Sayarah eejar]
reorganize [riː'ɔːgəˌnaɪz] *v* يُعْيد تنظيم [Yo'aeed tanḍheem]
rep [rɛp] *n* نسيج مضلع [Naseej moḍala'a]
repair [rɪ'pɛə] *n* تصليح [tasˤli:ħ] ▷ *v* يُصلح [jusˤliħu]; **repair kit** *n* عدة التصليح ['aodat altaṣleeh]; **Can you repair it?** هل يمكن تصليحها؟ [hal yamken taṣleeḥ-aha?]; **Can you repair my watch?** هل يمكن تصليح ساعتي؟ [hal yamken taṣleeḥ sa'aaty?]; **Can you repair this?** هل يمكن تصليح هذه؟ [hal yamken taṣleeḥ hadhy?]; **How long will it take to repair?** كم من الوقت يستغرق تصليحها؟ [kam min al-wa'qt yast-aghri'q taṣle-ḥaha?]; **How much will the repairs cost?** كم تكلفة التصليح؟ [kam taklifat al-taṣleeḥ?]; **Where can I get this repaired?** أين يمكنني تصليح هذه الحقيبة؟ [ayna yamken-any taṣleeḥ

hadhe al-ḥa'qeba?]
repay [rɪ'peɪ] *v* يَفي [jafi:]
repayment [rɪ'peɪmənt] *n* سَداد [sadda:d]
repeat [rɪ'pi:t] *n* تكرار [tikra:r] ▷ *v* يُعيد [juʕi:du]
repeatedly [rɪ'pi:tɪdlɪ] *adv* على نحو متكرر ['aala nahw motakarer]
repellent [rɪ'pɛlənt] *adj* طَارِد [tˤa:rid]; **insect repellent** *n* طارد للحَشرات [Ṭared lel-ḥasharat]
repercussions [ˌri:pə'kʌʃənz] *npl* تبعِيَّات [tabaʕijja:tun]
repetitive [rɪ'pɛtɪtɪv] *adj* تكراري [tikra:rij]
replace [rɪ'pleɪs] *v* يَستبدل [jastabdilu]
replacement [rɪ'pleɪsmənt] *n* استبدال [istibda:l]
replay *n* ['ri:ˌpleɪ]إعادة تشغيل [E'aadat tashgheel] ▷ *v* [ri:'pleɪ]يُعْيد تشغيل [Yo'aeed tashgheel]
replica ['rɛplɪkə] *n* نسخة مطابقة [Noskhah moṭe'qah]
reply [rɪ'plaɪ] *n* رَدّ [radd] ▷ *v* يُجيب [juʒi:bu]
report [rɪ'pɔ:t] *n* تقرير [taqri:r] ▷ *v* يُبْلغ [juballiɣu]; **report card** *n* تقرير مدرسي [Ta'qreer madrasey]
reporter [rɪ'pɔ:tə] *n* مُحَقّق [muħaqqiq]
represent [ˌrɛprɪ'zɛnt] *v* يُمَثل [jumaθθilu]
representative [ˌrɛprɪ'zɛntətɪv] *adj* نائب [na:ʔibb]
reproduction [ˌri:prə'dʌkʃən] *n* إعادة إنتاج [E'adat entaj]
reptile ['rɛptaɪl] *n* زواحف [zawa:ħif]
republic [rɪ'pʌblɪk] *n* جمهورية [ʒunmhu:rijjati]
repulsive [rɪ'pʌlsɪv] *adj* مثير للاشمئزاز [Mother lel-sheazaz]
reputable ['rɛpjʊtəbᵊl] *adj* حسن السمعة [Ḥasen al-som'aah]
reputation [ˌrɛpjʊ'teɪʃən] *n* سُمعة [sumʕa]
request [rɪ'kwɛst] *n* مطلب [matˤlab] ▷ *v* يَلْتَمِس [jaltamisu]
require [rɪ'kwaɪə] *v* يَتَطْلَب [jatatˤallabu]
requirement [rɪ'kwaɪəmənt] *n* مَطْلَب [matˤlab]
rescue ['rɛskju:] *n* إنقاذ [ʔinqa:ð] ▷ *v* يُنْقِذ [junqiðu]; **Where is the nearest mountain rescue service post?** أين يوجد أقرب مركز لخدمة الإنقاذ بالجبل؟ [ayna yujad a'qrab markaz le-khedmat al-en-'qaadh bil-jabal?]
research [rɪ'sɜ:tʃ; 'ri:sɜ:tʃ] *n* بَحْثٌ دراسي [Bahth derasy]; **market research** *n* دراسة السوق [Derasat al-soo'q]
resemblance [rɪ'zɛmbləns] *n* شبه [ʃibhu]
resemble [rɪ'zɛmbᵊl] *v* يُشْبه [juʃabbihu]
resent [rɪ'zɛnt] *v* يَمْتَعِض [jamtaʕidˤu]
resentful [rɪ'zɛntfʊl; re'sentful] *adj* مُستاء [musta:ʔ]
reservation [ˌrɛzə'veɪʃən] *n* تحَفُظ [taħafuzˤin]
reserve [rɪ'zɜ:v] *n (land)* مَحْمِيَّة [maħmijja], *(retention)* احتياطي [ʔiħtijja:tˤij] ▷ *v* يَحْتَفِظ [jaħtafizˤu]
reserved [rɪ'zɜ:vd] *adj* محجوز [maħʒu:z]
reservoir ['rɛzəˌvwɑ:] *n* خزان [xazza:nu]
resident ['rɛzɪdənt] *n* مُقيم [muqi:m]
residential [ˌrɛzɪ'dɛnʃəl] *adj* سَكني [sakanij]
resign [rɪ'zaɪn] *v* يَستقيل [jastaqi:l]
resin ['rɛzɪn] *n* مادة الراتينج [Madat al-ratenj]
resist [rɪ'zɪst] *v* يُقاوم [juqa:wimu]
resistance [rɪ'zɪstəns] *n* مقاومة [muqa:wama]
resit [ri:'sɪt] *v* يَجْلِس مرة أخرى [Yajles marrah okhra]
resolution [ˌrɛzə'lu:ʃən] *n* تصميم [tasˤmi:m]
resort [rɪ'zɔ:t] *n* منتجع [muntaʒaʕ]; **resort to** *v* لجأ إلى [Lajaa ela]
resource [rɪ'zɔ:s; -'sɔ:s] *n* مَورِد [mu:rad]; **natural resources** *npl* موارد طبيعية [Mawared ṭabe'aey]
respect [rɪ'spɛkt] *n* احترام [iħtira:m] ▷ *v* يَحَترم [jaħatarimu]
respectable [rɪ'spɛktəbᵊl] *adj* محترم

[muħtaram]
respectively [rɪˈspɛktɪvlɪ] *adv* على الترتيب [Ala altarteeb]
respond [rɪˈspɒnd] *v* يَستجيب [jastaʒiːbu]
response [rɪˈspɒns] *n* إستجابة [istiʒaːba]
responsibility [rɪˌspɒnsəˈbɪlɪtɪ] *n* مسؤولية [mas?uwlijja]
responsible [rɪˈspɒnsəbᵊl] *adj* مسؤول [mas?uːl]
rest [rɛst] *n* راحة [raːħa] ▷ *v* يَستريح [jastariːħu]; **the rest** *n* راحة [raːħatun]
restaurant [ˈrɛstəˌrɒŋ; ˈrɛstrɒŋ; -rɒnt] *n* مطعم [matˤʕam]
restful [ˈrɛstfʊl] *adj* مُريح [muriːħ]
restless [ˈrɛstlɪs] *adj* قلق [qalaq]
restore [rɪˈstɔː] *v* يَسْتَرِد [jastariddu]
restrict [rɪˈstrɪkt] *v* يُقَيِّد [juqajjidu]
restructure [riːˈstrʌktʃə] *v* يُعْيد إنشاء [juʕjidu ?inʃaː?a]
result [rɪˈzʌlt] *n* نتيجة [natiːʒa]; **result in** *v* يَنْجُم عن [Yanjam ʻan]
resume [rɪˈzjuːm] *v* يَستعيد [jastaʕiːdu]
retail [ˈriːteɪl] *n* بيع بالتجزئة [Bay'a bel- tajzeaah] ▷ *v* يَبْيع بالتجزئة [Yabea'a bel-tajzeaah]; **retail price** *n* سعر التجزئة [Se'ar al-tajzeah]
retailer [ˈriːteɪlə] *n* بائع تجزئة [Bae'a tajzeah]
retire [rɪˈtaɪə] *v* يَتقَاعد [jataqaːʕidu]
retired [rɪˈtaɪəd; reˈtired] *adj* متقاعد [mutaqaːʕid]
retirement [rɪˈtaɪəmənt] *n* تقاعد [taqaːʕud]
retrace [rɪˈtreɪs] *v* يعود من حيث أتى [jaʕuːdu min ħajθi ?ataː]
return [rɪˈtɜːn] *n (coming back)* عَوْدة [ʕawda], *(yield)* عائد [ʕaː?id] ▷ *vi* يُعْيد [juʕiːdu]; **day return** *n* تذكرة ذهاب وعودة في نفس اليوم [tadhkarat dhehab we-'awdah fee nafs al-yawm]; **return ticket** *n* تذكرة إياب [tadhkarat eyab]; **tax return** *n* إقرار ضريبي [E'qrar ḍareeby]
reunion [riːˈjuːnjən] *n* اجتماع الشمل [Ejtem'a alshaml]
reuse [riːˈjuːz] *v* يُعْيد استخدام [Yo'aeed estekhdam]
reveal [rɪˈviːl] *v* يبوح ب [Yabooḥ be]
revenge [rɪˈvɛndʒ] *n* انتقام [intiqaːm]
revenue [ˈrɛvɪˌnjuː] *n* إيراد [?iːraːd]
reverse [rɪˈvɜːs] *n* النقيض [anaqiːdˤu] ▷ *v* يَقْلِب [jaqlibu]
review [rɪˈvjuː] *n* اطلاع [itˤilaːʕ]
revise [rɪˈvaɪz] *v* يُراجِع [juraːʒiʕu]
revision [rɪˈvɪʒən] *n* مراجعة [muraːʒaʕa]
revive [rɪˈvaɪv] *v* يُنَشِط [junaʃʃitˤ]
revolting [rɪˈvəʊltɪŋ] *adj* ثائر [θaː?ir]
revolution [ˌrɛvəˈluːʃən] *n* ثورة [θawra]
revolutionary [ˌrɛvəˈluːʃənərɪ] *adj* ثوري [θawrij]
revolver [rɪˈvɒlvə] *n* سلاح ناري [Selaḥ narey]
reward [rɪˈwɔːd] *n* مكافأة [mukaːfa?a]
rewarding [rɪˈwɔːdɪŋ] *adj* مُجْزي [muʒziː]
rewind [riːˈwaɪnd] *v* يُعْيد اللف [juʕjidu allaf]
rheumatism [ˈruːməˌtɪzəm] *n* روماتيزم [ruːmaːtiːzmu]
rhubarb [ˈruːbɑːb] *n* عشب الراوند [ʻaoshb al-rawend]
rhyme [raɪm] *n*; **nursery rhyme** *n* أغنية أطفال [Aghzeyat aṭfaal]
rhythm [ˈrɪðəm] *n* الإيقاع [?al-?iːqaːʕu]
rib [rɪb] *n* ضِلْع [dˤilʕ]
ribbon [ˈrɪbᵊn] *n* وشاح [wiʃaːħ]
rice [raɪs] *n* أرْز [?urz]; **brown rice** *n* أرز أسمر [Orz asmar]
rich [rɪtʃ] *adj* غني [ɣanij]
ride [raɪd] *n* رَكْبَة [runkbatu] ▷ *v* يَركَب [jarkabu]
rider [ˈraɪdə] *n* راكب [raːkib]
ridiculous [rɪˈdɪkjʊləs] *adj* تافه [taːfih]
riding [ˈraɪdɪŋ] *n* ركوب [rukuːb]; **horse riding** *n* ركوب الخيل [Rekoob al-khayl]
rifle [ˈraɪfᵊl] *n* بندقية [bunduqijja]
rig [rɪg] *n* جهاز حفر [Jehaz hafr]; **oil rig** *n* جهاز حفر آبار النفط [Gehaz ḥafr abar al-naft]
right [raɪt] *adj (correct)* صحيح [sˤaħiːħ], *(not left)* يمين [jamiːn] ▷ *adv* بطريقة صحيحة [Be- ṭaree'qah ṣaḥeeḥah] ▷ *n* حق

[ħaq]; **civil rights** *npl* حقوق مدنية [Ḥo'qoo'q madaneyah]; **human rights** *npl* حقوق الإنسان [Ho'qoo'q al-ensan]; **right angle** *n* زاوية يُمنى [Zaweyah yomna]; **right of way** *n* حق المرور [Ha'q al-moror]; **Go right at the next junction** اتجه نحو اليمين عند التقاطع الثاني [Etajeh naḥw al-yameen]; **It wasn't your right of way** لم تكن تسير في الطريق الصحيح [lam takun ta-seer fee al-ṭaree'q al-ṣaheeḥ]; **Turn right** اتجه نحو اليمين [Etajeh anḥw al-yameen]
right-hand ['raɪtˌhænd] *adj* على اليمين [Ala al-yameen]; **right-hand drive** *n* عجلة القيادة اليمنى ['aajalat al-'qeyadah al-yomna]
right-handed ['raɪtˌhændɪd] *adj* أيمن [ʔajman]
rightly ['raɪtlɪ] *adv* بشكل صحيح [Beshakl ṣaheeh]
right-wing ['raɪtˌwɪŋ] *adj* جناح أيمن [Janah ayman]
rim [rɪm] *n* إطار [ʔitˤa:r]
ring [rɪŋ] *n* خاتم [xa:tam] ▷ *v* يَدُق [jaduqu]; **engagement ring** *n* خاتم الخطوبة [Khatem al-khotobah]; **ring binder** *n* ملف له حلقات معدنية لتثبيت الورق [Malaf lah ḥala'qaat ma'adaneyah letathbeet al-wara'q]; **ring road** *n* طريق دائري [Ṭaree'q dayery]; **wedding ring** *n* خاتم الزواج [Khatem al-zawaj]
ring back [rɪŋ bæk] *v* يَتَصِل ثانيةً [Yataṣel thaneyatan]
ringtone ['rɪŋˌtəʊn] *n* نغمة الرنين [Naghamat al-raneen]
ring up [rɪŋ ʌp] *v* يَتَّصِلُ هاتِفِيّا [Yataṣel hatefeyan]
rink [rɪŋk] *n* حلبة [ħalaba]; **ice rink** *n* حلبة من الجليد الصناعي [Ḥalabah men aljaleed alṣena'aey]; **skating rink** *n* حلبة تَزَلّج [Ḥalabat tazaloj]
rinse [rɪns] *n* شَطْف [ʃatˤf] ▷ *v* يَشْطُف [jaʃtˤufu]
riot ['raɪət] *n* شَغَبْ [ʃaɣab] ▷ *v* يُشاغِب [juʃa:ɣibu]
rip [rɪp] *v* يَشق [jaʃuqqu]
ripe [raɪp] *adj* ناضج [na:dˤiʒ]
rip off [rɪp ɒf] *v* يَسرِق عَلانيةً [Yasre'q 'alaneytan]
rip-off [rɪpɒf] *n* سرقة [sariqa]
rip up [rɪp ʌp] *v* يمزق [jumazziqu]
rise [raɪz] *n* صعود [sˤuʕu:d] ▷ *v* يَرْتَفِع [jartafiʕu]
risk [rɪsk] *n* مخاطرة [muxa:tˤara] ▷ *vt* يُجازف [juʒazifu]
risky ['rɪskɪ] *adj* محفوف بالمخاطر [Maḥfoof bel-makhaater]
ritual ['rɪtjʊəl] *adj* شعائري [ʃaʕa:ʔirij] ▷ *n* شَعيرة [ʃaʕi:ra]
rival ['raɪvəl] *adj* منافس [muna:fis] ▷ *n* خِصْم [xasˤm]
rivalry ['raɪvəlrɪ] *n* تنافس [tana:fus]
river ['rɪvə] *n* نهر [nahr]; **Can one swim in the river?** أيمكن السباحة في النهر؟ [a-yamkun al-sebaḥa fee al-naher?]
road [rəʊd] *n* طريق [tˤari:q]; **main road** *n* طريق رئيسي [ṭaree'q raeysey]; **ring road** *n* طريق دائري [Ṭaree'q dayery]; **road map** *n* خريطة الطريق [Khareeṭat al-ṭaree'q]; **road rage** *n* مشاحنات على الطريق [Moshahanaat ala al-ṭaree'q]; **road sign** *n* لافتة طريق [Lafetat ṭaree'q]; **road tax** *n* ضريبة طُرُق [Ḍareebat ṭoro'q]; **slip road** *n* طريق متصل بطريق سريع للسيارات أو منفصل عنه [ṭaree'q mataṣel be- ṭaree'q sarea'a lel-sayaraat aw monfaṣel 'anho]; **Are the roads icy?** هل توجد ثلوج على الطريق؟ [hal tojad thilooj 'ala al- ṭaree'q?]; **Do you have a road map of this area?** هل يوجد خريطة طريق لهذه المنطقة؟ [hal yujad khareeṭat ṭaree'q le-hadhy al-manṭa'qa?]; **I need a road map of...** أريد خريطة الطريق لـ... [areed khareeṭat al-ṭaree'q le...]; **Is the road to... snowed up?** هل توجد ثلوج على الطريق المؤدي إلى... [hal tojad thilooj 'ala al- ṭaree'q al-muad-dy ela...?]; **What is the speed limit on this road?** ما هي أقصى سرعة مسموح بها على هذا الطريق؟ [ma heya a'qṣa sur'aa masmooḥ beha 'aala hatha al-ṭaree'q?]; **Which road do I take for...?**

ما هو الطريق الذي يؤدي إلى... ؟ [ma howa al-ṭaree'q al-lathy yo-aady ela...?]
roadblock ['rəʊd,blɒk] *n* متراس [mutara:sin]
roadworks ['rəʊd,wɜːks] *npl* أعمال الطريق [a'amal alṭ aree'q]
roast [rəʊst] *adj* محمص [muħamasˤsˤ]
rob [rɒb] *v* يَسْلب [jaslubu]
robber [rɒbə] *n* سارق [sa:riq]
robbery ['rɒbərɪ] *n* سطو [satˤw]
robin ['rɒbɪn] *n* طائر أبو الحناء [Ṭaaer abo elḥnaa]
robot ['rəʊbɒt] *n* إنسان آلي [Ensaṇ aly]
rock [rɒk] *n* صخرة [sˤaxra] ▷ *v* يَتأرجح [jataʔarʒaħu]; **rock climbing** *n* تسلق الصخور [Tasalo'q alṣokhoor]
rocket ['rɒkɪt] *n* صاروخ [sˤa:ru:xin]
rod [rɒd] *n* قضيب [qadˤi:b]
rodent ['rəʊdᵊnt] *n* القارض [al-qa:ridˤi]
role [rəʊl] *n* دَور [dawr]
roll [rəʊl] *n* لَفّة [laffa] ▷ *v* يَلِف [jalifu]; **bread roll** *n* خبز ملفوف [Khobz malfoof]; **roll call** *n* تَفَقّد الحضور [Tafa'qod al-ḥoḍor]
roller ['rəʊlə] *n* اسطوانة [ustˤuwa:na]
rollercoaster ['rəʊlə,kəʊstə] *n* سكة حديد بالملاهي [Sekat ḥadeed bel-malahey]
rollerskates ['rəʊlə,skeɪts] *npl* مزلجة بعجل [Mazlajah be-'aajal]
rollerskating ['rəʊlə,skeɪtɪŋ] *n* تَزَلُّج على العجل [Tazaloj 'ala al-'ajal]
Roman ['rəʊmən] *adj* روماني [ru:ma:nij]; **Roman Catholic** *n* روماني كاثوليكي [Romaney katholeykey]شخص روماني , كاثوليكي [shakhṣ romaney katholeekey]
romance ['rəʊmæns] *n* رومانسية [ru:ma:nsijja]
Romanesque [,rəʊmə'nɛsk] *adj* طراز رومانسيكي [Ṭeraz romanseekey]
Romania [rəʊ'meɪnɪə] *n* رومانيا [ru:ma:njja:]
Romanian [rəʊ'meɪnɪən] *adj* روماني [ru:ma:nij] ▷ *n (language)* اللغة الرومانية [Al-loghah al-romanyah], *(person)* روماني الجنسية [Romaney al-jenseyah]
romantic [rəʊ'mæntɪk] *adj* رومانسي [ru:ma:nsij]
roof [ru:f] *n* سَطح المبنى [Saṭh al-mabna]
roof rack ['ru:f,ræk] *n* رَف السقف [Raf alsa'qf]
room [ru:m; rʊm] *n* غرفة [ɣurfa]; **changing room** *n* غرفة تبديل الملابس [Ghorfat tabdeel al-malabes]; **dining room** *n* غرفة طعام [ghorat ṭa'aam]; **double room** *n* غرفة مزدوجة [Ghorfah mozdawajah]; **fitting room** *n* غرفة القياس [ghorfat al-'qeyas]; **living room** *n* حجرة المعيشة [Ḥojrat al-ma'aeshah]; **room number** *n* رقم الغرفة [Ra'qam al-ghorfah]; **room service** *n* خدمة الغرف [Khedmat al-ghoraf]; **single room** *n* غرفة لشخص واحد [ghorfah le-shakhṣ wahed]; **sitting room** *n* غرفة المعيشة [ghorfat al-ma'aeshah]; **spare room** *n* غرفة إضافية [ghorfah eḍafeyah]; **twin room** *n* غرفة مزدوجة [Ghorfah mozdawajah]; **twin-bedded room** *n* غرفة مزودة بأسرة مزدوجة [Ghorfah mozawadah be-aserah mozdawajah]; **utility room** *n* غرفة خدمات [ghorfat khadamat]; **waiting room** *n* غرفة انتظار [Ghorfat enteḍhar]; **Can I see the room?** هل يمكن أن أرى الغرفة؟ [hal yamken an ara al-ghurfa?]; **Do you have a room for tonight?** هل لديكم غرفة شاغرة الليلة؟ [hal ladykum ghurfa shaghera al-layla?]; **Does the room have air conditioning?** هل هناك تكييف هواء بالغرفة [hal hunaka takyeef hawaa bil-ghurfa?]; **How much is the room?** كم تبلغ تكلفة الإقامة بالغرفة؟ [kam tablugh taklifat al-e'qama bil-ghurfa?]; **I need a room with wheelchair access** أحتاج إلى غرفة يمكن الوصول إليها بكرسي المقعدين المتحرك [aḥtaaj ela ghurfa yamkun al-wi-ṣool e-layha be-kursi al-mu'q'aadeen al-mutaḥarek]; **I want to reserve a double room** أريد حجز غرفة لشخصين [areed ḥajiz ghurfa le-shakhiṣ-yen]; **I'd like a no smoking room** أريد غرفة غير مسموح فيها بالتدخين

[areed ghurfa ghyer masmooḥ feeha bil-tadkheen]; **I'd like a room with a view of the sea** أريد غرفة تطل على البحر [areed ghurfa ta-ṭul 'aala al-baḥir]; **I'd like to rent a room** أريد غرفة للإيجار [areed ghurfa lil-eejar]; **The room is dirty** الغرفة متسخة [al-ghurfa mutaskha]; **The room is too cold** هذه الغرفة باردة أكثر من اللازم [hathy al-ghurfa barda ak-thar min al-laazim]

roommate ['ru:mˌmeɪt; 'rʊm-] *n* رفيق الحجرة [Refee'q al-hohrah]

root [ru:t] *n* جذر [ʒiðr]

rope [rəʊp] *n* حَبْل [ħabl]

rope in [rəʊp ɪn] *v* يَستَعين بمساعدة شخص ما [jastaʕi:nu bimusa:ʕadatin ʃaxsˤin ma:]

rose [rəʊz] *n* وردة [warda]

rosé ['rəʊzeɪ] *n* نبيذ أحمر [nabeedh aḥmar]

rosemary ['rəʊzmərɪ] *n* إكليل الجبل [Ekleel al-jabal]

rot [rɒt] *v* يَتْعِفَن [jataʕaffanu]

rotten ['rɒtᵊn] *adj* نتن [natin]

rough [rʌf] *adj* خشن [xaʃin]

roughly ['rʌflɪ; 'roughly] *adv* بقسوة [Be'qaswah]

roulette [ru:'lɛt] *n* روليت [ru:li:t]

round [raʊnd] *adj* مستدير [mustadi:r] ▷ *n (circle)* حلقة [ħalaqa], *(series)* دائرة [da:ʔira] ▷ *prep* حول [ħawla]; **paper round** *n* طريق توزيع الصحف [ṭaree'q tawze'a al-ṣohof]; **round trip** *n* رحلةانكفائية [Reḥlah enkefaeyah]

roundabout ['raʊndəˌbaʊt] *n* طريق ملتو [ṭaree'q moltawe]

round up [raʊnd ʌp] *v* يُجَمِع [juʒamiʕu]

route [ru:t] *n* مسلك [maslak]

routine [ru:'ti:n] *n* روتين [ru:ti:n]

row¹ [rəʊ] *n (line)* رُتبة [rutba] ▷ *v (in boat)* يُجدِف [juʒaddifu]

row² [raʊ] *n (argument)* مُشادَة [muʃa:da] ▷ *v (to argue)* يُجادِل [juʒa:dilu]

rowing [rəʊɪŋ] *n* تجديف [taʒdi:f]; **rowing boat** *n* قارب تجديف ['qareb tajdeef]

royal ['rɔɪəl] *adj* مَلَكي [milki:]

rub [rʌb] *v* يَحُكْ [jaħukku]

rubber ['rʌbə] *n* ممحاة [mimħa:t]; **rubber band** *n* شريط مطاطي [shareeṭ maṭaṭey]; **rubber gloves** *npl* قفازات مطاطية ['qoffazat maṭaṭeyah]

rubbish ['rʌbɪʃ] *adj* تافه [ta:fih] ▷ *n* هراء [hura:ʔ]; **rubbish dump** *n* مقلب النفايات [Ma'qlab al-nefayat]

rucksack ['rʌkˌsæk] *n* حقيبة ملابس تحمل على الظهر [Ha'qeebat malabes tohmal 'aala al-ḍhahr]

rude [ru:d] *adj* وقح [waqiħu]

rug [rʌg] *n* سجادة [saʒa:dda]

rugby ['rʌgbɪ] *n* رياضة الرَّكْبي [Reyaḍat al-rakbey]

ruin ['ru:ɪn] *n* خراب [xara:b] ▷ *v* يُدَمِر [judammir]

rule [ru:l] *n* حُكم [ħukm]

rule out [ru:l aʊt] *v* يستبعد [justabʕadu]

ruler ['ru:lə] *n (commander)* حاكم [ħa:kim], *(measure)* مسطرة [mistˤara]

rum [rʌm] *n* شراب الرّم [Sharab al-ram]

rumour ['ru:mə] *n* إشاعة [ʔiʃa:ʕa]

run [rʌn] *n* عَدْو [ʕaduww] ▷ *vi* يَجْري [jaʒri:] ▷ *vt* يُدير [judi:ru]

run away [rʌn ə'weɪ] *v* يَهْرُب [jahrubu]

runner ['rʌnə] *n* عدَّاء [ʕadda:ʔ]; **runner bean** *n* فاصوليا خضراء متعرشة [faṣoleya khadraa mota'aresha]

runner-up ['rʌnəʌp] *n* الحائز على المرتبة الثانية [Al-ḥaez ala al-martabah al-thaneyah]

running ['rʌnɪŋ] *n* ادارة, مستمر [mustamirr]

run out [rʌn aʊt] *v*; **The towels have run out** لقد استهلكت المناشف [la'qad istuh-lekat al-mana-shif]

run out of [rʌn aʊt ɒv] *v* يَستنفِذ [jastanfiðu]

run over [rʌn 'əʊvə] *v* يطفح [jatˤfaħu]

runway ['rʌnˌweɪ] *n* مَدرَج [madraʒ]

rural ['rʊərəl] *adj* ريفي [ri:fij]

rush [rʌʃ] *n* اندفاع [indifa:ʕ] ▷ *v* يَنْدَفِع [jandafiʕu]; **rush hour** *n* وَقْت الذروة

[Wa'qt al-dhorwah]
rusk [rʌsk] *n* بُقْسُماط [buqsuma:tˤin]
Russia ['rʌʃə] *n* روسيا [ru:sja:]
Russian ['rʌʃən] *adj* روسي [ru:sij] ▷ *n* *(language)* اللغة الروسية [Al-loghah al-roseyah], *(person)* روسي الجنسية [Rosey al-jenseyah]
rust [rʌst] *n* صدأ [sˤada]
rusty ['rʌstɪ] *adj* صدِئ [sˤadiʔ]
ruthless ['ru:θlɪs] *adj* قاس [qa:sin]
rye [raɪ] *n* نبات الجاودار [Nabat al-jawdar]

S

Sabbath ['sæbəθ] *n* يوم الراحة [Yawm al-rahah]
sabotage ['sæbə,tɑ:ʒ] *n* عمل تخريبي ['amal takhreeby] ▷ *v* يُخّرِب [juxxribu]
sachet ['sæʃeɪ] *n* ذرور معطر [Zaroor mo'aṭar]
sack [sæk] *n (container)* كيس [ki:s], *(dismissal)* كيس (فصل) [ki:s] ▷ *v* يَصْرِف من الخدمة [Yaṣref men al-khedmah]
sacred ['seɪkrɪd] *adj* ديني [di:nij]
sacrifice ['sækrɪ,faɪs] *n* يُضَحي [judˤaħħi:]
sad [sæd] *adj* حزين [ħazi:nu]
saddle ['sædᵊl] *n* سرج [sarʒ]
saddlebag ['sædᵊl,bæg] *n* حقيبة سِرْج الحصان [Ha'qeebat sarj al-hoṣan]
sadly [sædlɪ] *adv* بحُزْن [Beḥozn]
safari [sə'fɑ:rɪ] *n* رحلة سفاري [Reḥlat safarey]
safe [seɪf] *adj* آمِنْ [ʔa:mi] ▷ *n* خزينة [xazi:na]; **I have some things in the safe** لقد وضعت بعض الأشياء في الخزينة [la'qad waḍa'ato ba'aḍ al-ash-ya fe al-khazeena]; **I would like to put my jewellery in the safe** أريد أن أضع مجوهراتي في الخزينة [areed an aḍa'a mujaw-haraty fee al-khazeena]; **Put**

that in the safe, please ضع هذا في الخزينة من فضلك [ḍa'a hadha fee al-khazena, min faḍlak]
safety ['seɪftɪ] *n* سلامة [sala:ma]; **safety belt** *n* حزام الأمان [Hezam al-aman]; **safety pin** *n* دبوس أمان [Daboos aman]
saffron ['sæfrən] *n* نبات الزعفران [Nabat al-za'afaran]
Sagittarius [ˌsædʒɪ'tɛərɪəs] *n* كوكبة القوس والرامي [Kawkabat al-'qaws wa alramey]
Sahara [sə'hɑːrə] *n* الصحراء الكبرى [Al-ṣaḥraa al-kobraa]
sail [seɪl] *n* شِراع [ʃira:ʕ] ▷ *v* يُبحِر [jubħiru]
sailing ['seɪlɪŋ] *n* الإبحار [al-ʔibħa:ri]; **sailing boat** *n* قارب ابحار ['qareb ebḥar]
sailor ['seɪlə] *n* بحَّار [baħħa:r]
saint [seɪnt; sənt] *n* قدّيس [qiddi:s]
salad ['sæləd] *n* سَلاطة [sala:tˤa]; **mixed salad** *n* سلاطة مخلوطة [Salata makhloṭa]; **salad dressing** *n* صلصة السلطة [Ṣalṣat al-salata]
salami [sə'lɑːmɪ] *n* طعام السالامي [Ṭa'aam al-salamey]
salary ['sælərɪ] *n* راتب [ra:tib]
sale [seɪl] *n* بيع [bajʕ]; **sales assistant** *n* مساعد المبيعات [Mosa'aed al-mobee'aat]; **sales rep** *n* مندوب مبيعات [Mandoob mabee'aat]
salesman, salesmen ['seɪlzmən, 'seɪlzmɛn] *n* مندوب مبيعات [Mandoob mabee'aat]
salesperson ['seɪlzpɜːsᵊn] *n* مندوب مبيعات [Mandoob mabee'aat]
saleswoman, saleswomen ['seɪlzwʊmən, 'seɪlzwɪmɪn] *n* مندوبة مبيعات [Mandoobat mabee'aat]
saliva [sə'laɪvə] *n* لُعَاب [luʕa:b]
salmon ['sæmən] *n* سمك السلمون [Samak al-salmon]
salon ['sælɒn] *n*; **beauty salon** *n* صالون تجميل [Ṣalon ḥela'qa]
saloon [sə'luːn] *n* صالون [sˤa:lu:n]; **saloon car** *n* سيارة صالون [Sayarah ṣalon]
salt [sɔːlt] *n* مِلحْ [milħ]
saltwater ['sɔːltˌwɔːtə] *adj* ماء ملحي [Maa mel'ḥey]
salty ['sɔːltɪ] *adj* مملح [mumallaħ]
salute [sə'luːt] *v* يُحَيّي [juħajji:]
salve [sælv] *n*; **lip salve** *n* كريم للشفاه [Kereem lel shefah]
same [seɪm] *adj* عينه [ʕajinnat]
sample ['sɑːmpᵊl] *n* عينة [ʕajjina]
sand [sænd] *n* رمال [rima:l]; **sand dune** *n* كثبان رملية [Kothban ramleyah]
sandal ['sændᵊl] *n* (حذاء) صندل [sˤandal]
sandcastle [sændkɑːsᵊl] *n* قلعة من الرمال ['qal'aah men al-remal]
sandpaper ['sændˌpeɪpə] *n* ورق السنفرة [Wara'q al-sanfarah]
sandpit ['sændˌpɪt] *n* حفرة رملية [Hofrah ramleyah]
sandstone ['sændˌstəʊn] *n* حجر رملي [Hajar ramley]
sandwich ['sænwɪdʒ; -wɪtʃ] *n* سَندويتش [sandiwi:tʃ]
San Marino [ˌsæn mə'riːnəʊ] *n* سان مارينو [sa:n ma:ri:nu:]
sapphire ['sæfaɪə] *n* ياقوت أزرق [Ya'qoot azra'q]
sarcastic [sɑː'kæstɪk] *adj* ساخر [sa:xir]
sardine [sɑː'diːn] *n* سردين [sardi:nu]
satchel ['sætʃəl] *n* حقيبة للكتب المدرسية [Ha'qeebah lel-kotob al-madraseyah]
satellite ['sætᵊˌlaɪt] *n* قمر صناعي ['qamar ṣenaaey]; **satellite dish** *n* طبق قمر صناعي [Ṭaba'q ṣena'aey]
satisfaction [ˌsætɪs'fækʃən] *n* إشباع [ʔiʃba:ʕ]
satisfactory [ˌsætɪs'fæktərɪ; -trɪ] *adj* مرضٍ [maradˤ]
satisfied ['sætɪsˌfaɪd] *adj* راضٍ [ra:dˤin]; **I'm not satisfied with this** أنا لست راضية عن هذا [ana lastu raḍy-ya 'aan hadha]
sat nav ['sæt næv] *n* الاستدلال على الاتجاهات من الأقمار الصناعية [Al-estedlal ala al-etejahat men al-'qmar alṣena'ayah]

Saturday ['sætədɪ] *n* السبت [ʔa-sabti]; **last Saturday** يوم السبت الماضي [yawm al-sabit al-maḍy]; **next Saturday** يوم السبت القادم [yawm al-sabit al-'qadem]; **on Saturday** في يوم السبت [fee yawm al-sabit]; **on Saturdays** في أيام السبت [fee ayaam al-sabit]; **this Saturday** يوم السبت هذا [yawm al-sabit hadha]
sauce [sɔːs] *n* صلصة [sˤalsˤa]; **soy sauce** *n* صوص الصويا [Ṣoṣ al-ṣoyah]; **tomato sauce** *n* صلصة طماطم [Ṣalṣat ṭamaṭem]
saucepan ['sɔːspən] *n* مِقلاة (قِدر) [miqlaːt]
saucer ['sɔːsə] *n* صحن الفنجان [Ṣaḥn al-fenjaan]
Saudi ['sɔːdɪ; 'saʊ-] *adj* سعودي [saʕuːdij] ▷ *n* سعودي [saʕuːdij]
Saudi Arabia ['sɔːdɪ; 'saʊ-] *n* المملكة العربية السعودية [Al-mamlakah al-'aarabeyah al-so'aodeyah]
Saudi Arabian ['sɔːdɪ ə'reɪbɪən] *adj* السعودية [ʔa-saʕuːdijjatu] ▷ *n* مواطن سعودي [Mewaṭen saudey]
sauna ['sɔːnə] *n* حمام بخار [Hammam bokhar]
sausage ['sɒsɪdʒ] *n* سجق [saʒq]
save [seɪv] *v* يُحافِظ على [Yoḥafez 'aala]
save up [seɪv ʌp] *v* يُوَفِر [juwaffiru]
savings ['seɪvɪŋz] *npl* مُدّخَرَات [muddaxaraːtin]
savoury ['seɪvərɪ] *adj* سار [saːrr]
saw [sɔː] *n* منشار [minʃaːr]
sawdust ['sɔːˌdʌst] *n* نِشَارة [niʃaːra]
saxophone ['sæksəˌfəʊn] *n* آلة السكسية [Alat al-sekseyah]
say [seɪ] *v* يقول [jaquːlu]
saying ['seɪɪŋ] *n* قَوْل [qawl]
scaffolding ['skæfəldɪŋ] *n* سقالات [saqaːlaːt]
scale [skeɪl] *n* *(measure)* ميزان [miːzaːn], *(tiny piece)* ميزان [miːzaːn]
scales [skeɪlz] *npl* كفتي الميزان [Kafatay al-meezan]
scallop ['skɒləp; 'skæl-] *n* محار الاسقلوب [maḥar al-as'qaloob]
scam [skæm] *n* خِدَاع [xidaːʕ]
scampi ['skæmpɪ] *npl* جمبري كبير [Jambarey kabeer]
scan [skæn] *n* مسح ضوئي [Masḥ ḍawaey] ▷ *v* يمسح الكترونياً [Yamsaḥ elektroneyan]
scandal ['skændᵊl] *n* فضيحة [fadˤiːħa]
Scandinavia [ˌskændɪ'neɪvɪə] *n* إسكندنافيا [ʔiskundinaːfjaː]
Scandinavian [ˌskændɪ'neɪvɪən] *adj* اسكنديناڤي [ʔiskundinaːfjj]
scanner ['skænə] *n* ماسح ضوئي [Maaseh daweay]
scar [skɑː] *n* ندبة [nadba]
scarce [skɛəs] *adj* قليل [qaliːl]
scarcely ['skɛəslɪ] *adv* نادراً [naːdiran]
scare [skɛə] *n* ذُعْر [ðuʕr] ▷ *v* يُرَوْع [jurawwiʕu]
scarecrow ['skɛəˌkrəʊ] *n* خيال الظِل [Khayal al-ḍhel]
scared [skɛəd] *adj* خائف [xaːʔif]
scarf, scarves [skɑːf, skɑːvz] *n* وِشاح [wiʃaːħ]
scarlet ['skɑːlɪt] *adj* قرمزي [qurmuzij]
scary ['skɛərɪ] *adj* مخيف [muxiːf]
scene [siːn] *n* مشهد [maʃhad]
scenery ['siːnərɪ] *n* مَنْظَر [manzˤar]
scent [sɛnt] *n* عِطْر [ʕitˤr]
sceptical ['skɛptɪkᵊl; 'sceptical; 'skeptical] *adj* معتنق مذهب الشك [Mo'atane'q maḍhhab al-shak]
schedule ['ʃɛdjuːl; 'skɛdʒʊəl] *n* جدول زمني [Jadwal zamaney]
scheme [skiːm] *n* مخطط [muxatˤatˤ]
schizophrenic [ˌskɪtsəʊ'frɛnɪk; ˌschizo'phrenic] *adj* مريض بالفصَام [Mareeḍ bel-feṣaam]
scholarship ['skɒləʃɪp] *n* منحة تعليمية [Menḥah ta'aleemeyah]
school [skuːl] *n* مدرسة [madrasa]; **art school** *n* كلية الفنون [Koleyat al-fonoon]; **boarding school** *n* مدرسة داخلية [Madrasah dakheleyah]; **elementary school** *n* مدرسة نوعية [Madrasah naw'aeyah]; **infant school** *n* مدرسة أطفال [Madrasah aṭfaal]; **language**

school *n* مدرسة لغات [Madrasah lo-ghaat]; **law school** *n* كلية الحقوق [Kolayt al-ho'qooq]; **night school** *n* مدرسة ليلية [Madrasah layleyah]; **nursery school** *n* مدرسة الحضانة [Madrasah al-ḥaḍanah]; **primary school** *n* مدرسة إبتدائية [Madrasah ebtedaeyah]; **public school** *n* مدرسة عامة [Madrasah 'aamah]; **school uniform** *n* زي مدرسي موحد [Zey madrasey mowaḥad]; **secondary school** *n* مدرسة ثانوية [Madrasah thanaweyah]

schoolbag ['skuːlˌbæg] *n* حقيبة مدرسية [Ḥa'qeebah madraseyah]

schoolbook ['skuːlˌbʊk] *n* كتاب مدرسي [Ketab madrasey]

schoolboy ['skuːlˌbɔɪ] *n* تلميذ [tilmiːð]

schoolchildren ['skuːlˌtʃɪldrən] *n* طلاب المدرسة [Ṭolab al-madrasah]

schoolgirl ['skuːlˌɡɜːl] *n* تلميذة [tilmiːða]

schoolteacher ['skuːlˌtiːtʃə] *n* مُدَرِّس [mudarris]

science ['saɪəns] *n* عِلْم (المعرفة) [ʕilmu]; **science fiction** *n* خيال علمي [Khayal 'aelmey]

scientific [ˌsaɪən'tɪfɪk] *adj* علمي [ʕilmij]

scientist ['saɪəntɪst] *n* عَالِم [ʕaːlim]

scifi ['saɪˌfaɪ] *n* خيال علمي [Khayal 'aelmey]

scissors ['sɪzəz] *npl* مقص [miqasʕun]; **nail scissors** *npl* مقص أظافر [Ma'qaṣ aḍhafer]

sclerosis [sklɪə'rəʊsɪs] *n*; **multiple sclerosis** *n* تَلَيُّف عصبي متعدد [Talayof 'aaṣabey mota'aded]

scoff [skɒf] *v* يَسخَر من [Yaskhar men]

scold [skəʊld] *v* يُعَنِف [juʕannifu]

scooter ['skuːtə] *n* دراجة الرِجْل [Darrajat al-rejl]

score [skɔː] *n (game/match)* مجموع نقاط [Majmo'aat ne'qaaṭ], *(of music)* مجموع النقاط [Majmoo'a al-nekaṭ] ▷ *v* يُحْرِز [juħrizu]

Scorpio ['skɔːpɪˌəʊ] *n* العقرب [al-ʕaqrabi]

scorpion ['skɔːpɪən] *n* عقرب [ʕaqrab]

Scot [skɒt] *n* اسكتلاندي [iskutlaːndiː]

Scotland ['skɒtlənd] *n* اسكتلاندة [iskutlaːndatu]

Scots [skɒts] *adj* اسكتلانديون [iskutlaːndijuːna]

Scotsman, Scotsmen ['skɒtsmən, 'skɒtsmɛn] *n* اسكتلاندي [iskutlaːndiː]

Scotswoman, Scotswomen ['skɒtsˌwʊmən, 'skɒtsˌwɪmɪn] *n* اسكتلاندية [iskutlaːndijja]

Scottish ['skɒtɪʃ] *adj* اسكتلاندي [iskutlaːndiː]

scout [skaʊt] *n* كَشّاف [kaʃʃaːf]

scrap [skræp] *n (dispute)* عِراك [ʕiraːk], *(small piece)* فَضْلَة [fadˤla] ▷ *v* يتشاجر [jataʃaːʒaru]; **scrap paper** *n* ورق مسودة [Wara'q mosawadah]

scrapbook ['skræpˌbʊk] *n* سِجل القصاصات [Sejel al'qeṣaṣat]

scratch [skrætʃ] *n* خدش [xudʃu] ▷ *v* يَخدِش [jaxdiʃu]

scream [skriːm] *n* صراخ [sˤuraːx] ▷ *v* يصيح [jasˤiːħu]

screen [skriːn] *n* شاشة تليفزيون [Shashat telefezyoon]; **plasma screen** *n* شاشة بلازما [Shashah blazma]; **screen (off)** *v* يَحْجِب [jaħʒubu]

screen-saver ['skriːnseɪvər] *n* شاشة تَوقُف [Shashat taw'qof]

screw [skruː] *n* مسمار قلاووظ [Mesmar 'qalawooḍh]

screwdriver ['skruːˌdraɪvə] *n* مفك [mifakk]

scribble ['skrɪbᵊl] *v* يخربش [juxarbiʃu]

scrub [skrʌb] *v* يَفْرُك [jafruku]

sculptor ['skʌlptə] *n* مَثّال [maθθaːl]

sculpture ['skʌlptʃə] *n* فن النحت [Fan al-naḥt]

sea [siː] *n* بَحْر [baħr]; **North Sea** *n* البحر الشمالي [Al-baḥr al-Shamaley]; **Red Sea** *n* البحر الأحمر [Al-bahr al-ahmar]; **sea level** *n* مستوى سطح البحر [Mostawa saṭh al-bahr]; **sea water** *n* مياه البحر [Meyah al-baḥr]

seafood ['siː,fuːd] *n* الأطعمة البحرية [Al-aṭ'aemah al-baḥareyh]
seagull ['siː,gʌl] *n* نورس البحر [Nawras al-baḥr]
seal [siːl] *n (animal)* (حيوان) حيوان الفقمة [Ḥayawaan al-fa'qmah], *(mark)* خِتم [xitm] ▷ *v* يَختِم [jaxtimu]
seam [siːm] *n* ندبة [nadba]
seaman, seamen ['siːmən, 'siːmɛn] *n* جندي بحري [Jondey baharey]
search [sɜːtʃ] *n* بَحْث [baħθ] ▷ *v* يُفَتِش [jufattiʃu]; **search engine** *n* محرك البحث [moḥarek al-baḥth]; **search party** *n* فريق البحث [Faree'q al-bahth]
seashore ['siː,ʃɔː] *n* شاطئ البحر [Shaṭeya al-baḥr]
seasick ['siː,sɪk] *adj* مصاب بدوار البحر [Moṣab be-dawar al-baḥr]
seaside ['siː,saɪd] *n* ساحل البحر [saḥel al-baḥr]
season ['siːzᵊn] *n* موسم [mawsim]; **high season** *n* موسم ازدهار [Mawsem ezdehar]; **low season** *n* فترة ركود [Fatrat rekood]; **season ticket** *n* التذاكر الموسمية [Al-tadhaker al-mawsemeyah]
seasonal ['siːzənᵊl] *adj* موسمي [mawsimijjat]
seasoning ['siːzənɪŋ] *n* توابل [tawaːbil]
seat [siːt] *n (constituency)* عضوية في مجلس تشريعي ['aoḍweyah fee majles tashreaey], *(furniture)* مقعد [maqʕad]; **aisle seat** *n* كرسي بجوار الممر [Korsey be-jewar al-mamar]; **window seat** *n* مقعد بجوار النافذة [Ma'q'aad bejwar al-nafedhah]; **Excuse me, that's my seat** معذرة، هذا هو مقعدي؟ [ma'a-dhera, hadha howa ma'q'aady]; **I have a seat reservation** لقد قمت بحجز المقعد [la'qad 'qimto be-ḥajis al-ma'q'aad]; **I'd like a non-smoking seat** أريد مقعد في العربة المخصصة لغير المدخنين [areed ma'q'aad fee al-'aaraba al-mukhaṣaṣa le-ghyr al-mudakhineen]; **I'd like a seat in the smoking area** أريد مقعد في المكان المخصص للمدخنين [areed ma'q'ad fee al-makan al-mukhaṣaṣ lel -mudakhineen]; **I'd like a window seat** أريد مقعد بجوار النافذة [areed ma'q'aad be-jewar al-nafedha]; **Is this seat free?** هل يمكن الجلوس في هذا المقعد؟ [hal yamken al-jiloos fee hadha al-ma'q-'aad?]; **Is this seat taken?** هل هذا المقعد محجوز؟ [hal hadha al-ma'q'ad maḥjooz?]; **The seat is too high** المقعد مرتفع جدا [al-ma'q'ad mur-taf'a jedan]; **The seat is too low** المقعد منخفض جدا [al-ma'q'ad mun-khafiḍ jedan]; **We'd like to reserve two seats for tonight** نريد حجز مقعدين في هذه الليلة [nureed ḥajiz ma'q-'aad-ayn fee hadhy al-layla]
seatbelt ['siːt,bɛlt] *n* حزام الأمان المثبت في المقعد [Ḥezam al-aman al-mothabat fee al-ma'q'aad]
seaweed ['siː,wiːd] *n* طّحْلُب بحري [Ṭoḥleb baḥahrey]
second ['sɛkənd] *adj* الثاني [aθ-θaːniː] ▷ *n* ثَانِيَة [θaːnija]; **second class** *n* درجة ثانية [Darajah thaneyah]
second-class ['sɛkənd,klɑːs] *adj* مرتبة ثانية [Martabah thaneyah]
secondhand ['sɛkənd,hænd] *adj* مستعمل [mustaʕmal]
secondly ['sɛkəndlɪ] *adv* ثانياً [θaːniːan]
second-rate ['sɛkənd,reɪt] *adj* من الدرجة الثانية [Men al-darajah althaneyah]
secret ['siːkrɪt] *adj* سِريّ [sirij] ▷ *n* سِرّ [sirr]; **secret service** *n* خدمة سرية [Khedmah serreyah]
secretary ['sɛkrətrɪ] *n* سكرتير [sikirtiːr]
secretly ['siːkrɪtlɪ] *adv* سِراً [sirran]
sect [sɛkt] *n* طائفة [tˤaːʔifa]
section ['sɛkʃən] *n* قسم [qism]
sector ['sɛktə] *n* قطاع [qitˤaːʕ]
secure [sɪ'kjʊə] *adj* مُأمَّن [muʔamman]
security [sɪ'kjʊərɪtɪ] *n* الأمن [alʔamnu]; **security guard** *n* حارس الأمن [Ḥares al-amn]; **social security** *n* ضمان اجتماعي [Ḍaman ejtema'ay]
sedative ['sɛdətɪv] *n* عقار مسكن ['aa'qaar mosaken]
see [siː] *v* يرى [jaraː]

seed [siːd] *n* بِذْرة [biðra]
seek [siːk] *v* يَبْحَث عن [Yabḥath an]
seem [siːm] *v* يَبْدو [jabduː]
seesaw ['siːˌsɔː] *n* أرجوحة [ʔurʒuːħa]
see-through ['siːˌθruː] *adj* شَفّافة [ʃaffaːfat]
seize [siːz] *v* يستَولي على [Yastwley 'ala]
seizure ['siːʒə] *n* نوبة مرضية [Nawbah maraḍeyah]
seldom ['sɛldəm] *adv* نادرا ما [Naderan ma]
select [sɪ'lɛkt] *v* يَتخّير [jataxajjaru]
selection [sɪ'lɛkʃən] *n* اصطفاء [isˤtˤifaːʔ]
self-assured ['sɛlfə'ʃʊəd] *adj* واثق بنفسه [Wathe'q benafseh]
self-catering ['sɛlfˌkeɪtərɪŋ] *n* خدمة ذاتية [Khedmah ḍateyah]
self-centred ['sɛlfˌsɛntəd] *adj* مُحِب لنفسه [Moḥeb le-nafseh]
self-conscious ['sɛlfˌkɒnʃəs] *adj* خجول [xaʒuːl]
self-contained ['sɛlfˌkən'teɪnd] *adj* متميز بضبط النفس [Motameyez beḍṭ al-nafs]
self-control ['sɛlfˌkən'trəʊl] *n* ضبط النفس [Ḍabṭ al-nafs]
self-defence ['sɛlfˌdɪ'fɛns] *n* الدفاع عن النفس [Al-defaa'a 'aan al-nafs]
self-discipline ['sɛlfˌdɪsɪplɪn] *n* ضبط النفس [Ḍabṭ al-nafs]
self-employed ['sɛlɪm'plɔɪd] *adj* حُر المهنة [Ḥor al-mehnah]
selfish ['sɛlfɪʃ] *adj* أناني [ʔanaːnij]
self-service ['sɛlfˌsɜːvɪs] *adj* خدمة ذاتية [Khedmah ḍateyah]
sell [sɛl] *v* يَبْيع [jabiːʕu]; **sell-by date** *n* تاريخ انتهاء الصلاحية [Tareekh enthaa al-ṣalaḥeyah]; **selling price** *n* سعر البيع [Se'ar al-bay'a]
sell off [sɛl ɒf] *v* يَبْيع بالتصفية [Yabea'a bel-taṣfeyah]
Sellotape® ['sɛləˌteɪp] *n* شريط لاصق [Shreeṭ laṣe'q]
sell out [sɛl aʊt] *v* يَبْيع المخزون [Yabea'a al-makhzoon]
semester [sɪ'mɛstə] *n* فصل دراسي [Faṣl derasey]
semi ['sɛmɪ] *n* شبه [ʃibhu]
semicircle ['sɛmɪˌsɜːkᵊl] *n* نصف دائرة [Neṣf daaeyrah]
semicolon [ˌsɛmɪ'kəʊlən] *n* فصلة منقوطة [faṣelah man'qoṭa]
semifinal [ˌsɛmɪ'faɪnᵊl] *n* مباراة شبه نهائية [Mobarah shebh nehaeyah]
send [sɛnd] *v* يبْعَث ب [Yab'ath be]
send back [sɛnd bæk] *v* يُرْجِع [jurʒiʕu]
sender ['sɛndə] *n* مُرسِل [mursil]
send off [sɛnd ɒf] *v* يَطلُب الإرسال بالبريد [jatˤlubu alʔirsaːla bilbariːdi]
send out [sɛnd aʊt] *v* يَبعث ب [Tab'aath be]
Senegal [ˌsɛnɪ'gɔːl] *n* السنغال [as-siniɣaːlu]
Senegalese [ˌsɛnɪgə'liːz] *adj* سِنغالي [siniɣaːlij] ▷ *n* سنغالي [siniɣaːlij]
senior ['siːnjə] *adj* الأعلى مقاماً [Al a'ala ma'qaman]; **senior citizen** *n* شخص متقدم العمر [Shakhṣ mota'qadem al-'aomr]
sensational [sɛn'seɪʃənᵊl] *adj* مُثِير [muθiːr]
sense [sɛns] *n* حاسة [ħaːssa]; **sense of humour** *n* حس الفكاهة [Ḥes al-fokahah]
senseless ['sɛnslɪs] *adj* عديم الاحساس ['adeem al-ehsas]
sensible ['sɛnsɪbᵊl] *adj* محسوس [maħsuːs]
sensitive ['sɛnsɪtɪv] *adj* حساس [ħassaːs]
sensuous ['sɛnsjʊəs] *adj* حسي [ħissij]
sentence ['sɛntəns] *n* *(punishment)* حُكم [ħukm], *(words)* جملة [ʒumla] ▷ *v* يَحْكُم على [Yaḥkom 'ala]
sentimental [ˌsɛntɪ'mɛntᵊl] *adj* حساس [ħassaːs]
separate *adj* ['sɛpərɪt] منفصل [munfasˤil] ▷ *v* ['sɛpəˌreɪt] يُفَرق [jufarriqu]
separately ['sɛpərətlɪ] *adv* بصورة منفصلة [Beṣorah monfaṣelah]
separation [ˌsɛpə'reɪʃən] *n* انفصال [infisˤaːl]
September [sɛp'tɛmbə] *n* سبتمبر

[sibtumbar]
sequel ['siːkwəl] *n* نتيجة [natiːʒa]
sequence ['siːkwəns] *n* تسلسل [tasalsul]
Serbia ['sɜːbɪə] *n* الصرب [asˤ-sˤirbu]
Serbian ['sɜːbɪən] *adj* صربي [sˤirbij] ▷ *n* *(language)* اللغة الصربية [Al-loghah al-ṣerbeyah], *(person)* صربي [sˤirbij]
sergeant ['sɑːdʒənt] *n* ضابط رَقيب [Ḍabeṭ ra'qeeb]
serial ['sɪərɪəl] *n* حلقة مسلسلة [Ḥala'qah mosalsalah]
series ['sɪəriːz; -rɪz] *n* متتالية [mutataːlijja]
serious ['sɪərɪəs] *adj* جاد [ʒaːdd]
seriously ['sɪərɪəslɪ] *adv* جدياً [ʒiddiːan]
sermon ['sɜːmən] *n* موعظة [mawʕizˤa]
servant ['sɜːvᵊnt] *n* موظف حكومي [mowaḍhaf ḥokomey]; **civil servant** *n* موظف حكومة [mowaḍhaf hokomah]
serve [sɜːv] *n* مدة خدمة [Modat khedmah] ▷ *v* يَخدِم [jaxdimu]
server ['sɜːvə] *n (computer)* جهاز السيرفر [Jehaz al-servo], *(person)* خادم [xaːdim]
service ['sɜːvɪs] *n* خدمة [xidma] ▷ *v* يُزَوِد [juzawwidu]; **room service** *n* خدمة الغرف [Khedmat al-ghoraf]; **secret service** *n* خدمة سرية [Khedmah serreyah]; **service area** *n* منطقة تقديم الخدمات [Menta'qat ta'qdeem al- khadamat]; **service charge** *n* رَسْم الخدمة [Rasm al-khedmah]; **service station** *n* محطة الخدمة [Mahaṭat al-khedmah]; **social services** *npl* خدمات اجتماعية [Khadamat ejtem'aeyah]; **I want to complain about the service** أريد في تقديم شكاوى بشأن الخدمة [areed ta'q-deem shakawee be-shan al-khedma]; **Is service included?** هل الفاتورة شاملة الخدمة؟ [hal al-fatoora shamelat al-khidma?]; **Is there a charge for the service?** هل هناك مصاريف للحصول على الخدمة؟ [Hal honak maṣareef lel-ḥoṣol ala al-khedmah]; **Is there room service?** هل هناك خدمة للغرفة؟ [hal hunaka khidma lil-ghurfa?]; **The service was terrible** كانت الخدمة سيئة للغاية [kanat il-khidma say-ia el-ghaya]
serviceman, servicemen ['sɜːvɪsˌmæn; -mən, 'sɜːvɪsˌmɛn] *n* جندي [ʒundij]
servicewoman, servicewomen ['sɜːvɪsˌwʊmən, 'sɜːvɪsˌwɪmɪn] *n* امرأة ملتحقة بالقوات المسلحة [Emraah moltahe'qah bel-'qwat al-mosallaha]
serviette [ˌsɜːvɪ'ɛt] *n* منديل المائدة [Mandeel al-maaedah]
session ['sɛʃən] *n* جلسة [ʒalsa]
set [sɛt] *n* مجموعة كتب [Majmo'aat kotob] ▷ *v* يهيئ [juhajjiʔ]
setback ['sɛtbæk] *n* توقف [tawaqquf]
set menu [sɛt 'mɛnjuː] *n* قائمة مجموعات الأغذية ['qaemat majmo'aat al-oghneyah]
set off [sɛt ɒf] *v* يَبْدأ الرِّحْلَه [jabdaʔu arriħlata]
set out [sɛt aʊt] *v* يَعْرِض [jaʕridˤu]
settee [sɛ'tiː] *n* أريكة [ʔriːka]
settle ['sɛtᵊl] *v* يرسخ [jurassixu]
settle down ['sɛtᵊl daʊn] *v* يستقر [jastaqirru]
seven ['sɛvᵊn] *number* سبعة [sabʕatun]
seventeen ['sɛvᵊn'tiːn] *number* سبعة عشر [sabʕata ʕaʃara]
seventeenth ['sɛvᵊn'tiːnθ; 'seventeen'th] *adj* سابع عشر [saːbiʕa ʕaʃara]
seventh ['sɛvᵊnθ] *adj* سابع [saːbiʕu] ▷ *n* السابع [as-saːbiʕu]
seventy ['sɛvᵊntɪ] *number* سبعين [sabʕiːna]
several ['sɛvrəl] *adj* عديد [ʕadiːd] ▷ *pron* عِدَّة
sew [səʊ] *v* يُخِيط [juxiːtˤu]
sewer ['suːə] *n* بالوعة [baːluːʕa]
sewing ['səʊɪŋ] *n* خِيَاطة [xajaːtˤa]; **sewing machine** *n* ماكينة خياطة [Makenat kheyaṭah]
sew up [səʊ ʌp] *v* يُخيط تماما [Yokhayeṭ tamaman]
sex [sɛks] *n* جِنس [ʒins]

sexism ['sɛksɪzəm] *n* التفرقة العنصرية بحسب الجنس [Al-tafre'qa al'aonṣoreyah beḥasab al-jens]
sexist ['sɛksɪst] *adj* مؤيد للتفرقة العنصرية بحسب الجنس [Moaed lel-tare'qa al'aonṣeryah behasb aljens]
sexual ['sɛksjʊəl] *adj* جنسي [ʒinsij]; **sexual intercourse** *n* جماع [ʒima:ʕun]
sexuality [ˌsɛksjʊ'ælɪtɪ; ˌsexu'ality] *n* مَيْل جنسي [Mayl jensey]
sexy ['sɛksɪ] *adj* مثير جنسيا [Motheer jensyan]
shabby ['ʃæbɪ] *adj* بال [ba:lin]
shade [ʃeɪd] *n* ظل [zˤill]
shadow ['ʃædəʊ] *n* ظِل [zˤill]; **eye shadow** *n* ظل العيون [dhel al-'aoyoon]
shake [ʃeɪk] *vi* يَهتَز [jahtazzu] ▷ *vt* يَهُز [jahuzzu]
shaken ['ʃeɪkən] *adj* مهزوز [mahzu:zz]
shaky ['ʃeɪkɪ] *adj* متقلقل [mutaqalqil]
shallow ['ʃæləʊ] *adj* ضحل [dˤaħl]
shambles ['ʃæmbᵊlz] *npl* مجزر [maʒzarun]
shame [ʃeɪm] *n* خزي [xizj]
shampoo [ʃæm'pu:] *n* شامبو [ʃa:mbu:]; **Do you sell shampoo?** هل تبيع شامبوهات [hal tabee'a shambo-haat?]
shape [ʃeɪp] *n* مَظْهَر [mazˤhar]
share [ʃɛə] *n* سهم مالي [Sahm maley] ▷ *v* يُشارِك [juʃa:riku]
shareholder ['ʃɛəˌhəʊldə] *n* حامل أسهم [Hamel ashom]
share out [ʃɛə aʊt] *v* يُقَسِم [juqassimu]
shark [ʃɑ:k] *n* (سمك) سمك القرش [Samak al-'qersh]
sharp [ʃɑ:p] *adj* حاد [ħa:dd]
shave [ʃeɪv] *v* يَحْلِق [jaħliqu]; **shaving cream** *n* كريم الحلاقة [Kereem al-helaka]; **shaving foam** *n* رغوة الحلاقة [Raghwat ḥela'qah]
shaver ['ʃeɪvə] *n* ماكينة حِلاقَة [Makenat ḥela'qa]
shawl [ʃɔ:l] *n* شال [ʃa:l]
she [ʃi:] *pron* هي
shed [ʃɛd] *n* غُرفة خشبية [Ghorfah khashabeyah]
sheep [ʃi:p] *n* نعجة [naʕʒa]
sheepdog ['ʃi:pˌdɒg] *n* كلب الراعي [Kalb al-ra'aey]
sheepskin ['ʃi:pˌskɪn] *n* جلد الغنم [Jeld al-ghanam]
sheer [ʃɪə] *adj* مُطْلَق [mutˤlaq]
sheet [ʃi:t] *n* ملاءة [malla:ʔa]; **balance sheet** *n* ميزانية [mi:za:nijjatun]; **fitted sheet** *n* ملاءة مثبتة [Melaah mothabatah]
shelf, shelves [ʃɛlf, ʃɛlvz] *n* رَف [raff]
shell [ʃɛl] *n* محارة [maħa:ra]; **shell suit** *n* زي رياضي [Zey reyaḍey]
shellfish ['ʃɛlˌfɪʃ] *n* محار [maħa:r]; **I'm allergic to shellfish** عندي حساسية من المحار ['aendy ḥasas-eyah min al-maḥar]
shelter ['ʃɛltə] *n* ملتجأ [multaʒa]
shepherd ['ʃɛpəd] *n* راعي [ra:ʕi:]
sherry ['ʃɛrɪ] *n* خَمْر الشِري [Khamr alsherey]
shield [ʃi:ld] *n* حجاب واق [Hejab wa'q]
shift [ʃɪft] *n* تَغَيُر [taɣajjur] ▷ *v* يحول [juħawwilu]
shifty ['ʃɪftɪ] *adj* واسع الحيلة [Wase'a al-ḥeelah]
Shiite ['ʃi:aɪt] *adj* شيعي [ʃi:ʕij]
shin [ʃɪn] *n* قَصَبة الرِجْل ['qaṣabat al-rejl]
shine [ʃaɪn] *v* يَلْمَع [jalmaʕu]
shiny ['ʃaɪnɪ] *adj* لامع [la:miʕ]
ship [ʃɪp] *n* سَفينة [safi:na]
shipbuilding ['ʃɪpˌbɪldɪŋ] *n* بناء السفن [Benaa al-sofon]
shipment ['ʃɪpmənt] *n* شَحنة [ʃaxna]
shipwreck ['ʃɪpˌrɛk] *n* حطام السفينة [Hoṭam al-safeenah]
shipwrecked ['ʃɪpˌrɛkt] *adj* سفينة محطمة [Safeenah mohaṭamah]
shipyard ['ʃɪpˌjɑ:d] *n* تِرْسَانة السُفن [Yarsanat al-sofon]
shirt [ʃɜ:t] *n* قميص [qami:sˤ]; **polo shirt** *n* قميص بولو ['qameeṣ bolo]
shiver ['ʃɪvə] *v* يَرتعِش [jartaʕiʃu]
shock [ʃɒk] *n* صَدْمَة [sˤadma] ▷ *v* يَصْدِم [jasˤdimu]; **electric shock** *n* صَدْمَة كهربائية [Ṣadmah kahrbaeyah]
shocking ['ʃɒkɪŋ] *adj* مصدم [musˤdim]

shoe [ʃuː] *n* حذاء [ħiðaːʔ]; **shoe polish** *n* ورنيش الأحذية [Warneesh al-aḥdheyah]; **shoe shop** *n* محل أحذية [Maḥal aḥdheyah]; **Can you re-heel these shoes?** هل يمكن إعادة تركيب كعب لهذا الحذاء؟ [hal yamken e'aa-dat tarkeeb ka'ab le-hadha al-ḥedhaa?]; **Can you repair these shoes?** هل يمكن تصليح هذا الحذاء؟ [hal yamken taṣleeḥ hadha al-ḥedhaa?]
shoelace ['ʃuːˌleɪs] *n* رباط الحذاء [Rebaṭ al-hedhaa]
shoot [ʃuːt] *v* يُطْلِق [jutˤliqu]
shooting ['ʃuːtɪŋ] *n* إطلاق النار [Eṭla'q al nar]
shop [ʃɒp] *n* محل [maħall]; **antique shop** *n* متجر المقتنيات القديمة [Matjar al-mo'qtanayat al-'qadeemah]; **gift shop** *n* متجر هدايا [Matjar hadaya]; **shop assistant** *n* مساعد في متجر [Mosa'aed fee matjar]; **shop window** *n* واجهة العرض في المتجر [Wagehat al-'aarḍ fee al-matjar]; **What time do the shops close?** ما هو موعد إغلاق المحلات التجارية؟ [ma howa maw-'aid eghla'q al-maḥalat al-tejar-iya?]
shopkeeper ['ʃɒpˌkiːpə] *n* صاحب المتجر [Ṣaheb al-matjar]
shoplifting ['ʃɒpˌlɪftɪŋ; 'shopˌlifting] *n* سرقة السلع من المَتَاجِر [Sare'qat al-sela'a men al-matajer]
shopping ['ʃɒpɪŋ] *n* تسوق [tasawwuq]; **shopping bag** *n* كيس التسوق [Kees al-tasawo'q]; **shopping centre** *n* مركز تسوق [Markaz tasawe'q]; **shopping trolley** *n* ترولي التسوق [Trolley altasaw'q]
shore [ʃɔː] *n* ساحل [saːħil]
short [ʃɔːt] *adj* قصير [qasˤiːr]; **short story** *n* قصة قصيرة ['qeṣah 'qaṣeerah]
shortage ['ʃɔːtɪdʒ] *n* عجز [ʕaʒz]
shortcoming ['ʃɔːtˌkʌmɪŋ] *n* موطن ضعف [Mawṭen ḍa'af]
shortcut ['ʃɔːtˌkʌt] *n* طريق مختصر [ṭaree'q mokhtaṣar]
shortfall ['ʃɔːtˌfɔːl] *n* قلة [qilla]
shorthand ['ʃɔːtˌhænd] *n* اختزال [ixtizaːl]
shortlist ['ʃɔːtˌlɪst] *n* قائمة مرشحين ['qaemat morashaḥeen]
shortly ['ʃɔːtlɪ] *adv* قريباً [qariːban]
shorts [ʃɔːts] *npl* شورت [ʃuːrt]
short-sighted ['ʃɔːt'saɪtɪd] *adj* قصير النظر ['qaṣeer al-naḍhar]
short-sleeved ['ʃɔːtˌsliːvd] *adj* قصير الأكمام ['qaṣeer al-akmam]
shot [ʃɒt] *n* حقنة [ħuqna]; **I need a tetanus shot** أحتاج إلى حقنة تيتانوس [aḥtaaj ela ḥe'qnat tetanus]
shotgun ['ʃɒtˌgʌn] *n* بندقية رش [Bonde'qyat rash]
shoulder ['ʃəʊldə] *n* كتف [katif]; **hard shoulder** *n* كتف طريق صلب [Katef ṭaree'q ṣalb]; **shoulder blade** *n* لَوْح الكَتِف [Looh al-katef]; **I've hurt my shoulder** لقد أصبت في كتفي [la'qad oṣibto fee katfee]
shout [ʃaʊt] *n* صيحة [sˤajħa] ▷ *v* يصيح [jasˤiːħu]
shovel ['ʃʌvᵊl] *n* جاروف [ʒaːruːf]
show [ʃəʊ] *n* معرض [maʕridˤ] ▷ *v* يَعْرِض [jaʕridˤu]; **show business** *n* مجال الاستعراض [Majal al-este'araḍ]
shower ['ʃaʊə] *n* دُش [duʃʃ]; **shower cap** *n* غطاء الشعر للاستحمام [ghetaa al-sha'ar lel-estehmam]; **shower gel** *n* جل الاستحمام [Jel al-estehmam]
showerproof ['ʃaʊəˌpruːf] *adj* مقاوم للبلل [Mo'qawem lel-balal]
showing ['ʃəʊɪŋ] *n* مظهر [mazˤhar]
show off [ʃəʊ ɒf] *v* يَسعَى للفت الأنظار [Yas'aa lelaft alanḍhaar]
show-off [ʃəʊɒf] *n* المتفاخر [almutafaːxiru]
show up [ʃəʊ ʌp] *v* يَظْهر [jazˤharu]
shriek [ʃriːk] *v* يصرخ [jasˤruxu]
shrimp [ʃrɪmp] *n* جمبري [ʒambarij]
shrine [ʃraɪn] *n* ضريح [dˤariːħ]
shrink [ʃrɪŋk] *v* يَتقلَص [jataqallasˤu]
shrub [ʃrʌb] *n* شُجَيرة [ʃuʒajra]
shrug [ʃrʌg] *v* يهز كتفيه [Yahoz katefayh]
shrunk [ʃrʌŋk] *adj* متقلص [mutaqallisˤ]

shudder [ˈʃʌdə] *v* يَنتفض [jantafidˤu]
shuffle [ˈʃʌfᵊl] *v* يُلَخْبط [julaxbitˤu]
shut [ʃʌt] *v* يُغلِق [juɣliqu]
shut down [ʃʌt daʊn] *v* يَقْفِل [jaqfilu]
shutters [ˈʃʌtəz] *n* مصراع النافذة [meṣraa'a alnafedhah]
shuttle [ˈʃʌtᵊl] *n* مكوك [makku:k]
shuttlecock [ˈʃʌtᵊlˌkɒk] *n* كُرَة الريشة [Korat al-reeshaa]
shut up [ʃʌt ʌp] *v* يَسكُت [jaskutu]
shy [ʃaɪ] *adj* متحفظ [mutaħaffizˤ]
Siberia [saɪˈbɪərɪə] *n* سيبيريا [si:bi:rja:]
siblings [ˈsɪblɪŋz] *npl* أشقاء [ʔaʃʃiqa:ʔun]
sick [sɪk] *adj* عليل [ʕali:l]; **sick leave** *n* أجازة مَرضِيَّة [Ajaza maraḍeyah]; **sick note** *n* إذْن غياب مرضي [edhn gheyab maraḍey]; **sick pay** *n* الأجر المدفوع خلال الأجازة المرضية [Al-'ajr al-madfoo'a khelal al-'ajaza al-maraḍeyah]
sickening [ˈsɪkənɪŋ] *adj* مُمْرِض [mumridˤ]
sickness [ˈsɪknɪs] *n* سقم [saqam]; **morning sickness** *n* غثيان الصباح [Ghathayan al-ṣabaḥ]; **travel sickness** *n* دُوار السفر [Dowar al-safar]
side [saɪd] *n* جانب [ʒa:nib]; **side effect** *n* آثار جانبية [Aathar janeebyah]; **side street** *n* شارع جانبي [Share'a janebey]
sideboard [ˈsaɪdˌbɔːd] *n* بُوفيه [bu:fi:h]
sidelight [ˈsaɪdˌlaɪt] *n* ضوء جانبي [Ḍowa janebey]
sideways [ˈsaɪdˌweɪz] *adv* من الجنب [Men al-janb]
sieve [sɪv] *n* منخُل [manxal]
sigh [saɪ] *n* تنهيدة [tanhi:da] ▷ *v* يَتنهَد [jatanahhadu]
sight [saɪt] *n* رؤية [ruja]
sightseeing [ˈsaɪtˌsiːɪŋ] *n* زيارة المعالم السياحية [Zeyarat al-ma'aalem al-seyahyah]
sign [saɪn] *n* لافتة [la:fita] ▷ *v* يُوقِع [juwaqiʕu]; **road sign** *n* لافتة طريق [Lafetat ṭaree'q]; **sign language** *n* لغة الإشارة [Loghat al-esharah]
signal [ˈsɪɡnᵊl] *n* إشارة [ʔiʃa:ra] ▷ *v* يُومئ [ju:miʔu]; **busy signal** *n* إشارة إنشغال الخط [Esharat ensheghal al-khat]
signature [ˈsɪɡnɪtʃə] *n* توقيع [tawqi:ʕ]
significance [sɪɡˈnɪfɪkəns] *n* دِلالة [dala:la]
significant [sɪɡˈnɪfɪkənt] *adj* هام [ha:mm]
sign on [saɪn ɒn] *v* يَبْدأ التسجيل [jabdaʔu attasʒi:la]
signpost [ˈsaɪnˌpəʊst] *n* عمود الإشارة ['amood al-esharah]
Sikh [siːk] *adj* تابع للديانة السِيخِية [Tabe'a lel-zobabah al-sekheyah] ▷ *n* السيخي [assi:xijju]
silence [ˈsaɪləns] *n* صَمْت [sˤamt]
silencer [ˈsaɪlənsə] *n* كاتم للصوت [Katem lel-ṣawt]
silent [ˈsaɪlənt] *adj* صامت [sˤa:mit]
silk [sɪlk] *n* حرير [ħari:r]
silly [ˈsɪlɪ] *adj* أبْلَه [ʔablah]
silver [ˈsɪlvə] *n* فضة [fidˤdˤa]
similar [ˈsɪmɪlə] *adj* مماثل [muma:θil]
similarity [ˈsɪmɪˈlærɪtɪ] *n* تَشابُه [taʃa:buh]
simmer [ˈsɪmə] *v* يَغْلي برفق [Yaghley beref'q]
simple [ˈsɪmpᵊl] *adj* بسيط [basi:tˤ]
simplify [ˈsɪmplɪˌfaɪ] *v* يُبَسِط [jubassitˤu]
simply [ˈsɪmplɪ] *adv* ببساطة [Bebasata]
simultaneous [ˌsɪməlˈteɪnɪəs; ˌsaɪməlˈteɪnɪəs] *adj* متزامن [mutaza:min]
simultaneously [ˌsɪməlˈteɪnɪəslɪ] *adv* فوري [fawrijjun]
sin [sɪn] *n* خطيئة [xatˤi:ʔa]
since [sɪns] *adv* قديماً [qadi:man] ▷ *conj* منذ [Monz] ▷ *prep* مُنْذُ; **I've been sick since Monday** منذ يوم الاثنين وأنا أعاني من المرض [mundho yawm al-ithnayn wa ana o'aany min al-maraḍ]
sincere [sɪnˈsɪə] *adj* مُخْلِص [muxlisˤ]
sincerely [sɪnˈsɪəlɪ] *adv* بإخلاص [biʔixlasˤin]
sing [sɪŋ] *v* يُغَنِّي [juɣanni:]
singer [ˈsɪŋə] *n* مغني [muɣanni:]; **lead singer** *n* مُغَنّي حفلات [Moghaney ḥafalat]

singing ['sɪŋɪŋ] *n* غناء [ɣina:ʔ]
single ['sɪŋgᵊl] *adj* أعزب [ʔaʕzab] ▷ *n* فرد [fard]; **single bed** *n* سَرير فردي [Sareer fardey]; **single parent** *n* أحد الوالدين [Aḥad al-waledayn]; **single room** *n* غرفة لشخص واحد [ghorfah le-shakhṣ wahed]; **single ticket** *n* تذكرة فردية [tadhkarat fardeyah]; **I want to reserve a single room** أريد حجز غرفة لفرد واحد [areed ḥajiz ghurfa le-fard waḥid]
singles ['sɪŋgᵊlz] *npl* مباراة فردية [Mobarah fardeyah]
singular ['sɪŋgjʊlə] *n* مفرد [mufrad]
sinister ['sɪnɪstə] *adj* مَشْئوم [maʃʔwm]
sink [sɪŋk] *n* بالوعة [ba:lu:ʕa] ▷ *v* يغرق [jaɣraqu]
sinus ['saɪnəs] *n* تجويف [taʒwi:f]
sir [sɜː] *n* سيدي [sajjidi:]
siren ['saɪərən] *n* صَفَّارَة إنْذار [Ṣafarat enḍhar]
sister ['sɪstə] *n* أخت [ʔuxt]
sister-in-law ['sɪstə ɪn lɔː] *n* أخت الزوجة [Okht alzawjah]
sit [sɪt] *v* يَقْعُد [jaqʕudu]
sitcom ['sɪtˌkɒm] *n* كوميديا الموقف [Komedya al-maw'qf]
sit down [sɪt daʊn] *v* يَجْلِس [jaʒlisu]
site [saɪt] *n* موقع [mawqiʕ]; **building site** *n* موقع البناء [Maw'qe'a al-benaa]; **caravan site** *n* موقع المَقْطورَة [Maw'qe'a al-ma'qṭorah]
situated ['sɪtjʊˌeɪtɪd] *adj* كائن [ka:ʔin]
situation [ˌsɪtjʊ'eɪʃən] *n* وضع [wadˤʕ]
six [sɪks] *number* ستة [sittatun]
sixteen ['sɪks'tiːn] *number* ستة عشر [sittata ʕaʃara]
sixteenth ['sɪks'tiːnθ; 'six'teenth] *adj* السادس عشر [assa:disa ʕaʃara]
sixth [sɪksθ] *adj* السادس [as-sa:disu]
sixty ['sɪkstɪ] *number* ستون [sittu:na]
size [saɪz] *n* حجم [ħaʒm]
skate [skeɪt] *v* يَتَزلج [jatazallaʒu]
skateboard ['skeɪtˌbɔːd] *n* لوح التزلج [Lawh al-tazalloj]; **I'd like to go skateboarding** أريد ممارسة رياضة التزلج على لوح التزلج [areed mu-ma-rasat reyaḍat al-tazal-oj 'aala lawḥ al-tazal-oj]
skateboarding ['skeɪtˌbɔːdɪŋ] *n* تَزَلُج على اللوح [Tazaloj 'ala al-looh]
skates [skeɪts] *npl* زلاجات [zala:ʒa:tun]
skating ['skeɪtɪŋ] *n* تَزَلُج [tazaluʒ]; **skating rink** *n* حلبة تَزَلُج [Ḥalabat tazaloj]
skeleton ['skɛlɪtən] *n* هيكل عظمي [Haykal adḥmey]
sketch [skɛtʃ] *n* مُخَطَط [muxatˤtˤatˤ] ▷ *v* يُخَطِّط بدون تَفاصيل [Yokhaṭeṭ bedon tafaṣeel]
skewer ['skjʊə] *n* سيخ [si:x]
ski [skiː] *n* زلاجة [zala:ʒa] ▷ *v* يَتَزحلق على الثلج [Yatazahal'q ala al-thalj]; **ski lift** *n* مِصْعَد التَّزَلّج [Meṣ'aad al-tazalog]; **ski pass** *n* ممر التزحلق [Mamar al-tazahlo'q]; **I want to hire cross-country skis** أريد أن أؤجر زلاجة لمسافات طويلة; **I want to hire downhill skis** أريد أن أؤجر زلاجة لهبوط التل [areed an o-ajer zalaja le-hoboṭ al-tal]; **I want to hire skis** أريد أن أؤجر زلاجة [areed an o-ajer zalaja]
skid [skɪd] *v* يَنْزَلق [janzaliqu]
skier ['skiːə] *n* مُتَزَلِّج [mutazalliʒ]
skiing ['skiːɪŋ] *n* تَزْلُج [tazzaluʒ]
skilful ['skɪlfʊl] *adj* بارع [ba:riʕ]
skill [skɪl] *n* مهارة [maha:ra]
skilled [skɪld] *adj* ماهر [ma:hir]
skimpy ['skɪmpɪ] *adj* هزيل [hazi:l]
skin [skɪn] *n* جلد [ʒildu]
skinhead ['skɪnˌhɛd] *n* حليق الرأس [Halee'q al-raas]
skinny ['skɪnɪ] *adj* هزيل الجسم [Hazeel al-jesm]
skin-tight ['skɪn'taɪt] *adj* ضيق جدا [Ḍaye'q jedan]
skip [skɪp] *v* يَتخطى [jataxatˤtˤa:]
skirt [skɜːt] *n* جونلة [ʒawnala]
skive [skaɪv] *v* يَتَكاسَل [jataka:salu]
skull [skʌl] *n* جمجمة [ʒumʒuma]
sky [skaɪ] *n* سماء [sama:ʔ]
skyscraper ['skaɪˌskreɪpə] *n* ناطحة سحاب [Naṭehat saḥab]
slack [slæk] *adj* متوان [mitwa:n]

slam [slæm] *v* يُغْلِق الباب [Yoghle'q albab]
slang [slæŋ] *n* عامِّية [ʕa:mmija]
slap [slæp] *v* يُهْين [juhi:nu]يَصْفَع , [jasˤfaʕu]
slash [slæʃ] *n*; **forward slash** *n* شرطة مائلة للأمام [Sharṭah maelah lel-amam]
slate [sleɪt] *n* اردواز [ardwa:z]
slave [sleɪv] *n* عبد [ʕabd] ▷ *v* يَستعبد [jasataʕbidu]
sledge [slɛdʒ] *n* مزلجة [mizlaʒa]
sledging ['slɛdʒɪŋ] *n* تَزَلُّج [tazaluʒ]
sleep [sli:p] *n* نوم [nawm] ▷ *v* ينام [jana:mu]; **sleeping bag** *n* كيس النوم [Kees al-nawm]; **sleeping car** *n* عربة النوم ['arabat al-nawm]; **sleeping pill** *n* حبة نوم [Habit nawm]; **I can't sleep** لا أستطيع النوم [la asta-ṯee'a al-nawm]; **I can't sleep for the heat** لا يمكنني النوم بسبب حرارة الغرفة [la yam-kinuni al-nawm be-sabab ḥararat al-ghurfa]; **I can't sleep for the noise** لا استطيع النوم بسبب الضوضاء [la asta-ṭee'a al-nawm besa-bab al-ḍawḍaa]
sleeper ['sli:pə] *n*; **Can I reserve a sleeper?** هل يمكن أن أحجز عربة للنوم؟ [hal yamken an aḥjiz 'aaraba lel-nawm?]; **I want to book a sleeper to...** أريد حجز عربة للنوم بالقطار المتجه إلى... [ʔuri:du ħaʒza ʕarabata linnawmi bilqitˤa:ri almuttaʒihi ʔila]
sleep in [sli:p ɪn] *v* يتأخر في النوم في الصباح [Yataakhar fee al-nawm fee al-ṣabah]
sleepwalk ['sli:p,wɔ:k] *v* يَمشي أثناء نومه [Yamshee athnaa nawmeh]
sleepy ['sli:pɪ] *adj* نعسان [naʕsa:n]
sleet [sli:t] *n* مطر متجمد [Maṭar motajamed] ▷ *v* تمطر مطرا متجمدا [Tomṭer maṭran motajamedan]
sleeve [sli:v] *n* كم [kumm]
sleeveless ['sli:vlɪs] *adj* بدون أكمام [Bedon akmaam]
slender ['slɛndə] *adj* رفيع [rafi:ʕ]
slice [slaɪs] *n* شَريحة [ʃari:ħa] ▷ *v* يُقَطِّع إلى شرائح [Yo'qaṭe'a ela shraeḥ]
slick [slɪk] *n*; **oil slick** *n* طبقة زيت طافية على الماء [Ṭaba'qat zayt ṭafeyah alaa alma]
slide [slaɪd] *n* زِلاقَةٌ [zalla:qa] ▷ *v* ينزلق [janzaliqu]
slight [slaɪt] *adj* طفيف [tˤafi:f]
slightly ['slaɪtlɪ] *adv* بدرجة طفيفة [Bedarajah ṭafeefah]
slim [slɪm] *adj* نحيف [naħi:f]
sling [slɪŋ] *n* حَمَّالة [ħamma:la]
slip [slɪp] *n (mistake)* هفوة [hafwa], *(paper)* قصاصة [qusˤa:sˤa], *(underwear)* قميص تحتي ['qameeṣ taḥtey] ▷ *v* يَزِّل [jazillu]; **slip road** *n* طريق متصل بطريق سريع للسيارات أو منفصل عنه [ṭaree'q mataṣel be- ṭaree'q sarea'a lel-sayaraat aw monfaṣel 'anho]; **slipped disc** *n* إنزلاق غضروفي [Enzela'q ghodrofey]
slipper ['slɪpə] *n* شبشب حمام [Shebsheb ḥamam]
slippery ['slɪpərɪ; -prɪ] *adj* زَلق [zalaqa]
slip up [slɪp ʌp] *v* يَرْتَكِبُ خطأً [Yartekab khaṭaa]
slip-up [slɪpʌp] *n* خطأ [xatˤa]
slope [sləʊp] *n* منحدر [munħadir]; **nursery slope** *n* منحدر التزلج للمبتدئين [monḥadar al-tazaloj lel-mobtadeen]; **How difficult is this slope?** ما مدى صعوبة هذا المنحدر؟ [ma mada ṣo'aobat hatha al-mun-ḥadar?]; **Where are the beginners' slopes?** أين توجد منحدرات المبتدئين؟ [Ayn tojad monḥadrat al-mobtadean?]
sloppy ['slɒpɪ] *adj* قذر [qaðir]
slot [slɒt] *n* فَتْحة [fatħa]; **slot machine** *n* ماكينة الشقبية [Makenat al-sha'qabeyah]
Slovak ['sləʊvæk] *adj* سلوفاكي [slu:fa:kij] ▷ *n (language)* اللغة السلوفاكية [Al-logha al-slofakeyah], *(person)* مواطن سلوفاكي [Mowaṭen slofakey]
Slovakia [sləʊ'vækɪə] *n* سلوفاكيا [slu:fa:kija:]
Slovenia [sləʊ'vi:nɪə] *n* سلوفانيا [sluvi:f:nija:]
Slovenian [sləʊ'vi:nɪən] *adj* سلوفاني

[slu:fa:ni:] ▷ *n* *(language)* اللغة السلوفانية [Al-logha al-slofaneyah], *(person)* مواطن سلوفاني [Mowaṭen slofaney]
slow [sləʊ] *adj* بَطِيءٌ [batˁi:ʔ]
slow down [sləʊ daʊn] *v* يبُطئ [jubtˁiʔ]
slowly [sləʊlɪ] *adv* ببطء [Beboṭa]; **Could you speak more slowly, please?** هل يمكن أن تتحدث ببطء أكثر إذا سمحت؟ [hal yamken an tata-ḥadath be-buṭi akthar edha samaḥt?]
slug [slʌg] *n* يرقانة [jaraqa:na]
slum [slʌm] *n* حي الفقراء [Hay al-fo'qraa]
slush [slʌʃ] *n* طين رقيق القوام [Ṭeen ra'qee'q al'qawam]
sly [slaɪ] *adj* كتوم [katu:m]
smack [smæk] *v* يَصْفَع [jasˁfaʕu]
small [smɔ:l] *adj* صغير [sˁaɣi:r]; **small ads** *npl* إعلانات صغيرة [E'alanat ṣaghera]; **Do you have a small?** هل يوجد مقاسات صغيرة؟ [hal yujad ma'qaas-at ṣaghera?]; **It's too small** إنه صغير جدا [inaho ṣagheer jedan]; **The room is too small** الغرفة صغيرة جدا [al-ghurfa ṣagherah jedan]
smart [smɑ:t] *adj* ذكي [ðakij]; **smart phone** *n* هاتف ذكي [Hatef zaky]
smash [smæʃ] *v* يُهَشم [juhaʃʃimu]
smashing ['smæʃɪŋ] *adj* ساحِق [ṣa:ħiq]
smell [smɛl] *n* رائحة [ra:ʔiħa] ▷ *vi* يَبْعَثُ رائِحَةً [Yab'ath raeḥah] ▷ *vt* يَشم [jaʃummu]; **I can smell gas** أنني أشم رائحة غاز [ina-ny ashum ra-e-hat ghaaz]; **My room smells of smoke** هناك رائحة دخان بغرفتي [hunaka ra-eḥa dukhaan be-ghurfaty]; **There's a funny smell** توجد رائحة غريبة في الغرفة [toojad raeḥa ghareba fee al-ghurfa]
smelly ['smɛlɪ] *adj* كريه الرائحة [Kareeh al-raaehah]
smile [smaɪl] *n* ابتسامة [ʔibtisa:ma] ▷ *v* يبتسم [jabtasimu]
smiley ['smaɪlɪ] *n* (صورة الوجه المبتسم) سمايلي [(sˁu:ratu alwaʒhi almubtasimi) sma:jlijji]
smoke [sməʊk] *n* دخان [duxa:n] ▷ *v* يُدخِن [juðaxinu]; **smoke alarm** *n* كاشف الدُخان [Kashef al-dokhan]; **My room smells of smoke** هناك رائحة دخان بغرفتي [hunaka ra-eḥa dukhaan be-ghurfaty]
smoked ['sməʊkt] *adj* مُدَخِّنٌ [mudaxxin]
smoker ['sməʊkə] *n* مُدَخِن [muðaxxin]
smoking ['sməʊkɪŋ] *n* التدخين [Al-tadkheen]; **I'd like a no smoking room** أريد غرفة غير مسموح فيها بالتدخين [areed ghurfa ghyer masmooḥ feeha bil-tadkheen]; **I'd like a smoking room** أريد غرفة مسموح فيها بالتدخين [areed ghurfa masmooḥ feeha bil-tadkheen]
smoky ['sməʊkɪ] *adj*; **It's too smoky here** يوجد هنا الكثير من المدخنين [yujad huna al-kather min al-muda-khineen]
smooth [smu:ð] *adj* نعومة [nuʕu:mat]
SMS [ɛs ɛm ɛs] *n* خدمة الرسائل القصيرة [xidmatu arrasa:ʔili alqasˁi:rati]
smudge [smʌdʒ] *n* لَطْخَة [latˁxa]
smug [smʌg] *adj* مَزهُوٌّ بِنَفْسِه [Mazhowon benafseh]
smuggle ['smʌgᵊl] *v* يُهَرب [juharribu]
smuggler ['smʌglə] *n* مهرب بضائع [Moharreb badae'a]
smuggling ['smʌglɪŋ] *n* تهريب [tahri:bu]
snack [snæk] *n* وجبة خفيفة [Wajbah khafeefah]; **snack bar** *n* متجر الوجبات السريعة [Matjar al-wajabat al-sarey'aa]
snail [sneɪl] *n* حلزون [ħalazu:n]
snake [sneɪk] *n* ثعبان [θuʕba:n]
snap [snæp] *v* يَكْسِر [jaksiru]
snapshot ['snæp,ʃɒt] *n* لقطة فوتوغرافية [La'qṭah fotoghrafeyah]
snarl [snɑ:l] *v* يُشَابِك [juʃa:biku]
snatch [snætʃ] *v* يخْتَطِف [jixtatˁifu]
sneakers ['sni:kəz] *npl* زوج أحذية رياضية [Zawj ahzeyah Reyaḍeyah]
sneeze [sni:z] *v* يَعطس [jaʕtˁisu]
sniff [snɪf] *v* يَتنشَق [jatanaʃʃaqu]
snigger ['snɪgə] *v* يَضحَك ضحكاً نصف مكبوت [Yaḍḥak ḍeḥkan neṣf makboot]
snob [snɒb] *n* متكبر [mutakabbir]
snooker ['snu:kə] *n* لُعْبَةُ السُّنُوكِر [Lo'abat al-sonoker]
snooze [snu:z] *n* نومة خفيفة [Nomah

khafeefa] ▷ *v* يَغْفُو [jaɣfu]
snore [snɔː] *v* يَغُطْ في النوم [yaghoṭ fee al-nawm]
snorkel ['snɔːkᵊl] *n* سباحة تحت الماء [Sebaḥah taḥt al-maa]
snow [snəʊ] *n* ثلج [θalʒ] ▷ *v* تمطر ثلجا [Tomṭer thaljan]
snowball ['snəʊˌbɔːl] *n* كرة ثلج [Korat thalj]
snowboard ['snəʊˌbɔːd] *n*; **I want to hire a snowboard** أريد إيجار لوح تزلج [areed e-jar lawḥ tazaluj]
snowflake ['snəʊˌfleɪk] *n* كتلة ثلج رقيقة [Kotlat thalj ra'qee'qah]
snowman ['snəʊˌmæn] *n* رجل الثلج [Rajol al-thalj]
snowplough ['snəʊˌplaʊ] *n* محراث الثلج [Mehrath thalj]
snowstorm ['snəʊˌstɔːm] *n* عاصفة ثلجية ['aasefah thaljeyah]
so [səʊ] *adv* كذلك; **so (that)** *conj* وهكذا [wahakadha]
soak [səʊk] *v* ينقع [janqaʕu]
soaked [səʊkt] *adj* منقوع [manquːʕ]
soap [səʊp] *n* صابون [sˤaːbuːn]; **soap dish** *n* طبق صابون [Ṭaba'q ṣaboon]; **soap opera** *n* مسلسل درامي [Mosalsal deramey]; **soap powder** *n* مسحوق الصابون [Mashoo'q ṣaboon]; **There is no soap** لا يوجد صابون [la yujad ṣaboon]
sob [sɒb] *v* ينشج [janʃaʒʒu]
sober ['səʊbə] *adj* مقتصد [muqtasˤid]
sociable ['səʊʃəbᵊl] *adj* شخص اجتماعي [Shakhṣ ejtema'ay]
social ['səʊʃəl] *adj* اجتماعي [ʔiʒtimaːʕij]; **social security** *n* ضمان اجتماعي [Ḍaman ejtema'ay]; **social services** *npl* خدمات اجتماعية [Khadamat ejtem'aeyah]; **social worker** *n* أخصائي اجتماعي [Akhṣey ejtema'ay]
socialism ['səʊʃəˌlɪzəm] *n* اشتراكية [ʔiʃtiraːkijja]
socialist ['səʊʃəlɪst] *adj* اشتراكي [ʔiʃtiraːkij] ▷ *n* اشتراكي [ʔiʃtiraːkij]
society [sə'saɪətɪ] *n* مجتمع [muʒtamaʕ]
sociology [ˌsəʊsɪ'ɒlədʒɪ] *n* علم الاجتماع ['aelm al-ejtema'a]
sock [sɒk] *n* جورب قصير [Jawrab 'qaṣeer]
socket ['sɒkɪt] *n* مقبس [miqbas]; **Where is the socket for my electric razor?** أين المقبس الخاص بماكينة الحلاقة؟ [ayna al-ma'qbas al-khaaṣ be-makenat al-ḥelaa'qa?]
sofa ['səʊfə] *n* كَنَبَة [kanaba]; **sofa bed** *n* كنبة سرير [Kanabat sereer]
soft [sɒft] *adj* ناعم [naːʕim]; **soft drink** *n* مشروب غازي [Mashroob ghazey]
softener ['sɒfᵊnə; 'softener] *n*; **Do you have softener?** هل لديك مسحوق منعم للملابس؟ [hal ladyka mas-ḥoo'q mun-'aim lel-malabis?]
software ['sɒftˌwɛə] *n* برامج [baraːmiʒ]
soggy ['sɒgɪ] *adj* نَدِي [nadij]
soil [sɔɪl] *n* تربة [turba]
solar ['səʊlə] *adj* شمسي [ʃamsij]; **solar power** *n* طاقة شمسية [Ṭa'qah shamseyah]; **solar system** *n* نظام شمسي [neḍham shamsey]
soldier ['səʊldʒə] *n* جندي [ʒundij]
sold out [səʊld aʊt] *adj* مُبَاعٌ [mubaːʕ]
solicitor [sə'lɪsɪtə] *n* محامي ولاية [Moḥamey welayah]
solid ['sɒlɪd] *adj* صَلْب [sˤalb]
solo ['səʊləʊ] *n* عمل منفرد ['amal monfared]
soloist ['səʊləʊɪst] *n* مغني أو عازف منفرد [Moghaney aw 'aazef monfared]
soluble ['sɒljʊbᵊl] *adj* قابل للذوبان ['qabel lel-dhawaban]
solution [sə'luːʃən] *n* حل [ħall]; **cleansing solution for contact lenses** محلول مطهر للعدسات اللاصقة [maḥlool muṭaher lil-'aada-saat al-laṣi'qa]
solve [sɒlv] *v* يَحِل مشكلة [Taḥel al-moshkelah]
solvent ['sɒlvənt] *n* مذيب [muðiːb]
Somali [səʊ'mɑːlɪ] *adj* صومالي [sˤsˤuːmaːlij] ▷ *n (language)* اللغة الصومالية [Al-loghah al-Ṣomaleyah], *(person)* صومالي [sˤsˤuːmaːlij]
Somalia [səʊ'mɑːlɪə] *n* الصومال

[asˤ-sˤu:ma:lu]
some [sʌm; səm] *adj* بعض [baʕdˤu] ▷ *pron* البعض [Alba'aḍ]; **Could you lend me some money?** هل يمكن تسليفي بعض المال؟ [hal yamken tas-leefy ba'aḍ al-maal?]; **Here's some information about my company** تفضل بعض المعلومات المتعلقة بشركتي [tafaḍal ba'aḍ al-ma'a-lomaat al-muta'a-le'qa be-share-katy]; **There are some people injured** هناك بعض الأشخاص المصابين [hunaka ba'aḍ al-ash-khaaṣ al-muṣabeen]
somebody ['sʌmbədɪ] *pron* شخص ذو شأن [shakhṣdho shaan]
somehow ['sʌm,haʊ] *adv* بطريقة ما [ṭaree'qah ma]
someone ['sʌm,wʌn; -wən] *pron* شخص ما [Shakhṣ ma]
someplace ['sʌm,pleɪs] *adv* مكان ما [Makan ma]
something ['sʌmθɪŋ] *pron* شيء ما [Shaya ma]
sometime ['sʌm,taɪm] *adv* يوماً ما [Yawman ma]
sometimes ['sʌm,taɪmz] *adv* أحيانا [Aḥyanan]
somewhere ['sʌm,wɛə] *adv* مكان ما [Makan ma]
son [sʌn] *n* ابن [ʔibn]; **My son is lost** فقد ابني [fo'qeda ibny]; **My son is missing** إن ابني مفقود [enna ibny maf-'qood]
song [sɒŋ] *n* أغْنِيَّة [ʔuɣnijja]
son-in-law [sʌn ɪn lɔː] **(***pl* **sons-in-law)** *n* زوج الإبنة [Zawj al-ebnah]
soon [suːn] *adv* قريباً [qari:ban]
sooner ['suːnə] *adv* عاجلا [ʕa:ʒila:]
soot [sʊt] *n* سُخام [suxa:m]
sophisticated [sə'fɪstɪ,keɪtɪd] *adj* متكلف [mutakallif]
soppy ['sɒpɪ] *adj* مشبع بالماء [Moshaba'a bel-maa]
soprano [sə'prɑːnəʊ] *n* صوت السوبرانو [Ṣondok alsobrano]
sorbet ['sɔːbeɪ; -bɪt] *n* مثلجات الفاكهة [Mothalajat al-fakehah]
sorcerer ['sɔːsərə] *n* مُشعوذ [muʃaʕwið]
sore [sɔː] *adj* محزن [muħzin] ▷ *n* حُزْن [ħuzn]; **cold sore** *n* قرحة البرد حول الشفاة ['qorḥat al-bard ḥawl al-shefah]
sorry ['sɒrɪ] *interj*; **I'm sorry** أنا [ʔana]; **I'm sorry to trouble you** أناأسف للإزعاج [Ana asef lel-ez'aaj]; **I'm very sorry, I didn't know the regulations** أنا أسف لعدم معرفتي باللوائح [Ana aasef le'aadam ma'arefatey bel-lawaeah]; **Sorry we're late** أعتذر، فالوقت متأخر [ʔaʕtaðiru fa:lwaqtu mutaʔaxxirun]; **Sorry, I didn't catch that** أعتذر، لم ألاحظ ذلك [A'atadher, lam olaḥeḍh dhalek]; **Sorry, I'm not interested** معذرة، أنا غير مهتم بهذا الأمر [maʕðaratun ʔana: ɣajru muhtammin biha:ða: alʔamri]
sort [sɔːt] *n* صنف [sˤinf]
sort out [sɔːt aʊt] *v* يَفْرِز [jufrizu]
SOS [ɛs əʊ ɛs] *n* إشارة استغاثة [ʔiʃa:ratun istiɣa:θa]
so-so [səʊsəʊ] *adv* أقل من المقبول [A'qal men alma'qbool]
soul [səʊl] *n* نَفْس [nafsin]
sound [saʊnd] *adj* سليم [sali:m] ▷ *n* صوت [sˤawt]
soundtrack ['saʊnd,træk] *n* موسيقى تصويرية [Mose'qa taṣweereyah]
soup [suːp] *n* حساء [ħasa:ʔ]; **What is the soup of the day?** ما هو حساء اليوم؟ [ma howa ḥasaa al-yawm?]
sour ['saʊə] *adj* حامض [ħa:midˤ]
south [saʊθ] *adj* جنوبي [ʒanu:bij] ▷ *adv* جنوباً [ʒanu:ban] ▷ *n* جنوب [ʒanu:bu]; **South Africa** *n* جنوب أفريقيا [Janoob afree'qya]; **South African** *n* جنوب أفريقي [Janoob afree'qy]شخص من جنوب أفريقيا , [Shkhṣ men janoob afree'qya]; **South America** *n* أمريكا الجنوبية [Amrika al janobeyiah]; **South American** *n* جنوب أمريكي [Janoob amriky]شخص من أمريكا , الجنوبية [Shakhṣ men amreeka al-janoobeyah]; **South Korea** *n* كوريا الجنوبية [Korya al-janoobeyah]; **South Pole** *n* القطب الجنوبي [Al-k'qotb

al-janoobey]
southbound ['saʊθˌbaʊnd] *adj* متجه للجنوب [Motageh lel-janoob]
southeast [ˌsaʊθ'iːst; ˌsaʊ'iːst] *n* جنوب شرقي [Janoob shr'qey]
southern ['sʌðən] *adj* واقع نحو الجنوب [Wa'qe'a nahw al-janoob]
southwest [ˌsaʊθ'wɛst; ˌsaʊ'wɛst] *n* جنوب غربي [Janoob gharbey]
souvenir [ˌsuːvə'nɪə; 'suːvəˌnɪə] *n* تذكار [tiðkaːr]; **Do you have souvenirs?** هل يوجد لديكم هدايا تذكارية؟ [hal yujad laday-kum hada-ya tedhka-reya?]
soya ['sɔɪə] *n* صويا [sˤuːsˤu]
spa [spɑː] *n* منتجع صحي [Montaja'a ṣeḥey]
space [speɪs] *n* فضاء [fadˤaːʔ]
spacecraft ['speɪsˌkrɑːft] *n* سَفينة الفضاء [Safenat al-faḍaa]
spade [speɪd] *n* مجراف [miʒraːf]
spaghetti [spə'gɛtɪ] *n* مكرونة سباجتي [Makaronah spajety]
Spain [speɪn] *n* أسبانيا [ʔisbaːnjjaː]
spam [spæm] *n* رسائل غير مرغوبة [rasaːʔilu ɣajr marɣuːba]
Spaniard ['spænjəd] *n* أسباني [ʔisbaːnij]
spaniel ['spænjəl] *n* كلب السبنيلي [Kalb al-sebneeley]
Spanish ['spænɪʃ] *adj* أسباني [ʔisbaːnij] ▷ *n* أسباني [ʔisbaːnij]
spank [spæŋk] *v* يُوَبِخ بقسوة [Yowabekh be-'qaswah]
spanner ['spænə] *n* مفتاح ربط [Meftaḥ rabṭ]
spare [spɛə] *adj* احتياطي [ʔiħtijjaːtˤij] ▷ *v* يَجْتنب [jaʒtanibu]; **spare part** *n* قطع غيار ['qaṭa'a gheyar]; **spare room** *n* غرفة إضافية [ghorfah eḍafeyah]; **spare time** *n* وَقْت فراغ [Wa'qt faragh]; **spare tyre** *n* إطار إضافي [Eṭar eḍafy]; **spare wheel** *n* عجلة إضافية ['aagalh eḍafeyah]; **Is there any spare bedding?** هل يوجد مرتبة احتياطية؟ [hal yujad ferash iḥte-yaṭy?]
spark [spɑːk] *n* شرارة [ʃaraːra]; **spark plug** *n* شمعة إشعال [Sham'aat esh'aal]
sparrow ['spærəʊ] *n* عصفور [ʕusˤfuːr]
spasm ['spæzəm] *n* تقلص عضلي [Ta'qaloṣ 'aḍaley]
spatula ['spætjʊlə] *n* ملعقة البسط [Mel'a'qat al-bast]
speak [spiːk] *v* يتكلم [jatakalamu]
speaker ['spiːkə] *n* مكبر الصوت [Mokabber al-ṣawt]; **native speaker** *n* متحدث باللغة الأم [motaḥdeth bel-loghah al-om]
speak up [spiːk ʌp] *v* يتحدث بحرية وبدون تحفظ [yathadath be-ḥorreyah wa-bedon taḥaffoḍh]
special ['spɛʃəl] *adj* خاص [xaːsˤsˤ]; **special offer** *n* عرض خاص ['aarḍ khaṣ]
specialist ['spɛʃəlɪst] *n* متخصص [mutaxasˤsˤisˤ]
speciality [ˌspɛʃɪ'ælɪtɪ] *n* تَخَصُص [taxasˤusˤsˤ]
specialize ['spɛʃəˌlaɪz] *v* يَتَخصص [jataxasˤsˤasˤu]
specially ['spɛʃəlɪ] *adv* خاصة [xaːsˤsˤatu]
species ['spiːʃiːz; 'spiːʃɪˌiːz] *n* أنواع [ʔanwaːʕ]
specific [spɪ'sɪfɪk] *adj* محدد [muħadadd]
specifically [spɪ'sɪfɪklɪ] *adv* تحديداً [taħdiːdan]
specify ['spɛsɪˌfaɪ] *v* يحدد [juħaddidu]
specs [spɛks] *npl* نظارة [nazˤzˤaːratun]
spectacles ['spɛktəkᵊlz] *npl* نظارة [nazˤzˤaːratun]
spectacular [spɛk'tækjʊlə] *adj* مشهدي [maʃhadij]
spectator [spɛk'teɪtə] *n* مُشاهِد [muʃaːhid]
speculate ['spɛkjʊˌleɪt] *v* يَتَأَمل [jataʔammalu]
speech [spiːtʃ] *n* خُطبة [xutˤba]
speechless ['spiːtʃlɪs] *adj* فاقد القدرة على الكلام [Fa'qed al-'qodrah 'aala al-kalam]
speed [spiːd] *n* سرعة [surʕa]; **speed limit** *n* حد السرعة [Ḥad alsor'aah]; **What is the speed limit on this road?** ما هي أقصى سرعة مسموح بها على هذا الطريق؟ [ma heya a'qṣa sur'aa masmooḥ beha 'aala hatha al- ṭaree'q?]

speedboat ['spi:dˌbəʊt] *n* زورق بخاري سريع [Zawra'q bokharey sarea'a]
speeding ['spi:dɪŋ] *n* زيادة السرعة [Zeyadat alsor'aah]
speedometer [spɪ'dɒmɪtə] *n* عداد السرعة ['adaad al-sor'aah]
speed up [spi:d ʌp] *v* يُسْرِع [jusriʕu]
spell [spɛl] *n (magic)* نَوبة [nawba], *(time)* سحر [siħr] ▷ *v* يَسحِر [jasħiru]
spellchecker ['spɛlˌtʃɛkə] *n* مصحح التهجئة [Moṣaheh altahjeaah]
spelling ['spɛlɪŋ] *n* تهجئة [tahʒiʔa]
spend [spɛnd] *v* يَقْضِي [jaqdˁi:]
sperm [spɜ:m] *n* مَنيّ [manij]
spice [spaɪs] *n* توابل [tawa:bil]
spicy ['spaɪsɪ] *adj* متبل [mutabbal]; **The food is too spicy** الطعام متبل أكثر من اللازم [al-ṭa'aam mutabal akthar min al-laazim]
spider ['spaɪdə] *n* عنكبوت [ʕankabu:t]
spill [spɪl] *v* يُريق [juri:qu]
spinach ['spɪnɪdʒ; -ɪtʃ] *n* سبانخ [saba:nix]
spine [spaɪn] *n* عمود فقري ['amood fa'qarey]
spinster ['spɪnstə] *n* عانِس [ʕa:nis]
spire [spaɪə] *n* ورقة عشب [Wara'qat 'aoshb]
spirit ['spɪrɪt] *n* رَوح [ru:ħ]
spirits ['spɪrɪts] *npl* مشروبات روحية [Mashroobat rooḥeyah]
spiritual ['spɪrɪtjʊəl] *adj* رَوحي [ru:ħij]
spit [spɪt] *n* بُصاق [busˁa:q] ▷ *v* يبصق [jabsˁuqu]
spite [spaɪt] *n* ضغينة [dˁaɣi:na] ▷ *v* يَحْقِد على [yaḥ'qed 'alaa]
spiteful ['spaɪtfʊl; 'spiteful] *adj* حاقد [ħa:qid]
splash [splæʃ] *v* يَرُش [jaruʃʃu]
splendid ['splɛndɪd] *adj* مُدْهِش [mudhiʃ]
splint [splɪnt] *n* شريحة [ʃari:ħatt]
splinter ['splɪntə] *n* شظية [ʃazˁijja]
split [splɪt] *v* يَنْقَسِم [janqasim]
split up [splɪt ʌp] *v* يَنْفَصِل [janfasˁilu]
spoil [spɔɪl] *v* يُفسِد [jufsidu]
spoilsport ['spɔɪlˌspɔ:t] *n* مفسد المتعة [Mofsed al-mot'aah]
spoilt [spɔɪlt] *adj* مدلل [mudallal]
spoke [spəʊk] *n* مكبح العربة [Makbaḥ al-'arabah]
spokesman, spokesmen ['spəʊksmən, 'spəʊksmɛn] *n* مُتَحدِّث باسم [Motaḥadeth besm]
spokesperson ['spəʊksˌpɜrsən] *n* مُتَحدِّث باسم [Motaḥadeth besm]
spokeswoman, spokeswomen ['spəʊksˌwʊmən, 'spəʊksˌwɪmɪn] *n* مُتَحدِّثة باسم [Motaḥadethah besm]
sponge [spʌndʒ] *n (cake)* إسفنج [ʔisfanʒ], *(for washing)* إسفنجة [ʔisfanʒa]; **sponge bag** *n* حقيبة مبطنة [Ha'qeebah mobaṭanah]
sponsor ['spɒnsə] *n* راعي [ra:ʕi:] ▷ *v* يَرعَى [jarʕa:]
sponsorship ['spɒnsəʃɪp] *n* رعاية [riʕa:ja]
spontaneous [spɒn'teɪnɪəs] *adj* عفوي [ʕafawij]
spooky ['spu:kɪ; 'spooky] *adj* شَبحي [ʃabaħij]
spoon [spu:n] *n* ملعقة [milʕaqa]; **Could I have a clean spoon, please?** هل يمكنني الحصول على ملعقة نظيفة من فضلك؟ [hal yamken -any al-ḥuṣool 'aala mil-'aa'qa naḍheefa min faḍlak?]
spoonful ['spu:nˌfʊl] *n* مقدار ملعقة صغيرة [Me'qdar mel'a'qah ṣagheerah]
sport [spɔ:t] *n* رياضة [rija:dˁa]; **winter sports** *npl* رياضات شتوية [Reyḍat shetweyah]
sportsman, sportsmen ['spɔ:tsmən, 'spɔ:tsmɛn] *n* رجل رياضي [Rajol reyaḍey]
sportswear ['spɔ:tsˌwɛə] *n* ملابس رياضية [Malabes reyaḍah]
sportswoman, sportswomen ['spɔ:tsˌwʊmən, 'spɔ:tsˌwɪmɪn] *n* سيدة رياضية [Sayedah reyaḍah]
sporty ['spɔ:tɪ] *adj* (رياضي) متعلق بالألعاب الرياضية [(Reyaḍey) mota'ale'q bel-al'aab al-reyaḍah]

spot [spɒt] *n (blemish)* بُقْعَة [wasˤma], *(place)* مكان [maka:n] ▷ *v* يَستطِلع [jastatˤliʕu]
spotless ['spɒtlɪs; 'spotless] *adj* نظيف تماما [nadheef tamaman]
spotlight ['spɒt,laɪt] *n* ضوء مُسَلّط [Dawa mosalt]
spotty ['spɒtɪ] *adj* مرقط [muraqqatˤ]
spouse [spaʊs] *n* زوجة [zawʒa]
sprain [spreɪn] *n* التواء المفصل [El-tewaa al-mefṣal] ▷ *v* يلوي المفصل [Yalwey al-mefṣal]
spray [spreɪ] *n* رشاش [raʃʃa:ʃ] ▷ *v* يَنْثُر [janθuru]; **hair spray** *n* سْبراي الشعر [Sbray al-sha'ar]
spread [sprɛd] *n* انتشار [intiʃa:r] ▷ *v* ينتشر [jantaʃiru]
spread out [sprɛd aʊt] *v* ينتشر [jantaʃiru]
spreadsheet ['sprɛd,ʃi:t] *n* ورقة عمل [Wara'qat 'aamal]
spring [sprɪŋ] *n (coil)* زُنْبُرك [zunburk], *(season)* الربيع [arrabi:ʕu]; **spring onion** *n* بصل أخضر [Baṣal akhdar]
spring-cleaning ['sprɪŋ,kli:nɪŋ] *n* تنظيف شامل للمنزل بعد انتهاء الشتاء [tanḍheef shamel lel-manzel ba'ad entehaa al-shetaa]
springtime ['sprɪŋ,taɪm] *n* فصل الربيع [Faṣl al-rabeya]
sprinkler ['sprɪŋklə; 'sprinkler] *n* مرشة [miraʃʃa]
sprint [sprɪnt] *n* سباق قصير سريع [Seba'q 'qaṣer sare'a] ▷ *v* يَرْكُض بِسُرْعَه [Yrkoḍ besor'aah]
sprinter ['sprɪntə] *n* مُتَسابِق [mutasa:biq]
sprouts [spraʊts] *npl* براعم الورق [Bra'aem al-wara'q]; **Brussels sprouts** *npl* كرنب بروكسيل [Koronb brokseel]
spy [spaɪ] *n* جاسوس [ʒa:su:s] ▷ *v* يَتَجسس [jataʒassasu]
spying ['spaɪɪŋ] *n* تجسس [taʒassus]
squabble ['skwɒbᵊl] *v* يَتَخاصم [jataxa:sˤamu]
squander ['skwɒndə] *v* يُبَدِد [jubaddidu]
square [skwɛə] *adj* مربع الشكل [Moraba'a al-shakl] ▷ *n* ميدان [majda:n]
squash [skwɒʃ] *n* نبات القْرع [Nabat al-'qar'a] ▷ *v* يهرس [juharrisu]
squeak [skwi:k] *v* يَزْعَق [jazʕaqu]
squeeze [skwi:z] *v* يَعْصِر [jaʕsˤiru]
squeeze in [skwi:z ɪn] *v* يَحْشو [Yaḥsho]
squid [skwɪd] *n* حبار [ħabba:r]
squint [skwɪnt] *v* يَحْوِل عَيْنَه [Yoḥawel aynah]
squirrel ['skwɪrəl; 'skwɜ:rəl; 'skwʌr-] *n* سِنجاب [sinʒa:b]
Sri Lanka [,sri: 'læŋkə] *n* سِري لانكا [sri: la:nka:]
stab [stæb] *v* يطعن [jatˤʕanu]
stability [stə'bɪlɪtɪ] *n* استقرار [istiqra:r]
stable ['steɪbᵊl] *adj* مستقر [mustaqir] ▷ *n* اسطبل [istˤabl]
stack [stæk] *n* كومة منتظم [Komat montaḍhem]
stadium, stadia ['steɪdɪəm, 'steɪdɪə] *n* استاد [sta:d]
staff [stɑ:f] *n (stick or rod)* عارضة [ʕa:ridˤa], *(workers)* عاملين [ʕa:mili:na]
staffroom ['stɑ:f,ru:m] *n* غرفة العاملين [Ghorfat al'aameleen]
stage [steɪdʒ] *n* خشبة المسرح [Khashabat al-masrah]
stagger ['stægə] *v* يَتهادَى [jataha:da:]
stain [steɪn] *n* لطخة [latˤxa] ▷ *v* يُلَطِخ [julatˤtˤixu]; **stain remover** *n* مزيل البقع [Mozeel al-bo'qa,a]
staircase ['stɛə,keɪs] *n* دَرَج [durʒ]
stairs [stɛəz] *npl* سلالم [sala:limun]
stale [steɪl] *adj* مبتذل [mubtaðal]
stalemate ['steɪl,meɪt] *n* ورطة [wartˤa]
stall [stɔ:l] *n* مربط الجواد [Marbaṭ al-jawad]
stamina ['stæmɪnə] *n* قدرة على الاحتمال ['qodrah ala al-eḥtemal]
stammer ['stæmə] *v* يَتلْعثم [jatalaʕθamu]
stamp [stæmp] *n* دمغة [damɣa] ▷ *v* يَدوس [jadu:su]

stand [stænd] *v* يَقِفْ [jaqifu]
standard ['stændəd] *adj* قياسي [qija:sij] ▷ *n* مقياس [miqja:s]; **standard of living** *n* مستوى المعيشة [Mostawa al-ma'aeeshah]
stand for [stænd fɔ:] *v* يَرْمُز [jarmuzu]
stand out [stænd aʊt] *v* يَتمَيز [jatamajjazu]
standpoint ['stænd,pɔɪnt] *n* نقطة الاستشراف [No'qṭat al-esteshraf]
stands ['stændz] *npl* أجنحة عرض [Ajnehat 'arḍ]
stand up [stænd ʌp] *v* يَنْهَض [janhadˤu]
staple ['steɪpəl] *n (commodity)* إنْتاج رَئيسي [Entaj raaesey], *(wire)* رزَّة سلكية [Rozzah selkeyah] ▷ *v* يُدَبِّس الأوراق [Yodabes al-wra'q]
stapler ['steɪplə; 'stapler] *n* دَبَّاسَة [dabba:sa]
star [stɑ:] *n (person)* نجم [naʒm], *(sky)* نجمة [naʒma] ▷ *v* يُزَين بالنجوم [Yozaeyen bel-nejoom]; **film star** *n* نجم سينمائي [Najm senemaaey]
starch [stɑ:tʃ] *n* نشا [naʃa:]
stare [stɛə] *v* يُحملِق [juħamliqu]
stark [stɑ:k] *adj* صارم [sˤa:rim]
start [stɑ:t] *n* بَدْء [bad?] ▷ *vi* يبدأ [jabda?u] ▷ *vt* يَبْدأ [jabda?u]; **When does the film start?** متى يبدأ عرض الفيلم؟ [mata yabda 'aarḍ al-filim?]
starter ['stɑ:tə] *n* بادِئ [ba:di?]
startle ['stɑ:təl] *v* يُرَوْع فجأة [Yorawe'a fajaah]
start off [stɑ:t ɒf] *v* يَبْدأ الحركة والنشاط [Yabdaa alḥarakah wal-nashaṭ]
starve [stɑ:v] *v* يجوّع [jaʒu:ʕu]
state [steɪt] *n* حالة [ħa:la] ▷ *v* يُصَرح ب [Yoṣareh be]; **Gulf States** *npl* دُوَل الخلَيج العربي [Dowel al-khaleej al'arabey]
statement ['steɪtmənt] *n* بَيَانٌ [baja:n]; **bank statement** *n* كشف بنكي [Kashf bankey]
station ['steɪʃən] *n* محطة [maħatˤtˤa]; **bus station** *n* محطة أوتوبيس [Maḥaṭat otobees]; **metro station** *n* محطة مترو [Mahaṭat metro]; **petrol station** *n* محطة بنزين [Mahaṭat benzene]; **police station** *n* قسم شرطة ['qesm shorṭah]; **radio station** *n* محطة راديو [Mahaṭat radyo]; **railway station** *n* محطة سكك حديدية [Mahaṭat sekak ḥadeedeyah]; **service station** *n* محطة الخدمة [Mahaṭat al-khedmah]; **tube station** *n* محطة أنفاق [Mahaṭat anfa'q]; **How far are we from the bus station?** ما هي المسافة بيننا وبين محطة الأتوبيس؟ [ma heya al-masafa bay-nana wa bayn muḥaṭat al- baaṣ?]; **Is there a petrol station near here?** هل يوجد محطة بنزين قريبة من هنا؟ [hal yujad muḥaṭat banzeen 'qareeba min huna?]; **Where is the nearest tube station?** أين توجد أقرب محطة للمترو؟ [ayna tojad a'qrab muḥaṭa lel-metro?]
stationer's ['steɪʃənəz] *n* مكتبة لبيع الأدوات المكتبية [maktabatun libajʕi alʔadawa:ti almaktabijjati]
stationery ['steɪʃənərɪ] *n* أدوات مكتبية [Adawat maktabeyah]
statistics [stə'tɪstɪks] *npl* إحصائيات [ʔiħsˤa:ʔijja:tun]
statue ['stætju:] *n* تمثال [timθa:l]
status ['steɪtəs] *n*; **marital status** *n* الحالة الاجتماعية [Al-halah al-ejtemaayah]
status quo ['steɪtəs kwəʊ] *n* الوضع الراهن [Al-waḍ'a al-rahen]
stay [steɪ] *n* إقامة [ʔiqa:ma] ▷ *v* يُقْيم [juqimu]; **I want to stay from Monday till Wednesday** أريد الإقامة من يوم الاثنين إلى يوم الأربعاء [areed al-e'qama min yawm al-ithnayn ela yawm al-arbe'aa]; **I'd like to stay for two nights** أريد الإقامة لليلتين [areed al-e'qama le lay-la-tain]
stay in [steɪ ɪn] *v* يمْكُث [jamkuθu]
stay up [steɪ ʌp] *v* يَظَل [jazˤallu]
steady ['stɛdɪ] *adj* مطرد [mutˤrad]
steak [steɪk] *n* شَريحة لحم [Shareehat laḥm]; **rump steak** *n* شريحة من لحم البقر [Shreeḥa men laḥm al-ba'qar]
steal [sti:l] *v* يَسرِق [jasriqu]
steam [sti:m] *n* بُخَار [buxa:r]

steel [stiːl] *n* صُلْبْ [sˤalb]; **stainless steel** *n* صلب غير قابل للصدأ [Ṣalb ghayr 'qabel lel-ṣadaa]
steep [stiːp] *adj* شاهق [ʃaːhiq]
steeple ['stiːpᵊl] *n* بُرْج الكنيسة [Borj al-kaneesah]
steering ['stɪərɪŋ] *n* توجيه [tawʒiːh]; **steering wheel** *n* عجلة القيادة ['aagalat al-'qeyadh]
step [stɛp] *n* خطوة [xutˤwa]
stepbrother ['stɛpˌbrʌðə] *n* أخ من زوجة الأب أو زوج الأم [Akh men zawjat al ab]
stepdaughter ['stɛpˌdɔːtə] *n* رَبيبة [rabiːba]
stepfather ['stɛpˌfɑːðə] *n* زوج الأم [Zawj al-om]
stepladder ['stɛpˌlædə] *n* سُلَم نقال [Sollam na'q'qaal]
stepmother ['stɛpˌmʌðə] *n* زوجة الأب [Zawj al-aab]
stepsister ['stɛpˌsɪstə] *n* أخت من زوجة الأب أو زوج الأم [Okht men zawjat al ab aw zawj al om]
stepson ['stɛpˌsʌn] *n* رَبيب [rabiːb]
stereo ['stɛrɪəʊ; 'stɪər-] *n* ستريو [stirjuː]; **personal stereo** *n* جهاز الصوت المجسم الشخصي [Jehaz al-ṣawt al-mojasam al-shakhṣey]; **Is there a stereo in the car?** هل يوجد نظام ستريو بالسيارة؟ [hal yujad neḍham stereo bil-sayara?]
stereotype ['stɛrɪəˌtaɪp; 'stɪər-] *n* شكل نمطي [Shakl namaṭey]
sterile ['stɛraɪl] *adj* عقيم [ʕaqiːm]
sterilize ['stɛrɪˌlaɪz] *v* يُعَقِم [juʕaqqimu]
sterling ['stɜːlɪŋ] *n* الاسترليني [al-istirliːnijju]
steroid ['stɪərɔɪd; 'stɛr-] *n* سترودي [stirwudij]
stew [stjuː] *n* طعام مطهو بالغلي [ṭ a'aam maṭhoo bel-ghaley]
steward ['stjʊəd] *n* مُضيف [mudˤiːf]
stick [stɪk] *n* عصا [ʕasˤaː] ▷ *v* يَغْرُز [jaɣruzu]; **stick insect** *n* الحشرة العصوية [Al-hasherah al-'aodweia]; **walking stick** *n* عصا المشي ['asaa almashey]
sticker ['stɪkə] *n* ملصق [mulsˤaq]
stick out [stɪk aʊt] *v* يمكث [jamkuθu]
sticky ['stɪkɪ] *adj* لزج [laziʒ]
stiff [stɪf] *adj* قَاسْ [qaːsin]
stifling ['staɪflɪŋ] *adj* خانق [xaːniq]
still [stɪl] *adj* ثابت [θaːbit] ▷ *adv* لا يزال [La yazaal]
sting [stɪŋ] *n* لدغة [ladɣa] ▷ *v* يلدغ [jaldaɣu]
stingy ['stɪndʒɪ] *adj* قارص [qaːrisˤ]
stink [stɪŋk] *n* رائحة كريهة [Raaehah kareehah] ▷ *v* يَنْتِن [jantinu]
stir [stɜː] *v* يُقَلِب [juqallibu]
stitch [stɪtʃ] *n* ألم مفاجئ [Alam Mofajea] ▷ *v* يَدرُز [jadruzu]
stock [stɒk] *n* مخزون [maxzuːn] ▷ *v* يَخْزِن [jaxzunu]; **stock cube** *n* مكعب حساء [Moka'aab ḥasaa]; **stock exchange** *n* سُوق الأوراق المالية [Soo'q al-awra'q al-maleyah]; **stock market** *n* البورصة [al-buːrsˤatu]
stockbroker ['stɒkˌbrəʊkə] *n* سِمسار البورصة [Semsar al-borṣah]
stockholder ['stɒkˌhəʊldə] *n* مساهم [musaːhim]
stocking ['stɒkɪŋ] *n* جورب [ʒawrab]
stock up [stɒk ʌp] *v*; **stock up on** *v* يُجَهِّز بالسِّلَع [Yojahez bel-sela'a]
stomach ['stʌmək] *n* معدة [maʕida]
stomachache ['stʌməkˌeɪk] *n* ألم المَعِدة [Alam alma'aedah]
stone [stəʊn] *n* حجر [ħaʒar]
stool [stuːl] *n* كرسي بلا ظهر أو ذراعين [Korsey bela ḍhahr aw dhera'aayn]
stop [stɒp] *n* توقف [tawaqquf] ▷ *vi* يَتوَقف [jatawaqqafu] ▷ *vt* يوقف [juːqifu]; **bus stop** *n* موقف أوتوبيس [Maw'qaf otobees]; **full stop** *n* نُقْطَة [nuqtˤatun]; **Do we stop at...?** هل سنتوقف في... [hal sanata-wa'qaf fee...?]; **Does the train stop at...?** هل يتوقف القطار في...؟ [hal yata-wa'qaf al-'qeṭaar fee...?]; **My watch has stopped** لقد توقفت ساعتي [la'qad tawa-'qafat sa'aaty]; **When do we stop next?** متى سنتوقف في المرة التالية؟ [mata sa-nata-wa'qaf fee

al-murra al-taleya?]; **Where do we stop for lunch?** متى سنتوقف لتناول الغذاء؟ [mata sa-nata-wa'qaf le-tanawil al-ghadaa?]
stopover ['stɒpˌəʊvə] *n* توقف في رحلة [Tawa'qof fee rehlah]
stopwatch ['stɒpˌwɒtʃ] *n* ساعة الإيقاف [Saa'ah al-e'qaaf]
storage ['stɔːrɪdʒ] *n* مخزن [maxzan]
store [stɔː] *n* محل تجاري [Maḥal tejarey] ▷ *v* يُخزن [juxazzinu]; **department store** *n* محل مكون من أقسام [Maḥal mokawan men a'qsaam]
storm [stɔːm] *n* عاصفة [ʕaːsˤifa]
stormy ['stɔːmɪ] *adj* عاصف [ʕaːsˤif]; **It's stormy** الجو عاصف [al-jaw 'aaṣuf]
story ['stɔːrɪ] *n* قصة [qisˤsˤa]; **short story** *n* قصة قصيرة ['qeṣah 'qaṣeerah]
stove [stəʊv] *n* موقد [mawqid]
straight [streɪt] *adj* مستقيم [mustaqiːm]; **straight on** *adv* في خط مستقيم [Fee khad mosta'qeem]
straighteners ['streɪtᵊnəz] *npl* مواد أو أدوات الفرد [Mawaad aw adawaat alfard]
straightforward [ˌstreɪt'fɔːwəd] *adj* صريح [sˤariːħ]
strain [streɪn] *n* إرْهاق [ʔirhaːq] ▷ *v* يُوَتِّرُ [juwattiru]
strained [streɪnd] *adj* مرهق [murhiq]
stranded ['strændɪd] *adj* مجدول [maʒduːl]
strange [streɪndʒ] *adj* غريب [ɣariːb]
stranger ['streɪndʒə] *n* شخص غريب [Shakhṣ ghareeb]
strangle ['stræŋgᵊl] *v* يَخنِق [jaxniqu]
strap [stræp] *n* طوق [tˤawq]; **watch strap** *n* سُوَار الساعة [Sowar al-sa'aah]
strategic [strə'tiːdʒɪk] *adj* إستراتيجي [ʔistiraːtiːʒij]
strategy ['strætɪdʒɪ] *n* إستراتيجية [ʔistiraːtiːʒijja]
straw [strɔː] *n* قش [qaʃʃ]
strawberry ['strɔːbərɪ; -brɪ] *n* فراولة [faraːwla]
stray [streɪ] *n* ضَالٌ [dˤaːl]
stream [striːm] *n* جدول [ʒadwal]
street [striːt] *n* شارع [ʃaːriʕ]; **street map** *n* خارطة الشارع [khareṭat al-share'a]; **street plan** *n* خريطة الشارع [Khareeṭat al-share'a]
streetlamp ['striːtˌlæmp] *n* مصباح الشارع [Mesbaḥ al-share'a]
streetwise ['striːtˌwaɪz] *adj* محنك [muħannak]
strength [strɛŋθ] *n* قوة [quwwa]
strengthen ['strɛŋθən] *v* يَقْوي [juqawwiː]
stress [strɛs] *n* ضغط [dˤaɣtˤ] ▷ *v* يُؤَكِّد [juʔakkidu]
stressed ['strɛst] *adj* متوتر [mutawattir]
stressful ['strɛsfʊl] *adj* مسبب توتر [Mosabeb tawator]
stretch [strɛtʃ] *v* يمتد [jamtadu]
stretcher ['strɛtʃə] *n* نقالة [naqqaːla]
stretchy ['strɛtʃɪ] *adj* مطاطي [matˤaːtˤij]
strict [strɪkt] *adj* حازم [ħaːzim]
strictly [strɪktlɪ] *adv* بحزم [biħazmin]
strike [straɪk] *n* ضربة [dˤarba] ▷ *vi* يَرْتَطِم ب [Yartaṭem be], *(suspend work)* يُضرِب [judˤribu] ▷ *vt* يَضرب [jadˤribu]
striker ['straɪkə] *n* ضَارِب [dˤaːrib]
striking ['straɪkɪŋ] *adj* لافت للنظر [Lafet lel-nadhar]
string [strɪŋ] *n* سِلْك [silk]
strip [strɪp] *n* شريطة [ʃariːtˤa] ▷ *v* يُجَرِد [juʒarridu]
stripe [straɪp] *n* قماش مقلم ['qomash mo'qallem]
striped [straɪpt; striped] *adj* مقلم [muqallam]
stripper ['strɪpə] *n* راقصة تعري [Ra'qeṣat ta'arey]
stripy ['straɪpɪ] *adj* مقلم [muqallam]
stroke [strəʊk] *n* *(apoplexy)* جلطة [ʒaltˤa], *(hit)* جلطة [ʒaltˤa] ▷ *v* يُلاطِف [julaːtˤifu]
stroll [strəʊl] *n* تَجَوُّل [taʒawwul]
strong [strɒŋ] *adj* مركز [markazu]
strongly [strɒŋlɪ] *adv* بقوة [Be-'qowah]
structure ['strʌktʃə] *n* هيكل [hajkal]
struggle ['strʌgᵊl] *v* يُكافِح [jukaːfiħu]
stub [stʌb] *n* الجذل [al-ʒaðalu]

stubborn ['stʌbᵊn] *adj* عنيد [ʕani:d]
stub out [stʌb aʊt] *v* يَخمد [jaxmudu]
stuck [stʌk] *adj* محبوس [maħbu:sa]
stuck-up [stʌkʌp] *adj* مغرور [maɣru:r]
stud [stʌd] *n* مزرعة خيل استيلاد [Mazra'at khayl esteelaad]
student ['stju:dᵊnt] *n* طالب [tˤa:lib]; **student discount** *n* خصم للطلاب [Khaṣm lel-ṭolab]
studio ['stju:dɪˌəʊ] *n* استوديو [stu:dju:]; **studio flat** *n* شقة ستديو [Sha'qah stedeyo]
study ['stʌdɪ] *v* يَدْرِس [jadrusu]
stuff [stʌf] *n* حشوة [ħaʃwa]
stuffy ['stʌfɪ] *adj* غاضب [ɣa:dˤib]
stumble ['stʌmbᵊl] *v* يَتَعثر [jataʕaθθaru]
stunned [stʌnd] *adj* مذهول [maðhu:l]
stunning ['stʌnɪŋ] *adj* مذهل [muðhil]
stunt [stʌnt] *n* عمل مثير ['aamal Mother]
stuntman, stuntmen ['stʌntmən, 'stʌntmɛn] *n* رَجُل المخاطر [Rajol al-makhater]
stupid ['stju:pɪd] *adj* غبي [ɣabijju]
stutter ['stʌtə] *v* يُتمْتم [jutamtimu]
style [staɪl] *n* لِباس [liba:s]
styling ['staɪlɪŋ] *n*; **Do you sell styling products?** هل تبيع مستحضرات لتسريح الشعر؟ [hal tabee'a musta-ḥḍaraat le-tasreeḥ al-sha'air?]
stylist ['staɪlɪst] *n* مُصَمِم أزياء [Moṣamem azyaa]
subject ['sʌbdʒɪkt] *n* موضوع [mawdˤu:ʕ]
submarine ['sʌbməˌri:n; ˌsʌbmə'ri:n] *n* غواصة [ɣawwa:sˤa]
subscription [səb'skrɪpʃən] *n* اشتراك [iʃtira:k]
subsidiary [səb'sɪdɪərɪ] *n* شركة تابعة [Sharekah tabe'ah]
subsidize ['sʌbsɪˌdaɪz] *v* يُقَدِم العون المالي ل [juqadimu alʕawana alma:li: li]
subsidy ['sʌbsɪdɪ] *n* إعانة مالية [E'aanah maleyah]
substance ['sʌbstəns] *n* جوهر [ʒawhar]
substitute ['sʌbstɪˌtju:t] *n* تَبْدِيل [tabdi:l] ▷ *v* يَحل محل [Taḥel maḥal]
subtitled ['sʌbˌtaɪtᵊld] *adj* مزود بعنوان فرعي [Mozawad be'aonwan far'aey]
subtitles ['sʌbˌtaɪtᵊlz] *npl* عناوين فرعية ['anaween far'aeyah]
subtle ['sʌtᵊl] *adj* مُهذّب [muhaððab]
subtract [səb'trækt] *v* يُسقِط من [Yos'qeṭ men]
suburb ['sʌbɜ:b] *n* ضاحية [dˤa:ħija]
suburban [sə'bɜ:bᵊn] *adj* ساكن الضاحية [Saken al-ḍaheyah]
subway ['sʌbˌweɪ] *n* نفق [nafaq]
succeed [sək'si:d] *v* ينجح [janʒaħu]
success [sək'sɛs] *n* نجاح [naʒa:ħ]
successful [sək'sɛsfʊl] *adj* ناجح [na:ʒiħ]
successfully [sək'sɛsfʊlɪ] *adv* بنجاح [binaʒa:ħin]
successive [sək'sɛsɪv] *adj* مُتَعاقِب [mutaʕa:qib]
successor [sək'sɛsə] *n* وريث [wari:θ]
such [sʌtʃ] *adj* كبير [kabi:r] ▷ *adv* جداً [ʒidan]
suck [sʌk] *v* يَرضَع [jardˤaʕu]
Sudan [su:'dɑ:n; -'dæn] *n* السودان [as-su:da:nu]
Sudanese [ˌsu:dᵊ'ni:z] *adj* سوداني [su:da:nij] ▷ *n* سوداني [su:da:nij]
sudden ['sʌdᵊn] *adj* مفاجئ [mufa:ʒiʔ]
suddenly ['sʌdᵊnlɪ] *adv* فجأةً [faʒʔatun]
sue [sju:; su:] *v* يُقاضي [juqa:dˤi:]
suede [sweɪd] *n* جلد مزأبر [Jeld mazaabar]
suffer ['sʌfə] *v* يُعانْي [juʕa:ni:]
sufficient [sə'fɪʃənt] *adj* غير كافي [Ghayr kafey]
suffocate ['sʌfəˌkeɪt] *v* يَخنِق [jaxniqu]
sugar ['ʃʊgə] *n* سكر [sukar]; **icing sugar** *n* سكر ناعِم [Sokar na'aem]; **no sugar** بدون سكر [bedoon suk-kar]
sugar-free ['ʃʊgəfri:] *adj* خالي من السكر [Khaley men al-oskar]
suggest [sə'dʒɛst; səg'dʒɛst] *v* يَقْتَرِح [jaqtariħu]
suggestion [sə'dʒɛstʃən] *n* اقتراح [iqtira:ħ]
suicide ['su:ɪˌsaɪd; 'sju:-] *n* ينتحر [jantaħiru]; **suicide bomber** *n* مفجر انتحاري [Mofajer enteḥaarey]

suit [suːt; sjuːt] *n* دعوى [daʕwaː] ▷ *v* يُلائِم [julaːʔimu]; **bathing suit** *n* لباس الاستحمام [Lebas al-estehmam]; **shell suit** *n* زي رياضي [Zey reyaḍey]
suitable ['suːtəbᵊl; 'sjuːt-] *adj* ملائم [mulaːʔim]
suitcase ['suːtˌkeɪs; 'sjuːt-] *n* حقيبة سفر [Ha'qeebat al-safar]
suite [swiːt] *n* جناح في فندق [Janaḥ fee fond'q]
sulk [sʌlk] *v* يَحْرِد [jaħridu]
sulky ['sʌlkɪ] *adj* مقطب الجبين [Mo'qṭ ab al-jabeen]
sultana [sʌl'tɑːnə] *n* زَبِيب سلطانة [Zebeeb solṭanah]
sum [sʌm] *n* خلاصة [xulaːsˤa]
summarize ['sʌməˌraɪz] *v* يُلَخِص [julaxxisˤu]
summary ['sʌmərɪ] *n* ملخص [mulaxxasˤ]
summer ['sʌmə] *n* الصيف [asˤ-sˤajfu]; **summer holidays** *npl* الأجازات الصيفية [Al-ajazat al-ṣayfeyah]; **after summer** بعد فصل الصيف [ba'ad faṣil al-ṣayf]; **during the summer** خلال فصل الصيف [khelal faṣl al-ṣayf]; **in summer** في الصيف [fee al-ṣayf]
summertime ['sʌməˌtaɪm] *n* فصل الصيف [Faṣl al-ṣayf]
summit ['sʌmɪt] *n* مؤتمر قمة [Moatamar 'qemmah]
sum up [sʌm ʌp] *v* يجمع [juʒammiʕu]
sun [sʌn] *n* شَمْس [ʃams]
sunbathe ['sʌnˌbeɪð] *v* يَأخُذ حمام شمس [yaakhoḍ hammam shams]
sunbed ['sʌnˌbɛd] *n* حمام شمس [Ḥamam shams]
sunblock ['sʌnˌblɒk] *n* كريم للوقاية من الشمس [Kreem lel-we'qayah men al-shams]
sunburn ['sʌnˌbɜːn] *n* سَفْعَة شمس [Saf'aat ahams]
sunburnt ['sʌnˌbɜːnt] *adj* مسفوع بأشعة الشمس [Masfoo'a be-ashe'aat al-shams]
suncream ['sʌnˌkriːm] *n* كريم الشمس [Kreem shams]
Sunday ['sʌndɪ] *n* الأحد [al-ʔaħadu]; **on Sunday** في يوم الأحد [fee yawm al-aḥad]
sunflower ['sʌnˌflaʊə] *n* عباد الشمس ['aabaad al-shams]
sunglasses ['sʌnˌglɑːsɪz] *npl* نظارات شمسية [naḍharat shamseyah]
sunlight ['sʌnlaɪt] *n* ضوء الشمس [Ḍawa al-shams]
sunny ['sʌnɪ] *adj* مشمس [muʃmis]; **It's sunny** الجو مشمس [al-jaw mushmis]
sunrise ['sʌnˌraɪz] *n* شروق الشمس [Sheroo'q al-shams]
sunroof ['sʌnˌruːf] *n* فتحة سَقف [Fathat sa'qf]
sunscreen ['sʌnˌskriːn] *n* واقي الشمس [Wa'qey al-shams]
sunset ['sʌnˌsɛt] *n* غُروب [ɣuruːb]
sunshine ['sʌnˌʃaɪn] *n* أشعة الشمس [Ashe'aat al-shams]
sunstroke ['sʌnˌstrəʊk] *n* ضربة شمس [Ḍarbat shams]
suntan ['sʌnˌtæn] *n* سُمرة الشمس [Somrat al-shams]; **suntan lotion** *n* غسول سمرة الشمس [ghasool somrat al-shams]; **suntan oil** *n* زيت سمرة الشمس [Zayt samarat al-shams]
super ['suːpə] *adj* ممتاز جدا [Momtaaz jedan]
superb [sʊ'pɜːb; sjʊ-] *adj* فاتن [faːtin]
superficial [ˌsuːpə'fɪʃəl] *adj* سَطحي [satˤħij]
superior [suː'pɪərɪə] *adj* مكانة أعلى [Makanah a'ala] ▷ *n* أعلى مكانة [A'ala makanah]
supermarket ['suːpəˌmɑːkɪt] *n* سوبر ماركت [suːbr maːrkit]; **I need to find a supermarket** أريد الذهاب إلى السوبر ماركت [areed al-dhehaab ela al-subar market]
supernatural [ˌsuːpə'nætʃrəl; -'nætʃərəl] *adj* خارق للطبيعة [Khare'q lel-ṭabe'aah]
superstitious [ˌsuːpə'stɪʃəs] *adj* خرافي [xuraːfij]
supervise ['suːpəˌvaɪz] *v* يُشرف [juʃrifu]

supervisor [ˈsuːpəˌvaɪzə] *n* مشرف [muʃrif]
supper [ˈsʌpə] *n* عَشَاء [ʕaʃaːʔ]
supplement [ˈsʌplɪmənt] *n* مُكَمِّل [mukammill]
supplier [səˈplaɪə] *n* مورد [muwarrid]
supplies [səˈplaɪz] *npl* توريدات [tawriːdaːtun]
supply [səˈplaɪ] *n* إمداد [ʔimdaːd] ▷ *v* يُزَوِّد [juzawwidu]; **supply teacher** *n* مُدرِّس بديل [Modares badeel]
support [səˈpɔːt] *n* دعم [daʕm] ▷ *v* يدعم [jadʕamu]
supporter [səˈpɔːtə] *n* المؤيد [al-muajjidu]
suppose [səˈpəʊz] *v* يَظُن [jazˤunnu]
supposedly [səˈpəʊzɪdlɪ] *adv* على افتراض [Ala eftraḍ]
supposing [səˈpəʊzɪŋ] *conj* بافتراض [Be-efteraḍ]
surcharge [ˈsɜːˌtʃɑːdʒ] *n* ضريبة إضافية [Ḍareba eḍafeyah]
sure [ʃʊə; ʃɔː] *adj* متأكد [mutaʔakkid]
surely [ˈʃʊəlɪ; ˈʃɔː-] *adv* بالتأكيد [bi-at-taʔkiːdi]
surf [sɜːf] *n* ركوب الأمواج [Rokoob al-amwaj] ▷ *v* يَتَصَفح الانترنت [Yataṣafaḥ al-enternet]; **Where can you go surfing?** أين يمكنك ممارسة رياضة ركوب الأمواج؟ [ayna yamken-ak muma-rasat riyaḍat rokob al-amwaj?]
surface [ˈsɜːfɪs] *n* سَطح [satˤħ]
surfboard [ˈsɜːfˌbɔːd] *n* لوح الركمجة [Looḥ al-rakmajah]
surfer [ˈsɜːfə] *n* مُتَصّفِح الانترنت [Motaṣafeḥ al-enternet]
surfing [ˈsɜːfɪŋ] *n* الركمجة [ar-rakmaʒatu]
surge [sɜːdʒ] *n* مَوْجَة [mawʒa]
surgeon [ˈsɜːdʒən] *n* جراح [ʒarraːħ]
surgery [ˈsɜːdʒərɪ] *n (doctor's)* جراحة [ʒiraːħa], *(operation)* عملية جراحية [ʻamaleyah jeraheyah]; **cosmetic surgery** *n* جراحة تجميل [Jerahat tajmeel]; **plastic surgery** *n* جراحة تجميلية [Jerahah tajmeeleyah]
surname [ˈsɜːˌneɪm] *n* لقب [laqab]
surplus [ˈsɜːpləs] *adj* فائض [faːʔidˤ] ▷ *n* فَائِض [faːʔidˤ]
surprise [səˈpraɪz] *n* مفاجئة [mufaːʒaʔa]
surprised [səˈpraɪzd] *adj* متفاجئ [mutafaːʒiʔ]
surprising [səˈpraɪzɪŋ] *adj* مفاجئ [mufaːʒiʔ]
surprisingly [səˈpraɪzɪŋlɪ] *adv* على نحو مفاجئ [Ala naḥw mofaheya]
surrender [səˈrɛndə] *v* يُسَلِّم [jusallimu]
surround [səˈraʊnd] *v* يحيط [juħiːtˤu]
surroundings [səˈraʊndɪŋz] *npl* البيئة المُحِيطة [Al- beeaah almoheeṭah]
survey [ˈsɜːveɪ] *n* مسح [masħ]
surveyor [sɜːˈveɪə] *n* ماسح الأراضي [Maseh al-araaḍey]
survival [səˈvaɪvəl] *n* بَقَاء [baqaːʔ]
survive [səˈvaɪv] *v* ينجو من [janʒuː min]
survivor [səˈvaɪvə; surˈvivor] *n* نَاجٍ [naːʒin]
suspect *n* [ˈsʌspɛkt] مشْتبه به [Moshtabah beh] ▷ *v* [səˈspɛkt] يَشتبِه ب [Yashtabeh be]
suspend [səˈspɛnd] *v* يُرْجِئ [jurʒiʔ]
suspenders [səˈspɛndəz] *npl* حمالات البنطلون [Hammalaat al- banṭaloon]
suspense [səˈspɛns] *n* تشويق [taʃwiːq]
suspension [səˈspɛnʃən] *n* تعليق [taʕliːq]; **suspension bridge** *n* جسر معلق [Jesr mo'aala'q]
suspicious [səˈspɪʃəs] *adj* مشبوه [maʃbuːh]
swallow [ˈswɒləʊ] *n* طائر السنونو [Ṭaaer al-sonono] ▷ *vi* يبتلع [jabtaliʕu] ▷ *vt* يَبْلع [jablaʕu]
swamp [swɒmp] *n* أرض وحلة [Arḍ waḥelah]
swan [swɒn] *n* إوزة [ʔiwazza]
swap [swɒp] *v* يقُايِّض [juqujidˤu]
swat [swɒt] *v* يَضرِب ضربة عنيفة [Yaḍreb ḍarban ʻaneefan]
sway [sweɪ] *v* يَتمَايل [jatamaːjalu]
Swaziland [ˈswɑːzɪˌlænd] *n* سوازيلاند [swaːziːlaːnd]
swear [swɛə] *v* يَحلِف [jaħlifu]

swearword ['swɛəˌwɜːd] *n* شتيمة [ʃatiːma]
sweat [swɛt] *n* عرق [ʕirq] ▷ *v* يَعْرَق [jaʕraqu]
sweater ['swɛtə] *n* بلوفر [buluːfar]; **polo-necked sweater** *n* سُترة بولو برقبة [Sotrat bolo be-ra'qabah]
sweatshirt ['swɛtˌʃɜːt] *n* كنزة فضفاضة يرتديها الرياضيون [Kanzah fedfadh yartadeha al-reyadeyon]
sweaty ['swɛtɪ] *adj* مبلل بالعرق [Mobala bel-ara'q]
swede [swiːd] *n* اللّفْت السويدي [Al-left al-sweedey]
Swede [swiːd] *n* سويدي [swiːdij]
Sweden ['swiːdᵊn] *n* السويد [as-suwiːdu]
Swedish ['swiːdɪʃ] *adj* سويدي [swiːdij] ▷ *n* اللغة السويدية [Al-loghah al-sweedeyah]
sweep [swiːp] *v* يَكْنِس [jaknisu]
sweet [swiːt] *adj (pleasing)* عذب [ʕaðb], *(taste)* حلو [ħulw] ▷ *n* حلوى [ħalwaː]
sweetcorn ['swiːtˌkɔːn] *n* ذرة سكري [dhorah sokarey]
sweetener ['swiːtᵊnə] *n* مواد تحلية [mawaːdun taħlijja]
sweets ['swiːtz] *npl* حلويات [ħalawijaːtun]
sweltering ['swɛltərɪŋ] *adj* شديد الحر [Shadeed al-har]
swerve [swɜːv] *v* ينحرف [janħarifu]
swim [swɪm] *v* يَسبَح [jasbaħu]
swimmer ['swɪmə] *n* سابح [saːbiħ]
swimming ['swɪmɪŋ] *n* سباحة [sibaːħa]; **swimming costume** *n* زي السباحة [Zey sebaḥah]; **swimming pool** *n* حمام سباحة [Hammam sebaḥah]; **swimming trunks** *npl* سِروال سباحة [Serwl sebaḥah]; **Where is the public swimming pool?** أين يوجد حمام السباحة العام؟ [ayna yujad ḥamam al-sebaḥa al-'aam?]
swimsuit ['swɪmˌsuːt; -ˌsjuːt] *n* مَايوه [maːjuːh]
swing [swɪŋ] *n* تَأَرْجُح [taʔarʒuħ] ▷ *v* يتمايل [jatamaːjalu]
Swiss [swɪs] *adj* سويسري [swiːsrij] ▷ *n* سويسري [swiːsrij]
switch [swɪtʃ] *n* مفتاح كهربائي [Meftaḥ kahrabaey] ▷ *v* يُحَوِّل [juħawwilu]
switchboard ['swɪtʃˌbɔːd] *n* لوحة مفاتيح تحكم [Looḥat mafateeḥ taḥakom]
switch off [swɪtʃ ɒf] *v* يُطفِئ [jutˤfiʔ]
switch on [swɪtʃ ɒn] *v* يُشَغِّل [juʃaɣɣilu]
Switzerland ['swɪtsələnd] *n* سويسرا [swiːsraː]
swollen ['swəʊlən] *adj* منتفخ [muntafixx]
sword [sɔːd] *n* سيف [sajf]
swordfish ['sɔːdˌfɪʃ] *n* سمك سياف البحر [Samak aayaf al-baḥr]
swot [swɒt] *v* يَدْرُس بجد [Yadros bejed]
syllable ['sɪləbᵊl] *n* مقطع لفظي [Ma'qṭa'a lafḍhy]
syllabus ['sɪləbəs] *n* خلاصة بحث أو منهج دراسي [Kholaṣat bahth aw manhaj derasey]
symbol ['sɪmbᵊl] *n* رَمز [ramz]
symmetrical [sɪ'mɛtrɪkᵊl] *adj* متماثل [mutamaːθil]
sympathetic [ˌsɪmpə'θɛtɪk] *adj* متعاطف [mutaʕaːtˤif]
sympathize ['sɪmpəˌθaɪz] *v* يَتعاطف [jataʕaːtˤafu]
sympathy ['sɪmpəθɪ] *n* تعاطف [taʕaːtˤuf]
symphony ['sɪmfənɪ] *n* سِمفونية [samfuːnijja]
symptom ['sɪmptəm] *n* علامة [ʕalaːma]
synagogue ['sɪnəˌgɒg] *n* معبد اليهود [Ma'abad al-yahood]
syndrome ['sɪndrəʊm] *n*; **Down's syndrome** *n* متلازمة داون [Motalazemat dawon]
Syria ['sɪrɪə] *n* سوريا [suːrjaː]
Syrian ['sɪrɪən] *adj* سوري [suːrij] ▷ *n* سوري [suːrij]
syringe ['sɪrɪndʒ; sɪ'rɪndʒ] *n* حقنة [ħuqna]
syrup ['sɪrəp] *n* شراب [ʃaraːb]
system ['sɪstəm] *n* نظام [nizˤaːm];

immune system *n* جهاز المناعة [Jehaz al-mana'aa]; **solar system** *n* نظام شمسي [neḍham shamsey]; **systems analyst** *n* محلل نظم [Moḥalel noḍhom]
systematic [ˌsɪstɪˈmætɪk] *adj* نظامي [nizˤa:mij]

table [ˈteɪbᵊl] *n (chart)* جدول [ʒadwal], *(furniture)* منضدة [mindˤada]; **bedside table** *n* كومودينو [ku:mu:di:nu:]; **coffee table** *n* طاولة قهوة [Ṭawlat 'qahwa]; **dressing table** *n* طَاوِلَة زينة [Ṭawlat zeenah]; **table tennis** *n* كرة الطاولة [Korat al-ṭawlah]; **table wine** *n* خَمْر الطعام [Khamr al-ṭa'aam]
tablecloth [ˈteɪbᵊlˌklɒθ] *n* غطاء مائدة [Gheṭa'a maydah]
tablespoon [ˈteɪbᵊlˌspu:n] *n* ملعقة مائدة [Mel'a'qat maedah]
tablet [ˈtæblɪt] *n* لوحة [lawħa]
taboo [təˈbu:] *adj* معزول بوصفه محرما [Ma'azool bewaṣfeh moḥaraman] ▷ *n* محرمات مقدسات [moḥaramat mo'qadasat]
tackle [ˈtækᵊl; ˈteɪkᵊl] *n* عدة [ʕudda] ▷ *v* يُمْسِك ب [Yomsek be]; **fishing tackle** *n* معدات صيد السمك [Mo'aedat ṣayed al-samak]
tact [tækt] *n* لباقة [laba:qa]
tactful [ˈtæktfʊl] *adj* لبق [labiq]
tactics [ˈtæktɪks] *npl* تكتيكات [tikti:ka:tun]
tactless [ˈtæktlɪs] *adj* غير لبق [Ghaey labe'q]

tadpole ['tæd,pəʊl] *n* فرخ الضفدع [Farkh al-ḍofda'a]
tag [tæg] *n* علامة [ʕala:ma]
Tahiti [tə'hi:tɪ] *n* تاهيتي [ta:hi:ti:]
tail [teɪl] *n* ذَيّل [ðajl]
tailor ['teɪlə] *n* خَيَّاط [xajja:tˤ]
Taiwan ['taɪ'wɑ:n] *n* تايوان [ta:jwa:n]
Taiwanese [,taɪwɑ:'ni:z] *adj* تايواني [ta:jwa:nij] ▷ *n* تايواني [ta:jwa:nij]
Tajikistan [tɑ:,dʒɪkɪ'stɑ:n; -stæn] *n* طاجكستان [tˤa:ʒikista:n]
take [teɪk] *v* يَأخُذ [jaʔxuðu], *(time)* يَأخُذ [jaʔxuðu]
take after [teɪk 'ɑ:ftə] *v* يُشْبِه [juʃbihu]
take apart [teɪk ə'pɑ:t] *v* يُفَكِّك إلى أَجْزاء [Yo'fakek ela ajzaa]
take away [teɪk ə'weɪ] *v* ينقل [junqalu]
takeaway ['teɪkə,weɪ] *n* وجبات سريعة [Wajabat sarey'aa]
take back [teɪk bæk] *v* يَسحب كلامه [Yasḥab kalameh]
taken ['teɪkən] *adj*; **Is this seat taken?** هل هذا المقعد محجوز؟ [hal hadha al-ma'q'ad maḥjooz?]
take off [teɪk ɒf] *v* يَخلع ملابسه [Yakhla'a malabesh]
takeoff ['teɪk,ɒf] *n* إقلاع [ʔiqla:ʕ]
take over [teɪk 'əʊvə] *v* يَتَوَلّى [jatawalla:]
takeover ['teɪk,əʊvə] *n* استلام [ʔistila:m]
takings ['teɪkɪŋz] *npl* إيصالات [ʔi:sˤa:la:tun]
tale [teɪl] *n* حكاية [ħika:ja]
talent ['tælənt] *n* موهبة [mawhiba]
talented ['tæləntɪd] *adj* موهوب [mawhu:b]
talk [tɔ:k] *n* كلام [kala:m] ▷ *v* يتحدث [jataħaddaθu]; **talk to** *v* يتحدث إلى [yataḥdath ela]
talkative ['tɔ:kətɪv] *adj* ثرثار [θarθa:r]
tall [tɔ:l] *adj* طويل القامة [Ṭaweel al-'qamah]
tame [teɪm] *adj* مُرَوَض [murawwidˤ]
tampon ['tæmpɒn] *n* سِدادة [sadda:da]
tan [tæn] *n* سُمرة [sumra]
tandem ['tændəm] *n* دراجة ترادفية [Darrajah tradofeyah]
tangerine [,tændʒə'ri:n] *n* يوسفي [ju:sufij]
tank [tæŋk] *n* *(combat vehicle)* دبابة [dabba:ba], *(large container)* صهريج [sˤihri:ʒ]; **petrol tank** *n* خزان بنزين [Khazan benzeen]; **septic tank** *n* غُرفِة تَفتيش [Ghorfat tafteesh]
tanker ['tæŋkə] *n* ناقلة بترول [Na'qelat berool]
tanned [tænd] *adj* له جلد برونزي اللون [lahu ʒildun bru:nziji allawni]
tantrum ['tæntrəm] *n* نوبة غضب [Nawbat ghaḍab]
Tanzania [,tænzə'nɪə] *n* تنزانيا [tanza:nja:]
Tanzanian [,tænzə'nɪən] *adj* تانزاني [ta:nza:nij] ▷ *n* تانزاني [ta:nza:nij]
tap [tæp] *n* حنفية [ħanafijja]
tap-dancing ['tæp,dɑ:nsɪŋ] *n* رقص الكلاكيت [Ra'qṣ al-kelakeet]
tape [teɪp] *n* شريط [ʃari:tˤ] ▷ *v* يُسَجِّل على شريط [Yosajel 'aala shereeṭ]; **tape measure** *n* شريط قياس [Shreeṭ 'qeyas]; **tape recorder** *n* مسجل شرائط [Mosajal sharayeṭ]; **Can I have a tape for this video camera, please?** هل يمكن أن أحصل على شريط فيديو لهذه الكاميرا من فضلك؟ [hal yamken an aḥṣal 'aala shar-eeṭ video le- hadhy al-kamera min faḍlak?]
target ['tɑ:gɪt] *n* هَدَف [hadaf]
tariff ['tærɪf] *n* تعريفة [taʕri:fa]
tarmac ['tɑ:mæk] *n* طريق اسفلتي [ṭaree'q asfaltey]
tarpaulin [tɑ:'pɔ:lɪn] *n* تربولين: قماش مشمع [tarbawli:n: qumma:ʃun muʃmaʕ]
tarragon ['tærəgən] *n* عُشْب الطرخون ['aoshb al-ṭarkhoon]
tart [tɑ:t] *n* فَطيرَة مَحْشُوَّة [Faṭeerah maḥshowah]
tartan ['tɑ:tᵊn] *adj* زِيْ الطرطان الاسكتلندي [zijju atˤtˤartˤa:n ala:skutlandijji]
task [tɑ:sk] *n* مهمة [mahamma]
Tasmania [tæz'meɪnɪə] *n* تسمانيا

[tasma:nja:]
taste [teɪst] *n* طعم [tˁaʕm] ▷ *v* يَتَذَوق [jataðawwaqu]
tasteful ['teɪstfʊl] *adj* حسن الذوق [Hosn aldhaw'q]
tasteless ['teɪstlɪs] *adj* عديم الذوق ['aadeem al-dhaw'q]
tasty ['teɪstɪ] *adj* لذيذ المذاق [Ladheedh al-madha'q]
tattoo [tæ'tu:] *n* وَشْم [waʃm]
Taurus ['tɔ:rəs] *n* الثور [aθθawri]
tax [tæks] *n* ضريبة [dˁari:ba]; **income tax** *n* ضريبة دخل [Dareebat dakhl]; **road tax** *n* ضريبة طُرُق [Dareebat ṭoro'q]; **tax payer** *n* دافع الضرائب [Daafe'a al-ḍarayeb]; **tax return** *n* إقرار ضريبي [E'qrar ḍareeby]
taxi ['tæksɪ] *n* تاكسي [ta:ksi:]; **taxi driver** *n* سائق تاكسي [Sae'q taksey]; **taxi rank** *n* موقف سيارات تاكسي [Maw'qaf sayarat taksy]; **How much is the taxi fare into town?** ما هي أجرة التاكسي داخل البلد؟ [ma heya ejrat al-taxi dakhil al-balad?]; **I left my bags in the taxi** لقد تركت حقائبي في التاكسي [la'qad ta-rakto ḥa'qa-eby fee al-taxi]; **I need a taxi** أنا في حاجة إلى تاكسي [ana fee ḥaja ela taxi]; **Please order me a taxi for 8 o'clock** من فضلك احجز لي تاكسي في الساعة الثامنة [min faḍlak iḥjiz lee taxi fee al-sa'aa al-thamina]; **Where can I get a taxi?** أين يمكن استقلال التاكسي؟ [Ayn yomken este'qlal al-taksey?]; **Where is the taxi stand?** أين يوجد موقف التاكسي؟ [ayna maw'qif al-taxi?]
TB [ti: bi:] *n* سُلّ [sull]
tea [ti:] *n* شاي [ʃa:j]; **herbal tea** *n* شاى بالأعشاب [Shay bel-a'ashab]; **tea bag** *n* كيس شاي [Kees shaay]; **tea towel** *n* مَناشِف الصُّحون [Manashef al-ṣoḥoon]; **A tea, please** شاي من فضلك [shaay min faḍlak]; **Could we have another cup of tea, please?** هل يمكن من فضلك الحصول على كوب آخر من الشاي؟ [hal yamken min faḍlak al-ḥusool 'aala koob aakhar min al-shay?]
teach [ti:tʃ] *v* يُدَرِّس [judarrisu]
teacher ['ti:tʃə] *n* مدرس [mudarris]; **supply teacher** *n* مُدرّس بديل [Modares badeel]
teaching ['ti:tʃɪŋ] *n* تَعْليم [taʕli:m]
teacup ['ti:ˌkʌp] *n* فنجان شاي [Fenjan shay]
team [ti:m] *n* فريق [farjq]
teapot ['ti:ˌpɒt] *n* براد الشاي [Brad shaay]
tear[1] [tɪə] *n (from eye)* دَمْعَة [damʕa]
tear[2] [tɛə] *n (split)* تَمْزيق [tamzi:q] ▷ *v* يُمَزِّق [jumazziqu]; **tear up** *v* يَتَمْزَق [jatamzzaqu]
teargas ['tɪəˌgæs] *n* غاز مسيل للدموع [Ghaz moseel lel-domooa]
tease [ti:z] *v* يُضَايِق [judˁa:jiqu]
teaspoon ['ti:ˌspu:n] *n* ملعقة شاي [Mel'a'qat shay]
teatime ['ti:ˌtaɪm] *n* ساعة تناول الشاي [Saa'ah tanawol al-shay]
technical ['tɛknɪkᵊl] *adj* تقني [tiqnij]
technician [tɛk'nɪʃən] *n* فَنِّي [fannij]
technique [tɛk'ni:k] *n* أسلوب [ʔuslu:b]
techno ['tɛknəʊ] *n* تقني [tiqnij]
technological [tɛk'nɒlədʒɪkᵊl] *adj* تكنولوجي [tiknu:lu:ʒij]
technology [tɛk'nɒlədʒɪ] *n* تكنولوجيا [tiknu:lu:ʒja:]
tee [ti:] *n* الهدف في لعبة الجولف [Al-hadaf fy le'abat al-jolf]
teenager ['ti:nˌeɪdʒə] *n* بالغ [ba:liɣ]
teens [ti:nz] *npl* بالغون [baleghoon]
tee-shirt ['ti:ˌʃɜ:t] *n* تي شيرت [ti: ʃi:rt]
teethe [ti:ð] *v* يُسَنِّن [jusanninu]
teetotal [ti:'təʊtᵊl] *adj* لا يشرب الكحوليات [la: jaʃrabu alkuħu:lija:t]
telecommunications [ˌtɛlɪkəˌmju:nɪ'keɪʃənz] *npl* الاتصالات السلكية [Al-etṣalat al-selkeyah]
telegram ['tɛlɪˌgræm] *n* تلغراف [tiliɣra:f]; **Can I send a telegram from here?** هل يمكن إرسال تلغراف من هنا؟ [hal yamken ersaal tal-ghraf min huna?]
telephone ['tɛlɪˌfəʊn] *n* تليفون [tili:fu:n]; **telephone directory** *n* دليل

الهاتف [Daleel al-hatef]; **How much is it to telephone...?** كم تبلغ تكلفة المكالمة التليفونية إلى... [kam tablugh taklifat al-mukalama al-talefoniya ela...?]; **I need to make an urgent telephone call** أنا في حاجة إلي إجراء مكالمة تليفونية عاجلة [ana fee ḥaja ela ejraa mukalama talefoniya 'aajela]; **What's the telephone number?** ما هو رقم التليفون؟ [ma howa ra'qim al-talefon?]

telesales ['tɛlɪˌseɪlz] *npl* مبيعات بالتليفون [Mabee'aat bel-telefoon]

telescope ['tɛlɪˌskəʊp] *n* تليسكوب [tili:sku:b]

television ['tɛlɪˌvɪʒən] *n* تلفاز [tilfa:z]; **cable television** *n* وَصْلَة تلفزيونية [Wṣlah telefezyoneyah]; **colour television** *n* تليفزيون ملون [Telefezyon molawan]; **digital television** *n* تليفزيون رقمي [telefezyoon ra'qamey]; **Where is the television?** أين أجد جهاز التلفاز؟ [ayna ajid jehaz al-tilfaz?]

tell [tɛl] *v* يُخبِر [juxbiru]

teller ['tɛlə] *n* رَاوِي [ra:wi:]

tell off [tɛl ɒf] *v* يُوَبِخ [juwabbixu]

telly ['tɛlɪ] *n* تلفاز [tilfa:z]

temp [tɛmp] *n* عامِل مُؤَقّت ['aamel mowa'qat]

temper ['tɛmpə] *n* مِزَاج [miza:ʒ]

temperature ['tɛmprɪtʃə] *n* درجة الحرارة [Darajat al-haraarah]; **I'd like something for a temperature** أريد شيئًا للارتفاع درجة الحرارة [areed shyan le-irtifa'a darajat al-ḥarara]; **She has a temperature** إنها مصابة بارتفاع في درجة الحرارة [inaha muṣa-ba be-irtefa'a fee darajat al-ḥarara]

temple ['tɛmpᵊl] *n* معبد [muʕabbad]; **Is the temple open to the public?** هل المعبد مفتوح للجمهور؟ [hal al-ma'abad maf-tooḥa lel-jamhoor?]; **When is the temple open?** متى يُفتح المعبد؟ [mata yoftaḥ al-ma'abad?]

temporary ['tɛmpərərɪ; 'tɛmprərɪ] *adj* مُؤَقّت [muʔaqqat]

tempt [tɛmpt] *v* يُغْري [juɣri:]

temptation [tɛmp'teɪʃən] *n* إغراء [ʔiɣra:ʔ]

tempting ['tɛmptɪŋ] *adj* مغر [muɣrin]

ten [tɛn] *number* عشرة [ʕaʃaratun]

tenant ['tɛnənt] *n* مستأجر [mustaʔʒir]

tend [tɛnd] *v* يرعى [jarʕa:]

tendency ['tɛndənsɪ] *n* مَيل [majl]

tender ['tɛndə] *adj* لطيف [latˤi:f]

tendon ['tɛndən] *n* وتر [watar]

tennis ['tɛnɪs] *n* تنس [tinis]; **table tennis** *n* كرة الطاولة [Korat al-ṭawlah]; **tennis player** *n* لاعب تنس [La'aeb tenes]; **tennis racket** *n* مضرب تنس [Maḍrab tenes]; **How much is it to hire a tennis court?** كم يتكلف استئجار ملعب تنس؟ [kam yo-kalaf estl-Jar mal'aab tanis?]; **Where can I play tennis?** أين يمكنني أن ألعب التنس؟ [ayna yamken-any an al-'aab al-tanis?]

tenor ['tɛnə] *n* آلة التينور الموسيقية [aalat al teenor al mose'qeiah]

tense [tɛns] *adj* متوتر [mutawattir] ▷ *n* صيغة الفعل [Ṣeghat al-fe'al]

tension ['tɛnʃən] *n* توتر [tawattur]

tent [tɛnt] *n* خَيْمة [xajma]; **tent peg** *n* وتد الخيمة [Watad al-kheemah]; **tent pole** *n* عمود الخيمة ['amood al-kheemah]

tenth [tɛnθ] *adj* العاشر [al-ʕa:ʃiru] ▷ *n* العاشر [al-ʕa:ʃiru]

term [tɜːm] *n (description)* أَجَل [ʔaʒal], *(division of year)* فصل من فصول السنة [Faṣl men foṣol al-sanah]

terminal ['tɜːmɪnᵊl] *adj* طرفي [tˤarafajj] ▷ *n* طرف [tˤaraf]

terminally ['tɜːmɪnᵊlɪ] *adv* إلى النهاية [Ela al-nehayah]

terrace ['tɛrəs] *n* شُرفة مكشوفة [Shorfah makshofah]

terraced ['tɛrəst] *adj* مزود بشرفة [Mozawad be-shorfah]

terrible ['tɛrəbᵊl] *adj* مريع [muri:ʕ]

terribly ['tɛrəblɪ; 'terribly] *adv* بشكل مريع [Be-shakl moreeḥ]

terrier ['tɛrɪə] *n* كلب ترير [Kalb tereer]

terrific [tə'rɪfɪk] *adj* مُرَوِّع [murawwiʕ]

terrified ['tɛrɪˌfaɪd] *adj* مرعوب [marʕu:b]
terrify ['tɛrɪˌfaɪ] *v* يُخَيف [juxi:f]
territory ['tɛrɪtərɪ; -trɪ] *n* إقليم [iqli:m]
terrorism ['tɛrəˌrɪzəm] *n* إرهاب [ʔirha:b]
terrorist ['tɛrərɪst] *n* إرهابي [ʔirha:bij]; **terrorist attack** *n* هجوم إرهابي [Hojoom 'erhaby]
test [tɛst] *n* اختبار [ixtiba:r] ▷ *v* يَخْتَبِر [jaxtabiru]; **driving test** *n* اختبار القيادة [Ekhtebar al-'qeyadah]; **smear test** *n* فحص عنق الرحم [Faḥṣ 'aono'q al-raḥem]; **test tube** *n* أنبوب اختبار [Anbob ekhtebar]
testicle ['tɛstɪkᵊl] *n* خصية [xisˤja]
tetanus ['tɛtənəs] *n* تيتانوس [ti:ta:nu:s]; **I need a tetanus shot** أحتاج إلى حقنة تيتانوس [aḥtaaj ela ḥe'qnat tetanus]
text [tɛkst] *n* نص [nasˤsˤ] ▷ *v* يَضع نصا [Yaḍa'a naṣan]; **text message** *n* رسالة نصية [Resalah naṣeyah]
textbook ['tɛkstˌbʊk] *n* كتاب دراسي [Ketab derasey]
textile ['tɛkstaɪl] *n* نسيج [nasi:ʒ]
Thai [taɪ] *adj* تايلاندي [ta:jla:ndij] ▷ *n* *(language)* اللغة التايلاندية [Al-logha al-taylandeiah], *(person)* تايلاندي [ta:jla:ndij]
Thailand ['taɪˌlænd] *n* تايلاند [ta:jla:nd]
than [ðæn; ðən] *conj* مِنْ [min]
thank [θæŋk] *v* يَشكر [jaʃkuru]
thanks [θæŋks] *excl* شكرا! [Shokran!]
that [ðæt; ðət] *adj* هذا [haða:] ▷ *conj* جداً [ʒidan] ▷ *pron* ذَلِك, هذا [haða:]; **Does that contain alcohol?** هل يحتوى هذا على الكحول؟ [hal yaḥ-tawy hadha 'aala al-kiḥool?]
thatched [θætʃt] *adj* مسقوف بالقش [Mas'qoof bel-'qash]
thaw [θɔ:] *v*; **It's thawing** بدأ الدفء في الجو [Badaa al-defaa fee al-jaw]
the [ðə] *art* لام التعريف [liummi attaʕri:fi]
theatre ['θɪətə] *n* مسرح [masraħ]; **operating theatre** *n* غرفة عمليات [ghorfat 'amaleyat]; **What's on at the theatre?** ماذا يعرض الآن على خشبة المسرح؟ [madha yu'a-raḍ al-aan 'aala kha-shabat al-masraḥ?]
theft [θɛft] *n* سرقة [sariqa]; **identity theft** *n* سرقة الهوية [Sare'qat al-hawyiah]; **I want to report a theft** أريد التبليغ عن وقوع سرقة [areed al-tableegh 'an wi'qoo'a sare'qa]
their [ðɛə] *pron* ضمير الملكية للجمع
theirs [ðɛəz] *pron* مِلكهم
them [ðɛm; ðəm] *pron* ضمير الغائب للجمع
theme [θi:m] *n* موضوع [mawdˤu:ʕ]; **theme park** *n* حديقة ألعاب [Hadee'qat al'aab]
themselves [ðəm'sɛlvz] *pron* أنفسهم
then [ðɛn] *adv* آنذاك [ʔa:naða:ka] ▷ *conj* ثُم
theology [θɪ'ɒlədʒɪ] *n* لاهوت [la:hu:t]
theory ['θɪərɪ] *n* نظرية [nazˤarijja]
therapy ['θɛrəpɪ] *n* علاج [ʕila:ʒ]
there [ðɛə] *adv* هناك [huna:ka]; **How do I get there?** كيف يمكن أن أصل إلى هناك؟ [kayfa yamkin an aṣal ela hunaak?]; **It's over there** إنه هناك [inaho honaka]
therefore ['ðɛəˌfɔ:] *adv* لذلك [ledhalek]
thermometer [θə'mɒmɪtə] *n* ترمومتر [tirmu:mitir]
Thermos® ['θɜ:məs] *n* ثيرموس® [θi:rmu:s]
thermostat ['θɜ:məˌstæt] *n* ثرموستات [θirmu:sta:t]
these [ði:z] *adj* هؤلاء ▷ *pron* هؤلاء
they [ðeɪ] *pron* هُم
thick [θɪk] *adj* سَميك [sami:k]
thickness ['θɪknɪs] *n* سَماكة [sama:ka]
thief [θi:f] *n* لص [lisˤsˤ]
thigh [θaɪ] *n* فخذ [faxð]
thin [θɪn] *adj* نحيف [naħi:f]
thing [θɪŋ] *n* أمْر [ʔamr]
think [θɪŋk] *v* يُفَكِر [jufakkiru]
third [θɜ:d] *adj* ثالث [θa:liθ] ▷ *n* الثالث [aθ-θa:liθu]; **third-party insurance** *n* تأمين عن الطرف الثالث [Tameen lada algheer]; **Third World** *n* العالم الثالث [Al-'aalam al-thaleth]
thirdly [θɜ:dlɪ] *adv* ثالثاً [θa:liθan]

thirst [θɜːst] *n* ظمأ [zˤama]
thirsty ['θɜːstɪ] *adj* ظمآن [zˤamʔaːn]
thirteen ['θɜː'tiːn] *number* ثلاثة عشر [θalaːθata ʕaʃara]
thirteenth ['θɜː'tiːnθ; 'thir'teenth] *adj* ثالث عشر [θaːliθa ʕaʃara]
thirty ['θɜːtɪ] *number* ثلاثون [θalaːθuːna]
this [ðɪs] *adj* هذا [haðaː] ▷ *pron* هذا [haðaː]; **I'll have this** سوف أتناول هذا [sawfa ata-nawal hadha]; **What is in this?** ماذا يوجد في هذا؟ [madha yujad fee hadha?]
thistle ['θɪsᵊl] *n* شَوْك [ʃawk]
thorn [θɔːn] *n* شَوْكَة [ʃawka]
thorough ['θʌrə] *adj* شَامِل [ʃaːmil]
thoroughly ['θʌrəlɪ] *adv* بشكل شامل [Be-shakl shamel]
those [ðəʊz] *adj* هذه ▷ *pron* هؤلاء
though [ðəʊ] *adv* رغم ذلك [Raghm dhalek] ▷ *conj* ولو أن
thought [θɔːt] *n* تفكير [tafkiːr]
thoughtful ['θɔːtfʊl] *adj* مستغرق في التفكير [Mostaghre'q fee al-tafkeer]
thoughtless ['θɔːtlɪs] *adj* طائش [tˤaːʔiʃ]
thousand ['θaʊzənd] *number* ألف [ʔalfun]
thousandth ['θaʊzənθ; 'thousandth] *adj* الألف [al-ʔalfu] ▷ *n* جزء من ألف [Joza men al alf]
thread [θrɛd] *n* خَيْط [xajtˤ]
threat [θrɛt] *n* تهديد [tahdiːd]
threaten ['θrɛtᵊn] *v* يُهَدِد [juhaddidu]
threatening ['θrɛtᵊnɪŋ] *adj* تهديدي [tahdiːdij]
three [θriː] *number* ثلاثة [θalaːθatun]
three-dimensional [ˌθriːdɪ'mɛnʃənᵊl] *adj* ثلاثي الأبعاد [Tholathy al-ab'aaad]
thrifty ['θrɪftɪ] *adj* مزدهر [muzdahir]
thrill [θrɪl] *n* رعشة [raʕʃa]
thrilled [θrɪld] *adj* مُنتشي [muntaʃij]
thriller ['θrɪlə] *n* تَشْويق [taʃwiːq]
thrilling ['θrɪlɪŋ; 'thrilling] *adj* مُفرِح [mufriħ]
throat [θrəʊt] *n* حنجرة [ħanʒura]
throb [θrɒb] *v* يَخفِق [jaxfiqu]
throne [θrəʊn] *n* عرش [ʕarʃ]
through [θruː] *prep* خلال [xilaːla]
throughout [θruː'aʊt] *prep* طوال [tˤiwaːla]
throw [θrəʊ] *v* يَرمِي [jarmiː]
throw away [θrəʊ ə'weɪ] *v* يَتَخَلَّص [jataxallasˤu]
throw out [θrəʊ aʊt] *v* يَقْذِف [jaqðifu]
throw up [θrəʊ ʌp] *v* يقيء [jaqiːʔu]
thrush [θrʌʃ] *n* دُجّ [duʒʒ]
thug [θʌg] *n* سَفَّاح [saffaːħ]
thumb [θʌm] *n* إبهام اليد [Ebham al-yad]
thumb tack ['θʌmˌtæk] *n* مسمار صغير يدفع بالإبهام [Mesmar ṣagheer yodfa'a bel-ebham]
thump [θʌmp] *v* يجلد [juʒallidu]
thunder ['θʌndə] *n* رَعْد [raʕd]
thunderstorm ['θʌndəˌstɔːm] *n* عاصفة رعدية ['aasefah ra'adeyah]
thundery ['θʌndərɪ] *adj* مصحوب برعد [Maṣḥoob bera'ad]
Thursday ['θɜːzdɪ] *n* يوم الخميس [jawmul xamiːsi]; **on Thursday** في يوم الخميس [fee yawm al-khamees]
thyme [taɪm] *n* الزعتر [az-zaʕtari]
Tibet [tɪ'bɛt] *n* تيبت [tiːbit]
Tibetan [tɪ'bɛtᵊn] *adj* تيبيتي [tiːbiːtij] ▷ *n* *(language)* اللغة التيبتية [Al-loghah al-tebeteyah], *(person)* شخص تيبيتي [Shakhṣ tebetey]
tick [tɪk] *n* حشرة القرادة [Hashrat al-'qaradah] ▷ *v* يُتَكْتِك [jutaktiku]
ticket ['tɪkɪt] *n* تذكَرة [taðkira]; **bus ticket** *n* تذكرة أوتوبيس [tadhkarat otobees]; **one-way ticket** *n* تذكرة ذهاب [tadhkarat dhehab]; **parking ticket** *n* تذكرة الركن [tadhkarat al-rokn]; **return ticket** *n* تذكرة إياب [tadhkarat eyab]; **season ticket** *n* التذاكر الموسمية [Al-tadhaker al-mawsemeyah]; **single ticket** *n* تذكرة فردية [tadhkarat fardeyah]; **stand-by ticket** *n* تذكرة انتظار [tadhkarat enteḍhar]; **ticket barrier** *n* حاجز وضع التذاكر [Hajez wad'a al-tadhaker]; **ticket collector** *n* جامع التذاكر [Jame'a al-tadhaker]; **ticket**

inspector *n* مفتش التذاكر [Mofatesh taḍhaker]; **ticket machine** *n* ماكينة التذاكر [Makenat al-taḍhaker]; **ticket office** *n* مكتب التذاكر [Maktab al-taḍhaker]
tickle ['tɪkᵊl] *v* يُدَغدِغ [judaɣdiɣu]
ticklish ['tɪklɪʃ] *adj* سريع الغضب [Saree'a al-ghaḍab]
tick off [tɪk ɒf] *v* يَضَع عَلامَة صَح [Beḍa'a 'aalamat ṣaḥ]
tide [taɪd] *n* مد وجزر [Mad wa-jazr]
tidy ['taɪdɪ] *adj* مرتب [murattab] ▷ *v* يُرَتِّب [jurattibu]
tidy up ['taɪdɪ ʌp] *v* يُهَنْدِم [juhandimu]
tie [taɪ] *n* رباط العنق [Rebaṭ al-'aono'q] ▷ *v* يُقيِّد [juqajjidu]; **bow tie** *n* رباط عنق على شكل فراشة [Rebaṭ 'ala shakl frashah]
tie up [taɪ ʌp] *v* يَرْتَبِط مع [Yartabeṭ ma'aa]
tiger ['taɪɡə] *n* نمر مخطط [Namer mokhaṭaṭ]
tight [taɪt] *adj* مُحْكَم [muħkam]
tighten ['taɪtᵊn] *v* يُضَيْق [judˤajjiqu]
tights [taɪts] *npl* بنطلون ضيق [banṭaloon ḍaye'q]
tile [taɪl] *n* أنبوب فخاري [Onbob fokhary]
tiled ['taɪld] *adj* مكسو بالقرميد [Makso bel-'qarmeed]
till [tɪl] *conj* إلى أن ▷ *n* دُرج النقود [Dorj al-no'qood]
timber ['tɪmbə] *n* أشجار الغابات [Ashjaar al-ghabat]
time [taɪm] *n* وَقْت [waqt]; **closing time** *n* وَقْت الإغلاق [Wa'qt al-eghlaa'q]; **dinner time** *n* وَقْت العشاء [Wa'qt al-'aashaa]; **on time** *adj* في الموعد المحدد [Fee al-maw'aed al-moḥadad]; **spare time** *n* وَقْت فراغ [Wa'qt faragh]; **time off** *n* أجازة [ʔaʒa:zatun]; **time zone** *n* نطاق زمني [Neṭa'q zamaney]
time bomb ['taɪm,bɒm] *n* قنبلة موقوتة ['qonbolah maw'qota]
timer ['taɪmə] *n* ميقاتي [mi:qa:tij]
timeshare ['taɪm,ʃɛə] *n* مُشاركة في الوقت [Mosharakah fee al-wa'qt]
timetable ['taɪm,teɪbᵊl] *n* جدول زمني [Jadwal zamaney]
tin [tɪn] *n* صفيح [sˤafi:ħ]; **tin-opener** *n* فتاحة علب [fatta ḥat 'aolab]
tinfoil ['tɪn,fɔɪl] *n* ورق فضي [Wara'q feḍey]
tinned [tɪnd] *adj* معلب [muʕallab]
tinsel ['tɪnsəl] *n* أشرطة للزينة [Ashreṭah lel-zeena]
tinted ['tɪntɪd] *adj* ملون على نحو خفيف [Molawan ala naḥw khafeef]
tiny ['taɪnɪ] *adj* ضئيل [dˤaʔijl]
tip [tɪp] *n (end of object)* طرف مستدق [Ṭaraf mostabe'q], *(reward)* إكرامية [ʔikra:mijja], *(suggestion)* فكرة مفيدة [Fekrah mofeedah] ▷ *v (incline)* يَميل [jami:lu], *(reward)* يمنح بقشيشاً [Yamnaḥ ba'qsheeshan]
tipsy ['tɪpsɪ] *adj* مترنح [mutarannih]
tiptoe ['tɪp,təʊ] *n* رَأس إصبع القدم [Raas eṣbe'a al-'qadam]
tired ['taɪəd] *adj* متعب [mutʕab]
tiring ['taɪərɪŋ] *adj* منهك [munhak]
tissue ['tɪsju:; 'tɪʃu:] *n (anatomy)* نَسيج الجِسْم [Naseej al-jesm], *(paper)* منديل ورقي [Mandeel wara'qey]
title ['taɪtᵊl] *n* لَقَبْ [laqab]
to [tu:; tʊ; tə] *prep* إلى [ʔila:]; **Can I speak to Mr...?** هل يمكن أن أتحدث إلى السيد... [hal yamken an ata-ḥadath ela al-sayid...?]; **I need someone to look after the children tonight** أحتاج إلى شخص يعتني بالأطفال ليلًا [aḥtaaj ela shakhiṣ y'atany be-al-aṭfaal laylan]; **I need to get to...** أريد أن أذهب إلى... [Areed an adhhab ela...]; **I'm going to...** سوف أذهب إلى... [Sawf adhhab ela]; **When is the first bus to...?** ما هو موعد أول أتوبيس متجه إلى... [ma howa maw-'aid awal baaṣ mutajih ela...?]
toad [təʊd] *n* ضفدع الطين [Ḍofda'a al- ṭeen]
toadstool ['təʊd,stu:l] *n* فطر الغاريقون [Feṭr al-gharekoon]
toast [təʊst] *n (grilled bread)* خبز محمص [Khobz mohammṣ], *(tribute)* مشروب

النُّخْب [Mashroob al-nnkhb]
toaster ['təʊstə] *n* محمصة خبز كهربائية [Mohamaṣat khobz kahrobaeyah]
tobacco [tə'bækəʊ] *n* تبغ [tibɣ]
tobacconist's [tə'bækənɪsts] *n* مَتجر السجائر [Matjar al-sajaaer]
tobogganing [tə'bɒgənɪŋ] *n* تزلق [tazaluq]
today [tə'deɪ] *adv* اليَوْم [aljawma]
toddler ['tɒdlə] *n* طفل صغير عادة ما بين السنة الأولى والثانية [Ṭefl ṣagheer 'aaadatan ma bayn al-sanah wal- sana-tayen]
toe [təʊ] *n* إصبع القدم [Eṣbe'a al'qadam]
toffee ['tɒfɪ] *n* حلوى [ħalwa:]
together [tə'gɛðə] *adv* سويا [sawijjan]
Togo ['təʊgəʊ] *n* توجو [tu:ʒu:]
toilet ['tɔɪlɪt] *n* حمام [ħamma:m]; **toilet bag** *n* حقيبة أدوات الاستحمام [Ha'qeebat adwat al-estehmam]; **toilet paper** *n* ورق المرحاض [Wara'q al-merḥaḍ]; **toilet roll** *n* لفة ورق المرحاض [Lafat wara'q al-merhaḍ]; **Are there any accessible toilets?** هل توجد حمامات مناسبة للمعاقين؟ [hal tojad ḥama-maat muna-seba lel-mu'aa'qeen?]; **Can I use the toilet?** هل يمكن أن استعمل الحمام؟ [hal yamken an asta'a-mil al-ḥam-maam?]; **Is there a toilet on board?** هل هناك حمام في الأتوبيس؟ [hal hunaka ḥamaam fee al-oto-bees?]
toiletries ['tɔɪlɪtri:s] *npl* مستلزمات الحمام [Mostalzamat al-hammam]
token ['təʊkən] *n* علامة [ʕala:ma]
tolerant ['tɒlərənt] *adj* متسامح [mutasa:miħ]
toll [təʊl] *n* رسوم [rusu:m]; **Is there a toll on this motorway?** هل هناك رسوم يتم دفعها للمرور بهذا الطريق؟ [hal hunaka risoom yatim daf-'aaha lel-miroor be-hadha al- ṯaree'q?]; **Where can I pay the toll?** أين سأدفع رسوم المرور بالطريق؟ [ayna sa-adfa'a rosom al-miroor bil-ṯaree'q?]
tomato, tomatoes [tə'mɑːtəʊ, tə'mɑːtəʊz] *n* طماطم [tˤama:tˤim];
tomato sauce *n* صلصة طماطم [Ṣalṣat ṭamaṭem]
tomb [tuːm] *n* مقبرة [maqbara]
tomboy ['tɒm,bɔɪ] *n* فتاة متشبهة بالصبيان [fata:tun mutaʃabbihatun bisˤsˤabja:ni]
tomorrow [tə'mɒrəʊ] *adv* غداً [ɣadan]
ton [tʌn] *n* طُنْ [tˤunn]
tone [təʊn] *n*; **dialling tone** *n* نغمة الاتصال [Naghamat al-eteṣal]; **engaged tone** *n* رنين انشغال الخط [Raneen ensheghal al-khaṭ]
Tonga ['tɒŋgə] *n* مملكة تونجا [Mamlakat tonja]
tongue [tʌŋ] *n* لسان [lisa:n]; **mother tongue** *n* اللغة الأم [Al loghah al om]
tonic ['tɒnɪk] *n* دواء مُقَوِي [Dawaa mo'qawey]
tonight [tə'naɪt] *adv* في هذه الليلة [Fee hadheh al-laylah]
tonsillitis [,tɒnsɪ'laɪtɪs] *n* التهاب اللوزتين [Eltehab al-lawzateyn]
tonsils ['tɒnsəlz] *npl* لوزتين [lawzatajni]
too [tuː] *adv* أيضا [ʔajdˤan]
tool [tuːl] *n* أداة [ʔada:t]
tooth, teeth ['tuːθ, tiːθ] *n* سِن [sin]; **wisdom tooth** *n* ضرس العقل [Ḍers al-a'aql]
toothache ['tuːθ,eɪk] *n* وجع الأسنان [Waja'a al-asnaan]
toothbrush ['tuːθ,brʌʃ] *n* فرشاة الأسنان [Forshat al-asnaan]
toothpaste ['tuːθ,peɪst] *n* معجون الأسنان [ma'ajoon asnan]
toothpick ['tuːθ,pɪk] *n* عود الأسنان ['aood al-asnan]
top [tɒp] *adj* علوي [ʕulwij] ▷ *n* قمة [qima]
topic ['tɒpɪk] *n* موضوع مقالة أو حديث [Mawḍoo'a ma'qaalah aw hadeeth]
topical ['tɒpɪkᵊl] *adj* موضعي [mawdˤiʕij]
top-secret ['tɒp'siːkrɪt] *adj* سري للغاية [Serey lel-ghayah]
top up [tɒp ʌp] *v*; **Can you top up the windscreen washers?** هل يمكن أن تملئ خزان المياه لمساحات الزجاج؟ [hal yamken an tamlee khazaan al-meaah

le-massa-ḥaat al-zujaaj?]; **Where can I buy a top-up card?** أين يمكن أن أشتري كارت إعادة شحن [ayna yamken an ash-tary kart e-'aadat shaḥin?]
torch [tɔːtʃ] *n* كشاف كهربائي [Kashaf kahrabaey]
tornado [tɔːˈneɪdəʊ] *n* إعصار قمعي [E'aṣar 'qam'ay]
tortoise [ˈtɔːtəs] *n* سُلحفاة [sulħufa:t]
torture [ˈtɔːtʃə] *n* تعذيب [taʕði:b] ▷ *v* يُعَذِب [juʕaððibu]
toss [tɒs] *v* يقذف [jaqðifu]
total [ˈtəʊtᵊl] *adj* إجمالي [ʔiʒma:lij] ▷ *n* إجمالي [ʔiʒma:lij]
totally [ˈtəʊtᵊlɪ] *adv* بشكل كامل [Beshakl kaamel]
touch [tʌtʃ] *v* يَلْمِس [jalmisu]
touchdown [ˈtʌtʃˌdaʊn] *n* هبوط الطائرة [Hobooṭ al-ṭaerah]
touched [tʌtʃt] *adj* ممسوس [mamsu:s]
touching [ˈtʌtʃɪŋ] *adj* فيما يتعلق بـ [Feema yat'ala'q be]
touchline [ˈtʌtʃˌlaɪn] *n* خط التماس [Khaṭ al-tamas]
touchpad [ˈtʌtʃˌpæd] *n* لوحة اللمس [Lawḥat al-lams]
touchy [ˈtʌtʃɪ] *adj* سريع الانفعال [Saree'a al-enfe'aal]
tough [tʌf] *adj* قوي [qawij]
toupee [ˈtuːpeɪ] *n* خصلة شعر مستعار [khoṣlat sha'ar mosta'aar]
tour [tʊə] *n* جولة [ʒawla] ▷ *v* يَتَجوَل [jataʒawwalu]; **guided tour** *n* جولة إرشادية [Jawlah ershadeyah]; **package tour** *n* خطة رحلة شاملة الإقامة والانتقالات [Khotah rehalah shamelah al-e'qamah wal-ente'qalat]; **tour guide** *n* مرشد سياحي [Morshed seyaḥey]; **tour operator** *n* منظم رحلات [monaḍhem raḥalat]
tourism [ˈtʊərɪzəm] *n* سياحة [sija:ħa]
tourist [ˈtʊərɪst] *n* سائح [sa:ʔiħ]; **tourist office** *n* مكتب سياحي [Maktab seayaḥey]
tournament [ˈtʊənəmənt; ˈtɔː-; ˈtɜː-] *n* سلسلة مباريات [Selselat mobarayat]
towards [təˈwɔːdz; tɔːdz] *prep* تجاه
tow away [təʊ əˈweɪ] *v* يَجُر سيارة [Yajor sayarah]
towel [ˈtaʊəl] *n* منشفة [minʃafa]; **bath towel** *n* منشفة الحمام [Manshafah alḥammam]; **dish towel** *n* فوطة تجفيف الأطباق [Foṭah tajfeef al-aṭbaa'q]; **sanitary towel** *n* منشفة صحية [Manshafah ṣeḥeyah]; **tea towel** *n* مَناشِف الصُّحون [Manashef al-ṣoḥoon]
tower [ˈtaʊə] *n* بُرْج [burʒ]
town [taʊn] *n* بلدة [balda]; **town centre** *n* وَسَطْ المدينة [Wasaṭ al-madeenah]; **town hall** *n* دار البلدية [Dar al-baladeyah]; **town planning** *n* تخطيط المدينة [Takhṭeeṭ almadeenah]
toxic [ˈtɒksɪk] *adj* سُمي [summij]
toy [tɔɪ] *n* لعبة [luʕba]
trace [treɪs] *n* أثَر [ʔaθar]
tracing paper [ˈtreɪsɪŋ ˈpeɪpə] *n* ورق شفاف [Wara'q shafaf]
track [træk] *n* مسار [masa:r]
track down [træk daʊn] *v* يَتَتبع [jatatabbaʕu]
tracksuit [ˈtrækˌsuːt; -ˌsjuːt] *n* بدلة تدريب [Badlat tadreeb]
tractor [ˈtræktə] *n* جرار [ʒaraar]
trade [treɪd] *n* تجارة [tiʒa:ra]; **trade union** *n* نقابة العمال [Ne'qabat al-'aomal]; **trade unionist** *n* عضو نقابة عمالية ['aḍw ne'qabah a'omaleyah]
trademark [ˈtreɪdˌmɑːk] *n* علامة تجارية ['alamah tejareyah]
tradition [trəˈdɪʃən] *n* تقليد [taqli:d]
traditional [trəˈdɪʃənᵊl] *adj* تقليدي [taqli:dij]
traffic [ˈtræfɪk] *n* مُرور [muru:r]; **traffic jam** *n* ازدحام المرور [Ezdeḥam al-moror]; **traffic lights** *npl* إشارات المرور [Esharaat al-moroor]; **traffic warden** *n* شُرطي المرور [Shrṭey al-moror]
tragedy [ˈtrædʒɪdɪ] *n* مأساة [maʔsa:t]
tragic [ˈtrædʒɪk] *adj* مأساوي [maʔsa:wij]
trailer [ˈtreɪlə] *n* عربة مقطورة ['arabat ma'qtoorah]
train [treɪn] *n* قطار [qitˤa:r] ▷ *v* يُدرِب

[judarribu]; **Does the train stop at...?** هل يتوقف القطار في...؟ [hal yata-wa'qaf al-'qeṭaar fee...?]; **How frequent are the trains to...?** ما هي المدة الفاصلة بين القطارات؟ [Ma heya almodah alfaselah bayn al'qeṭaraat]; **I've missed my train** لم أتمكن من اللحاق بالقطار [lam atamakan min al-leḥa'q bil-'qeṭaar]; **Is the train wheelchair-accessible?** هل يمكن الوصول إلى القطار بالكراسي المتحركة؟ [hal yamken al-wiṣool ela al-'qeṭaar bel-karasi al-mutaḥarika?]; **Is this the train for...?** هل هذا هو القطار المتجه إلى...؟ [hal hadha howa al-'qeṭaar al-mutajeh ela...?]; **The next available train, please** ما هو موعد القطار التالي من فضلك؟ [ma howa maw-'aid al-'qeṭaar al-taaly min faḍlak?]; **What time does the train arrive in...?** ما هو موعد وصول القطار إلى... [ma howa maw-'aid wiṣool al-'qeṭaar ela...?]; **What time does the train leave?** ما هو موعد مغادرة القطار؟ [ma howa maw-'aid mughadarat al-'qeṭaar?]; **When is the first train to...?** ما هو موعد أول قطار متجه إلى...؟ [ma howa maw-'aid awal 'qeṭaar mutajih ela...?]; **When is the next train to...?** ما هو موعد القطار التالي المتجه إلى...؟ [ma howa maw-'aid al-'qeṭaar al-taaly al-mutajih ela...?]; **Where can I get a train to...?** كيف يمكن أن أركب القطار المتجه إلى... [kayfa yamkin an arkab al-'qetaar al-mutajih ela...?]; **Which platform does the train leave from?** على أي رصيف يغادر القطار؟ ['ala ay raṣeef yo-ghader al-'qeṭaar?]

trained ['treɪnd] *adj* مُدَرَب [mudarrib]

trainee [treɪ'niː] *n* متدرب [mutadarrib]

trainer ['treɪnə] *n* مُدَرِب [mudarrib]

trainers ['treɪnəz] *npl* مدربون [mudarribu:na]

training ['treɪnɪŋ] *n* تدريب [tadri:b]; **training course** *n* دروة تدريبية [Dawrah tadreebeyah]

tram [træm] *n* ترام [tra:m]

tramp [træmp] *n (beggar)* مُتَسَوِّل [mutasawwil], *(long walk)* رحلة سيرًا على الأقدام [rehalah sayran ala al-a'qdam]

trampoline ['træmpəlɪn; -ˌliːn] *n* منصة البهلوان [Manaṣat al-bahlawan]

tranquillizer ['træŋkwɪˌlaɪzə] *n* مُهَدّئ [muhaddi?]

transaction [træn'zækʃən] *n* مُعَاملة [muʕa:mala]

transcript ['trænskrɪpt] *n* سجل مدرسي [Sejel madrasey]

transfer *n* ['trænsfɜː]تحويل [taħwi:l] ▷ *v* [træns'fɜː]تحويل [taħwi:lun]; **How long will it take to transfer?** كم يستغرق التحويل؟ [kam yasta-ghri'q al-taḥweel?]; **I would like to transfer some money from my account** أريد تحويل بعض الأموال من حسابي [areed taḥweel ba'aḍ al-amwal min ḥesaaby]; **Is there a transfer charge?** هل يحتسب رسم تحويل؟ [hal yoḥ-tasab rasim taḥ-weel?]

transform [træns'fɔːm] *v* يُبَدِل [jubaddilu]

transfusion [træns'fjuːʒən] *n* نقل الدم [Na'ql al-dam]; **blood transfusion** *n* نقل الدم [Na'ql al-dam]

transistor [træn'zɪstə] *n* ترانزستور [tra:nzistu:r]

transit ['trænsɪt; 'trænz-] *n* عبور [ʕubu:r]; **transit lounge** *n* صالة العبور [Ṣalat al'aoboor]

transition [træn'zɪʃən] *n* انتقال [intiqa:l]

translate [træns'leɪt; trænz-] *v* يُتَرجم [jutarʒimu]

translation [træns'leɪʃən; trænz-] *n* ترجمة [tarʒama]

translator [træns'leɪtə; trænz-; trans'lator] *n* مترجم [muntarʒim]

transparent [træns'pærənt; -'pɛər-] *adj* شَفّاف [ʃaffa:f]

transplant ['træns,plɑːnt] *n* زرع الأعضاء [Zar'a al-a'aḍaa]

transport *n* ['træns,pɔːt]نقل [naql] ▷ *v* [træns'pɔːt]ينقل [junqalu]; **public transport** *n* نقل عام [Na'ql 'aam]

transvestite [trænz'vɛstaɪt] *n* المخنث [al-muxannaθu]

trap [træp] *n* مصيدة [misˤjada]
trash [træʃ] *n* قمامة [quma:ma]
traumatic ['trɔːməˌtɪk] *adj* جرحي [ʒarħij]
travel ['trævᵊl] *n* سِفر [safar] ▷ *v* يُسافر [jusa:firu]; **travel agency** *n* وكالة سفريات [Wakalat safareyat]; **travel agent's** *n* مكتب وكيل السفريات [Maktab wakeel al-safareyat]; **travel sickness** *n* دُوار السفر [Dowar al-safar]
traveller ['trævələ; 'trævlə] *n* مسافر [musa:fir]; **traveller's cheque** *n* شِيك سياحي [Sheek seyahey]
travelling ['trævᵊlɪŋ] *n* سَفَر [safar]
tray [treɪ] *n* صينية [sˤi:nijja]
treacle ['triːkᵊl] *n* دِبْس السكُر [Debs al-sokor]
tread [trɛd] *v* يَدوس [jadu:su]
treasure ['trɛʒə] *n* كنز [kanz]
treasurer ['trɛʒərə] *n* أمين الصندوق [Ameen alṣondoo'q]
treat [triːt] *n* دعوة إلى طعام أو شراب [Dawah elaa ṭa'aam aw sharaab] ▷ *v* يَستضيف [jastadˤi:fu]
treatment ['triːtmənt] *n* معاملة [muʕa:mala]
treaty ['triːtɪ] *n* معاهدة [muʕa:hada]
treble ['trɛbᵊl] *v* يَزداد ثلاثة أضعاف [Yazdad thalathat aḍ'aaaf]
tree [triː] *n* شجرة [ʃaʒara]
trek [trɛk] *n* رحلة بعربة ثيران [Rehlah be-arabat theran] ▷ *v* يُسافِر سَفْرَة طَويلَة [jusa:firu safratan tˤawi:latan]
trekking ['trɛkɪŋ] *n*; **I'd like to go pony trekking** أود أن أقوم بنزهة على ظهر الخيول؟ [awid an a'qoom be-nozha 'aala ḍhahir al-khiyool]
tremble ['trɛmbᵊl] *v* يَرتعِد [jartaʕidu]
tremendous [trɪ'mɛndəs] *adj* هائل [ha:ʔil]
trench [trɛntʃ] *n* خَنْدَق [xandaq]
trend [trɛnd] *n* نزعة [nazʕa]
trendy ['trɛndɪ] *adj* مواكب للموضة [Mowakeb lel-moḍah]
trial ['traɪəl] *n* محاكمة [muħa:kama]; **trial period** *n* فترة المحاكمة [Fatrat al-moḥkamah]
triangle ['traɪˌæŋgᵊl] *n* مثلث [muθallaθ]
tribe [traɪb] *n* قبيلة [qabi:la]
tribunal [traɪ'bjuːnᵊl; trɪ-] *n* محكمة [maħkama]
trick [trɪk] *n* خدعة [xudʕa] ▷ *v* يْوهم [juhimu]
tricky ['trɪkɪ] *adj* مخادع [muxa:diʕ]
tricycle ['traɪsɪkᵊl] *n* دراجة ثلاثية [Darrajah tholatheyah]
trifle ['traɪfᵊl] *n* تَافِه [ta:fih]
trim [trɪm] *v* يُزَين [juzajjinu]
Trinidad and Tobago ['trɪnɪˌdæd ænd tə'beɪgəʊ] *n* جمهورية ترينيداد وتوباغو [ʒumhu:rijjatu tri:ni:da:d wa tu:ba:ɣu:]
trip [trɪp] *n* رحلة قصيرة [Rehalh 'qaṣeerah]; **business trip** *n* رحلة عمل [Reḥlat 'aamal]; **round trip** *n* رحلةانكفائية [Reḥlah enkefaeyah]; **trip (up)** *v* يَتَعَثَّر [jataʕaθθaru]
triple ['trɪpᵊl] *adj* ثلاثي [θula:θij]
triplets ['trɪplɪts] *npl* ثُلاثِي [θula:θijjun]
triumph ['traɪəmf] *n* انتصار [intisˤa:r] ▷ *v* يَنْتَصر [jantasˤiru]
trivial ['trɪvɪəl] *adj* تَافِه [ta:fih]
trolley ['trɒlɪ] *n* عربة الترولي ['arabat al-troley]; **luggage trolley** *n* عربة حقائب السفر ['arabat ḥa'qaaeb al-safar]; **shopping trolley** *n* ترولي التسوق [Trolley altasaw'q]
trombone [trɒm'bəʊn] *n* ترومبون [tru:mbu:n]
troops ['truːps] *npl* فرق كشافة [Fear'q kashafah]
trophy ['trəʊfɪ] *n* تذكار انتصار [tedhkaar enteṣar]
tropical ['trɒpɪkᵊl] *adj* استوائي [istiwa:ʔij]
trot [trɒt] *v* يَخِبُّ الفَرَس [Yakheb al-faras]
trouble ['trʌbᵊl] *n* قلق [qalaq]
troublemaker ['trʌbᵊlˌmeɪkə] *n* مثير المتاعب [Mother al-mataa'aeb]
trough [trɒf] *n* جُرن [ʒurn]
trousers ['traʊzəz] *npl* بَنطلون [bantˤalu:nun]
trout [traʊt] *n* سمك السَّلْمون المُرَقَّط

[Samak al-salamon almora'qaṭ]
trowel ['traʊəl] *n* مسطرين [mistˤarajni]
truant ['tru:ənt] *n*; **play truant** *v* يتغَيب [jataɣajjabu]
truce [tru:s] *n* هدنة [hudna]
truck [trʌk] *n* شاحِنة [ʃa:ħina]; **breakdown truck** *n* شاحنة قَطْر [Shaḥenat 'qaṭr]; **truck driver** *n* سائق شاحنة [Sae'q shahenah]
true [tru:] *adj* حقيقي [ħaqi:qij]
truly ['tru:lɪ] *adv* بحَقْ [biħaqqin]
trumpet ['trʌmpɪt] *n* بُوق [bu:q]
trunk [trʌŋk] *n* جِذْع [ʒiðʕ]; **swimming trunks** *npl* سِروال سباحة [Serwl sebaḥah]
trunks [trʌŋks] *npl* بنطلون قصير [Banṭaloon 'qaṣeer]
trust [trʌst] *n* ائتمان [iʔtima:n] ▷ *v* يَثِق ب [Yathe'q be]
trusting ['trʌstɪŋ] *adj* مؤتمن [muʔtaman]
truth [tru:θ] *n* حقيقة [ħaqi:qa]
truthful ['tru:θfʊl] *adj* صادق [sˤa:diq]
try [traɪ] *n* تجربة [taʒriba] ▷ *v* يُجَرب [juʒarribu]
try on [traɪ ɒn] *v* يَقْيس ثوباً [Ya'qees thawban]
try out [traɪ aʊt] *v* يَضع تحت الاختبار [Yada'a taḥt al-ekhtebar]
T-shirt ['ti:ˌʃɜ:t] *n* قميص قصير الكمين ['qameeṣ 'qaṣeer al-kmayen]
tsunami [tsʊ'næmɪ] *n* تسونامي [tsu:na:mi:]
tube [tju:b] *n* أنبوبة [ʔunbu:ba]; **inner tube** *n* أنبوب داخلي [Anboob dakheley]; **test tube** *n* أنبوب اختبار [Anbob ekhtebar]; **tube station** *n* محطة أنفاق [Mahaṭat anfa'q]
tuberculosis [tjʊˌbɜ:kjʊ'ləʊsɪs] *n* سُلٌ [sull]
Tuesday ['tju:zdɪ] *n* يوم الثلاثاء [Yawm al-tholathaa]; **Shrove Tuesday** *n* ثلاثاء المرافع [Tholathaa almrafe'a]; **on Tuesday** في يوم الثلاثاء [fee yawm al-thalathaa]
tug-of-war ['tʌgɒv'wɔ:] *n* صراع عنيف [Ṣera'a 'aneef]
tuition [tju:'ɪʃən] *n* تعليم [taʕli:m]; **tuition fees** *npl* رسوم التعليم [Rasm al-ta'aleem]
tulip ['tju:lɪp] *n* توليب [tawli:bu]
tummy ['tʌmɪ] *n* بطن [batˤn]
tumour ['tju:mə] *n* وَرَمْ [waram]
tuna ['tju:nə] *n* سمك التونة [Samak al-tonah]
tune [tju:n] *n* مقطوعة موسيقية [Ma'qtoo'aah moose'qeyah]
Tunisia [tju:'nɪzɪə; -'nɪsɪə] *n* تونس [tu:nus]
Tunisian [tju:'nɪzɪən; -'nɪsɪən] *adj* تونسي [tu:nusij] ▷ *n* تونسي [tu:nusij]
tunnel ['tʌnəl] *n* نفق [nafaq]
turbulence ['tɜ:bjʊləns] *n* اضطراب [idˤtˤira:b]
Turk [tɜ:k] *n* تُركي [turkij]
turkey ['tɜ:kɪ] *n* ديِّك رومي [Deek roomey]
Turkey ['tɜ:kɪ] *n* تركيا [turkija:]
Turkish ['tɜ:kɪʃ] *adj* تركي [turkij] ▷ *n* تُركي [turkij]
turn [tɜ:n] *n* دَوْرَة [dawra] ▷ *v* يَدْوُر [jadu:ru]
turn around [tɜ:n ə'raʊnd] *v* يَبْرُم [jabrumu]
turn back [tɜ:n bæk] *v* يَرجِع [jarʒiʕu]
turn down [tɜ:n daʊn] *v* يُقَلِّل [juqallilu]
turning ['tɜ:nɪŋ] *n* منعطف [munʕatˤaf]; **Is this the turning for...?** هل هذا هو المنعطف الذي يؤدي إلى...؟ [hal hadha howa al-mun'aa-ṭaf al-ladhy yo-addy ela...?]; **Take the first turning on your right** أتجه نحو أول منعطف على اليمين [ʔattaʒihu naħwa ʔawwali munʕatˤafi ʕala: aljami:ni]; **Take the second turning on your left** اتجه نحو المنعطف الثاني على اليسار [Etajeh naḥw almon'ataf althaney ala alyasaar]
turnip ['tɜ:nɪp] *n* نبات اللفت [Nabat al-left]
turn off [tɜ:n ɒf] *v* يُطْفِئ [jutˤfiʔ]
turn on [tɜ:n ɒn] *v* يُشْعِل [juʃʕilu]
turn out [tɜ:n aʊt] *v* يوقِف [ju:qifu]
turnover ['tɜ:nˌəʊvə] *n* انقلاب [inqila:b]

turn round [tɜːn raʊnd] *v* يَبْرُم [jabrumu]
turnstile ['tɜːn,staɪl] *n* بوابة متحركة [Bawabah motaharekah]
turn up [tɜːn ʌp] *v* يَظْهَر [jazˤharu]
turquoise ['tɜːkwɔɪz; -kwɑːz] *adj* فيروزي [fajruːzij]
turtle ['tɜːtᵊl] *n* سُلحفاة [sulħufaːt]
tutor ['tjuːtə] *n* مدرس خصوصي [Modares khoṣooṣey]
tutorial [tjuː'tɔːrɪəl] *n* درس خصوصي [Dars khoṣoṣey]
tuxedo [tʌk'siːdəʊ] *n* بذلة غامقة اللون للرجال [Badlah ghame'qah al-loon lel-rejal]
TV [tiː viː] *n* تليفزيون [tiliːfizjuːn]; **plasma TV** *n* تليفزيون بلازما [Telefezyoon ra'qamey]; **reality TV** *n* تلفزيون الواقع [Telefezyon al-wa'qe'a]; **Does the room have a TV?** هل يوجد تليفزيون بالغرفة [hal yujad tali-fizyon bil-ghurfa?]
tweezers ['twiːzəz] *npl* ملاقط صغيرة [Mala'qeṭ ṣagheerah]
twelfth [twɛlfθ] *adj* ثاني عشر [θaːnija ʕaʃara]
twelve [twɛlv] *number* اثنا عشر [iθnataː ʕaʃara]
twentieth ['twɛntɪɪθ; 'twentieth] *adj* العشرون [al-ʕiʃruːna]
twenty ['twɛntɪ] *number* عشرون [ʕiʃruːna]
twice [twaɪs] *adv* مرتين [marratajni]
twin [twɪn] *n* توأم [tawʔam]; **twin beds** *npl* سريرين منفصلين [Sareerayn monfaṣelayen]; **twin room** *n* غرفة مزدوجة [Ghorfah mozdawajah]; **twin-bedded room** *n* غرفة مزودة بأسرة مزدوجة [Ghorfah mozawadah be-aserah mozdawajah]
twinned ['twɪnd] *adj* مزدوج [muzdawaʒ]
twist [twɪst] *v* يلوي [jalwiː]
twit [twɪt] *n* يَسْخَر من [Yaskhar men]
two [tuː] *num* اثنين [iθnajni]
type [taɪp] *n* نوع [nawʕ] ▷ *v* يُصَنِف [jusˤannifu]; **Have you cut my type of hair before?** هل قمت من قبل بقص شعري من نوع شعري [hal 'qumt min 'qabil be-'qaṣ sha'ar min naw'a sha'ary?]
typewriter ['taɪp,raɪtə] *n* آلة كاتبة [aala katebah]
typhoid ['taɪfɔɪd] *n* مرض التيفود [Maraḍ al-tayfood]
typical ['tɪpɪkᵊl] *adj* نموذجي [namuːðaʒij]
typist ['taɪpɪst] *n* تايبِسْتْ [taːjbist]
tyre ['taɪə] *n* إطار العجلة [Eṭar al ajalah]; **spare tyre** *n* إطار إضافي [Eṭar eḍafy]

UFO ['juːfəʊ] *abbr* جسم غامض [ʒismun ɣaːmidˤun]
Uganda [juː'gændə] *n* أوغندا [ʔuːɣandaː]
Ugandan [juː'gændən] *adj* أوغندي [ʔuːɣandij] ▷ *n* أوغندي [ʔuːɣandij]
ugly ['ʌglɪ] *adj* قبيح [qabiːħ]
UK [juː keɪ] *n* المملكة المتحدة [Al-mamlakah al-motahedah]
Ukraine [juː'kreɪn] *n* أوكرانيا [ʔuːkraːnjaː]
Ukrainian [juː'kreɪnɪən] *adj* أوكراني [ʔuːkraːnij] ▷ *n (language)* اللغة الأوكرانية [Al loghah al okraneiah], *(person)* أوكراني [ʔuːkraːnij]
ulcer ['ʌlsə] *n* قرحة [qurħa]
Ulster ['ʌlstə] *n* مقاطعة أولستر [muqaːtˤaʕatun ʔuːlstr]
ultimate ['ʌltɪmɪt] *adj* أقصى [ʔaqsˤaː]
ultimately ['ʌltɪmɪtlɪ] *adv* حتمياً [ħatmiːan]
ultimatum [ˌʌltɪ'meɪtəm] *n* إنذار [ʔinðaːr]
ultrasound ['ʌltrəˌsaʊnd] *n* موجات فوق صوتية [mawʒaːtun fawqa sˤawtijjatin]
umbrella [ʌm'brɛlə] *n* مظلة [mizˤalla]
umpire ['ʌmpaɪə] *n* حَكَم [ħakam]
UN [juː ɛn] *abbr* الأمم المتحدة [Al-omam al-motahedah]
unable [ʌn'eɪbəl] *adj*; **unable to** *adj* عاجز [ʕaːʒizun]
unacceptable [ˌʌnək'sɛptəbəl] *adj* غير مقبول [Ghayr ma'qool]
unanimous [juː'nænɪməs] *adj* إجماعي [ʔiʒmaːʕij]
unattended [ˌʌnə'tɛndɪd] *adj* بدون مُرافق [Bedon morafe'q]
unavoidable [ˌʌnə'vɔɪdəbəl] *adj* متعذر تجنبه [Mota'adhar tajanobah]
unbearable [ʌn'bɛərəbəl] *adj* لا يحتمل [La yaḥtamel]
unbeatable [ʌn'biːtəbəl] *adj* لا يقهر [La yo'qhar]
unbelievable [ˌʌnbɪ'liːvəbəl] *adj* لايصدق [laːjusˤaddaq]
unbreakable [ʌn'breɪkəbəl] *adj* غير قابل للكسر [Ghayr 'qabel lelkasr]
uncanny [ʌn'kænɪ] *adj* غريب [ɣariːb]
uncertain [ʌn'sɜːtən] *adj* غير واثق [Ghayr wathe'q]
uncertainty [ʌn'sɜːtəntɪ] *n* عدم التأكد ['adam al-taakod]
unchanged [ʌn'tʃeɪndʒd] *adj* غير متغير [Ghayr motaghayer]
uncivilized [ʌn'sɪvɪˌlaɪzd] *adj* غير متحضر [ghayer motahaḍer]
uncle ['ʌŋkəl] *n* عَمّ [ʕamm]
unclear [ʌn'klɪə] *adj* غير واضح [Ghayr waḍeḥ]
uncomfortable [ʌn'kʌmftəbəl] *adj* غير مريح [Ghaeyr moreeḥ]
unconditional [ˌʌnkən'dɪʃənəl] *adj* غير مشروط [Ghayr mashrooṭ]
unconscious [ʌn'kɒnʃəs] *adj* فاقد الوعي [Fa'qed al-wa'aey]
uncontrollable [ˌʌnkən'trəʊləbəl] *adj* متعذر التحكم فيه [Mota'adher al-tahakom feeh]
unconventional [ˌʌnkən'vɛnʃənəl] *adj* غير تقليدي [Gheer ta'qleedey]
undecided [ˌʌndɪ'saɪdɪd] *adj* غير مفصول فيه [Ghaey mafṣool feeh]
undeniable [ˌʌndɪ'naɪəbəl] *adj* لا يمكن

إنكاره [La yomken enkareh]
under ['ʌndə] *prep* تحت [taħta]
underage [ˌʌndər'eɪdʒ] *adj* قاصر [qaːsˁir]
underestimate [ˌʌndərɛstɪ'meɪt] *v* يَسْتَخِف [jastaxiffu]
undergo [ˌʌndə'gəʊ] *v* يَتحمل [jataħammalu]
undergraduate [ˌʌndə'grædjʊɪt] *n* طالب لم يتخرج بعد [ṭ aleb lam yatakharaj ba'aad]
underground *adj* ['ʌndəˌgraʊnd]تحت سطح الأرض [Taht saṭh al arḍ] ▷ *n* ['ʌndəˌgraʊnd]سكة حديد تحت الأرض [Sekah hadeed taht al-arḍ]
underline [ˌʌndə'laɪn] *v* يَرسِم خطا تحت [Yarsem khaṭan taḥt]
underneath [ˌʌndə'niːθ] *adv* في الأسفل [Fee al-asfal] ▷ *prep* أسفل
underpaid [ˌʌndə'peɪd] *adj* مدفوع بأقل من القيمة [Madfoo'a be-a'qal men al-q'eemah]
underpants ['ʌndəˌpænts] *npl* سِروال تحتي [Serwaal taḥtey]
underpass ['ʌndəˌpɑːs] *n* مَمَر سُفْلِي [Mamar sofley]
underskirt ['ʌndəˌskɜːt] *n* تنورة تحتية [Tanorah taḥteyah]
understand [ˌʌndə'stænd] *v* يَفْهَم [jafhamu]
understandable [ˌʌndə'stændəbᵊl] *adj* مفهوم [mafhuːm]
understanding [ˌʌndə'stændɪŋ] *adj* متفهم [mutafahhim]
undertaker ['ʌndəˌteɪkə] *n* حانوتي [ħaːnuːtij]
underwater ['ʌndə'wɔːtə] *adv* تحت الماء [Taḥt al-maa]
underwear ['ʌndəˌwɛə] *n* ملابس داخلية [Malabes dakheleyah]
undisputed [ˌʌndɪ'spjuːtɪd] *adj* مُسَلّم به [Mosalam beh]
undo [ʌn'duː] *v* يَفُكُّ [jafukku]
undoubtedly [ʌn'daʊtɪdlɪ; un'doubtedly] *adv* يَقْيناً [jaqiːnan]
undress [ʌn'drɛs] *v* يُعَرّي [juʕarriː]
unemployed [ˌʌnɪm'plɔɪd] *adj* عاطل عن العمل ['aatel 'aan al-'aamal]
unemployment [ˌʌnɪm'plɔɪmənt] *n* بطالة [bitˁaːla]
unexpected [ˌʌnɪk'spɛktɪd] *adj* غير متوقع [Ghayer motwa'qa'a]
unexpectedly [ˌʌnɪk'spɛktɪdlɪ] *adv* على نحو غير متوقع [Ala naḥw motawa'qa'a]
unfair [ʌn'fɛə] *adj* جائر [ʒaːʔir]
unfaithful [ʌn'feɪθfʊl] *adj* خائن [xaːʔin]
unfamiliar [ˌʌnfə'mɪljə] *adj* غير مألوف [Ghayer maaloof]
unfashionable [ʌn'fæʃənəbᵊl] *adj* غير مواكب للموضة [Ghayr mowakeb lel-moḍah]
unfavourable [ʌn'feɪvərəbᵊl; -'feɪvrə-] *adj* معاد [muʕaːd]
unfit [ʌn'fɪt] *adj* غير صالح [Ghayer Ṣaleḥ]
unforgettable [ˌʌnfə'gɛtəbᵊl] *adj* لا يمكن نسيانه [La yomken nesyanh]
unfortunately [ʌn'fɔːtʃənɪtlɪ] *adv* لسوء الحظ [Le-soa al-haḍh]
unfriendly [ʌn'frɛndlɪ] *adj* غير ودي [Ghayr wedey]
ungrateful [ʌn'greɪtfʊl] *adj* عاق [ʕaːqq]
unhappy [ʌn'hæpɪ] *adj* تعيس [taʕiːs]
unhealthy [ʌn'hɛlθɪ] *adj* غير صحي [Ghayr ṣshey]
unhelpful [ʌn'hɛlpfʊl] *adj* غير مفيد [Ghayr mofeed]
uni ['juːnɪ] *n* أحادي [ʔuħaːdij]
unidentified [ˌʌnaɪ'dɛntɪˌfaɪd] *adj* غير محدد الهوية [Ghayr mohadad al-haweyah]
uniform ['juːnɪˌfɔːm] *n* زي رسمي [Zey rasmey]; **school uniform** *n* زي مدرسي موحد [Zey madrasey mowaḥad]
unimportant [ˌʌnɪm'pɔːtᵊnt] *adj* غير هام [Ghayr ham]
uninhabited [ˌʌnɪn'hæbɪtɪd] *adj* غير مسكون [Ghayr maskoon]
unintentional [ˌʌnɪn'tɛnʃənᵊl] *adj* غير متعمد [Ghayr mota'amad]
union ['juːnjən] *n* اتحاد [ittiħaːd];

European Union *n* الاتحاد الأوروبي [Al-tehad al-orobey]; **trade union** *n* نقابة العمال [Ne'qabat al-'aomal]
unique [juːˈniːk] *adj* فريد [fariːd]
unit [ˈjuːnɪt] *n* وحدة [waħda]
unite [juːˈnaɪt] *v* يُوحد [juwaħħidu]
United Kingdom [juːˈnaɪtɪd ˈkɪŋdəm] *n* المملكة المتحدة [Al-mamlakah al-motahedah]
United States [juːˈnaɪtɪd steɪts] *n* الولايات المتحدة [Al-welayat al-motḥedah al-amreekeyah]
universe [ˈjuːnɪˌvɜːs] *n* كَوْن [kawn]
university [ˌjuːnɪˈvɜːsɪtɪ] *n* جامعة [ʒaːmiʕa]
unknown [ʌnˈnəʊn] *adj* غير معروف [Gheyr ma'aroof]
unleaded [ʌnˈlɛdɪd] *n* خلو من الرصاص [Khelow men al-raṣaṣ]; **unleaded petrol** *n* بنزين خالي من الرصاص [Benzene khaly men al- raṣaṣ]
unless [ʌnˈlɛs] *conj* إلا إذا [Elaa edha]
unlike [ʌnˈlaɪk] *prep* مختلف عن [Mokhtalef an]
unlikely [ʌnˈlaɪklɪ] *adj* غير محتمل [Ghaeyr moḥtamal]
unlisted [ʌnˈlɪstɪd] *adj* غير مُدرّج [Ghayer modraj]
unload [ʌnˈləʊd] *v* يُفْرِغ حمولة [Yofaregh ḥomolah]
unlock [ʌnˈlɒk] *v* يَفْتَح القفل [Yaftaḥ al-'qafl]
unlucky [ʌnˈlʌkɪ] *adj* غير محظوظ [Ghayer mahḍhooḍh]
unmarried [ʌnˈmærɪd] *adj* غير متزوج [Ghayer motazawej]
unnecessary [ʌnˈnɛsɪsərɪ; -ɪsrɪ] *adj* غير ضروري [Ghayer ḍarorey]
unofficial [ˌʌnəˈfɪʃəl] *adj* غير رسمي [Ghayer rasmey]
unpack [ʌnˈpæk] *v* يَفُك [jafuku]
unpaid [ʌnˈpeɪd] *adj* غير مسدد [Ghayr mosadad]
unpleasant [ʌnˈplɛzᵊnt] *adj* غير سار [Ghayr sar]
unplug [ʌnˈplʌg] *v* يَنزَع القابس الكهربائي [janzaʕu alqaːbusi alkahrabaːʔijji]
unpopular [ʌnˈpɒpjʊlə] *adj* غير محبوب [Ghaey maḥboob]
unprecedented [ʌnˈprɛsɪˌdɛntɪd] *adj* جديد [ʒadiːd]
unpredictable [ˌʌnprɪˈdɪktəbᵊl] *adj* لا يمكن التنبؤ به [La yomken al-tanaboa beh]
unreal [ʌnˈrɪəl] *adj* غير حقيقي [Ghayer ha'qee'qey]
unrealistic [ˌʌnrɪəˈlɪstɪk] *adj* غير واقعي [Ghayer wa'qe'aey]
unreasonable [ʌnˈriːznəbᵊl] *adj* غير معقول [Ghear ma'a'qool]
unreliable [ˌʌnrɪˈlaɪəbᵊl] *adj* غير جدير بالثقة [Ghaayr jadeer bel-the'qa]
unroll [ʌnˈrəʊl] *v* يَبْسِط [jabsitˤu]
unsatisfactory [ˌʌnsætɪsˈfæktərɪ; -trɪ] *adj* غير مرضي [Ghayr marḍa]
unscrew [ʌnˈskruː] *v* يَفُكّ اللولب [Yafek al-lawlab]
unshaven [ʌnˈʃeɪvᵊn] *adj* غير حليق [Ghayr ḥalee'q]
unskilled [ʌnˈskɪld] *adj* غير بارع [gheer bare'a]
unstable [ʌnˈsteɪbᵊl] *adj* غير مستقر [Ghayr mosta'qer]
unsteady [ʌnˈstɛdɪ] *adj* متقلب [mutaqalibb]
unsuccessful [ˌʌnsəkˈsɛsfʊl] *adj* غير ناجح [ghayr najeḥ]
unsuitable [ʌnˈsuːtəbᵊl; ʌnˈsjuːt-] *adj* غير مناسب [Ghayr monaseb]
unsure [ʌnˈʃʊə] *adj* غير متأكد [Ghayer moaakad]
untidy [ʌnˈtaɪdɪ] *adj* غير مُرتب [Ghayer moratb]
untie [ʌnˈtaɪ] *v* يحُل [jaħullu]
until [ʌnˈtɪl] *conj* حتى [ħattaː] ▷ *prep* إلى أنْ
unusual [ʌnˈjuːʒʊəl] *adj* غير معتاد [Ghayer mo'ataad]
unwell [ʌnˈwɛl] *adj* معتل [muʕtal]
unwind [ʌnˈwaɪnd] *v* يَفُكّ [jafukku]
unwise [ʌnˈwaɪz] *adj* غير حكيم [Ghayer hakeem]

unwrap [ʌn'ræp] *v* يَفُض [jafudˤdˤu]
unzip [ʌn'zɪp] *v* يفتح النشاط [Yaftah nashaṭ]
up [ʌp] *adv* عالياً [ʕa:lijan]
upbringing ['ʌp,brɪŋɪŋ] *n* تربية [tarbija]
update *n* ['ʌp,deɪt]يَجعَله عصريا [Tej'aalah 'aṣreyan] ▷ *v* [ʌp'deɪt]يَجعَله عصريا [Tej'aalah 'aṣreyan]
upgrade [ʌp'greɪd] *n*; **I want to upgrade my ticket** أريد تغيير تذكرتي إلى درجة أعلى [areed taghyeer tadhkeraty ela daraja a'ala]
uphill ['ʌp'hɪl] *adv* قائم على مرتفع ['qaem ala mortafa'a]
upper ['ʌpə] *adj* فوقي [fawqi:]
upright ['ʌp,raɪt] *adv* عموديا [ʕamu:dijan]
upset *adj* [ʌp'sɛt]قَلِق [qalaq] ▷ *v* [ʌp'sɛt]يَنْقَلِب [janqalibu]
upside down ['ʌp,saɪd daʊn] *adv* مقلوب رأسا على عقب [Ma'qloob raasan 'ala 'aa'qab]
upstairs ['ʌp'stɛəz] *adv* بالأعلى [Bel'aala]
uptight [ʌp'taɪt] *adj* عصبي جداً ['aṣabey jedan]
up-to-date [ʌptʊdeɪt] *adj* مُحَدَث [muħaddiθ]
upwards ['ʌpwədz] *adv* صاعداً [sˤa:ʕidan]
uranium [jʊ'reɪnɪəm] *n* يورانيوم [ju:ra:nju:mi]
urgency ['ɜ:dʒənsɪ] *n* أهمية مُلحة [Ahameiah molehah]
urgent ['ɜ:dʒənt] *adj* مُلِحْ [milħ]
urine ['jʊərɪn] *n* بُوْل [bawl]
URL [ju: ɑ: ɛl] *n* محدد مكان الموارد الموحد [muħaddidun maka:n almuwa:rid almuwaħħad]
Uruguay ['jʊərə,gwaɪ] *n* أوروجواي [uwru:ʒwa:j]
Uruguayan [,jʊərə'gwaɪən] *adj* أوروجواياني [ʔu:ru:ʒwa:ja:ni:] ▷ *n* الأوروجواياني [al-ʔu:ru:ʒwa:ja:ni:]
us [ʌs] *pron* نا [na:]; **We'd like to see nobody but us all day!** لا نريد أن نرى أي شخص آخر غيرنا طوال اليوم! [la nureed an nara ay shakhṣ akhar ghyrana ṭewaal al-yawm!]
US [ju: ɛs] *n* الولايات المتحدة [Al-welayat al-motḥedah al-amreekeyah]
USA [ju: ɛs eɪ] *n* الولايات المتحدة الأمريكية [Alwelayat almotahdah al amrikiyah]
use *n* [ju:s]استخدام [istixda:mu] ▷ *v* [ju:z]يَستخدِم [jastaxdimu]; **It is for my own personal use** إنه للاستخدام الشخصي [inaho lel-estikhdam al-shakhṣi]
used [ju:zd] *adj* مُستَخدَم [mustaxdamu]
useful ['ju:sfʊl] *adj* نافع [na:fiʕ]
useless ['ju:slɪs] *adj* عديم الجدوى ['aadam al-jadwa]
user ['ju:zə] *n* مُستَخْدِم [mustaxdim]; **Internet user** *n* مُستَخدِم الانترنت [Mostakhdem al-enternet]
user-friendly ['ju:zə,frɛndlɪ] *adj* سهل الاستخدام [Sahl al-estekhdam]
use up [ju:z ʌp] *v* يَستهلك كليةً [Yastahlek koleyatan]
usual ['ju:ʒʊəl] *adj* معتاد [muʕta:d]; **Is it usual to give a tip?** هل من المعتاد إعطاء بقشيش؟ [hal min al-mu'a-taad e'aṭaa ba'q-sheesh?]
usually ['ju:ʒʊəlɪ] *adv* عادة [ʕa:datun]
U-turn ['ju:,tɜ:n] *n* ملف على شكل حرف U [Malaf 'ala shakl ḥarf U]
Uzbekistan [,ʌzbɛkɪ'stɑ:n] *n* أوزباكستان [ʔu:zba:kista:n]

vacancy ['veɪkənsɪ] *n* عطلة [ʕutˁla]
vacant ['veɪkənt] *adj* شاغِر [ʃa:ɣir]
vacate [və'keɪt] *v* يجلو عن مكان [Yajloo 'an al-makaan]
vaccinate ['væksɪˌneɪt] *v* يُلَقِح [julaqqiħu]
vaccination [ˌvæksɪ'neɪʃən] *n* تلقيح [talqi:ħ]
vacuum ['vækjʊəm] *v* يُنَظِف بمكنسة كهربائية [junazˁzˁifu bimiknasatin kahraba:ʔijjatin]; **vacuum cleaner** *n* مكنسة كهربائية [Meknasah kahrobaeyah]
vague [veɪg] *adj* مبهم [mubham]
vain [veɪn] *adj* تافه [ta:fih]
valid ['vælɪd] *adj* مَشروع [maʃru:ʕ]
valley ['vælɪ] *n* وادي [wa:di:]
valuable ['væljʊəbᵊl] *adj* نفيس [nafi:s]
valuables ['væljʊəbᵊlz] *npl* نَفَائِس [nafa:ʔisun]
value ['vælju:] *n* قيمة [qi:ma]
vampire ['væmpaɪə] *n* مصاص دماء [Maṣaṣ demaa]
van [væn] *n* جناح [ʒana:ħ]; **breakdown van** *n* عربة الأعطال ['arabat al-a'ataal]; **removal van** *n* شاحِنة نقل [Shahenat na'ql]
vandal ['vændᵊl] *n* مخرب [muxarrib]
vandalism ['vændəˌlɪzəm] *n* تَخْريب [taxri:b]
vandalize ['vændəˌlaɪz] *v* يُخَّرِب المَمتلكات العامة والخاصة عن عمد [Yokhareb al-momtalakat al-'aaamah 'an 'amd]
vanilla [və'nɪlə] *n* فانيليا [fa:ni:lja:]
vanish ['vænɪʃ] *v* يَغيب عن الأنظار [Yagheeb 'an al-anḍhaar]
variable ['vɛərɪəbᵊl] *adj* قابل للتغيير ['qabel lel-tagheyer]
varied ['vɛərɪd] *adj* معدل [muʕaddal]
variety [və'raɪɪtɪ] *n* تنوع [tanawwuʕ]
various ['vɛərɪəs] *adj* مختلف [muxtalif]
varnish ['vɑ:nɪʃ] *n* ورنيش [warni:ʃu] ▷ *v* يُصْقِل [jasˁqulu]; **nail varnish** *n* طلاء أظافر [Telaa aḍhafer]
vary ['vɛərɪ] *v* يُغَيْر [juɣajjiru]
vase [vɑ:z] *n* زهرية [zahrijja]
VAT [væt] *abbr* ضريبة القيمة المضافة [dˁari:batu alqi:mati almudˁa:fati]; **Is VAT included?** هل يكون شاملاً ضريبة القيمة المضافة؟ [hal yakoon sha-melan ḍare-bat al-'qema al-muḍafa?]
Vatican ['vætɪkən] *n* الفاتيكان [al-fa:ti:ka:ni]
vault [vɔ:lt] *n*; **pole vault** *n* قفز بالزانة ['qafz bel-zanah]
veal [vi:l] *n* لحم عجل [Laḥm 'aejl]
vegan ['vi:gən] *n* نباتي [naba:tij]; **Do you have any vegan dishes?** هل يوجد أي أطباق نباتية؟ [hal yujad ay aṭbaa'q nabat-iya?]
vegetable ['vɛdʒtəbᵊl] *n* خضار [xudˁa:r]
vegetarian [ˌvɛdʒɪ'tɛərɪən] *adj* نباتي [naba:tij] ▷ *n* نباتي [naba:tij]; **Do you have any vegetarian dishes?** هل يوجد أي أطباق نباتية؟ [hal yujad ay aṭbaa'q nabat-iya?]
vegetation [ˌvɛdʒɪ'teɪʃən] *n* حياة نباتية [Hayah Nabateyah]
vehicle ['vi:ɪkᵊl] *n* عَرَبة [ʕaraba]
veil [veɪl] *n* خمار [xima:r]
vein [veɪn] *n* وريد [wari:d]
Velcro® ['vɛlkrəʊ] *n* فيلكرو® [fi:lkru:]
velvet ['vɛlvɪt] *n* نُعُومة [nuʕu:ma]

vendor ['vɛndɔː] *n* بائع [baːʔiʕ]
Venezuela [ˌvɛnɪ'zweɪlə] *n* فنزويلا [finzwiːlaː]
Venezuelan [ˌvɛnɪ'zweɪlən] *adj* فنزويلي [finizwiːliː] ▷ *n* فنزويلي [finizwiːliː]
venison ['vɛnɪzᵊn; -sᵊn] *n* لحم غزال [Laḥm ghazal]
venom ['vɛnəm] *n* سُمّ [summ]
ventilation [ˌvɛntɪ'leɪʃən] *n* تهوية [tahwijatin]
venue ['vɛnjuː] *n* مكان الحوادث [Makan al-ḥawadeth]
verb [vɜːb] *n* فعل [fiʕl]
verdict ['vɜːdɪkt] *n* حُكم المحلفين [Hokm al-mohallefeen]
versatile ['vɜːsəˌtaɪl] *adj* متعدد الجوانب [Mota'aded al-jawaneb]
version ['vɜːʃən; -ʒən] *n* نسخة [nusxa]
versus ['vɜːsəs] *prep* ضد [dˤiddun]
vertical ['vɜːtɪkᵊl] *adj* رَأسي [raʔsij]
vertigo ['vɜːtɪˌɡəʊ] *n* دُوار [duwaːr]
very ['vɛrɪ] *adv* جداً [ʒidan]
vest [vɛst] *n* صدرة [sˤadra]
vet [vɛt] *n* طبيب بيطري [Ṭabeeb bayṭareey]
veteran ['vɛtərən; 'vɛtrən] *adj* محنك [muħannak] ▷ *n* محارب قديم [Moḥareb 'qadeem]
veto ['viːtəʊ] *n* حق الرفض [Ha'q al-rafḍ]
via ['vaɪə] *prep* عن طريق [An ṭaree'q al-khaṭaa]
vicar ['vɪkə] *n* قِسْ [qiss]
vice [vaɪs] *n* رذيلة [raðiːla]
vice versa ['vaɪsɪ 'vɜːsə] *adv* والعكس كذلك [Wal-'aaks kaḍalek]
vicinity [vɪ'sɪnɪtɪ] *n* منطقة مجاورة [Menta'qat mojawerah]
vicious ['vɪʃəs] *adj* أثيم [ʔaθiːm]
victim ['vɪktɪm] *n* ضحية [dˤaħijja]
victory ['vɪktərɪ] *n* نصر [nasˤr]
video ['vɪdɪˌəʊ] *n* فيديو [fiːdjuː]; **video camera** *n* كاميرا فيديو [Kamera fedyo]
videophone ['vɪdɪəˌfəʊn] *n* هاتف مرئي [Hatef mareay]
Vietnam [ˌvjɛt'næm] *n* فيتنام [fiːtnaːm]
Vietnamese [ˌvjɛtnə'miːz] *adj* فيتنامي [fiːtnaːmij] ▷ *n* *(language)* اللغة الفيتنامية [Al-loghah al-fetnameyah], *(person)* شخص فيتنامي [Shakhṣ fetnamey]
view [vjuː] *n* منظر [manzˤar]
viewer ['vjuːə] *n* مشاهد التلفزيون [Moshahadat al-telefezyon]
viewpoint ['vjuːˌpɔɪnt] *n* وجهة نظر [Wejhat naḍhar]
vile [vaɪl] *adj* وَضيع [wadˤiːʕ]
villa ['vɪlə] *n* فيلا [fiːlaː]; **I'd like to rent a villa** أريد فيلا للإيجار [areed villa lil-eejar]
village ['vɪlɪdʒ] *n* قرية [qarja]
villain ['vɪlən] *n* شِرّير [ʃirriːr]
vinaigrette [ˌvɪneɪ'ɡrɛt] *n* صَلْصَة السَّلَطَة [sˤalsˤatu assalatˤati]
vine [vaɪn] *n* كَرْمَة العنب [Karmat al'aenab]
vinegar ['vɪnɪɡə] *n* خل [xall]
vineyard ['vɪnjəd] *n* كَرْم [karam]
viola [vɪ'əʊlə] *n* آلة الفيولا الموسيقية [aalat al veiola al mose'qeiah]
violence ['vaɪələns] *n* عنف [ʕunf]
violent ['vaɪələnt] *adj* عنيف [ʕaniːf]
violin [ˌvaɪə'lɪn] *n* آلة الكَمَان الموسيقية [Aalat al-kaman al-moose'qeyah]
violinist [ˌvaɪə'lɪnɪst] *n* عازف الكمان ['aazef al-kaman]
virgin ['vɜːdʒɪn] *n* عذراء [ʕaðraːʔ]
Virgo ['vɜːɡəʊ] *n* العذراء [al-ʕaðraːʔi]
virtual ['vɜːtʃʊəl] *adj* واقعي [waːqiʕij]; **virtual reality** *n* واقع افتراضي [Wa'qe'a eftraḍey]
virus ['vaɪrəs] *n* فيروس [fiːruːs]
visa ['viːzə] *n* فيزا [fiːzaː]
visibility [ˌvɪzɪ'bɪlɪtɪ] *n* وضوح [wudˤuːħ]
visible ['vɪzɪbᵊl] *adj* مرئي [marʔij]
visit ['vɪzɪt] *n* زيارة [zijaːra] ▷ *v* يَزُور [jazuːru]; **visiting hours** *npl* ساعات الزيارة [Sa'at al-zeyadah]; **Can we visit the castle?** أيمكننا زيارة القلعة؟ [a-yamkun-ana zeyarat al-'qal'aa?]; **Do we have time to visit the town?** هل الوقت متاح لزيارة المدينة؟ [hal al-wa'qt muaaḥ le-ziyarat al-madeena?]; **I'm here visiting friends** أنا هنا لزيارة أحد الأصدقاء [ʔanaː hunaː lizijaːratin ʔaħada

alʔasˤdiqa:ʔa]; **We'd like to visit...** نريد زيارة... [nureed ze-yarat...]
visitor ['vɪzɪtə] *n* زائر [za:ʔir]; **visitor centre** *n* مركز زائري [Markaz zaerey]
visual ['vɪʒʊəl; -zjʊ-] *adj* بصري [basˤarij]
visualize ['vɪʒʊəˌlaɪz; -zjʊ-] *v* يَتَصور [jatasˤawwaru]
vital ['vaɪtᵊl] *adj* حيوي [ħajawij]
vitamin ['vɪtəmɪn; 'vaɪ-] *n* فيتامين [fi:ta:mi:n]
vivid ['vɪvɪd] *adj* لامِع [la:miʕ]
vocabulary [və'kæbjʊlərɪ] *n* مُفردات اللغة [Mofradat Al-loghah]
vocational [vəʊ'keɪʃənᵊl] *adj* مهني [mihanij]
vodka ['vɒdkə] *n* فودكا [fu:dka:]
voice [vɔɪs] *n* صوت [sˤawt]
voicemail ['vɔɪsˌmeɪl] *n* بريد صوتي [Bareed ṣawṭey]
void [vɔɪd] *adj* باطل [ba:tˤil] ▷ *n* فَراغ [fara:ɣ]
volcano, volcanoes [vɒl'keɪnəʊ, vɒl'keɪnəʊz] *n* بركان [burka:n]
volleyball ['vɒlɪˌbɔ:l] *n* كرة طائرة [Korah Ṭaayeara]
volt [vəʊlt] *n* حركة دائرية [ħarakatun da:ʔirijja]
voltage ['vəʊltɪdʒ] *n* جهد كهربي [Jahd kahrabey]
volume ['vɒlju:m] *n* حَجْم [ħaʒm]
voluntarily ['vɒləntərɪlɪ] *adv* بشكل متعمد [Be-shakl mota'amad]
voluntary ['vɒləntərɪ; -trɪ] *adj* طَوْعي [tˤawʕij]
volunteer [ˌvɒlən'tɪə] *n* متطوع [mutatˤawwiʕ] ▷ *v* يتطوع [jatatˤawwaʕu]
vomit ['vɒmɪt] *v* يَتقيأ [jataqajjaʔu]
vote [vəʊt] *n* تصويت [tasˤwi:t] ▷ *v* يُصَوِت [jusˤawwitu]
voucher ['vaʊtʃə] *n* إيصال [ʔi:sˤa:l]; **gift voucher** *n* قسيمة هدية ['qaseemat hadeyah]
vowel ['vaʊəl] *n* حرف متحرك [ħurfun mutaħarrik]
vulgar ['vʌlgə] *adj* سُوقي [su:qij]
vulnerable ['vʌlnərəbᵊl] *adj* قابل للجرح ['qabel lel-jarh]
vulture ['vʌltʃə] *n* نسر [nasr]

W

wafer ['weɪfə] *n* رقاقة [ruqa:qa]
waffle ['wɒfᵊl] *n* وَافِل [wa:fil] ▷ *v* يَرغي في الكلام [Yarghey fel kalaam]
wage [weɪdʒ] *n* أجْر [ʔaʒr]
waist [weɪst] *n* خَصر [xasˤr]
waistcoat ['weɪs,kəʊt] *n* صدرية [sˤadrijja]
wait [weɪt] *v* يَتَوَقَّع [jatawaqqaʕu]; **wait for** *v* ينتظر [jantazˤiru]; **waiting list** *n* قائمة انتظار ['qaemat enteḍhar]; **waiting room** *n* غرفة انتظار [Ghorfat enteḍhar]
waiter ['weɪtə] *n* نادل [na:dil]
waitress ['weɪtrɪs] *n* نادلة [na:dila]
wait up [weɪt ʌp] *v* يُطيل السهر [Yoṭeel alsaḥar]
waive [weɪv] *v* يَتنازَل عن [Tetnazel 'an]
wake up [weɪk ʌp] *v* يَستيقظ [jastajqizˤu]
Wales [weɪlz] *n* ويلز [wi:lzu]
walk [wɔːk] *n* مُشْوار [miʃwa:r] ▷ *v* يَمْشي [jamʃi:]
walkie-talkie [ˌwɔːkɪ'tɔːkɪ] *n* جهاز راديو للإرسال والاستقبال [ʒiha:zu ra:diju: lil?irsa:li wa ali:stiqba:li]
walking ['wɔːkɪŋ] *n* مَشْي [maʃj]; **walking stick** *n* عصا المشي ['asaa almashey]
walkway ['wɔːkˌweɪ] *n* ممشى [mamʃa:]
wall [wɔːl] *n* جدار [ʒida:r]
wallet ['wɒlɪt] *n* محفظة [miħfazˤa]; **My wallet has been stolen** لقد سرقت محفظة نقودي [la'qad sore'qat meḥ-faḍhat ni-'qoody]
wallpaper ['wɔːlˌpeɪpə] *n* ورق حائط [Wara'q ḥaeṭ]
walnut ['wɔːlˌnʌt] *n* جوز [ʒawz]
walrus ['wɔːlrəs; 'wɒl-] *n* حيوان الفَظّ [Ḥayawan al-fadh]
waltz [wɔːls] *n* رقصة الفالس [Ra'qṣat al-fales] ▷ *v* يَرقص الفالس [Yar'qos al-fales]
wander ['wɒndə] *v* يتجول [jataʒawwalu]
want [wɒnt] *v* يُريد [juri:du]
war [wɔː] *n* حرب [ħarb]; **civil war** *n* حرب أهلية [Ḥarb ahleyah]
ward [wɔːd] *n (area)* دائرة من مدينة [Dayrah men madeenah], *(hospital room)* جناح من مستشفى [Janah men al-mostashfa]
warden ['wɔːdᵊn] *n* وَصِيّ [wasˤij]; **traffic warden** *n* شُرطي المرور [Shrṭey al-moror]
wardrobe ['wɔːdrəʊb] *n* خزانة الثياب [Khezanat al-theyab]
warehouse ['wɛəˌhaʊs] *n* مستودع [mustawdaʕu]
warm [wɔːm] *adj* دافئ [da:fiʔ]
warm up [wɔːm ʌp] *v* يُسَخِّن [jusaxxinu]
warn [wɔːn] *v* يُحذِر [juħaððiru]
warning ['wɔːnɪŋ] *n* تحذير [taħði:r]; **hazard warning lights** *npl* أضواء التحذير من الخطر [Aḍwaa al-tahdheer men al-khaṭar]
warranty ['wɒrəntɪ] *n* كفالة [kafa:la]
wart [wɔːt] *n* نتوء صغير [Netoa ṣagheer]
wash [wɒʃ] *v* يَغْسِل [jaɣsilu]; **car wash** *n* غسيل سيارة [ghaseel sayaarah]
washable ['wɒʃəbᵊl] *adj*; **machine washable** *adj* قابل للغسل في الغسالة ['qabel lel-ghaseel fee al-ghassaalah]; **Is it washable?** هل هذا يمكن غسله؟ [hal hadha yamken ghas-loho?]
washbasin ['wɒʃˌbeɪsᵊn] *n* حوض الغسل

[Hawḍ al-ghaseel]
washing ['wɒʃɪŋ] *n* غسيل [ɣassi:l]; **washing line** *n* خط الغسيل [Khat al-ghaseel]; **washing machine** *n* غسَّالَة [ɣassa:latun]; **washing powder** *n* مسحوق الغسيل [Mashoo'q alghaseel]; **Do you have washing powder?** هل لديك مسحوق غسيل [hal ladyka mas-ḥoo'q ghaseel?]
washing-up ['wɒʃɪŋʌp] *n* غسيل الأطباق [ghaseel al-atba'q]; **washing-up liquid** *n* سائل غسيل الأطباق [Saael ghaseel al-aṭba'q]
wash up [wɒʃ ʌp] *v* يَغْسِل الأطباق [Yaghsel al-aṭbaa'q]
wasp [wɒsp] *n* دبور [dabu:r]
waste [weɪst] *n* فضلات [fadˤala:t] ▷ *v* يُبَدِد [jubaddidu]
watch [wɒtʃ] *n* ساعة يدوية [Saa'ah yadaweyah] ▷ *v* يُشاهد [juʃa:hidu]; **digital watch** *n* ساعة رقمية [Sa'aah ra'qameyah]
watch out [wɒtʃ aʊt] *v* يَحترِس [jaħtarisu]
water ['wɔːtə] *n* مياه [mijja:hu] ▷ *v* يَروي [jarwi:]; **drinking water** *n* مياه الشرب [Meyah al-shorb]; **mineral water** *n* مياه معدنية [Meyah ma'adaneyah]; **sea water** *n* مياه البحر [Meyah al-baḥr]; **sparkling water** *n* مياه فوارة [Meyah fawarah]; **watering can** *n* رشاش مياه [Rashah meyah]; **How deep is the water?** كم يبلغ عمق المياه؟ [kam yablugh 'aom'q al-meah?]; **Is hot water included in the price?** هل يشمل السعر توفير المياه الساخنة؟ [hal yash-mil al-si'ar taw-feer al-me-yah al-sakhina?]; **There is no hot water** لا توجد مياه ساخنة [La tojad meyah sakhena]
watercolour ['wɔːtəˌkʌlə] *n* لون مائي [Lawn maaey]
watercress ['wɔːtəˌkrɛs] *n* قرة العين ['qorat al-'ayn]
waterfall ['wɔːtəˌfɔːl] *n* شَلّال [ʃalla:l]
watermelon ['wɔːtəˌmɛlən] *n* بطيخة [batˤi:xa]
waterproof ['wɔːtəˌpruːf] *adj* مقاوم للمياه [Mo'qawem lel-meyah]
water-skiing ['wɔːtəˌskiːɪŋ] *n* تَزَلُج على المياه [Tazaloj 'ala al-meyah]
wave [weɪv] *n* موجة [mawʒa] ▷ *v* يُلَوِح [julawwiħu]
wavelength ['weɪvˌlɛŋθ] *n* طول الموجة [Ṭool al-majah]
wavy ['weɪvɪ] *adj* متموج [mutamawwiʒ]
wax [wæks] *n* شمع [ʃamʕ]
way [weɪ] *n* سبيل [sabi:l]; **right of way** *n* حق المرور [Ha'q al-moror]
way in [weɪ ɪn] *n* ممر دخول [Mamar dokhool]
way out [weɪ aʊt] *n* منفذ خروج [Manfaz khoroj]
we [wiː] *pron* نحن
weak [wiːk] *adj* ضعيف [dˤaʕi:f]
weakness ['wiːknɪs] *n* ضعف [dˤiʕfa]
wealth [wɛlθ] *n* ثروة [θarwa]
wealthy ['wɛlθɪ] *adj* ثري [θarij]
weapon ['wɛpən] *n* سلاح [sila:ħ]
wear [wɛə] *v* يَرتدي [jartadi:]
weasel ['wiːzᵊl] *n* ابن عرسة [ibnu ʕarusatin]
weather ['wɛðə] *n* طقس [tˤaqs]; **weather forecast** *n* توقعات حالة الطقس [Tawa'qo'aat ḥalat al-ṭaqs]; **What awful weather!** ما هذا الطقس السيئ [Ma hadha al-ṭa'qs al-sayea]
web [wɛb] *n* شبكة عنكبوتية [Shabakah 'ankaboteyah]; **web address** *n* عنوان الويب ['aonwan al-web]; **web browser** *n* متصفح شبكة الإنترنت [Motaṣafeḥ shabakat al-enternet]
webcam ['wɛbˌkæm] *n* كاميرا الانترنت [Kamera al-enternet]
webmaster ['wɛbˌmɑːstə] *n* مُصَمِم موقع [Moṣamem maw'qe'a]
website ['wɛbˌsaɪt] *n* موقع الويب [Maw'qe'a al-weeb]
webzine ['wɛbˌziːn] *n* منشور الكتروني [Manshoor elektrooney]
wedding ['wɛdɪŋ] *n* زِفَاف [zifa:f]; **wedding anniversary** *n* عيد الزواج

['aeed al-zawaj]; **wedding dress** *n* فستان الزفاف [Fostaan al-zefaf]; **wedding ring** *n* خاتم الزواج [Khatem al-zawaj]

Wednesday ['wɛnzdɪ] *n* الأربعاء [al-ʔarbiʕaːʔi]; **Ash Wednesday** *n* أربعاء الرماد [Arba'aa alramad]; **on Wednesday** في يوم الأربعاء [fee yawm al-arbe-'aa]

weed [wiːd] *n* عشبة ضارة ['aoshabah ḍarah]

weedkiller ['wiːdˌkɪlə] *n* مبيد الأعشاب الضارة [Mobeed al'ashaab al-ḍarah]

week [wiːk] *n* أسبوع [ʔusbuːʕ]; **a week ago** منذ أسبوع [mundho isboo'a]; **How much is it for a week?** كم تبلغ التكلفة الأسبوعية؟ [kam tablugh al-taklifa al-isboo-'aiya?]; **last week** الأسبوع الماضي [al-esboo'a al-maaḍy]; **next week** الأسبوع التالي [al-esboo'a al-taaly]

weekday ['wiːkˌdeɪ] *n* يوم في الأسبوع [Yawm fee al-osboo'a]

weekend [ˌwiːk'ɛnd] *n* عطلة أسبوعية ['aoṭlah osboo'ayeah]

weep [wiːp] *v* يَنْتَحب [jantaħibu]

weigh [weɪ] *v* يَزِن [jazinu]

weight [weɪt] *n* وَزْن [wazn]

weightlifter ['weɪtˌlɪftə] *n* رافع الأثقال [Rafe'a al-ath'qaal]

weightlifting ['weɪtˌlɪftɪŋ] *n* رفع الأثقال [Raf'a al-th'qaal]

weird [wɪəd] *adj* عجيب [ʕaʒiːb]

welcome ['wɛlkəm] *n* ترحيب [tarħiːb] ▷ *v* يَحْتَفي بـ [Yaḥtafey be]; **welcome!** *excl* مرحبا [marħaban]

well [wɛl] *adj* حَسَن [ħasan] ▷ *adv* كُلِيَةً [kulijjatun] ▷ *n* بئر [biʔr]; **oil well** *n* بئر بترول [Beear betrol]

well-behaved ['wɛl'bɪ'heɪvd] *adj* حسن السلوك [Ḥasen al-solook]

wellies ['wɛlɪz] *npl* حذاء برقبة [Hedhaa be-ra'qabah]

wellingtons ['wɛlɪŋtənz] *npl* حذاء برقبة [Hedhaa be-ra'qabah]

well-known ['wɛl'nəʊn] *adj* مشهور [maʃhuːr]

well-off ['wɛl'ɒf] *adj* حسن الأحوال [Hosn al-ahwaal]

well-paid ['wɛl'peɪd] *adj* حسن الدخل [Hosn al-dakhl]

Welsh [wɛlʃ] *adj* ويلزي [wiːlzij] ▷ *n* ويلزي [wiːlzij]

west [wɛst] *adj* غربي [ɣarbij] ▷ *adv* غرباً [ɣarban] ▷ *n* غَرْب [ɣarb]; **West Indian** *n* ساكن الهند الغربية [Saken al-hend al-gharbeyah]; **West Indies** *npl* جزر الهند الغربية [Jozor al-hend al-gharbeyah]

westbound ['wɛstˌbaʊnd] *adj* متجه غرباً [Motajeh gharban]

western ['wɛstən] *adj* غربي [ɣarbij] ▷ *n* وسترن [Western]

wet [wɛt] *adj* مبتل [mubtal]

wetsuit ['wɛtˌsuːt] *n* بدلة الغوص [Badlat al-ghawṣ]

whale [weɪl] *n* حوت [ħuːt]

what [wɒt; wət] *adj* أيّ ▷ *pron* ما [maː]; **What do you do?** ماذا تعمل؟ [madha ta'amal?]; **What is it?** ما هذا؟ [ma hatha?]; **What is the word for...?** ما هي الكلمة التي تعني... [ma heya al-kalema al-laty ta'any...?]

wheat [wiːt] *n* قمح [qamħ]; **wheat intolerance** *n* حساسية القمح [Ḥasaseyah al-'qamḥ]

wheel [wiːl] *n* عجلة [ʕaʒala]; **spare wheel** *n* عجلة إضافية ['aagalh eḍafeyah]; **steering wheel** *n* عجلة القيادة ['aagalat al-'qeyadh]

wheelbarrow ['wiːlˌbærəʊ] *n* عجلة اليد ['aagalat al-yad]

wheelchair ['wiːlˌtʃɛə] *n* كرسي بعجلات [Korsey be-'ajalat]

when [wɛn] *adv* متى [mataː] ▷ *conj* عندما; **When does it begin?** متى يبدأ العمل هنا؟ [mata yabda al-'aamal huna?]; **When does it finish?** متى ينتهي العمل هنا؟ [mata yan-tahy al-'aamal huna?]; **When is it due?** متى سيحين الموعد؟ [mata sa-ya-ḥeen al-maw'aid?]

where [wɛə] *adv* أين [ʔajna] ▷ *conj* حيث [ħajθu]; **Where are we?** أين نحن الآن؟

[ayna naḥno al-aan?]; **Where are you from?** من أين أنت؟ [min ayna anta?]; **Where are you staying?** أين تقيم؟ [Ayn to'qeem?]; **Where can we meet?** أين يمكن أن نتقابل؟ [ayna yamken an nata-'qabal?]; **Where can you go...?** أين يمكن الذهاب لـ...؟ [ayna yamken al-dhehaab le...?]; **Where do I pay?** أين يتم الدفع؟ [ayna yatim al-daf'a?]; **Where do I sign?** أين مكان التوقيع؟ [ayna makan al-taw'qe'a?]; **Where is...?** أين يوجد... [ayna yujad...?]; **Where is the gents?** أين يوجد حمام الرجال؟ [Ayn yojad ḥamam al-rejal]

whether ['wɛðə] *conj* سواء

which [wɪtʃ] *pron* أيّ, أيَّة [ayyat]

while [waɪls] *conj* حينما ▷ *n* فترة وجيزة [Fatrah wajeezah]

whip [wɪp] *n* سَوط [sawtˤ]; **whipped cream** *n* كريمة مخفوقة [Keremah makhfoo'qah]

whisk [wɪsk] *n* مَضْرَب [midˤrabu]

whiskers ['wɪskəz] *npl* شَوَارِب [ʃawa:ribun]

whisky ['wɪskɪ] *n* وِسْكي [wiski:]; **malt whisky** *n* ويسكي الشَعير المجفف [Weskey al-she'aeer al-mojafaf]

whisper ['wɪspə] *v* يهمس [jahmisu]

whistle ['wɪsᵊl] *n* صُفَّارة [sˤaffa:ra] ▷ *v* يُصَفِر [jusˤaffiru]

white [waɪt] *adj* أبيض [ʔabjadˤ]; **egg white** *n* بياض البيض [Bayaḍ al-bayḍ]; **a carafe of white wine** دورق من النبيذ الأبيض [dawra'q min al-nabeedh al-abyaḍ]

whiteboard ['waɪt,bɔːd] *n* لوحة بيضاء [Looḥ bayḍaa]

whitewash ['waɪt,wɒʃ] *v* يبيض [jubajjidˤu]

whiting ['waɪtɪŋ] *n* سمك الأبيض [Samak al-abyaḍ]

who [huː] *pron* مَنْ [man]

whole [həʊl] *adj* سليم [sali:m] ▷ *n* وحدة كاملة [Weḥdah kamelah]

wholefoods ['həʊl,fuːdz] *npl* أغذية متكاملة [Aghzeyah motakamelah]

wholemeal ['həʊl,miːl] *adj* طحين الاسمر [tˤaħi:nu ila:smari]

wholesale ['həʊl,seɪl] *adj* جملي [ʒumalij] ▷ *n* بيع بالجملة [Bay'a bel-jomlah]

whom [huːm] *pron* مَنْ [man]

whose [huːz] *adj* خاص به [Khaṣ beh] ▷ *pron* لمن

why [waɪ] *adv* لماذا [lemadha]

wicked ['wɪkɪd] *adj* كريه [kari:h]

wide [waɪd] *adj* عريض [ʕari:dˤ] ▷ *adv* عريضا [ʕari:dˤun]

widespread ['waɪd,sprɛd] *adj* منتشر [muntaʃir]

widow ['wɪdəʊ] *n* أرملة [ʔarmala]

widower ['wɪdəʊə] *n* أرمل [ʔarmal]

width [wɪdθ] *n* اتساع [ittisa:ʕ]

wife, wives [waɪf, waɪvz] *n* زوجة [zawʒa]

WiFi [waɪ faɪ] *n* ماركة واي فاي خاصة بالتكنولوجيا التحتية للشبكات المحلية اللاسلكية [ma:rikatun wa ajji fa:j xa:sˤatin bittiknu:lu:ʒija: attaħtijjati liʃʃabakti almaħallijjati alla:silkijjati]

wig [wɪg] *n* باروكة [ba:ru:ka]

wild [waɪld] *adj* بري [barij]

wildlife ['waɪld,laɪf] *n* حياة برية [Hayah bareyah]

will [wɪl] *n (document)* وَصْية [wasˤijja], *(motivation)* إرادة [ʔira:da]

willing ['wɪlɪŋ] *adj* مستعد [mustaʕidd]

willingly ['wɪlɪŋlɪ] *adv* عن طيب خاطر [An ṭeeb khaṭer]

willow ['wɪləʊ] *n* شجرة الصِفْصَاف [Shajart al-ṣefṣaf]

willpower ['wɪl,paʊə] *n* قوة الإرادة ['qowat al-eradah]

wilt [wɪlt] *v* يَذبُل [jaðbulu]

win [wɪn] *v* يفوز [jafu:zu]

wind¹ [wɪnd] *n* رياح [rijja:ħ] ▷ *vt (with a blow etc.)* يُهَوي [juhawi:]

wind² [waɪnd] *v (coil around)* يُهَوي [juhawi:]

windmill ['wɪnd,mɪl; 'wɪn,mɪl] *n* طاحونة هواء [ṭaḥoonat hawaa]

window ['wɪndəʊ] *n* نافذة [na:fiða];

shop window *n* واجهة العرض في المتجر [Wagehat al-'aarḍ fee al-matjar]; **window pane** *n* لوح زجاجي [Loḥ zojajey]; **window seat** *n* مقعد بجوار النافذة [Ma'q'aad bejwar al-nafedhah]; **I can't open the window** لا يمكنني فتح النافذة [la yam-kinuni faitḥ al-nafitha]; **I'd like a window seat** أريد مقعد بجوار النافذة [areed ma'q'aad be-jewar al-nafedha]; **May I close the window?** هل يمكن أن أغلق النافذة؟ [hal yamken an aghli'q al-nafidha?]; **May I open the window?** هل يمكن أن أفتح النافذة؟ [hal yamken an aftaḥ al-nafidha?]

windowsill ['wɪndəʊˌsɪl] *n* عتبة النافذة ['aatabat al-nafedhah]

windscreen ['wɪndˌskriːn] *n* الزجاج الأمامي [Al-zojaj al-amamy]; **windscreen wiper** *n* ماسحة زجاج السيارة [Masehat zojaj sayarh]; **Could you clean the windscreen?** أيمكنك تنظيف الزجاج الأمامي من فضلك؟ [a-yamkun-ika tanḍheef al-zujaj al-ama-me min faḍlak?]; **The windscreen is broken** لقد تحطم الزجاج الأمامي [la'qad taḥa-ṭama al-zujaj al-amamy]

windsurfing ['wɪndˌsɜːfɪŋ] *n* تَزَلُج شِرَاعِي [Tazaloj shera'aey]

windy ['wɪndɪ] *adj* مذرو بالرياح [Madhro bel-reyah]

wine [waɪn] *n* خمر [xamr]; **house wine** *n* خمر هاوس واين [Khamr hawees wayen]; **red wine** *n* نبيذ أحمر [nabeedh aḥmar]; **table wine** *n* خَمْر الطعام [Khamr al-ṭa'aam]; **wine list** *n* قائمة خمور ['qaemat khomor]; **This stain is wine** هذه البقعة بقعة خمر [hathy al-bu'q-'aa bu'q-'aat khamur]; **This wine is not chilled** هذا الخمر ليس مثلج [hatha al-khamur lysa muthal-laj]

wineglass ['waɪnˌglɑːs] *n* زجاجة الخمر [Zojajat al-khamr]

wing [wɪŋ] *n* جناح [ʒanaːħ]; **wing mirror** *n* مرآة جانبية [Meraah janebeyah]

wink [wɪŋk] *v* يَغْمِز [jaɣmizu]

winner ['wɪnə] *n* شخص فائز [Shakhṣ faaez]

winning ['wɪnɪŋ] *adj* فائز [faːʔiz]

winter ['wɪntə] *n* الشتاء [aʃ-ʃitaːʔi]; **winter sports** *npl* رياضات شتوية [Reyḍat shetweyah]

wipe [waɪp] *v* يَمْسَح [jamsaħu]; **baby wipe** *n* منديل أطفال [Mandeel aṭfaal]

wipe up [waɪp ʌp] *v* يَمْسَح [jamsaħu]

wire [waɪə] *n* سِلْك [silk]; **barbed wire** *n* سِلك شائك [Selk shaaek]

wisdom ['wɪzdəm] *n* حِكمة [ħikma]; **wisdom tooth** *n* ضرس العقل [Ḍers al-a'aql]

wise [waɪz] *adj* حكيم [ħakiːm]

wish [wɪʃ] *n* أمنية [ʔumnijja] ▷ *v* يَتمَنى [jatamannaː]

wit [wɪt] *n* فِطْنَة [fitˤna]

witch [wɪtʃ] *n* ساحرة [saːħira]

with [wɪð; wɪθ] *prep* مع [maʕa]; **Can I leave a message with his secretary?** هل يمكنني ترك رسالة مع السكرتير الخاص به؟ [hal yamken -any tark resala ma'aa al-sikertair al-khaṣ behe?]; **It's been a pleasure working with you** من دواعي سروري العمل معك [min dawa-'ay siro-ry al-'aamal ma'aak]

withdraw [wɪð'drɔː] *v* يَسحَب [jasħabu]

withdrawal [wɪð'drɔːəl] *n* إنسِحاب [ʔinsiħaːb]

within [wɪ'ðɪn] *prep (space)* داخل [Dakhel], *(term)* داخل [Dakhel]

without [wɪ'ðaʊt] *prep* بدون [biduːni]; **I'd like it without..., please** أحب تناوله بدون...من فضلك [aḥib tana-wilaho be-doon... min faḍlak]

witness ['wɪtnɪs] *n* شاهد [ʃaːhid]; **Jehovah's Witness** *n* طائفة شهود يهوه المسيحية [Ṭaaefat shehood yahwah al-maseyheyah]

witty ['wɪtɪ] *adj* فَطِن [fatˤin]

wolf, wolves [wʊlf, wʊlvz] *n* ذئب [ðiʔb]

woman, women ['wʊmən, 'wɪmɪn] *n* امرأة [imraʔa]

wonder ['wʌndə] *v* يَتَعجب [jataʕaʒʒabu]

wonderful ['wʌndəfʊl] *adj* عجيب

[ʕaʒiːb]
wood [wʊd] *n (forest)* غابة [ɣaːba], *(material)* خشب [xaʃab]
wooden ['wʊdᵊn] *adj* خشبي [xaʃabij]
woodwind ['wʊd,wɪnd] *n* آلة نفخ موسيقية [Aalat nafkh mose'qeyah]
woodwork ['wʊd,wɜːk] *n* أعمال الخشب [A'amal al khashab]
wool [wʊl] *n* صوف [sˤuːf]; **cotton wool** *n* قطن طبى ['qoṭn ṭebey]
woollen ['wʊlən] *adj* صوفي [sˤuːfij]
woollens ['wʊlənz] *npl* أنسجة صوفية [Ansejah ṣoofeyah]
word [wɜːd] *n* كلمة [kalima]; **all one word** كلمة واحدة فقط [kilema waḥeda fa'qaṭ]; **What is the word for...?** ما هي الكلمة التي تعني... [ma heya al-kalema al-laty ta'any...?]
work [wɜːk] *n* عمل [ʕamal] ▷ *v* يَعمَل [jaʕmalu]; **work experience** *n* خبرة العمل [Khebrat al'aamal]; **work of art** *n* عمل فني ['amal faney]; **work permit** *n* تصريح عمل [Taṣreeh 'amal]; **work station** *n* محطة عمل [Mahaṭat 'aamal]; **How does the ticket machine work?** كيف تعمل ماكينة التذاكر؟ [kayfa ta'amal makenat al-tathaker?]; **How does this work?** كيف يعمل هذا؟ [Kayfa ya'amal hatha?]; **I hope we can work together again soon** أتمنى أن نستطيع معاودة العمل سويًا في وقت قريب [ata-mana an nasta-ṭee'a mo'aawadat al-'aamal sa-waian fee wa'qt 'qareeb]; **I work in a factory** أعمل في أحد المصانع [A'amal fee aḥad al-maṣaane'a]; **I'm here for work** أنا هنا للعمل [ana huna lel-'aamal]; **The... doesn't work properly** إن... لا يعمل كما ينبغي [enna... la ya'amal kama yanbaghy]; **The air conditioning doesn't work** التكيف لا يعمل [al-tak-yeef la ya'amal]; **The brakes don't work** الفرامل لا تعمل [Al-faramel la ta'amal]; **The flash is not working** إن الفلاش لا يعمل [enna al-flaash la ya'amal]; **The gears are not working** ناقل السرعات لا يعمل [na'qil al-sur'aat la ya'amal]; **This doesn't work** هذا لا يعمل كما ينبغي [hatha la-ya'amal kama yan-baghy]; **Where do you work?** أين تعمل؟ [ayna ta'amal?]
worker ['wɜːkə] *n* عامل [ʕaːmil]; **social worker** *n* أخصائي اجتماعي [Akhṣey ejtema'ay]
workforce ['wɜːk,fɔːs] *n* قوة العاملة ['qowah al-'aamelah]
working-class ['wɜːkɪŋklɑːs] *adj* طبقة عاملة [Ṭaba'qah 'aaamelah]
workman, workmen ['wɜːkmən, 'wɜːkmɛn] *n* عَامِل [ʕaːmil]
work out [wɜːk aʊt] *v* يَحُل [jaħullu]
workplace ['wɜːk,pleɪs] *n* محل العمل [Maḥal al-'aamal]
workshop ['wɜːk,ʃɒp] *n* ورشة العمل [Warshat al-'aamal]
workspace ['wɜːk,speɪs] *n* مكان العمل [Makan al-'amal]
workstation ['wɜːk,steɪʃən] *n* مكان عمل [Makan 'aamal]
world [wɜːld] *n* عالم [ʕaːlam]; **Third World** *n* العالم الثالث [Al-'aalam al-thaleth]; **World Cup** *n* كأس العالم [Kaas al-'aalam]
worm [wɜːm] *n* دُودَة [duːda]
worn [wɔːn] *adj* رَثّ [raθθ]
worried ['wʌrɪd] *adj* قَلِق [qalaq]
worry ['wʌrɪ] *v* يَقْلَق [jaqlaqu]
worrying ['wʌrɪɪŋ] *adj* مقلق [muqliq]
worse [wɜːs] *adj* أسوأ [ʔaswaʔ] ▷ *adv* على نحو أسوأ [Ala nahw aswaa]
worsen ['wɜːsᵊn] *v* يَجعله أسوأ [Tej'aalah aswaa]
worship ['wɜːʃɪp] *v* يَعَبُد [jaʕbudu]
worst [wɜːst] *adj* الأسوأ [Al-aswaa]
worth [wɜːθ] *n* قيمة مالية ['qeemah maleyah]
worthless ['wɜːθlɪs] *adj* عديم القيمة ['adeem al-'qeemah]
would [wʊd; wəd] *v*; **I would like to wash the car** أريد أن أغسل السيارة [areed an aghsil al-sayara]; **We would like to go cycling** أريد ممارسة رياضة

ركوب الدراجات [areed mu-ma-rasat reyaḍat rikoob al-darrajaat]
wound [wuːnd] *n* جرح [ʒurħ] ▷ *v* يجرح [jaʒraħu]
wrap [ræp] *v* يُغَلِف [juɣallifu]; **wrapping paper** *n* ورق التغليف [Wara'q al-taghleef]
wrap up [ræp ʌp] *v* يُغَلِف [juɣallifu]
wreck [rɛk] *n* خراب [xaraːb] ▷ *v* يُحطِم [juħatˤimu]
wreckage ['rɛkɪdʒ] *n* حطام [ħutˤaːm]
wren [rɛn] *n* طائر الغِطاس [Ṭaayer al-ghaṭas]
wrench [rɛntʃ] *n* مفتاح ربط وفك الصواميل [Meftaḥ rabṭ wafak al-ṣawameel] ▷ *v* يُحَرِف [juħarrifu]
wrestler ['rɛslə] *n* مُصارع [musˤaːriʕ]
wrestling ['rɛslɪŋ] *n* مصارعة [musˤaːraʕa]
wrinkle ['rɪŋkəl] *n* تجعيد [taʒʕiːd]
wrinkled ['rɪŋkəld] *adj* متجعد [mutaʒaʕid]
wrist [rɪst] *n* معصم [miʕsˤam]
write [raɪt] *v* يَكْتُب [jaktubu]
write down [raɪt daʊn] *v* يُدَوِن [judawwinu]
writer ['raɪtə] *n* الكاتب [Al-kateb]
writing ['raɪtɪŋ] *n* كتابة [kitaːba]; **writing paper** *n* ورقة كتابة [Wara'qat ketabah]
wrong [rɒŋ] *adj* خاطئ [xaːtˤiʔ] ▷ *adv* على نحو خاطئ [Ala nahwen khaṭea]; **wrong number** *n* رقم خطأ [Ra'qam khaṭaa]

Xmas ['ɛksməs; 'krɪsməs] *n* كريسماس [kriːsmaːs]
X-ray [ɛksreɪ] *n* صورَةٌ شُعاعِيَّة [Ṣewar sho'aeyah] ▷ *v* يصور بأشعة إكس [jasˤuːru biʔaʃʕati ʔiks]
xylophone ['zaɪlə,fəʊn] *n* آلة الإكسيليفون الموسيقية [aalat al ekseelefon al mose'qeiah]

yacht [jɒt] *n* يخت [jaxt]
yard [jɑːd] *n (enclosure)* حظيرة [ħazˤiːra], *(measurement)* ياردة [jaːrda]
yawn [jɔːn] *v* يتَثَاءب [jataθaːʔabu]
year [jɪə] *n* سَنَة [sana]; **academic year** *n* عام دراسي [ʻaam derasey]; **financial year** *n* سَنة مالية [Sanah maleyah]; **leap year** *n* سَنة كبيسة [Sanah kabeesah]; **New Year** *n* رَأس السَنَة [Raas alsanah]
yearly [ˈjɪəlɪ] *adj* كل سنة [Kol sanah] ▷ *adv* سنويا [sanawijan]
yeast [jiːst] *n* خَمِيرَة [xamiːra]
yell [jɛl] *v* يَهْتِف [jahtifu]
yellow [ˈjɛləʊ] *adj* أصفر [ʔasˤfar]; **Yellow Pages®** *npl* ®يلوبيدجز [bloobeedjez®]
Yemen [ˈjɛmən] *n* اليَمَنْ [al-jamanu]
yes [jɛs] *excl* نعم [niʕma]
yesterday [ˈjɛstədɪ; -ˌdeɪ] *adv* أمس [ʔamsun]; **the day before yesterday** أمس الأول [ams al-a-wal]
yet [jɛt] *adv (interrogative)* حتى الآن [Ḥata alaan], *(with negative)* حتى الآن [Ḥata alaan] ▷ *conj (nevertheless)* حتى الآن [Ḥata alaan]
yew [juː] *n* شجر الطقسوس [Shajar al-ṭa'qsoos]
yield [jiːld] *v* يَهبْ [jahibu]
yoga [ˈjəʊɡə] *n* يُوجَا [juːʒaː]
yoghurt [ˈjəʊɡət; ˈjɒɡ-] *n* زبادي [zabaːdij]
yolk [jəʊk] *n* صفار [sˤafaːr]
you [juː; jʊ] *pron (plural)* أنت [ʔanta], *(singular polite)* أنت [ʔanta], *(singular)* أنت [ʔanta]; **Are you alright?** هل أنت على ما يرام [hal anta ʻaala ma yoraam?]
young [jʌŋ] *adj* شَاب [ʃaːbb]
younger [jʌŋə] *adj* أصغر [ʔasˤɣaru]
youngest [jʌŋɪst] *adj* الأصغر [al-ʔasˤɣaru]
your [jɔː; jʊə; jə] *adj (plural)* الخاص بك [alxaːsˤ bik], *(singular polite)* الخاص بك [alxaːsˤ bik], *(singular)* الخاص بك [alxaːsˤ bik]
yours [jɔːz; jʊəz] *pron (plural)* لك [lak], *(singular polite)* لك [lak], *(singular)* لك [lak]
yourself [jɔːˈsɛlf; jʊə-] *pron* نفسك [Nafsek], *(intensifier)* نفسك [Nafsek], *(polite)* نفسك [Nafsek]
yourselves [jɔːˈsɛlvz] *pron (intensifier)* أنفسكم [Anfosokom], *(polite)* أنفسكم [Anfosokom], *(reflexive)* أنفسكم [Anfosokom]
youth [juːθ] *n* شباب [ʃabaːb]; **youth club** *n* نادي الشباب [Nadey shabab]; **youth hostel** *n* دار الشباب [Dar al-shabab]

Z

Zambia ['zæmbɪə] *n* زامبيا [za:mbja:]
Zambian ['zæmbɪən] *adj* زامبي [za:mbij] ▷ *n* زامبي [za:mbij]
zebra ['zi:brə; 'zɛbrə] *n* الحمار الوحشي [Al-hemar al-wahshey]; **zebra crossing** *n* ممر للمشاة ملون بالأبيض والأسود [Mamar lel-moshah molawan bel-abyaḍ wal-aswad]
zero, zeroes ['zɪərəʊ, 'zɪərəʊz] *n* صفر [sˤifr]
zest [zɛst] *n* *(excitement)* نَكْهة [nakha], *(lemon-peel)* نَكْهَة [nakha]
Zimbabwe [zɪm'bɑ:bwɪ; -weɪ] *n* زيمبابوي [zi:mba:bwij]
Zimbabwean [zɪm'bɑ:bwɪən; -weɪən] *adj* دولة زيمبابوي [Dawlat zembabway] ▷ *n* مواطن زيمبابوي [Mewaṭen zembabway]
zinc [zɪŋk] *n* زنك [zink]
zip [zɪp] *n* حيوية [ħajawijja]; **zip (up)** *v* يُغْلِق زِمام البنطلون [yoghle'q zemam albantaaloon]
zit [zɪt] *n* بثرة [baθra]
zodiac ['zəʊdɪ,æk] *n* دائرة البروج [Dayrat al-boroj]
zone [zəʊn] *n* منطقة [mintˤaqa]; **time zone** *n* نطاق زمني [Neṭa'q zamaney]
zoo [zu:] *n* حديقة الحيوان [Hadee'qat al-hayawan]
zoology [zəʊ'ɒlədʒɪ; zu:-] *n* علم الحيوان ['aelm al-hayawan]
zoom [zu:m] *n*; **zoom lens** *n* عدسة تكبير ['adasah mokaberah]
zucchini [tsu:'ki:nɪ; zu:-] *n* كوسة [ku:sa]

Arabic Grammar

Contents

Arabic grammar is often found to be difficult and complicated. Like most languages, it adheres to grammatical rules. Below are some important features of Arabic grammar. In order to make things as clear as possible, Romanized transcriptions are given next to the Arabic characters throughout this grammar supplement.

Adjectives

In English there is only one type of adjective for masculine and feminine.

In Arabic there are two types of adjectives – one for masculine and one for feminine.

We form the feminine adjectives by adding ة **taa marboota** to the masculine adjectives.

English	Feminine Adjective		Masculine Adjective	
tall/long	**taweela**	طويلة	**taweel**	طويل
short	**qaseera**	قصيرة	**qaseer**	قصير
heavy	**thaqeela**	ثقيلة	**thaqeel**	ثقيل
light	**khafeefa**	خفيفة	**khafeef**	خفيف
new	**jadeeda**	جديدة	**jadeed**	جديد
old	**qadeema**	قديمة	**qadeem**	قديم
beautiful	**jameela**	جميلة	**jameel**	جميل
ugly	**qabeeha**	قبيحة	**qabeeh**	قبيح
big/large	**kabeera**	كبيرة	**kabeer**	كبير
small	**sagheera**	صغيرة	**sagheer**	صغير
rich	**ghaneyya**	غنية	**ghaney**	غني
poor	**faqeera**	فقيرة	**faqeer**	فقير

In English, adjectives are usually used before the nouns they describe. For example:

<u>big</u> garden

In Arabic, adjectives are usually used after the nouns they describe and must agree with the noun. This means if the noun is singular, masculine, feminine, indefinite or definite, then the adjective must be the same.

walad waseem ولد وسيم
a handsome boy

madeena kabeera مدينة كبيرة
a big city

alwalad alwaseem الولد الوسيم
the handsome boy

Adjectives are also used as the predicate **الخبر** **alkhabar** of a nominative sentence: the predicate is the part of the sentence which tells you about the subject.

alwalad waseem الولد وسيم
The boy is handsome

almadeena kabeera المدينة كبيرة
The city is big

The adjectives here are used as predicates as they are indefinite and the subject is definite.

When a noun has a possessive ending, as in **كتابي** **ketabi** (*my book*), the adjective must be definite with **ال** **al**. Nouns with the possessive ending are considered definite since we know what is being referred to.

ketabi aljadeed كتابي الجديد
my new book

haqeebati alkabeera حقيبتي الكبيرة
my big bag

If there is more than one adjective, they all come after the noun they describe with **و** **wa** (*and*) between them.

walad waseem <u>wa</u> mo'addab ولد وسيم ومؤدب
a handsome and polite boy

almadeena alkabeera <u>wa</u> aljameela
المدينة الكبيرة و الجميلة
the big and beautiful city

When we use the demonstratives **هذا hatha** / **هذه hathehe** we use them like this.

walad waseem ولد وسيم
a handsome boy

alwalad alwaseem الولد الوسيم
the handsome boy

alwalad waseem الولد وسيم
the boy is handsome

<u>hatha</u> walad waseem هذا ولد وسيم
this is a handsome boy

<u>hatha</u> alwalad alwaseem mo'addab هذا الولد الوسيم مؤدب
this handsome boy is polite

<u>hatha</u> alwalad waseem هذا الولد وسيم
this boy is handsome

Plural adjectives are used only with people as non-human plural nouns are described by feminine singular adjective.

mommaththeloon <u>mashhorroon</u> ممثلون مشهورون
famous actors

mo'tamar <u>kabeer</u> مؤتمر كبير
a big conference

mo'tamarat <u>kabeera</u> مؤتمرات كبيرة
big conferences

alghassala <u>aljadeeda</u> الغسالة الجديدة
the new washing machine

alghassalat <u>aljadeeda</u> الغسالات الجديدة
the new washing machines

The plural adjectives which are used to describe people can often be formed using the sound masculine and the sound feminine plurals.

mudarrisoon amrekeyyun مدرسون أمريكيون
American male teachers

mudarrisat britaneyyat مدرسات بريطانيات
British female teachers

Some of the basic adjectives have broken (irregular) plurals which should be learned individually.

mudarrisoon jodod مُدَرِّسُونْ جُدُدْ
new teachers

mudarrisat maherat مُدَرِّسَاتْ مَاهِرَاتْ
clever female teachers

All the colours are considered adjectives. Basic colour feminine adjectives can be formed by moving the ء **hamza** from the beginning to the end as follows:

ENGLISH	FEMININE		MASCULINE	
red	**hamraa**	حمراء	**ahmar**	أحمر
blue	**zarqaa**	زرقاء	**azraq**	أزرق
green	**khadraa**	خضراء	**akhdar**	أخضر
black	**sawdaa**	سوداء	**aswad**	أسود
white	**baydaa**	بيضاء	**abyad**	أبيض
yellow	**safraa**	صفراء	**asfar**	أصفر

ketab akhdar كتاب أخضر
a green book

sayyara hamraa سيارة حمراء
a red car

kotob khadraa كتب خضراء
green books

sayyarat hamraa سيارات حمراء
red cars

Note that we use singular feminine adjectives when we describe plural non-human nouns.

Definite Article

There is no indefinite article in the Arabic language for ***a*** or ***an***. So a word without ال **al** is indefinite.

ketab كتاب
a book

bayda بيضة
an egg

The definite article in the Arabic language is ال **al** which means ***the*** and is always attached to the noun.

alketab الكتاب
the book

albayda البيضة
the egg

Indefinite Article			Definite Article		
a chair	**korsi**	كرسي	*the chair*	**alkorsi**	الكرسي
a pen	**qalam**	قلم	*the pen*	**alqalam**	القلم
a house	**bayt**	بيت	*the house*	**albayt**	البيت
a train	**qetar**	قطار	*the train*	**alqetar**	القطار

Demonstratives

Demonstratives are those words which are used for *this* and *that* in English.

this	**hatha**	هذا
this	**hathehe**	هذه

that	**thalik**	**ذلك**
that	**tilka**	**تلك**

هذا hatha / **ذلك thalik** refer to masculine nouns.

هذه hathehe / **تلك tilka** refer to feminine nouns.

The demonstratives go before the nouns with the article **ال al**:

hathehe almar'a هذه المرأة
this woman/girl

thalika aljabal ذلك الجبل
that mountain

The demonstrative can also be used with an indefinite noun without **ال al** to form a sentence:

hatha modarris هذا مدرس
This is a teacher

tilka madrasa تلك مدرسة
That is a school

Remember that the Arabic language has no indefinite article *a* and *an* and no verb *to be* in the present tense.

This means that **ال al** indicates the difference between the two examples below

hatha rajol هذا رجل
This is a man

hatha alrajol هذا الرجل
This man

If we want to say *This is the man/woman*, we need to use **هو hoa** (masculine) or **هي heya** (feminine) after the demonstrative.

hatha hoa alrajol هذا هو الرجل
This is the man

hathehe <u>heya</u> almara'a هذه هي المرأة
This is the woman

If we want to say something about the person we follow that with an indefinite word.

hatha alrajal <u>amrekey</u> هذا الرجل أمريكي
This man is American

hathehe almara'a <u>masreyya</u> هذه المرأة مصرية
This woman is Egyptian

There is a big difference between human and non-human plurals. Human plurals are formed either by adding an **ون** **un** to the masculine noun or **ات** **at** to the feminine noun.

Non-human plurals are grammatically feminine singular. Therefore, the demonstratives will be the same as the feminine singular **تلك** **tilka** and **هذه** **hathehe**.

<u>hathehe</u> hayawanat هذه حيوانات
These are animals

When we talk about people, we use the following plural demonstratives.

ha'ula' هؤلاء
these

ula'ika أولئك
those

<u>ha'ula'</u> alrejal هؤلاء الرجال
These men

<u>ula'ika</u> hum alrejal أولئك هم الرجال
Those are the men

Gender: Masculine and Feminine

In Arabic, nouns (words that name people, objects and ideas) are either masculine or feminine.

haqeeba (feminine) حقيبة
bag

ketab (masculine) كتاب
book

It is easy to tell if the word is masculine or feminine. Feminine words have two types:

1. Words with the feminine ending ة **taa marbuta**

    tawela طاولة
    table

    sura صورة
    picture

2. Words which refer to females but do not end in ة **taa marbuta**.

    bint بنت
    girl

    umm أم
    mother

However, there are a small number of words which are considered feminine and don't belong to either of the feminine types. Most are names of countries, natural features or parts of the body (which are one of a pair).

qatar قطر
Qatar

shams شمس
sun

yad يد
hand

Personal Pronouns

Pronouns are words such as *I*, *you*, *he*, *it* which replace names or nouns in a sentence.

Arabic has more pronouns than English as it has different versions for masculine and feminine, singular, dual (two people) and plural.

			Masculine		Feminine	
Singular	First Person	*I*	**ana**	أَنَا	**ana**	أَنَا
	Second Person	*you*	**anta**	أَنْتَ	**anti**	أَنْتِ
	Third Person	*he / she*	**hoa**	هُو	**heya**	هِيَ
	First Person	*we*	**nahnu**	نَحْنُ	**nahnu**	نَحْنُ
Dual	Second Person	*you*	**antoma**	أَنْتُمَا	**antoma**	أَنْتُمَا
	Third Person	*they*	**homa**	هُمَا	**homa**	هُمَا
	First Person	*we*	**nahnu**	نَحْنُ	**nahnu**	نَحْنُ
Plural	Second Person	*you*	**antom**	أَنْتُمْ	**antonna**	أَنْتُنَّ
	Third Person	*they*	**homm**	هُمْ	**honna**	هُنَّ

Personal Pronouns (Object)

In English the object pronouns such as *me*, *him*, *us*, *them* are used separately and there are only singular and plural forms of personal pronouns.

In Arabic there are singular, dual (two people) and plural forms.

			Masculine		Feminine	
Singular	First Person	*me*	**- ni**	ني	**- ni**	ني
	Second Person	*you*	**- ka**	كَ	**- ki**	كِ
	Third Person	*him / her*	**- oh**	ه	**- ha**	هَا
	First Person	*us*	**- na**	نا	**- na**	نا
Dual	Second Person	*you*	**- koma**	كُمَا	**- koma**	كُمَا
	Third Person	*them*	**- homa**	هما	**- homa**	هما
	First Person	*us*	**- na**	نا	**- na**	نا
Plural	Second Person	*you*	**- kom**	كُمْ	**- konna**	كُنَّ
	Third Person	*them*	**- hom**	هُمْ	**- honna**	هُنَّ

In Arabic the personal pronoun objects are attached to the verbs as shown in the examples.

> **hoa zarani ams** هو زارني أمس
> *He visited me yesterday*
>
> **ana oqabelha koll asoboo'a** أنا اقابلها كل أسبوع
> *I meet her every week*

Plural Nouns

Arabic nouns are formed in three different ways:

1. If the singular noun is masculine, then the letters **ون un** are to be added to the singular noun.

   modarris مدرس
   male teacher

mudarris<u>un</u> مدرسون
male teachers

2. If the singular noun is feminine, then the letters ات **at** are to be added to the singular nouns after taking the ة **taa marboota** off.

modarrisa مدرسة
female teacher

mudarris<u>at</u> مدرسات
female teachers

If the singular noun ends with ة **taa marboota** this should be removed before the ات **at** is added.

faranseyy<u>a</u> فرنسية
French female

faranseyy<u>at</u> فرنسيات
French females

The sound feminine plural is usually used with a variety of masculine and feminine nouns which refer to objects and ideas.

ijtemaa' اجتماع
meeting

ijtemaa'<u>at</u> اجتماعات
meetings

hayawan حيوان
animal

hayawan<u>at</u> حيوانات
animals

3. The third type of plural in the Arabic language is called **جمع تكسير jamaa' takseer**. This is an irregular plural as it is formed in different ways, like some plurals in English. For example, the plural of *mouse* is *mice* and the plural of *woman* is *women*.

ketab كتاب
a book

<u>kotob</u> كتب
books

walad ولد
a boy

<u>a'wlad</u> أولاد
boys

You need to learn these plurals as there is no rule for forming them.

Plural pronouns such as **هُمْ** **hum** and **هُنَّ** **hunna** are only used when we refer to people.

<u>hum</u> amrekeyyiun هم أمريكيون
They are American males

<u>hunna</u> amrekeyyat هن أمريكيات
They are American females

When we refer to non-human plurals, we use the feminine singular pronoun.

assayyarat fi almera'b السيارات في المرآب
The cars in the garage

<u>heya</u> fi almera'b هي في المرآب
They are in the garage

Questions

In Arabic there are two types of questions.

1. Yes/No questions
2. Question words

Yes/No questions are formed by using **هل** **hal** or **أ** **a** at the beginning of a statement.

<u>hal</u> almodarris fi alfasl? هل المدرس في الفصل؟
Is the teacher in the class?

<u>a</u> hatha ketab? أهذا كتاب؟
Is this a book?

We can simply add a question mark at the end of a statement with a change of intonation to make a yes/no question. This is less formal.

hatha ketab Ahmed? هذا كتاب أحمد؟
Is this Ahmed's book?

Question Words

The other type of questions start with a question word such as:

What + verb?	**matha**	ماذا + فعل؟
What + noun?	**ma**	ما + اسم؟
Where?	**ayna**	أين؟
How?	**kayfa**	كيف؟
Why?	**lematha**	لماذا؟
Who?	**man**	مَنْ؟
When?	**mata**	متى؟
How many/much?	**kam**	كم؟
How much (price)?	**bekam**	بكم؟
From where?	**min ayna**	من أين؟
Which	**ayy**	أي؟

<u>ayna</u> alqalam? أين القلم؟
Where is the pen?

<u>ma</u> ismok? ما اسمك؟
What's your name?

Sun letters and Moon letters

The pronunciation of ال **al** (the definite article) usually changes when it is followed by some letters. The ل **lam** is not pronounced when the word starts with these letters and the first letter of the noun is stressed.

The letters which cause this pronunciation are called 'sun letters' (**الحروف الشمسية alhuroof ash-shamseyya**). As ش **shin** is one of these letters it is only the pronunciation which changes but the spelling remains the same.

ash-shams الشمس
the sun

as-samaa السماء
the sky

The rest of the letters are called the 'moon letters' (**الحروف القمرية alhuroof alqamareyya**) and the letter ق **qaf** is one of these letters.

alqamar القمر
the moon

alketab الكتاب
the book

MOON LETTERS الحروف القمرية			SUN LETTERS الحروف الشمسية		
أ ب ج ح خ ع غ ف ق ك م ه و ى			ت ث د ذ ر ز س ش ص ض ط ظ ل ن		
the son	**al-ibn**	الإبن	*the crown*	**at-taj**	التاج
the door	**al-bab**	الباب	*the price*	**ath-thaman**	الثمن
the camel	**al-jamal**	الجمل	*the lesson*	**ad-dars**	الدرس
the war	**al-harb**	الحرب	*the corn*	**adh-dhora**	الذرة
the bread	**al-khobz**	الخبز	*the message*	**ar-resala**	الرسالة
the eye	**al-ayn**	العين	*the time*	**az-zaman**	الزمن
the west	**al-gharb**	الغرب	*the peace*	**as-salam**	السلام
the dawn	**al-fajr**	الفجر	*the sun*	**ash-shams**	الشمس
the pen	**al-qalam**	القلم	*the morning*	**as-sabah**	الصباح
the book	**al-ketab**	الكتاب	*the fog*	**add-ddabab**	الضباب
the money	**al-mal**	المال	*the tomatoes*	**at-tamatem**	الطماطم
the pyramid	**al-haram**	الهرم	*the darkness*	**ath-thalam**	الظلام
the weight	**al-wazn**	الوزن	*the night*	**al-layl**	الليل
the hand	**al-yad**	اليد	*the people*	**an-nas**	الناس

ARABIC-ENGLISH

عربي - إنجليزي

ائتمان credit, trust *n* [iʔtima:n]

كارت ائتمان

[Kart eateman] *n* credit card

أب dad *n* [ʔab]

أب روحي

[Af rooḥey] *n* godfather *(baptism)*

زوجة الأب

[Zawj al-aab] *n* stepmother

إباحي pornographic *adj* [ʔiba:ħij]

فن إباحي

[Fan ebaḥey] *n* pornography

ابتاع purchase *v* [ʔebta:ʕa]

ابتدائي initial *adj* [ibtida:ʔij]

ابتز blackmail *v* [ʔebtazza]

ابتزاز blackmail *n* [ʔibtiza:z]

ابتسامة smile *n* [ʔibtisa:ma]

ابتسامة عريضة

[Ebtesamah areeḍah] *n* grin

ابتسم smile *v* [ʔebtasama]

ابتعِد *v* [ʔebtaʕida]

يبتعِد عن

[Yabta'aed 'an] *v* keep out

ابتكار innovation *n* [ibtika:r]

ابتكاري innovative *adj* [ibtika:rij]

ابتكر devise *v* [ʔebtakara]

ابتلع swallow *vi* [ʔebtalaʕa]

ابتهاج cheer *n* [ibtiha:ʒ]

إبتهج cheer *v* [ʔebtahiʒa]

ابجدية alphabet *n* [ʔabaʒadijja]

إبحار *n* [ʔibħa:r]

ما هو موعد الإبحار؟

[ma howa maw-'aid al-ebḥar?] When do we sail?

أبحر sail *v* [ʔabħara]

أبخِرَة fumes *npl* [ʔabxiratun]

أبدًا always *adv* [ʔabadan]

أنا لا أشرب الخمر أبدا

[ana la ashrab al-khamr abadan] I never drink wine

ابداء display *n* [ibda:ʔ]

إبداع creation *n* [ʔibda:ʕ]

أبْدِع create *v* [ʔabdaʕa]

أبدي present *v* [ʔabda:]

إبر *n* [ʔibar]

وخز بالإبر

[Wakhz bel-ebar] *n* acupuncture

إبرة needle *n* [ʔibra]

إبرة خياطة

[Ebrat khayṭ] *n* knitting needle

هل يوجد لديك إبرة وخيط؟

[hal yujad ladyka ebra wa khyṭ?] Do you have a needle and thread?

أبرشية parish *n* [ʔabraʃijja]

أبرم turn round *v* [ʔabarama]

أبريق pitcher *n* [ibri:qu]

أبريق القهوة

[Abreeq al-'qahwah] *n* coffeepot

إبريق jug *n* [ibri:q]

أبريل April *n* [ʔabri:l]

يوم كذبة أبريل

[yawm kedhbat abreel] *n* April Fools' Day

إبزيم buckle *n* [ʔibzi:m]

إبط armpit *n* [ʔibitˤ]

أبطأ slow down *v* [ʔabtˤaʔa]

أبْطل cancel *vt* [ʔabtˤala]

أبْعد relegate *v* [ʔabʕada]

أبكم dummy *n* [ʔabkam]

أبْلغ report *v* [ʔablaɣa]

يُبْلغ عن

[Yoballegh an] *v* inform

أبْلَه silly *adj* ◃ idiot *n* [ʔablah]

ابن son *n* [ʔibn]

ابن الإبن
[Ebn el-ebn] *n* grandson
ابن الأخ
[Ebn al-akh] *n* nephew
زوجة الابن
[Zawj al-ebn] *n* daughter-in-law
إن ابني مفقود
[enna ibny maf-'qood] My son is missing
فقد ابني
[fo'qeda ibny] My son is lost
اِبْنَةٌ *n* [ʔibna]
فقدت ابنتي
[fo'qedat ibnaty] My daughter is lost
ابنة daughter *n* [ibna]
إبنة daughter *n* [ʔibna]
زوج الإبنة
[Zawj al-ebnah] *n* son-in-law
إبهام *n* [ʔibha:m]
إبهام اليد
[Ebham al-yad] *n* thumb
أبو ظبي Abu Dhabi *n* [ʔabu zˤabj]
أَبَى reject *v* [ʔaba:]
أبيض blank *n* ◃ white *adj* [ʔabjadˤ]
اتبِع follow *vt* [ʔetbaʕa]
اتجِه *v* [ʔettaʒaha]
من فضلك، أي الأتوبيسات يتجه إلى...؟
[Men faḍlek, ay al-otobeesaat yatjeh ela...] Excuse me, which bus goes to...?
هل يتجه هذا الأتوبيس إلى...؟
[hal yata-jih hadha al-baaṣ ela...?] Does this bus go to...?
هل يوجد أتوبيس يتجه إلى المطار؟
[Hal yojad otobees yatjeh ela al-maṭaar?] Is there a bus to the airport?
اتحاد union *n* [ittiħa:d]
الاتحاد الأوروبي
[Al-tehad al-orobey] *n* European Union
اتساع width *n* [ittisa:ʕ]
اتصال communication, *n* [ittisˤa:l] contact
اتصال هاتفي
[Eteṣal hatefey] *n* phonecall
كود الاتصال بمنطقة أو بلد
[Kod al-eteṣal bemanṭe'qah aw balad] *n* dialling code
نغمة الاتصال
[Naghamat al-eteṣal] *n* dialling tone
نظام الاتصال الداخلي
[nedhaam aleteṣaal aldakheley] *n* intercom
أين يمكنني الاتصال بك؟
[ayna yamken-any al-etiṣal beka?] Where can I contact you?
من الذي يمكن الاتصال به في حالة حدوث أي مشكلات؟
[man allaði: jumkinu alittisˤa:lu bihi fi: ħa:latin ħudu:θin ʔajji muʃkila:tin] Who do we contact if there are problems?
إتصال connection *n* [ʔittisˤsˤl]
الاتصالات السلكية
[Al-etṣalat al-selkeyah] *npl* telecommunications
اتصل contact, dial *v* [ʔettasˤala]
يَتَصِل بـ
[Yataṣel be] *v* communicate
سوف أتصل بك غدا
[sawfa ataṣil beka ghadan] I'll call back tomorrow
من فضلك، اتصل بخدمة الأعطال
[min faḍlak, itaṣil be-khidmat al-e'ṭaal] Call the breakdown service, please
هل لي أن اتصل بالمنزل؟
[hal lee an ataṣil bil-manzil?] May I phone home?
إتفاق agreement *n* [ʔittifa:q]
أتْقن master *v* [ʔatqana]
اتكأ lean *v* [ʔettakaʔa]
يَتَكِئ على
[Yatakea ala] *v* lean out
يَتَكِئ للأمام
[Yatakea lel-amam] *v* lean forward
أتم *v* [ʔatamma]
أن يتم تقديم الإفطار
[An yatem ta'qdeem al-efṭaar] Where is breakfast served?
هل يتم أخذ الدولارات؟
[hal yatum akhidh al-dolar-aat?] Do you take dollars?
هل يتم قبول بطاقات الائتمان؟

[hal yatum 'qubool be-ṭa'qaat al-eeteman?] Do you take credit cards?
اتِهام accusation *n* [ittiha:m]
اتّهم charge *vt* ◁ accuse *v* [ʔettahama] *(accuse)*
أتوبيس coach *n* [ʔatu:bi:s]
أتوبيس المطار
[Otobees al-maṭar] *n* airport bus
أين توجد أقرب محطة للأتوبيس؟
[Ayn tojad a'qrab maḥaṭah lel-otobees] Where is the nearest bus stop?
أين توجد محطة الأتوبيس؟
[ayna tojad muḥaṭat al-baaṣ?] Where is the bus station?
أين يمكن استقلال الأتوبيس إلى...؟
[Ayn yomken este'qlal al-otobees ela...?] Where do I get a bus for...?
ما هو موعد الأتوبيس المتجه إلى المدينة؟
[ma howa maw-'aid al-baaṣ al-mutajih ela al-madena?] When is the bus tour of the town?
ما هي المسافة بيننا وبين محطة الأتوبيس؟
[ma heya al-masafa bay-nana wa bayn muḥaṭat al- baaṣ?] How far are we from the bus station?
من فضلك، أي الأتوبيسات يتجه إلى...؟
[Men faḍlek, ay al-otobeesaat yatjeh ela...] Excuse me, which bus goes to...?
أتى come *v* [ʔata:]
يَأتي من
[Yaatey men] *v* come from
أثاث furniture *n* [ʔaθa:θ]
آثار *n* [ʔa:θa:r]
عالم آثار
['aalem aathar] *n* archaeologist
عِلم الآثار
['Aelm al-aathar] *n* archaeology
إثبات proof *(for checking)* *n* [ʔiθba:t]
أثبت prove *v* [ʔaθbata]
أثبَط *v* [ʔaθbatˤa]
يُثبَط من الهمة
[yothabeṭ men al-hemah] *v* discourage
آثر *n* [ʔa:θar]
آثار جانبية
[Aathar janeebyah] *n* side effect
أثر effect, trace, influence *n* [ʔaθar]
أثر القدم
[Athar al'qadam] *n* footprint
أثّر affect *v* [ʔaθθara]
يُؤثِر فى
[Yoather fee] *v* impress, influence
أثري archaeological *adj* [ʔaθarij]
نقوش أثرية
[No'qoosh athareyah] *npl* graffiti
اثنا عشر *number* [iθnata: ʕaʃara] twelve
أثْني *v* [ʔaθna:]
يُثني على
[Yothney 'aala] *v* praise
إثنين two *number* [iθnajni]
أثيم vicious *adj* [ʔaθi:m]
إثيوبي Ethiopian *adj* [ʔiθju:bij]
مواطن إثيوبي
[Mowaṭen ethyobey] *n* Ethiopian
إثيوبيا Ethiopia *n* [ʔiθju:bja:]
أجاب must *v* [ʔajaʒaba]
يَجِب عليه
[Yajeb alayh] *v* have to
ما الذي يجب أن ألبسه؟
[ma al-lathy yajib an al-basaho?] What should I wear?
أجاب answer, reply *v* [ʔaʒa:ba]
إجابة answer *n* [ʔiʒa:ba]
هل يمكن أن ترسل لي الإجابة في رسالة؟
[hal yamken an tarsil lee al-ejaba fee resala?] Can you text me your answer?
أجازة time off, holiday *n* [ʔaʒa:za]
أجازة رعاية طفل
[ajaazat re'aayat al ṭefl] *n* paternity leave
أجازة عامة
[ajaaza a'mah] *n* public holiday
أجازة لممارسة الأنشطة
[ajaaza lemomarsat al 'anshe ṭah] *n* activity holiday
أجازة مَرضِيَّة
[Ajaza maraḍeyah] *n* sick leave
أجازة وضع

[Ajazat wad'a] *n* maternity leave
أجازة سعيدة
[ejaaza sa'aeeda] Enjoy your holiday!
أنا أقضي أجازة هنا
[ana a'q-ḍy ejaza huna] I'm on holiday here
أنا هنا في أجازة
[ana huna fee ejasa] I'm here on holiday
إجازة leave *n* [ʔiʒaːza]
أجْبر force *v* [ʔaʒbara]
اجْتاز pass, go through *vt* [ʔeʒtaːza]
اجتماع assembly, *n* [ʔiʒtimaːʕ] meeting
علم الاجتماع
['aelm al-ejtema'a] *n* sociology
اجتماع الشمل
[Ejtem'a alshaml] *n* reunion
اجتماعي social *adj* [ʔiʒtimaːʕij]
أخصائي اجتماعي
[Akhṣey ejtema'ay] *n* social worker
ضمان اجتماعي
[Ḍaman ejtema'ay] *n* social security
خدمات اجتماعية
[Khadamat ejtem'aeyah] *npl* social services
الحالة الاجتماعية
[Al-halah al-ejtemaayah] *n* marital status
شخص اجتماعي
[Shakhṣ ejtema'ay] *adj* sociable
شخص اجتماعي
[Shakhṣ ejtema'ay] *adj* joiner
اجتمع get together, *v* [ʔeʒtamaʕa] gather, meet up
اجْتنب spare *v* [ʔeʒtanaba]
إجْحاف prejudice *n* [ʔiʒħaːf]
إجر fee (رسم) *n* [ʔaʒr]
أجّر hire *(rental)* *n* [ʔaʒʒara]
أجْر wage *n* [ʔaʒr]
وُجر rent *v* [ʔaʒʒara]
يُؤَجِر منقولات
[Yoajer man'qolat] *v* lease
هل يمكن أن نؤجر أدوت التزلج هنا؟
[hal yamken an no-ajer adawat al-tazal-oj huna?] Can we hire skis here?
إجراء *n* [ʔiʒraːʔu]
أريد إجراء مكالمة تليفونية
[areed ejraa mukalama talefonia] I want to make a phonecall
هل يمكن أن أقوم بإجراء مكالمة تليفونية من هنا؟
[hal yamken an a'qoom be-ijraa mukalama talefonia min huna?] Can I phone from here?
أجرة rental, price *n* [ʔuʒra]
سيارة أجرة صغيرة
[Sayarah ojrah ṣagherah] *n* minicab
أجرة السفر
[Ojrat al-safar] *n* fare
أجرة البريد
[ojrat al bareed] *n* postage
ما هي أجرة التاكسي للذهاب إلى المطار؟
[ma heya ejrat al-taxi lel-thehaab ela al-maṭaar?] How much is the taxi to the airport?
أجرم penalize, convict *v* [ʔaʒrama]
أجرَى *v* [ʔaʒraː]
يُجرَي عملية جراحية
[Yojrey 'amaleyah jeraḥeyah] *v* operate *(to perform surgery)*
أجل *n* [ʔaʒl]
ماذا يوجد هناك لأجل الأطفال؟
[madha yujad hunaka le-ajel al-aṭfaal?] What is there for children to do?
أجل postpone *v* [aʒʒala]
أجَل term *(description)* *n* [ʔaʒal]
أجلى polish *v* [ʔaʒla]
يجلو عن مكان
[Yajloo 'an al-makaan] *v* vacate
إجماع consensus *n* [ʔiʒmaːʕ]
إجماعي unanimous *adj* [ʔiʒmaːʕij]
إجمالي total *n* ◁ total *adj* [ʔiʒmaːlij]
اجمع collect, sum *v* [ʔeʒmmaʕa] up, add up
أجمع round up *v* [ʔaʒamaʕ]
أجنبي alien, foreign *adj* [ʔaʒnabij] foreigner *n* ◁
أجنحة *npl* [ʔaʒniħatu]
أجنحة عرض

[Ajnehat 'arḍ] *n* stands
إجهاض abortion *n* [ʔiʒha:dˤ]
إجهاض تلقائي
[Ejhaḍ tel'qaaey] *n* miscarriage
أجوف hollow *adj* [ʔaʒwaf]
إحادي university *adj* [ʔuħa:dij]
إحاط surround *v* [ʔaħa:tˤa]
أحب *v* [ʔaħaba]
أحبك
[aḥibak] I love you
أنا أحب...
[ana aḥib] I love...
أنا لا أحب...
[ana la oḥibo...] I don't like...
أحبّ like *v* [ʔaħabba]
إحباط depression *n* [ʔiħba:tˤ]
أحبك crochet *v* [ʔaħabaka]
احتاج *v* [ʔeħta:ʒa]
يَحتاج إلى
[Taḥtaaj ela] *v* need
احتاج إلى *v* [ʔiħta:ʒa ʔila]
أحتاج إلى الذهاب إلى طبيب أسنان
[aḥtaaj ela al-dhehaab ela ṭabeeb asnaan] I need a dentist
أحتاج إلى شخص يعتني بالأطفال ليلًا
[aḥtaaj ela shakhiṣ y'atany be-al-aṭfaal laylan] I need someone to look after the children tonight
هل تحتاج إلى أي شيء؟
[hal taḥtaaj ela ay shay?] Do you need anything?
احتجاج protest *n* [iħtiʒa:ʒ]
احتجاز detention *n* [iħtiʒa:z]
احتراف *n* [iħtira:f]
باحتراف
[Beḥteraaf] *adv* professionally
احتراق five *n* [ʔiħtira:q]
شعلة الاحتراق
[Sho'alat al-eḥtera'q] *n* pilot light
احترام respect *n* [iħtira:m]
احترس watch out *v* [ʔeħtarasa]
احترَق *v* [ʔeħtaraqa]
يَحترق عن آخره
[Yaḥtare'q 'an aakherh] *vt* burn down
احترم respect *v* [ʔeħtarama]
احتفاظ keeping, *n* [ʔiħtifa:zˤ]
guarding
هل يمكنني الاحتفاظ بمفتاح؟
[hal yamken -any al-eḥtefaaḍh be-muftaaḥ?] Can I have a key?
هل يمكنني الاحتفاظ بها؟
[hal yamken -any al-eḥtefaaḍh beha?] May I keep it?
احتفال celebration *n* [iħtifa:l]
احتفظ reserve *v* [ʔiħtafizˤa]
يَحتَفظ ب
[taḥtafeḍh be] *vt* hold
احتفظ بالباقي
[iḥ-tafuḍh bil-ba'qy] Keep the change
لا تحتفظ بشحنها
[la taḥtafiḍh be-shaḥ-neha] It's not holding its charge
هل يمكنك أن تحتفظ لي بذلك؟
[hal yamken -aka an taḥ-tafeḍh lee be-dhalik?] Could you hold this for me?
احْتفل celebrate *v* [ʔeħtafala]
احْتَفي *v* [ʔeħtafa:]
يَحْتَفي بـ
[Yaḥtafey be] *n* welcome
احتقار contempt *n* [iħtiqa:r]
احتقان congestion *n* [iħtiqa:n]
احتقر despise *v* [ʔeħtaqara]
احتكار monopoly *n* [iħtika:r]
احتل occupy *v* [ʔeħtalla]
احتلال occupation *n* [iħtila:l] *(invasion)*
احتمالية probability *n* [iħtima:lijja]
احتمل *v* [ʔiħtamala]
لا يحتمل
[La yaḥtamel] *adj* unbearable
احتوي contain *v* [ʔeħtawa:]
احتياطي *n* ⊲ spare *adj* [ʔiħtijja:tˤij] reserve *(retention)*
احتيال fraud *n* [iħtija:l]
إحجام negative *n* [ʔiħʒa:mu]
أحد anyone *n* [ʔaħad]
أحدث modernize *v* [juħaddiθu]
أحد عشر *number* [ʔaħada ʕaʃar] eleven
أحْرز score *v* [ʔaħraza]
إحسان charlty *n* [ʔiħsa:n]
أحسن improve *v* [ʔaħsana]

إحصاء [ʔiħsˤa:ʔ] *n*
إحصاء رسمي
[Ehṣaa rasmey] *n* census
إحصائيات [ʔiħsˤa:ʔijja:t] *n* statistics
أحفاد [ʔaħfa:dun] *npl* grandchildren
أحقاً [ħaqqan] *adv* really
إحكام [ʔiħka:mu] *n* precision, accuracy
هل يمكنك إحكام الأربطة لي من فضلك؟
[hal yamken -aka eḥkaam al-arbe-ṭa lee min faḍlak?] Can you tighten my bindings, please?
أحل [ʔaħalla] *v* untie
أحل [ʔaħala] *v*
يَحِل مشكلة
[Taḥel al-moshkelah] *v* solve
أحمر [ʔaħmar] *adj* red
أحمر خدود
[Ahmar khodod] *n* blusher
أحمر شفاه
[Ahmar shefah] *n* lipstick
عنب أحمر
[ʻaenab aḥmar] *n* redcurrant
الصليب الأحمر
[Al-Ṣaleeb al-aḥmar] *n* Red Cross
البحر الأحمر
[Al-bahr al-ahmar] *n* Red Sea
شَعْر أحمر
[Sha'ar ahmar] *n* redhead
لحم أحمر
[Laḥm aḥmar] *n* red meat
نبيذ أحمر
[nabeedh aḥmar] *n* rosé
هل يمكن أن ترشح لي نوع جيد من النبيذ الأحمر
[hal yamken an tura-shiḥ lee naw'a jayid min al-nabeedh al-aḥmar] Can you recommend a good red wine?
أحمق [ʔaħmaq] *adj* idiotic, daft
أحيا [ʔaħjja:] *v* salute
أخ [ʔax] *n* brother
أخ من زوجة الأب أو زوج الأم
[Akh men zawjat al ab] *n* stepbrother
ابن الأخ
[Ebn al-akh] *n* nephew

أخاف [ʔaxa:fa] *v* terrify
أخبار [ʔaxba:run] *npl* news
تى تعرض الأخبار؟
[Tee ta'areḍ alakhbaar] When is the news?
أخبر [ʔaxbara] *vt* tell
أخت [ʔuxt] *n* sister
أخت الزوجة
[Okht alzawjah] *n* sister-in-law
أخت من زوجة الأب أو زوج الأم
[Okht men zawjat al ab aw zawj al om] *n* stepsister
بَنْت الأخت
[Bent al-okht] *n* niece
اختار [ʔexta:ra] *v* choose ◁ *vt* pick
اختَبئ [ʔextabaʔ] *vi* hide
اختبار [ixtiba:r] *n* test
أنبوب اختبار
[Anbob ekhtebar] *n* test tube
اختبار الدم
[Ekhtebar al-dam] *n* blood test
اختبار القيادة
[Ekhtebar al-'qeyadah] *n* driving test
اختبار موجز
[ekhtebar mojaz] *n* quiz
اخْتَبر [ʔextabara] *v* test
اختَتَم [ʔextatama] *vt* conclude, finish
اختراع [ixtira:ʕ] *n* invention
اخترع [ʔextaraʕa] *v* invent
اختزال [ixtiza:l] *n* shorthand
اختصار [ixtisˤa:r] *n* abbreviation
باختصار
[bekhteṣaar] *adv* briefly
اختطف [ʔextatˤafa] *v* hijack, kidnap
اخْتَطف [ʔextatˤafa] *v* snatch
اختفاء [ixtifa:ʔ] *n* disappearance
اختفي [ʔextafa:] *v* disappear
اختلاف [ixtila:f] *n* difference
اختلاف الرأى
[Ekhtelaf al-raaey] *n* disagreement
اخْتَلق [ʔextalaqa] *v* make up
اختنَق [ʔextanaqa] *vi* choke
اختيار [ixtija:r] *n* choice
إختياري [ixtija:rij] *adj* optional
أخدود [ʔuxdu:d] *n* pothole
أخذ [ʔaxaða] *vt* take

هل يمكن أن تأخذ مقاسي من فضلك؟
[hal yamken an takhudh ma'qa-see min faḍlak?] Can you measure me, please?
هل يمكنك أن تأخذ بيدي من فضلك؟
[hal yamken -aka an takhudh be-yady min faḍlak?] Can you guide me, please?
آخر *adj* [ʔa:xar]
فى مكان آخر
[Fee makaan aakhar] *adv* elsewhere
ما هو آخر موعد للمركب المتجه إلى...؟
[ma howa aakhir maw'aid lel-markab al-mutajeh ela...?] When is the last sailing to...?
ما هو موعد آخر قطار متجه إلى...؟
[ma howa maw-'aid aakhir 'qeṭaar mutajih ela...?] When is the last train to...?
هل لديكم أي شيء آخر؟
[hal ladykum ay shay aakhar?] Have you anything else?
آخَر another *n* [ʔa:xaru]
أخر put off *v* [aʔaxara]
أخر other *adj* [ʔaxar]
آخراً last *adv* [ʔa:xiran]
أخرق clumsy, awkward *adj* [ʔaxraq]
أخرى other *pron* [ʔuxra:]
متى ستتحرك السيارات مرة أخرى؟
[mata satata-ḥarak al-saya-raat murra ukhra?] When will the road be clear?
هل لديك أي غرف أخرى؟
[hal ladyka ay 'quraf okhra?] Do you have any others?
أخصائي *adj* [ʔaxisˤa:ʔijju]
أخصائي العلاج الطبيعي
[Akeṣaaey al-elaj al-ṭabeaey] *n* physiotherapist
أخضر green *(colour) adj* [ʔaxdˤar] green *n* ◁
أخطأ mistake *v* [ʔaxtˤʔa]
يُخطئ في الحكم على
[yokhṭea fee al-ḥokm ala] *v* misjudge
أخطأ mess up *v* [ʔaxtˤaʔa]
أخطبوط octopus *n* [ʔuxtˤubu:tˤ]
أخفى hide *vt* [ʔaxfa:]
إخلاص loyalty *n* [ʔixla:sˤ]
أخلاق character *n* [ʔaxla:q]

دَمِث الأخلاق
[Dameth al-akhla'q] *adj* good-natured
أخلاقي moral (معنوي) *adj* [ʔaxla:qij]
أخلاقي مِهَنِي
[Akhla'qy mehany] *adj* ethical
لا أخلاقي
[La Akhla'qy] *adj* immoral
أخلاقيات morals *npl* [ʔaxla:qijja:tun]
أخلى evacuate *v* [ʔaxla:]
أخير last *adj* [ʔaxi:r]
قبل الأخير
['qabl al akheer] *adj* penultimate
أخيراً lastly *adv* [ʔaxi:ran]
أداء performance *n* [ʔada:ʔ]
أداة tool, instrument *n* [ʔada:t]
أدوات الإسعافات الأولية
[Adawat al-es'aafaat al-awaleyah] *n* first-aid kit
أدار run *vt* ◁ manage *v* [ʔada:ra]
إدارة administration, *n* [ʔida:ra] management
إدارة الحوادث والطوارئ
[Edarat al-hawadeth wa-al-tawarea] *n* accident & emergency department
مدير الإدارة التنفيذية
[Modeer el-edarah al-tanfeedheyah] *n* CEO
إداري administrative *adj* [ʔida:rij]
أداع let *v* [ʔada:ʕa]
أدان owe, condemn *v* [ʔada:na]
إدب literature *n* [dab]
أدَب culture *n* [ʔadab]
بأدَب
[Beadab] *adv* politely
إدخر save *(money) v* [ʔeddaxara]
أدخل enter *vt* [ʔadxala]
إدراك comprehension *n* [ʔidra:k]
أدْرك realize *v* [ʔadraka]
أدرَياتيكي Adriatic *adj* [ʔadrija:ti:ki:]
البحر الأدرياتيكي
[Albahr al adriateky] *n* Adriatic Sea
إدّعاء allegation *n* [ʔiddiʕa:ʔ]
أدنى lower, minimal *adj* [ʔadna:] *v* ◁ minimum
أدنى درجة
[Adna darajah] *n* inferior

حد أدنى
[Had adna] *n* minimum
astonish *v* [ʔadhaʃa] **أدهش**
perform *v* [ʔadda] **أدى**
if *conj* [ʔiða:] **إذا**
dissolve, melt *vt* [ʔaða:ba] **أذاب**
advertise *v* [ʔaða:ʕa] **أذاع**
broadcast *v* [ʔaða:ʕa] **أذاع**
broadcast *n* [ʔiða:ʕa] **إذاعة**
Azerbaijan *n* [ʔaðarbajʒa:n] **أذربيجان**
adj [ʔaðarbi:ʒa:nij] **أذربيجاني**
Azerbaijani
Azerbaijani *n* ◁
panic *v* [ʔaðʕara] **أذْعَر**
permission *n* [ʔiðn] **اذن**
اذن بالدخول
[Edhn bel-dekhool] *n* admittance
ear *n* [ʔuðun] **أذن**
سماعات الأذن
[Sama'at al-odhon] *npl* earphones
سِدادات الأذن
[Sedadat alodhon] *npl* earplugs
ألم الأذُن
[Alam al odhon] *n* earache
طبلة الأذن
[Ṭablat alozon] *n* eardrum
permission *n* [ʔiðn] **إذن**
amaze *v* [ʔaðhala] **أذهل**
hurt *v* [ʔaðja] **أذى**
want *v* [ʔara:da] **أراد**
أريد... من فضلك
[areed... min faḍlak] I'd like..., please
أريد أن أتركها في...
[Areed an atrokha fee...] I'd like to leave it in...
أريد أن أتحدث مع... من فضلك
[areed an ataḥad-ath ma'aa... min faḍlak] I'd like to speak to..., please
أريد أن أذهب إلى...
[Areed an adhhab ela...] I need to get to...
.أريد تذكرتين من فضلك
[Areed tadhkaratayn men faḍlek.] I'd like two tickets, please
أريد التسجيل في الرحلة من فضلك
[areed al-tasjeel fee al-reḥla min faḍlak] I'd like to check in, please
أريد الذهاب إلى السوبر ماركت
[areed al-dhehaab ela al-subar market] I need to find a supermarket
will *(motivation) n* [ʔira:da] **إرادة**
spill *vt* [ʔara:qa] **إراق**
four *number* [ʔarbaʕatun] **أربعة**
number [ʔarbaʕata ʕaʃr] **أربعة عشر**
fourteen
forty *number* [ʔarbaʕu:na] **أربعون**
confuse, rave *v* [ʔarbaka] **أربك**
doubt *v* [ʔerta:ba] **ارتاب**
engagement *n* [irtiba:tˤ] **ارتباط**
muddle *n* [irtiba:k] **ارتباك**
v [ʔertabatˤa] **ارتبط**
يَرْتَبِط مع
[Yartabeṭ ma'aa] *v* tie up
shock *n* [rtiʒa:ʒ] **ارتجاج**
ارتجاج في المخ
[Ertejaj fee al-mokh] *n* concussion
bounce *vi* [ʔertadda] **ارتدّ**
wear *vt* [ʔartada:] **ارتدى**
v [ʔertatˤama] **ارتطم**
يَرْتَطِم ب
[Yartaṭem be] *vi* strike
tremble *v* [ʔertaʕada] **ارتعد**
shiver *v* [ʔertaʕaʃa] **ارتعش**
height *n* [irtifa:ʕ] **ارتفاع**
climb, go up, rise *v* [ʔertafaʕa] **ارتفع**
commit *v* [ʔertakaba] **ارتكب**
يَرْتَكِبُ خطأ
[Yartekab khaṭaa] *v* slip up
suspend *v* [ʔarʒaʔa] **أرْجَأ**
back, put back, *v* [ʔarʒaʕa] **ارجع**
send back
Argentine *adj* [ʔarʒunti:nij] **أرجنتيني**
Argentinian *(person) n* ◁
purple *adj* [urʒuwa:nij] **أرجواني**
seesaw *n* [ʔurʒu:ħa] **أرجوحة**
الأرجوحة الشبكية
[Al orjoha al shabakiya] *n* hammock
please! *excl* [ʔarʒu:ka] **أرجوك**
buttocks *npl* [ʔarda:fun] **أرْداف**
n ◁ Jordanian *adj* [unrdunij] **أردني**
Jordanian
slate *n* [ardwa:z] **اردواز**

أرز rice *n* [ʔurz]
أرز أسمر
[Orz asmar] *n* brown rice
إرسال sending, shipping *n* [irsa:l]
جهاز إرسال الإشعاع
[Jehaz esrsaal al-esh'aaa'a] *n* radiator
أريد إرسال فاكس
[areed ersaal fax] I want to send a fax
أين يمكن إرسال هذه الكروت؟
[ayna yamken ersaal hadhy al-korot?] Where can I post these cards?
كم تبلغ تكلفة إرسال هذا الطرد؟
[kam tablugh taklifat ersal hadha al-ṭard?] How much is it to send this parcel?
لقد قمت بإرسال حقائبي مقدما
[la'qad 'qimto be-irsaal ḥa'qa-eby mu-'qadaman] I sent my luggage on in advance
من أين يمكنني إرسال تلغراف؟
[min ayna yamken -ini ersaal tal-ighraaf?] Where can I send a telegram from?
أرسل forward *v* [ʔarsala]
يُرسِل رسالة بالفاكس
[Yorsel resalah bel-fax] *v* fax
يُرْسِل بريدا إلكترونيا
[Yorsel bareedan electroneyan] *v* email
إرشادي guide *adj* [ʔirʃa:dijjat]
جولة إرشادية
[Jawlah ershadeyah] *n* guided tour
أرشيف archive *n* [ʔarʃi:f]
أرض land *n* [ʔardˁ]
صاحب الأرض
[Ṣaheb ardh] *n* landlord
سَطح الأرض
[Saṭh alarḍ] *n* ground
أرض سبخة
[Arḍ sabkha] *n* moor
أرض خضراء
[Arḍ khaḍraa] *n* meadow
أرض المعارض
[Arḍ al ma'ariḍ] *n* fairground
تحت سطح الأرض
[Taht saṭh al arḍ] *adv* underground
مالك الأرض
[Malek al-arḍ] *n* landowner
إرضاع breast-feeding *n* [ʔirdˁa:ʕ]
هل يمكنني إرضاعه هنا؟
[hal yamken -any erḍa-'aaho huna?] Can I breast-feed here?
أرضي *adj* [ʔardˁij]
الدور الأرضي
[Aldoor al-arḍey] *n* ground floor
الكرة الأرضية
[Al-korah al-ardheyah] *n* globe
أرضية floor *n* [ʔardˁijja]
أرْعب frighten *v* [ʔarʕaba]
أرْغن organ *(music)* *n* [ʔurɣun]
آلة الأرْغن الموسيقية
[Aalat al-arghan al-moseeqeyah] *n* organ *(music)*
أرْفق attach *v* [ʔarfaqa]
أرق insomnia *n* [ʔaraq]
أرمل widower *n* [ʔarmal]
أرملة widow *n* [ʔarmala]
أرمني Armenian *adj* [ʔarminij]
⊲ Armenian *(person)* *n*
اللغة الأرمنية
[Al-loghah al-armeeneyah] *(language)* *n* Armenian
أرمنيا Armenia *n* [ʔarminja:]
أرنب hare, rabbit *n* [ʔarnab]
إرهاب terrorism *n* [ʔirha:b]
إرهابي terrorist *n* [ʔirha:bij]
هجوم إرهابي
[Hojoom 'erhaby] *n* terrorist attack
إرْهاق strain *n* [ʔirha:q]
إريتريا Eritrea *n* [ʔiri:tirja:]
أريكة settee *n* [ʔri:ka]
أزال remove *v* [ʔaza:la]
يُزيل الغموض
[Yozeel al-ghmooḍ] *v* clear up
إزالة removal *n* [ʔiza:la]
ازداد *v* [ʔezda:da]
يَزداد ثلاثة أضعاف
[Yazdad thalathat aḍ'aaaf] *v* triple
ازدحام crowd *n* [izdiħa:m]
ازدحام المرور
[Ezdeḥam al-moror] *n* traffic jam
هل هناك طريق بعيد عن ازدحام المرور؟

[hal hunaka ṭaree'q ba'aeed 'aan izde-ḥam al-miroor?] Is there a route that avoids the traffic?

ازدهار bloom, flourishing *n* [izdiha:r]

موسم ازدهار
[Mawsem ezdehar] *n* high season

إزدهار prosperity *n* [ʔizdiha:r]

أزرق blue *adj* [ʔazraq]

أزرق داكن
[Azra'q daken] *n* navy-blue

إزعاج mischief, nuisance *n* [ʔizʕa:ʒ]

إزعَج disturb *v* [ʔazʕaʒa]

أزل slip *vi* [ʔazalla]

أزمة crisis *n* [ʔazma]

أزمة قلبية
[Azmah 'qalbeyah] *n* heart attack

إزمِيل chisel *n* [ʔizmi:l]

إزهَر flower, blossom *v* [ʔazhara]

أساء *v* [ʔasaʔa]

يُسِئ فهم
[Yoseea fahm] *v* misunderstand

أساء *v* [ʔasa:ʔa]

يُسيء إلى
[Yoseea ela] *v* offend

يُسيء استخدام
[Yosea estekhdam] *v* abuse

إساءة offence *n* [ʔisa:ʔa]

أساس basis *n* [ʔasa:s]

أساسات *npl* [ʔasa:sa:tun] foundations

أساسي basic, main, *adj* [ʔasa:sij] major

بصورة أساسية
[Beṣorah asasiyah] *adv* primarily

بشكل أساسي
[Beshkl asasy] *adv* basically

أساسيات basics *npl* [ʔasa:sijja:tun]

أسباني *n* ◃ Spanish *adj* [ʔisba:nij] Spaniard, Spanish

أسبانيا Spain *n* [ʔisba:njja:]

أسبرين aspirin *n* [ʔasbiri:n]

أريد بعض الأسبرين
[areed ba'aḍ al-asbereen] I'd like some aspirin

أسبوع week *n* [ʔusbu:ʕ]

أريد تذكرة تزلج لمدة أسبوع
[areed tadhkera tazaluj le-mudat isboo'a] I'd like a ski pass for a week

الأسبوع التالي
[al-esboo'a al-taaly] next week

الأسبوع الذي يلي الأسبوع المقبل
[al-esboo'a al-ladhy yalee al-esboo'a al-mu'qbil] the week after next

الأسبوع الماضي
[al-esboo'a al-maaḍy] last week

الأسبوع قبل الماضي
[al-esboo'a 'qabil al-maaḍy] the week before last

في غضون أسبوع
[fee ghoḍon isboo'a] a week from today

كم تبلغ تكلفة الإقامة الأسبوعية بالغرفة؟
[kam tablugh taklifat al-e'qama al-isbo-'aiya bil-ghurfa?] How much is it per week?

منذ أسبوع
[mundho isboo'a] a week ago

أسبوعي weekly *adj* [ʔusbu:ʕij]

كم تبلغ التكلفة الأسبوعية؟
[kam tablugh al-taklifa al-isboo-'aiya?] How much is it for a week?

استئجار rent *n* [isti:ʒa:r]

استئجار سيارة
[isti-jar sayara] *n* rental car

أريد استئجار موتوسيكل
[Oreed esteajaar motoseekl] I want to rent a motorbike

إستأجر hire *(people)* *v* [ʔestaʔʒara]

أستاذ *n* [ʔusta:ð]

أستاذ جامعي
[Ostaz jame'aey] *n* professor

استئناف appeal *n* [ʔistiʔna:f]

استأنف continue *vi* [ʔestaʔnafa]

يَستأنِف حكما
[Yastaanef al-hokm] *v* appeal

استبدال replacement *n* [istibda:l]

استبدل replace *v* [ʔestabdala]

استبعد rule out, *v* [ʔestabʕada] exclude, leave out

استبيان questionnaire *n* [istibja:n]

استثمار [istiθma:r] *n* investment
استثمر [ʔestaθmara] *v* invest
استثناء [istiθna:ʔ] *n* exception
استثنائي [istiθna:ʔij] *adj* exceptional, extraordinary
إستجابة [istiʒa:ba] *n* response
أستجدى [ʔestaʒda:] *v* beg
استجواب [istiʒwa:b] *n* inquest
استجوب [ʔestaʒwaba] *v* interrogate, question
استجيب [ʔestaʒa:ba] *v* respond
استحق [ʔestaħaqqa] *v* deserve
متى يستحق الدفع؟
[mata yasta-ḥl'q al-daf'a?] When is it due to be paid?
استحم [ʔestaħamma] *v* swim
استحمام [istiħma:m] *n* bathing
سائل استحمام
[Saael estehmam] *n* bubble bath
غطاء الشعر للاستحمام
[ghetaa al-sha'ar lel-estehmam] *n* shower cap
جل الاستحمام
[Jel al-estehmam] *n* shower gel
حقيبة أدوات الاستحمام
[Ha'qeebat adwat al-estehmam] *n* toilet bag
أين توجد أماكن الاستحمام؟
[ayna tojad amaken al-estiḥmam?] Where are the showers?
استحى [ʔestaħa:] *v* blush
استخدام [istixda:mu] *n* use
سهل الاستخدام
[Sahl al-estekhdam] *adj* user-friendly
استخدام الحاسب الآلي
[Estekhdam al-haseb al-aaly] *n* computing
يُسيء استخدام
[Yosea estekhdam] *v* abuse
يُفضل استخدامه قبل التاريخ المُحدد
[Yofaḍḍal estekhdamoh 'qabl al-tareekh al-mohaddad] *adj* best-before date
إنه للاستخدام الشخصي
[inaho lel-estikhdam al-shakhṣi] It is for my own personal use
هل يمكنني استخدام تليفوني من فضلك؟
[hal yamken -any estl-khdaam talefonak min faḍlak?] Can I use your phone, please?
هل يمكنني استخدام بطاقتي في ماكينة الصرف الآلي هذه؟
[hal yamken -any esti-khdaam beṭa-'qatee fee makenat al-ṣarf al-aaly hadhy?] Can I use my card with this cash machine?
استخدم [ʔestaxdama] *v* use
استخرج [ʔestaxraʒa] *v*
يستخرج نسخة
[Yastakhrej noskhah] *v* photocopy
اسْتخف [ʔestaxaffa] *v* underestimate
استدان [ʔestada:na] *v* borrow
استدعى [ʔestadʕa:] *v* page, call
استدلال [ʔistidla:l] *n* guidance
الاستدلال على الاتجاهات من الأقمار الصناعية
[Al-estedlal ala al-etejahat men al-'qmar alṣena'ayah] *n* sat nav
إستراتيجي [ʔistira:ti:ʒij] *adj* strategic
إستراتيجية [ʔistira:ti:ʒijja] *n* strategy
استراح [ʔestara:ħa] *vi* rest
استراحة [istira:ħa] *n* rest, break
استراحة غداء
[Estrahet ghadaa] *n* lunch break
أسترالي [ʔustra:lij] *adj* Australian ◁ Australian *n*
أستراليا [ʔustra:lija:] *n* Australia
استرخاء [istirxa:ʔ] *n* relaxation
استرخى [ʔestarxa:] *vi* relax
استرد [ʔestarada] *v*
أريد أن أسترد نقودي
[areed an asta-rid ni'qodi] I want my money back
هل يمكن أن أسترد المال مرة أخرى؟
[hal yamken an asta-rid al-maal marra okhra?] Can I have a refund?
اسْترد [ʔestaradda] *v* restore, get back
استرليني [ʒunajh] *n*
جنيه استرليني

[Jeneh esterleeney] *n* pound sterling
استسلم [ʔestaslama] *v* give in
استشار [ʔestaʃa:ra] *v* consult
استضاف [ʔestadˤa:fa] *v* treat, entertain (يسلي)
استطاع [ʔestatˤa:ʕa] *v*
لا يستطع التنفس
[la ystạ-ṯee'a al-tanaf-uss] He can't breathe
استطاع [ʔestatˤa:ʕa] *v* can
استطلاع [istitˤla:ʕ] *n* study
استطلاع الرأي
[Eateṭla'a al-ray] *n* opinion poll
محب للاستطلاع
[Moḥeb lel-esteṭlaa'a] *adj* curious
استطلع [ʔestatˤlaʕa] *v* spot
يَستطلع الرأي
[Yastaṭle'a al-ray] *v* canvass
استعاد [ʔestaʕa:da] *v* regain, resume
استعبد [ʔesataʕbada] *v* slave
استعجال [istiʕʒa:l] *n* hurry
استعجِل [ʔestaʕʒala] *v* hurry up
استعراض [istiʕra:dˤ] *n* parade
استعراضات القفز
[Este'araḍat al-'qafz] *n* show-jumping
مجال الاستعراض
[Majal al-este'araḍ] *n* show business
استعلام [istiʕla:m] *n* inquiry
استعلامات [istiʕla:ma:tun] *npl*
مكتب الاستعلامات
[Maktab al-este'alamaat] *n* enquiry desk
استعَلم عن [ʔestaʕlama ʕan] *v* inquire
استعمال [stiʕma:lin] *n*
سوء استعمال
[Sooa este'amal] *v* abuse
ما هي طريقة استعماله؟
[ma heya ṯaree-'qat esti-'amal-uho?] How should I take it?
استغرق [ʔestaɣraqa] *v*
كم من الوقت يستغرق تصليحها؟
[kam min al-wa'qt yast-aghri'q taṣle-ḥaha?] How long will it take to repair?
ما الفترة التي سأستغرقها للوصول إلى...؟
[Ma al-fatrah alatey sastaghre'qha lel-woṣool ela...] How long will it take to get to...?
ما هي المدة التي يستغرقها العبور؟
[ma heya al-mudda al-laty yasta-ghri'q-uha al-'auboor?] How long does the crossing take?
استغلّ [ʔestaɣalla] *v* exploit
استغلال [istiɣla:l] *n* exploitation
استغني [ʔestaɣna:] *v*
يَستغني عن
[Yastaghney 'aan] *v* do without
استفاد [ʔestafa:da] *v* benefit
استفاق [ʔestafa:qa] *v* come round
استفهم [ʔestafhama] *v* query
استقال [ʔestaqa:l] *v* resign
استقبال [istiqba:l] *n* reception
جهاز الاستقبال
[Jehaz alest'qbal] *n* receiver *(electronic)*
موظف الاستقبال
[mowadhaf al-este'qbal] *n* receptionist
استقر [ʔestaqarra] *v* settle down
استقرار [istiqra:r] *n* stability
استقلال [istiqla:lu] *n* independence
استكشف [ʔestakʃafa] *v* explore
استلام [ʔistila:m] *n* takeover
استلام الأمتعة
[Estelam al-amte'aah] *n* baggage reclaim
استلم [ʔestalama] *v* receive
استمارة [istima:ra] *n*
استمارة مطالبة
[Estemarat moṭalabah] *n* claim form
استماع [ʔistima:ʕ] *n* listening
أين يمكننا الاستماع إلى عازفين محليين يعزفون الموسيقى؟
[ayna yamken-ana al-istima'a ela 'aazifeen ma-ḥaliyeen y'azifoon al-mose'qa?] Where can we hear local musicians play?
استمتاع [ʔistimta:ʕ] *n* pleasure
نتمنى الاستمتاع بوجبتك
[nata-mana al-estim-ta'a be-waj-bataka] Enjoy your meal!
استمتع [ʔestamtaʕa] *v*
هل تستمتع بهذا العمل؟

[Hal tastamte'a behadha al-'amal] Do you enjoy it?
هل استمتعت؟
[hal istam-ta'at?] Did you enjoy yourself?
استمتع ب [ʔestamtaʕa bi] *v* enjoy
استمر [ʔestamarra] *v* go on, carry continue *vt* ◁ on, last
استمع [ʔestamaʕa] *v* listen
يَستمِع إلى
[Yastame'a ela] *v* listen to
استند [ʔestanada] *v*
يَستنِد على
[Yastaned 'ala] *v* lean on
استنساخ [istinsa:x] *n* clone
اسْتَنْسخ [ʔestansax] *v* clone
استنشق [ʔestanʃaqa] *v* breathe in
استنفذ [ʔestanfaða] *v* run out of
استهلك [ʔestahlaka] *v*
يَستهلك كلية
[Yastahlek koleyatan] *v* use up
استواء [istiwa:ʔ] *n*
غابات المطر بخط الاستواء
[Ghabat al-maṭar be-khaṭ al-estwaa] *n* rainforest
خط الاستواء
[Khaṭ al-estwaa] *n* equator
استوائي [istiwa:ʔij] *adj* tropical
استوديو [stu:dju:] *n* studio
استورد [ʔestawrada] *v* Import
استَولى [ʔestawla:] *v*
يستَولي على
[Yastwley 'ala] *v* seize
إستوني [ʔistu:nij] *adj* Estonian ◁ *n* Estonian *(person)*
اللغة الإستوانية
[Al-loghah al-estwaneyah] *(language) n* Estonian
إستونيا [ʔistu:nja:] *n* Estonia
استيراد [istijra:d] *n* import
إستيقظ [ʔestajqazˤa] *v* wake up
إسد [ʔasad] *n* lion
اسِر [ʔasira] *v* capture
إسرائيل [ʔisra:ʔijl] *n* Israel
إسرائيلي [ʔisra:ʔi:lij] *adj* Israeli ◁ *n* Israeli

أسرة [ʔusra] *n* family
هل توجد أسرة للأطفال؟
[hal tojad a-serra lil-aṭfaal?] Do you have a cot?
هل يوجد لديكم أسرة فردية بدورين؟
[Hal yoojad ladaykom aserah fardeyah bedoorayen?] Do you have any single sex dorms?
أسْرع [ʔasraʕa] *v* accelerate, hurry, speed up
اسطبل [istˤabl] *n* stable
اسطوانة [ustˤuwa:na] *n* cylinder, CD, roller
اسطوانة دى في دي
[Esṭwanah DVD] *n* DVD
مشغل اسطوانات دى في دي
[Moshaghel esṭwanat D V D] *n* DVD player
ناسخ لاسطوانات دى في دي
[Nasekh le-sṭewanat D V D] *n* DVD burner
هل يمكنك وضع هذه الصور على اسطوانة من فضلك؟
[hal yamken -aka waḍi'a hadhy al-ṣowar 'aala eṣṭi-wana min faḍlak?] Can you put these photos on CD, please?
اسطورة [ʔustˤu:ra] *n* legend, myth
علم الأساطير
['aelm al asateer] *n* mythology
أسطول [ʔustˤu:l] *n* navy
إسعاف [ʔisʕa:f] *n* help
سيارة إسعاف
[Sayarat es'aaf] *n* ambulance
اتصل بعربة الإسعاف
[itaṣel be-'aarabat al-es'aaaf] Call an ambulance
أسعد [ʔasʕada] *v*
يسعدني أن التقي بك أخيرًا
[yas-'aedny an al-ta'qy beka akheran] I'm delighted to meet you at last
أسف [ʔasaf] *n* sorrow, regret
أناأسف للإزعاج
[Ana asef lel-ez'aaj] I'm sorry to trouble you
أسِف [ʔasfa] *v* regret
أسفَل [ʔasfala] *adv* underneath

في الأسفل [Fee al-asfal] *adv* underneath
أسفلُ [ʔasfalu] *adj* underneath ◁ *prep* beneath
إسفنج [ʔisfanʒ] *n* sponge
إسفنجة [ʔisfanʒa] *n* sponge (*for washing*)
أسقط [ʔasqatˤa] *v*
يُسقِط من [Yos'qeṭ men] *v* subtract
أسْقُف [asquf] *n* bishop
اسكتلاندة [iskutla:ndatu] *n* Scotland
اسكتلاندي [iskutla:ndi:] *adj* Scottish ◁ *n* Scot, Scotsman
اسكتلاندية [iskutla:ndijja] *n* Scotswoman
اسكتلانديون[iskutla:ndiju:na] Scots *adj*
إسكندنافيا [ʔiskundina:fja:] *n* Scandinavia
اسكندينافي [ʔiskundina:fjj] *adj* Scandinavian
إسلامي [ʔisla:mij] *adj* Islamic
أسلوب [ʔuslu:b] *n* technique
اسم [ism] *n* name, noun
اسم المرأة قبل الزواج [Esm al-marah 'qabl alzawaj] *n* maiden name
اسم مستعار [Esm mostaar] *n* alias
اسم مَسيحي [Esm maseeḥey] *n* first name
اسم مُستعار [Esm most'aar] *n* pseudonym
اسم مُختَصَر [Esm mokhtaṣar] *n* acronym
الاسم الأول [Al-esm al-awal] *n* first name
اسمي... [ismee..] My name is...
لقد قمت بحجز غرفة باسم... [La'qad 'qomt behajz ghorfah besm...] I booked a room in the name of...
ما اسمك؟ [ma ismak?] What's your name?

أسمر [ʔasmar] *adj* brown
أرز أسمر [Orz asmar] *n* brown rice
أسمر محمر [Asmar mehmer] *adj* auburn
خبز أسمر [Khobz asmar] *n* brown bread
إسمنت [ʔasmant] *n* cement
أسنان [ʔasna:nu] *npl* teeth
إسهاب [ʔisha:b] *n* (حشو) redundancy
إسهال [ʔisha:l] *n* diarrhoea
أعاني من الإصابة بالإسهال [o-'aany min al-eṣaaba bel-es-haal] I have diarrhoea
إسهام [ʔisha:m] *n* contribution
أسهم [ʔashama] *v* contribute
أسوأ [ʔaswaʔ] *adj* worse
الأسوأ [Al-aswaa] *adj* worst
أسود [ʔaswad] *adj* black
أسى [ʔasa:] *n* grief
آسيا [ʔa:sja:] *n* Asia
آسيوي [ʔa:sjawij] *adj* Asian, Asiatic ◁ *n* Asian
أشار [ʔeʃa:ra] *v* point
يُشير إلى [Yosheer ela] *v* refer
يشير إلى [Yosheer ela] *v* indicate
إشارة [ʔiʃa:ra] *n* signal
إشارة إنشغال الخط [Esharat ensheghal al-khat] *n* engaged tone
إشارات المرور [Esharaat al-moroor] *npl* traffic lights
عمود الإشارة ['amood al-esharah] *n* signpost
لغة الإشارة [Loghat al-esharah] *n* sign language
إشاعة [ʔiʃa:ʕa] *n* rumour
إشباع [ʔiʃba:ʕ] *n* satisfaction
أشبع [ʔaʃbaʕa] *v*
لقد شبعت [la'qad sha-be'ato] I'm full
أشْبه [ʔaʃabbah] *v* resemble
أشبِه [ʔaʃbbaha] *v* look like

اشتبِه [ʔeʃtabaha] *v*
يَشتَبِه ب
[Yashtabeh be] *v* suspect
اشتراك [iʃtira:k] *n* subscription
اشتراكي [ʔiʃtira:kij] *adj* socialist
◃ *n* socialist
اشتراكية [ʔiʃtira:kijja] *n* socialism
اشتَرك [ʔeʃtaraka] *v*
يَشتَرك في
[Yashtarek fee] *v* participate
اشتري [ʔeʃtara:] *v* buy
سوف أشتريه
[sawfa ashtareeh] I'll take it
أين يمكن أن أشتري خريطة للبلد؟
[ayna yamken an ash-tary khareeṭa lil-balad?] Where can I buy a map of the country?
أين يمكن أن أشتري الهدايا؟
[ayna yamken an ash-tary al-hadaya?] Where can I buy gifts?
اشتعال [iʃtiʕa:l] *n* ignition
قابل للاشتعال
['qabel lel-eshte'aal] *adj* flammable
اشتمل [ʔeʃtamila] *v*
هل يشتمل على خضروات؟
[hal yash-tamil 'aala khiḍra-waat?] Are the vegetables included?
إشراف [ʔiʃra:f] *n* supervision
أشرطة [ʔaʃritˤa] *n*
أشرطة للزينة
[Ashreṭah lel-zeena] *n* tinsel
إشعار [ʔiʃʕa:r] *n* notice *(note)*
إشعاع [ʔiʃʕa:ʕ] *n* radiation
إشعال [ʔiʃʕa:l] *n* making a fire
إشعال الحرائق
[Esha'aal alḥarae'q] *n* arson
إشعال النار
[Esh'aal al-naar] *n* bonfire
شمعة إشعال
[Sham'aat esh'aal] *n* spark plug
أشعة [ʔuʃiʕʕatu] *npl*
أشعة الشمس
[Ashe'aat al-shams] *n* sunshine
أشعَل [ʔaʃʕala] *v* turn on
أشفق [ʔaʃfaqa] *v*
يُشفق على
[Yoshfe'q 'aala] *v* pity
أشقاء [ʔaʃʃiqa:ʔun] *npl* siblings
أشقر [ʔaʃqar] *n* blonde
اشمئز [ʔeʃmaʔazza] *v*
يَشمئِز من
[Yashmaaez 'an] *v* loathe
أصاب [ʔasˤa:ba] *v* hit
لقد أصيب أحد الأشخاص
[la'qad oṣeba aḥad al-ash-khaaṣ] Someone is injured
إصابة [ʔisˤa:ba] *n* injury
إصابة بالإيدز- إيجابية
[Eṣaba bel edz – ejabeyah] *adj* HIV-positive
إصابة بالإيدز- سلبية
[Eṣaba bel edz – salbeyah] *adj* HIV-negative
أصبح [ʔasˤbaħa] *v* become
إصبَع [ʔisˤbaʕ] *n* finger
إصبع القدم
[Eṣbe'a al'qadam] *n* toe
إصدار [ʔisˤda:r] *n* issue
إصدار التعليمات
[Eṣdar al ta'alemat] *n* briefing
أصّر [ʔasˤarra] *v*
يُصِر على
[Yoṣṣer 'aala] *v* insist
اصطاد [ʔesˤtˤa:da] *v*
هل نستطيع أن نصطاد هنا؟
[hal nastạ-ṭee'a an naṣ-ṭaad huna?] Can we fish here?
اصطاد [ʔesˤtˤa:da] *vi* fish
اصْطَدم [ʔesˤtˤadama] *vi* clash
اصْطَف [ʔesˤtˤaffa] *v* queue
اصطفاء [isˤtˤifa:ʔ] *n* selection
إصطناعي [ʔisˤtˤina:ʕij] *adj* artificial
أصغر [ʔasˤɣaru] *adj* junior, younger
أصفر [ʔasˤfar] *adj* yellow
أصْقَل [ʔasˤqala] *v* varnish
أصل [ʔasˤl] *adj* pedigree ◃ *n* *(source)* origin
في الأصل
[Fee al aṣl] *adv* originally
إصلاح [ʔisˤla:ħ] *n* repair
أين توجد أقرب ورشة لإصلاح الدراجات؟
[ayna tojad a'qrab warsha le-eṣlaḥ

al-darrajaat?] Where is the nearest bike repair shop?

أين توجد أقرب ورشة لإصلاح الكراسي المتحركة؟

[ayna tojad a'qrab warsha le-eṣlaḥ al-karasy al-mutaḥarika?] Where is the nearest repair shop for wheelchairs?

هل يمكن أن أحصل على عدة الإصلاح؟

[Hal yomken an aḥsol ala 'aedat eṣlaḥ] Can I have a repair kit?

أصلح repair, fix *v* [ʔasˤlaħa]

أصلع bald *adj* [ʔasˤlaʕ]

أصلي genuine, principal *adj* [ʔasˤlij]

موطن أصلي

[Mawṭen aṣley] *n* homeland

أصم deaf *adj* [ʔasˤamm]

أصهار in-laws *npl* [ʔasˤha:run]

أصيل original *adj* [ʔasˤi:l]

أضاء light *v* [ʔadˤa:ʔa]

إضاءة lighting *n* [idˤa:ʔa]

أضاف add *v* [ʔadˤa:fa]

إضافة addition *n* [ʔidˤa:fatan]

بالإضافة إلى

[Bel-edafah ela] *adv* besides

إضَافة additive *n* [ʔidˤa:fa]

إضافي additional *adj* [ʔidˤa:fij]

إطار إضافي

[Eṭar eḍafy] *n* spare tyre

ضريبة إضافية

[Ḍareba eḍafeyah] *n* surcharge

عجلة إضافية

['aagalh eḍafeyah] *n* spare wheel

غرفة إضافية

[ghorfah eḍafeyah] *n* spare room

إضراب strike *n* [ʔidˤra:b]

بسبب وجود إضراب

[besabab wijood eḍraab] Because there was a strike

أضرِب strike (*suspend vi* [ʔadˤraba] *work*)

اضطراب turbulence *n* [idˤtˤira:b]

اضطهد prosecute, *v* [ʔedˤtˤahada] persecute

إطار frame, rim *n* [ʔitˤa:r]

إطار إضافي

[Eṭar eḍafy] *n* spare tyre

إطار الصورة

[Eṭar al ṣorah] *n* picture frame

إطار العجلة

[Eṭar al ajalah] *n* tyre

أطاع obey *v* [ʔatˤa:ʕa]

أطال *v* [ʔatˤa:la]

يُطيل السهر

[Yoṭeel alsahar] *v* wait up

أطرى flatter, applaud *v* [ʔatˤra:]

أطعم feed *vt* [ʔatˤʕama]

أطعمة food *n* [ʔatˤʕima]

الأطعمة البحرية

[Al-aṭ'aemah al-baḥareyh] *n* seafood

أطفأ turn off *v* [ʔatˤfaʔa]

اطلاع review *n* [itˤila:ʕ]

إطلاق release *n* [ʔitˤla:q]

إطلاق سراح مشروط

[Eṭla'q ṣarah mashrooṭ] *n* parole

إطلاق النار

[Eṭla'q al nar] *n* shooting

أطلق launch, shoot *vt* [ʔatˤlaqa]

يُطلق سراح

[Yoṭle'q sarah] *v* release

أطلنطي Atlantic *n* [ʔatˤlantˤij]

أطول longer *adv* [ʔatˤwalu]

أعاد bring back, return, *v* [ʔaʕa:da] repeat

يُعْيد عمل الشيء

[Yo'aeed 'aamal al-shaya] *v* redo

يُعْيد تزيين

[Yo'aeed tazyeen] *v* redecorate

يُعْيد تشغيل

[Yo'aeed tashgheel] *v* replay

يُعْيد تنظيم

[Yo'aeed tanḍheem] *v* reorganize

يُعْيد تهيئة

[Yo'aeed taheyaah] *v* format

يُعْيد استخدام

[Yo'aeed estekhdam] *v* recycle, reuse

يُعْيد النظر في

[Yo'aeed al-naḍhar fee] *v* reconsider

يُعْيد بناء

[Yo'aeed benaa] *v* rebuild

يُعْيد شحن بطارية

[Yo'aeed shaḥn baṭareyah] *v* recharge

يُعْيد طَمْأنَته

[Yo'aeed ṭomaanath] v reassure
يُعْيد ملء
[Yo'aeed mela] v refill
هل يجب أن أعيد السيارة إلى هنا مرة أخرى؟
[hal yajib an a'aeed al-sayarah ela huna marra okhra?] Do I have to return the car here?
إعادة returning, restoring n [ʔiʕaːda]
إعادة صُنْع
[E'aadat taṣnea'a] n remake
إعادة تصنيع
[E'aadat taṣnee'a] n recycling
إعادة تشغيل
[E'aadat tashgheel] n replay
إعادة دفع
[E'aadat daf'a] n refund
رجاء إعادة إرسال الفاكس
[rejaa e-'aadat ersaal al-fax] Please resend your fax
أين يمكن أن أشتري كارت إعادة شحن
[ayna yamken an ash-tary kart e-'aadat shaḥin?] Where can I buy a top-up card?
إعاقة disability n [ʔiʕaːqa]
أعال provide for v [ʔaʕaːla]
إعانة help, aid n [ʔiʕaːna]
إعانة بَطَالة
[E'anat baṭalah] n dole
إعانة مالية
[E'aanah maleyah] n subsidy
اعتبر regard v [ʔeʕtabara]
اعتدال moderation n [iʕtidaːl]
اعتذار apology n [ʔiʕtiðaːr]
اعتذر apologize v [ʔaʕtaðara]
اعتراض objection n [iʕtiraːdˤ]
اعتراف acknowledgement, admission n [iʕtiraːf]
اعترض protest v [ʔeʕtaradˤa]
اعترَف confess v [ʔeʕtarafa]
اعْتَزم intend to v [ʔeʕtazama]
اعتقاد belief n [ʕtiqaːd]
اعتقال arrest n [ʔiʕtiqaːl]
اعتقد v [ʔeʕtaqada]
أعتقد أنه سوف يكون هناك رعدا
[a'ata'qid anna-ho sawfa yakoon hunaka ra'adan] I think it's going to thunder
اعتماد n [ʕtimaːd]
أوراق اعتماد
[Awra'q e'atemaad] n credentials
اعتمد v [ʔeʕtamada]
يعتمد على
[jaʕtamidu ʕalaː] v count on
اعتمد على v [ʔeʕtamada ʕalaː] depend
يعتمد على
[jaʕtamidu ʕalaː] v count on
اعتنى care v [ʔeʕtanaː]
يعتني بـ
[Ya'ataney be] v look after
إعجاب admiration n [ʔiʕʒaːb]
أعجب ب v [ʔoʕʒiba bi]
يُعجب بـ
[Yo'ajab be] v admire
أعد prepare v [ʔaʕada]
أعدّ calculate v [ʔaʕadda]
إعداد preparation n [ʔiʕdaːd]
أعدم execute v [ʔaʕdama]
أعزب bachelor n ◁ single adj [ʔaʕzab]
أعسر left-hand, left-handed adj [ʔaʕsar]
أعشاب herbs npl [ʔaʕʃaːbun]
شاى بالأعشاب
[Shay bel-a'ashab] n herbal tea
إعصار hurricane n [ʔiʕsˤaːr]
إعصار قمعي
[E'aṣar 'qam'ay] n tornado
إعطاء giving n [ʔiʕtˤaːʔ]
اعتقد أنه قد تم إعطاء الباقي لك خطأً
[a'ata'qid an-naka a'aṭytani al-baa-'qy kḥaṭa-an] I think you've given me the wrong change
أعْطى give vt [ʔaʕtˤaː]
إعلام information n [ʔiʕlaːm]
وَسائِل الإعلام
[Wasaael al-e'alaam] npl media
إعلان advert, advertisement, announcement n [ʔiʕlaːn]
صناعة الإعلان
[Ṣena'aat al e'alan] n advertising
إعلان تجارى
[E'alaan tejarey] n commercial

إعلان ملصق
[E'alan Molṣa'q] *n* poster
إعلانات صغيرة
[E'alanat ṣaghera] *npl* small ads
إعلاني advertising *adj* [ʔiʕlaːniː]
فاصل إعلاني
[Faṣel e'alaany] *n* commercial break
أعلم instruct, notify *v* [ʔaʕallama]
أعلن announce, declare *v* [ʔaʕlana]
أعلى higher *adj* [ʔaʕlaː]
أعلى مكانة
[A'ala makanah] *n* superior
الأعلى مقاماً
[Al a'ala ma'qaman] *adj* senior
بالأعلى
[Bel'aala] *adv* upstairs
أعْلى raise *v* [ʔaʕlaː]
أعمال work *n* [ʔaʕmaːl]
رَجُل أعمال
[Rajol a'amal] *n* businessman
سيدة أعمال
[Sayedat a'amaal] *n* businesswoman
أعمال تجارية
[A'amaal tejareyah] *n* business
أعمال الخشب
[A'amal al khashab] *npl* woodwork
أعمال الطريق
[a'amal alṭ aree'q] *n* roadworks
أعمال منزلية
[A'amaal manzelyah] *n* housework
جدول أعمال
[Jadwal a'amal] *n* agenda
درجة رجال الأعمال
[Darajat rejal ala'amal] *n* business class
اغتسال *n* [ʔiɣtisaːl]
هل يوجد أماكن للاغتسال؟
[hal yujad amakin lel-ightisaal?] Are there showers?
اغتصاب rape *(sexual n* [iɣtisˤaːb] *attack)*
لقد تعرضت للاغتصاب
[la'qad ta-'aaraḍto lel-ighti-ṣaab] I've been raped
إغتصب rape (يسلب) *v* [ʔeɣtasˤaba]
أغذية food *n* [ʔaɣðijjat]
أغذية متكاملة
[Aghzeyah motakamelah] *npl* wholefoods
إغْراء temptation *n* [ʔiɣraːʔ]
إغْرى tempt *v* [ʔaɣraː]
اغسطس August *n* [ʔuɣustˤus]
إغلاق closure *n* [ʔiɣlaːq]
وَقت الإغلاق
[Wa'qt al-eghlaa'q] *n* closing time
أغلب most *adj* [ʔaɣlab]
في الأغلب
[Fee al-aghlab] *adv* mostly
أغلق shut, close *v* [ʔaɣlaqa]
يُغْلِق الباب
[Yoghle'q albab] *v* slam
إغماء faint *n* [ʔiɣmaːʔ]
يُصَاب بإغماء
[yoṣab be-eghmaa] faint
أغْمَى *v* [ʔaɣmaː]
يُغْمَى عليه
[Yoghma alayh] *v* pass out
أغنَى sing *v* [ʔaɣnaː]
أغنية song *n* [ʔuɣnija]
أغنية أطفال
[Aghzeyat aṭfaal] *n* nursery rhyme
أغنية مرحة
[oghneyah mareha] *n* carol
أُغْنيَّة song *n* [ʔuɣnijja]
إفادَة notice, *n* [ʔifaːda] communication
الإفادة بالرأي
[Al-efadah bel-raay] *n* feedback
أفَاق awake *v* [ʔafaːqa]
افتراض assumption *n* [iftiraːdˤ]
على افتراض
[Ala eftraḍ] *adv* supposedly
بافتراض
[Be-efteraḍ] *conj* supposing
افتراضي *n* [iftiraːdˤij]
واقع افتراضي
[Wa'qe'a eftraḍey] *n* virtual reality
افْترض assume *v* [ʔeftaradˤa]
افتقد miss *vt* [ʔeftaqada]
افراط excess *n* [ifraːtˤ]
افراط السحب على البنك
[Efraṭ al-saḥb ala al-bank] *n* overdraft
أفريقي African *adj* [ʔifriːqij]

جنوب أفريقي
[Janoob afree'qy] *adj* South African
أفريقيا [ʔifri:qija:] *n* Africa
جمهورية أفريقيا الوسطى
[Jomhoreyat afre'qya al-wosṭa] *n* Central African Republic
جنوب أفريقيا
[Janoob afree'qya] *n* South Africa
شخص من جنوب أفريقيا
[Shkhṣ men janoob afree'qya] *n* South African
شمال أفريقيا
[Shamal afreekya] *n* North Africa
إفريقيا [ʔifri:qja:] *n* Africa
شخص من شمال إفريقيا
[Shakhs men shamal afree'qya] *n* North African
من شمال إفريقيا
[Men shamal afree'qya] *adv* North African
أفريكاني [ʔafri:ka:nij] *n*
اللغة الأفريكانية
[Al-loghah al-afreekaneyah] *n* Afrikaans
أفسد [ʔafsada] *vt* spoil
أفشى [ʔafʃa:] *v* disclose
أفضل [ʔafdˤalu] *adj* best, better
من الأفضل
[Men al-'afḍal] *adv* preferably
إفطار [ʔiftˤa:r] *n* breakfast
إفطار كونتيننتال
[Efṭaar kontenental] *n* continental breakfast
مبيت وإفطار
[Mabeet wa efṭaar] *n* bed and breakfast, B&B
غير شاملة للإفطار
[gheyr shamela lel-efṭaar] without breakfast
شاملة الإفطار
[shamelat al-efṭaar] with breakfast
ما هو موعد الإفطار
[ma howa maw-'aid al-efṭaar?] What time is breakfast?
هل يمكن أن أتناول الإفطار داخل غرفتي؟
[hal yamken an ata-nawal al-efṭaar dakhil ghurfaty?] Can I have breakfast in my room?
أفعى [ʔafʕa:] *n*
الأفعى ذات الأجراس
[Al-af'aa dhat al-ajraas] *n* rattlesnake
افغانستان [ʔafɣa:nista:n] *n* Afghanistan
أفغاني [ʔafɣa:nij] *adj* Afghan ◁ *n* Afghan
أُفُقِي [ʔufuqij] *adj* horizontal
أفوكاتو [ʔafu:ka:tu:] *n* solicitor, avocado
ثمرة الأفوكاتو
[Thamarat al-afokatoo] *n* avocado
أقام [ʔaqama] *v* stay
إقامة [ʔiqa:ma] *n* stay
أريد الإقامة لليلتين
[areed al-e'qama le lay-la-tain] I'd like to stay for two nights
اقتباس [iqtiba:s] *n* quote
علامات الاقتباس
['aalamat al-e'qtebas] *n* quotation marks
اقتبِس [ʔeqtabasa] *v* quote
اقتحام [iqtiħa:m] *n* break-in
اقتراح [iqtira:ħ] *n* offer, suggestion
اقتراع [iqtira:ʕ] *n* poll
اقترب [ʔeqtaraba] *v* approach
اقترَح [ʔeqtaraħa] *v* propose, suggest
اقتصاد [iqtisˤa:d] *n* economy
علم الاقتصاد
['aelm al-e'qtesad] *npl* economics
اقتصادي [iqtisˤa:dij] *adj* economic
عالم اقتصادي
['aaalem e'qteṣaadey] *n* economist
اقْتَصد [ʔeqtasˤada] *v* economize
اقْتَطع [ʔeqtatˤaʕa] *v* deduct
اِقتَلع [ʔeqtalaʕa] *v* pull out
أقحُوان [ʔuqħuwa:n] *n* daisy, chamomile
زهرة الأقحُوان
[Thamrat al-o'qḥowan] *n* daisy
أقدام [ʔaqda:mun] *npl* feet
إقدام [ʔiqda:m] *n* courage
أقدم [aqdam] *adv* earlier
أقر [ʔaqara] *v* admit *(confess)*

يُقِر ب
[Yo'qarreb] v own up
confession n [ʔiqrar] إقرار
إقرار ضريبي
[E'qrar ḍareeby] n tax return
n [ʔaqra:sˤ] أقراص
لا أتناول الأقراص
[la ata-nawal al-a'qraaṣ] I'm not on the pill
loan v [ʔaqradˤa] أقرض
يُقرِض مالا
[Yo'qred malan] v loan
part, npl [ʔaqsa:mun] أقسام
department
محل مكون من أقسام
[Maḥal mokawan men a'qsaam] n department store
vt ◁ share out v [ʔaqassama] أقسَم
divide
maximum, most, adj [ʔaqsˤa:] أقصى
ultimate
أقصى عقوبة
[A'qsa 'aoqobah] n capital punishment
fewer adj [ʔaqallu] أقل
على الأقل
['ala ala'qal] adv at least
الأقل
[Al'aqal] adj least
takeoff n [ʔiqla:ʕ] إقلاع
v [ʔaqalaʕa] أقلع
يُقلِع عن
[Yo'qle'a 'aan] vt quit
v [ʔaqlaʕa] أقْلع
يُقلِع عن
[Yo'qle'a an] v give up
minority n [ʔaqallija] أقلية
region, territory n [iqli:m] إقليم
regional adj [iqli:mij] إقليمي
v [ʔaqnaʕa] أقنع
يُقنِع بـ
[Yo'qn'a be] v convince
brackets npl [ʔaqwa:sun] أقواس
(round)
academic adj [ʔaka:di:mij] أكاديمي
academy n [ʔaka:di:mijja] أكاديمية
bigger adj [ʔakbaru] أكبر

depression n [iktiʔa:b] اكتئاب
مضاد للاكتئاب
[Moḍad lel-ekteaab] n antidepressant
obtain, earn v [ʔektasaba] اكْتسب
discover, v [ʔektaʃafa] اكْتشف
find out
October n [ʔuktu:bar] أكتوبر
best, adv ◁ more adj [ʔakθaru] أكثر
better
multiply v [ʔakθara] أكْثر
emphasize v [ʔakadda] أكدّ
يُؤَكِد على
[Yoaked ala] v confirm
stress v [ʔakkada] أكِّد
acre n [ʔakr] أكْر
tip (reward) n [ʔikra:mijja] إكرامية
acrobat n [ʔakru:ba:t] أكروبات
eczema n [ikzi:ma:] إكزيما
oxygen n [ʔuksiʒi:n] أكسجين
n [ʔakl] أكل
صالح للأكل
[Ṣaleḥ lel-aakl] adj edible
شراهة الأكل
[Sharahat alakal] n bulimia
eat vt [ʔakala] أكل
n [ʔikli:l] إكليل
إكليل الجبل
[Ekleel al-jabal] n rosemary
accordion n [ʔaku:rdju:n] أكورديون
porn n [al-ʔiba:ħijatu] الإباحية
sailing n [al-ʔibħa:ri] الإبحار
Monday n [al-ʔiθnajni] الاثنين
في يوم الاثنين
[fee yawm al-ithnayn] on Monday
يوم الاثنين الموافق 15 يونيو
[yawm al-ithnain al-muwa-fi'q 15 yon-yo] It's Monday fifteenth June
rental n [alʔuʒrati] الأجرة
Sunday n [al-ʔaħadu] الأحد
يوم الأحد الموافق الثالث من أكتوبر
[yawm al-aḥad al- muwa-fi'q al-thalith min iktobar] It's Sunday third October
Wednesday n [al-ʔarbiʕa:ʔi] الأربعاء
في يوم الأربعاء
[fee yawm al-arbe-'aa] on Wednesday
n [ʔal-ʔarʒunti:n] الأرجنتين

Argentina
الأردن Jordan *n* [al-ʔurd]
الأرض earth *n* [al-ʔardˤi]
الاسترليني *n* [al-istirli:nijju] sterling
الإسلام Islam *n* [al-ʔisla:mu]
الأصغر youngest *adj* [al-ʔasˤɣaru]
الأطلس atlas *n* [ʔal-ʔatˤlasu]
الأغلبية majority *n* [al-ʔaɣlabijjatu]
الأفق horizon *n* [al-ʔufuqi]
الاقحوان *n* [al-uqħuwa:nu] chrysanthemum
الأقحوان *n* [al-ʔuqħuwa:nu] marigold
الإكوادور Ecuador *n* [al-ikwa:du:r]
الألف thousandth *adj* [al-ʔalfu]
الألفية millennium *n* [al-ʔalfijjatu]
الآلية machinery *n* [al-ajjatu]
آلام *n* [a:la:m]
مسكن آلام
[Mosaken lel-alam] *n* painkiller
الأمن security *n* [alʔamnu]
الآن now *adv* [ʔal-ʔa:n]
من فضلك هل يمكنني الآن أن أطلب ما أريده؟
[min faḍlak hal yamkin-ani al-aan an aṯlib ma areed-aho?] Can I order now, please?
الانترنت Internet *n* [al-intirnit]
الأنثروبولوجيا [ʔal-anthropology *n*ʔanθiru:bu:lu:ʒja:]
الإنجيل Bible *n* [al-ʔinʒi:lu]
الأوبرا opera *n* [ʔal-ʔu:bira:]
الأوركسترا *n* [ʔal-ʔu:rkistra:] orchestra
الأوروجواياني *n* [al-ʔu:ru:ʒwa:ja:ni:] Uruguayan
الأوزون ozone *n* [ʔal-ʔu:zu:ni]
الأومليت omelette *n* [ʔal-ʔu:mli:ti]
الأونس ounce *n* [ʔal-ʔu:nsu]
الإيقاع rhythm *n* [ʔal-ʔi:qa:ʕu]
البابا pope *n* [al-ba:ba:]
ألباني *n* ◃ Albanian *adj* [ʔalba:nij] Albanian *(person)*
ألبانيا Albania *n* [ʔalba:nja:]
البحرين Bahrain *n* [al-baħrajni]
البرازيل Brazil *n* [ʔal-bara:zi:lu]
البربادوس *n* [ʔalbarba:du:s] Barbados
البرتغال Portugal *n* [al-burtuɣa:l]
ألبسة clothing *n* [ʔalbisa]
البندق hazelnut *n* [al-bunduqi]
البوذية Buddhism *n* [al-bu:ðijjatu]
البورصة stock *n* [al-bu:rsˤatu] market
البوسنة Bosnia *v* [ʔal-bu:snatu]
البوسنة والهرسك [ʔal-bu:snatu Bosnia and *n*wa ʔal-hirsik] Herzegovina
ألبوم album *n* [ʔalbu:m]
ألبوم الصور
[Albom al ṣewar] *n* photo album
آلة machine *n* [a:la]
آلة الصنج الموسيقية
[Alat al-ṣanj al-mose'qeyah] *npl* cymbals
آلة الإكسيليفون الموسيقية
[aalat al ekseelefon al mose'qeiah] *n* xylophone
آلة التينور الموسيقية
[aalat al teenor al mose'qeiah] *n* tenor
آلة الفيولا الموسيقية
[aalat al veiola al mose'qeiah] *n* viola
آلة حاسبة
[Aalah ḥasbah] *n* calculator
آلة كاتبة
[aala katebah] *n* typewriter
آلة كشف الشذوذ الجنسي
[aalat kashf al sheḍhoḍh al jensy] *n* fruit machine
التاسع عشر *adj* [atta:siʕa ʕaʃara] nineteenth
التذكرة memento *n* [at-taðkiratu]
التفاف *n* [iltifa:f]
التفاف إبهام القدم
[Eltefaf ebham al-'qadam] *n* bunion
التقط *v* [ʕeltaqatˤa]
هل يمكن أن تلتقط لنا صورة هنا من فضلك؟
[hal yamken an talta-'qiṭ lana ṣoora min faḍlak?] Would you take a picture of us, please?
الْتَقى *v* [ʔeltaqa:]

يَلْتَقي ب
[Yalta'qey be] *v* meet up
petition *n* [iltima:s] **اِلْتماس**
request *v* [ʔeltamasa] **اِلْتَمس**
inflammation *n* [ʔiltiha:b] **التهاب**
التهاب السحايا
[Eltehab al-sahaya] *n* meningitis
التهاب الغدة النكفية
[Eltehab alghda alnokafeyah] *n* mumps
التهاب الحنجرة
[Eltehab al-hanjara] *n* laryngitis
التهاب الكبد
[El-tehab al-kabed] *n* hepatitis
التهاب المثانة
[El-tehab al-mathanah] *n* cystitis
التهاب المفاصل
[Eltehab al-mafaṣel] *n* arthritis
التهاب شُعَبي
[Eltehab sho'aaby] *n* bronchitis
n [ʔiltiha:bun] **إِلتِهاب**
التهاب الزائدة
[Eltehab al-zaedah] *n* appendicitis
bend *n* [ʔiltiwa:ʔ] **التواء**
third *n* [aθ-θa:liθu] **الثالث**
eighth *adj* [aθθa:min] **الثامن**
adj [aθ-θa:min ʕaʃar] **الثامن عشر**
eighteenth
second *adj* [aθ-θa:ni:] **الثاني**
n [aθ-θula:θa:ʔu] **الثلاثاء**
في يوم الثلاثاء
[fee yawm al-thalathaa] on Tuesday
Taurus *n* [aθθawri] **الثور**
Gabon *n* [al-ʒa:bu:n] **الجابون**
Capricorn *n* [alʒadjju] **الجَدي**
npl [al-ʒaddajni] **الجدين**
grandparents
stub *n* [al-ʒaðalu] **الجذل**
Algeria *n* [ʔal-ʒaza:ʔiru] **الجزائر**
Friday *n* [al-ʒumuʕatu] **الجمعة**
في يوم الجمعة
[fee yawm al-jum'aa] on Friday
يوم الجمعة الموافق الحادي والثلاثين من ديسمبر
[yawm al-jum'aa al- muwa-fi'q al-ḥady waal-thalatheen min desambar] on Friday, December thirty-first

Gemini *n* [al-ʒawza:ʔu] **الجوزاء**
number [al-ħa:di: ʕaʃar] **الحادي عشر**
الحادي عشر
[al-ħa:di: ʕaʃar] *adj* eleventh
npl [ʔal-ħa:dˤiri:na] **الحاضرين**
attendance
pilgrimage *n* [al-ħaʒʒu] **الحج**
mother-in-law *n* [al-ħama:tu] **الحماة**
father-in-law *n* [alħamu:] **الحمو**
Pisces *n* [al-ħu:tu] **الحوت**
pelvis *n* [alħawdˤi] **الحوض**
etc *abbr* [ʔilax] **إلخ**
loser *n* [al-xa:siru] **الخاسر**
adj [al-xa:mis ʕaʃar] **الخامس عشر**
fifteenth
mole *(mammal)* *n* [al-xuldu] **الخُلْد**
n [al-xami:su] **الخميس**
في يوم الخميس
[fee yawm al-khamees] on Thursday
n [ad-da:nma:rk] **الدانمارك**
Denmark
who, that, which *pron* [al-laði:] **الذي**
ما الذي بك؟
[ma al-lathy beka?] What's wrong?
adj [ar-ra:biʕu ʕaʃari] **الرابع عشر**
fourteenth
spring *(season)* *n* [arrabi:ʕu] **الربيع**
kneecap *n* [aradˤfatu] **الرضفة**
surfing *n* [ar-rakmaʒatu] **الركمجة**
compulsory *adj* [ʔilza:mij] **إلزامي**
dustman *n* [az-zabba:lu] **الزَّبّال**
thyme *n* [az-zaʕtari] **الزعتر**
seventh *n* [as-sa:biʕu] **السابع**
sixth *adj* [as-sa:disu] **السادس**
[assa:disa ʕaʃara] **السادس عشر**
sixteenth *adj*
Saturday *n* [ʔa-sabti] **السبت**
في يوم السبت
[fee yawm al-sabit] on Saturday
lizard *n* [as-siħlijjatu] **السِحلية**
Saudi *adj* [ʔa-saʕu:dijjatu] **السعودية**
Arabian
Senegal *n* [as-siniɣa:lu] **السنغال**
n [as-sunu:nu:] **السنونو**
طائر السنونو
[Ṭaaer al-sonono] *n* swallow

السودان Sudan *n* [as-su:da:nu]
السوق marketplace *n* [as-su:qi]
السويد Sweden *n* [as-suwi:du]
السيخي Sikh *n* [assi:xijju]
تابع للديانة السِيخِية
[Tabe'a lel-zobabah al-sekheyah] *adj* Sikh
السيد Mr *n* [asajjidu]
السيدة Mrs *n* [asajjidatu]
الشتاء winter *n* [aʃ-ʃita:ʔi]
الشيشان Chechnya *n* [aʃ-ʃi:ʃa:n]
الصرب Serbia *n* [asˤ-sˤirbu]
الصومال Somalia *n* [asˤ-sˤu:ma:lu]
الصيف summer *n* [asˤ-sˤajfu]
الصين China *n* [asˤ-sˤi:nu]
ألعاب القوى [ʔalʕa:bun ʔalqiwa:] athletics *npl*
العاشر *n* ◁ tenth *adj* [al-ʕa:ʃiru] tenth
العذراء Virgo *n* [al-ʕaðra:ʔi]
العراق Iraq *n* [al-ʕira:qi]
العشرون twentieth *adj* [al-ʕiʃru:na]
العقرب Scorpio *n* [al-ʕaqrabi]
إلغاء abolition, cancellation *n* [ʔilɣa:ʔ]
الغوص diving *n* [al-ɣawsˤu]
ألغى abolish *v* [ʕalɣa:]
ألف thousand *number* [ʔalfun]
جزء من ألف
[Joza men al alf] *n* thousandth
الفاتيكان Vatican *n* [al-fa:ti:ka:ni]
الفاحص examiner *n* [al-fa:ħisˤu]
القارض rodent *n* [al-qa:ridˤi]
القرآن Koran *n* [al-qurʔa:nu]
ألقى *v* [ʔalqa:]
يُلقي بضغط
[Yol'qy be-ḍaght] *v* pressure
يُلْقي الضوء على
[Yol'qy al-ḍawa 'aala] *v* highlight
يُلْقي النفايات
[Yol'qy al-nefayat] *v* dump
القيود handcuffs *npl* [al-quju:du]
الكاميرون *n* [al-ka:mi:ru:n] Cameroon
الكتروني *adj* [iliktru:nijjat] electronic
بريد الكتروني
[Bareed elektrooney] *n* email
كتاب الكتروني
[Ketab elektrooney] *n* e-book
لعبة الكترونية
[Lo'abah elektroneyah] *n* computer game
إلكتروني electronic *adj* [ʔiliktru:ni:]
هل تلقيت أي رسائل بالبريد الإلكتروني؟
[hal tala-'qyto ay rasa-el bil-bareed al-alekitrony?] Is there any mail for me?
الكترونيات *npl* [ilikturu:nijja:tun] electronics
الكترونية *n* [ilikturu:nijja]
تجارة الكترونية
[Tejarah elektroneyah] *n* e-commerce
إلكترونيةّ *adj* [ʔilikturu:nijjat]
تذكرة إلكترونية
[Tadhkarah elektroneyah] *n* e-ticket
الكونغو Congo *n* [al-ku:nɣu:]
الكويت Kuwait *n* [al-kuwi:tu]
الكياسة politeness *n* [al-kija:satu]
الله Allah, God *n* [allahu]
آلم ache *v* [ʔalama]
ألم pain *n* [ʔalam]
ألم الأذُن
[Alam al odhon] *n* earache
ألم المَعِدة
[Alam alma'aedah] *n* stomachache
ألم مفاجئ
[Alam Mofajea] *n* stitch
أَلَمْ الظهر
[Alam al-ḍhahr] *n* back pain
إن ظهري به آلام
[enna ḍhahry behe aa-laam] My back is sore
أريد أخذ حقنة لتخفيف الألم
[areed akhdh ḥu'qna le-takhfeef al-alam] I want an injection for the pain
أعاني من ألم في صدري
[o-'aany min alam fee ṣadry] I have a pain in my chest
أشعر بألم هنا
[ash-'aur be-alam huna] It hurts here
موضع الألم هنا
[mawḍi'a al-alam huna] It hurts here

هل يمكنك إعطائي شيئًا لتخفيف الألم؟ [hal yamken -aka e'aṭa-ee shay-an le-takhfeef al-alam?] Can you give me something for the pain?
الماركسية [al-maːrkisijjatu] n Marxism
إلماع [ʔilmaːʕ] n cue
المؤلف [ʔal-muallifu] n author
ألماني [ʔalmaːnij] adj German ◁ n German (person)
اللغة الألمانية [Al loghah al almaniyah] (language) n German
حصبة ألمانية [Haṣbah al-maneyah] n German measles
ألمانيا [ʔalmaːnijjaː] n Germany
المؤيد [al-muajjidu] n supporter
المتبجح [al-mutabaʒʒiħ] n bouncer
المتفاخر [almutafaːxiru] n show-off
المجر [al-maʒari] n Hungary
المحيط الهادي [al-moḥeeṭ l-haadey] n Pacific
المخنث [al-muxannaθu] n transvestite
المَسِيح [al-masiːħu] n Christ
المَسيحية [al-masiːħijjatu] n Christianity
المَشرِق [ʔalmaʃriqi] n Far East
المغرِب [almaɣribu] n Morocco
المكسيك [al-miksiːku] n Mexico
الموظفين [almuwazˤzˤafiːna] n personnel
الميزان [al-miːzaːnu] n Libra
النجدة [al-naʒdati] excl help!
النرويج [ʔan-narwiːʒ] n Norway
النقص [an-naqsˤu] n decrease
النقيض [anaqiːdˤu] n reverse
النِمْس [an-nimsu] n ferret
النَمسا [ʔa-nnamsaː] n Austria
النَوْع [an-nawʕu] n gender
النيجر [an-niːʒar] n Niger
إله [ʔilah] n god
الهند [al-hindi] n India
الهندوراس [al-handuːraːsi] n Honduras
الومونيوم [ʔaluːminjuːm] n aluminium
آلي [ajj] adj automatic
إليّ [ʔilajja] pron me
إلى [ʔilaː] prep to
آليا [ajjan] adv automatically
اليابان [al-jaːbaːnu] n Japan
اليابسة [al-jaːbisatu] n mainland
ألياف [ʔaljaːf] n fibre
أليف [ʔaliːf] adj
حيوان أليف [Ḥayawaan aleef] n pet
اليَمَنْ [al-jamanu] n Yemen
اليَوْم [aljawma] adv today
اليونان [al-juːnaːni] n Greece
أم [ʔumm] n mother
أم الأب أو الأم [Om al-ab aw al-om] n grandmother
الأم البديلة [al om al badeelah] n surrogate mother
الأم المُربية [al om almorabeyah] n godmother
اللغة الأم [Al loghah al om] n mother tongue
زوج الأم [Zawj al-om] n stepfather
متعلق بالأم [Mota'ale'q bel om] adj maternal
إمارة [ʔimaːra] n emirate
إمارة أندورة [ʔimaːratu ʔanduːrata] n Andorra
أمام [ʔamaːma] adv before ◁ prep before
إلى الأمام [Ela al amam] adv forward
أمامي [ʔamaːmij] adj front ◁ n foreground
أمان [ʔamaːn] n safety, security
حزام الأمان المثبت في المقعد [Ḥezam al-aman al-mothabat fee al-ma'q'aad] n seatbelt
أمانة [ʔamaːna] n honesty
إمبراطور [ʔimbaraːtˤuːr] n emperor
إمبراطورية [ʔimbaraːtˤuːrijja] n empire
أمبير [ʔambiːr] n amp

أمة nation *n* [ʔumma]
الأمم المتحدة
[Al-omam al-motahedah] *n* United Nations
امتحان exam *n* [imtiħa:n]
امتد stretch *vi* [ʔemtada]
امتداد extension (توسع) *n* [imtida:d]
امتطي *v* [ʔemtatˤa:]
هل يمكننا أن نمتطي الجياد؟
[hal yamken -ana an namta-ṭy al-ji-yaad?] Can we go horse riding?
أمتعة baggage *n* [ʔamtiʕa]
أمتعة محمولة في اليد
[Amte'aah maḥmoolah fee al-yad] *n* hand luggage
أمتعة مُخزّنة
[Amte'aah mokhazzanah] *n* left-luggage
استلام الأمتعة
[Estelam al-amte'aah] *n* baggage reclaim
مكتب الأمتعة
[Makatb al amte'aah] *n* left-luggage office
وَزْن الأمتعة المسموح به
[Wazn al-amte'aah al-masmooh beh] *n* baggage allowance
امْتَعض resent *v* [ʔemtaʕadˤa]
امتلك possess, own *v* [ʔemtalaka]
امتياز concession, *n* [imtija:z] privilege
أمحى erase *v* [ʔamħa:]
إمداد supply *n* [ʔimda:d]
أمر thing *n* [ʔamr]
أمر دفع شهري
[Amr daf'a shahrey] *n* standing order
أمر order *v* [ʔamara]
امرأة woman *n* [imraʔa]
امرأة ملتحقة بالقوات المسلحة
[Emraah moltahe'qah bel-'qwat al-mosallaha] *n* servicewoman
أمريكا America *n* [ʔamri:ka:]
أمريكا الجنوبية
[Amrika al janobeyiah] *n* South America
أمريكا الشمالية
[Amreeka al- Shamaleyah] *n* North America
أمريكا اللاتينية
[Amreeka al-lateeneyah] *n* Latin America
أمريكا الوسطى
[Amrika al wostaa] *n* Central America
شخص من أمريكا الشمالية
[Shkhṣ men Amrika al shamalyiah] *n* North American
من أمريكا الشمالية
[men Amrika al shamalyiah] *adv* North American
من أمريكا اللاتينية
[men Amrika al lateniyah] *adj* Latin American
أمريكي *n* ◁ American *adj* [ʔamri:kij] American
جنوب أمريكي
[Janoob amriky] *adj* South American
الولايات المتحدة الأمريكية
[Alwelayat almotahdah al amrikiyah] *n* USA
كرة القدم الأمريكية
[Korat al-'qadam al-amreekeyah] *n* American football
أمس yesterday *adv* [ʔamsun]
أمس الأول
[ams al-a-wal] the day before yesterday
منذ الأمس وأنا أعاني من المرض
[mundho al-ams wa ana o'aany min al-maraḍ] I've been sick since yesterday
امساك stopping *n* [imsa:k]
مصاب بالامساك
[Moṣab bel-emsak] *adj* constipated
أمسك *v* [ʔamasaka]
يُمْسِك ب
[Yomsek be] *v* tackle ◁ *vt* catch
يمسك بإحكام
[Yamsek be-ehkam] *v* grip
أمطر rain *v* [ʔamtˤara]
تمطر ثلجا
[Tomṭer thaljan] *v* snow
تمطر مطرا متجمدا
[Tomṭer maṭran motajamedan] *v* sleet
إمكانية possibility, *n* [ʔimka:nijja] potential
أمكن *v* [ʔamkana]

أين يمكنني كيّ هذا؟
[Ayna yomkenaney kay hadhah] Where can I get this ironed?
هل هذا يمكن غسله؟
[hal hadha yamken ghas-loho?] Is it washable?
هل يمكن أن أجربها
[hal yamken an ajar-rebha] Can I try it on?
هل يمكن أن نتقابل فيما بعد؟
[hal yamken an nta'qabal fema ba'ad?] Shall we meet afterwards?
هل يمكن تصليح هذه؟
[hal yamken taṣleeḥ hadhy?] Can you repair this?
هل يمكنك كتابة ذلك على الورق إذا سمحت؟
[hal yamken -aka ketabat dhaleka 'aala al-wara'q edha samaḥt?] Could you write it down, please?
أمل hope *n* [ʔamal]
خيبة الأمل
[Khaybat al-amal] *n* disappointment
مفعم بالأمل
[Mof-'am bel-amal] *adv* hopefully
أمل hope *v* [ʔamela]
إملاء dictation *n* [ʔimla:ʔ]
أمْلى *v* [ʔamla:]
يُمْلي عليه
[Yomely 'aleyh] *v* boss around
أمِّم nationalize *v* [ʔammama]
آمن safety, security *n* [ʔa:min]
غير آمن
[Ghayr aamen] *adj* insecure
هل هذا المكان آمن للسباحة؟
[hal hadha al-makaan aamin lel-sebaḥa?] Is it safe to swim here?
هل هو آمن للأطفال
[hal howa aamin lil-ạṭfaal?] Is it safe for children?
هل هو آمن للأطفال؟
[hal howa aamin lil-ạṭfaal?] Is it safe for children?
آمن reckon *v* [ʔamana]
آمِنْ safe *adj* [ʔa:mi]
أمن safety, security *n* [ʔamn]

حارس الأمن
[Ḥares al-amn] *n* security guard
أمّن insure *v* [ʔammana]
إمنية wish *n* [ʔumnijja]
أمواج waves *npl* [ʔamwa:ʒun]
ركوب الأمواج
[Rokoob al-amwaj] *n* surf
أمي illiterate *adj* [ʔumijju]
أمير prince *n* [ʔami:r]
أميرة princess *n* [ʔami:ra]
أميري fiscal *adj* [ʔami:rij]
أمين honest *adj* [ʔami:n]
أمين الصندوق
[Ameen alṣondoo'q] *n* treasurer
أمين المكتبة
[Ameen al maktabah] *n* librarian
غير أمين
[Gheyr amen] *adj* dishonest
أن if, that, a,though *conj* [ʔanna]
لأن
[liʔanna] *conj* because
أنّ groan *v* [ʔanna]
أنا I *pron* [ʔana]
إناء pot *n* [ʔina:ʔ]
أناناس pineapple *n* [ʔana:na:s]
أناني selfish *adj* [ʔana:nij]
إنْبَعج dent *v* [ʔenbaʕaʒa]
أنبوب jet, tube, pipe *n* [ʔunbu:b]
أنبوب اختبار
[Anbob ekhtebar] *n* test tube
أنبوب التصريف
[Anboob altaṣreef] *n* drainpipe
أنبوب فخاري
[Onbob fokhary] *n* tile
أنبوبة tube *n* [ʔunbu:ba]
أنت you *pron* [ʔanta]
انتاج production *n* [inta:ʒ]
تخفيض الانتاج
[Takhfeeḍ al-entaj] *n* cutback
إنتاج production *n* [ʔinta:ʒ]
إعادة إنتاج
[E'adat entaj] *n* reproduction
إنْتاج رَئيسي
[Entaj raaesey] *v* staple *(commodity)*
إنتاجية productivity *n* [ʔinta:ʒijja]
انتباه attention *n* [ʔintiba:h]

شديد الانتباه
[shaded al-entebah] *adj* observant
produce *v* [ʔantaʒa] **أنْتِج**
weep *v* [ʔentaħaba] **انْتَحب**
suicide *v* [ʔetaħara] **انتحر**
election *n* [intixa:b] **انتخاب**
n [intixa:ba:t] **انتخابات**
انتخابات عامة
[Entekhabat 'aamah] *n* general election
electoral *adj* [intixa:bijjat] **انتخابي**
دائرة انتخابية
[Daaera entekhabeyah] *n* constituency
elect *v* [ʔentaxaba] **انتخب**
delegate *n* [intida:b] **انتداب**
delegate *v* [ʔantadaba] **انتدب**
Internet *n* [intirnit] **انترنت**
جرائم الكمبيوتر والانترنت
[Jraem al-kmobyoter wal-enternet] *n* cybercrime
مقهى الانترنت
[Ma'qha al-enternet] *n* cybercafé
Internet *n* [ʔintirnit] **إنترنت**
متصلا بالإنترنت
[Motaṣelan bel-enternet] *adv* online
هل هناك اتصال لاسلكي بالإنترنت داخل الحجرة
[hal hunak ite-ṣaal la-silki bel-internet dakhil al-ḥijra?] Does the room have wireless internet access?
هل يوجد أي مقهى للإنترنت هنا؟
[hal yujad ay ma'qha lel-internet huna?] Are there any Internet cafés here?
spread *n* [intiʃa:r] **انتشار**
vt ◂ spread out *v* [ʔentaʃara] **انتشر** spread
triumph *n* [intisˤa:r] **انتصار**
تذكار انتصار
[tedhkaar enteṣar] *n* trophy
triumph *v* [ʔentasˤara] **انْتَصر**
waiting *n* [intizˤa:r] **انتظار**
غرفة انتظار
[Ghorfat enteḍhar] *n* waiting room
مكان انتظار
[Makan enteḍhar] *n* layby
هل يوجد مكان انتظار للسيارات بالقرب من هنا؟
[hal yujad makan inti-ḍhar lil-sayaraat bil-'qurb min huna?] Is there a car park near here?
order *n* [intizˤa:m] **انتظام**
بانتظام
[benteḍham] *adv* regularly
hang on, *v* [ʔentazˤara] **انتظر** wait for
ينتظر قليلا
[yantḍher 'qaleelan] *v* hold on
انتظرني من فضلك
[intaḍhirny min faḍlak] Please wait for me
هل يمكن أن تنتظر هنا دقائق قليلة؟
[hal yamken an tanta-ḍher huna le-da'qa-e'q 'qalela?] Can you wait here for a few minutes?
shudder *v* [ʔentafadˤa] **انتفض**
pick *n* [intiqa:ʔ] **انتقاء**
critical *adj* [intiqa:dij] **انتقادي**
shift, transition *n* [intiqa:l] **انتقال**
revenge *n* [intiqa:m] **انتقام**
criticize *v* [ʔentaqada] **انتقد**
move in *v* [ʔentaqala] **انتقل**
pick out *v* [ʔentaqa:] **انتقى**
relapse *n* [intika:sa] **انتكاسة**
membership *n* [ntima:ʔ] **انتماء**
الانتماء الوطني
[Al-entemaa alwaṭaney] *n* citizenship
v [ʔentama:] **انتمي**
ينتمي إلى
[Yantamey ela] *v* belong to
ending *n* [intiha:ʔ] **انتهاء**
تاريخ الانتهاء
[Tareekh al-entehaa] *n* expiry date
موعد الانتهاء
[Maw'aed al-entehaa] *n* deadline
end *v* [ʔentaha:] **إنْتَهى**
female *n* [ʔunθa:] **أنثى**
achievement *n* [ʔinʒa:z] **إنجاز**
drift *vi* [ʔenʒarafa] **إنْجَرف**
fulfil *v* [ʔanʒaza] **أنْجز**
England *n* [ʔinʒiltira:] **إنجَلترا**
English *adj* [inʒili:zij] **أنجليزي**
n ◂ English *adj* [ʔinʒili:zij] **إنجليزي** English

مواطنة إنجليزية [Mowaṭenah enjlezeyah] *n* Englishwoman
هل يوجد لديكم كتيب باللغة الإنجليزية؟ [hal yujad laday-kum kuty-ib bil-lugha al-injile-ziya?] Do you have a leaflet in English?
إنجليزية [ʔinʒali:zijja] *n*
هل تتحدث الإنجليزية [hal tata- ḥadath al-injileez-iya?] Do you speak English?
أنجولا [ʔanʒu:la:] Angola *n*
أنجولي [ʔanʒu:lij] Angolan *adj* ◁ *n* Angolan
إنجيل [ʔinʒi:l] gospel *n*
انحدار [ʔinħida:r] slope, decline *n*
هل هو شديد الانحدار؟ [hal howa shadeed al-inḥi-daar?] Is it very steep?
انحدر [ʔenħadara] descend *v*
انحراف [inħira:f] diversion *(road)* *n*
انحرف [ʔenħarafa] swerve *v*
انحناء [inħina:ʔ] bow *n*
انحنى [ʔenħana:] bend over *v*
انخفض [ʔenxafadˤa] lower, come down *v*
اندفاع [indifa:ʕ] rush *n*
إندفع [ʔandafaʕa] dash, rush *vi*
أندونيسي [ʔandu:ni:sij] *n* Indonesian *(person)* ◁ Indonesian *adj*
أندونيسيا [ʔandu:ni:sjja:] *n* Indonesia
إنذار [ʔinða:r] alarm, notice *n* *(termination)*, ultimatum
إنذار سرقة [endhar sare'qa] *n* burglar alarm
إنذار حريق [endhar Haree'q] *n* fire alarm
إنذار كاذب [endhar kadheb] *n* false alarm
آنذاك [ʔa:naða:ka] then *adv*
أنْذر [ʔanðara] notice *v*
إنزلاق [ʔinzila:q] slipping *n*
إنزلاق غضروفي [Enzela'q ghodrofey] *n* slipped disc
انزلق [ʔenzalaqa] slide, skid *v*
إنسان [ʔinsa:n] human being *n*
إنسان آلي [Ensan aly] *n* robot
حقوق الإنسان [Ho'qoo'q al-ensan] *npl* human rights
من صنع الإنسان [Men ṣon'a al-ensan] *adj* man-made
إنساني [ʔinsa:nij] human *adj*
ضمير إنساني [Ḍameer ensaney] *n* conscience
آنسة [ʔa:nisa] Miss *n*
انسحاب [insiħa:b] recession *n*
إنسِحاب [ʔinsiħa:b] withdrawal *n*
أنسحب [ʔensaħaba] drag *vt*
إنسداد [insida:d] blockage *n*
إنسولين [ʔansu:li:n] insulin *n*
أنْشأ [ʔanʃaʔa] construct *v*
إنشاء [ʔinʃa:ʔ] construction *n*
أنشوجة [ʔunʃu:da] anchovy *n*
انْصَرف [ʔensˤarafa] get away *v*
انطباع [intˤibba:ʕ] impression *n*
إنطلق [ʔentˤalaqa] go ahead *v*
أنْعش [ʔanʕaʃa] freshen up *v*
انعكاس [inʕika:s] reflection *n*
انعكاسي [inʕika:sij] *adj*
رد انعكاسي [Rad en'aekasey] *n* reflex
أَنْف [ʔanf] nose *n*
انفجار [infiʒa:r] explosion *n*
انفجار عاطفي [Enfejar 'aatefy] *n* gust
انفجر [ʔenfaʒara] blow up, burst *v*
لقد انفجر إطار السيارة [la'qad infajara eṭar al-sayara] The tyre has burst
انفراد [ʔinfira:d] isolation *n*
هل يمكنني التحدث إليك على انفراد؟ [hal yamken -any al-taḥaduth elayka 'aala enfi-raad?] Can I speak to you in private?
إنفِصال [infisˤa:l] separation *n*
انْفصل [ʔenfasˤala] split up *v*
انفعال [infiʕa:l] *n*
سريع الانفعال [Saree'a al-enfe'aal] *adj* touchy

إنفلوانزا [ʔinfilwa:nza:] *n* flu
إنفلوانزا الطيور
[Enfelwanza al-ṭeyor] *n* bird flu
أنفلونزا [ʔanfluwanza:] *n* influenza
إنقاذ [ʔinqa:ð] *n* rescue
عامل الإنقاذ
[ʻaamel alen'qaḍh] *n* lifeguard
حبل الإنقاذ
[Habl elen'qadh] *n* helpline
أين يوجد أقرب مركز لخدمة الإنقاذ بالجبل؟
[ayna yujad a'qrab markaz le-khedmat al-en-'qaadh bil-jabal?] Where is the nearest mountain rescue service post?
أَنْقَذ [ʔanqaða] *v* rescue
إنْقَسم [ʔenqasama] *vt* split
أنقص [ʔanqasˤa] *v* decrease
انقطاع [inqitˤa:ʕ] *n* disruption
انقطاع التيار الكهربي
[En'qetaa'a al-tayar alkahrabey] *n* power cut
انقطع [ʔenqatˤaʕa] *v* go off
انقلاب [inqila:b] *n* turnover
انقلب [ʔenqalaba] *v* capsize, upset
انقياد [inqija:d] *n*
سهل الانقياد
[Sahl al-en'qyad] *adj* easy-going
إنكار [ʔinka:ruhu] *n* denial
لا يمكن إنكاره
[La yomken enkareh] *adj* undeniable
أنكر [ʔankara] *v* deny
انكسر [ʔenkasara] *v*
لقد انكسرت علبة التروس
[la'qad inkasarat ʻailbat al-tiroos] The gearbox is broken
انهار [ʔenha:ra] *v* collapse
انْهَمك [ʔenhamaka] *v*
يَنْهَمك في القيل والقال
[Yanhamek fee al-'qeel wa al-'qaal] *v* gossip
أنْهى [ʔanha:] *v* finalize
انهيار [ʔinhija:r] *n* avalanche, crash, collapse
انهيار أرضي
[Enheyar ardey] *n* landslide
إنهيار عصبي
[Enheyar aṣabey] *n* nervous breakdown
أنواع [ʔanwa:ʕ] *npl* species
آنية [ʔa:nija] *n*
آنية من الصيني
[Aaneyah men al-ṣeeney] *n* china
أنيق [ʔani:q] *adj* elegant
أنيميا [ʔani:mja:] *n* anaemia
مُصاب بالأنيميا
[Moṣaab bel-aneemeya] *n* anaemic
أهان [ʔaha:na] *v* insult, slap
إهانة [ʔiha:na] *n* insult
اهتَز [ʔehtazza] *vi* shake
اهتم [ʔehtamma] *vi* mind
اهتمام [ihtima:m] *n* concern, interest *(curiosity)*, regard
يُثير اهتمام
[yotheer ehtemam] *v* interest
اهتياج [htija:ʒ] *n* agitation
شديد الاهتياج
[Shdeed al-ehteyaj] *adj* frantic
أهْدر [ʔahdara] *v* growl
أهل [ʔahl] *n* family
أهل البيت
[Ahl al-bayt] *n* household
أهّل [ʔahala] *v* qualify
أهلا [ʔahlan] *excl* hello!
أهلي [ʔahlij] *adj* family
حرب أهلية
[Ḥarb ahleyah] *n* civil war
إهمال [ʔihma:l] *n* neglect
أهْمَل [ʔahmala] *v* neglect
أهمية [ʔahamijja] *n* importance
أهمية مُلحة
[Ahameiah molehah] *n* urgency
أوبوا [ʔu:bwa:] *n* oboe
أوتوبيس [ʔu:tu:bi:s] *n* coach
تذكرة أوتوبيس
[tadhkarat otobees] *n* bus ticket
محطة أوتوبيس
[Mahaṭat otobees] *n* bus station
موقف أوتوبيس
[Maw'qaf otobees] *n* bus stop
أوتوجراف [ʔu:tu:ʒra:f] *n* autograph
أوثق [ʔawθaqa] *v* moor
أوركيد [ʔu:rki:d] *n*
زهرة الأوركيد

[Zahrat al-orkeed] *n* orchid
Europe *n* [ʔu:ru:bba:] **أوروبا**
European *adj* [ʔu:ru:bij] **أوروبي**
الاتحاد الأوروبي
[Al-tehad al-orobey] *n* European Union
شخص أوروبي
[Shakhs orobby] *n* European
Uruguay *n* [uwru:ʒwa:j] **أوروجواي**
adj [ʔu:ru:ʒwa:ja:ni:] **اوروجواياني**
Uruguayan
n [ʔu:zba:kista:n] **أوزباكستان**
Uzbekistan
goose, swan *n* [ʔiwazza] **إوزة**
n [ʔu:zu:n] **أوزون**
طبقة الأوزون
[Taba'qat al-odhoon] *n* ozone layer
n [ʔu:stra:la:sja:] **أوسترالاسيا**
Australasia
mid *adj* [ʔawsatˤ] **أوسط**
Oceania *n* [ʔu:sja:nja:] **أوسيانيا**
recommend *v* [ʔawsˤa:] **أوصى**
point out *v* [ʔawdˤaħa] **أوضح**
clarify *v* [ʔawdˤaħa] **أوضح**
Uganda *n* [ʔu:ɣanda:] **أوغندا**
n ◃ Ugandan *adj* [ʔu:ɣandij] **أوغندي**
Ugandan
sign *v* [ʔawaqaʕa] **أوقَع**
stop, turn out *v* [ʔawqafa] **أوقف**
يُوْقِف السيارة
[Yo'qef sayarah] *v* pullover
n ◃ Ukrainian *adj* [ʔu:kra:nij] **أوكراني**
Ukrainian *(person)*
اللغة الأوكرانية
[Al loghah al okraneiah] *(language) n*
Ukrainian
Ukraine *n* [ʔu:kra:nja:] **أوكرانيا**
first *n* ◃ first *adj* [ʔawwal] **أول**
الاسم الأول
[Al-esm al-awal] *n* first name
ما هو موعد أول قطار متجه إلى...؟
[ma howa maw-'aid awal 'qeṭaar mutajih ela...?] When is the first train to...?
first, firstly *adv* [ʔawwala:] **أولًا**
priority *n* [ʔawlawijja] **أولوية**
primary *adj* [ʔawwalij] **أولي**
الأحرف الأولى
[Al-aḥrof al-ola] *npl* initials
في الدرجة الأولى
[Fee al darajah al ola] *adv* mainly
إسعافات أولية
[Es'aafat awaleyah] *n* first aid
signal *v* [ʔawmaʔa] **أومأ**
يُومئ برأسه
[Yomea beraaseh] *v* nod
trick *v* [ʔewhama] **أوهم**
any *adj* [ʔajju] **أي**
أي شخص
[Ay shakhṣ] *pron* anybody
أي شيء
[Ay shaya] *n* anything
أي من
[Ay men] *pron* any
على أي حال
[Ala ay ḥal] *adv* anyway
بأي طريقة
[Be-ay ṭaree'qah] *adv* anyhow
في أي مكان
[Fee ay makan] *adv* anywhere
positive *adj* [ʔi:ʒa:bij] **إيجابي**
rent *n* [ʔjʒa:r] **إيجار**
ideology *n* [ʔajdu:lu:ʒijja] **أيدولوجية**
revenue *n* [ʔi:ra:d] **إيراد**
Iran *n* [ʔi:ra:n] **إيران**
n ◃ Iranian *adj* [ʔi:ra:nij] **إيراني**
Iranian *(person)*
Ireland *n* [ʔajrlanda:] **أيرلندا**
n [ʔajrlanda] **أيرلندة**
أيرلندة الشمالية
[Ayarlanda al-shamaleyah] *n* Northern Ireland
Irish *adj* [ajrlandij] **أيرلندي**
الأيرلندي
[Alayarlandey] *n* Irish
adj [ijrlandij] **إيرلندي**
رَجُل إيرلندي
[Rajol ayarlandey] *n* Irishman
Irishwoman *n* [ijrlandijja] **إيرلندية**
n [ʔa:js] **آيس**
ستيك الآيس كريم
[Steek al-aayes kreem] *n* ice lolly
آيس كريم
[aayes kreem] *n* ice cream

أيسلاندي Icelandic *adj* [ʔajslaːndiː]
الأيسلندي
[Alayeslandey] *n* Icelandic
أيسلندا Iceland *n* [ʔajslandaː]
إيصال voucher *n* [ʔiːsˤaːl]
إيصالات takings *npl* [ʔiːsˤaːlaːtun] *(money)*
أيضا also, else, too *adv* [ʔajdˤan]
إيضاحي *adj* [ʔiːdˤaːħijjat]
تجربة إيضاحية
[Tajrebah eeḍaheyah] *n* demonstration
إيطالي *n* ◁ Italian *adj* [ʔiːtˤaːlij]
Italian *(person)*
اللغة الإيطالية
[alloghah al eṭaleyah] *(language) n* Italian
إيطاليا Italy *n* [ʔiːtˤaːljjaː]
إيقاف stopping *n* [ʔiːqaːf]
لا يمكنني إيقاف تشغيله
[la yam-kinuni e-'qaaf tash-ghe-lehe] I can't turn the heating off
لن أقوم بإيقاف تشغيله
[Lan a'qoom be-ee'qaf tashgheeleh] It won't turn off
هل يمكن إيقاف السيارة بالقرب منا؟
[hal yamken e'qaaf al-sayara bil-'qurb min-na?] Can we park by our site?
أيقونة icon *n* [ʔajquːna]
أيْل deer *n* [ʔajl]
إيماءة gesture *n* [ʔiːmaːʔa]
إيمان faith *n* [ʔiːmaːn]
أيمن right-handed *adj* [ʔajman]
أين where *adv* [ʔajna]
أين تسكن؟
[ayna taskun?] Where do you live?
أين تقيم؟
[Ayn to'qeem?] Where are you staying?
أين يمكن أن نتقابل؟
[ayna yamken an nata-'qabal?] Where can we meet?
أين يمكنني إرضاع الرضيع؟
[ayna yamken-any erḍa'a al-raḍee'a?] Where can I breast-feed the baby?
أين يوجد قسم الشرطة؟
[ayna yujad 'qisim al- shurṭa?] Where is the police station?
من أين أنت؟
[min ayna anta?] Where are you from?
إيوَاء lodging *n* [ʔiːwaːʔ]
دَار إيوَاء
[Dar eewaa] *n* dormitory *(large bedroom)*

in, on, with, by *prep* [bi] **ب**

بجانب

[Bejaneb] *prep* beside

vendor *n* [ba:ʔiʕ] **بائع**

بائع تجزئة

[Bae'a tajzeah] *n* retailer

بائع زهور

[Bae'a zohor] *n* florist

door *n* [ba:b] **باب**

جرس الباب

[Jaras al-bab] *n* doorbell

درجة الباب

[Darajat al-bab] *n* doorstep

مقبض الباب

[Me'qbaḍ al-bab] *n* door handle

أين يوجد باب الخروج...؟

[Ayn yojad bab al-khoroj...] Which exit for...?

أين يوجد مفتاح الباب الأمامي؟

[ayna yujad muftaaḥ al-baab al-ama-my?] Which is the key for the front door?

أين يوجد مفتاح الباب الخلفي؟

[ayna yujad muftaaḥ al-baab al-khalfy?] Which is the key for the back door?

أين يوجد مفتاح هذا الباب؟

[ayna yujad muftaaḥ hadha al-baab?] Which is the key for this door?

اترك الباب مغلقا

[itruk al-baab mughla'qan] Keep the door locked

الباب لا يُغلَق

[al-baab la yoghla'q] The door won't close

الباب لا يُقفَل

[al-baab la yo'qfal] The door won't lock

لقد أوصد الباب وأنا بخارج الغرفة

[la'qad o-ṣeda al-baab wa ana be kharej al-ghurfa] I have locked myself out of my room

daddy *n* [ba:ba:] **بابا**

n [buʔbuʔ] **بُؤبُؤ**

بُؤبُؤ العَيْن

[Boaboa al-'ayn] *n* pupil *(eye)*

neatly *adv* [biʔitqa:nin] **بإتقان**

v [ba:ħa] **باح**

يبوح ب

[Yabooḥ be] *v* reveal

close *adv* [biʔiħka:min] **بإحكام**

n [baxira] **باخِرَة**

باخِرَة رُكّاب

[Bakherat rokkab] *n* liner

sincerely *adv* [biʔixlasˤin] **بإخلاص**

starter *n* [ba:diʔ] **بادئ**

aubergine *n* [ba:ðinʒa:n] **باذنجان**

bar *(alcohol)* *n* [ba:r] **بار**

ساقي البار

[Sa'qey al-bar] *n* bartender

well *n* [biʔr] **بئر**

Paraguay *n* [ba:ra:ʒwa:j] **باراجواي**

شخص من باراجواي

[Shakhṣ men barajway] *n* Paraguayan

من باراجواي

[Men barajway] *adj* Paraguayan

n [ba:ra:si:ta:mu:l] **باراسيتامول**

أريد باراسيتامول

[areed barasetamol] I'd like some paracetamol

paraffin *n* [ba:ra:fi:n] **بارافين**

focus *n* [buʔra] **بؤرة**

ثنائي البؤرة

[Thonaey al-booarah] *npl* bifocals

cold *adj* [ba:rid] **بارد**

إن الطعام بارد أكثر من اللازم
[enna al-ṭa'aam bared akthar min al-laazim] The food is too cold
إن اللحم باردة
[En al-laḥm baredah] The meat is cold
الحمامات باردة
[al-doosh bared] The showers are cold
هذه الغرفة باردة أكثر من اللازم
[hathy al-ghurfa barda ak-thar min al-laazim] The room is too cold
بارز outstanding *adj* [ba:riz]
بارع skilful *adj* [ba:riʕ]
غير بارع
[gheer bare'a] *adj* unskilled
بارك bless *v* [ba:raka]
باروكة wig *n* [ba:ru:ka]
بأس *adj* [baʔs]
لا بأس
[la baas] No problem
لا بأس من أخذ الأطفال
[la baas min akhth al-aṭfaal] Is it OK to take children?
بؤس misery *n* [buʔs]
باستا pasta *n* [ba:sta:]
باستمرار *adv* [bistimrarin] continually
باسكي *n* ◁ Basque *adj* [ba:ski:] Basque *(person)*
باص *n* [ba:sˤ]
ميني باص
[Meny baas] *n* minibus
باض whitewash, bleach *v* [ba:dˤa]
باطل void *adj* [ba:tˤil]
باطني inner *adj* [ba:tˤinij]
باع sell *v* [ba:ʕa]
يَبْيع المخزون
[Yabea'a al-makhzoon] *v* sell out
يَبْيع بالتصفية
[Yabea'a bel-taṣfeyah] *v* sell off
يَبْيع بالتجزئة
[Yabea'a bel-tajzeaah] *v* retail
هل تبيع كروت التليفون؟
[hal tabee'a kroot al-talefon?] Do you sell phonecards?
باعِث incentive *n* [ba:ʕiθ]
بَاقَة bouquet *n* [ba:qa]

باكراً early *adv* [ba:kiran]
باكستان Pakistan *n* [ba:kista:n]
باكستاني Pakistani *adj* [ba:kista:nij] Pakistani *n* ◁
بال shabby *adj* [ba:lin]
بالبَيْت at home *adv* [bi-al-bajti]
بالتأكيد surely *adv* [bi-at-taʔki:di]
بالتحديد precisely *adv* [bi-at-taħdi:di]
بالتدريج gradually *adv* [bi-at-tadri:ʒi]
بالحاح instantly *adv* [bi-ilħa:ħin]
بالضرورة *adv* [bi-adˤ-dˤaru:rati] necessarily
بالغ grown-up, teenager *n* [ba:liɣ]
بالغ exaggerate *v* [ba:laɣa]
بالفعل already *adv* [bi-al-fiʕli]
بالكَاد hardly *adv* [bil-ka:di]
بالكامل completely *adv* [bialka:mili]
بالمائة per cent *adv* [biʕalmiʕati]
بالوعة sewer, washbasin *n* [ba:lu:ʕa]
بالون balloon *n* [ba:lu:n]
لبان بالون
[Leban balloon] *n* bubble gum
باليه ballet *n* [ba:li:h]
راقص باليه
[Ra'qeṣ baleeh] *n* ballet dancer
راقصة باليه
[Ra'ṣat baleeh] *n* ballerina
أين يمكنني أن أشتري تذاكر لعرض الباليه؟
[ayna yamken-any an ashtray tadhaker le-'aarḍ al-baleh?] Where can I buy tickets for the ballet?
بأمانة honestly *adv* [biʔama:nati]
بانجو *n* [ba:nʒu:]
آلة البانجو الموسيقية
[Aalat al-banjoo al-mose'qeyah] *n* banjo
بإنْصَاف fairly *adv* [bi-ʔinsˤa:fin]
باهت dim *adj* [ba:hit]
باينت pint *n* [ba:jant]
ببغاء parrot *n* [babbaɣa:ʔ]
بترول petroleum *n* [bitru:l]
بئر بترول
[Beear betrol] *n* oil well
بتسوانا Botswana *n* [butswa:na:]
بثَبات constantly *adv* [biθaba:tin]
بَثْرة pimple, blister *n* [baθra]

bajaʕa [bazaʕa] n pelican بَجَعَة

بجنون [biʒunu:nin] adv madly

بحّار [baħħa:r] n sailor

بحث [baħθ] n search

محب للبحث والتحقيق
[moḥeb lel-baḥth wal-taḥ'qeeq] adj inquisitive

بَحْث دراسي
[Bahth derasy] n research

بحث [baħaθa] v

يَبْحَث عن
[Yabḥath an] v look for, seek

إننا نبحث عن...
[ena-na nabḥath 'aan...] We're looking for...

أنا أبحث عن بطاقات بريدية
[ana abḥath 'aan beṭa-'qaat baree-diya] I'm looking for postcards

أنا أبحث هدية لطفلي
[Ana abḥath ḥadeyah leṭfley] I'm looking for a present for a child

نحن نبحث عن أحد الفنادق
[naḥno nabḥath 'aan aḥad al-fanadi'q] We're looking for a hotel

بحر [baħr] n sea

ساحل البحر
[saḥel al-baḥr] n seaside

عبر البحار
['abr al-behar] adv overseas

البحر الأحمر
[Al-bahr al-ahmar] n Red Sea

البحر الشمالي
[Al-baḥr al-Shamaley] n North Sea

البحر الكاريبي
[Al-baḥr al-kareebey] n Caribbean

البحر المتوسط
[Al-bahr al-motawaseṭ] n Mediterranean

مستوى سطح البحر
[Mostawa saṭh al-bahr] n sea level

مياه البحر
[Meyah al-baḥr] n sea water

أريد غرفة تطل على البحر
[areed ghurfa ta-ṭul 'aala al-baḥir] I'd like a room with a view of the sea

أعاني من دوار البحر
[o-'aany min dawaar al-baḥar] I get travel-sick

هل تظهر هنا قناديل البحر؟
[hal taḍhhar huna 'qana-deel al-baḥir?] Are there jellyfish here?

هل البحر مرتفع اليوم؟
[hal al-baḥr murta-fi'a al-yawm?] Is the sea rough today?

بحري [baħrij] adj maritime, naval

رحلة بحرية
[Rehalh bahreyah] n cruise

جندي بحري
[Jondey baharey] n seaman

الأطعمة البحرية
[Al-aṭ'aemah al-baḥareyh] n seafood

بحزم [biħazmin] adv strictly

بحَق [biħaqqin] adv truly

بُحَيْرة [buħajra] n lake, lagoon

بحيوية [biħajawijjatin] adj lively

بَخّاخ [baxxa:x] n inhaler

بُخَار [buxa:r] n steam

بَخْس [baxs] adj inexpensive

بَخيل [baxi:l] adj miser

بدا [bada:] v seem

بَدْء [badʔ] n start

بدأ [badaʔa] v begin, start

يَبْدأ الحركة والنشاط
[Yabdaa alḥarakah wal-nashaṭ] v start off

متى يبدأ العرض؟
[mata yabda al-'aarḍ?] When does the performance begin?

متى يبدأ العمل هنا؟
[mata yabda al-'aamal huna?] When does it begin?

بدائي [bida:ʔij] adj primitive

بداخل [bida:xili] prep into

بداية [bida:ja] n beginning

في بداية شهر يونيو
[fee bedayat shaher yon-yo] at the beginning of June

بَدد [baddada] v squander, waste

بَدْر [badr] n full moon

بدروم [bidru:m] n basement

بدل [baddala] v

أين أستطيع أن أبدل ملابسي؟
[ayna astaṭe'a an abid-il mala-bisy]

Where do I change?
هل يمكن أن أبدل الغرف
[hal yamken an abad-il al-ghuraf?] Can I switch rooms?
alter, transform *v* [baddala] **بَدّل**
instead of *prep* [badalan] **بدلا**
بدلًا من ذلك
[Badalan men ḍhalek] *adv* instead of that
fancy dress, outfit *n* [badla] **بدلة**
بدلة تدريب
[Badlat tadreeb] *n* tracksuit
بدلة العمل
[Badlat al-'aamal] *n* overalls
بدلة الغوص
[Badlat al-ghawṣ] *n* wetsuit
physical *adj* [badanij] **بدني**
عقوبة بدنية
['ao'qoba badaneyah] *n* corporal punishment
without *prep* [bidu:ni] **بدون**
بدون توقف
[Bedon tawa'qof] *adv* non-stop
magnificent *adj* [badi:ʕ] **بديع**
alternative *n* [badi:l] **بديل**
fat *n* ◁ obese *adj* [badi:n] **بَدِين**
seed *n* [biðra] **بِذرة**
suit *n* [baðla] **بَذلة**
بذلة غامقة اللون للرجال
[Badlah ghame'qah al-loon lel-rejal] *n* tuxedo
innocent *adj* [bari:ʔ] **بريء**
n ◁ Brazilian *adj* [bara:zi:lij] **برازيلي** Brazilian
flower *n* [bara:ʕim] **براعم**
براعم الورق
[Bra'aem al-wara'q] *n* sprouts
software *n* [bara:miʒ] **برامج**
brandy *n* [bra:ndi:] **براندي**
سأتناول براندي
[sa-ata-nawal brandy] I'll have a brandy
Portuguese *adj* [burtuɣa:lij] **برتغالي**
Portuguese *(person)* *n* ◁
اللغة البرتغالية
[Al-loghah al-bortoghaleyah] *(language)* *n* Portuguese

orange *(fruit)* *n* [burtuqa:l] **برتقال**
عصير برتقال
[Aṣeer borto'qaal] *n* orange juice
orange *n* [burtuqa:la] **برتقالة**
orange *adj* [burtuqa:lij] **برتقالي**
Puerto *n* [burtu: ri:ku:] **برتو ريكو** Rico
tower *n* [burʒ] **برج**
برج محصن
[Borj mohaṣṣan] *n* dungeon
بُرج كهرباء
[Borj kahrbaa] *n* pylon
بُرْج الكنيسة
[Borj al-kaneesah] *n* steeple
cold *n* [bard] **برد**
أريد شيئًا للبرد
[areed shyan lel-bard] I'd like something for a cold
أعاني من البرد
[o-'aany min al-barid] I have a cold
أشعر بالبرد
[ash-'aur bil-bard] I'm cold
v [brada] **برد**
يبرد بمبرد
[Yobared bemobared] *v* file *(smoothing)*
chill *v* [barrada] **برّد**
n [bardaqu:ʃ] **بَرْدَقوش**
عُشب البَرْدَقُوش
['aoshb al-barda'qoosh] *n* marjoram
account for *v* [barara] **برر**
v [baroza] **برُز**
يَبْرُز من
[Yabroz men] *v* come out
jar *n* [bartˤama:n] **برطمان**
flea *n* [barɣu:θ] **برغوث**
lightning *n* [barq] **بَرْق**
plum, prune *n* [barqu:q] **برقوق**
volcano *n* [burka:n] **بركان**
volcanic *adj* [burka:nijjat] **بركانية**
الحمم البركانية
[Al-ḥemam al-borkaneyah] *n* lava
pond, puddle *n* [birka] **بِرْكَة**
parliament *n* [barlama:n] **بَرلمان**
programme *v* [barmaʒ] **بَرمج**
programming *n* [barmaʒa] **برمجة**
barrel *n* [birmi:l] **برميل**

برنامج programme, *n* [barnaːmaʒ] *(computer)* programme
برنامج حواري
[Barnamaj hewary] *n* chat show
بَرْهن demonstrate *v* [barhana]
بروتستانتي *adj* [bruːtistaːntij] Protestant
Protestant *n* ◁
بروتين protein *n* [bruːtiːn]
برودة cold *n* [buruːda]
شديد البرودة
[Shadeedat al-broodah] *adj* freezing
بروش brooch *n* [bruːʃ]
بروفة rehearsal, test *n* [bruːfa]
بروكسيل *n* [bruːksiːl]
كرنب بروكسيل
[Koronb brokseel] *n* Brussels sprouts
برونز bronze *n* [bruːnz]
بري wild *adj* [barrij]
بريد post *n* [bariːd]
صندوق البريد
[Ṣondo'q bareed] *n* postbox
عنوان البريد الإلكتروني
['aonwan al-bareed al-electrooney] *n* email address
بريد غير مرغوب
[Bareed gheer marghoob] *n* junk mail
بريد جوي
[Bareed jawey] *n* airmail
بريد الكتروني
[Bareed elektrooney] *n* email
يُرْسِل بريدا إلكترونيا
[Yorsel bareedan electroneyan] *v* email
ما المدة التي يستغرقها بالبريد العادي؟
[ma al-mudda al-laty yasta-ghru'qoha bil-bareed al-al-'aadee?] How long will it take by normal post?
بريدي postal *adj* [bariːdij]
نظام بريدي
[nedham bareedey] *n* post *(mail)*
هل يمكن أن أحصل على طوابع لأربعة كروت بريدية؟
[hal yamken an aḥṣal 'aala ṭawa-bi'a le-arba'aat kiroot baree-diya?] Can I have stamps for four postcards to...

بريطاني British *adj* [briːtˤaːnij]
British *n* ◁
بريطانيا Britain *n* [briːtˤaːnjaː]
بريطانيا العظمى
[Beretanyah al-'aoḍhma] *n* Great Britain
بستان orchard *n* [bustaːn]
بُستاني gardener *n* [bustaːnij]
بَسْتَنة gardening *n* [bastana]
بسِط unroll *v* [basitˤa]
بَسَط simplify *v* [basatˤa]
بسكويت biscuit *n* [baskawiːt]
بسِلّة peas *n* [bisalati]
بَسَلّة mangetout *n* [bisallatin]
بَسهولة easily *adv* [bisuhuːlatin]
بسيط plain, simple *adj* [basiːtˤ]
ببساطة
[Bebasata] *adv* simply
بشر *v* [baʃara] (يحك بسطح خشن) grate
بَشرَة complexion *n* [baʃra]
بشري human *adj* [baʃarijjat]
قوة بشرية
['qowah bashareyah] *n* manpower
بشرية mankind *n* [baʃarijja]
بَشِع hideous *adj* [baʃiʕ]
بُصاق spit *n* [busˤaːq]
بصِدق faithfully *adv* [bisˤidqin]
بصر vision *n* [basˤar]
أعاني من ضعف البصر
[o-'aany min ḍu'auf al-baṣar] I'm visually impaired
بصري visual *adj* [basˤarij]
بصق spit *v* [bsˤaqa]
بصل onion *n* [basˤal]
بصل أخضر
[Baṣal akhdar] *n* spring onion
بصلة *n* [basˤala]
بصلة النبات
[baṣalat al-nabat] *n* bulb *(electricity)*
بصمة imprint *n* [basˤma]
بصمة الإصبع
[Baṣmat al-eṣba'a] *n* fingerprint
بصمة كربونية
[Baṣma karbonyah] *n* carbon footprint
بضائع goods *npl* [badˤaːʔiʕun]
بطء slowness *n* [butˤʔ]

ببطء
[Beboṭa] *adv* slowly
هل يمكن أن تتحدث ببطء أكثر إذا سمحت؟
[hal yamken an tata-ḥadath be-buṭi akthar edha samaḥt?] Could you speak more slowly, please?
بطارية battery *n* [batˤtˤaːrijja]
أريد بطارية جديدة
[areed baṭaariya jadeeda] I need a new battery
هل لديك أي بطاريات كهربية لهذه الكاميرا؟
[hal ladyka ay baṭa-reyaat le-hadhy al-kamera?] Do you have batteries for this camera?
بطاطس potato *n* [batˤaːtˤis]
بطاطس بالفرن
[Baṭaṭes bel-forn] *npl* jacket potato
بطاطس مشوية بقشرها
[Baṭaṭes mashweiah be'qshreha] *n* jacket potato
بطاطس مهروسة
[Baṭaṭes mahrosah] *n* mashed potatoes
شرائح البطاطس
[Sharaeh al- baṭaṭes] *npl* crisps
بطاقة card *n* [bitˤaːqa]
بطاقة عضوية
[Beṭaqat 'aodweiah] *n* membership card
بطاقة تهنئة
[Beṭaqat tahneaa] *n* greetings card
بطاقة بريدية
[Beṭaqah bareedyah] *n* postcard
بطاقة شخصية
[beṭ a'qah shakhṣeyah] *n* identity card, ID card
بطاقة لعب
[Beṭaqat la'aeb] *n* playing card
لقد سرقت بطاقتي
[la'qad sore'qat be-ṭa'qaty] My card has been stolen
هل لديك بطاقة تجارية؟
[hal ladyka beṭa'qa tejar-eya?] Do you have a business card?
هل يتم قبول بطاقات الخصم؟
[hal yatum 'qubool be-ṭa'qaat al-khaṣim?] Do you take debit cards?
هل يمكنني الدفع ببطاقة الائتمان؟
[hal yamken -any al-daf'a be- beṭa-'qat al-etemaan?] Can I pay by credit card?
هل يمكنني الحصول على سلفه نقدية ببطاقة الائتمان الخاصة بي؟
[hal yamken -any al-ḥuṣool 'aala silfa na'qdiya be- beṭa-'qat al-etemaan al-khaṣa bee?] Can I get a cash advance with my credit card?
بطالة unemployment *n* [bitˤaːla]
بَطَالة *n* [batˤaːla]
إعانة بَطَالة
[E'anat baṭalah] *n* dole
بطَانَة lining *n* [batˤaːna]
بَطانية blanket *n* [batˤaːnijja]
بطانية كهربائية
[Baṭaneyah kahrobaeyah] *n* electric blanket
من فضلك أريد بطانية إضافية
[min faḍlak areed baṭa-nya eḍa-fiya] Please bring me an extra blanket
بطة duck *n* [batˤtˤa]
بطريق penguin *n* [bitˤriːq]
بطل champion *(competition)*, *n* [batˤal] hero *(novel)*
بَطَلة heroine *n* [batˤala]
بطن stomach *n* [batˤn]
سُرَّة البطن
[Sorrat al-batn] *n* belly button
بَطنِيّ coeliac *adj* [batˤnij]
بطولة championship *n* [butˤuːla]
بَطيءٌ slow *adj* [batˤiːʔ]
بِطيخة watermelon *n* [batˤiːxa]
بَعَث *v* [baʕaθa]
يبْعَث ب
[Yab'ath be] *v* send
يَبعث ب
[Tab'aath be] *v* send out
يَبْعَثُ رائِحَة
[Yab'ath raeḥah] *vi* smell
بِعْثَة expedition *n* [biʕθa]
بَعد after, *prep* ◁ after *conj* [baʕda] besides
بَعْد ذلك
[Ba'ad dhalek] *adv* afterwards

بَعْدَما
[Ba'dama] *prep* after
بعد الميلاد
[Ba'ad al-meelad] *abbr* AD
فيما بعد
[Feema baad] *adv* later
بُعْد [buʕd] *n* dimension
عن بُعْد
['an bo'ad] *adv* remotely
بعض [baʕdˤu] *adj* few, some
أي يمكن أن أشتري بعض البطاقات البريدية؟
[ʔajji jumkinu ʔan ʔaʃtari: baʕdˤa albitˤa:qa:ti albari:dijjati] Where can I buy some postcards?
هناك بعض الأشخاص المصابين
[hunaka ba'aḍ al-ash-khaaṣ al-muṣabeen] There are some people injured
بعمق [biʕumqin] *adv* deeply
بعوضة [baʕu:dˤa] *n* mosquito
بعيد [baʕi:d] *adj* distant, far, out
المسافة ليست بعيدة
[al-masaafa laysat ba'aeeda] It's not far
هل المسافة بعيدة؟
[hal al-masafa ba'aeda?] Is it far?
بعيدا [baʕi:dan] *adv* off, away
بغبغاء [babbaɣa:ʔ] *n* budgerigar, budgie
بغِض [buɣdˤ] *n* hatred
بغْض [baɣadˤa] *v* hate
بَغل [baɣl] *n* mule
بغيض [baɣi:dˤ] *adj* obnoxious
بفظاظة [bifazˤa:zˤatin] *adv* grossly
بفعالية [bifaʕa:lijjatin] *adv* effectively
بَقّاء [baqa:ʔ] *n* survival
بَقّال [baqqa:l] *n* grocer
بقالة [baqa:la] *n* groceries
بَقايا [baqa:ja:] *npl* remains
بقِة [baqqa] *n* bug
بَقدونِس [baqdu:nis] *n* parsley
بقر [baqar] *n* cattle
راعى البقر
[Ra'aey al-ba'qar] *n* cowboy
بقرة [baqara] *n* cow

بُقسماط [buqsuma:tˤ] *n*
بُقسماط مطحون
[Bo'qsomat maṭḥoon] *n* breadcrumbs
بُقْسُماط [buqsuma:tˤin] *n* rusk
بقشيش [baqʃi:ʃan] *n* tip
يمنح بقشيشاً
[Yamnaḥ ba'qsheeshan] *vt* tip *(reward)*
هل من المعتاد إعطاء بقشيش؟
[hal min al-mu'a-taad e'aṭaa ba'q-sheesh?] Is it usual to give a tip?
بقع [buqaʕ] *n* stain
مزيل البقع
[Mozeel al-bo'qa,a] *n* stain remover
بُقْعَة [wasˤma] *n* spot *(blemish)*
بقِي [baqa:] *v* remain
بُكَاء [buka:ʔ] *n* cry
بكتريا [baktirja:] *npl* bacteria
قابل للتحلل بالبكتريا
['qabel lel-tahalol bel-bekteriya] *n* biodegradable
بَكَرَة [bakara] *n* reel
بكسل [biksil] *n* pixel
بَكفاءة [bikafa:ʔatin] *adv* efficiently
بكين [biki:n] *n* Beijing
بلاتين [bla:ti:n] *n* platinum
بلاستيك [bla:sti:k] *n* plastic
بلاستيكي [bla:sti:kij] *adj* plastic
كيس بلاستيكي
[Kees belasteekey] *n* plastic bag
بلاط [bala:tˤ] *n*
بلاط القصر
[Balaṭ al-'qaṣr] *n* court
بلاك بيري® [bla:k bi:ri:] *n* BlackBerry®
بلايستيشن® [bla:jsiti:ʃn] *n* PlayStation®
بلجيكا [bilʒi:ka:] *n* Belgium
بلجيكي [bilʒi:kij] *adj* Belgian ◁ *n* Belgian
بلد [balad] *n* country, city, village
بَلَد نام
[Baladen namen] *n* developing country
ما هي أجرة التاكسي داخل البلد؟
[ma heya ejrat al-taxi dakhil al-balad?] How much is the taxi fare into town?
ما هي المسافة بيننا وبين وسط البلد؟

[ma heya al-masafa bay-nana wa bayn waṣaṭ al-balad?] How far are we from the town centre?
town *n* [balda] **بلدة**
هل يوجد لديكم أي شيء يحمل طابع هذه البلدة؟
[hal yujad laday-kum ay shay yaḥmil ṭabi'a hadhy al-balda?] Have you anything typical of this town?
native *adj* [baladij] **بلدي**
axe *n* [baltˤa] **بَلْطَة**
bully *n* [baltˤaʒij] **بلطجي**
gently *adv* [bilutˤfin] **بلطف**
swallow *vt* [balaʕa] **بلع**
v [balaɣa] **بلغ**
كم يبلغ سعر ذلك؟
[kam yablugh si'ar thalik?] How much does that come to?
كم يبلغ عمق المياه؟
[kam yablugh 'aom'q al-meah?] How deep is the water?
كم يبلغ ثمن تذكرة الذهاب فقط؟
[Kam yablogh thaman tadhkarat aldhehab fa'qaṭ?] How much is a single ticket?
كم يبلغ البقشيش الذي علي أن أدفعه؟
[Kam yablogh al-ba'qsheesh aladhey 'alay an adfa'aoh?] How much should I give as a tip?
كم يبلغ زمن العرض؟
[kam yablugh zamin al-'aarḍ?] How long does the performance last?
كم يبلغ طولك؟
[kam yablugh ṭoolak?] How tall are you?
كم يبلغ وزنك؟
[kam yablugh waznak?] How much do you weigh?
reach *v* [balaɣa] **بلّغ**
Bulgarian *adj* [balɣa:ri:] **بلغاري**
◁ Bulgarian *(person) n*
اللغة البلغارية
[Al-loghah al-balghareyah] *(language) n* Bulgarian
Bulgaria *n* [bulɣa:rja:] **بلغاريا**
Balkan *adj* [balqa:nij] **بلقاني**
drench *v* [balala] **بَلل**

crystal *n* [billawr] **بُلّور**
blouse *n* [blu:za] **بلوزة**
oak *n* [ballu:tˤ] **بَلوط**
sweater *n* [bulu:far] **بلوفر**
n [bilaja:rdu:] **بلياردو**
لعبة البلياردو
[Lo'abat al-belyardo] *n* billiards
blazer *n* [blajzir] **بليزر**
coffee *n* [bunn] **بن**
حبوب البن
[Ḥobob al-bon] *n* coffee bean
building *n* [bina:ʔ] **بناء**
بناء على
[Benaa ala] *adv* accordingly
موقع البناء
[Maw'qe'a al-benaa] *n* building site
bricklayer, builder *n* [banna:ʔ] **بنَّاء**
◁ constructive *adj*
block *(buildings) n* [bina:ja] **بِنَايَة**
بِنَايَة عالية
[Benayah 'aaleyah] *n* high-rise
lass *n* [bint] **بَنْت**
بَنْت الأخت
[Bent al-okht] *n* niece
successfully *adv* [binaʒa:ħin] **بنجاح**
beetroot *n* [banʒar] **بنجر**
Bangladesh *n* [banʒla:di:ʃ] **بنجلاديش**
adj [banʒla:di:ʃij] **بنجلاديشي** Bangladeshi
◁ Bangladeshi *n*
n [banʒu:] **بنجو**
لعبة البنجو
[Lo'abat al-benjo] *n* bingo
item *n* [bund] **بَنْد**
panda *n* [banda:] **بَندَا**
gun, rifle *n* [bunduqijja] **بندقية**
بندقية رش
[Bonde'qyat rash] *n* shotgun
petrol *n* [binzi:n] **بنزين**
خزان بنزين
[Khazan benzeen] *n* petrol tank
بنزين خالي من الرصاص
[Benzene khaly men al- raṣaṣ] *n* unleaded petrol
محطة بنزين
[Mahaṭat benzene] *n* petrol station

بنسلين penicillin *n* [binisili:n]
بنطلون trousers *npl* [bantˤalu:n]
بنطلون صيق
[Banṭaloon ṣaye'q] *npl* leggings
بنطلون ضيق
[banṭaloon ḍaye'q] *n* tights
بنطلون قصير
[Banṭaloon 'qaṣeer] *npl* trunks
حمالات البنطلون
[Hammalaat al- banṭaloon] *npl* suspenders
هل يمكن أن أجرب هذا البنطلون؟
[hal yamken an ajar-reb hadha al-ban-taloon?] Can I try on these trousers?
بنفسجي mauve *adj* [banafsaʒij]
بنك bank *(finance) n* [bank]
بنك تجاري
[Bank Tejarey] *n* merchant bank
موظف بنك
[mowaḍhaf bank] *n* banker
ما هي المسافة بينا وبين البنك؟
[Ma heya al-masafa bayna wa been al-bank?] How far is the bank?
هل يوجد بنك هنا؟
[hal yujad bank huna?] Is there a bank here?
بنكي *adj* [bankij]
حساب بنكي
[Hesab bankey] *n* bank account
كشف بنكي
[Kashf bankey] *n* bank statement
مصاريف بنكية
[Maṣareef Bankeyah] *npl* bank charges
بنما Panama *n* [banama:]
بني build *vt* [bana:]
بُنِّي brown *adj* [bunnij]
بِنْيَة structure *n* [binja]
بِنْيَة أساسية
[Benyah asaseyah] *n* infrastructure
بهجة delight, joy *n* [bahʒa]
بهدوء quietly *adv* [bihudu:ʔin]
بهيج jolly, merry *adj* [bahi:ʒ]
بواب doorman *n* [bawwa:b]
بوابة gate *n* [bawwa:ba]
بوابة متحركة
[Bawabah motaharekah] *n* turnstile
بواسطة by *prep* [biwa:sitˤati]
بودرة powder *n* [bu:dra]
بودكاست podcast *n* [bu:dka:st]
بودل *n* [bu:dal]
كلب البودل
[Kalb al-boodel] *n* poodle
بودينج *n* [bu:di:nʒ]
حلوى البودينج
[Ḥalwa al-boodenj] *n* sweet
بوذا Buddha *n* [bu:ða:]
بوذي *n* ◁ Buddhist *adj* [bu:ðij] ▷ Buddhist
بورما Burma *n* [bu:rma:]
بورمي *n* ◁ Burmese *adj* [bu:rmij] Burmese *(person)*
اللغة البورمية
[Al-loghah al-bormeyah] *(language) n* Burmese
بوسني Bosnian *(person) n* [bu:snij]
بوصة inch *n* [bawsˤa]
بوصلة compass *n* [bawsˤala]
بوضوح clearly *adv* [biwudˤu:ħin]
بوفيه sideboard *n* [bu:fi:h]
عربة البوفيه
['arabat al-boofeeh] *n* dining car
بوق trumpet, cornet, horn *n* [bu:q]
بوكر *n* [bu:kar]
لُعبَة البوكَر
[Lo'abat al-bookar] *n* poker
بُوْل urine *n* [bawl]
بولندة Poland *n* [bu:landat]
بولندي *n* ◁ Polish *adj* [bu:landij] Pole, Polish
بولنسي Polynesian *adj* [bu:linisij]
بوليصة *n* [bu:li:sˤa]
بوليصة تأمين
[Booleeṣat taameen] *n* insurance policy
بوليفي *n* ◁ Bolivian *adj* [bu:li:fij] Bolivian
بوليفيا Bolivia *n* [bu:lijfja:]
بولينسيا Polynesia *n* [bu:li:nisja:]
بولينيسي Polynesian *n* [bu:li:ni:sij] *(person)*
اللغة البولينيسية
[Al- loghah al-bolenseyah] *(language) n*

Polynesian
بومة owl *n* [buːma]
بيئة environment *n* [biːʔit]
صديق للبيئة
[Ṣadeek al-beeaah] *adj* environmentally friendly
علم البيئة
['aelm al-beeah] *n* ecology
البيئة المُحِيطة
[Al- beeaah almoheeṭah] *npl* surroundings
بيأس desperately *adv* [bijaʔsin]
بياضات bedding *npl* [bajjaːdˤaːtun]
بياضات الأسرّة
[Bayaḍat al-aserah] *n* bed linen
بيان account (بالأسباب) *n* [bajaːn] *(report)*
بيانات data *npl* [bajaːnaːtun]
بيانو piano *n* [bijaːnuː]
لاعب البيانو
[La'aeb al-beyano] *n* pianist
بيئي ecological, *adj* [biːʔij] environmental
بيت house *n* [bajt]
أهل البيت
[Ahl al-bayt] *n* household
بيت من طابق واحد
[Bayt men ṭabe'q wahed] *n* bungalow
بيتزا pizza *n* [biːtzaː]
بيجْ beige *n* [biːʒ]
بِيجامة pyjamas *n* [biːʒaːma]
بيرة beer *n* [biːra]
مصنع البيرة
[maṣna'a al-beerah] *n* brewery
كأس آخر من البيرة
[kaas aakhar min al-beera] another beer
بيرو Peru *n* [biːruː]
بيرو® Biro® *n* [biːruː]
بيروفي *n* ◁ Peruvian *adj* [biːruːfij] Peruvian
بيروقراطية *n* [biːruːqraːtˤijjati] bureaucracy
بيريه beret *n* [biːriːh]
بيسبول baseball *adj* [biːsbuːl]
بيض egg *n* [bajdˤ]
بيض عيد الفصح
[Bayḍ 'aeed al-feṣh] *n* Easter egg
بيض مخفوق
[Bayḍ makhfou'q] *n* scrambled eggs
لا أستطيع تناول البيض النيئ
[la astạ-ṯee'a ta-nawil al-bayḍ al-nee] I can't eat raw eggs
بيضة egg *n* [bajdˤa]
صفار البيض
[Ṣafar al-bayḍ] *n* egg yolk
بيضة مسلوقة
[Bayḍah maslo'qah] *n* boiled egg
بياض البيض
[Bayaḍ al-bayḍ] *n* egg white
كأس البيضة
[Kaas al-bayḍah] *n* eggcup
بيضوي oval *adj* [bajdˤawij]
بيع sale *n* [bajʕ]
الأكثر مبيعا
[Al-akthar mabe'aan] *adj* bestseller
بيع بالتجزئة
[Bay'a bel- tajzeaah] *n* retail
بيع بالجملة
[Bay'a bel-jomlah] *n* wholesale
طاولة بيع
[Ṭawelat bey'a] *n* counter
بِيع *v* [beeːʕa]
أين تُباع التذاكر؟
[ayna tuba'a al-tadhaker?] Where can I get tickets?, Where do I buy a ticket?
بيكيني bikini *n* [biːkiːniː]
بيلاروسي Belarussian, *n* [biːlaːruːsij] Belarussian *(person)*
اللغة البيلاروسية
[Al-loghah al-belaroseyah] *(language) n* Belarussian
بين between *prep* [bajna]
بينما
[bajnamaː] *conj* as
بينما while, *conj* [bajnamaː] whereas, as
بينما
[bajnamaː] *conj* as
بيوتر *n* [bijuːtar]
سبيكة البيوتر
[Sabeekat al-beyooter] *n* pewter

biological *adj* [bju:lu:ʒij] **بيولوجي**
بيولوجي إحصائي
[Bayology ehṢaey] *adj* biometric
biology *n* [bju:lu:ʒja:] **بيولوجيا**

lost *adj* [ta:ʔih] **تائه**
following *n* [ta:biʕa] **تابع**
شركة تابعة
[Sharekah tabe'ah] *n* subsidiary
coffin, box, case *n* [ta:bu:t] **تابوت**
impact *n* [taʔθi:r] **تأثير**
crown *n* [ta:ʒ] **تاج**
dealer *n* [ta:ʒir] **تاجر**
تاجر الأسماك
[Tajer al-asmak] *n* fishmonger
تاجر مخدرات
[Tajer mokhaddrat] *n* drug dealer
rental, lease *n* [taʔʒi:r] **تأجير**
تأجير سيارة
[Taajeer sayarah] *n* car rental
هل تقومون بتأجير أجهزة DVD؟
[Hal ta'qomoon betaajeer ajhezat DVD?]
Do you rent DVDs?
هل يمكن تأجير عربات للأطفال؟
[hal yamken ta-jeer 'aarabat lil-aṭfaal?]
Do you hire push-chairs?
delay *n* [taʔʒi:l] **تأجيل**
لقد تم تأجيل موعد الرحلة
[la'qad tum-a ta-jeel maw-'aid al-reḥla]
The flight has been delayed
delay *v* [taʔaxxara] **تأخر**
يتأخر في النوم في الصباح

[Yataakhar fee al-nawm fee al-ṣabah] *v* sleep in

هل تأخر القطار عن الموعد المحدد؟

[hal ta-akhar al-'qiṭaar 'aan al-maw'aid al-muḥadad?] Is the train running late?

تأخير delay *n* [taʔxi:r]

تأديب discipline *n* [taʔdi:b]

تأرجح rock *v* [taʔarʒaħa]

تَأرْجُح swing *n* [taʔarʒuħ]

تاريخ date, history *n* [ta:ri:x]

تاريخ الانتهاء

[Tareekh al-entehaa] *n* expiry date

متعلق بما قبل التاريخ

[Mota'ale'q bema 'qabl al-tareekh] *adj* prehistoric

يُفضل استخدامه قبل التاريخ المُحدد

[Yofaḍḍal estekhdamoh 'qabl al-tareekh al-mohaddad] *adj* best-before date

ما هو التاريخ؟

[ma howa al-tareekh?] What is the date?

تاريخي historical *adj* [ta:ri:xij]

تاسع ninth *n* ◁ ninth *adj* [ta:siʕ]

تأشيرة visa *n* [taʔʃi:ra]

لدي تأشيرة دخول

[la-daya ta-sherat dikhool] I have an entry visa

هذه هي التأشيرة

[hathy heya al-taa-sheera] Here is my visa

تافه trivial, rubbish, *adj* [ta:fih] trifle *n* ◁ ridiculous, vain

تاكسي taxi *n* [ta:ksi:]

موقف سيارات تاكسي

[Maw'qaf sayarat taksy] *n* taxi rank

أنا في حاجة إلى تاكسي

[ana fee ḥaja ela taxi] I need a taxi

أين يمكن استقلال التاكسي؟

[Ayn yomken este'qlal al-taksey?] Where can I get a taxi?

لقد تركت حقائبي في التاكسي

[la'qad ta-rakto ḥa'qa-eby fee al-taxi] I left my bags in the taxi

من فضلك احجز لي تاكسي

[min faḍlak iḥjiz lee taxi] Please order me a taxi

تأكيد confirmation *n* [taʔki:d]

بكل تأكيد

[Bekol taakeed] *adv* absolutely, definitely

تالٍ next *adv* [ta:lin]

تَألّف *v* [taʔallafa]

يَتَألف من

[Yataalaf men] consist of

تالي further, next *adj* [ta:li:]

متى سنتوقف في المرة التالية؟

[mata sa-nata-wa'qaf fee al-murra al-taleya?] When do we stop next?

ما هو الموعد التالي للأتوبيس المتجه إلى...؟

[ma howa al-maw'aid al-taaly lel-baaṣ al-mutajeh ela...?] When is the next bus to...?

ما هو موعد القطار التالي من فضلك؟

[ma howa maw-'aid al-'qeṭaar al-taaly min faḍlak?] The next available train, please

تام perfect *adj* [ta:mm]

تآمر plot *(secret plan)* *v* [taʔa:mara]

تَأمل speculate *v* [taʔammala]

تَأمُّل meditation *n* [taʔammul]

تأمين insurance *n* [taʔmi:n]

تأمين سيارة

[Taameen sayarah] *n* car insurance

تأمين ضد الحوادث

[Taameen ḍed al-hawaadeth] *n* accident insurance

تأمين على الحياة

[Taameen 'ala al-hayah] *n* life insurance

تأمين السفر

[Taameen al-safar] *n* travel insurance

تأمين عن الطرف الثالث

[Tameen lada algheer] *n* third-party insurance

بوليصة تأمين

[Booleeṣat taameen] *n* insurance policy

شهادة تأمين

[Shehadat taameen] *n* insurance certificate

أحتاج إلى إيصال لأجل التأمين

[aḥtaaj ela eṣaal leajl al-taameen] I need a receipt for the insurance

تفضل هذه هي بيانات التأمين الخاص بي
[Tafaḍal hadheh heya beyanaat altaameen alkhaṣ bee] Here are my insurance details
لدي تأمين صحي خاص
[la-daya ta-meen ṣiḥy khaṣ] I have private health insurance
ليس لدي تأمين في السفر
[laysa la-daya ta-meen lel-safar] I don't have travel insurance
هل ستدفع لك شركة التأمين مقابل ذلك
[hal sa-tadfaa laka share-kat al-tameen ma'qabil dhalik?] Will the insurance pay for it?
هل لديك تأمين؟
[hal ladyka ta-meen?] Do you have insurance?
تانزاني [ta:nza:nij] *adj* Tanzanian ◁ *n* Tanzanian
تَأَنق [taʔannaqa] *v* dress up
تاهيتي [ta:hi:ti:] *n* Tahiti
تايبِسْت [ta:jbist] *n* typist
تايلاند [ta:jla:nd] *n* Thailand
تايلاندي [ta:jla:ndij] *adj* Thai ◁ *n* Thai *(person)*
اللغة التايلاندية
[Al-logha al-taylandeiah] *(language) n* Thai
تايوان [ta:jwa:n] *n* Taiwan
تايواني [ta:jwa:nij] *adj* Taiwanese ◁ *n* Taiwanese
تَبَادل [taba:dala] *v* exchange
تَبَاهى [taba:ha:] *v* boast
تباين [taba:jun] *n* contrast
تبديل [tabdi:l] *n* change, substitute
أين غرف تبديل الملابس؟
[ayna ghuraf tabdeel al-malabis?] Where are the clothes lockers?
تَبْرع [tabarraʕa] *v* donate
تبعيَّات [tabaʕijja:t] *n* repercussions
تبغ [tibɣ] *n* tobacco
تبن [tibn] *n* hay
تَبَنّي [tabanni:] *n* adoption
تَبَنى [tabanna:] *v* (يُقر) adopt

تبين [tabajjana] *v* figure out
تَتَبع [tatabbaʕa] *v* track down
تَثَاءب [taθa:ʔaba] *v* yawn
تثقيفي [taθqi:fij] *adj* informative
تجارب [taʒa:rib] *n* experiment
حقل للتجارب
[Ha'ql lel-tajareb] *n* guinea pig *(for experiment)*
تجارة [tiʒa:ra] *n* trade
تجارة الكترونية
[Tejarah elektroneyah] *n* e-commerce
تجاري [tiʒa:rij] *adj* commercial
إعلان تجارى
[E'alaan tejarey] *n* commercial
أعمال تجارية
[A'amaal tejareyah] *n* business
فاتورة تجارية
[Fatoorah tejareyah] *n* invoice
ما هو موعد إغلاق المحلات التجارية؟
[ma howa maw-'aid eghla'q al-maḥalat al-tejar-iya?] What time do the shops close?
تجَاه [tiʒa:ha] *adv* opposite
تَجاهل [taʒa:hala] *v* ignore
تجاوز [taʒa:waza] *v* pass *(on road)*, go past
تجديد [taʒdi:d] *n*
ممكن تجديده
[Momken tajdedoh] *adj* renewable
تجديف [taʒdi:f] *n* canoeing, rowing
أين يمكن أن أمارس رياضة التجديف بالقوارب الصغيرة؟
[ayna yamken an omares riyaḍat al-tajdeef bil- 'qawareb al-ṣaghera?] Where can we go canoeing?
أين يمكننا أن نذهب للتجديف؟
[ʔajna jumkinuna: ʔan naðhabu littaʒdi:fi] Where can we go rowing?
تجربة [taʒriba] *n* experiment, try
تجربة إيضاحية
[Tajrebah eeḍaheyah] *n* demo
تجسس [taʒassus] *n* spying
تَجسس [taʒassasa] *vi* spy
تجشأ [taʒaʃʃaʔa] *vi* burp
تَجَشؤ [taʒaʃʃuʔ] *n* burp
تجعيد [taʒʕi:d] *n* wrinkle

ماكينة تجعيد الشعر
[Makeenat taj'aeed sha'ar] *n* curler
تجفيف drying *n* [taʒfi:f]
تجفيف الشعر
[Tajfeef al-saha'ar] *n* blow-dry
لوحة تجفيف
[Lawhat tajfeef] *n* draining board
هل يمكنك من فضلك تجفيفه؟
[hal yamken -aka min faḍlak taj-fefaho?] Can you dye my hair, please?
هل يوجد مكان ما لتجفيف الملابس؟
[hal yujad makan ma le-tajfeef al-malabis?] Is there somewhere to dry clothes?
تجمد freezing *n* [taʒammud]
مانع للتجمد
[Mane'a lel-tajamod] *n* antifreeze
تَجمد freeze *vi* [taʒammada]
تجمع meeting *n* [taʒammuʕ]
متى يحين موعد التجمع؟
[mata yaḥeen maw'aid al-tajamu'a?] When is mass?
تجميل *n* [taʒmi:l]
جراحة تجميل
[Jerahat tajmeel] *n* plastic surgery
مستحضرات التجميل
[Mostahdraat al-tajmeel] *n* make-up
تجميلي cosmetic *adj* [taʒmi:lij]
مادة تجميلية تبرز الملامح
[Madah tajmeeleyah tobrez al-malameḥ] *n* highlighter
تَجنب avoid *v* [taʒanabba]
تجول wander, tour *v* [taʒawwala]
تَجَوَّل stroll *n* [taʒawwul]
تجويف sinus *n* [taʒwi:f]
تَحَالف alliance *n* [taħa:luf]
تحت below *prep* ◁ below *adv* [taħta]
تحتي lower *adj* [taħtij]
سِروال تحتي
[Serwaal taḥtey] *n* underpants
تحدّ challenge *n* [taħaddin]
تحدث talk *vi* [taħaddaθa]
يتحدث إلى
[yataḥdath ela] *v* talk to
يتحدث بحرية وبدون تحفظ
[yathadath be-ḥorreyah wa-bedon taḥaffoḍh] *v* speak up
تحدى challenge *v* [taħadda:]
تحديداً specifically *adv* [taħdi:dan]
تحذير warning *n* [taħði:r]
أضواء التحذير من الخطر
[Aḍwaa al-tahdheer men al-khaṭar] *npl* hazard warning lights
تحرري liberal *adj* [taħarurij]
تحرك movement *n* [taħaruk]
لا يمكنها التحرك
[la yam-kinuha al-taḥaruk] She can't move
تحرّك *v* [taħarraka]
متى يتحرك أول ناقل للمتزلجين؟
[mata yata-ḥarak awal na'qil lel-muta-zalijeen?] When does the first chair-lift go?
تَحرك shift *vi* [taħarraka]
يَتَحرك إلى الأمام
[Yatḥarak lel-amam] *v* move forward
يَتَحرك للخلف
[Yatḥarak lel-khalf] *v* move back
تحرير liberation *n* [taħri:r]
تحريك moving *n* [taħri:k]
هل يمكنك تحريك سيارتك من فضلك؟
[hal yamken -aka taḥreek saya-ratuka min faḍlak?] Could you move your car, please?
تحسّن *v* [taħassana]
أتمني أن تتحسن حالة الجو
[ata-mana an tata-ḥasan ḥalat al-jaw] I hope the weather improves
تَحَسُن advance *n* [taħassun]
تحسين improvement *n* [taħsi:n]
تَحَطَّم wreck, crash *v* [taħatˤtˤama]
تَحَطُّم wreck *n* [taħatˤum]
تحَفظ reservation *n* [taħafuzˤin]
تحفيز motivation *n* [taħfi:z]
تحقيق investigation *n* [taħqi:qu]
تحكم control *n* [taħakkum]
التحكم عن بعد
[Al-taḥakom an bo'ad] *n* remote control
وحدة التحكم في ألعاب الفيديو
[Wehdat al-tahakom fee al'aab al-vedyoo] *n* games console
لقد تعطلت مفاتيح التحكم عن العمل

هل هناك تخفيض للأشخاص المعاقين؟
[hal hunaka takhfeeḍ lel-ash-khaṣ al-mu'aa-'qeen?] Is there a reduction for people with disabilities?
هل يوجد أي تخفيضات لطلبة؟
[hal yujad ay takhfeeḍ-aat lel-ṯalaba?] Are there any reductions for students?
هل يوجد أي تخفيضات للأطفال؟
[hal yujad ay takhfeeḍ-aat lil-ạṭfaal?] Are there any reductions for children?
تخفيف [taxfi:f] *n* relief
لا أريد أخذ حقنة لتخفيف الألم
[la areed akhith ḥu'qna li-takhfeef al-alam] I don't want an injection for the pain
تخلص [taxallusˤ] *n*
ممكن التخلص منه
[Momken al-takhalos menh] *adj* disposable
تَخَلَّص [taxallasˤa] *v* throw away
تخلف [taxallafa] *v* lag behind
تخلّف [taxallafa] *v*
لقد تخلفت عنه
[la'qad takha-lafto 'aanho] I've been left behind
تخلى [taxalla:] *v*
يَتخلى عن
[Yatkhala an] *v* let down
يَتَخَلّى عن
[Yatkhala 'an] *v* part with
تخم [tuxm] *n* frontier
تخمين [taxmi:n] *n* guess
تخّير [taxajjara] *v* select
تَخَيَل [taxajjala] *v* imagine, fancy
تَخَيُلي [taxajjulij] *adj* imaginary
تدخل [tadaxxala] *v* go in
تدخين [tadxi:n] *n* smoking
التدخين
[Al-tadkheen] *n* smoking
أريد غرفة مسموح فيها بالتدخين
[areed ghurfa masmooḥ feeha bil-tadkheen] I'd like a smoking room
تدرج [tadruʒ] *n*
طائر التدرج
[Ṭaear al-tadraj] *n* pheasant
تدريب [tadri:b] *n* training

[la'qad ta-'aaṭalat mafa-teeḥ al-taḥa-kum 'aan al-'aamal] The controls have jammed
تحكم [taħakkama] *v*
يَتحكم ب
[Yataḥkam be] *v* overrule
تحكيم [taħki:m] *n* arbitration
تحلية [taħlija] *n* sweet
تحليق [taħli:q] *n*
التحليق في الجو
[Al-taḥlee'q fee al-jaw] *n* gliding
تحليل [taħli:l] *n* analysis
تحمل [taħammala] *v* undergo
تحميل [taħmi:l] *n* download
تحول [taħawwul] *n* diversion
تحول في المظهر
[taḥawol fee almaḍhhar] *n* makeover
تحّول [taħawwala] *v* convert
تحويل [taħwi:l] *n* transfer
قابل للتحويل
['qabel lel-taḥweel] *adj* convertible
كم يستغرق التحويل؟
[kam yasta-ghri'q al-taḥweel?] How long will it take to transfer?
تحية [taħijja] *n* greeting
تَخاصم [taxa:sˤama] *v* squabble
تخْرج [taxarruʒ] *n* graduation
تَخْريب [taxri:b] *n* vandalism
تخريبي [taxri:bij] *adj* destructive
عمل تخريبي
['amal takhreeby] *n* sabotage
تَخصص [taxasˤsˤasˤa] *v* specialize
تَخَصُص [taxasˤusˤsˤ] *n* speciality
تخطى [taxatˤtˤa:] *vt* skip
تخطيط [taxtˤi:tˤ] *n* planning
تخطيط المدينة
[Takhṭeeṭ almadeenah] *n* town planning
تخطيط بياني
[Takhṭeeṭ bayany] *n* graph
تخفيض [taxfi:dˤ] *n* reduction
تخفيض الانتاج
[Takhfeeḍ al-entaj] *n* cutback
تخفيض قيمة العملة
[Takhfeeḍ 'qeemat al'aomlah] *n* devaluation

تدريجي [tadri:ʒij] gradual *adj*
تدريس [tadri:s] teaching *n*
هل تقومون بالتدريس؟
[hal ta'qo-moon bil-tadrees?] Do you give lessons?
تدريم [tadri:m] *n*
تدريم الأظافر
[Tadreem al-aḍhaafe] *n* manicure
تدفئة [tadfiʔa] heating *n*
تدفئة مركزية
[Tadfeah markazeyah] *n* central heating
إن نظام التدفئة لا يعمل
[enna neḍham al-tad-fe-a la ya'amal] The heating doesn't work
تدفق [tadaffuq] current *(flow)* *n*
تدفق [tadaffaqa] flow *v*
تدليك [tadli:k] massage *n*
تدمير [tadmi:r] destruction *n*
تدوير [tadwi:ru] cycling *n*
تذكار [tiðka:r] souvenir *n*
تَذكر [taðakkara] remember *v*
تذكرة [taðkira] ticket, pass *n*
تذكرة إلكترونية
[Tadhkarah elektroneyah] *n* e-ticket
تذكرة إياب
[tadhkarat eyab] *n* return ticket
تذكرة أوتوبيس
[tadhkarat otobees] *n* bus ticket
تذكرة الركن
[tadhkarat al-rokn] *n* parking ticket
تذكرة انتظار
[tadhkarat enteḍhar] *n* stand-by ticket
تذكرة ذهاب
[tadhkarat dhehab] *n* single ticket
تذكرة ذهاب وعودة في نفس اليوم
[tadhkarat dhehab we-'awdah fee nafs al-yawm] *n* day return
تذكرة فردية
[tadhkarat fardeyah] *n* single ticket
شباك التذاكر
[Shobak al-taḍhaker] *n* box office
ماكينة التذاكر
[Makenat al-taḍhaker] *n* ticket machine
تذكرة طفل
[tadhkerat ṭifil] a child's ticket
كم يبلغ ثمن تذكرة الذهاب والعودة؟
[Kam yablogh thaman tadhkarat al-dhab wal-'awdah?] How much is a return ticket?
لقد ضاعت تذكرتي
[la'qad ḍa'aat taḍhkeraty] I've lost my ticket
ما هو ثمن تذكرة التزلج؟
[ma howa thaman tathkarat al-tazal-oj?] How much is a ski pass?
من أين يمكن شراء تذكرة الأتوبيس؟
[Men ayen yomken sheraa tadhkarat al otoobees?] Where can I buy a bus card?
هل يمكن أن أشتري التذاكر هنا؟
[hal yamken an ashtary al-tadhaker huna?] Can I buy the tickets here?
تَذَوق [taðawwaqa] taste *v*
تراجع عن [tara:ʒaʕa ʕan] back out *v*
ترام [tra:m] tram *n*
ترانزستور [tra:nzistu:r] transistor *n*
تَراوح [tara:waħa] range *v*
تربة [turba] soil *n*
تربوي [tarbawij] educational *adj*
تربية [tarbija] upbringing *n*
ترتيب [tarti:b] arrangement *n*
على الترتيب
[Ala altarteeb] *adv* respectively
ترجم [tarʒama] translate *v*
هل يمكن أن تترجم لي من فضلك؟
[hal yamken an tutar-jim lee min faḍlak?] Could you act as an interpreter for us, please?
ترجمة [tarʒama] translation *n*
ترحيب [tarħi:b] welcome *n*
تردد [taraddud] frequency *n*
تَردد [taraddada] hesitate *v*
ترشيح [tarʃi:ħ] nomination *n*
جهاز ترشيح
[Jehaz tarsheeh] *n* filter
ترفيه [tarfi:h] *n*
هل يوجد ملهي للترفيه هنا؟
[hal yujad mula-hee lel-tarfeeh huna?] Is there a play park near here?
تُرْقُوة [turquwa] collarbone *n*
ترك [taraka] leave *v*
أين يمكن أن أترك متعلقاتي الثمينة؟

[ayna yamken an atruk muta-'ala'qaty al-thameena?] Where can I leave my valuables?
focus *v* [tarakkaza] **تَرَكَز**
Turkish *adj* [turkij] **تركي**
Turkey *n* [turkija:] **تركيا**
composition, *n* [tarki:b] **تركيب** instalment
concentration *n* [tarki:z] **تركيز**
n [tirmu:mitir] **ترمومتر** thermometer
hum *v* [tarannama] **تَرنم**
hymn *n* [tarni:ma] **ترنيمة**
promotion *n* [tarwi:ʒ] **ترويج**
antidote *n* [tirja:q] **ترياق**
coincidence *n* [taza:mana] **تزامن**
coincide *v* [taza:mana] **تَزامن**
sledging, *n* [tazaħluq] **تزحلق** skating, rolling, sliding
ممر التزحلق
[Mamar al-tazahlo'q] *n* ski pass
تَزَلُج على العجل
[Tazaloj 'ala al-'ajal] *n* rollerskating
تَزَلُج على الجليد
[Tazaloj 'ala al-jaleed] *n* ice-skating
تَزَلُج على اللوح
[Tazaloj 'ala al-looh] *n* skateboarding
تَزَلُج على المياه
[Tazaloj 'ala al-meyah] *n* water-skiing
تَزَلُج شِرَاعِي
[Tazaloj shera'aey] *n* windsurfing
حلبة تَزَلُّج
[Ḥalabat tazaloj] *n* skating rink
أين يمكنك ممارسة رياضة التزحلق على الماء؟
[ayna yamken-ak muma-rasat riyaḍat al-tazaḥlu'q 'ala al-maa?] Where can you go water-skiing?
lead *vt* [tzaʕʕama] **تزَعَم**
n [tazaluʒ] **تزلج**
لوح التزلج
[Lawh al-tazalloj] *n* skateboard
أريد إيجار عصي تزلج
[areed e-jar 'aoṣy tazaluj] I want to hire ski poles
أين يمكن أن نؤجر معدات التزلج؟
[ayna yamken an noa-jer mo'aedat al-tazal-oj?] Where can I hire skiing equipment?
أين يمكن أن نذهب للتزلج على الجليد؟
[ayna yamken an nadhhab lel-tazaluj 'ala al-jaleed?] Where can we go ice-skating?
ما هي أسهل ممرات التزلج؟
[ma heya as-hal mama-raat al-tazal-oj?] Which are the easiest runs?
من أين يمكن أن نشتري تذاكر التزلج؟
[min ayna yamken an nash-tary tadhaker al-tazal-oj?] Where can I buy a ski pass?
skate *v* [tazallaʒa] **تزلج**
أين يمكن أن نتزلج على عربات التزلج؟
[ayna yamken an natazalaj 'ala 'aarabat al-tazal-oj?] Where can we go sledging?
skiing *n* [tazzaluʒ] **تَزَلُّج**
tobogganing *n* [tazaluq] **تزلق**
marry *v* [tazawwaʒa] **تَزوج**
يَتَزوج ثانية
[Yatazawaj thaneyah] *v* remarry
forgery *n* [tazwi:r] **تزوير**
n [tazji:nu] **تَزيين**
تَزْيين الحلوى
[Tazyeen al-ḥalwa] *n* icing
query *n* [tasa:ʔul] **تساؤل**
race *vi* [tasa:baqa] **تَسابق**
v [tasaʒʒala] **تسجل**
يتسجل فى فندق
[Yatasajal fee fondo'q] *v* check in
registration *n* [tasʒi:lu] **تسجيل**
عملية التسجيل
['amalyat al-tasjeel] *n* recording
جهاز التسجيل
[Jehaz al-tasjeel] *n* recorder *(music)*
التسجيل فى فندق
[Al-tasjeel fee fondo'q] *n* check-in
ماكينة تسجيل الكاش
[Makenat tasjeel al-kaash] *n* till
مكتب التسجيل
[Maktab al-tasjeel] *n* registry office
heating *n* [tasxi:n] **تسخين**
leak *n* [tasarrub] **تَسَرُب**
n [tasri:ħ] **تسريح**

هل تبيع مستحضرات لتسريح الشعر؟ [hal tabee'a musta-ḥḍaraat le-tasreeḥ al-sha'air?] Do you sell styling products?

تسريحة hairstyle *n* [tasri:ħa]

أريد تسريحة جديدة تمامًا [areed tas-reeḥa jadeeda ta-maman] I want a completely new style

هذه التسريحة من فضلك [hathy al-tasreeḥa min faḍlak] This style, please

تسريع acceleration *n* [tasri:ʕ]

تسعة nine *number* [tisʕatun]

تسعة عشر *number* [tisʕata ʕaʃara] nineteen

تسعين ninety *number* [tisʕi:nun]

تسلسل sequence *n* [tasalsul]

تسلق climbing *n* [tasalluq]

تسلق الصخور [Tasalo'q alṣokhoor] *n* rock climbing

تسلق الجبال [Tasalo'q al-jebal] *n* mountaineering

أود أن أذهب للتسلق؟ [awid an adhhab lel tasalo'q] I'd like to go climbing

تسلق climb *v* [tasallaqa]

تَسلل hack (كمبيوتر) *v* [tasallala]

تسلية pastime *n* [taslija]

تسليم delivery *n* [tasli:m]

تسمانيا Tasmania *n* [tasma:nja:]

تسمم poisoning *n* [tasammum]

تسمم الدم [Tasamom al-dam] *n* blood poisoning

التسمم الغذائي [Al-tasmom al-ghedhaaey] *n* food poisoning

تسهيل *n* [tashi:l]

ما هي التسهيلات التي تقدمها للمعاقين؟ [ma heya al-tas-helaat al-laty tu'qadem-ha lel-mu'aa'qeen?] What facilities do you have for people with disabilities?

تسوق shopping *n* [tasawwuq]

ترولي التسوق [Trolley altasaw'q] *n* shopping trolley

تسونامي tsunami *n* [tsu:na:mi:]

تسوية compromise *n* [taswija]

تسويق marketing *n* [taswi:qu]

تَشابُه similarity *n* [taʃa:buh]

تشاجر scrap, fall out *v* [taʃa:ʒara]

يتشاجر مع [Yatashajar ma'a] *v* row

تشاد Chad *n* [tʃa:d]

تشبث hug *n* [taʃabbuθ]

تشجيع encouragement *n* [taʃʒi:ʕ]

تشخيص diagnosis *n* [taʃxi:sˤ]

تشريع legislation *n* [taʃri:ʕ]

تشغيل working, functioning *n* [taʃɣi:l]

إعادة تشغيل [E'aadat tashgheel] *n* replay

لا يمكنني تشغيله [la yam-kinuni tash-gheloho] I can't turn the heating on

لن أقوم بتشغيله [Lan a'qoom betashgheeloh] It won't turn on

تشوش muddle, mix-up *n* [taʃawwuʃ]

تشويق suspense, thriller *n* [taʃwi:q]

تشيكي Czech *adj* [tʃi:kij]

اللغة التشيكية [Al-loghah al-teshekeyah] *(language) n* Czech

شخص تشيكي [Shakhṣ tesheekey] *(person) n* Czech

تشيلي Chilean *adj* [tʃi:lij]

دولة تشيلي [Dawlat tesheeley] *n* Chile

مواطن تشيلي [Mowaṭen tsheeley] *n* Chilean

تصادف *v* [tasˤa:dafa]

يتصادف مع [Yataṣaadaf ma'a] *v* bump into

تصادم collision *n* [tasˤa:dum]

تصادم collide *v* [tasˤa:dama]

تصحيح correction *n* [tasˤħi:ħ]

تصديق *n* [tasˤdi:q]

غير قابل للتصديق [Ghayr 'qabel leltaṣdee'q] *adj* fabulous

تَصَرف behave *v* [tasˤarrafa]

تصريح permission, permit [tasˤri:ħ]

تصريح عمل
[Taṣreeh 'amal] *n* work permit
تصريح خروج
[Taṣreeh khoroj] *n* Passover
تصريح الركوب
[Taṣreeh al-rokob] *n* boarding pass
هل أنت في احتياج إلى تصريح بالصيد؟
[hal anta fee iḥti-yaj ela taṣreeḥ bil-ṣayd?] Do you need a fishing permit?
هل يوجد أي تخفيضات مع هذا التصريح؟
[hal yujad ay takhfeeḍ-aat ma'aa hadha al-taṣ-reeḥ?] Is there a reduction with this pass?
تصريف *n* [tasˤriːf]
أنبوب التصريف
[Anboob altaṣreef] *n* drainpipe
تصريف الأفعال
[Taṣreef al-afaal] *n* conjugation
تصّفح browse *vt* [tassˤaffaħa]
يَتَصَفح الانترنت
[Yataṣafaḥ al-enternet] *v* surf
تصفيف alignment *n* [tasˤfiːf]
تصفيف الشعر
[taṣfeef al-sha'ar] *n* hairstyle
تصفيق applause *n* [tasˤfiːq]
تصليح repair *n* [tasˤliːħ]
عدة التصليح
['aodat altaṣleeh] *n* repair kit
أين يمكنني تصليح هذه الحقيبة؟
[ayna yamken-any taṣleeḥ hadhe al-ḥa'qeba?] Where can I get this repaired?
كم تكلفة التصليح؟
[kam taklifat al-taṣleeḥ?] How much will the repairs cost?
هل تستحق أن يتم تصليحها؟
[hal tasta-ḥi'q an yatum taṣle-ḥaha?] Is it worth repairing?
هل يمكن تصليح ساعتي؟
[hal yamken taṣleeḥ sa'aaty?] Can you repair my watch?
تصميم design, *n* [tasˤmiːm] resolution
تصنيف assortment *n* [tasˤniːf]

تَصور visualize *v* [tasˤawwara]
تصويت vote *n* [tasˤwiːt]
تصوير drawing, *n* [tasˤwiːr] photography
التصوير الفوتوغرافي
[Al-taṣweer al-fotoghrafey] *n* photography
ماكينة تصوير
[Makenat taṣweer] *n* photocopier
أين يوجد أقرب محل لبيع معدات التصوير الفوتوغرافي؟
[Ayn yoojad a'qrab mahal lebay'a mo'aedat al-taṣweer al-fotoghrafey] Where is the nearest place to buy photography equipment?
هل يمكنني القيام بالتصوير السينمائي هنا؟
[hal yamken -any al-'qeyaam bil-taṣ-weer al-sena-maiy huna?] Can I film here?
تَضَخُّم inflation *n* [tadˤaxxum]
تَضمن include *v* [tadˤammana]
تطرف extremism *n* [tatˤarruf]
تطريز embroidery *n* [tatˤriːz]
تطعيم vaccination *n* [tatˤʕiːm]
أنا أحتاج إلى تطعيم
[ana aḥtaaj ela ṭaṭ-'aeem] I need a vaccination
تَطَلّب require *v* [tatˤallaba]
تطور development *n* [tatˤawwur]
تطور develop *vi* [tatˤawwara]
تطوع volunteer *v* [tatˤawwaʕa]
تظاهر pretend *v* [tazˤaːhara]
تعادل *v* [taʕaːdala]
يتعادل مع
[Yata'aaadal ma'a] *v* tie *(equal with)*
تعارَض disagree *v* [taʕaːradˤa]
تعاطف sympathy *n* [taʕaːtˤuf]
تعاطف sympathize *v* [taʕaːtˤafa]
تعاون cooperation *n* [taʕaːwun]
تعاون collaborate *v* [taʕaːwana]
تعب exhaustion *n* [taʕib]
تعب بعد السفر بالطائرة
[Ta'aeb ba'ad al-safar bel-ṭaerah] *n* jetlag
أشعر بالتعب

[ash-'aur bil-ta'aab] I'm tired
تعبئة packaging *n* [taʕbiʔit]
تعبير expression *n* [taʕbi:r]
تعتيم blackout *n* [taʕti:m]
تَعَثّر trip, stumble *v* [taʕaθθara]
تَعجب wonder *v* [taʕaʒʒaba]
تعديل modification *n* [taʕdi:l]
تعدين mining *n* [taʕdi:n]
تعذيب torture *n* [taʕði:b]
تعرض *v* [taʕarradˤa]
لقد تعرضت حقائبي للضرر
[la'qad ta-'aaraḍat ḥa'qa-eby lel-ḍarar] My luggage has been damaged
تَعَرف *v* [taʕarrafa]
يَتْعَرف على
[Yata'araf 'ala] *v* recognize
تَعَرُّق perspiration *n* [taʕarruq]
تعري *adj* [taʕarri:]
راقصة تعري
[Ra'qeṣat ta'arey] *n* stripper
تعريف definition, *n* [taʕri:f] description
تعريف الهوية
[Ta'areef al-haweyah] *n* identification
تعريفة tariff, notice *n* [taʕri:fa]
تعشيقة gear *(mechanism)* *n* [taʕʃi:qa]
تعطل break down *v* [taʕatˤtˤala]
لقد تعطلت سيارتي
[la'qad ta-'aaṭalat sayaraty] My car has broken down
ماذا أفعل إلى تعطلت السيارة؟
[madha af'aal edha ta'aa-ṭalat al-sayara?] What do I do if I break down?
تَعَطُّل breakdown *n* [taʕatˤul]
تعفن decay, rot *v* [taʕaffana]
تعقل discretion *n* [taʕaqqul]
تعقيد complication *n* [taʕqi:d]
تعلق *v* [taʕallaqa]
فيما يتعلق بـ
[Feema yat'ala'q be] *adj* moving
تعلم learn *v* [taʕallama]
تعليق caption, *n* [taʕli:q] commentary, suspension
تعليم teaching, *n* [taʕli:m] education, tuition
تعليم عالى
[Ta'aleem 'aaaly] *n* higher education
تعليم الكبار
[Ta'aleem al-kebar] *n* adult education
نظام التعليم الإضافي
[neḍham al-ta'aleem al-eḍafey] *n* higher education *(lower-level)*
تعليمات *npl* [taʕli:ma:tun] instructions
تعليمي educational *adj* [taʕli:mijjat]
منحة تعليمية
[Menḥah ta'aleemeyah] *n* scholarship
تعميد *n* [tʕmi:d]
حفلة التعميد
[Ḥaflat alt'ameed] *n* christening
تعويض compensation *n* [taʕwi:dˤ]
تعيس miserable, *adj* [taʕi:s] unhappy
تغذية nutrition *n* [taɣðija]
سوء التغذية
[Sooa al taghdheyah] *n* malnutrition
تغطية coverage *n* [taɣtˤija]
تغطية الكيك
[taghṭeyat al-keek] *n* frosting
تَغلب *v* [taɣallaba]
يَتَغلب على
[Yatghalab 'ala] *v* get over
يَتَغْلَب على
[Yatghalab 'ala] *v* overcome
يَتَغْلَب على
[Yatghalab 'ala] *v* cope
تغَيّب play truant *v* [taɣajjaba]
تغير shift, change *n* [taɣajjur]
تغير المناخ
[Taghyeer almonakh] *n* climate change
تغَير change *vi* [taɣajjara]
تغيير change *n* [taɣji:r]
قابل للتغيير
['qabel lel-tagheyer] *adj* changeable, variable
أريد تغيير تذكرتي
[areed taghyeer tadhkeraty] I want to change my ticket
أين يمكنني تغيير ملابس الرضيع؟
[ayna yamken-any taghyeer ma-labis al-raḍee'a?] Where can I change the

[Mata sanata'qabal] Where shall we meet?
تقاطع junction, way out *n* [taqa:tˤuʕ]
اتجه نحو اليمين عند التقاطع الثاني
[Etajeh naḥw al-yameen] Go right at the next junction
السيارة بالقرب من التقاطع رقم...
[al-sayara bil-'qurb min al-ta'qa-ṭu'a ra'qim...] The car is near junction number...
ما هو التقاطع الذي يوصل إلى...؟
[ma howa al-ta'qa-ṭu'a al-lathy yo-waṣil ela...?] Which junction is it for...?
تقاعد retirement *n* [taqa:ʕud]
تقاعد *v* [taqa:ʕada]
لقد تقاعدت عن العمل
[Le'qad ta'qa'adt 'an al-'amal] I'm retired
تقَاعِد retire *v* [taqa:ʕada]
تقدّم progress *n* [taqaddum]
تقدم advance *v* [taqadama]
تقدير estimate *n* [taqdi:r]
تقديم presentation *n* [taqdi:m]
تقديم الهدايا
[Ta'qdeem al-hadayah] *n* prize-giving
تقريبا approximately, *adv* [taqri:ban] almost
تقريبي approximate *adj* [taqri:bij]
تقرير report *n* [taqri:r]
تقرير مدرسي
[Ta'qreer madrasey] *n* report card
تقسيم division *n* [taqsi:m]
تقشير peeling *n* [taqʃi:r]
جهاز تقشير البطاطس
[Jehaz ta'qsheer al-baṭaṭes] *n* potato peeler
تقطير filtration, *n* [taqtˤi:r] distillation
معمل التقطير
[Ma'amal alta'qṭeer] *n* distillery
تقلص contraction *n* [taqallunsˤ]
تقلص عضلي
[Ta'qaloṣ 'aḍaley] *n* spasm
تقلَص shrink *v* [taqallasˤa]
تقليد tradition *n* [taqli:d]
تقليدي conventional, *adj* [taqli:dij] traditional

baby?
هل من المتوقع أن يحدث تغيير في حالة الجو
[Hal men al-motwa'qa'a an yahdoth tagheer fee ḥalat al-jaw] Is the weather going to change?
تفاؤل optimism *n* [tafa:ʔul]
تفاح apple *n* [tuffa:ħ]
عصير تفاح
['aaṣeer tofaḥ] *n* cider
فطيرة التفاح
[Faṭeerat al-tofaaḥ] *n* apple pie
تفاحة apple *n* [tuffa:ħa]
تفادى flee *v* [tafa:da:]
تفاعل react *v* [tafaaʕala]
تَفاعُل reaction *n* [tafa:ʕul]
تفاهم *n* [tafa:hum]
هناك سوء تفاهم
[hunaka so-i tafa-hum] There's been a misunderstanding
تفاوَض negotiate *v* [tafa:wadˤa]
تَفتِيش *n* [tafti:ʃ]
غُرفة تَفتيش
[Ghorfat tafteesh] *n* septic tank
تفجير bombing *n* [tafʒi:r]
تَفحَص (يستجوب) *v* [tafaħħasˤa] examine
تفريغ unpacking *n* [tafri:ɣ]
يحب على تفريغ الحقائب
[yajib 'aala-ya taf-reegh al-ḥa'qaeb] I have to unpack
تفصيل detail *n* [tafsˤi:l]
تفضيل preference *n* [tafdˤi:l]
تفقد *v* [tafaqqada]
أين يمكن أن أتفقد حقائبي؟
[ayna yamken e-da'a ḥa'qa-eby?] Where do I check in my luggage?
تَفَقّد review, inspection *n* [tafaqqud]
تَفَقُّد الحضور
[Tafa'qod al-ḥoḍor] *n* roll call
تفكير thought *n* [tafki:r]
مستغرق في التفكير
[Mostaghre'q fee al-tafkeer] *adj* thoughtful
تقابل *v* [taqa:bala]
متى سنتقابل

غير تقليدي
[Gheer ta'qleedey] *adj* unconventional
تقليل reduction *n* [taqli:l]
تقني technical *adj* [tiqnij]
techie *n* ◁
تقنية mechanism *n* [tiqnija]
تقويم calendar *n* [taqwi:m]
تقيأ vomit *v* [taqajjaʔa]
تَكاسَل skive *v* [taka:sala]
تكبير enlargement *n* [takbi:r]
تَكْتَك tick *v* [taktaka]
تكتيكات tactics *npl* [takti:ka:tun]
تكثيف condensation *n* [takθi:f]
تكدس pile-up *n* [takaddus]
تكرار repeat *n* [tikra:r]
تكراري repetitive *adj* [tikra:rij]
تكريس dedication *n* [takri:s]
تكلفة cost *n* [taklufa]
تكلفة المعيشة
[Taklefat al-ma'aeeshah] *n* cost of living
كم تبلغ تكلفة المكالمة التليفونية إلى...؟
[kam tablugh taklifat al-mukalama al-talefoniya ela...?] How much is it to telephone...?
كم تبلغ تكلفة ذلك؟
[kam tablugh taklifat dhalik?] How much does that cost?
هل يشمل ذلك تكلفة الكهرباء؟
[hal yash-mil dhalik tak-lifat al-kah-rabaa?] Is the cost of electricity included?
تكلم speech *n* [takallum]
عسر التكلم
['aosr al-takalom] *n* dyslexia
تكلم speak *v* [takalama]
تكنولوجي *adj* [tiknu:lu:ʒij] technological
تكنولوجيا *n* [tiknu:lu:ʒja:] technology
تَكَيف adapt *v* [takajjafa]
تكييف regulation, *n* [takji:fu] adjusting
تكييف الهواء
[Takyeef al-hawaa] *n* air conditioning
هل هناك تكييف هواء بالغرفة
[hal hunaka takyeef hawaa bil-ghurfa?] Does the room have air conditioning?
تل hill *n* [tall]
تلاءم *v* [tala:ʔama]
يَتلائم مع
[Yatalaam ma'a] *v* fit in
تلْخبط mess about *v* [talaxbatˤa]
تلْعثم stammer *v* [talaʕθama]
تلغراف telegram *n* [tiliɣra:f]
أريد إرسال تلغراف
[areed ersaal tal-ghraaf] I want to send a telegram
هل يمكن إرسال تلغراف من هنا؟
[hal yamken ersaal tal-ghraf min huna?] Can I send a telegram from here?
تلفاز television, TV *n* [tilfa:z]
أين أجد جهاز التلفاز؟
[ayna ajid jehaz al-tilfaz?] Where is the television?
تلفزيون television *n* [tilifiziju:n]
تلفزيون الواقع
[Telefezyon al-wa'qe'a] *n* reality TV
وَصْلَة تلفزيونية
[Wṣlah telefezyoneyah] *n* cable television
هل يوجد قاعة لمشاهدة التلفزيون؟
[hal yujad 'qa'aa le-musha-hadat al-tali-fizyon?] Is there a television lounge?
تلفزيوني *adj* [tilifizju:nij]
دائرة تلفزيونية مغلقة
[Daerah telefezyoneyah moghla'qa] *n* CCTV
تَلَقف grab *v* [talaqqafa]
تلقى *v* [talaqqa:]
يتلقى حملا
[Yatala'qa ḥemlan] *v* load
تلقيح vaccination *n* [talqi:ħ]
تلَمس *v* [talammasa]
يَتلَمس طريقه في الظلام
[Yatalamas ṭaree'qah fee al-ḍhalam] *v* grope
تلميح hint *n* [talmi:ħ]
تلميذ, تلميذة, [tilmi:ðun, tilmi:ða, pupil, schoolboy, *n*tilmi:ða] schoolgirl

تلميذ داخلي
[telmeedh dakhely] *n* boarder
schoolgirl *n* [tilmi:ða] **تلميذة**
pollution *n* [talawwuθ] **تلوث**
colouring *n* [talwi:n] **تلوين**
telescope *n* [tili:sku:b] **تليسكوب**
chairlift *n* [tili:fri:k] **تليفريك**
TV *n* [tili:fizju:n] **تليفزيون**
تليفزيون رقمي
[telefezyoon ra'qamey] *n* digital television
تليفزيون بلازما
[Telefezyoon ra'qamey] *n* plasma TV
تليفزيون ملون
[Telefezyon molawan] *n* colour television
شاشة تليفزيون
[Shashat telefezyoon] *n* screen
هل يوجد تليفزيون بالغرفة
[hal yujad tali-fizyon bil-ghurfa?] Does the room have a TV?
telephone *n* [tili:fu:n] **تليفون**
رقم التليفون
[Ra'qm al-telefone] *n* phone number
تليفون المدخل
[Telefoon al-madkhal] *n* entry phone
تليفون بكاميرا
[Telefoon bekamerah] *n* camera phone
تليفون مزود بوظيفة الرد الآلي
[Telephone mozawad be-waḍheefat al-rad al-aaley] *n* answerphone
كارت تليفون
[Kart telefone] *n* cardphone, phonecard
كابينة تليفون
[Kabeenat telefoon] *n* phonebox
adj [tili:fu:nij] **تليفوني**
يجب أن أقوم بإجراء مكالمة تليفونية
[yajib an a'qoom be-ijraa mukalama talefonia] I must make a phonecall
fully, *adv* [tama:man] **تماما**
altogether, exactly
swing, sway *vi* [tama:jala] **تمايل**
stutter *v* [tamtama] **تمْتم**
statue *n* [timθa:l] **تمثال**
acting *n* [tamθi:ll] **تمثيل**
التمثيل الصامت
[altamtheel al-ṣamet] *n* pantomime
n [tamri:dˤ] **تمريض**
دار التمريض
[Dar al-tamreeḍ] *n* nursing home
exercise *n* [tamri:n] **تمرين**
تمرين الضغط
[Tamreen al- Ḍaghṭ] *n* push-up
tear up *v* [tamzzaqa] **تَمزَق**
tear *(split)* *n* [tamzi:q] **تَمْزيق**
crocodile *n* [timsa:ħ] **تمساح**
تمساح أمريكي
[Temsaah amreekey] *n* alligator
تمساح نهري أسيوي
[Temsaah nahrey asyawey] *n* mugger
wish *v* [tamanna:] **تَمَنى**
n [tamwi:ʒu] **تمويج**
تمويج الشعر
[Tamweej al-sha'ar] *n* perm
finance *n* [tamwi:l] **تمويل**
stand out *v* [tamajjaza] **تَمَيز**
discrimination *n* [tamji:z] **تمييز**
تمييز عنصري
[Tamyeez 'aonory] *n* racism
ممكن تمييزه
[Momken tamyezoh] *adj* recognizable
waiver, surrender, *n* [tana:zul] **تنازل**
fight
أريد عمل الترتيبات الخاصة بالتنازل عن تعويض التصادم
[areed 'aamal al-tar-tebaat al-khaṣa bil-tanazul 'aan ta'aweeḍ al-ta-ṣadum] I'd like to arrange a collision damage waiver
v [tana:zala] **تنازَل**
يَتنازَل عن
[Tetnazel 'an] *v* waive
breed *v* [tana:sala] **تناسل**
rivalry *n* [tana:fus] **تنافس**
compete *v* [tana:fasa] **تنافس**
competitive *adj* [tana:fusij] **تنافسي**
contradiction *n* [tana:qudˤ] **تناقض**
relay *n* [tana:wub] **تناوب**
taking, having *n* [tana:wul] **تناول**
أحب تناوله بدون...من فضلك
[aḥib tana-wilaho be-doon... min faḍlak] I'd like it without..., please

أحب تناوله وبه...زائد من فضلك
[aḥib tana-wilaho be-zeyaada... min faḍlak] I'd like it with extra..., please
لا يمكنني تناول الأسبرين
[la yam-kinuni tanawil al-asbireen] I can't take aspirin
ماذا تريد تناوله في الإفطار
[madha tureed tana-wilho fee al-efṯaar?] What would you like for breakfast?
تناول v [tana:wala]
سوف أتناول هذا
[sawfa ata-nawal hadha] I'll have this
ماذا تريد أن تتناول؟
[madha tureed an tata-nawal?] What would you like to eat?
هل يمكن أن أتناول أحد المشروبات؟
[Hal yomken an atanaawal aḥad al-mashroobat?] Can I get you a drink?
هل يمكن أن أتناول الإفطار داخل غرفتي؟
[hal yamken an ata-nawal al-efṭaar dakhil ghurfaty?] Can I have breakfast in my room?
تنبأ predict v [tanabbaʔa]
يتنَبأ ب
[Yatanabaa be] v foresee
تنبؤ forecast n [tanabuʔ]
لا يمكن التنبؤ به
[La yomken al-tanaboa beh] adj unpredictable
تنجيم n [tanʒi:m]
علم التنجيم
[A'elm al-tanjeem] n astrology
تنزانيا Tanzania n [tanza:nija:]
تنزه hill-walking n [tanazzuh]
التنزه بين المرتفعات
[Altanazoh bayn al-mortaf'aat] n hill-walking
تنس tennis n [tinis]
تنس الريشة
[Tenes al-reshah] n badminton
لاعب تنس
[La'aeb tenes] n tennis player
مضرب تنس
[Maḍrab tenes] n tennis racket
ملعب تنس
[Mal'aab tenes] n tennis court
نود أن نلعب التنس؟
[nawid an nal'aab al-tanis] We'd like to play tennis
تنسِيق format n [tansi:q]
تنشق sniff v [tanaʃʃaqa]
تنظيف cleaning n [tanzˤi:f]
تنظيف شامل للمنزل بعد انتهاء الشتاء
[tanḍheef shamel lel-manzel ba'ad entehaa al-shetaa] n spring-cleaning
خادم للتنظيف
[Khadem lel-tanḍheef] n cleaner
محل التنظيف الجاف
[Mahal al- tanḍheef al-jaf] n dry-cleaner's
تنظيم regulation n [tanzˤi:m]
تنظيم المعسكرات
[Tanṭeem al-mo'askarat] n camping
تنظيم النسل
[tanḍheem al-nasl] n birth control
تنفس breathing n [tanaffus]
تنفس breathe v [tanafasa]
تنفيذ execution n [tanfi:ð]
تنفيذي executive adj [tanfi:ðijjat]
سُلطة تنفيذية
[Soltah tanfeedheyah] (مدير) n executive
تنكَر disguise v [tanakkara]
تنهَد sigh v [tanahhada]
تنهيدة sigh n [tanhi:da]
تنوب n [tannu:b]
شجر التنوب
[Shajar al-tanob] n fir (tree)
تنورة n [tannu:ra]
تنورة تحتية
[Tanorah taḥteyah] n underskirt
تنورة قصيرة بها ثنيات واسعة
[Tannorah 'qaṣeerah beha thanayat wase'aah] n kilt
تنوع variety n [tanawwuʕ]
تنين dragon n [tinni:n]
تهادي stagger v [taha:da:]
تهجئة spelling n [tahʒiʔa]
مصحح التهجئة
[Moṣaheh altahjeaah] n spellchecker
تهديد threat n [tahdi:d]

threatening *adj* [tahdi:dij] **تهديدي**
smuggling *n* [tahri:bu] **تهريب**
ironic *adj* [tahakumij] **تهكمي**
charge *(accusation) n* [tuhma] **تهمة**
congratulations *npl* [tahniʔat] **تهنئة**
ventilation *n* [tahwijatin] **تهوية**
lullaby *n* [tahwi:da] **تهويدة**
soon *adv* [tawwan] **توا**
seasoning, spice *n* [tawa:bil] **توابل**
balance *n* [tawa:zun] **توازن**
n [tawa:lajtu] **تواليت**
السيفون لا يعمل في التواليت
[al-seefon la ya'amal fee al-toilet] The toilet won't flush
twin *n* [tawʔam] **توأم**
berry, raspberry *n* [tu:tt] **توت**
توت برى
[Toot barrey] *n* cranberry
تُوتْ أزرق
[Toot azra'q] *n* blueberry
tension *n* [tawattur] **توتر**
مسبب توتر
[Mosabeb tawator] *adj* stressful
documentation *n* [tawθi:q] **توثيق**
Togo *n* [tu:ʒu:] **توجو**
direction, steering *n* [tawʒi:h] **توجيه**
npl [tawʒi:ha:tun] **توجيهات** directions
flush (يتدفق) *v* [tawarrada] **تَورد**
v [tawarratˤa] **تَورط**
يَتوَرط في
[Yatawaraṭ fee] *v* get into
supply *n* [tawri:d] **توريد**
توريد الطعام
[Tarweed al-ṭa'aam] *n* catering
supplies *npl* [tawri:da:tun] **توريدات**
n [tawzi:ʕ] **توزيع**
صُنبور توزيع
[Ṣonboor twazea'a] *n* dispenser
طريق توزيع الصحف
[ṭaree'q tawze'a al-ṣohof] *n* paper round
recommendation *n* [tawsˤijja] **توصية**
conveyance *n* [tawsˤi:l] **توصيل**
طلب التوصيل
[Ṭalab al-tawseel] *n* hitchhiking
أريد إرسال ساعي لتوصيل ذلك
[areed ersaal sa'ay le-tawṣeel hadha] I want to send this by courier
هل يمكن توصيل حقائبي إلى أعلى؟
[hal yamken tawṣeel ḥa'qa-ebee ela a'ala?] Could you have my luggage taken up?
n [tawsˤi:la] **توصيلة**
توصيلة مجانية
[tawṣeelah majaneyah] *n* ride *(free ride)*
illustration *n* [tawdˤi:ħ] **توضيح**
recruitment *n* [tawzˤi:f] **توظيف**
availability *n* [tawaffur] **تَوَفّرٌ**
n [tawq] **توق**
توق شديد
[Too'q shaded] *n* anxiety
v [tawaqa] **تْوق**
يَتوق إلى
[Yatoo'q ela] *v* long
expect, wait *v* [tawaqqaʕa] **تَوَقَع**
prospect *n* [tawaqqaʕa] **تَوَقّع**
setback, stop *n* [tawaqquf] **توقف**
توقف في رحلة
[Tawa'qof fee rehlah] *n* stopover
شاشة تَوَقُف
[Shashat taw'qof] *n* screen-saver
v [tawaqafa] **توقف**
هل سنتوقف في ...؟
[hal sanata-wa'qaf fee...?] Do we stop at...?
هل يتوقف القطار في...؟
[hal yata-wa'qaf al-'qeṭaar fee...?] Does the train stop at...?
stop *vi* [tawaqqafa] **تَوَقف**
signature *n* [tawqi:ʕ] **توقّيع**
take over *v* [tawalla:] **تَوَلّى**
tulip *n* [tawli:bu] **توليب**
reproduction, midwifery *n* [tawli:d] **توليد**
مستشفى توليد
[Mostashfa tawleed] *n* maternity hospital
n [tu:nʒa:] **تونجا**
مملكة تونجا
[Mamlakat tonja] *n* Tonga
Tunisia *n* [tu:nus] **تونس**
n ◁ Tunisian *adj* [tu:nusij] **تونسي**

Tunisian
current *(electricity)* *n* [tajja:r] **تيار**
Tibet *n* [ti:bit] **تيبت**
adj [ti:bitij] **تيبتي**
اللغة التيبتية
[Al-loghah al-tebeteyah] *(language)* *n* Tibetan
Tibetan *adj* [ti:bi:tij] **تيبيتي**
شخص تيبيتي
[Shakhṣ tebetey] *(person)* *n* Tibetan
tetanus *n* [ti:ta:nu:s] **تيتانوس**
v [tajjamma] **تيَّم**
يُتَيمّ ب
[Yotayam be] *v* love
fig *n* [ti:n] **تين**

rebellious, furious *adj* [θa:ʔir] **ثائر**
fixed, still *adj* [θa:bit] **ثابت**
persevere *v* [θa:bara] **ثابر**
thirdly *adv* [θa:liθan] **ثالثاً**
adj [θa:liθa ʕaʃara] **ثالث عشر** thirteenth
minor *adj* [θa:nawij] **ثانوي**
next, second *adj* [θa:ni:] **ثاني**
اتجه نحو اليسار عند التقاطع الثاني
[Etajh naḥw al-yasar 'aend al-ta'qato'a al-thaney] Go left at the next junction
secondly *adv* [θa:ni:an] **ثانياً**
second *n* [θa:nija] **ثانِيَة**
twelfth *adj* [θa:nija ʕaʃara] **ثانِي عشر**
do up, fix *v* [θabbata] **ثبّت**
breast *n* [θadjj] **ثدي**
talkative *adj* [θarθa:r] **ثرثار**
n [θirmu:sta:t] **ثرموستات** thermostat
wealth *n* [θarwa] **ثروة**
wealthy *adj* [θarij] **ثري**
snake *n* [θuʕba:n] **ثعبان**
fox *n* [θaʕlab] **ثعلب**
ثعلب الماء
[Tha'alab al-maaa] *n* otter
culture *n* [θaqa:fa] **ثقافة**
cultural *adj* [θaqa:fij] **ثقافى**

ثقالة [θaqqa:la] *n* weight
ثقالة الورق
[Na'qalat al-wara'q] *n* paperweight
ثقب [θuqb] *n* aperture, puncture, piercing
ثقْب [θaqaba] *v* prick, bore
يَثقب بمثقاب
[Yath'qob bemeth'qaab] *vt* drill
ثقة [θiqa] *n* confidence *(secret)*, confidence *(trust)*
غير جدير بالثقة
[Ghaayr jadeer bel-the'qa] *adj* unreliable
ثقة بالنفس
[The'qah bel-nafs] *n* confidence *(self-assurance)*
ثقيل [θaqi:l] *adj* heavy
إنه ثقيل جدا
[inaho tha'qeel jedan] This is too heavy
ثلاث [θala:θun] *number*
عندي ثلاثة أطفال
['aendy thalathat aṭfaal] I have three children
ثلاثاء [θula:θa:ʔ] *n* Tuesday
ثلاثاء المرافع
[Tholathaa almrafe'a] *n* Shrove Tuesday
ثلاثة [θala:θatun] *number* three
ثلاثة عشر [θala:θata ʕaʃara] *number* thirteen
ثلاثون [θala:θu:na] *number* thirty
ثلاثي [θula:θij] *adj* triple
ثلاثي الأبعاد
[Tholathy al-ab'aaad] *adj* three-dimensional
ثُلاثِي [θula:θijjun] *npl* triplets
ثلاجَة [θalla:ʒa] *n* fridge, refrigerator
ثلاجة صغيرة
[Thallaja ṣagheerah] *n* minibar
ثلج [θalʒ] *n* snow
رجل الثلج
[Rajol al-thalj] *n* snowman
صندوق الثلج
[Ṣondoo'q al-thalj] *n* icebox
ثلج أسود
[thalj aswad] *n* black ice
كرة ثلج
[Korat thalj] *n* snowball
كتلة ثلج رقيقة
[Kotlat thalj ra'qee'qah] *n* snowflake
محراث الثلج
[Mehrath thalj] *n* snowplough
مكعب ثلج
[Moka'aab thalj] *n* ice cube
يَتَزحلق على الثلج
[Yatazahal'q ala al-thalj] *v* ski
تتساقط الثلوج
[tata-sa'qaṭ al-tholooj] It's snowing
الثلوج كثيفة جدا
[al- tholoj kathefa jedan] The snow is very heavy
هل تعتقد أن الثلوج سوف تتساقط؟
[hal ta'ata-'qid an-na al-thilooj sawfa tata-sa'qaṭ?] Do you think it will snow?
ثلوج [θulu:ʒ] *n*
ماكينة إزالة الثلوج
[Makenat ezalat al-tholo'j] *n* de-icer
ثمانون [θama:nu:na] *number* eighty
ثمانية [θama:nijatun] *number* eight
ثمانية عشر [θama:nijata ʕaʃara] eighteen *number*
ثمرة [θamara] *n* fruit
ثمرة العُليق
[Thamrat al-'alay'q] *n* blackberry
ثمرة البلوط
[Thamarat al-balooṭ] *n* acorn
ثمرة الكاجو
[Thamarat al-kajoo] *n* cashew
ثَمِل [θamil] *adj* drunk
ثمن [θaman] *n* cost, value
مرتفع الثمن
[mortafe'a al-thaman] *adj* expensive
كم يبلغ الثمن لكل ساعة
[kam yablugh al-thaman le-kul layla?] How much is it per night?
لقد طلب مني ثمنًا باهظًا
[la'qad ṭuleba min-y thamanan ba-heḍhan] I've been overcharged
ما هو ثمن التذاكر؟
[Ma hwa thamn al-tadhaker?] How much are the tickets?
ثمّن [θammana] *v* rate
ثمن [θumun] *n* eighth
ثمين [θami:n] *adj* valuable

أريد أن أضع بعض الأشياء الثمينة في الخزينة
[areed an aḍa'a ba'aḍ al-ashiaa al-thameena fee al-khazeena] I'd like to put my valuables in the safe
bend *v* [θana:] **ثني**
crease *n* [θanja] **ثنية**
garment *n* [θawb] **ثوب**
ثوب الراقص أو البهلوان
[Thawb al-ra'qes aw al-bahlawan] *n* leotard
ثوب فضفاض
[Thawb feḍeaḍ] *n* negligee
bull *n* [θawr] **ثور**
revolution *n* [θawra] **ثورة**
revolutionary *adj* [θawrij] **ثوري**
garlic *n* [θu:m] **ثوم**
ثوم معمر
[Thoom mo'aamer] *npl* chives
هل به ثوم؟
[hal behe thoom?] Is there any garlic in it?
clothing *n* [θija:b] **ثياب**
ثياب النوم
[Theyab al-noom] *n* nightdress
أيجب أن نرتدي ثيابًا خاصة؟
[ayajib an nartady the-aban khaṣa?] Is there a dress-code?
Thermos® *n* [θi:rmu:s] **ثيرموس®**

unfair *adj* [ʒa:ʔir] **جائر**
award, prize *n* [ʒa:ʔiza] **جائزة**
الفائز بالجائزة
[Al-faez bel-jaaezah] *n* prizewinner
gateau *n* [ʒa:tu:] **جاتوه**
serious *adj* [ʒa:dd] **جاد**
argue, row *(to argue)* *v* [ʒa:dala] **جادل**
attraction *n* [ʒa:ðibijja] **جاذبية**
neighbour *n* [ʒa:r] **جار**
shovel *n* [ʒa:ru:f] **جاروف**
jazz *n* [ʒa:z] **جاز**
موسيقى الجاز
[Mosey'qa al-jaz] *n* jazz
risk *v* [ʒazafa] **جازف**
spy *n* [ʒa:su:s] **جاسوس**
espionage *n* [ʒa:su:sijja] **جاسوسية**
dry *adj* [ʒa:ff] **جاف**
تنظيف جاف
[tanḍheef jaf] *n* dry-cleaning
جاف تماماً
[Jaf tamaman] *n* bone dry
أنا شعري جاف
[ana sha'ary jaaf] I have dry hair
كأس من مشروب الشيري الجاف من فضلك
[Kaas mashroob al-sheery al-jaf men faḍlek] A dry sherry, please

جاكت [ʒa:kit] *n* jacket
جاكت العشاء
[Jaket al-'aashaa] *n* dinner jacket
جاكيت ثقيل
[Jaket tha'qeel] *n* anorak
جالس [ʒa:lasa] *v*
يُجالس الأطفال
[Yojales al-aṭfaal] *v* babysit
جاليري [ʒa:li:ri:] *n* gallery
جامايكي [ʒa:ma:jkij] *adj* Jamaican
◃ *n* Jamaican
جامبيا [ʒa:mbija:] *n* Gambia
جامع [ʒa:miʕ] *adj* inclusive ◃ *n* mosque
جامع التذاكر
[Jame'a al-tadhaker] *n* ticket collector
جامع الجوز
[Jame'a al-jooz] *n* nutter
جامعة [ʒa:miʕa] *n* university
جامعي [ʒa:miʕij] *adj* academic
الحرم الجامعي
[Al-ḥaram al-jame'aey] *n* campus
جامل [ʒa:mala] *v* compliment
جاموسة [ʒa:mu:sa] *n* buffalo
جانب [ʒa:nib] *n* side
بجانب
[Bejaneb] *prep* beside
جانبي [ʒa:nibij] *adj*
ضوء جانبي
[Ḍowa janebey] *n* sidelight
آثار جانبية
[Aathar janeebyah] *n* side effect
شارع جانبي
[Share'a janebey] *n* side street
جاهز [ʒa:hiz] *adj* bought
جاهزة [ʒa:hizat] *adj*
السيارة ستكون جاهزة
[al-sayara sa-ta-koon ja-heza] When will the car be ready?
متى ستكون جاهزة للتشغيل؟
[mata sata-koon jaheza lel-tash-gheel?] When will it be ready?
جاهل [ʒa:hil] *adj* ignorant
جبال [ʒiba:l] *npl* mountains
جبال الألب
[ʒiba:lu al-ʔalbi] *npl* Alps
جبال الأنديز
[ʒiba:lu al-ʔandi:zi] *npl* Andes
جبل
[ʒabal] *n* mountain
جبل جليدي
[Jabal jaleedey] *n* iceberg
دراجة الجبال
[Darrajah al-jebal] *n* mountain bike
أريد غرفة مطلة على الجبال
[areed ghurfa muṭella 'aala al-jebaal] I'd like a room with a view of the mountains
أين يوجد أقرب كوخ بالجبل؟
[ayna yujad a'qrab kookh bil-jabal?] Where is the nearest mountain hut?
جبان [ʒaba:n] *adj* cowardly ◃ *n* coward
جبد [ʒabad] *adj* fit
جبلي [ʒabalij] *adj* mountainous
جبن [ʒubn] *n* cheese
جبن قريش
[Jobn 'qareesh] *n* cottage cheese
ما نوع الجبن؟
[ma naw'a al-jibin?] What sort of cheese?
جبهة [ʒabha] *n* forehead
جثة [ʒuθθa] *n* corpse
جحيم [ʒaħi:m] *n* hell
جد [ʒadd] *n* granddad, grandfather, grandpa
الجَدّ الأكبر
[Al-jad al-akbar] *n* great-grandfather
جداً [ʒidan] *adv* very
مسرور جداً
[Masroor jedan] *adj* delighted
إلى جد بعيد
[Ela jad ba'aeed] *adv* most
جدار [ʒida:r] *n* wall
الجدار الواقي
[Al-jedar al-wa'qey] *n* firewall
جدة [ʒadda] *n* grandma, granny
الجدة الأكبر
[Al-jaddah al-akbar] *n* great-grandmother
جَدد [ʒaddada] *v* renew
جدف [ʒaddafa] *v* row (*in boat*)
جَدَلي [ʒadalij] *adj* controversial

جدول [ʒadwal] *n* stream, table *(chart)*
جدول أعمال
[Jadwal a'amal] *n* agenda
جدول زمني
[Jadwal zamaney] *n* schedule, timetable
جدياً [ʒiddi:an] *adv* seriously
جديد [ʒadi:d] *adj* new, unprecedented
جدير [ʒadi:r] *adj* worthy
جدير بالذكر
[Jadeer bel-dhekr] *adj* particular
جدير بالملاحظة
[Jadeer bel-molahaḍhah] *adj* remarkable
جذاب [ʒaððа:b] *adj* attractive
جذب [ʒaðaba] *v* pull *vt* ◁ attract
جِذر [ʒiðr] *n* root
جِذع [ʒiðʕ] *n* trunk
جَذف [ʒaððafa] *vi* paddle
جر [ʒarra] *v*
يَجُر سيارة
[Yajor sayarah] *v* tow away
جرأ [ʒaraʔa] *v* dare
جرئ [ʒariʔ] *adj* daring
جراب [ʒira:b] *n* bag, holdall
جراج [ʒara:ʒ] *n* garage
جراح [ʒarra:ħ] *n* surgeon
جراحة [ʒira:ħa] *n* surgery
جراحة تجميل
[Jerahat tajmeel] *n* plastic surgery
جراحة تجميلية
[Jerahah tajmeeleyah] *n* plastic surgery
جراد [ʒara:d] *n*
جراد الجندب
[Jarad al-jandab] *n* grasshopper
جراد البحر
[Jarad al-bahr] *n* crayfish
جَرَاد البحر
[Garad al-baḥr] *n* lobster
جرار [ʒaraar] *n* tractor
جرافة [ʒarra:fa] *n* bulldozer
جرافيك [ʒara:fi:k] *n*
رسوم جرافيك
[Rasm jrafek] *npl* graphics
جرام [ʒra:m] *n* gramme
جرانيت [ʒara:ni:t] *n*
حجر الجرانيت
[Ḥajar al-jraneet] *n* granite
جرب [ʒarraba] *v* try
هل يمكن أن أجربها من فضلك؟
[hal yamken an ajar-rebha min faḍlak?] Can I test it, please?
جرثومة [ʒurθu:ma] *n* germ
جرح [ʒurħ] *n* injury, wound
قابل للجرح
['qabel lel-jarh] *adj* vulnerable
جرح [ʒaraħa] *v* injure, wound
جرحي [ʒarħij] *adj* traumatic
جَرِد [ʒarrada] *v* strip
جرَذ [ʒurð] *n* rat
جرس [ʒaras] *n* bell
جرس الباب
[Jaras al-bab] *n* doorbell
جرعة [ʒurʕa] *n* dose
جرعة زائدة
[Jor'aah zaedah] *n* overdose
جرف [ʒurf] *n* drift, cliff
جرم [ʒurm] *n* crime
جرائم الكمبيوتر والانترنت
[Jraem al-kmobyoter wal-enternet] *n* cybercrime
جُرن [ʒurn] *n* trough
جرو [ʒarw] *n* puppy
جرى [ʒara:] *v* run
يَجْري بالفرس
[Yajree bel-faras] *v* gallop
جريدة [ʒari:da] *n* newspaper
أين يمكن أن أشتري الجرائد الإخبارية؟
[Ayn yomken an ashtray al-jraaed al-yawmeyah] Where can I buy a newspaper?
أين يوجد أقرب محل لبيع الجرائد؟
[Ayn yojad a'qrab mahal leby'a aljraaed?] Where is the nearest shop which sells newspapers?
هل يوجد لديكم جرائد إخبارية؟
[hal yujad laday-kum jara-ed ekhbar-iya?] Do you have newspapers?
جريمة [ʒari:ma] *n* crime
شريك في جريمة
[Shareek fee jareemah] *n* accomplice
جرينلاند [ʒri:nala:ndi] *n* Greenland

mow v [ʒazza] جزًّ
part n [ʒuzʔ] جزء
جزء صغير
[Joza ṣagheer] n bit
جزء ذو أهمية خاصة
[Joza dho ahammeyah khaṣah] n highlight
لا يعمل هذا الجزء كما ينبغي
[la ya'amal hatha al-juz-i kama yan-baghy] This part doesn't work properly
break up v [ʒazzaʔa] جَزأ
penalty n [ʒaza:ʔ] جزَاء
Algerian adj [ʒaza:ʔirij] جزائري
شخص جزائري
[Shakhṣ jazayry] n Algerian
butcher n [ʒazza:r] جزار
mower n [ʒazza:zatu] جزازة
جزازة العشب
[Jazazt al-'aoshb] n lawnmower
partial adj [ʒuzʔij] جزئي
بدوام جزئي
[Bedwam jozay] adv part-time
partly adv [ʒuzʔijan] جزئياً
carrot n [ʒazar] جزر
جزر أبيض
[Jazar abyad] n parsnip
جزر الهند الغربية
[Jozor al-hend al-gharbeyah] n West Indies
[ʒuzuru ʔal-ba:ha:ma:] جزر الباهاما Bahamas npl
molecule n [ʒuzajʔ] جزيء
island n [ʒazi:ra] جزيرة
جزيرة استوائية غير مأهولة
[Jozor ghayr maahoolah] n desert island
شبه الجزيرة
[Shebh al-jazeerah] n peninsula
bridge, embankment n [ʒisr] جسر
جسر معلق
[Jesr mo'aala'q] n suspension bridge
body n [ʒism] جسم
جسم السفينة
[Jesm al-safeenah] n hull
جسم مضاد
[Jesm moḍad] n antibody

greedy adj [ʒaʃiʕ] جشع
plaster (for wall) n [ʒibsˤ] جص
n [ʒunʕʕa] جعة
جعة معتقة
[Jo'aah mo'ata'qah] n lager
v [ʒaʕala] جعَل
يَجعَله عصريا
[Tej'aalah 'aṣreyan] v update
geography n [ʒuɣra:fja:] جغرافيا
drought n [ʒafa:f] جفاف
dry v [ʒaffafa] جَفف
eyelid n [ʒafn] جفن
gel n [ʒil] جَل
جل الشعر
[Jel al-sha'ar] n hair gel
majesty n [ʒala:la] جلالة
fetch, pick up v [ʒlaba] جلب
fuss n [ʒalaba] جَلَبة
skin n [ʒildu] جلد
جلد الغنم
[Jeld al-ghanam] n sheepskin
جلد مدبوغ
[Jeld madboogh] n leather
جلد مزأبر
[Jeld mazaabar] n suede
قشعريرة الجلد
['qash'aarerat al-jeld] n goose pimples
thump v [ʒalada] جلد
v [ʒalasa] جلس
هل يمكن أن نجلس معا؟
[hal yamken an najlis ma'aan?] Can we have seats together?
sit down v [jaʒlasa] جلس
يَجْلِس مرة أخرى
[Yajles marrah okhra] v resit
session n [ʒalsa] جلسة
stroke n [ʒaltˤa] جلطة
gluten n [ʒlu:ti:n] جلوتين
sitting n [ʒulu:s] جلوس
حجرة الجلوس
[Hojrat al-joloos] n lounge
أين يمكنني الجلوس؟
[ayna yamken-any al-jiloos?] Where can I sit down?
هل يوجد مكان يمكنني الجلوس فيه؟
[hal yujad makan yamken -ini al-juloos

feehe?] Is there somewhere I can sit down?
جلوكوز glucose *n* [ʒluku:z]
جَلّي obvious *adj* [ʒalij]
جليد ice *n* [ʒali:d]
جليدي icy *adj* [ʒali:dij]
نهر جليدي
[Nahr jaleedey] *n* glacier
جليس companion *(male)* *n* [ʒali:s]
جليس أطفال
[Jalees aṭfaal] *n* babysitter
جليسة companion *(female)* *n* [ʒali:sa]
جليسة أطفال
[Jaleesat aṭfaal] *n* nanny
جليل glorious *adj* [ʒali:l]
جماع sexual intercourse *n* [ʒima:ʕ]
جماعة lot *n* [ʒama:ʕa]
جماعي collective *adj* [ʒama: ʕij]
جمال beauty *n* [ʒama:l]
جمانزيوم gym *n* [ʒimna:zju:mi]
أخصائي الجمنازيوم
[akheṣaaey al-jemnazyom] *n* gymnast
تدريبات الجمنازيوم
[Tadreebat al-jemnazyoom] *npl* gymnastics
جمبري shrimp *n* [ʒambarij]
جمبري كبير
[Jambarey kabeer] *n* scampi
جمجمة skull *n* [ʒumʒuma]
جمركي *adj* [ʒumrukij]
رسوم جمركية
[Rosoom jomrekeyah] *npl* customs
جمع plural *n* [ʒamʕ]
جمعة Friday *n* [ʒumuʕa]
الجمعة العظيمة
[Al-jom'ah al-'aaḍheemah] *n* Good Friday
جمعية association *n* [ʒamʕijja]
جمل camel *n* [ʒamal]
جملة sentence *(words)* *n* [ʒumla]
جملي wholesale *adj* [ʒumalij]
جمهور audience *n* [ʒumhu:r]
جمهور الناخبين
[Jomhoor al-nakhebeen] *n* electorate
جمهورية republic *n* [ʒunmhu:rijjati]
جمهورية أفريقيا الوسطى
[Jomhoreyat afre'qya al-wosṭa] *n* Central African Republic
جمهورية التشيك
[Jomhoreyat al-tesheek] *n* Czech Republic
جمهورية الدومنيكان
[Jomhoreyat al-domenekan] *n* Dominican Republic
جميع all *adj* [ʒami:ʕ]
جميل beautiful *adj* [ʒami:l]
على نحو جميل
[Ala nahw jameel] *adv* prettily
بشكل جميل
[Beshakl jameel] *adv* beautifully
جنائي criminal *adj* [ʒina:ʔij]
جناح van, wing *n* [ʒana:ħ]
جناح أيسر
[Janah aysar] *adj* left-wing
جناح أيمن
[Janah ayman] *adj* right-wing
جناح من مستشفى
[Janah men al-mostashfa] *n* ward *(hospital room)*
جنازة funeral *n* [ʒana:za]
جنب side *n* [ʒanbun]
من الجنب
[Men al-janb] *adv* sideways
جنة paradise, heaven *n* [ʒanna]
جندي serviceman, soldier *n* [ʒundij]
جندي بحري
[Jondey baharey] *n* seaman
جنس category, class, *n* [ʒins] gender, sex
مؤيد للتفرقة العنصرية بحسب الجنس
[Moaed lel-tare'qa al'aonṣeryah behasb aljens] *n* sexist
مشته للجنس الآخر
[Mashtah lel-jens al-aakahar] *adj* heterosexual
جنسي sexual *adj* [ʒinsij]
مثير جنسيا
[Motheer jensyan] *adj* sexy
مُثير للشهوة الجنسية
[Motheer lel shahwah al-jenseyah] *adj* erotic
مَيْل جِنسي

[Mayl jensey] *n* sexuality
جنسية [ʒinsijja] *n* nationality
جنوب [ʒanu:bu] *n* south
جنوب أفريقيا
[Janoob afree'qya] *n* South Africa
جنوب شرقي
[Janoob shr'qey] *n* southeast
متجه للجنوب
[Motageh lel-janoob] *adj* southbound
واقع نحو الجنوب
[Wa'qe'a nahw al-janoob] *adj* southern
جنوباً [ʒanu:ban] *adv* south
جنوبي [ʒanu:bij] *adj* south
القارة القطبية الجنوبية
[Al-'qarah al-'qoṭbeyah al-janoobeyah] *n* Antarctic
القطب الجنوبي
[Al-k'qotb al-janoobey] *n* South Pole
شخص من أمريكا الجنوبية
[Shakhṣ men amreeka al-janoobeyah] *n* South American
قطبي جنوبي
['qoṭbey janoobey] *adj* Antarctic
كوريا الجنوبية
[Korya al-janoobeyah] *n* South Korea
جنون [ʒunu:n] *n* madness
جنية [ʒinnija] *n* fairy
جنين [ʒani:n] *n* foetus
جنيني [ʒani:nijjun] *adv* antenatal
جنيه [ʒunajh] *n*
جنيه استرليني
[Jeneh esterleeney] *n* pound sterling
جهاز [ʒiha:z] *n* apparatus, gear *(equipment)*, appliance
جهاز الرد الآلي
[Jehaz al-rad al-aaly] *n* answerphone
جهاز المناعة
[Jehaz al-mana'aa] *n* immune system
جهاز النداء الآلي
[Jehaz al-nedaa al-aaley] *n* bleeper
جهاز حفر
[Jehaz hafr] *n* rig
جهد [ʒuhd] *n* effort
جهد كهربي
[Jahd kahrabey] *n* voltage
بجهد شديد
[Bejahd shaded] *adv* barely
جهّز [ʒahhaza] *v* (يوفر) accommodate
يُجَهِّز بالسِّلَع
[Yojahez bel-sela'a] *v* stock up on
جهل [ʒahl] *n* ignorance
جو [ʒaww] *n* weather, air, atmosphere
الجو شديد البرودة
[al-jaw shaded al-boroda] It's freezing cold
الجو شديد الحرارة
[al-jaw shaded al-ḥarara] It's very hot
كيف ستكون حالة الجو غدا؟
[kayfa sata-koon ḥalat al-jaw ghadan?] What will the weather be like tomorrow?
ما هي حالة الجو المتوقعة غدا؟
[ma heya ḥalat al-jaw al-muta-wa'qi'aa ghadan?] What's the weather forecast?
هل من المتوقع أن يحدث تغيير في حالة الجو
[Hal men al-motwa'qa'a an yahdoth tagheer fee ḥalat al-jaw] Is the weather going to change?
جواتيمالا [ʒwa:ti:ma:la:] *n* Guatemala
جواد [ʒawa:d] *n*
جواد السباق
[Jawad al-seba'q] *n* racehorse
جواز [ʒawa:z] *n* permit
جواز سفر
[Jawaz al-safar] *n* passport
جواز مرور
[Jawaz moror] *n* pass *(permit)*
الأطفال مقيدون في هذا الجواز
[Al-aṭfaal mo'aydoon fee hadha al-jawaz] The children are on this passport
لقد سرق جواز سفري
[la'qad sure'qa jawaz safary] My passport has been stolen
لقد ضاع جواز سفري
[la'qad ḍa'aa jawaz safary] I've lost my passport
لقد نسيت جواز سفري

[la'qad nasyto jawaz safary] I've forgotten my passport

jeweller *n* [ʒawa:hirʒi:] **جواهرجي**

محل جواهرجي

[Maḥal jawaherjey] *n* jeweller's

quality *n* [ʒawda] **جودة**

Judo *n* [ʒu:du:] **جودو**

stocking *n* [ʒawrab] **جورب**

جورب قصير

[Jawrab 'qaṣeer] *n* sock

Georgian *adj* [ʒu:rʒij] **جورجي**

مواطن جورجي

[Mowaṭen jorjey] *n* Georgian *(person)*

Georgia *(country)* *n* [ʒu:rʒja:] **جورجيا**

ولاية جورجيا

[Welayat jorjeya] *n* Georgia *(US state)*

walnut *n* [ʒawz] **جوز**

جامع الجوز

[Jame'a al-jooz] *n* nutter

حساسية الجوز

[Hasaseyat al-joz] *n* nut allergy

nut *(food)* *n* [ʒawza] **جوزة**

جوزة الهند

[Jawzat al-hend] *n* coconut

hunger *n* [ʒu:ʕ] **جوع**

starve *v* [ʒu:ʕa] **جوّع**

hungry *adj* [ʒawʕa:n] **جوعان**

choir *n* [ʒawqa] **جَوْقة**

jockey *n* [ʒu:kij] **جوكي**

tour *n* [ʒawla] **جولة**

جولة إرشادية

[Jawlah ershadeyah] *n* guided tour

n [ʒu:lf] **جولف**

رياضة الجولف

[Reyadat al-jolf] *n* golf

ملعب الجولف

[Mal'aab al-jolf] *n* golf course

نادي الجولف

[Nady al-jolf] *n* golf club *(game)*

أين يمكنني أن ألعب الجولف؟

[ayna yamken-any an al-'aab al-jolf?] Where can I play golf?

skirt *n* [ʒawnala] **جونلة**

جونلة قصيرة

[Jonelah 'qaṣeerah] *n* miniskirt

substance *n* [ʒawhar] **جوهر**

jewel *n* [ʒawhara] **جوهرة**

essential *adj* [ʒawharij] **جَوهَري**

air *adj* [ʒawwij] **جوي**

ما المدة التي يستغرقها بالبريد الجوي؟

[ma al-mudda al-laty yasta-ghru'qoha bil-bareed al-jaw-wy?] How long will it take by air?

n [ʒawijja] **جوية**

أريد تغيير رحلتي الجوية

[areed taghyeer reḥlaty al-jaw-wya] I'd like to change my flight

Guyana *n* [ʒuja:na:] **جيانا**

pocket *n* [ʒajb] **جيب**

guitar *n* [ʒi:ta:r] **جيتار**

good, excellent *adj* [ʒajjid] **جيد**

إنه جيد جدًا

[inaho jayed jedan] It's quite good

هل يوجد شواطئ جيدة قريبة من هنا؟

[hal yujad shawaṭee jayida 'qareeba min huna?] Are there any good beaches near here?

well *adv* [ʒajjidan] **جيدًا**

مذاقه ليس جيدًا

[madha-'qaho laysa jay-edan] It doesn't taste very nice

هل نمت جيدًا؟

[hal nimt jayi-dan?] Did you sleep well?

lime *(compound)* *n* [ʒi:r] **جير**

n [ʒi:ra:nju:mi] **جيرانيوم**

نبات الجيرانيوم

[Nabat al-jeranyom] *n* geranium

army *n* [ʒajʃ] **جيش**

generation *n* [ʒi:l] **جيل**

jelly *n* [ʒi:li:] **جيلي**

n [ʒi:n] **جين**

جين وراثي

[Jeen werathey] *n* gene

n [ʒi:nz] **جينز**

ملابس الجينز

[Malabes al-jeenz] *npl* jeans

genetic *adj* [ʒi:nnij] **جيني**

geology *n* [ʒju:lu:ʒja:] **جيولوجيا**

حائز n [ħa:ʔiz]
الحائز على المرتبة الثانية
[Al-ḥaez ala al-martabah al-thaneyah] n runner-up
حائط wall n [ħa:ʔitˤ]
ورق حائط
[Wara'q ḥaeṭ] n wallpaper
حَاجّ pilgrim n [ħa:ʒʒ]
حاجب eyebrow, janitor n [ħa:ʒib]
حاجة need n [ħa:ʒa]
حاجة ملحة
[Hajah molehah] n demand
إننا في حاجة إلى مفتاح آخر
[ena-na fee ḥaja ela muftaaḥ aakhar] We need a second key
أنا في حاجة إلى مكواة
[ana fee ḥaja ela muk-wat] I need an iron
نحن في حاجة إلى المزيد من المفارش
[naḥno fee ḥaja ela al-mazeed min al-mafa-rish] We need more sheets
حاجز barrier n [ħa:ʒiz]
حاجز الأمواج
[Hajez al-amwaj] n mole *(infiltrator)*
حاجز الماء
[Hajez al-maa] n jetty
حاجز حجرى
[Hajez hajarey] n kerb
حاجز وضع التذاكر
[Hajez wad'a al-tadhaker] n ticket barrier
حاخام rabbi n [ħa:xa:m]
حاد sharp *adj* [ħa:dd]
حادث accident n [ħa:diθ]
إدارة الحوادث والطوارئ
[Edarat al-hawadeth wa-al-tawarea] n accident & emergency department
تأمين ضد الحوادث
[Taameen ḍed al-hawaadeth] n accident insurance
تعرضت لحادث
[ta'aar-ḍto le-ḥadith] I've had an accident
لقد وقع لي حادث
[la'qad wa'qa lee ḥadeth] I've been in an accident
ماذا أفعل عند وقوع حادث؟
[madha af'aal 'aenda wi-'qoo'a ḥadeth?] What do I do if I have an accident?
حادثة n [ħa:diθa]
كانت هناك حادثة
[kanat hunaka ḥadetha] There's been an accident!
حار hot *adj* [ħa:rr]
فلفل أحمر حار
[Felfel aḥmar ḥar] n chilli
هذه الغرفة حارة أكثر من اللازم
[hathy al-ghurfa ḥara ak-thar min al-laazim] The room is too hot
حارب fight v [ħa:raba]
حارَة n [ħa:ra]
أنت تسير في حارة غير صحيحة
[Anta taseer fee ḥarah gheyr ṣaheehah] You are in the wrong lane
حارس guard n [ħa:ris]
حارس الأمن
[Ḥares al-amn] n security guard
حارس المرمى
[Hares al-marma] n goalkeeper
حارس شخصي
[ḥares shakhṣ] n bodyguard
حازم strict *adj* [ħa:zim]
حاسب calculator, n [ħa:sib]

computer
علوم الحاسب الآلي
['aoloom al-ḥaseb al-aaly] *n* computer science
استخدام الحاسب الآلي
[Estekhdam al-haseb al-aaly] *n* computing
حاسبة [ħa:siba] *n*
آلة حاسبة
[Aalah ḥasbah] *n* calculator
آلة حاسبة للجيب
[Alah haseba lel-jeeb] *n* pocket calculator
حاسة [ħa:ssa] *n* sense
حاسة السمع
[Hasat al-sama'a] *n* audition
حاسم [ħa:sim] *adj* decisive
غير حاسم
[Gahyr hasem] *adj* indecisive
حاشية [ħa:ʃijja] *n* border
حاضر [ħa:dˤir] *adj* present ◁ *n* present *(time being)*
حاضر [ħa:dˤara] *v* lecture
حافة [ħa:ffa] *n* edge
حافز [ħa:fiz] *n* motive
حافظ [ħa:fizˤa] *n* guardian
مادة حافظة
[Madah ḥafeḍhah] *n* preservative
حافظ [ħa:fazˤa] *v*
يُحافِظ على
[Yoḥafez 'aala] *v* save
حافظة [ħa:fizˤa] *n* folder, wallet
حافلة [ħa:fila] *n* carriage *(train)*
حاقد [ħa:qid] *adj* spiteful
حاكم [ħa:kim] *n* ruler *(commander)*
حاكم [ħa:kama] *v* judge
حال [ħa:l] *n* situation
على أي حال
[Ala ay ḥal] *adv* anyway
فى الحال
[Fee al-hal] *adv* immediately
هل يجب علي دفعها في الحال؟
[hal yajib 'aala-ya daf'aa-ha fee al-ḥaal?] Do I have to pay it straightaway?
هل يمكنك تصليحها في الحال؟
[hal yamken -aka taṣlee-ḥaha fee al-ḥaal?] Can you do it straightaway?
حالًا [ħa:la:] *adv* readily
حالة [ħa:la] *n* state, situation, condition
الحالة الاجتماعية
[Al-halah al-ejtemaayah] *n* marital status
حالة طارئة
[Ḥalah ṭareaa] *n* emergency
حالة مزاجية
[Halah mazajeyah] *n* mood
حالي [ħa:lij] *adj* current
حاليا [ħa:lijjan] *adv* currently
حامض [ħa:midˤ] *adj* sour
حامل [ħa:mil] *n* rack
حامل أسهم
[Hamel ashom] *n* shareholder
حامل حقائب السفر
[Hamel ha'qaeb al-safar] *n* luggage rack
حامل حقيبة الظهر
[Hamel ha'qeebat al-ḍhahr] *n* backpacker
حانة [ħa:na] *n* pub
صاحب حانة
[Ṣaheb hanah] *n* publican
حانوتي [ħa:nu:tij] *n* undertaker
حاول [ħa:wala] *v* attempt
حاوِية [ħa:wija] *n* container
حب [ħubb] *n* love
حب الأطفال
[Hob al-atfaal] *n* paedophile
حب الشباب
[Hob al-shabab] *n* acne
حبار [ħabba:r] *n* squid
حبة [ħabba] *n* grain, seed, tablet
حبة الحمص
[Habat al-hommoṣ] *n* chickpea
حبة نوم
[Habit nawm] *n* sleeping pill
حبر [ħibr] *n* ink
حَبْس [ħabs] *n* prison
حَبك [ħibk] *n* knitting
حبل [ħabl] *n* cord, rope
الحبل الشوكي
[Al-ḥabl alshawkey] *n* spinal cord

حبل الغسيل
[ḥ abl al-ghaseel] *n* washing line
حَبلى [ħubla:] *adj* pregnant
حبوب [ħubu:b] *n* cereal
حبوب البن
[Ḥobob al-bon] *n* coffee bean
حبيب [ħabi:b] *n* darling
حبيبة [ħabi:ba] *n*
حبيبات خشنة
[Ḥobaybat khashabeyah] *npl* grit
حتمياً [ħatmi:an] *adv* ultimately
حتى [ħatta:] *adv* even
حث [ħaθθa] *v* persuade
حثالة [ħuθa:la] *n* refuse
حجاب [ħiʒa:b] *n* veil, cover
حجاب واقى
[Ḥejab wara'qey] *n* dashboard
حجاب واق
[Hejab wa'q̄] *n* shield
حجب [ħaʒaba] *v* screen
حجة [ħuʒʒa] *n* argument, document, pretext
حجر [ħaʒar] *n* stone
أحجار الدومينو
[Ahjar al-domino] *npl* dominoes
حجر رملي
[Hajar ramley] *n* sandstone
حجر الجرانيت
[Ḥajar al-jraneet] *n* granite
حجر الجير
[Hajar al-jeer] *n* limestone
حجر كريم
[Ajar kareem] *n* gem
حَجْر صحي
[Ḥajar ṣeḥey] *n* quarantine
حجرة [ħuʒra] *n* room
حجرة دراسية
[Ḥojrat derasah] *n* classroom
حجرة لحفظ المعاطف
[Hojarah le-hefḍh al-ma'atef] *n* cloakroom
هل هناك تدفئة بالحجرة
[hal hunaka tad-fiaa bil-ḥijra?] Does the room have heating?
هل يوجد وصلة إنترنت داخل الحجرة
[hal yujad wṣlat internet dakhil al-ḥijra?] Is there an Internet connection in the room?
حجز [ħaʒz] *n* reservation
حجز مقدم
[Hajz mo'qadam] *n* advance booking
لدي حجز
[la-daya ḥajiz] I have a reservation
لقد أكدت حجزي بخطاب
[la'qad akad-to ḥajzi bekhe-ṭab] I confirmed my booking by letter
هل يمكن أن أغير الحجز الذي قمت به؟
[hal yamken an aghyir al-ḥajiz al-ladhy 'qumt behe?] Can I change my booking?
حجز [ħʒiza] *v* reserve
أريد حجز غرفة لشخص واحد
[areed ḥajiz ghurfa le-shakhiṣ waḥid] I'd like to book a double room, I'd like to book a single room
أين يمكنني أن أحجز ملعبًا؟
[ayna yamken-any an aḥjiz mal-'aaban?] Where can I book a court?
حجم [ħaʒm] *n* size, volume
حُجَيْرَة [ħuʒajra] *n*
حُجَيْرَةُ الطَّيّار
[Ḥojayrat al-ṭayar] *n* cockpit
حد [ħadd] *n* boundary
حد أقصى
[Had a'qsa] *n* maximum
حداد [ħida:d] *n* mourning
حدث [ħadaθ] *n* event
حدث عرضي
[Hadth 'aradey] *n* incident
حدث [ħadaθa] *v*
ماذا حدث
[madha ḥadatha?] What happened?
من الذي يحدثني؟
[min al-ladhy yoḥadi-thny?] Who am I talking to?
حدث [ħadaθa] *v* happen
حدد [ħaddada] *v* specify
حَدَسْ [ħads] *n* intuition
حدق [ħaddaqa] *v* gaze
يُحَدِق بإمعان
[Yoḥade'q be-em'aaan] *v* pry
حدوث [ħudu:θ] *n* occurrence

n [ħaddu:q] **حدوق**
سمك الحدوق
[Samak al-ḥadoo'q] *n* haddock
recent *adj* [ħadi:θ] **حديث**
recently *adv* [ħadi:θan] **حديثاً**
n [ħadi:θa] **حديثة**
لغات حديثة
[Loghat hadethah] *npl* modern languages
iron *n* [ħadi:d] **حديد**
سكة حديد تحت الأرض
[Sekah hadeed taht al-arḍ] *n* underground
محل تاجر الحديد والأدوات المعدنية
[Maḥal tajer alḥadeed wal-adwat al-ma'adaneyah] *n* ironmonger's
iron *adj* [ħadi:dijjat] **حديدي**
قضبان السكة الحديدية
['qoḍban al-sekah al-ḥadeedeyah] *n* rail
garden *n* [ħadi:qa] **حديقة**
حديقة ألعاب
[Hadee'qat al'aab] *n* theme park
حديقة الحيوان
[Hadee'qat al-hayawan] *n* zoo
حديقة وطنية
[Hadee'qah waṭaneyah] *n* national park
shoe *n* [ħiða:ʔ] **حذاء**
حذاء عالي الساق
[hedhaa 'aaley al-sa'q] *n* boot
حذاء الباليه
[hedhaa al-baleeh] *npl* ballet shoes
حذاء برقبة
[Hedhaa be-ra'qabah] *npl* wellingtons
زوج أحذية رياضية
[Zawj ahzeyah Reyaḍeyah] *n* sneakers
هل يمكن إعادة تركيب كعب لهذا الحذاء؟
[hal yamken e'aa-dat tarkeeb ka'ab le-hadha al-ḥedhaa?] Can you re-heel these shoes?
هل يمكن تصليح هذا الحذاء؟
[hal yamken taṣleeḥ hadha al-ḥedhaa?] Can you repair these shoes?
cautious *adj* [ħaðir] **حذر**
بحذر
[beḥadhar] *adv* cautiously

توخي الحذر
[ta-wakhy al-ḥadhar] Take care
warn *v* [ħaððara] **حذّر**
caution *n* [ħaðar] **حَذَر**
careful *adj* [ħaðir] **حَذِرٌ**
eliminate *v* [ħðefa] **حذف**
delete *v* [ħaðafa] **حذف**
cute *adj* [ħaðiq] **حَذِق**
free *(no restraint)* *adj* [ħurr] **حر**
شديد الحر
[Shadeed al-har] *adj* sweltering
يعمل بشكل حر
[Ya'amal beshakl ḥor] *adj* freelance
adj [ħurru] **حُر**
حُر المهنة
[Ḥor al-mehnah] *adj* self-employed
heat *n* [ħara:ra] **حرارة**
درجة الحرارة
[Darajat al-haraarah] *n* temperature
درجة حرارة سلزيوس
[Darajat ḥararah selezyos] *n* degree Celsius
درجة حرارة فهرنهايتي
[Darjat hararh ferhrenhaytey] *n* degree Fahrenheit
لا يمكنني النوم بسبب حرارة الغرفة
[la yam-kinuni al-nawm be-sabab ḥararat al-ghurfa] I can't sleep because of the heat
war *n* [ħarb] **حرب**
حرب أهلية
[Ḥarb ahleyah] *n* civil war
n [ħura] **حرة**
أين يوجد السوق الحرة؟
[ayna tojad al-soo'q al-ḥorra?] Where is the duty-free shopping?
plough *vt* [ħaraθa] **حرث**
sulk *v* [ħarada] **حرد**
free *v* [ħarrara] **حَرَّر**
guard *v* [ħarasa] **حرَس**
letter *(a, b, c)* *n* [ħarf] **حرف**
حرف ساكن
[ḥarf saken] *n* consonant
حرف عطف
[Harf 'aaṭf] *n* conjunction
wrench *v* [ħarrafa] **حَرَّف**

craft *n* [ħirfa] **حرفة**
craftsman *n* [ħirafij] **حِرَفي**
literally *adv* [ħarfijjan] **حَرفياً**
burn *n* [ħuriqa] **حرق**
burn *vt* [ħaraqa] **حرق**
burning *n* [ħurqa] **حرقة**
حرقة في فم المعدة
[Ḥor'qah fee fom al-ma'adah] *n* heartburn
shift *vt* [ħarraka] **حَرّك**
movement *n* [ħaraka] **حركة**
حركة مفاجئة
[Ḥarakah mofajeah] *n* hitch
n [ħaram] **حرم**
الحرم الجامعي
[Al-ḥaram al-jame'aey] *n* campus
v [ħarrama] **حرِّم**
يُحرِم شخصاً من الدخول
[Yoḥrem shakhṣan men al-dokhool] *v* lock out
forbid *v* [ħarrama] **حَرَّم**
freedom *n* [ħurrijja] **حرية**
silk *n* [ħari:r] **حرير**
sack *n* [ħari:q] **حريق**
سُلَم النجاة من الحريق
[Solam al-najah men al-ḥaree'q] *n* fire escape
طفاية الحريق
[Ṭafayat ḥaree'q] *n* fire extinguisher
belt *n* [ħiza:m] **حزام**
حزام الأمان
[Hezam al-aman] *n* safety belt
حزام النجاة من الغرق
[Hezam al-najah men al-ghar'q] *n* lifebelt
حزام لحفظ المال
[Hezam lehefḍh almal] *n* money belt
party *(group)* *n* [ħizb] **حزب**
n [ħuzam] **حزم**
أنا في حاجة لحزم أمتعتي الآن
[ana fee ḥaja le-ḥazem am-te-'aaty al-aan] I need to pack now
pack *vt* [ħazama] **حَزم**
bunch, parcel *n* [ħuzma] **حِزْمة**
sorrow, sore *n* [ħuzn] **حُزْن**
بحُزْن
[Beḥozn] *adv* sadly
sad *adj* [ħazi:nu] **حزين**
sense, feeling *n* [ħiss] **حِس**
الحِس العام
[Al-ḥes al-'aaam] *n* common sense
soup *n* [ħasa:ʔ] **حساء**
ما هو حساء اليوم؟
[ma howa ḥasaa al-yawm?] What is the soup of the day?
account *(in bank)* *n* [ħisa:b] **حساب**
رقم الحساب
[Ra'qm al-hesab] *n* account number
حساب جاري
[Hesab tejarey] *n* current account
حساب بنكي
[Hesab bankey] *n* bank account, bank balance
حساب مشترك
[Hesab moshtarak] *n* joint account
يخصم مباشرةً من حساب العميل
[Yokhṣam mobasharatan men hesab al'ameel] *n* direct debit
المشروبات على حسابي
[al-mashro-baat 'ala ḥesaby] The drinks are on me
sensitive, *adj* [ħassa:s] **حساس** sentimental
غير حساس
[Ghayr hasas] *adj* insensitive
allergy *n* [ħasa:sijja] **حساسية**
حساسية تجاه الفول السوداني
[Hasaseyah tejah al-fool alsodaney] *n* peanut allergy
حساسية الجوز
[Hasaseyat al-joz] *n* nut allergy
reckon *v* [ħsaba] **حسب**
count *v* [ħasaba] **حسَب**
calculation *n* [ħusba:n] **حُسبان**
envy *n* [ħasad] **حسد**
envy *v* [ħasada] **حسد**
rebate *n* [ħasm] **حَسْم**
well *adj* [ħasan] **حَسَن**
حسن الاطلاع
[Hosn al-etela'a] *adj* knowledgeable
حسن المظهر
[Hosn al-maḍhar] *adj* good-looking

حُسْن [ħusn] *n* excellence, beauty
حسن السلوك
[Ḥasen al-solook] *adj* well-behaved
حسن الأحوال
[Hosn al-ahwaal] *adj* well-off
حسن الدخل
[Hosn al-dakhl] *adj* well-paid
لحسن الطالع
[Le-hosn alṭale'a] *adj* luckily
حسناً [ħasanan] *excl* okay!, OK!
حسود [ħasu:d] *adj* envious
حسي [ħissij] *adj* sensuous
حشد [ħaʃd] *n* crowd, presenter (multitude)
حشرة [ħaʃara] *n* insect
الحشرة العصوية
[Al-hasherah al-'aodweia] *n* stick insect
حشرة صرار الليل
[Hashrat ṣarar al-layl] *n* cricket (insect)
حشرة القرادة
[Hashrat al-'qaradah] *n* tick
حشو [ħaʃw] *n* filling
لقد تآكل الحشو
[la'qad ta-aa-kala al-ḥasho] A filling has fallen out
هل يمكنك عمل حشو مؤقت؟
[hal yamken -aka 'aamal ḥasho mo-a'qat?] Can you do a temporary filling?
حشوة [ħaʃwa] *n* stuffing
حشي [ħaʃeja] *vi* swot, charge (electricity)
حشية [ħiʃja] *n* mattress
حشيش [ħaʃi:ʃ] *n* cannabis
حشيش مخدر
[Hashesh mokhader] *n* marijuana
حصاة [ħasˤa:t] *n* pebble
حصاة المرارة
[Haṣat al-mararah] *n* gallstone
حصاد [ħasˤa:d] *n* harvest
حصالة [ħasˤsˤa:la] *n*
حصالة على شكل خنزير
[Ḥaṣalah ala shakl khenzeer] *n* piggybank
حصان [ħisˤa:n] *n* horse
حصان خشبي هزاز
[Heṣan khashabey hazaz] *n* rocking horse
حدوة الحصان
[Hedawat heṣan] *n* horseshoe
حصبة [ħasˤaba] *n* measles
حصبة ألمانية
[Haṣbah al-maneyah] *n* German measles
حصة [ħisˤsˤa] *n* portion
حصد [ħasˤada] *v* harvest
حصل [jaħsˤala] *v*
يَحصُل على
[Tahṣol 'ala] *v* get
هل يمكن أن أحصل على جدول المواعيد من فضلك؟
[hal yamken an aḥṣal 'aala jadwal al-mawa-'aeed min faḍlak?] Can I have a timetable, please?
حصن [ħisˤn] *n* fort
حصول [ħusˤu:l] *n* acquisition
أرغب في الحصول على خمسمائة...
[Arghab fee al-ḥoṣol alaa khomsamah...] I'd like five hundred...
أريد الحصول على أرخص البدائل
[areed al-ḥuṣool 'aala arkhaṣ al-badaa-el] I'd like the cheapest option
كيف يمكن لنا الحصول على التذاكر؟
[kayfa yamkun lana al-ḥuṣool 'aala al-tadhaker?] Where can we get tickets?
هل يمكنني استخدام بطاقتي للحصول على أموال نقدية؟
[hal yamken -any esti-khdaam beṭa-'qatee lil-ḥiṣool 'aala amwaal na'qdiya?] Can I use my card to get cash?
هل يمكنني الحصول على شوكة نظيفة من فضلك؟
[hal yamken -any al-ḥuṣool 'aala shawka naḍhefa min faḍlak?] Could I have a clean fork please?
حصى [ħasˤa:] *n* gravel
حضارة [ħadˤa:ra] *n* civilization
حضانة [ħadˤa:na] *n* nursery
حضانة أطفال
[Haḍanat aṭfal] *n* crêche

حضر *n* [ħadˤr]

حضر التجول

[haḍr al-tajawol] *n* curfew

حضر *v* [ʔeħadˤara]

يَحضر حفل

[Taḥḍar ḥafl] *v* party

حضّر attend, bring *v* [ħadˤdˤara]

حضن lap *n* [ħudˤn]

حضور presence *n* [ħudˤu:r]

حطام wreckage *n* [ħutˤa:m]

سفينة محطمة

[Safeenah mohaṭamah] *adj* shipwrecked

حطام السفينة

[Hoṭam al-safeenah] *n* shipwreck

حُطام النيزك

[Ḥoṭaam al-nayzak] *n* meteorite

حطم wreck *v* [ħatˤama]

حظ luck *n* [ħazˤzˤ]

حظ سعيد

[haḍh sa'aeed] *n* fortune

لسوء الحظ

[Le-soa al-haḍh] *adv* unfortunately

لحسن الحظ

[Le-hosn al-haḍh] *adv* fortunately

حظر ban *n* [ħazˤr]

حظر prohibit *v* [ħazˤara]

حظيرة yard *(enclosure)* *n* [ħazˤi:ra]

حفار digger *n* [ħaffa:r]

حفر dig *vt* [ħafara]

حفرة hole *n* [ħufra]

حفرة رملية

[Hofrah ramleyah] *n* sandpit

حَفّز prompt *v* [ħaffaza]

حفظ keep *vt* ◁ memorize *v* [ħafazˤa]

يَحفَظ في ملف

[yahfaḍh fee malaf] *v* file *(folder)*

حفل gathering, event *n* [ħafl]

حفل راقص

[Half ra'qeṣ] *n* ball *(dance)*

أين يمكنني شراء تذاكر الحفل الغنائي؟

[ayna yamken-any sheraa tadhaker al-ḥafil al-ghenaee?] Where can I buy tickets for the concert?

نحن هنا لحضور حفل زفاف

[naḥno huna le-ḥiḍor ḥafil zafaaf] We are here for a wedding

حفلة party *(social gathering)* *n* [ħafla]

حفلة عشاء

[Ḥaflat 'aashaa] *n* dinner party

حفلة موسيقية

[Haflah mose'qeyah] *n* concert

حفيد grandchild *n* [ħafi:d]

حفيدة granddaughter *n* [ħafi:da]

حق right *n* [ħaq]

حق الرفض

[Ha'q al-rafḍ] *n* veto

حق المرور

[Ha'q al-moror] *n* right of way

حقوق الإنسان

[Ho'qoo'q al-ensan] *npl* human rights

حقوق الطبع والنشر

[Ho'qoo'q al-ṭab'a wal-nashr] *n* copyright

حقوق مدنية

[Ḥo'qoo'q madaneyah] *npl* civil rights

حقاً right *excl* ◁ indeed *adv* [ħaqqan]

حقد *v* [ħaqada]

يَحْقِد على

[yaḥ'qed 'alaa] *v* spite

حقق achieve *v* [ħaqqaqa]

حقل field *n* [ħaql]

حقل النشاط

[Ha'ql al-nashaṭ] *n* career

حقل للتجارب

[Ha'ql lel-tajareb] *n* guinea pig *(for experiment)*

حقن injection *n* [ħaqn]

حقن inject *v* [ħaqana]

حقنة shot, syringe *n* [ħuqna]

أحتاج إلى حقنة تيتانوس

[aḥtaaj ela ḥe'qnat tetanus] I need a tetanus shot

حقوق law *npl* [ħuqu:qun]

كلية الحقوق

[Kolayt al-ho'qooq] *n* law school

حقيبة bag *n* [ħaqi:ba]

حقيبة صغيرة

[Ha'qeebah ṣagheerah] *n* bum bag

حقيبة سِرْج الحصان

[Ha'qeebat sarj al-hoṣan] *n* saddlebag

حقيبة أوراق

[Ha'qeebat awra'q] *n* portfolio

حقيبة أوراق جلدية
[Ha'qeebat awra'q jeldeyah] *n* briefcase
حقيبة الظهر
[Ha'qeebat al-ḍhahr] *n* rucksack
حقيبة للرحلات القصيرة
[Ha'qeebah lel-rahalat al-'qaṣeerah] *n* overnight bag
حقيبة للكتب المدرسية
[Ha'qeebah lel-kotob al-madraseyah] *n* satchel
حقيبة مبطنة
[Ha'qeebah mobaṭanah] *n* sponge bag
حقيبة ملابس تحمل على الظهر
[Ha'qeebat malabes tohmal 'aala al-ḍhahr] *n* rucksack
حقيبة من البوليثين
[Ha'qeebah men al-bolytheleyn] *n* polythene bag
حقيبة يد
[Ha'qeebat yad] *n* handbag
شكرًا لا أحتاج إلى حقيبة
[shukran la aḥtaj ela ḥa'qeba] I don't need a bag, thanks
من فضلك هل يمكنني الحصول على حقيبة أخرى؟
[min faḍlak hal yamkin-ani al-ḥuṣool 'aala ḥa'qeba okhra?] Can I have an extra bag, please?
حقير [ħaqi:r] *adj* stingy
حقيقة [ħaqi:qa] *n* fact, truth
حقيقي [ħaqi:qij] *adj* true
غير حقيقي
[Ghayer ha'qee'qey] *adj* unreal
حك [ħakka] *n* scratching
يَتَطلب الحك
[yataṭalab al-hak] *adj* itchy
حكّ [ħakka] *v* rub
حكاية [ħika:ja] *n* tale
إحدى حكايات الجان
[Aḥad ḥekayat al-jan] *n* fairytale
حكم [ħakama] *v*
يَحْكُم على
[Yaḥkom 'ala] *v* sentence
حَكَم [ħakam] *n* umpire
حَكَم مباريات رياضية
[Hosn almaḍhar] *n* referee
حُكم [ħukm] *n* rule, sentence (*punishment*)
حُكم المحلفين
[Hokm al-mohallefeen] *n* verdict
حُكْم ذاتي
[ḥokm ḍhatey] *n* autonomy
حِكمة [ħikma] *n* wisdom
حَكومة [ħukuwamt] *n* government
موظف حكومة
[mowaḍhaf hokomah] *n* civil servant
حكومي [ħuku:mij] *adj* governmental
موظف حكومي
[mowaḍhaf ḥokomey] *n* servant
حكيم [ħaki:m] *adj* wise
غير حكيم
[Ghayer hakeem] *adj* unwise
حل [ħall] *n* solution
حل [ħalla] *v*
يَحل محل
[Taḥel maḥal] *v* substitute
حلّ [ħalla] *v* work out
حلاق [ħalla:q] *n* shaving, barber
ماكينة حلاقة
[Makeenat ḥelaqah] *npl* clippers
صالون حلاقة
[Ṣalon ḥelaqah] *n* hairdresser's
شفرة حلاقة
[Shafrat hela'qah] *n* razor blade
ماكينة حِلاقَة
[Makenat ḥela'qa] *n* shaver
موسى الحلاقة
[Mosa alḥela'qah] *n* razor
حلب [ħalaba] *v* milk
حلبة [ħalaba] *n* rink
حلبة تَزَلُّج
[Ḥalabat tazaloj] *n* skating rink
حلبة السباق
[ḥ alabat seba'q] *n* racetrack
حلبة من الجليد الصناعي
[Ḥalabah men aljaleed alṣena'aey] *n* ice rink
حلزون [ħalazu:n] *n* snail
حلف [ħalafa] *v* swear
حلق [ħalaqa] *v* shave
حلقة [ħalaqa] *n* round, circle, ring

analyse v [ħallala] حلل
dream n [ħulm] حلم
dream v [ħalama] حلم
sweet (taste) adj [ħulw] حلو
sweet, toffee n [ħalwa:] حلوى
حلوى البودينج
[Ḥalwa al-boodenj] n sweet
قائمة الحلوى من فضلك
['qaemat al-ḥalwa min faḍlak] The dessert menu, please
sweets npl [ħalawija:tun] حلويات
milk n [ħali:b] حليب
حليب منزوع الدسم
[Haleeb manzoo'a al-dasam] n skimmed milk
حليب نصف دسم
[Haleeb nesf dasam] n semi-skimmed milk
بالحليب دون خلطه
[bil ḥaleeb doon khal-ṭuho] with the milk separate
ornament n [ħilijja] حلية
حلية متدلية
[Halabh motadaleyah] n pendant
ally n [ħali:f] حليف
shaved adj [ħali:q] حليق
غير حليق
[Ghayr ḥalee'q] adj unshaven
donkey n [ħima:r] حمار
الحمار الوحشي
[Al-hemar al-wahshey] n zebra
enthusiasm n [ħama:sa] حماسة
chickenpox n [ħumq] حُماق
braces, sling n [ħamma:la] حمالة
حمالة ثياب
[Hammalt theyab] n hanger
حَمَّالة صَدْر
[Hammalat ṣadr] n bra
bath, loo, toilet n [ħamma:m] حمام
بُرْنس حمام
[Bornos hammam] n dressing gown
حمام بخار
[Hammam bokhar] n sauna
مستلزمات الحمام
[Mostalzamat al-hammam] npl toiletries
منشفة الحمام
[Manshafah alḥammam] n bath towel
يَاخُذ حمام شمس
[yaakhoḍ hammam shams] v sunbathe
الحمام تغمره المياه
[al-ḥamaam taghmurho al-me-aa] The bathroom is flooded
هل يوجد حمام خاص داخل الحجرة
[hal yujad ḥamam khaṣ dakhil al-ḥujra?] Does the room have a private bathroom?
baths npl [ħamma:ma:tun] حمامات
pigeon n [ħama:ma] حمامة
protection n [ħima:ja] حماية
acid n [ħimdˁ] حمض
adj [ħimdˁijjat] حمضي
أمطار حمضية
[Amṭar ḥemdeyah] n acid rain
pregnancy n [ħaml] حمل
عازل طبى لمنع الحمل
['aazel ṭebey le-man'a al-haml] n condom
حمل حقيبة الظهر
[Hamal ha'qeebat al-ḍhahr] n backpacking
منع الحمل
[Man'a al-ḥml] n contraception
مواد مانعة للحمل
[Mawad mane'aah lel-haml] n contraceptive
download v [ħammala] حمل
carry vt [ħamala] حمل
lamb n [ħiml] حَمَل
pregnancy n [ħaml] حَمْل
load n [ħiml] حِمل
campaign n [ħamla] حَملة
stare, v [ħamlaqa] حملق
glare (يسطع)
cargo n [ħumu:la] حُمولة
fever n [ħumma:] حمى
protect v [ħama:] حمى
close, intimate adj [ħami:m] حميم
n [ħinθ] حنث
الحنث باليمين
[Al-ḥanth bel-yameen] n perjury
throat n [ħanʒura] حنجرة
tap n [ħanafijja] حنفية

حنون [ħanu:n] *adj* affectionate, kind
حنين [ħani:n] *adj* longing
حنين إلى الوطن
[Ḥaneem ela al-waṭan] *adj* homesick
حوار [ħiwa:ru] *n* dialogue
حوالة [ħawa:la] *n*
حوالة مالية
[Ḥewala maleyah] *n* postal order
حوالي [ħawa:laj] *prep* about
حَوَّامَة [ħawwa:ma] *n* hovercraft
حوت [ħu:t] *n* whale
حور [ħu:r] *n* poplar
خشب الحور
[Khashab al-ḥoor] *n* poplar, wood
حورية [ħu:rijja] *n*
حورية الماء
[Ḥooreyat al-maa] *n* mermaid
حوض [ħawdˤdˤ] *n* basin, pool
حوض سمك
[Hawḍ al-samak] *n* aquarium
حوض استحمام
[Hawḍ estehmam] *n* bathtub
حوض السفن
[Hawḍ al-sofon] *n* dock
حوض الغسل
[Hawḍ al-ghaseel] *n* washbasin
حوض مرسى السفن
[Hawḍ marsa al-sofon] *n* marina
حوض منتج للنفط
[Hawḍ montej lel-nafṭ] *n* pool *(resources)*
حوض نباتات
[Hawḍ nabatat] *n* plant pot
حَوض [ħawdˤ] *n* pool *(water)*
حَوض سباحة للأطفال
[Ḥaeḍ sebaha lel-aṭfaal] *n* paddling pool
حول [ħawla] *prep* round
حوّل [ħawwala] *v*
يَحْول عَيْنَه
[Yoḥawel aynah] *v* squint
حَوّل [ħawwala] *v* switch
حي [ħajj] *adj* live
حي الفقراء
[Hay al-fo'qraa] *n* slum
حياة [ħaja:t] *n* life
على قيد الحياة
[Ala 'qayd al-hayah] *adj* alive
حياة برية
[Hayah bareyah] *n* wildlife
مُنقذ للحياة
[Mon'qedh lel-ḥayah] *adj* life-saving
نمط حياة
[Namaṭ hayah] *n* lifestyle
حيادي [ħija:dij] *n* neutral
حيازة [ħija:za] *n* possession
حيث [ħajθu] *conj* where
حيث أن
[Hayth ann] *adv* as, because
حيثما [ħajθuma:] *adv* everywhere
حيطة [ħi:tˤa] *n* precaution
حيوان [ħajawa:n] *n* animal
حيوان أليف
[Ḥayawaan aleef] *n* pet
حيوان الغُرَير
[Ḥayawaan al-ghoreer] *n* badger
حيوان الهمستر
[Heyawaan al-hemester] *n* hamster
حيوي [ħajawij] *adj* vital
مضاد حيوي
[Moḍad ḥayawey] *n* antibiotic
حيوية [ħajawijja] *n* zip

بالخارج
[Bel-kharej] *adv* abroad
خارجاً [xa:riʒan] *adv* out, outside
خارجي [xa:riʒij] *adj* exterior, outside
أريد إجراء مكالمة خارجية، هل يمكن أن تحول لي أحد الخطوط؟
[areed ejraa mukalama kharij-iya, hal yamkin an it-ḥawil le aḥad al-khiṭooṭ?] I want to make an outside call, can I have a line?
خارطة [xa:ritˤatu] *n* map, chart
خارطة الشارع
[khareṭat al-share'a] *n* street map
خارق [xa:riq] *adj* out-of-the-ordinary
خارق للطبيعة
[Khare'q lel-ṭabe'aah] *adj* supernatural
خازوق [xa:zu:q] *n* pole
خاص [xa:sˤsˤ] *adj* special
عرض خاص
['aarḍ khaṣ] *n* special offer
خاصة [xa:sˤsˤatan] *adv* specially
خاط [xa:tˤa] *v* sew
خاطئ [xa:tˤiʔ] *adj* incorrect, wrong
على نحو خاطئ
[Ala nahwen khaṭea] *adv* wrong
خاطر [xa:tˤir] *n* thought, wish
عن طيب خاطر
[An ṭeeb khaṭer] *adv* willingly
خاطف [xa:tˤif] *adj* momentary
خاف [xa:fa] *v* fear
خالٍ [xa:lin] *adj* empty
خال [xa:l] *n* mole *(skin)*
خالد [xa:lid] *adj* eternal
خالي [xa:li:] *adj* free (of)
خالى من الرصاص
[Khaley men al-raṣaṣ] *adj* lead-free
هل توجد أطباق خالية من الجلوتين؟
[hal tojad aṭba'q khaleya min al-jiloteen?] Do you have gluten-free dishes?
هل توجد أطباق خالية من منتجات الألبان؟
[hal tojad aṭba'q khaleya min munta-jaat al-albaan?] Do you have dairy-free dishes?
هل يمكن إعداد وجبة خالية من

خائر [xa:ʔir] *adj* excellent
خائر القوى
[Khaaer al-'qowa] *adj* faint
خائف [xa:ʔif] *adj* afraid, apprehensive, scared
خائف من الأماكن المغلقة
[Khaef men al-amaken al-moghla'ah] *adj* claustrophobic
خائن [xa:ʔin] *adj* unfaithful
خاتم [xa:tam] *n* ring
خاتم الخطوبة
[Khatem al-khotobah] *n* engagement ring
خاتم البريد
[Khatem al-bareed] *n* postmark
خاتم الزواج
[Khatem al-zawaj] *n* wedding ring
خاتمة [xa:tima] *n* conclusion
خادم [xa:dim] *n* server *(person)*, servant
خادمة [xa:dima] *n* maid
خادمة فى فندق
[Khademah fee fodo'q] *n* maid
خارج [xa:riʒ] *n* outside
خارج النطاق المُحَدد
[Kharej al-neta'q al-mohadad] *adv* offside

الجلوتين؟
[hal yamken e'adad wajba khaliya min al-jilo-teen?] Could you prepare a meal without gluten?
خام [xa:m] adj raw
خامة [xa:ma] n
ماهي خامة؟
[ma heya khamat al-ṣuni'a?] What is the material?
خامس [xa:mis] adj fifth
خان [xa:na] n inn
خان [xa:na] v betray
خانق [xa:niq] adj stifling
خبّ [xabba] v
يَخِبُّ الفَرَس
[Yakheb al-faras] v trot
خباز [xabba:z] n baker
خبرة [xibra] n experience
خبرة العمل
[Khebrat al'aamal] n work experience
قليل الخبرة
['qaleel al-khebrah] adj inexperienced
خبز [xubz] n bread, baking
خبز أسمر
[Khobz asmar] n brown bread
خبز محمص
[Khobz mohammṣ] n toast *(grilled bread)*
خبز ملفوف
[Khobz malfoof] n roll
كِسْرة خبز
[Kesrat khobz] n crumb
محمصة خبز كهربائية
[Mohamaṣat khobz kahrobaeyah] n toaster
من فضلك أحضر لي المزيد من الخبز
[min faḍlak iḥḍir lee al-mazeed min al-khibz] Please bring more bread
هل تريد بعض الخبز؟
[hal tureed ba'aḍ al-khubz?] Would you like some bread?
خبز [xabaza] v bake
خبل [xabil] adj mad *(insane)*
خبيث [xabi:θ] adj malicious, malignant
خبير [xabi:r] n expert
ختم [xatama] v seal
خِتم [xitm] n seal *(mark)*
خَجلان [xaʒla:n] n ashamed
خجول [xaʒu:l] adj self-conscious
خد [xadd] n cheek
خِداع [xida:ʕ] n scam
خَدِر [xadir] adj numb
خدش [xudʃu] n scratch
خدش [xadaʃa] v scratch
خدَع [xadaʕa] v bluff, kid
خدعة [xudʕa] n trick
خدم [xadama] v serve
خدمة [xidma] n service
خدمة رسائل الوسائط المتعددة
[Khedmat rasael al-wasaaeṭ almota'aadedah] n MMS
خدمة سرية
[Khedmah serreyah] n secret service
خدمة الغرف
[Khedmat al-ghoraf] n room service
خدمة ذاتية
[Khedmah ḍateyah] n self-service, self-catering *(lodging)*
مدة خدمة
[Modat khedmah] n serve
محطة الخدمة
[Mahaṭat al-khedmah] n service station
أريد في تقديم شكاوى بشأن الخدمة
[areed ta'q-deem shakawee be-shan al-khedma] I want to complain about the service
أي الصيدليات تقدم خدمة الطوارئ؟
[ay al-ṣyda-lyaat to'qadem khidmat al-ṭawa-ree] Which pharmacy provides emergency service?
كانت الخدمة سيئة للغاية
[kanat il-khidma say-ia el-ghaya] The service was terrible
هل هناك مصاريف للحصول على الخدمة؟
[Hal honak maṣareef lel-ḥoṣol ala al-khedmah] Is there a charge for the service?
خديعة [xadi:ʕa] n bluff
خراب [xara:b] n ruin, wreck
خراج [xura:ʒ] n abscess
أعاني من وجود خراج

[o-'aany min wijood khuraaj] I have an abscess

خُرَّاج abscess *n* [xurra:ʒ]

خرافي superstitious *n* [xura:fij]

خرّب sabotage *v* [xxarraba]

خرّب *v* [xarraba]

يُخَرِّب الممتلكات العامة والخاصة عن عمد

[Yokhareb al-momtalakat al-'aaamah 'an 'amd] *v* vandalize

خربش scribble *v* [xarbaʃa]

خرج *v* [xraʒa]

متى سيخرج من المستشفى؟

[mata sa-yakhruj min al-mus-tashfa?] When will he be discharged?

خرج get out *v* [xaraʒa]

خرخر purr *v* [xarxara]

خُردة junk *n* [xurda]

خردل mustard *n* [xardal]

خرزة bead *n* [xurza]

خرشوف artichoke *n* [xarʃu:f]

خرصانة concrete *n* [xarasˤa:na]

خرطوشة cartridge *n* [xartˤu:ʃa]

خرطوم hose *n* [xurtˤu:m]

خرطوم المياه

[Kharṭoom al-meyah] *n* hosepipe

خرق pierce *v* [xaraqa]

خرقة rag *n* [xirqa]

خرّم punch *v* [xarrama]

خروج way out, departure *n* [xuru:ʒ]

أين يوجد باب الخروج؟

[ayna yujad bab al-khorooj?] Where is the exit?

خروف sheep *n* [xaru:f]

صوف الخروف

[Ṣoof al-kharoof] *n* fleece

خريج graduate *n* [xirri:ʒ]

خريطة map *n* [xari:tˤa]

خريطة البروج

[khareeṭat al-brooj] *n* horoscope

خريطة الطريق

[Khareeṭat al-ṭaree'q] *n* road map

أريد خريطة الطريق لـ...

[areed khareeṭat al-ṭaree'q le...] I need a road map of...

أين يمكن أن أشتري خريطة للمنطقة؟

[ayna yamken an ash-tary khareeṭa lil-manṭa'qa?] Where can I buy a map of the region?

هل لديكم خريطة لمحطات المترو؟

[hal ladykum khareeṭa le-muḥaṭ-aat al-metro?] Do you have a map of the tube?

هل يمكن أن أري مكانه على الخريطة؟

[Hal yomken an ara makanah ala al-khareeṭah] Can you show me where it is on the map?

هل يمكنني الحصول على خريطة المترو من فضلك؟

[hal yamken -any al-ḥuṣool 'aala khareeṭat al-mitro min faḍlak?] Could I have a map of the tube, please?

هل يوجد لديك خريطة... ؟

[hal yujad ladyka khareeṭa...?] Have you got a map of...?

خريف *n* [xari:f]

الخريف

[Al-khareef] *n* autumn

خزان reservoir *n* [xazza:nu]

خزان بنزين

[Khazan benzeen] *n* petrol tank

خزانة safe, closet, cabinet *n* [xiza:na]

خزانة الأمتعة المتروكة

[Khezanat al-amte'ah al-matrookah] *n* left-luggage locker

خزانة الثياب

[Khezanat al-theyab] *n* wardrobe

خزانة بقفل

[Khezanah be-'qefl] *n* locker

خزانة كتب

[Khezanat kotob] *n* bookcase

خزانة للأطباق والكؤوس

[Khezanah lel aṭba'q wal-koos] *n* cupboard

خزانة ملابس بأدراج

[Khezanat malabes be-adraj] *n* chest of drawers

خزفي ceramic *adj* [xazafij]

خزن stock *v* [xazana]

خزّن store *v* [xazzana]

خزي shame *n* [xizj]

خزينة safe *n* [xazi:na]

أريد أن أضع مجوهراتي في الخزينة [areed an aḍa'a mujaw-haraty fee al-khazeena] I would like to put my jewellery in the safe
ضع هذا في الخزينة من فضلك [ḍa'a hadha fee al-khazena, min faḍlak] Put that in the safe, please
خَسْ lettuce *n* [xussu]
خسارة loss *n* [xasa:ra]
خسر lose *vt* [xasara]
خسيس rubbish *adj* [xasi:s]
خشب wood *(material) n* [xaʃab]
خشب أبلكاج [Khashab ablakaj] *n* plywood
خشبة *n* [xaʃabatu]
خشبة المسرح [Khashabat al-masrah] *n* stage
خشبي wooden *adj* [xaʃabij]
خشخاش poppy *n* [xaʃxa:ʃ]
خشخيشة *n* [xaʃxi:ʃa]
خشخيشة الأطفال [Khashkheeshat al-aṭfaal] *n* rattle
خشن harsh, rough *adj* [xaʃin]
خص belong *v* [xasˤsˤa]
خِصب fertile *adj* [xisˤb]
خَصر waist *n* [xasˤr]
خصص privatize *v* [xasˤsˤasˤa]
خُصلة *n* [xusˤla]
خُصلة شعر [Khoṣlat sha'ar] *n* lock *(hair)*
خصم discount *n* [xasˤm]
خصم للطلاب [Khaṣm lel-ṭolab] *n* student discount
هل يتم قبول بطاقات الخصم؟ [hal yatum 'qubool be-ṭa'qaat al-khaṣim?] Do you take debit cards?
خَصْم adversary, opponent, *n* [xasˤm] rival
خصوص *n* [xusˤu:sˤ]
على وجه الخصوص [Ala wajh al-khoṣoṣ] *adv* particularly
خصوصاً especially *adv* [xusˤwusˤan]
خصوصي private *adj* [xusˤu:sˤij]
خصية testicle *n* [xisˤja]
خضار vegetable *n* [xudˤa:r]
خضر vegetables *npl* [xudˤar]
متجر الخضر والفاكهة [Matjar al-khoḍar wal-fakehah] *n* greengrocer's
خط queue *n* [xatˤtˤu]
إشارة إنشغال الخط [Esharat ensheghal al-khat] *n* engaged tone
خط أنابيب [Khaṭ anabeeb] *n* pipeline
خط التماس [Khaṭ al-tamas] *n* touchline
خط الاستواء [Khaṭ al-estwaa] *n* equator
خط طول [Khaṭ ṭool] *n* longitude
ما هو الخط الذي يجب أن أستقله؟ [ma howa al-khaṭ al-lathy yajeb an asta'qil-uho?] Which line should I take for...?
خطأ mistake *n* [xatˤa]
رقم خطأ [Ra'qam khaṭaa] *n* wrong number
خطأ فادح [Khata fadeh] *n* blunder
خطأ مطبعي [Khata matba'aey] *n* misprint
خطاب letter, message, *n* [xitˤa:b] speech, address
أريد أن أرسل هذا الخطاب [areed an arsil hadha al-kheṭab] I'd like to send this letter
خُطاف crook *n* [xutˤa:f]
خُطبة speech *n* [xutˤba]
خطة scheme *n* [xutˤtˤa]
خطر danger *n* [xatˤar]
هل يوجد خطر من وجود الكتلة الجليدية المنحدرة؟ [hal yujad khatar min wijood al-kutla al-jalee-diya al-muḥadera?] Is there a danger of avalanches?
خطَف abduct *v* [xatˤafa]
خطوة step *n* [xutˤwa]
خطيئة sin *n* [xatˤi:ʔa]
خطيب fiancé *n* [xatˤi:b]
خطيبة fiancée *n* [xatˤi:ba]
خطير dangerous *adj* [xatˤi:r]

n [xalnaʒ] خَلَنج
نبات الخَلَنج
[Nabat al-khalnaj] n heather
bat (mammal) n [xuffa:ʃ] خُفّاش
guard n [xafar] خفر
خفر السواحل
[Khafar al-ṣawaḥel] n coastguard
reduce v [xaffadˤa] خَفَض
dilute, relieve v [xafaffa] خفف
throb v [xafaqa] خفق
hidden adj [xafij] خفي
light (not dark), light adj [xafi:f] (not heavy) خفيف
vinegar n [xall] خل
summary n [xula:sˤa] خلاصة
خلاصة بحث أو منهج دراسي
[Kholaṣat bahth aw manhaj derasey] n syllabus
mixer n [xala:atˤ] خلاط
خلاط كهربائي
[Khalaṭ kahrabaey] n liquidizer
contrast, difference n [xila:f] خلاف
بخلاف
[Be-khelaf] prep apart from
creative adj [xalla:q] خلاق
through prep [xila:la] خلال
خلال ذلك
[Khelal dhalek] adv meanwhile
mix up v [xalatˤa] خلط
v [xalaʕa] خلع
يَخلع ملابسه
[Yakhla'a malabesh], take off
behind adv [xalfa] خلف
للخلف
[Lel-khalf] adv backwards
rear adj [xalfij] خلفي
متجه خلفاً
[Motajeh khalfan] adj back
background n [xalfijja] خلفية
marinade v [xallala] خلّل
eternity n [xulu:d] خُلود
n [xulu:l] خُلول
أم الخُلول
[Om al-kholool] n mussel
outdoor adj [xalawij] خلوي
cell n [xalijja] خلية

bay n [xali:ʒ] خليج
دُوَل الخليج العربي
[Dowel al-khaleej al'arabey] npl Gulf States
mixture n [xali:tˤ] خليط
mistress n [xali:la] خليلة
veil n [xima:r] خمار
five-part adj [xuma:sij] خماسي
مباراة خماسية
[Mobarah khomaseyah] n pentathlon
stub out v [xamada] خمد
wine n [xamr] خمر
خَمْر الشِري
[Khamr alsherey] n sherry
خَمْر الطعام
[Khamr al-ṭa'aam] n table wine
هذا الخمر ليس مثلج
[hatha al-khamur lysa muthal-laj] This wine is not chilled
هذه البقعة بقعة خمر
[hathy al-bu'q-'aa bu'q-'aat khamur] This stain is wine
five number [xamsatun] خَمْسة
number [xamsata ʕaʃar] fifteen خَمْسة عشر
fifty number [xamsu:na] خَمْسُون
guess v [xammana] خمّن
yeast n [xami:ra] خَمِيرَة
trench n [xandaq] خَنْدَق
خَنْدَق مائي
[Khanda'q maaey] n moat
pig n [xinzi:r] خنزير
خنزير غينيا
[Khnzeer ghemyah] n guinea pig (rodent)
فخذ الخنزير المدخن
[Fakhdh al-khenzeer al-modakhan] n ham
لحم خنزير
[Lahm al-khenzeer] n pork
لحم خنزير مقدد
[Laḥm khanzeer me'qaded] n bacon
beetle n [xunfusa:ʔ] خُنفَساء
خُنفُساء الدَعْسُوقَة
[Khonfesaa al-da'aso'qah] n ladybird
strangle, suffocate v [xanaqa] خنق

nectarine, peach *n* [xu:x] **خُوخ**
helmet *n* [xuwða] **خوذة**
هل يمكن أن أحصل على خوذة؟
[hal yamken an aḥṣal 'aala khoo-dha?] Can I have a helmet?
fear *n* [xawf] **خوف**
خوف مرضي
[Khawf maraḍey] *n* phobia
intimidate *v* [xawwafa] **خوّف**
cucumber, option *n* [xija:r] **خِيَار**
tailor *n* [xajja:tˤ] **خَيَّاط**
sewing *n* [xija:tˤa] **خياطة**
ماكينة خياطة
[Makenat kheyaṭah] *n* sewing machine
sewing *n* [xaja:tˤa] **خِيَاطة**
imagination *n* [xaja:l] **خَيال**
خيال علمي
[Khayal 'aelmey] *n* science fiction
خيال الظِل
[Khayal al-ḍhel] *n* scarecrow
fantastic *adj* [xaja:lij] **خَيَالِي**
n [xajba] **خيب**
خيبة الأمل
[Khaybat al-amal] *n* disappointment
disappoint *v* [xajjaba] **خيّب**
good *adj* [xajr] **خير**
بخير، شكرا
[be-khair, shukran] Fine, thanks
bamboo *n* [xajzura:n] **خَيْزُرَان**
v [xajatˤa] **خيط**
يُخيط تماما
[Yokhayeṭ tamaman] *v* sew up
thread *n* [xajtˤ] **خَيْط**
خَيْط تنظيف الأسنان
[Khayṭ tandheef al-asnan] *n* dental floss
horse *n* [xajl] **خيل**
ركوب الخيل
[Rekoob al-khayl] *n* horse riding
دوامة الخيل
[Dawamat al-kheel] *n* merry-go-round
أود أن أشاهد سباقًا للخيول؟
[awid an oshahed seba'qan lil-khiyool] I'd like to see a horse race
أود أن أقوم بنزهة على ظهر الخيول؟
[awid an a'qoom be-nozha 'aala ḍhahir al-khiyool] I'd like to go pony trekking

هيا نذهب لركوب الخيل
[hya nadhhab le-rikoob al-khayl] Let's go horse riding
camp *v* [xajjama] **خيم**
tent *n* [xajma] **خيمة**
عمود الخيمة
['amood al-kheemah] *n* tent pole
نريد موقع لنصب الخيمة
[nureed maw'qi'a le-naṣib al-khyma] We'd like a site for a tent
هل يمكن أن ننصب خيمتنا هنا؟
[Hal yomken an nansob khaymatna hona?] Can we pitch our tent here?

داء [daːʔ] *n* illness
داء البواسير
[Daa al-bawaseer] *n* piles
داء الكلب
[Daa al-kalb] *n* rabies
دائرة [daːʔira] *n* (*series*) circle, round
دائرة تلفزيونية مغلقة
[Daerah telefezyoneyah moghla'qa] *n* CCTV
دائرة البروج
[Dayrat al-boroj] *n* zodiac
دائرة انتخابية
[Daaera entekhabeyah] *n* constituency, precinct
دائرة من مدينة
[Dayrah men madeenah] *n* ward (*area*)
الدائرة القطبية الشمالية
[Al-daerah al'qoṭbeyah al-Shamaleyah] *n* Arctic Circle
دائري [daːʔirij] *adj* circular
طريق دائري
[Ṭaree'q dayery] *n* ring road
دائم [daːʔim] *adj* permanent
بشكل دائم
[Beshakl daaem] *adv* permanently
دائما [daːʔiman] *adv* always
دَاخِل [daːxila] *n* inside
دَاخِلٌ [daːxil] *n* interior
داخلًا [daːxilaː] *adv* inside
داخلي [daːxilij] *adj* domestic, indoor, internal
أنبوب داخلي
[Anboob dakheley] *n* inner tube
تلميذ داخلي
[telmeedh dakhely] *n* boarder
لباس داخلي
[Lebas dakhely] *n* panties
مدرسة داخلية
[Madrasah dakheleyah] *n* boarding school
ملابس داخلية
[Malabes dakheleyah] *n* underwear
مُصَمِم داخلي
[Moṣamem dakheley] *n* interior designer
نظام الاتصال الداخلي
[nedhaam aleteṣaal aldakheley] *n* intercom
ما الأنشطة الرياضية الداخلية المتاحة؟
[ma al-anshiṭa al-reyaḍya al-dakhiliya al-mutaḥa?] What indoor activities are there?
داخلياً [daːxilijjan] *adv* indoors
دار [daːr] *n* house, building
دار سك العملة
[Daar ṣaak al'aomlah] *n* mint (*coins*)
دار ضيافة
[Dar eḍafeyah] *n* guesthouse
دار البلدية
[Dar al-baladeyah] *n* town hall
دار الشباب
[Dar al-shabab] *n* youth hostel
دار المجلس التشريعى
[Dar al-majles al-tashre'aey] *n* council house
ماذا يعرض الآن في دار الأوبرا؟
[madha yu'a-raḍ al-aan fee daar al-obera?] What's on tonight at the opera?
دارة [daːra] *n* circuit
داس [daːsa] *vt* stamp ◁ *v* step on
دافئ [daːfiʔ] *adj* warm
دافع [daːfiʕ] *n*

دافع الضرائب
[Daafe'a al-ḍarayeb] *n* tax payer
defend *v* [da:fasa] **دافع**
Danish *adj* [da:nma:rkij] **دانماركي**
Dane *n* ◁
adj [da:nmarkijjat] **دانمركي**
اللغة الدانمركية
[Al-loghah al-danmarkeyah] *(language) n* Danish
bear *n* [dubb] **دُبّ**
دُب تيدي بير
[Dob tedey beer] *n* teddy bear
tank *(combat vehicle) n* [dabba:ba] **دبابة**
stapler *n* [dabba:sa] **دَبَّاسَة**
v [dabbasa] **دَبَّس**
يُدَبِّس الأوراق
[Yodabes al-wra'q] *v* staple
n [dibs] **دِبْس**
دِبْس السكَر
[Debs al-sokor] *n* treacle
diploma *n* [diblu:ma:] **دبلوما**
adj [diblu:ma:sij] **دبلوماسي** diplomatic
diplomat *n* ◁
wasp *n* [dabu:r] **دبور**
pin *n* [dabbu:s] **دبوس**
دبوس أمان
[Daboos aman] *n* safety pin
دبوس تثبيت اللوائح
[Daboos tathbeet al-lawaeh] *n* drawing pin
دبوس شعر
[Daboos sha'ar] *n* hairgrip
أحتاج إلى دبوس آمن
[aḥtaaj ela dub-boos aamin] I need a safety pin
thrush *n* [duʒʒ] **دُجّ**
hen, chicken *n* [daʒa:ʒa] **دجاجة**
juggler *n* [daʒʒa:l] **دَجَّال**
smoke *n* [duxa:n] **دخان**
كاشف الدُخان
[Kashef al-dokhan] *n* smoke alarm
هناك رائحة دخان بغرفتي
[hunaka ra-eḥa dukhaan be-ghurfaty] My room smells of smoke
income *n* [daxl] **دخل**

ضريبة دخل
[Ḍareebat dakhl] *n* income tax
access, come in *v* [daxala] **دَخل**
income *n* [daxla] **دَخْل**
v [daxxin] **دخن**
أين يمكن أن أدخن؟
[ayna yamken an adakhin?] Where can I smoke?
هل أنت ممن يدخنون؟
[hal anta me-man yoda-khinoon?] Do you smoke?
smoke *v* [daxana] **دخّن**
entry (مادة) *n* [duxu:l] **دخول**
رَسْم الدخول
[Rasm al-dokhool] *n* entrance fee
يَسمَح بالدخول
[Yasmaḥ bel-dokhool] *v* admit *(allow in)*
exotic, alien *adj* [daxi:l] **دخيل**
banister *n* [dara:bizi:n] **درابزين**
npl [dara:bzi:na:tun] **درابَزينات** railings
cycle *n* [darra:ʒa] **دراجة**
راكب الدراجة
[Rakeb al-darrajah] *n* cyclist
دراجة ترادفية
[Darrajah tradofeyah] *n* tandem
دراجة آلية
[darrajah aaleyah] *n* moped
دراجة الرِجْل
[Darrajat al-rejl] *n* scooter
دراجة الجبال
[Darrajah al-jebal] *n* mountain bike
دراجة بخارية
[Darrajah bokhareyah] *n* cycle *(bike)*
دراجة بمحرك
[Darrajah be-moharrek] *n* motorbike
دراجة نارية
[Darrajah narreyah] *n* motorcycle
دراجة هوائية
[Darrajah hawaeyah] *n* bike
منفاخ دراجة
[Monfakh draajah] *n* bicycle pump
study *n* [dira:sa] **دراسة**
دراسة السوق
[Derasat al-soo'q] *n* market research
لا زلت في الدراسة

[la zilto fee al-deraasa] I'm still studying
دراسي academic *adj* [dira:sij]
عام دراسي
['aam derasey] *n* academic year
حجرة دراسية
[Ḥojrat derasah] *n* classroom
كتاب دراسي
[Ketab derasey] *n* textbook
منهج دراسى
[Manhaj derasey] *n* curriculum
دراما drama *n* [dra:ma:]
درامي dramatic *adj* [dra:mij]
درب driveway *n* [darb]
درّب train *vt* [darraba]
دَرَج staircase *n* [daraʒ]
دُرج drawer *n* [durʒ]
دُرج الأسطوانات المدمجة
[Dorj al-esṭewanaat al-modmajah] *n* CD-ROM
دُرج العربة
[Dorj al-'aarabah] *n* glove compartment
دُرج النقود
[Dorj al-no'qood] *n* till
درجة degree, class *n* [daraʒa]
إلى درجة فائقة
[Ela darajah fae'qah] *adv* extra
درجة رجال الأعمال
[Darajat rejal ala'amal] *n* business class
درجة سياحية
[Darjah seyaḥeyah] *n* economy class
درجة أولى
[Darajah aula] *adj* first-class
درجة ثانية
[Darajah thaneyah] *n* second class
درجة الباب
[Darajat al-bab] *n* doorstep
درجة الحرارة
[Darajat al-haraarah] *n* temperature
درجة حرارة سلزيوس
[Darajat ḥararah selezyos] *n* degree Celsius
درجة حرارة فهرنهايتي
[Darjat hararh ferhrenhaytey] *n* degree Fahrenheit
درجة حرارة مئوية
[Draajat ḥaraarah meaweyah] *n* degree centigrade
بدرجة أقل
[Be-darajah a'qal] *adv* less
بدرجة أكبر
[Be-darajah akbar] *adv* more
بدرجة كبيرة
[Be-darajah kabeerah] *adv* largely
من الدرجة الثانية
[Men al-darajah althaneyah] *adj* second-rate
دردار elm *n* [darda:r]
شجر الدردار
[Shajar al-dardaar] *n* elm tree
دردش chat *v* [dardaʃa]
دردشة chat *n* [dardaʃa]
درز stitch *v* [daraza]
درس study *v* [darasa]
يَدْرُس بِجِد
[Yadros bejed] *v* swot *(study)*
دَرس teach *v* [darrasa]
دَرْس lesson *n* [dars]
درس خصوصي
[Dars khoṣoṣey] *n* tutorial
دَرْس القيادة
[Dars al-'qeyadah] *n* driving lesson
هل يمكن أن نأخذ دروسا؟
[hal yamken an nakhudh di-roosan?] Can we take lessons?
دِرْع armour *n* [dirʕ]
درم do one's nails *v* [darrama]
دروة *n* [dirwa]
دروة تدريبية
[Dawrah tadreebeyah] *n* training course
دستة dozen *n* [dasta]
دستور constitution *n* [dustu:r]
دسم fat *n* [dasam]
قليل الدسم
['qaleel al-dasam] *adj* low-fat
الطعام كثير الدسم
[al-ṯa'aam katheer al-dasim] The food is very greasy
دش shower *n* [duʃʃ]
الدش لا يعمل
[al-doosh la ya'amal] The shower doesn't work
الدش متسخ

[al-doosh mutasikh] The shower is dirty

دعا invite *v* [daʕa:]

يَدْعو إلى

[Yad'aoo ela] *v* call for

دِعائم piles *npl* [daʕa:ʔimun]

دُعَابة humour *n* [duʕa:ba]

دعامة pier, pillar, *n* [daʕa:ma] support

دِعَايَة propaganda *n* [diʕa:jat]

دَعم support, backing *n* [daʕm]

دعم back up *v* ◁ support *n* [dʕama]

دعوة invitation *n* [daʕwa]

دعوة إلى طعام أو شراب

[Dawah elaa ṭa'aam aw sharaab] *n* treat

دعوى suit *n* [daʕwa:]

دعوى قضائية

[Da'awa 'qaḍaeyah] *n* proceedings

دَغدغ tickle *v* [daɣdaɣa]

دغِل jungle *n* [daɣl]

دَغَل bush *(thicket)* *n* [daɣal]

دفء warmth *n* [difʔ]

بدأ الدفء في الجو

[Badaa al-defaa fee al-jaw] It's thawing

دفاع defence *n* [difa:ʕ]

الدفاع عن النفس

[Al-defaa'a 'aan al-nafs] *n* self-defence

دفتر notebook *n* [diftar]

دفتر صغير

[Daftar ṣagheer] *n* notepad

دفتر العناوين

[Daftar al-'aanaaween] *n* address book

دفتر الهاتف

[Daftar al-hatef] *n* phonebook

دفتر شيكات

[Daftar sheekaat] *n* chequebook

دفتر تذاكر من فضلك

[daftar tadhaker min faḍlak] A book of tickets, please

دفع payment *n* [dafʕ]

دفع بالغيبة

[Dafa'a bel-ghaybah] *n* alibi

واجب دفعه

[Wajeb daf'aaho] *adj* payable

أين يتم الدفع؟

[ayna yatim al-daf'a?] Where do I pay?

هل سيكون الدفع واجبًا علي؟

[hal sayakon al-dafi'a wajeban 'aalya?] Will I have to pay?

هل يجب الدفع مقدما؟

[hal yajib al-dafi'a mu'qad-aman?] Do I pay in advance?

دفع pay, push *v* [dfaʕa]

متى أدفع؟

[mata adfa'a?] When do I pay?

هل هناك أية إضافة تدفع؟

[hal hunaka ayaty eḍafa tudfa'a?] Is there a supplement to pay?

هل يمكن أن تدفع سيارتي

[hal yamken an tadfa'a sayaraty?] Can you give me a push?

يجب أن تدفع لي

[yajib an tad-fa'a lee...] You owe me...

دفن bury *v* [dafana]

دقّ ring *v* [daqqa]

دقة *n* [daqqa]

دقة قديمة

[Da'qah 'qadeemah] *adj* old-fashioned

دِقّة accuracy *n* [diqqa]

بِدِقّة

[Bedae'qah] *adv* accurately

دقق *v* [daqqaqa]

يدقق الحسابات

[Yoda'qe'q al-ḥesabat] *v* audit

دقيق accurate *adj* [daqi:q]

غير دقيق

[Ghayer da'qee'q] *adj* inaccurate

دقيق الحجم

[Da'qee'q al-hajm] *adj* minute

دقيق الشوفان

[Da'qee'q al-shofaan] *n* porridge

دقيق طحين

[Da'qee'q ṭaheen] *n* flour

دقيقة minute *n* [daqi:qa]

من فضلك، هل يمكن أن أترك حقيبتي معك لدقيقة واحدة؟

[min faḍlak, hal yamkin an atrik ḥa'qebaty ma'aak le-da'qe'qa waḥeda?] Could you watch my bag for a minute, please?

هناك أتوبيس يغادر كل 20 دقيقة

[Honak otobees yoghader kol 20 da'qee'qa] The bus runs every twenty

minutes
دكتاتوري [dikta:tu:rij] *n* bossy
دِلالة [dala:la] *n* significance
دَلايَة [dala:ja] *n* locket
دلو [dalw] *n* pail, bucket
دليل [dali:l] *n* directory, evidence, handbook, proof
دليل التشغيل
[Daleel al-tashgheel] *n* manual
دليل الهاتف
[Daleel al-hatef] *n* telephone directory
استعلامات دليل الهاتف
[Este'alamat daleel al-hatef] *npl* directory enquiries
ما هو رقم استعلامات دليل التليفون؟
[ma howa ra'qim esti'a-lamaat daleel al-talefon?] What is the number for directory enquiries?
دم [dam] *n* blood
ضغط الدم
[ḍaghṭ al-dam] *n* blood pressure
تسمم الدم
[Tasamom al-dam] *n* blood poisoning
اختبار الدم
[Ekhtebar al-dam] *n* blood test
فصيلة دم
[faṣeelat dam] *n* blood group
نقل الدم
[Na'ql al-dam] *n* blood transfusion, transfusion
هذه البقعة بقعة دم
[hathy al-bu'q-'aa bu'q-'aat dum] This stain is blood
دمار [dama:r] *n* destruction
مسبب لدمار هائل
[Mosabeb ledamar haael] *adj* devastating
دِمَاغ [dima:ɣ] *n* brain
دَمِث [damiθ] *adj*
دَمِث الأخلاق
[Dameth al-akhla'q] *adj* good-natured
دِمج [damaʒa] *v* merge
دَمْج [damʒ] *n* merger
دِمّر [dammara] *v* destroy
دَمّر [dammara] *v* ruin
دَمْعَة [damʕa] *n* tear *(from eye)*
دِمغة [damɣa] *n* stamp
دُمّل [dumul] *n* pimple
دموي [damawij] *n* bloody
دمية [dumja] *n* doll
دمية متحركة
[Domeyah motaḥarekah] *n* puppet
دنيم [dani:m] *n*
قماش الدنيم القطنى
['qomash al-deneem al-'qotney] *n* denim
دِنيم [dini:mi] *n*
سروال من قماش الدِنيم القطنى
[Serwal men 'qomash al-deneem al-'qotney] *n* jeans
دِهَان [diha:n] *n* paint
دُهْني [duhnij] *adj* greasy
دواء [dawa:ʔ] *n* remedy, medicine
دواء مُقَوي
[Dawaa mo'qawey] *n* tonic
حبة دواء
[Habbat dawaa] *n* tablet
دوار [duwa:ru] *n* vertigo, motion sickness
دوار الجو
[Dawar al-jaw] *n* airsick
دُوار [duwa:r] *n* vertigo ◁ *adj* dizzy
دَوّاسة [dawwa:sa] *n* pedal
دوام [dawa:m] *n* length of time
دوام كامل
[Dawam kamel] *adj* full-time
دوخة [du:xa] *n* vertigo, nausea
أعاني من الدوخة
[o-'aany min al-dokha] I suffer from vertigo
أشعر بدوخة
[ash-'aur be-dowkha] I feel dizzy
لا زلت أعاني من الدوخة
[la zilto o'aany min al-dokha] I keep having dizzy spells
دُودَة [du:da] *n* worm
دور [dawr] *n* round, floor, role
دَور رئيسي
[Dawr raaesey] *n* lead *(in play/film)*
على من الدور؟
[Ala man al-door?] Whose round is it?
في أي دور تقع هذه الغرفة
[fee ay dawr ta'qa'a hadhy al-ghurfa?]

What floor is it on?
في أي دور توجد محلات الأحذية؟ [fee ay dawr tojad maḥa-laat al-aḥ-dhiyah?] Which floor are shoes on?
دور [dawara] *v* turn, cycle
السيارة لا تدور [al-sayara la tadoor] The car won't start
يجب أن تدور إلى الخلف [yajib an tadoor ela al-khalf] You have to turn round
دَوَران [dawara:n] *n* circulation
دورة [dawra] *n* cycle *(recurring period)*, turn
دورة تنشيطية [Dawrah ṭansheeṭeyah] *n* refresher course
دَوْرَة تعليمية [Dawrah ta'aleemeyah] *n* course
دورق [dawraq] *n* carafe, flask
دورق من النبيذ الأبيض [dawra'q min al-nabeedh al-abyaḍ] a carafe of white wine
دَورية [dawrijja] *n* patrol
دولاب [du:la:b] *n*
أي من دولاب من هذه الدواليب يخصني؟ [ay doolab lee?] Which locker is mine?
دُولَار [du:la:r] *n* dollar
دولة [dawla] *n* country
دولة تشيلي [Dawlat tesheeley] *n* Chile
دُولفين [du:lfi:n] *n* dolphin
دولي [dawlij] *adj* international
أين يمكن أن أقوم بإجراء مكالمة دولية؟ [ayna yamken an a'qoom be-ijraa mukalama daw-liya?] Where can I make an international phonecall?
هل تبيع كروت المكالمات الدولية التليفونية؟ [hal tabee'a kroot al-muka-lamat al-daw-liya al-talefoniya?] Do you sell international phonecards?
دومنيكان [du:mini:ka:n] *adj* Dominican
جمهورية الدومنيكان [Jomhoreyat al-domenekan] *n* Dominican Republic
دومينو [du:mi:nu:] *n*
أحجار الدومينو [Ahjar al-domino] *npl* dominoes
لعبة الدومينو [Loabat al-domeno] *n* domino
دوّن [dawwana] *v* note down, blog, write down
دير [dajr] *n* monastery
دَيْر الراهبات [Deer al-rahebat] *n* convent
دَيْر الرهبان [Deer al-rohban] *n* abbey, monastery
هل الدير مفتوحة للجمهور؟ [Hal al-deer maftoḥah lel-jomhoor?] Is the monastery open to the public?
ديزيل [di:zi:l] *n*
وقود الديزيل [Wa'qood al-deezel] *n* diesel
ديسكو [di:sku:] *n* disco
ديسمبر [di:sambar] *n* December
دى في دي [di:fi: di:] *n*
اسطوانة دى في دي [Esṭwanah DVD] *n* DVD
ديك [di:k] *n* cock
دِيك رومي [Deek roomey] *n* turkey
دِيك صغير [Deek ṣagheer] *n* cockerel
ديكتاتور [di:kta:tu:r] *n* dictator
ديمقراطي [di:muqra:tˤij] *adj* democratic
ديمقراطية [di:muqra:tˤijja] *n* democracy
دَيْن [dajn] *n* debt
دِينْ [dajn] *n* religion
دَيناصور [di:na:sˤu:r] *n* dinosaur
ديناميكي [di:na:mi:kajj] *adj* dynamic
ديني [di:nij] *adj* religious, sacred

ذِرَاع [ðiraːʕ] *n* arm
ذِراع الفتيس
[dhera'a al-fetees] *n* gearshift
لا يمكنني تحريك ذراعي
[la yam-kinuni taḥreek thera-'ay] I can't move my arm
لقد جرح ذراعه
[la'qad jara-ḥa thera-'aehe] He has hurt his arm
ذرة [ðura] *n*
ذرة سكري
[dhorah sokarey] *n* sweetcorn
نشا الذرة
[Nesha al-zorah] *n* cornflour
ذَرَّة [ðarra] *n* atom
ذُرَة [ðura] *n* corn
رقائق الذُرَة
[Ra'qae'a al-dorrah] *npl* cornflakes
ذروة [ðirwa] *n* peak
ساعات الذروة
[Sa'aat al-dhorwah] *npl* peak hours
في غير وقت الذروة
[Fee ghaeyr wa'qt al-dhorwah] *adv* off-peak
ذرور [ðuruːr] *n*
ذرور معطر
[Zaroor mo'aṭar] *n* sachet
ذَرِي [ðarij] *adj* atomic
ذُعْر [ðuʕr] *n* panic, scare
ذقن [ðaqn] *n* chin
ذكاء [ðakaːʔ] *n* intelligence
شخص متقد الذكاء
[shakhṣ mota'qed al-dhakaa] *n* brilliant
ذَكَّر [ðakkara] *v* remind
ذَكَر [ðkara] *v* mention
ذَكَر [ðakar] *n* male
ذَكَرِي [ðakarij] *adj* male
ذِكْرَى [ðikraː] *n* memory, remembrance
ذِكْرى سنوية
[dhekra sanaweyah] *n* anniversary
ذكي [ðakij] *adj* brainy, smart, intelligent
ذنب [ðanab] *n* tail
نجم ذو ذنب
[Najm dho dhanab] *n* comet

ذاب [ðaːba] *vi* melt
ذئب [ðiʔb] *n* wolf
ذاتي [ðaːtij] *adj* personal
سيرة ذاتية
[Seerah dhateyah] *n* CV
حُكْم ذاتي
[ḥokm ḍhatey] *n* autonomy
ذاق [ðaːqa] *v*
هل يمكنني تذوقها؟
[hal yamken -any tadha-we'qha?] Can I taste it?
ذَاكِرة [ðaːkira] *n* memory
ذاهب [ðaːhib] *n*
نحن ذاهبون إلى...
[naḥno dhahe-boon ela...] We're going to...
ذُبَابَة [ðubaːba] *n* fly
ذُبَابَة صغيرة
[Dhobabah ṣagheerah] *n* midge
ذبحة [ðabħa] *n*
ذبحة صدرية
[dhabhah ṣadreyah] *n* angina
ذَبُل [ðabula] *v* wilt
ذَخِيرة [ðaxiːra] *n* ammunition
ذخيرة حربية
[dhakheerah ḥarbeyah] *n* magazine *(ammunition)*

ذَنْب guilt *n* [ðanb]
ذهاب going *n* [ðaha:b]
أريد الذهاب للتزلج
[areed al-dhehaab lil-tazal-oj] I'd like to go skiing
أين يمكن الذهاب لـ...؟
[ayna yamken al-dhehaab le...?] Where can you go...?
أين يمكنني الذهاب للعدو؟
[ayna yamken-any al-dhehab lel-'aado?] Where can I go jogging?
نريد الذهاب إلى...
[nureed al-dhehaab ela...] We'd like to go to...
هل يمكن أن تقترح بعض الأماكن الشيقة التي يمكن الذهاب إليها؟
[hal yamken an ta'qta-reḥ ba'aḍ al-amakin al-shay-i'qa al-laty yamken al- dhehaab elay-ha?] Can you suggest somewhere interesting to go?
ذهب gold *n* [ðahab]
مطلي بالذهب
[Maṭley beldhahab] *adj* gold-plated
ذهب go *v* [ðahaba]
يَذهَب بسرعة
[yaḍhab besor'aa] *v* go away
سوف أذهب إلى...
[Sawf adhhab ela] I'm going to...
لم أذهب أبدا إلى...
[lam athhab abadan ela...] I've never been to...
لن أذهب
[Lan adhhab] I'm not coming
هل ذهبت إلى...
[hal dhahabta ela...?] Have you ever been to...?
ذهبي golden *adj* [ðahabij]
سمك ذهبي
[Samak dhahabey] *n* goldfish
ذهن mind *n* [ðihn]
شارِد الذهن
[Shared al-dhehn] *adj* absent-minded
ذوبان dissolving, *n* [ðawaba:n] melting
قابل للذوبان
['qabel lel-dhawaban] *adj* soluble
ذوق taste *n* [ðawq]
عديم الذوق
['aadeem al-dhaw'q] *adj* tasteless
حسن الذوق
[Hosn aldhaw'q] *adj* tasteful
ذِوى fade *v* [ðawwa:]
ذَيِّل tail *n* [ðajl]

راجع [raːʒaʕa] v revise
راحة [raːħa] n leisure, relief, rest
راحة اليد
[Rahat al-yad] n palm *(part of hand)*
أسباب الراحة
[Asbab al-rahah] n amenities
وسائل الراحة الحديثة
[Wasael al-rahah al-hadethah] *npl* mod cons
يساعد على الراحة
[Yosaed ala al-rahah] *adj* relaxing
يوم الراحة
[Yawm al-raḥah] n Sabbath
راحل [raːħil] *adj* gone
رادار [raːdaːr] n radar
راديو [raːdjuː] n radio
راديو رقمي
[Radyo ra'qamey] n digital radio
محطة راديو
[Mahaṭat radyo] n radio station
هل يمكن أن أشغل الراديو؟
[hal yamken an osha-ghel al-radio?] Can I switch the radio on?
هل يمكن أن أطفئ الراديو؟
[hal yamken an aṭfee al-radio?] Can I switch the radio off?
رأس [raʔs] n head
رأس البرعم القطني
[Raas al-bor'aom al-'qaṭaney] n cotton bud
سماعات الرأس
[Samaat al-raas] *npl* headphones
عصابة الرأس
['eṣabat al-raas] n hairband
غطاء للرأس والعنق
[Gheṭa'a lel-raas wal-a'ono'q] n hood
حليق الرأس
[Halee'q al-raas] n skinhead
وشاح غطاء الرأس
[Weshaḥ gheṭaa al-raas] n headscarf
رَأس إصبع القدم
[Raas eṣbe'a al-'qadam] n tiptoe
رَأس السَنَة
[Raas alsanah] n New Year
هل توجد سماعات رأس؟
[hal tojad simma-'aat raas?] Does it

رائحة [raːʔiħa] n smell
رائحة كريهة
[Raaehah kareehah] n stink
كريه الرائحة
[Kareeh al-raaehah] *adj* smelly
مزيل رائحة العرق
[Mozeel raaehat al-'aara'q] n deodorant
أنني أشم رائحة غاز
[ina-ny ashum ra-e-hat ghaaz] I can smell gas
توجد رائحة غريبة في الغرفة
[toojad raeḥa ghareba fee al-ghurfa] There's a funny smell
رائع [raːʔiʕ] *adj* amazing, picturesque, fine (رقيق)
على نحو رائع
[Ala nahw rae'a] *adv* fine
رائعاً [raːʔiʕan] *adv* remarkably
رائعة [raːʔiʕa] n masterpiece
رابط [raːbitˤ] n link
رَابطة [raːbitˤa] n connection
رابِع [raːbiʕu] *adj* fourth
رئة [riʔit] n lung
راتب [raːtib] n salary
راتينج [raːtiːnʒ] n
مادة الراتينج
[Madat al-ratenj] n resin

have headphones?

رأس [raʔasa] v head
رإسخ [raːsix] adj firm
رإسمالية [raʔsumaːlijja] n capitalism
رَأسي [raʔsij] adj vertical
راشد [raːʃid] adj adult
طالب راشد
[Ṭaleb rashed] n mature student
راض [raːdˤin] adj satisfied
غير راض
[Ghayr raḍ] adj dissatisfied
راعي [raːʕiː] n shepherd, sponsor
راعى البقر
[Ra'aey al-ba'qar] n cowboy
رافع [raːfiʕ] n
رافع الأثقال
[Rafe'a al-ath'qaal] n weightlifter
رافعة [raːfiʕa] n crane (bird), jack
رافق [raːfaqa] v escort, accompany
راقص [raːqisˤu] nm dancer
راقص باليه
[Ra'qeṣ baleeh] n ballet dancer
راقصة [raːqisˤa] nf dancer
راقصة باليه
[Ra'ṣat baleeh] n ballerina
راكب [raːkib] n passenger, rider
راكب الدراجة
[Rakeb al-darrajah] n cyclist
راكون [raːkuːn] n
حيوان الراكون
[Ḥayawaan al-rakoon] n racoon
راكيت [raːkiːt] n
مضرب الراكيت
[Maḍrab alrakeet] n racquet
رام [raːma] v
على ما يُرام
['aala ma yoram] adv all right
إنه ليس على ما يرام
[inaho laysa 'aala ma you-ram] He's not well
راهب [raːhib] n monk
راهبة [raːhiba] n nun
راهن [raːhin] adj current
الوضع الراهن
[Al-waḍ'a al-rahen] n status quo
راهن [raːhana] vi bet

راوغ [raːwaɣa] v dodge
راوند [raːwand] n
عشب الراوند
['aoshb al-rawend] n rhubarb
رَاوي [raːwiː] n teller
رأيْ [raʔj] n option
الرأي العام
[Al-raaey al-'aam] n public opinion
ما رأيك في الخروج وتناول العشاء
[Ma raaek fee al-khoroj wa-tanawol al-'aashaa] Would you like to go out for dinner?
رَأي [raʔjj] n opinion
رأى [raʔa] vt see
نريد أن نرى النباتات والأشجار المحلية
[nureed an nara al-naba-taat wa al-ash-jaar al-maḥali-ya] We'd like to see local plants and trees
رؤية [ruʔja] n sight
رئيس [raʔijs] n captain, president
رئيس أساقفة
[Raees asa'qefah] n archbishop
رئيس عصابة
[Raees eṣabah] n godfather (criminal leader)
رئيس الطهاة
[Raees al-ṭohah] n chef
رئيس المجلس
[Raees al-majlas] n chairman
رئيس الوزراء
[Raees al-wezaraa] n prime minister
نائب الرئيس
[Naeb al-raaes] n deputy head
رئيسي [raʔiːsij] adj chief
صفحة رئيسية
[Ṣafḥah raeseyah] n home page
دَور رئيسي
[Dawr raaesey] n lead (in play/film)
طريق رئيسي
[ṭaree'q raeysey] n main road
طبق رئيسي
[Ṭaba'q raeesey] n main course
مراكز رئيسية
[Marakez raeaseyah] npl headquarters
مقال رئيسي فى صحيفة
[Ma'qal raaeaey fee ṣaheefah] n lead

(position)
مكتب رئيسي
[Maktab a'ala] n head office
band (strip) n [riba:tˤ] رباط
رباط عنق على شكل فراشة
[Rebaṭ 'ala shakl frashah] n bow tie
رباط العنق
[Rebaṭ al-'aono'q] n tie
رباط الحذاء
[Rebaṭ al-hedhaa] n shoelace
رباط مطاطي
[rebaṭ maṭaṭey] n rubber band
quartet n [ruba:ʕijjatu] رباعية
quarter n [rubba:n] ربان
ربان الطائرة
[Roban al-ṭaaerah] n pilot
lady, owner n [rabba] رَبّة
رَبّة المنزل
[Rabat al-manzel] n housewife
gain vt [rabaħa] ربَح
profit n [ribħ] ربْح
crouch down v [rabadˤa] ربَض
join vt [rabatˤa] ربَط
attachment n [rabtˤ] رَبْط
quarter n [rubʕ] ربع
سباق الدور رُبع النهائي
[Seba'q al-door roba'a al-nehaaey] n quarter final
الساعة الثانية إلا ربع
[al-sa'aa al-thaneya ella rubu'a] It's quarter to two
maybe adv [rubbama:] رُبما
n [rabw] ربو
الربو
[Al-rabw] n asthma
أعاني من مرض الربو
[o-'aany min maraḍ al-raboo] I suffer from asthma
bring up v [rabba:] ربى
godchild, godson, stepson n [rabi:b] ربيب
goddaughter, stepdaughter n [rabi:ba] ربيبة
spring n [rabi:ʕ] ربيع
زهرة الربيع
[Zahrat al-rabee'a] n primrose
فصل الربيع
[Faṣl al-rabeya] n springtime
arrange, rank v [rattaba] رتّب
row (line) n [rutba] رُتبة
drab adj [rati:b] رَتيب
worn adj [raθθ] رَث
men npl [riʒa:lun] رجال
دَوْرة مياه للرجال
[Dawrat meyah lel-rejal] n gents'
turn back, go back v [raʒaʕa] رجع
man n [raʒul] رجُل
رَجُل أعمال
[Rajol a'amal] n businessman
رَجُل المخاطر
[Rajol al-makhater] n stuntman
أنا رجل أعمال
[ana rajul a'amaal] I'm a businessman
leg n [riʒl] رِجل
return n [ruʒu:ʕ] رُجوع
أود الرجوع إلى البيت
[awid al-rijoo'a ela al-bayt] I'd like to go home
v [raħħaba] رحّب
يُرحِب ب
[Yoraḥeb bee] v greet
depart v [raħala] رحل
journey, passage (musical) n [riħla] رحلة
رحلة سيرًا على الأقدام
[rehalah sayran ala al-a'qdam] n tramp (long walk)
رحلة على الجياد
[Rehalah ala al-jeyad] n pony trekking
رحلة عمل
[Reḥlat 'aamal] n business trip
رحلة جوية
[Rehalah jaweyah] n flight
رحلة جوية مُؤجَرة
[Rehalh jaweyah moajarah] n charter flight
رحلة بعربة ثيران
[Rehlah be-arabat theran] n trek
رحلة بحرية
[Rehalh bahreyah] n cruise
رحلة قصيرة
[Rehalh 'qaṣeerah] n trip
رحلةانكفائية

[Reḥlah enkefaeyah] *n* round trip
خطة رحلة شاملة الإقامة والانتقالات
[Khotah rehalah shamelah al-e'qamah wal-ente'qalat] *n* package tour
womb *n* [raħim] **رحم**
فحص عنق الرحم
[Faḥṣ 'aono'q al-raḥem] *n* smear test
mercy *n* [raħma] **رحمة**
nectar *n* [raħi:q] **رحيق**
شجيرة غنية بالرحيق
[Shojayrah ghaneyah bel-raḥee'q] *n* honeysuckle
parting *n* [raħi:l] **رحيل**
marble *n* [ruxa:m] **رُخَام**
licence *n* [ruxsˁa] **رخصة**
رُخْصَة القيادة
[Rokhṣat al-'qeyadah] *n* driving licence
رُخصَة بيع الخمور لتناولها خارج المحل
[Rokhṣat baye'a al-khomor letnawolha kharej al-maḥal] *n* off-license
رقم رخصة قيادتي هو...
[ra'qim rikhṣat 'qeyad-aty howa...] My driving licence number is...
أحمل رخصة قيادة، لكنها ليست معي الآن
[Aḥmel rokhṣat 'qeyadah, lakenaha laysat ma'aey al-aan] I don't have my driving licence on me
flabby *adj* [raxw] **رَخو**
cheap *adj* [raxi:sˁ] **رخيص**
هل هناك أي رحلات جوية رخيصة؟
[hal hunaka ay reḥ-laat jaw-wya rakheṣa?] Are there any cheap flights?
return, response, reply *n* [radd] **رد**
رد انعكاسي
[Rad en'aekasey] *n* reflex
تليفون مزود بوظيفة الرد الآلي
[Telephone mozawad be-waḍheefat al-rad al-aaley] *n* answerphone
جهاز الرد الآلي
[Jehaz al-rad al-aaly] *n* answerphone
give back *v* [radda] **رد**
مال يرد بعد دفعه
[Maal yorad daf'ah] *n* drawback
hallway *n* [radha] **رُدهَة**
drizzle *n* [raða:ð] **رذاذ**

vice *n* [raði:la] **رذيلة**
n [razza] **رزّة**
رزّة سلكية
[Rozzah selkeyah] *n* staple *(wire)*
living *n* [rizq] **رزق**
pack, packet *n* [ruzma] **رَزمة**
message *n* [risa:la] **رسالة**
رسالة تذكير
[Resalat tadhkeer] *n* reminder
هل وصلتكم أي رسائل من أجلي؟
[hal waṣal-kum ay rasaa-el min ajlee?] Are there any messages for me?
هل يمكن أن أترك رسالة؟
[hal yamken an atruk resala?] Can I leave a message?
painter *n* [rassa:m] **رسام**
settle *v* [rassixa] **رسخ**
n [rusɣ] **رُسغ**
رُسغ القدم
[rosgh al-'qadam] *n* ankle
charge *(price)*, drawing *n* [rasm] **رسم**
رسم بياني
[Rasm bayany] *n* chart, diagram
رسم بياني دائري
[Rasm bayany daery] *n* pie chart
رسوم جمركية
[Rosoom jomrekeyah] *npl* customs
رسوم التعليم
[Rasm al-ta'aleem] *npl* tuition fees
رسوم متحركة
[Rosoom motaharekah] *npl* cartoon
رَسْم الدخول
[Rasm al-dokhool] *n* entrance fee
رَسْم الخدمة
[Rasm al-khedmah] *n* service charge
رَسْم الالتحاق
[Rasm al-elteha'q] *n* admission charge
هل يحتسب رسم تحويل؟
[hal yoḥ-tasab rasim taḥ-weel?] Is there a transfer charge?
draw *(sketch)* *v* [rasama] **رسم**
يَرسِم خطا تحت
[Yarsem khaṭan taḥt] *v* underline
هل يمكن أن ترسم لي خريطة للاتجاهات؟
[Hal yomken an tarsem le khareeṭah

lel-etejahaat?] Can you draw me a map with directions?
رسمي official *adj* [rasmij]
غير رسمي
[Ghayer rasmey] *adj* unofficial
غير رسمي
[Ghayer rasmey] *adj* informal
زي رسمي
[Zey rasmey] *n* uniform
شكل رسمي
[Shakl rasmey] *n* formality
رسول messenger *n* [rasu:l]
رسوم toll *n* [rusu:m]
أين سأدفع رسوم المرور بالطريق؟
[ayna sa-adfa'a rosom al-miroor bil-ṭaree'q?] Where can I pay the toll?
هل هناك رسوم يتم دفعها للمرور بهذا الطريق؟
[hal hunaka risoom yatim daf-'aaha lel-miroor be-hadha al-ṭaree'q?] Is there a toll on this motorway?
رش splash *v* [raʃʃa]
رشاد *n* [raʃa:d]
نبات رشاد
[Nabat rashad] *n* cress
رشاش machine gun, spray *n* [raʃʃa:ʃ]
رشاش مياه
[Rashah meyah] *n* watering can
رشح *v* [raʃaħa]
ماذا ترشح لنا؟
[madha tura-shiḥ lana?] What do you recommend?
هل يمكن أن ترشح لي أحد الأطباق المحلية؟
[hal yamken an tura-shiḥ lee aḥad al-aṭbaa'q al-maḥa-leya?] Can you recommend a local dish?
هل يمكن أن ترشح لي نوع جيد من النبيذ الوردي؟
[hal yamken an tura-shiḥ lee naw'a jayid min al-nabeedh al-wardy?] Can you recommend a good rosé wine?
رَشّح nominate *v* [raʃʃaħa]
رشوة bribery *n* [raʃwa]
رصاص lead *n* [rasˤa:sˤa]
خلو من الرصاص
[Khelow men al-raṣaṣ] *n* unleaded
رصاصة bullet *n* [rasˤa:sˤa]
رصيف pavement *n* [rasˤi:fu]
رصيف الميناء
[Raṣeef al-meenaa] *n* quay
رضا content *n* [ridˤa:]
رضع nursing *n* [rudˤdˤaʕ]
هل توجد تسهيلات لمن معهم أطفالهم الرضع؟
[hal tojad tas-heelat leman ma-'aahum aṭfaal-ahum al-ruḍa'a?] Are there facilities for parents with babies?
رضِع breast-feed *v* [radˤaʕa]
رضَع suck *v* [radˤaʕa]
رطب humid *adj* [ratˤb]
الجو رطب
[al-jaw raṭb] It's muggy
رطل pound *n* [ratˤl]
رطوبة humidity *n* [rutˤu:ba]
رعاية sponsorship *n* [riʕa:ja]
رعاية الأطفال
[Re'aayat al-aṭfal] *n* childcare
رُعْب fright *n* [ruʕb]
رعد thunder *n* [raʕd]
مصحوب برعد
[Maṣḥoob bera'ad] *adj* thundery
رعديّ *adj* [raʕdij]
عاصفة رعدية
['aasefah ra'adeyah] *n* thunderstorm
رعشة thrill *n* [raʕʃa]
رعى tend, sponsor *v* [raʕa:]
رغب desire *v* [raɣaba]
رغبة desire *n* [raɣba]
رغب في *v* [rɣeba fi:]
أرغب في ترتيب إجراء اجتماع مع.....؟
[arghab fee tar-teeb ejraa ejtemaa ma'aa...] I'd like to arrange a meeting with...
من فضلك أرغب في التحدث إلى المدير
[min faḍlak arghab fee al-taḥaduth ela al-mudeer] I'd like to speak to the manager, please
هل ترغب في تناول أحد المشروبات؟
[hal tar-ghab fee tanawil aḥad al-mashro-baat?] Would you like a drink?

رغم despite *prep* [raɣma]
بالرغم من
[Bel-raghm men] *conj* although
رغوة foam *n* [raɣwa]
رغوة الحلاقة
[Raghwat ḥela'qah] *n* shaving foam
رغيف loaf *n* [raɣi:f]
رف shelf *n* [raffu]
رف المستوقد
[Raf al-mostaw'qed] *n* mantelpiece
رَف السقف
[Raf alsa'qf] *n* roofrack
رَف الكُتُب
[Raf al-kotob] *n* bookshelf
رفاق companion, lot *npl* [rifa:qun]
الرفاق الموجودون في الأسرة المجاورة يسببسبون إزعاجا شديدا
[al-osrah al-mojawera ḍajeej-oha sha-deed] My roommates are very noisy
رفاهية luxury *n* [rafa:hijja]
رفرف lifting *n* [rafraf]
رفرف العجلة
[Rafraf al-'ajalah] *n* mudguard
رفرف flap *v* [rafrafa]
رَفِض refuse *v* [rafadˤa]
رَفض refusal *n* [rafdˤ]
رفع lifting *n* [rafʕ]
رفع الأثقال
[Raf'a al-th'qaal] *n* weightlifting
رفع lift *v* [rafaʕa]
يَرفع بصره
[Yarfa'a baṣarah] *v* look up
من فضلك، ارفع صوتك في الحديث
[min faḍlak, irfa'a ṣawtak fee al-ḥadeeth] Could you speak louder, please?
رفيع slender *adj* [rafi:ʕ]
رفيق boyfriend, mate *n* [rafi:q]
رفيق الحجرة
[Refee'q al-hohrah] *n* roommate
رقابة *n* [riqa:ba]
الرقابة على جوازات السفر
[Al-re'qabah ala jawazat al-safar] *n* passport control
رقاقة chip *(small piece)*, *n* [ruqa:qa] wafer
رقائق الذُرَة
[Ra'qae'a al-dorrah] *npl* cornflakes
رقاقة معدنية
[Re'qaeq ma'adaneyah] *n* foil
رَقَبَة neck *n* [raqaba]
رقص dancing *n* [raqsˤ]
رقص ثنائي
[Ra'qṣ thonaaey] *n* ballroom dancing
رقص الكلاكيت
[Ra'qṣ al-kelakeet] *n* tap-dancing
أين يمكننا الذهاب للرقص؟
[ayna yamken-ana al-dhehaab lel-ra'qṣ?] Where can we go dancing?
هل تحب الرقص؟
[hal taḥib al-ra'qiṣ?] Would you like to dance?
.يتملكني شعور بالرغبة في الرقص
[yatamal-akany shi'aoor bil-raghba fee al-ri'qṣ] I feel like dancing
رقص dance *v* [raqasˤa]
يَرقص الفالس
[Yar'qos al-fales] *v* waltz
رقصة dance *n* [raqsˤa]
رقصة الفالس
[Ra'qṣat al-fales] *n* waltz
رقعة patch *n* [ruqʕa]
رقم figure, number *n* [raqm]
رقم الغرفة
[Ra'qam al-ghorfah] *n* room number
رقم التليفون
[Ra'qm al-telefone] *n* phone number
رقم الحساب
[Ra'qm al-hesab] *n* account number
رقم المحمول
[Ra'qm almahmool] *n* mobile number
رقم مرجعي
[Ra'qm marje'ay] *n* reference number
ما هو رقم تليفونك المحمول؟
[ma howa ra'qim talefonak al-maḥmool?] What is the number of your mobile?
ما هو رقم التليفون؟
[ma howa ra'qim al-talefon?] What's the telephone number?
ما هو رقم الفاكس؟
[ma howa ra'qim al-fax?] What is the fax number?

مفتاح الغرفة رقم مائتين واثنين
[muftaaḥ al-ghurfa ra'qim ma-atyn wa ithnayn] the key for room number two hundred and two
هل يمكن أن أحصل على رقم تليفونك؟
[hal yamken an aḥṣal 'aala ra'qm talefonak?] Can I have your phone number?
رقمي [raqmij] *adj* digital
راديو رقمي
[Radyo ra'qamey] *n* digital radio
ساعة رقمية
[Sa'aah ra'qameyah] *n* digital watch
تليفزيون رقمي
[telefezyoon ra'qamey] *n* digital television
كاميرا رقمية
[Kameera ra'qmeyah] *n* digital camera
أريد كارت ذاكرة لهذه الكاميرا الرقمية من فضلك
[areed kart dhakera le-hadhy al-kamera al-ra'qm-eya min faḍlak] A memory card for this digital camera, please
رقيق [raqi:q] *adj* delicate
طين رقيق القوام
[Ṭeen ra'qee'q al'qawam] *n* slush
زُكَام [ruka:m] *n*
زُكَام مُبَعثَر
[Rokaam moba'athar] *n* litter *(trash)*
رَكِب [rakaba] *v* get in, get on, put in
رَكِب [rakaba] *vt* ride
رَكْبَة [runkbatu] *n* ride
رُكْبَة [rukba] *n* knee
رَكبي [rakbi:] *n*
رياضة الرَّكْبي
[Reyaḍat al-rakbey] *n* rugby
رَكّز [rakkaza] *v* concentrate
ركض [rakadˤa] *v*
يَرْكض بِسُرْعَه
[Yrkoḍ besor'aah] *v* sprint
رَكع [rakaʕa] *v* kneel
ركل [rakala] *vt* kick
ركلة [rakla] *n* kick
الركلة الأولى
[Al-raklah al-ola] *n* kick-off
ركوب [ruku:b] *n* riding
تصريح الركوب
[Taṣreeh al-rokob] *n* boarding pass
رم [ramm] *n*
شراب الرّم
[Sharab al-ram] *n* rum
رمادي [rama:dij] *adj* grey
رِمال [rima:l] *n* sand
رُمَّان [rumma:n] *n* pomegranate
رُمْح [rumħ] *n* javelin
رمز [ramz] *n* symbol, code
رمز بريدي
[Ramz bareedey] *n* post code
رمز [ramaza] *v* stand for
يَرْمُز إلى
[Yarmoz ela] *v* hint
رِمش [rimʃ] *n*
رِمش العين
[Remsh al'ayn] *n* eyelash
رَمَضَانْ [ramadˤa:n] *n* Ramadan
رملي [ramlij] *adj*
حجر رملي
[Hajar ramley] *n* sandstone
كثبان رملية
[Kothban ramleyah] *n* sand dune
رمم [rammam] *v* renovate
رمى [rama:] *vt* throw, pitch
رَمْيَة [ramja] *n* pitch *(sport)*
رِنجَة [ranʒa] *n*
سمك الرِنجَة
[Samakat al-renjah] *n* herring
رنين [rani:nu] *n* sound
رنين انشغال الخط
[Raneen ensheghal al-khaṭ] *n* engaged tone
رِهان [riha:n] *n* bet
رَهْن [rahn] *n* mortgage
رهيب [rahi:b] *adj* horrendous, horrible
رهينة [rahi:na] *n* hostage
رُوَائي [riwa:ʔij] *n* novelist
رواق [riwa:q] *n* porch, corridor
رِواية [riwa:ja] *n* novel
رُوب [ru:b] *n*
رُوب الحَمَّام
[Roob al-ḥamam] *n* dressing gown
رُوبيَان [ru:bja:n] *n* shrimp

روتين routine *n* [ru:ti:n]
روّج promote *v* [rawwaʒa]
رَوح spirit *n* [ru:ħ]
روحي spiritual *adj* [ru:ħij]
أب روحي
[Af rooḥey] *n* godfather *(baptism)*
روسي Russian *adj* [ru:sij]
روسي الجنسية
[Rosey al-jenseyah] *(person) n* Russian
اللغة الروسية
[Al-loghah al-roseyah] *(language) n* Russian
روسيا Russia *n* [ru:sja:]
روسيا البيضاء [ru:sja: ʔal-bajdˤa:ʔu] Belarus *n*
رَوّع scare *v* [rawwaʕa]
يُرَوْع فجأة
[Yorawe'a fajaah] *v* startle, surprise
روليت roulette *n* [ru:li:t]
روماتيزم *n* [ru:ma:ti:zmu] rheumatism
رومانسي romantic *adj* [ru:ma:nsij]
رومانسية romance *n* [ru:ma:nsijja]
رومانسيكي *adj* [ru:ma:nsi:kij]
طراز رومانسيكي
[Ṭeraz romanseekey] *adj* Romanesque
روماني Roman, *adj* [ru:ma:nij] Romanian
روماني الجنسية
[Romaney al-jenseyah] *(person) n* Romanian
اللغة الرومانية
[Al-loghah al-romanyah] *(language) n* Romanian
شخص روماني كاثوليكي
[shakhṣ romaney katholeekey] *n* Roman Catholic
رومانيا Romania *n* [ru:ma:nja:]
روى water *v* [rawa:]
رياح wind *n* [rijja:ħ]
مذرو بالرياح
[Madhro bel-reyah] *adj* windy
رياضة sport *n* [rija:dˤa]
رياضة دموية
[Reyaḍah damaweyah] *n* blood sports
رياضة الطائرة الشراعية الصغيرة
[Reyadar al-Ṭaayearah al-ehraeyah al-ṣagherah] *n* hang-gliding
رياضي *adj* [rija:dˤij]
رجل رياضي
[Rajol reyaḍey] *n* sportsman
رياضي) متعلق بالرياضة البدنية)
[(Reyaḍy) mota'ale'q bel- Reyaḍah al-badabeyah] *adj* athletic
رياضي) متعلق بالألعاب الرياضية)
[(Reyaḍey) mota'ale'q bel- al'aab al-reyaḍah] *adj* sporty
سيدة رياضية
[Sayedah reyaḍah] *n* sportswoman
زي رياضي
[Zey reyaḍey] *n* tracksuit
ملابس رياضية
[Malabes reyaḍah] *n* sportswear
إلى أي الأحداث الرياضية يمكننا أن نذهب؟
[Ela ay al-aḥdath al-reyaḍiyah yamkuno-na an nadhhab?] Which sporting events can we go to?
كيف نصل إلى الإستاد الرياضي؟
[kayfa naṣil ela al-istad al-riyaḍy?] How do we get to the stadium?
ما الخدمات الرياضية المتاحة؟
[ma al-khadamat al-reyaḍya al-mutaḥa?] What sports facilities are there?
رياضيات *npl* [rija:dˤijja:tun] mathematics
علم الرياضيات
['aelm al-reyaḍeyat] *npl* maths
ريح wind *n* [ri:ħ]
ريح موسمية
[Reeḥ mawsemeyah] *adj* monsoon
ريح هوجاء
[Reyḥ ḥawjaa] *n* gale
رَيحان basil *n* [rajħa:nn]
ريشة feather, pen *n* [ri:ʃa]
كُرَة الريشة
[Korat al-reeshaa] *n* shuttlecock
ريف countryside *n* [ri:f]
رَيفي rural *adj* [ri:fij]
قصر ريفي
['qaṣr reefey] *n* stately home

angle, corner *n* [za:wija] **زاوية**

زاوية يُمنى

[Zaweyah yomna] *n* right angle

(at auction) bid *vi* [za:jada] **زايد**

yoghurt *n* [zaba:dij] **زبادي**

butter *n* [zubda] **زُبْدَة**

زُبْدَة الفستق

[Zobdat al-fosto'q] *n* peanut butter

client *n* [zabu:n] **زبون**

currant, raisin *n* [zabi:b] **زبيب**

glass *n* [zuʒa:ʒ] **زجاج**

الزجاج الأمامي

[Al-zojaj al-amamy] *n* windscreen

زجاج مُعَشَّق

[Zojaj moasha'q] *n* stained glass

طبقتين من الزجاج

[Ṭaba'qatayen men al-zojaj] *n* double glazing

مادة ألياف الزجاج

[Madat alyaf alzojaj] *n* fibreglass

لقد تحطم الزجاج الأمامي

[la'qad taḥa-ṯama al-zujaj al-amamy] The windscreen is broken

هل يمكن أن تملئ خزان المياه لمساحات الزجاج؟

[hal yamken an tamlee khazaan al-meaah le-massa-ḥaat al-zujaaj?] Can you top up the windscreen washers?

bottle *n* [zuʒa:ʒa] **زجاجة**

زجاجة رضاعة الطفل

[Zojajat reḍa'aat al-ṭefl] *n* baby's bottle

زجاجة الخمر

[Zojajat al-khamr] *n* wineglass

زجاجة من النبيذ الأحمر

[zujaja min al-nabeedh al-aḥmar] a bottle of red wine

زجاجة مياه معدنية

[zujaja meaa ma'adan-iya] a bottle of mineral water

معي زجاجة للمشروبات الروحية

[ma'ay zujaja lil-mashroobat al-roḥiya] I have a bottle of spirits to declare

من فضلك أحضر لي زجاجة أخرى

[min faḍlak iḥḍir lee zujaja okhra] Please bring another bottle

[za:ʔidun] **زائد**

زائد الطهو

[Zaed al-ṭahw] *adj* overdone

زائد الوزن

[Zaed alwazn] *adj* overweight

extra *adj* [za:ʔid] **زَائِد**

visitor *n* [za:ʔir] **زائِر**

fake (مدعٍ) *n* ◁ false *adj* [za:ʔif] **زائف**

mercury *n* [ziʔbaq] **زئبق**

adj [za:xir] **زاخر**

زاخر بالأحداث

[Zakher bel-aḥdath] (خطير) *adj* eventful

increase *v* [za:da] **زاد**

يزيد من

[Yazeed men] *v* mount up, accumulate

هذا يزيد عن العداد

[hatha yazeed 'aan al-'aadad] It's more than on the meter

visit *v* [za:ra] **زار**

forge *v* [za:ra] **زار**

v [za:la] **زال**

لا يزال

[La yazaal] *adv* still

n ◁ Zambian *adj* [za:mbij] **زامبي**

Zambian

Zambia *n* [za:mbja:] **زامبيا**

زجاجي *adj* [zuʒaːʒij]
لوح زجاجي
[Loḥ zojajey] *n* window pane
زحف [zaħafa] *v* crawl
زخرف [zaxrafa] *v* decorate
زرّ [zirr] *n* button
زرار [ziraːr] *n* button
أزرار كم القميص
[Azrar kom al'qameeṣ] *npl* cufflinks
زراعة [ziraːʕa] *n* farming, agriculture
زراعي [ziraːʕij] *adj* agricultural
زرافة [zaraːfa] *n* giraffe
زرع [zarʕ] *n* seed, planting
زرع الأعضاء
[Zar'a al-a'aḍaa] *n* transplant
زرع [zaraʕa] *v* plant
زعانف *npl* [zaʕaːnifun]
زعانف الغطس
[Za'aanef al-ghaṭs] *npl* flippers
زَعْتَر *n* [zaʕtar]
زَعْتَر بَري
[Za'atar barey] *n* oregano
زعرور *n* [zaʕruːr]
زعرور بلدي
[Za'aroor baladey] *n* hawthorn
زعفران [zaʕfaraːn] *n* crocus
نبات الزعفران
[Nabat al-za'afaran] *n* saffron
زعَق [zaʕaqa] *v* squeak
زعيم [zaʕiːm] *n* boss
زُغطة [zuɣtˤatun] *npl* hiccups
زفاف [zifaːf] *n* wedding
زَفر [zafara] *v* breathe out
زقاق [zuqaːq] *n* alley, lane
زُقاق دائري
[Zo'qa'q daerey] *n* cycle lane
زكام [zukaːm] *n* cold
زلابية [zalaːbijja] *n* doughnut, dumpling
زلاجات [zalaːʒaːtun] *npl* skates
زلاجة [zalaːʒa] *n* ski
أريد أن أؤجر زلاجة
[areed an o-ajer zalaja] I want to hire skis
زلاقة [zallaːqa] *n* slide
زَلزال [zilzaːl] *n* earthquake
زَلق [zalaqa] *adj* slippery
زمن [zaman] *n* time
عقد من الزمن
['aa'qd men al-zaman] *n* decade
زمني *adj* [zamanij]
جدول زمني
[Jadwal zamaney] *n* timetable
زميل [zamiːl] *n* colleague
زميل الفصل
[Zameel al-faṣl] *n* classmate
زُنْبُرك [zunburk] *n* spring *(coil)*
زَنبَق *n* [zanbaq]
زَنْبَق الوادي
[Zanba'q al-wadey] *n* lily of the valley
زنبقة [zanbaqa] *n* lily
زَنْجَبيل [zanʒabiːl] *n* ginger
زنجية *n* [zinʒijja]
زنجية عجوز
[Enjeyah 'aajooz] *n* auntie
زنك [zink] *n* zinc
زهرة [zahra] *n* flower
زهرة الشجرة المثمرة
[Zahrat al-shajarah al-mothmerah] *n* blossom
زهرية [zahrijja] *n* vase
زواج [zawaːʒ] *n* marriage
عقد زواج
['aa'qd zawaj] *n* marriage certificate
عيد الزواج
['aeed al-zawaj] *n* wedding anniversary
زواحف [zawaːħif] *n* reptile
زَوْبَعة [zawbaʕa] *n* cyclone
زوج [zawʒ] *n* husband
زوج سابق
[Zawj sabe'q] *n* ex-husband
زوج الإبنة
[Zawj al-ebnah] *n* son-in-law
زوج الأخت
[zawj alokht] *n* brother-in-law
زوج الأم
[Zawj al-om] *n* stepfather
أنا أبحث عن هدية لزوجي
[ana abḥath 'aan hadiya le-zawjee] I'm looking for a present for my husband
هذا زوجي
[hatha zawjee] This is my husband

زوجان [zawʒa:ni] *n* couple, pair
زوجة [zawʒa] *n* wife
أخت الزوجة
[Okht alzawjah] *n* sister-in-law
زوجة سابقة
[Zawjah sabe'qah] *n* ex-wife
زوجة الأب
[Zawj al-aab] *n* stepmother
زوجة الابن
[Zawj al-ebn] *n* daughter-in-law
هذه زوجتي
[hathy zawjaty] This is my wife
زود [zawwada] *v* provide, service, supply
زورق [zawraq] *n* boat
زورق صغير
[Zawra'q ṣagheer] *n* pram
زورق تجديف
[Zawra'q] *n* dinghy
زورق بخاري مخصص لقائد الأسطول
[Zawra'q bokharee mokhaṣaṣ le-'qaaed al-osṭool] *n* barge
زورق بمحرك
[Zawra'q be-moḥ arek] *n* motorboat
استدعي زورق النجاة
[istad'ay zawra'q al-najaat] Call out the lifeboat!
زي [zij] *n* clothing, outfit
زي رياضي
[Zey reyaḍey] *n* tracksuit
زي تنكري
[Zey tanakorey] *n* fancy dress *(party)*
زي مدرسي موحد
[Zey madrasey mowaḥad] *n* school uniform
زي [zajj] *n* fancy dress
زيادة [zija:da] *n* increase
زيادة السرعة
[Zeyadat alsor'aah] *n* speeding
زيارة [zija:ra] *n* visit
ساعات الزيارة
[Sa'at al-zeyadah] *n* visiting hours
زيارة المعالم السياحية
[Zeyarat al-ma'aalem al-seyahyah] *n* sightseeing
أنا هنا لزيارة أحد الأصدقاء
[?ana: huna: lizija:ratin ?aħada al?asˤdiqa:?a] I'm here visiting friends
أيمكننا زيارة الحدائق؟
[a-yamkun-ana zeyarat al-ḥada-e'q?] Can we visit the gardens?
متى تكون ساعات الزيارة؟
[mata takoon sa'aat al-zeyara?] When are visiting hours?
نريد زيارة...
[nureed ze-yarat...] We'd like to visit...
هل الوقت متاح لزيارة المدينة؟
[hal al-wa'qt muaaḥ le-ziyarat al-madeena?] Do we have time to visit the town?
زيت [zajt] *n*
زيت سمرة الشمس
[Zayt samarat al-shams] *n* suntan oil
زيت الزيتون
[Zayt al-zaytoon] *n* olive oil
طبقة زيت طافية على الماء
[Ṭaba'qat zayt ṭafeyah alaa alma] *n* oil slick
معمل تكرير الزيت
[Ma'amal takreer al-zayt] *n* oil refinery
هذه البقعة بقعة زيت
[hathy al-bu'q-'aa bu'q-'aat zayt] This stain is oil
زيتون [zajtu:n] *n* olive
زيت الزيتون
[Zayt al-zaytoon] *n* olive oil
شجرة الزيتون
[Shajarat al-zaytoon] *n* olive tree
زيمبابوي [zi:mba:bwij] *n* Zimbabwe
دولة زيمبابوي
[Dawlat zembabway] *adj* Zimbabwean
مواطن زيمبابوي
[Mewaṭen zembabway] *n* Zimbabwean
زَيّن [zajjana] *v* embroider, trim
يُزَين بالنجوم
[Yozaeyen bel-nejoom] *v* star

[Sael tanḍheef] *n* cleansing lotion
سائل استحمام
[Saael estehmam] *n* bubble bath
سائل متقطّر
[Sael mota'qaṭer] *n* drop
سُؤال [sua:l] *n* question
سابح [sa:biħ] *n* swimmer
سابع [sa:biʕu] *adj* seventh
سابع عشر [sa:biʕa ʕaʃara] *adj* seventeenth
سابق [sa:biq] *adj* former
زوج سابق
[Zawj sabe'q] *n* ex-husband
سابقاً [sa:biqan] *adv* formerly
ساحة [sa:ħa] *n*
ساحة الدار
[Sahat al-dar] *n* courtyard
ساحر [sa:ħir] *adj* charming, magic
◁ *n* magician
ساحرة [sa:ħira] *n* witch
ساحِق [sa:ħiq] *adj* terrific
ساحَل [sa:ħil] *n* coast, shore
ساخر [sa:xir] *adj* sarcastic
ساخن [sa:xinat] *adj* hot
زجاجة مياه ساخنة
[Zojajat meyah sakhenah] *n* hot-water bottle
إن الطعام ساخن أكثر من اللازم
[enna al-ṭa'aam sakhen akthar min al-laazim] The food is too hot
أهو مسبح ساخن؟
[a-howa masbaḥ sakhin?] Is the pool heated?
لا توجد مياه ساخنة
[La tojad meyah sakhena] There is no hot water
ساذَج [sa:ðaʒ] *adj* naïve
سار [sa:rr] *adj* pleasant, savoury
سار جداً
[Sar jedan] *adj* delightful
غير سار
[Ghayr sar] *adj* unpleasant
سار [sa:ra] *v* march
سارق [sa:riq] *n* robber
ساطع [sa:tˤiʕ] *adj* bright, glaring
ساعة [sa:ʕa] *n* hour

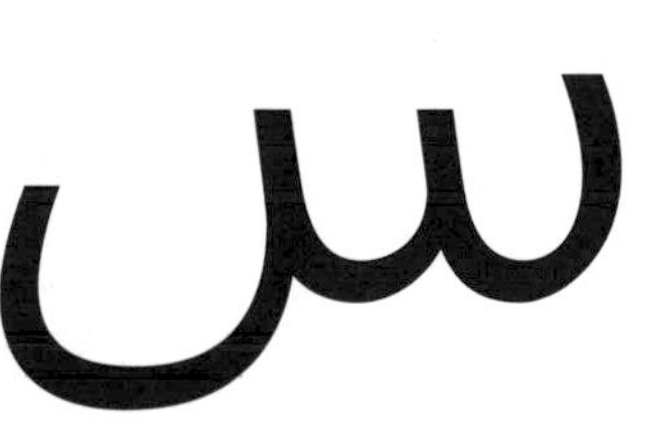

سائح [sa:ʔiħ] *n* tourist
دليل السائح
[Daleel al-saaeh] *n* itinerary
سائس [sa:ʔis] *n*
سائس خيل
[Saaes kheel] *n* groom
سائق [sa:ʔiq] *n* driver
سائق سيارة
[Saae'q sayarah] *n* chauffeur, motorist
سائق سيارة سباق
[Sae'q sayarah seba'q] *n* racing driver
سائق تاكسي
[Sae'q taksey] *n* taxi driver
سائق دراجة بخارية
[Sae'q drajah bokhareyah] *n* motorcyclist
سائق شاحنة
[Sae'q shahenah] *n* truck driver
سائق لوري
[Sae'q lorey] *n* lorry driver
سائق مبتدئ
[Sae'q mobtadea] *n* learner driver
سائل [sa:ʔil] *n* liquid
سائل غسيل الأطباق
[Saael ghaseel al-aṭba'q] *n* washing-up liquid
سائل تنظيف

ساعة رقمية
[Sa'aah ra'qameyah] *n* digital watch
ساعة تناول الشاي
[Saa'ah tanawol al-shay] *n* teatime
ساعة الإيقاف
[Saa'ah al-e'qaaf] *n* stopwatch
ساعة حائط
[Saa'ah ḥaaeṭ] *n* clock
ساعة يدوية
[Saa'ah yadaweyah] *n* watch
عكس عقارب الساعة
['aaks 'aa'qareb al-saa'ah] *n* anticlockwise
باتجاه عقارب الساعة
[Betejah a'qareb al-saa'ah] *adv* clockwise
شؤون الساعة
[Sheoon al-saa'ah] *npl* current affairs
كل ساعة
[Kol al-saa'ah] *adv* hourly
محسوب بالساعة
[Mahsoob bel-saa'ah] *adj* hourly
نصف ساعة
[Neṣf saa'aah] *n* half-hour
كم تبلغ تكلفة الدخول على الإنترنت لمدة ساعة؟
[kam tablugh taklifat al-dikhool 'ala al-internet le-mudat sa'aa?] How much is it to log on for an hour?
كم يبلغ الثمن لكل ساعة؟
[kam yablugh al-thaman le-kul sa'a a?] How much is it per hour?
ساعد [sa:ʕada] *vt* help
ساعي [sa:ʕi:] *n* courier
ساعي البريد
[Sa'aey al-bareed] *n* postwoman
ساعية [sa:ʕijatu] *n (female)* courier
ساعية البريد
[Sa'aeyat al-bareed] *n* postwoman
سافر [sa:fira] *v* travel
يُسافر متطفلا
[Yosaafer motaṭafelan] *v* hitchhike
يُسافر يومياً من وإلى مكان عمله
[Yosafer yawmeyan men wa ela makan 'amaleh] *v* commute
أنا أسافر بمفردي
[ana asaafir be-mufrady] I'm travelling alone
ساكن [sa:kin] *adj* calm, motionless
▷ *n* inhabitant
حرف ساكن
[ḥarf saken] *n* consonant
سأل [saʔala] *v* ask
يَسأل عن
[Yasaal 'an] *v* inquire
سالامي [sa:la:mi:] *n*
طعام السالامي
[Ṭa'aam al-salamey] *n* salami
سالِف [sa:lif] *adj* preceding
سامّ [sa:mm] *adj* poisonous
سَأم [saʔam] *n* boredom
سَئِمَ [saʔima] *adj* fed up
سان مارينو [sa:n ma:ri:nu:] *n* San Marino
ساوم [sa:wama] *v* haggle
ساوَى [sa:wa:] *v* equal
يُساوي بين
[Yosawey bayn] *v* equalize
إنه يساوي...
[Enah yosaawey...] It's worth...
كم يساوي؟
[kam yusa-wee?] How much is it worth?
سبابة [sabba:ba] *n*
اصبع السبابة
[Eṣbe'a al-sababah] *n* index finger
سباحة [siba:ħa] *n* swimming
سباحة تحت الماء
[Sebaḥah taḥt al-maa] *n* snorkel
سباحة الصدر
[Sebaḥat al-ṣadr] *n* breaststroke
سِروال سباحة
[Serwl sebaḥah] *n* swimming trunks
حمام سباحة
[Hammam sebaḥah] *n* swimming pool
زي السباحة
[Zey sebaḥah] *n* swimming costume
أين يمكنني أن أذهب للسباحة؟
[ayna yamken-any an adhhab lel-sebaḥa?] Where can I go swimming?
هل يوجد حمام سباحة؟

[hal yujad ḥamam sebaḥa?] Is there a swimming pool?
هيا نذهب للسباحة
[hya nadhhab lil-sebaḥa] Let's go swimming
سباق race *(contest)* *n* [siba:q]
سباق سيارات
[Seba'q sayarat] *n* motor racing
سباق الراليات
[Seba'q al-raleyat] *n* rally
سباق الضاحية
[Seba'q al-ḍaheyah] *n* cross-country
سباق الخيول
[Seba'q al-kheyol] *n* horse racing
سباق قصير سريع
[Seba'q 'qaṣer sare'a] *n* sprint
حلبة السباق
[ḥ alabat seba'q] *n* racetrack
سباك plumber *n* [sabba:k]
سِبَاكة plumbing *n* [siba:ka]
سبانخ spinach *n* [saba:nix]
سبب cause *(ideals)*, cause *n* [sabab] *(reason)*
ما السبب في هذا الوقوف؟
[ma al-sabab fee hatha al-wi'qoof?] What is causing this hold-up?
سبب cause *v* [abbaba]
يُسبِب الملل
[Yosabeb al-malal] *v* bored
سبتمبر September *n* [sibtumbar]
سبَح swim *vi* [sabaħa]
سبخة marsh *n* [sabxa]
سبعة seven *number* [sabʕatun]
سبعة عشر *number* [sabʕata ʕaʃara] seventeen
سبعين seventy *number* [sabʕi:na]
سبورة blackboard *n* [sabu:ra]
سبيل path, way *n* [sabi:l]
على سبيل المثال
['ala sabeel al-methal] *n* e.g.
ستارة curtain *n* [sita:ra]
ستارة النافذة
[Setarat al-nafedhah] *n* blind
ستارة مُعتِمة
[Setarah mo'atemah] *n* Venetian blind
ستة six *number* [sittatun]
ستة عشر *number* [sittata ʕaʃara] sixteen
سترة coat, jacket *n* [sutra]
سترة صوفية
[Sotrah ṣofeyah] *n* cardigan
سُترة النجاة
[Sotrat al-najah] *n* life jacket
سُترة بولو برقبة
[Sotrat bolo be-ra'qabah] *n* polo-necked sweater
ستيرودي steroid *n* [stirwudij]
ستريو stereo *n* [stirju:]
ستون sixty *number* [sittu:na]
سجائر *n* [saʒa:ʔir]
هل يمكنني الحصول على طفاية للسجائر؟
[hal yamken -any al-ḥuṣool 'aala ṭafa-ya lel-saja-er?] May I have an ashtray?
سجاد *n* [saʒʒa:d]
سجاد مثبت
[Sejad mothabat] *n* fitted carpet
سجادة carpet, rug *n* [saʒa:dda]
سجد kneel down *v* [saʒada]
سجق sausage *n* [saʒq]
سجل register *n* [siʒʒil]
سجل مدرسي
[Sejel madrasey] *n* transcript
سِجل القصاصات
[Sejel al'qeṣaṣat] *n* scrapbook
سجَّل record, register *v* [saʒʒala]
يُسجِل الدخول
[Yosajel al-dokhool] *v* log in
يُسجِل الخروج
[Yosajel al-khoroj] *v* log off
يُسَجِّل على شريط
[Yosajel 'aala shereeṭ] *v* tape
سجن jail *n* [siʒn]
ضابط سجن
[Ḍabeṭ sejn] *n* prison officer
سجِن jail *v* [saʒana]
سجين prisoner *n* [saʒi:n]
سحاب cloud *n* [saħa:b]
ناطحة سحاب
[Naṭehat saḥab] *n* skyscraper
سحابة cloud *n* [saħa:ba]
سحب draw, withdrawing *n* [saħb]

كارت سحب
[Kart sahb] *n* debit card
withdraw, pull up *v* [saħaba] **سحَب**
يَسحب كلامه
[Yasḥab kalameh] *v* take back
spell, magic *n* [siħr] **سحر**
spell *v* [jasħiru] **سحر**
magical *adj* [siħrij] **سِحري**
crush *v* [saħaqa] **سحق**
soot *n* [suxa:m] **سُخام**
heater *n* [saxxa:n] **سخان**
v [saxara] **سخَر**
يَسخَر من
[Yaskhar men] *v* scoff
irony *n* [suxrijja] **سُخرية**
heat up *v* [saxxana] **سَخّن**
heat, warm up *v* [saxxana] **سَخّن**
generous *adj* [saxij] **سخي**
absurd *adj* [saxi:f] **سَخيف**
dam *n* [sadd] **سد**
repayment *n* [sadda:d] **سَداد**
tampon *n* [sidda:da] **سِدادة**
pay back *v* [saddada] **سَدَّد**
secret *n* [sirr] **سِرّ**
secretly *adv* [sirran] **سِراً**
n [sara:xis] **سَراخس**
نبات السراخس
[Nabat al-sarakhes] *n* fern
pavilion *n* [sara:diq] **سُرادق**
leak *vi* [sarraba] **سرّب**
flock *n* [sirb] **سِرب**
navel *n* [surra] **سُرَّة**
سُرَّة البطن
[Sorrat al-baṭn] *n* belly button
saddle *n* [sarʒ] **سرج**
lay off *v* [sarraħa] **سَرَّح**
sardine *n* [sardi:nu] **سردين**
n [saratˤa:n] **سرطان**
حيوان السرطان
[Ḥayawan al-saraṭan] *n* crab
مرض السرطان
[Maraḍ al-saraṭan] *n* cancer *(illness)*
speed *n* [surʕa] **سرعة**
سرعة السير
[Sor'aat al-seer] *n* pace
بسرعة
[Besor'aah] *adv* fast
حد السرعة
[Ḥad alsor'aah] *n* speed limit
ذراع نقل السرعة
[Dhera'a na'ql al-sor'aah] *n* gearshift
steal *v* [saraqa] **سرق**
يَسرِق عَلانية
[Yasre'q 'alaneytan] *v* rip off
لقد سرق شخص ما حقيبتي
[la'qad sara'qa shakh-ṣon ma ḥa'qebaty] Someone's stolen my bag
rip-off, theft *n* [sariqa] **سرقة**
سرقة السلع من المَتَاجِر
[Sare'qat al-sela'a men al-matajer] *n* shoplifting
سرقة الهوية
[Sare'qat al-hawyiah] *n* identity theft
أريد التبليغ عن وقوع سرقة
[areed al-tableegh 'an wi'qoo'a sare'qa] I want to report a theft
pants *npl* [sirwa:l] **سروال**
سروال تحتي قصير
[Serwal taḥtey 'qaṣeer] *n* briefs
سروال قصير
[Serwal 'qaṣeer] *n* knickers
سروال من قماش الدِنيم القطنى
[Serwal men 'qomash al-deneem al-'qotney] *n* jeans
pleasure *n* [suru:r] **سرور**
بكل سرور
[bekul siroor] With pleasure!
من دواعي سروري العمل معك
[min dawa-'ay siro-ry al-'aamal ma'aak] It's been a pleasure working with you
n [suru:rij] **سروري**
من دواعي سروري أن التقي بك
[min dawa-'ay siro-ry an al-ta'qy bik] It was a pleasure to meet you
adj [sirrij] **سري**
سري للغاية
[Serey lel-ghayah] *adj* top-secret
confidential, secret *adj* [sirij] **سِريّ**
privacy *n* [sirrija] **سَرية**
bed *n* [sari:r] **سرير**
سرير محمول للطفل
[Sareer maḥmool lel-ṭefl] *n* carrycot

سريرين منفصلين
[Sareerayn monfaṣ elayen] *npl* twin beds
بياضات الأسرّة
[Bayaḍat al-aserah] *n* bed linen
سَرير رحلات
[Sareer raḥalat] *n* camp bed
سَرير بدورين
[Sareer bedoreen] *n* bunk beds
سَرير فردي
[Sareer fardey] *n* single bed
سَرير مبيت
[Sareer mabeet] *n* bunk
سَرير مُزدوج
[Sareer mozdawaj] *n* double bed
أريد سرير بدورين
[Areed sareer bedoreen] I'd like a dorm bed
أريد غرفة بسرير مزدوج
[areed ghurfa be-sareer muzdawaj] I'd like a room with a double bed
السرير ليس مريحًا
[al-sareer laysa mureeḥan] The bed is uncomfortable
هل يجب علي البقاء في السرير؟
[hal yajib 'aala-ya al-ba'qaa fee al-sareer?] Do I have to stay in bed?
سريع fast, quick *adj* [sariːʕ]
سريع الغضب
[Saree'a al-ghaḍab] *adj* ticklish
زورق بخاري سريع
[Zawra'q bokharey sarea'a] *n* speedboat
سريعاً quickly *adv* [sariːʕan]
سِري لانكا Sri Lanka *n* [sriː laːnkaː]
سَطح surface *n* [satˤħ]
سَطح المبنى
[Saṭh al-mabna] *n* roof
سَطح مستوي
[Saṭ mostawey] *n* plane *(surface)*
أيمكننا أن نخرج إلى سطح المركب؟
[a-yamkun-ana an nakhruj ela saṭ-ḥ al-markab?] Can we go out on deck?
سطحي external, *adj* [satˤħij] superficial
سطو robbery, burglary *n* [satˤw]
سطو مُسلح
[Saṭw mosalaḥ] *n* hold-up
سطو burgle *v* [satˤwaː]
يسطو على
[Yasṭo 'ala] *v* break in
سَعادة happiness *n* [saʕaːda]
بسعادة
[Besa'aaadah] *adv* happily
سُعال cough *n* [suʕaːl]
سعة capacity *n* [siʕa]
سعر price *n* [siʕr]
سعر التجزئة
[Se'ar al-tajzeah] *n* retail price
سعر البيع
[Se'ar al-bay'a] *n* selling price
بنصف السعر
[Be-nesf al-se'ar] *adv* half-price
رجاء كتابة السعر
[rejaa ketabat al-si'ar] Please write down the price
كم سعره؟
[kam si'aroh?] How much is it?
ما هو سعر الصرف؟
[ma howa si'ar al-ṣarf?] What's the exchange rate?
ما هو سعر الوجبة الشاملة؟
[ma howa si'ar al-wajba al-shamela?] How much is the set menu?
ما هي الأشياء التي تدخل ضمن هذا السعر؟
[ma heya al-ashyaa al-laty tadkhul ḍimn hatha al-si'ar?] What is included in the price?
هل لديكم أشياء أقل سعرا؟
[hal ladykum ashyaa a'qal si'aran?] Do you have anything cheaper?
سُعْر *n* [suʕr]
سُعْر حراري
[So'ar hararey] *n* calorie
سِعر price *n* [siʕr]
سِعر الصرف
[Se'ar al-ṣ arf] *n* exchange rate, rate of exchange
سعل cough *vi* [saʕala]
سعودي Saudi *n* ◁ Saudi *adj* [saʕuːdij]
المملكة العربية السعودية
[Al-mamlakah al-'aarabeyah

al-so'aodeyah] *n* Saudi Arabia
مواطن سعودي
[Mewaṭen saudey] *n* Saudi Arabian
سعَى *v* [saʕa:]
يَسعَى إلى
[Yas'aaa ela] *n* aim
يَسعَى وراء
[Yas'aa waraa] *v* pursue, follow
سعيد fortunate, glad, *adj* [saʕi:d] happy
حظ سعيد
[haḍh sa'aeed] *n* fortune
سفاح killer, thug *n* [saffa:ħ]
سفارة embassy *n* [sifa:ra]
أريد الاتصال بسفارة بلادي
[areed al-etiṣal be-safaarat belaady] I'd like to phone my embassy
أحتاج إلى الاتصال بسفارة بلادي
[aḥtaaj ela al-iteṣaal be-safaarat belaady] I need to call my embassy
سفاري *n* [safa:ri:]
رحلة سفاري
[Reḥlat safarey] *n* safari
سفر trip, travel, travelling *n* [safar]
أجرة السفر
[Ojrat al-safar] *n* fare
دُوار السفر
[Dowar al-safar] *n* travel sickness
حقائب السفر
[ḥa'qaeb al-safar] *n* luggage
حقيبة سفر
[Ha'qeebat al-safar] *n* suitcase
أريد السفر في الدرجة الأولى
[areed al-safar fee al-daraja al-oola] I would like to travel first-class
لم تصل حقائب السفر الخاصة بي بعد
[Lam taṣel ḥa'qaeb al-safar al-khaṣah bee ba'ad] My luggage hasn't arrived
هذا هو جواز السفر
[hatha howa jawaz al-safar] Here is my passport
سُفرة snack bar *n* [sufra]
سَفعَة *n* [safʕa]
سَفعَة شمس
[Saf'aat ahams] *n* sunburn
سُفلى downstairs *adj* [sufla:]

سفلياً downstairs *adv* [suflijjan]
سفن ships *npl* [sufun]
تِرْسَانة السُفن
[Yarsanat al-sofon] *n* shipyard
بناء السفن
[Benaa al-sofon] *n* shipbuilding
حوض السفن
[Hawḍ al-sofon] *n* dock
سَفير ambassador *n* [safi:r]
سَفينة ship *n* [safi:na]
سَفينة حربية
[Safeenah ḥarbeyah] *n* battleship
سقالات scaffolding *npl* [saqa:la:tun]
سقط drop, fall down *v* [saqatˤa]
سقطت
[sa'qaṭat] She fell
لقد سقط مقبض الباب
[la'qad sa'qaṭa me-'qbaḍ al-baab] The handle has come off
هل تظن أن المطر سوف يسقط؟
[hal taḍhun ana al-maṭar sawfa yas'qiṭ?] Do you think it's going to rain?
سقف roof, ceiling *n* [saqf]
يوجد تسرب في السقف
[yujad tasa-rub fee al-sa'qf] The roof leaks
سقم sickness *n* [saqam]
سُقوط fall *n* [suqu:tˤ]
سقيم ill *adj* [saqi:m]
سكان population *n* [sukka:n]
سكب pour *vt* [sakaba]
سكت shut up *v* [sakata]
سكة road *n* [sikka]
سكة حديد بالملاهي
[Sekat ḥadeed bel-malahey] *n* rollercoaster
سكة حديدية
[Sekah haedeedyah] *n* railway
قضبان السكة الحديدية
['qoḍban al-sekah al-ḥadeedeyah] *n* rail
سكر sugar *n* [sukar]
سكر ناعِم
[Sokar na'aem] *n* icing sugar
خالي من السكر
[Khaley men al-oskar] *adj* sugar-free
مرض السكر

[Maraḍ al-sokar] *n* diabetes
بدون سكر
[bedoon suk-kar] no sugar
سكران [sakra:n] *n* drunk
سكرتير [sikirti:r] *n* secretary
هل يمكنني ترك رسالة مع السكرتير الخاص به؟
[hal yamken -any tark resala ma'aa al-sikertair al-khaṣ behe?] Can I leave a message with his secretary?
سكري [sukkarij] *adj*
شخص مصاب بالبول السكرى
[Shakhṣ moṣaab bel-bol al-sokarey] *n* diabetic
مصاب بالسكري
[Moṣab bel sokkarey] *adj* diabetic
سكسية [saksijja] *n*
آلة السكسية
[Alat al-sekseyah] *n* saxophone
سكن [sakana] *v*
أسكن في...
[askun fee..] We live in...
أسكن في...
[askun fee..] I live in...
سَكني [sakanij] *adj* residential
سكير [sikki:r] *n* alcoholic
سكين [sikki:n] *n* knife
سكين القلم
[Sekeen al-'qalam] *n* penknife
سَكاكين المائدة
[Skakeen al-maeadah] *n* cutlery
سِكينة [sikki:na] *n* knife
سُل [sull] *n* tuberculosis
سلاح [sila:ħ] *n* weapon
سلاح الطيران
[Selaḥ al-ṭayaran] *n* Air Force
سلاح المُشاة
[Selaḥ al-moshah] *n* infantry
سلاح ناري
[Selaḥ narey] *n* revolver
سلاطة [sala:tˤa] *n* salad
سَلاطة خضراء
[Salaṭat khadraa] *n* green salad
سلاطة مخلوطة
[Salata makhloṭa] *n* mixed salad
سَلاطة الكرنب والجزر
[Salaṭ at al-koronb wal-jazar] *n* coleslaw
سَلاطة فواكه
[Salaṭat fawakeh] *n* fruit salad
سلالة [sula:la] *n* race *(origin)*
سلام [sala:m] *n* peace
سلامة [sala:ma] *n* safety
سلب [salaba] *v* rob
سلبي [silbij] *adj* negative, passive
سلة [salla] *n* basket
سلة الأوراق المهملة
[Salat al-awra'q al-mohmalah] *n* wastepaper basket
سلة المهملات
[Salat al-mohmalat] *n* litter bin
كرة السلة
[Korat al-salah] *n* basketball
سُلحفاة [sulħufa:t] *n* tortoise, turtle
سلزيوس [silizju:s] *n*
درجة حرارة سلزيوس
[Darajat ḥararah selezyos] *n* degree Celsius
سَلس [salis] *adj* (فصيح) fluent
سِلسة [silsila] *n* chain
سلسلة رسوم هزلية
[Selselat resoom hazaleyah] *n* comic strip
سلسلة جبال
[Selselat jebal] *n* range *(mountains)*
سلسلة متتابعة
[Selselah motatabe'ah] *n* episode
سلسلة مباريات
[Selselat mobarayat] *n* tournament
سلطانة [sultˤa:na] *n* sultana
زَبيب سلطانة
[Zebeeb solṭanah] *n* sultana
سُلطانية [sultˤa:nijja] *n* bowels
سلطة [sultˤa] *n* command, power
سلف [salaf] *n* predecessor, ancestor
سلق [slaqa] *vi* boil
سِلك [silk] *n* string, wire
سِلك شائك
[Selk shaaek] *n* barbed wire
سلكي [silkij] *n*
لا سلكي
[La-selkey] *adj* cordless
سلم [sullam] *n* stair, staircase

سلم متحرك
[Solam motaḥarek] *n* escalator
سُلَم نقال
[Sollam na'q'qaal] *n* stepladder
سلالم
[sala:lim] *n* stairs
سَلَّم [sallama] *v* hand, surrender
◁ *vt* deliver
يُسَلِم ب
[Yosalem be] *v* presume
سُلَم *n* ladder
سلمون [salamu:n] *n*
سمك السلمون
[Samak al-salmon] *n* salmon
ذَكَر سمك السلمون
[Dhakar samak al-salamon] *n* kipper
سلوفاكي [slu:fa:kij] *adj* Slovak
اللغة السلوفاكية
[Al-logha al-slofakeyah] *(language) n* Slovak
مواطن سلوفاكي
[Mowaṭen slofakey] *(person) n* Slovak
سلوفاكيا [slu:fa:kija:] *n* Slovakia
سلوفاني [slu:fa:ni:] *adj* Slovenian
اللغة السلوفانية
[Al-logha al-slofaneyah] *(language) n* Slovenian
مواطن سلوفاني
[Mowaṭen slofaney] *(person) n* Slovenian
سلوفانيا [slu:fa:nija:] *n* Slovenia
سلوك [sulu:k] *n* behaviour, manner
سلوكي [sulu:kij] *adj*
عادة سلوكية
['aadah selokeyah] *n* habit
سلوكيات [sulu:kijja:tun] *npl* manners
سَلَّى [salla:] *v* amuse
سليم [sali:m] *adj* intact, sound, whole
سُمّ [summ] *n* poison, venom
سماء [sama:ʔ] *n* sky
سماد [sama:d] *n* manure, fertilizer
سماد عضوي
[Semad 'aodwey] *n* manure
سِمَاد طبيعي
[Semad ṭabe'ay] *n* peat

سماعات [samma:ʕa:t] *n* hands-free kit
سَماكة [sama:ka] *n* thickness
سِمَّان [simma:n] *n*
طائر السِمَّان
[Ṭaaer al-saman] *n* quail
سمة [sima] *n* characteristic, feature
سمَح [samaħa] *v* allow
سُمرة [sumra] *n* tan
سُمرة الشمس
[Somrat al-shams] *n* suntan
سِمسار [samsa:r] *n* broker
سِمسار عقارات
[Semsaar a'qarat] *n* estate agent
سِمسار البورصة
[Semsar al-borṣah] *n* stockbroker
سَمْع [samʕ] *n* hearing
سمعة [sumʕa] *n* reputation
حسن السمعة
[Ḥasen al-som'aah] *adj* reputable
سَمعي [samʕij] *adj* acoustic
سِمفونية [samfu:nijja] *n* symphony
سَمك [samak] *n* fish
صياد السمك
[Ṣayad al-samak] *n* fisherman
سمك سياف البحر
[Samak aayaf al-baḥr] *n* swordfish
سمك السَّلْمون المُرَقَّط
[Samak al-salamon almora'qaṭ] *n* trout
سمك الأبيض
[Samak al-abyaḍ] *n* whiting
سمك التونة
[Samak al-tonah] *n* tuna
سمك الشص
[Samak al-shaṣ] *n* fisherman
سمك القد
[Samak al'qad] *n* cod
سمك ذهبي
[Samak dhahabey] *n* goldfish
سوف أتناول سمك
[sawfa ata-nawal samak] I'll have the fish
لا أتناول الأسماك
[la ata-nawal al-asmaak] I don't eat fish
ماذا يوجد من أطباق السمك؟
[madha yujad min aṭbaa'q al-samak?]

What fish dishes do you have?
هل يمكن إعداد وجبة خالية من الأسماك؟
[hal yamken e'adad wajba khaliya min al-asmaak?] Could you prepare a meal without fish?
سَمك fish *n* [samaka]
سَمكة مياه عذبة
[Samakat meyah adhbah] *n* freshwater fish
سَمكة الأنقليس
[Samakat al-anfalees] *n* eel
سَمَّم poison *v* [sammama]
سَمْن butter *n* [samn]
سَمْن نباتي
[Samn nabatey] *n* margarine
سَمندل salamander *n* [samandal]
سَمندل الماء
[Samandal al-maa] *n* newt
سُمي toxic *adj* [summij]
سَميك thick *adj* [sami:k]
سَمين fat *adj* [sami:n]
سن tooth *n* [sinn]
أطقم أسنان صناعية
[Aṭ'qom asnan ṣena'aeyah] *npl* dentures
أكبر سِنّاً
[Akbar senan] *adj* elder
خَيْط تنظيف الأسنان
[Khayṭ tandheef al-asnan] *n* dental floss
الأكبر سناً
[Al-akbar senan] *adj* eldest
طبيب أسنان
[Ṭabeeb asnan] *n* dentist
متعلق بطب الأسنان
[Mota'ale'q be-ṭeb al-asnan] *adj* dental
عندي وجع في الأسنان
['aendy waja'a fee al-as-nan] I have toothache
لقد كسرت سنتي
[la'qad kasarto sin-ny] I've broken a tooth
ليس لدي تأمين صحي لأسناني
[laysa la-daya ta-meen ṣiḥee le-asnany] I don't have dental insurance
هذا السن يؤلمني
[haḍha al-sen yoelemoney] This tooth hurts
سِن tooth *n* [sin]
سِن المرء
[Sen al-mara] *n* age
سِن المراهقة
[Sen al-moraha'qah] *n* adolescence
حد السّن
[Had alssan] *n* age limit
سناد brace *n* [sana:d]
سِنارة fishing rod *n* [sˤanna:ra]
سِنت cent, penny *n* [sint]
سَنة year *n* [sana]
سنة ضريبية
[Sanah ḍareebeyah] *n* fiscal year
سَنة كبيسة
[Sanah kabeesah] *n* leap year
سَنة مالية
[Sanah maleyah] *n* financial year
رَأس السَنَة
[Raas alsanah] *n* New Year
كل سنة
[Kol sanah] *adj* yearly
سنتيمتر centimetre *n* [santi:mitar]
سِنجاب squirrel *n* [sinʒa:b]
سَند bond *n* [sanad]
سَندويتش sandwich *n* [sandiwi:tʃ]
سِنغالي Senegalese *n* [siniɣa:lij]
سَنَّن teethe *v* [sannana]
سنُوكِر *n* [snu:kar]
لُعْبَة السُّنوكِر
[Lo'abat al-sonoker] *n* snooker
سنوي annual *adj* [sanawij]
سنوياً yearly *adv* [sanawijan]
سهرة *n* [sahra]
ملابس السهرة
[Malabes al-sahrah] *npl* evening dress
سهل easy, flat *adj* [sahl]
سهل الانقياد
[Sahl al-en'qyad] *adj* easy-going
سهل الوصول
[Sahl al-woṣool] *adj* accessible
سهم arrow, dart *n* [sahm]
سهم مالي
[Sahm maley] *n* share
لعبة رمي السهام
[Lo'abat ramey al-seham] *npl* darts

سهو oversight *(mistake)* *n* [sahw]
سوء misfortune *n* [suːʔ]
سوء الحظ
[Soa al-ḥaḍh] *n* misfortune
سوء فهم
[Soa fahm] *n* misunderstanding
سوء معاملة الأطفال
[Soo mo'aamalat al-aṭfaal] *n* child abuse
سُوَار bracelet *n* [suwaːr]
سُوَار الساعة
[Sowar al-sa'aah] *n* watch strap
سوازيلاند Swaziland *n* [swaːziːlaːnd]
سوداني *n* ◁ Sudanese *adj* [suːdaːnij] Sudanese
سوري Syrian *n* ◁ Syrian *adj* [suːrij]
سوريا Syria *n* [suːrjaː]
سَوط whip *n* [sawtˤ]
سوق market, market place *n* [suːq]
سوق خيرية
[Soo'q khayreyah] *n* fair
سُوق الأوراق المالية
[Soo'q al-awra'q al-maleyah] *n* stock exchange
سُوق للسلع الرخيصة
[Soo'q lel-sealaa al-ṣgheerah] *n* flea market
متى يبدأ العمل في السوق؟
[mata yabda al-'aamal fee al-soo'q?] When is the market on?
سُوقي vulgar *adj* [suːqij]
سولار *n* [suːlaːr]
سولار من فضلك...
[Solar men faḍlek…] ... worth of diesel, please
سويا together *adv* [sawijjan]
سويدي *n* ◁ Swedish *adj* [swiːdij] Swede
اللغة السويدية
[Al-loghah al-sweedeyah] *n* Swedish
اللّفت السويدي
[Al-left al-sweedey] *n* swede
سويسرا Switzerland *n* [swiːsraː]
سويسري *n* ◁ Swiss *adj* [swiːsrij] Swiss
سيء bad *adj* [sajjiʔ]
على نحو سيء
[Ala nahw saye] *adv* badly
أسوأ
[ʔaswaʔun] *adj* worse
على نحو أسوأ
[Ala nahw aswaa] *adv* worse
الأسوأ
[Al-aswaa] *adj* worst
سياج fence *n* [sijaːʒ]
سياج نقال
[Seyaj na'qal] *n* hurdle
سِياج من الشجيرات
[Seyaj men al-shojayrat] *n* hedge
سياحة tourism *n* [sijaːħa]
سياحي *adj* [sijaːħij]
درجة سياحية
[Darjah seyaḥeyah] *n* economy class
مرشد سياحي
[Morshed seyaḥey] *n* tour guide
مكتب سياحي
[Maktab seayaḥey] *n* tourist office
لقد سرق شخص ما الشيكات السياحية الخاصة بي
[la'qad sara'qa shakh-ṣon ma al-shaikaat al-seyaḥiya al-khaṣa be] Someone's stolen my traveller's cheques
هل يتم قبول الشيكات السياحية؟
[hal yatum 'qubool al-shaikaat al-seyaḥiya?] Do you accept traveller's cheques?
سيارة carriage *n* [sajjaːra]
إيجار سيارة
[Ejar sayarah] *n* car rental
سائق سيارة
[Saae'q sayarah] *n* chauffeur
سيارة صالون
[Sayarah ṣalon] *n* saloon car
سيارة إسعاف
[Sayarat es'aaf] *n* ambulance
سيارة إيجار
[Sayarah eejar] *n* rental car
سيارة أجرة
[Sayarah ojarah] *n* cab
سيارة السباق
[Sayarah al-seba'q] *n* racing car
سيارة الشركة

[Sayarat al-sharekah] *n* company car
سيارة بصالون متحرك المقاعد
[Sayarah be-ṣalon motaḥarek al-ma'qaed] *n* estate car
سيارة بباب خلفي
[Sayarah be-bab khalfey] *n* hatchback
سيارة كوبيه
[Sayarah kobeeh] *n* convertible
سيارة مستأجرة
[Sayarah mostaajarah] *n* hired car
غسيل سيارة
[ghaseel sayaarah] *n* car wash
تأجير سيارة
[Taajeer sayarah] *n* car rental
تأمين سيارة
[Taameen sayarah] *n* car insurance
استئجار سيارة
[isti-jar sayara] *n* rental car
أريد أن استأجر سيارة
[areed an asta-jer sayara] I want to hire a car
الأطفال في السيارة
[al-aṭfaal fee al-sayara] My children are in the car
كم تبلغ مصاريف سيارة لشخصين؟
[kam tablugh ma-ṣareef sayarah le-sha-khṣyn?] How much is it for a car for two people?
لقد صدمتُ سيارتي
[la'qad ṣadamto sayaraty] I've crashed my car
متى ستغادر السيارة في الصباح؟
[mata satu-ghader al-sayarah fee al-ṣabaaḥ?] When does the coach leave in the morning?
هل يمكن أن أوقف السيارة هنا؟
[hal yamken an o'qef al- sayara huna?] Can I park here?
هل يمكنك توصيلي بالسيارة؟
[hal yamken -aka taw-ṣeely bil-sayara?] Can you take me by car?
هل يمكنك جر سيارتي إلى ورشة السيارات؟
[Hal yomkenak jar sayaratey ela warshat al-sayarat?] Can you tow me to a garage?

هناك ثقب في رادياتير السيارة
[Honak tho'qb fee radyateer al-sayarah] There is a leak in the radiator
politics *npl* [sija:sa] **سياسة**
رجل سياسة
[Rajol seyasah] *n* politician
علم السياسة
['aelm alseyasah] *n* political science
political *adj* [sija:sij] **سياسي**
context *n* [sija:q] **سياق**
Siberia *n* [si:bi:rja:] **سيبيريا**
cigar *n* [si:ʒa:r] **سيجار**
cigarette *n* [si:ʒa:ra] **سيجارة**
skewer *n* [si:x] **سيخ**
chief *n* [sajjid] **سيد**
lady *n* [sajjida] **سيدة**
سيدة أعمال
[Sayedat a'amaal] *n* businesswoman
sir *n* [sajjidi:] **سيدي**
belt, march *n* [sajr] **سير**
سرعة السير
[Sor'aat al-seer] *n* pace
سير المروحة
[Seer almarwaha] *n* fan belt
سير متحرك
[Sayer motaḥrrek] *n* conveyor belt
أريد صعود التل سيرا على الأقدام
[areed ṣi'aood al-tal sayran 'aala al-a'qdaam] I'd like to go hill walking
هل يمكن السير هناك؟
[hal yamken al-sayr hunak?] Can I walk there?
هل يوجد أي جولات للسير مع أحد المرشدين؟
[hal yujad ay jaw-laat lel-sayer ma'aa aḥad al-murshid-een?] Are there any guided walks?
biography *n* [si:ra] **سيرة**
سيرة ذاتية
[Seerah dhateyah] *n* autobiography, CV
n [si:rfar] **سيرفر**
جهاز السيرفر
[Jehaz al-servo] *n* server *(computer)*
circus *n* [si:rk] **سيرك**
sword *n* [sajf] **سيف**
adj [sajku:lu:ʒij] **سيكولوجي**

psychological

سَيْل downpour *n* [sajl]

سينما cinema *n* [siːnimaː]

ماذا يعرض الآن على شاشات السينما؟

[madha yu'a-raḍ al-aan 'aala sha-shaat al-senama?] What's on at the cinema?

سينمائي *adj* [siːnimaːʔij]

نجم سينمائي

[Najm senemaaey] *n* film star

شائع common *adj* [ʃaːʔiʕ]

شائك prickly *adj* [ʃaːʔiku]

نبات شائك الأطراف

[Nabat shaek al-aṭraf] *n* holly

شائِن disgraceful *adj* [ʃaːʔin]

شاب young *adj* [ʃaːbb]

شابك snarl *v* [ʃaːbaka]

شاة ewe *n* [ʃaːt]

شاحب pale *adj* [ʃaːħib]

شاحِن charger *n* [ʃaːħin]

شاحنة truck *n* [ʃaːħina]

شاحِنة لوري

[Shaḥenah loorey] *n* truck

شاحنة قَطْر

[Shaḥenat 'qaṭr] *n* breakdown truck

شاحِنة نقل

[Shahenat na'ql] *n* removal van

شاذ odd *adj* [ʃaːðð]

شارب moustache *n* [ʃaːrib]

شارَة badge *n* [ʃaːra]

شارع street *n* [ʃaːriʕ]

شارع جانبي

[Share'a janebey] *n* side street

خريطة الشارع

[Khareeṭat al-share'a] *n* street plan

أريد خريطة لشوارع المدينة

[areed khareeṭa le-shawari'a al-madena]

I want a street map of the city

شارك share *v* [ʃaːraka]

شاشة monitor *n* [ʃaːʃa]

شاشة بلازما

[Shashah blazma] *n* plasma screen

شاشة مسطحة

[Shasha mosṭahah] *adj* flat-screen

شاطئ beach *n* [ʃaːtˤiʔ]

شاطئ البحر

[Shaṭeya al-baḥr] *n* seashore

سوف أذهب إلى الشاطئ

[sawfa adhab ela al-shaṭee] I'm going to the beach

ما هي المسافة بيننا وبين الشاطئ؟

[ma heya al-masafa bay-nana wa bayn al-shaṭee?] How far are we from the beach?, How far is the beach?

هل يوجد أتوبيس إلى الشاطئ؟

[Hal yojad otobees elaa al-shaṭea?] Is there a bus to the beach?

شاطر clever *adj* [ʃaːtˤir]

شاعر intuitive *adj* ◃ poet *n* [ʃaːʕir]

شاعر بالإطراء

[Shaa'aer bel-eṭraa] *adj* flattered

شاغب riot *v* [ʃaːɣaba]

شاغر vacant *adj* [ʃaːɣir]

شاكوش hammer *n* [ʃaːkuːʃ]

شال shawl *n* [ʃaːl]

شامبانيا champagne *n* [ʃaːmbaːnijaː]

شامبو shampoo *n* [ʃaːmbuː]

هل تبيع شامبوهات

[hal tabee'a shambo-haat?] Do you sell shampoo?

شامة beauty spot *n* [ʃaːma]

شامل comprehensive, *adj* [ʃaːmil] thorough

بشكل شامل

[Be-shakl shamel] *adv* thoroughly

شأن affair *n* [ʃaʔn]

شؤون الساعة

[Sheoon al-saa'ah] *npl* current affairs

شاهد witness *n* [ʃaːhid]

شاهد watch *v* [ʃaːhada]

أنا أشاهد فقط

[ana ashahid fa'qaṭ] I'm just looking

شاهق steep, high *adj* [ʃaːhiq]

شاي tea *n* [ʃaːj]

براد الشاي

[Brad shaay] *n* teapot

فنجان شاي

[Fenjan shay] *n* teacup

كيس شاي

[Kees shaay] *n* tea bag

ملعقة شاي

[Mel'a'qat shay] *v* teaspoon

شاي من فضلك

[shaay min faḍlak] A tea, please

هل يمكن من فضلك الحصول على كوب آخر من الشاي؟

[hal yamken min faḍlak al-ḥusool 'aala koob aakhar min al-shay?] Could we have another cup of tea, please?

شباب youth *n* [ʃabaːb]

بيت الشباب

[Bayt al-shabab] *n* hostel

شباك *n* [ʃubbaːk]

شباك التذاكر

[Shobak al-taḍhaker] *n* box office

شبح ghost *n* [ʃabaħ]

شبحي spooky *adj* [ʃabaħij]

شبشب flip-flops *n* [ʃubʃub]

شبشب حمام

[Shebsheb ḥamam] *n* slipper

شبكة net, network *n* [ʃabaka]

شبكة عنكبوتية

[Shabakah 'ankaboteyah] *n* web

شبكة داخلية

[Shabakah dakheleyah] *n* intranet

كرة الشبكة

[Korat al-shabakah] *n* netball

شبكة قضبان مُتصالِبة

[Shabakat 'qodban motaṣalebah] *n* grid

لا أستطيع الوصول إلى الشبكة

[la astạ-ṭee'a al-wiṣool ela al-shabaka] I can't get a network

شِبْل cub *n* [ʃibl]

شِبه semi-detached house, *n* [ʃibhu] resemblance

شَبُّورة mist *n* [ʃabuwra]

شتوي winter *adj* [ʃitwijjat]

رياضات شتوية

[Reyḍat shetweyah] *npl* winter sports

شتيمة [ʃatiːma] *n* swearword, insult
شجار [ʃiʒaːr] *n* row
شجاع [ʃuʒaːʕ] *n* brave
شجاعة [ʃaʒaːʕa] *n* bravery
شجر [ʃaʒar] *n* tree
شجر البتولا
[Ahjar al-betola] *n* birch
شجر الطقسوس
[Shajar al-ṭa'qsoos] *n* yew
أشجار الغابات
[Ashjaar al-ghabat] *n* timber
شجرة [ʃaʒara] *n* tree
شجرة عيد الميلاد
[Shajarat 'aeed al-meelad] *n* Christmas tree
شجرة الصنوبر
[Shajarat al-ṣonobar] *n* pine
شجرة الصنوبر المخروطية
[Shajarat al-ṣonobar al-makhrooṭeyah] *n* conifer
شجرة الصِفْصَاف
[Shajart al-ṣefṣaf] *n* willow
شجرة الزان
[Shajarat al-zaan] *n* beech (tree)
شجَّع [ʃaʒʒaʕa] *v* encourage
شجَيْرَة [ʃuʒajra] *n* bush *(shrub)*
شحرور [ʃaħruːr] *n* blackbird
شحم [ʃaħm] *n* grease
شحن [ʃaħn] *n* charge *(electricity)*
إنها لا تقبل الشحن
[inaha la ta'qbal al-shaḥin] It's not charging
شحنة [ʃuħna] *n* freight
شخص [ʃaxsˤun] *n* person, character
أي شخص
[Ay shakhṣ] *pron* anybody
شخص عربي
[Shakhṣ 'arabey] *(person) adj* Arab
شخص جزائري
[Shakhṣ jazayry] *n* Algerian
كم تبلغ تكلفة عربة مجهزة للمخيمات لأربعة أشخاص؟
[kam tablugh taklifat 'aaraba mujahaza lel-mukhyamat le-arba'aat ash-khaṣ?] How much is it for a camper with four people?
هل هذا مناسب للأشخاص النباتيين
[hal hadha munasib lel-ash-khaaṣ al-nabat-iyen?] Is this suitable for vegetarians?
شخصي [ʃaxsˤij] *adj* personal
بطاقة شخصية
[beṭ a'qah shakhṣeyah] *n* identity card
حارس شخصي
[ḥares shakhṣ] *n* bodyguard
أريد عمل الترتيبات الخاصة بالتأمين ضد الحوادث الشخصية
[areed 'aamal al-tar-tebaat al-khaṣa bil-taameen ḍid al-ḥawadith al-shakhṣiya] I'd like to arrange personal accident insurance
شخصياً [ʃaxsˤiːan] *adv* personally
شخصية [ʃaxsˤijja] *n* character, personality
شَحنة [ʃaxna] *n* shipment
شديد [ʃadiːd] *adj* extreme, intensive
بدرجة شديدة
[Bedarajah shadeedah] *adv* extremely
شَذا [ʃaðaː] *n* odour
شراء [ʃiraːʔ] *n* purchase
شراء كامل
[Sheraa kaamel] *n* buyout
أين يمكن شراء الطوابع؟
[ayna yamken sheraa al-ṯawabi'a?] Where can I buy stamps?
هل يجب شراء تذكرة لإيقاف السيارة؟
[hal yajib al-sayarah tadhkara] Do I need to buy a car-parking ticket?
شرائح [ʃaraːʔiħun] *npl* chips
شراب [ʃaraːb] *n* drink, syrup
إسراف في الشراب
[Esraf fee alsharab] *n* booze
الإفراط في تناول الشراب
[Al-efraaṭ fee tanawol alsharab] *n* binge drinking
شراب الجين المُسكِر
[Sharaab al-jobn al-mosaker] (محلج القطن) *n* gin
شراب البَنْش المُسكِر
[Sharaab al-bensh al-mosker] *n* punch *(hot drink)*
شراب مُسكِر

[Sharaab mosker] *n* nappy
spark *n* [ʃaraːra] **شرارة**
bedding *n* [ʃaraːʃif] **شراشف**
sail *n* [ʃiraːʕ] **شِراع**
drinking *n* [ʃurb] **شُرب**
مياه الشرب
[Meyah al-shorb] *n* drinking water
drink *v* [ʃareba] **شرِب**
.أنا لا أشرب
[ana la ashrab] I'm not drinking
أنا لا أشرب الخمر أبدا
[ana la ashrab al-khamr abadan] I never drink wine
أنا لا أشرب الكحول
[ana la ashrab al-koḥool] I don't drink alcohol
هل أنت ممن يشربون اللبن؟
[hal anta me-man yash-raboon al-laban?] Do you drink milk?
drink *vt* [ʃaraba] **شرب**
explain *v* [ʃaraħa] **شرح**
هل يمكن أن تشرح لي ما الذي بي؟
[hal yamken an tash-raḥ lee ma al-ladhy be?] Can you explain what the matter is?
explanation *n* [ʃarħ] **شَرح**
bad-tempered *adj* [ʃaris] **شَرِس**
condition *n* [ʃartˤ] **شَرَط**
police *n* [ʃurtˤa] **شرطة**
ضابط شرطة
[Ḍabeṭ shorṭah] *n* policeman
شرطة سرية
[Shorṭah serryah] *n* detective
شرطة قصيرة
[Sharṭah 'qaṣeerah] *n* hyphen
شرطة مائلة للأمام
[Sharṭah maelah lel-amam] *n* forward slash
شرطة مائلة للخلف
[Sharṭah maelah lel-khalf] *n* backslash
قسم شرطة
['qesm shorṭah] *n* police station
سوف يجب علينا إبلاغ الشرطة
[sawfa yajeb 'aalyna eb-laagh al-shurṭa] We will have to report it to the police
أريد الذهاب إلى قسم الشرطة؟
[areed al-dhehaab ela 'qism al-shurṭa] I need to find a police station
ارغب في التحدث إلى أحد رجال الشرطة
[arghab fee al-taḥaduth ela shurṭia] I want to speak to a policewoman
اتصل بالشرطة
[itaṣel bil-shurṭa] Call the police
احتاج إلي عمل محضر في الشرطة لأجل التأمين
[aḥtaaj ela 'aamal maḥḍar fee al-shurṭa le-ajl al-taameen] I need a police report for my insurance
cop *n* [ʃurtˤij] **شِرطي**
provisional *adj* [ʃartˤij] **شَرطي**
adj [ʃurtˤijju] **شُرطي**
شرطي المرور
[Shrṭey al-moror] *n* traffic warden
legal, kosher *adj* [ʃarʕij] **شَرْعِيّ**
supervise *v* [ʃarrafa] **شَرَّف**
honour *n* [ʃaraf] **شرف**
balcony *n* [ʃurfa] **شرفة**
مزود بشرفة
[Mozawad be-shorfah] *adj* terraced *(row houses)*
شرفة مكشوفة
[Shorfah makshofah] *n* terrace
هل يمكن أن أتناول طعامي في الشرفة؟
[hal yamken an ata-nawal ṭa'aa-mee fee al-shur-fa?] Can I eat on the terrace?
east *n* [ʃarq] **شرق**
الشرق الأقصى
[Al-shar'q al-a'qsa] *n* Far East
الشرق الأوسط
[Al-shar'q al-awṣaṭ] *n* Middle East
east *adv* [ʃarqan] **شرقاً**
متجه شرقاً
[Motajeh sharqan] *adj* eastbound
east, eastern *adj* [ʃarqij] **شرقي**
جنوب شرقي
[Janoob shr'qey] *n* southeast
شمال شرقي
[Shamal shar'qey] *n* northeast
company *n* [ʃarika] **شركة**
سيارة الشركة
[Sayarat al-sharekah] *n* company car

شركة تابعة
[Sharekah tabe'ah] *n* subsidiary
شركة طيران
[Sharekat ṭayaraan] *n* airline
شركة متعددة الجنسيات
[Shreakah mota'adedat al-jenseyat] *n* multinational
أريد الحصول على بعض المعلومات عن الشركة
[areed al-ḥuṣool 'aala ba'aḍ al-ma'aloomat 'an al-shareka] I would like some information about the company
تفضل بعض المعلومات المتعلقة بشركتي
[tafaḍal ba'aḍ al-ma'a-lomaat al-muta'a-le'qa be-share-katy] Here's some information about my company
شروق *n* [ʃuru:q]
شروق الشمس
[Sheroo'q al-shams] *n* sunrise
شريان artery *n* [ʃurja:n]
شريحة chip *(electronic)*, *n* [ʃari:ħatt] splint
شريحة صغيرة
[Shareehat ṣagheerah] *n* microchip
شريحة السليكون
[Shreeḥah men al-selekoon] *n* silicon chip
شريحة لحم مخلية من العظام
[Shreeḥat laḥm makhleyah men al-eḍham] (عصابة رأس) *n* fillet
شريحة من لحم البقر
[Shreeḥa men laḥm al-ba'qar] *n* rump steak
شَرِيحة slice *n* [ʃari:ħa]
شريحة لحم
[Shareehat laḥm] *n* steak
شريحة لحم خنزير
[Shareehat laḥm khenzeer] *n* pork chop
شريحة لحم مشوية
[Shareehat laḥm mashweyah] *n* cutlet
شريد homeless *adj* [ʃari:d]
شرير evil, villain *adj* [ʃirri:r]
شريط tape *n* [ʃari:tˤ]
شريط الحذاء
[Shreeṭ al-ḥedhaa] *n* lace
شريط قياس
[Shreeṭ 'qeyas] *n* tape measure
شريطة strip *n* [ʃari:tˤa]
شريعة sharia *n* [ʃari:ʕa]
هل توجد أطباق مباح أكلها في الشريعة الإسلامية؟
[hal tojad aṭba'q mubaḥ akluha fee al-sharee-'aa al-islam-iya?] Do you have halal dishes?
شريك partner *n* [ʃari:k]
شريك السكن
[Shareek al-sakan] *n* inmate
شريك حياة
[Shareek al-ḥayah] *n* match *(partnership)*
شريك في جريمة
[Shareek fee jareemah] *n* accomplice
شطب cross out *v* [ʃatˤaba]
شطرنج chess *n* [ʃatˤranʒ] *npl* ◁ draughts
شِطِف rinse *v* [ʃatˤafa]
شطف rinse *n* [ʃatˤf]
شظية splinter *n* [ʃazˤijja]
شعائري ritual *adj* [ʃaʕa:ʔirij]
شِعَار logo *n* [ʃiʕa:r]
شُعاعِيّ *adj* [ʃuʕa:ʕij]
صورَةٌ شُعاعِيَّة
[Ṣewar sho'aeyah] *v* X-ray
شعب public *n* [ʃaʕb]
شعبي popular, public *adj* [ʃaʕbij]
موسيقى شعبية
[Mose'qa sha'abeyah] *n* folk music
شِعبية popularity *n* [ʃaʕbijjit]
شعْبيّة publicity *n* [ʃaʕbijja]
شعر hair *n* [ʃaʕr]
رمادي الشعر
[Ramadey al-sha'ar] *adj* grey-haired
سْبِراي الشعر
[Sbray al-sha'ar] *n* hair spray
أحمر الشعر
[Aḥmar al-sha'ar] *adj* red-haired
تسريحة الشعر
[Tasreehat al-sha'ar] *n* hairdo
جل الشعر
[Jel al-sha'ar] *n* hair gel
خصلة شعر مستعار

[khoṣlat sha'ar mosta'aar] *n* toupee
قصة شعر قصيرة
['qaṣat sha'ar] *n* crew cut
كثير الشعر
[Katheer sha'ar] *adj* hairy
ماكينة تجعيد الشعر
[Makeenat taj'aeed sha'ar] *n* curler
يَعْقِص الشعر
[Ya'aqeṣ al-sha'ar] *n* curl
إن شعري مصبوغ
[enna sha'ary maṣboogh] My hair is highlighted
أنا في حاجة إلى مجفف شعر
[ana fee ḥaja ela mujaf-if sh'aar] I need a hair dryer
شعري أشقر بطبيعته
[sha'ary ash'qar beṭa-be'aatehe] My hair is naturally blonde
هل تبيع بلسم مرطب للشعر؟
[hal tabee'a balsam mura-ṯib lil-sha'air?] Do you sell conditioner?
هل يمكن أن تصبغ لي جذور شعري من فضلك؟
[hal yamken an taṣbugh lee jidhoor sha'ary min faḍlak?] Can you dye my roots, please?
هل يمكن أن تقص أطراف شعري؟
[hal yamken an ta'quṣ aṭraaf sha'ary?] Can I have a trim?
شعر [ʃaʕura] *v* feel
كيف تشعر الآن
[kayfa tash-'aur al-aan?] How are you feeling now?
شَعْر [ʃiʕr] *n* poetry
شَعر ب [ʃaʕura bi] *v*
أشعر بهرش في قدمي
[ash-'aur be-harsh fee sa'qy] My leg itches
شُعور [ʃuʕuːr] *n* feeling
شعير [ʃaʕiːrr] *n* barley
شِعيرة [ʃaʕiːra] *n* ritual
شِغَبْ [ʃaɣab] *n* riot
شغَّل [ʃaɣɣala] *v* turn on, operate *(to function)*
شِفاء [ʃifaːʔ] *n* cure, recovery
شفاف [ʃaffaːf] *adj* transparent
شفاه [ʃifaːh] *n* lip
شفرة [ʃafra] *n* blade, edge
شفرة حلاقة
[Shafrat hela'qah] *n* razor blade
شفقة [ʃafaqa] *n* pity
شفهي [ʃafahij] *adj* oral
فحص شفهي
[Faḥṣ shafahey] *n* oral
شفى [ʃafaː] *v* heal, recover
شقّ [ʃaqqa] *vt* rip
شقة [ʃaqqa] *n*
شقة ستديو
[Sha'qah stedeyo] *n* studio flat
شقة بغرفة واحدة
[Sh'qah be-ghorfah waḥedah] *n* studio flat
إننا نبحث عن شقة
[ena-na nabḥath 'aan shu'qa] We're looking for an apartment
لقد قمنا بحجز شقة باسم...
[la'qad 'qimto be- ḥajis shu'qa be-isim...] We've booked an apartment in the name of...
هل يمكن أن نرى الشقة؟
[hal yamken an naraa al-shu'qa?] Could you show us around the apartment?
شقي [ʃaqij] *adj* mischievous
شك [ʃakk] *n* doubt
معتنق مذهب الشك
[Mo'atane'q maḍhhab al-shak] *adj* sceptical
شكْ [ʃak] *n* doubt
بلا شكْ
[Bela shak] *adv* certainly
شكا [ʃakaː] *v* complain
شكر [ʃakara] *v* thank
شكرا [ʃukran] *excl* thanks!
!شكرا
[Shokran!] *excl* thanks!
شكرا جزيلا
[shukran jazeelan] Thank you very much
شكرا لك
[Shokran lak] That's very kind of you
شكل [ʃakl] *n* form
بشكل صحيح

[Beshakl ṣaheeh] *adv* correctly
بشكل سيء
[Be-shakl sayea] *adj* unwell
بشكل كامل
[Beshakl kaamel] *adv* totally
بشكل مُنفَصِل
[Beshakl monfaṣel] *adv* apart
شكل رسمي
[Shakl rasmey] *n* formality
ما هو شكل الثلوج؟
[ma howa shakl al-thilooj?] What is the snow like?
شَكَّل [ʃakkala] *v* model
شكوى [ʃakwa:] *n* complaint, grouse *(complaint)*
إني أرغب في تقديم شكوى
[inny arghab fee ta'qdeem shakwa] I'd like to make a complaint
شِكِيمة [ʃaki:ma] *n* kerb
شَلَّال [ʃalla:l] *n* waterfall
شَلّال كبير
[Shallal kabeer] *n* cataract *(waterfall)*
شلل [ʃalal] *n*
شلل أطفال
[Shalal aṭfaal] *n* polio
شمّ [ʃamma] *vt* smell
شماعة [ʃamma:ʕa] *n*
شماعة المعاطف
[Shama'aat al-ma'aatef] *n* coathanger
شمال [ʃama:l] *n* north
شمال أفريقيا
[Shamal afreekya] *n* North Africa
شمال غربي
[Shamal gharbey] *n* northwest
شمال شرقي
[Shamal shar'qey] *n* northeast
شمالا [ʃama:lan] *adv* north
متجه شمالًا
[Motajeh shamalan] *adj* northbound
شمالي [ʃama:lij] *n* north ◁ *adj* northern
أمريكا الشمالية
[Amreeka al- Shamaleyah] *n* North America
أيرلندة الشمالية
[Ayarlanda al-shamaleyah] *n* Northern Ireland
الدائرة القطبية الشمالية
[Al-daerah al'qoṭbeyah al-Shamaleyah] *n* Arctic Circle
البحر الشمالي
[Al-baḥr al-Shamaley] *n* North Sea
القطب الشمالي
[A'qoṭb al-shamaley] *n* North Pole
المحيط القطبي الشمالي
[Al-moḥeeṭ al-'qoṭbey al-shamaley] *n* Arctic Ocean
كوريا الشمالية
[Koreya al-shamaleyah] *n* North Korea
شمَّام [ʃamma:m] *n* melon
شمبانزي [ʃamba:nzij] *n* chimpanzee
شمر [ʃamar] *n*
نبات الشمر
[Nabat al-shamar] *n* fennel
شمس [ʃams] *n* sun
عباد الشمس
['aabaad al-shams] *n* sunflower
حمام شمس
[Ḥamam shams] *n* sunbed
كريم الشمس
[Kreem shams] *n* sunscreen
كريم للوقاية من الشمس
[Kreem lel-we'qayah men al-shams] *n* sunblock
مسفوع بأشعة الشمس
[Masfoo'a be-ashe'aat al-shams] *adj* sunburnt
أعاني من حروق من جراء التعرض للشمس
[O'aaney men ḥoro'q men jaraa al-ta'aroḍ lel-shams] I am sunburnt
شمسي [ʃamsij] *adj* solar
طاقة شمسية
[Ṭa'qah shamseyah] *n* solar power
نظارات شمسية
[naḍharat shamseyah] *npl* sunglasses
نظام شمسي
[neḍham shamsey] *n* solar system
شمع [ʃamʕ] *n* wax
شمعة [ʃamʕa] *n* candle
شمعدان [ʃamʕada:n] *n* candlestick
شمل [ʃamela] *v* involve

هل يشمل السعر عصي التزلج
[hal yash-mil al-si'ar 'aoṣy al-tazal-oj?] Does the price include poles?
هل يشمل ذلك الإفطار؟
[hal yash-mil dhalik al-iftaar?] Is breakfast included?
شنّ v [ʃanna]
يَشن غارة
[Yashen gharah] v raid
شنق hang vt [ʃanaqa]
شنيع awful, outrageous adj [ʃaniːʕ]
شهادة certificate n [ʃahaːda]
شهادة تأمين
[Shehadat taameen] n insurance certificate
شهادة طبية
[Shehadah ṭebeyah] n medical certificate
شهادة ميلاد
[Shahadat meelad] n birth certificate
هل يمكنني الإطلاع على شهادة التأمين من فضلك؟
[hal yamken -any al-eṭla'a 'aala sha-hadat al-tameen min faḍlak?] Can I see your insurance certificate please?
شهر month n [ʃahr]
شهْر العسل
[Shahr al-'asal] n honeymoon
في غضون شهر
[fee ghoḍon shahr] a month from now
في نهاية شهر يونيو
[fee nehayat shahr yon-yo] at the end of June
من المقرر أن أضع في غضون خمسة أشهر
[min al-mu'qarar an aḍa'a fee ghiḍoon khamsat ash-hur] I'm due in five months
منذ شهر
[mundho shahr] a month ago
شهْرَة celebrity n [ʃuhra]
شهري monthly adj [ʃahrij]
شهوة lust n [ʃahwa]
شهي delicious adj [ʃahij]
شهية appetite n [ʃahijja]
شهيد martyr n [ʃahiːd]
شهير renowned adj [ʃahiːr]
الشهير بـ
[Al-shaheer be-] adj alias
شوا grill v [ʃawaː]
شواء n [ʃiwaːʔu]
شواء اللحم
[Shewaa al-lahm] n barbecue
شَوَارِب whiskers npl [ʃawaːribun]
شواية grill n [ʃawwaːja]
شورت shorts n [ʃuːrt]
شورت بوكسر
[Short boksar] n boxer shorts
شوفان oats n [ʃuːfaːn]
دقيق الشوفان
[Da'qee'q al-shofaan] n porridge
شوْك thistle n [ʃawk]
شوكة thorn, fork n [ʃawkatu]
شوكة طعام
[Shawkat ṭa'aaam] n fork
شوكولاتة chocolate n [ʃuːkuːlaːta]
شيء object, thing n [ʃajʔun]
أي شيء
[Ay shaya] n anything
شيء ما
[Shaya ma] pron something
لا شيء
[La shaya] n nothing, zero
شَيَّال porter n [ʃajjaːl]
شيخ n [ʃajx]
طب الشيخوخة
[Ṭeb al-shaykhokhah] n geriatric
شيخوخي geriatric adj [ʃajxuːxij]
شيطان devil n [ʃajtˤaːn]
شيعي Shiite adj [ʃiːʕij]
شيك tick n [ʃiːk]
دفتر شيكات
[Daftar sheekaat] n chequebook
شيك على بياض
[Sheek ala bayad] n blank cheque
شِيك سياحي
[Sheek seyahey] n traveller's cheque
شِيك بنكي
[Sheek bankey] n tick
أريد صرف شيكًا من فضلك
[areed ṣarf shaikan min faḍlak?] I want to cash a cheque, please

هل يمكنني الدفع بشيك؟
[hal yamken -any al-daf'a be- shaik?]
Can I pay by cheque?
شيكولاتة [ʃi:ku:la:ta] *n*
شيكولاتة سادة
[Shekolatah sada] *n* plain chocolate
شيكولاتة باللبن
[Shekolata bel-laban] *n* milk chocolate
كريمة شيكولاتة
[Kareemat shekolatah] *n* mousse
شيوعي [ʃuju:ʕij] *adj* communist ◁ *n* communist
شيوعية [ʃuju:ʕijja] *n* communism

صابون [sˤa:bu:n] *n* soap
طبق صابون
[Ṭaba'q ṣaboon] *n* soap dish
مسحوق الصابون
[Masḥoo'q ṣaboon] *n* washing powder
لا يوجد صابون
[la yujad ṣaboon] There is no soap
صاح [sˤa:ħa] *v* scream, shout
صاحب [sˤa:ħib] *n* companion
صاحب الأرض
[Ṣaheb ardh] *n* landlord
صاحب العمل
[Ṣaheb 'aamal] *n* employer
صَاحب [sˤa:ħaba] *v* escort
صاد [sˤa:da] *v* hunt
صادِر [sˤa:dir] *n* (تصدير) export
صادق [sˤa:diq] *adj* truthful
صَارخ [sˤa:rix] *adj* blatant
صارَم [sˤa:rim] *adj* stark
صاروخ [sˤa:ru:xin] *n* rocket
صاري [sˤa:ri:] *n* mast
صاعداً [sˤa:ʕidan] *adv* upwards
صافي [sˤa:fi:] *adj* net
صالة [sˤa:la] *n*
صالة العبور
[Ṣalat al'aoboor] *n* transit lounge
صالة المغادرة

[Ṣalat al-moghadarah] *n* departure lounge
أين توجد صالة الألعاب الرياضية؟
[ayna tojad ṣalat al-al'aab al-reyaḍeya?] Where is the gym?
fitting, good *adj* [sˤa:liħ] **صالح**
صالح للأكل
[Ṣaleḥ lel-aakl] *adj* edible
غير صالح
[Ghayer Ṣaleḥ] *adj* unfit
saloon car *n* [sˤa:lu:n] **صالون**
صالون تجميل
[Ṣalon ḥela'qa] *n* beauty salon
صالون حلاقة
[Ṣalon ḥelaqah] *n* hairdresser's
silent *adj* [sˤa:mit] **صامت**
bolt *n* [sˤa:mu:la] **صامولة**
maintain *v* [sˤa:na] **صان**
maker *n* [sˤa:niʕ] **صانع**
morning *n* [sˤaba:ħ] **صباح**
غثيان الصباح
[Ghathayan al-ṣabaḥ] *n* morning sickness
صباح الخير
[ṣabaḥ al-khyer] Good morning
سوف أغادر غدا في الساعة العاشرة صباحا
[sawfa oghader ghadan fee al-sa'aa al-'aashera ṣaba-han] I will be leaving tomorrow morning at ten a.m.
غدًا في الصباح
[ghadan fee al-ṣabaḥ] tomorrow morning
في الصباح
[fee al-ṣabaḥ] in the morning
منذ الصباح وأنا أعاني من المرض
[mundho al-ṣabaah wa ana o'aany min al-maraḍ] I've been sick since this morning
هذا الصباح
[hatha al-ṣabaḥ] this morning
morning *adj* [sˤaba:ħan] **صباحا**
cactus *n* [sˤabba:r] **صبار**
patience *n* [sˤabr] **صبر**
بدون صبر
[Bedon ṣabr] *adv* impatiently
نفاذ الصبر
[nafadh al-ṣabr] *n* impatience
dye *v* [sˤabaɣa] **صبغ**
dye *n* [sˤibɣa] **صبغة**
patient *adj* [sˤabu:r] **صبور**
lad *n* [sˤabij] **صبي**
journalism *n* [sˤaħa:fa] **صحافة**
health *n* [sˤiħħa] **صحة**
correct *v* [sˤaħħaħa] **صحح**
desert *n* [sˤaħra:ʔu] **صحراء**
الصحراء الكبرى
[Al-ṣaḥraa al-kobraa] *n* Sahara
journalist *n* [sˤaħafij] **صحفي**
dish *n* [sˤaħn] **صحن**
صحن الفنجان
[Ṣaḥn al-fenjaan] *n* saucer
healthy *adj* [sˤiħij] **صحي**
غير صحي
[Ghayr ṣshey] *adj* unhealthy
منتجع صحي
[Montaja'a ṣeḥey] *n* spa
correct, right *adj* [sˤaħi:ħ] **صحيح** *(correct)*
بشكل صحيح
[Beshakl ṣaheeh] *adv* correctly, rightly
لم تكن تسير في الطريق الصحيح
[lam takun ta-seer fee al-ṭaree'q al-ṣaḥeeḥ] It wasn't your right of way
ليس مطهي بشكل صحيح
[laysa maṭ-hee be-shakel ṣaḥeeḥ] This isn't cooked properly
newspaper, plate *n* [sˤaħi:fa] **صحيفة**
rock *n* [sˤaxra] **صخرة**
rust *n* [sˤada] **صدأ**
rusty *adj* [sˤadiʔ] **صدئ**
headache *n* [sˤuda:ʕ] **صداع**
صداع النصفي
[Ṣoda'a al-naṣfey] *n* migraine
أريد شيئًا للصداع
[areed shyan lel-ṣuda'a] I'd like something for a headache
friendship *n* [sˤada:qa] **صداقة**
export *v* [sˤaddara] **صَدَّر**
bust, chest *(body part)* *n* [sˤadr] **صَدر**
vest *n* [sˤadra] **صدرة**
waistcoat *n* [sˤadrijja] **صدرية**

صدرية طفل
[Ṣadreyat ṭefl] *n* bib
crack *vi* [sˤadaʕa] صدع
crack *(fracture)* *n* [sˤadʕ] صَدْع
oyster *n* [sˤadafa] صَدَفَة
n [sˤudfa] صُدْفَة
بالصُدْفَة
[Bel-ṣodfah] *adv* accidentally
v [sˤddaqa] صدّق
لا يصدق
[La yoṣda'q] *adj* incredible
reckon *vt* [sˤaddaqa] صدّق
shock *v* [sˤadama] صدم
يَصْدِم بقوة
[Yaṣdem be'qowah] *v* ram
shock *n* [sˤadma] صَدْمَة
صَدْمَة كهربائية
[Ṣadmah kahrbaeyah] *n* electric shock
echo *n* [sˤada:] صَدَى
friend, pal *n* [sˤadi:q] صديق
صديق بالمراسلة
[Ṣadeek belmoraslah] *n* penfriend
صديق للبيئة
[Ṣadeek al-beeaah] *adj* ecofriendly
أنا هنا مع أصدقائي
[ana huna ma'aa aṣde'qa-ee] I'm here with my friends
friend, girlfriend *n* [sˤadi:qa] صديقة
clarity *n* [sˤara:ħa] صراحة
بصراحة
[Beṣarahah] *adv* frankly
scream *n* [sˤura:x] صراخ
conflict *n* [sˤira:ʕ] صراع
صراع عنيف
[Ṣera'a 'aneef] *n* tug-of-war
cashier *n* [sˤarra:f] صَرَّاف
banking *n* [sˤira:fa] صرافة
ماكينة صرافة
[Makenat ṣerafah] *n* cash dispenser
مكتب صرافة
[Maktab ṣerafah] *n* bureau de change
أريد الذهاب إلى مكتب صرافة
[areed al-dhehaab ela maktab ṣerafa] I need to find a bureau de change
متى يبدأ مكتب الصرافة عمله؟
[mata yabda maktab al-ṣirafa 'aamalaho?] When is the bureau de change open?
Serbian *n* ◁ Serbian *adj* [sˤirbij] صربي *(person)*
اللغة الصربية
[Al-loghah al-ṣerbeyah] *(language)* *n* Serbian
v [sˤarraħa] صَرِّح
يُصَرِح ب
[Yoṣareh be] *v* state
shriek, cry *v* [sˤraxa] صرخ
cockroach *n* [sˤarsˤu:r] صرصور
n [sˤaraʕ] صرع
نوبة صرع
[Nawbat ṣar'a] *n* epileptic fit
knock down *v* [sˤaraʕa] صرَع
n [sˤarafa] صرف
لقد ابتلعت ماكينة الصرف الآلي بطاقتي
[la'qad ibtal-'aat makenat al-ṣarf al-aaly be-ṭa'qaty] The cash machine swallowed my card
هل توجد ماكينة صرف آلي هنا؟
[hal tojad makenat ṣarf aaly huna?] Is there a cash machine here?
هل يمكنني صرف شيك؟
[hal yamken -any ṣarf shaik?] Can I cash a cheque?
dismiss *v* [sˤarafa] صرف
يَصْرِف من الخدمة
[Yaṣref men al-khedmah] *v* sack
v [sˤarrafa] صَرّف
يُصَرّف ماءً
[Yoṣṣaref maae] *vt* plughole
outspoken, *adj* [sˤari:ħ] صريح straightforward
challenging, *adj* [sˤaʕb] صعب difficult, hard *(difficult)*
صَعْب الإرضاء
[Ṣa'ab al-erḍaa] (منمق) *adj* fussy
difficulty *n* [sˤuʕu:ba] صعوبة
rise *n* [sˤuʕu:d] صعود
little, small *adj* [sˤaɣi:r] صغير
شريحة صغيرة
[Shareehat ṣagheerah] *n* microchip
إنه صغير جدا

[inaho ṣagheer jedan] It's too small
الغرفة صغيرة جدا
[al-ghurfa ṣagherah jedan] The room is too small
هل يوجد مقاسات صغيرة؟
[hal yujad ma'qaas-at ṣaghera?] Do you have a small?
صف rank *(line)* *n* [sˁaff]
صف مسائي
[Ṣaf masaaey] *n* evening class
صَف queue *n* [sˁaf]
صفار yolk *n* [sˁafa:r]
صَفَّارَة whistle *n* [sˁaffa:ra]
صَفَّارَة إنْذار
[Ṣafarat enḍhar] *n* siren
صفة adjective *n* [sˁifa]
صفحة page *n* [sˁafħa]
صفحة رئيسية
[Ṣafḥah raeseyah] *n* home page
صِفر zero *n* [sˁifr]
صَفِر whistle *v* [sˁaffara]
صفع slap, smack *v* [sˁafaʕa]
صَفق clap *vi* [sˁaffaqa]
صفقة bargain, deal *n* [sˁafqa]
صَفى filter *v* [sˁaffa:]
صفيح tin *n* [sˁafi:ħ]
صقيع frost *n* [sˁaqi:ʕ]
تَكَوّنْ الصقِيع
[Takawon al-sa'qee'a] *adj* frosty
صلاة prayer *n* [sˁala:t]
صلب hard, steel, solid *adj* [sˁalb]
صلب غير قابل للصدأ
[Ṣalb ghayr 'qabel lel-ṣadaa] *n* stainless steel
صلصال clay *n* [sˁalsˁa:l]
صلصة sauce *n* [sˁalsˁa]
صلصة السلطة
[Ṣalṣat al-salata] *n* salad dressing
صلصة طماطم
[Ṣalṣat ṭamaṭem] *n* tomato sauce
صَلى pray *v* [sˁala:]
صليب cross *n* [sˁali:b]
الصليب الأحمر
[Al-Ṣaleeb al-aḥmar] *n* Red Cross
صمام *n* [sˁamma:m]
صمام كهربائي
[Ṣamam kahrabaey] *n* fuse
صَمْت silence *n* [sˁamt]
صمد bear up *v* [sˁamada]
صمّم design *v* [sˁammama]
صمولة nut *(device)* *n* [sˁamu:la]
صناعة industry *n* [sˁina:ʕa]
صناعي industrial *adj* [sˁina:ʕij]
أطقم أسنان صناعية
[Aṭ'qom asnan ṣena'aeyah] *npl* dentures
عقارات صناعية
['aa'qarat ṣenaeyah] *n* industrial estate
قمر صناعي
['qamar ṣenaaey] *n* satellite
صُنبور *n* [sˁunbu:r]
صُنبور توزيع
[Ṣonboor twazea'a] *n* dispenser
صنج *n* [sˁanʒ]
آلة الصنج الموسيقية
[Alat al-ṣanj al-mose'qeyah] *npl* cymbals
صندل canoe,| *n* [sˁandal] sandal (حذاء)
صندوق box, chest *n* [sˁundu:q] *(storage)*, bin
صندوق العدة
[Ṣondok al-'aedah] *n* kit
صندوق الخطابات
[Ṣondok al-kheṭabat] *n* postbox
صندوق القمامة
[Ṣondok al-'qemamah] *n* dustbin
صندوق الوارد
[Ṣondok alwared] *n* inbox
صنع manufacture, making *n* [sˁunʕ]
من صنع الإنسان
[Men ṣon'a al-ensan] *adj* man-made
صنَع make *v* [sˁanaʕa]
صنَّع manufacture *v* [sˁanaʕa]
صنف sort, kind *n* [sˁinf]
صَنّف type *v* [sˁannafa]
صهريج tank *(large* *n* [sˁihri:ʒ] *container)*
صوبة *n* [sˁu:bba]
صوبة زراعية
[Ṣobah zera'aeyah] *n* greenhouse
صوت sound, voice *n* [sˁawt]
صوت السوبرانو
[Ṣondok alsobrano] *n* soprano

جهاز الصوت المجسم الشخصي [Jehaz al-ṣawt al-mojasam al-shakhṣey] *n* personal stereo
بصوت مرتفع [Beṣot mortafe'a] *adv* aloud
كاتم للصوت [Katem lel-ṣawt] *n* silencer
مكبر الصوت [Mokabber al-ṣawt] *n* speaker
صَوّت vote *v* [sˤawwata]
صوَتي *adj* [sˤawtij]
بريد صوتي [Bareed ṣawṭey] *n* voicemail
صوّر *v* [sˤawwara]
يُصور فوتوغرافيا [Yoṣawer fotoghrafeyah] *v* photograph
صورة image, picture *n* [sˤuːra]
صورة عارية [Ṣoorah 'aareyah] *n* nude
صورة فوتوغرافية [Ṣorah fotoghrafeyah] *n* photo, photograph
صورة للوجه [Ṣorah lel-wajh] *n* portrait
صوص soya *n* [sˤuːsˤu]
صوص الصويا [Ṣoṣ al-ṣoyah] *n* soy sauce
صوف wool *n* [sˤuːf]
شال من الصوف الناعم [Shal men al-Ṣoof al-na'aem] *n* cashmere
صوفي woollen *adj* [sˤuːfij]
صَوْم frost *n* [sˤawm]
الصَوْم الكبير [Al-ṣawm al-kabeer] *n* Lent
صومالي *n* ◁ Somali *adj* [sˤsˤuːmaːlij] *(person)* Somali
اللغة الصومالية [Al-loghah al-Ṣomaleyah] *n* *(language)* Somali
صويا soy *n* [sˤuːjaː]
صوص الصويا [Ṣoṣ al-ṣoyah] *n* soy sauce
صياد hunter *n* [sˤajjaːd]
صيانة maintenance *n* [sˤijaːna]
صيحة shout *n* [sˤajħa]
صيد hunting *n* [sˤajd]
صيد السمك [Ṣayd al-samak] *n* fishing
صيد بالسِنّارة [Ṣayd bel-sayarah] *n* fishing
قارب صيد ['qareb ṣayd] *n* fishing boat
صيدلي pharmacist *n* [sˤajdalij]
صيدلية pharmacy *n* [sˤajdalijja]
صيغة formula *n* [sˤiːɣa]
صيغة الفعل [Ṣeghat al-fe'al] *n* tense
صيف summer *n* [sˤajf]
بعد فصل الصيف [ba'ad faṣil al-ṣayf] after summer
في الصيف [fee al-ṣayf] in summer
قبل الصيف ['qabl al-ṣayf] before summer
صيفي summer *adj* [sˤajfij]
الأجازات الصيفية [Al-ajazat al-ṣayfeyah] *npl* summer holidays
منزل صيفى [Manzel ṣayfey] *n* holiday home
صيني *n* ◁ Chinese *adj* [sˤiːnij] Chinese *(person)*
آنية من الصيني [Aaneyah men al-ṣeeney] *n* china
اللغة الصينية [Al-loghah al-ṣeeneyah] *(language)* *n* Chinese
اللغة الصينية الرئيسية [Al-loghah al-Ṣeneyah alraeseyah] *n* mandarin *(official)*
صينية tray *n* [sˤiːnijja]

annoy, pester, tease *v* [dˤa:jaqa] **ضايق**
remote, tiny *adj* [dˤaʔijl] **ضئيل**
fog *n* [dˤaba:b] **ضباب**
misty, foggy *adj* [dˤaba:bij] **ضبابي**
control, adjustment *n* [dˤabtˤ] **ضبط**
على وجه الضبط
[Ala wajh al-ḍabṭ] *adv* just
يُمْكِن ضبطه
[Yomken ḍabṭoh] *adj* adjustable
هل يمكنك ضبط الأربطة لي من فضلك؟
[hal yamken -aka ḍabṭ al-arbe-ṭa lee min faḍlak?] Can you adjust my bindings, please?
control, adjust *v* [dˤabatˤa] **ضبط**
bang *n* [dˤaʒʒa] **ضجّة**
din *n* [dˤaʒi:ʒ] **ضجيج**
laugh *v* [dˤaħaka] **ضحَك**
يَضحَك ضحكاً نصف مكبوت
[Yaḍḥak ḍeḥkan neṣf makboot] *v* snigger
laugh *n* [dˤaħka] **ضحكة**
ضَحِك
[dˤaħik] *n* laughter
shallow *adj* [dˤaħl] **ضحل**
victim *n* [dˤaħijja] **ضحِيّة**
pump *v* [dˤaxxa] **ضخّ**
enormous, massive *adj* [dˤaxm] **ضخم**
against *prep* [dˤiddun] **ضد**
damage, harm *v* [dˤarra] **ضرّ**
beat *(strike)*, strike *v* [dˤaraba] **ضرب**
يَضْرِب ضربة عنيفة
[Yaḍreb ḍarban 'aneefan] *v* swat
يَضرِب بعنف
[Yaḍreb be'aonf] *v* bash
bash, hit, strike, bump *n* [dˤarba] **ضربة**
ضربة عنيفة
[Ḍarba 'aneefa] *n* knock
ضربة خلفية
[Ḍarba khalfeyah] *n* backstroke
ضربة حرة
[Ḍarba ḥorra] *n* free kick
ضربة شمس
[Ḍarbat shams] *n* sunstroke

officer *n* [dˤa:bitˤ] **ضابط**
ضابط رَقِيب
[Ḍabeṭ ra'qeeb] *n* sergeant
ضابط سجن
[Ḍabeṭ sejn] *n* prison officer
ضابط شرطة
[Ḍabeṭ shorṭah] *n* police officer
police, officer *(female)* *n* [dˤa:bitˤa] **ضابطة**
ضابطة شرطة
[Ḍaabeṭ shorṭah] *n* policewoman
suburb *n* [dˤa:ħija] **ضاحية**
ساكن الضاحية
[Saken al-ḍaheyah] *adj* suburban
سباق الضاحية
[Seba'q al-ḍaheyah] *n* cross-country
striker *n* [dˤa:rib] **ضَارب**
misplace, lose *v* [dˤa:ʕa] **ضاعَ**
لقد ضاع جواز سفري
[la'qad ḍa'aa jawaz safary] I've lost my passport
double *vt* [dˤa:ʕafa] **ضاعف**
stray *n* [dˤa:l] **ضَالّ**
sheep *n* [dˤaʔn] **ضأن**
لحم ضأن
[Lahm ḍaan] *n* mutton
match *vt* [dˤa:ha:] **ضاهى**

ضرر [dˤarar] *n* damage
ضرورة [dˤaru:ra] *n* necessity
ضروري [dˤaru:rij] *adj* necessary
غير ضروري
[Ghayer ḍarorey] *adj* unnecessary
ضريبة [dˤari:ba] *n* tax
ضريبة دخل
[Ḍareebat dakhl] *n* income tax
ضريبة طُرُق
[Ḍareebat ṭoro'q] *n* road tax
ضريبي [dˤari:bij] *adj*
مَعْفِي من الضرائب
[Ma'afey men al-ḍaraaeb] *n* duty-free
ضريح [dˤari:ħ] *n* shrine, grave, tomb
ضرير [dˤari:r] *adj* blind
ضعف [dˤiʕfa] *n* weakness
ضعيف [dˤaʕi:f] *adj* mad, weak
ضغط [dˤaɣtˤ] *n* stress, pressure
ضغط الدم
[ḍaghṭ al-dam] *n* blood pressure
تمرين الضغط
[Tamreen al- Ḍaghṭ] *n* push-up
ضغط [dˤaɣatˤa] *v* press
ضغينة [dˤaɣi:na] *n* grudge, spite
ضفة [dˤiffa] *n* bank *(ridge)*, shore
ضفدع [dˤifdaʕ] *n* frog
ضفدع الطين
[Ḍofda'a al- ṭeen] *n* toad
ضفيرة [dˤafi:ra] *n* pigtail, ponytail
ضِلْع [dˤilʕ] *n* rib
ضَلل [dˤallala] *v*
لقد ضللنا الطريق
[la'qad ḍalalna al-ṭaree'q] We're lost
ضمادة [dˤamma:da] *n* plaster
أريد ضمادة جروح
[areed ḍimadat jirooḥ] I'd like a bandage
أريد ضمادة جديدة
[areed ḍimada jadeeda] I'd like a fresh bandage
ضمان [dˤama:n] *n* guarantee
ضمن [dˤamana] *v* guarantee
ضمير [dˤami:r] *n* pronoun
ضمير إنساني
[Ḍameer ensaney] *n* conscience
حى الضمير
[Hay al-Ḍameer] *adj* conscientious
ضوء [dˤawʔ] *n* light
ضوء الشمس
[Ḍawa al-shams] *n* sunlight
ضوء مُسَلّط
[Dawa mosalṭ] *n* spotlight
هل يمكن أن أشاهدها في الضوء؟
[hal yamken an osha-heduha fee al-ḍoe?] May I take it over to the light?
ضواح [dˤawa:ħin] *npl* outskirts
ضوضاء [dˤawdˤa:ʔ] *adj* noisy ◃ *n* clutter, noise
ضيافة [dˤija:fa] *n*
حُسن الضيافة
[Ḥosn al-ḍeyafah] *n* hospitality
ضيف [dˤajf] *n* guest
ضيق [dˤajjiq] *adj* narrow
ضيق جدا
[Ḍaye'q jedan] *adj* skin-tight
ضَيّق الأُفُق
[Ḍaye'q al-ofo'q] *adj* narrow-minded
ضَيّق [dˤajjiqa] *v* tighten

طائر bird *n* [tˤaːʔir]
طائر أبو الحناء
[Ṭaaer abo elḥnaa] *n* robin
طائر الرفراف
[Ṭaayer alrafraf] *n* kingfisher
طائر الغِطاس
[Ṭaayer al-ghaṭas] *n* wren
طائر الحَجل
[Ṭaayer al-hajal] *n* partridge
طائر الكناري
[Ṭaaer al-kanarey] *n* canary
طائر الوقواق
[Ṭaaer al-wa'qwa'q] *n* cuckoo
طائرة aircraft, plane *n* [tˤaːʔira] *(airplane)*, plane *(tool)*
رياضة الطائرة الشراعية الصغيرة
[Reyadar al-Ṭaayearah al-ehraeyah al-ṣagherah] *n* hang-gliding
طائرة شراعية
[Ṭaayearah ehraeyah] *n* glider
طائرة نفاثة
[Ṭaayeara nafathah] *n* jumbo jet
طائرة ورقية
[Ṭaayeara wara'qyah] *n* kite
كرة طائرة
[Korah Ṭaayeara] *n* volleyball
مضيف الطائرة
[moḍeef al-ṭaaerah] *n* flight attendant
طائش thoughtless *adj* [tˤaːʔiʃ]
طائفة sect *n* [tˤaːʔifa]
طائفة شهود يهوه المسيحية
[Ṭaaefat shehood yahwah al-maseyheyah] *n* Jehovah's Witness
طابع stamp *n* [tˤaːbaʕ]
أين يوجد أقرب محل لبيع الطوابع؟
[ayna yujad a'qrab maḥal le-bay'a al-ṭawabi'a?] Where is the nearest shop which sells stamps?
هل تبيعون الطوابع؟
[hal tabee'a-oon al-ṭawa-bi'a] Do you sell stamps?
هل يوجد لديكم أي شيء يحمل طابع هذه المنطقة؟
[hal yujad laday-kum ay shay yaḥmll ṭabi'a hadhy al- manṭa'qa?] Do you have anything typical of this region?
طابعة printer *(person)*, *n* [tˤaːbiʕa] printer *(machine)*
هل توجد طابعة ملونة؟
[hal tojaḍ ṭabe-'aa mulawa-na?] Is there a colour printer?
طابق story *(building)* *n* [tˤaːbaq]
طابق علوي
[Ṭabe'q 'aolwei] *n* loft
طاجكستان *n* [tˤaːʒikistaːn] Tajikistan
طاحونة mill *n* [tˤaːħuːna]
طار fly *vi* [tˤaːra]
طارئ casual, accidental *adj* [tˤaːriʔ]
حالة طارئة
[Ḥalah ṭareaa] *n* emergency
طارئة accident *n* [tˤaːriʔit]
أحتاج إلى الذهاب إلى قسم الحوادث الطارئة
[aḥtaaj ela al-dhehaab ela 'qisim al-ḥawadith al-ṭaa-reaa] I need to go to casualty
طارد expulsion, repellent *n* [tˤaːrid]
طارد للحشرات
[Ṭared lel-ḥasharat] *n* insect repellent
هل لديك طارد للحشرات؟
[hal ladykạ ṭared lel-ḥasha-raat?] Do you have insect repellent?

طارد chase v [tˤa:rada]
طازج fresh adj [tˤa:zaʒ]
هل الخضروات طازجة أم مجمدة؟
[hal al-khiḍ-rawaat ṭazija amm mujam-ada?] Are the vegetables fresh or frozen?
هل يوجد بن طازج؟
[hal yujad buṇ ṯaazij?] Have you got fresh coffee?
طاقة energy n [tˤa:qa]
طاقة شمسية
[Ṭa'qah shamseyah] n solar power
ملئ بالطاقة
[Maleea bel-ṭa'qah] adj energetic
طاقم crew n [tˤa:qam]
طالب student n [tˤa:lib]
طالب راشد
[Ṭaleb rashed] n mature student
طالب عسكري
[Ṭaleb 'askarey] n cadet
طالب لجوء سياسي
[ṭ aleb lejoa seyasy] n asylum seeker
طالب لم يتخرج بعد
[ṭ aleb lam yatakharaj ba'aad] n undergraduate
طالب claim v [tˤa:laba]
يُطَالِب ب
[Yoṭaleb be] v demand
طاولة n [tˤa:wila]
طاولة بيع
[Ṭawelat bey'a] n counter
طاولة قهوة
[Ṭawlat 'qahwa] n coffee table
كرة الطاولة
[Korat al-ṭawlah] n table tennis
لعبة طاولة
[Lo'abat ṭawlah] n board game
طَاولَة زينة
[Ṭawlat zeenah] n dressing table
طاووس peacock n [tˤa:wu:s]
طَبَّاخ cook n [tˤabba:x]
طباشير chalk n [tˤaba:ʃi:r]
طبال drummer n [tˤabba:l]
طبخ cooking n [tˤabx]
فن الطبخ
[Fan al-ṭabkh] n cookery

طبع temper, character n [tˤabʕ]
سَئ الطبع
[Sayea al-ṭabe'a] adj grumpy
طبَع print v [tˤabaʕa]
طبعة edition n [tˤabʕa]
طبق dish n [tˤabaq]
طبق رئيسي
[Ṭaba'q raeesey] n main course
طبق صابون
[Ṭaba'q ṣaboon] n soap dish
طبق قمر صناعي
[Ṭaba'q ṣena'aey] n satellite dish
ما الذي في هذا الطبق؟
[ma al-lathy fee hatha aḷ-ṭaba'q?] What is in this dish?
ما هو طبق اليوم
[ma howạ ṯaba'q al-yawm?] What is the dish of the day?
طبقة layer, level, class n [tˤabaqa]
طبقة صوت
[Ṭabaqat ṣawṭ] n pitch (sound)
طبقة عاملة
[Ṭaba'qah 'aaamelah] adj working-class
طبقة الأوزون
[Taba'qat al-odhoon] n ozone layer
طبقتين من الزجاج
[Ṭaba'qatayen men al-zojaj] n double glazing
من الطبقة الوسطى
[men al-Ṭaba'qah al-wosṭa] adj middle-class
طبلة drum n [tˤabla]
طبلة الأذن
[Ṭablat alozon] n eardrum
طبلة كبيرة رنانة غليظة الصوت
[Ṭablah kabeerah rannanah ghaleeḍhat al-ṣawt] n bass drum
طبي medical adj [tˤibbij]
فحص طبي شامل
[Fahṣ ṭebey shamel] n physical
طبيب doctor n [tˤabi:b]
طبيب أسنان
[Ṭabeeb asnan] n dentist
طبيب أمراض نساء
[Ṭabeeb amraḍ nesaa] n gynaecologist
طبيب بيطري

[Ṭabeeb bayṭareey] *n* vet
طبيب مساعد
[Ṭabeeb mosaa'aed] *n* paramedic
طبيب نفساني
[Ṭabeeb nafsaaney] *n* psychiatrist
أرغب في استشارة طبيب
[arghab fee es-ti-sharaṭ ṯabeeb] I'd like to speak to a doctor
أحتاج إلى طبيب
[aḥtaaj ela ṯabeeb] I need a doctor
اتصل بالطبيب
[itaṣel bil-ṯabeeb] Call a doctor!
هل يمكنني تحديد موعد مع الطبيب؟
[hal yamken -any taḥdeed maw'aid ma'aa al-ṯabeeb?] Can I have an appointment with the doctor?
هل يوجد طبيب هنا يتحدث الإنجليزية؟
[hal yujad ṭabeeb huna yata-ḥadath al-injile-ziya?] Is there a doctor who speaks English?
طبيبة doctor *(female)* *n* [tˤabiːba]
أرغب في استشارة طبيبة
[arghab fee es-ti-sharaṭ ṯabeeba] I'd like to speak to a female doctor
طبيعة nature *n* [tˤabiːʕa]
طبيعي natural, normal *adj* [tˤabiːʕij]
naturally *adv* ◁
علاج طبيعي
['aelaj ṭabeye] *n* physiotherapy
غير طبيعي
[Ghayer ṭabe'aey] *adj* abnormal
بصورة طبيعية
[beṣoraten ṭabe'aey] *adv* normally
موارد طبيعية
[Mawared ṭabe'aey] *npl* natural resources
طُحْلُب *n* [tˤuħlub]
طُحْلب بحري
[Toḥleb baḥahrey] *n* seaweed
طُحْلُب moss *n* [tˤuħlub]
طحَن grind *vt* [tˤaħana]
طراز model, kind *n* [tˤiraːz]
قديم الطراز
['qadeem al-ṭeraz] *adj* naff
طرَح lay *vt* [tˤaraħa]
يَطرَح جانبا
[Yaṭraḥ janeban] *v* fling
طرد parcel *n* [tˤard]
أريد أن أرسل هذا الطرد
[areed an arsil hadha al-ṯard] I'd like to send this parcel
طرد expel *v* [tˤarada]
طرف terminal *n* [tˤaraf]
طرف مستدق
[Ṭaraf mostabe'q] *n* tip *(end of object)*
طرفي terminal *adj* [tˤarafij]
طرق corridor, aisle *n* [tˤuruq]
طرق متقاطعة
[Ṭaree'q mot'qat'ah] *n* crossroads
طرقة *n* [tˤarqa]
أريد مقعد بجوار الطرقة
[Oreed ma'q'aad bejwar al-ṭor'qah] I'd like an aisle seat
طريدة quarry *n* [tˤariːda]
طريف quaint, odd *adj* [tˤariːf]
طريق road *n* [tˤariːq]
عن طريق الخطأ
[Aan ṭaree'q al-khataa] *adv* mistakenly
طريق رئيسي
[ṭaree'q raeysey] *n* main road
طريق اسفلتي
[ṭaree'q asfaltey] *n* tarmac
طريق السيارات
[ṭaree'q alsayaraat] *n* motorway
طريق مسدود
[Taree'q masdood] *n* dead end
طريق متصل بطريق سريع للسيارات أو منفصل عنه
[ṭaree'q mataṣel be- ṭaree'q sarea'a lel-sayaraat aw monfaṣel 'anho] *n* slip road
طريق مختصر
[ṭaree'q mokhtaṣar] *n* shortcut
طريق مزدوج الاتجاه للسيارات
[Taree'q mozdawaj al-etejah lel-sayarat] *n* dual carriageway
طريق مشجر
[ṭaree'q moshajar] *n* avenue
طريق ملتو
[ṭaree'q moltawe] *n* roundabout
مشاحنات على الطريق
[Moshahanaat ala al-ṭaree'q] *n* road

rage
ما هو الطريق الذي يؤدي إلى... ؟
[ma howa al-ṭaree'q al-lathy yo-aady ela...?] Which road do I take for...?
هل يوجد خريطة طريق لهذه المنطقة؟
[hal yujad khareeṭat ṭaree'q le-hadhy al-manṭa'qa?] Do you have a road map of this area?
طريقة method *n* [tˤariːqa]
بأي طريقة
[Be-ay ṭaree'qah] *adv* anyhow
بطريقة صحيحة
[Be- ṭaree'qah ṣaḥeeḥah] *adv* right
بطريقة أخرى
[ṭaree'qah okhra] *adv* otherwise
طعام food *n* [tˤaʕaːm]
عربة تناول الطعام في القطار
['arabat tanawool al-ṭa'aaam fee al-'qeṭar] *n* dining car
غرفة طعام
[ghorat ṭa'aam] *n* dining room
توريد الطعام
[Tarweed al-ṭa'aam] *n* catering
بقايا الطعام
[Ba'qaya ṭ a'aam] *npl* leftovers
طعام مطهو بالغلي
[ṭ a'aam maṭhoo bel-ghaley] *n* stew
وجبة طعام خفيفة
[Wajbat ṭ a'aam khafeefah] *n* refreshments
وَجْبَة الطعام
[Wajbat al-ṭa'aam] *n* dinner
الطعام متبل أكثر من اللازم
[al-ṭa'aam mutabal akthar min al-laazim] The food is too spicy
هل تقدمون الطعام هنا؟
[hal tu'qa-dimoon al-ṭa'aam huna?] Do you serve food here?
طعم taste *n* [tˤaʕm]
أطعمة معلبة
[a ṭ'aemah mo'aalabah] *n* delicatessen
طعن stab *v* [tˤʕana]
طفا float *vi* [taˤfaː]
طفاية *n* [tˤaffaːja]
طفاية السجائر
[Ṭafayat al-sajayer] *n* ashtray
طفاية الحريق
[Ṭafayat ḥaree'q] *n* extinguisher
طفح rash *n* [tˤafħ]
طفح جلدي
[Ṭafh jeldey] *n* rash
أعاني من طفح جلدي
[O'aaney men ṭafḥ jeldey] I have a rash
طفح run over *v* [tˤafaħa]
طفل child, baby *n* [tˤifl]
سرير محمول للطفل
[Sareer maḥmool lel-ṭefl] *n* carrycot
طفل رضيع
[Ṭefl readea'a] *n* baby
طفل صغير عادة ما بين السنة الأولى والثانية
[Ṭefl ṣagheer 'aaadatan ma bayn al-sanah wal- sanatayen] *n* toddler
طفل حديث الولادة
[Ṭefl ḥadeeth alweladah] *n* newborn
طفل متبنى
[Ṭefl matabanna] *n* foster child
طفل مزعج
[Ṭefl moz'aej] *n* brat
عندي طفل واحد
['aendy ṭifil waḥid] I have one child
الطفل مقيد في هذا الجواز
[Al- ṭefl mo'qayad fee hadha al-jawaz] The child is on this passport
ليس لدي أطفال
[laysa la-daya ̣aṭfaal] I don't have any children
هل توجد أنشطة للأطفال
[hal tojad anshi-ṭa lil-aṭfaal?] Do you have activities for children?
هل يمكن أن ترشح لي أحد أطباء الأطفال؟
[hal yamken an tura-shiḥ lee aḥad aṭebaa al-aṭfaal?] Can you recommend a paediatrician?
هل يوجد لديك مقعد للأطفال؟
[hal yujad ladyka ma'q'aad lil-aṭfaal?] Do you have a child's seat?
طفولة childhood *n* [tˤufuːla]
طفوليّ childish *adj* [tˤufuːlij]
طفيف slight *adj* [tˤafiːf]
بدرجة طفيفة

[Bedarajah ṭafeefah] *adv* slightly
طقس weather *n* [tˤaqs]
توقعات حالة الطقس
[Tawa'qo'aat ḥalat al-ṭaqs] *npl* weather forecast
ما هذا الطقس السيئ
[Ma hadha al-ṭa'qs al-sayea] What awful weather!
طقم set *n* [tˤaqm]
هل يمكنك إصلاح طقم أسناني؟
[hal yamken -aka eṣlaaḥ ṭa'qum asnany?] Can you repair my dentures?
طلّ *v* [tˤalla]
يَطلّ على
[Ya'aṣeb al-'aynayn] *v* overlook
طلا paint *vt* [tˤala:]
طلاء coating *n* [tˤila:ʔ]
طلاء أظافر
[Ṭelaa aḍhafer] *n* nail varnish
طلاء المينا
[Ṭelaa al-meena] *n* enamel
طلاق divorce *n* [tˤala:q]
طلب application, order *n* [tˤalab]
مُقدم الطلب
[Mo'qadem al-ṭalab] *n* applicant
نموذج الطلب
[Namozaj al-ṭalab] *n* application form
يَتقَدم بطلب
[Yata'qadam be-ṭalab] *n* apply
طلب ask for *v* [tˤalaba]
هل تطلب عمولة؟
[hal ṭaṭlub 'aumoola?] Do you charge commission?
طلع come up *v* [tˤalaʕa]
طماطم tomato *n* [tˤama:tˤim]
طَمئِن assure *v* [tˤmaʔana]
طَمْث menstruation *n* [tˤamθ]
طَموح ambitious *adj* [tˤumu:ħ]
طُموح ambition *n* [tˤamu:ħ]
طنْ ton *n* [tˤunn]
طها cook *v* [tˤaha:]
طهي *v* [tˤahja:]
كيف يطهي هذا الطبق؟
[Kayfa yoṭhaa hadha alṭaba'q] How do you cook this dish?
طَهْيْ cooking *n* [tˤahj]
طوارئ emergency *n* [tˤawa:riʔ]
مخرج طوارئ
[Makhraj ṭawarea] *n* emergency exit
طوال throughout, durring [tˤiwa:la]
طوال شهر يونيو
[ṭewal shahr yon-yo] all through June
طوبة brick *n* [tˤu:ba]
طوّر develop *vt* [tˤawwara]
طَوْعي voluntary *adj* [tˤawʕij]
طَوْف raft *n* [tˤawf]
طوفان flood *n* [tˤu:fa:n]
طوق strap, necklace *n* [tˤawq]
طول length *n* [tˤu:l]
على طول
[Ala ṭool] *prep* along
طول الموجة
[Ṭool al-majah] *n* wavelength
هذا الطول من فضلك
[hatha al-ṭool min faḍlak] This length, please
طويل long *adj* [tˤawi:l]
طويل القامة
[Ṭaweel al-'qamah] *adj* tall
طويل مع هزال
[Ṭaweel ma'aa hozal] *adj* lanky
طويلًا long *adv* [tˤawi:la:an]
طي fold (حظيرة خراف) *n* [tˤajj]
طيب goodness *n* [tˤi:bu]
جوزة الطيب
[Jozat al-ṭeeb] *n* nutmeg
طية plait *n* [tˤajja]
طير bird *n* [tˤajr]
طيور جارحة
[Ṭeyoor jareḥah] *n* bird of prey
طيران flying *n* [tˤajara:n]
شركة طيران
[Sharekat ṭayaraan] *n* airline
أود أن أمارس رياضة الطيران الشراعي؟
[awid an oma-ris reyaḍat al- ṭayaran al-shera'ay] I'd like to go hang-gliding
طين mud, soil *n* [tˤi:n]
طيهوج *n* [tˤajhu:ʒ]
طائر الطيهوج
[Ṭaaer al-ṭayhooj] *n* grouse *(game bird)*

turn up
ظَهر back *n* [zˤahr]
أَلَمْ الظهر
[Alam al-ḍhahr] *n* backache
ظهر المركب
[ḍhahr al-mrkeb] *n* deck
لقد أصيب ظهري
[la'qad oṣeba ḍhahry] I've got a bad back
لقد جرحت في ظهري
[la'qad athayto ḍhahry] I've hurt my back
ظُهر noon *n* [zˤuhr]
بَعْد الظهر
[Ba'ada al-ḍhohr] *n* afternoon
الساعة الثانية عشر ظهرًا
[al-sa'aa al-thaneya 'aashar ḍhuhran] It's twelve midday
كيف يمكن الوصول إلى السيارة على ظهر المركب؟
[kayfa yamkin al-wiṣool ela al-sayarah 'ala ḍhahr al-markab?] How do I get to the car deck?
هل المتحف مفتوح بعد الظهر؟
[hal al-mat-ḥaf maf-tooḥ ba'ad al-ḍhihir?] Is the museum open in the afternoon?
ظهيرة noon *n* [zˤahiːra]
أوقات الظهيرة
[Aw'qat aldhaherah] *npl* sweet
غدًا في فترة بعد الظهيرة
[ghadan ba'ad al-ḍhuhr] tomorrow afternoon
في فترة ما بعد الظهيرة
[ba'ada al-ḍhuhr] in the afternoon

ظاهر apparent *adj* [zˤaːhir]
ظاهرة phenomenon *n* [zˤaːhira]
ظاهرة الاحتباس الحراري
[dhaherat al-eḥtebas al-ḥararey] *n* global warming
ظبي antelope *n* [zˤabjj]
ظرف adverb *n* [zˤarf]
ظروف circumstances *npl* [zˤuruːfun]
ظفر fingernail, claw *n* [zˤufr]
ظل shade, shadow *n* [zˤill]
ظل العيون
[ḍhel al-'aoyoon] *n* eye shadow
ظل stay up *v* [zˤalla]
إلى متى ستظل هكذا؟
[ela mata sa-taḍhil hakadha] How long will it keep?
أتمنى أن يظل الجو على ما هو عليه
[ata-mana an yaḍhil al-jaw 'aala ma howa 'aa-ly-he] I hope the weather stays like this
ظلام dark *n* [zˤalaːm]
ظُلم injustice *n* [zˤulm]
ظُلْمَة darkness *n* [zˤulma]
ظمأ thirst *n* [zˤama]
ظمآن thirsty *adj* [zˤamʔaːn]
ظنّ suppose *v* [zˤanna]
ظهر show up, appear, *v* [zˤahara]

ع

عائد return *(yield)* *n* [ʕa:ʔid]
عائدات proceeds *npl* [ʕa:ʔida:tun]
عائلة family *n* [ʕa:ʔila]
أقرب أفراد العائلة
[A'qrab afrad al-'aaleah] *n* next-of-kin
أنا هنا مع عائلتي
[ana huna ma'aa 'aa-elaty] I'm here with my family
عاثر *n* [ʕa:θir]
حظ عاثر
[Ḥadh 'aaer] *n* mishap
عاج ivory *n* [ʕa:ʒ]
عاجز disabled, unable to *adj* [ʕa:ʒiz]
عاجل immediate *adj* [ʕa:ʒil]
أنا في حاجة إلى إجراء مكالمة تليفونية عاجلة
[ana fee ḥaja ela ejraa mukalama talefoniya 'aajela] I need to make an urgent telephone call
هل يمكنك الترتيب للحصول على بعض الأموال التي تم إرسالها بشكل عاجل؟
[hal yamken -aka tarteeb ersaal ba'aḍ al-amwaal be-shakel 'aajil?] Can you arrange to have some money sent over urgently?
عاجلا sooner, *adv* [ʕa:ʒila:] immediately

عاد come back *v* [ʕa:da]
عادة custom, practise *n* [ʕa:datun]
عادة سلوكية
['aadah selokeyah] *n* habit
عادة من الماضى
['aadah men al-maḍey] *n* hangover
عادةً generally, usually *adv* [ʕa:datan]
عادل fair *(reasonable)* *adj* [ʕa:dil]
عادم waste, exhaust *n* [ʕa:dim]
أدخنة العادم
[Adghenat al-'aadem] *npl* exhaust fumes
ماسورة العادم
[Masorat al-'aadem] *n* exhaust pipe
لقد انكسرت ماسورة العادم
[Le'aad enkasarat masoorat al-'adem] The exhaust is broken
عادي ordinary *adj* [ʕa:dij]
عادى antagonize *v* [ʕa:da:]
عار naked *adj* [ʕa:r]
عارض oppose *v* [ʕa:radˤa]
عَارَض *adj* [ʕa:ridˤ]
بَشكل عَارِض
[Beshakl 'aareḍ] *n* casually
عارضة staff *(stick or rod)*, *n* [ʕa:ridˤa] post, beam
عَارِضَةٌ خَشَبِيَّةٌ
['aareḍeh khashabeyah] *n* beam
عاري naked *adj* [ʕa:ri:]
صورة عارية
[Ṣoorah 'aareyah] *n* nude
عَازَل insulation *n* [ʕa:zil]
عاش live *v* [ʕa:ʃa]
يعيش سوياً
[Ya'aeesh saweyan] *v* live together
يعيش على
[Ya'aeesh ala] *v* live on
عاصف stormy *adj* [ʕa:sˤif]
الجو عاصف
[al-jaw 'aaṣuf] It's stormy
عاصفة storm *n* [ʕa:sˤifa]
عاصفة ثلجية
['aasefah thaljeyah] *n* snowstorm
عاصفة ثلجية عنيفة
['aasefah thaljeyah 'aneefah] *n* blizzard
هل تتوقع هبوب أية عواصف؟

[Hal tatawa'q'a hobob 'awasef?] Do you think there will be a storm?
capital *n* [ʕaːsˤima] **عاصمة**
disobedient *adj* [ʕaːsˤiː] **عاصي**
emotion, affection *n* [ʕaːtˤifa] **عاطفة**
emotional, affectionate *adj* [ʕaːtˤifij] **عاطفي**
jobless, idle *adj* [ʕaːtˤil] **عاطل**
عاطل عن العمل
['aatel 'aan al-'aamal] *adj* unemployed
ungrateful, disrespectful *adj* [ʕaːqq] **عاق**
obstruct *v* [ʕaːqa] **عاق**
punish *v* [ʕaːqaba] **عَاقب**
consequence *n* [ʕaːqiba] **عاقبة**
high *adj* [ʕaːlin] **عال**
بصوت عال
[Besot 'aaley] *adv* loudly
cure *vt* ◁ deal with *v* [ʕaːlaʒa] **عالج**
يُعالِج باليد
[Yo'aalej bel-yad] *v* manipulate
adj [ʕaːliq] **عالق**
درج الملابس عالق
[durj al-malabis 'aali'q] The drawer is jammed
world *n* [ʕaːlam] **عالم**
العالم الثالث
[Al-'aalam al-thaleth] *n* Third World
scientist *n* [ʕaːlim] **عَالِم**
عالم آثار
['aalem aathar] *n* archaeologist
عالم اقتصادي
['aaalem e'qteṣaadey] *n* economist
عالم لغويات
['aalem laghaweyat] *n* linguist
global *adj* [ʕaːlamij] **عالمي**
high *adj* [ʕaːlijju] **عالي**
قفزة عالية
['qafzah 'aaleyah] *n* high jump
كعوب عالية
[Ko'aoob 'aleyah] *npl* high heels
up *adv* [ʕaːlijan] **عالياً**
general, public *adj* [ʕaːm] **عام**
عام دراسي
['aam derasey] *n* academic year
الحِس العام
[Al-ḥes al-'aaam] *n* common sense
كل عام
[Kol-'aaam] *adv* annually
مصاريف عامة
[Maṣareef 'aamah] *n* overheads
نقل عام
[Na'ql 'aam] *n* public transport
worker, labourer, workman *n* [ʕaːmil] **عامل**
عامل مناجم
['aaamel manajem] *n* miner
v [ʕaːmala] **عامل**
يُعامِل معاملة سيئة
[Yo'aamal mo'aamalh sayeah] *v* abuse
handle *v* [ʕaːmala] **عَامَل**
worker *(female)* *n* [ʕaːmila] **عاملة**
عاملة النظافة
['aamelat al-nadhafah] *n* cleaning lady
staff *(workers)* *n* [ʕaːmiliːna] **عاملين**
غرفة العاملين
[Ghorfat al'aameleen] *n* staffroom
slang *n* [ʕaːmmija] **عامِّية**
spinster *n* [ʕaːnis] **عانس**
cuddle, hug *v* [ʕaːnaqa] **عانَق**
suffer *v* [ʕaːnaː] **عانى**
أنه يعاني من الحمى
[inaho yo-'aany min al- ḥomma] He has a fever
prostitute *n* [ʕaːhira] **عاهرة**
v [ʕaːwada] **عاود**
يُعَاوِد الاتصال
[Yo'aaawed al-eteṣaal] *v* ring back
gauge *v* [ʕaːjara] **عايَر**
burden *n* [ʕibʔ] **عبء**
phrase *n* [ʕibaːra] **عبارة**
slave *n* [ʕabd] **عبد**
worship *v* [ʕabada] **عبد**
across *prep* [ʕabra] **عبر**
cross *vt* [ʕabara] **عَبر**
يُعَبِر عن
[Yo'aber 'an] *v* express
Jewish *adj* [ʕibriː] **عِبري**
frown *v* [ʕabasa] **عَبَس**
ingenious *adj* [ʕabqarij] **عبقري**
شخص عبقري
[Shakhṣ'ab'qarey] *n* genius

عبور crossing, transit *n* [ʕubu:r]
كان العبور صعبا
[kan il-'aobor ṣa'aban] The crossing was rough
عبير aroma *n* [ʕabi:r]
عتلة lever *n* [ʕatla]
عتيق antique *adj* [ʕati:q]
عثة moth *n* [ʕaθθa]
عُجالة *n* [ʕuʒa:la]
في عُجالة
[Fee 'aojalah] *adv* hastily
عجز disability, shortage *n* [ʕaʒz]
عجز فى الميزانية
['ajz fee- almezaneyah] *n* deficit
عجل calf *n* [ʕiʒl]
عجلة wheel *n* [ʕaʒala]
عجلة إضافية
['aagalh eḍafeyah] *n* spare wheel
عجلة القيادة
['aagalat al-'qeyadh] *n* steering wheel
عجلة اليد
['aagalat al-yad] *n* wheelbarrow
عجوز old *adj* [ʕaʒu:z]
عجيب weird, wonderful *adj* [ʕaʒi:b]
عَجِيزَةٌ bum *n* [ʕaʒi:za]
عجينة dough *n* [ʕaʒi:na]
عجينة الباف باستري
['ajeenah aleyaf bastrey] *n* puff pastry
عجينة الكريب
['aajenat al-kreeb] *n* batter
عدّاء runner *n* [ʕadda:ʔ]
عدائي hostile *adj* [ʕida:ʔij]
عداد metre *n* [ʕadda:d]
عداد السرعة
['adaad al-sor'aah] *n* speedometer
عداد الأميال المقطوعة
['adaad al-amyal al-ma'qto'aah] *n* mileometer
عداد وقوف السيارة
['adaad wo'qoof al-sayarah] *n* parking meter
أين يوجد عداد الكهرباء؟
[ayna yujad 'aadad al-kah-raba?] Where is the electricity meter?
من فضلك قم بتشغيل العداد
[Men fadlek 'qom betashgheel al'adaad] Please use the meter
هل لديك عداد؟
[hal ladyka 'aadaad?] Do you have a meter?
عَدَالة justice *n* [ʕada:la]
عدة tackle *n* [ʕudda]
عدد quantity, amount *n* [ʕadad]
كما عدد المحطات الباقية على الوصول إلى ...؟
[kam 'aadad al-muḥaṭaat al-ba'qiya lel-wiṣool ela...?] How many stops is it to...?
عدس lentils *n* [ʕadas]
نبات العدس
[Nabat al-'aads] *npl* lentils
عدسة lens *n* [ʕadasa]
عدسة تكبير
['adasah mokaberah] *n* zoom lens
عدسة مكبرة
['adasat takbeer] *n* magnifying glass
أنني استعمل العدسات اللاصقة
[ina-ny ast'amil al-'aadasaat al-laṣi'qa] I wear contact lenses
محلول مطهر للعدسات اللاصقة
[maḥlool muṭaher lil-'aada-saat al-laṣi'qa] cleansing solution for contact lenses
عدل fairness *n* [ʕadl]
عدّل rectify *v* [ʕaddala]
عَدّل modify *v* [ʕadala]
عدم lack, absence *n* [ʕadam]
عدم التأكد
['adam al-taakod] *n* uncertainty
عدم الثبات
['adam al-thabat] *n* instability
عدم المُلاءمة
['adam al-molaamah] *n* inconvenience
أنا أسف لعدم معرفتي باللوائح
[Ana aasef le'aadam ma'arefatey bel-lawaeah] I'm very sorry, I didn't know the regulations
عدو enemy, run *n* [ʕaduww]
عدواني aggressive *adj* [ʕudwa:nij]
عدوى infection *n* [ʕadwa:]
ناقل للعدوى
[Na'qel lel-'aadwa] *adj* contagious

عديد several *adj* [ʕadi:d]
عديم lacking *adj* [ʕadi:m]
عديم الجدوى
['aadam al-jadwa] *adj* useless
عديم الاحساس
['adeem al-ehsas] *adj* senseless
عديم القيمة
['adeem al-'qeemah] *adj* worthless
عذِب sweet *(pleasing)* *adj* [ʕaðb]
عَذّب torture *v* [ʕaððaba]
عذر excuse, pardon *n* [ʕuðran]
عذر excuse *v* [ʕaðara]
عذراء virgin, Virgo *n* [ʕaðra:ʔ]
عراء *n* [ʕara:ʔ]
في العراء
[Fee al-'aaraa] *adv* outdoors
عراقي Iraqi *n* ◁ Iraqi *adj* [ʕira:qij]
عِراك scrap *(dispute)* *n* [ʕira:k]
عَربة trolley, vehicle *n* [ʕaraba]
عربة صغيرة خفيفة
['arabah ṣagheerah khafeefah] *n* buggy
عربة تناول الطعام في القطار
['arabat tanawool al-ṭa'aaam fee al-'qeṭar] *n* dining car
عربة الأعطال
['arabat al-a'ataal] *n* breakdown truck
عربة الترولي
['arabat al-troley] *n* trolley
عربة البوفيه
['arabat al-boofeeh] *n* dining car
عربة النوم
['arabat al-nawm] *n* sleeping car
عربة حقائب السفر
['arabat ḥa'qaaeb al-safar] *n* luggage trolley
عربة طفل
['arabat ṭefl] *n* pushchair
عربة مقطورة
['arabat ma'qtoorah] *n* trailer
هل يوجد عربة متنقلة لحمل الحقائب؟
[hal yujad 'aaraba muta-na'qela leḥaml al-ḥa'qaeb?] Are there any luggage trolleys?
عربي Arabic, Arab *adj* [ʕarabij]
عربي الجنسية
['arabey al-jenseyah] *adj* Arab
الإمارات العربية المتحدة
[Al-emaraat al'arabeyah al-motaḥedah] *npl* United Arab Emirates
اللغة العربية
[Al-loghah al-arabeyah] *(language)* *n* Arabic
المملكة العربية السعودية
[Al-mamlakah al-'aarabeyah al-so'aodeyah] *n* Saudi Arabia
عرج limp *v* [ʕaraʒa]
عرش throne *n* [ʕarʃ]
عرض proposal *n* [ʕardˤ]
عرض أسعار
['aarḍ as'aar] *n* quotation
جهاز عرض
[Jehaz 'ard] *n* projector
جهاز العرض العلوي
[Jehaz al-'ard al-'aolwey] *n* overhead projector
خط العرض
[Khaṭ al-'arḍ] *n* latitude
عرض *v* [ʕaradˤa]
أي فيلم يعرض الآن على شاشة السينما؟
[ay filim ya'aruḍ al-aan 'ala sha-shat al-senama?] Which film is on at the cinema?
عرِض display, set out, *v* [ʕaradˤa] show
عَرِّض *v* [ʕarradˤa]
يُعَرِض للخطر
[Yo'areḍ lel-khaṭar] *v* endanger
عرضي accidental *adj* [ʕaradˤij]
عرف custom *n* [ʕurf]
عرف know, define *v* [ʕarafa]
لا أعرف
[la a'arif] I don't know
هل تعرفه؟
[hal ta'a-rifuho?] Do you know him?
عُرفي formal *adj* [ʕurafij]
عرق sweat *n* [ʕirq]
مبلل بالعرق
[Mobala bel-ara'q] *adj* sweaty
عرَق sweat *v* [ʕaraqa]
عرقي ethnic *adj* [ʕirqij]
عروس bride *n* [ʕaru:s]

وصيفة العروس
[Waṣeefat al-'aroos] *n* bridesmaid
عُرْي *n* [ʕurj]
مُناصر للعُرْي
[Monaṣer lel'aory] *n* nudist
عَرّى undress *v* [ʕarraː]
عريس bridegroom *n* [ʕariːs]
إشبين العريس
[Eshbeen al-aroos] *n* best man
عريض large, wide *adj* [ʕariːdˤ]
ابتسامة عريضة
[Ebtesamah areeḍah] *n* grin
عريضا wide *adv* [ʕariːdˤun]
عريف corporal *n* [ʕariːf]
عِزبة estate *n* [ʕizba]
عزز foster, boost (يتبنى) *v* [ʕazzaza]
عزف play *(music)* *vt* [ʕazafa]
عَزْف *n* [ʕazf]
آلة عَزْف
[Aalat 'aazf] *n* player *(instrumentalist)*
عزم determination *n* [ʕazm]
عاقد العزم
['aaa'qed al-'aazm] *adj* determined
عزيز dear *(loved)* *adj* [ʕaziːz]
عزيزي dear *(expensive)* *adj* [ʕaziːziː]
عسر difficulty *n* [ʕusr]
عسر التكلم
['aosr al-takalom] *n* dyslexia
عسر الهضم
['aosr al-haḍm] *n* indigestion
عسكري military *adj* [ʕaskarij]
طالب عسكري
[Ṭaleb 'askarey] *n* cadet
عسل honey *n* [ʕasal]
عش nest *n* [ʕuʃ]
عشاء dinner, supper *n* [ʕaʃaːʔ]
حفلة عشاء
[Ḥaflat 'aashaa] *n* dinner party
متناول العشاء
[Motanawal al-'aashaa] *n* diner
كان العشاء شهيا
[kan il-'aashaa sha-heyan] The dinner was delicious
ما رأيك في الخروج وتناول العشاء
[Ma raaek fee al-khoroj wa-tanawol al-'aashaa] Would you like to go out for dinner?
ما هو موعد العشاء؟
[ma howa maw-'aid al-'aashaa?] What time is dinner?
عشب grass *(plant)* *n* [ʕuʃb]
عُشب الحَوْذان
['aoshb al-hawdhan] *n* buttercup
عُشب الطرخون
['aoshb al-ṭarkhoon] *n* tarragon
عشبة *n* [ʕuʃba]
عشبة ضارة
['aoshabah ḍarah] *n* weed
عشر ten *number* [ʕaʃar]
أحد عشر
[ʔaħada ʕaʃar] *number* eleven
الحادي عشر
[al-ħaːdiː ʕaʃar] *adj* eleventh
لقد تأخرنا عشرة دقائق
[la'qad ta-akharna 'aashir da-'qae'q] We are ten minutes late
عشرة ten *number* [ʕaʃaratun]
عشرون twenty *number* [ʕiʃruːna]
عشري decimal *adj* [ʕuʃarij]
عشق passion *n* [ʕiʃq]
فاكهة العشق
[Fakehat al-'aesh'q] *n* passion fruit
عشق adore *v* [ʕaʃaqa]
عشوائي random *adj* [ʕaʃwaːʔij]
عشية eve *n* [ʕaʃijja]
عشية عيد الميلاد
['aasheyat 'aeed al-meelad] *n* Christmas Eve
عصا stick *n* [ʕasˤaː]
عصا القيادة
['aaṣa al-'qeyadh] *n* joystick
عصا المشي
['asaa almashey] *n* walking stick
عصابة gang, band *n* [ʕisˤaːba]
عصابة الرأس
['eṣabat al-raas] *n* hairband
معصوب العينين
[Ma'aṣoob al-'aainayn] *adj* blindfold
عصابي neurotic *adj* [ʕisˤaːbij]
عصب nerve *(to/from brain)* *n* [ʕasˤab]
عصب *v* [ʕasˤaba]
يَعْصِبُ العينين

[Ya'aṣeb al-ozonayn] v blindfold
nervous *adj* [ʕasˤabij] **عصبي**
عصبي جداً
['aṣabey jedan] *adj* uptight
عصبي المزاج
['aṣabey] *adj* nervous
squeeze *v* [ʕasˤara] **عصر**
modern *adj* [ʕasˤrij] **عصري**
sparrow *n* [ʕusˤfuːr] **عصفور**
disobey *v* [ʕasˤaː] **عصى**
crucial *adj* [ʕasˤiːb] **عصيب**
porridge *n* [ʕasˤiːda] **عصيدة**
juice *n* [ʕasˤiːru] **عصير**
عصير الفاكهة
['aṣeer fakehah] *n* fruit juice
عصير برتقال
[Aṣeer borto'qaal] *n* orange juice
muscle *n* [ʕadˤala] **عضلة**
muscular *adj* [ʕadˤalij] **عضلي**
member *n* [ʕudˤw] **عضو**
عضو في عصابة
['aoḍw fee eṣabah] *n* gangster
عضو في الجسد
['aoḍw fee al-jasad] *n* organ *(body part)*
عضو مجلس
['aodw majles] *n* councillor
عضو مُنتَدب
['aḍow montadab] *n* president *(business)*
عضو نقابة عمالية
['aḍw ne'qabah a'omaleyah] *n* trade unionist
هل يجب أن تكون عضوا؟
[hal yajib an takoon 'auḍwan?] Do you have to be a member?
هل يجب علي أن أكون عضوا؟
[hal yajib 'aala-ya an akoon 'auḍwan?] Do I have to be a member?
organic *adj* [ʕudˤwij] **عضوي**
سماد عضوي
[Semad 'aodwey] *n* manure
غير عضوي
[Ghayer 'aoḍwey] *adj* mineral
membership *n* [ʕudˤwijja] **عضوية**
عضوية في مجلس تشريعي
['aoḍweyah fee majles tashreaey] *n* seat *(constituency)*

perfume, scent *n* [ʕitˤr] **عطر**
أشعر بالعطش
[ash-'aur bil-'aaṭash] I'm thirsty
sneeze *v* [ʕatˤasa] **عطس**
holiday, *n* [ʕutˤla] **عطلة** unemployment
عطلة أسبوعية
['aoṭlah osboo'ayeah] *n* weekend
عطلة نصف الفصل الدراسي
['aoṭlah neṣf al-faṣl al-derasey] *n* half-term
خطة عطلة شاملة الإقامة والانتقال
[Khoṭ at 'aoṭlah shamelat al-e'qamah wal-ente'qal] *n* package tour
bone *n* [ʕazˤm] **عظم**
عظم الوجنة
[aḍhm al-wajnah] *n* cheekbone
bone *n* [ʕazˤama] **عظمة**
grand, great *adj* [ʕazˤiːm] **عظيم**
الجمعة العظيمة
[Al-jom'ah al-'aaḍheemah] *n* Good Friday
mould *(fungus)* *n* [ʕafan] **عفن**
spontaneous *adj* [ʕafawij] **عفوي**
punishment *n* [ʕiqaːb] **عقاب**
eagle *n* [ʕuqaːb] **عُقاب**
medication, drug *n* [ʕaqaːr] **عقار**
عقار مسكن
['aa'qaar mosaken] *n* sedative
عقار مخدر موضعي
['aa'qar mokhader mawde'aey] *n* local anaesthetic
end *n* [ʕaqib] **عقب**
مقلوب رأسا على عقب
[Ma'qloob raasan 'ala 'aa'qab] *adv* upside down
obstacle *n* [ʕaqaba] **عقبة**
contract *n* [ʕaqd] **عقد**
عقد إيجار
['aa'qd eejar] *n* lease
عقد من الزمن
['aa'qd men al-zaman] *n* decade
knit *v* [ʕaqada] **عقد**
knot *n* [ʕuqda] **عقدة**
scorpion, Scorpio *n* [ʕaqrab] **عقرب**
v [ʕaqasˤa] **عقص**

يَعْقِص الشعر
[Ya'aqeṣ al-sha'ar] *n* curl
عَقْعَق [ʕaqʕaq] *n*
طائر العَقْعَق
[Ṭaaer al'a'qa'q] *n* magpie
عقل [ʕaqil] *n* mind, intelligence
ضرس العقل
[Ḍers al-a'aql] *n* wisdom tooth
عقلاني [ʕaqla:nij] *adj* rational
عقلي [ʕaqlij] *adj* mental
عقلية [ʕaqlijja] *n* mentality
عَقَم [ʕaqqama] *v* sterilize
عقوبة [ʕuqu:ba] *n* punishment
أقصى عقوبة
[A'qsa 'aoqobah] *n* capital punishment
عقوبة بدنية
['ao'qoba badaneyah] *n* corporal punishment
عقيفة [ʕaqi:fa] *n* hook
عقيم [ʕaqi:m] *adj* sterile
عكاز [ʕukka:z] *n* crutch
عكس [ʕaks] *n* reverse, reversal
عكس عقارب الساعة
['aaks 'aa'qareb al-saa'ah] *n* anticlockwise
والعكس كذلك
[Wal-'aaks kaḍalek] *adv* vice versa
عكس [ʕakasa] *v* reflect
علاج [ʕila:ʒ] *n* therapy, treatment
علاج بالعطور
['aelaj bel-oṭoor] *n* aromatherapy
علاج طبيعي
['aelaj ṭabeye] *n* physiotherapy
علاج نفسي
['aelaj nafsey] *n* psychotherapy
مُركّب لعلاج السعال
[Morakab le'alaaj also'aal] *n* cough mixture
علاقة [ʕala:qa] *n* relation, relationship
علاقات عامة
['ala'qat 'aamah] *npl* public relations
آسف، أنا على علاقة بأحد الأشخاص
[ʔa:sifun ʔana: ʕala: ʕila:qatin biʔaħadin alʔaʃxa:sˤi] Sorry, I'm in a relationship
عَلاَقَة [ʕala:qatu] *n*
عَلاَقَة مفاتيح
['aalaqat mafateeḥ] *n* keyring
علامة [ʕala:ma] *n* mark, symptom, tag, token
علامة تعجب
['alamah ta'ajob] *n* exclamation mark
علامة تجارية
['alamah tejareyah] *n* trademark
علامة استفهام
['alamat estefham] *n* question mark
علامة مميزة
['alamah momayazah] *n* bookmark
العلامة التجارية
[Al-'alamah al-tejareyah] *n* brand name
يَضَع عَلامَة صَح
[Beḍa'a 'aalamat ṣaḥ] *v* tick off
علاوة [ʕala:wa] *n* bonus
علاوة على ذلك
['aelawah ala ḍalek] *adv* further
علب [ʕulab] *npl* cans
فتاحة علب
[fatta ḥat 'aolab] *n* tin opener
علبة [ʕulba] *n* parcel
علبة صغيرة
['aolbah ṣagherah] *n* canister
علبة التروس
['aolbat al-teroos] *n* gear box
علبة الفيوز
['aolbat al-feyoz] *n* fuse box
علبة كارتون
['aolbat kartoon] *n* carton
عَلّق [ʕallaqa] *vt* hang
يُعَلِق على
[Yo'alle'q ala] *v* comment
علكة [ʕilka] *n* chewing gum
عَلّل [ʕallala] *v* justify
علم [ʕilm] *n* knowledge, science
علم التنجيم
[A'elm al-tanjeem] *n* astrology
علم الاقتصاد
['aelm al-e'qtesad] *npl* economics
علم البيئة
['aelm al-beeah] *n* ecology
علم الحيوان
['aelm al-hayawan] *n* zoology
علم الفلك
['aelm al-falak] *n* astronomy

علم النحو والصرف
['aelm al-naḥw wal-ṣarf] *n* grammar
علوم الحاسب الآلى
['aoloom al-ḥaseb al-aaly] *n* computer science
عَلَم flag *n* [ʕalam]
عِلم *n* [ʕilm]
عِلم الآثار
['Aelm al-aathar] *n* archaeology
عِلْم science (المعرفة) *n* [ʕilmu]
عِلمي scientific *adj* [ʕilmij]
خيال علمي
[Khayal 'aelmey] *n* scifi
عُلُوّ altitude *n* [ʕuluww]
علوي top *adj* [ʕulwij]
على above *adv* ⊲ on *prep* [ʕala:]
على طول
[Ala ṭool] *prep* along
عِلية loft *n* [ʕilja]
عَليل sick *adj* [ʕali:l]
عم uncle *n* [ʕamm]
ابن العم
[Ebn al-'aam] *n* cousin
عمارة building *n* [ʕima:ra]
فن العمارة
[Fan el-'aemarah] *n* architecture
عمال labour *n* [ʕumma:l]
عمان Oman *n* [ʕuma:n]
عمة aunt (خالة) *n* [ʕamma]
عمر age *n* [ʕumur]
شخص متقدم العمر
[Shakhṣ mota'qadem al-'aomr] *n* senior citizen
إنه يبلغ من العمر عشرة أعوام
[inaho yabligh min al-'aumr 'aashrat a'a-wam] He is ten years old
أبلغ من العمر خمسين عاماً
[ablugh min al-'aumr khamseen 'aaman] I'm fifty years old
كم عمرك؟
[kam 'aomrak?] How old are you?
عمق depth *n* [ʕumq]
عمل work *n* [ʕamal]
رحلة عمل
[Reḥlat 'aamal] *n* business trip
ساعات عمل مرنة
[Sa'aat 'aamal marenah] *n* flexitime
ساعات العمل
[Sa'aat al-'amal] *npl* office hours, opening hours
مكان العمل
[Makan al-'amal] *n* workspace
أنا هنا للعمل
[ana huna lel-'aamal] I'm here for work
عمل work *v* [ʕamala]
يعمل بشكل حر
[Ya'amal beshakl ḥor] *adj* freelance
سيارة تعمل بنظام نقل السرعات اليدوي من فضلك
[sayara ta'amal be-neḍham na'qil al-sur'aat al-yadawy, min faḍlak] A manual, please
أعمل لدى...
[a'amal lada...] I work for...
أين تعمل؟
[ayna ta'amal?] Where do you work?
التكيف لا يعمل
[al-tak-yeef la ya'amal] The air conditioning doesn't work
المفتاح لا يعمل
[al-muftaaḥ la ya'amal] The key doesn't work
كيف يعمل هذا؟
[Kayfa ya'amal hatha?] How does this work?
ماذا تعمل؟
[madha ta'amal?] What do you do?
ماكينة التذاكر لا تعمل
[makenat al-tadhaker la-ta'amal] The ticket machine isn't working
هذا لا يعمل كما ينبغي
[hatha la-ya'amal kama yan-baghy] This doesn't work
عملاق giant, gigantic *adj* [ʕimla:q]
عملة currency, pay *n* [ʕumla]
عملة معدنية
[Omlah ma'adaneyah] *n* coin
عملة متداولة
[A'omlah motadawlah] *n* currency
تخفيض قيمة العملة
[Takhfeeḍ 'qeemat al'aomlah] *n* devaluation

دار سك العملة
[Daar ṣaak al'aomlah] *n* mint *(coins)*
عملي [ʕamalij] *adj* feasible, practical
غير عملي
[Ghayer 'aamaley] *adj* impractical
عمليا [ʕamalijan] *adv* practically
عملية [ʕamalijja] *n* operation *(undertaking)*, process
عملية جراحية
['amaleyah jeraheyah] *n* operation *(surgery)*, surgery *(operation)*
عملية الأيض
['amaleyah al-abyaḍ] *n* metabolism
عَمَّم [ʕammama] *v* generalize
عمود [ʕamu:d] *n* column, post *(stake)*
عمود النور
['amood al-noor] *n* lamppost
عمود فقري
['amood fa'qarey] *n* backbone, spine
عموديا [ʕamu:dijan] *adv* upright
عمولة [ʕumu:la] *n* commission
ما هي العمولة؟
[ma heya al-'aumola?] What's the commission?
عموما [ʕumu:man] *adv* overall
عمى [ʕama:] *n* blind
مصاب بعمى الألوان
[Moṣaab be-'ama al-alwaan] *adj* colour-blind
عميق [ʕami:q] *adj* deep
واد عميق وضيق
[Wad 'amee'q wa-ḍaye'q] *n* ravine
عميل [ʕami:l] *n* customer, client, agent
عن [ʕan] *prep* about, from
عناق [ʕina:q] *n* cuddle
عناية [ʕina:ja] *n* care
بعناية
[Be-'aenayah] *n* carefully
عنب [ʕinab] *n* grape
عنب أحمر
['aenab aḥmar] *n* redcurrant
كَرْمَة العنب
[Karmat al'aenab] *n* vine
عنبر [ʕanbar] *n* hospital ward
في أي عنبر يوجد......؟
[fee ay 'aanbar yujad...?] Which ward is... in?
عند [ʕinda] *prep* at
عنصر [ʕunsˤur] *n* element
عنصري [ʕunsˤurij] *adj* racial ⊲ *n* racist
التفرقة العنصرية بحسب الجنس
[Al-tafre'qa al'aonṣoreyah beḥasab al-jens] *n* sexism
عنف [ʕunf] *n* violence
عَنّف [ʕannafa] *v* scold
عنكبوت [ʕankabu:t] *n* spider
بيت العنكبوت
[Bayt al-'ankaboot] *n* cobweb
عنوان [ʕunwa:n] *n* address *(location)*
عنوان البريد الإلكتروني
['aonwan al-bareed al-electrooney] *n* email address
عنوان المنزل
['aonwan al-manzel] *n* home address
عنوان الويب
['aonwan al-web] *n* web address
دفتر العناوين
[Daftar al-'aanaaween] *n* address book
عُنوان رئيسي
['aonwan raaesey] *n* headline
عنوان موقع الويب هو...
['ainwan maw-'q i'a al-web howa...] The website address is...
ما هو عنوان بريدك الالكتروني؟
[ma howa 'ain-wan bareed-ak al-alikit-rony?] What is your email address?
من فضلك قم بتحويل رسائلي إلى هذا العنوان
[min faḍlak 'qum be-taḥweel rasa-ely ela hadha al-'ainwan] Please send my mail on to this address
هل يمكن لك أن تدون العنوان، إذا تفضلت؟
[hal yamken laka an tudaw-win al-'aenwaan, edha tafaḍalt?] Will you write down the address, please?
عنيد [ʕani:d] *adj* stubborn
عنيف [ʕani:f] *adj* drastic, violent
عهد [ʕahd] *n* promise

منذ عهد قريب
[mondh 'aahd 'qareeb] *adv* lately
عوامة float, buoy *n* [ʕawa:ma]
عود stick *n* [ʕu:d]
عود الأسنان
['aood al-asnan] *n* toothpick
عودة return *n* [ʕawda]
تذكرة ذهاب وعودة في نفس اليوم
[tadhkarat dhehab we-'awdah fee nafs al-yawm] *n* day return
رجاء العودة بحلول الساعة الحادية عشر مساءً
[rejaa al-'aawda beḥilool al-sa'aa al-ḥade-a 'aashar masa-an] Please come home by 11p.m.
ما هو موعد العودة؟
[ma howa maw-'aid al-'aawda?] When do we get back?
يمكنك العودة وقتما رغبت ذلك
[yam-kunaka al-'aawda wa'qt-ama raghabta dhalik] Come home whenever you like
عوّض compensate *v* [ʕawwadˤa]
يُعوّض عن
[Yo'awed 'an] *v* reimburse
عَوَّل *v* [ʕawwala]
يُعَوِل على
[yo'awel 'ala] *v* rely on
عَوْلَمَة globalization *n* [ʕawlama]
عون aid *n* [ʕawn]
عوى howl *v* [ʕawa:]
عيادة clinic *n* [ʕija:da]
عيب defect, fault, *n* [ʕajb] disadvantage
عيد festival, holiday *n* [ʕi:d]
عيد الحب
['aeed al-ḥob] *n* Valentine's Day
عيد الفصح
['aeed al-fesḥ] *n* Easter
عيد الميلاد المجيد
['aeed al-meelad al-majeed] *n* Christmas
عيد ميلاد
['aeed al-meelad] *n* birthday
عيش *n* [ʕajʃ]
عيش الغراب
['aaysh al-ghorab] *n* mushroom
عين eye *n* [ʕajn]
إن عيناي ملتهبتان
[enna 'aynaya multa-hebatan] My eyes are sore
يوجد شيء ما في عيني
[yujad shay-un ma fee 'aynee] I have something in my eye
عيّن appoint *v* [ʕajjana]
يُعَيِّنُ الهويَّة
[Yo'aeyen al-haweyah] *b* identify
عينة sample *n* [ʕajjina]
عينه same *adj* [ʕajinnat]

من أي مكان يغادر المركب؟
[min ay makan yoghader al-markab?] Where does the boat leave from?

هل هذا هو الرصيف الذي يغادر منه القطار المتجه إلى...؟
[hal hadha howa al-raṣeef al-ladhy yoghader minho al-'qeṭaar al-mutajeh ela...?] Is this the right platform for the train to...?

غادِر [ɣa:dir] *adj* foul

غار [ɣa:r] *n*

ورق الغار
[Wara'q alghaar] *n* bay leaf

غارة [ɣa:ra] *n* raid

غاز [ɣa:z] *n* gas

غاز طبيعي
[ghaz ṭabeeaey] *n* natural gas

غاز مسيل للدموع
[Ghaz moseel lel-domooa] *n* teargas

موقد يعمل بالغاز للمعسكرات
[Maw'qed ya'amal bel-ghaz lel-mo'askarat] *n* camping gas

أين يوجد عداد الغاز؟
[ayna yujad 'aadad al-ghaz?] Where is the gas meter?

هل يمكنك إعادة ملء الولاعة بالغاز؟
[hal yamken -aka e'aadat mil-e al-walla-'aa bil-ghaz?] Do you have a refill for my gas lighter?

غَازَل [ɣa:zala] *v* flirt

غاضِب [ɣa:dˤib] *adj* angry, stuffy

غاظ [ɣa:zˤa] *v* fret

غالباً [ɣa:liban] *adv* often

غالي [ɣa:li:] *adj*

إنه غالي جدا ولا يمكنني شراؤه
[Enaho ghaley gedan wala yomken sheraaoh] It's too expensive for me

إنه غالي بالفعل
[inaho ghalee bil-fi'ail] It's quite expensive

غالى [ɣa:la:] *v*

يغالي في الثمن
[Yoghaley fee al-thaman] *v* overcharge

يُغَالي في التقدير
[Yoghaley fee al-ta'qdeer] *v* overestimate

غائب [ɣa:ʔibb] *adj* absent

غائم [ɣa:ʔim] *adj* cloudy, foggy

غاب [ɣa:ba] *v*

يَغيب عن الأنظار
[Yagheeb 'an al-anḍhaar] *v* vanish

غابة [ɣa:ba] *n* forest, woods

غابات المطر بخط الاستواء
[Ghabat al-maṭar be-khaṭ al-estwaa] *n* rainforest

غادر [ɣa:dara] *v*

سوف أغادر غداً
[Yoghader al-fodo'q] *v* check out

يُغادِر المكان
[Yoghader al-makanan] *v* go out

يُغَادر مكانا
[Yoghader makanan] *v* go away

سوا أغادر غدا
[Sawa oghader ghadan] I'm leaving tomorrow

أين نترك المفتاح عندما نغادر؟
[ayna natruk al-muftaaḥ 'aendama nughader?] Where do we hand in the key when we're leaving?

على أي رصيف يغادر القطار؟
['ala ay raṣeef yo-ghader al-'qeṭaar?] Which platform does the train leave from?

غامض mysterious *adj* [ɣa:midˤ]
غانا Ghana *n* [ɣa:na:]
غاني Ghanaian *adj* [ɣa:nij]
مواطن غاني
[Mowaṭen ghaney] *n* Ghanaian
غبار dust *n* [ɣuba:r]
غبي stupid *adj* [ɣabijju]
غثيان nausea *n* [ɣaθaja:n]
غَجَريّ gypsy *n* [ɣaʒarij]
غد *n* [ɣad]
أريد أن توقظني بالتليفون في الساعة السابعة من صباح الغد
[areed an to'qeḍhaney bel-telefone fee al-sa'aah al-sabe'aah men ṣabaḥ al-ghad] I'd like a wake-up call for tomorrow morning at seven o'clock
بعد غد
[ba'ad al-ghad] the day after tomorrow
غداً tomorrow *adv* [ɣadan]
هل هو مفتوح غدا؟
[hal how maftooḥ ghadan?] Is it open tomorrow?
هل يمكن أن أتصل بك غدا؟
[hal yamken an ataṣel beka ghadan?] May I call you tomorrow?
غداء lunch *n* [ɣada:ʔ]
غدة gland *n* [ɣuda]
غذاء *n* [ɣaða:ʔ]
وجبة الغذاء المعبأة
[Wajbat al-ghezaa al-mo'abaah] *n* packed lunch
كان الغذاء رائعا
[kan il-ghadaa ra-e'aan] The lunch was excellent
متى سنتوقف لتناول الغذاء؟
[mata sa-nata-wa'qaf le-tanawil al-ghadaa?] Where do we stop for lunch?
متى سيتم تجهيز الغذاء؟
[mata sayatim taj-heez al-ghadaa?] When will lunch be ready?
غذائي *adj* [ɣiða:ʔij]
التسمم الغذائي
[Al-tasmom al-ghedhaaey] *n* food poisoning
نظام غذائي
[Neḍhaam ghedhey] *v* diet
غر child *n* [ɣirr]
غراء glue *n* [ɣira:ʔ]
غراب crow *n* [ɣura:b]
غراب أسود
[Ghorab aswad] *n* raven
غرّافة carafe *n* [ɣarra:fa]
غرامة fine *n* [ɣara:ma]
أين تدفع الغرامة؟
[ayna tudfa'a al-gharama?] Where do I pay the fine?
كم تبلغ الغرامة؟
[kam tablugh al-gharama?] How much is the fine?
غرب *n* [ɣarban]
متجه غرباً
[Motajeh gharban] *adj* westbound
غَرْب west *n* [ɣarb]
غرباً west *adv* [ɣarban]
غربي west, western *adj* [ɣarbij]
ساكن الهند الغربية
[Saken al-hend al-gharbeyah] *n* West Indian
جنوب غربي
[Janoob gharbey] *n* southwest
شمال غربي
[Shamal gharbey] *n* northwest
غرز stick *vi* [ɣaraza]
غرض purpose *n* [ɣaradˤ]
غرفة room *n* [ɣurfa]
رقم الغرفة
[Ra'qam al-ghorfah] *n* room number
غرفة إضافية
[ghorfah eḍafeyah] *n* spare room
غرفة عمليات
[ghorfat 'amaleyat] *n* operating theatre
غرفة تبديل الملابس
[Ghorfat tabdeel al-malabes] *n* fitting room
غرفة خدمات
[ghorfat khadamat] *n* utility room
غرفة القياس
[ghorfat al-'qeyas] *n* fitting room
غرفة المعيشة
[ghorfat al-ma'aeshah] *n* sitting room
غرفة النوم

[Ghorfat al-noom] *n* bedroom
غرفة طعام
[ghorat ṭa'aam] *n* dining room
غرفة لشخص واحد
[ghorfah le-shakhṣ wahed] *n* single room
غرفة محادثة
[ghorfat mohadathah] *n* chatroom
غرفة مزدوجة
[Ghorfah mozdawajah] *n* double room, twin room
غُرفة خشبية
[Ghorfah khashabeyah] *n* shed
أريد غرفة أخرى غيرها
[areed ghurfa ukhra ghyraha] I'd like another room
أريد غرفة للإيجار
[areed ghurfa lil-eejar] I'd like to rent a room
أريد حجز غرفة عائلية
[areed ḥajiz ghurfa 'aa-e-liya] I'd like to book a family room
أريد حجز غرفة لشخصين
[areed ḥajiz ghurfa le-shakhiṣ-yen] I want to reserve a double room
أيمكنني الحصول على أحد الغرف؟
[a-yamkun-iny al-ḥuṣool 'ala aḥad al-ghuraf?] Do you have a room?
أين توجد غرفة الكمبيوتر؟
[ayna tojad ghurfat al-computer] Where is the computer room?
الغرفة ليست نظيفة
[al-ghurfa laysat naḍhefa] The room isn't clean
الغرفة متسخة
[al-ghurfa mutaskha] The room is dirty
هل هناك خدمة للغرفة؟
[hal hunaka khidma lil-ghurfa?] Is there room service?
هل يمكن أن أرى الغرفة؟
[hal yamken an ara al-ghurfa?] Can I see the room?
هناك ضوضاء كثيرة جدا بالغرفة
[hunaka ḍaw-ḍaa kathera jedan bil-ghurfa] The room is too nolsy
غرق [ɣaraqa] *vi* washbasin, drown

غُروب [ɣuru:b] *n* sunset
غرَّى [ɣarra:] *v* glue
غريب [ɣari:b] *adj* strange, spooky
شخص غريب
[Shakhṣ ghareeb] *n* stranger
غُرَير [ɣuṛajr] *n*
حيوان الغُرير
[Ḥayawaan al-ghoreer] *n* badger
غريزة [ɣari:za] *n* instinct
غزل [ɣazl] *n* (حركة خاطفة) flirt
غزل البنات
[Ghazl al-banat] *n* candyfloss
غزى [ɣaza:] *v* invade, conquer
غسالة [ɣassa:la] *n* washing machine
غسالة أطباق
[ghasalat aṭba'q] *n* dishwasher
غَسَقٌ [ɣasaq] *n* dusk
غسل [ɣasl] *n*
قابل للغسل في الغسالة
['qabel lel-ghaseel fee al-ghassaalah] *adj* machine washable
أرغب في غسل هذه الأشياء
[arghab fee ghasil hadhy al-ashyaa] I'd like to get these things washed
غسل [ɣasala] *v* wash
يَغْسِل الأطباق
[Yaghsel al-aṭbaa'q] *v* wash up
أريد أن أغسل السيارة
[areed an aghsil al-sayara] I would like to wash the car
أين يمكن أن أغسل يدي؟
[ayna yamken an aghsil yady?] Where can I wash my hands?
هل يمكنك من فضلك غسله
[hal yamken -aka min faḍlak ghaslaho?] Could you wash my hair, please?
غسول [ɣasu:l] *n* cleanser
غسول سمرة الشمس
[ghasool somrat al-shams] *n* suntan lotion
غسيل [ɣassi:l] *n* washing
غسيل سيارة
[ghaseel sayaarah] *n* car wash
غسيل الأطباق
[ghaseel al-atba'q] *n* washing-up
خط الغسيل

[Khat al-ghaseel] *n* washing line
حبل الغسيل
[ḥ abl al-ghaseel] *n* washing line
مسحوق الغسيل
[Mashoo'q alghaseel] *n* washing powder
مشبك الغسيل
[Mashbak al-ghaseel] *n* clothes peg
cheat *n* [ɣaʃʃa] **غش**
deceive, cheat *v* [ɣaʃʃa] **غش**
anger *n* [ɣadˤab] **غضب**
سريع الغضب
[Saree'a al-ghaḍab] *adj* irritable
غضب شديد
[ghaḍab shaded] *n* rage
مثير للغضب
[Mother lel-ghaḍab] *adj* infuriating
v [ɣutˤtˤa] **غطّ**
يَغُطْ في النوم
[yaghoṭ fee al-nawm] *v* snore
cover, lid *n* [ɣitˤaːʔ] **غطاء**
غطاء سرير
[Gheṭa'a sareer] *n* bedspread
غطاء المصباح
[Gheṭaa almeṣbaḥ] *n* lampshade
غطاء الوسادة
[gheṭaa al-wesadah] *n* pillowcase
غطاء قنينة
[Gheṭa'a 'qeneenah] *n* cap
غطاء للرأس والعنق
[Gheṭa'a lel-raas wal-a'ono'q] *n* hood
غطاء للوقاية أو الزينة
[Gheṭa'a lel-we'qayah aw lel-zeenah] *n* hubcap
غطاء مخملي
[Gheṭa'a makhmaley] *n* duvet
غطاء مائدة
[Gheṭa'a maydah] *n* tablecloth
diver *n* [ɣatˤtˤaːs] **غطاس**
dive *n* [ɣatˤasa] **غطس**
لوح غطس
[Looḥ ghaṭs] *n* diving board
dive *v* [ɣatˤisa] **غطس**
plunge *v* [ɣatˤasa] **غطّس**
cover *v* [ɣatˤtˤaː] **غطّى**
snooze *v* [ɣafa] **غفا**
forgive *v* [ɣafara] **غفر**
nap *n* [ɣafwa] **غفوة**
kid *n* [ɣulaːm] **غلام**
kettle *n* [ɣallaːja] **غلاية**
mistake *v* [ɣalatˤun] **غلط**
error *n* [ɣaltˤa] **غلطة**
wrap, wrap up *v* [ɣallafa] **غلّف**
هل يمكن أن تغلفه من فضلك؟
[hal yamken an tugha-lifho min faḍlak?] Could you wrap it up for me, please?
n [ɣalaqa] **غلق**
ما هو ميعاد الغلق هنا؟
[ma howa me-'aad al-ghali'q huna?] When does it close?
boil *vi* [ɣalaː] **غلي**
boiling *n* [ɣalajaːn] **غليان**
flood *vt* [ɣamara] **غمر**
wink *v* [ɣamaza] **غمز**
dip *vt* [ɣamasa] **غمس**
dip *(food/sauce)* *n* [ɣams] **غَمْس**
mutter *v* [ɣamɣama] **غَمْغَم**
mystery *n* [ɣumuːdˤ] **غموض**
singing *n* [ɣinaːʔ] **غناء**
غِنَاء مع الموسيقى
[Ghenaa ma'a al-mose'qa] *n* karaoke
adj [ɣinaːʔijjat] **غنائي**
قصائد غنائية
['qaṣaaed ghenaaeah] *npl* lyrics
n [ɣanam] **غنم**
جلد الغنم
[Jeld al-ghanam] *n* sheepskin
rich *adj* [ɣanij] **غني**
غني بالألوان
[Ghaney bel-alwaan] ﻘﻔﺺ colourful
submarine *n* [ɣawwaːsˤa] **غواصة**
gorilla *n* [ɣuːriːlaː] **غوريلا**
diving *n* [ɣawsˤ] **غوص**
غوص بأجهزة التنفس
[ghawṣ beajhezat altanafos] *n* scuba diving
أين يمكننا أن نجد أفضل مناطق الغوص؟
[ayna yamken-ana an najed afḍal manaṭi'q al-ghawṣ?] Where is the best place to dive?
absence *n* [ɣijaːb] **غياب**

n [ɣijjaːr] **غيار**
هل لديك قطع غيار لماركة تويوتا
[hal ladyka 'qiṭa'a gheyaar le-markat toyota?] Do you have parts for a Toyota?
n [ɣajba] **غيبة**
دفع بالغيبة
[Dafa'a bel-ghaybah] *n* alibi
n [ɣajbuːba] **غيبوبة**
غيبوبة عميقة
[Ghaybobah 'amee'qah] *n* coma
not *adj* [ɣajru] **غير**
غير صبور
[Ghaeyr ṣaboor] *adj* impatient
غير معتاد
[Ghayer mo'ataad] *adj* unusual
غير مُرتّب
[Ghayer moratb] *adj* untidy
vary, change *v* [ɣajjara] **غَيّر**
Guinea *n* [ɣiːnjaː] **غينيا**
[ɣiːnjaː al-**غينيا الاستوائية**
Equatorial Guinea *n*istiwaːʔijjatu]
jealous *adj* [ɣajuːr] **غيور**

ف

benefit *n* [faːʔida] **فائدة**
معدل الفائدة
[Moaadal al-faaedah] *n* interest rate
winning *adj* [faːʔiz] **فائز**
شخص فائز
[Shakhṣ faaez] *n* winner
surplus *adj* [faːʔidˤ] **فائض**
adj [faːʔiq] **فائق**
فائق الجمال
[Faae'q al-jamal] *adj* gorgeous
category *n* [fiʔa] **فئة**
fair *(light colour)* *adj* [faːtiħ] **فاتح**
dull, lukewarm *adj* [faːtir] **فاتر**
catching, glamorous, *adj* [faːtin] **فاتن**
superb, fascinating
n [faːtuːra] **فاتورة**
فاتورة رسمية
[Fatoorah rasmeyah] *n* note *(account)*
فاتورة تجارية
[Fatoorah tejareyah] *n* invoice
فاتورة تليفون
[Fatoorat telefon] *n* phone bill
يُعِد فاتورة
[Yo'aed al-fatoorah] *v* invoice
قم بإضافته إلى فاتورتي
['qim be-iḍa-fatuho ela foatoraty] Put it on my bill

قم بإعداد الفاتورة من فضلك
['qim be-i'adad al-foatora min faḍlak] Please prepare the bill
من فضلك أحضر لي الفاتورة
[min faḍlak iḥḍir lee al-fatora] Please bring the bill
هل لي أن أحصل على فاتورة مفصلة؟
[hal lee an aḥṣil 'aala fatoora mufa-ṣala?] Can I have an itemized bill?
فاحش [fa:ħiʃ] *adj* obscene
فأر [faʔr] *n* mouse
فارسي [fa:risij] *adj* Persian
فارغ [fa:riɣ] *adj* blank
فارق [fa:riq] *n* distinction
فاز [fa:za] *v* win
فاسد [fa:sid] *adj* corrupt
فاصل [fa:sˤil] *n* interval
فاصل إعلاني
[Faṣel e'alaany] *n* commercial break
فاصلة [fa:sˤila] *n* comma
فاصلة علوية
[Faṣela a'olweyah] *n* apostrophe
فاصوليا [fa:sˤu:lja:] *n*
فاصوليا خضراء متعرشة
[faṣoleya khadraa mota'aresha] *n* runner bean
فاصوليا خضراء
[Faṣoleya khaḍraa] *npl* French beans
فاض [fa:dˤa] *vi* flood
فاكس [fa:ks] *n* fax
هل يوجد فاكس؟
[hal yujad fax?] Do you have a fax?
فاكهة [fa:kiha] *n* fruit
عصير الفاكهة
['aṣeer fakehah] *n* fruit juice
متجر الخضر والفاكهة
[Matjar al-khoḍar wal-fakehah] *n* greengrocer's
مثلجات الفاكهة
[Mothalajat al-fakehah] *n* sorbet
فانيلة [fa:ni:la] *n*
صوف فانيلة
[Ṣoof faneelah] *n* flannel
فانيليا [fa:ni:lja:] *n* vanilla
فبراير [fabra:jir] *n* February
فتاة [fata:t] *n* lass
فتاحة [fatta:ħa] *n*
فتاحة علب
[fatta ḥat 'aolab] *n* tin opener
فتاحة علب التصبير
[Fatahat 'aolab al-taṣdeer] *n* tin opener
فتاحة الزجاجات
[Fatahat al-zojajat] *n* bottle-opener
فتح [fataħa] *n*
أريد أن أبدأ بالمكرونة لفتح شهيتي
[areed an abda bil-makarona le-fatiḥ sha-heiaty] I'd like pasta as a starter
ما هو ميعاد الفتح هنا؟
[ma howa me-'aad al-fatiḥ huna?] When does it open?
فتح [fataħa] *vt* open
يفتح النشاط
[Yaftah nashaṭ] *v* unzip
يَفتَح القفل
[Yaftaḥ al-'qafl] *v* unlock
الباب لا يُفتح
[al-baab la yoftaḥ] The door won't open
متى يُفتح القصر؟
[mata yoftaḥ al-'qaṣir?] When is the palace open?
متى يُفتح المعبد؟
[mata yoftaḥ al-ma'abad?] When is the temple open?
فتحة [fatħa] *n* slot
فتحة سقف السيارة
[fatḥ at saa'qf al-sayaarah] *n* headroom
فتحة سَقف
[Fathat sa'qf] *n* sunroof
فتحة الأنف
[Fathat al-anf] *n* nostril
فتحة التوصيل
[Fathat al-tawṣeel] *n* plughole
فترة [fatra] *n*
فترة راحة
[Fatrat raaḥ a] *n* break
فترة ركود
[Fatrat rekood] *n* low season
فترة المحاكمة
[Fatrat al-moḥkamah] *n* trial period
فترة النهار
[Fatrat al-nehaar] *n* daytime
فترة وجيزة

[Fatrah wajeezah] *n* while
إنها لا تزال داخل فترة الضمان
[inaha la tazaal dakhel fatrat al-ḍaman] It's still under guarantee
لقد ظللنا منتظرين لفترة طويلة
[La'qad ḍhallalna montaḍhereen le-fatrah ṭaweelah] We've been waiting for a very long time
ما الفترة التي سأستغرقها للوصول إلى هناك؟
[Ma alfatrah alaty saastaghre'qha lel-woṣool ela honak?] How long will it take to get there?
search *v* [fattaʃa] **فَتّش**
hernia *n* [fatq] **فتق**
charm *n* [fitna] **فِتنة**
guy *n* [fataː] **فتى**
crude *adj* [faʒʒ] **فج**
suddenly *adv* [faʒʔatun] **فجأة**
explode *v* [faʒʒara] **فَجّر**
dawn *n* [faʒr] **فجر**
radish *n* [fiʒl] **فجل**
فجل حار
[Fejl ḥar] *n* horseradish
gap *n* [faʒwa] **فجوة**
tick, examination *n* [faħsˤ] **فحص**
فحص طبى عام
[Faḥṣ ṭebey 'aam] *n* check-up
هل تسمح بفحص إطارات السيارة؟
[hal tasmaḥ be-faḥṣ eṭaraat al-sayarah?] Can you check the tyres, please?
tick, inspect *vt* [faħasˤa] **فحص**
coal *n* [faħm] **فحم**
منجم فحم
[Majam fahm] *n* colliery
فَحْم نباتي
[Faḥm nabatey] *n* charcoal
n [faxxaːr] **فخار**
مصنع الفخار
[Maṣna'a al-fakhaar] *n* pottery
thigh *n* [faxð] **فخذ**
pride *n* [faxr] **فخر**
proud *adj* [faxuːr] **فخور**
ransom *n* [fidja] **فدية**
escape *vi* [farra] **فر**

bed *n* [firaːʃ] **فراش**
فراش كبير الحجم
[Ferash kabeer al-ḥajm] *n* king-size bed
عند العودة سوف نكون في الفراش
['aenda al-'aoda sawfa nakoon fee al-feraash] We'll be in bed when you get back
butterfly, moth *n* [faraːʃa] **فراشة**
void *n* [faraːɣ] **فراغ**
وَقت فراغ
[Wa'qt faragh] *n* spare time
brake *n* [faraːmil] **فرامل**
الفرامل لا تعمل
[Al-faramel la ta'amal] The brakes are not working, The brakes don't work
هل يوجد فرامل في الدراجة؟
[hal yujad fara-mil fee al-darraja?] Does the bike have brakes?
strawberry *n* [faraːwla] **فراولة**
n [farx] **فرخ**
فرخ الضفدع
[Farkh al-ḍofda'a] *n* tadpole
single, person *n* [fard] **فرد**
أقرب أفراد العائلة
[A'qrab afrad al-'aaleah] *n* next-of-kin
individual *adj* [fardijjat] **فردي**
مباراة فردية
[Mobarah fardeyah] *n* singles
sort out *v* [faraza] **فرز**
mare *n* [faras] **فرَس**
عدو الفرس
[adow al-faras] (جري) *n* gallop
فرس النهر
[Faras al-nahr] *n* hippo
فَرَس قزم
[Faras 'qezm] *n* pony
brush *n* [furʃaːt] **فرشاة**
فرشاة أظافر
[Forshat aḍhafer] *n* nailbrush
فرشاة الأسنان
[Forshat al-asnaan] *n* toothbrush
فرشاة الدهان
[Forshat al-dahaan] *n* paintbrush
فرشاة الشعر
[Forshat al-sha'ar] *n* hairbrush
يُنَظِف بالفرشاة

[yonaḍhef bel-forshah] *v* brush
opportunity *n* [fursˤa] **فرصة**
branch *n* [farʕ] **فرع**
عناوين فرعية
['anaween far'aeyah] *npl* subtitles
adj [farʕijji] **فرعي**
مزود بعنوان فرعي
[Mozawad be'aonwan far'aey] *adj* subtitled
empty *vt* [farraɣa] **فرَّغ**
يُفرِغ حمولة
[Yofaregh ḥomolah] *v* unload
n [firaq] **فرق**
فرق كشافة
[Fear'q kashafah] *npl* troops
separate *vt* [farraqa] **فَرَّق**
n [firqa] **فرقة**
فرقة الآلات النحاسية
[Fer'qat al-aalat al-naḥaseqeyah] *n* brass band
فرقة مطافيء
[Fer'qat maṭafeya] *n* fire brigade
فرقة موسيقية
[Fer'qah mose'qeyah] *n* band *(musical group)*
من فضلك اتصل بفرقة المطافئ
[min faḍlak itaṣil be-fir'qat al-maṭa-fee] Please call the fire brigade
scrub *v* [faraka] **فرك**
chop *n* [faram] **فرم**
chop *v* [farama] **فَرم**
brake *v* [farmala] **فرْمَل**
n [farmala] **فرملة**
فرملة يَدّ
[Farmalat yad] *n* handbrake
oven *n* [furn] **فرن**
France *n* [faransaː] **فرنسا**
French *adj* [faransij] **فرنسي**
اللغة الفرنسية
[All-loghah al-franseyah] *adj* French
بوق فرنسي
[Boo'q faransey] *n* French horn
مواطن فرنسي
[Mowaṭen faransey] *n* Frenchman
مواطنة فرنسية
[Mowaṭenah faranseyah] *n* Frenchwoman
fur *n* [farw] **فرو**
peculiar, unique *adj* [fariːd] **فريد**
freezer *n* [friːzar] **فريزر**
prey *n* [fariːsa] **فريسة**
team *n* [farjq] **فريق**
فريق البحث
[Faree'q al-bahth] *n* search party
horror *n* [fazaʕ] **فَزَع**
corruption *n* [fasaːd] **فساد**
dress *n* [fustaːn] **فستان**
فستان الزفاف
[Fostaan al-zefaf] *n* wedding dress
هل يمكن أن أجرب هذا الفستان؟
[hal yamken an ajar-reb hadha al-fustaan?] Can I try on this dress?
deteriorate *v* [fasada] **فسَد**
interpret *v* [fassara] **فسّر**
mosaic *n* [fusajfisaːʔ] **فسيفساء**
popcorn *n* [fuʃaːr] **فشار**
failure *n* [faʃal] **فشل**
fail *vi* [faʃala] **فشل**
n [fasˤsˤ] **فص**
فص ثوم
[Faṣ thawm] *n* clove
n [fisˤaːm] **فصَام**
مريض بالفصَام
[Mareeḍ bel-feṣaam] *adj* schizophrenic
chapter *n* [fasˤl] **فصل**
فصل دراسي
[Faṣl derasey] *n* semester
فصل الربيع
[Faṣl al-rabeya] *n* springtime
فصل الصيف
[Faṣl al-ṣayf] *n* summertime
فصل من فصول السنة
[Faṣl men foṣol al-sanah] *n* term *(division of year)*
disconnect *v* [fasˤala] **فصل**
n [fasˤla] **فصلة**
فصلة منقوطة
[faṣelah man'qoṭa] *n* semicolon
n [fasˤiːla] **فصيلة**
فصيلة دم
[faṣeelat dam] *n* blood group
فصيلة دمي 0 موجب

[faṣeelat damey 0 mojab] My blood group is O positive
فضّ unwrap *v* [fadˤdˤa]
فضاء space *n* [fadˤaːʔ]
رائد فضاء
[Raeed faḍaa] *n* astronaut
سَفينة الفضاء
[Safenat al-faḍaa] *n* spacecraft
فضة silver *n* [fidˤdˤa]
فضفاض loose *adj* [fadˤfaːdˤ]
كنزة فضفاضة يرتديها الرياضيون
[Kanzah feḍfaḍh yartadeha al-reyadeyon] *n* sweatshirt
فضل *n* [fadˤl]
غير المدخنين من فضلك
[gheyr al-mudakhin-een min faḍlak] Non-smoking, please
.في الأمام من فضلك
[Fee al-amaam men faḍlek] Facing the front, please
من فضلك أخبرني عندما نصل إلى...
[min faḍlak ikh-birny 'aindama naṣal ela...] Please let me know when we get to...
فضل *v* [fadˤala]
أفضل أن تكون الرحلة الجوية في موعد أقرب
[ofaḍel an takoon al-reḥla al-jaw-wya fee maw-'aed a'qrab] I would prefer an earlier flight
أنا أفضل...
[ana ofaḍel...] I like..., I prefer to...
من فضلك
[min faḍlak] Please
فَضَّل prefer *v* [fadˤdˤala]
فضِلات waste *n* [fadˤalaːt]
فَضْلَة scrap *(small piece)* *n* [fadˤla]
فضولي nosy *adj* [fudˤuːlij]
فضيحة scandal *n* [fadˤiːħa]
فطر *n* [fatˤara]
فطر الغاريقون
[Feṭr al-gharekoon] *n* toadstool
فَطِن witty *adj* [fatˤin]
فِطْنَة wit *n* [fitˤna]
فَطير *adj* [fatˤiːratu]
فطيرة التفاح
[Faṭeerat al-tofaaḥ] *n* apple pie
فطيرة pie *n* [fatˤiːra]
فطيرة فْلَان
[Faṭerat folan] *n* flan
فطيرة محلاة
[Faṭerah moḥalah] *n* pancake
فطيرة هَشة
[Faṭerah hashah] *n* shortcrust pastry
فطيرَة مَحْشوَّة
[Faṭeerah maḥshowah] *n* tart
فظ coarse *adj* [fazˤzˤ]
حيوان الفَظّ
[Ḥayawan al-fadh] *n* walrus
فظاعة *n* [fazˤaːʕa]
بفظاعة
[befaḍha'aah] *adv* awfully
فعال effective *adj* [faʕʕaːl]
غير فعال
[Ghayer fa'aal] *adj* inefficient
فعل verb, act, action *n* [fiʕl]
فعل do *v* [faʕala]
ما الذي يمكن أن نفعله هنا؟
[ma al-lathy yamkin an naf-'aalaho hona?] What is there to do here?
فعلا quite *adv* [fiʕlan]
فِعلي actual *n* [fiʕlij]
فقاعة bubble *n* [fuqaːʕa]
فقدان *n* [fuqdaːn]
فقدان الشهية
[Fo'qdaan al-shaheyah] *n* anorexia
فَقر poverty *n* [faqr]
فقرة paragraph *n* [faqra]
فقط only *adv* [faqatˤ]
فقمة *n* [fuqma]
حيوان الفقمة
[Ḥayawaan al-fa'qmah] (حيوان) *n* seal *(animal)*
فقيد late *(dead)* *adj* [faqiːd]
فقير poor *adj* [faqiːr]
فك jaw *n* [fakk]
فكّ unpack *v* [fakka]
فكّ unwind, undo *vt* [fakka]
يَفكّ اللولب
[Yafek al-lawlab] *v* unscrew
فكاهة *n* [fukaːha]
حس الفكاهة

[Ḥes al-fokahah] *n* sense of humour
فكاهي [fuka:hij] *adj* humourous
فكّة [fakkat] *n*
معذرة، ليس لدي أية فكّة
[Ma'adheratan, lays laday ay fakah] Sorry, I don't have any change
هل يمكن إعطائي بعض الفكّة من فضلك؟
[Hal yomken e'ataaey ba'aḍ alfakah men faḍlek] Can you give me some change, please?
فَكَّر [fakkara] *v* think
يُفَكِر في
[Yofaker fee] *vi* consider
فكرة [fikra] *n* idea
فكرة عامة
[Fekrah 'aamah] *n* general
فكرة مفيدة
[Fekrah mofeedah] *n* tip *(suggestion)*
فِكْري [fikrij] *adj* intellectual ◁ *n* intellectual
فَكَّكَ [fakkaka] *v*
يُفَكِّك إلى أجْزاء
[Yo'fakek ela ajzaa] *v* take apart
فلاش [fla:ʃ] *n*
إن الفلاش لا يعمل
[enna al-flaash la ya'amal] The flash is not working
فلامنجو [fla:minʒ] *n*
طائر الفلامنجو
[Ṭaaer al-flamenjo] *n* flamingo
فلبيني [filibbi:nij] *adj* Filipino
مواطن فلبيني
[Mowaṭen felebeeney] *n* Filipino
فلسطين [filastˤi:nu] *n* Palestine
فلسطيني [filastˤi:nij] *adj* Palestinian ◁ *n* Palestinian
فلسفة [falsafa] *n* philosophy
فلفل [fulful] *n* pepper
فلفل أحمر حار
[Felfel aḥmar ḥar] *n* chilli
مطحنة الفلفل
[maṭḥanat al-felfel] *n* peppermill
فُلْفُل مطحون
[Felfel maṭhoon] *n* paprika
فلك [falak] *n*
علم الفلك
['aelm al-falak] *n* astronomy
فلوت [flu:t] *n*
آلة الفلوت
[Aalat al-felot] *n* flute
فلوري [flu:rij] *adj* fluorescent
فلين [filli:n] *n* cork
فم [fam] *n* mouth
غسول الفم
[Ghasool al-fam] *n* mouthwash
فن [fann] *n* (مهارة) art
فناء [fana:ʔ] *n*
فناء مرصوف
[Fenaa marṣoof] *n* patio
فنان [fanna:n] *n* artist
فنان متسول
[Fanan motasawol] *n* busker
فنان مشترك في حفلة عامة
[Fanan moshtarek fe ḥaflah 'aama] *n* (فنان) entertainer
فنجان [finʒa:n] *n* cup
صحن الفنجان
[Ṣaḥn al-fenjaan] *n* saucer
فنجان شاي
[Fenjan shay] *n* teacup
هل يمكن الحصول على فنجان آخر من القهوة من فضلك؟
[hal yamken al-ḥuṣool 'aala fin-jaan aakhar min al-'qahwa min faḍlak?] Could we have another cup of coffee, please?
فندق [funduq] *n* hotel
جناح في فندق
[Janaḥ fee fond'q] *n* suite
يغادر الفندق
[Yoghader al-fodo'q] *v* check out
يتسجل فى فندق
[Yatasajal fee fondo'q] *v* check in
أنا مقيم في فندق
[ana mu'qeem fee finda'q] I'm staying at a hotel
أيمكنك أن تحجز لي بالفندق؟
[a-yamkun-ika an taḥjuz lee bil-finda'q?] Can you book me into a hotel?
ما هو أفضل طريق للذهاب إلى هذا

الفندق
[Ma howa afḍal taree'q lel-dhehab ela al-fondo'q] What's the best way to get to this hotel?

ما هي أجرة التاكسي للذهاب إلى هذا الفندق؟
[ma heya ejrat al-taxi lel-thehaab ela hatha al-finda'q?] How much is the taxi fare to this hotel?

هل يمكن أن تنصحني بأحد الفنادق؟
[hal yamken an tan-ṣaḥny be-aḥad al-fana-di'q] Can you recommend a hotel?

هل يمكن الوصول إلى الفندق بكراسي المقعدين المتحركة؟
[hal yamken al-wiṣool ela al-finda'q be-karasi al-mu'q'aadeen al-mutaḥarika?] Is your hotel wheelchair accessible?

Venezuela *n* [finzwi:la:] **فنزويلا**

Venezuelan *adj* [finizwi:li:] **فنزويلي** Venezuelan *n* ◂

Finland *n* [finlanda:] **فنلندا**

Finnish *adj* [fanlandij] **فنلندي**

مواطن فنلندي
[Mowaṭen fenlandey] *n* Finn

artistic *adj* [fanij] **فني**

عمل فني
['amal faney] *n* work of art

جاليري فني
[Jalery faney] *n* art gallery

technician *n* [fannij] **فَنِّي**

index *(list)*, index *n* [fahras] **فهرس** *(numerical scale)*

n [fahranha:jti:] **فهرنهايتي**

درجة حرارة فهرنهايتي
[Darjat hararh ferhrenhaytey] *n* degree Fahrenheit

n [fahm] **فهم**

سوء فهم
[Soa fahm] *n* misunderstanding

understand *v* [fahama] **فهم**

أفهمت؟
[a-fa-hemt?] Do you understand?

فهمت
[fahamto] I understand

لم أفهم
[lam afham] I don't understand

fizzy *adj* [fuwa:r] **فوار**

npl [fawa:sˤilun] **فواصل**

فواصل معقوفة
[Fawaṣel ma'a'qoofah] *npl* quotation marks

n [fu:tu:ɣra:fijja] **فوتوغرافي**

صورة فوتوغرافية
[Ṣorah fotoghrafeyah] *n* photo

كم تبلغ تكلفة الصور الفوتوغرافية؟
[kam tablugh taklifat al-ṣowar al-foto-ghrafiyah?] How much do the photos cost?

regiment *n* [fawʒu] **فوج**

vodka *n* [fu:dka:] **فودكا**

promptly *adv* [fawran] **فورا**

adv ◂ immediate *adj* [fawrij] **فوري** simultaneously

authorize *v* [fawwadˤa] **فَوَّض**

messy *adj* [fawdˤawij] **فوضوي**

chaos, mess *n* [fawdˤa:] **فوضى**

n [fu:tˤa] **فوطة**

فوطة تجفيف الأطباق
[Foṭah tajfeef al-aṭbaa'q] *n* tea towel

above *prep* [fawqa] **فوق**

فوق ذلك
[Faw'q dhalek] *adv* neither

upper *adj* [fawqi:] **فوقي**

broad bean, bean *n* [fu:l] **فول**

حبة فول سوداني
[Ḥabat fool sodaney] *n* peanut

براعم الفول
[Braa'em al-fool] *npl* beansprouts

folklore *n* [fu:lklu:r] **فولكلور**

in *prep* [fi:] **في**

vitamin *n* [fi:ta:mi:n] **فيتامين**

Vietnam *n* [fi:tna:m] **فيتنام**

Vietnamese *adj* [fi:tna:mij] **فيتنامي**

اللغة الفيتنامية
[Al-loghah al-fetnameyah] *(language)* *n* Vietnamese

شخص فيتنامي
[Shakhṣ fetnamey] *(person)* *n* Vietnamese

Fiji *n* [fi:ʒi:] **فيجي**

فيديو video *n* [fiːdjuː]
كاميرا فيديو نقال
[Kamera fedyo na'q'qaal] *n* camcorder
هل يمكنني تشغيل ألعاب الفيديو؟
[hal yamken -any tash-gheel al-'aab al-video?] Can I play video games?
فيروزي turquoise *adj* [fajruːzij]
فيروس virus *n* [fiːruːs]
مضاد للفيروسات
[Modad lel-fayrosat] *n* antivirus
فيزا visa *n* [fiːzaː]
فيزياء physics *n* [fiːzjaːʔ]
فيزيائي physicist *n* [fiːzjaːʔij]
فيضان flooding *n* [fajadˤaːn]
فيل elephant *n* [fiːl]
فيلا villa *n* [fiːlaː]
أريد فيلا للإيجار
[areed villa lil-eejar] I'd like to rent a villa
فيلم movie *n* [fiːlm]
فيلم رعب
[Feelm ro'ab] *n* horror film
فيلم وثائقي
[Feel wathaae'qey] *n* documentary

قاء throw up *v* [qaːʔa]
قائد (قائدة)*n* [qaːʔidun, qaːʔida] principal *(principal)*, leader
قائد فرقة موسيقية
['qaaed fer'qah mose'qeyah] *n* conductor
قائم *adj* [qaːʔim]
القائم برحلات يومية من وإلى عمله
[Al-'qaem berahlaat yawmeyah men wa ela 'amaleh] *n* commuter
قائم على مرتفع
['qaem ala mortafa'a] *adv* uphill
قائمة list *n* [qaːʔima]
قائمة أسعار
['qaemat as'aar] *n* price list
قائمة خمور
['qaemat khomor] *n* wine list
قائمة انتظار
['qaemat entedhar] *n* waiting list
قائمة بريد
['qaemat bareed] *n* mailing list
قائمة طعام
['qaemat ta'aam] *n* menu
قائمة مرشحين
['qaemat morashaheen] *n* short list
قائمة مجموعات الأغذية
['qaemat majmo'aat al-oghneyah] *n* set

menu
قابِس plug *n* [qa:bis]
قابَض clutch *n* [qa:bidˤ]
قابل *adj* [qa:bil]
قابل للتغيير
['qabel lel-tagheyer] *adj* changeable
قابل للتحويل
['qabel lel-taḥweel] *adj* convertible
قابل للطي
['qabel lel-ṭay] *adj* folding
قابل للمقارنة
['qabel lel-mo'qaranah] *adj* comparable
قابَل interview, meet up *v* [qa:bala]
قابَلة midwife *n* [qa:bila]
قاتِل murderer *n* [qa:til]
قاحل infertile *adj* [qa:ħil]
قاد drive *v* [qa:da]
كان يقود السيارة بسرعة كبيرة
[ka:na jaqu:du assajja:rata bisurʕatin kabi:ratin] He was driving too fast
قادِر able *adj* [qa:dir]
قادِم *adj* [qa:dim]
أريد تذكرتين للجمعة القادمة
[areed tadhkeara-tayn lel-jum'aa al-'qadema] I'd like two tickets for next Friday
ما هي المحطة القادمة؟
[ma heya al-muḥaṭa al-'qadema?] What is the next stop?
هل المحطة القادمة هي محطة...؟
[Hal al-maḥaṭah al-'qademah hey maḥṭat...?] Is the next stop...?
يوم السبت القادم
[yawm al-sabit al-'qadem] next Saturday
قارِئ reader *n* [qa:riʔ]
قارئ الأخبار
['qarey al-akhbar] *n* newsreader
قارِب *adj* [qa:rib]
قارب صيد
['qareb ṣayd] *n* fishing boat
قارب تجديف
['qareb tajdeef] *n* rowing boat
قارب ابحار
['qareb ebḥar] *n* sailing boat
قارب نجاة
['qareb najah] *n* lifeboat
قارة continent *n* [qa:rra]
قارص stingy *adj* [qa:risˤ]
قارن compare *v* [qa:rana]
قاروس *n* [qa:ru:s]
سمك القاروس
[Samak al-faros] *n* bass
قاس ruthless, stiff *adj* [qa:sin]
قاسْ measure *v* [qasa]
يَقْيس ثوباً
[Ya'qees thawban] *v* try on
يَقْيس مقدار
[Ya'qees me'qdaar] *v* quantify
قاسي cruel *adj* [qa:si:]
قاصر underage *adj* [qa:sˤir]
شخص قاصر
[Shakhṣ 'qaṣer] *n* minor
قاضِي judge, magistrate *n* [qa:dˤi:]
قاضَى sue *v* [qa:dˤa:]
قاطِع edgy, keen *adj* [qa:tˤiʕ]
قاطَع interrupt *v* [qa:tˤaʕa]
قاع bottom *n* [qa:ʕ]
قاعة hall *n* [qa:ʕa]
قاعة إعداد الموتى
['qaat e'adad al-mawta] *n* funeral parlour
ماذا يعرضون هذه الليلة في قاعة الحفلات الغنائية؟
[madha ya'a-reḍoon hadhehe al-layla fee 'qa'aat al-ḥaf-laat al-ghena-eya?] What's on tonight at the concert hall?
قاعدة base *n* [qa:ʕida]
قاعدة بيانات
['qaedat bayanat] *n* database
قافلة fleet *n* [qa:fila]
قال say *v* [qa:la]
قالب mould *(shape)* *n* [qa:lab]
قالب مستطيل
['qaleb mostaṭeel] *n* bar *(strip)*
قامِ ب *v* [qa:ma bi ʕamalin]
يَقوم بعمل
[Ya'qoom be] *v* act
قامر gamble *v* [qa:mara]
قاموس dictionary *n* [qa:mu:s]
قانون law *n* [qa:nu:n]
مشروع قانون

[Mashroo'a 'qanooney] *n* note *(legislation)*
legal *adj* [qa:nu:nij] **قانوني**
غير قانوني
[Ghayer 'qanooney] *adj* illegal
resist *v* [qa:wama] **قاوم**
swap *v* [qa:jadˤa] **قايَض**
grave *n* [qabr] **قبر**
شاهد القبر
[Shahed al-'qabr] *n* gravestone
Cyprus *n* [qubrusˤ] **قبرص**
n ◁ Cypriot *adj* [qubrusˤij] **قبرصي** Cypriot *(person)*
v [qabadˤa] **قبِض**
يَقْبِض على
[jaqbudˤu ʕala:] *v* grasp
fist *n* [qabdˤa] **قبضة**
arrest *v* [qabadˤa ʕala:] **قبِض على**
hat *n* [qubaʕa] **قبَعة**
n [qubbaʕa] **قبَعة**
قبَعة البيسبول
['qoba'at al-beesbool] *n* baseball cap
clog *n* [qubqa:b] **قبقاب**
prep [qabla] **قبل**
من قبل
[Men 'qabl] *adv* previously
accept *v* ◁ agree *n* [qabbala] **قَبَل**
kiss *v* [qabbala] **قبّل**
kiss *n* [qibla] **قبلة**
cellar *n* [qabw] **قبو**
ugly *adj* [qabi:ħ] **قبيح**
tribe *n* [qabi:la] **قبيلة**
fight, fighting *n* [qita:l] **قتال**
n [qatl] **قتل**
جريمة قتل
[Jareemat 'qatl] *n* murder
kill *v* [qatala] **قتل**
يقتل عمداً
[Ya'qtol 'aamdan] *v* murder
cigarette lighter, *n* [qadda:ħa] **قداحة** lighter
mass *(church)* *n* [qudda:s] **قُدّاس**
afford, appreciate *v* [qadara] **قَدِر**
destiny, fate *n* [qadar] **قدَر**
ability *n* [qudra] **قدرة**
القدرة الفنية
[Al'qodarh al-faneyah] *n* know-how
قدرة على الاحتمال
['qodrah ala al-eḥtemal] *n* stamina
foot *n* [qadam] **قدم**
أثر القدم
[Athar al-'qadam] *n* footstep
حافي القدمين
[Ḥafey al-'qadameyn] *adv* barefoot
لاعب كرة قدم
[La'eb korat 'qadam] *n* footballer
مُعَالِج القدم
[Mo'aaleg al-'qadam] *n* chiropodist
إن قدماي تؤلمني
[enna 'qadam-aya to-al-imany] My feet are sore
مقاس قدمي ستة
[ma'qas 'qadamy sit-a] My feet are a size six
offer, introduce, *v* [qaddama] **قدم** put forward
كيف يقدم هذا الطبق؟
[kayfa yu'qadam hatha al-ṭaba'q?] How is this dish served?
ahead *adv* [qudumaan] **قُدُماً**
saint *n* [qiddi:s] **قدّيس**
ancient *adj* [qadi:m] **قديم**
since *adv* [qadi:man] **قديماً**
dirt *n* [qaða:ra] **قذارة**
filthy, sloppy *adj* [qaðir] **قذر**
toss, throw out *v* [qaðafa] **قذف**
n [qaði:fa] **قذيفة**
قذيفة صاروخية
['qadheefah ṣarookheyah] *n* missile
read *v* [qaraʔa] **قرَأ**
يَقرَأ الشفاه
[Ya'qraa al-shefaa] *v* lip-read
يَقْرَأ بصوت مرتفع
[Ya'qraa beṣawt mortafe'a] *v* read out
reading *n* [qira:ʔa] **قراءة**
proximity *n* [qura:ba] **قرابة**
decision *n* [qara:r] **قرار**
n [qara:sˤina] **قراصنة**
قراصنة الكمبيوتر
['qaraṣenat al-kombyotar] (كمبيوتر) *n* hacker
n [qurb] **قرب**

هل توجد مغسلة آلية بالقرب من هنا؟
[hal tojad maghsala aalya bil-'qurb min huna?] Is there a launderette near here?
هل هناك أي أماكن شيقة للمشي بالقرب من هنا؟
[hal hunaka ay amakin shay-i'qa lel-mashy bil-'qurb min huna?] Are there any interesting walks nearby?
هل يوجد بنك بالقرب من هنا؟
[hal yujad bank bil-'qurb min huna?] Is there a bank nearby?
هل يوجد ورشة سيارات بالقرب من هنا؟
[hal yujad warshat sayaraat bil-'qurb min huna?] Is there a garage near here?
قُرب [qurba] *adv* near
قرة [qurra] *n*
قرة العين
['qorat al-'ayn] *n* watercress
قرحة [qurħa] *n* ulcer
قرحة البرد حول الشفاة
['qorḥat al-bard ḥawl al-shefah] *n* cold sore
قرد [qird] *n* monkey
قرر [qarrara] *v* opt out, decide
قرش [qirʃ] *n*
سمك القرش
[Samak al-'qersh] (سمك) *n* shark
قرص [qursˤ] *n* disc
سواقة أقراص
[Sowa'qat a'qraṣ] *n* disk drive
قرص صغير
['qorṣ ṣagheyr] *n* diskette
قرص صلب
['qorṣ ṣalb] *n* hard disk
قرص مرن
['qorṣ maren] *n* floppy disk
قرص مضغوط
['qorṣ maḍghooṭ] *n* compact disc
قرص [qarasˤa] *vt* pinch
قُرْصان [qursˤa:n] *n* pirate
قرض [qardˤ] *n* loan
قرط [qirtˤ] *n* earring
قَرَع [qaraʕa] *v* knock
قَرْع [qarʕ] *n* pumpkin
نبات القرع
[Nabat al-'qar'a] *n* squash
قرفة [qirfa] *n* cinnamon
قرمزي [qurmuzij] *adj* scarlet
قرميد [qarmi:d] *n*
مكسو بالقرميد
[Makso bel-'qarmeed] *adj* tiled
قرن [qarn] *n* century, centenary
قرنبيط [qarnabi:tˤ] *n* broccoli
قريب [qari:b] *adj* near ◁ *n* relative
على نحو قريب
[Ala naḥw 'qareeb] *adv* nearby
قريب من
['qareeb men] *adj* close by
قريباً [qari:ban] *adv* shortly, soon
أراكم قريبا
[arakum 'qareeban] See you soon
قرية [qarja] *n* village
قزحية [quzaħijja] *n*
قزحية العين
['qazeḥeyat al-'ayn] *n* iris
قزم [qazam] *n* dwarf
قسّ [qiss] *n* vicar
قسم [qism] *n* section, oath, department
قسوة [qaswa] *n* cruelty
بقسوة
[Be'qaswah] *adv* roughly
يُوَبِخ بقسوة
[Yowabekh be-'qaswah] *v* spank
قسيس [qasi:s] *n* priest
قسيمة [qasi:ma] *n*
قسيمة هدية
['qaseemat hadeyah] *n* gift voucher
قش [qaʃʃ] *n* straw
كومة مضغوطة من القش
[Kawmah maḍghoṭah men al-'qash] *n* haystack
مسقوف بالقش
[Mas'qoof bel-'qash] *adj* thatched
قشدة [qiʃda] *n* cream
قشر [qaʃʃara] *vt* peel
قشرة [qiʃritu] *n*
قشرة الرأس
['qeshart al-raas] *n* dandruff
قشعريرة [quʃaʕri:ratun] *npl*
قشعريرة الجلد

['qash'aarerat al-jeld] *n* goose pimples
قص *n* [qasˤsˤ]
من فضلك أريد قص شعري وتجفيفه
[min faḍlak areed 'qaṣ sha'ary wa taj-fefaho] A cut and blow-dry, please
قصاصة slip *(paper)* *n* [qusˤaːsˤa]
قصبة reed *n* [qasˤaba]
قَصَبة الرِجْل
['qaṣabat al-rejl] *n* shin
قصة story *n* [qisˤsˤa]
قصة خيالية
['qeṣah khayaleyah] *n* fiction
قصة الشعر
['qaṣat al-sha'ar] *n* haircut
قصة شعر قصيرة
['qaṣat sha'ar] *n* crew cut
قصة قصيرة
['qeṣah 'qaṣeerah] *n* short story
قِصد mean *v* [qasˤada]
قَصْد *n* [qasˤd]
بدون قَصْد
[Bedoon 'qaṣd] *adv* inadvertently
قصر palace *n* [qasˤr]
بلاط القصر
[Balaṭ al-'qaṣr] *n* court
قصر ريفي
['qaṣr reefey] *n* stately home
هل القصر مفتوح للجمهور؟
[hal al-'qaṣir maf-tooḥ lel-jamhoor?] Is the palace open to the public?
قصف bomb *vt* [qasˤafa]
قصيدة poem *n* [qasˤiːda]
قصير short *adj* [qasˤiːr]
قصير الأكمام
['qaṣeer al-akmam] *adj* short-sleeved
قضائي *n* [qadˤaːʔijja]
دعوى قضائية
[Da'awa 'qaḍaeyah] *n* proceedings
قضمة bite *n* [qadˤma]
قضى spend *v* [qadˤaː]
قضيب rod *n* [qadˤiːb]
قضيب قياس العمق
['qaḍeeb 'qeyas al-'aom'q] *n* dipstick
قضية case *n* [qadˤijja]
قطار train *n* [qitˤaːr]
بطاقة للسفر بالقطار
[Beṭa'qah lel-safar bel-kharej] *n* railcard
كيف يمكن أن أركب القطار المتجه إلى...
[kayfa yamkin an arkab al- 'qetaar al-mutajih ela...?] Where can I get a train to...?
لم أتمكن من اللحاق بالقطار
[lam atamakan min al-leḥa'q bil-'qeṭaar] I've missed my train
متى يحين موعد القطار؟
[mata yaḥeen maw'aid al-'qeṭaar?] When is the train due?
ما هو أفضل طريق للذهاب إلى محطة القطار
[Ma howa af ḍal ṭaree'q lel-dhehab ela maḥaṭat al-'qeṭaar] What's the best way to get to the railway station?
ما هو موعد القطار التالي المتجه إلى...؟
[ma howa maw-'aid al-'qeṭaar al-taaly al-mutajih ela...?] When is the next train to...?
هل هذا هو القطار المتجه إلى...؟
[hal hadha howa al-'qeṭaar al-mutajeh ela...?] Is this the train for...?
قطاع sector *n* [qitˤaːʕ]
قطب pole *n* [qutˤb]
القطب الشمالي
[A'qoṭb al-shamaley] *n* North Pole
قطبي polar *adj* [qutˤbij]
الدب القطبي
[Al-dob al-shamaley] *n* polar bear
القارة القطبية الجنوبية
[Al-'qarah al-'qoṭbeyah al-janoobeyah] *n* Antarctic
قطبي جنوبي
['qoṭbey janoobey] *adj* Antarctic
قطبي شمالي
['qoṭbey shamaley] *adj* Arctic
قطة cat *n* [qitˤa]
قطر Qatar *n* [qatˤar]
قِطر drip *v* [qatˤara]
قَطْر *n* [qatˤr]
شاحنة قَطْر
[Shaḥenat 'qaṭr] *n* breakdown truck
قُطْر diameter *n* [qutˤr]
قطرة drop *n* [qatˤra]

قطرة للعين
['qaṭrah lel-'ayn] *n* eye drops
قطري [qutˤrij] *adj* diagonal
قطع [qitˤaʕ] *n* cutting
قطع غيار
['qaṭa'a gheyar] *n* spare part
قطع [qatˤaʕa] *v* cut
قطّع [qatˤtˤaʕa] *v*
يُقَطّع إلى شرائح
[Yo'qaṭe'a ela shraeḥ] *v* slice
يُقَطّع إلى شرائح
[Yo'qaṭe'a ela shraeḥ] *v* fillet
قطعة [qitˤʕa] *n* piece
قطعة أرض
['qeṭ'aat arḍ] *n* plot *(piece of land)*
قطعة غليظة قصيرة
['qet'aah ghaleḍhah] *n* chunk
قطن [qutˤn] *n* cotton wool
قطن طبى
['qoṭn ṭebey] *n* cotton wool
قطني [qutˤnijju] *adj*
رأس البرعم القطني
[Raas al-bor'aom al-'qaṭaney] *n* cotton bud
قعد [qaʕada] *vi* sit
قفاز [quffa:z] *n* glove
قفاز فرن
['qoffaz forn] *n* oven glove
قفاز يغطي الرسغ
['qoffaz yoghaṭey al-rasgh] *n* mitten
قفز [qafaza] *n* pop-up
قفز بالحبال
['qafz bel-ḥebal] *n* bungee jumping
قفز بالزانة
['qafz bel-zanah] *n* pole vault
قفز [qafaza] *vi* jump
قفزة [qafza] *n*
قفزة عالية
['qafzah 'aaleyah] *n* high jump
قفزة طويلة
['qafzah ṭaweelah] *n* long jump
قفص [qafasˤ] *n* cage
قفل [qufl] *n* padlock
قفل [qafala] *v* shut down ⊲ *vt* lock
قلادة [qila:da] *n* necklace, plaque
قلادة قصيرة
['qeladah 'qaṣeerah] *n* collar
قلاووظ [qala:wu:zˤ] *n*
لقد انفك المسمار القلاووظ
[La'qad anfak al-mesmar al-'qalawoḍh] The screw has come loose
قلاية [qala:jja] *n* frying pan
قلب [qalb] *n* heart
واقع في قلب المدينة
[Wa'qe'a fee 'qalb al-madeenah] *adv* downtown
أعاني من حالة مرضية في القلب
[o-'aany min ḥala maraḍiya fee al-'qalb] I have a heart condition
قلب [qalaba] *v* reverse
قلّب [qallaba] *vt* stir
قلبي [qalbijjat] *adj*
أزمة قلبية
[Azmah 'qalbeyah] *n* heart attack
قِلة [qilla] *n* shortfall
قلّد [qallada] *v* imitate
قلعة [qalʕa] *n* castle
قلعة من الرمال
['qal'aah men al-remal] *n* sandcastle
أيمكننا زيارة القلعة؟
[a-yamkun-ana zeyarat al-'qal'aa?] Can we visit the castle?
قلق [qalaq] *adj* restless, upset, worried ⊲ *n* trouble
قلق [qalaqa] *vi* worry, bother
قلل [qallala] *v* diminish, turn down
قلم [qalam] *n* pen
أقلام ملونة
[A'qlaam molawanah] *n* crayon
قلم رصاص
['qalam raṣaṣ] *n* pencil
قلم تحديد العينين
['qalam taḥdeed al-'ayn] *n* eyeliner
قلم حبر
['qalam ḥebr] *n* fountain pen
قلم حبر جاف
['qalam ḥebr jaf] *n* Biro®
قلم ذو سن من اللباد
['qalam dho sen men al-lebad] *n* felt-tip pen
هل يمكن أن أستعير منك أحد الأقلام؟
[hal yamken an asta-'aeer minka aḥad

al-a'qlaam?] Do you have a pen I could borrow?

قلنسوة hood *(car)* *n* [qulunsuwa]

قلى deep-fry, fry *v* [qala:]

قليل scarce *adj* [qali:l]

قماش cloth, fabric *n* [quma:ʃ]

قماش الرسم
['qomash al-rasm] *n* canvas

قماش الدنيم القطنى
['qomash al-deneem al-'qotney] *n* denim

قماش قطنى متين
['qomash 'qoṭ ney mateen] *n* corduroy

قماش مقلم
['qomash mo'qallem] *n* stripe

قماشة لغسل الأطباق
['qomash le-ghseel al-aṭbaa'q] *n* dishcloth

قمامة trash *n* [quma:ma]

أين تُوضع القمامة؟
[ayna toḍa'a al-'qemama?] Where do we leave the rubbish?

قمة peak, top *n* [qima]

مؤتمر قمة
[Moatamar 'qemmah] *n* summit

قمح wheat *n* [qamħ]

حساسية القمح
[Ḥasaseyah al-'qamḥ] *n* wheat intolerance

قمر moon *n* [qamar]

قمر صناعي
['qamar ṣenaaey] *n* satellite

قمع funnel *n* [qamʕ]

قمل lice *npl* [qamlun]

قميص shirt *n* [qami:sˤ]

أزرار كم القميص
[Azrar kom al'qameeṣ] *npl* cufflinks

قميص تحتي
['qameeṣ taḥtey] *n* slip *(underwear)*

قميص بولو
['qameeṣ bolo] *n* polo shirt

قميص قصير الكمين
['qameeṣ 'qaṣeer al-kmayen] *n* T-shirt

قميص من الصوف
['qameeṣ men al-ṣoof] *n* jersey

قميص نوم نسائي
['qamees noom nesaaey] *n* nightie

قناة canal *n* [qana:t]

قناع mask *n* [qina:ʕ]

قنبلة bomb *n* [qunbula]

قنبلة ذرية
['qobelah dhareyah] *n* atom bomb

قنبلة موقوتة
['qonbolah maw'qota] *n* timebomb

قنبيط cauliflower *n* [qanbi:tˤ]

قندس beaver *n* [qundus]

قنديل *n* [qindi:l]

قنديل البحر
['qandeel al-baḥr] *n* jellyfish

قنصل consul *n* [qunsˤul]

قنصلية consulate *n* [qunsˤulijja]

قنطرة arch *n* [qantˤara]

قنفذ hedgehog *n* [qunfuð]

قهر *v* [qahara]

لا يقهر
[La yo'qhar] *adj* unbeatable

قَهْقه giggle *v* [qahqaha]

قهوة coffee *n* [qahwa]

أبريق القهوة
[Abreeq al-'qahwah] *n* coffeepot

طاولة قهوة
[Ṭawlat 'qahwa] *n* coffee table

قهوة سادة
['qahwa sadah] *n* black coffee

قهوة منزوعة الكافيين
['qahwa manzo'aat al-kafayen] *n* decaffeinated coffee

قهوة باللبن من فضلك
['qahwa bil-laban min faḍlak] A white coffee, please

قهوة من فضلك
['qahwa min faḍlak] A coffee, please

هذه البقعة بقعة قهوة
[hathy al-bu'q-'aa bu'q-'aat 'qahwa] This stain is coffee

قوّا strengthen *v* [qawwa:]

قوة power, strength *n* [quwwa]

بقوة
[Be-'qowah] *adv* hard, strongly

قوة عسكرية
['qowah askareyah] *n* force

قوة الإرادة
['qowat al-eradah] *n* willpower

قوة العاملة
['qowah al-'aamelah] *n* workforce
قوة بشرية
['qowah bashareyah] *n* manpower
bow *(weapon)* *n* [qaws] **قوس**
قوس قزح
['qaws 'qazh] *n* rainbow
Caucasus *n* [qu:qa:z] **قُوقاز**
saying *n* [qawl] **قَوْل**
colon *n* [qu:lu:n] **قولون**
v [qawwama] **قوم**
هل يمكن أن أقوم بإجراء مكالمة دولية من هنا؟
[hal yamken an a'qoom be-ijraa mukalama dawleya min huna?] Can I phone internationally from here?
هل يمكن أن نقوم بعمل مخيم للمبيت هنا؟
[hal yamken an na'qoom be-'aamal mukhyam lel-mabeet huna?] Can we camp here overnight?
national *adj* [qawmijju] **قومي**
nationalism *n* [qawmijja] **قَوْمِيّة**
powerful, tough *adj* [qawij] **قوِي**
lead *(metal)* *n* [qija:da] **قيادة**
رُخْصَة القيادة
[Rokhṣat al-'qeyadah] *n* driving licence
سهل القيادة
[Sahl al-'qeyadah] *adj* manageable
عجلة القيادة اليمنى
['aajalat al-'qeyadah al-yomna] *n* right-hand drive
دَرْس القيادة
[Dars al-'qeyadah] *n* driving lesson
اختبار القيادة
[Ekhtebar al-'qeyadah] *n* driving test
القيادة تحت تأثير الكحول
[Al-'qeyadh taḥt taatheer al-koḥool] *n* drink-driving
معلم القيادة
[Mo'alem al-'qeyadh] *n* driving instructor
n [qija:s] **قياس**
وحدة قياس
[Weḥdat 'qeyas] *n* module
measurements *n* [qija:sa:t] **قياسات**
standard *adj* [qija:sij] **قياسي**
n [qija:m] **قيام**
أيمكنك القيام بذلك وأنا معك هنا؟
[a-yamkun-ika al-'qeyam be-dhalek wa ana ma'aka huna?] Can you do it while I wait?
نعم، أحب القيام بذلك
[na'aam, aḥib al-'qiyam be-dhalik] Yes, I'd love to
هل تفضل القيام بأي شيء غدا؟
[Hal tofaḍel al-'qeyam beay shaya ghadan?] Would you like to do something tomorrow?
harp *n* [qi:θa:ra] **قيثار**
pus *n* [qajħ] **قيح**
limit *n* [qajd] **قيد**
tie, restrict *v* [qajjada] **قيَّد**
carat *n* [qi:ra:tˤ] **قيراط**
n [qajqab] **قيقب**
أشجار القيقب
[Ashjaar al-'qay'qab] *n* maple
estimate *v* [qajjama] **قيَّم**
value *n* [qi:ma] **قيمة**
قيمة مالية
['qeemah maleyah] *n* worth

ك

ك [ka] *pron*

كما

[kama:] *prep* as

كائن [ka:ʔin] *adj* situated

كآبة [kaʔa:ba] *n* blues

كابل [ka:bil] *n* cable

كابوس [ka:bu:s] *n* nightmare

كابينة [ka:bi:na]

كابينة تليفون

[Kabeenat telefoon] *n* phonebox

كابينة الطاقم

[Kabbenat al-ṭa'qam] *n* cabin crew

كابينة من الدرجة الأولى

[kabeena min al-daraja al-o-la] a first-class cabin

كابينة من الدرجة العادية

[kabeena min al-daraja al-'aadiyah] a standard class cabin

كاتب [ka:tib] *n*

الكاتب

[Al-kateb] *n* writer

كاتب مسرحي

[Kateb masrḥey] *n* playwright

كاتدرائية [ka:tidra:ʔijja] *n* cathedral

متى تفتح الكاتدرائية؟

[mata tuftaḥ al-katid-ra-eya?] When is the cathedral open?

كاتشب [ka:tʃub] *n* ketchup

كاثوليكي [ka:θu:li:kij] *adj* Catholic

روماني كاثوليكي

[Romaney katholeykey] *adj* Roman Catholic

شخص كاثوليكي

[Shakhṣ katholeykey] *n* Catholic

كَارْبُوهَيْدْرَات [ka:rbu:hajdra:t] *n* carbohydrate

كارت [ka:rt] *n*

كارت إعادة الشحن

[Kart e'aadat shaḥn] *n* top-up card

كارت سحب

[Kart sahb] *n* debit card

كارت تليفون

[Kart telefone] *n* cardphone

كارت ائتمان

[Kart eateman] *n* credit card

كارت الكريسماس

[Kart al-kresmas] *n* Christmas card

كارت ذاكرة

[Kart dhakerah] *n* memory card

أريد كارت للمكالمات الدولية من فضلك

[areed kart lel-mukalamat al-dawleya min faḍlak] An international phonecard, please

أين يمكن أن اشتري كارت للهاتف؟

[ayna yamken an ash-tary kart lil-haatif?] Where can I buy a phonecard?

كارتون [ka:rtu:n] *n*

علبة كارتون

['aolbat kartoon] *n* carton

كارثه [ka:riθa] *n* disaster

كارثي [ka:riθij] *adj* disastrous

كاري [ka:ri:] *n* curry

مسحوق الكاري

[Masḥoo'q alkaarey] *n* curry powder

كاريبي [ka:rajbi:] *adj* Caribbean

البحر الكاريبي

[Al-baḥr al-kareebey] *n* Caribbean

كازاخستان [ka:za:xista:n] *n* Kazakhstan

كازينو [ka:zi:nu:] *n* casino

كأس [kaʔs] *n*
كأس العالم
[Kaas al-'aalam] *n* World Cup
كأس من البيرة من فضلك
[kaas min al-beera min faḍlak] A draught beer, please
كاسيت [ka:si:t] *n* cassette
كاش [ka:ʃ] *n*
ماكينة تسجيل الكاش
[Makenat tasjeel al-kaash] *n* till
كاف [ka:fin] *adj* efficient, enough
كافح [ka:faħa] *v* struggle
كافي [ka:fi:] *adj*
غير كافي
[Ghayr kafey] *adj* insufficient
كافيتريا [kafijtirja:] *n* cafeteria
كافين [ka:fi:n] *n* caffeine
كافيين [ka:faji:n] *n*
منزوع منه الكافيين
[Manzoo'a menh al-kafayeen] *adj* decaffeinated
كاكاو [ka:ka:w] *n* cocoa
كالسيوم [ka:lsju:m] *n* calcium
كامبوديا [ka:mbu:dja:] *n* Cambodia
كامل [ka:mil] *adj* complete
على نحو كامل
[Ala naḥw kaamel] *adv* perfectly
بدوام كامل
[Bedawam kaamel] *adv* full-time
بشكل كامل
[Beshakl kaamel] *adv* entirely
شراء كامل
[Sheraa kaamel] *n* buyout
كاميرا [ka:mi:ra:] *n* camera
كاميرا رقمية
[Kameera ra'qmeyah] *n* digital camera
كاميرا الانترنت
[Kamera al-enternet] *n* webcam
كاميرا فيديو
[Kamera fedyo] *n* video camera
كاميرا فيديو نقال
[Kamera fedyo na'q'qaal] *n* camcorder
هل يمكن أن أحصل على شريط فيديو لهذه الكاميرا من فضلك؟
[hal yamken an aḥṣal 'aala shar-eeṭ video le- hadhy al-kamera min faḍlak?] Can I have a tape for this video camera, please?
هناك التصاق بالكاميرا
[hunaka el-tiṣaa'q bel-kamera] My camera is sticking
كان [ka:na] *v* be
كاهن [ka:hin] *n* minister *(clergy)*
كئيب [kaʔijb] *adj* gloomy
كِباب [kaba:b] *n* kebab
كَبْح [kabħ] *n* inhibition
كبد [kabid] *n* liver
التهاب الكبد
[El-tehab al-kabed] *n* hepatitis
كبسولة [kabsu:la] *n* capsule
كبش [kabʃ] *n* ram
كبير [kabi:r] *adj* big, mega
إنه كبير جدا
[inaho kabeer jedan] It's too big
كتاب [kita:b] *n* book
كتاب دراسي
[Ketab derasey] *n* textbook
كتاب العبارات
[Ketab al-'aebarat] *n* phrasebook
كتاب الكتروني
[Ketab elektrooney] *n* e-book
كتاب طهى
[Ketab ṭahey] *n* cookery book
كتاب مدرسي
[Ketab madrasey] *n* schoolbook
كتاب هزلي
[Ketab hazaley] *n* comic book
كتاب ورقي الغلاف
[Ketab wara'qey al-gholaf] *n* paperback
كتابة [kita:ba] *n* writing
كتالوج [kata:lu:ʒ] *n* catalogue
أريد مشاهدة الكتالوج
[areed mu-shahadat al-kataloj] I'd like a catalogue
كتان [katta:n] *n* linen
كتب [kataba] *v* write
كتب بسرعة
[Katab besor'aah] *v* jot down
كتف [katif] *n* shoulder
كتف طريق صلب
[Katef ṭaree'q ṣalb] *n* hard shoulder
لَوْح الكَتِف

[Looh al-katef] *n* shoulder blade
لقد أصبت في كتفي
[la'qad oṣibto fee katfee] I've hurt my shoulder
كتكوت chick *n* [kutku:t]
كتلة block *(solid piece)* *n* [kutla]
كُتلة خشبية أو حجرية
[Kotlah khashebeyah aw hajareyah] *n* block *(obstruction)*
كتوم sly *adj* [katu:m]
كتيب pamphlet, booklet *n* [kutajjib]
كتيب إعلاني
[Kotayeb e'alaaney] *n* leaflet
كتيب ملاحظات
[Kotayeb molaḥaḍhat] *n* notepad
كُتَيِّب الإرشادات
[Kotayeb al-ershadat] *n* guidebook
كثافة density *n* [kaθa:fa]
كثير many, much *adj* [kaθi:r]
لا تقم بقص الكثير منه
[la ta'qum be-'qaṣ al-katheer minho] Don't cut too much off
يوجد به الكثير من...
[yujad behe al-kather min...] There's too much... in it
كثيرا much *adv* [kaθi:ran]
كثيف dense *adj* [kaθi:f]
كحة *n* [kuħħa]
أعاني من الكحة
[o-'aany min al-kaḥa] I have a cough
كحول alcohol *n* [kuħu:l]
خالي من الكحول
[Khaley men al-koḥool] *adj* alcohol-free
القيادة تحت تأثير الكحول
[Al-'qeyadh taḥt taatheer al-koḥool] *n* drink-driving
قليلة الكحول
['qaleelat al-koḥool] *adj* low-alcohol
أنا لا أشرب الكحول
[ana la ashrab al-koḥool] I don't drink alcohol
معي كمية من الكحول لا تزيد عن الكمية المصرح بها
[ma'ay kam-iya min al-kuḥool la tazeed 'aan al-kam-iya al-muṣa-raḥ beha] I have the allowed amount of alcohol to declare
هل يحتوى هذا على الكحول؟
[hal yaḥ-tawy hadha 'aala al-kiḥool?] Does that contain alcohol?
كحولي alcoholic *adj* [kuħu:lij]
كدح fag *n* [kadaħ]
كدمة bruise *n* [kadama]
كذّاب liar *n* [kaða:b]
كذّب lie *v* [kaððaba]
كذبة lie *n* [kiðba]
كراتيه karate *n* [kara:ti:h]
كرامة dignity *n* [kara:ma]
كربون carbon *n* [karbu:n]
كربونات *n* [karbu:na:t]
ثاني كربونات الصوديوم
[Thaney okseed al-karboon] *n* bicarbonate of soda
كرة ball *(toy)* *n* [kura]
الكرة الأرضية
[Al-korah al-ardheyah] *n* globe
كرة صغيرة
[Korat ṣagheerah] *n* pellet
كرة السلة
[Korat al-salah] *n* basketball
كرة الشبكة
[Korat al-shabakah] *n* netball
كرة القدم
[Korat al-'qadam] *n* football
كرة القدم الأمريكية
[Korat al-'qadam al-amreekeyah] *n* American football
كرة اليد
[Korat al-yad] *n* handball
كرة لحم
[Korat laḥm] *n* meatball
كرر *v* [karrara]
كرر ما قلت، إذا سمحت
[kar-ir ma 'qulta, edha samaḥt] Could you repeat that, please?
كَرر rehearse *v* [karara]
كرَز cherry *n* [karaz]
كرسي chair *(furniture)* *n* [kursij]
كرسي بعجلات
[Korsey be-'ajalat] *n* wheelchair
كرسي بجوار الممر
[Korsey be-jewar al-mamar] *n* aisle seat

كرسي بلا ظهر أو ذراعين
[Korsey bela ḍhahr aw dhera'aayn] *n* stool
كرسي مريح
[Korsey moreeḥ] *n* easy chair
كرسي مزود بذراعين
[Korsey mozawad be-dhera'aayn] *n* armchair
كرسي هَزَّاز
[Korsey hazzaz] *n* rocking chair
كُرْسي مُرتَفِع
[Korsey mortafe'a] *n* highchair
هل توجد كراسي عالية للأطفال؟
[hal tojad kursy 'aaleya lil-aṭfaal?] Do you have a high chair?
كرفس [kurfus] *n* celery
كَرَم [karam] *n* generosity
كَرْم [karm] *n* vineyard
كرميل [karami:l] *n* caramel
كرنب [kurnub] *n* cabbage
كرنب بروكسيل
[Koronb brokseel] *n* Brussels sprouts
كرنفال [karnafa:l] *n* carnival
كره [kareha] *v* dislike
كرواتي [kruwa:tijjat] *adj* Croatian
⊲ *n* *(person)* Croatian
اللغة الكرواتية
[Al-loghah al-korwateyah] *n* *(language)* Croatian
كرواتيا [karwa:tja:] *n* Croatia
كريسماس [kri:sma:s] *n* Xmas
كريكيت [kri:ki:t] *n*
لعبة الكريكيت
[Lo'abat al-kreeket] *n* cricket *(game)*
كريم [kri:m] *n*
كريم الحلاقة
[Kereem al-helaka] *n* shaving cream
كريم للشفاه
[Kereem lel shefah] *n* lip salve
أريد تناول آيس كريم
[areed tanawil ice kreem] I'd like an ice cream
كريمة [kri:matu] *n*
كريمة شيكولاتة
[Kareemat shekolatah] *n* mousse
كريمة مخفوقة
[Keremah makhfoo'qah] *n* whipped cream
كريمي [kri:mi:] *adj* cream
كريه [kari:ħ] *adj* nasty, wicked
كزبرة [kuzbara] *n* coriander *(seed)*
كسارة [kassa:ra] *n*
كسارة الجوز
[Kasarat al-jooz] *n* cracker
كِسترد [kustard] *n* custard
كَسْتِناء [kastana:ʔ] *n* chestnut
كسر [kasr] *n* fracture
غير قابل للكسر
[Ghayr 'qabel lelkasr] *adj* unbreakable
قابل للكسر
['qabel lel-kassr] *adj* fragile
كسر [kasara] *vt* break, snap
كِسْرة [kisra] *n*
كِسْرة خبز
[Kesrat khobz] *n* crumb
كسرولة [kasru:latu] *n* casserole
كسول [kasu:l] *adj* lazy
كسيح [kasi:ħ] *adj* lame
كشاف [kaʃʃa:f] *n* scout
كشاف كهربائي
[Kashaf kahrabaey] *n* torch
كشر [kaʃʃara] *v* grin
كشف [kaʃf] *n*
كشف بنكي
[Kashf bankey] *n* bank statement
كشف [kzʃafa] *v*
يَكْشِف عن
[Yakshef 'an] *v* bare
كشك [kiʃk] *n* kiosk
كشمش [kuʃmuʃ] *n* gooseberry
كِشمِش [kiʃmiʃ] *n*
كِشمِش أسود
[Keshmesh aswad] *n* blackcurrant
كعب [kaʕb] *n* heel
كعب عالى
[Ka'ab 'aaaley] *adj* high-heeled
كعوب عالية
[Ko'aoob 'aleyah] *npl* high heels
كعك [kaʕk] *n* cake
كعكة [kaʕka] *n* bun
كعكات محلاة مقلية
[Ka'akat moḥallah ma'qleyah] *n*

doughnut
كف [kaff] n
كف الحيوان
[Kaf al-ḥayawaan] n paw
كفؤ [kufuʔ] adj
غير كفؤ
[Ghayr kofa] adj incompetent
كفاح [kifa:ħ] n struggle
كفالة [kafa:la] n bail, warranty
كفتي [kafatajj] adj
كفتي الميزان
[Kafatay al-meezan] n scales
كفل [kafala] v ensure
كفى [kafa:] v
هذا يكفي شكرًا لك
[hatha ykfee shukran laka] That's enough, thank you
كل [kulla] pron all
بكل تأكيد
[Bekol taakeed] adv absolutely
كل يوم سبت
[kul yawm sabit] every Saturday
كلًا [kula:an] adj
كلًا من
[Kolan men] adj both
كلارينت [kla:ri:nit] n clarinet
كلاسيكي [kla:si:kij] adj classic,
classic n ◁ classical
كلام [kala:m] n talk
فاقد القدرة على الكلام
[Fa'qed al-'qodrah 'aala al-kalam] adj speechless
كلاهما [kila:huma:] pron both
كلب [kalb] n dog, bitch (female dog)
كلب ترير
[Kalb tereer] n terrier
كلب اسكتلندى ضخم
[Kalb eskotalandey dakhm] n collie
كلب الراعي
[Kalb al-ra'aey] n sheepdog
كلب السبنيلي
[Kalb al-sebneeley] n spaniel
كلب بِكِيني
[Kalb bekkeeney] n Pekinese
كلب هادي مدرب للمكفوفين
[Kalb hadey modarab lel-makfoofeen] n guide dog
وجار الكلب
[Wejaar alkalb] n kennel
لدي كلب يرشدني في السير
[la-daya kalb yar-shidiny fee al-sayr] I have a guide dog
كَلّف [kallafa] v cost
كلمة [kalima] n word
كلمة السر
[Kelmat al-ser] n password
كلمة واحدة فقط
[kilema waḥeda fa'qaṭ] all one word
ما هي الكلمة التي تعني...؟
[ma heya al-kalema al-laty ta'any...?] What is the word for...?
كلور [klu:r] n chlorine
كلية [kulijja] n
كلية الحقوق
[Kolayt al-ho'qooq] n law school
كلية الفنون
[Koleyat al-fonoon] n art school
كُلِيَة [kulijjatan] adv well
كُلِية [kulijja] n college
كُلْيَة [kilja] n kidney
كم [kumm] n sleeve
بدون أكمام
[Bedon akmaam] adj sleeveless
كما [kama:] conj
كما
[kama:] prep as
كمَّاشة [kamma:ʃa] n pliers
كمال [kama:l] n
كمال الأجسام
[Kamal al-ajsaam] npl bodybuilding
كماليات [kama:lijja:t] n accessory
كمان [kama:n] n violin
عازف الكمان
['aazef al-kaman] n violinist
آلة الكَمَان الموسيقية
[Aalat al-kaman al-moose'qeyah] n violin
كمبودي [kambu:dij] adj Cambodian
شخص كمبودي
[Shakhṣ kamboodey] (person) n Cambodian
كمبيوتر [kumbiju:tar] n computer

هل لي أن استخدم الكمبيوتر الخاص بك؟
[hal lee an astakhdim al-computer al-khaaṣ bik?] May I use your computer?
كُمِّثري pear *n* [kummiθra:]
كمنجة violin *n* [kamanʒa]
كمنجة كبيرة
[Kamanjah kabeerah] *n* cello
كَمّون cumin *n* [kammu:n]
كمية quantity *n* [kammija]
كمين ambush *n* [kami:n]
كناري canary *adj* [kana:rij]
طائر الكناري
[Ṭaaer al-kanarey] *n* canary
طيور الكناري
[tˤuju:ru al-kana:rijji] *n* Canaries
كناسة *n* [kanna:sati]
جاروف الكناسة
[Jaroof al-kannasah] *n* dustpan
كنبة sofa *n* [kanaba]
كنبة سرير
[Kanabat sereer] *n* sofa bed
كندا Canada *n* [kanada:]
كندي Canadian *n* [kanadij]
شخص كندي
[Shakhṣ kanadey] *n* Canadian
كنز treasure *n* [kanz]
كنس sweep *v* [kanasa]
يَكْنِس بالمكنسة الكهربائية
[Yaknes bel-maknasah al-kahrabaeyah] *v* vacuum
كُنْغُر kangaroo *n* [kanɣur]
كنية nickname *n* [kinja]
كنيسة church *n* [kani:sa]
كنيسة صغيرة
[Kanesah ṣagherah] *n* chapel
كنيسة معمدانية
[Kaneesah me'amedaneyah] *n* Baptist
أيمكننا زيارة الكنيسة؟
[a-yamkun-ana zeyarat al-kaneesa] Can we visit the church?
كهرباء electricity *n* [kahraba:ʔ]
مشتغل بالكهرباء
[Moshtaghel bel-kahrabaa] *n* electrician
لا توجد كهرباء
[la tojad kah-rabaa] There is no electricity
هل يحب علينا دفع مصاريف إضافية للكهرباء؟
[hal yajib 'aala-yna daf'a maṣa-reef eḍafiya lel-kah-rabaa?] Do we have to pay extra for electricity?
كهربائي electrical *adj* [kahraba:ʔij]
صَدْمَة كهربائية
[Ṣadmah kahrbaeyah] *n* electric shock
سِلك كهربائي
[Selk kahrabaey] (لي) *n* flex
بطانية كهربائية
[Baṭaneyah kahrobaeyah] *n* electric blanket
كهربي *adj* [kahrabij]
انقطاع التيار الكهربي
[En'qetaa'a al-tayar alkahrabey] *n* power cut
أين توجد علبة المفاتيح الكهربية
[ayna tojad 'ailbat al-mafateeḥ al-kahraba-eya?] Where is the fusebox?
هل لديك أي بطاريات كهربية؟
[hal ladyka ay baṭa-reyaat?] Do you have any batteries?
هناك خطأ ما في الوصلات الكهربية
[hunaka khaṭaa ma fee al-waslaat al-kah-rabiya] There is something wrong with the electrics
كهرمان amber *n* [kahrama:n]
كهف cave *n* [kahf]
كهل middle-aged *adj* [kahl]
كهنوت ministry *(religion)* *n* [kahnu:t]
كهولي elderly *adj* [kuhu:lij]
كوب *n* [ku:b]
كوب من الماء
[koob min al-maa] a glass of water
كوبا Cuba *n* [ku:ba:]
كوبي Cuban *n* ◁ Cuban *adj* [ku:bij]
كوخ cabin, hut *n* [ku:x]
كوخ لقضاء العطلة
[Kookh le-'qadaa al-'aotlah] *n* cottage
كود *n* [ku:du]
كود الاتصال بمنطقة أو بلد
[Kod al-eteṣal bemanṭe'qah aw balad] *n* dialling code

كُروم [ku:ru:mu] *n* chrome
كوري [ku:rijjat] *adj* Korean ◁ *n* Korean *(person)*
اللغة الكورية
[Al-loghah al-koreyah] *(language) n* Korean
كوريا [ku:rja:] *n* Korea
كوريا الشمالية
[Koreya al-shamaleyah] *n* North Korea
كوسة [ku:sa] *n* zucchini
كوستاريكا [ku:sta:ri:ka:] *n* Costa Rica
كوسوفو [ku:su:fu:] *n* Kosovo
كوكايين [ku:ka:ji:n] *n* cocaine
كوكب [kawkab] *n* planet
كوكبة [kawkaba] *n*
كوكبة القوس والرامي
[Kawkabat al-'qaws wa alramey] *n* Sagittarius
كوكتيل [ku:kti:l] *n* cocktail
أتقدمون الكوكتيلات؟
[a-tu'qade-moon al-koktailaat?] Do you sell cocktails?
كولِسْتِرُول [ku:listiru:l] *n* cholesterol
كولومبي [ku:lu:mbi:] *adj* Colombian
شخص كولومبي
[Shakhṣ kolombey] *n* Colombian
كولومبيا [ku:lu:mbija:] *n* Colombia
كولونيل [ku:lu:ni:l] *n* colonel
كومة [ku:ma] *n* heap
كومة منتظم
[Komat montaḍhem] *n* stack
كومودينو [ku:mu:di:nu:] *n* bedside table
كوميديا [ku:mi:dja:] *n* comedy
كوميديا الموقف
[Komedya al-maw'qf] *n* sitcom
كَوْن [kawn] *n* universe
كونتينتال [ku:nti:nunta:l] *adj*
إفطار كونتينتال
[Efṭaar kontenental] *n* continental breakfast
كوى [kawa:] *v* iron
كويتي [kuwajtij] *adj* Kuwaiti ◁ *n* Kuwaiti
كيّ [kajj] *n*
كيّ الملابس
[Kay almalabes] *n* ironing
لوح الكي
[Looḥ alkay] *n* ironing board
كيرجستان [ki:raʒista:n] *n* Kyrgyzstan
كيروسين [ki:runwsi:n] *n* kerosene
كيس [ki:s] *n* sack *(container)*
كيس التسوق
[Kees al-tasawo'q] *n* shopping bag
كيس النوم
[Kees al-nawm] *n* sleeping bag
كيس بلاستيكي
[Kees belasteekey] *n* plastic bag
كيس مشتريات
[Kees moshtarayat] *n* shopping bag
كيف [kajfa] *adv* how
كيف حالك؟
[kayfa ḥaluka?] How are you?
كيف يمكن أن أصل إلى هناك؟
[kayfa yamkin an aṣal ela hunaak?] How do I get there?
كيلو [ki:lu:] *n* kilo
كيلومتر [ki:lu:mitr] *n* kilometre
كيمياء [ki:mija:ʔ] *n* chemistry
كيمياء حيوية
[Kemyaa ḥayaweyah] *n* biochemistry
كيميائي [ki:mija:ʔij] *adj* pharmacist
معمل كيميائي
[M'amal kemyaeay] *n* pharmacy
مادة كيميائية
[Madah kemyaeyah] *n* chemical
كيني [ki:nij] *adj* Kenyan
شخص كيني
[Shakhs keeny] *n* Kenyan
كينيا [ki:nja:] *n* Kenya
كيوي [ki:wi:] *n*
طائر الكيوي
[Ṭaarr alkewey] *n* kiwi

ل [li] *prep*
لأن
[liʔanna] *conj* because
لا [laː] *adv* no, not
لائم [laːʔama] *v* suit
لاتيفي [laːtiːfiː] *adj* Latvian
اللغة اللاتيفية
[Al-loghah al-atefeyah] *(language) n* Latvian
شخص لاتيفي
[Shakhs lateefey] *(person) n* Latvian
لاتيفيا [laːtiːfjaː] *n* Latvia
لاتيني [laːtiːniː] *adj* Latin ⊲ *n* Latin
أمريكا اللاتينية
[Amreeka al-lateeneyah] *n* Latin America
لاجئ [laːʒiʔ] *n* refugee
لأجل [liʔaʒli] *prep* for
لاحظ [laːħazˤa] *v* observe
أعتذر، لم ألاحظ ذلك
[A'atadher, lam olaḥeḍh dhalek] Sorry, I didn't catch that
لاحق [laːħiq] *adj* following
سوف أتصل بك لاحقا
[sawfa ataṣil beka laḥi'qan] I'll call back later
هل يجب أن أدفع الآن أم لاحقا؟
[hal yajib an adfa'a al-aan am la-ḥe'qan?] Do I pay now or later?
هل يمكن أن أعود في وقت لاحق؟
[hal yamken an a'aood fee wa'qt la-ḥi'q?] Shall I come back later?
لاحق [laːħaqa] *v* pursue
يلاحق خطوة بخطوة
[Yolaḥek khoṭwa bekhoṭwah] *v* keep up
لاحقاً [laːħiqan] *adv* eventually
لاصق [laːsˤiq] *adj*
شريط لاصق
[Shreeṭ laṣe'q] *n* Sellotape®
لاصقة [laːsˤiqa] *n*
أريد بعض اللاصقات الطبية
[areed ba'aḍ al-laṣi-'qaat al-ṭub-iya] I'd like some plasters
لاطَف [laːtˤafa] *v* stroke
لاعب [laːʕib] *n* player *(of a sport)*
لاعب رياضي
[La'aeb reyaḍey] *n* athlete
لاعب كرة القدم
[La'aeb korat al-'qadam] *n* footballer
لافت [laːfit] *adj*
لافت للنظر
[Lafet lel-nadhar] *adj* striking
لافتة [laːfita] *n* sign
لافتة طريق
[Lafetat ṭaree'q] *n* road sign
لافندر [laːfandar] *n* lavender
لؤلؤة [luʔluʔa] *n* pearl
لام [laːm] *v* blame
لامع [laːmiʕ] *adj* shiny, vivid
لأن [liʔanna] *conj*
لأن
[liʔanna] *conj* because
لاهوت [laːhuːt] *n* theology
لاووس [laːwuːs] *n*
جمهورية لاووس
[Jomhoreyat lawoos] *n* Laos
لايصدق [laːjusˤaddaq] *adj* unbelievable
لإيْلاكْ [laːjlaːk] *n* lilac
لُبّ [lubb] *n* core
لبؤة [labuʔa] *n* lioness
لباد [libaːd] *n* felt
لباس [libaːs] *n* style
لباس الاستحمام
[Lebas al-estehmam] *n* swimming

costume
لباقة tact *n* [laba:qa]
لبس dress *vi* [labasa]
لبق tactful, graceful *adj* [labiq]
غير لبق
[Ghaey labe'q] *adj* tactless
لبْلاب ivy *n* [labla:b]
لَبن *n* [laban]
لبن أطفال
[Laban aṭfaal] *n* formula
لبن مبستر
[Laban mobaster] *n* UHT milk
مصنع منتجات الألبان
[maṣna'a montajat al-alban] *n* dairy
منتجات الألبان
[Montajat al-baan] *npl* dairy products
إنه منتج بلبن غير مبستر
[inaho muntaj be-laban ghayr mubastar] Is it made with unpasteurised milk?
لبنان Lebanon *n* [lubna:n]
لبناني Lebanese *adj* [lubna:nij]
لبون mammal *n* [labu:n]
لتر litre *n* [litr]
لَثة gum *n* [laθatt]
لثتي تنزف
[lathaty tanzuf] My gums are bleeding
لجأ *v* [laʒaʔa]
لجأ إلى
[Lajaa ela] *v* resort to
لجَام reins *n* [liʒa:m]
لَجنة committee *n* [laʒna]
لَحاء bulb *(plant)* *n* [liħa:ʔ]
لحاف quilt *n* [liħa:f]
لحظة moment *n* [laħzˤa]
كل لحظة
[Kol laḥḍhah] *adv* momentarily
لحظة واحدة من فضلك
[laḥḍha waheda min faḍlak] Just a moment, please
لحق ب catch up *n* [laħiqa bi]
لحم meat *n* [laħm]
شرائح اللحم البقري المشوي
[Shraeḥ al-laḥm al-ba'qarey al-mashwey] *n* beefburger
كرة لحم
[Korat laḥm] *n* meatball
لحم أحمر
[Laḥm aḥmar] *n* red meat
لحم ضأن
[Lahm ḍaan] *n* mutton
لحم عجل
[Laḥm 'aejl] *n* veal
لحم غزال
[Laḥm ghazal] *n* venison
لحم خنزير مقدد
[Laḥm khanzeer me'qaded] *n* bacon
لحم بقري
[Laḥm ba'qarey] *n* beef
لحم مفروم
[Laḥm mafroom] *n* mince
لا أتناول اللحوم الحمراء
[la ata- nawal al-liḥoom al-ḥamraa] I don't eat red meat
لا أحب تناول اللحوم
[la aḥib ta-nawal al-liḥoom] I don't like meat
لا أكل اللحوم
[la aakul al-liḥoom] I don't eat meat
ما هي الأطباق التي لا تحتوي على لحوم أو أسماك؟
[ma heya al-aṭba'q al-laty la taḥtawy 'aala liḥoom aw asmak?] Which dishes have no meat / fish?
لحن melody *n* [laħn]
لحن منفرد
[Laḥn monfared] *n* concerto
لِحية beard *n* [liħja]
لَخْبط shuffle *v* [lxbatˤa]
لختنشتاين *n* [lixtunʃta:jan] Liechtenstein
لَخّص summarize *v* [laxxasˤa]
لدغ sting *v* [ladaɣa]
لقد لدغت
[la'qad lode'q-to] I've been stung
لدغة sting *n* [ladɣa]
لذيذ *adj* [laði:ð]
لذيذ المذاق
[Ladheedh al-madha'q] *adj* tasty
كان مذاقه لذيذًا
[kan madha-'qoho ladhe-dhan] That was delicious
كان هذا لذيذًا

[kan hadha ladhe-dhan] That was delicious
لزج sticky *adj* [laziʒ]
لسان tongue *n* [lisaːn]
لسع bite *v* [lasaʕa]
لص thief *n* [lisˤsˤ]
لص المنازل
[Leṣ al-manazel] *n* burglar
لصقة *n* [lasˤqa]
لصقة طبية
[Laṣ'qah ṭebeyah] *n* Band-Aid
لَطخ stain *v* [latˤtˤaxa]
لطخة stain, smudge *n* [latˤxa]
لطف kindness *n* [lutˤf]
لطفاً kindly *adv* [lutˤfan]
لطمة blow *n* [latˤma]
لطيف mild, nice, tender *adj* [latˤiːf]
لُعَاب saliva *n* [luʕaːb]
لعب play *n* [laʕib]
لعب play *(in sports)* *vt* [laʕaba]
أين يمكنني أن ألعب التنس؟
[ayna yamken-any an al-'aab al-tanis?] Where can I play tennis?
لعبة toy *n* [luʕba]
لعبة رمي السهام
[Lo'abat ramey al-seham] *npl* darts
لعبة ترفيهية
[Lo'abah trafeheyah] *n* amusement arcade
لعبة الاستغماية
[Lo'abat al-estoghomayah] *n* hide-and-seek
لعبة البولنغ العشرية
[Lo'aba al-boolenj al-'ashreyah] *n* tenpin bowling
لعبة البولينج
[Lo'aba al-boolenj] *n* tenpin bowling
لعبة الكريكيت
[Lo'abat al-kreeket] *n* cricket *(game)*
لعبة الكترونية
[Lo'abah elektroneyah] *n* computer game
لعبة طاولة
[Lo'abat ṭawlah] *n* board game
لعَق lick *v* [laʕaqa]
لَعَّل perhaps *adv* [laʕalla]
لعنة curse *n* [laʕna]
لعوب cheerful *adj* [laʕuːb]
لعين damn *adj* [laʕiːnu]
لغة language *n* [luɣa]
اللغة الصينية
[Al-loghah al-ṣeeneyah] *(language)* *n* Chinese
اللغة الأرمنية
[Al-loghah al-armeeneyah] *(language)* *n* Armenian
اللغة الألبانية
[Al-loghah al-albaneyah] *(language)* *n* Albanian
اللغة العربية
[Al-loghah al-arabeyah] *(language)* *n* Arabic
اللغة التشيكية
[Al-loghah al-teshekeyah] *(language)* *n* Czech
اللغة الباسكية
[Al-loghah al-bakestaneyah] *(language)* *n* Basque
اللغة البلغارية
[Al-loghah al-balghareyah] *(language)* *n* Bulgarian
اللغة البورمية
[Al-loghah al-bormeyah] *(language)* *n* Burmese
اللغة البيلاروسية
[Al-loghah al-belaroseyah] *(language)* *n* Belarussian
اللغة الفنلندية
[Al-loghah al-fenlandeyah] *n* Finnish
اللغة الكرواتية
[Al-loghah al-korwateyah] *(language)* *n* Croatian
مُفردات اللغة
[Mofradat Al-loghah] *npl* vocabulary
لغز puzzle *n* [luɣz]
لغوي linguistic *adj* [luɣawij]
لفّ roll *vi* [laffa]
لفّ go round *v*
لفاع scarf *n* [lifaːʕ]
لفت turnip *n* [laft]
نبات اللفت
[Nabat al-left] *n* rape *(plant)*
لَفّة roll *n* [laffa]

لفحة [lafħa] n blast
لقاء [liqa:ʔ] n
إلى اللقاء
[ela al-le'qaa] excl bye-bye!
إلى اللقاء
[ela al-le'qaa] Goodbye
لقاح [liqa:ħ] n pollen
لِقب [laqab] n surname, title
لَقّح [laqqaħa] v vaccinate
لقطة [laqtˤa] n
لقطة فوتوغرافية
[La'qṭah fotoghrafeyah] n snapshot
لكسمبورغ [luksambu:rɣ] n Luxembourg
لكل [likulli] prep per
لكم [lakama] v poke
لمبة [lamba] n
اللمبة لا تضئ
[al-lumbah la-tuḍee] The lamp is not working
لمح [lamaħa] v glance
لمحة [lamħa] n glance
لمس [lams] n
لوحة اللمس
[Lawḥat al-lams] n touchpad
لمس [lamasa] v touch
لمَع [lamaʕa] v shine
لندن [lund] n London
لهب [lahab] n flame
لهجة [lahʒa] n dialect
لِهو [lahw] n fun
لَوّث [lawwaθa] v pollute
لوح [lawħ] n board (wood)
لوح صلب
[Looḥ ṣolb] n hardboard
لوح غطس
[Looḥ ghaṭs] n diving board
لوح الركمجة
[Looḥ al-rakmajah] n surfboard
لوح الكي
[Looḥ alkay] n ironing board
لَوّح [lawwaħa] v wave
لوحة [lawħa] n tablet, painting
لوحة الأرقام
[Looḥ al-ar'qaam] n number plate
لوحة الفأرة
[Looḥat al-faarah] n mouse mat
لوحة الملاحظات
[Looḥat al-molahḍhat] n notice board
لوحة النشرات
[Looḥat al-nasharaat] n notice board
لوحة بيضاء
[Looḥ bayḍaa] n whiteboard
لوحة مفاتيح
[Looḥat mafateeḥ] n keyboard
لوحة مفاتيح تحكم
[Looḥat mafateeḥ taḥakom] n switchboard
لوري [lu:ri:] n
شاحِنة لوري
[Shaḥenah loorey] n truck
لوز [lawz] n almond
لوزة [lawza] n
التهاب اللوزتين
[Eltehab al-lawzateyn] n tonsillitis
لوزتين [lawzatajni] npl tonsils
لوشن [lawʃan] n
لوشن بعد التعرض للشمس
[Loshan b'ad al-t'aroḍ lel shams] n after-sun lotion
لوكيميا [lu:ki:mja:] n leukaemia
لوم [lawm] n blame
لون [lawn] n colour
لون مائي
[Lawn maaey] n watercolour
أنا لا أحب هذا اللون
[ana la oḥibo hadha al-lawn] I don't like the colour
بالألوان
[bil-al-waan] in colour
هذا اللون من فضلك
[hatha al-lawn min faḍlak] This colour, please
هل يوجد لون آخر غير ذلك اللون؟
[hal yujad lawn aakhar ghayr dhalika al-lawn?] Do you have this in another colour?
لوى [lawa:] vt twist
يلوي المفصل
[Yalwey al-mefṣal] v sprain
ليبي [li:bij] n ◁ Libyan adj Libyan
ليبيا [li:bja:] n Libya

ليبيري n ⊲ Liberian *adj* [liːbiːrij] Liberian
ليبيريا Liberia *n* [liːbiːrjaː]
ليتواني Lithuanian *adj* [liːtwaːnij]
اللغة الليتوانية
[Al-loghah al-letwaneyah] *(language) n* Lithuanian
شخص ليتواني
[shakhṣ letwaneyah] *(person) n* Lithuanian
ليتوانيا Lithuania *n* [liːtwaːnjaː]
ليزر laser *n* [lajzar]
ليس *adv* [lajsa]
ليس لدي أية فكّة أصغر
[Laysa laday ay fakah aṣghar] I don't have anything smaller
ليل night *n* [lajl]
منتصف الليل
[montaṣaf al-layl] *n* midnight
غدًا في الليل
[ghadan fee al-layl] tomorrow night
ليلًا at night *adv* [lajlaː]
ليلة night *n* [lajla]
في هذه الليلة
[Fee hadheh al-laylah] *adv* tonight
.أريد تذكرتين لحفلة الليلة، إذا تفضلت
[areed tadhkara-tayn le-ḥaflat al-layla, edha tafaḍalt] Two tickets for tonight, please
أريد تذكرتين لهذه الليلة
[areed tadhkeara-tayn le-hadhy al-layla] I'd like two tickets for tonight
أريد البقاء لليلة أخرى
[areed al-ba'qaa le-layla ukhra] I want to stay an extra night
أريد حجز مائدة لثلاثة أشخاص هذه الليلة
[areed ḥajiz ma-e-da le-thalathat ashkhaaṣ hadhy al-layla] I'd like to reserve a table for three people for tonight
الليلة الماضية
[al-laylah al-maaḍiya] last night
كم تبلغ تكلفة الإقامة في الليلة الواحدة؟
[kam tablugh taklifat al-e'qama fee al-layla al-waḥida?] How much is it per night?
كم تبلغ تكلفة الخيمة في الليلة الواحدة؟
[kam tablugh taklifat al-khyma fee al-layla al-waḥida?] How much is it per night for a tent?
ليلة سعيدة
[layla sa'aeeda] Good night
ما المكان تفضل الذي الذهاب إليه الليلة؟
[ma al-makan aladhy tofaḍel al-dhehab wlayhe al-laylah?] Where would you like to go tonight?
ماذا يعرض الليلة على شاشة السينما؟
[madha yu'a-raḍ al-layla 'aala sha-shat al-senama?] What's on tonight at the cinema?
نريد حجز مقعدين في هذه الليلة
[nureed ḥajiz ma'q-'aad-ayn fee hadhy al-layla] We'd like to reserve two seats for tonight
هل سيكون الجو باردا الليلة؟
[hal sayakon al-jaw baredan al-layla?] Will it be cold tonight?
هل لديكم غرفة شاغرة الليلة؟
[hal ladykum ghurfa shaghera al-layla?] Do you have a room for tonight?
ليلي nighttime *adj* [lajlij]
الخدمات الترفيهية الليلية
[Alkhadmat al-tarfeeheyah al-layleyah] *n* nightlife
مدرسة ليلية
[Madrasah layleyah] *n* night school
نادي ليلي
[Nadey layley] *n* nightclub
نوبة ليلية
[Noba layleyah] *n* nightshift
ليموزين limousine *n* [liːmuːziːn]
ليمون lemon, lime *(fruit) n* [lajmuːn]
عصير الليمون المحلى
['aaṣeer al-laymoon al-moḥala] *n* lemonade
بالليمون
[bil-laymoon] with lemon
ليو Leo *n* [lijuː]

ما [ma:] *pron* what
كما
[kama:] *prep* as
ما الذي بك؟
[ma al-lathy beka?] What's the matter?
ماء [ma:ʔ] *n* water
تحت الماء
[Taḥt al-maa] *adv* underwater
ماء ملحي
[Maa mel'ḥey] *adj* saltwater
إبريق من الماء
[ebree'q min al-maa-i] a jug of water
أتسمح بفحص الماء بالسيارة؟
[a-tas-maḥ be-faḥiṣ al-maa-i bil-sayara?] Can you check the water, please?
.أود أن أسبح تحت الماء
[Owad an asbaḥ taḥt al-maa.] I'd like to go snorkelling
مائة [ma:ʔitun] *number* hundred
...أرغب في تغيير مائة... إلى
[arghab fee taghyeer ma-a... ela...] I'd like to change one hundred... into...
أرغب في الحصول على مائتي...
[arghab fee al-ḥuṣool 'aala ma-a-tay...] I'd like two hundred...
مائدة [ma:ʔida] *n*
سَكاكين المائدة
[Skakeen al-maeadah] *n* cutlery
أريد حجز مائدة لشخصين في ليلة الغد
[areed ḥajiz ma-e-da le-shakhṣiyn fee laylat al-ghad] I'd like to reserve a table for two people for tomorrow night
من فضلك أريد مائدة لأربعة أشخاص
[min faḍlak areed ma-eda le-arba'aat ash-khaṣ] A table for four people, please
مائِل [ma:ʔil] *adj*
مائِل للبرودة
[Mael lel-brodah] *adj* cool *(cold)*
مؤامرة [muʔa:mara] *n* conspiracy
مات [ma:ta] *v* die
مؤتمر [muʔtamar] *n* conference
مؤتمر صحفي
[Moatamar ṣaḥafey] *n* press conference
مؤتمن [muʔtaman] *adj* trusting
مؤثر [muʔaθir] *adj* impressive
مؤخرًا [muʔaxxaran] *adv*
أصبت مؤخرًا بمرض الحصبة
[oṣebtu mu-akharan be-maraḍ al-ḥaṣba] I had measles recently
مُؤَخِرَّةٌ [muʔaxirra] *n* backside
مؤخرة الجيش
[Mowakherat al-jaysh] *n* rear
مُؤَخَّرَه [muʔaxxirra] *n* behind
مؤدب [muʔaddab] *adj* polite
مادة [ma:dda] *n* clause, material
مادة سائلة
[madah saaelah] *n* liquid
مادة غير عضوية
[Madah ghayer 'aodweyah] *n* mineral
مادة تلميع
[Madah talmee'a] *adj* polish
مادة كيميائية
[Madah kemyaeyah] *n* chemical
مادة لاصقة
[Madah laṣe'qah] *n* plaster *(for wound)*
مادة مركبة
[Madah morakabah] *n* complex
مادة مسيلة
[Madah moseelah] *n* liquidizer
مادة متفجرة
[Madah motafajerah] *n* explosive

مادة منظفة
[Madah monadhefah] *n* detergent
مادة منكهة
[Madah monakahah] *n* flavouring
مادي adj [maːdijat]
مكونات مادية
[Mokawenat madeyah] *n* hardware
مؤذ mischievous *adj* [muʔðin]
غير مؤذ
[Ghayer modh] *adj* harmless
ماذا *pron* [maːðaː]
ماذا أفعل؟
[madha af'aal?] What do I do?
ماذا يوجد في هذا؟
[madha yujad fee hadha?] What is in this?
ماذا؟
[Madeyah] Pardon?
مؤذي *v* ◁ harmful *adj* [muʔðiː] abusive
مارثون *n* [maːraθuːn]
سباق المارثون
[Seba'q al-marathon] *n* marathon
مُؤرِّخ historian *n* [muʔarrix]
مارد giant *n* [maːrid]
مارس March *n* [maːris]
مارس practise *v* [maːrasa]
يُمارِس رياضة العدو
[Yomares reyaḍat al-'adw] *vi* jog
.أود أن أمارس رياضة ركوب الأمواج
[Awad an omares reyaḍat rekob al-amwaj.] I'd like to go wind-surfing
أين يمكن أن نمارس رياضة التزلج بأحذية التزلج؟
[ayna yamken an nomares riyaḍat al-tazal-oj be-aḥdheat al-tazal-oj?] Where can we go roller skating?
ماركة make *n* [maːrka]
ماركة جديدة
[Markah jadeedah] *n* brand-new
ماريجوانا *n* [maːriːʒwaːnaː] marijuana
مئزر pinafore *n* [miʔzar]
مأزق ordeal *n* [maʔziq]
ماس diamond *n* [maːs]
مأساة tragedy *n* [maʔsaːt]
مأساوي tragic *adj* [maʔsaːwij]
ماسح *n* [maːsiħ]
ماسح ضوئي
[Maaseh daweay] *n* scanner
ماسح الأراضي
[Maseh al-araaḍey] *n* surveyor
ماسحة *n* [maːsiħa]
ماسحة زجاج السيارة
[Masehat zojaj sayarh] *n* windscreen wiper
مؤسس *adj* [muʔassas]
مؤسس على
[Moasas ala] *adj* based
مؤسسة firm, *n* [muʔassasa] institution
ماسكارا mascara *n* [maːskaːraː]
ماسورة pipe *n* [maːsuːra]
مُؤَشر cursor, indicator *n* [muʔaʃʃir]
ماشية cattle *npl* [maːʃijjatun]
ماضي past *n* [maːdˤiː]
ماعِز goat *n* [maːʕiz]
مُؤَقت temporary *adj* [muʔaqqat]
عامِل مُؤَقّت
['aamel mowa'qat] *n* temp
ماكر cunning *adj* [maːkir]
ماكريل *n* [maːkiriːli]
سمك الماكريل
[Samak al-makreel] *n* mackerel
ماكينة machine *n* [maːkiːna]
ماكينة صرافة
[Makenat ṣerafah] *n* cash dispenser
ماكينة تسجيل الكاش
[Makenat tasjeel al-kaash] *n* till
ماكينة الشقبية
[Makenat al-sha'qabeyah] *n* vending machine
ماكينة بيع
[Makenat bay'a] *n* vending machine
أين توجد ماكينة التذاكر؟
[ayna tojad makenat al-tadhaker?] Where is the ticket machine?
هل توجد ماكينة فاكس يمكن استخدامها؟
[hal tojad makenat fax yamken istekh-damuha?] Is there a fax machine I can use?

مال [ma:l] *n* money
مال يرد بعد دفعه
[Maal yorad daf'ah] *n* drawback
أريد تحويل بعض الأموال من حسابي
[areed taḥweel ba'aḍ al-amwal min ḥesaaby] I would like to transfer some money from my account
ليس معي مال
[laysa ma'ay maal] I have no money
هل يمكن تسليفي بعض المال؟
[hal yamken tas-leefy ba'aḍ al-maal?] Could you lend me some money?
مال [ma:la] *v* tip *(incline)*, bend down
مالح [ma:liħ] *adj*
ماء مالح
[Maa maleḥ] *n* marinade
مالطة [ma:ltˤa] *n* Malta
مالطي [ma:ltˤij] *adj* Maltese ◁ *n* Maltese *(person)*
اللغة المالطية
[Al-loghah al-malṭeyah] *(language) n* Maltese
مؤلف [muʔallif] *n* author
مؤلف موسيقى
[Moaalef mosee'qy] *n* composer
مالك [ma:lik] *n* owner
مالك الأرض
[Malek al-arḍ] *n* landowner
مالك الحزين
[Malek al ḥazeen] *n* heron
من فضلك هل يمكنني التحدث إلى المالك؟
[min faḍlak hal yamkin-ani al-taḥaduth ela al-maalik?] Could I speak to the owner, please?
مالكة [ma:lika] *n*
مالكة الأرض
[Malekat al-arḍ] *n* landlady
مؤلم [mulim] *adj* painful
مألوف [maʔlu:f] *adj* familiar
غير مألوف
[Ghayer maaloof] *adj* unfamiliar
مالي [ma:lij] *adj* financial
سَنة مالية
[Sanah maleyah] *n* financial year
موارد مالية
[Mawared maleyah] *npl* funds
ورقة مالية
[Wara'qah maleyah] *n* note
ماليزي [ma:li:zij] *adj* Malaysian
شخص ماليزي
[shakhṣ maleezey] *n* Malaysian
ماليزيا [ma:li:zja:] *n* Malaysia
ماما [ma:ma:] *n* mum, mummy *(mother)*
مُأَمَّن *adj* secure
مؤمن [muʔamman] *n*
مؤمن عليه
[Moaman 'aalayh] *adj* insured
أنا مؤمن عليّ
[ana mo-aaman 'aalya] I have insurance
ماموث [ma:mu:θ] *n* mammoth
مؤنث [muʔannaθ] *adj* feminine, female
مَانح [ma:niħ] *n* donor
مانَع [ma:niʕ] *n*
هل لديك مانع في أن أدخن؟
[Hal ladayk mane'a fee an adakhan?] Do you mind if I smoke?
مانع [ma:naʕa] *v*
أنا لا أمانع
[ana la omani'a] I don't mind
هل تمانع؟
[hal tumani'a?] Do you mind?
ماهر [ma:hir] *adj* skilled
مؤهل [moahhal] *n* capable
مُؤهَل [muahhal] *adj* qualified
مُؤهل [muahhil] *n* qualification
ماهَوجني [ma:hu:ʒnij] *adj*
خشب الماهوجني
[Khashab al-mahojney] *n* mahogany
ماوري [ma:wrij] *adj* Maori
اللغة الماورية
[Al-loghah al-mawreyah] *(language) n* Maori
شخص ماوري
[Shakhṣ mawrey] *(person) n* Maori
مئوية [miʔiwijja] *n*
درجة حرارة مئوية
[Draajat ḥaraarah meaweyah] *n* degree centigrade
ما يرام [ma: jura:m] *adv*

أشعر أنني لست على ما يرام
[ash-'aur enna-nee lasto 'aala ma yo-raam] I feel sick
هل أنت على ما يرام
[hal anta 'aala ma yoraam?] Are you alright?
مايو May *n* [ma:ju:]
مَايوه swimsuit *n* [ma:ju:h]
مبادرة initiative *n* [muba:dara]
مباراة game, match *n* [muba:ra:t] *(sport)*
مباراة الإياب فى ملعب المضيف
[Mobarat al-eyab fee mal'aab al-moḍeef] *n* home match
مباراة الذهاب
[Mobarat al-dhehab] *n* away match
مباراة كرة قدم
[Mobarat korat al-'qadam] *n* football match
مباشر direct *adj* [muba:ʃir]
غير مباشر
[Ghayer mobasher] *adj* indirect
أفضل الذهاب مباشرة
[ofaḍel al-dhehaab muba-sharatan] I'd prefer to go direct
هل يتجه هذا القطار مباشرة إلى...؟
[hal yata-jih hadha al-'qeṭaar muba-sha-ratan ela...?] Is it a direct train?
مباشرةً directly *adv* [muba:ʃaratan]
مُبَاعٌ sold out *adj* [muba:ʕ]
مبالغ *adj* [muba:laɣ]
مبالغ فيه
[mobalagh feeh] *adj* overdrawn
مبالغة exaggeration *n* [muba:laɣa]
مباني *npl* [maba:ni:]
مباني وتجهيزات
[Mabaney watajheezaat] *n* plant *(site/equipment)*
مبتدئ *adj* [mubtadiʔ]
المبتدئ
[Almobtadea] *n* beginner
أين توجد منحدرات المبتدئين؟
[Ayn tojad monḥadrat al-mobtadean?] Where are the beginners' slopes?
مبتذل stale *adj* [mubtaðal]
مبتسر premature *adj* [mubatasir]
مبتل wet *adj* [mubtal]
مُبْتَل moist *adj* [mubtall]
مبدأ principle *n* [mabdaʔ]
مبدئياً initially *adv* [mabdaʔijjan]
مبدع ingenious *adj* [mubdiʕ]
مبراة pencil sharpener *n* [mibra:t]
مبرد *n* [mibrad]
مبرد أظافر
[Mabrad aḍhafer] *n* nailfile
مُبّرر reason *n* [mubbarir]
مُبَرْمِج programmer *n* [mubarmiʒ]
مبستر pasteurized *adj* [mubastar]
مُبَشر missionary *n* [mubaʃʃir]
مُبطئ late *(delayed)* *adj* [mubtˤiʔ]
مبكر early *adj* [mubakkir]
مبكرًا *adv* [mubakiran]
لقد وصلنا مبكرًا
[la'qad waṣalna mu-bakiran] We arrived early/late
مبلغ amount *n* [mablaɣ]
مبلل *adj* [muballal]
مبلل بالعرق
[Mobala bel-ara'q] *adj* sweaty
مبنى *n* [mabna:]
المبنى والأراضي التابعه له
[Al-mabna wal-aradey al-taabe'ah laho] *n* premises
مبنى نُصُب تذكاري
[Mabna noṣob tedhkarey] *n* monument
مبهج cheerful *adj* [mubhaʒ]
مبهم vague *adj* [mubham]
مبيت *n* [mabi:t]
مبيت وإفطار
[Mabeet wa efṭaar] *n* bed and breakfast, B&B
هل يجب علي المبيت؟
[hal yajib 'aala-ya al-mabeet?] Do I have to stay overnight?
مبيد *n* [mubi:d]
مبيد الأعشاب الضارة
[Mobeed al'ashaab al-ḍarah] *n* weedkiller
مبيد الجراثيم
[Mobeed al-jaratheem] *n* disinfectant
مبيد حشرات

[Mobeed hasharat] *n* pesticide
bleached *adj* [mubajjidˁ] **مُبَيَّض**
ovary *n* [mabiːdˁ] **مِبْيَض**
n [mubiːʕ] **مبيع**
مبيعات بالتليفون
[Mabee'aat bel-telefoon] *npl* telesales
مندوب مبيعات
[Mandoob mabee'aat] *n* sales rep
impressed *adj* [mutaʔaθirr] **متأثر**
delayed *adj* [mutaʔaxxir] **متأخر**
late *adv* [mutaʔaxiran] **متأخراً**
npl [mutaʔaxxiraːtun] **متأخرات** arrears
sure *adj* [mutaʔakkid] **متأكد**
غير متأكد
[Ghayer moaakad] *adj* unsure
dressed *adj* [mutaʔanniq] **متأنق**
ready *adj* [mutaʔahib] **متأهب**
maze *n* [mataːha] **متاهة**
mutual *adj* [mutabaːdal] **متبادل**
n [mutabarriʕ] **متبرع**
محل لبضائع متبرع بها لجهة خيرية
[Maḥal lebaḍae'a motabar'a beha lejahah khayryah] *n* charity shop
remaining *adj* [mutabaqij] **متبقي**
spicy *adj* [mutabbal] **متبل**
blunt *adj* [mutaballid] **متبلد**
متبلد الحس
[Motabled al-ḥes] *adj* cool *(stylish)*
adopted *adv* [mutabannaː] **مُتَبَنَّى**
adj [mutataːbiʕ] **متتابع**
سلسلة متتابعة
[Selselah motatabe'ah] *n* episode
series *n* [mutataːlijja] **متتالية**
n [matʒar] **متجر**
صاحب المتجر
[Ṣaheb al-matjar] *n* shopkeeper
متجر البقالة
[Matjar al-be'qalah] *n* grocer's
متجر المقتنيات القديمة
[Matjar al-mo'qtanayat al-'qadeemah] *n* antique shop
متجر كبير جداً
[Matjar kabeer jedan] *n* hypermarket
متجر هدايا
[Matjar hadaya] *n* gift shop

واجهة العرض في المتجر
[Wagehat al-'aarḍ fee al-matjar] *n* shop window
مَتجر السجائر
[Matjar al-sajaaer] *n* tobacconist's
wrinkled *adj* [mutaʒaʕid] **متجعد**
frozen *adj* [mutaʒammid] **متجمد**
مطر متجمد
[Maṭar motajamed] *n* sleet
adj [muttaʒih] **متجه**
ما هو الموعد التالي للمركب المتجه إلى...؟
[ma howa al-maw'aid al-taaly lel-markab al-mutajeh ela...?] When is the next sailing to...?
rambler *n* [mutaʒawwil] **مُتَجوِّل**
prejudiced *adj* [mutaħaːmil] **متحامل**
petrified *adj* [mutaħaʒʒir] **متحجر**
united *adj* [muttaħid] **متحد**
الإمارات العربية المتحدة
[Al-emaraat al'arabeyah al-motaḥedah] *npl* United Arab Emirates
الأمم المتحدة
[Al-omam al-motahedah] *n* United Nations
المملكة المتحدة
[Al-mamlakah al-motahedah] *n* UK
الولايات المتحدة
[Al-welayat al-motḥedah al-amreekeyah] *n* United States, US
adj [mutaħaddiθ] **متحدث**
متحدث باللغة الأم
[motaḥdeth bel-loghah al-om] *n* native speaker
مُتَحدِّث باسم
[Motaḥadeth besm] *n* spokesman, spokesperson
n [mutaħddiθa] **مُتَحدِّثة**
مُتَحدِّثة باسم
[Motaḥadethah besm] *n* spokeswoman
moving *adj* [mutaħarriki] **متحرك**
سلم متحرك
[Solam motaḥarek] *n* escalator
سير متحرك
[Sayer motaḥrrek] *n* conveyor belt
mobile *adj* [mutaħarrik] **مُتَحَرِّكٌ**

متحضر [mutaħadˤdˤir] *adj*
غير متحضر
[ghayer motahaḍer] *adj* uncivilized
متحف [matħaf] *n* museum
متى يُفتح المتحف؟
[mata yoftaḥ al-matḥaf?] When is the museum open?
هل المتحف مفتوح في الصباح؟
[hal al-mat-ḥaf maf-tooḥ fee al-ṣabaḥ] Is the museum open in the morning?
متحفظ [mutaħaffizˤ] *adj* shy
متحكم [mutaħakkim] *adj*
متحكم به عن بعد
[Motaḥkam beh an bo'ad] *adj* radio-controlled
متحمس [mutaħammis] *adj* keen
متحير [mutaħajjir] *adj* baffled, bewildered
متحيز [mutaħajjiz] *adj* biased
غير متحيز
[Ghayer motaḥeyz] *adj* impartial
متحيز عنصريا
[Motaḥeyz 'aonṣoreyan] *n* racist
متخصص [mutaxasˤsˤisˤ] *n* specialist
متخلف [mutaxaliff] *adj* out-of-date
متداول [mutada:walat] *adj*
عملة متداولة
[A'omlah motadawlah] *n* currency
متدرب [mutadarrib] *n* trainee
متر [mitr] *n* metre
متراس [mutara:sin] *n* roadblock
متراكز [mutara:kiz] *adj*
لا متراكز
[La motrakez] *adj* eccentric
مترجم [muntarʒim] *n* translator
مترف [mutraf] *adj* luxurious
مترنح [mutaranniħ] *adj* tipsy
مترو [mitru:] *n*
محطة مترو
[Mahaṭat metro] *n* tube station
أين توجد أقرب محطة للمترو؟
[ayna tojad a'qrab muḥaṭa lel-metro?] Where is the nearest tube station?
متري [mitrij] *adj* metric
متزامن [mutaza:min] *adj* simultaneous
متزايد [mutaza:jid] *adj*
بشكل متزايد
[Beshakl motazayed] *adv* increasingly
مُتَزَلِّج [mutazalliʒ] *n* skier
متزوج [mutazawwiʒ] *adj* married
غير متزوج
[Ghayer motazawej] *adj* unmarried
مُتَسابِق [mutasa:biq] *n* sprinter
متسامِح [mutasa:miħ] *adj* tolerant
متسخ [muttasix] *adj*
إنها متسخة
[inaha mutasikha] It's dirty
متسلق [mutasalliq] *n*
متسلق الجبال
[Motasale'q al-jebaal] *n* mountaineer
متسلق الجبال
[Motasale'q al-jebaal] *n* climber
متسول [mutasawwil] *n* tramp *(beggar)*
المتسول
[Almotasawel] *n* beggar
فنان متسول
[Fanan motasawol] *n* busker
متشائم [mutaʃa:ʔim] *adj* pessimistic, pessimist
متصدع [mutasˤaddiʕ] *adj* cracked
متصفح [mutasˤaffiħ] *n* browser
متصفح شبكة الإنترنت
[Motaṣafeḥ shabakat al-enternet] *n* web browser
مُتَصِّفِح الانترنت
[Motaṣafeḥ al-enternet] *n* surfer
متصل [muttasˤil] *adj*
غير متصل بالموضوع
[Ghayr motaṣel bel-maeḍo'a] *adj* irrelevant
متصل بالإنترنت
[motaṣel bel-enternet] *adj* online
من المتصل؟
[min al-mutaṣil?] Who's calling?
متضارب [mutadˤa:rib] *adj* inconsistent
متطابق [mutatˤa:biq] *adj* identical
متطرف [mutatˤarrif] *n* extremist
متطفل [mutatˤafil] *n* intruder
متطوع [mutatˤawwiʕ] *n* volunteer

متعاطف adj [mutaʕa:tˤif] sympathetic
متعاقب adj [mutaʕa:qib] consecutive, successive
متعب tired adj [mutʕab]
متعجرف arrogant adj [mutaʕaʒrif]
متعدد numerous adj [mutaʕaddid]
تَلَيُّف عصبي متعدد
[Talayof 'aaṣabey mota'aded] n multiple sclerosis
متعدد الجنسيات
[Mota'aded al-jenseyat] adj multinational
متعدد الجوانب
[Mota'aded al-jawaneb] n versatile
متعذر adj [mutaʕaððir]
متعذر تجنبه
[Mota'adhar tajanobah] adj unavoidable
متعذر التحكم فيه
[Mota'adher al-tahakom feeh] adj uncontrollable
متعسر adj [mutaʕassir]
شخص متعسر النطق
[Shakhṣ mota'aser al-noṭ'q] n dyslexic
متعصب adj [mutaʕasˤsˤib]
شخص متعصب
[Shakhṣ motaṣeb] n fanatic
مُتَعصِب intolerant adj [mutaʕasˤibb]
متعفن mouldy adj [mutaʕaffin]
متعلق adj [mutaʕalliq]
متعلق بالعملة
[Mota'ale'q bel-'omlah] adj monetary
متعلق بالبدن
[Mota'ale'q bel-badan] n physical
متعلق بالقرون الوسطى
[Mot'aale'q bel-'qroon al-wosṭa] adj mediaeval
متعلقات npl [mutaʕalliqa:tun] belongings
متعلِم educated adj [mutaʕallim]
مُتَعَلِّم learner n [mutaʕallinm]
متعمد adj [mutaʕammad] deliberate
غير متعمد
[Ghayr mota'amad] adj unintentional
بشكل متعمد
[Be-shakl mota'amad] adv deliberately
متغضن creased adj [mutaɣadˤdˤin]
متغير adj [mutaɣajjir]
غير متغير
[Ghayr motaghayer] adj unchanged
متفائل optimistic, adj [mutafa:ʔil] optimist
متفاجئ surprised adj [mutafa:ʒiʔ]
متفرغ dedicated adj [mutafarriɣ]
غِير مُتَفرِغ
[Ghayr motafaregh] part-time
مُتفق adj [muttafaq]
مُتفق عليه
[Moṭafa'q 'alayeh] adj agreed
متفهم adj [mutafahhim] understanding
متقاطع adj [mutaqa:tˤiʕat]
طرق متقاطعة
[Ṭaree'q mot'qat'ah] n crossroads
كلمات متقاطعة
[Kalemat mota'qat'aa] n crossword
مُتَقَاطِع cross adj [mutaqa:tˤiʕ]
متقاعد retired adj [mutaqa:ʕid]
متقدم advanced adj [mutaqaddim]
شخص متقدم العمر
[Shakhṣ mota'qadem al-'aomr] n senior citizen
متقلب unsteady adj [mutaqalibb]
متقلب المزاج
[Mota'qaleb al-mazaj] adj moody
متقلص shrunk adj [mutaqallisˤ]
متقلقل shaky adj [mutaqalqil]
متكبر snob n [mutakabbir]
متكرر frequent, adj [mutakarrir] recurring
على نحو متكرر
['aala nahw motakarer] adv repeatedly
سُؤال مُتكرر
[Soaal motakarer] n FAQ
متكلف adj [mutakallif] sophisticated
متلازمة n [mutala:zima]
متلازمة داون
[Motalazemat dawon] n Down's syndrome
مُتَلقِ recipient n [mutalaqi]

متماثل [mutama:θil] *adj* symmetrical
متماسك [mutama:sik] *adj* consistent
متمتّع [mutamattiʕ] *adj*
متمتّع بحُكْم ذاتي [Motamet'a be-ḥokm dhatey] *adj* autonomous
متمرد [mutamarrid] *adj* rebellious
متمم [mutammim] *adj* complementary
متموج [mutamawwiʒ] *adj* wavy
مُتَناوب [mutana:wibb] *adj* alternate
متناول [mutana:wil] *n*
في المتناول [Fee almotanawal] *adj* convenient
متنزه [mutanazzah] *n* park
متنقل [mutanaqil] *n*
هل يمكن أن نوقف عربة النوم المتنقلة هنا؟ [hal yamken an nuwa-'qif 'aarabat al-nawm al-muta-na'qila huna?] Can we park our caravan here?
متنكر [mutanakkir] *adj* masked
متنوع [mutanawwiʕ] *adj* miscellaneous
متهم [muttaham] *n* accused
متوازن [mutawa:zinn] *adj* balanced
متوازي [mutawa:zi:] *adj* parallel
متواصل [mutawasˤil] *adj* continual
متواضع [mutawa:dˤiʕ] *adj* humble
متوافق [mutawa:fiq] *adj* compatible
متوافِق مع المعايير [Motawaf'q fee al-m'aayeer] *n* pass *(meets standard)*
متوان [mitwa:n] *adj* slack
متوتر [mutawattir] *adj* stressed, tense
متوحد [mutawaħħid] *adj* lonely
متورم [mutawarrim] *adj* bigheaded
متوسط [mutawassitˤ] *adj* average, moderate
متوسط الحجم [Motawaseṭ al-hajm] *adj* medium-sized
متوسطي [mutawassitˤij] *n* Mediterranean

متوفر [mutawaffir] *adj* available
متوفى [mutawaffin] *adj* dead
متوقع [mutawaqqaʕ] *adj* predictable
على نحو غير متوقع [Ala naḥw motawa'qa'a] *adv* unexpectedly
غير متوقع [Ghayer motwa'qa'a] *adj* unexpected
متى [mata:] *adv* when
متى ستنتهي من ذلك؟ [mata satan-tahe min dhalik?] When will you have finished?
متى حدث ذلك؟ [mata ḥadatha dhalik?] When did it happen?
مُثار [muθa:r] *adj* excited
مثال [miθa:l] *n* example
على سبيل المثال ['ala sabeel al-methal] *n* e.g.
مَثّال [maθθa:l] *n* sculptor
مثالي [miθa:lij] *adj* ideal, model
بشكل مثالي [Be-shakl methaley] *adv* ideally
مِثاليّة [miθa:lijja] *n* perfection
مَثانة [maθa:na] *n* bladder, cyst
التهاب المثانة [El-tehab al-mathanah] *n* cystitis
مثقاب [miθqa:b] *n* drill
مثقاب هوائي [Meth'qaab hawaey] *n* pneumatic drill
مثقب [miθqab] *n* punch *(blow)*
مثقوب [maθqu:b] *adj* pierced
مَثَل [maθal] *n* proverb
مَثّل [maθθala] *v* represent
مثلث [muθallaθ] *n* triangle
مثلج [muθliʒ] *adj*
هل النبيذ مثلج؟ [hal al-nabeedh mutha-laj?] Is the wine chilled?
مُثلّج [muθallaʒ] *adj* chilly
مثلي [miθlij] *adj*
العلاج المِثْلي [Al-a'elaj al-methley] *n* homeopathy
معالج مثلي [Moalej methley] *adj* homeopathic
مثير [muθi:r] *adj* exciting, gripping,

criminal *n* [muʒrim] **مجرم**
injured *adj* [maʒruːħ] **مجروح**
Hungarian *adj* [maʒrij] **مجري**
Hungarian *adj* [maʒarij] **مَجَري**
مَجَري الجنسية
[Majra al-jenseyah] *(person) n* Hungarian
n [maʒraː] **مجرى**
مجرى نهر
[Majra nahr] *n* channel
shambles *n* [maʒzar] **مجزر**
rewarding *adj* [muʒziː] **مُجْزي**
dried, *adj* [muʒaffif] **مجفف**
dehydrated, dryer
مجفف ملابس
[Mojafef malabes] *n* tumble dryer
مُجَفِف دوار
[Mojafef dwar] *n* spin drier
مُجَفِف الشعر
[Mojafef al-sha'ar] *n* hairdryer
magazine *n* [maʒalla] **مجلة**
(periodical)
أين يمكن أن أشتري المجلات؟
[ayna yamken an ash-tary al-majal-aat?] Where can I buy a magazine?
council *n* [maʒlis] **مجلس**
رئيس المجلس
[Raees al-majlas] *n* chairman
عضو مجلس
['aodw majles] *n* councillor
دار المجلس التشريعى
[Dar al-majles al-tashre'aey] *n* council house
adj [muʒammad] **مجمد**
هل السمك طازج أم مجمد؟
[hal al-samaḳ ṭazij amm mujam-ad?] Is the fish fresh or frozen?
هل الخضروات طازجة أم مجمدة؟
[hal al-khiḍ-rawaat ṭazija amm mujam-ada?] Are the vegetables fresh or frozen?
n [maʒmuːʕ] **مجموع**
مجموع مراهنات
[Majmoo'a morahnaat] *n* jackpot
مجموع نقاط
[Majmo'aat ne'qaaṭ] *n* score *(game/*

sensational
عمل مثير
['aamal Mother] *n* stunt
مثير المتاعب
[Mother al-mataa'aeb] *n* troublemaker
مثير للغضب
[Mother lel-ghaḍab] *adj* infuriating, irritating
مثير للاشمئزاز
[Mother lel-sheazaz] *adj* disgusting, repulsive
مثير للحساسية
[Mother lel-hasaseyah] *adj* allergic
مثير للحزن
[Mother lel-ḥozn] *adj* pathetic
mug *n* [maʒʒ] **مَجّ**
pass *(in mountains) n* [maʒaːz] **مجاز**
famine *n* [maʒaːʕa] **مجاعة**
area *n* [maʒaːl] **مجال**
مجال جوي
[Majal jawey] *n* airspace
مجال البصر
[Majal al-baṣar] *n* eyesight
n [muʒaːlisa] **مجالسة**
مجالسة الأطفال
[Mojalasat al-atfaal] *n* babysitting
adj [muʒaːmil] **مُجامِل**
complimentary
compliment *n* [muʒaːmala] **مجاملة**
free *(no cost) adj* [maʒʒaːnij] **مجاني**
adjacent, *adj* [muʒaːwir] **مجاور**
nearby
n [muʒaːwira] **مُجَاورة**
neighbourhood
society, *n* [muʒtamaʕ] **مجتمع**
community
glory *n* [maʒd] **مجد**
oar *n* [miʒdaːf] **مجداف**
adj [muʒaddid] **مُجدد**
مُجدد للنشاط
[Mojaded lel-nashaṭ] *adj* refreshing
stranded *adj* [maʒduːl] **مجدول**
maniac *n* [maʒðuːb] **مجذوب**
spade *n* [miʒraːf] **مِجراف**
experienced *adj* [muʒarrib] **مُجَرِّب**
mere, bare *adj* [muʒarrad] **مجرد**

match)
مجموعة collection *n* [maʒmuːʕa]
مجموعة قوانين السير في الطرق السريعة
[Majmo'aat 'qwaneen al-sayer fee al-ṭoro'q al-saree'aah] *n* Highway Code
مجموعة كتب
[Majmo'aat kotob] *n* set
مجموعة لعب
[Majmo'aat le'aab] *n* playgroup
مجموعة مؤتلفة
[Majmo'aah moatalefa] *n* combination
مجنون insane, mad *adj* [maʒnuːn]
(angry)
madman *n* ◁
مجهد intense *adj* [muʒhid]
مجهز equipped *adj* [muʒahhaz]
مجوهرات jewelry *n* [muʒawharaːt]
محادثة conversation *n* [muħaːdaθa]
محار shellfish *n* [maħaːr]
محار الاسقلوب
[maḥar al-as'qaloob] *n* scallop
محارب *n* [muħaːrib]
محارب قديم
[Moḥareb 'qadeem] *n* veteran
محارة shell *n* [maħaːra]
محاسب accountant *n* [muħaːsib]
مُحَاسَبَة accountancy *n* [muħaːsaba]
محاضر lecturer *n* [muħaːdˤir]
محاضرة lecture *n* [muħaːdˤara]
محافظ mayor *n* [muħaːfizˤ]
شخص محافظ
[Shakhṣ moḥafeḍh] *adj* conservative
مُحافظة *n* [muħaːfazˤa]
المُحافظة على الموارد الطبيعية
[Al-moḥafadhah ala al-mawared al-ṭabe'aeyah] *n* conservation
محاكاة imitation *n* [muħaːkaːt]
محاكمة trial *n* [muħaːkama]
محامي solicitor *n* [muħaːmij]
محامي ولاية
[Moḥamey welayah] *n* solicitor
محاور interviewer *n* [muħaːwir]
محاولة attempt *n* [muħaːwala]
محايد *adj* [muħaːjid]
شخص محايد
[Moḥareb moḥayed] *n* neutral
محب *adj* [muħibb]
محب للاستطلاع
[Moḥeb lel-esteṭlaa'a] *adj* curious
مُحِب lover *n* [muħib]
مُحِب لنفسه
[Moḥeb le-nafseh] *adj* self-centred
مُحبب lovely *adj* [muħabbab]
محبط depressed, disappointed *adj* [muħbatˤ]
مُحبِط disappointing *adj* [muħbitˤ]
محبوب *adj* [maħbuːb]
غير محبوب
[Ghaey maḥboob] *adj* unpopular
محبوس stuck *adj* [maħbuːsa]
محترف professional *n* [muħtarif]
محترم respectable *adj* [muħtaram]
محتمل likely, probable *adj* [muħtamal]
غير محتمل
[Ghaeyr moḥtamal] *adj* unlikely
بصورة محتملة
[be ṣorah moḥtamalah] *adv* presumably
محتوم inevitable *adj* [maħtuːm]
محتويات *npl* [muħtawajaːtun] contents
محجوز reserved *adj* [maħʒuːz]
مُحَدَث up-to-date *adj* [muħaddiθ]
محدد certain, specific *adj* [muħadadd]
في الموعد المحدد
[Fee al-maw'aed al-moḥadad] *adj* on time
محراث plough *n* [miħraːθ]
محراك paddle *n* [miħraːk]
مُحرَج embarrassed *adj* [muħraʒ]
مُحرِج embarrassing *adj* [muħriʒ]
مُحَرِر editor *n* [muħarrir]
مَحْرَقة crematorium *n* [maħraqa]
محرك engine *n* [muħarrik]
محرك البحث
[moḥarek al-baḥth] *n* search engine
المحرك حرارته مرتفعه
[al-muḥar-ik ḥarara-tuho murtafe'aa] The engine is overheating
محرم banned *adj* [muħarram]

معزول بوصفه محرما
[Ma'azool bewaṣfeh moḥaraman] *adj* taboo
محرمات مقدسات
[moḥaramat mo'qadasat] *n* taboo
محزن depressing, sore *adj* [muħzin]
مُحسِن humanitarian *adj* [muħsin]
محسوس sensible *adj* [maħsu:s]
محشو crammed *adj* [maħʃuww]
مُحصِّل collector *n* [muħasˤsˤil]
محصول crop *n* [maħsˤu:l]
محضر record *n* [maħdˤar]
محضر الطعام
[Moḥder al-ṭa'aam] *n* food processor
محطة station *n* [maħatˤtˤa]
محطة راديو
[Mahaṭat radyo] *n* radio station
محطة سكك حديدية
[Mahaṭat sekak ḥadeedeyah] *n* railway station
محطة أنفاق
[Mahaṭat anfa'q] *n* tube station
محطة أوتوبيس
[Mahaṭat otobees] *n* bus station
محطة عمل
[Mahaṭat 'aamal] *n* work station
محطة الخدمة
[Mahaṭat al-khedmah] *n* service station
محطة بنزين
[Mahaṭat benzene] *n* petrol station
محطة مترو
[Mahaṭat metro] *n* tube station
أين توجد أقرب محطة للمترو؟
[ayna tojad a'qrab muḥaṭa lel-metro?] Where is the nearest tube station?
أين توجد محطة الأتوبيس؟
[ayna tojad muḥaṭat al-baaṣ?] Where is the bus station?
كيف يمكن أن أصل إلى أقرب محطة مترو؟
[Kayf yomken an aṣel ela a'qrab maḥaṭat metro?] How do I get to the nearest tube station?
ما هو أفضل طريق للذهاب إلى محطة القطار
[Ma howa af ḍal ṭaree'q lel-dhehab ela maḥaṭat al-'qeṭaar] What's the best way to get to the railway station?
هل يوجد محطة بنزين قريبة من هنا؟
[hal yujad muḥaṭat banzeen 'qareeba min huna?] Is there a petrol station near here?
محظور prohibited *adj* [maħzˤu:r]
محظوظ lucky *adj* [maħzˤu:zˤ]
غير محظوظ
[Ghayer mahḍhooḍh] *adj* unlucky
محفز motivated *adj* [muħaffiz]
محفظة wallet *n* [miħfazˤa]
لقد سرقت محفظة نقودي
[la'qad sore'qat meḥ-faḍhat ni-'qoody] My wallet has been stolen
لقد ضاعت محفظتي
[la'qad ḍa'aat meḥ-faḍhaty] I've lost my wallet
محفوف *adj* [maħfu:f]
محفوف بالمخاطر
[Maḥfoof bel-makhaater] *adj* risky
مُحَقق reporter *n* [muħaqqiq]
مُحكم precise, tight *adj* [muħkam]
مُحكم الغلق
[Moḥkam al-ghal'q] *n* airtight
محكمة tribunal *n* [maħkama]
محل store *n* [maħall]
محل أحذية
[Maḥal aḥdheyah] *n* shoe shop
محل تجاري
[Maḥal tejarey] *n* store
محل تاجر الحديد والأدوات المعدنية
[Maḥal tajer alḥadeed wal-adwat al-ma'adaneyah] *n* ironmonger's
محل العمل
[Maḥal al-'aamal] *n* workplace
محل الجزار
[Maḥal al-jazar] *n* butcher's
محل الميلاد
[Mahal al-meelad] *n* birthplace
محل لبضائع متبرع بها لجهة خيرية
[Maḥal lebaḍae'a motabar'a beha lejahah khayryah] *n* charity shop
محل مكون من أقسام
[Maḥal mokawan men a'qsaam] *n* department store

محلل n [muħallil]
محلل نظم
[Moḥalel noḍhom] n systems analyst
محلي local adj [maħalij]
أريد أن أجرب أحد الأشياء المحلية من فضلك
[areed an ajar-rub aḥad al-ashyaa al-maḥal-lya min faḍlak] I'd like to try something local, please
ما هو الطبق المحلي المميز؟
[ma howa al-ṭaba'q al-maḥa-ly al-muma-yaz?] What's the local speciality?
محمص roast adj [muħamasˤsˤ]
محمول portable adj [maħmu:l]
كمبيوتر محمول
[Kombeyotar maḥmool] n laptop
مَحْمِيَّة reserve (land) n [maħmijja]
محنَك streetwise, adj [muħannak] veteran
محور n [miħwar]
محور الدوران
[Meḥwar al-dawaraan] n axle
محول n [muħawwil]
محول إلى منطقة مشاه
[Meḥawel ela manṭe'qat moshah] adj pedestrianized
مُحَوِّل كهربي
[Moḥawel kahrabey] n adaptor
مُحير puzzling adj [muħajjir]
محيَط ocean n [muħi:tˤ]
المحيط القطبي الشمالي
[Al-moḥeeṭ al-'qoṭbey al-shamaley] n Arctic Ocean
المحيط الهادي
[Al-moḥeeṭ al-haadey] n Pacific
المحيط الهندي
[Almoḥeeṭ alhendey] n Indian Ocean
مخادع tricky adj [muxa:diʕ]
مخاطِرة risk n [muxa:tˤara]
مخالفة foul n [muxa:lafa]
مخبز bakery n [maxbaz]
مخبوز baked adj [maxbu:z]
مختار chosen adj [muxta:r]
مُختَبَر laboratory n [muxtabar]
مُختَبَر اللغة
[Mokhtabar al-loghah] n language laboratory
مُختَرِع inventor n [muxtaraʕ]
مختَص competent adj [muxtasˤsˤ]
مُختَطِف hijacker n [muxtatˤif]
مختلَف different, adj [muxtalif] various
مٌخَدر n [muxadirru]
مٌخَدِر كلي
[Mo-khader koley] n general anaesthetic
مُخَدِر crack (cocaine), n [muxaddir] anaesthetic
مخدرات drug n [muxaddira:t]
مخرب vandal n [muxarrib]
مخرج way out n [maxraʒ]
مخرج طوارئ
[Makhraj ṭawarea] n emergency exit
مخروط cone n [maxru:tˤ]
مخزن storage n [maxzan]
مخزن حبوب
[Makhzan ḥoboob] n barn
مخزون inventory, stock n [maxzu:n]
مخطئ mistaken adj [muxtˤiʔ]
مخطط scheme, layout n [muxatˤatˤ]
مخطط تمهيدي
[Mokhaṭaṭ tamheedey] n outline
مُخَطَّط sketch n [muxatˤtˤatˤ]
مخطوطة manuscript n [maxtˤu:tˤa]
مخفف diluted adj [muxaffaf]
مخفف الصدمات
[Mokhafef al-ṣadamat] n cushion
مخفوق n [maxfu:q]
مخفوق الحليب
[Makhfoo'q al-ḥaleeb] n milkshake
مخلص faithful, sincere adj [muxlisˤ]
مخلوط mixed adj [maxlu:tˤ]
مخلوق creature n [maxlu:q]
مخيب frustrated adj [muxajjib]
مخيف scary adj [muxi:f]
مد n [madd]
مد وجزر
[Mad wa-jazr] n tide
متى يعلو المد؟
[mata ya'alo al-mad?] When is high tide?
مُدَافِع defender n [muda:fiʕ]

مدالية [mida:lijja] *n*
مدالية كبيرة
[Medaleyah kabeerah] *n* medallion
مدة [mudda] *n* period, duration
مُدّخَرَات [muddaxara:tin] *npl* savings
مدخل [madxal] *n* way in
مدخن [mudaxxin] *n*
أريد مقعد في المكان المخصص للمدخنين
[areed ma'q'ad fee al-makan al-mukhaṣaṣ lel -mudakhineen] I'd like a seat in the smoking area
مُدَخِن [muðaxxin] *n* smoker
غير مُدَخِن
[Ghayr modakhen] *n* non-smoking
شخص غير مُدَخِن
[Shakhṣ Ghayr modakhen] *n* non-smoker
مَدخَنة [midxana] *n* chimney
مدرب [mudarrib] *n* coach *(trainer)*, trained, trainer
مدربون [mudarribu:na] *npl* trainers
مَدْرَج [madraʒ] *n* runway
مُدرَّج [mudarraʒ] *adj* registered
غير مُدرّج
[Ghayer modraj] *adj* unlisted
مدرس [mudarris] *n* master, teacher, schoolteacher
مدرس أول
[Modares awal] *n* principal
مدرس خصوصي
[Modares khoṣooṣey] *n* tutor
مُدرّس بديل
[Modares badeel] *n* supply teacher
مدرسة [madrasa] *n* school
طلاب المدرسة
[Ṭolab al-madrasah] *n* schoolchildren
مدرسة إبتدائية
[Madrasah ebtedaeyah] *n* primary school
مدرسة أطفال
[Madrasah aṭfaal] *n* infant school
مدرسة عامة
[Madrasah 'aamah] *n* public school
مدرسة ثانوية
[Madrasah thanaweyah] *n* secondary school
مدرسة داخلية
[Madrasah dakheleyah] *n* boarding school
مدرسة الحضانة
[Madrasah al-ḥaḍanah] *n* nursery school
مدرسة لغات
[Madrasah lo-ghaat] *n* language school
مدرسة ليلية
[Madrasah layleyah] *n* night school
مدرسة نوعية
[Madrasah naw'aeyah] *n* primary school
مدير مدرسة
[Madeer madrasah] *n* principal
مدرسي [madrasij] *adj*
حقيبة مدرسية
[Ḥa'qeebah madraseyah] *n* schoolbag
زي مدرسي موحد
[Zey madrasey mowaḥad] *n* school uniform
كتاب مدرسي
[Ketab madrasey] *n* schoolbook
مدرك [mudrik] *adj* aware
مدعي [muddaʕi:] *adj*
مدعي العلم بكل شيء
[Moda'aey al'aelm bel-shaya] *n* know-all
مُدَعى [mudaʕʕa:] *adj*
مُدَعى عليه
[Moda'aa 'aalayh] *n* defendant
مدغشقر [madaɣaʃqar] *n* Madagascar
مدفأة [midfaʔa] *n*
كيف تعمل المدفأة؟
[kayfa ta'amal al-madfaa?] How does the heating work?
مدفع [midfaʕu] *n*
مدفع الهاون
[Madafa'a al-hawon] *n* mortar *(military)*
مدفن [madfan] *n* graveyard
مدفوع [madfu:ʕ] *adj*
مدفوع بأقل من القيمة
[Madfoo'a be-a'qal men al-q'eemah] *adj* underpaid

مدفوع مسبقا
[Madfo'a mosba'qan] *adj* prepaid
مدلل spoilt *adj* [mudallal]
مدمر devastated *adj* [mudammar]
مدمن addict, addicted *n* [mudmin]
مدمن مخدرات
[Modmen mokhadarat] *n* drug addict
مدني *n* ◁ civilian *adj* [madanijjat] civilian
حقوق مدنية
[Ḥo'qoo'q madaneyah] *npl* civil rights
مدهش marvellous, *adj* [mudhiʃ] splendid
مدو loud *adj* [mudawwin]
مُدَوَّنة blog *n* [mudawwana]
مدى extent, range *(limits)* *n* [mada:]
مدير manageress, director *n* [mudi:r]
مدير الإدارة التنفيذية
[Modeer el-edarah al-tanfeedheyah] *n* CEO
مدير مدرسة
[Madeer madrasah] *n* principal
مديرة manageress *n* [mudi:ra]
مَدين debit *n* [madi:n]
مدينة city *n* [madi:na]
وسط المدينة
[Wasaṭ al-madeenah] *n* town centre
واقع في قلب المدينة
[Wa'qe'a fee 'qalb al-madeenah] *adv* downtown
وَسَطْ المدينة
[Wasaṭ al-madeenah] *n* town centre
أين يمكن أن أشتري خريطة للمدينة؟
[ayna yamken an ash-tary khareeṭa lil-madena?] Where can I buy a map of the city?
هل يوجد أتوبيس إلى المدينة؟
[Hal yojad otobees ela al-madeenah?] Is there a bus to the city?
مذبح *n* [maðbaħ]
مذبح الكنيسة
[madhbaḥ al-kaneesah] *n* altar
مذبحة massacre *n* [maðbaħa]
مذكر masculine *adj* [muðakkar]
مذكرة memo *n* [muðakkira]
مذنب guilty, culprit *adj* [muðnib]

مذهل astonishing, *adj* [muðhil] stunning
مذهول astonished, *adj* [maðhu:l] stunned
مذيب solvent *n* [muði:b]
مر bitter *adj* [murr]
مرّ pass *vi* ◁ go by *v* [marra]
مرآة mirror *n* [mirʔa:t]
مرآة جانبية
[Meraah janebeyah] *n* wing mirror
مرآة الرؤية الخلفية
[Meraah al-roayah al-khalfeyah] *n* rear-view mirror
مرأة *n* [marʔa]
اسم المرأة قبل الزواج
[Esm al-marah 'qabl alzawaj] *n* maiden name
شخص موال لمساواة المرأة بالرجل
[Shakhṣ mowal le-mosawat al-maraah bel-rajol] *n* feminist
مراجع *n* [mura:ʒiʕ]
مراجع حسابات
[Moraaje'a ḥesabat] *n* auditor
مراجعة revision *n* [mura:ʒaʕa]
مراجعة حسابية
[Moraj'ah ḥesabeyah] *n* audit
مَرَارَة gall bladder *n* [marra:ra]
مُرَاسِل correspondent *n* [mura:sil]
مراسَلة *n* [mura:salatu] correspondence
مراسم ceremony *n* [mara:sim]
مرافق associate, *n* [mura:fiq] companion
بدون مُرافق
[Bedon morafe'q] *adj* unattended
مراقب observer, *n* [mura:qib] invigilator
نقطة مراقبة
[No'qtat mora'qabah] *n* observatory
مراقبة *n* [mura:qaba]
مراقبة جوية
[Mora'qabah jaweyah] *n* air-traffic controller
مراهق adolescent *n* [mura:hiq]
مراهنة betting *n* [mura:hana]
مرؤوس inferior *n* [marʔuws]

مرئي visible *adj* [marʔij]
مربح lucrative, *adj* [murbiħ] profitable
مربط *n* [marbatˤu]
مربط الجواد
[Marbaṭ al-jawad] *n* stall
مربع *adj* [murabbaʕ]
ذو مربعات
[dho moraba'aat] *adj* checked
مربع الشكل
[Moraba'a al-shakl] *adj* square
مُربك confusing *adj* [murbik]
مربّى jam *n* [murabba:]
وعاء المربّى
[We'aaa almorabey] *n* jam jar
مربية nanny *n* [murabbija]
مرّة once *adv* [marratan]
مرة ثانية
[Marrah thaneyah] *n* again
مرّة *n* [mara]
مرة واحدة
[Marah waḥedah] *n* one-off
مرتاح relieved *adj* [murta:ħ]
مرتب tidy *adj* [murattab]
مرتبة *n* [martaba]
مرتبة ثانية
[Martabah thaneyah] *adj* second-class
هل يوجد مرتبة احتياطية؟
[hal yujad ferash iḥte-yaṭy?] Is there any spare bedding?
مرتبط related *adj* [murtabitˤ]
مرتبك puzzled, *adj* [murtabik] confused
مُرْتَجِل pedestrian *n* [murtaʒil]
مرتفع high *adv* [murtafiʕun]
بصوت مرتفع
[Beṣot mortafe'a] *adv* aloud
مرتفع الثمن
[mortafe'a al-thaman] *adj* expensive
المقعد مرتفع جدا
[al-ma'q'ad mur-taf'a jedan] The seat is too high
مرتين twice *adv* [marratajni]
مرج lawn *n* [marʒ]
مُرجان coral *n* [marʒa:n]
مرجع reference *n* [marʒaʕin]
مرجل boiler *n* [mirʒal]
مرح hilarious *adj* [marañ]
مرحاض lavatory, loo *n* [mirħa:dˤ]
لفة ورق المرحاض
[Lafat wara'q al-merhaḍ] *n* toilet roll
مرحبا welcome! *excl* [marħaban]
مرحبا!
[marħaban] *excl* hi!
مرحلة instance *n* [marħala]
مَرْزيبان marzipan *n* [marzi:ba:n]
مرساة anchor *n* [mirsa:t]
مُرسِل sender *n* [mursil]
مرسى berth *n* [marsa:]
مرشة sprinkler *n* [miraʃʃa]
مُرَشح candidate *n* [muraʃʃaħ]
مرشد guide *n* [murʃid]
مرشد سياحي
[Morshed seyaḥey] *n* tour guide
في أي وقت تبدأ الرحلة مع المرشد؟
[fee ay wa'qit tabda al-reḥla m'aa al-murshid?] What time does the guided tour begin?
هل يوجد أي رحلات مع مرشد يتحدث بالإنجليزية؟
[hal yujad ay reḥlaat ma'aa murshid yata-ḥadath bil-injile-ziya?] Is there a guided tour in English?
هل يوجد لديكم مرشد لجولات السير المحلية؟
[hal yujad laday-kum murshid le-jaw-laat al-sayr al-maḥal-iya?] Do you have a guide to local walks?
مرض disease *n* [maradˤ]
مرض تصلب الأنسجة المتعددة
[Maraḍ taṣalob al-ansejah al-mota'adedah] *n* MS
مرض السرطان
[Maraḍ al-saraṭan] *n* cancer *(illness)*
مرض السكر
[Maraḍ al-sokar] *n* diabetes
مرض التيفود
[Maraḍ al-tayfood] *n* typhoid
مرض الزهايمر
[Maraḍ al-zehaymar] *n* Alzheimer's disease
مرض حمى القش

[Maraḍ ḥomma al-'qash] *n* hay fever
مرض ذات الرئة
[Maraḍ dhat al-re'aa] *n* pneumonia
مرضي disease-related *adj* [maradˤij]
إذن غياب مرضي
[edhn gheyab maraḍey] *n* sick note
أجازة مَرضِيَّة
[Ajaza maraḍeyah] *n* sick leave
غير مرضي
[Ghayr marḍa] *adj* unsatisfactory
الأجر المدفوع خلال الأجازة المرضية
[Al-'ajr al-madfoo'a khelal al-'ajaza al-maraḍeyah] *n* sick pay
مرطب moisturizer *n* [muratˤtˤib]
مرعب frightening, *adj* [murʕib] horrifying, alarming
مرعوب frightened, *adj* [marʕu:b] terrified
مُرفق included *adj* [murfiq]
مِرفق elbow *n* [mirfaq]
مرق broth *n* [maraq]
مرقة *n* [marqatu]
مرقة اللحم
[Mara'qat al-laḥm] *n* gravy
مرقط spotty *adj* [muraqqatˤ]
مرقع patched *adj* [muraqqaʕ]
مَركب boat *n* [markab]
ظهر المركب
[ḍhahr al-mrkeb] *n* deck
ما هو موعد آخر مركب؟
[ma howa maw-'aid aakhir markab?] When is the last boat?
مُركّب medication *n* [murakkab]
مُركّب لعلاج السعال
[Morakab le'alaaj also'aal] *n* cough mixture
مُرَكّب complex *adj* [markab]
مَركَبَة coach *(vehicle)* *n* [markaba]
مركز strong *adj* [markazu]
مراكز رئيسية
[Marakez raeaseyah] *npl* headquarters
مركز ترفيهي
[Markaz tarfehy] *n* leisure centre
مركز تسوق
[Markaz tasawe'q] *n* shopping centre
مركز العمل
[markaz al-'aamal] *n* job centre
مركز الاتصال
[Markaz al-eteṣal] *n* call centre
مركز زائري
[Markaz zaerey] *n* visitor centre
مركز موسيقى
[Markaz mose'qa] *n* stereo
مركزي central *adj* [markazijjat]
تدفئة مركزية
[Tadfeah markazeyah] *n* central heating
مرن flexible *adj* [marin]
غير مَرِن
[Ghayer maren] *adj* stubborn
مرهق exhausted, *adj* [murhiq] strained
مرهق الأعصاب
[Morha'q al-a'aṣaab] *adj* nerve-racking
مرهم ointment *n* [marhamun]
مُرهن pawnbroker *n* [murhin]
مرهَوظ baggy *adj* [marhu:zˤ]
مروحة fan *n* [mirwaħa]
هل يوجد مروحة بالغرفة
[hal yujad mirwa-ḥa bil-ghurfa?] Does the room have a fan?
مُرور traffic *n* [muru:r]
مُرَوّض tame *adj* [murawwidˤ]
مروع appalling, *adj* [murawwiʕ] grim, terrific
مريب dubious *adj* [muri:b]
مريح comfortable, *adj* [muri:ħ] restful
غير مريح
[Ghaeyr moreeḥ] *adj* uncomfortable
دافئ ومريح
[Dafea wa moreeḥ] *adj* cosy
كرسي مريح
[Korsey moreeḥ] *n* easy chair
مريض invalid, patient *n* [mari:dˤ]
مريع terrible *adj* [muri:ʕ]
بشكل مريع
[Be-shakl moreeḥ] *adv* terribly
مريلة *n* [marjala]
مريلة مطبخ
[Maryalat maṭbakh] *n* apron
مِزَاج temper *n* [miza:ʒ]

مزاد auction *n* [maza:d]
مزارع farmer *n* [maza:riʕ]
مزج mix *vt* [maziʒa]
مزح joke *v* [mazaħa]
مزحة prank *n* [mazħa]
مزحي fun *adj* [mazħij]
مُزْخَرَف painter *(in house)* *n* [muzaxraf]
مزدحم crowded *adj* [muzdaħim]
مزدهر lush, thrifty *adj* [muzdahir]
مزدوج twinned *adj* [muzdawaʒ]
غرفة مزدوجة
[Ghorfah mozdawajah] *n* double room
طريق مزدوج الاتجاه للسيارات
[Taree'q mozdawaj al-etejah lel-sayarat] *n* dual carriageway
مزرعة farm *n* [mazraʕa]
مزرعة خيل استيلاد
[Mazra'at khayl esteelaad] *n* stud
مزعج *adj* [muzʕiʒ]
طفل مزعج
[Ṭefl moz'aej] *n* brat
مَزْعوم alleged *adj* [mazʕu:m]
مزق rip up, disrupt, tear *v* [mazzaqa]
مزلجة sledge *n* [mizlaʒa]
مزلجة بعجل
[Mazlajah be-'aajal] *n* rollerskates
مزلقان level crossing *n* [mizlaqa:n]
مزلقة toboggan *n* [mizlaqa]
مزمار bassoon *n* [mizma:r]
مزامير القربة
[Mazameer al-'qarbah] *npl* bagpipes
مزمن chronic *adj* [muzmin]
مَزهُوّ *adj* [mazhuww]
مَزهُوّ بنَفْسِه
[Mazhowon benafseh] *adj* smug
مزود *n* [muzawwad]
مزود بخدمة الإنترنت
[Mozawadah be-khedmat al-enternet] *n* ISP
مُزَوَر mock *adj* [muzawwir]
مزيج mix *n* [mazi:ʒ]
مزيد *adj* [mazi:d]
من فضلك أحضر لي المزيد من الماء
[min faḍlak iḥḍir lee al-mazeed min al-maa] Please bring more water
نحن في حاجة إلى المزيد من أواني الطهي
[naḥno fee ḥaja ela al-mazeed min awany al-ṭahy] We need more crockery
نحن في حاجة إلى المزيد من البطاطين
[Naḥn fee ḥajah ela al-mazeed men al-baṭaṭeen] We need more blankets
مُزَيَّف fake *adj* [muzajjaf]
مزيل *n* [muzi:l]
مزيل رائحة العرق
[Mozeel raaehat al-'aara'q] *n* deodorant
مزيل طلاء الأظافر
[Mozeel ṭalaa al-aḍhafer] *n* nail-polish remover
مساء evening *n* [masa:ʔ]
في المساء
[fee al-masaa] in the evening
مساء الخير
[masaa al-khayer] Good evening
ما الذي ستفعله هذا المساء
[ma al-lathy sataf-'aalaho hatha al-masaa?] What are you doing this evening?
ماذا يمكن أن نفعله في المساء؟
[madha yamken an naf-'aalaho fee al-masaa?] What is there to do in the evenings?
هذه المائدة محجوزة للساعة التاسعة من هذا المساء
[hathy al-ma-eda maḥjoza lel-sa'aa al-tase'aa min hatha al-masaa] The table is reserved for nine o'clock this evening
مساءً p.m. *adv* [masa:ʔun]
مسائي *adj* [masa:ʔij]
صف مسائي
[Ṣaf masaaey] *n* evening class
مُسَابِق racer *n* [musa:biq]
مسابَقة contest *n* [musa:baqa]
مسار track *n* [masa:r]
مسار كرة البولينج
[Maser korat al-boolenj] *n* bowling alley
مساعد *n* ◁ associate *adj* [musa:ʕid] assistant
مساعد اللبس
[Mosa'aed al-lebs] *n* dresser

مساعد المدرس
[Mosa'aed al-modares] *n* classroom assistant
مساعد المبيعات
[Mosa'aed al-mobee'aat] *n* sales assistant
مساعد شخصي
[Mosa'aed shakhṣey] *n* personal assistant
مساعد في متجر
[Mosa'aed fee matjar] *n* shop assistant
مساعدة assistance, *n* [musa:ʕada] help
وسائل المساعدة السمعية
[Wasael al-mosa'adah al-sam'aeyah] *n* hearing aid
سرعة طلب المساعدة
[isri'a bẹ-ṭalab al-musa-'aada] Fetch help quickly!
أحتاج إلى مساعدة
[aḥtaaj ela musa-'aada] I need assistance
هل يمكن مساعدتي
[hal yamken musa-'aadaty?] Can you help me?
هل يمكنك مساعدتي في الركوب من فضلك؟
[hal yamken -aka musa-'aadaty fee al-rikoob min faḍlak?] Can you help me get on, please?
هل يمكنك مساعدتي من فضلك؟
[hal yamken -aka musa-'aadaty min faḍlak?] Can you help me, please?
مسافة distance *n* [masa:fa]
على مسافة بعيدة
[Ala masafah ba'aedah] *adv* far
مسافة بالميل
[Masafah bel-meel] *n* mileage
مسافر traveller *n* [musa:fir]
مسافر يوقف السيارات ليركبها مجانا
[Mosafer yo'qef al-sayarat le-yarkabha majanan] *n* hitchhiker
مسألة matter *n* [masʔala]
مسالم peaceful *adj* [musa:lim]
مساهم stockholder *n* [musa:him]
مساو equal *adj* [musa:win]
مساواة equality *n* [musa:wa:t]
مسؤول accountable, *adj* [masʔu:l] responsible
غير مسئول
[Ghayr maswool] *adj* irresponsible
مسئول الجمرك
[Masool al-jomrok] *n* customs officer
مسؤولية *n* [masʔuwlijja] responsibility
مُساوي equivalent *n* [musa:wi:]
مسبب *adj* [musabbibu]
مسبب الصمم
[Mosabeb lel-ṣamam] *adj* deafening
مسبح *n* [masbaħ]
هل يوجد مسبح؟
[hal yujad masbaḥ?] Is there a swimming pool?
مستاء hurt, resentful *adj* [musta:ʔ]
مستأجر tenant *n* [mustaʔʒir]
مُسْتَثمر investor *n* [mustaθmir]
مستحسن *adj* [mustaħsan]
من مستحسن
[Men al-mostahsan] *adj* advisable
مستحضر *n* [mustaħdˤara:t]
مستحضرات تزيين
[Mostaḥdarat tazyeen] *npl* cosmetics
مُستحضر *n* [mustaħdˤar]
مُستحضر سائل
[Mostḥdar saael] *n* lotion
مستحق *adj* [mustaħaqq]
مستحق الدفع
[Mostaḥa'q al-daf'a] *adj* due
مستحيل impossible *adj* [mustaħi:l]
مُستَخدم used *adj* [mustaxdamu]
مُستَخدِم user *n* [mustaxdim]
مُستَخدِم الانترنت
[Mostakhdem al-enternet] *n* internet user
مستدير round *adj* [mustadi:r]
مسترخي laid-back *adj* [mustarxi:]
مستريح relaxed *adj* [mustri:ħ]
مستشار specialist *n* [mustaʃa:r] *(physician)*
مستشفى hospital *n* [mustaʃfa:]
مستشفى أمراض عقلية
[Mostashfa amraḍ 'aa'qleyah] *n* mental

hospital
مستشفى توليد
[Mostashfa tawleed] *n* maternity hospital
أعمل في أحد المستشفيات
[A'amal fee aḥad al-mostashfayat] I work in a hospital
أين توجد المستشفى؟
[ayna tojad al-mustashfa?] Where is the hospital?
علينا أن ننقله إلى المستشفى
['alayna an nan-'quloho ela al-mustashfa] We must get him to hospital
كيف يمكن أن أذهب إلى المستشفى؟
[kayfa yamkin an athhab ela al-mustashfa?] How do I get to the hospital?
مستطيل [mustatˤiːl] *n* rectangle
مستطيل الشكل
[Mostaṭeel al-shakl] *adj* oblong, rectangular
مُستعار [mustaʕaːr] *adj*
اسم مُستعار
[Esm most'aar] *n* pseudonym
مستعد [mustaʕidd] *adj* willing
مستعص [mustaʕsˤin] *adj* obstinate
مستعمل [mustaʕmal] *adj* secondhand
مُستَغِل [mustaɣill] *adj* extortionate
مستقَبل [mustaqbal] *n* future
مستقبلي [mustaqbalij] *adj* future
مستقر [mustaqirr] *adj* stable
غير مستقر
[Ghayr mosta'qer] *adj* unstable
مستَقل [mustaqil] *adj* independent
مُستَقل [mustaqilin] *adj*
بشكل مُستَقل
[Beshakl mosta'qel] *adv* freelance
مستقيم [mustaqiːm] *adj* straight
في خط مستقيم
[Fee khad mosta'qeem] *adv* straight on
مستكشف [mustakʃif] *n* (مسبار) explorer
مُستَكمَل [mustakmal] *adj* done
مُستَلِم [mustalim] *n* receiver *(person)*

مستمر [mustamirr] *adj* constant, running *n* ◁ continuous
مستمع [mustamiʕ] *n* listener
مستنبت زجاجي [mustanbatun zuʒaːʒijjun] conservatory
مستند [mustanad] *n* document
أريد نسخ هذا المستند
[areed naskh hadha al-mustanad] I want to copy this document
مستندات [mustanada:tun] *npl* documents
مستنقع [mustanqaʕ] *n* bog
مُستَهل [mustahall] *n* outset
مُستَهلِك [mustahlik] *n* consumer
مستو [mustawin] *adj* even
مستودع [mustawdaʕu] *n* warehouse
مستودع الزجاجات
[Mostawda'a al-zojajat] *n* bottle bank
مستوقد [mustawqid] *n* fireplace
مستوى [mustawa:] *n*
مستوى المعيشة
[Mostawa al-ma'aeeshah] *n* standard of living
مُستيقظ [mustajqizˤ] *adj* awake
مسجد [masʒid] *n*
هل يوجد هنا مسجد؟
[hal yujad huna masjid?] Where is there a mosque?
مسجل [musaʒʒal] *adj*
مسجل شرائط
[Mosajal sharayeṭ] *n* tape recorder
ما المدة التي يستغرقها بالبريد المسجل؟
[ma al-mudda al-laty yasta-ghru'qoha bil-bareed al-musajal?] How long will it take by registered post?
مُسَجَل [mussaʒal] *adj* registered
مُسَجِّل [musaʒʒal] *n* recorder *(scribe)*
مسح [masħ] *n* survey
مسح ضوئي
[Masḥ ḍawaey] *n* scan
مسح [masaħa] *v* mop up, wipe, wipe up
يمسح الكترونياً
[Yamsaḥ elektroneyan] *v* scan

مسحوق n [masħu:q]
مسحوق خبز
[Masḥoo'q khobz] n baking powder
مسحوق الكاري
[Masḥoo'q alkaarey] n curry powder
مَسْحوق الطَّلْق
[Masḥoo'q al-ṭal'q] n talcum powder
مسخ monster n [masx]
مسدد paid adj [musaddad]
غير مسدد
[Ghayr mosadad] adj unpaid
مسدس pistol n [musaddas]
مسدود blocked n [masdu:d]
طريق مسدود
[Taree'q masdood] n dead end
مسرح theatre n [masraħ]
ماذا يعرض الآن على خشبة المسرح؟
[madha yu'a-raḍ al-aan 'aala kha-shabat al-masraḥ?] What's on at the theatre?
مسرحي adj [masraħij]
متى يمكننا أن نذهب لمشاهدة عرضًا مسرحيًا؟
[mata yamkin-ona an nadhab le-musha-hadat 'aarḍan masra-ḥyan?] Where can we go to see a play?
مسرحية n [masraħijja]
مسرحية موسيقية
[Masraḥeyah mose'qeya] n musical
مسرف extravagant adj [musrif]
مسرور pleased adj [masru:r]
مسرور جداً
[Masroor jedan] adj delighted
مُسَطَّح flat n [musatˁtˁaħ]
مسطرة ruler (*measure*) n [mistˁara]
مسطرين trowel n [mistˁarajni]
مُسكِر liqueur n [muskir]
مسكَن n [maskan] accommodation
مسكون n [masku:n]
غير مسكون
[Ghayr maskoon] adj uninhabited
مسل entertaining adj [musallin]
مُسلح armed adj [musallaħ]
مسلسل n [musalsal]
حلقة مسلسلة
[Ḥala'qah mosalsalah] n serial
مسلسل درامي
[Mosalsal deramey] n soap opera
مسلك route n [maslak]
مُسلِم Moslem, Muslim adj [muslim] ◁ n Muslim
مُسَلَّم intact, adj [musallam] accepted
مُسَلَّم به
[Mosalam beh] adj undisputed
مسلوق poached adj [maslu:q] (*simmered gently*)
مسمار nail n [misma:r]
مسمار صغير يدفع بالإبهام
[Mesmar ṣagheer yodfa'a bel-ebham] n thumb tack
مسمار قلاووظ
[Mesmar 'qalawooḍh] n screw
مسموح adj [masmu:ħ]
أريد غرفة غير مسموح فيها بالتدخين
[areed ghurfa ghyer masmooḥ feeha bil-tadkheen] I'd like a non-smoking room
أمسموح لي أن أصطاد هنا؟
[amasmooḥ lee an aṣ-ṭad huna?] Am I allowed to fish here?
ما هو الحد المسموح به من الحقائب؟
[ma howa al-ḥad al-masmooḥ behe min al-ḥa'qaeb?] What is the baggage allowance?
ما هي أقصى سرعة مسموح بها على هذا الطريق؟
[ma heya a'qṣa sur'aa masmooḥ beha 'aala hatha al- ṭaree'q?] What is the speed limit on this road?
مسمى adj [musamma:]
غير مسمى
[ghayr mosama] adj anonymous
مُسِن aged adj [musinn]
مسودة draught n [muswadda]
مسيء offensive adj [musi:ʔ]
مسيح n [masi:ħ]
نزول المسيح
[Nezool al-maseeḥ] n advent
مَسيحي Christian adj [masi:ħij] ◁ n Christian

اسم مَسيحي
[Esm maseeḥey] *n* Christian name
n [muʃa:dda] **مشادة**
مشادة كلامية
[Moshadah kalameyah] *n* argument
row *(argument)* *n* [muʃa:da] **مُشادَة**
n [muʃa:rika] **مُشاركة**
مُشاركة في الوقت
[Mosharakah fee al-wa'qt] *n* timeshare
communion *n* [muʃa:raka] **مُشاركَة**
n [maʃa:ʕir] **مشاعر**
مُراعٍ لمشاعر الآخرين
[Moraa'a le-masha'aer al-aakhareen] *adj* considerate
spectator, *n* [muʃa:hid] **مشاهد** onlooker
مشاهد التلفزيون
[Moshahadat al-telefezyon] *n* viewer
n [muʃa:hada] **مشاهدة**
متى يمكننا أن نذهب لمشاهدة فيلمًا سينمائيا؟
[Mata yomkenona an nadhab le-moshahadat feelman senemaeyan] Where can we go to see a film?
هل يمكن أن نذهب لمشاهدة الغرفة؟
[hal yamken an nadhhab le-musha-hadat al-ghurfa?] Could you show me please?
sinister *adj* [maʃʔwm] **مَشؤوم**
adj [muʃbaʕ] **مشبع**
مشبع بالماء
[Moshaba'a bel-maa] *adj* soppy
clip *n* [maʃbak] **مشبك**
مشبك الغسيل
[Mashbak al-ghaseel] *n* clothes peg
مشبك ورق
[Mashbak wara'q] *n* paperclip
suspicious *adj* [maʃbu:h] **مشبوه**
suspect *n* [muʃtabah] **مشتبه**
مشتبه به
[Moshtabah beh] *v* suspect
joint *adj* [muʃtarak] **مشترك**
buyer *n* [muʃtari:] **مشتري**
inflamed *adj* [muʃtaʕil] **مشتعل**
n [muʃtaɣil] **مشتغل**
مشتغل بالكهرباء
[Moshtaghel bel-kahrabaa] *n* electrician
garden centre *n* [maʃtal] **مشتل**
encouraging *adj* [muʃaʒʒiʕ] **مشجع**
morgue *n* [maʃraħa] **مشرحة**
supervisor *n* [muʃrif] **مشرف**
مشرف على بيت
[Moshref ala bayt] *n* caretaker
far-eastern, *adj* [maʃriqij] **مَشرِقي** oriental
drink *n* [maʃru:b] **مشروب**
مشروب غازي
[Mashroob ghazey] *n* soft drink
مشروب النَّخْب
[Mashroob al-nnkhb] *n* toast *(tribute)*
مشروب فاتح للشهية
[Mashroob fateḥ lel shaheyah] *n* aperitif
مشروبات روحية
[Mashroobat rooḥeyah] *npl* spirits
أي المشروبات لديك رغبة في تناولها؟
[ay al-mash-roobat la-dyka al-raghba fee tana-wilha?] What would you like to drink?
ما هو مشروبك المفضل
[ma howa mashro-bak al-mufaḍal?] What is your favourite drink?
ماذا يوجد من المشروبات المسكرة المحلية؟
[madha yujad min al-mash-robaat al-musakera al-maḥa-leya?] What liqueurs do you have?
هل لديك رغبة في تناول مشروب؟
[hal ladyka raghba fee tanawil mash-roob?] Would you like a drink?
conditional *adj* [maʃru:tˤ] **مشروط**
غير مشروط
[Ghayr mashrooṭ] *adj* unconditional
valid *adj* ◁ project *n* [maʃru:ʕ] **مشروع**
comb *n* [muʃtˤ] **مشط**
comb *v* [maʃatˤa] **مشط**
radioactive *adj* [muʃiʕʕ] **مشع**
sorcerer, *n* [muʃaʕwið] **مُشعوذ** juggler
operator *n* [muʃaɣɣil] **مشغل**
مشغل اسطوانات دى في دي
[Moshaghel esṭwanat D V D] *n* DVD player

مشغل الأغنيات المسجلة
[Moshaghel al-oghneyat al-mosajalah] *n* disc jockey
مشغل الاسطوانات
[Moshaghel al-esṭewanat] *n* CD player
MP3 مشغل ملفات
[Moshaghel malafat MP3] *n* MP3 player
MP4 مشغل ملفات
[Moshaghel malafat MP4] *n* MP4 player
مشغول busy, engaged *adj* [maʃɣu:l]
مشغول البال
[Mashghool al-bal] *adj* preoccupied
إنه مشغول
[inaho mash-ghool] It's engaged
مَشفى infirmary *n* [maʃfa:]
مشكلة problem *n* [muʃkila]
هناك مشكلة ما في الغرفة
[Honak moshkelatan ma fel-ghorfah] There's a problem with the room
هناك مشكلة ما في الفاكس
[Honak moshkelah ma fel-faks] There is a problem with your fax
مشكوك *adj* [maʃku:k]
مشكوك فيه
[Mashkook feeh] *adj* doubtful
مشلول paralysed *adj* [maʃlu:l]
مشمئز disgusted *adj* [muʃmaʔizz]
مشمس sunny *adj* [muʃmis]
الجو مشمس
[al-jaw mushmis] It's sunny
مشمش apricot *n* [miʃmiʃ]
مشمع *n* [muʃammiʕ]
مشمع الأرضية
[Meshama'a al-arḍeyah] *n* lino
مشهد scene *n* [maʃhad]
مشهدي spectacular *adj* [maʃhadij]
مشهور known, well- *adj* [maʃhu:r] known, famous
مُشوار walk *n* [miʃwa:r]
مشوش chaotic *adj* [muʃawwaʃ]
مُشوق interesting *adj* [muʃawwiq]
مشوَي grilled *adj* [maʃwij]
مَشي walking *n* [maʃj]
مشى walk *v* [maʃa:]
يَمشي أثناء نومه
[Yamshee athnaa nawmeh] *v* sleepwalk

مشيخي Presbyterian *adj* [maʃjaxij]
كَنِيسة مَشيَخِيَّة
[Kaneesah mashyakheyah] *n* Presbyterian
مصاب casualty *adj* [musˁa:b]
مصاب بدوار البحر
[Moṣab be-dawar al-baḥr] *adj* seasick
مصاب بالسكري
[Moṣab bel sokkarey] *adj* diabetic
مصاب بالامساك
[Moṣab bel-emsak] *adj* constipated
إنها مصابة بالدوار
[inaha muṣa-ba bel-dawar] She has fainted
مصادفة chance *n* [musˁa:dafa]
مُصارع wrestler *n* [musˁa:riʕ]
مصارَعة wrestling *n* [musˁa:raʕa]
مصاريف *n* [masˁa:ri:f]
هل يوجد مصاريف للحجز؟
[hal yujad maṣareef lel-ḥajz?] Is there a booking fee?
مصاص *n* [masˁsˁa:sˁ]
مصاص دماء
[Maṣaṣ demaa] *n* vampire
مَصّاصَه lolly *n* [masˁsˁasˁa]
مصباح lamp *n* [misˁba:ħ]
مصباح أمامى
[Mesbaḥ amamey] *n* headlight
مصباح علوي
[Mesbaḥ 'aolwey] *n* headlight
مصباح اضاءة
[Mesbaḥ eḍaah] *n* light bulb
مصباح الضباب
[Mesbaḥ al-ḍabab] *n* fog light
مصباح الشارع
[Mesbaḥ al-share'a] *n* streetlamp
مصباح الفرامل
[Mesbaḥ al-faramel] *n* brake light
مِصْبَاح بِسَرِير
[Meṣbaaḥ besareer] *n* bedside lamp
مصد bumper *n* [musˁidd]
مَصْدر infinitive *n* [masˁdar]
مصدم shocking *adj* [musˁdim]
مصر Egypt *n* [misˁru]
مُصِر persistent *adj* [musˁirru]
مصراع *n* [misˁra:ʕ]

مصراع النافذة
[meṣraa'a alnafedhah] *n* shutters
مصرف [masˤrif] *n* ditch
المصاريف المدفوعة مقدما
[Al-maṣaareef al-madfoo'ah mo'qadaman] *n* cover charge
مصرف للمياه
[Maṣraf lel-meyah] *n* plughole
مصرف النفايات به انسداد
[muṣraf al-nifayaat behe ensi-dad] The drain is blocked
مصروف [masˤru:f] *n*
مصروف الجيب
[Maṣroof al-jeeb] *n* pocket money
مصري [misˤrij] *adj* Egyptian ◁ *n* Egyptian
مصعد [misˤʕad] *n* lift *(up/down)*
مِصْعَد التَّزَلُّج
[Meṣ'aad al-tazalog] *n* ski lift
أين يوجد المصعد؟
[ayna yujad al-maṣ'aad?] Where is the lift?
هل يوجد مصعد في المبنى؟
[hal yujad maṣ'aad fee al-mabna?] Is there a lift in the building?
مُصَغَر [musˤaɣɣar] *adj* miniature
شَكْل مُصَغَر
[Shakl moṣaghar] *n* miniature
مصفاة [misˤfa:t] *n* colander
مصفاة معمل التكرير
[Meṣfaah ma'amal al-takreer] *n* refinery
مُصفف [musˤaffif] *n*
مُصفف الشعر
[Moṣafef al-sha'ar] *n* hairdresser
مصلحة [masˤlaħa] *n* interest *(income)*
مُصَمِم [musˤammim] *n* designer
مُصَمِم أزياء
[Moṣamem azyaa] *n* stylist
مُصَمِم داخلي
[Moṣamem dakheley] *n* interior designer
مُصَمِم موقع
[Moṣamem maw'qe'a] *n* webmaster
مصنع [masˤnaʕ] *n* factory
صاحب المصنع
[Ṣaheb al-maṣna'a] *n* manufacturer
مصنع البيرة
[maṣna'a al-beerah] *n* brewery
مصنع منتجات الألبان
[maṣna'a montajat al-alban] *n* dairy
مصنع منزلياً
[Maṣna'a manzeleyan] *adj* home-made
أعمل في أحد المصانع
[A'amal fee aḥad al-maṣaane'a] I work in a factory
مصور [musˤawwir] *n* cameraman
مصور فوتوغرافي
[moṣawer fotoghrafey] *n* photographer
مصيدة [misˤjada] *n* trap
مضاد [mudˤa:d] *adj* opposite
جسم مضاد
[Jesm moḍad] *n* antibody
مضاد حيوي
[Moḍad ḥayawey] *n* antibiotic
مضاد لإفراز العرق
[Moḍad le-efraz al-'aar'q] *n* antiperspirant
مضاد للفيروسات
[Moḍad lel-fayrosat] *n* antivirus
مضارب [mudˤa:rib] *n*
هل يؤجرون مضارب الجولف؟
[hal yo-ajeroon maḍarib al-jolf?] Do they hire out golf clubs?
هل يقومون بتأجير مضارب اللعب؟
[hal ya'qo-moon be-ta-jeer maḍarib al-li'aib?] Do they hire out rackets?
مضاعف [mudˤa:ʕaf] *adj* double
مضاعفة [mudˤa:ʕafa] *n* multiplication
مضايق [mudˤa:jiq] *adj* annoying
مُضايقة [mudˤa:jaqa] *n* harassment
مضبوط [madˤbu:tˤ] *adj* exact
مضجع [madˤʒaʕ] *n* settee
مضجع صغير
[Maḍja'a ṣagheer] *n* couchette
مضحك [mudˤħik] *adj* funny
مضخة [midˤaxxa] *n* pump
المضخة رقم ثلاثة من فضلك
[al-maḍakha ra'qum thalath min faḍlak] Pump number three, please
مضرب [midˤrab] *n* bat *(with ball)*
مضرب كرة الطاولة

[Maḍrab korat al-ṭawlah] *n* racquet
مَضْرَب [midˤrabu] *n* whisk
مضغ [madˤaɣa] *v* chew
مضغوط [madˤɣu:tˤ] *adj* compact, jammed
قرص مضغوط
['qorṣ maḍghooṭ] *n* compact disc
مُضَلِل [mudˤallil] *adj* misleading
مضيف [mudˤi:f] *n* presenter (entertains), steward
مضيف الطائرة
[moḍeef al-ṭaaerah] *n* flight attendant
مضيف بار
[Moḍeef bar] *n* bartender
مضيفة [mudˤi:fa] *n*
مضيفة جوية
[Moḍeefah jaweyah] *n* flight attendant
مضيفة بار
[Moḍeefat bar] *n* bartender
مطار [matˤa:r] *n* airport
أتوبيس المطار
[Otobees al-maṭar] *n* airport bus
كيف يمكن أن أذهب إلى المطار
[Kayf yomken an adhhab ela al-maṭar] How do I get to the airport?
مُطَارَد [mutˤa:rad] *adj* haunted
مطاردة [mutˤa:rada] *n* chase
مطاط [matˤtˤa:tˤ] *n* rubber band
مطاطي [matˤa:tˤij] *adj* stretchy
شريط مطاطي
[shareeṭ maṭaṭey] *n* rubber band
قفازات مطاطية
['qoffazat maṭaṭeyah] *n* rubber gloves
مطافئ [matˤa:fiʔ] *adj*
رَجُل المطافئ
[Rajol al-maṭafeya] *n* fireman
مطالب [matˤa:lib] *adj*
كثير المطالب
[Katheer almaṭaleb] *adj* demanding
مطالبة [mutˤa:laba] *n* claim
مطبخ [matˤbax] *n* kitchen
مطبخ مجهز
[Maṭbakh mojahaz] *n* fitted kitchen
مطبوع [matˤbu:ʕ] *adj*
هل يوجد لديكم أي مطبوعات عن ...؟
[hal yujad laday-kum ay maṭ-bo'aat 'aan...?] Do you have any leaflets about...?
مطبوعات [matˤbu:ʕa:tun] *npl* printout
مطحنة [mitˤħanatu] *n*
مطحنة الفلفل
[maṭḥanat al-felfel] *n* peppermill
مطر [matˤar] *n* rain
أمطار حمضية
[Amṭar ḥemdeyah] *n* acid rain
هل تظن أن المطر سوف يسقط؟
[hal taḍhun ana al-maṭar sawfa yas'qiṭ?] Do you think it's going to rain?
مطرد [mutˤrad] *adj* steady
مطعم [matˤʕam] *n* cafeteria, restaurant
هل يمكن أن تنصحني بمطعم جيد؟
[hal yamken an tan-ṣaḥny be-maṭ'aam jayid?] Can you recommend a good restaurant?
هل يوجد أي مطاعم نباتية هنا؟
[hal yujad ay maṭa-'aem nabat-iya huna?] Are there any vegetarian restaurants here?
مطل [matall] *n* outlook
مطلب [matˤlab] *n* request, requirement
مُطَلَق [mutˤallaq] *adj* divorced
مُطْلَق [mutˤlaq] *adj* sheer
مُطمئِن [mutˤmaʔin] *adj* reassuring
مطنب [mutˤanabb] *adj* redundant
مُطهر [mutˤahhir] *n* antiseptic
مطهو [matˤhuww] *adj* ready-cooked
مطيع [mutˤi:ʕ] *adj* obedient
مُظَاهرة [muzˤa:hara] *n* demonstration
مظلة [mizˤalla] *n* umbrella, parachute
مظلم [muzˤlim] *adj* dark
مظهر [mazˤhar] *n* appearance, showing, shape
مع [maʕa] *prep* with
معاد [muʕa:d] *adj* unfavourable
مُعادلة [muʕa:dala] *n* equation
معارِض [muʕa:ridˤ] *adj* opposing
مُعارضة [muʕa:radˤa] *n* opposition

معاش [maʕaːʃ] *n* pension
صاحب المعاش
[Ṣaheb al-ma'aash] *n* senior
صاحب معاش كبير السن
[Ṣaheb ma'aash kabeer al-sen] *n* senior citizen
معاصر [muʕaːsˤiru] *adj* contemporary
معاق [muʕaːq] *adj* disabled
مُعَاق [muʕaːqun] *npl* disabled people
مُعَاكس [muʕaːkis] *n* contrary
مُعَالِج [muʕaːliʒ] *n*
مُعَالِج القدم
[Mo'aaleg al-'qadam] *n* chiropodist
معالم [maʕaːlim] *n*
ما هي المعالم التي يمكن أن نزورها هنا؟
[ma heya al-ma'aalim al-laty yamken an nazo-raha huna?] What sights can you visit here?
معاملة [muʕaːmala] *n* treatment, transaction
سوء معاملة الأطفال
[Soo mo'aamalat al-aṭfaal] *n* child abuse
معاهدة [muʕaːhada] *n* treaty
معبد [muʕabbad] *n* temple
معبد اليهود
[Ma'abad al-yahood] *n* synagogue
معتاد [muʕtaːd] *adj* usual, regular
معتدل [muʕtadil] *adj* medium (*between extremes*), modest
معتل [muʕtal] *adj* unwell
معتم [muʕtim] *adj* overcast
معجزة [muʕʒiza] *n* miracle
معجل [muʕaʒʒil] *n* accelerator
معجنات [muʕaʒʒanaːt] *n* pastry
معجون [maʕʒuːn] *n* paste
معجون الأسنان
[ma'ajoon asnan] *n* toothpaste
مُعَد [muʕadd] *adj* prepared
مُعْد [muʕdin] *adj* infectious
معدات [muʕidaːt] *n*
هل يمكن أن نؤجر المعدات؟
[hal yamken an no-ajer al-mu'ae-daat?] Can we hire the equipment?
مُعدات [muʕaddaːt] *n* equipment, outfit
معدة [maʕida] *n* stomach
مُعَدَّة [muʕadda] *n* device
معدل [muʕaddal] *adj* varied ◃ *n* average, rate
معدل وراثيا
[Mo'aaddal weratheyan] *adj* genetically-modified
معدن [maʕdin] *n* metal
معدني [maʕdinij] *adj*
زجاجة من المياه المعدنية غير الفوارة
[zujaja min al-meaa al-ma'adan-iya gher al-fawara] a bottle of still mineral water
معدي [muʕddiː] *adj*
هل هو معدي؟
[hal howa mu'ady?] Is it infectious?
معدية [muʕdija] *n* ferry
معدية سيارات
[Me'adeyat sayarat] *n* car-ferry
معذرة [maʕðiratun] *excl*
معذرة، هذا هو مقعدي؟
[ma'a-dhera, hadha howa ma'q'aady] Excuse me, that's my seat
معرض [maʕridˤ] *n* exhibition, show
معرفة [maʕrifa] *n* knowledge
معركة [maʕraka] *n* battle
معروف [maʕruːf] *n* favour
غير معروف
[Gheyr ma'aroof] *adj* unknown
معزول [maʕzuːl] *adj* isolated
معسر [muʕassir] *adj* drunk
معسكر [muʕaskar] *n* camp, camper
تنظيم المعسكرات
[Tanṭeem al-mo'askarat] *n* camping
موقد يعمل بالغاز للمعسكرات
[Maw'qed ya'amal bel-ghaz lel-mo'askarat] *n* camping gas
معصم [miʕsˤam] *n* wrist
معضلة [muʕdˤila] *n* dilemma
معطف [miʕtˤaf] *n* overcoat
معطف المطر
[Me'ataf lel-maṭar] *n* raincoat
معطف فرو
[Me'ataf farw] *n* fur coat
معطف واق من المطر

[Me'ataf wa'qen men al-maarṭar] *n* raincoat

معطل broken down *adj* [muʕatˤtˤal]

عداد موقف الانتظار معطل

['adad maw'qif al-entiḍhar mo'ạaṭal] The parking meter is broken

العداد معطل

[al-'aadad mu'ạaṭal] The meter is broken

معفى *adj* [muʕfaː]

معفى من الرسوم الضريبية

[Ma'afee men al-rosoom al-ḍareebeyah] *adj* duty-free

معقد complicated *adj* [muʕaqqad]

معقوص curly *adj* [maʕquːsˤ]

معقول reasonable *adj* [maʕquːlin]

إلى حد معقول

[Ela ḥad ma'a'qool] *adv* pretty

على نحو معقول

[Ala naḥw ma'a'qool] *adv* reasonably

غير معقول

[Ghear ma'a'qool] *adj* unreasonable

معلب tinned *adj* [muʕallab]

معلق outstanding *adj* [muʕallaq]

مُعلق commentator *n* [muʕalliq]

معلَم *n* [muʕallim]

معلم القيادة

[Mo'alem al-'qeyadh] *n* driving instructor

مَعلَم landmark *n* [maʕlam]

مُعَلم instructor *n* [muʕallim]

معلَومات *n* [amaʕluːmaːt] information

أريد الحصول على بعض المعلومات عن...

[areed al-ḥuṣool 'aala ba'aḍ al-ma'aloomat 'an...] I'd like some information about...

معلومة *n* [maʕluːma]

معلومات عامة

[Ma'aloomaat 'aamah] *npl* general knowledge

معماري architect *n* [miʕmairjj]

معمداني *n* [maʕmadaːnijja]

كنيسة معمدانية

[Kaneesah me'amedaneyah] *n* Baptist

معمل lab *n* [maʕmal]

معمل كيميائي

[M'amal kemyaeay] *n* pharmacy

معنويات *npl* [maʕnawijjaːtun] morale

مَعنيّ concerned *adj* [maʕnij]

معنى meaning *n* [maʕnaː]

معهد institute *n* [maʕhad]

معي gut *n* [maʕjj]

معيار criterion *n* [miʕjir]

معيد demonstrator *n* [muʕiːd]

معيشة *n* [maʕiːʃa]

تكلفة المعيشة

[Taklefat al-ma'aeeshah] *n* cost of living

حجرة المعيشة

[Ḥojrat al-ma'aeshah] *n* sitting room

معيوب faulty *adj* [maʕjuːb]

مغادرة departure *n* [muɣaːdara]

مغادرة الفندق

[Moghadarat al-fondo'q] *n* checkout

مُغامر adventurous *adj* [muɣaːmir]

مغامرة adventure *n* [muɣaːmara]

مغبر dusty *adj* [muɣbarr]

مُغتصب rapist *n* [muɣtasˤib]

مغذِي nutritious *adj* [muɣaððij]

مادة مغذية

[Madah moghadheyah] *n* nutrient

مغر tempting *adj* [muɣrin]

مغربي Moroccan *adj* [maɣribij] ◁ *n* Moroccan

مغرفة ladle *n* [miɣrafa]

مغرور stuck-up *adj* [maɣruːr]

مغزى moral *n* [maɣzan]

بلا مغزى

[Bela maghdha] *adj* pointless

مغسلة laundry *n* [miɣsala]

مغفل naive, daft *adj* [muɣaffal]

مُغَفل fool *n* [muɣaffl]

مغلف packed *adj* [muɣallaf] ◁ *n* envelope

مغلق closed *adj* [muɣlaq]

مغلقا closely *adv* [muɣlaqan]

مغلي boiled *adj* [maɣlij]

مغناطيس magnet *n* [miɣnaːtˤiːs]

مغناطيسي *adj* [miɣnaːtˤiːsij] magnetic

مغني singer *n* [muɣanniː]

مغني أو عازف منفرد
[Moghaney aw 'aazef monfared] *n* soloist
مُغَنّي حفلات
[Moghaney ḥafalat] *n* lead singer
مُغَيِّر [muɣajjir] *n*
مُغَيِّر السرعة
[Moghaey al-sor'aah] *n* gearshift
مفاجئ [mufa:ʒiʔ] *adj* sudden, abrupt, surprising
على نحو مفاجئ
[Ala naḥw mofaheya] *adv* surprisingly
بشكل مفاجئ
[Be-sakl mofajeya] *adv* abruptly
حركة مفاجئة
[Ḥarakah mofajeah] *n* hitch
مفَاجئة [mufa:ʒaʔa] *n* surprise
مُفَاعِل [mufa:ʕil] *n* reactor
مفاوض [mufa:widˤ] *n* negotiator
مفاوضات [mufa:wadˤa:tun] *npl* negotiations
مفتاح [mifta:ħ] *n* key *(for lock)*
صانع المفاتيح
[Ṣaane'a al-mafateeḥ] *n* locksmith
مفتاح ربط
[Meftaḥ rabṭ] *n* wrench
مفتاح ربط وفك الصواميل
[Meftaḥ rabṭ wafak al-ṣawameel] *n* wrench
مفتاح كهربائي
[Meftaḥ kahrabaey] *n* switch
مفتاح لغز
[Meftaḥ loghz] *n* clue
مفاتيح السيارة
[Meftaḥ al-sayarah] *n* car keys
أين يمكن أن أحصل على المفتاح...؟
[ayna yamken an naḥṣal 'ala al-muftaaḥ...?] Where do we get the key...?
أين يوجد مفتاح ...
[le-ay ghurfa hadha al-muftaaḥ?] What's this key for?
أين يوجد مفتاح الجراج؟
[ayna yujad muftaaḥ al-jaraj?] Which is the key for the garage?
المفتاح لو سمحت
[al-muftaaḥ law samaḥt] The key, please
لقد نسيت المفتاح
[la'qad nasyto al-muftaaḥ] I've forgotten the key
مفترس [muftaris] *adj* fierce, ravenous
مفتش [mufattiʃʃ] *n* inspector
مفتش التذاكر
[Mofatesh taḍhaker] *n* ticket inspector
مفتوح [maftu:ħ] *adj* open
هل المعبد مفتوح للجمهور؟
[hal al-ma'abad maf-tooḥa lel-jamhoor?] Is the temple open to the public?
هل المتحف مفتوح أيام السبت؟
[hal al-mat-ḥaf maf-tooḥ ayaam al-sabit?] Is the museum open on Sundays?
مفجر [mufaʒʒir] *n*
مفجر انتحاري
[Mofajer enteḥaarey] *n* suicide bomber
مفر [mafarr] *adj*
لا مفر منه
[La mafar menh] *adj* indispensable
مُفرِح [mufriħ] *adj* thrilling
مفرَد [mufrad] *n* singular
مفرط [mufritˤ] *adj* excessive
مفروش [mafru:ʃ] *adj* furnished
مفروض [mafru:dˤ] *adj*
هل هناك رسوم مفروضة على كل شخص؟
[hal hunaka risoom maf-rooḍa 'aala kul shakhiṣ?] Is there a cover charge?
مفزع [mufziʕ] *adj* dreadful
مفسد [mufsid] *n*
مفسد المتعة
[Mofsed al-mot'aah] *n* spoilsport
مُفَسِّر [mufassir] *n* interpreter
مفصل [mifsˤal] *adj*
التواء المفصل
[El-tewaa al-mefṣal] *n* sprain
مُفَصّل [mufasˤsˤal] *adj* detailed
مْفصَل [mafsˤal] *n* joint *(meat)*
مِفصلة [mifsˤala] *n* hinge
مفصول [mafsˤu:l] *adj*
غير مفصول فيه
[Ghaey mafṣool feeh] *adj* undecided

مفضل favourite *adj* [mufadˤdˤal]
مُفقِد *n* [mufqid]
مُفَقِد للشهية
[Mof'qed lel-shaheyah] *adj* anorexic
مفقود missing *adj* [mafqu:d]
مفقودات وموجودات
[maf'qodat wa- mawjoodat] *n* lost-and-found
إن ابنتي مفقودة
[enna ibnaty maf-'qoda] My daughter is missing
مفك screwdriver *n* [mifakk]
مفكرة notebook *n* [mufakkira]
مفلس broke, bankrupt *adj* [muflis]
مفهوم *adj* [mafhu:m] understandable
مُفوّض *adj* [mufawwdˤ]
تلميذ مُفوّض
[telmeedh mofawaḍ] *n* prefect
مفيد helpful *adj* [mufi:d]
غير مفيد
[Ghayr mofeed] *adj* unhelpful
مقابل opposed *adj* [muqa:bil]
مقابلة interview *n* [muqa:bala]
مقارنة comparison *n* [muqa:rana]
قابل للمقارنة
['qabel lel-mo'qaranah] *adj* comparable
مقاس *n* [maqa:s]
مقاس كبير
[Ma'qaas kabeer] *adj* outsize
هل يوجد مقاس أصغر من ذلك؟
[hal yujad ma'qaas aṣghar min dhalik?] Do you have this in a smaller size?
هل يوجد مقاس أكبر من ذلك؟
[hal yujad ma'qaas akbar min dhalik?] Do you have this in a bigger size?
هل يوجد مقاس كبير جدا؟
[hal yujad ma'qaas kabeer jedan?] Do you have an extra large?
مقاطعة interruption *n* [muqa:tˤaʕa]
مقال essay *n* [maqa:l]
مقالة article *n* [maqa:la]
مقام *adj* [maqa:m]
هل يوجد أية حفلات غنائية ممتعة مقامة حاليًا؟
[hal yujad ayat ḥaf-laat ghena-eya mumti'aa mu'qama ḥaleyan?] Are there any good concerts on?
مقامر gambler *n* [muqa:mir]
مقامرة gambling *n* [muqa:mara]
مقاول contractor *n* [muqa:wil]
مقاوم *adj* [muqa:wim]
مقاوم لحرارة الفرن
[Mo'qawem le-ḥarart al-forn] *adj* ovenproof
مقاوم للبلل
[Mo'qawem lel-balal] *adj* showerproof
مقاوم للمياه
[Mo'qawem lel-meyah] *adj* waterproof
مقاومة resistance *n* [muqa:wama]
مقبرة cemetery, tomb *n* [maqbara]
مقبس socket *n* [miqbas]
مقبض handle, knob *n* [miqbadˤ]
مقبض الباب
[Me'qbaḍ al-bab] *n* door handle
لقد سقط مقبض الباب
[la'qad sa'qaṭa me-'qbaḍ al-baab] The door handle has come off
مقبل coming *n* [muqbil]
مقبول acceptable, *adj* [maqbu:l] okay
غير مقبول
[Ghayr ma'qool] *adj* unacceptable
مقتصد sober, *adj* [muqtasˤid] economical
مقدار *n* [miqda:r]
مقدار كبير
[Me'qdaar kabeer] *n* mass *(amount)*
مِقدام courageous *adj* [miqda:m]
مَقدس holy *adj* [muqadas]
مقدم presenter *n* [muqaddim]
مقدم برامج
[Mo'qadem bramej] *n* compere
مُقدم الطلب
[Mo'qadem al-ṭalab] *n* applicant
مقدماً *adv* [muqaddaman] beforehand
مقدمة introduction *n* [muqadima]
مُقَرّب intimate, close *adj* [muqarrab]
شخص مُقَرّب
[Shakhṣ mo'qarab] *n* favourite
مقروء legible *adj* [maqru:ʔ]

غير مقروء
[Ghayr ma'qrooa] *adj* illegible
مقص scissors *n* [miqasˤ]
مقص أظافر
[Ma'qaṣ aḍhafer] *n* nail scissors
مَقصَد destination *n* [maqsˤid]
مقصود intentional *adj* [maqsˤu:d]
مقصورة compartment *n* [maqsˤu:ra]
مقطب *n* [muqatˤtˤab]
مقطب الجبين
[Mo'qṭ ab al-jabeen] *adj* sulky
مقطع *n* [maqtˤaʕ]
مقطع لفظي
[Ma'qṭa'a lafḍhy] *n* syllable
مَقطُورَة trailer *n* [maqtˤu:ra]
موقع المَقطُورَة
[Maw'qe'a al-ma'qṭorah] *n* caravan site
مقطوعة *n* [maqtˤunwʕa]
مقطوعة موسيقية
[Ma'qṭoo'aah moose'qeyah] *n* tune
مقعد seat *(furniture)* *n* [maqʕad]
مقعد بجوار النافذة
[Ma'q'aad bejwar al-nafedhah] *n* window seat
أريد حجز مقعد في العربة المخصصة لغير المدخنين
[areed ḥajiz ma'q'ad fee al-'aaraba al-mukhaṣaṣa le-ghyr al-mudakhin-een] I want to reserve a seat in a non-smoking compartment
أريد مقعد في العربة المخصصة لغير المدخنين
[areed ma'q'aad fee al-'aaraba al-mukhaṣaṣa le-ghyr al-mudakhineen] I'd like a non-smoking seat
أريد مقعد لطفل عمره عامين
[areed ma'q'ad le-ṯifil 'aumro 'aam-yin] I'd like a child seat for a two-year-old child
المقعد منخفض جدا
[al-ma'q'ad mun-khafiḍ jedan] The seat is too low
لقد قمت بحجز المقعد
[la'qad 'qimto be-ḥajis al-ma'q'aad] I have a seat reservation
هل يمكن الجلوس في هذا المقعد؟
[hal yamken al-jiloos fee hadha al-ma'q-'aad?] Is this seat free?
مقلاة pan, saucepan *n* [miqla:t]
مقلب *n* [muqallib]
مقلب النفايات
[Ma'qlab al-nefayat] *n* rubbish dump
مقلق worrying *adj* [muqliq]
مقلم stripy *adj* [muqallam]
مقلمة pencil case *n* [miqlama]
مقلي fried *adj* [maqlij]
مقنع convincing, *adj* [muqniʕ] persuasive
مقهى café *n* [maqha:]
مقهى الانترنت
[Ma'qha al-enternet] *n* cybercafé, internet café
مقود handlebars *n* [miqwad]
سيارة مقودها على الجانب الأيسر
[Sayarh me'qwadoha ala al-janeb al-aysar] *n* left-hand drive
مقياس gauge, standard *n* [miqja:s]
مقيم resident *n* [muqi:m]
أجنبي مقيم
[Ajnabey mo'qeem] *n* au pair
مكاتب office *n* [maka:tib]
أعمل في أحد المكاتب
[A'amal fee aḥad al-makateb] I work in an office
مكاسب earnings *npl* [maka:sibun]
مكافئ matching *adj* [muka:fiʔ]
مكافأة reward *n* [muka:faʔa]
مكالمة call *n* [muka:lama]
أين يمكن أن أقوم بإجراء مكالمة تليفونية؟
[ayna yamken an a'qoom be-ijraa mukalama talefoniya?] Where can I make a phonecall?
مكان location, place, *n* [maka:n] spot *(place)*
في أي مكان
[Fee ay makan] *adv* anywhere
ليس في أي مكان
[Lays fee ay makan] *adv* nowhere
مكان عمل
[Makan 'aamal] *n* workstation
مكان الحوادث

[Makan al-ḥawadeth] *n* venue
مكان الميلاد
[Makan al-meelad] *n* place of birth
أتعرف مكانا جيدا يمكن أن أذهب إليه؟
[a-ta'aruf makanan jayidan yamkin an adhhab e-lay-he?] Do you know a good place to go?
أنا في المكان ...
[ana fee al-makaan...] My location is...
مكانة position, rank *n* [maka:na] *(status)*
مكانة أعلى
[Makanah a'ala] *n* superior
مكبح *n* [makbaħ]
مكبح العربة
[Makbaḥ al-'arabah] *n* spoke
مكْبر amplifier *n* [mukabbir]
مِكْبَس piston *n* [mikbas]
مَكة Mecca *n* [makkatu]
مكتب desk, disk, office *n* [maktab]
مكتب رئيسي
[Maktab a'ala] *n* head office
مكتب صرافة
[Maktab ṣerafah] *n* bureau de change
مكتب التسجيل
[Maktab al-tasjeel] *n* registry office
مكتب التذاكر
[Maktab al-taḍhaker] *n* ticket office
مكتب الاستعلامات
[Maktab al-este'alamaat] *n* enquiry desk
مكتب البريد
[maktab al-bareed] *n* post office
مكتب الحجز
[Maktab al-ḥjz] *n* ticket office
مكتب المراهنة
[Maktab al-morahanah] *n* betting shop
مكتب المفقودات
[Maktab al-maf'qodat] *n* lost-property office
مكتب وكيل السفريات
[Maktab wakeel al-safareyat] *n* travel agent's
أين يوجد مكتب السياحة؟
[ayna maktab al-siyaḥa?] Where is the tourist office?
هل لديك مكتب إعلامي؟
[hal ladyka maktab e'a-laamy?] Do you have a press office?
هل لي أن أستخدم المكتب الخاص بك؟
[hal lee an astakhdim al-maktab al-khaaṣ bik?] May I use your desk?
مكتبة library *n* [maktaba]
مكتبة لبيع الكتب
[Maktabah le-bay'a al-kotob] *n* bookshop
مكتبي *adj* [maktabij]
أعمال مكتبية
[A'amaal maktabeyah] *npl* paperwork
أدوات مكتبية
[Adawat maktabeyah] *n* stationery
مكث stick out, stay in *v* [makaθa]
مُكَثّف *adj* [mukaθθaf]
بصورة مُكَثّفة
[Beṣorah mokathafah] *adv* heavily
مكربن *n* [mukarban]
المكربن
[Al-makreen] *n* carburettor
مكرس devoted *adj* [mukarras]
مكرونة *npl* [makaru:natun] macaroni
مكرونة سباجتي
[Makaronah spajety] *n* spaghetti
مكرونة اسباجتي
[Makaronah spajety] *n* noodles
مَكْسَب gain *n* [maksab]
مكسور broken *adj* [maksu:r]
مكسور القلب من شدة الحزن
[Maksoor al-'qalb men shedat al-ḥozn] *adj* heartbroken
إنها مكسورة
[inaha maksoora] This is broken
القفل مكسور
[al-'qiful maksoor] The lock is broken
مكسيكي Mexican *adj* [miksi:kij] Mexican *n* ◁
مكعب cube *n* ◁ cubic *adj* [mukaʕʕab]
مكعب ثلج
[Moka'aab thalj] *n* ice cube
مكعب حساء
[Moka'aab ḥasaa] *n* stock cube
مُكَمِّل supplement *n* [mukammill]
مكنسة broom *n* [miknasatu]

مكنسة كهربائية
[Meknasah kahrobaeyah] *n* vacuum cleaner
مكهرب electric *adj* [mukahrab]
مكوك shuttle *n* [makku:k]
مكون component *adj* [mukawwin] ◃ component *n*
مُكَوِّن ingredient *n* [mukawwan]
ملأ *v* [malaʔa]
يَملأ ب
[Yamlaa be] *v* fill up
ملأ fill *vt* [malaʔa]
يَمْلأ الفراغ
[Yamlaa al-faragh] *v* fill in
ملئ *adj* [malʔ]
ملئ بالطاقة
[Maleea bel-ṭa'qah] *adj* energetic
ملاءة sheet *n* [malla:ʔa]
ملاءة مثبتة
[Melaah mothabatah] *n* fitted sheet
ملائم appropriate, *adj* [mula:ʔim] suitable
غير ملائم
[Ghayr molaem] *adj* inadequate, inconvenient
ملابس clothes *npl* [mala:bisun]
غرفة تبديل الملابس
[Ghorfat tabdeel al-malabes] *n* fitting room
ملابس داخلية
[Malabes dakheleyah] *n* lingerie
ملابس السهرة
[Malabes al-sahrah] *npl* evening dress
ملابس قطنية خشنة
[Malabes 'qotneyah khashenah] *npl* dungarees
ملابسي بها بلل
[mala-bisy beha balal] My clothes are damp
ملاحظة comment, *n* [mula:ħazˤa] note *(message)*, remark
ملاحظة الطيور
[molaḥaḍhat al-ṭeyoor] *n* birdwatching
ملاحقة pursuit *n* [mula:ħaqa]
ملاريا malaria *n* [mala:rja:]
ملازم *n* [mula:zim]
ملازم أول
[Molazem awal] *n* lieutenant
ملاط mortar *(plaster)* *n* [mala:tˤ]
ملاقط *n* [mala:qitˤ]
ملاقط صغيرة
[Mala'qeṭ ṣagheerah] *npl* tweezers
ملاك angel *n* [mala:k]
ملاكم boxer *n* [mula:kim]
ملاكمة boxing *n* [mula:kama]
ملاهي funfair *n* [mala:hijju]
ملاوي Malawi *n* [mala:wi:]
ملتجأ shelter *n* [multaʒa]
ملتجأ آمن
[Moltajaa aamen] *n* asylum
مُلتحٍ bearded *adj* [multaħin]
ملتهَب *adj* [multahib]
لثتي ملتهبة
[lathaty multaheba] My gums are sore
ملجأ refuge *n* [malʒa]
ملح instant, urgent *adj* ◃ salt *n* [milħ]
مُلحِد atheist *n* [mulħid]
ملحق attached *adj* [mulħaq]
ملحوظ noticeable *n* [malħu:zˤ]
ملحي *adj* [milħij]
ماء ملحي
[Maa mel'ḥey] *adj* saltwater
ملخص *n* ◃ brief *adj* [mulaxxasˤ] summary
ملصق sticker *n* [mulsˤaq]
ملصق بيانات
[Molsa'q bayanat] *n* label
ملطف conditioner *n* [mulatˤtˤif]
ملعب playground *n* [malʕab]
مباراة الإياب فى ملعب المضيف
[Mobarat al-eyab fee mal'aab al-moḍeef] *n* home match
ملعب رياضي
[Mal'aab reyady] *n* playing field
ملعب الجولف
[Mal'aab al-jolf] *n* golf course
ملعقة spoon *n* [milʕaqa]
مقدار ملعقة صغيرة
[Me'qdar mel'a'qah ṣagheerah] *n* spoonful
ملعقة البسط
[Mel'a'qat al-bast] *n* spatula

ملعقة الحلويات
[Mel'a'qat al-ḥalaweyat] *n* dessert spoon
ملعقة شاي
[Mel'a'qat shay] *v* teaspoon
ملعقة مائدة
[Mel'a'qat maedah] *n* tablespoon
ملف file *(folder)*, file *(tool)* *n* [milaff]
ملف PDF
[Malaf PDF] ی PDF
ملف على شكل حرف U
[Malaf 'ala shakl ḥarf U] *n* U-turn
ملف له حلقات معدنية لتثبيت الورق
[Malaf lah ḥala'qaat ma'adaneyah letathbeet al-wara'q] *n* ring binder
ملك king, monarch *n* [milk]
ملك have *v* [malaka]
ملكة queen *n* [malika]
ملكه own *adj* [mulkahu]
مَلَكي royal *adj* [milki:]
مِلكية property *n* [milkijja]
مِلكِية خاصة
[Melkeyah khaṣah] *n* private property
ملل *n* [malal]
يُسبِب الملل
[Yosabeb al-malal] *v* bored
ملوث dirty, polluted *adj* [mulawwaθ]
ملون *adj* [mulawwan]
تليفزيون ملون
[Telefezyon molawan] *n* colour television
ملون على نحو خفيف
[Molawan ala naḥw khafeef] *adj* tinted
أرجو الحصول على نسخة ضوئية ملونة من هذا المستند
[arjo al-ḥuṣool 'aala nuskha mu-lawana min hadha al-mustanad min faḍlak] I'd like a colour photocopy of this, please
فيلم ملون من فضلك
[filim mola-wan min faḍlak] A colour film, please
مِلْيَار billion *n* [milja:r]
مليمتر millimetre *n* [mili:mitr]
ملين *n* [mulajjin]
ملين الأمعاء
[Molayen al-am'aa] *n* laxative
مليون million *n* [milju:n]
مليونير millionaire *n* [milju:ni:ru]
مماثل similar *adj* [muma:θil]
ممارسة practise *n* [muma:rasa]
ممانع reluctant *adj* [muma:niʕ]
ممتاز excellent *adj* [mumta:z]
ممتاز جدا
[Momtaaz jedan] *adj* super
ممتد extensive *adj* [mumtadd]
ممتع enjoyable *adj* [mumtiʕ]
ممتلئ chubby *adj* [mumtaliʔ]
ممتلئ الجسم
[Momtaleya al-jesm] *adj* plump
ممتلیء full *adj* [mumtali:ʔʔ]
ممتن grateful *adj* [mumtann]
ممثل actor (عامل) *n* [mumaθθil]
ممثل هزلي
[Momthel hazaley] *n* comedian
ممثلة actress *n* [mumaθθila]
ممحاة rubber *n* [mimħa:t]
ممر passage *(route)* *n* [mamarr]
ممر جانبي
[Mamar janebey] *n* bypass
مَمَر سُفلِي
[Mamar sofley] *n* underpass
ممر دخول
[Mamar dokhool] *n* way in
ممر خاص لعبور المشاه
[Mamar khaṣ leaboor al-moshah] *n* pedestrian crossing
ممر الدراجات
[Mamar al-darajat] *n* cycle path
ممر المشاة
[mamar al-moshah] *n* footpath
مُمْرِض sickening *adj* [mumridˤ]
ممرَضة nurse *n* [mumarridˤa]
أرغب في استشارة ممرضة
[arghab fee es-ti-sharat mu-mareḍa] I'd like to speak to a nurse
ممسحة *n* [mimsaħa]
ممسحة أرجل
[Memsahat arjol] *n* mat
ممسحة تنظيف
[Mamsaḥat tanḍheef] *n* mop
ممسوس touched *adj* [mamsu:s]
ممشى aisle, walkway *n* [mamʃa:]
مُمطر rainy *adj* [mumtˤir]

ممكن [mumkin] *adj* possible, potential
من الممكن
[Men al-momken] *adv* possibly
ممل [mumill] *adj* boring, monotonous
مملح [mumallaħ] *adj* salty
مملكة [mamlaka] *n* kingdom
المملكة العربية السعودية
[Al-mamlakah al-'aarabeyah al-so'aodeyah] *n* Saudi Arabia
المملكة المتحدة
[Al-mamlakah al-motahedah] *n* United Kingdom
مملكة تونجا
[Mamlakat tonja] *n* Tonga
ممنوع [mamnu:ʕ] *adj* forbidden
مميت [mumi:t] *adj* (مقدر) fatal
مميز [mumajjaz] *adj* distinctive
من [min] *prep* from
أي من
[Ay men] *pron* any
أنا من ...
[ana min...] I'm from...
من هذا؟
[man hadha?] Who is it?
مَنْ [man] *pron* who
مِنْ [min] *prep* from
مناخ [muna:x] *n* climate
منارة [mana:ra] *n* lighthouse
مُنازع [muna:ziʕ] *n* contestant
مناسِب [muna:sib] *adj* convenient, proper
غير مناسب
[Ghayr monaseb] *adj* unsuitable
بشكل مناسب
[Be-shakl monaseb] *adv* properly
مناسبة [muna:saba] *n* occasion
هل توجد حمامات مناسبة للمعاقين؟
[hal tojad ḥama-maat muna-seba lel-mu'aa'qeen?] Are there any accessible toilets?
مناسبي [muna:sabij] *adj* occasional
مناشف [mana:ʃif] *n*
مَناشِف الصُّحون
[Manashef al-ṣoḥoon] *n* tea towel
لقد استهلكت المناشف
[la'qad istuh-lekat al-mana-shif] The towels have run out
هل يمكن أن أقترض منك أحد المناشف؟
[hal yamken an a'qta-reḍ minka aḥad al-mana-shif?] Could you lend me a towel?
مُناصر [muna:sˤir] *n*
مُناصر للطبيعة
[monaṢer lel-ṭabe'aah] *n* naturalist
مُنَاصر للقومية
[Monaṣer lel-'qawmeyah] *n* nationalist
مناصفة [muna:sˤafatan] *adv* fifty-fifty
مقسم مناصفة
[Mo'qassam monaṣafah] *adj* fifty-fifty
مناظر [mana:zˤir] *n*
نريد أن نشاهد المناظر المثيرة
[nureed an nusha-hid al-manaḍhir al-muthera] We'd like to see spectacular views
منافس [muna:fis] *adj* rival, competitor
منافسة [muna:fasa] *n* competition
منافق [muna:fiq] *adj* insincere
مناقشة [muna:qaʃa] *n* debate, discussion
مناقصة [muna:qasˤa] *n* bid
منبسط [munbasitˤ] *adj* flat, level
level *n* ◁
منبه [munabbih] *n* alarm clock
منبوذ [manbu:ð] *adj* maroon
منتبه [muntabih] *adj* alert
منتج [muntaʒ] *n*
منتج ألبان
[Montej albaan] *npl* dairy products
منتجات الألبان
[Montajat al-baan] *npl* dairy products
منتَج [mantu:ʒ] *n* product
مُنتِج [muntiʒ] *n* producer
منتَجع [muntaʒaʕ] *n* resort
منتسب [muntasib] *adj*
منتسب لجماعة الأصحاب
[Montaseb le-jama'at al-aṣḥaab] *n* Quaker
منتشر [muntaʃir] *adj* widespread

مُنتشي thrilled *adj* [muntaʃij]
منتصف *n* [muntasˤaf]
إلى منتصف المسافة
[Ela montaṣaf al-masafah] *adv* halfway
منتصف الليل
[montaṣaf al-layl] *n* midnight
منتصف اليوم
[Montaṣaf al-yawm] *n* noon
منتظم *adj* [muntazˤim]
غير منتظم
[Ghayr montaḍhem] *adj* irregular
منتفخ swollen *adj* [muntafixx]
منتهي over *adj* [muntahij]
منثني bent *(not adj* [munθanij] *straight)*
مَنجا mango *n* [manʒa:]
مُنجَز finished *adj* [munʒaz]
منجم mine *n* [manʒam]
منح *v* [manaħa]
يمنح بقشيشاً
[Yamnaḥ ba'qsheeshan] *vt* tip *(reward)*
منحة grant *n* [minħa]
منحة تعليمية
[Menḥah ta'aleemeyah] *n* scholarship
منحدر slope *n* [munħadir]
طريق منحدر
[Ṭaree'q monḥadar] *n* ramp
منحدر التزلج للمبتدئين
[monḥadar al-tazaloj lel-mobtadeen] *n* nursery slope
منحدر النهر
[Monḥadar al-nahr] *n* rapids
منحني bent *adj* [munħanij] *(dishonest)*, reclining
منخفض low *adj* [munxafidˤ]
منخفضاً low *adv* [munxafadˤan]
منخل sieve *n* [manxal]
مندهش amazed *adj* [mundahiʃ]
مندوب *n* [mandu:b]
مندوب مبيعات
[Mandoob mabee'aat] *n* salesman, shop assistant
مندوبة *n* [mandu:ba]
مندوبة مبيعات
[Mandoobat mabee'aat] *n* saleswoman
منديل hankie *n* [mindi:l]
منديل أطفال
[Mandeel aṭfaal] *n* baby wipe
منديل المائدة
[Mandeel al-maaedah] *n* serviette
منديل قماش
[Mandeel 'qomash] *n* handkerchief
منزل home *n* [manzil]
منزل ريفي
[Mazel reefey] *n* farmhouse
منزل صيفى
[Manzel ṣayfey] *n* villa
منزل فخم
[Mazel fakhm] *n* stately home
منزل متحرك
[Mazel motaḥarek] *n* mobile home
منزل منفصل
[Manzel monfaṣelah] *n* house
منزل نصف متصل
[Mazel neṣf motaṣel] *n* semi-detached house
مَنْزِلة mark *n* [manzila]
منزلي *adj* [manzilijjat]
أعمال منزلية
[A'amaal manzelyah] *n* housework
منسي forgotten *adj* [mansijju]
منشأ *n* [manʃa]
منشأ السلعة المصنوعة
[Manshaa al-sel'aah al-maṣno'aah] *n* make
منشآت (تسهيلات) *npl* [munʃaʔa:tun] facilities
منشار saw *n* [minʃa:r]
منشار المنحنيات
[Menshar al-monḥanayat] *n* jigsaw
منشفة towel *n* [minʃafa]
منشفة صحية
[Manshafah ṣeḥeyah] *n* sanitary towel
منشفة الحمام
[Manshafah alḥammam] *n* bath towel
مِنشَفة الوجه
[Menshafat al-wajh] *n* flannel
منشور publication *n* [manʃu:r]
منشور الكتروني
[Manshoor elektrooney] *n* webzine
منصة platform *n* [minasˤsˤa]
منصة البهلوان

منعزل bleak *adj* [munʕazil]
منعطف turning *n* [munʕatˤaf]
هل هذا هو المنعطف الذي يؤدي إلى...؟
[hal hadha howa al-mun'aa-ṭaf al-ladhy yo-addy ela...?] Is this the turning for...?
منغولي Mongolian *adj* [manɣu:lij]
Mongolian *(person) n* ◁
اللغة المنغولية
[Al-koghah al-manghooleyah] *(language) n* Mongolian
منغوليا Mongolia *n* [manɣu:lja:]
منفاخ *n* [minfa:x]
منفاخ دراجة
[Monfakh draajah] *n* bicycle pump
هل لديك منفاخ؟
[hal ladyka minfaakh?] Do you have a pump?
منفذ *n* [manfað]
منفذ جوي أو بحري
[manfaḍh jawey aw baḥrey] *n* port *(ships)*
منفذ خروج
[Manfaz khoroj] *n* way out
منفرد *adj* [munfarid]
عمل منفرد
['amal monfared] *n* solo
لحن منفرد
[Laḥn monfared] *n* concerto
منفصل separate *adj* [munfasˤil]
بصورة منفصلة
[Beṣorah monfaṣelah] *adv* separately
منزل منفصل
[Manzel monfaṣelah] *n* house
بشكل مُنفَصِل
[Beshakl monfaṣel] *adv* apart
فواتير منفصلة من فضلك
[fawateer mufa-ṣa-lah min faḍlak] Separate bills, please
منفى exile *n* [manfa:]
منقار beak *n* [minqa:r]
مُنقذ *adj* [munqið]
مُنقذ للحياة
[Mon'qedh lel-ḥayah] *adj* life-saving
منقرض extinct *adj* [munqaridˤ]
منقوع soaked *adj* [manqu:ʕ]

[Manaṣat al-bahlawan] *n* trampoline
منصرف outgoing *adj* [munsˤarif]
منصرم past, *adj* [munsˤarim] previous
مُنْضَبِط punctual *adj* [mundˤabitˤ]
منضَدة table *(furniture) n* [mindˤada]
منطقة district, zone *n* [mintˤaqa]
منطقة تقديم الخدمات
[Menta'qat ta'qdeem al- khadamat] *n* service area
منطقة مجاورة
[Menta'qat mojawerah] *n* vicinity
منطقة مشاه
[Menta'qat moshah] *n* precinct
منطقي logical *adj* [mantˤiqij]
منظار binoculars *n* [minzˤa:r]
منظر view, scenery *n* [manzˤar]
منظر طبيعى
[manḍhar ṭabe'aey] *n* landscape
منظف *adj* [munazˤzˤif]
مادة منظفة
[Madah monaḍhefah] *n* detergent
منظم *n* [munazˤzˤim]
منظم رحلات
[monaḍhem raḥalat] *n* tour operator
منظم الضارة
[monaḍhem al-ḍarah] *n* catalytic converter
منظم الخطوات
[monaḍhem al-khaṭawat] *n* pacemaker
منظم شخصي
[monaḍhem shakhṣey] *n* personal organizer
منظمة *n* [munazˤzˤama] organization
منظمة تعاونية
[monaḍhamah ta'aaweneyah] *n* collective
منظور perspective *n* [manzˤu:r]
غير منظور
[Ghayr monaḍhoor] *adj* invisible
منع *n* [manʕ]
منع الحمل
[Man'a al-ḥml] *n* contraception
مَنع prevent *v* [manaʕa]
منَع ban *v* [manaʕa]

مِنْك [mink] n
حيوان المِنْك
[Ḥayawaan almenk] n mink
منهج [manhaʒ] n
منهج دراسى
[Manhaj derasey] n curriculum
منهجي [manhaʒij] adj Methodlst
منهك [munhak] adj tiring
مَنيّ [manij] n sperm
مهاجر [muha:ʒir] adj migrant
مهارة [maha:ra] n skill
مهتاج [muhta:ʒ] adj furious
مهتم [muhttam] adj interested
مهتم بالآخرين
[Mohtam bel-aakhareen] n caring
معذرة، أنا غير مهتم بهذا الأمر
[maʕðaratun ʔana: ɣajru muhtammin biha:ða: alʔamri] Sorry, I'm not interested
مهجور [mahʒu:r] adj lonesome, obsolete
مهد [mahd] n cot, cradle
مُهَدّئ [muhaddiʔ] n tranquillizer
مهذب [muhaððab] adj decent, subtle
مهر [mahr] n foal
مهرب [muharrib] n
مهرب بضائع
[Moharreb baḍae'a] n smuggler
مهرج [muharriʒ] n clown
مهرجان [mihraʒa:n] n festival
مهزوز [mahzu:zz] adj shaken
مهمة [mahamma] n assignment, task
مهمل [muhmil] adj careless, neglected
مهنة [mihna] n occupation (work)
مهندس [muhandis] n engineer
مهني [mihanij] adj vocational
مهني مبتدئ
[Mehaney mobtadea] n apprentice
مهووس [mahwu:s] adj obsessed
مَهيب [mahi:b] adj prestigious
موَاطن [muwa:tˤin] n citizen
مواطن إثيوبي
[Mowaṭen ethyobey] n Ethiopian
مواطن تشيلي
[Mowaṭen tsheeley] n Chilean
مواطن انجليزي
[mowaṭen enjeleezey] n Englishman
مواطنة إنجليزية
[Mowaṭenah enjlezeyah] n Englishwoman
موافقة [muwa:faqa] n approval
مواكب [muwa:kib] adj
مواكب للموضة
[Mowakeb lel-moḍah] adj trendy
مَوْت [mawt] n death
موتور [mawtu:r] n motor
مُوثّق [muwaθθiq] adj authentic
موثوق [mawθu:q] adj
موثوق به
[Mawthoo'q beh] adj reliable
موثوق فيه
[Mawthoo'q beh] adj credible
موجة [mawʒa] n wave, surge
موجز [mu:ʒaz] adj concise
موجود [mawʒu:d] adj
ما هي النكهات الموجودة؟
[Ma hey al-nakhaat al-mawjoodah] What flavours do you have?
هل... موجود؟
[hal... mawjood?] Is... there?
موحد [muwaħħad] adj
الفاتورة موحدة من فضلك
[al-fatoorah mowaḥada min faḍlak] All together, please
موحش [mu:ħiʃ] adj dismal
موحل [mu:ħil] adj muddy
مودم [mu:dim] n modem
مورد [muwarrid] n supplier
مَورِد [mu:rad] n resource
مورَس [mu:ris] n Morse
مورفين [mu:rfi:n] n morphine
موروث [mawru:θ] n heritage
موريتاني [mu:ri:ta:nij] n Mauritius
موريتانيا [mu:ri:ta:nja:] n Mauritania
موز [mawz] n banana
موزع [muwazziʕ] n distributor
موزمبيق [mu:zambi:q] n Mozambique

مُوَسَّع adj [muwassaʕ]
بشكل مُوَسَّع
[Beshakl mowasa'a] adv extensively
موسم season n [mawsim]
موسم راكد
[Mawsem raked] adj off-season
موسمي seasonal adj [mawsimijjat]
التذاكر الموسمية
[Al-tadhaker al-mawsemeyah] n season ticket
موسوعة n [mawsu:ʕa] encyclopaedia
موسى adj [mu:sa:]
موسى الحلاقة
[Mosa alḥela'qah] n razor
موسيقي musical adj [mu:si:qij]
آلة موسيقية
[Aala mose'qeyah] n musical instrument
حفلة موسيقية
[Haflah mose'qeyah] n concert
قائد فرقة موسيقية
['qaaed fer'qah mose'qeyah] n conductor
مسرحية موسيقية
[Masraḥeyah mose'qeya] n musical
موسيقى music n [mu:si:qa:]
عازف موسيقى
['aazef mose'qaa] n musician
مركز موسيقى
[Markaz mose'qa] n stereo
مؤلف موسيقى
[Moaalef mosee'qy] n composer
موسيقى تصويرية
[Mose'qa taṣweereyah] n soundtrack
موسيقى شعبية
[Mose'qa sha'abeyah] n folk music
أين يمكننا الاستماع إلى موسيقى حية؟
[ayna yamken-ana al-istima'a ela mose'qa ḥay-a?] Where can we hear live music?
موصل sweater n [mu:sˤil]
موضة fashion (نمط) n [mu:dˤa]
غير مواكب للموضة
[Ghayr mowakeb lel-moḍah] adj unfashionable
مواكب للموضة
[Mowakeb lel-moḍah] adj fashionable
موضع post (position) n [mawdˤiʕ]
موضع لحفظ الأطعمة
[Mawḍe'a lehafḍh al-aṭ'aemah] n larder
موضعي topical adj [mawdˤiʕij]
موضوع subject, theme n [mawdˤu:ʕ]
موضوع مقالة أو حديث
[Mawḍoo'a ma'qaalah aw hadeeth] n topic
موضوعي adj [mawdˤu:ʕij] impersonal, objective
موطن n [mawtˤin]
موطن أصلي
[Mawṭen aṣley] n homeland
موطن ضعف
[Mawṭen ḍa'af] n shortcoming
موظف employee n [muwazˤzˤaf]
موظف بنك
[mowaḍhaf bank] n banker
موظف حكومة
[mowaḍhaf hokomah] n civil servant
موعد appointment, n [mawʕid] rendezvous
فات موعد استحقاقه
[Fat maw'aed esteḥ'qa'qh] adj overdue
موعد الانتهاء
[Maw'aed al-entehaa] n deadline
أود في تحديد موعد
[awid fee taḥdeed maw'aid] I'd like to make an appointment
لدي موعد مع.....؟
[la-daya maw-'aid m'aa...] I have an appointment with...
هل تحدد لك موعدًا؟
[hal taḥa-dada laka maw'aid?] Do you have an appointment?
موعظة sermon n [mawʕizˤa]
موقد stove n [mawqid]
موقد يعمل بالغاز
[Maw'qed ya'amal bel-ghaz] n gas cooker
موقد يعمل بالغاز للمعسكرات
[Maw'qed ya'amal bel-ghaz lel-mo'askarat] n camping gas
مَوْقِد stove n [mu:qid]

موقع [mawqiʕ] *n* site
موقع البناء
[Maw'qe'a al-benaa] *n* building site
موقع المعسكر
[Maw'qe'a al-mo'askar] *n* campsite
موقع المَقْطُورَة
[Maw'qe'a al-ma'qṭorah] *n* caravan site
موقع الويب
[Maw'qe'a al-weeb] *n* website
موقف [mawqif] *n* attitude
موقف سيارات
[Maw'qaf sayarat] *n* parking
موقف أوتوبيس
[Maw'qaf otobees] *n* bus stop
موقف انتظار
[Maw'qaf entedhar] *n* car park
أين يوجد موقف التاكسي؟
[ayna maw'qif al-taxi?] Where is the taxi stand?
هل معك نقود فكه لعداد موقف الانتظار؟
[Hal ma'ak ne'qood fakah le'adad maw'qaf al-ente ḍhar?] Do you have change for the parking meter?
موكب [mawkib] *n* convoy, procession
مَول [mawwala] *v* finance
مولد [muwalid] *n* generator
مولدافي [mu:lda:fij] *adj* Moldovan
▷ *n* Moldovan
مولدافيا [mu:lda:fja:] *n* Moldova
مولود [mawlu:d] *n* born
مومياء [mu:mja:ʔ] *n* mummy *(body)*
موناكو [mu:na:ku:] *n* Monaco
موهبة [mawhiba] *n* talent
موهوب [mawhu:b] *adj* gifted, talented
ميانمار [mija:nma:r] *n* Myanmar
مياه [mijja:hu] *n* water
زجاجة مياه ساخنة
[Zojajat meyah sakhenah] *n* hot-water bottle
مياه البحر
[Meyah al-baḥr] *n* sea water
مياه الشرب
[Meyah al-shorb] *n* drinking water
مياه بيضاء
[Meyah bayḍaa] *n* cataract *(eye)*
مياه فوارة
[Meyah fawarah] *adj* sparkling water
مياه معدنية
[Meyah ma'adaneyah] *n* mineral water
زجاجة من المياه المعدنية الفوارة
[zujaja min al-meaa al-ma'adan-iya al-fawara] a bottle of sparkling mineral water
كيف يعمل سخان المياه؟
[kayfa ya'amal sikhaan al-meaah?] How does the water heater work?
لا توجد مياه ساخنة
[La tojad meyah sakhena] There is no hot water
هل يشمل السعر توفير المياه الساخنة؟
[hal yash-mil al-si'ar taw-feer al-me-yah al-sakhina?] Is hot water included in the price?
ميدالية [mi:da:lijja] *n* medal
ميدان [majda:n] *n* square
ميراث [mi:ra:θ] *n* inheritance
ميرنجو [mi:rinʒu:] *n* meringue
مَيَّز [majjaza] *v* distinguish
ميزان [mi:za:n] *n* scale *(measure)*, scale *(tiny piece)*
كفتي الميزان
[Kafatay al-meezan] *n* scales
ميزانية [mi:za:nijja] *n* balance sheet, budget
ميزة [mi:za] *n* advantage
ميعاد [mi:ʕa:d] *n*
ما ميعاد استيقاظك؟
[ma me-'aad iste'qa-ḍhak?] What time do you get up?
ميقاتي [mi:qa:tij] *n* timer
ميكانيكي [mi:ka:ni:kij] *adj* mechanical
▷ *n* mechanic
ميكانيكي السيارات
[Mekaneekey al-sayarat] *n* motor mechanic
هل يمكن أن ترسل لي ميكانيكي؟
[hal yamken an tarsil lee meka-neeky?] Can you send a mechanic?

ن

ميكروسكوب [mi:kuru:sku:b] *n* microscope

ميكروفون [mi:kuru:fu:n] *n* microphone, mike

هل يوجد ميكروفون؟
[hal yujad mekro-fon?] Does it have a microphone?

ميكروويف [majkuru:wi:f] *n*

فرن الميكروويف
[Forn al-maykroweef] *n* microwave oven

مَيل [majl] *n* tendency

مَيْل جِنسي
[Mayl jensey] *n* sexuality

مِيل [mi:l] *n* mile

ميلاد [mi:la:d] *n* birth

عشية عيد الميلاد
['aasheyat 'aeed al-meelad] *n* Christmas Eve

عيد الميلاد المجيد
['aeed al-meelad al-majeed] *n* Christmas

عيد ميلاد
['aeed al-meelad] *n* birthday

بعد الميلاد
[Ba'ad al-meelad] *abbr* AD

شجرة عيد الميلاد
[Shajarat 'aeed al-meelad] *n* Christmas tree

شهادة ميلاد
[Shahadat meelad] *n* birth certificate

قبل الميلاد
['qabl al-meelad] *adv* BC

محل الميلاد
[Mahal al-meelad] *n* birthplace

ميناء [mi:na:ʔ] *n* harbour

ميني [mi:ni:] *adj*

ميني باص
[Meny baas] *n* minibus

ميوسلي [miju:sli:] *n*

حبوب الميوسلي
[Ḥoboob al-meyosley] *npl* muesli

ميونيز [maju:ni:z] *n* mayonnaise

نا [na:] *pron* us

نائب [na:ʔibb] *adj* acting, representative

نائب الرئيس
[Naeb al-raaes] *n* deputy head

نائم [na:ʔim] *adj* asleep

ناتج [na:tiʒ] *n* outcome

نَاج [na:ʒin] *n* survivor

ناجح [na:ʒiħ] *adj* successful

غير ناجح
[ghayr najeḥ] *adj* unsuccessful

ناحية [na:ħija] *n* aspect

نادر [na:dir] *adj* rare *(uncommon)*, rare *(undercooked)*

نادرا [na:diran] *adv* rarely, scarcely

نادرا ما
[Naderan ma] *adv* seldom

نادل [na:dil] *n* waiter

نادلة [na:dila] *n* waitress

نادي [na:di:] *n* club *(group)*

نادي الجولف
[Nady al-jolf] *n* golf club *(society)*

نادي الشباب
[Nadey shabab] *n* youth club

نادي ليلي
[Nadey layley] *n* nightclub

هل يوجد نادي جيدة؟

[Hal yojad nady jayedah] Where is there a good club?
sack *n* [na:ru] **نار**
إشعال النار
[Esh'aal al-naar] *n* bonfire
وَقْف إطلاق النار
[Wa'qf eṭlaa'q al-naar] *n* ceasefire
adj [na:rijjat] **ناري**
ألعاب نارية
[Al-'aab nareyah] *npl* fireworks
people *npl* [na:s] **ناس**
fit *vt* [nasaba] **ناسَب**
n [na:six] **ناسخ**
ناسخ الاسطوانة
[Nasekh al-esṭewanah] *n* CD burner
ناسخ لاسطوانات دى في دي
[Nasekh le-sṭewanat D V D] *n* DVD burner
publisher *n* [na:ʃir] **ناشر**
mature, ripe *adj* [na:dˤiʒ] **ناضج**
غير ناضج
[Ghayr naḍej] *adj* immature
adj [na:tˤiq] **ناطق**
ناطق بلغتين
[Naṭe'q be-loghatayn] *adj* bilingual
soft *adj* [na:ʕim] **ناعم**
window *n* [na:fiða] **نافذة**
عتبة النافذة
['aatabat al-nafedhah] *n* windowsill
أريد مقعد بجوار النافذة
[areed ma'q'aad be-jewar al-nafedha] I'd like a window seat
النافذة لا تُفتح
[al-nafidhah la tuftaḥ] The window won't open
لا يمكنني فتح النافذة
[la yam-kinuni faitḥ al-nafitha] I can't open the window
لقد كسرت النافذة
[la'qad kasarto al-nafe-tha] I've broken the window
هل يمكن أن أغلق النافذة؟
[hal yamken an aghli'q al-nafidha?] May I close the window?
هل يمكن أن أفتح النافذة؟
[hal yamken an aftaḥ al-nafidha?] May I open the window?
useful *adj* [na:fiʕ] **نافع**
fountain *n* [na:fu:ra] **نافورة**
critic *n* [na:qid] **نَاقد**
debate, discuss *v* [na:qaʃa] **ناقَش**
incomplete, nude *adj* [na:qisˤ] **ناقص**
contradict *v* [na:qadˤa] **ناقض**
adj [na:qil] **ناقل**
ناقل للعدوى
[Na'qel lel-'aadwa] *adj* contagious
ناقل السرعات لا يعمل
[na'qil al-sur'aat la ya'amal] The gears are not working
n [na:qila] **ناقلة**
ناقلة بترول
[Na'qelat berool] *n* tanker
adj [na:min] **نام**
بَلَد نام
[Baladen namen] *n* developing country
sleep *v* [na:ma] **نام**
nylon *n* [na:jlu:n] **نايلون**
plant *n* [naba:t] **نبات**
نبات رشاد
[Nabat rashad] *n* cress
نبات الجاودار
[Nabat al-jawdar] *n* rye
نبات اللفت
[Nabat al-left] *n* turnip
نبات الهندباء البرية
[Nabat al-hendbaa al-bareyah] *n* dandelion
نبات ذو وبر شائك
[Nabat dho wabar shaek] *n* nettle
نبات يزرع في حاوية
[Nabat yozra'a fee ḥaweyah] *n* pot plant
n ◁ vegetarian *adj* [naba:tij] **نباتي**
vegan, vegetarian
حياة نباتية
[Hayah Nabateyah] *n* vegetation
هل يوجد أي أطباق نباتية؟
[hal yujad ay aṭbaa'q nabat-iya?] Do you have any vegan dishes?
bark *v* [nabaħa] **نبح**
pulses *npl* [nabadˤa:tun] **نبضات**
beat, pulse *n* [nabdˤa] **نبضة**
alert *v* [nabbaha] **نَبِّه**

نبيذ n [nabi:ð]
نبيذ أحمر
[nabeedh aḥmar] n red wine
دورق من النبيذ الأحمر
[dawra'q min al-nabeedh al-aḥmar] a carafe of red wine
زجاجة من النبيذ الأبيض
[zujaja min al-nabeedh al-abyaḍ] a bottle of white wine
قائمة النبيذ من فضلك
['qaemat al-nabeedh min faḍlak] The wine list, please
هل يمكن أن ترشح لي نوع جيد من النبيذ الأبيض؟
[hal yamken an tura-shiḥ lee naw'a jayid min al-nabeedh al-abyaḍ?] Can you recommend a good white wine?
نبيل adj [nabi:l]
رَجُل نبيل
[Rajol nabeel] n gentleman
نبيل المحتد
[Nabeel al-moḥtad] adj gentle
نتن rotten adj [natin]
نتن stink v [natina]
نتَوء n [nutu:ʔ]
نتوء صغير
[Netoa ṣagheer] n wart
نتيجة result, sequel n [nati:ʒa]
نثر spray v [naθara]
نجاح success n [naʒa:ħ]
نجار joiner n [naʒʒa:r]
نجارة carpentry n [niʒʒa:ra]
نجح succeed v [naʒaħa]
نجم star (person) n [naʒm]
نجم سينمائي
[Najm senemaaey] n film star
نجم ذو ذنب
[Najm dho dhanab] n comet
نَجم v [naʒama]
يَنْجُم عن
[Yanjam 'an] v result
نجمة star (sky) n [naʒma]
نحاس copper n [nuħa:s]
نحاس أصفر
[Nahas aṣfar] n brass
نحت n [naħt]
فن النحت
[Fan al-naḥt] n sculpture
نحت carve vt [naħata]
نحلة bee n [naħla]
نحلة ضخمة
[Naḥlah ḍakhmah] n bumblebee
نحوي grammatical adj [naħwij]
نحيف slim, thin adj [naħi:f]
نخاع n [nuxa:ʕu]
نخاع العظم
[Nokhaa'a al-'aḍhm] n marrow
نُخالة bran n [nuxa:la]
نخلة palm (tree) n [naxla]
نداء n [nida:ʔ]
جهاز النداء
[Jehaaz al-nedaa] n pager
جهاز النداء الآلي
[Jehaz al-nedaa al-aaley] n bleeper
نداء استغاثة
[Nedaa esteghathah] n alarm call
نداوة moisture n [nada:wa]
ندب moan v [nadaba]
ندبة scar, seam n [nadba]
ندم remorse n [nadam]
نَدَم regret n [nadima]
نَدِي damp, soggy adj [nadij]
نرجس daffodil n [narʒis]
نَرْد dice n [nard]
نرويجي Norwegian adj [narwi:ʒij]
Norwegian (person) n ◁
اللغة النرويجية
[Al-loghah al-narwejeyah] (language) n Norwegian
نزعة trend n [nazʕa]
نزف bleed vi [nazafa]
نزل get off, go down v [nazala]
يَنزِل في مكان
[Yanzel fee makaan] v put up
يَنْزِلُ البَرَد
[Yanzel al-barad] v hail
نَزْلَة catarrh n [nazla]
نزهة outing, promenade n [nuzha]
نزهة في سيارة
[Nozhah fee sayarah] n drive
نزهة في الهواء الطلق
[Nozhah fee al-hawaa al-ṭal'q] n picnic

نزول n [nuzu:l]
ما هي المحطة النزول للذهاب إلى ...
[ma heya muḥaṭat al-nizool lel-thehaab ela...?] Which stop is it for...?
من فضلك أريد النزول الآن
[min faḍlak areed al-nizool al-aan] Please let me off
من فضلك أخبرني عندما يأتي موعد النزول
[Men faḍlek akhberney 'aendama yaatey maw'aed al-nozool] Please tell me when to get off
نزيف n [nazi:f]
نزيف الأنف
[Nazeef al-anf] n nosebleed
نزيل lodger n [nazi:l]
نساء n [nisa:ʔ]
طبيب أمراض نساء
[Ṭabeeb amraḍ nesaa] n gynaecologist
نسائي adj [nisa:ʔij]
قميص نوم نسائي
['qamees noom nesaaey] n nightie
نسبة proportion, ratio n [nisba]
نسبة مئوية
[Nesbah meaweyah] n percentage
نسبي proportional adj [nisbij]
نسبيا comparatively adv [nisbijjan]
نسبيًا relatively adv [nisbijan]
نسج n [nasʒ]
أنسجة صوفية
[Ansejah ṣoofeyah] npl woollens
نسخ copy *(reproduction)* n [nasx]
أين يمكنني الحصول على بعض النسخ؟
[Ayn yomken al-ḥoṣool ala ba'aḍ al-nosakh?] Where can I get some photocopying done?
نسخ copy v [nasaxa]
هل يمكنك نسخ هذا من أجلي؟
[hal yamken -aka nasikh hadha min ajlee?] Can you copy this for me?
نسخة copy *(written text)*, n [nusxa] version
نسخة ضوئية
[niskha ḍaw-iyaa] n photocopy
نسخة احتياطية
[Noskhah eḥteyaṭeyah] n backup
نسخة مطابقة
[Noskhah moṭe'qah] n replica
نسر vulture n [nasr]
نسل breed n [nasl]
نسى forget v [nasa:]
نسيان n [nisja:nuhu]
لا يمكن نسيانه
[La yomken nesyanh] adj unforgettable
نسيج textile n [nasi:ʒ]
نسيج مضلع
[Naseej moḍala'a] n representative
نَسيج الجِسْم
[Naseej al-jesm] n tissue
نسيم breeze n [nasi:m]
نشا starch n [naʃa:]
نشا الذرة
[Nesha al-zorah] n cornflour
نشابة breadbin, rolling n [naʃʃa:ba] pin
نِشارة sawdust n [niʃa:ra]
نَشاط activity n [naʃa:tˁ]
نَشال pickpocket n [naʃʃa:l]
نشج sob v [naʃaʒa]
نشر press n [naʃr]
حقوق الطبع والنشر
[Ho'qoo'q al-ṭab'a wal-nashr] n copyright
نشر publish v [naʃara]
نشرة leaflet n [naʃra]
نشرة دعائية
[Nashrah de'aeyah] n prospectus
نشرة مطبوعة
[Nashrah maṭbo'aah] n print
نَشط revive v [naʃʃtˁa]
نشوء evolution n [nuʃwuʔ]
نشوب outbreak n [nuʃu:b]
نشوي ecstasy n [naʃawij]
نشيد anthem n [naʃi:d]
نشيد وطني
[Nasheed waṭney] n national anthem
نشيط active adj [naʃi:tˁ]
نص text n [nasˁsˁ]
يَضع نصا
[Yaḍa'a naṣan] v text
نُصب n [nusˁub]
نُصب تذكاري

[Noṣob tedhkarey] *n* memorial
نصح advise *v* [nasˤaħa]
نصر victory *n* [nasˤr]
نصف half *n* [nisˤf]
نصف إقامة
[Neṣf e'qamah] *n* half board
نصف ساعة
[Neṣf saa'aah] *n* half-hour
نصف دائرة
[Neṣf daaeyrah] *n* semicircle
نصف السعر
[Neṣf al-se'ar] *adj* half-price
نِصْف الوقت
[Nesf al-wa'qt] *n* half-time
نصفي half *adj* [nisˤfaj]
نصفياً half *adv* [nisˤfijja:]
نصل blade *n* [nasˤl]
نصّي *adj* [nasˤsˤij]
رسالة نصية
[Resalah naṣeyah] *n* text message
نصيب lot, quota *n* [nasˤi:b]
نصيحة advice *n* [nasˤi:ħa]
نضارة flush *n* [nadˤdˤa:ra]
نضج grow up *v* [nadˤaʒa]
نضد bench *n* [nadˤad]
نطاق *n* [nitˤa:q]
نطاق زمني
[Neṭa'q zamaney] *n* time zone
نطاق واسع
[Neṭ'q wase'a] *n* broadband
نطق *n* [nutˤqin]
متعسر النطق
[Mota'aer alnoṭ'q] *adj* dyslexic
نطق pronounce *v* [natˤaqa]
كيف تنطق هذه الكلمة؟
[kayfa tanṭu'q hathy al-kalema?] How do you pronounce it?
نُطق pronunciation *n* [nutˤq]
نظاراتي optician *n* [nazˤzˤa:ra:ti:]
نظارة glasses, specs, *n* [nazˤzˤa:ra] spectacles
نظارة واقية
[naḍharah wa'qeyah] *n* goggles
هل يمكن تصليح نظارتي؟
[hal yamken taṣleeḥ naḍharaty] Can you repair my glasses?

نظافة hygiene *n* [nazˤa:fa]
عاملة النظافة
['aamelat al-nadhafah] *n* cleaning lady
نظام system *n* [nizˤa:m]
نظام غذائي
[Neḍhaam ghedhey] *v* diet
نظام شمسي
[neḍham shamsey] *n* solar system
نظامي systematic *adj* [nizˤa:mij]
نظر *n* [nazˤr]
قريب النظر
['qareeb al- naḍhar] *adj* near-sighted
قصير النظر
['qaṣeer al-naḍhar] *adj* near-sighted
أعاني من طول النظر
[o-'aany min bu'ad al-naḍhar] I'm long-sighted
أعاني من قصر النظر
[o-'aany min 'quṣr al-naḍhar] I'm short-sighted
نظر look *vi* [nazˤara]
ينظر إلى
[yanḍhor ela] *v* look at
نظرة look *n* [nazˤra]
نظري abstract *adj* [nazˤarij]
نظّرية theory *n* [nazˤarijja]
نَظّف clean *vt* [nazˤzˤafa]
نَظّم organize *v* [nazˤzˤama]
نظيف clean, neat *adj* [nazˤi:f]
نظيف تماما
[naḍheef tamaman] *adj* spotless
هل يمكنني الحصول على كوب نظيف من فضلك؟
[hal yamken -any al-ḥuṣool 'aala koob naḍheef min faḍlak?] Can I have a clean glass, please?
هل يمكنني الحصول على ملعقة نظيفة من فضلك؟
[hal yamken -any al-ḥuṣool 'aala mil-'aa'qa naḍheefa min faḍlak?] Could I have a clean spoon, please?
نعامة ostrich *n* [naʕa:ma]
نعجة sheep *n* [naʕʒa]
نعس doze *v* [naʕasa]
نعسان drowsy, sleepy *adj* [naʕsa:n]
نعم yes! *excl* [niʕma]

نعناع [naʕnaːʕ] *n* mint *(herb/sweet)*, peppermint
نعومة [nuʕuːma] *n* smooth, velvet
نَعْي [naʕj] *n* obituary
نعيم [naʕiːm] *n* bliss
نغمة [naɣama] *n* note *(music)*
نغمة الرنين [Naghamat al-raneen] *n* ringtone
نغمة الاتصال [Naghamat al-eteṣal] *n* dialling tone
نغمة مميزة [Naghamaah momayazah] *n* key *(music/computer)*
نَفَائس [nafaːʔisun] *npl* valuables
نفايَة [nufaːja] *n* dump, garbage
نفخ [nafx] *adj*
آلة نفخ موسيقية [Aalat nafkh mose'qeyah] *n* woodwind
قابل للنفخ ['qabel lel-nafkh] *adj* inflatable
نفّخ [nafaxa] *v* pump up
نَفّذ [naffaða] *v* carry out
نفس [nafs] *n* breath
أنفسكم [Anfosokom] *pron* yourselves
ضبط النفس [Ḍabṭ al-nafs] *n* self-control, self-discipline
علم النفس ['aelm al-nafs] *n* psychology
ثقة بالنفس [The'qah bel-nafs] *n* confidence *(self-assurance)*
افعلها بنفسك [Ef'alhaa be-nafsek] *n* DIY
متميز بضبط النفس [Motameyez bedṭ al-nafs] *adj* self-contained
نفسك [Nafsek] *pron* yourself
لقد جرحت نفسها [la'qad jara-ḥat naf-saha] She has hurt herself
نفساني [nafsaːnij] *adj*
طبيب نفساني [Ṭabeeb nafsaaney] *n* psychiatrist
نفسي [nafsij] *adj* psychiatric
عالم نفسي ['aaalem nafsey] *n* psychologist
نفض [nafadˤa] *vt* dust
نفط [naftˤ] *n* (زيت) oil
جهاز حفر آبار النفط [Gehaz ḥafr abar al-nafṭ] *n* oil rig
نفق [nafaq] *n* tunnel, underpass
نفقات [nafaqaːtun] *npl* expenses
نَفَقة [nafaqa] *n* expenditure
نفي [nafaː] *v* deport
نفيس [nafiːs] *adj* valuable *n* ◁ precious
نقابة [niqaːba] *n*
نقابة العمال [Ne'qabat al-'aomal] *n* trade union
نقالة [naqqaːla] *n* stretcher
نقانق [naqaːniq] *n*
نقانق ساخنة [Na'qane'q sakhenah] *n* hot dog
نَقْد [naqd] *n* cash, criticism
نقدي [naqdijjat] *adj*
ليس معي أية أموال نقدية [laysa ma'ay ayat amwaal na'q-diya] I don't have any cash
نقّر [naqara] *v* click
نَقر [naqr] *n* percussion
نقرة [naqra] *n* click
نقش [naqʃ] *n* inscription
نقش [naqaʃa] *v* engrave
نقص [naqsˤ] *n* flaw, lack
نقطة [nuqtˤa] *n* dot, point, period *(punctuation)*
مجموع النقاط [Majmoo'a al-nekaṭ] *n* score *(of music)*
نقطة الاستشراف [No'qṭat al-esteshraf] *n* standpoint
نقع [naqaʕa] *v* soak
نقل [naql] *n* transport
قابل للنقل ['qabel lel-na'ql] *adj* removable
نقل عام [Na'ql 'aam] *n* public transport
نقل الدم [Na'ql al-dam] *n* blood transfusion
نقل [naqala] *v* take away, transport

n [nuqu:d] **نقود**

حافظة نقود

[ḥafedhat ne'qood] *n* purse

أين يمكنني تغيير بعض النقود؟

[ayna yamken-any taghyeer ba'aḍ al-ni'qood?] Where can I change some money?

هل لديك فكّة أصغر من النقود؟

[Hal ladayk fakah aṣghar men alno'qood?] Do you have any small change?

هل يمكن إعطائي فكّة من النقود تبلغ...؟

[Hal yomken e'aṭaey fakah men alno'qood tablogh...?] Could you give me change of...?

هل يمكن أن أسترد نقودي مرة أخرى؟

[hal yamken an asta-rid ni-'qoody marra okhra?] Can I have my money back?

pure *adj* [naqij] **نقي**

catastrophe *n* [nakba] **نكبة**

joke *n* [nukta] **نكتة**

flavour, zest *(lemon-peel)*, zest *(excitement)* *n* [nakha] **نكهة**

panther *n* [namir] **نمر**

نمر مخطط

[Namer mokhaṭaṭ] *n* tiger

نمر منقط

[Nemr men'qaṭ] *n* leopard

Austrian *adj* [namsa:wij] **نمساوي**
Austrian *n* ◃

freckles *n* [namʃ] **نمش**

pattern *n* [namatˤ] **نمط**

adj [namatˤij] **نمطي**

شكل نمطي

[Shakl namaṭey] *n* stereotype

ant *n* [namla] **نملة**

growth *n* [numuww] **نمو**

n [namu:ðaʒ] **نموذج**

نموذج طلبية

[Namodhaj ṭalabeyah] *n* order form

typical *adj* [namu:ðaʒij] **نموذجي**

grow *v* [nama:] **نَمى**

gossip *n* [nami:ma] **نَميمة**

final *n* ◃ final *adj* [niha:ʔij] **نهائي**

لا نهائي

[La nehaaey] *adj* endless

مباراة شبه نهائية

[Mobarah shebh nehaeyah] *n* semifinal

n [nha:r] **نهار**

فترة النهار

[Fatrat al-nehaar] *n* daytime

end, finish *n* [niha:ja] **نهاية**

إلى النهاية

[Ela al-nehayah] *adv* terminally

river *n* [nahr] **نهر**

فرس النهر

[Faras al-nahr] *n* hippopotamus

أيمكن السباحة في النهر؟

[a-yamkun al-sebaḥa fee al-naher?] Can one swim in the river?

هل يوجد أي رحلات بالمراكب في النهر؟

[hal yujad ay reḥlaat bil-markab fee al-nahir?] Are there any boat trips on the river?

get up, stand up *v* [nahadˤa] **نهض**

fit, spell *(magic)* *n* [nawba] **نوبة**

نوبة صرع

[Nawbat ṣar'a] *n* epileptic fit

نوبة غضب

[Nawbat ghaḍab] *n* tantrum

نوبة مرضية

[Nawbah maraḍeyah] *n* seizure

light *n* [nu:r] **نور**

النور لا يُضاء

[al-noor la yo-ḍaa] The light doesn't work

هل يمكن أن أشغل النور؟

[hal yamken an osha-ghel al-noor?] Can I switch the light on?

هل يمكن أن أطفئ النور؟

[hal yamken an aṭfee al-noor?] Can I switch the light off?

n [nawras] **نورس**

نورس البحر

[Nawras al-baḥr] *n* seagull

kind, type, gender *n* [nawʕ] **نوع**

ما نوع الساندويتشات الموجودة؟

[ma naw'a al-sandweshaat al-maw-jooda?] What kind of sandwiches do you have?

هل قمت من قبل بقص شعري من نوع

شعري
[hal 'qumt min 'qabil be-'qaṣ sha'ar min naw'a sha'ary?] Have you cut my type of hair before?

نوعي [nawʕij] *adj*

مدرسة نوعية
[Madrasah naw'aeyah] *n* primary school

نوفمبر [nu:fumbar] *n* November

نوم [nawm] *n* sleep

غرفة النوم
[Ghorfat al-noom] *n* bedroom

ثياب النوم
[Theyab al-noom] *n* nightdress

وَقْت النوم
[Wa'qt al-nawm] *n* bedtime

لا أستطيع النوم
[la asta-ṯee'a al-nawm] I can't sleep

لا استطيع النوم بسبب الضوضاء
[la asta-ṭee'a al-nawm besa-bab al-ḍawḍaa] I can't sleep for the noise

نومة [nawma] *n*

نومة خفيفة
[Nomah khafeefa] *n* snooze

نونية [nu:nijja] *n*

نونية للأطفال
[Noneyah lel-aṭfaal] *n* potty

نووي [nawawij] *adj* nuclear

نيبال [ni:ba:l] *n* Nepal

نية [nijja] *n* intention

نيتروجين [ni:tru:ʒi:n] *n* nitrogen

نيجيري [ni:ʒi:rij] *n* Nigerian

نيجيريا [ni:ʒi:rja:] *n* Nigeria

نيكاراجاو [ni:ka:ra:ʒwa:] *n*

من نيكاراجاو
[Men nekarajwa] *adj* Nicaraguan

نيكاراجاوي [ni:ka:ra:ʒa:wi:] *n* Nicaraguan

نيكاراجوا [ni:ka:ra:ʒwa:] *n* Nicaragua

نيكوتين [ni:ku:ti:n] *n* nicotine

نيوزلندا [nju:zilanda:] *n* New Zealand

نيوزلندي [nju:zilandi:] *n* New Zealander

نيون [niju:n] *n*

غاز النيون
[Ghaz al-neywon] *n* neon

هائل [ha:ʔil] *adj* gross, huge, tremendous

مسبب لدمار هائل
[Mosabeb ledamar haael] *adj* devastating

هاتف [ha:tif] *n* ring up

دفتر الهاتف
[Daftar al-hatef] *n* phonebook

هاتف عمومي
[Hatef 'aomoomy] *n* payphone

هاتف جوال
[Hatef jawal] *n* mobile phone

هاتف ذكي
[Hatef zaky] *n* smart phone

هاتف مرئي
[Hatef mareay] *n* videophone

أريد بعض العملات المعدنية من أجل الهاتف من فضلك
[areed ba'aḍ al-'aimlaat al-ma'a-danya min ajil al-haatif min faḍlak] I'd like some coins for the phone, please

هل يمكن أن أستخدم هاتفك؟
[hal yamken an asta-khdim ha-tifak?] May I use your phone?

هناك مشكلة في الهاتف
[hunaka mushkila fee al-haatlf] I'm having trouble with the phone

هاتفي adj [ha:tifij]
اتصال هاتفي
[Eteṣal hatefey] n phonecall
هاجر emigrate v [ha:ʒara]
هاجس n [ha:ʒis]
هاجس داخلي
[Hajes dakheley] n premonition
هاجم attack vt [ha:ʒama]
يهاجم بقصد السرقة
[Yohajem be'qaṣd al-sare'qah] v mug
هادئ quiet adj [ha:diʔ]
أفضل أن تكون الغرفة هادئة
[ofaḍel an takoon al-ghurfa hade-a] I'd like a quiet room
هل يوجد شواطئ هادئ قريب من هنا؟
[hal ju:ʒadu ʃawa:tˤiʔa ha:diʔi qari:bun min huna:] Is there a quiet beach near here?
هام important, significant adj [ha:mm]
غير هام
[Ghayr ham] adj unimportant
هام جداً
[Ham jedan] adj momentous
هامبرجر hamburger n [ha:mbarʒar]
هامش margin n [ha:miʃ]
هاو amateur n [ha:win]
هايتي Haiti n [ha:jti:]
هبّ blow vi [habba]
هبّ yield v [haba]
هباء n [haba:ʔ]
هباء جوي
[Habaa jawey] n aerosol
هبة gift n [hiba]
هبط land vi [hsbstˤa]
هبوط landing n [hubu:tˤ]
هبوط اضطراري
[Hobooṭ eḍṭerary] n emergency landing
هبوط الطائرة
[Hobooṭ al-ṭaerah] n touchdown
هتف yell v [hatafa]
هجر abandon v [haʒara]
هجرة migration, immigration n [hiʒra]
هجوم attack n [huʒu:m]
هجوم إرهابي
[Hojoom 'erhaby] n terrorist attack
هجوم للسرقة
[Hojoom lel-sare'qah] n mugging
لقد تعرضت لهجوم
[la'qad ta-'aaraḍto lel-hijoom] I've been attacked
هجين mongrel n [haʒi:n]
هُداب fringe (hair) n [huda:b]
هُدَال n [huda:l]
نبات الهُدَال
[Nabat al-hoddal] n mistletoe
هَدَد threaten v [haddada]
هدف aim, goal, target n [hadaf]
الهدف في لعبة الجولف
[Al-hadaf fy le'abat al-jolf] n tee
هدم demolish, pull down v [hadama]
هدنة truce n [hudna]
هدية present (gift) n [hadijja]
قسيمة هدية
['qaseemat hadeyah] n gift voucher
أنا أبحث عن هدية لزوجتي
[ana abḥath 'aan hadiya le-zawjatee] I'm looking for a present for my wife
هذا that, this adj [haða:]
هذيان rave n [haðaja:n]
هراء nonsense, trash n [hura:ʔ]
هراوة club (weapon) n [hara:wa]
هرب run away v [haraba]
يَهْرُب مسرعا
[Yahrab mosre'aan] v fly away
هَرَّب smuggle v [harraba]
هرة n [hira]
هرة صغيرة
[Herah ṣagheerah] n kitten
هرس squash v [harrisa]
هرم pyramid n [haram]
هرمون hormone n [hurmu:n]
هرمونيكا n [hirmu:ni:ka:]
آلة الهرمونيكا الموسيقية
[Alat al-harmoneeka al-mose'qeyah] n mouth organ
هروب escape n [huru:b]
هَرْوَلة jogging n [harwala]
هز shake v [hazza]
يهز كتفيه
[Yahoz katefayh] v shrug

هزأ v [hazaʔabi]
يَهزأ ب
[Yah-zaa be] *v* mock
هزة *n* [haza]
هزة الجماع
[Hezat al-jemaa'a] *n* orgasm
هزلي comic *n* [hazlijja]
سلسلة رسوم هزلية
[Selselat resoom hazaleyah] *n* comic strip
كتاب هزلي
[Ketab hazaley] *n* comic book
ممثل هزلي
[Momthel hazaley] *n* comedian
هزم defeat, beat *(outdo)* *v* [hazima]
هزيل skimpy *adj* [hazi:l]
هزيل الجسم
[Hazeel al-jesm] *adj* skinny
هزيمة defeat *n* [hazi:munt]
هستامين *n* [hista:mi:n]
مضاد للهستامين
[Moḍad lel-hestameen] *n* antihistamine
هش crisp, crispy *adj* [haʃʃ]
هَشم smash *vt* [haʃʃama]
هضم digestion *n* [hadˤm]
هضم digest *v* [hadˤama]
هفوة slip *(mistake)* *n* [hafwa]
هلام *n* [hala:mu]
هلام الفاكهة
[Holam al-fakehah] *n* marmalade
هم matter *v* [hamma]
لا يهم
[la yahim] It doesn't matter
همجي barbaric *adj* [hamaʒij]
همس whisper *v* [hamasa]
هنا here *adv* [huna:]
هنّأ congratulate *v* [hannaʔa]
هناك there *adv* [huna:ka]
إنه هناك
[inaho honaka] It's over there
هند *n* [hind]
ساكن الهند الغربية
[Saken al-hend al-gharbeyah] *n* West Indian
هندباء *n* [hindaba:ʔi]
نبات الهندباء البرية
[Nabat al-hendbaa al-bareyah] *n* dandelion
هندسة engineering *n* [handasa]
هَنْدَم tidy up *v* [handama]
هندوسي Hindu *adj* [hindu:sij]
Hindu *n* ◁
هندوسية Hinduism *n* [hindu:sijja]
هندي Indian *n* ◁ Indian *adj* [hindij]
المحيط الهندي
[Almoḥeeṭ alhendey] *n* Indian Ocean
هواء air *n* [hawa:ʔ]
طاحونة هواء
[ṭaḥoonat hawaa] *n* windmill
في الهواء الطلق
[Fe al-hawaa al-ṭal'q] *adv* outdoors
مُكيف الهواء
[Mokaeyaf al-hawaa] *adj* air-conditioned
هوائي aerial *adj* [hawa:ʔij]
هواية hobby *n* [hiwa:ja]
هَوَس mania *n* [hawas]
هوكي *n* [hu:ki:]
لعبة الهوكي على الجليد
[Lo'abat alhookey 'ala aljaleed] *n* ice hockey
لعبة الهوكي
[Lo'abat alhookey] *n* hockey
هولندا Holland, *n* [hu:landa:] Netherlands
هولندي *n* ◁ Dutch *adj* [hu:landij] Dutch
رَجُل هولندي
[Rajol holandey] *n* Dutchman
هولندية *n* [hu:landijja] Dutchwoman
هَوي wind *(coil around)* *v* [hawa:]
هوية *n* [huwijja]
غير محدد الهوية
[Ghayr mohadad al-haweyah] *adj* unidentified
هَوية personality *n* [hawijja]
هَويّة identity *n* [huwijja]
هويس lock *(door)* *n* [huwajs]
هيئ set *v* [hajjaʔa]
هيئة board *(meeting)* *n* [hajʔa]
هيئة المحلفون

[Hayaat moḥalefeen] *n* jury
هيبةْ prestige *n* [hajba]
هيبزْ hippie *n* [hi:biz]
هَيدَروجين hydrogen *n* [hi:dru:ʒi:n]
هيروين heroin *n* [hi:rwi:n]
هيكل structure *n* [hajkal]
هيكل عظمي
[Haykal aḍhmey] *n* skeleton
هيلكوبتر helicopter *n* [hi:liku:btir]

و and *conj* [wa]
واثق confident *adj* [wa:θiq]
غير واثق
[Ghayr wathe'q] *adj* uncertain
واثق بنفسه
[Wathe'q benafseh] *adj* self-assured
واجب duty *n* [wa:ʒib]
واجب منزلى
[Wajeb manzeley] *n* homework
واجه face *v* [wa:ʒaha]
واجهة front *n* [wa:ʒiha]
واحة oasis *n* [wa:ħa]
واحد one *number* ◁ ace *n* [wa:ħid]
وادي valley *n* [wa:di:]
واسع broad *adj* [wa:siʕ]
واسع الأفق
[Wase'a al-ofo'q] *adj* broad-minded
واسع الحيلة
[Wase'a al-ḥeelah] *adj* shifty
واشي grass *(informer)* *n* [wa:ʃi:]
واضح clear, definite *adj* [wa:dˤiħ]
غير واضح
[Ghayr waḍeḥ] *adj* unclear
بشكل واضح
[Beshakl waḍeḥ] *adv* obviously
من الواضح
[Men al-waḍeḥ] *adv* apparently

واع [waːʕin] *adj* conscious
واعد [waːʕada] *v* promise
واعَد [waːʕada] *adj* promising
واعِد [waːʕid] *adj* hopeful
وَافِد [waːfid] *n* immigrant, newcomer
وافق [waːfaqa] *v* approve
وَافِل [waːfil] *n* waffle
واقِع [waːqiʕ] *n* reality
تلفزيون الواقع [Telefezyon al-wa'qe'a] *n* reality TV
في الواقع [Fee al-wa'qe'a] *adv* actually
واقعي [waːqiʕij] *adj* real, realistic, virtual
غير واقعي [Ghayer wa'qe'aey] *adj* unrealistic
واقي [waːqij] *n*
نظارة واقية [naḍharah wa'qeyah] *n* goggles
واقي الشمس [Wa'qey al-shams] *n* sunscreen
والد [waːlidajni] *n* parent, father
أحد الوالدين [Aḥad al-waledayn] *n* single parent ◁ *npl* parents
والِد أو والدة [Waled aw waledah] *n* parent *n*
واهِن [waːhin] *adj* frail
وايَن [waːjn] *n*
خمر هاوس واين [Khamr hawees wayen] *n* house wine
وباء [wabaːʔ] *n* epidemic, pest
وَبَّخ [wabbaxa] *v* tell off
وتد [watad] *n* peg
وتد الخيمة [Watad al-kheemah] *n* tent peg
وتر [watar] *n* tendon
وَتَّر [wattara] *v* strain
وثائقي [waθaːʔiqij] *adj*
فيلم وثائقي [Feel wathaae'qey] *n* documentary
وثب [waθaba] *v* leap
وثِق [waθiqa] *v*
يَثِق ب [Yathe'q be] *n* trust

وثيق [waθiːq] *adj*
على نحو وثيق ['aala naḥwen wathee'q] *adv* nearly
وثيق الصلة [Wathee'q al-ṣelah] *adj* relevant
وجبة [waʒba] *n* meal
متجر الوجبات السريعة [Matjar al-wajabat al-sarey'aa] *n* snack bar
وجبة خفيفة [Wajbah khafeefah] *n* snack
وجبات سريعة [Wajabat sarey'aa] *n* takeaway
وَجْبَة الطعام [Wajbat al-ṭa'aam] *n* dinner
كانت الوجبة شهية [kanat il-wajba sha-heyah] The meal was delicious
وجد [waʒada] *v* exist
وجِد [waʒada] *v* find
وجع [waʒaʕ] *n*
وجع الأسنان [Waja'a al-asnaan] *n* toothache
وجنة [waʒna] *n*
عظم الوجنة [aḍhm al-wajnah] *n* cheekbone
وجه [waʒh] *n* face
على وجه الحصر ['ala wajh al-ḥaṣr] *adv* exclusively
تدليك الوجه [Tadleek al-wajh] *n* facial
وجّه [waʒʒaha] *vt* direct
وجهة [wiʒha] *n*
وجهة نظر [Wejhat naḍhar] *n* viewpoint
وجهي [waʒhij] *adj* facial
وحّد [waħħada] *v* combine, unite
وحدة [waħda] *n* unit, loneliness
وحدة إضاءة كشافة [Weḥdah eḍafeyah kashafah] *n* floodlight
وحدة العناية المركزة [Weḥdat al-'aenayah al-morkazah] *n* intensive care unit
وحدة كاملة [Weḥdah kamelah] *n* whole

وحشي brutal *adj* [waħʃij]
وحل *n* [waħil]
أرض وحلة
[Arḍ waḥelah] *n* swamp
وحيد alone *adj* [waħi:d]
وخز jab *n* [waxz]
وداعا goodbye! *excl* [wada:ʕan]
ودود friendly *adj* [wadu:d]
ودي *adj* [widij]
غير ودي
[Ghayr wedey] *adj* unfriendly
وراء beyond *prep* [wara:ʔa]
إلى الوراء
[Ela al-waraa] *adv* back
وراثة *n* [wira:θa]
علم الوراثة
[A'elm al-weratha] *n* genetics
وراثي hereditary *adj* [wira:θij]
ورث inherit *v* [wariθa]
وَردة rose *n* [warda]
وردي pink *adj* [wardij]
ورشة *n* [warʃatu]
ورشة العمل
[Warshat al-'aamal] *n* workshop
هل يمكن أن توصلني إلى ورشة السيارات؟
[hal yamken an tuwa-ṣilny ela warshat al-sayaraat?] Can you give me a lift to the garage?
ورطة stalemate *n* [wartˤa]
ورق *n* [waraq]
أوراق اعتماد
[Awra'q e'atemaad] *n* credentials
أوراق الشجر
[Awra'q al-shajar] *npl* leaves
ورق السنفرة
[Wara'q al-sanfarah] *n* sandpaper
ورق الغار
[Wara'q alghaar] *n* bay leaf
ورق التغليف
[Wara'q al-taghleef] *n* wrapping paper
ورق المرحاض
[Wara'q al-merḥaḍ] *n* toilet paper
ورق شفاف
[Wara'q shafaf] *n* tracing paper
ورق فضي
[Wara'q feḍey] *n* tinfoil
ورق مسودة
[Wara'q mosawadah] *n* scrap paper
ورق مقوى
[Wara'q mo'qawa] *n* cardboard
لا يوجد ورق تواليت
[la yujad wara'q toilet] There is no toilet paper
ورقة paper *n* [waraqa]
ورقة عشب
[Wara'qat 'aoshb] *n* spire
ورقة عمل
[Wara'qat 'aamal] *n* spreadsheet
ورقة كتابة
[Wara'qat ketabah] *n* writing paper
ورقة مالية
[Wara'qah maleyah] *n* note
ورقة ملاحظات
[Wara'qat molaḥadhaat] *n* notepaper
ورقة نبات
[Wara'qat nabat] *n* leaf
ورم lump, tumour *n* [waram]
ورنيش varnish *n* [warni:ʃu]
ورنيش الأحذية
[Warneesh al-aḥḍheyah] *n* shoe polish
ورنيش اللَك
[Warneesh al-llak] *n* lacquer
وريث heir, successor *n* [wari:θ]
وريثة heiress *n* [wari:θa]
وريد vein *n* [wari:d]
وِزارة ministry *(government)* *n* [wiza:ra]
وَزرة skirting board *n* [wizra]
وزع distribute, give out *v* [wazzaʕa]
وزن weight *n* [wazn]
وزن زائد للأمتعة
[Wazn zaed lel-amte'aah] *n* excess baggage
وَزْن الأمتعة المسموح به
[Wazn al-amte'aah al-masmooh beh] *n* baggage allowance
وزن weigh *v* [wazana]
وزِير minister *(government)* *n* [wazi:r]
وَسائِل means *npl* [wasa:ʔilun]
وسادة pillow *n* [wisa:da]
وِسَادة هوائية
[Wesadah hwaaeyah] *n* airbag

غطاء الوسادة
[gheṭaa al-wesadah] *n* pillowcase
وسادة رقيقة
[Wesadah ra'qee'qah] *n* pad
من فضلك أريد وسادة إضافية
[min faḍlak areed wesada eḍa-fiya] Please bring me an extra pillow
centre *n* [wasatˁ] **وسطٌ**
العصور الوسطى
[Al-'aoṣoor al-woṣṭa] *npl* Middle Ages
الشرق الأوسط
[Al-shar'q al-awṣaṭ] *n* Middle East
كيف يمكن أن أذهب إلى وسط ...
[kayfa yamkin an athhab ela wasaṭ...?] How do I get to the centre of...?
among *prep* [wasatˁa] **وسطِ**
middle *n* [wasatˁ] **وَسْط**
وَسَطْ المدينة
[Wasaṭ al-madeenah] *n* town centre
whisky *n* [wiski:] **وِسْكي**
mark *(make sign)* *v* [wasama] **وَسَم**
n [wasi:la] **وسيلة**
هل هناك وسيلة مواصلات إلى... تسمح بصعود الكراسي المتحركة؟
[hal hunaka waseelat muwa-ṣalaat ela... tasmaḥ beṣi-'aood al-karasi al-mutaḥarika?] Is there wheelchair-friendly transportation available to...?
handsome, pretty *adj* [wasi:m] **وسيم**
scarf, ribbon *n* [wiʃa:ħ] **وِشاح**
وشاح غطاء الرأس
[Weshaḥ gheṭaa al-raas] *n* headscarf
tattoo *n* [waʃm] **وَشْم**
custody *n* [wisˁa:ja] **وِصاية**
describe *v* [wasˁafa] **وَصف**
يصف علاجا
[Yaṣef 'aelagan] *v* prescribe
description *n* [wasˁf] **وَصف**
n [wasˁfa] **وصفة**
وصفة طبية
[Waṣfah ṭebeyah] *n* prescription
وصفة طهي
[Waṣfat ṭahey] *n* recipe
أين يمكنني إيجاد هذه الوصفة؟
[ayna yamken-any ejad hadhe al-waṣfa?] Where can I get this prescription made up?
arrive *v* [wasˁala] **وصل**
يَصل بين
[yaṣel bayn] *v* link
كيف يمكن أن أصل إلى ...
[kayfa yamkin an aṣal ela...?] How do I get to...?
متى يصل إلى ...
[mata yaṣil ela...?] When does it arrive in...?
conduct *vt* [wasˁala] **وصّل**
receipt *n* [wasˁl] **وَصْل**
junction, joint *n* [wasˁla] **وصلة** *(junction)*
وصلة بطارية السيارة
[Waṣlat baṭareyah al-sayarah] *npl* jump leads
وَصْلَة تلفزيونية
[Wṣlah telefezyoneyah] *n* cable television
وَصْلَة تمديد
[Waṣlat tamdeed] *n* extension cable
access, arrival *n* [wusˁu:l] **وصول**
سهل الوصول
[Sahl al-woṣool] *adj* accessible
بعلم الوصول
[Be-'aelm al-woṣool] *n* recorded delivery
warden *n* [wasˁij] **وَصِيّ**
will *(document)* *n* [wasˁijja] **وَصِّية**
n [wasˁi:fa] **وصيفة**
وصيفة العروس
[Waṣeefat al-'aroos] *n* bridesmaid
situation, placement *n* [wadˁʕ] **وضع**
أجازة وضع
[Ajazat waḍ'a] *n* maternity leave
وضع علامات الترقيم
[Waḍ'a 'alamaat al-tar'qeem] *n* punctuation
put *v* [wadˁaʕa] **وضع**
يَضع على الأرض
[Yaḍa'a ala al-arḍ] *v* ground
يَضع تحت الاختبار
[Yaḍa'a taḥt al-ekhtebar] *v* try out
يَضع في
[Yaḍa'a fee] *n* place
لقد وضعت بعض الأشياء في الخزينة

[la'qad waḍa'ato ba'aḍ al-ash-ya fe al-khazeena] I have some things in the safe
وضوح visibility *n* [wudˤu:ħ]
وَضِيع vile *adj* [wadˤi:ʕ]
وطَن *n* [watˤan]
حنين إلى الوطن
[Ḥaneem ela al-waṭan] *adj* homesick
وطني patriotic *adj* [watˤanij]
الانتماء الوطني
[Al-entemaa alwaṭaney] *n* citizenship
وظف employ *v* [wazˤzˤafa]
وظيفة employment, *n* [wazˤi:fa] profession, post
تليفون مزود بوظيفة الرد الآلي
[Telephone mozawad be-waḍheefat al-rad al-aaley] *n* answerphone
وَظيفة فى فترة الأجازة
[waḍheefah fee fatrat al-ajaazah] *n* holiday job
وِعاء bowl *n* [wiʕa:ʔ]
وَعِر bumpy *adj* [waʕir]
وعي *n* [waʕj]
فاقد الوعي
[Fa'qed al-wa'aey] *adj* unconscious
وَعى consciousness *n* [waʕa:]
وَفَر save up *v* [waffara]
وَفرة plenty *n* [wafra]
وفقاًلـ according to *adv* [wifqan-li]
وَفى repay *v* [wafa:]
وقاحة nerve *(boldness)* *n* [waqa:ħa]
وقاية prevention *n* [wiqa:ja]
وقت time *n* [waqt]
في أي وقت
[Fee ay wa'qt] *adv* ever
من وقت لآخر
[Men wa'qt le-aakhar] *adv* occasionally
وَقْت إضافي
[Wa'qt eḍafey] *n* overtime
وَقْت الإغلاق
[Wa'qt al-eghlaa'q] *n* closing time
وَقْت العشاء
[Wa'qt al-'aashaa] *n* dinner time
وَقْت الغداء
[Wa'qt al-ghadhaa] *n* lunchtime
وَقْت الذروة
[Wa'qt al-dhorwah] *n* rush hour
وَقْت الطعام
[Wa'qt al-ṭa'aaam] *n* mealtime
وَقْت اللعب
[Wa'qt al-la'aeb] *n* playtime
وَقْت النوم
[Wa'qt al-nawm] *n* bedtime
وَقْت بدل الضائع
[Wa'qt badal ḍaye'a] *n* injury time
وَقْت فراغ
[Wa'qt faragh] *n* spare time
أعتقد أن ساعتي متقدمة عن الوقت الصحيح
[a'ata'qid anna sa'aaty muta-'qadema] I think my watch is fast
أنا غير مشغول وقت الغذاء
[Ana ghayr mashghool waqt al-ghadaa] I'm free for lunch
تأخرنا قليلًا عن الوقت المحدد
[ta-akharna 'qale-lan 'aan al-wa'qt al-muḥadad] We are slightly behind schedule
في أقرب وقت ممكن
[fee a'qrab wa'qt mumkin] as soon as possible
في أي وقت سوف نصل إلى ...؟
[Fee ay wa'qt sawfa naṣel ela?...] What time do we get to...?
كم الوقت من فضلك؟
[kam al-wa'qt min faḍlak?] What time is it, please?
نقضي وقتا سعيدا
[na'qḍy wa'qtan sa'aedan] We are having a nice time
وقح rude *adj* [waqiħu]
وَقِح cheeky *adj* [waqiħ]
وقع occur, fall *v* [waqaʕa]
يقع في غرامها
[Ya'qah fee ghrameha] *v* fall for
وقف stand *v* [waqafa]
قف هنا من فضلك
['qif hona min faḍlak] Stop here, please
وَقْف *n* [waqf]
وَقْف إطلاق النار
[Wa'qf eṭlaa'q al-naar] *n* ceasefire
وَقْفَة pause *n* [waqfa]

وقواق [waqwa:q] *n*
طائر الوقواق
[Ṭaaer al-wa'qwa'q] *n* cuckoo
وقود [waqunwdu] *n* fuel
وقوف [wuqu:f] *n* halt
وكالة [wika:la] *n* agency
وكالة سفريات
[Wakalat safareyat] *n* travel agent's
وكيل [waki:l] *n* agent, attorney
وكيل سفريات
[Wakeel safareyat] *n* travel agent
وكيل أخبار
[Wakeel akhbaar] *n* newsagent
ولادة [wila:da] *n*
ولادة الحيوان
[Weladat al-ḥayawaan] *n* litter *(offspring)*
ولاية [wila:ja] *n* state
الولايات المتحدة
[Al-welayat al-motḥedah al-amreekeyah] *n* United States
ولاية جورجيا
[Welayat jorjeya] *n* Georgia *(US state)*
ولد [walad] *n* lad, child
وَلَع [walaʕ] *n* passion
ومض [w:madˤa] *vi* flash, blink
وميض [wami:dˤ] *n* flash, torch
ونش [winʃ] *n* crane *(for lifting)*
وَهج [wahaʒ] *n* blaze
وهم [wahm] *n* illusion
ويسكي [wi:ski:] *n* whisky
ويسكي الشعير المجفف
[Weskey al-she'aeer al-mojafaf] *n* malt whisky
سأتناول ويسكي
[sa-ata-nawal wisky] I'll have a whisky
ويسكي بالصودا
[wesky bil-ṣoda] a whisky and soda
ويلز [wi:lzu] *n* Wales
ويلزي [wi:lzij] *adj* Welsh ⊲ *n* Welsh

ي

يائس [ja:ʔis] *adj* hopeless
ياباني [ja:ba:ni:] *adj* Japanese ⊲ *n* Japanese *(person)*
اللغة اليابانية
[Al-lghah al-yabaneyah] *(language) n* Japanese
ياردة [ja:rda] *n (measurement)* yard
يأس [jaʔs] *n* despair
سِن اليأس
[Sen al-yaas] *n* menopause
ياقوت [ja:qu:tun] *v*
ياقوت أزرق
[Ya'qoot azra'q] *n* sapphire
يانسون [ja:nsu:n] *n* aniseed
يانصيب [ja:nasˤi:b] *n* lottery
بيع باليانصيب
[Bay'a bel-yanaṣeeb] *n* raffle
يئوس [jaʔu:s] *adj* desperate
يَتيم [jati:m] *n* orphan
يَجعل [jaʒʕaluhu] *v*
يَجعله أسوأ
[Tej'aalah aswaa] *v* worsen
يحاكِي [ħa:ka:] *v* mimic
يَحتمِل [juħtamalu] *n* bear
يحولَ [juħawwilu] *n* shift
يُحب [juħibu] *v*
يُحِب الفرس

[Yokheb al-faras] *v* canter
yacht *n* [jaxt] **يخت**
v ◁ scheme *n* [juxatˤtˤitˤu] **يُخطط**
يُخَطِّط بدون تَفاصيل
[Yokhaṭeṭ bedon tafaṣeel] *v* sketch
hand *n* [jadd] **يد**
خط اليد
[Khaṭ al-yad] *n* handwriting
كرة اليد
[Korat al-yad] *n* handball
v [jadawijjun] **يدوي**
غير يدوي
[Ghayr yadawey] *adj* hands-free
handmade *adj* [jadawij] **يَدوي**
gerbil *n* [jarbu:ʕ] **يَربوع**
bribe *n* [jarʃu:] **يَرشو**
jaundice *n* [jaraqa:n] **يرقان**
slug, caterpillar *n* [jaraqa:na] **يرقانة**
maggot *n* [jaraqa] **يَرَقَة**
يَرَقَة دودية
[Yara'qah doodeyah] *n* grub
mortgage *n* [jarhanu] **يَرْهن**
call off *n* [jazʒuru] **يَزجُر**
oil *n* [juzajjitu] **يُزيت**
left *n* [jasa:r] **يسار**
اتجه نحو اليسار
[Etajeh naḥw al-yasaar] Turn left
left *adv* [jasa:ran] **يساراً**
left *adj* [jasa:rij] **يساري**
v [jastaħikkuhu] **يستحك**
يستحكه جلده
[yastaḥekah jaldah] *v* itch
v [jasmaħu bidduxu:li] **يَسمَح ب**
يَسمَح بالدخول
[Yasmaḥ bel-dokhool] *v* admit *(allow in)*
hear *v* [jasmaʕu] **يسمع**
أنا لا أسمع
[ana la asma'a] I'm deaf
Jesus *n* [jasu:ʕ] **يسوع**
v [ʔeʃtahara] **يشتهر**
ما هو الطبق الذي يشتهر به المكان؟
[ma howa al-ṭaba'q al-lathy yashta-her behe al-makan?] What is the house speciality?
confiscate *n* [jusˤa:diru] **يُصادر**
clasp *n* [jusˤa:fiħu] **يُصافح**

cast *n* [jasˤubu] **يَصُبْ**
issue *n* [jasˤduru] **يَصْدر**
sacrifice *n* [judˤaħħi:] **يُضَحي**
fool *v* [jundˤallilu] **يُضَلل**
plaster *n* [judˤammidu] **يُضَمد**
dragonfly *n* [jaʕsu:b] **يَعْسُوب**
hold up *v* [junʕatˤtˤilu] **يُعَطِل**
v [qa:ma] **يقم**
لا تقم بتحريكه
[la ta'qum be-taḥ-rekehe] Don't move him
certainty *n* [jaqi:n] **يقين**
undoubtedly *adv* [jaqi:nan] **يَقيناً**
dove *n* [jama:ma] **يمامة**
right *(not left)* *adj* [jami:n] **يمين**
على اليمين
[Ala al-yameen] *adj* right-hand
الحنث باليمين
[Al-ḥanth bel-yameen] *n* perjury
اتجه نحو اليمين
[Etajeh anḥw al-yameen] Turn right
January *n* [jana:jiru] **يناير**
v [janbaɣi:] **ينبغي**
إن... لا يعمل كما ينبغي
[enna... la ya'amal kama yanbaghy] The... doesn't work properly
كم الكمية التي ينبغي على تناولها؟
[kam al-kamiyah al-laty yan-baghy 'ala tana-welaha?] How much should I take?
كم الكمية التي ينبغي علي إعطائها؟
[kam al-kamiyah al-laty yan-baghy 'aalaya e'aṭa-eha?] How much should I give?
expire *v* [janqadˤi:] **ينتهي**
nag *v* [janiqqu] **ينق**
calm down *n* [juhaddiʔu] **يَهْدأ**
Jew *n* [jahu:di:] **يهودي**
هل توجد أطباق مباح أكلها في الشريعة اليهودية؟
Do you have kosher dishes?
yoga *n* [ju:ʒa:] **يُوجَا**
deposit *n* [judiʕu] **يُوْدِع**
uranium *n* [ju:ra:nju:mi] **يورانيوم**
euro *n* [ju:ru:] **يورو**
أريد كارت تليفون بخمس وعشرين يورو

[areed kart talefon be-khams wa-'aishreen yoro] I'd like a twenty-five-euro phonecard

يوسفي [ju:sufij] *n* (*fruit*), mandarin tangerine

يوليو [ju:lju:] *n* July

يوم [jawm] *n* day

يوم الراحة [Yawm al-raḥah] *n* Sabbath

يوم الثلاثاء [Yawm al-tholathaa] *n* Tuesday

يوم الخميس [jawmul xami:si] *n* Thursday

يوم في الأسبوع [Yawm fee al-osboo'a] *n* weekday

أريد تذكرة تزلج ليوم واحد [areed tadhkera tazaluj le-yawm waḥid] I'd like a ski pass for a day

أي الأيام تكون اليوم؟ [ay al-ayaam howa al- yawm?] What day is it today?

لا نريد أن نرى أي شخص آخر غيرنا !طوال اليوم [la nureed an nara ay shakhṣ akhar ghyranạ ṯewaal al-yawm!] We'd like to see nobody but us all day!

!يا له من يوم جميل [ya laho min yawm jameel] What a lovely day!

يومان [jawma:ni] *n* fortnight

يَوْمي [jawmij] *adj* daily

يومياً [jawmijjaan] *adv* daily

يوميات [jawmijja:t] *n* diary (*appointments*)

يوناني [ju:na:nij] *adj* Greek ◃ *n* Greek (*person*)

اللغة اليونانية [Al-loghah al-yonaneyah] *n* (*language*) Greek

يونيو [ju:nju:] *n* June

قواعد الانجليزية

المحتويات

مثل كثير من اللغات تتبع اللغة الإنجليزية قواعد محددة. فيما يلي بعض القواعد الأساسية للغة الإنجليزية.

الأفعال الرئيسية **Main verbs**

هي أهم الأفعال في الجملة لأنه بدونها لاتكتمل الجملة ولها معنى خاصاً بها على خلاف الأفعال المساعدة. يمكن تفسيم الأفعال الأساسية إلى المجموعات التالية:

الأفعال المتعدية واللازمة **Transitive and intransitive verbs**

وهي التي تقبل مفعولاً به مباشراً، مثل:

اشترى غيتاراً *He bought a guitar*

الأفعال اللازمة والتي لا تأخذ مفعولاً به مباشراً، مثل:

أنا استيقظت *I woke up*

الكثير من الأفعال، مثل (**speak يتكلم**)، يمكن أن تكون متعدية أو لازمة. كما هو الحال في الأمثلة التالية:

متعدي**transitive**	لازم **intransitive**
He speaks Spanish	**John speaks fast**
يتحدث الإسبانية	جون يتحدث بسرعة

أفعال الربط **Linking verbs**

إن فعل الربط ليس له معنى خاصاً به بشكل عام. تربط هذه الأفعال الفاعل مع ماقيل عنه (**بقية الجملة**) . ويعبر فعل الربط عادة عن تغير إلى حالة أو مكان ما وغالباً مايتبع بصفة. إن فعل الربط هو دائماً لازم لكن

ليست كل الأفعال اللازمة أفعال ربط. أنظر الأمثلة التالية:

The book sounds interesting	**The sky looks cloudy**
يبدو الكتاب ممتعاً	تبدو السماء غائمة

الأفعال الديناميكية (الحركية) والحالة **Dynamic and stative verbs**

هنالك أفعال تصف الحركة وتسمى أفعال حركية، و تستعمل مع صيغ الأفعال المستمرة. من هذه الأفعال:

go	**run**	**hit**
يذهب	يجري	يضرب

وهنالك أفعال أخرى تصف الحالة وتدعى أفعال الحالة، و عادة لا تستعمل مع صيغ الأفعال المستمرة.

be	love	wish	see	include	need	resemble
يكون	يحب	يتمنى	يرى	يتضمن	يحتاج	يشبه

الأفعال المنتظمة و الشاذة Regular and irregular verbs

هذا متعلق بالمفردات أكثر منه بالقواعد. الاختلاف الحقيقي الوحيد بين الأفعال المنتظمة و الشاذة هو اختلاف نهايتها في أشكال التصريفين الثاني و الثالث. في حالة الأفعال النظامية، تكون نهاية التصريف الثاني و نهاية التصريف الثالث واحدة.ed- أما في حالة الأفعال الشاذة، فإن نهاية التصريف الثاني و نهاية التصريف الثالث متغيرة . لذا من الضروري أن نحفظها عن ظهر قلب.

الأفعال المنتظمة:

التصريف الأول	التصريف الثاني	التصريف الثالث
look ينظر	looked نظر	looked نظر
work يعمل	worked عمل	worked عمل

الأفعال الشاذة:

التصريف الأول	التصريف الثاني	التصريف الثالث
buy يشتري	bought اشترى	bought اشترى
do يعمل	did عمل	done عمل

في أغلب الأحيان التقسيمات أعلاه يمكن أن تخلط. على سبيل المثال، يمكن أن يكون فعل ما شاذ، متعد و حركي; فعل آخر يمكن أن يكون منتظم، متعد و حالة.

الأفعال المساعدة Auxiliary verbs

تستعمل الأفعال المساعدة مع الأفعال الرئيسية بغرض السماح لنا بالتحدث عن فترات زمنية مختلفة وتشكيل صيغ استفهام ونفي.

يمثل الفعلان (يكون be و (يملك have) الأفعال المساعدة الرئيسية. الغرض من الفعل المساعد الرئيسي تشكيل أزمنة مركبة. يستخدم (be) لتشكيل زمني المضارع المستمر والماضي المستمر ولتشكيل المبني للمجهول أيضاً، كما توضح الأمثلة التالية:

أنا أعمل.	I am working
كنا جميعاً نتساءل عن ذلك.	We were all wondering about that.
تم اعتقال مارتن واحتجازه طيلة الليل.	Martin was arrested and held overnight.

يستخدم (**have**) لتشكيل زمني المضارع التام والماضي التام:

Sara has finished fixing the car	لقد أنهت سارا إصلاح السيارة.
Amanda had already eaten when we arrived.	كانت أماندا قد فرغت من تناول الطعام عندما وصلنا.

يعد الفعل يفعل **Do** الفعل المساعد الداعم ويستخدم في تشكيل صيغ النفي والاستفهام والجمل التأكيدية:

I do not like meat at all.	أنا لا أحب اللحم على الإطلاق.
Do you like fish?	هل تحب السمك؟
You do like fish, don't you?	أنت تحب السمك، أليس كذلك؟

الأفعال الشكلية (الناقصة) Modal verbs

تستخدم الأفعال الشكلية قبل الأفعال الأخرى للتعبيرعن أفكار مثل المقدرة (**can**) والإمكانية (**may**) والوجوب (**must**) .

الأفعال الشكلية الأساسية هي:

should	would	will	shall	ought to	must	might	May	could	can

تختلف الأفعال الشكلية عن غيرها من الأفعال لأنها لاتغير شكلها:

يمكنني أن أمتطي الحصان *I can ride a horse*

يمكنها أن تمتطي الحصان *She can ride a horse*

ويتم صياغة النفي من الأفعال الشكلية كالتالي:

Short form الشكل المختصر للنفي	Negative النفي	Modal verb الفعل الشكلي
can't	cannot	can
couldn't	could not	could
(نادراً ماتستخدم mayn't)	may not	may
mightn't	might not	might
mustn't	must not	must
oughtn't to	ought not to	ought to
shan't	shall not	shall
shouldn't	should not	should
won't	will not	will
wouldn't	would not	would

غالباً مايتم اختصار الفعل الشكلي (**will** سوفٍ) إلى (**'ll**) وذلك أثناء الكلام والكتابة غير الرسمية، مثال: **I'll** ،**they'll** . ويتم أيضاً اختصار الفعل (**would**) إلى (**'d**)، مثال: **I'd** و **they'd** .

أشباه الجمل **Phrasal verbs**

إن شبه الجملة هي نوع من الأفعال التي تتشكل عندما يتم جمع فعل أساسي مع أي من:

- **حال** **adverb**

give in	take off	break in
تنازل/قدم	نزع/حلّق	اقتحم

- **حرف جر** **preposition**

get at (someone)	pick up
يصل/يشير إلى (شخص ما)	التقط/رفع

- **حال وحرف جر** **adverb+preposition**

put up with (insults)	get rid of
يحتمل (إهانة)	يتخلص من

إن المعنى الحقيقي غالباً لاعلاقة له بالمعنى الحرفي للفعل أو الأداة (الحال أو حرف الجر).

الأسماء **Nouns**

الأسماء هي الكلمات التي تدل على الأشياء والأفكار. ويمكن تصنيف الأسماء كما يلي:

أسماء العلم **Proper nouns**

وهي أسماء الأشخاص أوالأماكن أوالأشياء وجميعها يبدأ بحرف كبير:

Thursday	April	Mount Everest	Egypt	Victor Hugo
الثلاثاء	إبريل/ نيسان	جبل إفرست	مصر	فيكتور هوجو

الأسماء العامة **Common nouns**

وهي كل الأسماء الأخرى التي تشير إلى الأشياء والتي يمكن تقسيمها إلى المجموعات التالية:

الأسماء المجردة **Abstract nouns** والتي تشير إلى الأشياء التي لايمكنك رؤيتها أو لمسها، مثل:

time	idea	anger	honesty
وقت	فكرة	غضب	صدق

الأسماء المحسوسة **Concrete nouns**وهي التي تشير إلى الأشياء التي يمكنك رؤيتها أو لمسها، مثل:

teacher	stone	sugar	dog
مدرّس	حجر	سكر	كلب

الأسماء الجماعية**Compound nouns**

وهي تتكون من كلمتين أو أكثر. بعضها يكتب ككلمة واحدة والبعض الآخر ككلمتين منفصلتين أو بينهما واصلة (-). كما هو الحال في الأمثلة التالية:

teapot	washing machine	break-in
إبريق الشاي	غسالة	اقتحام

الأسماء المعدودة وغير المعدودة <u>**Countable and uncountable nouns**</u>

الأسماء المعدودة هي الأسماء التي تشير إلى الأشياء التي يمكن عدّها، مثل: بقرة واحدة

one cow ، بقرتان اثنتان **two cows**، سبع عشرة قطة **seventeen cats** ، ...إلخ. ولهذه الأسماء حالتان: الجمع والإفراد، وهي تظهر في طريقة الكتابة. يجب أن يسبقها أحد المحددات إذا كانت مفردة:

car/cars	apple/apples
سيارة/سيارات	تفاحة/تفاحات

الأسماء غير المعدودة وهي تشير إلى الأشياء التي لايمكن عدها: (**sugar** سكر) ، (**advice** نصيحة)

Sami asked me for some <u>advice</u>	<u>Sugar</u> is quite cheap
طلب سامي مني أن أسدي له بعض النصح	السكر رخيص جداً

لا تجمع عادة الأسماء غير المعدودة ويأتي بعدها أفعال تشير إلى المفرد. كما أنه من غير المألوف استخدامها مع أدوات التنكير. لايمكن التحدث عن (**an advice** نصيحة) أو (**a money** مال)

أسماء الكتلة **Mass nouns** وهي تشير إلى المواد التي يمكن تقسيمها أو قياسها ولكن لا يمكن عدها. ولا يوجد عادة قبلها أداة تنكير.

Sugar is quite cheap	Meat is usually more expensive than cheese
السكر رخيص جداً	اللحم عادة ثمنه أكثر من الجبن

يمكن أن تجمع أسماء الكتلة في حالات خاصة. على سبيل المثال، عندما تشير إلى نوع معين أو أنواع من المادة أو عندما تشير إلى تقديم مادة ما.

Two teas, please	Rose brought out a tempting selection of French cheeses
كوبان من الشاي، من فضلك	جلبت روز مجموعة مغرية من الأجبان الفرنسية

الضمائر **Pronouns**

الضمير هو كلمة يمكن أن تستخدم عوضاً عن الإسم أو العبارة الإسمية. وتستخدم الضمائر عندما لا نريد أن نكرر نفس الإسم في الجملة أو المقطع. كما هو الحال في المثال التالي:

Gary saw Sue so he asked her to help him

غاري قابل سو فسألها أن تساعده.

هنالك سبعة أنواع من الضمائر وهي تصنف تبعاً لمعانيها و استعمالاتها.

الضمائر الشخصية **Personal pronouns**

ويمكن أن تستخدم كفاعل أو مفعول به في الجمل.

We saw them both on Friday.	He gave her a box of chocolate.
رأينا كلاهما يوم الجمعة.	أعطاها علبة من الشوكولاتة.

الضمائر الإنعكاسية **Reflexive pronouns**

وتستخدم لتحل محل المفعول به وتعود على فاعل الجملة كما في المثال التالي:

I've just cut myself on a piece of glass.
لقد جرحت نفسي بقطعة من الزجاج

وتستعمل الضمائر الانعكاسية أيضاً للتأكيد على أمر ما كما يوضح المثال التالي:

Never mind. I'll do it myself.
لا تقلق. سوف أقوم بذلك بنفسي.

ضمائر الملكية **Possessive pronouns**

وهي تشير إلى ملكية الشيء:

Give it back, it's mine.
أعطنيه. إنه لي.

ضمائر الإشارة **Demonstrative pronouns**

وهي الضمائر التي تستخدم للدلالة على قرب الشيء أو بعده عنا كما يوضح المثال الآتي:

This is John's and that is Peter's.
هذا ملك لجون وذاك ملك لبيتر

ضمائر الوصل **Relative pronouns**

والغرض منها الربط مابين شبه جملة إيضاحية (وهي الجزء من الجملة الذي يعطي معلومات أكثر عن كلمة أو عبارة في الجملة ذاتها) وعبارة إسمية أو شبه جملة أخرى كما يوضح المثال التالي:

That's the girl <u>who</u> always comes top.
تلك هي الفتاة التي حدثتك عنها.

ضمائر الاستفهام **Interrogative pronouns**

وتستعمل للسؤال عن العبارة الإسمية التي تصفها كما هو الحال في المثال التالي:

<u>Who</u> was responsible?	<u>What</u> would you like for lunch?
من كان المسؤول؟	ما الذي ترغب بتناوله على وجبة الغداء؟

الضمائر غير المعرفة **Indefinite pronouns**

وهي الضمائر التي تستخدم على نطاق واسع للإشارة إلى شيء ما عندما لا يكون هناك حاجة أو إمكانية لاستخدام أحد الضمائر الشخصية، كما هو واضح في المثال التالي:

<u>Neither</u> wanted to give in and apologize.	<u>Everyone</u> had a compass and a whistle.
لا أحد منهما أراد أن يتنازل ويتقدم باعتذار.	كل شخص منهم يملك بوصلة وصفارة.

الضمائر الشخصية يمكن أن تحل محل الفاعل في الجملة (أنا، أنت، هو، هي، نحن، هم) أو محل المفعول به. ومن الصعب تحديد الصيغة التي يجب اعتمادها في بعض الأحيان وخاصة إذا ما كنا بصدد استعمال ضميرين في آن واحد أو اسماً شخصياً مرفقاً بضمير شخصي. وفيما يلي بعض القواعد التوضيحية:

- إذا كان الضميران المستخدمان يشكلان الفاعل المشترك للفعل، عندها يجب استخدام الضمير بصيغة الفاعل:

<u>Jerry</u> and <u>I</u> are going to paint the house ourselves.

سنقوم أنا وجيري بطلاء المنزل بأنفسنا

- إذا كان الضميران المستخدمان يشكلان المفعول به المشترك للفعل، عندها يجب استخدام الضمير بصيغة المفعول به:

I want to give you and him a present.	They decided to help Jane and me
أود تقديم هدية لك وله.	قررا بأن يساعدانني وجين.

- تستخدم صيغة المفعول به للضمائر بعد أحرف الجر:

Wasn't that kind of him?	Between you and me, I don't like this place
ألم يكن ذلك لطفاً منها؟	بيني وبينك، لا أحب هذا المكان.

الصفات Adjectives

تقوم الصفة بإعطاء معلومات عن الاسم وتصف إحدى خواص الاسم بشيء من التفصيل.

their new, wide-screen TV	a tall man
تلفازهم الجديد ذو الشاشة العريضة	رجل طويل

عندما يكون هنالك أكثر من صفة غالباً ما يتم استخدام الفواصل بينها، إلا أنه يمكن استخدام لائحة من الصفات المتتالية من دون فواصل بينها:

a happy young blonde German girl.
بنت ألمانية صغيرة شقراء سعيدة

وتستخدم الصيغة المقارنة **comparative** للصفة للمقارنة بين شخصين أو شيئين أو حالتين:

Ann is taller than Mary, but Mary is older
آن أطول من ماري لكن ماري أكبر سناً

في حين تستخدم الصيغة التفضيلية **superlative** لأكثر من شخصين أو شيئين أو حالتين وذلك عندما يكون أحدها لديه أهمية أو نوعية أفضل من الأخرى. عادة ما يأتي قبل هذه الصفاة التفضيلية أداة التعريف **the**.

Mike is the tallest student in the school.
مايك هو أطول طالب في المدرسة

هناك طريقتان يتم فيهما تشكيل الصيغ المقارنة والتفضيلية للصفات:

- نقوم بإضافة **er-** (المقارنة)، و **est-** (التفضيل) للصفة. الصفات ذات المقطع اللفظي الواحد تأخذ النهايات التالية:

التفضيلية superlative	المقارنة comparative	
the brightest الأكثر ذكاءً/سطوعاً	brighter أكثر ذكاءً/سطوعاً	bright ذكي/ ساطع
the longest الأكثر طولاً	longer أكثر طولاً	long طويل

إذا كانت الكلمة تنتهي بـ **(e) عندها يجب أن تترك ويتم إضافة (r) أو (st)**. أما إذا كانت تنتهي بـ **(y)** عادة يتم تغيير الـ **(y)** إلى **(i)** وإضافة **(er)** أو **(est)**.

التفضيلية superlative	المقارنة comparative	
the wisest الأكثر حكمة	wiser أكثر حكمة	wise حكيم
the prettiest الأكثر جمالاً	prettier أكثر جمالاً	pretty جميل

ملاحظة: عندما يتم إضافة **(er)** أو **(est)** للصفات ذات المقطع اللفظي الواحد والمنتهي بحرف صوتي يتبعه حرف صامت، يجب مضاعفة الحرف الصامت، مثل:
- أكبر **bigger**

الأكثر حزناً **saddest**

- نقوم بإضافة إحدى الكلمتين (**more** أكثر) أو (**most** الأكثر) قبل الصفات التي تتكون من ثلاثة مقاطع لفظية أو أكثر:

التفضيلية superlative	المقارنة comparative	
the most fortunate الأكثر حظاً	more fortunate أكثر حظاً	Fortunate محظوظ
the most beautiful الأكثر جمالاً	more beautiful أكثر جمالاً	Beautiful جميل

الصفات التي يتم صياغتها من اسم المفعول (**أحد أشكال الفعل**) تستخدم كلاً من **more** أو **most** أيضاً:

التفضيلية superlative	المقارنة comparative	
the most provoking الأكثر إزعاجاً	more provoking أكثر إزعاجاً	provoking مزعج
the most determined الأكثر تصميماً	more determined أكثر تصميماً	determined مصمم

الصفات ذات المقطعين اللفظيين بما فيها تلك التي تنتهي بـ **er-** يمكن أن تتبع أحد النمطين أو كلاهما أحياناً. في حال لم تكن متأكداً يمكنك عندئذ استخدام **more/most** مع الصفات ذات المقطعين اللفظيين.

	المقارنة **comparative**	التفضيلية **superlative**
shallow ضحل، قليل العمق	**shallower** أو **more shallow** أقل عمقاَ	**the shallowest** أو **the most shallow** الأقل عمقاً
Polite مهذب	**politer** أو **more polite** أكثر تهذيباً	**the politest** أو **the most polite** الأكثر تهذيباً

هنالك مجموعة من الصفات غير النظامية والتي لديها صياغة مختلفة في حالتي المقارنة والتفضيل:

	المقارنة **comparative**	التفضيلية **superlative**
good جيد	**better** أفضل	**the best** الأفضل
bad سيء	**worse** أسوأ	**the worst** الأسوأ
Far بعيد	**Further, farther** أبعد	**the furthest, the farthest** الأبعد

ويتم استخدام (**less** أقل) أو (**least** الأقل) للإشارة إلى عكس كلٍ من **(-er/-est)** و **(more/most)** وذلك عند المقارنة بين الأشياء أو الأشخاص.

	المقارنة **comparative**	التفضيلية **superlative**
sharp حاد/ذكي	**less sharp** أقل حدة/ذكاء	**the least sharp** الأقل حدة/ذكاء
interesting مشوّق	**less interesting** أقل تشويقاً	**the least interesting** الأقل تشويقاً

أحرف الجر **Prepositions**

حرف الجر هو كلمة تنتمي إلى مجموعة صغيرة ولكن شائعة من الكلمات التي تربط عناصر مختلفة ببعضها البعض. معظم أحرف الجر الانجليزية هي ذات معان متعددة ترتبط بحرف جر محدد. وتتكون أحرف الجر البسيطة من كلمة واحدة كما هو ملاحظ في الأمثلة التالية:

under	on	in
تحت	على	في

أما أحرف الجر المعقدة فتتكون من أكثر من كلمة واحدة كما هو مبين في الأمثلة التالية:

out of	in spite of	on top of	together with	due to
خارج	بالرغم من	بالإضافة إلى ذلك	بالاشتراك مع	بسبب

وتتضمن المجموعتان أدناه جميع أحرف الجر البسيطة. بعض الكلمات يمكن أن تكون أحرف جر أو أحوال، وهذا متعلق بكيفية استخدامها وبما يرتبط بها. يحتاج حرف الجر إلى مفعول به، حاله في ذلك كحال الفعل المتعدي.و سنجد بأن أحرف الجر التي يمكن أن تستخدم كأحوال أيضا تظهر في المجموعة الأولى بينما تتضمن المجموعة الثانية أحرف الجر التي لا تستخدم كأحوال:

المجموعة الأولى:
Aboard (على متن), **about** (بخصوص ،حول، عن), **above** (فوق), **across** (عبر), **after** (بعد، عقب), **along** (على طول، بمحاذاة), **alongside** (بمحاذاة), **around** (حول), **before** (قبل، أمام), **behind** (وراء), **below** (أسفل), **beneath** (تحت), **beside** (بجانب), **between** (بين), **beyond** (ماوراء), **by** (ب، بفعل، بالقرب من), **down** (تحت), **inside** (داخل), **near** (بالقرب من), **off** (عن), **opposite** (عكس), **outside** (خارج), **over** (فوق), **past** (إلى ماوراء، بعد), **round** (حول، طوال), **since** (منذ), **through** (خلال، بواسطة، طوال), **throughout** (طوال), **under** (تحت), **underneath** (تحت، في الأسفل), **pu** (فوق، نحو), **within** (داخل، ضمن), **without** (خارج، بدون).

المجموعة الثانية:
against (ضد ،عكس), **amid** (في خضم), **among** (بين), **as** (ك), **at** (عند), **atop** (في أعلى الشيء), **bar** (ماعدا), **despite** (على الرغم), **during** (خلال), **for** (لأجل، بسبب), **from** (من), **ni** (في), **into** (عبر، في), **like** (ك ، مثل), **of** (من), **on** (على), **onto** (على، فوق), **pending** (خلال), **per** (في، بواسطة), **prior** (سابق), **pro** (تأييداً ل), **re** (فيما يتعلق ب), **regarding** (بخصوص), **than** (من، غير، على أن، حتى), **till** (حتى), **to** (إلى), **towards** (نحو، من، حوالي، من أجل), **until** (إلى أن، حتى), **unto** (حتى، إلى), **upon** (حين، على وشك), **via** (بواسطة), **with** (مع، ب).

أدوات العطف **Conjunctions**

تقوم أداة العطف بربط اسمين (أو أكثر) أو عبارتين (أو أكثر) مع بعضهما البعض. وتسمى أدوات العطف أحياناً "كلمات الوصل".

I went to the shop and bought some bread.	I bought some bread but forgot to get the milk.
ذهبت إلى المتجر واشتريت بعض الخبز.	اشتريت بعض الخبز ولكن نسيت أن أجلب الحليب.

في أغلب الكتابة الرسمية لا يعتبر أسلوباً جيداً أن تبدأ الجملة بأداة عطف. ولكن في أسلوب الكتابة الأكثر ابداعاً يمكن القيام بذلك من أجل جعل الكتابة ذات تأثير.

الأزمنة الفعلية **Tenses**

تستخدم أشكال الأفعال الأزمنة للإشارة إلى الزمن الذي يمثل ما نتكلم عنه، سواء أكان ذلك في الماضي أو الحاضر أو المستقبل:

Jessica works in the post office.	Laurence worked in the post office over the Christmas holidays.
تعمل جيسيكا في مكتب البريد.	عمل لورنس في مكتب البريد خلال عطلة عيد الميلاد.

في اللغة الانجليزية، هناك نوعان من الأزمنة:

- الزمن البسيط: وهو مكون من كلمة واحدة.
- الأزمنة المركبة: ويتم تشكيل هذه الأزمنة باستخدام الشكل المضارع أو الماضي من الأفعال المساعدة مع فعل آخر منته ب (ing) أو (ed). وفيما يلي الأشكال المختلفة للأزمنة في اللغة الانجليزية:

المضارع البسيط **Present simple**

Manuela goes to school every day.	I go to college in London.
تذهب مانويلا إلى المدرسة كل يوم	أذهب إلى المعهد في لندن.

الماضي البسيط **Past simple**

He saw a tiger.	I cooked a meal.
رأى نمراً	طهوت وجبة.

المستقبل البسيط **Future simple**

Louise will phone you later.	We will give you the money tomorrow.
ستتصل لويز بك لاحقاً.	سوف نعطيك النقود غداً.

المضارع التام Present perfect

The illness has ruined my life.	I have ordered a new sofa.
لقد دمر المرض حياتي.	لقد طلبت أريكة جديدة.

الماضي التام Past perfect

She had visited Paris before.	They had noticed a strange smell.
كانت قد زارت باريس من قبل.	كانوا قد لاحظوا رائحة غريبة.

المستقبل التام Future perfect

Gary will have done his work by then.	We will have finished before dark.
سيكون غاري قد أتم عمله عندئذ.	سنكون قد انتهينا قبل حلول الظلام.

المضارع المستمر Present continuous

She is finishing her meal.	I am waiting for Jack.
إنها تنهي وجبتها.	أنا أنتظر جاك.

الماضي المستمر Past continuous

The man was waiting for the bus.	We were trying to see the queen.
كان الرجل ينتظر الحافلة.	كنا نحاول رؤية الملكة.

المستقبل المستمر Future continuous

Mum will be worrying about us.	We will be playing football with another school team.
سوف تقلق أمي علينا.	سوف نلعب كرة القدم مع فريق من مدرسة أخرى.

المضارع التام المستمر Present perfect continuous

The snow has been falling all night.	We have been trying to phone you all morning.
ظل الثلج يهطل طوال الليل.	ظللنا نحاول الاتصال بك طيلة فترة الصباح.

الماضي التام المستمر **Past perfect continuous**

The children <u>had been using</u> my computer.	Anna <u>had been sitting</u> there all day.
كان الأولاد يستعملون حاسبي الشخصي.	كانت آنا تجلس هناك طيلة اليوم.

المستقبل التام المستمر **Future perfect continuous**

On Sunday, we <u>will have been living</u> here for 10 years.	I <u>will have been working</u> on the project for over a year.
بحلول يوم الأحد، سيكون قد مر على حياتنا هنا عشر سنوات.	سيكون قد مر على عملي بهذا المشروع مايزيد عن عام.

الفعل والفاعل والمفعول به غير المباشر
Subject, object, and indirect object

إن الفاعل في الجملة هو الشخص أو الشيء الذي يقوم بالفعل. يمكن أن يكون الفعل إسماً أو عبارة إسمية أو ضمير. جميع الجمل بحاجة إلى فاعل.

<u>Her</u> car broke down.	<u>The man in the red coat</u> asked me some questions.	<u>Adam</u> played the piano.
تعطلت سيارتها.	الرجل ذو المعطف الأحمر سألني بضعة أسئلة.	عزف آدم على البيانو.

يأتي المفعول به في الجملة عادة بعد الفعل. ويمكن أن يكون اسماً أو عبارة إسمية أو ضمير.

I couldn't find <u>it</u>.	She saw <u>a large, black bird</u>.	I threw <u>the ball</u>.
لم أتمكن من إيجاده.	رأت طائراً أسود كبيراً.	رميت الكرة.

لايوجد لكل الجمل مفعول به.

Erica was writing a letter. (with object)	**Erica was writing.** (no object)
كانت إريكا تكتب رسالة. (مع مفعول به)	كانت إريكا تكتب. (بلا مفعول به)

كما يكون لبعض الأفعال أنواعاً أخرى من المفعول به وتسمى المفعول به غير المباشر. يسمي المفعول به غير المباشر الشخص الذي من أجله أو لأجله تم عمل شيء ما. وعادة ما يحتاج المفعول به غير المباشر إلى أفعال مثل: **give** يعطي – **find** يجد – **owe** يدين بكذا

Jonathan owes Tom <u>five pounds</u>.	Naveen gave me <u>a box of chocolate</u>.	Susan bought her cat <u>some more food</u>.
جوناثان مدين لتوم بخمسة	أعطتني نافين علبة من الشوكولاتة.	اشترت سوزان لقطتها المزيد من الطعام.

التوافق **Agreement**

التوافق يعني الحرص على جعل كل الكلمات والعبارات في جملة ما تأخذ الصيغة الصحيحة في علاقتها ببعضها البعض.

توافق الفاعل والفعل **Subject-verb agreement**

يجب أن تكون صيغة الفعل صحيحة لكي يتوافق مع الفاعل:

The stars are very bright (plural subject, plural verb)	**The house is very large.** (singular subject, singular verb)
النجوم ساطعة جداً (الفاعل جمع والفعل جمع)	المنزل كبير جداً (الفاعل مفرد والفعل مفرد)

في الجمل الطويلة جداً يكون من السهل ارتكاب خطأ ما وخاصة إذا ماكان الفعل بعيداً في موضعه في الجملة عن موضع الفاعل. إذا كان هناك فاعلان مفردان ويجمعهما حرف الوصل **and** ، يكون عندئذ من الضروري استخدام فعل بصيغة الجمع:

The table and the chair <u>need</u> cleaning.	**John and Larry <u>are</u> going on holiday.**
الطاولة والكرسي يحتاجان إلى تنظيف.	جون ولاري ذاهبان في عطلة.

ولكن عندما ينظر إلى شيئين تجمعهما **and** على أنهما شيء واحد نستعمل عندها فعلاً مفرداً:

Fish and chips <u>is</u> my favorite meal.
إن السمك وشرائح البطاطس المقلية هي وجبتي المفضلة

إذا كان الفاعل مسبوقاً ب **each** أو **every** أو **no**، فإن صيغة الفعل يجب أن تكون مفردة، والشيء ذاته ينطبق على **any** عندما تسبق فاعلاً مفرداً:

Each vase <u>holds</u> four or five roses.	**Every seat <u>was</u> taken already.**
كل مزهرية تحتوي على أربع أو خمس زهرات.	كل المقاعد كان قد تم حجزها مسبقاً.

إذا كان هناك فاعلان مفردان ويجمعهما **neither/nor** أو **either/or** أو

Not only/but also، نستعمل عندها فعلاً مفرداً كما في الأمثلة التالية:

Neither Blake nor Jones was available for comment.	Either Mrs Spiers or Mr Turner takes the children to football.
لا بليك ولا جونز كان موجوداً للتعليق.	إما السيدة سبيرز أو السيد تيرنر سيأخذ الأطفال ليلعبوا كرة القدم.

نستخدم فعلاً مفرداً مع عناوين الكتب والأفلام والأغاني، إلخ حتى لو كان العنوان نفسه بصيغة الجمع:

The Birds' is a really scary film.'
الطيور هو فيلم مخيف بالفعل.

توافق الضمير Pronoun agreement

يجب أن يكون للضمائر الصيغة الصحيحة في علاقتها بالأشياء التي تشير إليها. غالباً ما تشير الضمائر إلى جملة سبقتها:

The car started fine, but it broke down half way to Manchester.
عملت السيارة بشكل جيد في البداية

فاعل مفرد يتبعه ضمير بصيغة الجمع
Singular subject followed by plural pronoun

انظر الجملة التالية:

Any pupil who is going on the school trip should hand in their payment at the office.
أي تلميذ يرغب في الذهاب في الرحلة المدرسية يجب أن يدفع رسم الاشتراك في المكتب.

في هذه الجملة، **any pupil** هو تعبير مفرد ونلاحظ بأن الفعل **is** مفرد أيضاً ولكن الضمير **their** وهو بصيغة الجمع قد تم استخدامه هنا.

التوافق مع أسماء المجموعات Agreement with group nouns

أسماء المجموعات هي كلمات تشير إلى مجموعة أو كل الأفراد في تلك المجموعة:

Committee	Parliament
لجنة	برلمان، مجلس الشعب

في اللغة الانجليزية، يمكنك استخدام فعل مفرد أو جمع مع هذه الأسماء ولكن عليك أن تعتمد أسلوباً واحداً. انظر المثالين التاليين:

The army was marching towards us.	The army were marching towards us.
كان الجيش يتقدم نحونا.	كان أفراد الجيش يتقدمون نحونا.

توافق الأزمنة الفعلية **Tense agreement**

يجب عليك أن تحرص على جعل الأزمنة الفعلية في جملة تتوافق مع بعضها البعض بشكل صحيح:

While I was waiting, I seen a film. (incorrect)	**While I was waiting, I saw a film.** (correct)
بينما كنت أنتظر كنت قد أشاهد فيلماً (خاطئة)	بينما كنت أنتظر شاهدت فيلماً (صحيحة)

احذر عند استخدامك فعلين مساعدين أو فعلين شكليين معاً في جملة واحدة:

I can and I have done it. (incorrect)	**I can do it and I have done it.** (correct)
أنا أستطيع أن ولقد فعلتها (خاطئة)	أنا أستطيع أن أفعلها ولقد فعلتها (صحيحة)